T0295776

DATA SCIENCE, ANALYTICS AND MACHINE LEARNING WITH R

DATA SCIENCE, ANALYTICS AND MACHINE LEARNING WITH R

Luiz Paulo Fávero

Patrícia Belfiore

Rafael de Freitas Souza

Academic Press is an imprint of Elsevier
125 London Wall, London EC2Y 5AS, United Kingdom
525 B Street, Suite 1650, San Diego, CA 92101, United States
50 Hampshire Street, 5th Floor, Cambridge, MA 02139, United States
The Boulevard, Langford Lane, Kidlington, Oxford OX5 1GB, United Kingdom

Notices

Knowledge and best practice in this field are constantly changing. As new research and experience broaden our understanding, changes in research methods, professional practices, or medical treatment may become necessary.

Practitioners and researchers must always rely on their own experience and knowledge in evaluating and using any information, methods, compounds, or experiments described herein. In using such information or methods they should be mindful of their own safety and the safety of others, including parties for whom they have a professional responsibility.

To the fullest extent of the law, neither the Publisher nor the authors, contributors, or editors, assume any liability for any injury and/or damage to persons or property as a matter of products liability, negligence or otherwise, or from any use or operation of any methods, products, instructions, or ideas contained in the material herein.

ISBN: 978-0-12-824271-1

For information on all Academic Press publications
visit our website at https://www.elsevier.com/books-and-journals

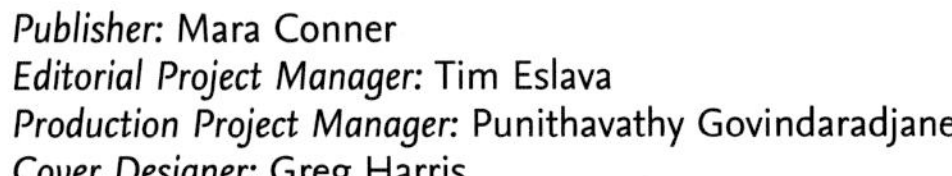

Publisher: Mara Conner
Editorial Project Manager: Tim Eslava
Production Project Manager: Punithavathy Govindaradjane
Cover Designer: Greg Harris

Typeset by STRAIVE, India

Dedication

To Leonor Lopes Fávero

Epigraph

Everything in us is mortal, except the gifts of the spirit and of intelligence.

Publius Ovidius Naso

Contents

19. Classification and regression trees

20. Boosting and bagging

21. Random forests

22. Artificial neural networks

VII

Spatial analysis

23. Working on shapefiles

24. Dealing with simple feature objects

25. Raster objects

26. Exploratory spatial analysis

VIII

Adding value to your work

27. Enhanced and interactive graphs

PART I

Introduction

CHAPTER

1

Overview of data science, analytics, and machine learning

Introduction

This chapter provides a brief introduction to data science, analytics, and machine learning, which will serve as a foundation for understanding the concepts and techniques covered throughout the book.

In this new millennium, in which it is estimated that more than 5 quintillion pieces of data are generated daily from social networks, the internet of things, digital photos, consumer monitoring, and other sources, the understanding of the importance of data science in its various aspects is of fundamental importance for scientific and technological advancement, economic and social development, environmental preservation, business success, the discovery and exploration of new areas of knowledge, understanding of historical events, and even the protection of life on our planet!

Data science is therefore naturally multidisciplinary. We found examples of data science applications in engineering, physics, medicine, biology, education, psychology, pedagogy, law, politics, public security, economics, sociology, business, marketing, astronomy, anthropology, human resources, meteorology, geography, and history. We will hardly be able to find a field of study in which it is not possible to investigate phenomena through the techniques and procedures of data science.

There are many aspects that data science encompasses. Many are the professions associated with these aspects because every day we witness the emergence of new terminologies and positions in the market and in the academic world. Examples include data scientist, data engineer, data architect, data analyst, business intelligence analyst, machine learning engineer, database administrator, computer engineer, information technology facilitator, edge computing master, cybercity analyst, personal data broker, machine manager, digital tailor, augmented reality (AR) journey builder, user experience (UX) writer, DevOps (developers and IT operation professionals), among many other professions. And these professionals work, as we mentioned, in the most diverse sectors! We find data engineers in the food and beverage industry as well as AR journey builders in the gaming industry.

Figure 1.1 provides an overview of the relationship among data science, analytics, and machine learning.

Data Science, Analytics and Machine Learning with R
https://doi.org/10.1016/B978-0-12-824271-1.00034-2

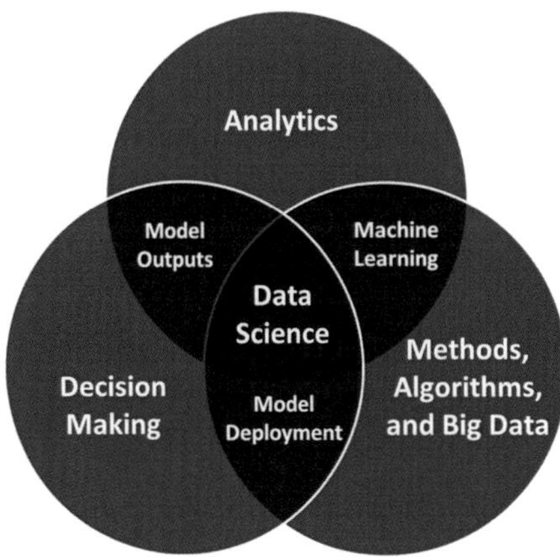

FIGURE 1.1 Overview of data science, analytics, and machine learning (Fávero and Belfiore, 2019).

Through Figure 1.1, it is possible to verify, therefore, that data science encompasses knowledge about data analysis (analytics) as well as knowledge about methods, algorithms, Big Data, and decision-making processes.

The Analytics pillar involves knowledge and fundamentals about measurement scales of variables, mathematics, statistics, calculus, linear algebra, operations research, geometry, and trigonometry. It is not possible to find a data scientist who does not present some solidity of knowledge in these fields; however, if you find one who identifies this way, this person will be, at most, a pusher of codes and buttons!

The pillar referring to methods, algorithms, and Big Data refers to the knowledge for implementing routines and codes from specific languages such as R, Python, Stata, Julia, SQL, Java, C/C++, Scala, SAS, Matlab, SPSS, among many others. Note that the implementation of routines necessarily involves knowledge about the fundamentals of Analytics so mistakes are not made when writing the codes. It is very common to find programmers who do not know the statistical foundations of a particular modeling technique and end up writing code that does not reflect, for example, the nature of the variables under study. The outputs obtained in this case will be, to say the least, inaccurate and sometimes completely wrong!

In this pillar, we can still find the fundamentals of Big Data, which correspond to the simultaneous occurrence of five characteristics, or dimensions of the data: **volume, speed, variety, variability,** and **complexity** of the data.

The exacerbated **volume** of data arises, among other reasons, from the increase in computational capacity and the increase in the monitoring of the most diverse phenomena. The **speed** with which data becomes available for treatment and analysis, due to new forms of collection that use, for example, electronic tags and radiofrequency systems, is also visible and vital for the decision-making processes. The **variety** refers to the different formats in which the data are accessed, such as texts, indicators, secondary bases, or even speeches, and a convergent analysis can also provide better decision making. The **variability** of the data is related, in addition to the three previous dimensions, with cyclical or seasonal phenomena, sometimes with high frequency, directly observable or not, and that a given treatment can generate differentiated information. Last, but not least, the **complexity** of the data, especially for large volumes, lies in the fact that many sources can be accessed with different codes, periodicities, or criteria, which requires a control process from the researcher (Fávero and Belfiore, 2019).

In this sense, the relationship between the Analytics pillar and the Methods, Algorithms, and Big Data pillar corresponds to what we call *machine learning,* which refers to the processes of pattern recognition in data from codes that "train the machine" for this purpose, that is, **a process for exploring data to discover meaningful patterns and rules.** Here are also deep learning algorithms, or deep pattern recognition from algorithms, for example, from neural networks for image recognition based on large amounts of data.

This processing flow cannot be supported without being accompanied by the improved professional software and increased processing capacity of increasingly gigantic datasets that are capable of supporting the elaboration of the most diverse tests and the estimation of the most varied models that should reflect the reality of each situation and according to what the researcher and the decision maker want.

These are the main reasons that have led organizations active in the most diverse sectors to invest in the structuring and development of multidisciplinary areas of data science that have the main objective of analyzing data and generating information, allowing the creation of pattern recognition and the establishment of real-time **predictive capability.** The emergence and improvement of complex computer systems, together with the reduction in costs for acquiring hardware and software, have made organizations increasingly store data in data warehouses, data lakes, virtual libraries, and the cloud (Fávero and Belfiore, 2019).

The direct acquisition of outputs from analytics tools and the deployment of models, which refers to a data engineering task focused on the production and availability, through APIs (Application Programming Interfaces), of models estimated in real time, generate subsidies for decision making. And, obviously, the decision-making process goes through aspects related to team management, resource allocation, and humanization of production processes!

In a cyclical way, understanding the business or the area of study can improve the acquisition of new data, increase the ability to prepare these data, and favor the development of new programming codes with a focus on the search for other machine learning models that eventually generate better adhesions between the real values of the phenomenon under study and the fitted values obtained. This can provide better results, which will favor an increase in the ability to understand the area of study and the business as a whole!

Overview of the book

The book is divided into 28 chapters, as follows:

Part I: Introduction
Chapter 1: Overview of data science, analytics, and machine learning
Chapter 2: Introduction to R-based language

Part II: Applied statistics and data visualization
Chapter 3: Types of variables, measurement scales, and accuracy scales
Chapter 4: Univariate descriptive statistics
Chapter 5: Bivariate descriptive statistics
Chapter 6: Hypotheses tests
Chapter 7: Data visualization and multivariate graphs

Part III: Data mining and preparation
Chapter 8: Webscraping and handcrafted robots
Chapter 9: Using application programming interfaces to collect data
Chapter 10: Managing data

Part IV: Unsupervised machine learning techniques
Chapter 11: Cluster analysis
Chapter 12: Principal component factor analysis
Chapter 13: Simple and multiple correspondence analysis

Part V: Supervised machine learning techniques
Chapter 14: Simple and multiple regression models
Chapter 15: Binary and multinomial logistic regression models
Chapter 16: Count-data and zero-inflated regression models
Chapter 17: Generalized linear mixed models

Part VI: Improving performance
Chapter 18: Support vector machines
Chapter 19: Classification and regression trees
Chapter 20: Boosting and bagging
Chapter 21: Random forests
Chapter 22: Artificial neural networks

Part VII: Spatial analysis
Chapter 23: Working on shapefiles
Chapter 24: Dealing with simple features objects
Chapter 25: Raster objects
Chapter 26: Exploratory spatial analysis

Part VIII: Adding value to your work
Chapter 27: Enhanced and interactive graphs
Chapter 28: Dashboards with R

It is important to emphasize that a version of this chapter, as well as Chapters 3 to 6 and 11 to 17, was previously published in the books *Manual de Análise de Dados/Handbook of Data Analysis* (Fávero and Belfiore, 2017, Portuguese Edition) and *Data Science for Business and Decision Making* (Fávero and Belfiore, 2019, English Edition; 2020, Korean Edition), published by Elsevier Academic Press. All the conceptual parts, the algebraic and mathematical developments, the datasets, the outputs and the discussions come from those books. Here only R codes are included.

Each chapter is structured in the same presentation didactical logic, which we believe favors learning. First, we offer applications and practical exercises in R, which will be presented and discussed through case studies with open real data from many fields (e.g., science, engineering, technology, and health care).

We believe that this logic facilitates the study and understanding of the correct use of each technique. Moreover, the practical application of the models in R also brings benefits to researchers as the results can be obtained through recent packages and functions.

At the end of most chapters, additional exercises are proposed along with solutions available online.

Final remarks

I believe this book is meant for researchers who, for different reasons, are specifically interested in data science, analytics, and machine learning as well as for those who want to deepen their knowledge by using R-based packages and codes.

This book is recommended to undergraduate and graduate students in the fields of sciences, engineering, technology, health care, psychology, actuarial sciences, statistics, economics, business, and other fields related to exact, biomedical, and human sciences. It is also meant for students taking extension, *lato sensu* postgraduation, and MBA courses as well as for company employees, consultants, and other researchers who have as their main objectives to treat and analyze data, aiming at preparing data models, creating information, and improving knowledge through decision-making processes.

First, I want to thank Professor Patrícia Belfiore immensely for our partnership and friendship. Our discussions and joint studies have been going on for more than twenty years. I remember, like it was yesterday, our first discussions about data analysis, multivariate modeling, and machine learning techniques. Our first book was published in 2007, and it has been 15 years now. Thank you so much for everything, Professor Patrícia!

I would also like to sincerely thank the professionals at Montvero Consulting and Training Ltd. and at Elsevier Academic Press, especially Mara E. Conner, Punithavathy Govindaradjane, Judith Clarisse Punzalan, Indhumathi Mani, and Andre Gerhard Wolff. Lastly, but not less important, I would like to thank the professors, students, and employees of the Economics, Business Administration and Accounting College of the University of Sao Paulo (FEA/USP) and of the Federal University of the ABC (UFABC).

Now it is time for you to get started! I would like to emphasize that any contributions, criticisms, and suggestions are always welcome so they may be later incorporated into this book and make it better.

Luiz Paulo Fávero

CHAPTER

2

Introduction to R-based language

AT THE END OF THIS CHAPTER, YOU WILL BE ABLE TO:

- Demonstrate the installation of R-based language and its integrated development environment (IDE), *RStudio* software.
- Introduce the grammar and some basic syntax of R-based language.
- Learn to work with objects, understand the need for functions and their arguments, and install and load packages.
- Introduce how to load, manipulate, and save datasets.

Don't forget to define the R working directory (the location where your datasets are installed):

```
setwd("C:/book/chapter2")
```

Introduction

The purpose of this chapter is to approach R-based language in an introductory way and to provide the reader with the basic knowledge necessary to use this book. This includes setting up how to use this work, installing R-based language, introducing the necessary software, and absorbing important concepts.

Although it is true that this section will start from the premise that the reader has never had contact with R, it is important to mention that, in the course of the other chapters of this book, more advanced features will be presented as they are needed. If the reader feels the need to go even deeper into R-based language, there are numerous possible readings in the bibliography of this book. In any case, we think that what is proposed in this work is enough for the reader to be able to enter the world of machine learning using R-based language. Even so, if a beginning reader feels the urge to delve into R-based language, we suggest two important readings:

- *Hands-On Programming with R* (Grolemund, 2014)
- *R for Data Science* (Wickham and Grolemund, 2017)

At the end of this chapter, the reader will be able to install R-based language on a computer and will be familiar with the main basic functionalities of the necessary software. This chapter will also help the reader internalize certain R concepts, install and use language packages, and open datasets, including those from other types of computer languages.

Data Science, Analytics and Machine Learning with R
https://doi.org/10.1016/B978-0-12-824271-1.00033-0

How to use this work

Throughout the book, we will treat the terms *R*, *Rstudio*, and *R-based language* as synonyms or sometimes as one thing, as a facilitator for the reader. We recognize that they are different things, despite working together in the course of this work.

The reader also must know that whenever something related to the R-based language environment is mentioned (e.g., an object, function, or argument), it will be written in a different typeface from the purely textual part of the work (e.g., `object`, `function()`, `argument =`). **We also think it is important not to worry about memorizing R commands because it would be impossible to memorize all of them.** Over time, some commands will actually be memorized, and others will trigger the reader's memory. This will remind the reader that almost anything is possible in R, leading him or her to look for solutions in this or other works or in specialized forums, and that is enough for us! **And believe me, it will suffice for the reader.**

Finally, from Chapter 4 onward, the reader will always come across an initial frame that will be a reminder to define the working directory and will provide information about packages that are used throughout the text.

Well, let's get to what really matters!

R-based language installation

In a conversation between friends, one of them says, "Hey, let's go." The other friend, already imbued with the context and having experience with the other person, will be fully capable of understanding what was asked, even with so many omissions of words in the sentence. The sentence "Hey, let's go" can mean "Let's go to a cafeteria," "Let's go to the club," or "Let's go to the gym." It does not matter because as a rule, the human receiving the message will know what it is about, but the machine will not. For the machine, in most cases, it will be necessary to say, in a logical order and with explicit details, where you go, how you go, with whom you go, and what time you go. Do you understand?

Be that as it may, this communication, even among friends, is only possible because there is a common language. The language that the reader will use to communicate with his or her computer while reading this book will therefore be R.

A fair question would be, **Did my computer come from the factory knowing how to "speak" and "understand" R?** It depends. There are some *Linux* distributions in which R is already present, however, as a rule, installation is required for all computers.

In order to "teach" the computer to "speak" and "understand" R, it is necessary to install R-based language, present on the R Project website, accessible at https://www.r-project.org.

On the R Project website, as shown in Figure 2.1, click on "CRAN" below the *Download* tab.

Depending on the reading date of the work, it is possible that the site presented by Figure 2.1 has undergone significant changes.

The next page, demonstrated by Figure 2.2, will be a list of servers from which R-based language can be downloaded. We advise downloading from servers that are in the country where the reader is located because of the chance of better download speed. Whichever the reader chooses, the downloaded language will be the same and by default it comes in English.

By clicking any of the links presented in Figure 2.2, the reader will be directed to a next page, as shown in Figure 2.3, in which he or she will need to point out the operating system used by the machine on which R is intended to run and the version of R-based language to be installed.

After that, the reader will choose the version of R-based language to download. At the time of editing this work, the most recent R version was 4.1.3, and we guarantee the functionality of the examples in this work for that version.

After downloading, the reader must install the downloaded application. Installation will take place as usual on the operating system used by the reader to install any other application. **We suggest that the installation defaults not be changed unless the reader knows exactly what he or she is doing.** For questions, just consult the R installation manual at https://cran.r-project.org/doc/manuals/r-release/R-admin.pdf.

After installation is done, it can be said that the reader's machine is already able to "speak" and "understand" R-based language. However, for a better conduct of the studies proposed by this work, we recommend installation of *RStudio* software.

[Home]

Download

CRAN 

R Project

About R
Logo
Contributors
What's New?
Reporting Bugs
Conferences
Search
Get Involved: Mailing Lists
Get Involved: Contributing
Developer Pages
R Blog

R Foundation

Foundation
Board
Members
Donors
Donate

Help With R

The R Project for Statistical Computing

Getting Started

R is a free software environment for statistical computing and graphics. It compiles and runs on a wide variety of UNIX platforms, Windows and MacOS. To **download R**, please choose your preferred CRAN mirror.

If you have questions about R like how to download and install the software, or what the license terms are, please read our answers to frequently asked questions before you send an email.

News

- **R version 4.2.0 (Vigorous Calisthenics) prerelease versions** will appear starting Tuesday 2022-03-22. Final release is scheduled for Friday 2022-04-22.
- **R version 4.1.3 (One Push-Up)** has been released on 2022-03-10.
- **R version 4.0.5 (Shake and Throw)** was released on 2021-03-31.
- Thanks to the organisers of useR! 2020 for a successful online conference. Recorded tutorials and talks from the conference are available on the R Consortium YouTube channel.
- You can support the R Foundation with a renewable subscription as a supporting member

News via Twitter

The R Foundation Retweeted

useR! 2022
@_useRconf
Registration for useR! 2022 is open! Before you sign up, please read through our tutorial offerings, since the form will ask you for your selections: user2022.r-project.org/program/tutori...

FIGURE 2.1 The home page of the R Project website.

CRAN Mirrors

The Comprehensive R Archive Network is available at the following URLs, please choose a location close to you. Some statistics on the status of the mirrors can be found here: main page, windows release, windows old release.

If you want to host a new mirror at your institution, please have a look at the CRAN Mirror HOWTO.

0-Cloud
- https://cloud.r-project.org/ — Automatic redirection to servers worldwide, currently sponsored by Rstudio

Argentina
- http://mirror.fcaglp.unlp.edu.ar/CRAN/ — Universidad Nacional de La Plata

Australia
- https://cran.csiro.au/ — CSIRO
- https://mirror.aarnet.edu.au/pub/CRAN/ — AARNET
- https://cran.ms.unimelb.edu.au/ — School of Mathematics and Statistics, University of Melbourne
- https://cran.curtin.edu.au/ — Curtin University

Austria
- https://cran.wu.ac.at/ — Wirtschaftsuniversität Wien

Belgium
- https://www.freestatistics.org/cran/ — Patrick Wessa
- https://ftp.belnet.be/mirror/CRAN/ — Belnet, the Belgian research and education network

Brazil
- https://cran-r.c3sl.ufpr.br/ — Universidade Federal do Parana
- https://cran.fiocruz.br/ — Oswaldo Cruz Foundation, Rio de Janeiro
- https://vps.fmvz.usp.br/CRAN/ — University of Sao Paulo, Sao Paulo
- https://brieger.esalq.usp.br/CRAN/ — University of Sao Paulo, Piracicaba

Bulgaria
- https://ftp.uni-sofia.bg/CRAN/ — Sofia University

FIGURE 2.2 Cut from the page with the list of servers from which R-based language can be downloaded.

The Comprehensive R Archive Network

Download and Install R

Precompiled binary distributions of the base system and contributed packages, **Windows and Mac** users most likely want one of these versions of R:

- Download R for Linux (Debian, Fedora/Redhat, Ubuntu)
- Download R for macOS
- Download R for Windows

R is part of many Linux distributions, you should check with your Linux package management system in addition to the link above.

Source Code for all Platforms

Windows and Mac users most likely want to download the precompiled binaries listed in the upper box, not the source code. The sources have to be compiled before you can use them. If you do not know what this means, you probably do not want to do it!

- The latest release (2021-11-01, Bird Hippie) R-4.1.2.tar.gz, read what's new in the latest version.
- Sources of R alpha and beta releases (daily snapshots, created only in time periods before a planned release).
- Daily snapshots of current patched and development versions are available here. Please read about new features and bug fixes before filing corresponding feature requests or bug reports.
- Source code of older versions of R is available here.
- Contributed extension packages

Questions About R

- If you have questions about R like how to download and install the software, or what the license terms are, please read our answers to frequently asked questions before you send an email.

FIGURE 2.3 Selection screen for choosing the machine's operating system.

Installing *RStudio*

RStudio is a free application that provides a friendly interface and with a greater power of control by the reader over everything that is happening while using R-based language. Nothing would prevent the reader from using only the application discussed earlier to continue reading, but we strongly recommend that *RStudio* be downloaded, installed, and used, especially for readers who are new to programming.

An important question would be, **Can I install only *RStudio* and disregard the previous instructions on the R Project website? The answer is no. It is imperative that the reader install the application discussed in earlier the "R-based language installation" section and then install *RStudio*.**

RStudio software can be downloaded from https://www.rstudio.com, as shown in Figure 2.4.

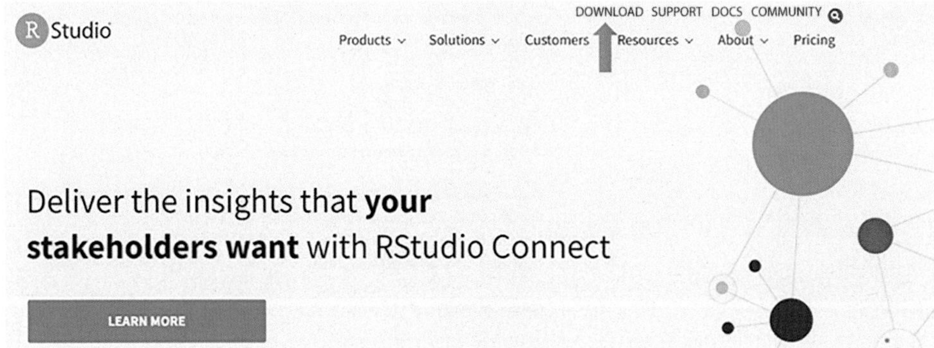

FIGURE 2.4 The *RStudio* website.

Following the arrow, purposely inserted in Figure 2.4, the reader must click on the *Download* option.

After that, a new screen will open that must be scrolled to the options present in Figure 2.5, where you must click on the *Download* button of the *RStudio Desktop* option.

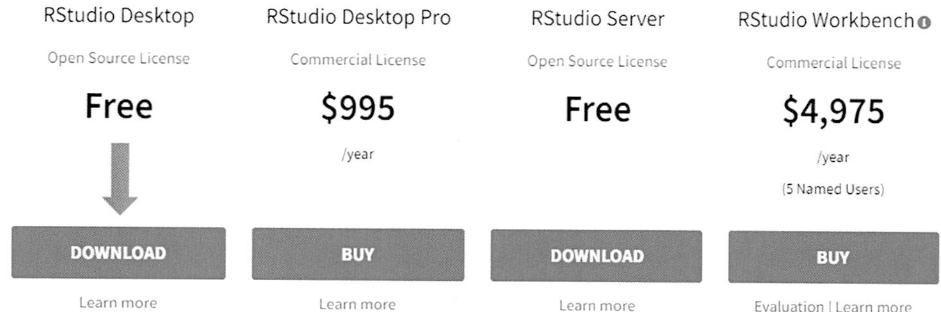

FIGURE 2.5 The RStudio website.

Finally, the reader will be taken to the screen presented in Figure 2.6, where he or she will have to choose the version of *RStudio* for the operating system present on his or her machine.

OS	Download	Size	SHA-256
Windows 10	RStudio-2021.09.1-372.exe	156.89 MB	1c3d27f5
macOS 10.14+	RStudio-2021.09.1-372.dmg	203.00 MB	daec6a40
Ubuntu 18/Debian 10	rstudio-2021.09.1-372-amd64.deb	117.89 MB	921b4f23
Fedora 19/Red Hat 7	rstudio-2021.09.1-372-x86_64.rpm	133.83 MB	f1be5848
Fedora 28/Red Hat 8	rstudio-2021.09.1-372-x86_64.rpm	133.85 MB	ba36870d
Debian 9	rstudio-2021.09.1-372-amd64.deb	118.10 MB	637cd465
OpenSUSE 15	rstudio-2021.09.1-372-x86_64.rpm	119.78 MB	678d020e

FIGURE 2.6 Clipping from the *RStudio* website; continuity of procedures for downloading *RStudio* software.

The download will start, and the installation will be performed as usual for any application on the reader's operating system. **We strongly recommend that none of the settings on the installation screens be changed.**

After the installation is complete, the *RStudio* software can be opened. Figure 2.7 presents its home screen.

Before we start presenting the application, it is very important that the reader click *File* > *New File* > *R Script*. Thus the *RStudio* interface will be similar to the one shown in Figure 2.8.

We emphasize that this work is not about teaching programming, but about teaching machine learning techniques using a type of programming language. Thus we will present the main points of interest of the work in the interface presented by Figure 2.8, without the intention of exhausting all capabilities of *RStudio*.

For didactic purposes, we propose that the reader understand *RStudio* subdivided into four screens called A, B, C, and D, as shown in Figure 2.9.

In Figure 2.9, Screen A refers to the *Script Editor;* Screen B concerns the *Console;* Screen C presents the *Environment, History, Connections,* and *Tutorial* tabs; and Screen D comprises the *Files, Plots, Packages, Help,* and *Viewer* tabs.

The Script Editor

In the Script Editor, readers will be able to write as many codes as they want, activate them at the time and in the desired order, add comments to them, and save and share them with whomever and in the way they want.

However, it is necessary to keep in mind that, in the case of Screen A (the window reserved for the *Script Editor*), the *Enter* key will only cause a change of lines. When you try to type, for example, `2+2` and press *Enter*, nothing interesting will happen; the big occurrence will be the cursor line change. That's all.

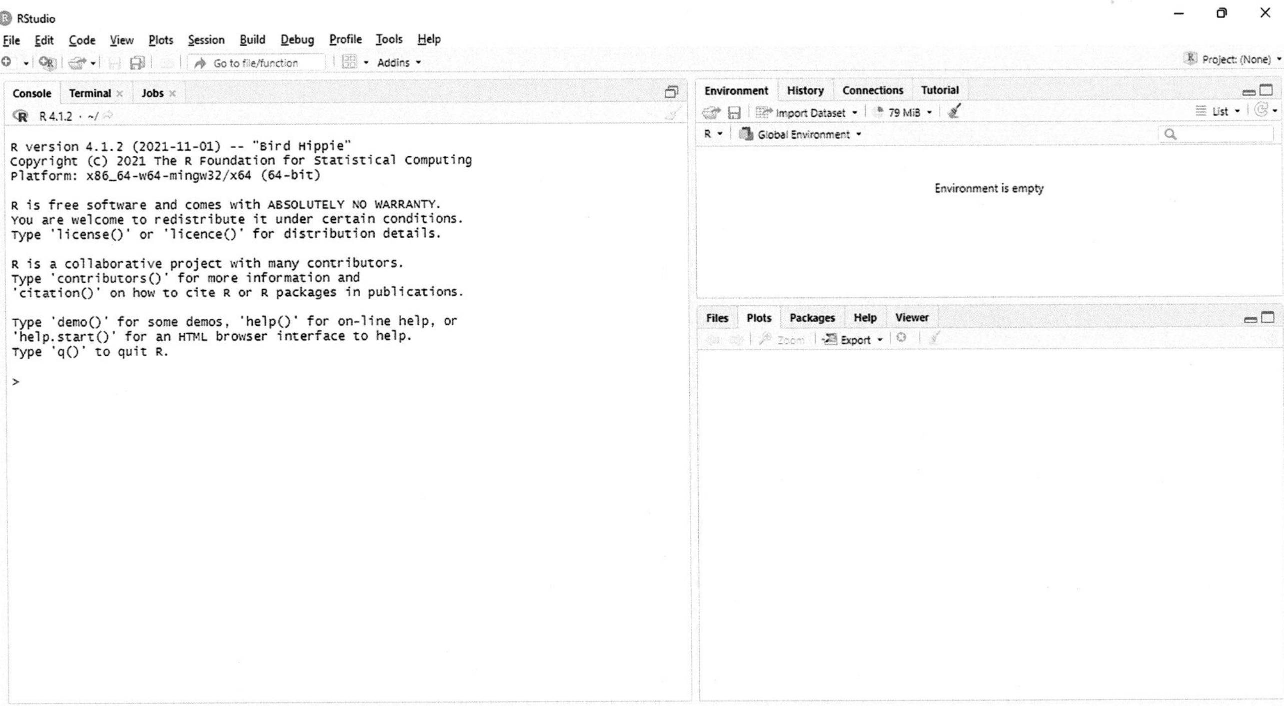

FIGURE 2.7 The RStudio software.

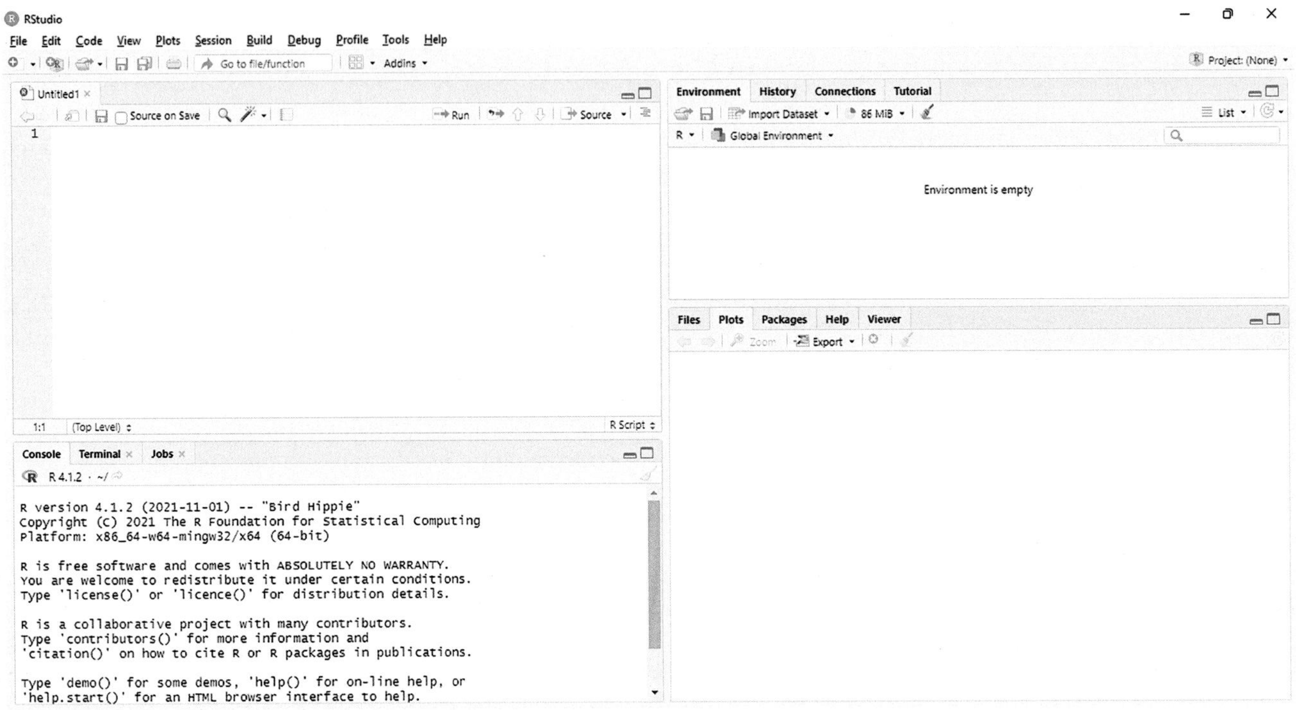

FIGURE 2.8 The *RStudio* interface that will be used throughout this work.

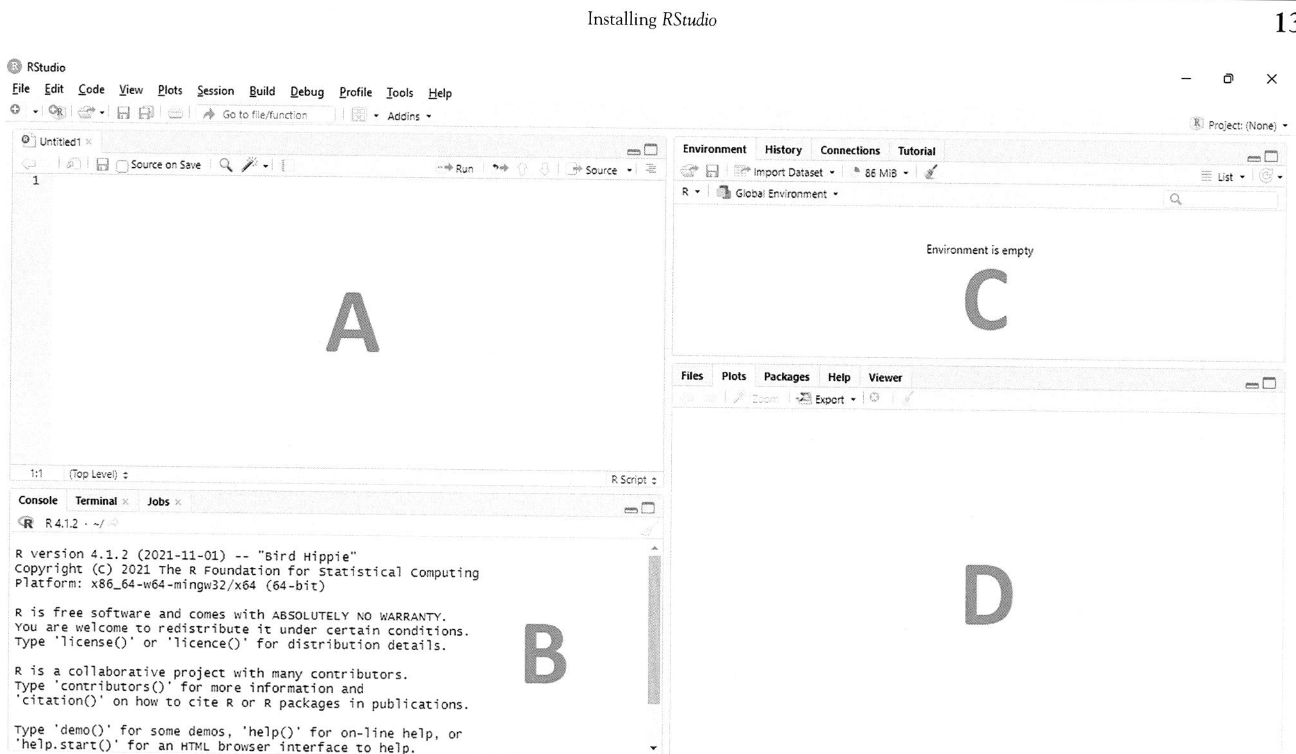

FIGURE 2.9 The *RStudio* software panels that will be used throughout this work.

Now try to return the cursor to the line where you typed `2+2` and press, together, the keys *Ctrl+Enter* (for *Windows* and *Linux* machines) or *Command+Enter* (for Apple machines). R will return the result 4 in the lower- left panel (Screen B). Did you notice one of the advantages of the *Script Editor?* You could have written code with several lines, for example, and if there was an error, it would just be corrected directly in the *Script Editor,* without having to type everything again. The command `2+2` is still there, and if the reader wants to replace one of the numbers (simulating a code correction), and press *Ctrl+Enter* or *Command+Enter,* a new result will appear.

The *Scripts Editor* even allows comments to be added to your code using the operator `#`. The operator `#` will tell R that, on that line, starting from the symbol `#`, all writing does not concern computer code and therefore should be ignored by the machine. The operator `#` therefore allows you to add comments to written routines, and this is a facilitator for the reader who will review the code at a later time after writing it and/or for a third party who will analyze the code in order to understand what was done, give suggestions, correct any errors, and/or replicate the research. Figure 2.10 demonstrates the operation of the operator `#`.

In Figure 2.10, when you command `2+2 #This is a sum` in the *Script Editor,* the result will still be 4 because the operator `#` told R to ignore everything else that came after that symbol on that line. A curious reader could edit the script and remove the operator `#`. In this case, R-based language would show an error because the words *This, is, a,* and *sum,* a priori, do not make sense for R-based language.

If the reader accidentally closes *RStudio,* no problem. When the application is opened again, it is normal that the previously opened scripts will continue there with the information assigned to them. **However, we always recommend saving information using the button located at the top of the *Script Editor.***

It is also interesting to note that some commands presented in this work will be long and will take some processing time. So if the reader wants to cancel the command, for some reason, he or she can just press the *Ctrl+C* or *Command+C* keys. By the way, if the reader wants access to the main keyboard shortcuts for commands in *RStudio,* he or she can just click *Help > Cheat Sheets > RStudio IDE Cheat Sheet.*

The console

Screen B, which is presented in Figure 2.9, is the *R Console.* It actually represents R-based language. The reader can type any valid command and simply press the *Enter* key to obtain the result. However, as the reader will notice, Screen B does not allow us to save or edit our commands or to facilitate revisiting of the given commands. We will

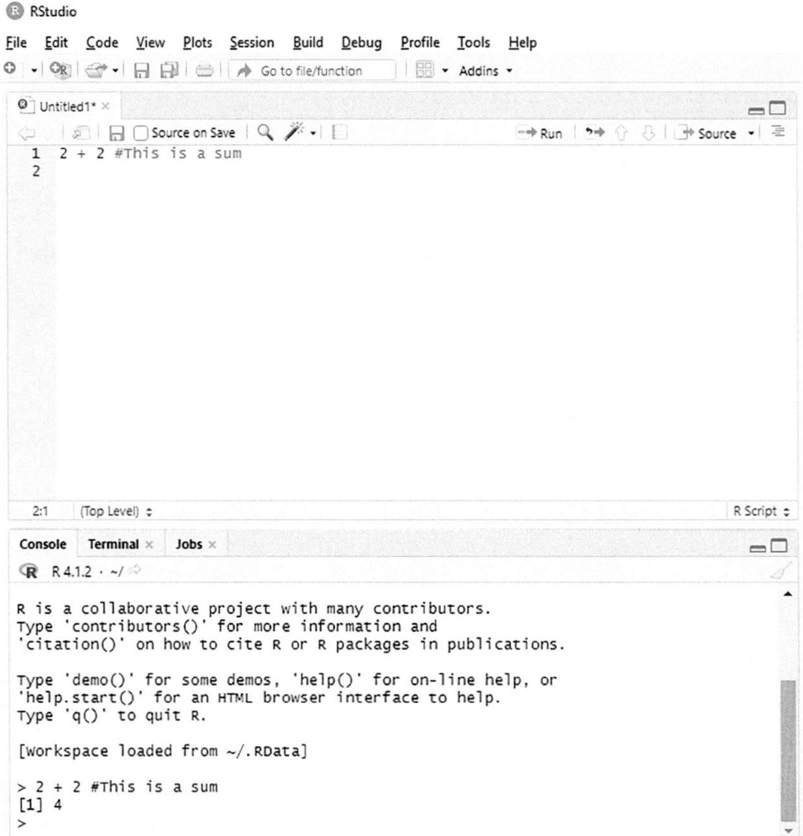

FIGURE 2.10 The operator #.

use Screen B as an output viewer. For the purposes of this work, with the exception of graphs and Help queries, all R results will be returned via the console. **It also strongly urges the reader to type the codes only in the *Script Editor* given the ease of editing, revisiting, and saving the codes.**

The *Environment*, *History*, *Connections*, and *Tutorial* tabs

Screen C, which comprises the *Environment* tab, contains the objects created by the reader, which we will discuss in the "Objects" section later in this chapter.

The *History* tab, on the other hand, contains a history of the commands performed by the reader. The *Connections* tab shows possible connections between the reader's machine and other computers. Finally, the *Tutorial* tab presents tutorials about some R-based language packages, which we will discuss in the "Packages" section later in this chapter.

For the purposes of this work, we will pay more attention to the *Environment* tab.

The *Files*, *Plots*, *Packages*, *Help*, and *Viewer* tabs

The *Files*, *Plots*, *Packages*, *Help*, and *Viewer* tabs are present on Screen D, as shown in Figure 2.9.

An attentive reader will notice that the *Files* tab allows us to browse the folders and files on our own computer. The *Plots* tab (still blank), will return the visualization of the two-dimensional graphics proposed by this work, which can be exported, if the reader wishes, to other software in different formats, including *.pdf, *.png, *.jpeg, *.bmp, and so on.

The *Packages* tab contains the R packages (discussed in the "Packages" section) installed on the reader's machine, allowing the reader to check which ones were loaded, for example. As a rule, we will do all of this with the use of codes.

The *Help* tab is a kind of library that contains help files about the features of R-based language commands. The help files come in English and, as a rule, will be enough for the reader to complement the readings about some features that we will learn. However, the reader may not be satisfied with the internal explanations of R. In this case, we inform that the community of R users is immense, and it is enough to use search portals to research the possible mishaps faced by the reader.

Finally, the *Viewer* tab, for this work, will present the visualization of three-dimensional graphics and some textual outputs more elegantly than those presented in the *Console* (Screen B).

Objects

R-based language is an object-oriented language, and this information generates somewhat complex definitions and concepts from computer science. For beginners in R-based language, we propose that you imagine an object in R-based language as a kind of box, in an organized way.

An object in R-based language can store everything that can be loaded or created with R-based language. In this way, a dataset can be stored in an object; a graph can be contained in an object, an algorithm can be placed inside an object, and so on. Therefore we will conclude that in R everything is an object.

So, let's create our first "box," that is, our first object in R-based language. To create objects in R, we must use the assignment operator, consisting of the less than and minus sign, together, without spaces: <-:

```
my_first_object <- 20
```

By doing this in the *Script Editor* and pressing the *Ctrl+Enter* or *Command+Enter* keys, the reader will notice that the *Console* will not return any information, but an attentive reader will see that something new has appeared in the *Environment* tab, as shown in Figure 2.11.

FIGURE 2.11 The presence of the object `my_first_object` in the *Environment* tab.

What we commanded in R, in terms of Figure 2.11, was to store the metric value 20 in a "box" that, with the use of the assignment operator `<-`, we assign the name `my_first_object`. So the result is our first object created.

A curious reader could retype `my_first_object` in the *Script Editor*, press *Ctrl+Enter* or *Command+Enter*, and verify that R will return the contents of this object (i.e., the value 20).

```
my_first_object
```

We can also say that the object `my_first_object` at this point contains an atomic vector. Vectors are one-dimensional structures, therefore of size $n \times 1$, where n points to the number of observations; atomic vectors are vectors that contain only one piece of data, such as the result object, that is, of size 1×1.

R objects are not intended to store only vectors. They can contain two-dimensional information, such as arrays and data frames. They can also, for example, contain lists, objects that can have multiple dimensions.

And what would happen if we commanded the following code?

```
my_first_object + 12
```

Yes! The result will be the value 32. And we can use other mathematical operators next to our object because it stores a metric value inside it. For example:

```
my_first_object * 3
```

For the previous declaration, R will return the value 60. The operator *, for metric values, proposes a multiplication.

Table 2.1 presents the most basic mathematical operators of R-based language that can be freely tested by the reader.

TABLE 2.1 Some mathematical operators in R-based language.

Mathematical operator	Common meaning	Example of use	Result
+	Addition	2 + 2	4
-	Subtraction	5 - 2	3
*	Multiplication	7 * 4	28
/	Division	1 / 2	0.5
^	Exponentiation	3 ^ 2	9

The second column of Table 2.1 is called *Common Meaning* because in R-based language, some operators mentioned can assume other functions, similar to homonymous words in a given language. For example, the operator - can assume the negation function, or the operator + can assume the function of the conjunction *and*.

If the intention is to store textual values, we must use quotation marks. It does not matter if they are single quotes or double quotes. What matters is that if the beginning of the declaration is with single quotes, the end must also be with single quotes; the same goes for the double quotes:

```
text_object <- "science"
```

Note that a new object called `text_object` has been added in the *Environment* tab. If the reader declares `text_object` to R, it will receive the stored textual value.

```
text_object
```

Note, however, that in R-based language it makes no sense to use the mathematical operators mentioned in Table 2.1 to, for example, try to multiply the object `text_object` by some value because it is a string.

In R-based language, it is also possible to create objects containing logical values, such as `TRUE` or `FALSE`:

```
logical_object <- TRUE
```

We just created a new object called `logical_object`. It contains the logical value `TRUE`, and the reader can see this by commanding the following:

```
logical_object
```

We ask the reader to be aware that the logical value `TRUE` has been declared in all capital letters. If the reader wants to save the logical value `FALSE`, he or she should also do so with all capital letters. One way to obtain similar results is to abbreviate the value `TRUE` with the capital letter `T`. Something similar goes for the value `FALSE`, but with the letter `F`, capitalized:

```
logical_object <- T
```

An attentive reader will notice that until now, we have created atomic vectors—objects with a single element. **However, how should we proceed to create objects with more than one element?**

For this, first of all, we will need to talk about a special type of object in R-based language: functions.

Functions and arguments

In R, so-called *functions* are equivalent to verbs that indicate an action; an order. Therefore they are algorithms. In other words, they are predefined objects that contain explicit, literal, limited, and systemic sequences of instructions and operations aimed at achieving a predefined objective.

Complex? Let's imagine that we want to round off a certain number. For this, we must use the function `round()`:

```
round(x = 3.141592)
```

Note that the value returned by the console was 3. Possible questions may be: (1) **How should I know that I was facing a function?** and (2) **How was rounding possible?**

First, as a rule, we will be facing a function when, right after its name (`round`, in this case) there are parentheses, that is, `round()`. That said, we can answer the second question. Inside the object `round` there are predefined instructions about rounding numbers. Therefore, the function `round()` is born.

At this moment, what will go inside the parentheses of the function `round()` will be called an *argument*, which will undergo numerical rounding. Therefore it is not enough to just command `round()` to R:

```
round()
```

Note that R returned the error `Error: 0 arguments passed to 'round' which requires 1 or 2 arguments`. In other words, R needs to know what will be rounded explicitly.

Another question could be, **What if I wanted to round to 3 decimal places?**

Well, for that we would need to declare a second argument:

```
round(x = 3.141592, digits = 3)
```

R will return the value of 3142 to the reader. Note that R works with statistical rounding, that is, whenever, there is a numeral greater than or equal to 5 after the decimal separator, the number before it will be rounded to the next subsequent one; when less than 5, the previous value will be maintained. Thus if we command `round(8.5)`, we will get the return 9; however, if we command `round(8.4)`, we will return the number 8. Here, a new question may also arise: **How will I know which arguments a function has?**

Functions have the most varied types of arguments, and at this point, the *Help* tab (discussed earlier in *"The Files, Plots, Packages, Help, and Viewer Tabs"*) is providential. When we do not know which arguments can be applied to a given function, we can type the operator `?` before the function name without parentheses and then press *Ctrl + Enter* or *Command + Enter*, as follows:

```
?round
```

The reader may have noticed that the *Help* tab was automatically highlighted, and in it there is usually a brief explanation about the function, its arguments, its possible applications, and some usage examples. Figure 2.12 demonstrates the *Help* tab, emphasizing the arguments of the function `round()`.

That said, we can go back to the question in the "Objects" section: **How should we proceed to create objects with more than one element?**

This task must be done using the concatenate function: `c()`. Therefore we propose the use of an object that contains the values 1, 7, 12, 30, 51, and 8:

```
my_first_object <- c(1, 7, 12, 30, 51, 8)
```

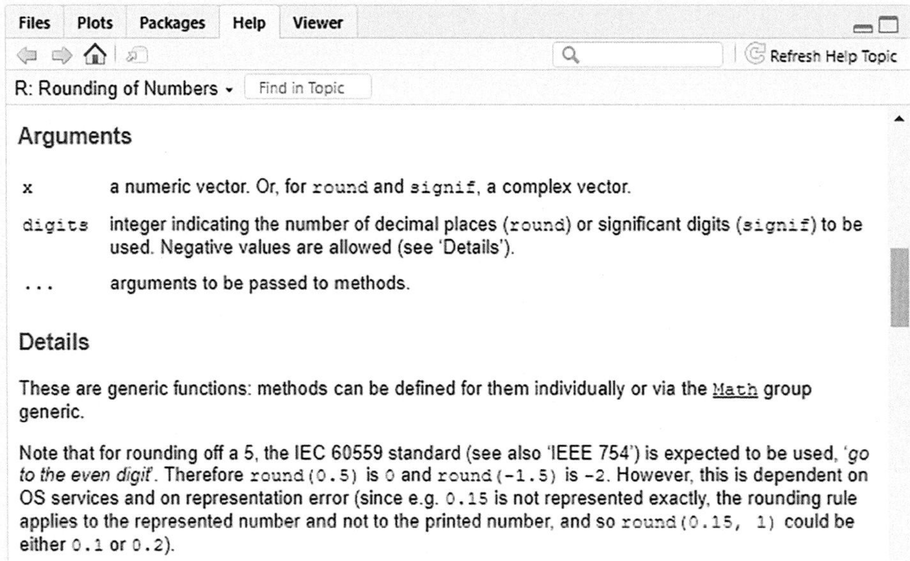

FIGURE 2.12 Example of using help functions of R-based language.

Notice that we told R to save the values 1, 7, 12, 30, 51, and 8 in the object `my_first_object`. We ask that the reader redeclare `my_first_object` to R:

```
my_first_object
```

R will respond with the values that were assigned to it, that is, `1, 7, 12, 30, 51,` and `8`. Also note that in the *Environment* tab the old value `20` for our object `my_first_object` was immediately replaced, without **any prior notice to the reader.** Thus we emphasize the care in creating homonymous objects. **We would also like to advise the reader to avoid creating objects that have capital letters because R is case-sensitive, which eventually can cause typing problems and even non-conformity of expected results for novice readers.** Furthermore, as Grolemund (2014) discusses, you cannot create objects whose naming starts with a number, nor can you name them using special characters such as !, ~, $, @, +, −, /, *.

Packages

The R-based language that we helped the reader install only has the so-called *base language* at this moment. The term *base language* is not exactly the best nomenclature for most purists. However, throughout this work, we will use the term to refer to functions that are already preinstalled in R-based language.

That said, what we call *base language* brings together a large number of functions, but they are not all we will need to work with the machine learning techniques of this work. Right now, there are a multitude of researchers developing new features for R in the most diverse fields of knowledge. Once these new features are tested and verified, they will be made available to the general public in the form of packages. From then on, we will be able to download these packages so our machines acquire new capabilities within R-based language.

Throughout this work, we will use the package `tidyverse`, which is extremely useful in handling, processing, and visualizing data. The installation of packages is done using the function `install.packages()`. The main—and often the only—argument of this function must be the name of the package to be installed, enclosed in quotes, respecting uppercase and lowercase letters. That said, to install the package `tidyverse`, we must command `install.packages("tidyverse")`.

Installation time will vary depending on the reader's Internet connection speed. After installation, it is imperative to say that the machine is not yet able to use the functions present in the downloaded package. It is necessary that this package be "called", that is, you tell the machine that you want to use it, and this is done by commanding the function `library()`. Thus to inform the computer that we want to use the features of the package `tidyverse`, we must command `library(tidyverse)`.

Two things still need to be said. The first is that when using the functions `install.packages()` and `library()`, it is common for the computer to display messages on the console. Therefore it is very important that the operator pays attention to these reports that may even contain an explanation of why, eventually, the machine has refused to install or call a package. The second thing to say is that every time the R or RStudio application is closed, you must command the package you want to use with the function `library()`. The package will forever remain installed, but it will not necessarily continue to be active.

Loading datasets

R has the ability to open datasets of the most different statistical analysis software available on the market. For example, to open a dataset saved in the *Stata, IBM SPSS,* or *SAS* software formats, you can use the package `haven`; for datasets in *.xls or *.xlsx format, typical of *Microsoft Excel,* the package `readxl` can be used. If the reader needs a dataset available only for a type of software not mentioned earlier, just seek help in some R language community with the help of Google. No doubt the reader will find the desired package!

Before we demonstrate how to open a dataset, we inform you that it is convenient and desirable for the reader to define a directory on his or her machine that will contain the dataset to be used. During the entire work, we will consider that the chosen directory will be called *book* and will be present directly on the hard disk of the reader's computer. If the reader wants to define another location, there will be no problem. First, we advise the reader to see which directory R is currently working in using the function `getwd()`, without the presence of any arguments.

```
getwd()
```

Figure 2.13 shows the execution of the function, assuming that the directory that R uses at this moment is the "Documents" folder present directly on the operator's hard disk.

```
[1] "C:/Documents"
```

FIGURE 2.13 The function `getwd()`.

The result shown in Figure 2.13 may seem natural for users of *Linux* distributions, but it can be quite counterintuitive, especially for beginning users of *Microsoft Windows.* By default, *Windows* indicates its directories with a backslash "\"; note that the forward slash returned by R is distinct from "/". Regardless of the reader's operating system, during commands in R-based language, spelling must be respected. So to change from the directory where we are (supposedly "Documents") to the proposed directory "data", we must use the slash "/", using the function `setwd()`, indicating as an argument the location we want to work, between quotes, as follows:

```
setwd("C:/book")
```

The directory change, if successful, can be verified with the function `getwd()`, as shown in Figure 2.14.

```
[1] "C:/book"
```

FIGURE 2.14 Verifying the working directory change.

In Figure 2.14, we command R to start working in the folder called "book", and "C:" would be the reader's hard disk. After that, we run the function `getwd()` once again to make sure that everything went as expected. **For the use of this work, it will be up to the reader to indicate the directory from which R should work. So if there is a subfolder called "chapter02" where the Chapter 02 study materials will be, the reader should set the directory to, for example, `setwd("C:/book/chapter02")`.**

Assuming that the reader has downloaded the datasets that will be used throughout this work and placed them in the directory defined by the instructions given, we will open the dataset `introduction.csv`.

In *RStudio*, there are two ways to import a dataset: using the mouse or writing a computational routine, that is, a code. We will cover both ways, starting with the use of the mouse.

Loading a dataset using the mouse

First, for the sake of organization, we ask the reader to clear the *Environment* tab using the button, which can be found on the *Environment* tab. Figure 2.15 shows what happens when we make a single click on the mentioned button.

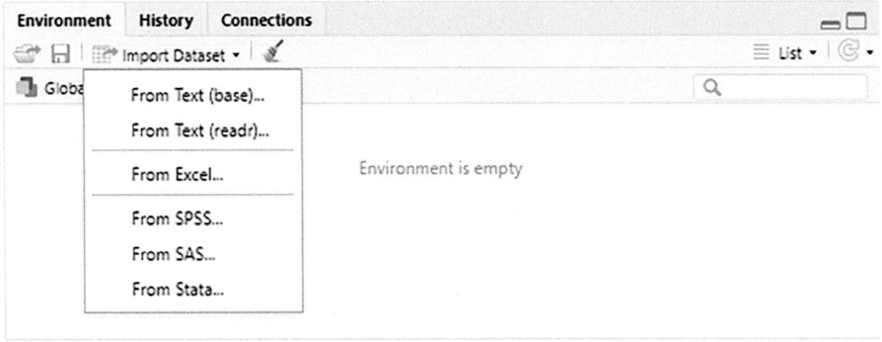

FIGURE 2.15 Importing datasets into *RStudio*.

The menu opened in Figure 2.15, by clicking the Import Dataset button, shows some possibilities for importing datasets with different extensions and software. The *From Text (base)* option is commonly used when the dataset to be imported is available in the *.txt extension. In the case of datasets available in the *.csv extension, we must click on the From Text (readr) option. Finally, to import data in the formats used by default by *Microsoft Excel, IBM SPSS, SAS,* and *Stata,* the other options in the menu shown in Figure 2.15 must be used.

Figure 2.16 shows the screen that opens when we click *From Text (readr).*

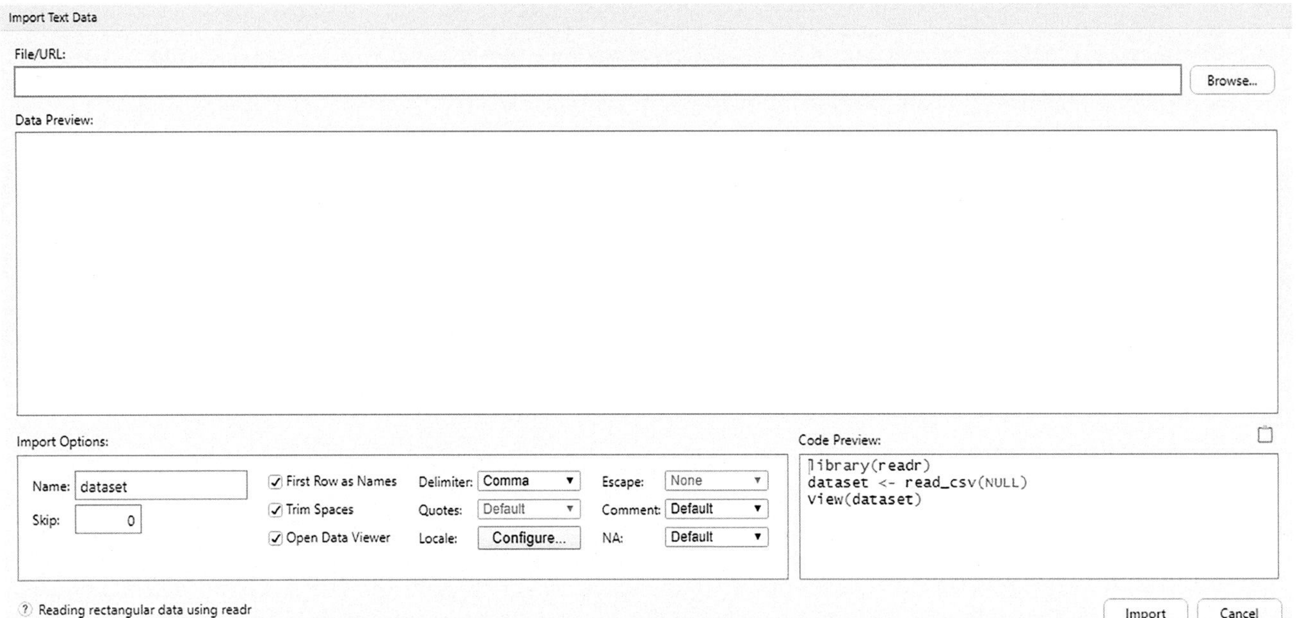

FIGURE 2.16 The *RStudio* imports panel for datasets in *.csv format.

Using the *Browse* button, we must navigate to the dataset `introduction.csv` and select it. If the reader followed the instructions at the beginning of the "Loading datasets" section, the file we are looking for will be seen immediately.

Figure 2.17 shows the changes that occurred in the screen shown in Figure 2.16 when we selected the dataset `introduction.csv`.

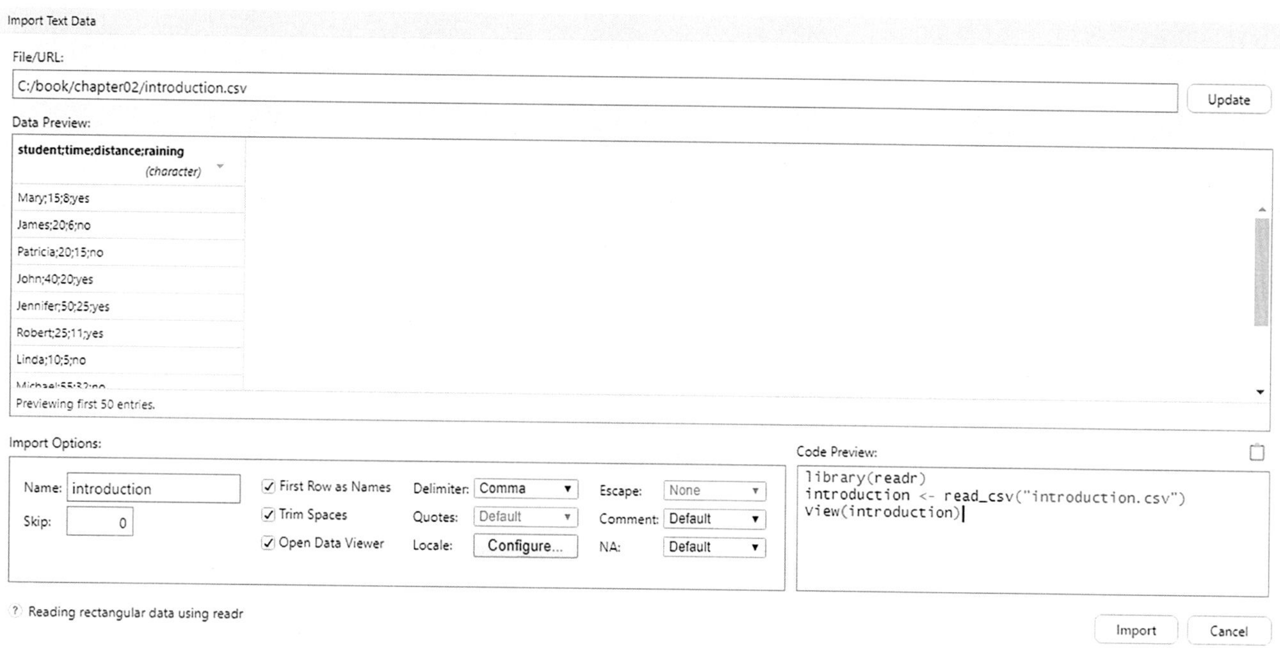

FIGURE 2.17 Initial instructions for importing the dataset `introduction.csv`.

In the case of Figure 2.17, we can see that for this csv file, what delimits the columns is the character ";". Thus we must click on the scroll box of the "Delimiter" option, and select the *Semicolon* option and then click on the *Import* button.

At that moment, the *Environment* tab will contain a new object called `introduction`, as shown in Figure 2.18.

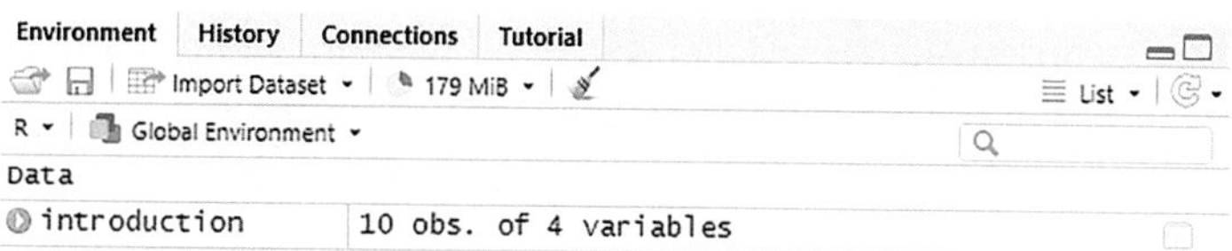

FIGURE 2.18 Initial instructions for importing the dataset `introduction.csv`.

In Figure 2.18, if the reader clicks on the ◎ button, it will automatically change to ◎, and some information, attributes, and values present in the introduction object will be displayed, as shown in Figure 2.19.

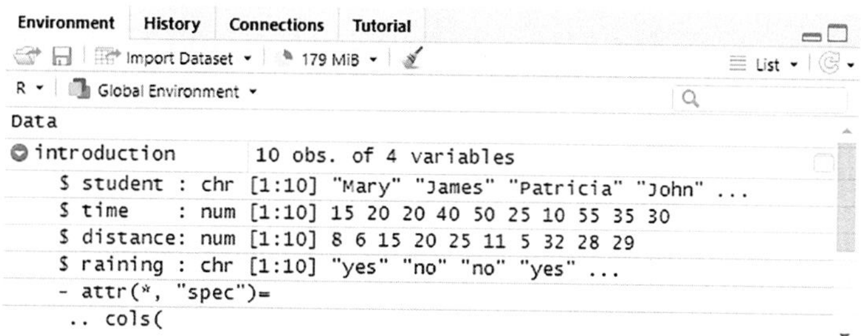

FIGURE 2.19 The usefulness of the ◎ button.

That said, we will present the procedures for importing the same dataset `introduction.csv` using only codes.

Loading a dataset using codes

To open the dataset `introduction.csv`, just use the routine present in the *Code Preview* field in Figure 2.17. However, initially we ask the reader to command `rm(introduction)`, removing the object created by the instructions in the "Loading a dataset using the mouse" section, so we can more precisely demonstrate the use of codes for importing datasets in R-based language. So first:

```
rm(introduction)
```

Then we will call the package `readr`, as it contains the function `read_csv()` that we will use to load the dataset. **If the version of R used by the reader accuses the inexistence of a package called *readr*, we ask that the "Packages" section be revised.**

```
library(readr)
```

Then:

```
introduction <- read_delim(file = "introduction.csv",
                           delim = ";",
                           escape_double = FALSE,
                           trim_ws = TRUE)
```

In the previous routine, there was creation of an object called `introduction`, and we know this because the name given to our object is to the left of the assignment operator `<-`. The function used to open the dataset is `read_delim ()`, whose arguments in this case were: `file` to determine the name of the file to be loaded; `delim` to point out which delimiter is used by the studied csv file; `escape_double` to indicate whether we should ignore the presence of quotes inside quotes; and, finally, `trim_ws` to determine whether we want to remove any excess spacing in the dataset.

At that moment, in the *Environment* tab, the object `introduction` has already appeared. To view its content, we can use the function `View()`, paying attention to the first capital letter, by commanding `View(introduction)`.

Sometimes we will suggest avoiding the use of the function `View()`, especially in the presence of large and therefore computationally demanding datasets. We suggest using the function `head()` instead. The function `head()` allows the reader to visualize the first observations in the dataset. He or she can just command:

```
head(introduction)
```

When we command `head(introduction)`, R returns the outcomes shown in Figure 2.20. In it, we have a brief, however more than necessary view of the dataset present in the object `introduction`. We can visualize the name and values present in the first six observations. The tags *<chr>* and *<dbl>* refer to the class of imported variables and are, respectively, abbreviations for character and doubles.

```
  student    time distance raining
  <chr>     <dbl>    <dbl> <chr>
1 Mary         15        8 yes
2 James        20        6 no
3 Patricia     20       15 no
4 John         40       20 yes
5 Jennifer     50       25 yes
6 Robert       25       11 yes
```

FIGURE 2.20 The use of the function `head()`.

Opening datasets present in R-based language

Yes, R-based language, as well as most of its packages, brings together datasets. The idea of using these datasets is aimed at training the R user in the treatment, manipulation, modeling, and plotting of data.

A dataset present in the base language is called `mtcars`. To access it, the reader only needs to declare his or her name; if you want to save it in an object, just use the function `data()`, as follows:

```
data(mtcars)
```

The base language of R, by itself, already brings an interesting amount of datasets that readers can use to improve their knowledge of programming and machine learning. The command `help(package = "datasets")` contains some datasets that can be commanded by the reader with the aid of the function `data()`.

Brief notion of data manipulation

In order to introduce the reader to introductory knowledge about data manipulation, we propose that the reader use the dataset `mtcars` that we have just loaded. Initially, we propose a quick visualization of the data with the function `head()`:

```
head(mtcars)
```

Figure 2.21 presents the proposed view of the object `mtcars`.

```
                   mpg cyl disp  hp drat    wt  qsec vs am gear carb
Mazda RX4         21.0   6  160 110 3.90 2.620 16.46  0  1    4    4
Mazda RX4 Wag     21.0   6  160 110 3.90 2.875 17.02  0  1    4    4
Datsun 710        22.8   4  108  93 3.85 2.320 18.61  1  1    4    1
Hornet 4 Drive    21.4   6  258 110 3.08 3.215 19.44  1  0    3    1
Hornet Sportabout 18.7   8  360 175 3.15 3.440 17.02  0  0    3    2
Valiant           18.1   6  225 105 2.76 3.460 20.22  1  0    3    1
```

FIGURE 2.21 The object `mtcars`.

A curious reader, when applying the function `class()` to our object `mtcars`, would receive the result *data frame* as a response from R. The data frames will be the kind of two-dimensional object that we will work with most of the time throughout this work. We prefer them over matrix objects because of their ease of data manipulation, even though we are forced to recognize that they demand greater computational power.

Our object `mtcars`, sized 32 × 11, concerns information about different vehicle models taken from a 1974 issue of *Motor Trend US* magazine. A curious reader can verify this information as well as the meaning of our dataset variables by commanding `?mtcars`.

That said, we thought it would be interesting to introduce the functionality of the operator `$` when handling data frames. The operator `$` allows us to individually access the variables present in a given data frame. A curious reader may have already noticed that it is no use to simply command the name of a variable from the dataset directly to R. In this way, if we wanted, for example, to access only the variable *mpg* present in the dataset contained by the object `mtcars`, it would suffice that we command `mtcars$mpg`. We recognize, however, that this type of approach using the operator `$` can sometimes be tedious and tiresome. Therefore we present the function `attach()`.

The function `attach()` reduces the hassle of having to constantly type the name of the object that contains the dataset, plus the operator `$`, finally adding the variable name. That said, after commanding `attach(mtcars)`, we can simply command directly the name of any variable present in our dataset, for example, `mpg`:

```
attach(mtcars)
```

Then:

```
mpg
```

Still using the dataset `mtcars`, we propose to the reader to demonstrate how we would visualize the values observed in the fifth line of the fourth column. We know that the dataset used is small, but imagine the difficulty in doing this when working with datasets with thousands or millions of rows.

The first information needed is that R understands the positioning of data in objects that contain datasets, indicating first the row and then the column. Therefore to know the value of the constant observation in $\mathtt{mtcars}_{5\times4}$, that is, in the dataset `mtcars`, in its 5th row and 4th column, we must use the operator `[,]`.

To use the operator[,], the first thing to do is to indicate the name of the object that contains the dataset to then inform the row and column that you want to access, separated by a comma:

```
mtcars[5,4]
```

R's response to the previous command will be 175.

In fact, when viewing the dataset mtcars, the constant value in the fifth row and fourth column is 175, present in the variable *hp*. If the reader only wants the values present in the third line, considering all the columns, he or she can just command mtcars[3,]. In this case, omission of the column coordinates leads the machine to understand that it wants to consider all of them:

```
mtcars[3,]
```

Figure 2.22 shows the outcome of the previous command.

```
            mpg cyl disp hp drat    wt  qsec vs am gear carb
Datsun 710 22.8   4  108 93 3.85 2.32 18.61  1  1    4    1
```

FIGURE 2.22 The object mtcars.

Similarly, we could proceed by highlighting only the sixth column, commanding mtcars[,6]:

```
mtcars[,6]
```

We propose the following exercise for the reader: Using the knowledge acquired so far, try to create a new dataset called new_mtcars that contains lines 1, 2, 3, 4, 7, and 10 and columns 1, 4, and 5 from the cars dataset. The answer can be obtained by the following command:

```
new_mtcars <- mtcars[c(1,2,3,4,7,10), c(1,4,5)]
```

Using the function head() for a short view on the created object new_mtcars will confirm the proposed solution.

Note that we created a new object, using the operator <-, called new_mtcars. After that, we tell R that the content of the object new_mtcars should be lines 1, 2, 3, 4, 7, and 10 and columns 1, 4, and 5 of the object cars. The function c() was used because we selected more than one thing; the one to the left of the operator [,] concerns the lines, and the one to the right of the operator [,] concerns the columns. Finally, the command head(new_mtcars) showed us the new created dataset of size 6 rows by 3 columns. There are even more far-fetched ways to do the same things. Without intending to exhaust the subject, we could also achieve the proposed commanding:

```
new_mtcars <- mtcars[c(1:4,7,10), c(1, 4:5)]
```

Comparing the commands used to establish the object new_mtcars, the big difference is the use of the operator :, which indicates to R the existence of a sequence. So, instead of telling R that we want lines 1, 2, 3, 4, 7, and 10, we indicate that we want the sequence of lines 1 to 4 and also lines 7 and 10. The same was done for columns, using the operator : in 4:5.

We also want to give the reader a practical way to exclude columns (variables) from datasets, if desired. In this case, the function rm() will not work because the variables present in the datasets will not be directly exposed in the *Environment* tab. Thus it will be useless, for example, to command rm(new_mtcars$drat) if you want to exclude the variable *drat*, present in the object new_mtcars.

On the other hand, what must be done to exclude a variable is to assign it the value NULL, in uppercase. So, to delete the drat variable from the dataset new_mtcars, we must command the following:

```
new_mtcars$drat <- NULL
```

The command will delete all observations for the variable *drat*, leaving the other columns unchanged. We can confirm the statement with the use of the function `head()`.

We also took the opportunity to introduce the function `write.csv()`, which will allow the reader to save the modified datasets in a new file in *.csv format, directly in the user-defined directory, as discussed at the beginning of the "Loading datasets" section.

So if we want to save the contents of the object `new_mtcars` in a *.csv file, we must command:

```
write.csv(x = new_mtcars,
          file = "new_mtcars.csv",
          row.names = FALSE)
```

In the previous command, as the first argument of the function `write.csv()`, we must indicate the object that contains the dataset that we want to save; next, the file argument must indicate, in quotes, the name we want to assign to this new file followed by the *.csv extension; finally, the argument `row.names = F` (ou `row.names = FALSE`) prevents a new column from being created in the file containing the row names. That said, to reopen the saved file, the reader must use the knowledge acquired in the "Loading a dataset using the mouse" and/or "Loading a dataset using codes" section. There is also the option of saving objects created in R with the *.RData extension. For that, we must command:

```
save(new_mtcars, file = "new_mtcars.RData")
```

To load what was saved in the file `new_cars.RData`, just command:

```
load(file = "new_mtcars.RData")
```

The reader will find most of the book's datasets in *.RData format.

Final remarks

The objective of this chapter was to familiarize the reader with the computational language R, its installation, the presentation of introductory constructions about its syntax, demonstration of its object-oriented behavior, and the purpose of using functions and arguments.

We also introduce the reader to the meaning and necessity of what R-based language understands by packages, as well as ways to load, manipulate, and save datasets.

Next, in Chapter 3, the last introductory section of this book, the reader will be introduced to types of variables along with measurement and accuracy scales.

Supplementary data sets

`new_cars.RData`

Please access supplementary data files here: https://doi.org/10.17632/55623jkwrp.3

PART II

Applied statistics and data visualization

CHAPTER

3

Types of variables, measurement scales, and accuracy scales*

AT THE END OF THIS CHAPTER, YOU WILL BE ABLE TO:

- Understand the types of variables and their scales of measurement for the preparation of research and for the treatment and analysis of data
- Establish differences between metric (quantitative) and nonmetric (qualitative) variables
- Identify the circumstances in which each type of variable should be used, depending on the research objectives
- Use the appropriate statistical treatment for each type of variable

Introduction

A variable is a characteristic of the population (or sample) being studied, and it is possible to measure, count, and categorize it.

The type of variable collected is crucial in the calculation of descriptive statistics and the graphical representation of results as well as in the selection of the statistical methods that will be used to analyze the data.

Statistical data are the raw materials of statistical research, always appearing in cases of measurement or record of observations.

This chapter discusses the existing types of variables (*metric* or *quantitative* and *nonmetric* or *qualitative*) and their respective scales of measurement (*nominal* and *ordinal* for qualitative variables, and *interval* and *ratio* for quantitative variables). Classifying the types of variables based on the number of categories and scales of accuracy is also discussed (*binary* and *polychotomous* for qualitative variables and *discrete* and *continuous* for quantitative variables).

Types of variables

Variables can be classified as nonmetric, also known as *qualitative* or *categorical*, or metric, also known as *quantitative* (Figure 3.1). Nonmetric or qualitative variables represent the characteristics of an individual, object, or element that cannot be measured or quantified. The answers are given in categories. In contrast, metric or quantitative variables represent the characteristics of an individual, object, or element that result from a count (a finite set of values) or measurement (an infinite set of values).

*Portions of this chapter were previously published in Fávero and Belfiore (2019).

https://doi.org/10.1016/B978-0-12-824271-1.00001-9

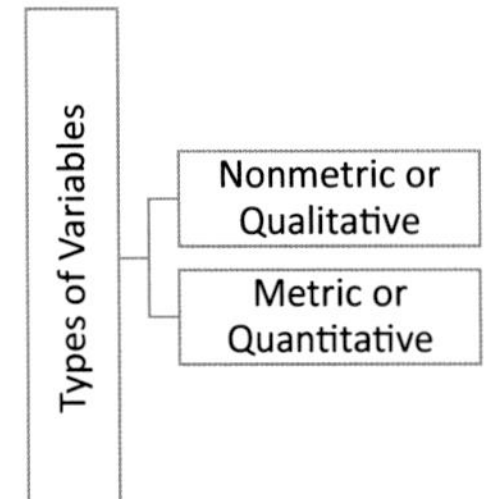

FIGURE 3.1 Types of variables.

Nonmetric or qualitative variables

As we are going to study in Chapter 4, the characteristics of nonmetric or qualitative variables can be represented with a frequency distribution table or a graph without having to calculate the measures of position, dispersion, and shape. The only exception is the mode, a measure that provides the variable's most frequent value, and it can also be applied to nonmetric variables.

Imagine that a questionnaire will be used to collect data on family income from a sample of consumers based on certain salary ranges. Table 3.1 shows the variable categories.

Note that both variables are qualitative because the data are represented by ranges. However, it is very common for researchers to classify them incorrectly, mainly when the variable has numerical values in the data. In this case, it is only possible to calculate the frequency and not the summary measures, such as the mean and standard deviation.

TABLE 3.1 Family income ranges and social class.

Class	Minimum wage salaries (MWS)	Family income (US$)
A	Above 20	Above $15,760
B	10 to 20	$7,880 to $15,760
C	4 to 10	$3,152 to $7,880
D	2 to 4	$1,576 to $3,152
E	Up to 2	Up to $1,576

The frequencies obtained for each income range are shown in Table 3.2.

TABLE 3.2 Frequency of family income ranges.

Frequency	Family income ($)
10%	Above $15,760
18%	$7,880 to $15,760
24%	$3,152 to $7,880
36%	$1,576 to $3,152
12%	Up to $1,576

A common error found in papers that use qualitative variables represented by numbers is the calculation of the sample mean or any other summary measure. The researcher calculates the mean of the limits of each range, assuming that this value corresponds to the real mean of the consumers found in that range. However, because the data distribution is not necessarily linear or symmetrical around the mean, this hypothesis is often violated.

The variable being studied must be quantitative for the researcher to be able to calculate summary measures such as the mean and standard deviation.

Metric or quantitative variables

Quantitative variables can be represented in a graphical way (line charts, scatter plots, histograms, stem-and-leaf plots, and box plots) using measures of position or location (mean, median, mode, quartile, decile, and percentile); measures of dispersion or variability (range, average deviation, variance, standard deviation, standard error, and coefficient of variation); or measures of shape such as skewness and kurtosis, as we are going to study in Chapter 4.

These variables can be discrete or continuous. Discrete variables can take on a finite set of values that frequently result from a count, such as the number of children in a family (0, 1, 2…). Conversely, continuous variables take on values that are in an interval with real numbers, such as an individual's weight or income.

Imagine a database with the name, age, weight, and height of 20 individuals, as shown in Table 3.3.

TABLE 3.3 Database with information on 20 individuals.

Name	Age (years)	Weight (kg)	Height (m)
Mary	48	62	1.60
James	41	56	1.62
Patricia	54	84	1.76
John	30	82	1.90
Jennifer	35	76	1.85
Robert	60	98	1.78
Linda	28	54	1.68
Michael	50	70	1.72
Elizabeth	40	75	1.68
William	24	50	1.59
Barbara	44	65	1.62
David	39	83	1.75
Susan	22	68	1.78
Richard	31	56	1.66
Jessica	45	60	1.64
Joseph	62	88	1.77
Sarah	24	80	1.92
Thomas	28	75	1.80
Karen	49	92	1.76
Charles	54	66	1.68

Types of variables and scales of measurement

Variables can also be classified according to the level or scale of measurement. *Measurement* is the process of assigning numbers or labels to objects, people, states, or events, based on specific rules, to represent the quantities or qualities of the attributes. A *rule* is a guide, method, or command that tells the researcher how to measure the attribute. A *scale* is a set of symbols or numbers that is based on a rule and applies to individuals or their behaviors or attitudes. An individual's position on the scale is based on whether or not he or she has the attribute the scale is measuring.

Several taxonomies are found in the existing literature to classify the scales of measurement for all types of variables (Stevens, 1946). We will discuss the Stevens classification scale because it is simple, it is widely used, and its nomenclature is used in statistical software.

According to Stevens (1946), the scales for measurement of nonmetric, categorical, or qualitative variables are classified as *nominal* and *ordinal* scales, and the metric or quantitative variables are classified as *interval* and *ratio* (or proportional) scales, as shown in Figure 3.2.

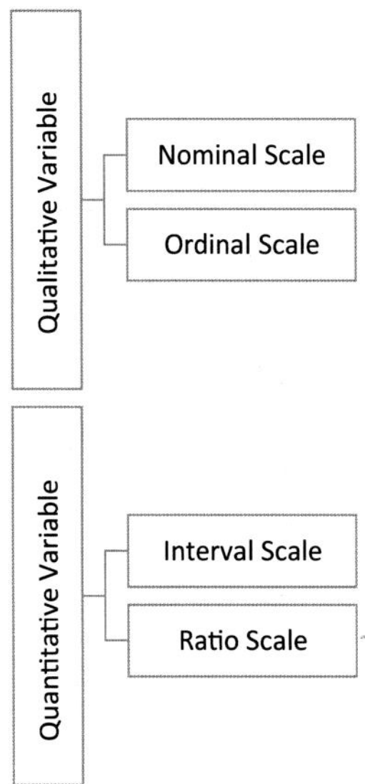

FIGURE 3.2 Types of Variables and Scales of Measurement.

Nonmetric variables: Nominal scale

The nominal scale classifies units into classes or categories regarding the characteristic represented without establishing any magnitude or order relationship. It is called *nominal* because the categories are only differentiated by their names.

We can assign numerical labels to the variable categories, but arithmetic operations (i.e., addition, subtraction, multiplication, and division) cannot be applied to these values. The nominal scale only allows some basic arithmetic operations. For instance, we can count the number of elements in each class or apply hypotheses tests regarding the distribution of population units in the classes. Thus, most of the usual statistics, such as the mean and standard deviation, do not make sense for nominal scale qualitative variables.

Examples of nonmetric variables on nominal scales include professions, religion, color, marital status, geographic location, and country of origin.

Imagine a nonmetric variable related to the country of origin of 10 large multinational companies. To represent the categories of the variable *(country of origin)*, we can use numbers, assigning value 1 to the United States, 2 to the Netherlands, 3 to China, 4 to the United Kingdom, and 5 to Brazil, as shown in Table 3.4. In this case, the numbers are only labels or tags to help identify and classify objects.

TABLE 3.4 Companies and country of origin.

Company	Country of origin
Exxon Mobil	1
JP Morgan Chase	1
General Electric	1
Royal Dutch Shell	2
Industrial and Commercial Bank of China	3
HSBC Holdings	4
PetroChina	3
Berkshire Hathaway	1
Wells Fargo	1
Petrobras	5

This scale of measurement is known as a *nominal scale,* that is, the numbers are randomly assigned to the object categories without any kind of order. To represent the behavior of nominal data, we can use descriptive statistics such as frequency distribution tables, bar or pie charts, or calculation of the mode (Chapter 4).

Descriptive statistics used to represent the behavior of a single qualitative variable and two qualitative variables will be studied in Chapter 4.

Nonmetric variables: Ordinal scale

A nonmetric variable on an ordinal scale classifies the units into classes or categories regarding the characteristic being represented, establishing an order between the units of the different categories. An ordinal scale is a scale on which data is shown to determine a relative position of classes according to one direction. Any set of values can be assigned to the variable categories as long as the order between them is respected.

As in the nominal scale, arithmetic operations (i.e., addition, subtraction, multiplication, and division) cannot be applied to these values. Thus the application of the usual descriptive statistics is also limited to nominal variables. Because the scale numbers are only meant to classify them, the descriptive statistics that can be used for ordinal data are frequency distribution tables, charts (including bar charts and pie charts), and calculation of the mode, as discussed in Chapter 4.

Examples of ordinal variables include consumers' opinions and satisfaction scales, educational level, social class, and age.

Imagine a nonmetric variable called *classification* that measures a group of consumers' preference regarding a certain wine brand. Creation of labels for each ordinal variable category is shown in Table 3.5. Value 1 is assigned to the worst classification, value 2 to the second worst, and so on, until value 5, which is the best classification.

TABLE 3.5 Consumers' classification of a certain wine brand.

Value	Label
1	Very bad
2	Bad
3	Average
4	Good
5	Very good

Instead of using scales from 1 to 5, we can assign any other numerical scale, as long as the order of classification is respected. Thus the numerical values do not represent a score of the product's quality; they are only meant to classify it. Therefore the difference between these values does not represent the difference of the attribute analyzed. This scale of measurement is known as an *ordinal scale.*

Quantitative variables: Interval scale

According to the Stevens classification (1946), metric or quantitative variables include data on an interval or ratio scale.

Besides ordering the units based on the characteristic being measured, the interval scale has a constant unit of measure. The origin or point zero of this scale of measurement is random, and it does not express an absence of quantity.

A classic example of an interval scale is temperature measured in Celsius (°C) or Fahrenheit (°F). Choosing temperature zero is random, and differences of equal temperatures are determined by identification of equal expansion volumes in the liquid inside the thermometer. Hence the interval scale allows us to infer differences between the units to be measured. However, we cannot state that a value in a specific interval of the scale is a multiple of another one. For instance, assume that two objects are measured at 15°C and 30°C, respectively. Measuring the temperature allows us to determine how much one object is hotter than the other. However, we cannot state that the object with 30°C is twice as hot as the one with 15°C.

The interval scale does not vary under positive linear transformation. Therefore an interval scale can be transformed into another one through positive linear transformation. Transforming degrees Celsius into degrees Fahrenheit is an example of linear transformation.

Most descriptive statistics can be applied to variable data with an interval scale, except statistics based on the ratio scale, such as the variation coefficient.

Quantitative variables: Ratio scale

Analogous to the interval scale, the ratio scale orders the units based on the characteristic measured and has a constant unit of measure. On the other hand, the origin (or point zero) is unique, and value zero expresses the absence of quantity. Therefore it is possible to know if a value in a specific interval of the scale is a multiple of another.

Equal ratios between values of the scale correspond to equal ratios between the units measured. Thus ratio scales do not vary under positive proportion transformations. For example, if a unit is 1 m high and the other 3 m high, we can say that the latter is three times higher than the former.

Among the scales of measurement, the ratio scale is the most complete because it allows us to use all arithmetic operations. In addition, all of the descriptive statistics can be applied to the data of a variable expressed on a ratio scale.

Examples of variables whose data can be on a ratio scale include income, age, how many units of a certain product were manufactured, and distance traveled.

Types of variables based on number of categories and scales of accuracy

Qualitative or categorical variables can also be classified based on the number of categories. A *dichotomous* or binary (dummy) variable only takes on two categories; a *polychotomous* variable takes on more than two categories.

On the other hand, metric or quantitative variables can also be classified based on the scale of accuracy: *discrete* or *continuous*.

This classification can be seen in Figure 3.3.

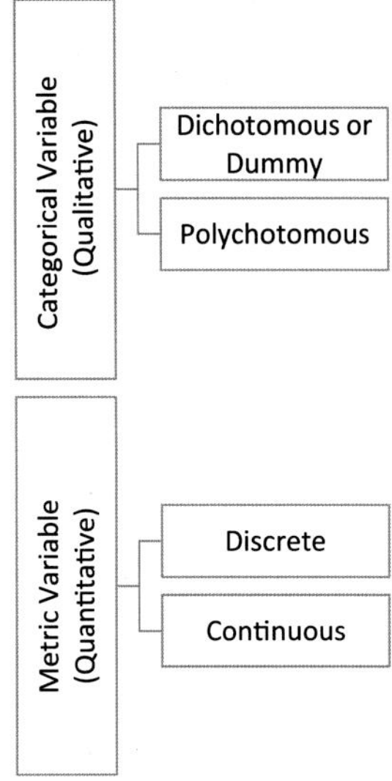

FIGURE 3.3 Qualitative Variables Based on Number of Categories and Quantitative Variables Based on Scales of Accuracy.

Dichotomous or binary variables: Dummy

A dichotomous or binary (dummy) variable can only take on two categories, and the values 0 or 1 are assigned to these categories. Value 1 is assigned when the characteristic of interest is present in the variable, and value 0 is assigned if the characteristic is not present. Examples are smokers (1) and nonsmokers (0); a developed country (1) and a developing country (0); and vaccinated patients (1) and nonvaccinated patients (0).

The main objective of multivariate dependence techniques is to specify a model that can explain and predict the behavior of one or more dependent variables through one or more explanatory variables. Many of these techniques, including simple and multiple regression analysis, binary and multinomial logistic regression, regression for count data, and canonical correlation, among others, can easily and coherently be applied with the use of nonmetric explanatory variables, as long as they are transformed into binary variables that represent the categories of the original qualitative variable. In this regard, a qualitative variable with n categories, for example, can be represented by $(n - 1)$ binary variables.

For instance, imagine a variable called *evaluation* that is expressed by the categories *good*, *average*, and *bad*. Thus, two binary variables may be necessary to represent the original variable, depending on the researcher's objectives, as shown in Table 3.6.

TABLE 3.6 Creating binary variables (dummies) for the variable *Evaluation*.

	Binary variables (dummies)	
Evaluation	D_1	D_2
Good	0	0
Average	1	0
Bad	0	1

Further details about the definition of dummy variables in dependence models are discussed in Chapter 13, including a presentation of the operations necessary to create them on software such as *Stata*.

Polychotomous variables

A qualitative variable can take on more than two categories, and in this case it is called *polychotomous*. Examples are social classes (lower, middle, and upper) and educational levels (elementary school, high school, college, and graduate school).

Discrete quantitative variables

As described in the "Metric or quantitative variables" section earlier in the chapter, discrete quantitative variables can take on a finite set of values that frequently result from a count such as number of children in a family (0, 1, 2...), number of senators elected, or number of cars manufactured in a certain factory.

Continuous quantitative variables

Continuous quantitative variables, on the other hand, are those whose possible values are in an interval with real numbers and result from a metric measurement such as an individual's weight, height, or salary (Bussab and Morettin, 2017).

Final remarks

When treated and analyzed using various statistical techniques, data are transformed into information and can support the decision-making process.

These data can be metric (quantitative) or nonmetric (categorical or qualitative). Metric data represent the characteristics of an individual, object, or element that result from a count or measurement (e.g., age, interest rate). In the case of nonmetric data, these characteristics cannot be measured or quantified. The answer is given in categories (e.g., educational level) or determined by a "yes" or "no."

According to Stevens (1946), the scales of measurement of nonmetric categorical or qualitative variables are classified as nominal and ordinal, while metric or quantitative variables are classified on interval and ratio scales (or proportional).

A great deal of data can be collected in both a metric and nonmetric way. Assume that we wish to assess the quality of a certain product. To do this, scores from 1 to 10 regarding certain attributes can be assigned, and a Likert scale can be created from information that has already been established. In general, and whenever possible, questions must be created in a quantitative way for the researcher not to lose data information.

Creating the questionnaire and defining the variable scales of measurement depends on several aspects including research objectives, modeling to be adopted to achieve the objectives, average time to apply the questionnaire, and how the data will be collected (Fávero et al., 2009). A database can present variables on metric and nonmetric scales; it is not restricted to only one type of scale. This combination can provide some interesting research, and with suitable modeling it can generate information aimed at assisting the decision-making process.

The type of variable collected is crucial in the calculation of descriptive statistics, the graphical representation of results, and the selection of statistical methods that will be used to analyze the data.

Exercises

(1) What is the difference between qualitative and quantitative variables?
(2) What are scales of measurement? What are the main types and the differences between them?
(3) What is the difference between a discrete and continuous variable?
(4) Classify the variables according to a nominal, ordinal, binary, discrete, or continuous scale.
   (a) A company's revenue
   (b) Performance rank: good, average, or bad
   (c) Time to process a part
   (d) Number of cars sold
   (e) Distance traveled in kilometers
   (f) Municipalities in the greater Sao Paulo area
   (g) Family income ranges
   (h) A student's grades: A, B, C, D
   (i) Hours worked
   (j) Region: North, Northeast, Center-West, South, or Southeast
   (k) Location: Sao Paulo or Seoul
   (l) Size of organization: small, medium, or large
   (m) Number of bedrooms
   (n) Classification of risk: high, average, speculative, or substantial
   (o) Married: yes or no
(5) A researcher wishes to study the impact of physical aptitude on the improvement of productivity in an organization. How would you describe the binary variables that would be included in this model so the variable *physical aptitude* can be represented? The possible variable categories are: *active and healthy; acceptable (could be better); not good enough;* and *sedentary.*

CHAPTER

4

Univariate descriptive statistics

AT THE END OF THIS CHAPTER, YOU WILL BE ABLE TO:

- Represent the frequency of occurrence of a set of observations using frequency distribution tables.
- Represent the distribution of a variable with graphs.
- Use measures of position or location (central trend and separatrices) to represent a set of data.
- Measure the variability of a set of data using dispersion measures.
- Use measures of skewness and kurtosis to characterize the distribution shape of the elements of the population sampled around the average.
- Generate tables, graphs, and summary measures using the R language.

R language packages used in this chapter

```
library(questionr)
library(e1071)
```

Don't forget to define the R working directory (the location where your datasets are installed):

```
setwd("C:/book/chapter4")
```

Introduction

In this chapter we study frequency distribution tables for qualitative and discrete variables and for continuous variables grouped into classes. We also present results in graphs, such as bar charts, pie charts, and pareto charts. For quantitative variables, we present graphical representations for quantitative variables, such as line graphs, scatter plots, histograms, stem-and-leaf plots, and boxplots. Finally, we show how to obtain the most common summary measures in univariate descriptive statistics.

Data Science, Analytics and Machine Learning with R
https://doi.org/10.1016/B978-0-12-824271-1.00002-0

Frequency distribution table

Frequency distribution table for qualitative variables

Example 4.1 (Fávero and Belfiore, 2019)

Saint August Hospital provides 3,000 blood transfusions to hospitalized patients every month. For the hospital to be able to maintain its stocks, 60 blood donations per day are necessary. Table 4.1 shows the total number of donors for each blood type on a certain day. Create a frequency distribution table for these data.

TABLE 4.1 Total number of donors of each blood type (Fávero and Belfiore, 2019).

Blood type	Donors
A+	15
A–	2
B+	6
B–	1
AB+	1
AB–	1
O+	32
O–	2

Solution

To create a frequency table for qualitative data in R, we must open the file **blood_donors.RData** (Fávero and Belfiore, 2019):

```
load("blood_donors.RData")
```

The quickest way to create a frequency table for qualitative data in R is to use the function `table()`. We also use the function `attach()` to facilitate the declaration of variables:

```
table(blood_type)
```

For establishment of the relative frequencies, we can use the nesting of the function `table()`, as shown by the previous routine, with the function `prop.table()`:

```
prop.table(table(blood_type))
```

If the interest is on the calculation of the cumulative frequencies, we can use the combination of the function `table()` and the function `cumsum()`, similarly to what was done previously:

```
cumsum(table(blood_type))
```

Finally, to calculate the cumulative relative frequencies, we nest the function `table()` with the function `prop.table()`. Then, we nest them to the function `cumsum()`:

```
cumsum(prop.table(table(blood_type)))
```

We can combine all results of the previous routines into a single dataset, similar to Table 4.1, using the function `cbind()`, as discussed in Chapter 2:

```
example4_1 <- cbind(table(blood_type),
                    prop.table(table(blood_type)),
                    cumsum(table(blood_type)),
                    cumsum(prop.table(table(blood_type))))
```

In addition, we could finally add the column names, as follows:

```
colnames(example4_1) <- c("F_i","Fr_i","F_ac","Fr_ac")
```

The reader can check the final result by declaring the name of the object `example4_1` to R and comparing it to Table 4.1.

A more elegant way of creating a frequency table can be done, for example, through the function `freq()` of the package `questionr`:

```
freq(blood_type, cum = TRUE, total = TRUE)
```

For the function `freq()`, we argue `cum = TRUE` so the cumulative sums of frequencies and relative frequencies appear. We can also argue `total = TRUE` to have access to a line of totals.

Figure 4.1 shows the final result. It is worth mentioning that the values present in the columns *val%* and *val%cum* refer, respectively, to the relative frequencies and the cumulative relative frequencies, disregarding any missing values.

```
       n     %  val%  %cum val%cum
a+    15  25.0  25.0  25.0    25.0
a-     2   3.3   3.3  28.3    28.3
b+     6  10.0  10.0  38.3    38.3
b-     1   1.7   1.7  40.0    40.0
ab+    1   1.7   1.7  41.7    41.7
ab-    1   1.7   1.7  43.3    43.3
o+    32  53.3  53.3  96.7    96.7
o-     2   3.3   3.3 100.0   100.0
Total 60 100.0 100.0 100.0   100.0
```

FIGURE 4.1 Frequency distribution table for qualitative data elaborated through the function `freq()`.

Frequency distribution table for discrete data

Example 4.2 (Fávero and Belfiore, 2019)

A Japanese restaurant is defining a new layout for its tables and has collected information on the number of people who have lunch and dinner at each table throughout 1 week. Table 4.2 shows the first 40 pieces of data collected. Create a frequency distribution table for these data.

TABLE 4.2 Number of people per table (Fávero and Belfiore, 2019).

2	5	4	7	4	1	6	2	2	5
4	12	8	6	4	5	2	8	2	6
4	7	2	5	6	4	1	5	10	2
2	10	6	4	3	4	6	3	8	4

Solution

Similar to our discussion in the "Frequency distribution table for qualitative variables" section earlier in the chapter, we can create a table of frequencies for discrete data with the function `freq()` of the package `questionr`. First, we will create an object that contains the data presented in Table 4.2:

```
example4_2 <- c(2,5,4,7,4,1,6,2,2,5,4,12,8,6,4,5,2,8,2,6,
                4,7,2,5,6,4,1,5,10,2,2,10,6,4,3,4,6,3,8,4)
```

Next, we must sort the observations with the function `sort()`:

```
example4_2 <- sort(example4_2)
```

Finally, we can use the function `freq()`:

```
freq(example4_2, cum = TRUE, total = TRUE)
```

Frequency distribution table for continuous data grouped into classes

Example 4.3 (Fávero and Belfiore, 2019)

Consider the data in Table 4.3 regarding the grades of 30 students enrolled in a financial market class. Create a frequency distribution table for these data.

TABLE 4.3 Grades of 30 students enrolled in a financial market class (Fávero and Belfiore, 2019).

4.2	3.9	5.7	6.5	4.6	6.3	8.0	4.4	5.0	5.5
6.0	4.5	5.0	7.2	6.4	7.2	5.0	6.8	4.7	3.5
6.0	7.4	8.8	3.8	5.5	5.0	6.6	7.1	5.3	4.7

Note: To determine the number of classes, use Sturges' rule.

Solution

In R, we can calculate the k number of classes using Sturges' rule, through the function `nclass.Sturges()`. So, initially, let's save the data in an object:

```
example4_3 <- c(4.2,3.9,5.7,6.5,4.6,6.3,8.0,4.4,5.0,5.5,6.0,
               4.5,5.0,7.2,6.4,7.2,5.0,6.8,4.7,3.5,6.0,7.4,
               8.8,3.8,5.5,5.0,6.6,7.1,5.3,4.7)
```

From the object `example4_3`, we can apply the function `nclass.Sturges()`:

```
nclass.Sturges(example4_3)
```

To calculate the interval between classes (h), it would be enough to combine the functions `min()` and `max()` with the function `nclass.Sturges()` to replicate the formula discussed in Step 3 of Example 4.3:

```
(max(example4_3) - min(example4_3)) / nclass.Sturges(example4_3)
```

Graphical representation of the results

Graphical representation for qualitative variables

Bar chart

Example 4.4 (Fávero and Belfiore, 2019)

A bank created a satisfaction survey to measure the degree of agility of its services (excellent, good, satisfactory, or poor) for 120 customers. The absolute frequency for each category is shown in Table 4.4. Create a vertical and horizontal bar chart for these data.

TABLE 4.4 Frequencies of occurrences per category (Fávero and Belfiore, 2019).

Satisfaction	Absolute frequency
Excellent	58
Good	18
Satisfactory	32
Poor	12

Solution

To load the file **satisfaction_survey.RData** (Fávero and Belfiore, 2019), we must command:

```
load("satisfaction_survey.RData ")
```

To replicate Table 4.4 in R, we must use the function `table()` applied to the variable *satisfaction* in the dataset `satisfaction_survey`. As discussed in Chapter 2, we can access a given variable from a dataset using the operator `$`, or we can declare it directly after applying the function `attach()` to the dataset (chosen path):

```
attach(satisfaction_survey)
table(satisfaction)
```

Figure 4.2 shows the result of the previous command, which is identical to Table 4.4.

```
        poor satisfactory         good    excellent
          12           32           18           58
```

FIGURE 4.2 R-based language response to the command `table()` applied to the object `satisfaction_survey`.

To create a bar graph in R language, we must use the function `barplot()`. We will explore more elaborate graphics from Chapter 7 onward. In the initial sections of this book, our goal is to make the reader comfortable with introductory topics in statistics.

That said, we can command:

```
barplot(table(satisfaction))
```

In the previous command, we used the output presented in Figure 4.2, that is, the one obtained by the routine `table(satisfaction)`, and from it, we asked R to create a bar graph, as shown in Figure 4.3.

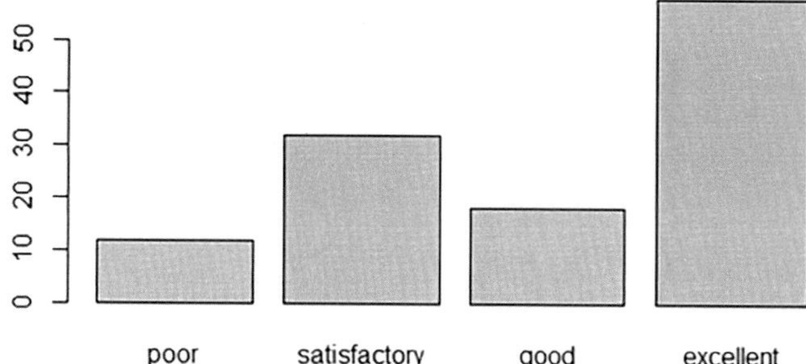

FIGURE 4.3 Vertical bar graph of absolute frequencies of the satisfaction variable created with R-based language.

As an example, we could create a more elegant graph for Figure 4.3, commanding:

```
barplot(table(satisfaction),
        xlab = "Satisfaction",
        ylab = "Frequency",
        col = "steelblue")
```

Have you noticed the expansion of the code? In addition to the indication of the dataset, we now inform that the bars of the graph must be filled in by the steelblue color, which is declared in quotation marks by the argument `col`. We also argue `xlab()` and `ylab()` to name the abscissa and ordinate axes, respectively. The graph created with the previous command is shown in Figure 4.4.

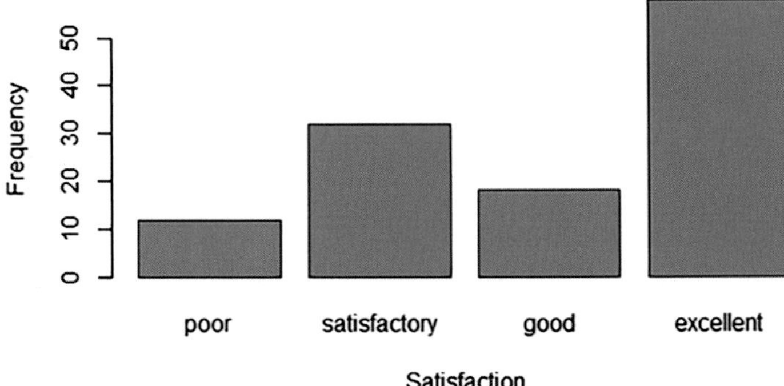

FIGURE 4.4 Vertical bar graph of absolute frequencies of the satisfaction variable created with R-based language.

A fair question would be, "What colors, exactly, could be used in graphics?" As a rule, the chosen colors should be reported to R in English (e.g., blue, red, green). We purposely adopted a color with a more elaborate nomenclature (steelblue) to generate this kind of doubt. In the Appendix of this chapter, we will present the main colors and color scales that can be used.

For construction of the horizontal bar graph, we must argue `horiz = TRUE`:

```
barplot(table(satisfaction),
        horiz = TRUE,
        xlab = "Frequency",
        ylab = "Satisfaction",
        col = "steelblue")
```

Figure 4.5 shows the graph created through the previous command:

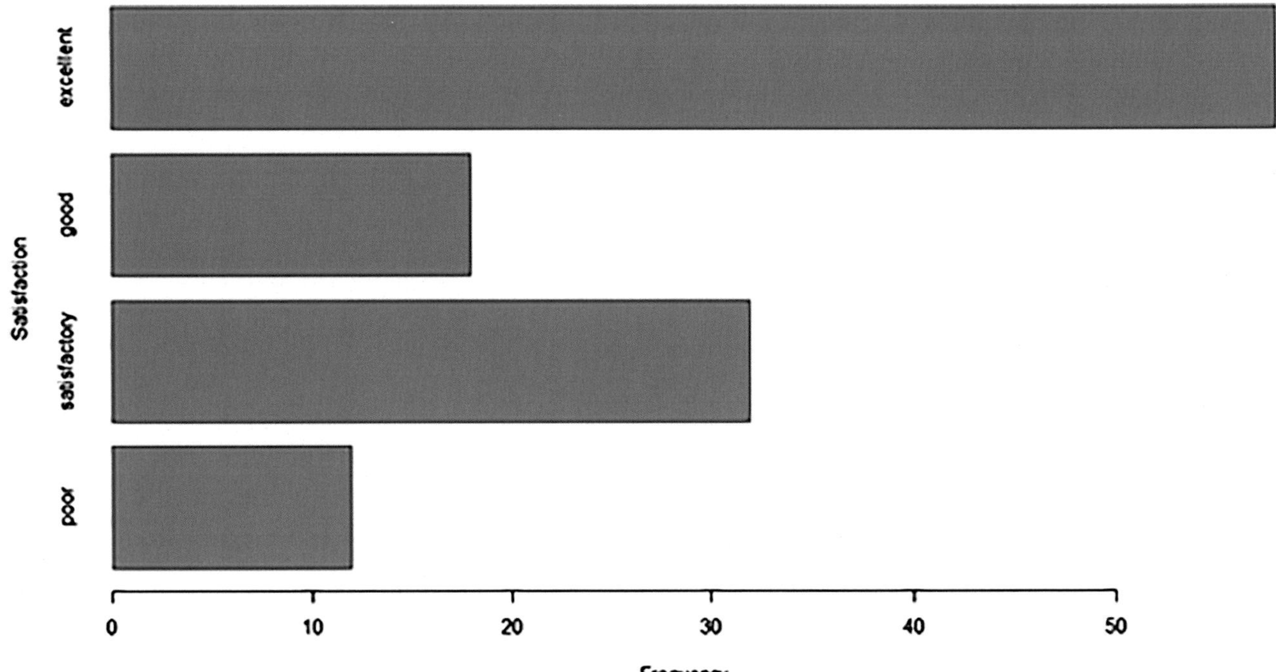

FIGURE 4.5 Horizontal bar graph of absolute frequencies of the satisfaction variable created with R-based language.

An attentive reader will notice that we inverted the labels identifying the axes of the graph in Figure 4.5 in the arguments `xlab()` and `ylab()` because we changed their position from vertical to horizontal.

The horizontal bar chart in Figure 4.5 represents the categories of the variable on the y-axis and their respective frequencies on the x-axis. For each variable category, we draw a bar with a length that corresponds to its frequency.

Therefore this chart only offers information related to the behavior of each category of the original variable and to the creation of investigations regarding the type of distribution, but it does not allow us to calculate position, dispersion, skewness, or kurtosis because the variable being studied is qualitative.

Pie chart

Example 4.5 (Fávero and Belfiore, 2019)

The city of Sao Paulo conducted an election poll to check voter preferences concerning the political parties running for mayor in the next election. The percentage of voters for each political party is shown in Table 4.5. Create a pie chart for Example 4.5.

TABLE 4.5 Percentage of voters per political party (Fávero and Belfiore, 2019).

Political party	Percentage
PMDB	18
PSDB	22
PDT	12.5
PT	24.5
PC do B	8
PV	5
Others	10

Solution

Let's create a pie chart for Example 4.5 in R. First, we must load the dataset **political_parties.RData** (Fávero and Belfiore, 2019).

```
load("political_parties.RData")
```

Next, let's activate the function `attach()`. We can use the function `pie()` to create a pie chart based on the values of the variable *percentage*:

```
attach(political_parties)
pie(percentage)
```

Figure 4.6 shows still unsatisfactory results because we still must identify the categories of the variable *political party* in the graph.

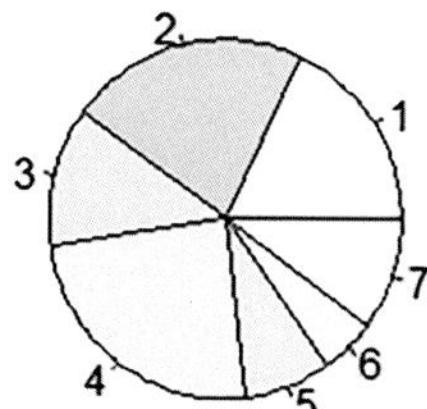

FIGURE 4.6 Pie chart created with R-based language.

To add identification labels for each political party and the percentage of votes reached in the election, we must use the functions `paste()` and `paste0()`, as already presented in Chapter 2:

```
pie(percentage,
    labels = paste(political_party,
                   paste0(percentage, "%")))
```

In the previous routine, we asked R to create a pie chart in which each sector refers to the values present in the variable *percentage*. Then, we informed that the argument `labels` would be composed of the junction of the acronyms of each political party, the percentage of votes reached, and the symbol `%`, using the nesting of the functions `paste()` and `paste0()`. The final result is shown in Figure 4.7.

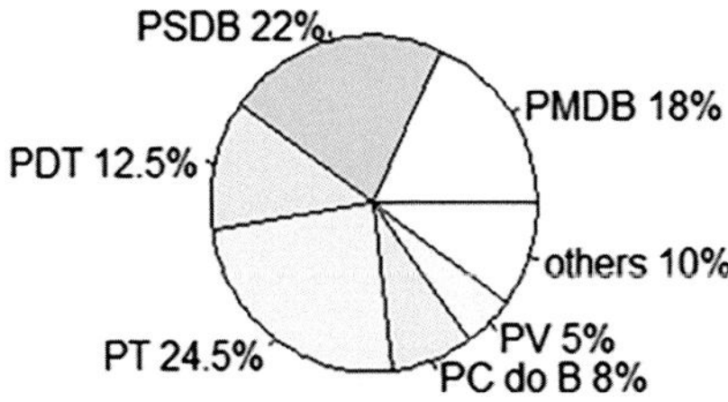

FIGURE 4.7 Pie chart created with R-based language.

Pareto chart

Example 4.6 (Fávero and Belfiore, 2019)

A manufacturer of credit and magnetic cards has as its main objective to reduce the number of defective cards. The quality inspector classified a sample of 1,000 cards collected during 1 week of production, according to the types of defects found, as shown in Table 4.6. Create a Pareto chart for these data.

TABLE 4.6 Frequencies of the occurrence of each defect (Fávero and Belfiore, 2019).

Type of defect	**Absolute frequency (F_i)**
Damaged/bent	71
Perforated	28
Illegible printing	12
Wrong characters	20
Wrong numbers	44
Others	6
Total	**181**

Solution

Let's now create a Pareto chart for Example 4.6 in R, using the data shown in Table 4.6. Initially, we must load the dataset **cards.RData** (Fávero and Belfiore, 2019):

```
load("cards.RData")
```

Then, we must sort the variable *type of defect* by reason of its absolute frequencies, from highest to lowest, using the function `order()` that will receive the argument `decreasing = TRUE`:

```
cards <- cards[order(cards$absolute_frequency, decreasing = TRUE),]
```

Do you remember what was discussed in Chapter 2? When we want to access the rows and columns of a dataset, we must use the operator `[,]`. Thus in the previous routine we declared the object `cards` that contains our dataset; then, as we want to order the rows of our dataset, we declare `[,]`, and inside the operator `[,]` we use the function `order()` before the comma because we want to sort the lines based on the variable *absolute frequency*. Internally to the function `order()`, we argue `decreasing = TRUE` because we are looking for a decreasing order of the number of occurrences of defects.

Thus for the first part of the Pareto chart, that is, to create a vertical bar graph, we must declare:

```
barplot(cards$absolute_frequency)
```

Figure 4.8 shows the first output of the construction of the Pareto chart.

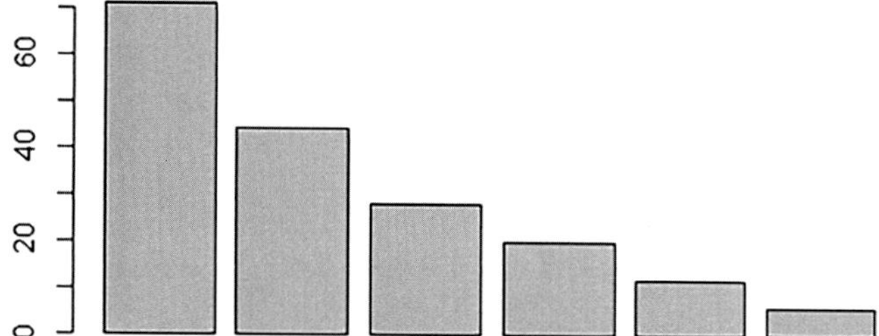

FIGURE 4.8 Vertical bar graph of absolute frequencies of the variable *type of defect*.

To add the name of each category of the variable *type of defect*, we must argue `names.arg`, as follows:

```
barplot(cards$absolute_frequency,
        names.arg = cards$type_of_defect,
        xlab = "Type of Defect",
        ylab = "Cumulative Count")
```

In the previous routine, the arguments `xlab` and `ylab` were also commanded so that the abscissa and ordinate axes were named, as shown in Figure 4.9.

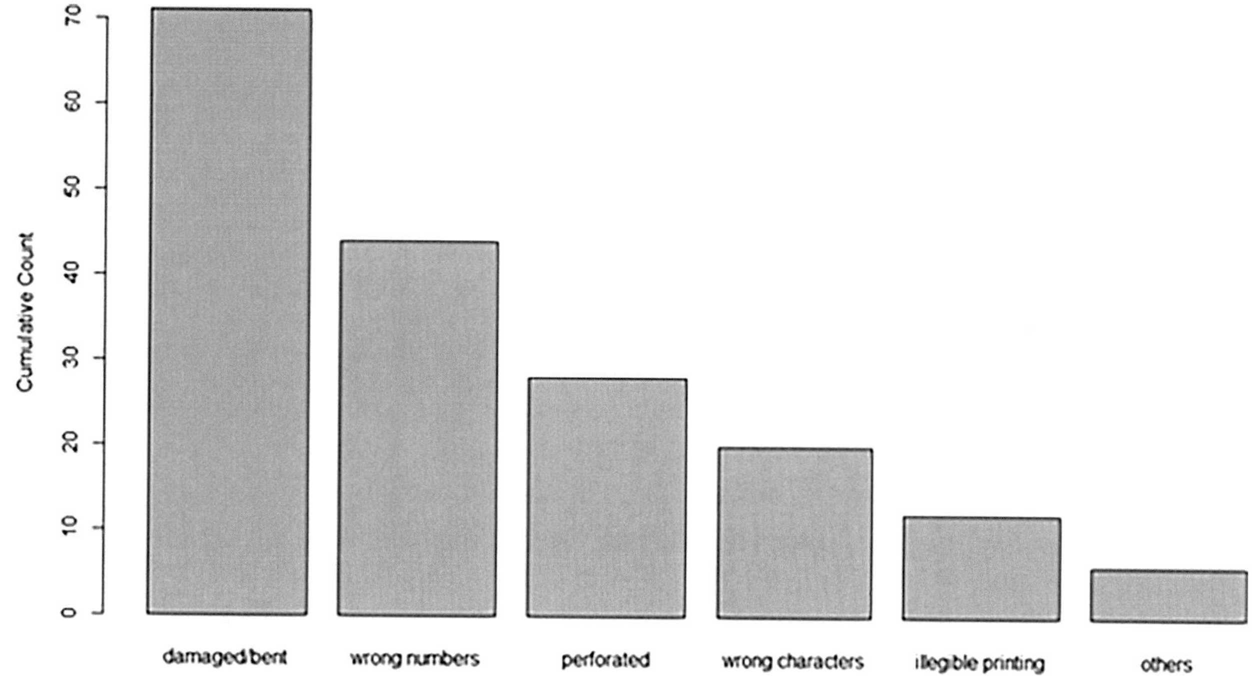

FIGURE 4.9 Vertical bar graph of absolute frequencies of the variable *type of defect*.

An attentive reader will notice that the name of the ordinate axis ("Cumulative Count") does not yet represent the real situation presented in Figure 4.10 because a line graph will do what we should observe on the y-axis. In this sense, we must create a new variable for our dataset that, in fact, contains the cumulative values of the defects of the studied cards.

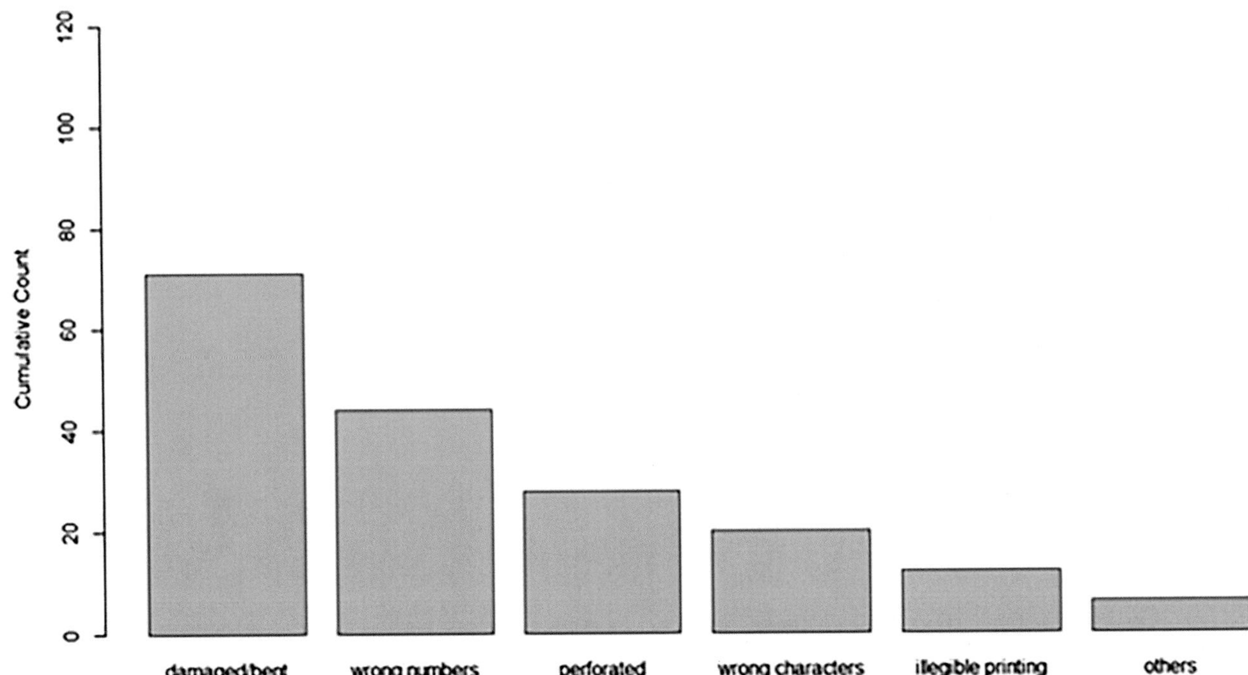

FIGURE 4.10 Vertical bar graph of absolute frequencies of the variable *type of defect*.

To achieve the proposed objective, we must use the functions `cumsum()` and `prop.table()`. The first function performs cumulative sums, while the second calculates the relative frequencies:

```
attach(cards)

cards["cumulative_count"] <- cumsum(
                                prop.table(absolute_frequency)
                                ) * 100
```

In the previous routine, we used the function `attach()` to facilitate the declaration of a variable, as studied in Chapter 2. An attentive reader will notice that a new variable concerning the relative cumulative sums of occurrence of defects has been added to the dataset `cards`.

Thus before creating the part that concerns the line graph, we must make an adjustment to the current bar graph so we can view the entire Pareto chart. The adjustment is similar to a "zoom out" so the line graph can fit on the screen:

```
barplot(cards$absolute_frequency,
        ylim = c(0, 1.7 * max(cards$absolute_frequency, na.rm = T)),
        ylab = "Cumulative Count",
        names.arg = cards$type_of_defect,
        col = "orange")
```

The reader can see that the adjustment comes from the argument `ylim` that points to the vertical adjustment of the graphs created in R-based language. In it, we have commanded that the screen space for the ordinate axis must be able to contain from 0% to 170% of the maximum value present in the variable *absolute frequency*. We also took the opportunity to add a new color to the graph bars (argument `col`), as shown in Figure 4.10.

Have you noticed the greater range of the y-axis? Now we are ready to generate the line graph for the final composition of the Pareto chart! Thus we ask the reader to use the function `lines()`, arguing to it the graph generated in Figure 4.10:

```
lines(barplot(cards$absolute_frequency,
              ylim = c(0, 1.7 * max(cards$absolute_frequency,
                                    na.rm = T)),
              ylab = "Cumulative Count",
              names.arg = cards$type_of_defect,
              col = "orange"),
      cards$cumulative_count,
      type = "b",
      pch = 19,
      col = "purple")
```

In the previous command, we also argued that the line chart should have the color purple (`col = "purple"`). In addition, the argument `pch` indicates a point shape (the Appendix of this chapter provides the reader with the codes of each used `pch`). Finally, the argument `type = "b"` allows plotting a line graph in which each segment of the line is joined by a point (`pch`, in this case).

Figure 4.11 shows the Pareto chart.

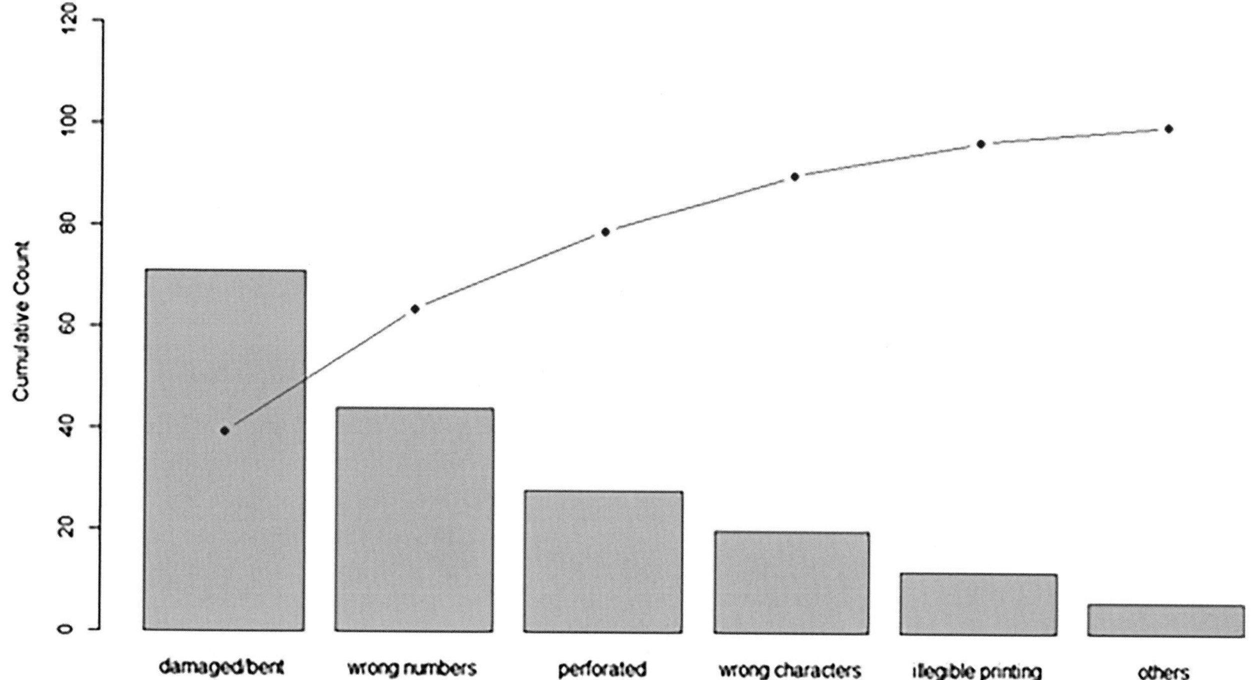

FIGURE 4.11 Pareto chart for Example 4.6.

Graphical representation for quantitative variables

Line graph

Example 4.7 (Fávero and Belfiore, 2019)

A supermarket wants to adopt new prevention measures after registering the percentage of losses it had in the past 12 months (Table 4.7). Create a line graph for Example 4.7.

TABLE 4.7 Percentage of losses in the past 12 months (Fávero and Belfiore, 2019).

Month	Losses (%)
January	0.42
February	0.38
March	0.12
April	0.34
May	0.22
June	0.15
July	0.18
August	0.31
September	0.47
October	0.24
November	0.42
December	0.09

Solution

To create the line graph for Example 4.7 in R, we must load the dataset **cheap_easy.RData** (Fávero and Belfiore, 2019):

```
load("cheap_easy.RData")
```

We can then use the function `plot()` arguing `type = "l"` to create a simple line graph, or `type = "b"` to create a line graph in which the union of the line segments is marked by a point shape (`pch`).

```
plot(cheap_easy$losses,
     type = "b",
     pch = 15,
     col = "darkgreen",
     xlab = "Months",
     ylab = "Losses %")
```

Figure 4.12 presents the preliminary result of the previous routine.

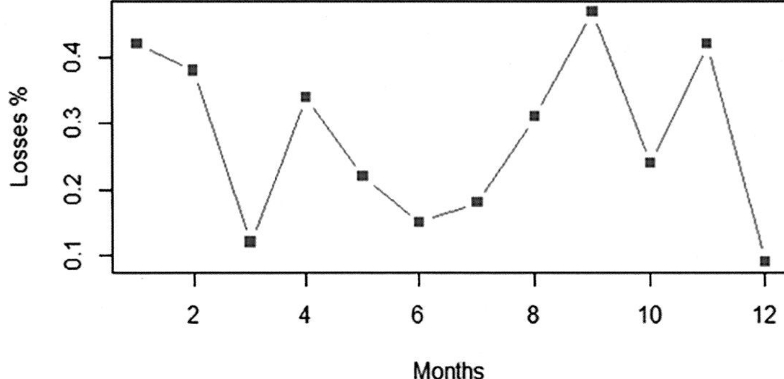

FIGURE 4.12 Line graph for Example 4.7.

As discussed earlier in this chapter, the arguments xlab and ylab refer to the names of the variables present, respectively, in the abscissa and ordinate axes, and the argument col indicates a color.

The reader will notice that the gradation of the x-axis is in numeric format, but the idea is that such a place should be occupied by the months of the year, as shown in Table 4.7. So, for the previous routine, we should argue xaxt = "n" to erase the markings on the abscissa axis:

```
plot(cheap_easy$losses,
     type = "b",
     pch = 15,
     xaxt = "n",
     col = "darkgreen",
     xlab = "Months",
     ylab = "Losses %")
```

Figure 4.13 shows the result obtained from the previous routine.

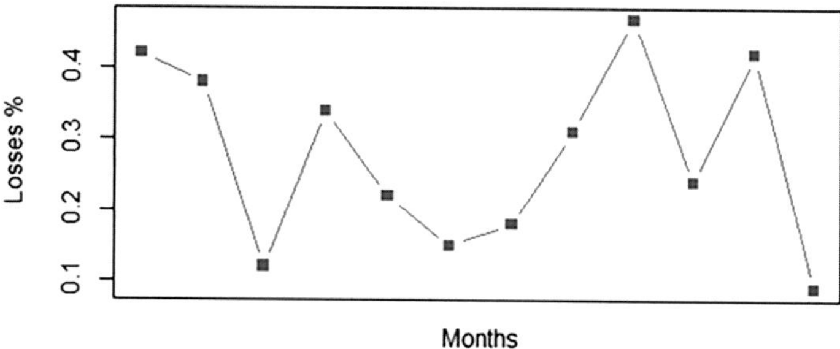

FIGURE 4.13 Line graph for Example 4.7.

Finally, we can plot the months of the year with the help of the function axis(), arguing side = 1 (1 = below, 2 = left, 3 = above, and 4 = right) to inform to R where the names of the months will go: labels = cheap_easy$month to tell R where the data for month names are coming from; and at = cheap_easy$month to inform to R that the number 1 in Figure 4.14 must be replaced by January, the number 2 by February, and so on.

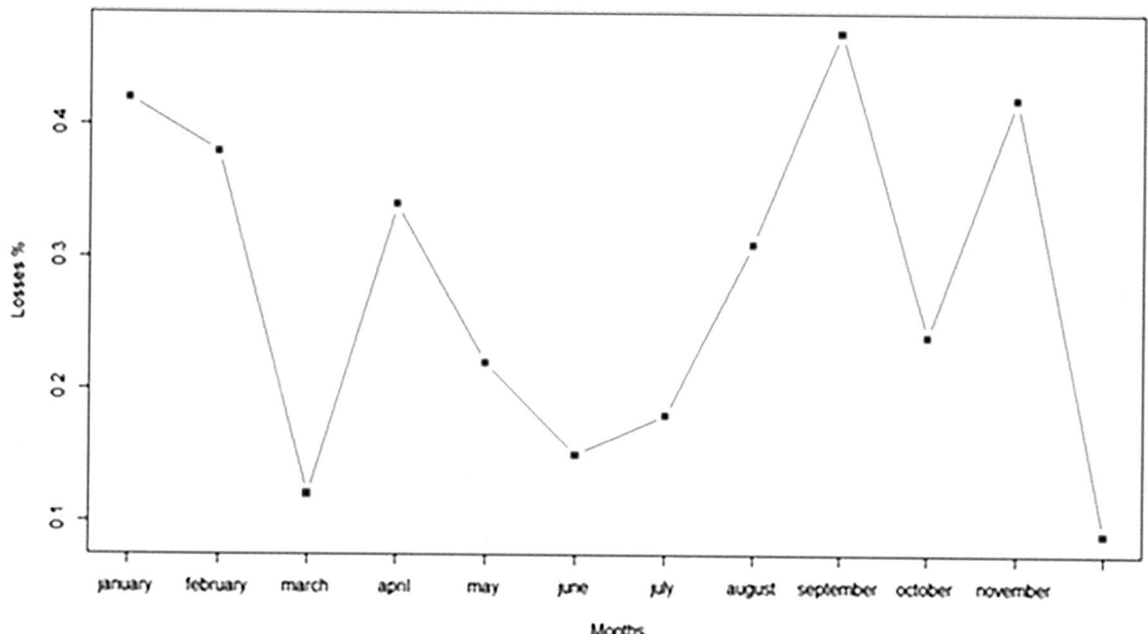

FIGURE 4.14 Line graph for Example 4.7.

```
axis(side = 1, labels = cheap_easy$month, at = cheap_easy$month)
```

Figure 4.14 presents the final result for our line graph.

Scatter plot

Example 4.8 (Fávero and Belfiore, 2019)

Papermisto is the supplier of three types of raw materials for the production of paper: cellulose, mechanical pulp, and trimmings. To maintain its quality standards, the factory carries out a rigorous inspection of its products during each production phase. At irregular intervals, an operator must verify the esthetic and dimensional characteristics of the product selected with specialized instruments. For instance, in the cellulose storage phase, the product must be piled up in bales of approximately 250 kg each. Table 4.8 shows the weight of the bales collected in the past 5 hours, at irregular intervals, varying between 20 and 45 minutes. Create a scatter plot for Example 4.8.

TABLE 4.8 Evolution of the weight of the bales throughout time (Fávero and Belfiore, 2019).

Time (min)	Weight (kg)
30	250
50	255
85	252
106	248
138	250
178	249
198	252
222	251
252	250
297	245

Solution

To create a scatter plot for Example 4.8 in R, we must load the dataset **papermisto.RData** (Fávero and Belfiore, 2019):

```
load("papermisto.RData")
```

After that, we can apply the function `plot()`, arguing which variables will be represented by the x- and y- axes. As discussed earlier in this chapter, we also argue for a point shape, colors, and the names of the axes:

```
plot(x = papermisto$weight_kg,
     y = papermisto$time_min,
     col = "firebrick",
     pch = 17,
     xlab = "Weight (kg)",
     ylab = "Time (min)")
```

Figure 4.15 presents the scatter plot created from the previous routine.

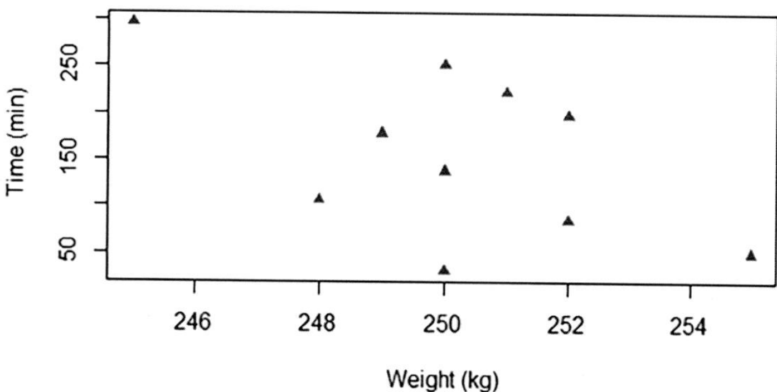

FIGURE 4.15 Type of scatter plot for Example 4.8.

Histogram

Example 4.9 (Fávero and Belfiore, 2019)

To improve their services, a national bank is hiring new managers to serve their corporate clients. Table 4.9 shows the number of companies the national bank deals with daily in one of their main branches in the capital. Create a histogram for these data using R.

TABLE 4.9 Number of companies the bank deals with daily (Fávero and Belfiore, 2019).

13	11	13	10	11	12	8	12	9	10
12	10	8	11	9	11	14	11	10	9

Solution

Let's load the file **bank.RData** (Fávero and Belfiore, 2019):

```
load("bank.RData")
```

After that, we can command the function `hist()` to plot a histogram:

```
hist(bank$number_of_companies,
     main = "Histogram",
     xlab = "Number of Companies",
     col = "slateblue1")
```

The arguments `xlab` and `col` are already known to the reader. The argument `main` makes it possible to define a title for the chart. Figure 4.16 shows the result obtained from the previous routine.

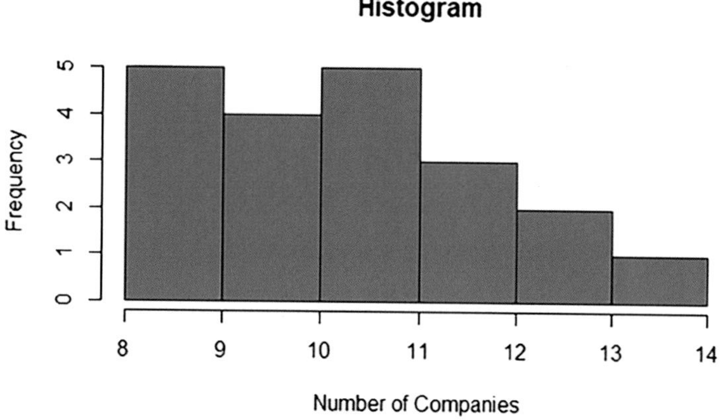

FIGURE 4.16 Histogram of absolute frequencies for Example 4.9.

The reader can establish the desired number of boxes in the histogram, arguing `breaks` to the function `hist()`:

```
hist(bank$number_of_companies,
     main = "Histogram",
     xlab = "Number of Companies",
     col = "slateblue1",
     breaks = c(7,8,9,10,11,12,13,14))
```

Figure 4.17 presents the result obtained from the previous routine.

FIGURE 4.17 Example of aesthetic refinement for the histogram.

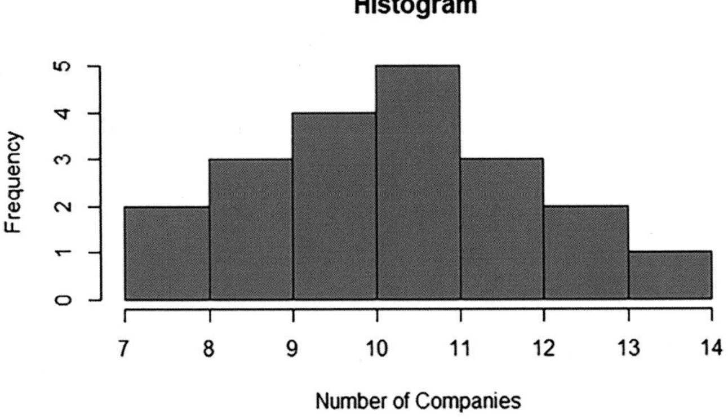

Stem-and-leaf plot

Example 4.10 (Fávero and Belfiore, 2019)

The average temperatures (in Celsius) registered in the past 40 days in Porto Alegre are shown in Table 4.10. Create a stem-and-leaf plot for Example 4.10.

TABLE 4.10 Average temperature in Celsius (Fávero and Belfiore, 2019).

8.5	13.7	12.9	9.4	11.7	19.2	12.8	9.7	19.5	11.5
15.5	16.0	20.4	17.4	18.0	14.4	14.8	13.0	16.6	20.2
17.9	17.7	16.9	15.2	18.5	17.8	16.2	16.4	18.2	16.9
18.7	19.6	13.2	17.2	20.5	14.1	16.1	15.9	18.8	15.7

Solution

To create a stem-and-leaf plot in R for Example 4.10, we must open the file **temperature.RData** (Fávero and Belfiore, 2019):

```
load("temperature.RData")
```

After that, we can command the function `stem()` on the variable of interest:

```
stem(temperature$average_temp)
```

Figure 4.18 shows the R outcomes.

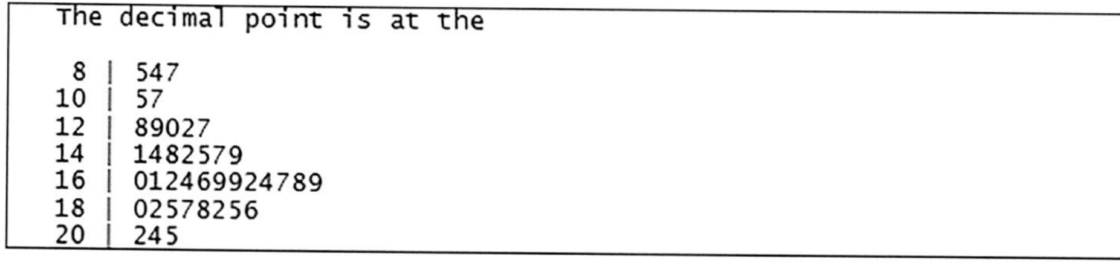

```
The decimal point is at the

  8 | 547
 10 | 57
 12 | 89027
 14 | 1482579
 16 | 012469924789
 18 | 02578256
 20 | 245
```

FIGURE 4.18 Stem-and-leaf plot resulting from not correctly arguing the function `stem()`.

By default, the function `stem()` groups the values of the observations of the variable of interest two by two, to the left of the bar "|" of the graph. The command must take into account the argument `scale`:

```
stem(temperature$average_temp, scale = 2)
```

Figure 4.19 presents the new stem-and-leaf plot.

```
The decimal point is at the

  8 | 5
  9 | 47
 10 |
 11 | 57
 12 | 89
 13 | 027
 14 | 148
 15 | 2579
 16 | 0124699
 17 | 24789
 18 | 02578
 19 | 256
 20 | 245
```

FIGURE 4.19 Stem-and-leaf plot for Example 4.10 created with R-based language.

Boxplot or box-and-whisker diagram

To create a boxplot, let's take the data shown in Example 4.7, Table 4.7, and the file **cheap_easy.RData** (Fávero and Belfiore, 2019):

```
load("cheap_easy.Rdata")
```

After that, we can command the function `boxplot()`, declaring the variable *losses*:

```
boxplot(cheap_easy$losses,
        ylab = "Losses %",
        col = "wheat")
```

Figure 4.20 shows the result. In Chapter 7, we will discuss how to produce graphics with greater visual appeal. In the initial sections of this book, our intention is to present introductory statistical concepts.

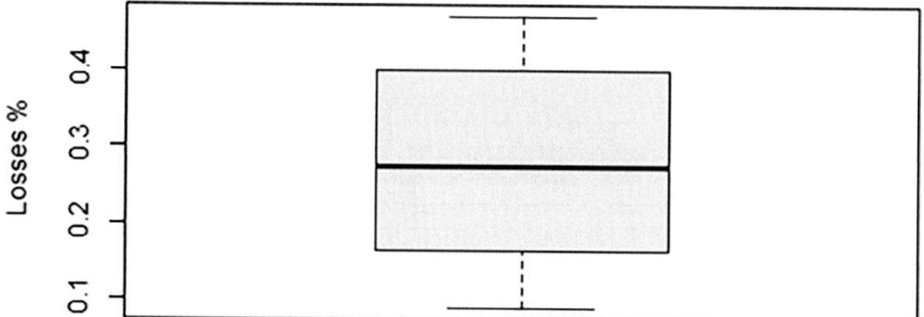

FIGURE 4.20 Boxplot for Example 4.7.

Example 4.11 (Fávero and Belfiore, 2019)

The production of carrots in a certain company is divided into five phases, including the post-harvest handling phase. Table 4.11 shows the average time the processing (in seconds) takes in this phase for 20 observations. Calculate the mode.

TABLE 4.11 Processing time in the post-harvest handling phase (in seconds) (Fávero and Belfiore, 2019).

45.0	44.5	44.0	45.0	46.5	46.0	45.8	44.8	45.0	46.2
44.5	45.0	45.4	44.9	45.7	46.2	44.7	45.6	46.3	44.9

In R-based language, the calculation of the quartiles, deciles, and percentiles of ungrouped discrete and continuous data can be done through the function `quantile()`. **However, we ask the reader to focus attention on the argument `type`!** According to Hyndman and Fan (1996), there are at least nine different methodologies for measuring the types of separatist measures discussed in this section. Following the authors' work, the calculation method that we present here is commonly mentioned in the literature as the fifth type.

Thus considering the vector of average processing times of carrots shown in Table 4.11, we have:

```
processing_time <- c(45.0, 44.5, 44.0, 45.0, 46.5, 46.0, 45.8, 44.8,
                     45.0, 46.2, 44.5, 45.0, 45.4, 44.9, 45.7, 46.2,
                     44.7, 45.6, 46.3, 44.9)
```

We can find the quartiles commanding:

```
quantile(processing_time, type = 5, na.rm = TRUE)
```

In the previous command, the argument `type = 5` determines to R that we want the quartiles to be measured based on the fifth definition of Hyndman and Fan (1996), that is, according to what has been discussed so far. The argument `na.rm = TRUE`, for this case, is a mere preciousness of the authors; it would disregard missing values, if they existed. We leave the tip as a contribution to the reader because **the function `quantile()` does not accept the presence of NA values.** Figure 4.21 shows the result of the previous command.

FIGURE 4.21 The quartile division of the object `processing_time`, according to the fifth definition of Hyndman and Fan (1996).

```
   0%   25%   50%   75%  100% 
44.00 44.85 45.00 45.90 46.50 
```

An attentive reader will notice that, in Figure 4.21, the label 25% refers to Q_1, while the label 75% refers to Q_3, whose values coincide with those previously calculated.

To calculate deciles and percentiles, we suggest the use of the function `seq()` internal to the argument `probs` of the function `quantile()`:

```
quantile(processing_time,
         probs = seq(from = 0, to = 1, by = 0.1),
         type = 5,
         na.rm = TRUE)
```

The argument `probs` calculates the occurrence probabilities of the values present in the object `processing_time`, varying from 0 to 1 (0% to 100%), segmenting them in every 0.1 (every 10%). Figure 4.22 shows the outcomes of the previous command.

```
   0%   10%   20%   30%   40%   50%   60%   70%   80%   90%  100%
44.00 44.50 44.75 44.90 45.00 45.00 45.50 45.75 46.10 46.25 46.50
```

FIGURE 4.22 The decile division of the object `processing_time`, according to the fifth definition of Hyndman and Fan (1996).

In Figure 4.22, the 10% label identifies D_1; the 20% label identifies D_2, and so on. **To measure the percentiles**, it must be argued that the breaks present in `probs` should vary in every 0.01, that is, 1%:

```
quantile(processing_time,
         probs = seq(from = 0, to = 1, by = 0.01),
         type = 5,
         na.rm = TRUE)
```

Finally, Figure 4.23 shows the percentiles of the values shown in Table 4.11, whose interpretation must be similar to that already presented.

```
   0%    1%    2%    3%    4%    5%    6%    7%    8%    9%   10%   11%   12%   13%
44.00 44.00 44.00 44.05 44.15 44.25 44.35 44.45 44.50 44.50 44.50 44.50 44.50 44.52
  14%   15%   16%   17%   18%   19%   20%   21%   22%   23%   24%   25%   26%   27%
44.56 44.60 44.64 44.68 44.71 44.73 44.75 44.77 44.79 44.81 44.83 44.85 44.87 44.89
  28%   29%   30%   31%   32%   33%   34%   35%   36%   37%   38%   39%   40%   41%
44.90 44.90 44.90 44.90 44.90 44.91 44.93 44.95 44.97 44.99 45.00 45.00 45.00 45.00
  42%   43%   44%   45%   46%   47%   48%   49%   50%   51%   52%   53%   54%   55%
45.00 45.00 45.00 45.00 45.00 45.00 45.00 45.00 45.00 45.00 45.00 45.04 45.12 45.20
  56%   57%   58%   59%   60%   61%   62%   63%   64%   65%   66%   67%   68%   69%
45.28 45.36 45.42 45.46 45.50 45.54 45.58 45.61 45.63 45.65 45.67 45.69 45.71 45.73
  70%   71%   72%   73%   74%   75%   76%   77%   78%   79%   80%   81%   82%   83%
45.75 45.77 45.79 45.82 45.86 45.90 45.94 45.98 46.02 46.06 46.10 46.14 46.18 46.20
  84%   85%   86%   87%   88%   89%   90%   91%   92%   93%   94%   95%   96%   97%
46.20 46.20 46.20 46.20 46.21 46.23 46.25 46.27 46.29 46.32 46.36 46.40 46.44 46.48
  98%   99%  100%
46.50 46.50 46.50
```

FIGURE 4.23 The percentile division of the object `processing_time`, according to the fifth definition of Hyndman and Fan (1996).

On the other hand, to calculate the quartiles, deciles, and percentiles of grouped discrete data, similarly to the what was studied for the arithmetic mean and the median, we suggest the nested use of the functions `rep()` and `quartile ()`—something like `quartile(rep(groups of discrete data here, discrete values of the variable to be measured here, the quantiles here), probs = the information on whether you want to calculate quartiles, deciles or percentiles here, type = 5, na.rm = TRUE)`.

Finally, for the measurement of quartiles, deciles, and percentiles of continuous data grouped into classes, there is no predefined function in R-based language.

Measures of dispersion or variability

Case 1: Average deviation of ungrouped discrete and continuous data

Example 4.12 (Fávero and Belfiore, 2019)

Table 4.12 shows the distances traveled (in kilometers) by a vehicle to deliver 10 packages throughout the day. Calculate the average deviation.

TABLE 4.12 Distances traveled (km) (Fávero and Belfiore, 2019).

12.4	22.6	18.9	9.7	14.5	22.5	26.3	17.7	31.2	20.4

Solution

The average deviation can be calculated in R by combining the functions `sum()`, `abs()` and `length()`. As discussed in Chapter 2, the function `sum()` performs the sum of a given vector; the function `abs()` represents the module operation; and the function `length()` refers to the size of a vector. Thus we can command:

```
distances <- c(12.4,22.6,18.9,9.7,14.5,22.5,26.3,17.7,31.2,20.4)
```

After that, we can check D_m commanding:

```
sum(abs(distances - mean(distances))) / length(distances)
```

Example 4.13 (Fávero and Belfiore, 2019)

Table 4.13 shows the number of goals scored by the D.C. soccer team in their last 30 games, with their respective absolute frequencies. Calculate the average deviation.

TABLE 4.13 Frequency distribution table for Example 4.13 (Fávero and Belfiore, 2019).

Number of goals	F_i
0	5
1	8
2	6
3	4
4	4
5	2
6	1
Sum	**30**

Solution

For the case of calculating the mean deviation for data grouped in R, in addition to combining the functions `sum()`, `abs()`, and `length()`, we must add the function `rep()` because there is a need to calculate the average for grouped data. Thus creating the vectors of goals and the frequencies of their occurrences, we have:

```
goals <- c(0, 1, 2, 3, 4, 5, 6)
frequencies <- c(5, 8, 6, 4, 4, 2, 1)
```

After that, we must command:

```
sum(abs(goals - mean(rep(goals, frequencies))) * frequencies) /
  sum(frequencies)
```

Example 4.14 (Fávero and Belfiore, 2019)

One of the phases in the preparation of concrete is mixing it in a concrete mixer. Tables 4.14 and 4.15 show the concrete mixing times (in seconds), considering a sample with 10 and 30 elements, respectively. Calculate the standard error for both cases and interpret the results.

TABLE 4.14 Concrete mixing time for a sample with 10 elements (Fávero and Belfiore, 2019).

124	111	132	142	108	127	133	144	148	105

TABLE 4.15 Concrete mixing time for a sample with 30 elements (Fávero and Belfiore, 2019).

125	102	135	126	132	129	156	112	108	134
126	104	143	140	138	129	119	114	107	121
124	112	148	145	130	125	120	127	106	148

Solution

Calculate the coefficient of variation for both samples of the previous example.

Solution

There is also no function for calculating the coefficient of variation in R-based language. We can inform the reader, for example, about the existence of the function `coefficient.variation()` of the package `FinCal` but, for the same reasons pointed out in the previous section, we believe it is faster that the reader uses the statistical fundamentals and functions already studied in the course of this book to calculate the coefficient of variation. Furthermore, the function `coefficient.variation()` of the package `FinCal` requires the reader to argue the standard deviation and the average of the data. If the reader already proposes to do this kind of calculation, it does not make much sense to download, install, and command a package for that. Thus we can command:

```
cv1 <- (sd(table4_39)/mean(table4_39)) * 100

cv2 <- (sd(table4_40)/mean(table4_40)) * 100
```

Objects `cv1` and `cv2` started to contain the coefficients of variation of the data present in Tables 4.14 and 4.15, respectively:

```
cv1

cv2
```

Coefficient of skewness in R

The calculation of skewness in the R language can be done in different ways (e.g. following the foundations proposed in earlier in this chapter along with the functions presented. Here, we separate, for example, the function `skewness()` from the package `e1071`.

The aforementioned function `skewness()` requires the declaration of three arguments: (1) `x`: a numeric vector that contains the data for which the skewness is to be verified; (2) `na.rm`: a logical value, `TRUE` or `FALSE`, in this case informing the algorithm whether or not missing values should be considered; and (3) `type`: a numeric value from 1 to 3 that informs the type of skewness measure to be calculated.

That said, we will demonstrate the use of the argument `type` of the function `skewness()`. Thus we will create the vector `processing_time` from the data shown in Table 4.11, commanding:

```
processing_time <- c(45.0, 44.5, 44.0, 45.0, 46.5, 46.0, 45.8, 44.8,
                     45.0, 46.2, 44.5, 45.0, 45.4, 44.9, 45.7, 46.2,
                     44.7, 45.6, 46.3, 44.9)
```

First Case: argument `type = 1`: R will calculate the coefficient of skewness from the second and third moments around the mean (M_2 and M_3), as follows:

$$G_{\text{type1}} = \frac{M_3}{M_2^{\frac{3}{2}}} \tag{4.1}$$

em que:

$$M_2 = \frac{\sum_{i=1}^{n} (X_i - \overline{X})^2}{n} \tag{4.2}$$

In this sense, we can command:

```
skewness(processing_time, na.rm = FALSE, type = 1)
```

Second Case: argument `type = 2`: R will calculate the Fisher's coefficient of skewness.

The command is:

```
skewness(processing_time, na.rm = FALSE, type = 2)
```

Third Case – argument `type = 3`: R will calculate the coefficient of skewness with the argument `type = 1`, but applying a correction factor, as follows:

$$G_{\text{type3}} = G_{\text{type1}} \cdot \left[\left(\frac{(n-1)}{n} \right) \right]^{\frac{3}{2}} \tag{4.3}$$

Thus it would suffice to command:

```
skewness(processing_time, na.rm = FALSE, type = 3)
```

Coefficient of kurtosis in R

The calculation of skewness in R can be done in several ways, and the same can be said about calculating kurtosis. As an example, we will use the function `kurtosis()` of the package `e1071`.

The function `kurtosis()`, as well as the function `skewness()`, requires the declaration of 3 arguments: a) `x`: a numeric vector that contains the data that the reader wants to check for kurtosis; b) `na.rm`: a logical value - `TRUE` or `FALSE`, in this case - informing the algorithm whether or not missing values should be considered; and c) `type`: a numeric value from 1 to 3, which informs the type of kurtosis measure to be calculated.

In this way, the use of the argument `type` of the function `kurtosis()` will be demonstrated. Thus we will create the vector `stocks` from the data shown in Table 4.16.

TABLE 4.16 Prices of stock Y throughout the month (Fávero and Belfiore, 2019).

18.7	18.3	18.4	18.7	18.8	18.8	19.1	18.9	19.1	19.9
18.5	18.5	18.1	17.9	18.2	18.3	18.1	18.8	17.5	16.9

In this sense, we can command:

```
stocks <- c(18.7, 18.3, 18.4, 18.7, 18.8, 18.8, 19.1, 18.9, 19.1,
            19.9, 18.5, 18.5, 18.1, 17.9, 18.2, 18.3, 18.1, 18.8,
            17.5, 16.9)
```

First Case: argument `type = 1`: R will calculate the coefficient of kurtosis from the second and fourth moments around the mean (M_2 and M_4), as follows:

$$K_{type1} = \frac{M_4}{M_2^2 - 3} \tag{4.4}$$

For that, we must command:

```
kurtosis(stocks, na.rm = FALSE, type = 1)
```

Second Case: argument `type = 2`: R will calculate the Fisher's coefficient of kurtosis. Thus the command must be:

```
kurtosis(stocks, na.rm = FALSE, type = 2)
```

Third Case: argument `type = 3`: R will calculate the coefficient of kurtosis with the argument `type = 1`, but applying a correction factor, as follows:

$$K_{type3} = \left(K_{type1} + 3\right) \cdot \left[\left(1 - \frac{1}{n}\right)^2 - 3\right] \tag{4.5}$$

In this sense, we can just command:

```
kurtosis(stocks, na.rm = FALSE, type = 3)
```

Final remarks

The descriptive statistics used to represent the behavior of a qualitative variable's data are frequency distribution tables and charts. The frequency distribution table for a qualitative variable represents the frequency in which each variable category occurs. The graphical representation of qualitative variables can be illustrated by bar charts (horizontal and vertical), pie charts, and Pareto charts (Fávero and Belfiore, 2019).

For quantitative variables, the most common descriptive statistics are charts and summary measures (measures of position or location, measures of dispersion or variability, and measures of shape). Frequency distribution tables can also be used to represent the frequency in which each possible value of a discrete variable occurs or to represent the frequency of continuous variables' data grouped into classes. Line graphs, dot or scatter plots, histograms, stem-and-leaf plots, and boxplots (or box-and-whisker diagrams) are normally used to graphically represent quantitative variables (Fávero and Belfiore, 2019).

Exercises

1. Table 4.17 shows the number of vehicles sold by a dealership in the past 30 days. Create a frequency distribution table for these data (Fávero and Belfiore, 2019).

TABLE 4.17 Number of vehicles sold.

7	5	9	11	10	8	9	6	8	10
8	5	7	11	9	11	6	7	10	9
8	5	6	8	6	7	6	5	10	8

2. A survey on patients' health was carried out and information regarding the weight of 50 patients was collected (Table 4.18). Create a frequency distribution table for these data (Fávero and Belfiore, 2019).

TABLE 4.18 Patients' weight.

60.4	78.9	65.7	82.1	80.9	92.3	85.7	86.6	90.3	93.2
75.2	77.3	80.4	62.0	90.4	70.4	80.5	75.9	55.0	84.3
81.3	78.3	70.5	85.6	71.9	77.5	76.1	67.7	80.6	78.0
71.6	74.8	92.1	87.7	83.8	93.4	69.3	97.8	81.7	72.2
69.3	80.2	90.0	76.9	54.7	78.4	55.2	75.5	99.3	66.7

3. At an electrical appliances factory, in the door component production phase, the quality inspector verifies the total number of parts rejected per type of defect (lack of alignment, scratches, deformation, discoloration, and oxygenation), as shown in Table 4.19 (Fávero and Belfiore, 2019).

TABLE 4.19 Total number of parts rejected per type of defect.

Type of defect	Total
Lack of alignment	98
Scratches	67
Deformation	45
Discoloration	28
Oxygenation	12
Total	**250**

We would like you to:

a. Create a frequency distribution table for these data.
b. Construct a pie chart and a Pareto chart.

4. A passenger collected the average travel times (in minutes) of a bus in Vila Mariana, on the Jabaquara route, for 120 days (Table 4.20) (Fávero and Belfiore, 2019).

TABLE 4.20 Average travel times in 120 days.

Time	Number of days
30	4
32	7
33	10
35	12
38	18
40	22
42	20
43	15
45	8
50	4

We would like you to:

a. Calculate the arithmetic mean, median, and mode.
b. Calculate Q_1, Q_3, D_4, P_{61}, and P_{84}.
c. Are there any outliers?
d. Calculate the range, variance, standard deviation, and standard error.
e. Calculate Fisher's coefficient of skewness (g_1) and Fisher's coefficient of kurtosis (g_2). Classify the symmetry and the flatness level of each distribution.
f. Construct a bar chart, histogram, stem-and-leaf plot, and boxplot.

5. To improve the quality of its services, a retail company collected the average service time, in seconds, of 250 employees. The data were grouped into classes, with their respective absolute and relative frequencies, as shown in Table 4.21 (Fávero and Belfiore, 2019).

TABLE 4.21 Average service time.

Class	F_i	Fr_i (%)
30 ├ 60	11	4.4
60 ├ 90	29	11.6
90 ├ 120	41	16.4
120 ├ 150	82	32.8
150 ├ 180	54	21.6
180 ├ 210	33	13.2
Sum	**250**	**100**

We would like you to:

a. Calculate the arithmetic mean, median, and mode.
b. Calculate Q_1, Q_3, D_2, P_{13}, and P_{95}.
c. Are there any outliers?
d. Calculate the range, variance, standard deviation, and standard error.
e. Calculate Pearson's first coefficient of skewness and the coefficient of kurtosis. Classify the symmetry and the flatness level of each distribution.
f. Construct a histogram.

Supplementary data sets

```
bank.RData
blood_donors.RData
cards.RData
cheap_easy.RData
dehydration.RData
papermisto.RData
patients_weight.RData
political_parties.RData
salaries.RData
satisfaction_survey.RData
services.RData
temperature.RData
```

Please access supplementary data files here: https://doi.org/10.17632/55623jkwrp.3

CHAPTER

5

Bivariate descriptive statistics

AT THE END OF THIS CHAPTER, YOU WILL BE ABLE TO:

- Study the associations between two qualitative variables using contingency tables and measures of association such as chi-square statistics (used for nominal and ordinal qualitative variables); the *Phi* coefficient, the contingency coefficient, and the Cramér's *V* coefficient (all based on chi-square and used for nominal variables); and Spearman's coefficient (used for ordinal qualitative variables).
- Study the correlation between two quantitative variables using joint frequency distribution tables; graphical representations such as a scatter plot; and measures of correlation such as covariance and Pearson's correlation coefficient.
- Implement the codes using R-based language.

R-based language packages used for this chapter

```
library(sjPlot)
library(DescTools)
```

Don't forget to define the R working directory (the location where your datasets are installed):

```
setwd("C:/book/chapter5")
```

Introduction

In this chapter we study the associations between two qualitative variables using contingency tables and measures of association, such as chi-square statistics (used for nominal and ordinal qualitative variables. We also study the correlation between two quantitative variables using joint frequency distribution tables, as well as graphical representations such as a scatter plots.

https://doi.org/10.1016/B978-0-12-824271-1.00003-2

Association between two qualitative variables

Joint frequency distribution tables (Fávero and Belfiore, 2019)

Example 5.1 (Fávero and Belfiore, 2019)

A study was done with 200 individuals to analyze the joint behavior of variable x (*health insurance agency*) with variable y (*level of satisfaction*). Table 5.1 shows the contingency table with the variables' joint absolute frequency distribution and the marginal totals. The data are available in the file `health_insurance.RData` (Fávero and Belfiore, 2019).

TABLE 5.1 Joint absolute frequency distribution of the variables being studied (Fávero and Belfiore, 2019).

	Level of satisfaction			
Agency	**Dissatisfied**	**Neutral**	**Satisfied**	**Total**
Live Life	32	24	16	**72**
Mena Health	24	32	4	**60**
Total Health	40	16	12	**68**
Total	**96**	**72**	**32**	**200**

Elaborating contingency tables in R

For the construction of a frequency table in R, we can, for example, use the function `table()`. We ask the reader to load the following dataset:

```
load("health_insurance.RData")
```

After that, we can prepare our frequency table, as follows:

```
table(health_insurance)
```

The result obtained from the previous command is shown in Figure 5.1:

```
                satisfaction_level
agency          dissatisfied neutral satisfied
  live life               32      24        16
  mena health             24      32         4
  total health            40      16        12
```

FIGURE 5.1 Example of a contingency table built in R.

To establish a joint relative frequency distribution of the variables being studied in relation to the general total, we must use the function `prop.table ()`:

```
prop.table(table(health_insurance))
```

Figure 5.2 shows the joint relative frequency distribution of the variables being studied, in relation to the general total, built in R.

```
                satisfaction_level
agency          dissatisfied neutral satisfied
  live life             0.16    0.12      0.08
  mena health           0.12    0.16      0.02
  total health          0.20    0.08      0.06
```

FIGURE 5.2 Joint relative frequency distribution of the variables being studied in relation to the general total.

If the intention is to establish a joint relative frequency distribution of the variables being studied in relation to the total of each row or in relation to the total of each column, we must use the argument `margin` in the function `prop.table()`, whose values will be 1 for the first case (row) or 2 for the second case (column).

Thus, to define a joint relative frequency distribution of the variables being studied in relation to the total of each row, we must command:

```
prop.table(table(health_insurance), margin = 1)
```

On the other hand, to define a joint relative frequency distribution of the variables being studied in relation to the total of each column, we must command:

```
prop.table(table(health_insurance), margin = 2)
```

Figure 5.3 summarizes the results of the previous commands.

```
#margin = 1

                satisfaction_level
agency           dissatisfied    neutral  satisfied
  live life        0.44444444 0.33333333 0.22222222
  mena health      0.40000000 0.53333333 0.06666667
  total health     0.58823529 0.23529412 0.17647059


#margin = 2

                satisfaction_level
agency          dissatisfied   neutral satisfied
  live life        0.3333333 0.3333333 0.5000000
  mena health      0.2500000 0.4444444 0.1250000
  total health     0.4166667 0.2222222 0.3750000
```

FIGURE 5.3 Joint relative frequency distribution of the variables being studied in relation to the total of each row and column, respectively.

If the reader wants a solution to the problem that contains all of the information present in Figures 5.1 and 5.3, we suggest using the function `sjt.xtab()` from the package `sjPlot`. In the aforementioned function, we must argue `var.row` and `var.col` as the variables that will be part of the contingency table and `show.row.prc = TRUE` and `show.col.prc = TRUE` to access the joint relative frequency distribution of the variables being studied in relation to the total of each row and column:

```
attach(health_insurance)

sjt.xtab(var.row = agency,
         var.col = satisfaction_level,
         show.row.prc = TRUE,
         show.col.prc = TRUE)
```

Figure 5.4 shows the result obtained from the previous proposed command.

	satisfaction_level			
agency	dissatisfied	neutral	satisfied	*Total*
live life	32 44.4 % 33.3 %	24 33.3 % 33.3 %	16 22.2 % 50 %	72 100 % 36 %
mena health	24 40 % 25 %	32 53.3 % 44.4 %	4 6.7 % 12.5 %	60 100 % 30 %
total health	40 58.8 % 41.7 %	16 23.5 % 22.2 %	12 17.6 % 37.5 %	68 100 % 34 %
Total	96 48 % 100 %	72 36 % 100 %	32 16 % 100 %	200 100 % 100 %

FIGURE 5.4 Outcome of the function `sjt.xtab()`.

Measures of association (Fávero and Belfiore, 2019)

Chi-square statistic

Example 5.2 (Fávero and Belfiore, 2019)
Calculate the χ^2 statistic for Example 5.1.

Solving the chi-square statistic in R

To calculate the χ^2 statistic in R, the function `chisq.test()` of the base language is used. Thus when we assume the data from Example 5.1, we must tab them with the function `table()` so we can apply the test:

```
chisq.test(table(health_insurance))
```

Figure 5.5 shows the result.

FIGURE 5.5 Chi-square statistic in R.

```
        Pearson's Chi-squared test

data:  table(health_insurance)
X-squared = 15.861, df = 4, p-value = 0.003212
```

If the reader is interested in viewing the expected values (E_{ij}) in R, it would be enough to save the above command in an object and explore its components with the operator `$`. Thus:

```
chi2 <- chisq.test(table(health_insurance))
```

So, to view the observed values:

```
chi2$observed
```

And to view the expected values:

```
chi2$expected
```

If the reader wants the value of the χ^2 statistic established in the object `chi2`, simply command:

```
chi2$statistic
```

Example 5.3 (Fávero and Belfiore, 2019)

To offer high-quality services and meet their customers' expectations, Ivanblue, a company in the male fashion industry, is investing in strategies to segment the market. Currently, the company has four stores in Campinas, located in the north, center, south and east regions of the city, and they sell four types of clothing: ties, shirts, polo shirts, and pants. Table 5.2 shows the purchase data for 20 customers, such as the type of clothing and the location of the store. Check if there is an association between the two variables using the *Phi* coefficient (Fávero and Belfiore, 2019).

TABLE 5.2 Purchase data for 20 customers.

Customer	Clothing	Region
1	Tie	South
2	Polo shirt	North
3	Shirt	South
4	Pants	North
5	Tie	South
6	Polo shirt	Center
7	Polo shirt	East
8	Tie	South
9	Shirt	South
10	Tie	Center
11	Pants	North
12	Pants	Center
13	Tie	Center
14	Polo shirt	East
15	Pants	Center
16	Tie	Center
17	Pants	South
18	Pants	North
19	Polo shirt	East
20	Shirt	Center

Solution: calculating *Phi*, contingency, and Cramér's *V* coefficients in R

As already stated, all measures of association discussed earlier in the "Other measures of association based on chi-square" section are derived from the χ^2 statistic. Thus the reader can establish his or her own formulas or functions because the fundamentals have already been established.

Even so, we will present some functions from the package `DescTools` because the R-based language does not have direct ways of calculating the studied measures. That said, we ask the reader to load the dataset `ivanblue.RData` (Fávero and Belfiore, 2019):

```
load("ivanblue.RData")
```

***Phi* Coefficient**: We suggest that the reader use the function `Phi()` from the package `DescTools`. To command it, we argue the used contingency table:

```
Phi(table(ivanblue[, 2:3]))
```

Contingency Coefficient (*C*): To calculate it directly in R, we must command the function `ContCoef()` from the package `Desctools`:

```
ContCoef(table(ivanblue[, 2:3]))
```

Cramér's *V* Coefficient: Finally, for the calculation of Cramér's *V* coefficient, with the aid of the package `DescTools`, we command the function `CramerV()`:

```
CramerV(table(ivanblue[, 2:3]))
```

Spearman's coefficient (Fávero and Belfiore, 2019)

Example 5.6 (Fávero and Belfiore, 2019)

The coordinator of a business administration course is analyzing if there is any association between the grades of 10 students in two different subjects: simulation and finance. The data regarding this problem are presented in Table 5.3. Calculate Spearman's coefficient for the data in Table 5.3.

TABLE 5.3 Grades in the subjects simulation and finance for 10 students being analyzed (Fávero and Belfiore, 2019).

	Grades	
Student	**Simulation**	**Finance**
1	4.7	6.6
2	6.3	5.1
3	7.5	6.9
4	5.0	7.1
5	4.4	3.5
6	3.7	4.6
7	8.5	6.8
8	8.2	7.5
9	3.5	4.2
10	4.0	3.3

Calculating Spearman's coefficient in R

To demonstrate calculation of Spearman's coefficient in R, we ask the reader to load the dataset `grades.RData` (Fávero and Belfiore, 2019):

```
load("grades.RData")
```

After that, we can use the function `cor.test()` present in the R-based language. We must argue the following to the function: *x*, which is the vector that contains one of the variables to be analyzed; *y*, which is another vector that contains the other variable to be studied; and `method = "spearman"`. Thus:

```
cor.test(x = grades$simulation,
         y = grades$finance,
         method = "spearman")
```

Figure 5.6 shows the solution for calculating the coefficient r_{sp} in R.

```
        Spearman's rank correlation rho

data:  grades$simulation and grades$finance
S = 40, p-value = 0.01592
alternative hypothesis: true rho is not equal to 0
sample estimates:
      rho
0.7575758
```

FIGURE 5.6 Spearman's coefficient in R.

The *P*-value = 0.016 < 0.05 (under the null hypothesis of non-relationship between the variables) indicates that there is a correlation between the grades in the subjects simulation and finance, with a confidence level of 95%.

Correlation between two quantitative variables

Constructing a scatter plot in R

Example 5.7

Let's open the file `income_education.RData` (Fávero and Belfiore, 2019) in R. The objective is to analyze the correlation between the variables *family income* and *years of education* using a scatter plot:

```
load("income_education.RData")
```

We can build a scatter plot with the function `plot()` using R-based language. In Chapter 7, we will present ways to create more elegant graphs with the package `ggplot2`.

```
plot(income_education$yearsofeducation,
     income_education$familyincome,
     col = "orange",
     xlab = "Years of Education",
     ylab = "Family Income")
```

Figure 5.7 shows our scatter plot.

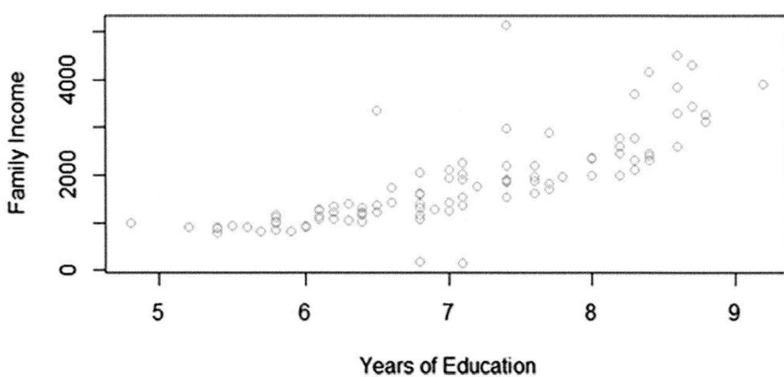

FIGURE 5.7 Scatter plot for variables family income and years of education.

Figure 5.7 shows a strong positive correlation between the variables *family income* and *years of education*. Therefore, the greater the number of years studied, the greater the family income, even if there is not necessarily a cause-and-effect relationship.

Solution (calculation of covariance and Pearson's correlation coefficient) in R

Still using the dataset in the file `income_education.RData`, we can use the function `cov()` to calculate the covariance and use the function `cor()` to calculate Pearson's correlation coefficient. Both commands are in R-based language, and their results are shown in Figure 5.8.

```
cov(income_education)

cor(income_education)
```

FIGURE 5.8 Functions `cov()` and `cor()` in R.

```
#covariance
                 familyincome yearsofeducation
familyincome       942403.015       761.336047
yearsofeducation      761.336         1.017895

#correlation
                 familyincome yearsofeducation
familyincome        1.0000000        0.7773322
yearsofeducation    0.7773322        1.0000000
```

Final remarks

The construction and interpretation of frequency distribution tables, graphical representations, and summary measures (measures of position or location and measures of dispersion or variability) provide the researcher a better understanding and clearer visualization of the data behavior for two variables simultaneously. More advanced techniques can be applied in the future to the same dataset so researchers can go deeper in their studies on bivariate analysis, with the aim of improving the quality of the decision-making process (Fávero and Belfiore, 2019).

Exercises

1. The file `motivation_companies.RData` contains a dataset with the variables *company* and *level of motivation* (*motivation*) that was obtained from a survey of 250 employees (50 respondents for each of the 5 companies surveyed) and aimed at assessing employees' level of motivation in relation to the companies (which were considered to be large firms) (Fávero and Belfiore, 2019). We would like you to:

a. Construct contingency tables of absolute frequencies, relative frequencies in relation to the general total, relative frequencies in relation to the total of each row, relative frequencies in relation to the total of each column, and expected frequencies;
b. Calculate the percentage of individuals who are very demotivated.
c. Calculate the percentage of individuals from Company A who are very demotivated.
d. Calculate the percentage of individuals from Company D who are motivated.
e. Calculate the percentage of individuals from Company C who are slightly motivated.
f. Among the individuals who are very motivated, determine the percentage of those who work for Company B.
g. Verify if there are indications of dependence between the variables.
h. Confirm the previous item using the χ^2 statistic.
i. Calculate the *Phi* coefficient, contingency coefficient, and Cramér's *V* coefficient, and confirm whether or not there is an association between the variables.

2. The file `students_evaluation.RData` contains the grades (from 0 to 10) of 100 students from a public university in relation to the following subjects: operational research, statistics, operations management, and finance. Construct a scatter plot and calculate Pearson's correlation coefficient to see if there is a correlation between the following pairs of variables (Fávero and Belfiore, 2019):
   a. Operational research and statistics
   b. Operations management and finance
   c. Operational research and operations management
3. The file `brazilian_supermarkets.RData` contains revenue data and the number of stores for the 20 largest Brazilian supermarket chains in a given year (source: The Brazilian Association of Supermarkets [ABRAS]). We would like you to (Fávero and Belfiore, 2019):
   a. Construct a scatter plot for the variables *revenue* × *number of stores*.
   b. Calculate Pearson's correlation coefficient between the two variables.
   c. Exclude the four largest supermarket chains in terms of revenue, and, once again, construct a scatter plot.
   d. Once again, calculate Pearson's correlation coefficient between the two variables being studied.

Supplementary data sets

```
brazilian_supermarkets.RData
default.RData
grades.RData
health_insurance.RData
income_education.RData
ivanblue.RData
motivation_companies.RData
students_evaluation.RData
```

Please access supplementary data files here: https://doi.org/10.17632/55623jkwrp.3

CHAPTER

6

Hypotheses tests

AT THE END OF THIS CHAPTER, YOU WILL BE ABLE TO:

- Study the main types of parametric hypotheses tests.
- Understand the assumptions inherent to each parametric test.
- Define in which situation each parametric test can be used.
- Solve each test analytically using R-based language, and interpret the obtained results.

R-based language packages used in this chapter

```
library(nortest)
library(outliers)
library(PMCMRplus)
library(car)
library(BSDA)
library(tidyverse)
```

Introduction

In this chapter we present how to apply and interpret hypotheses tests in R, such as univariate tests for normality, tests for homogeneity of variance, hypotheses tests regarding a population mean, tests to compare population means from random samples, analysis of variance to compare the means of more than two populations, and factorial ANOVA tests.

Univariate tests for normality

Example 6.1: Applying the Kolmogorov-Smirnov test (Fávero and Belfiore, 2019)

Table 6.1 shows the data for a company's monthly production of farming equipment in the past 36 months. Check if the data in Table 6.1 are drawn from a population that follows a normal distribution, considering that $\alpha = 5\%$.

TABLE 6.1 Production of farming equipment in the past 36 months.

52	50	44	50	42	30	36	34	48	40	55	40
30	36	40	42	55	44	38	42	40	38	52	44
52	34	38	44	48	36	36	55	50	34	44	42

Data Science, Analytics and Machine Learning with R
https://doi.org/10.1016/B978-0-12-824271-1.00004-4

Example 6.2: Applying the Shapiro-Wilk test (Fávero and Belfiore, 2019)

Table 6.2 shows the data for an aerospace company's monthly production of aircraft in the past 24 months. Check if the data in Table 6.2 are drawn from a population with a normal distribution, considering that $\alpha = 1\%$.

TABLE 6.2 Production of aircraft in the past 24 months.

28	32	46	24	22	18	20	34	30	24	31	29
15	19	23	25	28	30	32	36	39	16	23	36

Example 6.3: Applying the Shapiro-Francia test (Fávero and Belfiore, 2019)

Table 6.3 shows the data regarding a company's daily production of bicycles in the past 60 months. Check if the data are drawn from a population with a normal distribution, considering $\alpha = 5\%$.

TABLE 6.3 Production of bicycles in the past 60 months.

85	70	74	49	67	88	80	91	57	63	66	60
72	81	73	80	55	54	93	77	80	64	60	63
67	54	59	78	73	84	91	57	59	64	68	67
70	76	78	75	80	81	70	77	65	63	59	60
61	74	76	81	79	78	60	68	76	71	72	84

Solving tests for normality in R

The K-S normality test can be implemented using R-based language. The S-F test can be applied using the package `nortest`.

Consider the data in Example 6.1. The data are available in the file `production_farming_equipment.RData` (Fávero and Belfiore, 2019).

```
load("production_farming_equipment.RData")
```

To perform the K-S test in R, we must use the function `ks.test()`, declaring the dataset and a theoretical sample distribution with the same mean and standard deviation obtained from our data. Thus the following arguments must be declared to the function: *x*, which represents the observed dataset; *y*, which represents the theoretical sample distribution to be compared (a normal distribution in this case); `mean`, which represents the mean obtained from our observed data; and `sd`, which represents the standard deviation of the observed data. Thst said, we can command:

```
ks.test(x = production_farming_equipment$production,
        y = "pnorm",
        mean = mean(production_farming_equipment$production),
        sd = sd(production_farming_equipment$production))
```

Figure 6.1 shows the result obtained from the previous command. This allows us to conclude that the data distribution is normal at a confidence level of 95%. The warning message, in red, is recurrent in the chosen function when there are repeated data.

According to Figure 6.1, the result of the K-S statistic equals 0.118, which is similar to the value calculated in Example 6.1. Because the sample has more than 30 elements, we should only use the K-S test to verify the normality of the data (the S-W test was applied to Example 6.2).

```
        One-sample Kolmogorov-Smirnov test

data:  production_farming_equipment$production
D = 0.11843, p-value = 0.6936
alternative hypothesis: two-sided

Warning message:
In ks.test(x = production_farming_equipment$production, y = "pnorm",
:
  ties should not be present for the Kolmogorov-Smirnov test
```

FIGURE 6.1 The function `ks.test()`.

As presented in the introduction of this chapter, R calculates the *P*-value that corresponds to the lowest significance level observed that would lead to the rejection of the null hypothesis. For the K-S test, the *P*-value corresponds to the lowest value of *P* from which $D_{cal} > D_c$. Because $P > 0.05$, we do not reject the null hypothesis, which allows us to conclude with a 95% confidence level that the data distribution is normal. The S-W test also allows us to conclude that the data distribution follows a normal distribution.

To implement the S-W test, we will use the data from Example 6.2. The data are available in the file `production_aircraft.RData` (Fávero and Belfiore, 2019). Thus:

```
load("production_aircraft.RData")
```

The S-W test can be implemented using the function `shapiro.test()`, as follows:

```
shapiro.test(production_aircraft$production)
```

Figure 6.2 contains R's response to the previous command ($W_{cal}=0.978$).

```
        Shapiro-Wilk normality test

data:  production_aircraft$production
W = 0.97801, p-value = 0.8565
```

FIGURE 6.2 The function `shapiro.test()`.

Finally, to perform the S-F test in R, we will use the data from Example 6.3. The data are available in the file `production_bicycles.RData` (Fávero and Belfiore, 2019). Therefore we must command:

```
load("production_bicycles.RData")
```

The function `sf.test()`, from the package `nortest`, performs the S-F test. Thus:

```
sf.test(production_bicycles$production)
```

Figure 6.3 shows the results of the Shapiro-Francia test.

```
        Shapiro-Francia normality test

data:  production_bicycles$production
W = 0.98669, p-value = 0.6642
```

FIGURE 6.3 The function `sf.test()`.

Tests for homogeneity of variance

Example 6.4: Applying the Bartlett's χ2 test (Fávero and Belfiore, 2019)
A chain of supermarkets wishes to study the number of customers they serve every day to make strategic operational decisions. Table 6.4 shows the data for three stores throughout 2 weeks. Check if the variances between the groups are homogeneous. Consider $\alpha = 5\%$.

TABLE 6.4 Number of customers served per day and per store.

	Store 1	**Store 2**	**Store 3**
Day 1	620	710	924
Day 2	630	780	695
Day 3	610	810	854
Day 4	650	755	802
Day 5	585	699	931
Day 6	590	680	924
Day 7	630	710	847
Day 8	644	850	800
Day 9	595	844	769
Day 10	603	730	863
Day 11	570	645	901
Day 12	605	688	888
Day 13	622	718	757
Day 14	578	702	712
Standard deviation	**24.4059**	**62.2466**	**78.9144**
Variance	**595.6484**	**3,874.6429**	**6,227.4780**

Solution
If we apply the K-S test or the S-W test for normality to the data in Table 6.4, we can verify that their distribution shows adherence to normality with a 5% significance level; therefore the Bartlett's χ^2 test can be applied to compare the homogeneity of variances between the groups.

Step 1: Because the main goal is to compare the equality of the variances between the groups, we will use the Bartlett's χ^2 test.
Step 2: The Bartlett's χ^2 test hypotheses for this example are:
H_0: The population variances of all three groups are homogeneous.
H_1: The population variance of at least one group is different from the others.
Step 3: The significance level to be considered is 5%.
Step 4: The complete calculation of the Bartlett's χ^2 statistic is as follows. First, we calculate the value of S_p^2

$$S_p^2 = \frac{13 \times (595.65 + 3,874.64 + 6,227.48)}{42 - 3} = 3,565.92$$

Thus we can calculate q

$$q = 39 \cdot \ln(3,565.92) - 13 \cdot [\ln(595.65) + \ln(3,874.64) + \ln(6,227.48)] = 14.94$$

The correction factor c for q statistic is calculated as follows

$$c = 1 + \left(\frac{1}{3 \cdot (3-1)}\right) \cdot 3 \cdot \left(\frac{1}{13} - \frac{1}{42-3}\right) = 1.0256$$

Finally, we calculate B_{cal}:

$$B_{cal} = \frac{q}{c} = \frac{14.94}{1.0256} = 14.567$$

Example 6.5: Applying the Cochran's C test (Fávero and Belfiore, 2019)

Apply the Cochran's C test for the data in Example 6.4. The main objective is to compare the group with the highest variability in relation to the others.

Example 6.6: Applying the Hartley's F_{max} test (Fávero and Belfiore, 2019)

Apply the Hartley's F_{max} test for the data in Example 6.4. The main goal is to compare the group with the highest variability with the group with the lowest variability.

Example 6.7: Applying the Levene's test (Fávero and Belfiore, 2019)

Apply the Levene's test for the data in Example 6.4.

Solving tests for homogeneity of variance in R

The data in Example 6.4 are available in the file `customer_services_store.RData` (Fávero and Belfiore, 2019). To implement the Bartlett's χ^2 test, we must use the function `bartlett.test()`. Thus we ask the reader to load the dataset:

```
load("customer_services_store.RData")
```

And after that:

```
bartlett.test(formula = customer_services ~ store,
              data = customer_services_store)
```

In the previous command, we type the function `bartlett.test()`, declaring the metric variable *customer services* and indicating that it is grouped by *store*, so the operator ~ is followed by the categorical variable in the argument `formula`; finally, we declare the dataset used in the argument `data`. Figure 6.4 shows the result of the previous routine. An attentive reader will notice a slight difference in the value of Bartlett's χ^2 as a result of rounding.

```
        Bartlett test of homogeneity of variances

data:  customer_services by store
Bartlett's K-squared = 14.443, df = 2, p-value = 0.0007309
```

FIGURE 6.4 Bartlett's χ^2 test in R.

For the Cochran's C test for the data in Example 6.5, we will use the function `cochran.test()` from the package `outliers`. The syntax of the algorithm to be used is similar to the previous function, but now we will use the argument `object` for the vector of variables instead of the argument `formula`, as follows:

```
cochran.test(object = customer_services ~ store,
             data = customer_services_store)
```

Figure 6.5 shows the results obtained from the previous routine.

In R, Hartley's F_{max} test can be performed with the function `hartleyTest()` from the package `PMCMRplus`. Similar to the one applied so far, we can command it to solve Example 6.6:

```
hartleyTest(formula = customer_services ~ store,
            data = customer_services_store)
```

```
        Cochran test for outlying variance

data:  customer_services ~ store
C = 0.58213, df = 14, k = 3, p-value = 0.03794
alternative hypothesis: Group 3 has outlying variance
sample estimates:
        1         2         3
 595.6484 3874.6429 6227.4780
```

FIGURE 6.5 Cochran's C test in R.

The reader can check the result of the previous command in Figure 6.6.

```
        Hartley's maximum F-ratio test of homogeneity of variances

data:  customer_services by store
F Max = 10.455, df = 13, k = 3, p-value = 0.0005683
```

FIGURE 6.6 Hartley's F_{max} test in R.

Finally, for the solution of Example 6.7, we apply Levene's F test using the function `leveneTest()` from the package `car`. We ask the reader to take care not to use a very similar function called `levene.test()` that is also present in the package because it has been discontinued, even though it is still available in R.

The way to command the function `leveneTest()` is similar to the syntaxes used in Examples 6.4, 6.5, and 6.6. The differences are a result of the addition of the argument `center = mean` and the declaration of the argument `y` instead of the argument `formula` or `object`.

```
leveneTest(y = customer_services ~ store,
           data = customer_services_store,
           center = mean)
```

Figure 6.7 shows the result obtained from the previous command.

```
Levene's Test for Homogeneity of Variance (center = mean)
      Df F value    Pr(>F)
group  2  8.4267 0.0009085 ***
      39
---
Signif. codes:  0 '***' 0.001 '**' 0.01 '*' 0.05 '.' 0.1 ' ' 1
```

FIGURE 6.7 Levene's F test in R.

We can see that the result of F_{cal} makes us reject H_0, since $P < 0.05$.

Hypotheses tests regarding a population mean (μ) from one random sample

Example 6.8: Applying the z-test to one sample (Fávero and Belfiore, 2019)

A cereal manufacturer states that the average quantity of food fiber in each portion of its product is, at least, 4.2 g with a standard deviation of 1 g. A health care agency wishes to verify if this statement is true. Collecting a random sample of 42 portions, in which the average quantity of food fiber is 3.9 g. With a significance level equal to 5%, is there evidence to reject the manufacturer's statement?

Example 6.9: Applying the Student's t-test to one sample (Fávero and Belfiore, 2019)

The average processing time of a task using a certain machine has been 18 minutes. New concepts have been implemented to reduce the average processing time. Hence, after a certain period of time, a sample with 25 elements was collected, and an average time of 16.808 minutes was measured, with a standard deviation of 2.733 minutes. Check if this result represents an improvement in the average processing time. Consider $\alpha = 1\%$.

Solving the z-test and the Student's t-test for a single sample in R

For the application of the z-test when the population standard deviation (σ) is known and the distribution is normal, the function `z.test()` from the package `BSDA` can be used. We ask the reader to open the file `z_test_one_sample.RData` (Fávero and Belfiore, 2019), as follows:

```
load("z_test_one_sample.RData")
```

After that, we can command the following to obtain the solution for Example 6.8:

```
z.test(x = z_test_one_sample$production,
       mu = 4.2,
       sigma.x = 1,
       alternative = "less")
```

In the previous routine, we type `x = z_test_one_sample$production` to indicate the numeric vector for the application of the z-test. As we seek to verify that the average amount of food fiber in each product is 4.2 g, we must also type `mu = 4.2`. In addition, the argument `sigma.x` refers to the known standard deviation of the sample, which is 1. Finally, as we are looking for a left-tailed unilateral test, we type `alternative = "less"` (for a right-tailed unilateral test, we can type `alternative = "greater"` and, for a bilateral test, `alternative = "two.sided"`). Figure 6.8 shows the result of the command of the function `z.test()` applied to Example 6.8.

```
data:  z_test_one_sample$production
z = -1.9442, p-value = 0.02593
alternative hypothesis: true mean is less than 4.2
95 percent confidence interval:
       NA 4.153806
sample estimates:
mean of x
      3.9
```

FIGURE 6.8 Z-test in R for the case when the population standard deviation (σ) is known and the distribution is normal.

To implement the Student's t-test in the data of Example 6.9, we can use the function `t.test()` of R-base language, which has a syntax very close to the function previously studied. Initially, we must load the file `t_test_one_sample.RData` (Fávero and Belfiore, 2019).

```
load("t_test_one_sample.RData")
```

Thus we can command the function `t.test()`, declaring the numeric value to be studied to the argument `x`; the mean to the argument `mu`; and, finally, `alternative = "less"` because it is a left-tailed unilateral test.

```
t.test(x = t_test_one_sample$time,
       mu = 18,
       alternative = "less")
```

If the reader is interested in a right-tailed unilateral test, it would be enough to command `alternative = "greater"`. If the interest is in a bilateral test, then the reader would command `alternative = "two.sided"`.

Figure 6.9 shows the result of the Student's t-test for Example 6.9.

This figure shows the result of the t-test (similar to the value calculated in Example 6.9) and the associated probability (P-value) for a bilateral test. For a unilateral test, the associated probability is 0.0195 (we saw in Example 6.9 that this probability would be between 0.01 and 0.025). Because $0.0195 > 0.01$, we do not reject the null hypothesis, which allows us to conclude with a 99% confidence level that there was no improvement in average processing time.

```
        One Sample t-test

data:  t_test_one_sample$time
t = -2.1804, df = 24, p-value = 0.01963
alternative hypothesis: true mean is less than 18
95 percent confidence interval:
    -Inf 17.74331
sample estimates:
mean of x
   16.808
```

FIGURE 6.9 Student's *t*-test for Example 6.9.

Student's *t*-test to compare two population means from two independent random samples

Example 6.10: Applying the Student's *t*-test to two independent samples (Fávero and Belfiore, 2019)
A quality engineer believes that the average time to manufacture a certain plastic product may depend on the raw materials used, which come from two different suppliers. A sample with 30 observations from each supplier was collected for a test, and the results are shown in Tables 6.5 and 6.6. Check if there is any difference between the means ($\alpha = 5\%$).

TABLE 6.5 Manufacturing time using raw materials from supplier 1.

22.8	23.4	26.2	24.3	22.0	24.8	26.7	25.1	23.1	22.8
25.6	25.1	24.3	24.2	22.8	23.2	24.7	26.5	24.5	23.6
23.9	22.8	25.4	26.7	22.9	23.5	23.8	24.6	26.3	22.7

TABLE 6.6 Manufacturing time using raw materials from supplier 2.

26.8	29.3	28.4	25.6	29.4	27.2	27.6	26.8	25.4	28.6
29.7	27.2	27.9	28.4	26.0	26.8	27.5	28.5	27.3	29.1
29.2	25.7	28.4	28.6	27.9	27.4	26.7	26.8	25.6	26.1

Solving the Student's *t*-test for two independent samples in R

The data for Example 6.10 are available in the file `t_test_two_independent_samples.Rdata` (Fávero and Belfiore, 2019):

```
load("t_test_two_independent_samples.Rdata")
```

The *t*-test for two independent samples can also be calculated with the function `t.test()` in R-based language. Because the numeric data of the variable *time* are grouped by the categorical variable *supplier*, we must declare the situation with the operator ~ in the argument `formula`:

```
attach(t_test_two_independent_samples)

t.test(formula = time ~ supplier,
       alternative = "two.sided")
```

Figure 6.10 shows the result of the *t*-test for two independent samples for Example 6.10.

```
        Welch Two Sample t-test

data:  time by supplier
t = -9.7084, df = 57.679, p-value = 9.729e-14
alternative hypothesis: true difference in means is not equal to 0
95 percent confidence interval:
 -3.924197 -2.582469
sample estimates:
mean in group 1 mean in group 2
       24.27667        27.53000
```

FIGURE 6.10 Results of the *t*-test for two independent samples for Example 6.10 in R.

Student's *t*-test to compare two population means from two paired random samples

Example 6.11: Applying the Student's *t*-test to two paired samples (Fávero and Belfiore, 2019)

A group of 10 machine operators who are responsible for carrying out a certain task were trained to perform the task more efficiently. To verify if there is a reduction in the time taken to perform the task, we measured the time spent by each operator before and after the training course (Tables 6.7 and 6.8). Test the hypothesis that the population means of both paired samples are similar, that is, that there is no reduction in time taken to perform the task after the training course. Consider $\alpha = 5\%$.

TABLE 6.7 Time spent per operator before the training course.

3.2	3.6	3.4	3.8	3.4	3.5	3.7	3.2	3.5	3.9

TABLE 6.8 Time spent per operator after the training course.

3.0	3.3	3.5	3.6	3.4	3.3	3.4	3.0	3.2	3.6

Solving Student's *t*-test for two paired samples in R

The data for Example 6.11 are available in the file `t_test_two_paired_samples.RData` (Fávero and Belfiore, 2019):

```
load("t_test_two_paired_samples.RData")
```

Similar to the methods used earlier in the "Solving the Z-test and the Student's *t*-test for a single sample in R" section and the "Solving the Student's *t*-test for two independent samples in R" section, the *t*-test to compare the means of two paired groups can be implemented through the function `t.test()`. However, for Example 6.11, the reader must be careful and type `paired = TRUE`, as follows:

```
attach(t_test_two_paired_samples)

t.test(x = before,
       y = after,
       paired = TRUE,
       alternative = "two.sided")
```

Figure 6.11 shows the result obtained from the previous command.

```
        Paired t-test

data:  before and after
t = 4.3846, df = 9, p-value = 0.001759
alternative hypothesis: true difference in means is not equal to 0
95 percent confidence interval:
 0.09197323 0.28802683
sample estimates:
mean of the differences
                   0.19
```

FIGURE 6.11 Results of the Student's *t*-test for two paired samples for Example 6.11 in R.

The value of the t-test is 4.385, and the significance level observed for a bilateral test is 0.002 (a value less than 0.05), which leads us to reject the null hypothesis and allows us to conclude with a 95% confidence level that there is a significant difference between the times spent by the operators before and after the training course.

Analysis of variance to compare the means of more than two populations

Example 6.12: Applying the one-way ANOVA test (Fávero and Belfiore, 2019)

A sample with 32 products is collected to analyze the quality of the honey supplied by three different suppliers. One way to test the quality of the honey is to find out how much sucrose it contains, which usually varies between 0.25% and 6.5%. Table 6.9 shows the percentage of sucrose in the sample collected from each supplier. Check if there are differences in this quality indicator among the three suppliers, considering a 5% significance level.

TABLE 6.9 Percentage of sucrose for the three suppliers.

Supplier 1 ($n_1 = 12$)	Supplier 2 ($n_2 = 10$)	Supplier 3 ($n_3 = 10$)
0.33	1.54	1.47
0.79	1.11	1.69
1.24	0.97	1.55
1.75	2.57	2.04
0.94	2.94	2.67
2.42	3.44	3.07
1.97	3.02	3.33
0.87	3.55	4.01
0.33	2.04	1.52
0.79	1.67	2.03
1.24		
3.12.		
$\overline{Y}_1 = 1.316$	$\overline{Y}_2 = 2.285$	$\overline{Y}_3 = 2.338$
$S_1 = 0.850$	$S_2 = 0.948$	$S_3 = 0.886$

Solving the one-way ANOVA test in R

The data in Example 6.12 are identical to those presented in Table 6.9 and can be found in the file `one_way_ANOVA.RData` (Fávero and Belfiore, 2019).

```
load("one_way_ANOVA.RData")
```

ANOVA assumes adherence of the data to the normality. Thus as discussed in the "Univariate tests for normality" section earlier in this chapter, we will verify this situation with the S-W test applied to the variables *supplier 1*, *supplier 2*, and *supplier 3*, as shown in Table 6.9:

```
attach(one_way_ANOVA)

shapiro.test(supplier_1)
shapiro.test(supplier_2)
shapiro.test(supplier_3)
```

Table 6.10 summarizes the results of the previous commands.

TABLE 6.10 Results of the Shapiro-Wilk test for the observations in Table 6.9.

Variable	W_{cal}	*P-value*
Supplier 1	0.91486	0.2462
Supplier 2	0.92901	0.4382
Supplier 3	0.88312	0.1417

After that, we must verify the existence of homogeneity of variance between the groups of observations and, for that, we will use the Levene's test. However, there is a problem! The reader should remember that all tests presented earlier in the "Tests for homogeneity of variance" section had a categorical variable that identified which group each observation belonged to, and this is not the case with the data shown in Table 6.9.

To perform this transformation, we will use the function `gather()` from the package `tidyverse`. If the reader would like to transform the dataset the opposite way (i.e., from the long to the wide format), the function `spread()` from the package `tidyverse` can be used. Functions similar to those mentioned are `melt()` and `dcast()` from the package `reshape2`. We chose the package `tidyverse` for its timeliness and ease of syntax:

```
one_way_ANOVA_LONG <- gather(one_way_ANOVA)
```

The categorical variable that identifies the groupings is called *key*, and the metric variable is called *value*.

We can now apply the function `leveneTest()` to the new object `one_way_ANOVA_LONG` to verify the existence, or not, of homogeneity of variance between the groups of observations. The command is:

```
leveneTest(y = value ~ key,
           data = one_way_ANOVA_LONG,
           center = mean)
```

Figure 6.12 shows the result of the previous routine, as well as the warning message reported in red.

```
Levene's Test for Homogeneity of Variance (center = mean)
      Df F value Pr(>F)
group  2  0.3374 0.7164
      29
Warning message:
In leveneTest.default(y = y, group = group, ...) : group coerced to f
actor.
```

FIGURE 6.12 Result of the Levene's test in R.

In Figure 6.12, we can apply the ANOVA test to our data. In addition, the warning message only says that the function `leveneTest()` transformed the variable *key* of the object `one_way_ANOVA_LONG` into a categorical variable, automatically. As presented in Chapter 2, R calls categorical variables as *factor*.

Application of the ANOVA test for the comparison of means of more than two populations is done using the function `aov()` of R-based language. The function syntax requires that we define a metric variable in function of a categorical variable and that we declare in which dataset these variables are found. Thus we will use the object `one_way_ANOVA_LONG` for this:

```
example6_12 <- aov(formula = value ~ key,
                   data = one_way_ANOVA_LONG)
```

At this moment, the results of the ANOVA test are in the new created object, called `example6_12`. To access them, we must use the function `summary()`:

```
summary(example6_12)
```

The results are shown in Figure 6.13.

```
            Df Sum Sq Mean Sq F value Pr(>F)
key          2  7.449   3.725   4.676 0.0174 *
Residuals   29 23.100   0.797
---
Signif. codes:  0 '***' 0.001 '**' 0.01 '*' 0.05 '.' 0.1 ' ' 1
4 observations deleted due to missingness
```

FIGURE 6.13 Results of the one-way ANOVA test for Example 6.12 in R.

According to Table 6.10, we can verify that each group has data that follow a normal distribution. Moreover, from Figure 6.12, we can conclude that the variances between the groups are homogeneous.

From the ANOVA table (Figure 6.13), we can see that the value of the *F* test is 4.676 and the respective *P*-value is 0.017 (we saw in Example 6.12 that this value would be between 0.01 and 0.025), a value less than 0.05. This leads us to reject the null hypothesis and allows us to conclude with a 95% confidence level that at least one of the population means is different from the others (there are differences in the percentage of sucrose in the honey from the three suppliers).

Factorial ANOVA test

Example 6.13: Applying the two-way ANOVA test (Fávero and Belfiore, 2019)

A sample with 24 passengers who travel from Sao Paulo to Campinas in a certain week is collected. The following variables are analyzed (1) travel time in minutes, (2) bus company chosen, and (3) day of the week. The main objective is to verify if there is a relationship between the travel time and the bus company, between the travel time and the day of the week, and between the bus company and the day of the week. The levels considered in the variable bus company are Company A (1), Company B (2), and Company C (3). On the other hand, the levels regarding the day of the week are Monday (1), Tuesday (2), Wednesday (3), Thursday (4), Friday (5), Saturday (6), and Sunday (7). The results of the sample are shown in Table 6.11 and are available in the file `two_way_ANOVA.RData` (Fávero and Belfiore, 2019) as well. Test these hypotheses, considering a 5% significance level.

Solving the two-way ANOVA test in R

Let's load the file `two_way_ANOVA.RData` (Fávero and Belfiore, 2019), as follows:

```
load("two_way_ANOVA.RData")
```

First, we must verify if there is normality in the variable *time* (metric) in the model (as shown in Figure 6.14). According to this figure, we can conclude that variable *Time* follows a normal distribution, with a 95% confidence level.

```
shapiro.test(two_way_ANOVA$time)
```

Next, we must test for the existence of homogeneity of variance between groups. However, as we want to capture the existing interactions between two categorical variables (*company* and *day of the week*), we must use the operator * between them, as follows:

```
leveneTest(y = time ~ company * day_of_the_week,
           data = two_way_ANOVA,
           center = mean)
```

TABLE 6.11 Data from Example 6.13 (using the two-way ANOVA).

Time (min)	Company	Day of the week
90	2	4
100	1	5
72	1	6
76	3	1
85	2	2
95	1	5
79	3	1
100	2	4
70	1	7
80	3	1
85	2	3
90	1	5
77	2	7
80	1	2
85	3	4
74	2	7
72	3	6
92	1	5
84	2	4
80	1	3
79	2	1
70	3	6
88	3	5
84	2	4

```
        Shapiro-Wilk normality test

data:  two_way_ANOVA$time
W = 0.95639, p-value = 0.3702
```

FIGURE 6.14 Results of the normality test in R.

In Figure 6.15, we can see that the variances between the groups are homogeneous ($P = 0.451 > 0.05$).

```
Levene's Test for Homogeneity of Variance (center = mean)
      Df F value Pr(>F)
group 13  1.0957 0.4507
      10
```

FIGURE 6.15 Test for the homogeneity of variance in R.

The null hypothesis H_0 of the two-way ANOVA test for this example assumes that the population means of each level of the factor *company* and of each level of the factor *day_of_the_week* are equal, that is, $H_0^A: \mu_1 = \mu_2 = \mu_3$ and $H_0^B: \mu_1 = \mu_2 = \ldots = \mu_7$.

The null hypothesis H_0 also states that there is no interaction between the factor *company* and the factor *day_of_the_week*, that is, H_0: $\gamma_{ij} = 0$ for $i \neq j$. In this sense, we have:

```
example6_13 <- aov(time ~ company * day_of_the_week,
                   data = two_way_ANOVA)
```

To study the results of the applied technique, we must use the function `summary()` in the created object `example6_13`:

```
summary(example6_13)
```

Based on Figure 6.16, we can conclude that there are no significant differences between the travel times of the companies analyzed, that is, the factor *company* does not have a significant impact on the variable *time* ($P = 0.064 > 0.05$).

On the other hand, we can conclude that there are significant differences between the days of the week, that is, the factor *day_of_the_week* has a significant effect on the variable *time* ($P = 0.002 < 0.05$).

We finally conclude that there is no significant interaction, with a 95% confidence level, between the two factors *company* and *day_of_the_week* because $P = 0.898 > 0.05$.

```
                        Df Sum Sq Mean Sq F value Pr(>F)
company                  2  177.8   88.91   3.660 0.0642 .
day_of_the_week          6 1286.0  214.34   8.824 0.0016 **
company: day_of_the_week  5   37.2    7.44   0.306 0.8982
Residuals               10  242.9   24.29
---
Signif. codes:  0 '***' 0.001 '**' 0.01 '*' 0.05 '.' 0.1 ' ' 1
```

FIGURE 6.16 Results of the two-way ANOVA test for Example 6.13 in R.

Final remarks

We studied the tests for normality (Kolmogorov-Smirnov, Shapiro-Wilk, and Shapiro-Francia tests); tests for homogeneity of variance (Bartlett's χ^2, Cochran's C, Hartley's F_{max}, and Levene's F tests); the Student's t-test for one population mean, two independent means, and two paired means; and the ANOVA test and its extensions (Fávero and Belfiore, 2019).

Exercises

1. The monthly aircraft sales data throughout the past year are shown in the following table. Check if there is normality in the data. Consider $\alpha = 5\%$ (Fávero and Belfiore, 2019).

Jan.	Feb.	Mar.	Apr.	May	Jun.	Jul.	Aug.	Sept.	Oct.	Nov.	Dec.
48	52	50	49	47	50	51	54	39	56	52	55

2. Test the normality of the temperature data listed in the following table ($\alpha = 5\%$) (Fávero and Belfiore, 2019):

12.5	14.2	13.4	14.6	12.7	10.9	16.5	14.7	11.2	10.9	12.1	12.8
13.8	13.5	13.2	14.1	15.5	16.2	10.8	14.3	12.8	12.4	11.4	16.2
14.3	14.8	14.6	13.7	13.5	10.8	10.4	11.5	11.9	11.3	14.2	11.2
13.4	16.1	13.5	17.5	16.2	15.0	14.2	13.2	12.4	13.4	12.7	11.2

3. The following table shows the final grades of two students in nine subjects. Check if there is homogeneity of variance between the students ($\alpha = 5\%$) (Fávero and Belfiore, 2019).

Student 1	6.4	5.8	6.9	5.4	7.3	8.2	6.1	5.5	6.0
Student 2	6.5	7.0	7.5	6.5	8.1	9.0	7.5	6.5	6.8

4. To compare the average waiting time before being seen by a doctor (in minutes) in two hospitals, we collected a sample with 20 patients from each hospital. The data are available in the following tables. Check if there are differences between the average waiting times in both hospitals. Consider $\alpha = 1\%$ (Fávero and Belfiore, 2019).

Hospital 1

72	58	91	88	70	76	98	101	65	73
79	82	80	91	93	88	97	83	71	74

Hospital 2

66	40	55	70	76	61	53	50	47	61
52	48	60	72	57	70	66	55	46	51

5. An aerospace company produces civilian and military helicopters at its three factories. The following tables show the monthly production of helicopters in the past 12 months at each factory. Check if there is a difference between the population means. Consider $\alpha = 5\%$ (Fávero and Belfiore, 2019).

Factory 1

24	26	28	22	31	25	27	28	30	21	20	24

Factory 2

28	26	24	30	24	27	25	29	30	27	26	25

Factory 3

29	25	24	26	20	22	22	27	20	26	24	25

Supplementary data sets

```
customer_services_store.RData
one_way_ANOVA.RData
production_aircraft.RData
production_bicycles.RData
production_farming_equipment.RData
t_test_one_sample.RData
t_test_two_independent_samples.Rdata
t_test_two_paired_samples.RData
two_way_ANOVA.RData
z_test_one_sample.RData
```

Please access supplementary data files here: https://doi.org/10.17632/55623jkwrp.3

CHAPTER

7

Data visualization and multivariate graphs

AT THE END OF THIS CHAPTER, YOU WILL BE ABLE TO:

- Understand the basic syntax of the package `ggplot2`
- Learn to blend graphics layers with the package `ggplot2`
- Build graphics in R-based language with the package `ggplot2`

R-based language packages used in this chapter

```
library(plotly)
library(tidyverse)
library(ggrepel)
```

Don't forget to define the R working directory (the location where your datasets are installed):

```
setwd("C:/book/chapter7")
```

Introduction

In Chapter 4, in addition to studying univariate descriptive statistics, we proposed some graphics, but in the base language of R. These graphics, as useful and commonly used as they are, do not represent the state of the art of the R language respect of bidimensional graphics.

Furthermore, when we abuse our creativity in the process of creating a graphic that uses the base language, command syntaxes quickly become difficult, especially for beginners.

Throughout this work, for two-dimensional graphs, we will emphasize the package `ggplot2`, which we will discuss in this chapter, and the package `tmap`, which we will present in Chapter 23, when we begin to discuss spatial analysis. The package `ggplot2` is also capable of generating maps, being an alternative choice for authors who prefer a lighter syntax for readers.

In this section, we will revisit the types of graphs studied throughout Chapter 4 and discuss the syntaxes of the package `ggplot2`, but not to exhaust the subject. The real intention is to introduce the reader to this kind of graphics

Data Science, Analytics and Machine Learning with R
https://doi.org/10.1016/B978-0-12-824271-1.00019-6

library, with routines that resemble recipes, so the reader feels comfortable exploring the graphic routines proposed throughout the work.

The library `ggplot2`

The library `ggplot2` is the main R-based language package when it comes to drawing two-dimensional graphics, with high customization capabilities and a reasonably simple syntax. Figure 7.1 summarizes the simplest structure of its commands.

```
ggplot(data = insert your database here) +
  geom_insert the chosen geometry here (aes(insert the main elements of the chart here))
```

FIGURE 7.1 Explanation of the most basic theoretical syntax of the library `ggplot2`.

From Figure 7.1, it follows that in its most basic form, a command of a graph created via `ggplot2` requires at least the declaration of three functions: (1) the function `ggplot()`, which, in short, tells R that a graph will be elaborated using the library `ggplot2` from a given dataset; (2) some geometry function—`geom_something()`—where the word *something* will be replaced (e.g., by the word *point* if the intention is a point graph or by the word *line* if the intention is a line graph); and (3) the function `aes()` nested to the function `ggplot()` or to some geometry function, where *aes* is an abbreviation for *aestethics*—in it we will minimally declare which variables will be represented on the abscissa axes and of the ordinates—that is, we will give instructions about the coordinates of x and y.

You will also notice in Figure 7.1 that the function `ggplot()` and the subsequent geometry function are connected by the operator +, which in this case means something like the additive conjunction *and*. In this sense, Figure 7.1 can be read in human language as: (a) first line of Figure 7.1: "R, I want a graph, and..."; (b) second line of Figure 7.1: "[...] the graph must be of points (or lines, or a boxplot, and so on), where the variable M will be on the abscissa axis, and the variable N will be on the axis of the ordinates."

That said, it is necessary to point out that for the argument `data` in which we will declare a dataset, **this dataset must necessarily be a data frame or a tibble.** Tibbles, visually speaking, are identical to data frames, the difference is that they are unmodifiable and we will not emphasize them in this work.

As much as Figure 7.1 has its value from a didactic point of view, it is limited in a number of aspects. For example, Figure 7.1 might mistakenly lead the reader to think that it is not possible to mix geometries or that it is not possible to mix different colors or to stratify observations because of their characteristics. All of this is possible with the package `ggplot2`, as we will see later in this chapter.

What we must make clear is that this chapter is not intended to explore all of the nuances and capabilities of the package `ggplot2`. The intention of this chapter is to equip the reader so, as reading progresses, he or she does not feel lost or bothered by the syntaxes regarding the graphics of this work, which, for the most part, were elaborated with the package `ggplot2`. On the other hand, if the reader's intention is to deepen the use of this powerful graphics library, we suggest the work *R Graphics Cookbook* (Chang, 2013) or the work *ggplot2* (Wickham, 2009).

It should be clarified that the package `ggplot2` does not have its own geometry for pie charts. This does not mean that it is not possible to create them by adapting the use of other geometry functions. We will pay attention to how to generate these kinds of graphs with `ggplot2` in the appendix of this chapter.

Stem-and-leaf plots also do not have a dedicated geometry function, however, unlike pie charts, we will not discuss their creation with the package `ggplot2` because the work expended by the reader in counterpoint to visual gain simply does not pay off.

That said, we will return to the charts established in Chapter 4 of this work. The first kind of chart we studied in Chapter 4 was the bar chart, which we will discuss in the following section.

Bar chart with `ggplot2`

In the "Graphical representation for qualitative variables" section in Chapter 4, we used the dataset present in the file `satisfaction_survey.RData` (Fávero and Belfiore, 2019) to create a bar chart. We will use it again here. We ask the reader to load the dataset as follows:

```
load("satisfaction_survey.RData")
```

The variables present in the object were presented in Table 4.9, which is replicated here.

Following what Figure 7.1 proposes, to create a bar graph with the package `ggplot2`, we could command the following:

```
ggplot(data = satisfaction_survey) +
  geom_bar(aes(x = satisfaction))
```

Figure 7.2 shows the result obtained from the previous command.

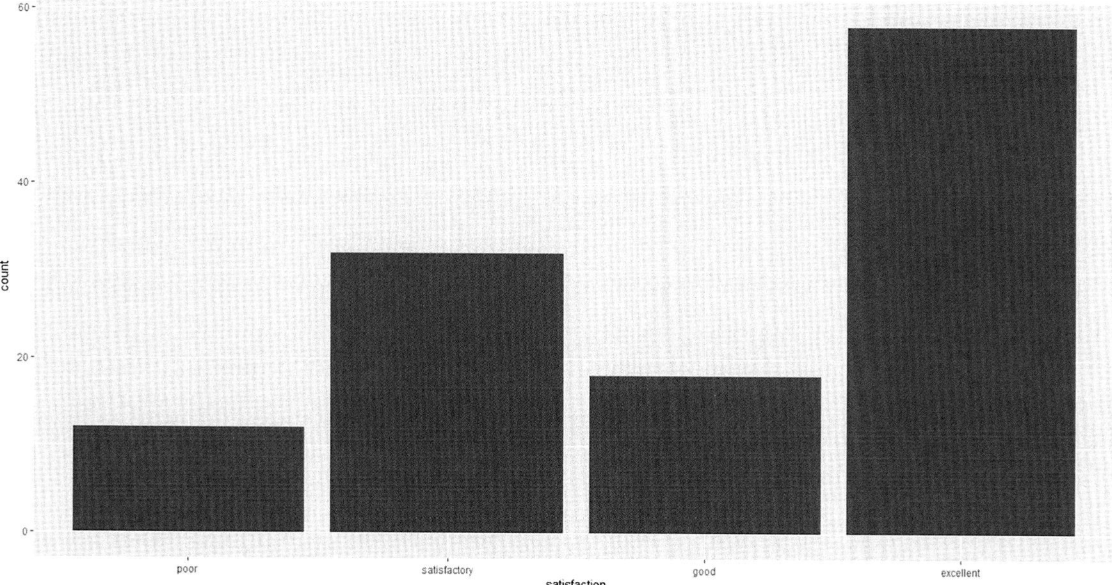

FIGURE 7.2 Vertical bar graph of the absolute frequencies of the variable *satisfaction* created with the package `ggplot2`.

Briefly, what happened in the previous code was the command of the function `ggplot()`, arguing that the dataset we want to use is called `satisfaction_survey`. Then, using the operator `+`, we define the bar graph geometry with the function `geom_bar()`; and with the function `aes()` (short for aesthetics), we define that the variable of interest is the variable *satisfaction*.

In Figure 7.2, two considerations are necessary: (1) the graphic is ugly, and (2) an attentive reader will notice that a variable was not declared for the ordinate axis.

As for the graphic's elegance, we will explore many options in the lines that follow. As for the lack of an explicit variable for the ordinate axis, we ask the reader to reread the "Graphical representation for qualitative variables" section in Chapter 4 to understand that, as a rule, a bar graph is a frequency graph of categorical variables. Therefore R knows how to act in the situation.

Let's proceed by adding colors to our graphic in Figure 7.2. For this, we must argue `fill` for the chosen geometry. The results are shown in Figure 7.3.

```
ggplot(data = satisfaction_survey) +
  geom_bar(aes(x = satisfaction), fill = "orange")
```

Easy, right? The code for the construction of Figure 7.3 is the same as that used for the construction of Figure 7.2, with the only exception of the addition of the argument `fill` to the geometry function. Note that colors must be declared in quotes, regardless of whether they are single quotes or double quotes. It is also possible to declare colors in hexadecimal form, also enclosed in quotation marks whose hexadecimal code is preceded by the character #. **In the appendix of this chapter, there is a table containing the main colors used in R-based language.** As a rule, names of colors declared in English will be accepted.

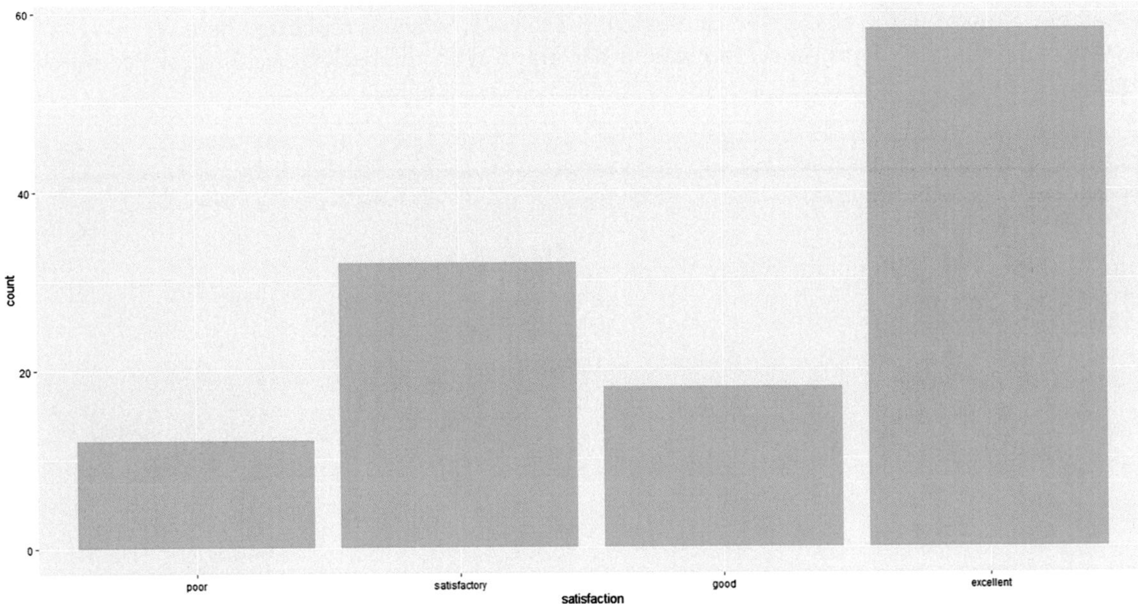

FIGURE 7.3 Vertical bar graph of the absolute frequencies of the variable *satisfaction* created with the package `ggplot2`.

A curious reader may be wondering why the argument `fill`, which is aesthetic, is outside the function `aes()`. Another reader may be wondering how to define different colors for each stratum of the variable *satisfaction*. The two doubts will lead to the same place.

When we want a unique color for the geometry, the argument about that color must be placed outside the function `aes()`, but inside the geometry function, obviously. On the other hand, to stratify observations with colors, we must position the argument about colors internally to the function `aes()`:

```
ggplot(data = satisfaction_survey) +
  geom_bar(aes(x = satisfaction, fill = satisfaction))
```

An attentive reader will notice that in the previous codes, the argument `fill` did not explicitly receive a color name; however, it received the name of the variable that will stratify the observations, as shown in Figure 7.4.

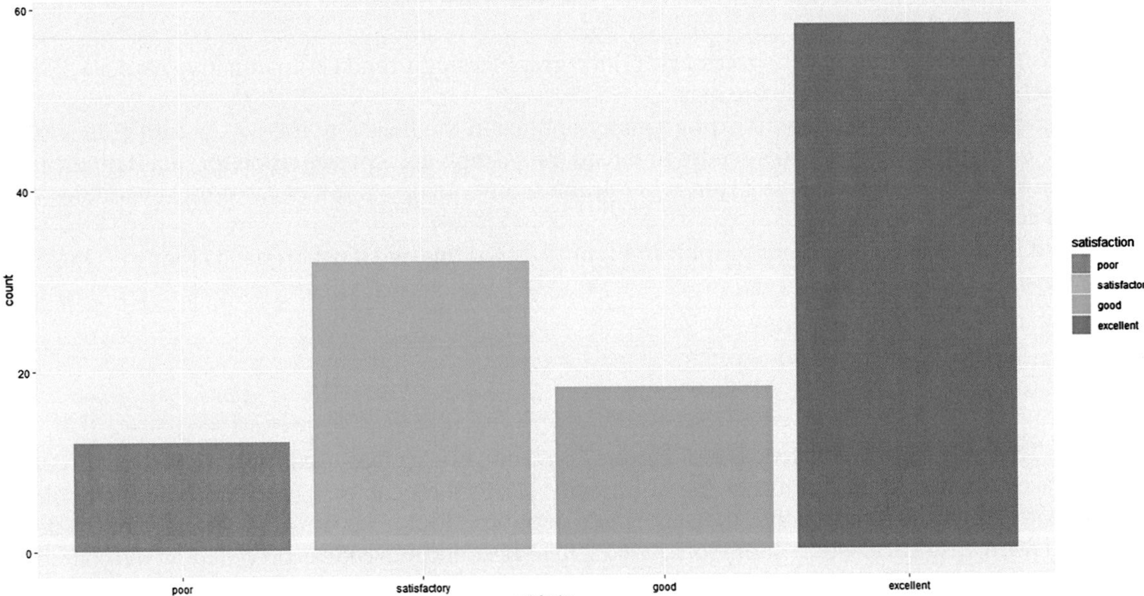

FIGURE 7.4 Vertical bar graph of the absolute frequencies of the variable *satisfaction* created with the package `ggplot2`.

In Figure 7.4, if the color blindness of the receiver of the graphic information is a limiting factor for the absorption of information about each color, we suggest that the reader explore the package `viridis` or declare friendly colors to this type of audience with the use of functions like `scale_fill_manual()` (to see the function documentation, just command `?scale_fill_manual`).

To add the names of the graph's axes, we will use the function `labs()`:

```
ggplot(data = satisfaction_survey) +
  geom_bar(aes(x = satisfaction), fill = "orange") +
  labs(x = "Customer Satisfaction Level",
       y = "Absolute Observed Frequencies")
```

Figure 7.5 shows the graph created earlier.

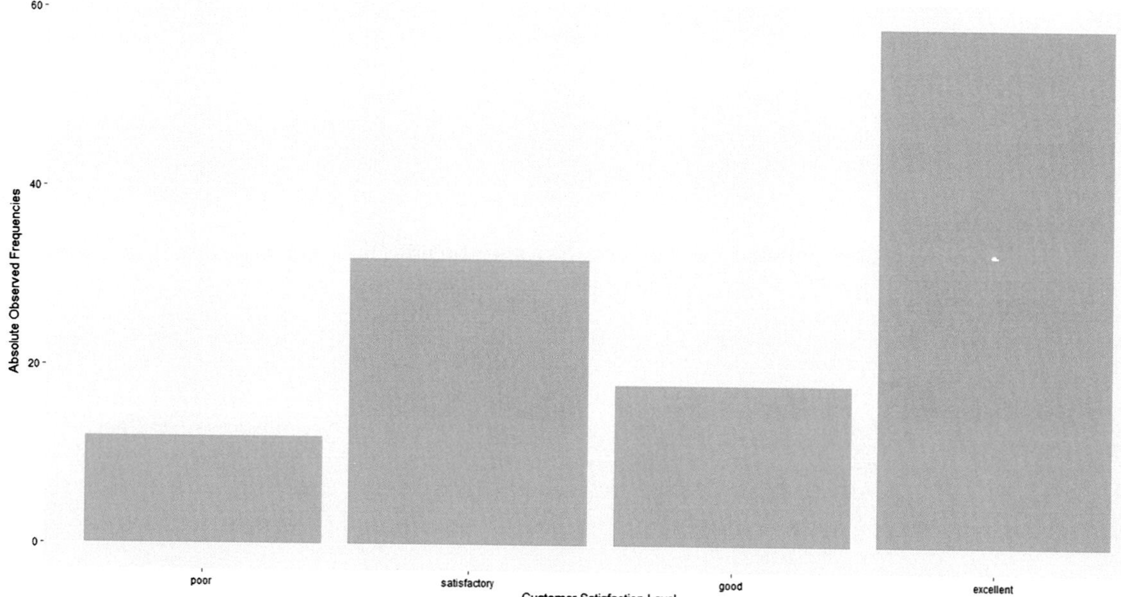

FIGURE 7.5 Vertical bar graph of the absolute frequencies of the variable *satisfaction* created with the package `ggplot2`.

Note in Figure 7.5 that the arguments *x* and *y* of the function `labs()` refer, respectively, to the abscissa and ordinate axes. Note also that as axis descriptions are textual elements, they must be declared in quotation marks.

We can also use the function to add a title to our graph in Figure 7.5:

```
ggplot(data = satisfaction_survey) +
  geom_bar(aes(x = satisfaction), fill = "orange") +
  labs(x = "Customer Satisfaction Level",
       y = "Absolute Observed Frequencies",
       title = "Consumer Profile")
```

Figure 7.6 shows the results obtained from the previous commands.

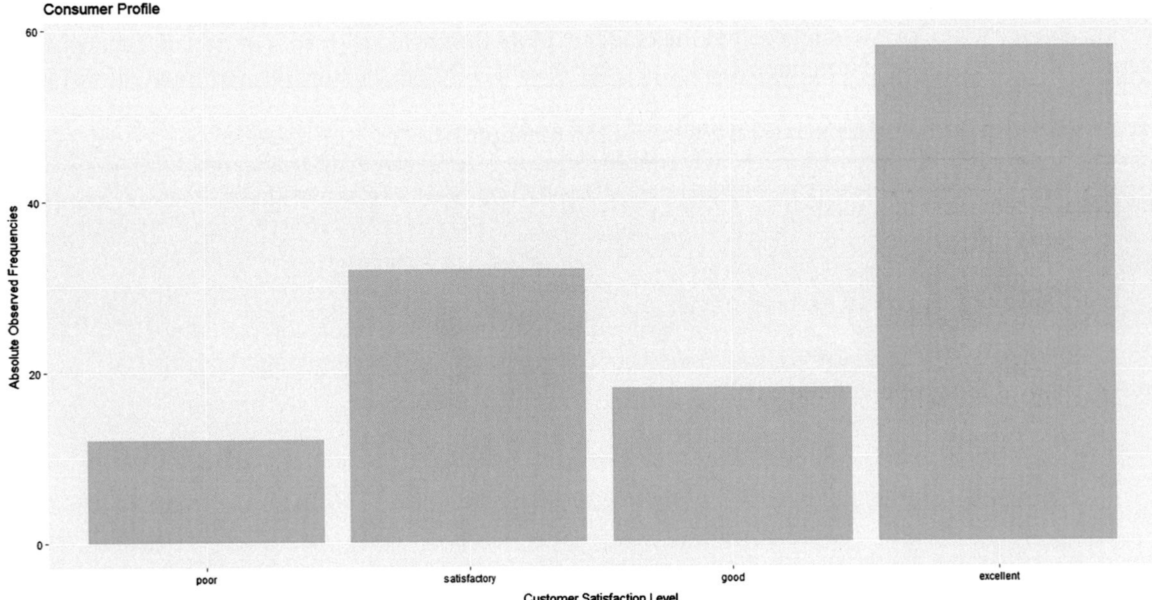

FIGURE 7.6 Vertical bar graph of the absolute frequencies of the variable *satisfaction* created with the package `ggplot2`.

We can go further with the function `labs()` and determine a subtitle with the argument `subtitle` and a caption with the argument `caption`, as explained in Figure 7.7. Simple, right?

```
ggplot(data = satisfaction_survey) +
  geom_bar(aes(x = satisfaction), fill = "orange") +
  labs(x = "Customer Satisfaction Level",
       y = "Absolute Observed Frequencies",
       title = "Consumer Profile")
```

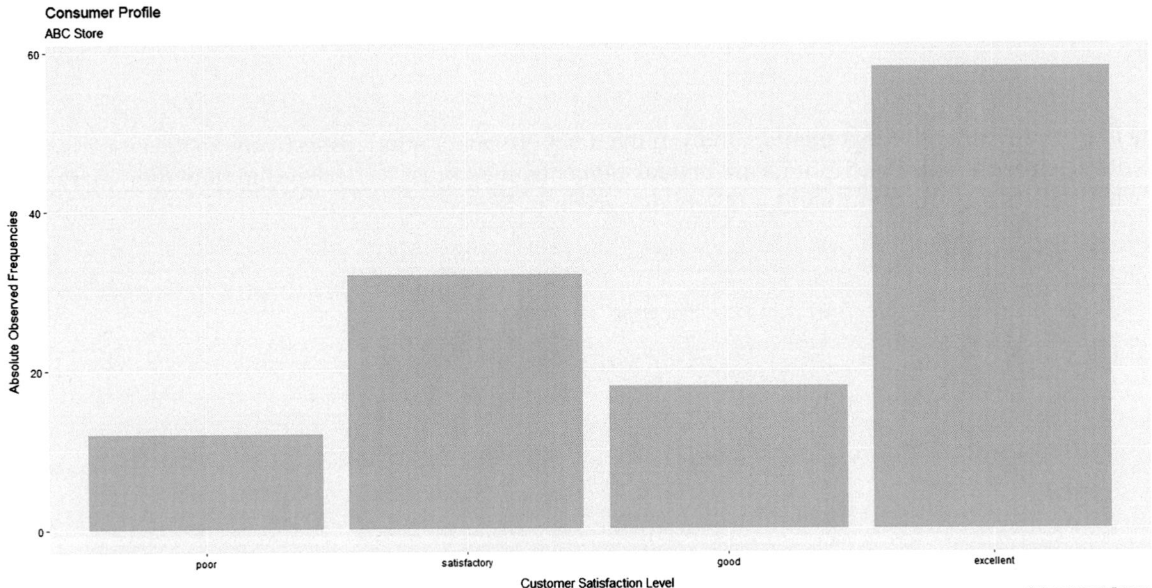

FIGURE 7.7 Vertical bar graph of the absolute frequencies of the variable *satisfaction* created with the package `ggplot2`.

You may want to add the existing customer count in each category of the variable *satisfaction*. The way out to the challenge is neither the easiest nor the most intuitive of all.

First, we must use a new geometry function called `geom_bar()` that makes bar graphs (that's all). To insert texts in graphics, we must use the function `geom_label()` or the function `geom_text()`.

Note that `ggplot2` is a two-dimensional graphics library and, as such, is oriented in a two-dimensional way. **As obvious as the comment sounds, most of the command errors in the package `ggplot2` stem from inattention to this statement.**

We can use the function `geom_label()`, or we can use `geom_text()` with no problem. According to the previous comment and Figure 7.1, we must declare coordinates so it is oriented. So for the function `geom_label()`, there will also be a function `aes()`. For this new function `aes()`, which is in conjunction with bar geometry, we must repoint the variable that will appear on the abscissa axis and argue `label`. However, we do not have a variable in our dataset `satisfaction_survey` that explicitly shows the count of each category which, even though it is being executed in the background by the function `geom_bar()`, will be made explicit in our chart by the function `geom_label()`. Therefore we will use a special variable called `..count..` to indicate explicit counts for each category of the variable *satisfaction*. We will not use many of these special variables in this work—only `..count..` and `..density..`; we will use the latter for disclosure of the probability density values of the variables.

Then, externally to the function `aes()` but internally to the function `geom_label()`, we will use the argument `stat`. The argument `stat` is very common, as a rule, when we want to break R's default connection for a given axis. Note that the counting done by R in the case of bar graphs is automatic, dispensing with the declaration of a variable on the y axis and using the geometry function `geom_bar()`. However, here we are replacing this default R connection by the special variable `..count..` so the counts are made explicit through the geometry function `geom_label()`.

```
ggplot(data = satisfaction_survey) +
  geom_bar(aes(x = satisfaction), fill = "orange") +
  geom_label(aes(x = satisfaction, label = ..count..),
             stat = "count") +
  labs(x = "Customer Satisfaction Level",
       y = "Absolute Observed Frequencies",
       title = "Consumer Profile",
       subtitle = "ABC Store",
       caption = "Reference Month: February")
```

Figure 7.8 shows the result obtained from the previous commands.

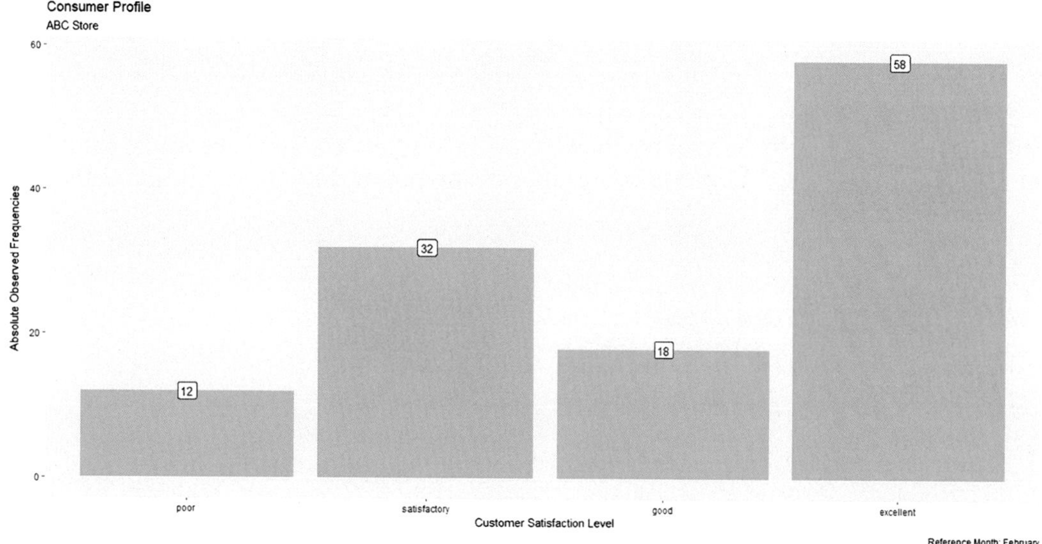

FIGURE 7.8 Vertical bar graph of the absolute frequencies of the variable *satisfaction* created with the package `ggplot2`.

In Figure 7.8, it may be that the position of the labels does not please the reader. Thus, we could argue `vjust` (for vertical adjustments) and `hjust` (for horizontal adjustments) internally to the function `geom_label()`, but externally to the function `aes()`. As the graph is constructed in Figure 7.8, declaring positive values for the argument `vjust` would cause the labels to be drawn toward the abscissa axis; the declared negative values would do the opposite. Similarly, for the argument `hjust`, declaring positive values would position the labels closer to the ordinate axis; declaring negative values would obviously do the opposite:

```
ggplot(data = satisfaction_survey) +
  geom_bar(aes(x = satisfaction), fill = "orange") +
  geom_label(aes(x = satisfaction, label = ..count..),
             stat = "count",
             vjust = 1.3) +
  labs(x = "Customer Satisfaction Level",
       y = "Absolute Observed Frequencies",
       title = "Consumer Profile",
       subtitle = "ABC Store",
       caption = "Reference Month: February")
```

Figure 7.9 shows the result obtained from the previous commands.

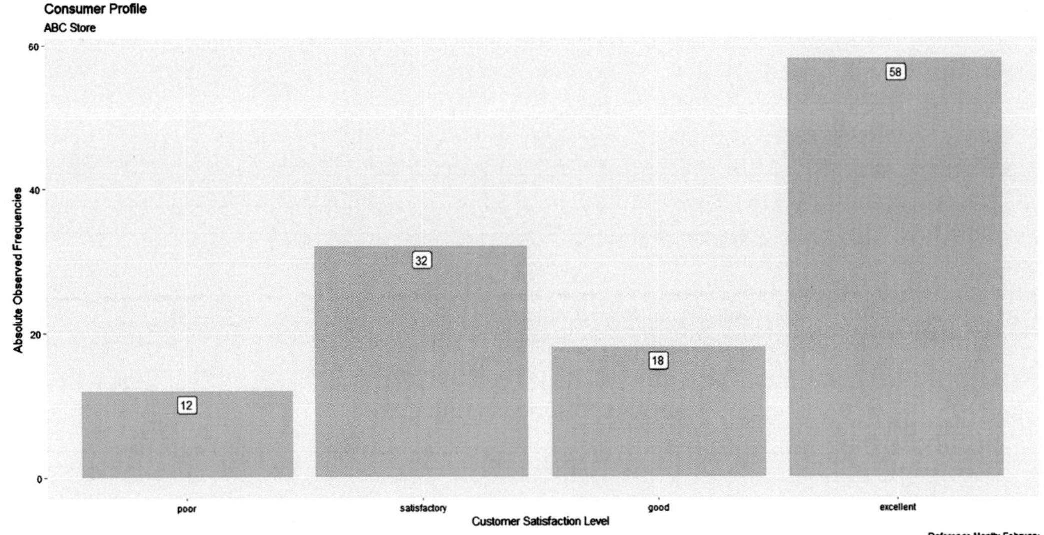

FIGURE 7.9 Vertical bar graph of the absolute frequencies of the variable *satisfaction* created with the package `ggplot2`.

If we want a bar graph similar to the one shown in Figure 7.9, but rotated (i.e., a horizontal bar graph), we must use the function `coord_flip()`. Figure 7.10 shows the results obtained from the following commands:

```
ggplot(data = satisfaction_survey) +
  geom_bar(aes(x = satisfaction), fill = "orange") +
  geom_label(aes(x = satisfaction, label = ..count..),
             stat = "count",
             hjust = 1.3) +
  labs(x = "Customer Satisfaction Level",
       y = "Absolute Observed Frequencies",
       title = "Consumer Profile",
       subtitle = "ABC Store",
       caption = "Reference Month: February") +
  coord_flip()
```

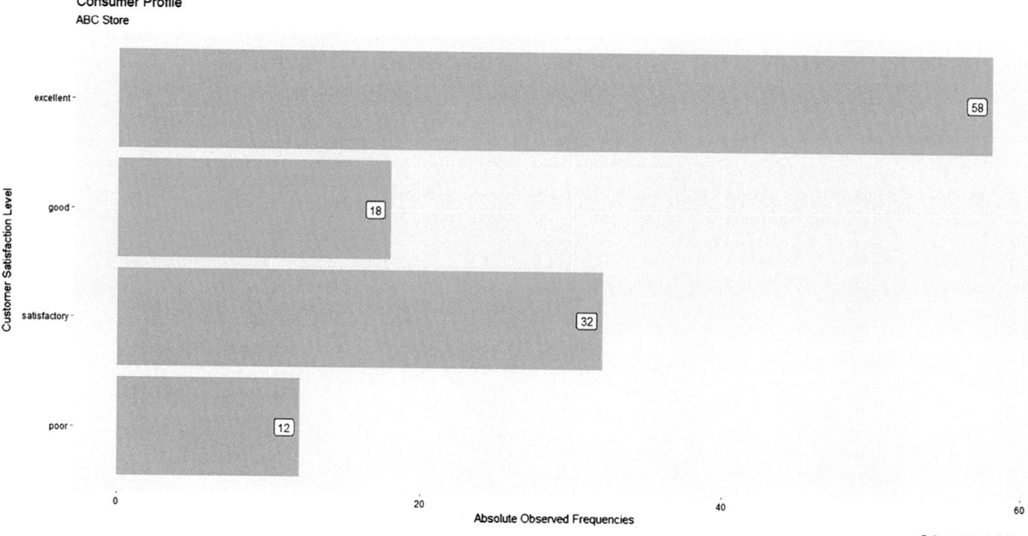

FIGURE 7.10 Horizontal bar graph of the absolute frequencies of the variable *satisfaction* created with the package `ggplot2`.

In Figure 7.10, an attentive reader will notice that regarding its commands, in addition to the use of the function `coord_flip()`, there was the use of the argument `hjust` instead of `vjust` inside the function `geom_label()`. This adjustment was necessary because, in comparison to Figure 7.9, what was on the abscissa axis now occupies a place on the ordinate axis.

Finally, depending on the work done by the reader, the gray background present in Figures 7.2 to 7.10, the absence or presence of grids in the graph, the absence of borders, and the typography used may not be the most adequate. To access such levels of personalization, the reader must use the function `theme()`. However, the package `ggplot2` comes with predefined forms of the function `theme()`, such as `theme_bw()`, `theme_classic()`, and `theme_dark()`, which, as a rule, meet most of the needs mentioned. We advise the reader to explore the function `theme()` with the command `?theme` as well as test its predefined forms. Next, we will present the use of the predefined form `theme_bw()`, whose resulting graphic is shown in Figure 7.11.

```
ggplot(data = satisfaction_survey) +
  geom_bar(aes(x = satisfaction), fill = "orange") +
  geom_label(aes(x = satisfaction, label = ..count..),
             stat = "count",
             hjust = 1.3) +
  labs(x = "Customer Satisfaction Level",
       y = "Absolute Observed Frequencies",
       title = "Consumer Profile",
       subtitle = "ABC Store",
       caption = "Reference Month: February") +
  coord_flip() +
  theme_bw()
```

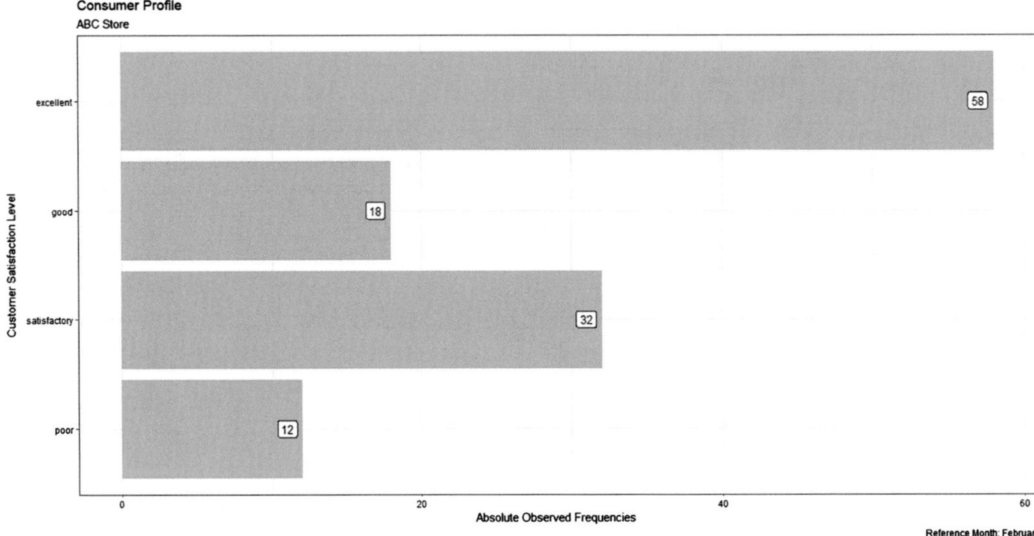

FIGURE 7.11 Horizontal bar graph of the absolute frequencies of the variable *satisfaction* created with the package `ggplot2`.

Pareto chart with `ggplot2`

As studied in the "Pie chart" section in Chapter 4, a Pareto graph is a combination of a bar graph and a line graph in which the bars represent the absolute frequencies of occurrences of problems and the lines represent the relative cumulative frequencies.

Following the logic of this chapter, we will use the same dataset presented in Chapter 4 to build this kind of graph. So, we ask the reader to open the file `cards.RData` (Fávero and Belfiore, 2019):

```
load("cards.RData")
```

The data present in the object `cards` were already presented in Table 4.11, which, for the reader's comfort, is replicated here.

First of all, we must organize the dataset in descending order of occurrences, as seen in the "Pareto chart" section in Chapter 4:

```
cards <- cards[order(cards$absolute_frequency, decreasing = TRUE),]
```

Once this is done, we will start with what we learned the "Bar chart with `ggplot2`" section earlier in this chapter, that is, with the bar graph:

```
ggplot(data = cards) +
  geom_bar(aes(x = type_of_defect))
```

The graph in Figure 7.12 makes it clear that something really went wrong, even though we apparently followed the instructions given in the "Bar chart with `ggplot2`" section earlier in this chapter.

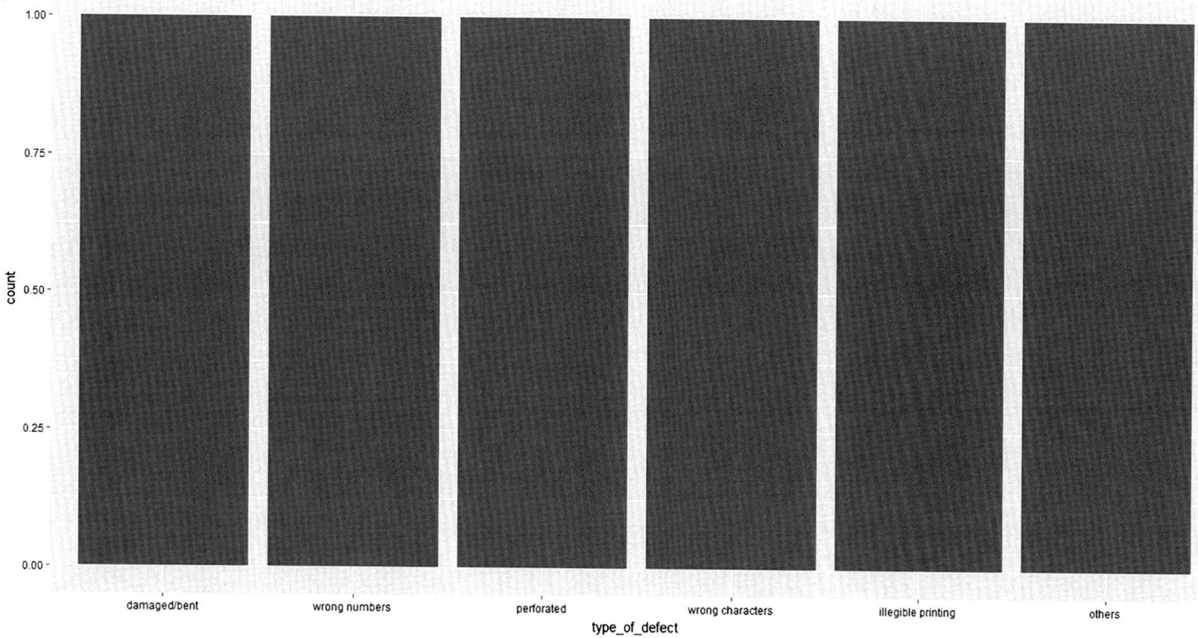

FIGURE 7.12 Vertical bar graph created with the package `ggplot2`.

The graphic shown in Figure 7.12 did not work because of the structure of the dataset `cards`. When we compare it with the dataset `satisfaction_survey`, we notice that the object `cards` already contains a table of observed frequencies (variable *absolute_frequency*). However, the geometry function `geom_bar()` counted the frequency of occurrence of each category as present in the variable *type_of_defect*. Nevertheless, the counts should respect what is presented in the variable *absolute_frequency*.

That said, it is obvious that we will need to declare a variable for the ordinate axis in the function `geom_bar()`. The problem is that, by default, such geometry does not accept the presence of a variable for the y axis. In the "Bar chart with `ggplot2`" section earlier in this chapter, we explained to the reader how to break the connections of the geometry function `geom_bar()` by using the argument `stat`. In this way, we can command the following:

```
ggplot(data = cards) +
  geom_bar(aes(x = type_of_defect, y = absolute_frequency),
           stat = "identity")
```

Earlier in this chapter, we argued `stat = "count"` for the function `geom_label()` to understand the counts for each category. Now, we argue `stat = "identity"` so the function `geom_bar()` understands that we are defining who the ordinate axis variable will be. Figure 7.13 shows the graph obtained from the previous commands.

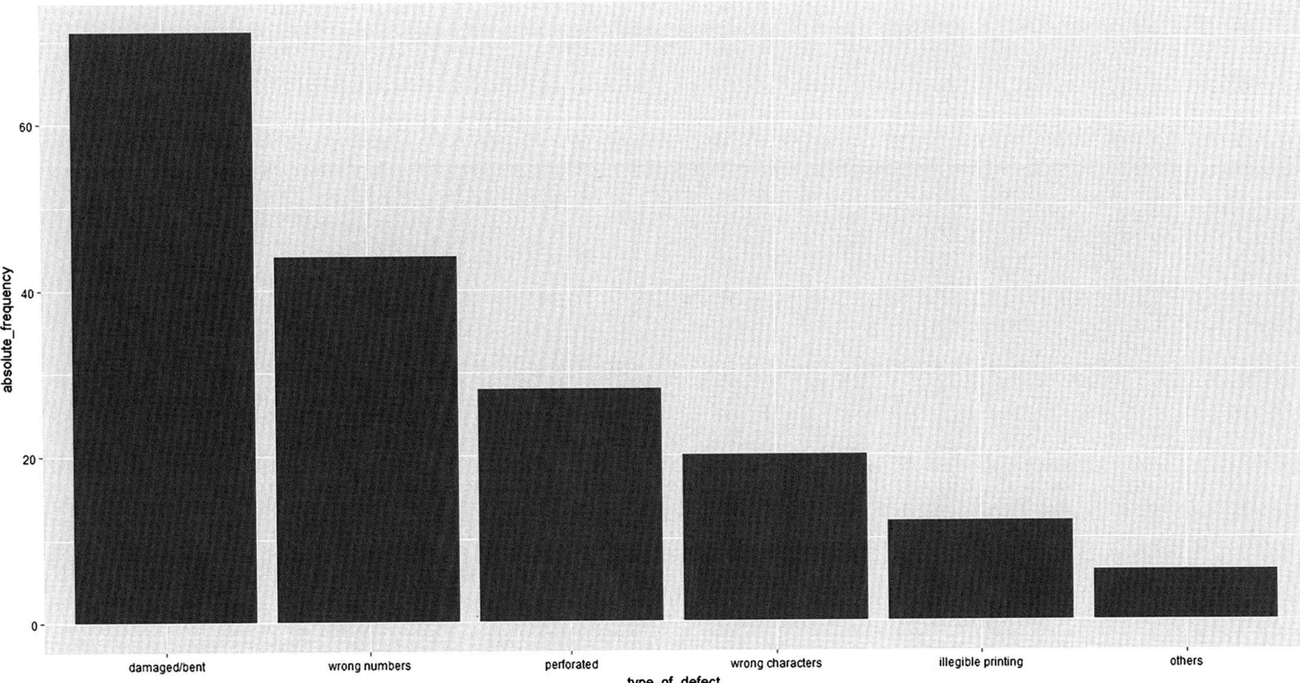

FIGURE 7.13 Vertical bar graph of absolute frequencies created with the package `ggplot2`.

The lines are still missing! Let's start by marking the points where these lines should intersect using the geometry function `geom_point()`. But first, it is necessary to remember that the lines represent cumulative relative frequencies. In this way, we will create the variable *cumulative_count* in an analogous way to what was proposed in The "Pareto chart" section in Chapter 4:

```
cards["cumulative_count"] <- cumsum(
  prop.table(cards$absolute_frequency)
  ) * 100
```

Now we can use the function `geom_point()`. In this geometry function, the ordinate axis variable will be the new variable *cumulative_count:*

```
ggplot(data = cards) +
  geom_bar(aes(x = type_of_defect, y = absolute_frequency),
           stat = "identity") +
  geom_point(aes(x = type_of_defect, y = cumulative_count))
```

Figure 7.14 shows the graph obtained from the previous commands.

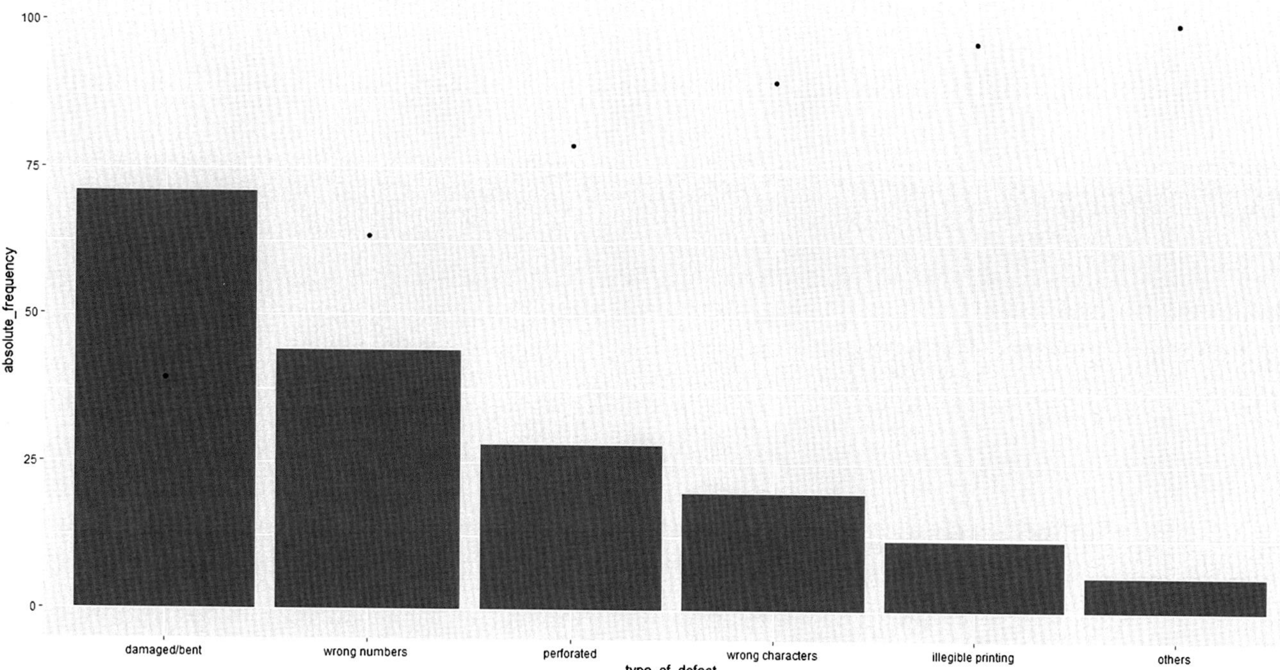

FIGURE 7.14 Vertical bar graph of absolute frequencies created with the package ggplot2.

Now we can insert the lines with the geometry function geom_line():

```
ggplot(data = cards) +
  geom_bar(aes(x = type_of_defect, y = absolute_frequency),
           stat = "identity") +
  geom_point(aes(x = type_of_defect,
                 y = cumulative_count)) +
  geom_line(aes(x = type_of_defect,
                y = cumulative_count,
                group = TRUE))
```

An attentive reader will notice that we argued for the function geom_line() that the lines should follow the ordinate axis coordinates with respect to the variable *cumulative_count*. We also argued that group = TRUE so the package ggplot2 understood that there was a continuity, that is, so the points could be interconnected. Figure 7.15 demonstrates the Pareto graph resulting from the previous command.

Finally, we can name the axes, add colors, and add a function of the theme type according to what we learned in the "Bar chart with ggplot2" section earlier in this chapter. The results are shown in Figure 7.16.

```
ggplot(data = cards) +
  geom_bar(aes(x = type_of_defect, y = absolute_frequency),
           stat = "identity",
           fill = "orange") +
  geom_point(aes(x = type_of_defect,
                 y = cumulative_count)) +
  geom_line(aes(x = type_of_defect,
                y = cumulative_count,
                group = TRUE),
            color = "darkorchid") +
  labs(x = NULL,
       y = "Cumulative Count") +
  theme_bw()
```

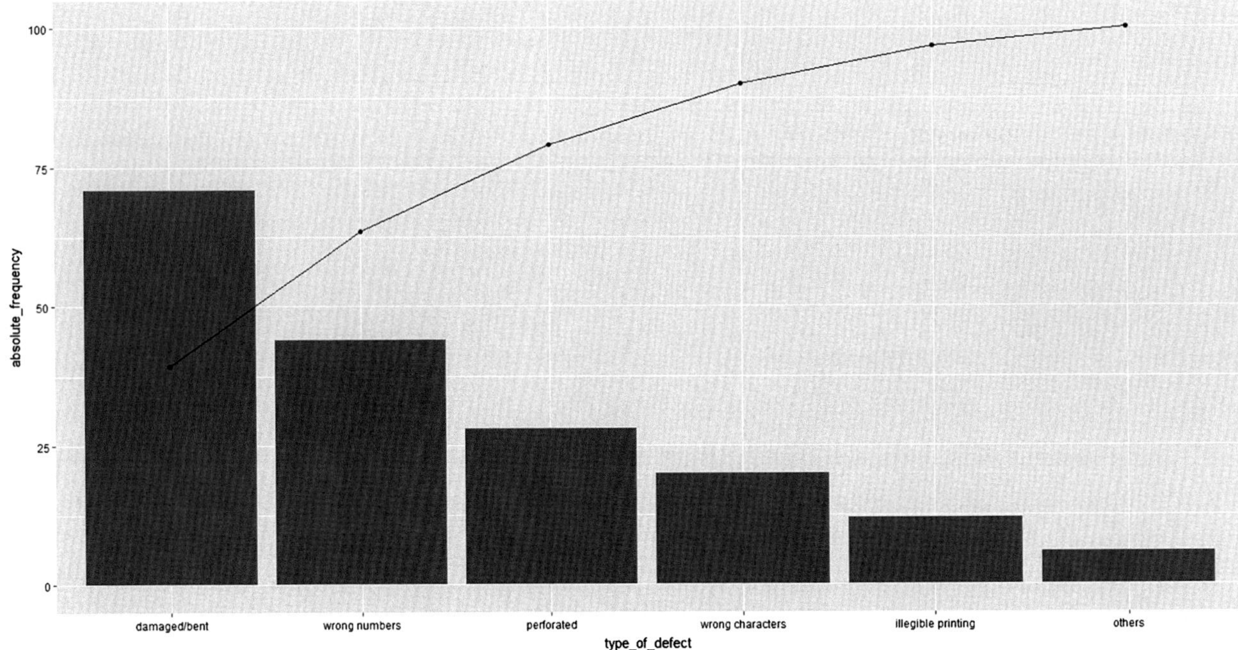

FIGURE 7.15 Pareto graph created with the package `ggplot2`.

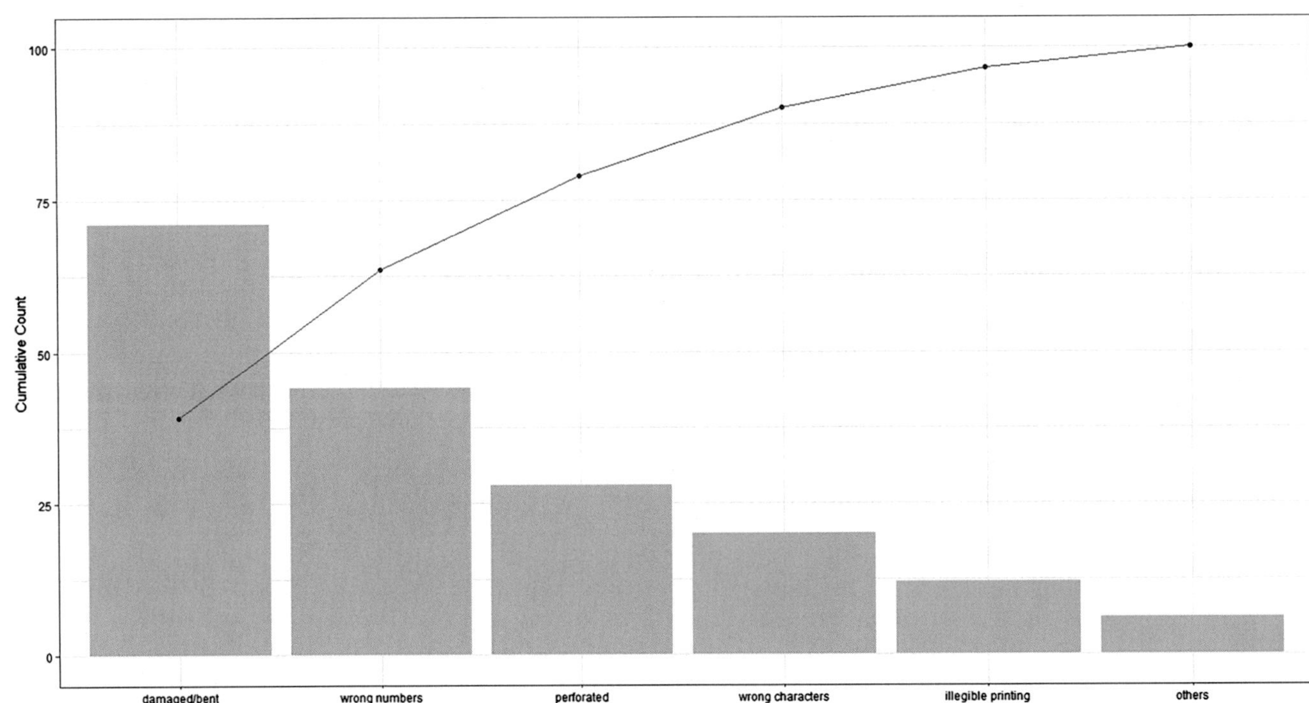

FIGURE 7.16 Pareto graph created with the package `ggplot2`.

Line graph with ggplot2

For the construction of a line graph, we will again use the geometric function `geom_line()` presented in the "Pareto chart with `ggplot2`" section earlier in this chapter. To meet this objective, we will use the dataset present in the file `cheap_easy.RData` (Fávero and Belfiore, 2019), which we studied in the "Line graph" section in Chapter 4 and whose information is presented in Table 4.13.

To load the data from Table 4.13, we can command the following:

```
load("cheap_easy.RData")
```

The creation of the line graph follows the ideas studied in the previous sections, as the following codes demonstrate:

```
ggplot(cheap_easy) +
  geom_line(aes(x = month, y = losses, group = TRUE))
```

Figure 7.17 shows the result obtained from the previous command.

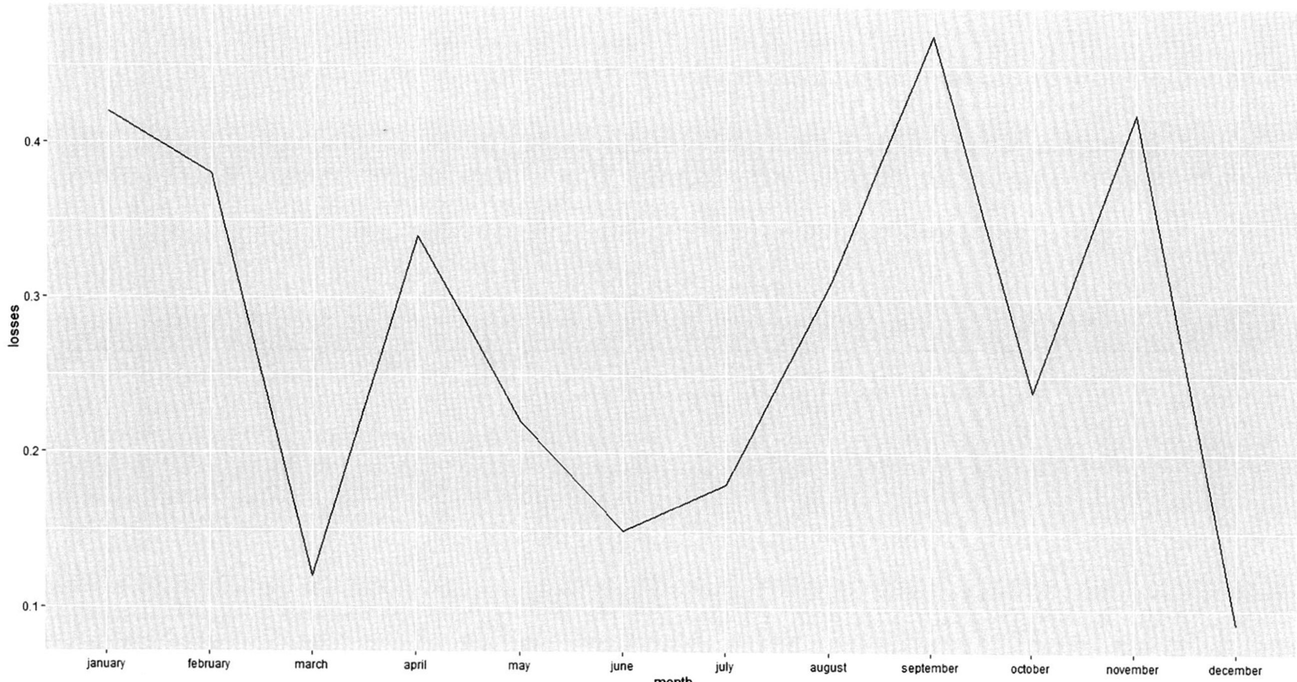

FIGURE 7.17 Line graph created with the package `ggplot2`.

If the reader wants to add an arrow that indicates the current trend of the chart, he or she can do so with the function `arrow()` declared to the function `geom_line()`, as shown in Figure 7.18:

```
ggplot(cheap_easy) +
  geom_line(aes(x = month, y = losses, group = TRUE))

ggplot(cheap_easy) +
  geom_line(aes(x = month, y = losses, group = TRUE),
            arrow = arrow(type = "closed",
                          length = unit(x = 0.1, units = "inches")))
```

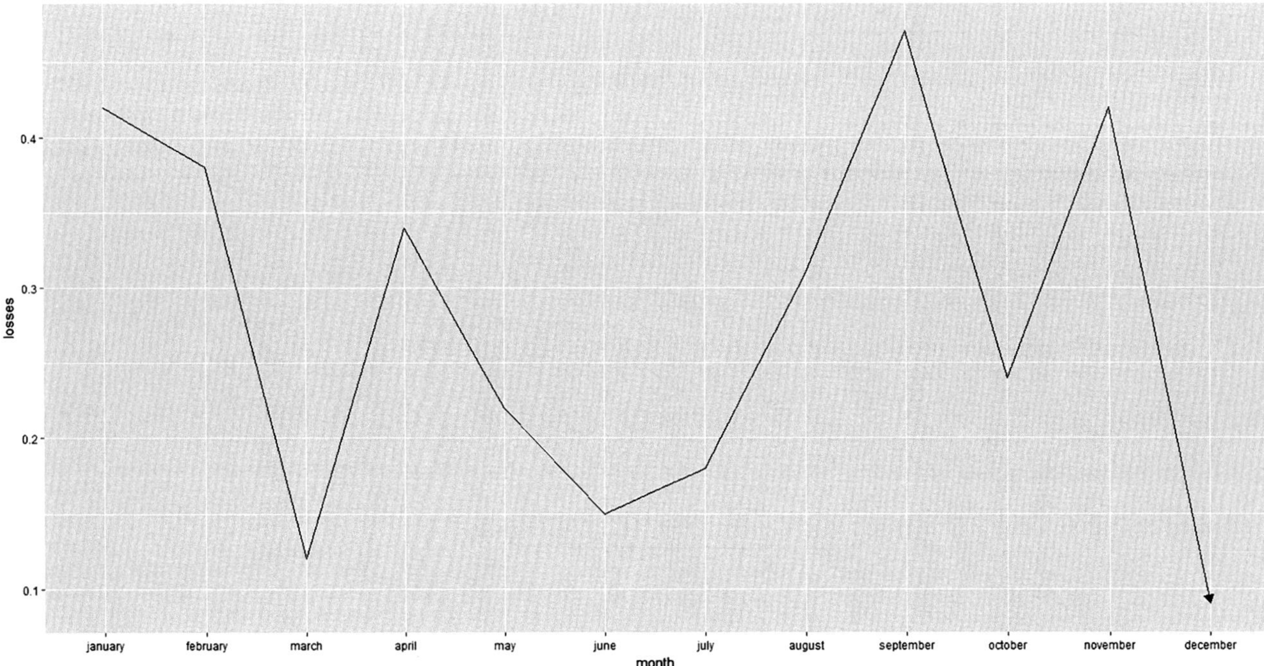

FIGURE 7.18 Line graph created with the package `ggplot2`.

Instead of a trending arrow, the reader may also want to add dots that indicate the monthly results of the graph shown in Figure 7.18. To do this, the reader can add a new layer with the help of the function `geom_point()`:

```
ggplot(cheap_easy) +
  geom_line(aes(x = month, y = losses, group = TRUE)) +
  geom_point(aes(x = month, y = losses))
```

Figure 7.19 shows the result obtained from the previous code.

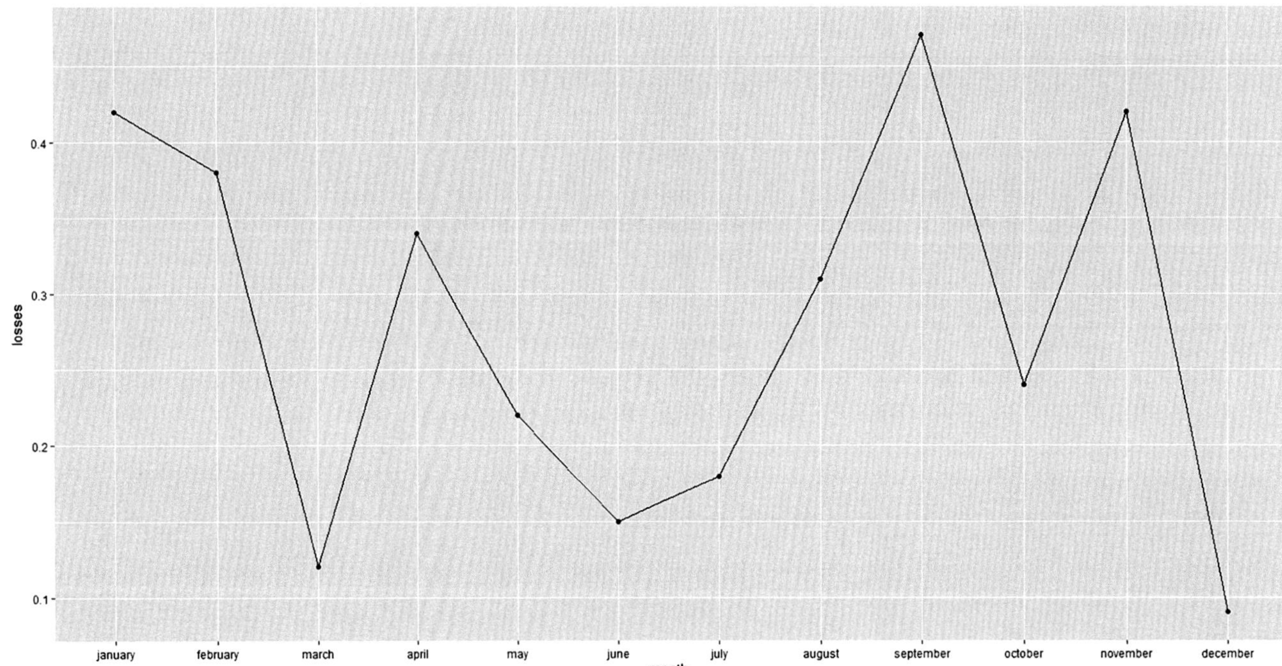

FIGURE 7.19 Line graph created with the package `ggplot2`.

It is also possible to add the values corresponding to each month, explicitly, using the geometry functions `geom_label()` or `geom_text()`. However, if the reader did this in this graph, he or she would see an overlap between the points of the geometry `geom_point()` and the values evidenced by the functions `geom_label()` or `geom_text()`. When this situation occurs, we recommend using the functions `geom_label_repel()` or `geom_text_repel()`, both from the package `ggrepel`. The algorithms of the package `ggrepel` try to find the best possible point to make some text explicit in a given graphic, mitigating the overlapping problems. Figure 7.20 shows the graph obtained from the following commands.

```
ggplot(cheap_easy) +
  geom_line(aes(x = month, y = losses, group = TRUE)) +
  geom_point(aes(x = month, y = losses)) +
  geom_text_repel(aes(x = month,
                      y = losses,
                      label = paste0(losses * 100, "%")),
                  size = 3)
```

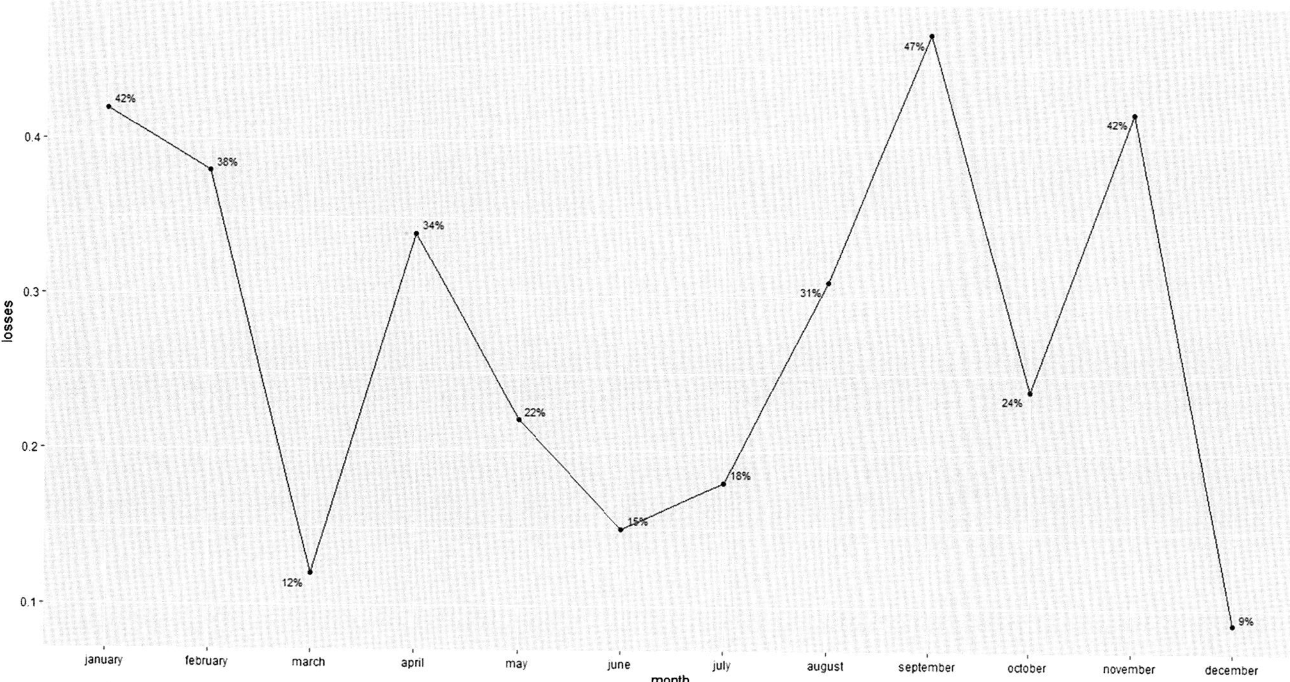

FIGURE 7.20 Line graph created with the package `ggplot2`.

In Figure 7.20, an attentive reader will notice the use of the function `paste0()`. This function is great for concatenating vectors by forcing them to become string type, so there is no space between the concatenated elements. Note that we command `paste0(losses * 100, "%"))`, first making the values of the variable *losses* multiplied by 100 and then adding the percent sign to the result. If the reader wants to concatenate vectors, forcing them to become of the string type, but with spacing between the concatenated elements, they must use the function `paste()`.

Finally, as we learned earlier, we can make the graph more elegant by adding colors and naming the axes. The final result is shown in Figure 7.21.

```
ggplot(cheap_easy) +
  geom_line(aes(x = month,
                y = losses,
            group = TRUE),
            color = "darkgreen") +
  geom_point(aes(x = month, y = losses)) +
  geom_text_repel(aes(x = month,
                      y = losses,
                      label = paste0(losses * 100, "%")),
                  size = 3) +
  labs(x = "Months",
       y = "Losses %") +
  theme_light()
```

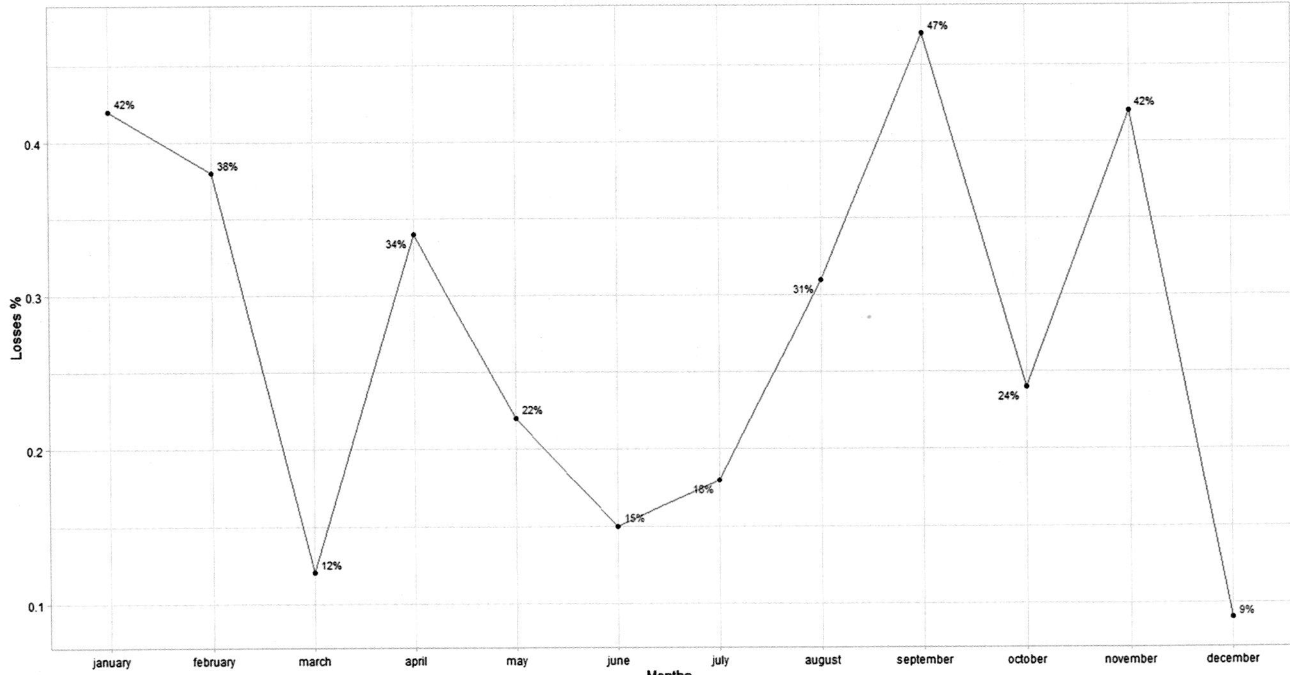

FIGURE 7.21 Line graph created with the package `ggplot2`.

Scatter plot with `ggplot2`

As an attentive reader may already know, a scatter plot can be constructed with the help of the geometry function `geom_point()`. To prepare it, we will use the same dataset present in the "Scatter plot" section in Chapter 4, which is available in the file `papermisto.RData`. The dataset variables are presented in Table 4.14.

As usual, to load the file `papermisto.RData` (Fávero and Belfiore, 2019), we must type the following command:

```
load("papermisto.RData")
```

The creation of a scatter plot follows the logic studied earlier in this chapter:

```
ggplot(data = papermisto) +
  geom_point(aes(x = time_min, y = weight_kg))
```

Figure 7.22 shows the graph obtained from the previous command.

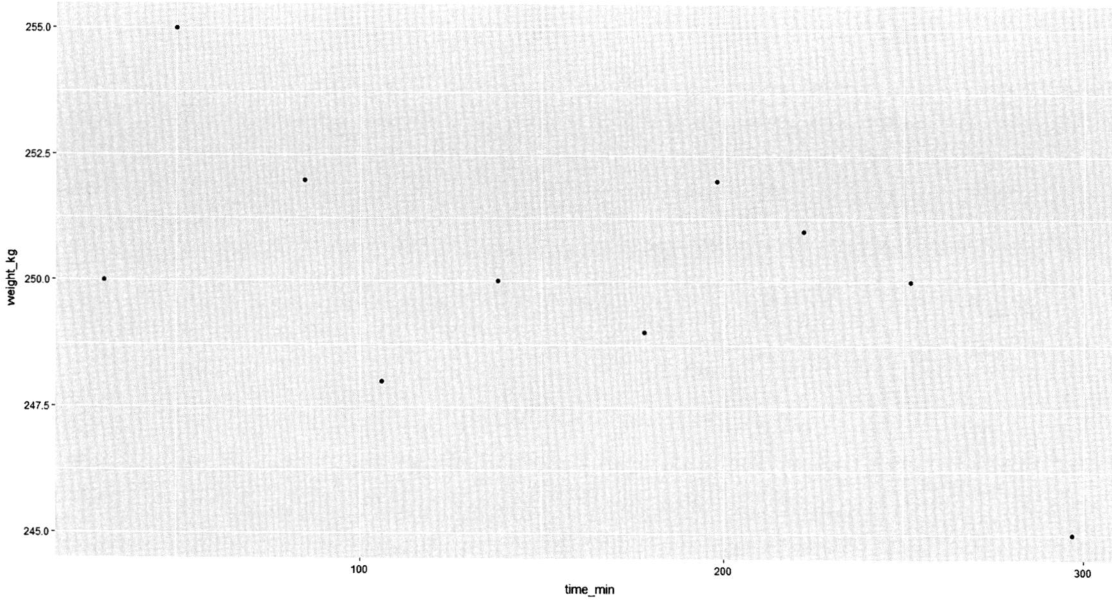

FIGURE 7.22 Scatter plot created with the package ggplot2.

As discussed earlier in this chapter, we can make the chart more elegant by adding colors and naming the axes with the following codes. The result is shown in Figure 7.23.

```
ggplot(data = papermisto) +
  geom_point(aes(x = time_min, y = weight_kg), color = "darkblue") +
  labs(x = "Time (min)",
       y = "Weight (kg)") +
  theme_minimal()
```

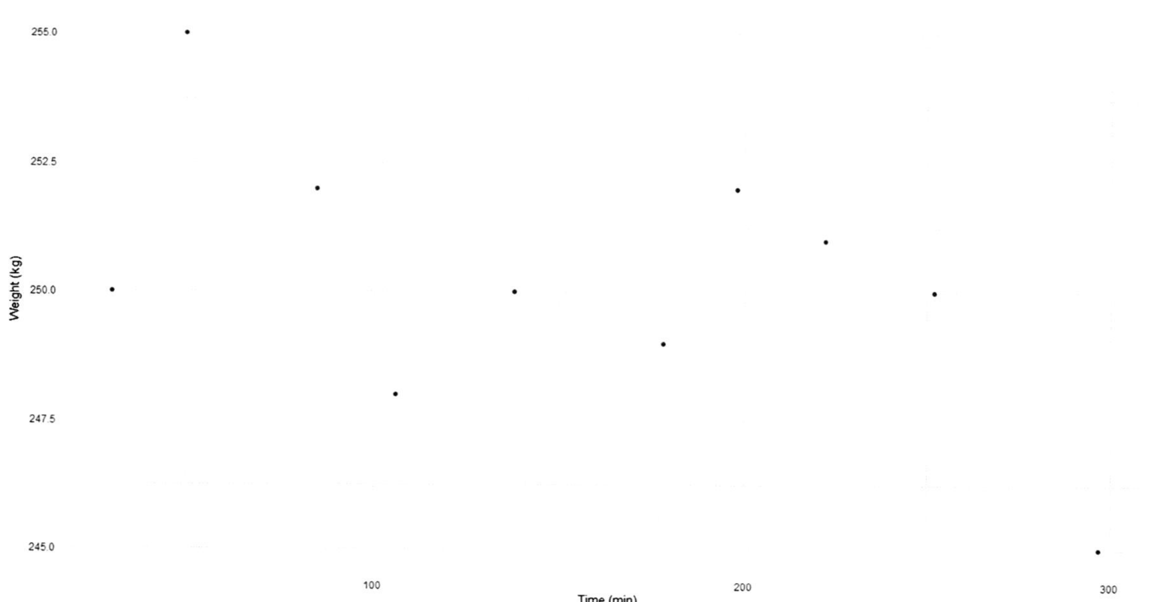

FIGURE 7.23 Scatter plot created with the package ggplot2.

If we wanted to, we could stratify the observations with respect to a given categorical variable (if it existed in the dataset) or from a threshold of a metric variable, arguing `size` internally to the function `aes()`:

```
ggplot(data = papermisto) +
  geom_point(aes(x = time_min,
                 y = weight_kg,
                 size = weight_kg > 250),
             color = "darkblue") +
  labs(x = "Time (min)",
       y = "Weight (kg)") +
  theme_minimal()
```

Figure 7.24 shows the graph obtained from the previous command.

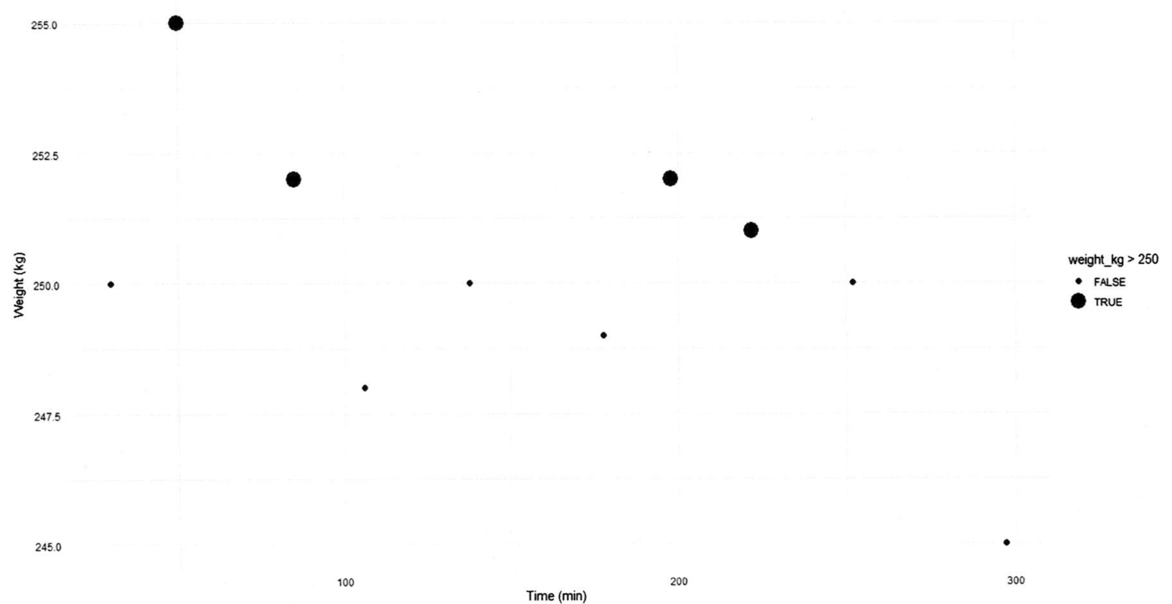

FIGURE 7.24 Scatter plot created with the package `ggplot2`.

We could even stratify the observations as follows using different shapes or colors from a given categorical variable or threshold of a metric variable, the result of which is shown in Figure 7.25.

```
ggplot(data = papermisto) +
  geom_point(aes(x = time_min,
                 y = weight_kg,
                 size = weight_kg > 250,
                 color = weight_kg < 252,
                 shape = weight_kg > 251)) +
  labs(x = "Time (min)",
       y = "Weight (kg)") +
  theme_minimal()
```

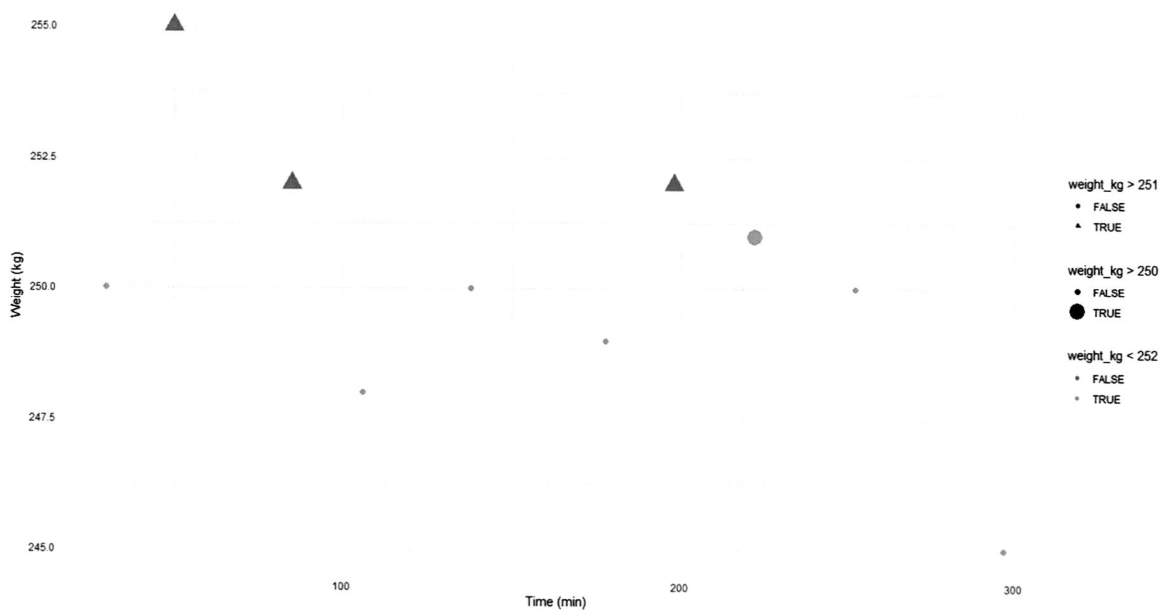

FIGURE 7.25 Scatter plot created with the package `ggplot2`.

Histogram with `ggplot2`

Building a histogram with the library `ggplot2` uses the function `geom_histogram()`. The dataset we will use is in the file `bank.RData` (Fávero and Belfiore, 2019), whose data are presented in Table 4.15.

```
load("bank.RData")
```

After loading the file `bank.RData`, we can command the following. Figure 7.26 shows the histogram obtained from this routine.

```
ggplot(data = bank) +
  geom_histogram(aes(x = number_of_companies))
```

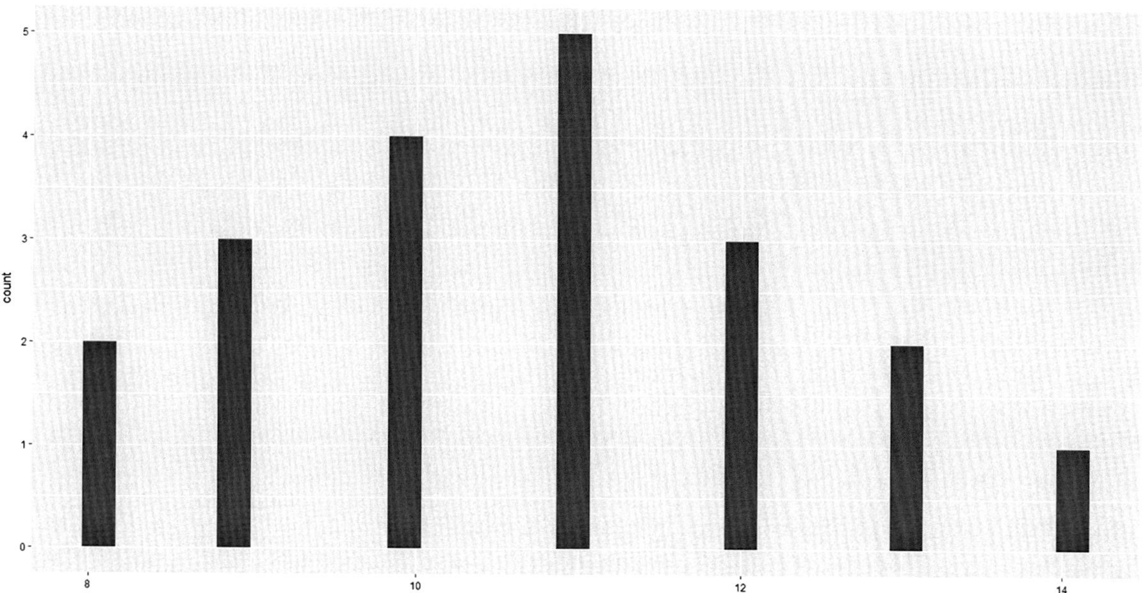

FIGURE 7.26 Histogram created with the package `ggplot2`.

An attentive reader will notice that R also returned the following warning: **"`stat_bin()` using `bins = 30`. Pick better value with `binwidth`."**. By default, the package ggplot2 uses 30 boxes in its histograms.

To obtain a histogram similar to Figure 4.18 in the "Histogram" section in Chapter 4, we must argue bins = 7. Figure 7.27 shows the result of the following command.

```
ggplot(data = bank) +
  geom_histogram(aes(x = number_of_companies), bins = 7)
```

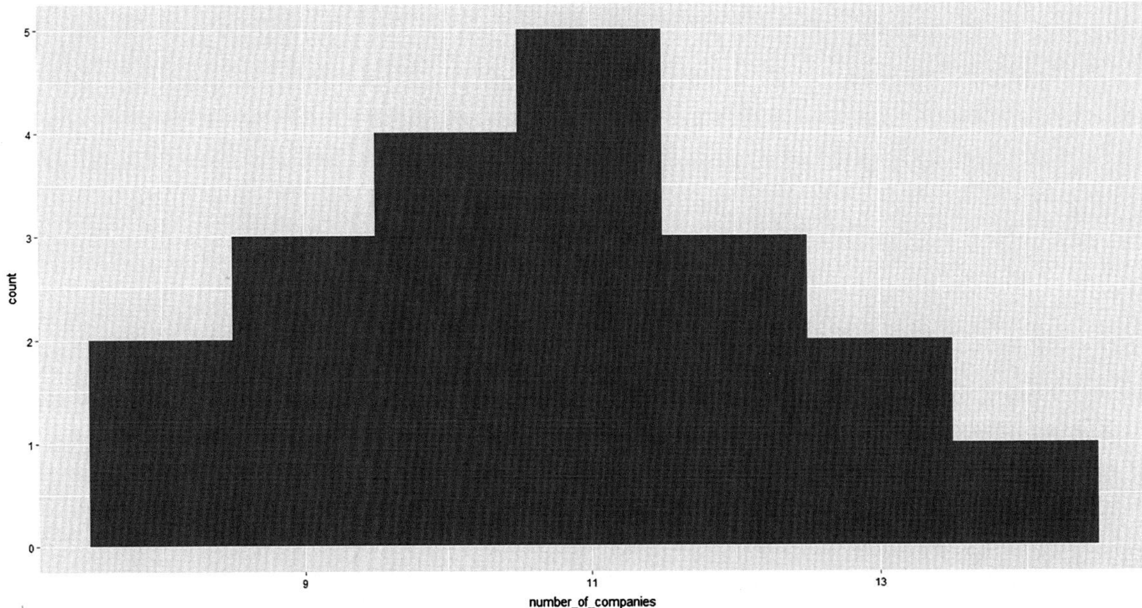

FIGURE 7.27 Histogram created with the package ggplot2.

To make the histogram in Figure 7.27 more elegant, we can use the graphical elements discussed earlier in this chapter:

```
ggplot(data = bank) +
  geom_histogram(aes(x = number_of_companies),
                 bins = 7,
                 fill = "brown",
                 color = "black") +
  geom_text(aes(x = number_of_companies,
                label = ..count..),
            stat = "count",
            vjust = -0.5) +
 labs(x = "Number of Companies",
      y = "Count") +
 theme_bw()
```

Figure 7.28 shows the result obtained from the previous commands.

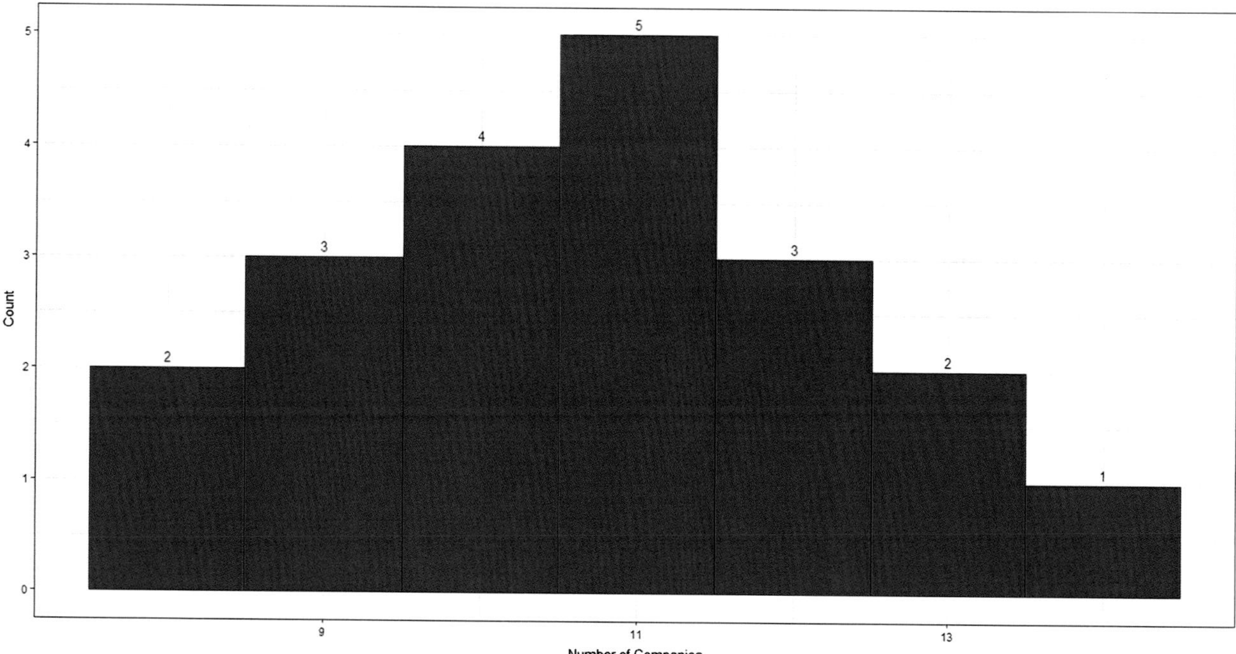

FIGURE 7.28 Histogram created with the package `ggplot2`.

Boxplot with ggplot2

To create a boxplot with the package `ggplot2`, we will again use the data from the file `cheap_easy.RData` (Fávero and Belfiore, 2019), which are presented in the "Line graph with ggplot2" section earlier in this chapter and the "Line graph" section in Chapter 4 and whose variables are shown in Table 4.13.

To load the dataset to be used, we can command the following:

```
load("cheap_easy.RData")
```

The geometry function for constructing a boxplot with the library `ggplot2` is `geom_boxplot()`:

```
ggplot(data = cheap_easy) +
  geom_boxplot(aes(y = losses))
```

An attentive reader will notice that, in place of a variable on the abscissa axis, we declared a variable on the ordinate axis. If the reader used only the declaration of a variable for the abscissa axis, there would be no serious problems; the point is that the boxplot would be constructed horizontally. Figure 7.29 shows the boxplot obtained from the previous commands.

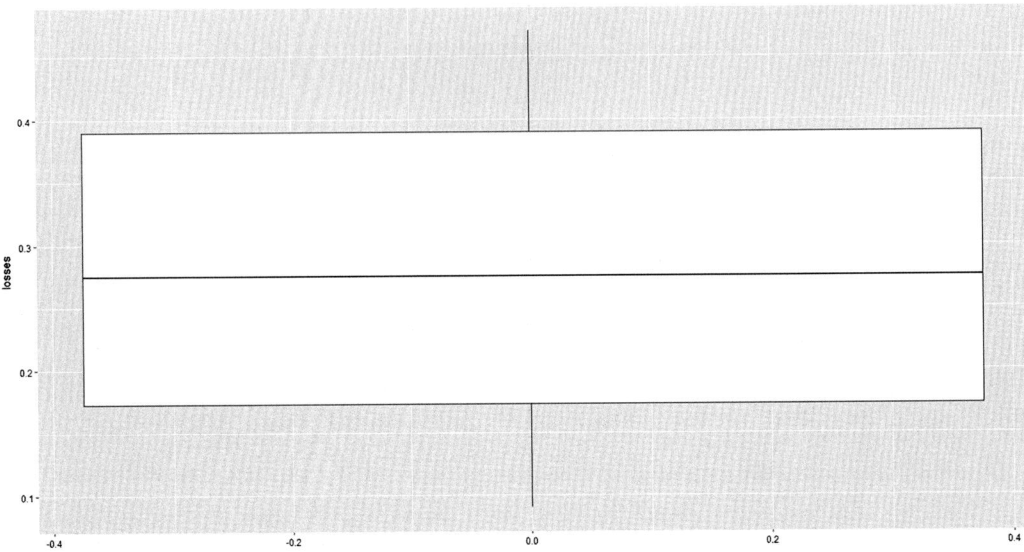

FIGURE 7.29 Boxplot created with the package ggplot2.

To make the graphic in Figure 7.29 more elegant, we can follow what we have learned so far, declaring to R, for example:

```
ggplot(data = cheap_easy) +
  geom_boxplot(aes(y = losses),
               fill = "cadetblue4") +
  labs(x = NULL,
       y = "Losses (%)") +
  theme(axis.text.x = element_text(color = "white"),
        axis.ticks.x = element_line(color = "white"),
        panel.background = element_rect(color = "black",
                                        fill = "white"),
        panel.grid = element_line("gray90"))
```

This time, we will not use a predefined function of "theme" type. We make voice so the reader can learn to customize the graphics using the function theme(). On the other hand, if the reader wants to explore more predefined functions of the "theme" type, we suggest the packages ggthemes and ggthemr. Figure 7.30 shows the result obtained from the previous command.

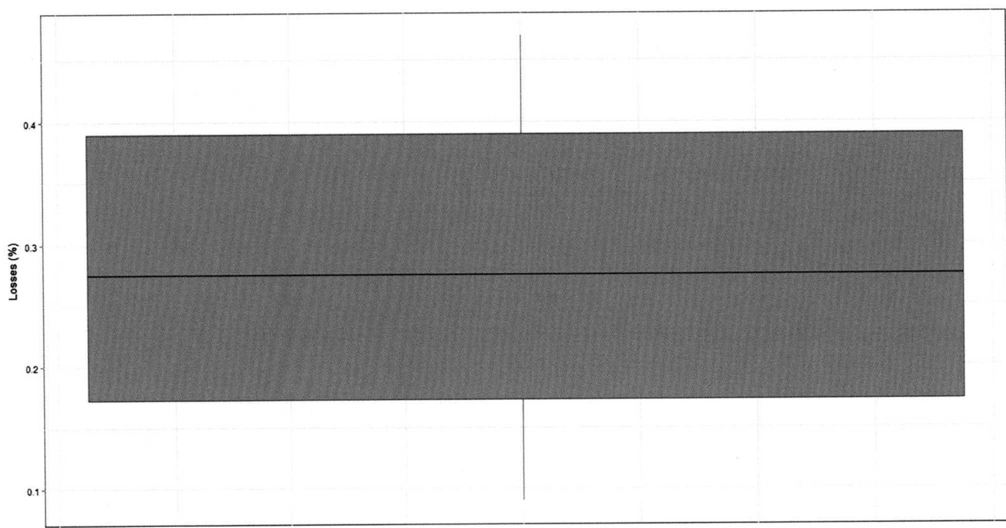

FIGURE 7.30 Boxplot created with the package ggplot2.

It is also important for the reader to know that all of the graphs presented have important interactions with the function ggplotly() from the package plotly. This function has the ability to make most of the geometries in the package ggplot2 behave interactively with the reader through the use of a mouse:

```
ggplotly(
  ggplot(data = cheap_easy) +
    geom_boxplot(aes(y = losses),
                 fill = "cadetblue4") +
    labs(x = NULL,
         y = "Losses (%)") +
    theme(axis.text.x = element_text(color = "white"),
          axis.ticks.x = element_line(color = "white"),
          panel.background = element_rect(color = "black",
                                          fill = "white"),
          panel.grid = element_line("gray90"))
)
```

Regarding the previous routine, an attentive reader will notice that we declared exactly the same code that generated Figure 7.30 internally to the function ggplotly(). We agree that the function may not make much sense for printed reports, but it is a powerful tool for creating dashboards (see Chapter 28) and creating web pages with R. Figure 7.31 shows the result obtained from the previous command. We encourage the reader to test the function ggplotly() with the graphs generated in this chapter.

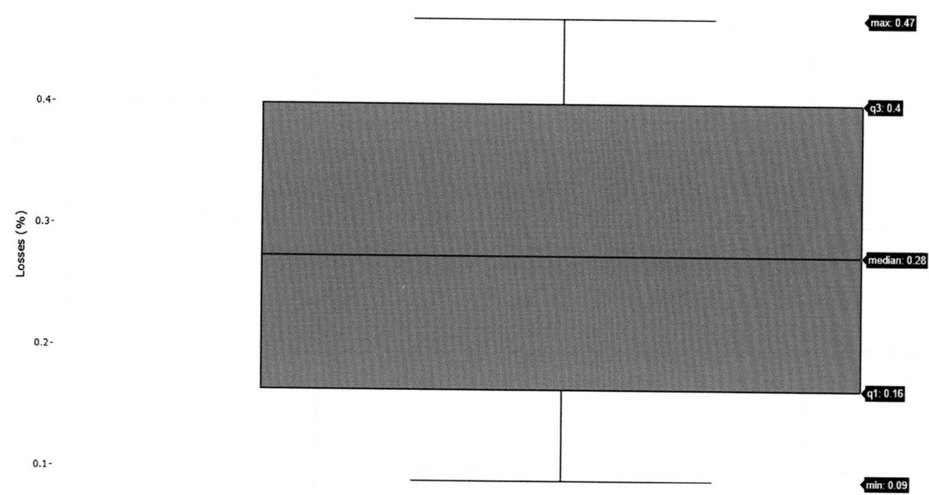

FIGURE 7.31 Boxplot created with the package ggplot2.

Final remarks

In this chapter, the main focus was to present, although superficially, some commands from the library ggplot2 so the reader can become familiar with most of the graphics used from now on.

An in-depth look at all of the features of the package ggplot2 would require the entire space of a book. In fact, in the introduction to this section, we recommend two entire works on the subject alone. Furthermore, even considering the two recommended books, they do not cover, for example, direct interactions between the package ggplot2 and the packages plotly and rayshader, which allow for a three-dimensional expansion for most of the graphics presented in this section.

Additionally, we will use the package plotly in some chapters of this work, but in these chapters we will provide direct explanations for all of the steps in the construction of graphs with this package. In the appendix, we will demonstrate the simplified construction of a pie chart with this library.

Exercises

(1) To preserve *açaí*, it is necessary to carry out several procedures, such as whitening, pasteurization, freezing, and dehydration. The file `dehydration.RData` shows the processing times (in seconds) in the dehydration phase throughout 100 periods. We would like you to create a histogram and a boxplot for the variable being studied with the library `ggplot2` (Fávero and Belfiore, 2019).

(2) At a certain bank branch, we collected the average service time (in minutes) from a sample with 50 customers regarding three types of services. The data can be found in the file `services.RData`. We would like you to create a histogram, a line graph, and a boxplot for each of the variables (Fávero and Belfiore, 2019).

Appendix

Main colors and color range accepted by R-based language

The main scale of colors allowed for figures (e.g., maps and graphs) established in R-based language can be checked by the function `colors()`, whose result is shown in Table 7.1:

```
colors()
```

TABLE 7.1 The main colors established by R-based language.

[1]	"white"	"aliceblue"	"antiquewhite"
[4]	"antiquewhite1"	"antiquewhite2"	"antiquewhite3"
[7]	"antiquewhite4"	"aquamarine"	"aquamarine1"
[10]	"aquamarine2"	"aquamarine3"	"aquamarine4"
[13]	"azure"	"azure1"	"azure2"
[16]	"azure3"	"azure4"	"beige"
[19]	"bisque"	"bisque1"	"bisque2"
[22]	"bisque3"	"bisque4"	"black"
[25]	"blanchedalmond"	"blue"	"blue1"
[28]	"blue2"	"blue3"	"blue4"
[31]	"blueviolet"	"brown"	"brown1"
[34]	"brown2"	"brown3"	"brown4"
[37]	"burlywood"	"burlywood1"	"burlywood2"
[40]	"burlywood3"	"burlywood4"	"cadetblue"
[43]	"cadetblue1"	"cadetblue2"	"cadetblue3"
[46]	"cadetblue4"	"chartreuse"	"chartreuse1"
[49]	"chartreuse2"	"chartreuse3"	"chartreuse4"
[52]	"chocolate"	"chocolate1"	"chocolate2"

TABLE 7.1 The main colors established by R-based language—cont'd

[55]	"chocolate3"	"chocolate4"	"coral"
[58]	"coral1"	"coral2"	"coral3"
[61]	"coral4"	"cornflowerblue"	"cornsilk"
[64]	"cornsilk1"	"cornsilk2"	"cornsilk3"
[67]	"cornsilk4"	"cyan"	"cyan1"
[70]	"cyan2"	"cyan3"	"cyan4"
[73]	"darkblue"	"darkcyan"	"darkgoldenrod"
[76]	"darkgoldenrod1"	"darkgoldenrod2"	"darkgoldenrod3"
[79]	"darkgoldenrod4"	"darkgray"	"darkgreen"
[82]	"darkgrey"	"darkkhaki"	"darkmagenta"
[85]	"darkolivegreen"	"darkolivegreen1"	"darkolivegreen2"
[88]	"darkolivegreen3"	"darkolivegreen4"	"darkorange"
[91]	"darkorange1"	"darkorange2"	"darkorange3"
[94]	"darkorange4"	"darkorchid"	"darkorchid1"
[97]	"darkorchid2"	"darkorchid3"	"darkorchid4"
[100]	"darkred"	"darksalmon"	"darkseagreen"
[103]	"darkseagreen1"	"darkseagreen2"	"darkseagreen3"
[106]	"darkseagreen4"	"darkslateblue"	"darkslategray"
[109]	"darkslategray1"	"darkslategray2"	"darkslategray3"
[112]	"darkslategray4"	"darkslategrey"	"darkturquoise"
[115]	"darkviolet"	"deeppink"	"deeppink1"
[118]	"deeppink2"	"deeppink3"	"deeppink4"
[121]	"deepskyblue"	"deepskyblue1"	"deepskyblue2"
[124]	"deepskyblue3"	"deepskyblue4"	"dimgray"
[127]	"dimgrey"	"dodgerblue"	"dodgerblue1"
[130]	"dodgerblue2"	"dodgerblue3"	"dodgerblue4"
[133]	"firebrick"	"firebrick1"	"firebrick2"
[136]	"firebrick3"	"firebrick4"	"floralwhite"
[139]	"forestgreen"	"gainsboro"	"ghostwhite"
[142]	"gold"	"gold1"	"gold2"
[145]	"gold3"	"gold4"	"goldenrod"
[148]	"goldenrod1"	"goldenrod2"	"goldenrod3"
[151]	"goldenrod4"	"gray"	"gray0"
[154]	"gray1"	"gray2"	"gray3"
[157]	"gray4"	"gray5"	"gray6"
[160]	"gray7"	"gray8"	"gray9"
[163]	"gray10"	"gray11"	"gray12"
[166]	"gray13"	"gray14"	"gray15"
[169]	"gray16"	"gray17"	"gray18"
[172]	"gray19"	"gray20"	"gray21"

Continued

TABLE 7.1 The main colors established by R-based language—cont'd

[175]	"gray22"	"gray23"	"gray24"
[178]	"gray25"	"gray26"	"gray27"
[181]	"gray28"	"gray29"	"gray30"
[184]	"gray31"	"gray32"	"gray33"
[187]	"gray34"	"gray35"	"gray36"
[190]	"gray37"	"gray38"	"gray39"
[193]	"gray40"	"gray41"	"gray42"
[196]	"gray43"	"gray44"	"gray45"
[199]	"gray46"	"gray47"	"gray48"
[202]	"gray49"	"gray50"	"gray51"
[205]	"gray52"	"gray53"	"gray54"
[208]	"gray55"	"gray56"	"gray57"
[211]	"gray58"	"gray59"	"gray60"
[214]	"gray61"	"gray62"	"gray63"
[217]	"gray64"	"gray65"	"gray66"
[220]	"gray67"	"gray68"	"gray69"
[223]	"gray70"	"gray71"	"gray72"
[226]	"gray73"	"gray74"	"gray75"
[229]	"gray76"	"gray77"	"gray78"
[232]	"gray79"	"gray80"	"gray81"
[235]	"gray82"	"gray83"	"gray84"
[238]	"gray85"	"gray86"	"gray87"
[241]	"gray88"	"gray89"	"gray90"
[244]	"gray91"	"gray92"	"gray93"
[247]	"gray94"	"gray95"	"gray96"
[250]	"gray97"	"gray98"	"gray99"
[253]	"gray100"	"green"	"green1"
[256]	"green2"	"green3"	"green4"
[259]	"greenyellow"	"grey"	"grey0"
[262]	"grey1"	"grey2"	"grey3"
[265]	"grey4"	"grey5"	"grey6"
[268]	"grey7"	"grey8"	"grey9"
[271]	"grey10"	"grey11"	"grey12"
[274]	"grey13"	"grey14"	"grey15"
[277]	"grey16"	"grey17"	"grey18"
[280]	"grey19"	"grey20"	"grey21"
[283]	"grey22"	"grey23"	"grey24"
[286]	"grey25"	"grey26"	"grey27"
[289]	"grey28"	"grey29"	"grey30"
[292]	"grey31"	"grey32"	"grey33"

TABLE 7.1 The main colors established by R-based language—cont'd

[295]	"grey34"	"grey35"	"grey36"
[298]	"grey37"	"grey38"	"grey39"
[301]	"grey40"	"grey41"	"grey42"
[304]	"grey43"	"grey44"	"grey45"
[307]	"grey46"	"grey47"	"grey48"
[310]	"grey49"	"grey50"	"grey51"
[313]	"grey52"	"grey53"	"grey54"
[316]	"grey55"	"grey56"	"grey57"
[319]	"grey58"	"grey59"	"grey60"
[322]	"grey61"	"grey62"	"grey63"
[325]	"grey64"	"grey65"	"grey66"
[328]	"grey67"	"grey68"	"grey69"
[331]	"grey70"	"grey71"	"grey72"
[334]	"grey73"	"grey74"	"grey75"
[337]	"grey76"	"grey77"	"grey78"
[340]	"grey79"	"grey80"	"grey81"
[343]	"grey82"	"grey83"	"grey84"
[346]	"grey85"	"grey86"	"grey87"
[349]	"grey88"	"grey89"	"grey90"
[352]	"grey91"	"grey92"	"grey93"
[355]	"grey94"	"grey95"	"grey96"
[358]	"grey97"	"grey98"	"grey99"
[361]	"grey100"	"honeydew"	"honeydew1"
[364]	"honeydew2"	"honeydew3"	"honeydew4"
[367]	"hotpink"	"hotpink1"	"hotpink2"
[370]	"hotpink3"	"hotpink4"	"indianred"
[373]	"indianred1"	"indianred2"	"indianred3"
[376]	"indianred4"	"ivory"	"ivory1"
[379]	"ivory2"	"ivory3"	"ivory4"
[382]	"khaki"	"khaki1"	"khaki2"
[385]	"khaki3"	"khaki4"	"lavender"
[388]	"lavenderblush"	"lavenderblush1"	"lavenderblush2"
[391]	"lavenderblush3"	"lavenderblush4"	"lawngreen"
[394]	"lemonchiffon"	"lemonchiffon1"	"lemonchiffon2"
[397]	"lemonchiffon3"	"lemonchiffon4"	"lightblue"
[400]	"lightblue1"	"lightblue2"	"lightblue3"
[403]	"lightblue4"	"lightcoral"	"lightcyan"
[406]	"lightcyan1"	"lightcyan2"	"lightcyan3"
[409]	"lightcyan4"	"lightgoldenrod"	"lightgoldenrod1"
[412]	"lightgoldenrod2"	"lightgoldenrod3"	"lightgoldenrod4"

Continued

TABLE 7.1 The main colors established by R-based language—cont'd

[415]	"lightgoldenrodyellow"	"lightgray"	"lightgreen"
[418]	"lightgrey"	"lightpink"	"lightpink1"
[421]	"lightpink2"	"lightpink3"	"lightpink4"
[424]	"lightsalmon"	"lightsalmon1"	"lightsalmon2"
[427]	"lightsalmon3"	"lightsalmon4"	"lightseagreen"
[430]	"lightskyblue"	"lightskyblue1"	"lightskyblue2"
[433]	"lightskyblue3"	"lightskyblue4"	"lightslateblue"
[436]	"lightslategray"	"lightslategrey"	"lightsteelblue"
[439]	"lightsteelblue1"	"lightsteelblue2"	"lightsteelblue3"
[442]	"lightsteelblue4"	"lightyellow"	"lightyellow1"
[445]	"lightyellow2"	"lightyellow3"	"lightyellow4"
[448]	"limegreen"	"linen"	"magenta"
[451]	"magenta1"	"magenta2"	"magenta3"
[454]	"magenta4"	"maroon"	"maroon1"
[457]	"maroon2"	"maroon3"	"maroon4"
[460]	"mediumaquamarine"	"mediumblue"	"mediumorchid"
[463]	"mediumorchid1"	"mediumorchid2"	"mediumorchid3"
[466]	"mediumorchid4"	"mediumpurple"	"mediumpurple1"
[469]	"mediumpurple2"	"mediumpurple3"	"mediumpurple4"
[472]	"mediumseagreen"	"mediumslateblue"	"mediumspringgreen"
[475]	"mediumturquoise"	"mediumvioletred"	"midnightblue"
[478]	"mintcream"	"mistyrose"	"mistyrose1"
[481]	"mistyrose2"	"mistyrose3"	"mistyrose4"
[484]	"moccasin"	"navajowhite"	"navajowhite1"
[487]	"navajowhite2"	"navajowhite3"	"navajowhite4"
[490]	"navy"	"navyblue"	"oldlace"
[493]	"olivedrab"	"olivedrab1"	"olivedrab2"
[496]	"olivedrab3"	"olivedrab4"	"orange"
[499]	"orange1"	"orange2"	"orange3"
[502]	"orange4"	"orangered"	"orangered1"
[505]	"orangered2"	"orangered3"	"orangered4"
[508]	"orchid"	"orchid1"	"orchid2"
[511]	"orchid3"	"orchid4"	"palegoldenrod"
[514]	"palegreen"	"palegreen1"	"palegreen2"
[517]	"palegreen3"	"palegreen4"	"paleturquoise"
[520]	"paleturquoise1"	"paleturquoise2"	"paleturquoise3"
[523]	"paleturquoise4"	"palevioletred"	"palevioletred1"
[526]	"palevioletred2"	"palevioletred3"	"palevioletred4"
[529]	"papayawhip"	"peachpuff"	"peachpuff1"
[532]	"peachpuff2"	"peachpuff3"	"peachpuff4"

TABLE 7.1 The main colors established by R-based language—cont'd

[535]	"peru"	"pink"	"pink1"
[538]	"pink2"	"pink3"	"pink4"
[541]	"plum"	"plum1"	"plum2"
[544]	"plum3"	"plum4"	"powderblue"
[547]	"purple"	"purple1"	"purple2"
[550]	"purple3"	"purple4"	"red"
[553]	"red1"	"red2"	"red3"
[556]	"red4"	"rosybrown"	"rosybrown1"
[559]	"rosybrown2"	"rosybrown3"	"rosybrown4"
[562]	"royalblue"	"royalblue1"	"royalblue2"
[565]	"royalblue3"	"royalblue4"	"saddlebrown"
[568]	"salmon"	"salmon1"	"salmon2"
[571]	"salmon3"	"salmon4"	"sandybrown"
[574]	"seagreen"	"seagreen1"	"seagreen2"
[577]	"seagreen3"	"seagreen4"	"seashell"
[580]	"seashell1"	"seashell2"	"seashell3"
[583]	"seashell4"	"sienna"	"sienna1"
[586]	"sienna2"	"sienna3"	"sienna4"
[589]	"skyblue"	"skyblue1"	"skyblue2"
[592]	"skyblue3"	"skyblue4"	"slateblue"
[595]	"slateblue1"	"slateblue2"	"slateblue3"
[598]	"slateblue4"	"slategray"	"slategray1"
[601]	"slategray2"	"slategray3"	"slategray4"
[604]	"slategrey"	"snow"	"snow1"
[607]	"snow2"	"snow3"	"snow4"
[610]	"springgreen"	"springgreen1"	"springgreen2"
[613]	"springgreen3"	"springgreen4"	"steelblue"
[616]	"steelblue1"	"steelblue2"	"steelblue3"
[619]	"steelblue4"	"tan"	"tan1"
[622]	"tan2"	"tan3"	"tan4"
[625]	"thistle"	"thistle1"	"thistle2"
[628]	"thistle3"	"thistle4"	"tomato"
[631]	"tomato1"	"tomato2"	"tomato3"
[634]	"tomato4"	"turquoise"	"turquoise1"
[637]	"turquoise2"	"turquoise3"	"turquoise4"
[640]	"violet"	"violetred"	"violetred1"
[643]	"violetred2"	"violetred3"	"violetred4"
[646]	"wheat"	"wheat1"	"wheat2"
[649]	"wheat3"	"wheat4"	"whitesmoke"
[652]	"yellow"	"yellow1"	"yellow2"
[655]	"yellow3"	"yellow4"	"yellowgreen"

Every time the reader wants to use any of the colors presented in Table 7.1, he or she must discuss it in full and in quotation marks. However, this is not the only way to declare a color in R-based language! In addition to specific packages, such as the package `viridis` and the package `RColorBrewer` that will be used from Chapter 23 onward, we can use hexadecimal script to command some color in R.

Therefore we suggest that the reader visit the RapidTables website (https://www.rapidtables.com/web/color/RGB_Color.html). In a very intuitive way, you can create the desired color, and the site will provide the hexadecimal encoding to be declared to R. The reader should be careful to declare the encoding in quotes and start with the character # (e.g., "`#551B1B`").

Pie charts with `ggplot2` and an easier solution

There is no geometry function for building a pie chart with the package `ggplot2`. This does not mean, however, that it is impossible to build these kinds of graphics with the library `ggplot2`. The task, however, is not the simplest.

Thus, we will demonstrate the creation of a pie chart with the package `ggplot2` and, later, a possible more direct and easier solution with the package `plotly`. To achieve this objective, we will use the file `notebooks.RData` (Fávero and Belfiore, 2019):

```
load("notebooks.RData")
```

Table 7.2 presents the data contained in the file `notebooks.RData`, which refers to five brands of notebooks and their respective market shares.

TABLE 7.2 Data of the object `notebooks`.

Brand	**Market share (%)**
Tech A	40.4%
Robot	25.0%
Rainbow One	17.3%
Pear	3.8%
LapTop	13.5%

If the intention is to build a pie chart with the package `ggplot2`, the first step is to create a bar chart without declaring the variable of interest to the abscissa axis, but declaring it to the ordinate axis. As discussed in the "Bar chart with `ggplot2`" section earlier in this chapter, `geom_bar()` dispenses with the existence of a variable on its y axis by default, therefore we should argue `stat = "identity"` for the same reasons explained in the "Pareto chart with `ggplot2`" section earlier in this chapter:

```
ggplot(data = notebooks) +
  geom_bar(aes(x = "", y = market_share, fill = brand),
           stat = "identity")
```

Figure 7.32 shows the result obtained from the previous command.

FIGURE 7.32 First step for creating a pie chart with the package ggplot2.

The reader may find it completely counterintuitive to attempt to establish a pie chart with a stacked bar chart as a first step. But what we will do next is use the function coord_polar() to join the two ends of Figure 7.32 so it looks like a circle. Figure 7.33 shows the result of the following command:

```
ggplot(data = notebooks) +
  geom_bar(aes(x = "", y = market_share, fill = brand),
           stat = "identity") +
  coord_polar(theta = "y", start = 0) +
  theme_void()
```

In the next step, we will try to enter the values for each market share of each notebook brand in Figure 7.33. We will use the function geom_text(), but we could use the function geom_label(), depending on the reader's taste, as discussed earlier in this chapter:

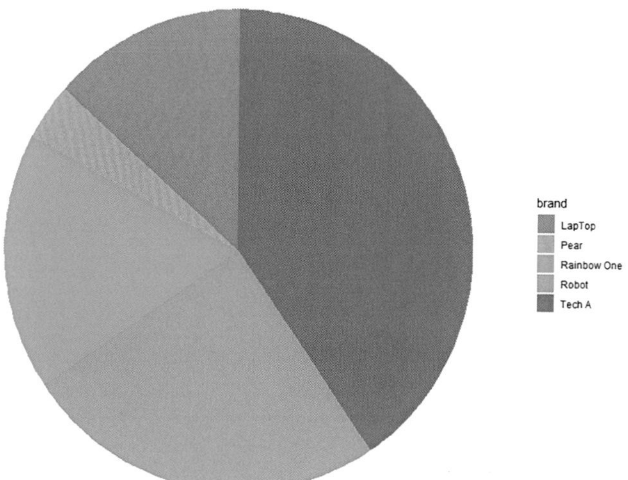

FIGURE 7.33 Second step for creating a pie chart with the package ggplot2.

```
ggplot(data = notebooks) +
  geom_bar(aes(x = "", y = market_share, fill = brand),
           stat = "identity") +
  geom_text(aes(x = "", y = market_share, label = market_share)) +
  coord_polar(theta = "y", start = 0) +
  theme_void()
```

As Figure 7.34 denounces, the proposed task is, in fact, not the easiest.

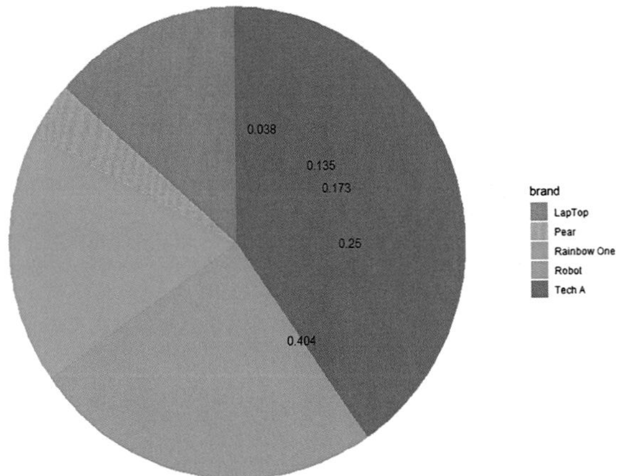

FIGURE 7.34 Third step for creating a pie chart with the package `ggplot2`.

Remember that it was said that the package `ggplot2` will always be oriented in a Cartesian way, that is, in a two-dimensional way? So the reader will need to know the x and y coordinates to get his or her bearings. So let's repeat the creation routine in Figure 7.34, but abandon the function `coord_polar()` for a moment. Figure 7.35 shows the result obtained from this command:

```
ggplot(data = notebooks) +
  geom_bar(aes(x = "", y = market_share, fill = brand),
           stat = "identity") +
  geom_text(aes(x = "", y = market_share, label = market_share))
```

Figure 7.35 shows us that our challenge will be to correctly place the market share value labels about each brand on a stacked bar chart.

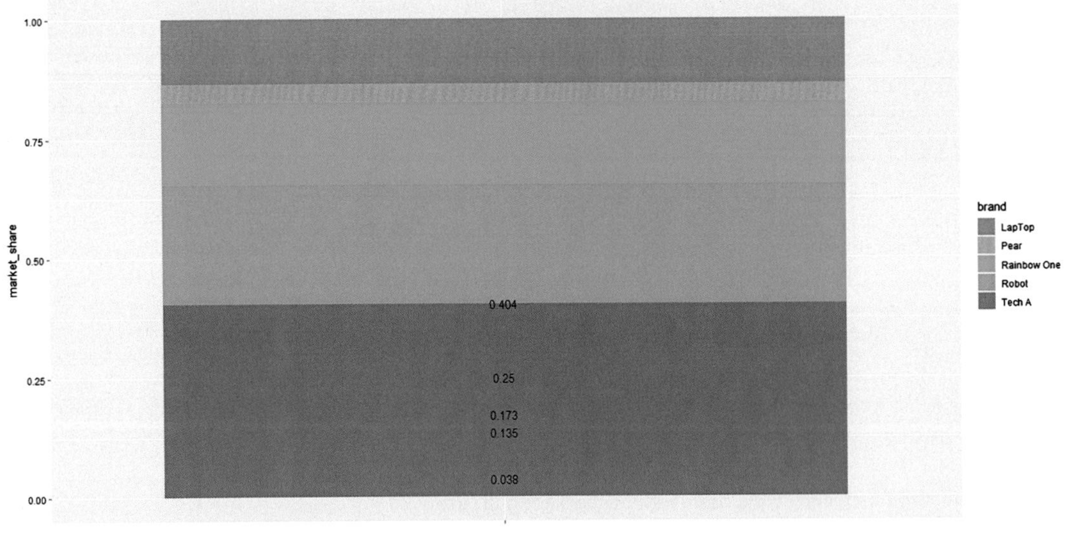

FIGURE 7.35 Fourth step for creating a pie chart with the package `ggplot2`.

Knowing this and knowing that `ggplot2` needs x and y coordinates, we will create the variable that will appear on the ordinate axis to guide the labels regarding the market share values.

Looking at the ordinate axis of Figure 7.35, the reader will agree that it actually represents the cumulative sum of each brand's market shares. Therefore the new variable must be obtained by the cumulative sum of the market share values multiplied by 0.5 and subsequently subtracted from the market share values of each brand. This procedure will no doubt make each value label appear in the middle of each stacked bar for each brand. We will call this new variable *position:*

```
notebooks["position"] <- cumsum(notebooks$market_share) - 0.5 *
  notebooks$market_share
```

That said, let's orient the function `geom_text()` with the help of the new variable *position*:

```
ggplot(data = notebooks) +
  geom_bar(aes(x = "", y = market_share, fill = brand),
           stat = "identity") +
  geom_text(aes(x = "", y = position, label = market_share),
            size = 3)
```

Figure 7.36 shows the result obtained from the previous command.

Finally, it will be enough for us to use the function `coord_polar()` again. The final result of a pie chart with the package `ggplot2` is shown in Figure 7.37.

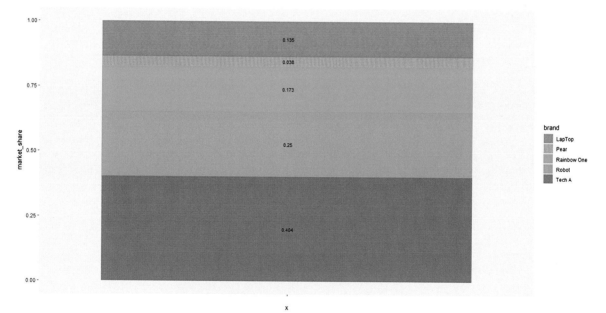

FIGURE 7.36 Fifth step for creating a pie chart with the package `ggplot2`.

```
ggplot(data = notebooks) +
  geom_bar(aes(x = "", y = market_share, fill = brand),
           stat = "identity") +
  geom_text(aes(x = "", y = position, label = market_share),
            size = 3) +
  coord_polar(theta = "y", start = 0) +
  theme_void()
```

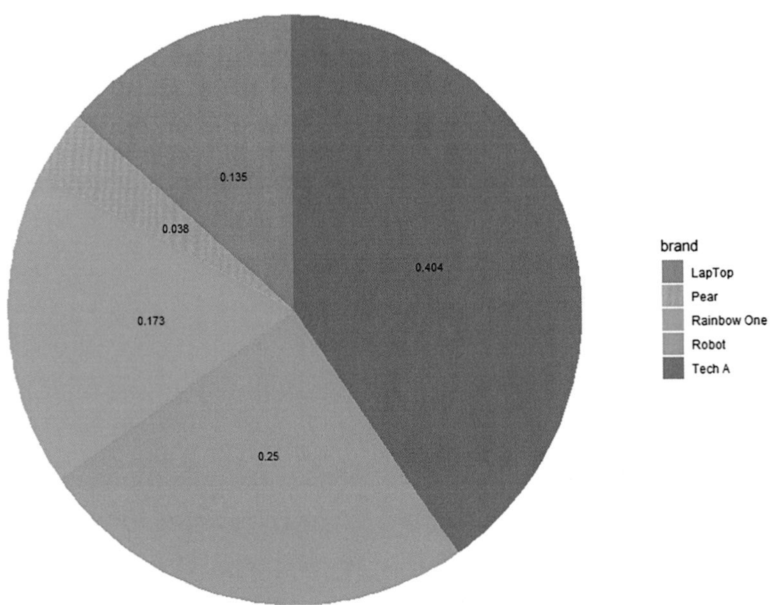

FIGURE 7.37 Final result obtained from creating a pie chart with the package `ggplot2`.

A faster and more practical alternative to creating a pie chart can be applying the function `plot_ly()` from the package `plotly`:

```
plot_ly(data = notebooks,
        labels = ~brand,
        values = ~market_share,
        type = "pie",
        textinfo = "label+percent",
        showlegend = FALSE)
```

As stated in this chapter, the package `plotly` will be used in this work with an emphasis on its three-dimensional capabilities, but we will pay attention to other applications in Chapter 27. Figure 7.38 shows the graph obtained from the previous commands.

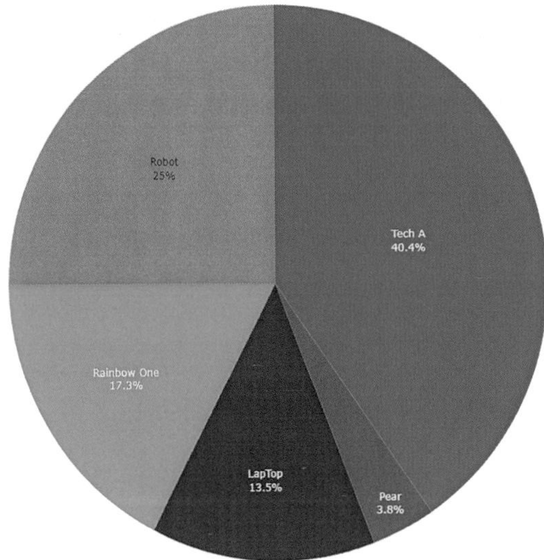

FIGURE 7.38 Final result obtained from creating a pie chart with the package `plotly`.

Supplementary data sets

```
satisfaction_survey.RData
cards.RData
cheap_easy.RData
papermisto.RData
bank.RData
dehydration.RData
services.RData
notebooks.RData
```

Please access supplementary data files here: https://doi.org/10.17632/55623jkwrp.3

PART III

Data mining and preparation

CHAPTER

8

Webscraping and handcrafted robots

AT THE END OF THIS CHAPTER, YOU WILL BE ABLE TO:

- Instruct the reader regarding the scraping of purely textual data present on the Internet
- Teach the reader to proceed with scraping data previously tabulated on web pages
- Present automation suggestions for data collection on the Internet
- Demonstrate to the reader how to create handcrafted robots for collecting data from the Internet

R language packages used in this chapter

```
library(rvest)
library(RSelenium)
library(data.table)
```

Don't forget to define the R working directory (the location where your datasets are installed):

```
setwd("C:/book/chapter8")
```

Introduction

One of the crucial points in data analysis is the obvious assumption that data are needed. In the algorithms and techniques discussed in this work, the reader has already found and will continue to find datasets that are properly organized and ready for training. However, in the world outside of this work, things do not happen in such a linear way.

It is true that in recent years the amount of organized datasets available to Internet users has increased a lot, which makes the task easier. However, there are many fields of human knowledge, and the different types of phenomena that science can study are infinite. As such, this increase in the availability of properly organized data cannot keep up with the speed of the need for information.

For example, a political scientist may want to elaborate, in real time, an analysis of feelings about posts made during an electoral campaign by politicians on social networks about the most different topics of interest to a given electorate. A linguist may want to study the similarities and differences between certain speeches about a topic in a classroom. A historian may be interested in a spatial analysis of a given excavation at a newly discovered archaeological site. As the reader

Data Science, Analytics and Machine Learning with R
https://doi.org/10.1016/B978-0-12-824271-1.00022-6

must have already noticed, for the narrated examples, there will hardly be datasets organized and ready for public access on these very specific subjects and, according to the references of these researchers, so recent.

Phenomena can be so specific that sometimes they cannot be measured directly, requiring "approximations"—the so-called *proxies*. The construction of these proxies commonly permeates not only a scientific theory, but also the researcher's creativity based on his or her previous experiences.

Taking into account the issues of the specificity of the phenomenon and creativity for the elaboration of a given proxy, another common obstacle is that all of the variables necessary for a good model are not always (read: *almost never*) available in the same place and explicit for download.

Take, for example, a scholar of law who wants to research an eventual legal system of Byzantine civilization. If this researcher had to start from scratch, he or she may have to digitize the regulations on the desired subject, apply some optical character recognition (OCR) algorithm, make the necessary translations regarding the topics of interest, categorize these topics, and then apply a textual analysis technique to continue the studies. The reader may also note that many of the steps narrated in this example were abbreviated. For example, it is necessary to gain access to these historical works, to obtain permission to download if they are already digitized in a museum, to have the technical ability to translate the language, and so on. In fact, the paths that permeate the topics of data science, analytics, and machine learning are far from being effortless.

For this chapter, we will dedicate ourselves to instructing the reader to capture information from secondary sources, in this case, Internet pages.

The proposed objective, when the subject is R-based language, invariably leads to the study of two main packages: `rvest` and `RSelenium`. Both packages deal with computational languages that extrapolate R-based language (i.e., HTML language and Java language), but the interesting part is that R will make the necessary translations between these languages as necessary, leaving the reader to be concerned with R-based language. It is obvious that if the reader has prior knowledge of HTML and Java as well as web page structures, there will be an advantage; however, as we said, it is not mandatory.

Next, we will equip the reader with the necessary concepts and some accessory tools to continue reading this chapter.

CSS selector and XPATH

By already having a certain command of R-based language, the reader must have already realized that, basically, if something is digital, then it is maintained by codes.

When the reader turns on a smart TV and sees a nice splash screen and a series of apps, he or she must have already noticed that this nice splash screen is generated by a series of codes as well as, of course, the functionalities of the applications installed on the smart TV.

The same can be said about the operating system installed on the reader's computer; the same can be said for the reader's smart phone. Likewise, the same can be said of the Internet pages.

When we enter a web page, we expect a pleasant and functional environment. Take, for example, the web page reserved for the Jet Propulsion Laboratory on Wikipedia, shown in Figure 8.1.

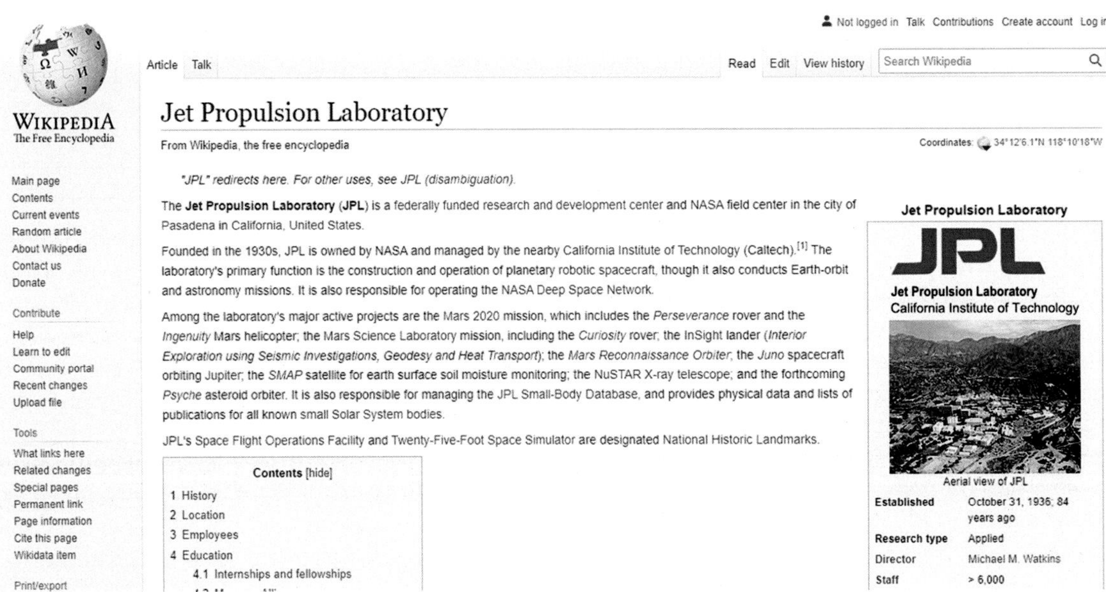

FIGURE 8.1 Wikipedia clipping about the Jet Propulsion Laboratory.

The web page shown in Figure 8.1 has images, links, a survey form, and text. Behind all of this, in fact, there is a tangle of code from one or more programming languages. As a general rule, on a given web page, the reader can access these codes by right-clicking on an area with no links, forms, or images and then searching for an option close to something like "inspect" (the functionality nomenclature may vary depending on the browser used by the reader). Figure 8.2 presents one possible result when using the Google Chrome browser.

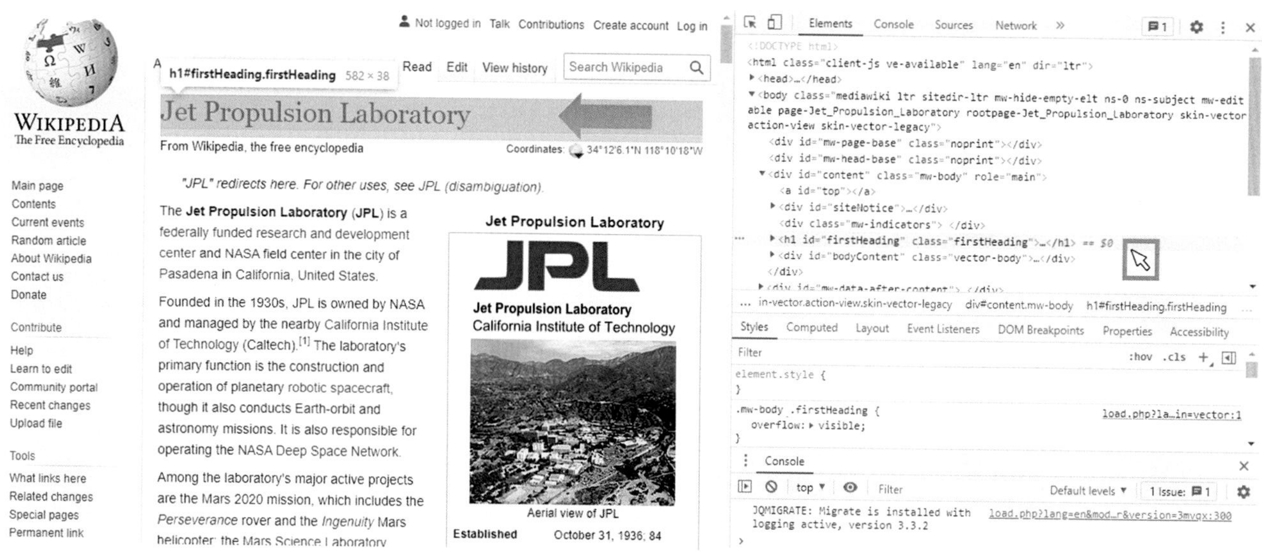

FIGURE 8.2 Wikipedia clipping on the Jet Propulsion Laboratory, highlighting the web page's source code.

In the previous paragraph, we pointed out that Figure 8.2 presents "one possible result" because web pages are absolutely dynamic. Depending on when the reader had access to this work, the administrators of a certain website may have already made substantial changes to the page's source codes, modifying not only its background, but also its appearance and browsing experience.

In any case, an attentive reader will notice two highlights in Figure 8.2: (1) a highlight regarding the mouse position in the source code inspection window of the studied web page and (2) a highlight regarding an automatic selection made in the Internet browser that presents the web page studied per se.

An attentive reader will also notice that, depending on where the mouse cursor rests on the inspection page, new selections are made on the web page simultaneously with the mouse movement. This proves what we said earlier, that is, everything, strictly everything presented on a web page, comes down to codes.

Remembering the beginning of Chapter 2, the reader should already be figuring out that to collect data from the web, we must be absolutely precise and unambiguous about our commands for R. Plus, each set of codes (those exposed in Figure 8.2) that caused a selection on the web page will represent these explicit and unambiguous paths. If the reader imagined this, he or she would be correct!

The point is that these codes that indicate elements of interest (data that we will collect), as shown in Figure 8.2, can be very extensive, generating a relevant workload for the reader. In this sense, to make the reader's work easier, we would like to talk about XPath and CSS Selector tags.

Codes regarding XPath and CSS Selector paths are useful tools for web developers to style web pages. For us, these codes will be seen as shortcut paths to search/select what we want R to access.

Each code highlighted in Figure 8.2 has its respective XPath or CSS Selector. Assuming that the reader's mouse was exactly where the authors' mouse was in Figure 8.2, in relation to the same web page, it would be enough to right-click on the code that makes selecting the data of interest and then going to the "Copy" option (or a similar option) and choosing something like "Copy CSS Selector" or "Copy Selector" or "Copy XPath" (or a similar option; it all depends on the browser that the reader uses).

Assuming that the reader opts for the CSS Selector, when pasting the information, the reader would have a result similar to the following: `#firstHeading`. If the reader chooses XPath, when pasting the copied information, the result would be similar to the following: `//*[@id="firstHeading"]`.

There is no need to use CSS Selector and XPath at the same time. As a rule, the reader will choose only one of them. In general, readers tend to opt for the CSS Selector.

Next, we will demonstrate a lightweight and free solution for capturing CSS Selector and XPath paths from web pages in a simplified way.

The tool SelectorGadget

The SelectorGadget solution is a lightweight and free application available for most web browsers to capture CSS Selector and XPath paths. To download the tool, the reader can go to the website https://selectorgadget.com/. Figure 8.3 demonstrates the interface at https://selectorgadget.com/.

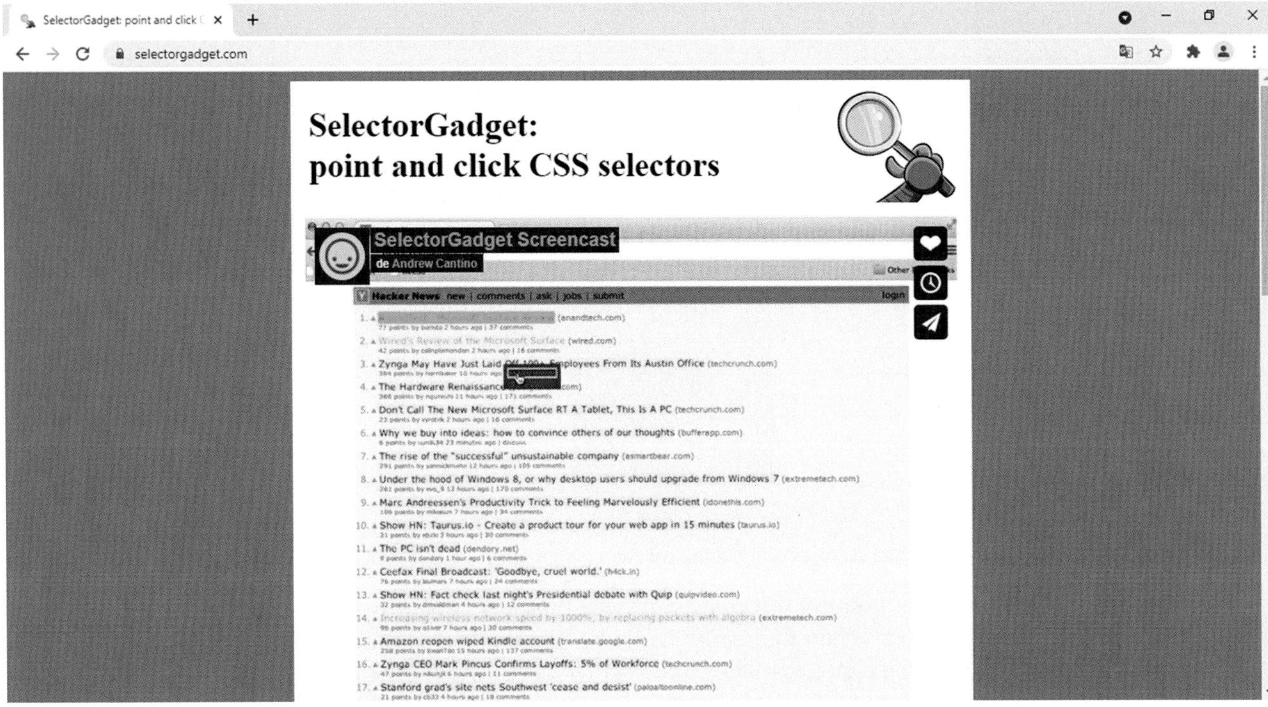

FIGURE 8.3 The SelectorGadget website home page.

Next, the reader must scroll the web page exposed in Figure 8.3 to the end. Figure 8.4 demonstrates this proposal.

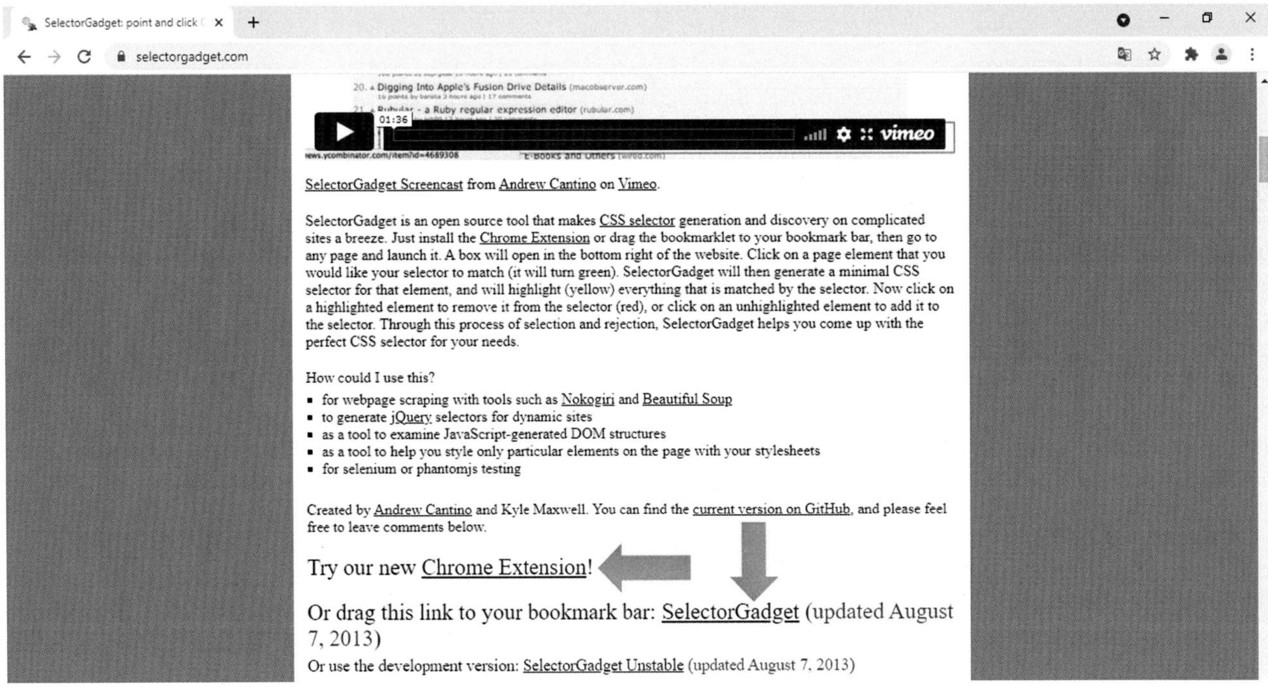

FIGURE 8.4 The SelectorGadget web page.

In Figure 8.4, two arrows were purposely placed: one horizontal and one vertical. If the reader is using the Google Chrome browser, he or she can choose to use the link pointed by the horizontal arrow; for other browsers, the reader should choose the link suggested by the vertical arrow. Regardless of the path taken by the reader, from a practical point of view, the results will be the same.

Due to the figures to come, the reader should be aware that the authors used the Google Chrome browser to carry out the proposed tasks together with the packages `rvest` and `RSelenium`.

The library `rvest`

The package `rvest` is the library with the largest number of tutorials available on the Internet. It has powerful tools for so-called *webscraping* and, as a rule, will solve many of the reader's demands regarding data collection. Installation and loading follow the general instructions for installing and loading packages presented in Chapter 2.

Along with the commands resulting from the use of the package `rvest` (and `RSelenium`), the SelectorGadget tool will have a fundamental role providing the arguments of the functions of these libraries (such arguments will concern the CSS Selector or XPath paths). **Therefore if the reader has not done the installation of the SelectorGadget application, we suggest reviewing "The tool SelectorGadget" section earlier in this chapter.**

To start demonstrating the functionalities of the package `rvest`, we propose two examples: (1) suppose the interest of assembling a dataset containing titles of scientific articles about the search for a given keyword, arranged in strings; (2) we will assume the interest in capturing information about some universities arranged in tables.

Example 1: Using the Function `HTML_TEXT()`

For the first example, that is, the interest of assembling a dataset containing titles of scientific articles regarding the search for a given keyword, as a rule, we will use the function `html_text()` because the results reported are usually strings.

In this task, we will search for publications regarding the term *sustainability index*. In fact, we could be using any search term in any search portal, be it journalistic, governmental, scientific, and so on. The idea in this example is to search for a given term (*sustainability index*, in this case) and collect the results presented in n pages of search results.

Thus we propose that the reader go to the Google Scholar website (https://scholar.google.com) and, in the search field, type the term *sustainability index*. The authors' SelectorGadget solution was already active, as shown in Figure 8.5.

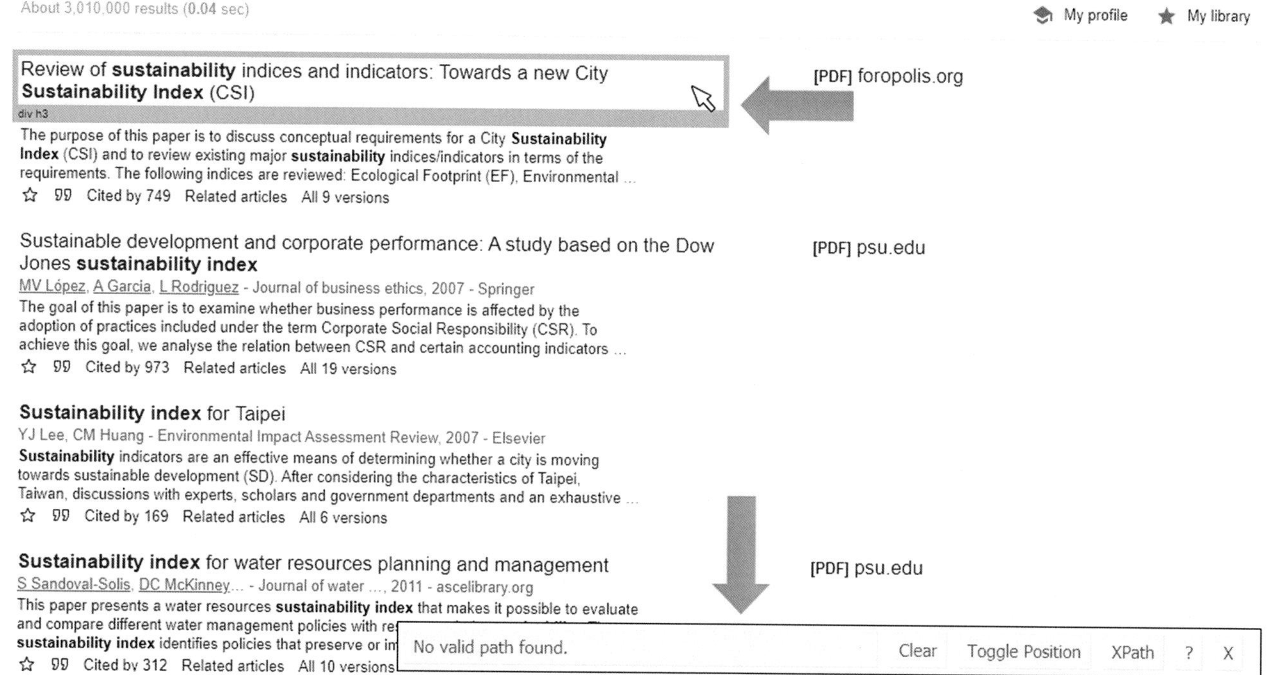

FIGURE 8.5 Using the SelectorGadget tool.

In Figure 8.5, once again, we placed two arrows, and there is a quadrilateral that surrounds the title of an article that exists due to the action of the SelectorGadget tool in function of the authors' mouse position. The horizontal arrow indicates the position of the authors' mouse cursor, and an attentive reader will notice that, depending on where your mouse cursor is on the web page, different quadrilaterals will be established by the SelectorGadget application. The vertical arrow points to the active SelectorGadget solution; it will be in this form that we will receive the CSS Selector paths of each point of interest on the web page we browse. The message "No valid path found" is displayed because we have not clicked anywhere yet. **Again, we make the reservation that the image in Figure 8.5 will not necessarily represent the same web page, with the same results, found by the authors, depending on the date of reading of this work.**

Following the proposed example that we want to build a dataset containing scientific articles as well as some of its characteristics, regarding the term *sustainability index*, let's start by capturing the CSS Selector regarding the titles of these articles. Thus with the mouse cursor generating the same selection as the title of publications shown in Figure 8.5, we ask the reader to press the left mouse button. The result of this action is shown in Figure 8.6.

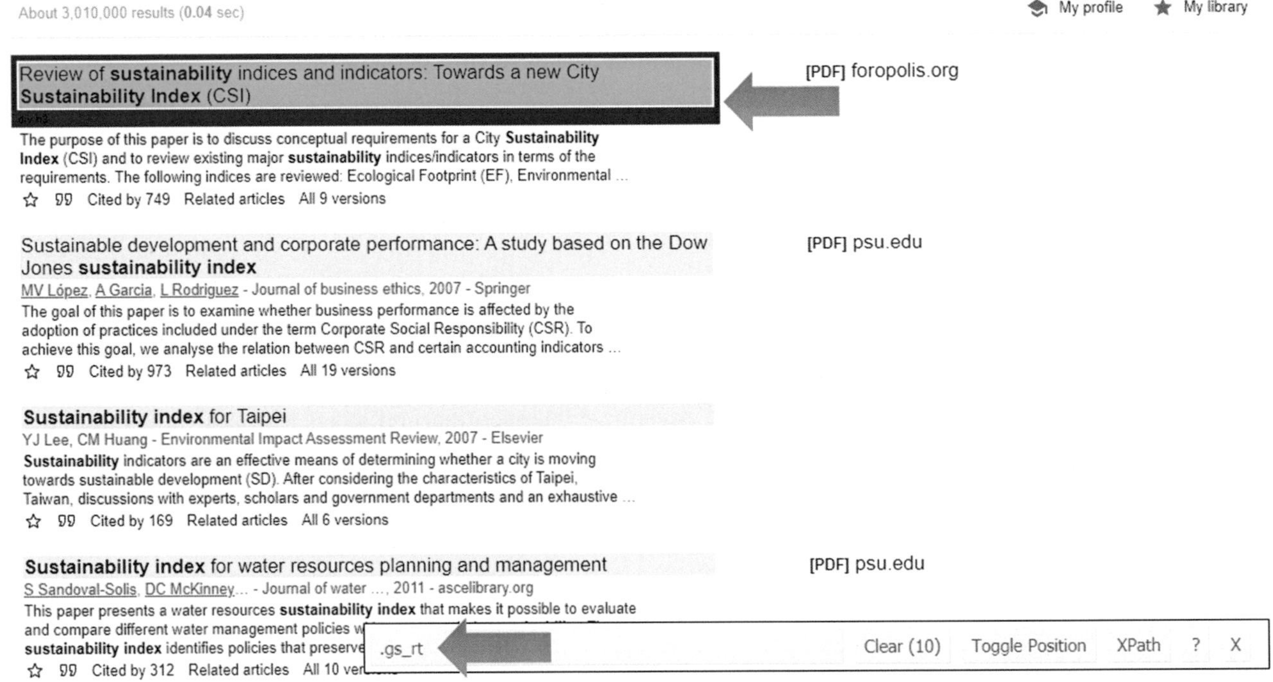

FIGURE 8.6 Using the SelectorGadget tool.

Following the previous steps, as shown in Figure 8.6, the area of the web page now selected will be in green color, outlined by the red color. Two arrows, purposely placed by the authors, indicate where the mouse click occurred as well as the result `.gs_rt` generated by the SelectorGadget solution; this is the CSS Selector path; if the reader wants the XPath path, he or she can just click on the homonym button.

The reader will also notice that, in Figure 8.6, in addition to the selection triggered by our mouse click, other selections (in yellow) were made. These selections refer to titles from other publications, the result of our research on Google Scholar. This indicates that the CSS Selector `.gs_rt` will take us to all of these titles at once.

Let's start using R to collect and organize the information of interest so far. The first step will be to save the precise address of the web page that presented the results about the articles returned from the search term *sustainability index* in Google Scholar. In our case, the URL reported by our browser was the following: https://scholar.google.com/scholar?hl=en&as_sdt=0%2C5&q=sustainability+index&btnG=.

```
url_gs <- "https://scholar.google.com/scholar?hl=en&as_sdt=0%2C5&q=sustainability+index&btnG="
```

Note that in the previous command we created an object called `url_gs` that will contain the Internet address that has the information present in Figures 8.5 and 8.6. Also note that the Internet address was declared in quotes.

The first step will be to have R capture relevant information regarding the coding of that web page. To do so, we will use the function `read_html()`, arguing the object that contains the address of the web page we want to analyze (`url_gs` s, in this case):

```
web_info_gs <- read_html(x = url_gs)
```

From the previous command, the object `web_info_gs` will be created, which will be of the type *list,* whose exploration is not of interest to the scope of this work, but which is very similar to that shown in Figure 8.2; that is, R captured the page structure of the analyzed web and saved it in an object.

Next, we will use the function `html_elements()` to access elements that are important to our work, that is, the structures of the web page where the search results of our interest appear because we will argue the CSS Selector path provided by the SelectorGadget tool:

```
title_elements_gs <- html_elements(x = web_info_gs,
                                   css = ".gs_rt")
```

After this, extraction of the titles of articles reported by Google Scholar, due to the search for the term *sustainability index,* can be done with the function `html_text()`:

```
titles <- html_text(x = title_elements_gs)
```

Ready! We already have the titles of the works presented on the first page! To access this information, the reader simply declares to R the name of the object `titles` and will have answers, as shown in Figure 8.7.

```
 [1] "Review of sustainability indices and indicators: Towards a new
City Sustainability Index (CSI)"
 [2] "Sustainable development and corporate performance: A study based
on the Dow Jones sustainability index"
 [3] "Sustainability index for Taipei"
 [4]  "Sustainability   index   for   water   resources   planning   and
management"
 [5] "In search of a natural systems sustainability index"
 [6] "Environmental Sustainability Index"
 [7]   "A   generalized   environmental   sustainability   index   for
agricultural systems"
 [8] "Creating a farmer sustainability index: a Malaysian case study"
 [9] "Transport sustainability index: Melbourne case study"
[10] "Proposal of a sustainability index for the automotive industry"
```

FIGURE 8.7 The object `titles`.

We insist that the image shown in Figure 8.7 will not necessarily contain the same web page, with the same results, found by the authors, depending on the date of reading of this work.

It is also important to note that the 10 article titles captured here must be the same 10 article titles displayed by Google Scholar on the date of the reader's search, however, they will not necessarily be presented in the same sequential order adopted by the browser!

Another point to clarify is that, for now, we are capturing the results present on the first page. Next, we will discuss routines to automatically scrape a larger number of web pages.

Even though we captured the information as proposed, there are numerous other pages reported by Google Scholar that contain articles on *sustainability index*. Let's assume, for educational purposes, that our interest focuses on capturing the titles of articles from the first 10 pages.

At this point, we ask the reader to click on the responsible links to access the tenth page, the second page, and the first page **(the reader must click on the links; it is not useful to observe the URL, for example, of the first page after replying to the Google Scholar search):**

- **Tenth page:**

  https://scholar.google.com/scholar?**start=90**&q=sustainability+index&hl=pt-BR&as_sdt=0,5

- **Second page:**

  https://scholar.google.com/scholar?**start=10**&q=sustainability+index&hl=pt-BR&as_sdt=0,5

- **First page:**

  https://scholar.google.com/scholar?**start=0**&q=sustainability+index&hl=pt-BR&as_sdt=0,5

The reader must have noticed that there is a pattern evidenced by the part of the links purposely bolded by the authors. The first page has the term start=0 in its URL; the second page has start=10, and the tenth page has start=90. This pattern leads us to think that the third page will have the term start=20 in its URL, the fourth page will have start=30, and so on.

So, to collect the results of the first 10 pages regarding the titles of articles reported by Google Scholar, after searching for the expression *sustainability index*, we must inform R the pattern perceived in the construction of the pages of this search portal. Then, for each page, we must apply what was taught in this section.

Now we need to join what we have learned so far with an algorithm that makes R understand that we want all of the results of those 10 pages (could be infinite pages). So it is true to say that we already have all the knowledge we need to do all of this: we have just gained some interesting knowledge about `rvest`, and in Chapter 2 we learned about manipulating variables and loops.

Thus the first step will be to replace the existing numbers after **start=** to something that R uses as a wildcard, as follows:

```
url <- "https://scholar.google.com/scholar?start=PGNUM&q=sustainability+index&hl=pt-BR&as_sdt=0,5"
```

In the previous routine, an attentive reader will notice that in the URL https://scholar.google.com/scholar?start=0&q=sustainability+index&hl=pt-BR&as_sdt=0,5, we replaced the numeric value 0 with the wildcard PGNUM (something like the abbreviation for page number). The reader can use whichever wildcards he or she wants, **as long as the textual pattern does not exist in the URL worked.**

The aforementioned information is important because in the subsequent steps, we will make R understand that the **PGNUM** value must be replaced by 0, then by 10, then by 20, 30... even 90. It could even be the final number of pages ideal for the reader. To substitute values, let's use the function `gsub()` studied in Chapter 2.

Next, let's make it clear to R which web pages we want to download. There are 10, right? However, the values range from 0 to 90, changing from 10 to 10 in a simple arithmetic progression. Therefore we will create a sequence of numbers that respects the logic described, using the function `seq()`:

```
pages_index <- seq(from = 0, to = 90, by = 10)
```

Next, we will create an empty object of type *list* to contain the data frame regarding the first page of results. *List*-type objects are not part of the scope of this work, however their understanding is not that complex.

In Chapter 2 we said that an object works like a box and that in that box we can store things created in R. Following this analogy, *list*-type objects would be boxes with internal compartments. Thus in the same object of type *list*, we can save a dataset in one of its compartments, a model in another compartment, a text in a third compartment, another dataset in a fourth compartment, and so on.

In an object of type *list*, we have access to compartments using the operator `[[]]` and declaring which compartment we want to access. For example, if our object of type *list* is called *recipe*, then we should declare `recipe[[1]]` to access its first compartment, `recipe[[2]]` to access the second compartment, and so on.

```
gs_data <- list()
```

We already have everything we need. From here, we will command the iterative function `for()`, indicating that R should do everything we learned with the package `rvest` for the first page, expanding those same commands to the other pages. Inside the function `for()`, we will explain to R that at each iterative step, it should replace the **PGNUM** value by 0, then by 10, 20, 30, up to 90. After that, the algorithm for each page of result should sequentially apply the functions `read_html()`, `html_elements()`, and `html_text()`. Finally, the results of each iterative step must be saved in a compartment of the *list*-type object that has been called `gs_data`.

However, before commanding the algorithm, the reader must be presented with the function `Sys.sleep()`. We make a voice so the reading of the following lines is not ignored.

Before proceeding, we feel obliged to familiarize the reader with the spurious kind of hacker conduct called Denial of Service (DoS).

A DoS-type attack is an attempt to make data from a particular server unavailable to users who try to access it. This behavior, in short, causes a certain computer to purposely overload another machine, causing it a kind of "confusion." For educational purposes, try to imagine yourself in a crowd where each person, at the same time, asks you to do something different. You will probably understand one or another request, and, no doubt, you will become confused as you answer them. When the machine becomes confused, it stops serving you because all of its memory is overloaded or because the communication path (i.e., the network bandwidth) is obstructed, preventing communication with other users.

DoS is not an invasion, but it is considered a kind of hacker attack because it can even bring down a web server; therefore, it is a kind of virtual crime. Precisely to avoid damages of this kind (whether for the reader or the maintainer of the website), the function `Sys.sleep()` makes sense in the construction of robots. Obviously Google's servers would not go down so easily with attacks of this kind, but the reader could get some kind of access ban of a few hours or days.

The function `Sys.sleep()` determines a pause, established in the seconds metric, between one command and another. Thus we will use the function `Sys.sleep()` to not overload the studied website.

Disclaimer, the proposed command follows:

```
for(i in pages_index){

        #First step: replacing the PGN pattern with the page numbers
        new_url <- gsub("PGNUM", i, url)

        #Second step: collecting information from web pages
        page_info <- read_html(new_url)

        #Third step: reading CSS Selector elements
        elements_info <- html_elements(x = page_info,
                                       css = ".gs_rt")

        #Fourth step: giving a break to the web server
        Sys.sleep(1.5)

        #Fifth step: saving the collected data in the object gs_data
        gs_data[[(i / 10) + 1]] <- html_text(elements_info)

        #Miscellaneous: displaying a progress message
        message("Saving page with term start=", i)
}
```

The reader may find it strange to create an object following the routine `gs_data[[(i / 10) + 1]]`. The reader should remember that the first page of results has in its URL the term start=0, therefore in the first iterative step, `i` will assume the value of `0`, following the order proposed by the object `pages_index`. However, the indexing of R starts at number 1, that is, there is no way to index the data inside the object `gs_data` from 0. There is no way to exist `gs_data[[0]]`, hence, `[[(i / 10) + 1]]`. This way, the URL data that contains the term start=0 will be saved in `gs_data[[1]]`; similarly, when the URL contains the term start=10, your data will be saved in `gs_data[[2]]`, and so on.

After the previous routines, to save the data regarding the 10 pages of results about the article titles reported by Google Scholar, we can command:

```
gs_df <- data.frame(titles = unlist(gs_data))
```

The object gs_df must be a data frame that contains the search results of the first 10 pages of the Google Scholar website about the *sustainability index* theme.

Next, we will demonstrate how to handle the features of the package rvest when the data is arranged in a table.

Example 2: Using the Function html_table()

In this second example, we will demonstrate the use of the function html_table(). It will be useful when we are interested in capturing data already properly tabulated present in web pages. For the task, we will use the information from the Webometrics Ranking of World Universities (Webometrics) website.

Webometrics is a ranking of higher education institutions that contains information on more than 30,000 organizations of this kind. For the English version, the email address is https://www.webometrics.info/en.

If the reader decides to access this website, he or she will find that navigation is very easy and intuitive, and the site is able to stratify higher education institutions by geographic regions. As it is a website about a ranking, its rankings obviously have subjectivities, arbitrariness, premises, and scores for the ordering of these educational institutions. **This work does not have the purpose of advertising gyms or dissemination of Webometrics, much less the goal of assuming Webometrics as a perfect metric. Our intention is regarding the collection of data available on the Internet—that and that's it.**

Let's assume that our researcher is interested in South African higher education institutions. When browsing the Webometrics page about these South African organizations, the reader will find a table similar to the one proposed in Figure 8.8.

ranking	World Rank	University	Det.	Impact Rank*	Openness Rank*	Excellence Rank*
1	264	University of Cape Town		409	232	249
2	382	University of the Witwatersrand		657	417	354
3	419	Stellenbosch University		668	355	458
4	442	University of Pretoria		652	461	501
5	586	University of Kwazulu Natal		1305	520	521
6	711	University of Johannesburg		2167	711	504
7	871	University of South Africa		1161	978	1025
8	913	University of the Western Cape		1288	874	1137
9	1039	Rhodes University		1518	1061	1266
10	1189	University of the Free State		2951	1120	1133

FIGURE 8.8 Clipping from Webometrics website on South African higher education institutions.

Figure 8.8 represents a cut of 10 higher education institutions present in the results reported by Webometrics. The reader will notice that there are at least two pages of results in his or her web browser.

If we wanted the complete table, whose cutout is shown in Figure 8.8, the first step would be to inform R where these data can be found:

```
url_webo <- "https://www.webometrics.info/en/Africa/South%20Africa"
```

Note that, similar to what we discussed earlier in the "Example 1: Using the Function `html_text()`" section, we created an object in the previous command called `url_webo`, which will contain the Internet address that has the information presented in Figure 8.8.

As follows from the reading of Example 1: Using the Function `html_text()`" section, the first step will be to use the function `read_html()`:

```
web_info_webo <- read_html(x = url_webo)
```

After creating the object `web_info_webo`, which contains the structure of the entire web page with information about some South African higher education institutions present in Figure 8.8, we can use the SelectorGadget tool to capture the CSS Selector path with respect to the ranking table of interest. Figure 8.9 demonstrates the web page of interest with the SelectorGadget tool active as well as the approximate position of the mouse cursor that enables selection of the interest table on the rankings of South African educational institutions.

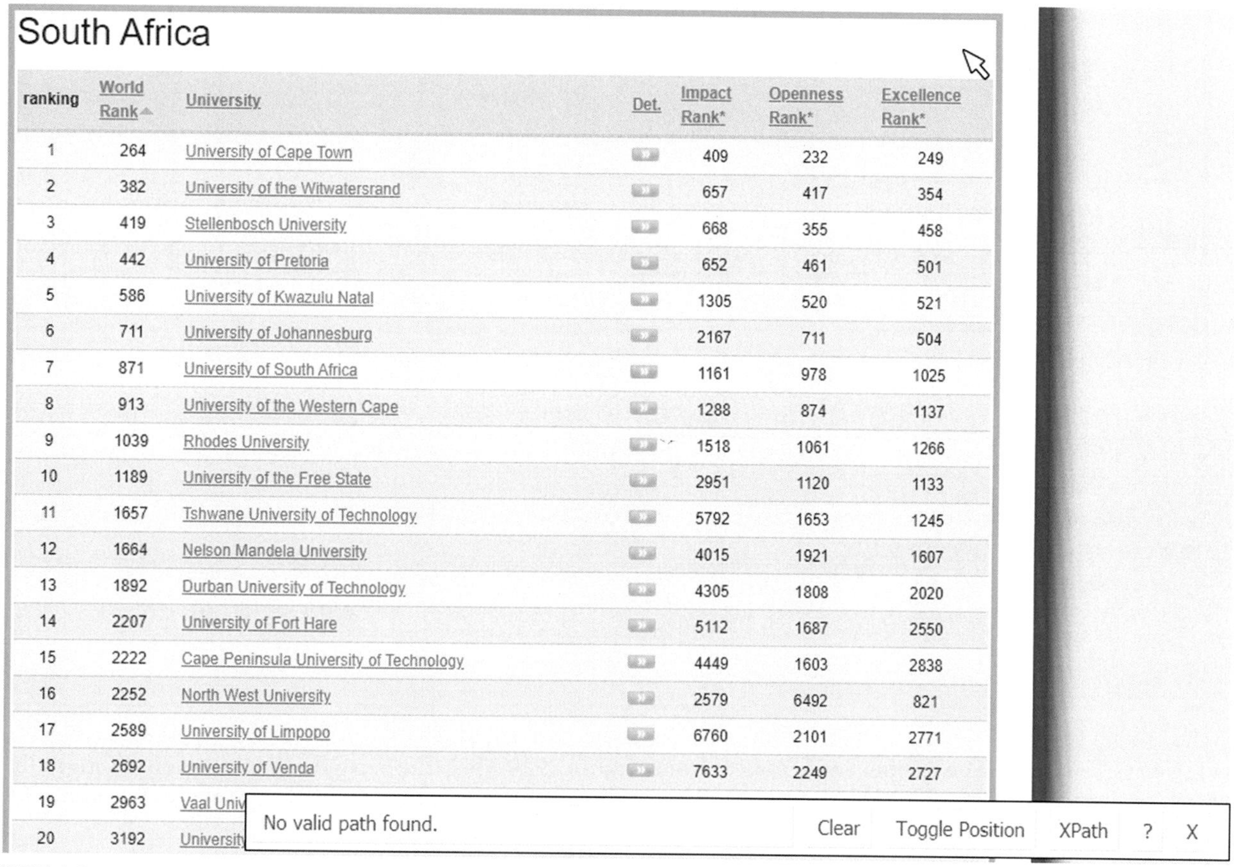

South Africa

ranking	World Rank	University	Det.	Impact Rank*	Openness Rank*	Excellence Rank*
1	264	University of Cape Town		409	232	249
2	382	University of the Witwatersrand		657	417	354
3	419	Stellenbosch University		668	355	458
4	442	University of Pretoria		652	461	501
5	586	University of Kwazulu Natal		1305	520	521
6	711	University of Johannesburg		2167	711	504
7	871	University of South Africa		1161	978	1025
8	913	University of the Western Cape		1288	874	1137
9	1039	Rhodes University		1518	1061	1266
10	1189	University of the Free State		2951	1120	1133
11	1657	Tshwane University of Technology		5792	1653	1245
12	1664	Nelson Mandela University		4015	1921	1607
13	1892	Durban University of Technology		4305	1808	2020
14	2207	University of Fort Hare		5112	1687	2550
15	2222	Cape Peninsula University of Technology		4449	1603	2838
16	2252	North West University		2579	6492	821
17	2589	University of Limpopo		6760	2101	2771
18	2692	University of Venda		7633	2249	2727
19	2963	Vaal Univ				
20	3192	Universit				

No valid path found. Clear Toggle Position XPath ? X

FIGURE 8.9 Using the SelectorGadget tool.

As the reader can already imagine, the next step will be the left-click for the SelectorGadget solution to present the CSS Selector path corresponding to the information we want to collect. Figure 8.10 shows the result of the proposed action.

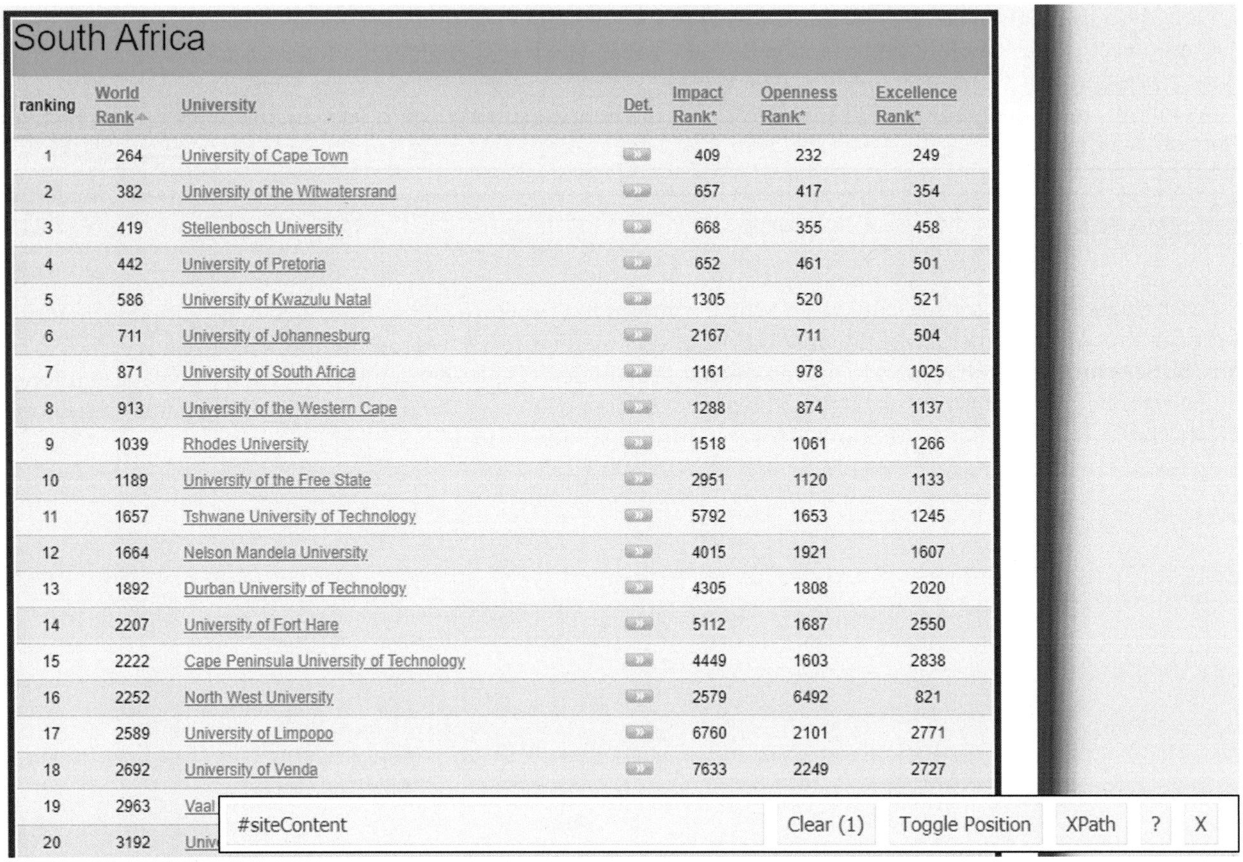

South Africa

ranking	World Rank	University	Det.	Impact Rank*	Openness Rank*	Excellence Rank*
1	264	University of Cape Town		409	232	249
2	382	University of the Witwatersrand		657	417	354
3	419	Stellenbosch University		668	355	458
4	442	University of Pretoria		652	461	501
5	586	University of Kwazulu Natal		1305	520	521
6	711	University of Johannesburg		2167	711	504
7	871	University of South Africa		1161	978	1025
8	913	University of the Western Cape		1288	874	1137
9	1039	Rhodes University		1518	1061	1266
10	1189	University of the Free State		2951	1120	1133
11	1657	Tshwane University of Technology		5792	1653	1245
12	1664	Nelson Mandela University		4015	1921	1607
13	1892	Durban University of Technology		4305	1808	2020
14	2207	University of Fort Hare		5112	1687	2550
15	2222	Cape Peninsula University of Technology		4449	1603	2838
16	2252	North West University		2579	6492	821
17	2589	University of Limpopo		6760	2101	2771
18	2692	University of Venda		7633	2249	2727
19	2963	Vaal				
20	3192	Univ				

#siteContent Clear (1) Toggle Position XPath ? X

FIGURE 8.10 Using the SelectorGadget tool.

Note that the CSS Selector path highlighted in Figure 8.10 was `#siteContent`. Each web page will have its own CSS Selector or XPath naming.

As the reader may already suspect, the next step will be to use the function `html_elements()`, arguing to her the CSS Selector path shown in Figure 8.10.

```
elements_webo <- html_elements(x = web_info_webo,
                               css = "#siteContent")
```

The final step, however, differs from the solution presented in the "Example 1: Using the Function `html_text()`" section. The reader will notice from Figure 8.10 that the searched data, even though they are textual, are properly tabulated on the website. Thus instead of the function `html_text()`, we will use the function `html_table()`:

```
ranking_webo <- html_table(x = elements_webo)
```

An attentive reader will notice that the object `ranking_webo` has a data frame contained in an object of type *list*. If the reader declares to R the created object `ranking_webo`, he or she will receive as output the same cutout of institutions present in Figure 8.8, but with the information that the object discussed contains data about 90 other organizations.

As already said, it is not the purpose of this work to study objects of type *list*, but we think that it is interesting for the reader to explore the object `ranking_webo`.

In RStudio, on the *Global Environment* tab, if the reader clicks on the object `ranking_webo`, a window will open in the script editor, whose content is shown in Figure 8.11.

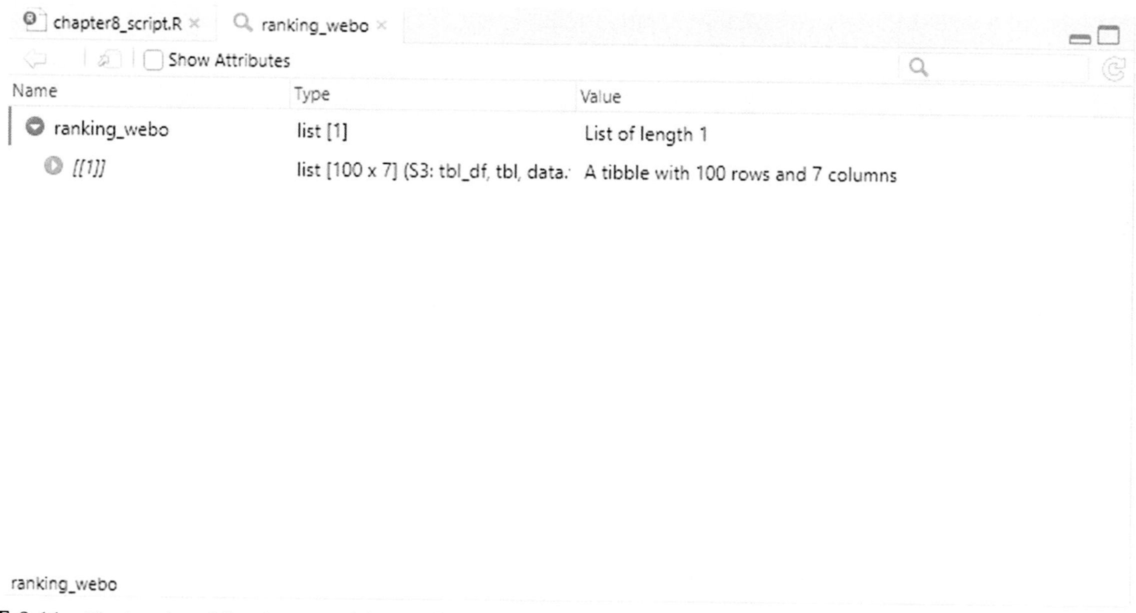

FIGURE 8.11 The interior of the object `ranking_webo`.

Taken carelessly, Figure 8.11 looks pretty uninteresting, but this reasoning is a serious misnomer. Note that there are two blue icons: , which is to the left of the object name `ranking_webo`, and , which is to the left of something called `[[1]]`.

The icon means the disclosure of the content of something. In this case, internal to the object `ranking_webo`, there is another object called `[[1]]`. It turns out that `[[1]]` is the indexing tag of a given component of a list. In `[[1]]`, there is our data frame about the first 100 observations from South African higher education institutions (tibbles are sorts of data frames). If there was another data frame (it could be anything created in R) internal to the object `ranking_webo`, it would be indexed in a different indexer (e.g., `[[2]]`). The reader can try the command `ranking_webo[[1]]` to see what happens.

Still discussing Figure 8.11, the icon indicates that something is not being made explicit to the reader. The reader simply clicks on the icon , and it changes its shape to . The reader will notice that Figure 8.11 has changed, and now the content observed by the reader will be present in Figure 8.12.

chapter8_script.R | ranking_webo | Show Attributes

Name	Type	Value
ranking_webo	list [1]	List of length 1
[[1]]	list [100 x 7] (S3: tbl_df, tbl, data.	A tibble with 100 rows and 7 columns
ranking	integer [100]	1 2 3 4 5 6 ...
World Rank	integer [100]	264 382 419 442 586 711 ...
University	character [100]	'University of Cape Town' 'University of the Witwatersrand' 'Stel...
Det.	logical [100]	NA NA NA NA NA NA ...
Impact Rank*	integer [100]	409 657 668 652 1305 2167 ...
Openness Rank*	integer [100]	232 417 355 461 520 711 ...
Excellence Rank*	integer [100]	249 354 458 501 521 504 ...

ranking_webo

FIGURE 8.12 Expansion of the visualization inside the object `ranking_webo`.

The reader will notice from Figure 8.12 that, inside the indexing `[[1]]`, in fact, there is the data frame that we are looking for, having been highlighted, at that moment, each of its variables.

If the reader wanted to save the content of this data frame in a new object, he or she could command as follows:

```
df_webo <- ranking_webo[[1]]
```

However, the previous command may represent a limitation for a researcher who is not satisfied with only the first page of the results of the studied website.

At this moment, similar to what we proposed in the "Example 1: Using the Function `html_text()`" section, it is extremely important that the reader navigate to the Webometrics website and go to the section corresponding to South African educational institutions. When scrolling the page, the reader will notice at least two pages of content. The reader will also be sure that the object `df_webo` contains only the higher education institutions contained in the first page of results. At the time of publication of this work, the address is https://www.webometrics.info/en/Africa/South%20Africa.

We ask the reader to navigate to the second page of results regarding South African higher education institutions and note the URL present in his or her web browser. At the time of publication of this work, the address is https://www.webometrics.info/en/Africa/South%20Africa?page=11.

An attentive reader will notice that when comparing the URLs discussed and switching to the second page, the term **?page = 1** was added. Now, if **page = 1** represents the second page of results, most likely, **page = 0** will return us to the previous page of results—the first page. The reader can change **page = 1** to **page = 0** and will see that, in fact, the browser will return to the home page about South African higher education institutions.

Therefore what we need to do is join what we have learned so far with an algorithm that makes R understand that we want all of the results of these two pages (could be infinite pages), similar to the one studied in the "Example 1: Using the function `html_text()`" section.

The first step will be to replace the existing numbers after **page =** to something that R uses as a wildcard, as follows:

```
url <- "https://www.webometrics.info/en/Africa/South%20Africa?page=PGNUM"
```

In the previous routine, an attentive reader will notice that at the URL https://www.webometrics.info/en/Africa/South%20Africa?page=1, we replaced the numeric value 1 with the wildcard **PGNUM** (something like the abbreviation of page number). We repeat that the reader can use whichever wildcards he or she wants, **as long as the textual pattern does not exist in the URL worked.**

The aforementioned information is important because in the subsequent steps we will make R understand that the **PGNUM** value must be replaced by **0** and then by **1**. It could be up to the final number of pages ideal for the reader. To substitute values, let's use the function `gsub()`, already studied in Chapter 2.

Next, let's make it clear to R which web pages we want to download. There are two, whose values range from 0 to 1. Therefore we will create a sequence of integers between 0 and 1. We will download page 0 (page = 0, **the first page of results regarding South African higher education institutions**); then we will download page 1 (page = 1, **the second page of results regarding South African higher education institutions**).

```
pages_index <- seq(from = 0, to = 1, by = 1)
```

Next, we will create an empty object of type *list* to contain the data frame about the first page of results in indexing `[[1]]` and to contain the data frame about the second page of results in indexing `[[2]]`:

```
webometrics_data <- list()
```

All ready! We will again resort to the iterative function `for()`, indicating that R should do what we learned from the package `rvest` for the first and second page of results on South African higher education institutions.

Inside the function `for()`, we will explain to R that at each iterative step, it should replace the **PGNUM** value by 0 and then by 1. After this, the algorithm for each result page should sequentially apply the functions `read_html()`, `html_elements()`, and `html_table()`. Finally, the results of each iterative step must be saved in a object compartment of type *list* called webometrics_data. We also remind the reader not to forget to use the function Sys.sleep(). See the "Example 1: Using the Function html_text()" section. That said, the proposed command follows:

```
for(i in pages_index){

        #First step: replacing the PGN pattern with the page numbers
        new_url <- gsub("PGN", i, url)

        #Second step: collecting information from web pages
        page_info <- read_html(new_url)

        #Third step: giving a break to the web server
        Sys.sleep(1.5)

        #Fourth step: saving the collected data in the object
        #webometrics_data
        webometrics_data[i+1] <- html_table(page_info)

        #Miscellaneous: displaying a progress message
        message("Saving page=", i)
}
```

After the previous routines, to save the data regarding the two pages of results about the institutions of higher education in South Africa in a single data frame, the reader could command the following:

```
df_webometrics <- rbind(webometrics_data[[1]],
                        webometrics_data[[2]])
```

Next, we will instruct the reader about the package RSelenium. This library aims to create robots for data collection on the web and is useful in situations in which the package rvest has limited performance.

The library RSelenium

The package RSelenium is an extremely useful tool when there is a need to interpose the automation of mimetic behaviors exercised by the machine. Here, we are talking about a robot for data collection.

Although it is possible to establish robots that automate the behavior that occurs internally to a computer or in a small business network, we will teach the use of this tool in the collection of existing data on the Internet.

That said, it must be made clear that the robots established by RSelenium are mimetic creations; that is, they perform **pre-established tasks**, behaving as a human would behave for these mentioned tasks. **Therefore if an event not previously predicted arises,** the robot will not know how to behave, and, consequently, the data will not be collected as it should or even will not be collected. In other words, the robot will only do what it has been precisely instructed to do—nothing more.

To exemplify what is guaranteed, if we want to gather some news about the behavior of some stocks on a stock exchange, we should instruct the robot informing which Internet browser it should use, which site it should go to, whether or not there will be opening of pop-up windows and what to do with them, and which sections of the site the robot must click on or which forms it must fill out, until we get to the information about the actions we want. After this, we should define what data would be collected.

Given the aforementioned, we also think it is necessary to say that instruments to verify the use of robots are common on the Internet. We have probably all visited web pages that ask the user to type one or more words, click on certain images, or solve simple arithmetic calculations to continue browsing. In this case, there is one more difficulty that will not be resolved by RSelenium. We think that the narrated situation goes beyond the scope of this work, but we leave the suggestion that the reader should train an algorithm for image recognition and combine it with the robot commands implemented by RSelenium.

A fair question could be, "Web pages, as a rule, are established in HTML coding, and therefore do I need to have this kind of knowledge?" Obviously, this knowledge would be an enabling asset, but for this specific case, there is no need to know HTML language, and the SelectorGadget tool will continue to help us (see "The Tool SelectorGadget" earlier in this chapter).

Requirements necessary for using `RSelenium`

In addition to R-based language and *RStudio* facilitator software, it is imperative that the reader has Java language plug-ins installed on his or her machine. **For beginners, we think it is necessary that the reader's computer has another Internet browser in addition to the one he or she usually uses.**

`RSelenium` is a derivative of *Selenium* software, written entirely in Java and created primarily for the automation of Internet browsers. It was noticed over time that it also had the ability to collect data, being soon spread to other programming languages. In any case, when using `RSelenium`, it will not be necessary to know how to program in any computer language other than R-based language.

Installing the Java language brings a very important detail for users of *Microsoft Windows* and *Linux* distributions! The architecture of R-based language installed on the reader's machine must be the same as the Java language installed so both can communicate correctly. In insisting on the use of different architectures, the package `RSelenium` can even be installed, but it will not perform any operation.

Most likely, the R-based language that the reader uses has two possible architectures installed: 32-bit (×86) and 64-bit (×64), and the command `R.version()` can therefore give dubious answers. So, for greater security, we ask the reader to use, in *RStudio*, the menu *Help>>About RStudio*. Figure 8.13 demonstrates the architecture used.

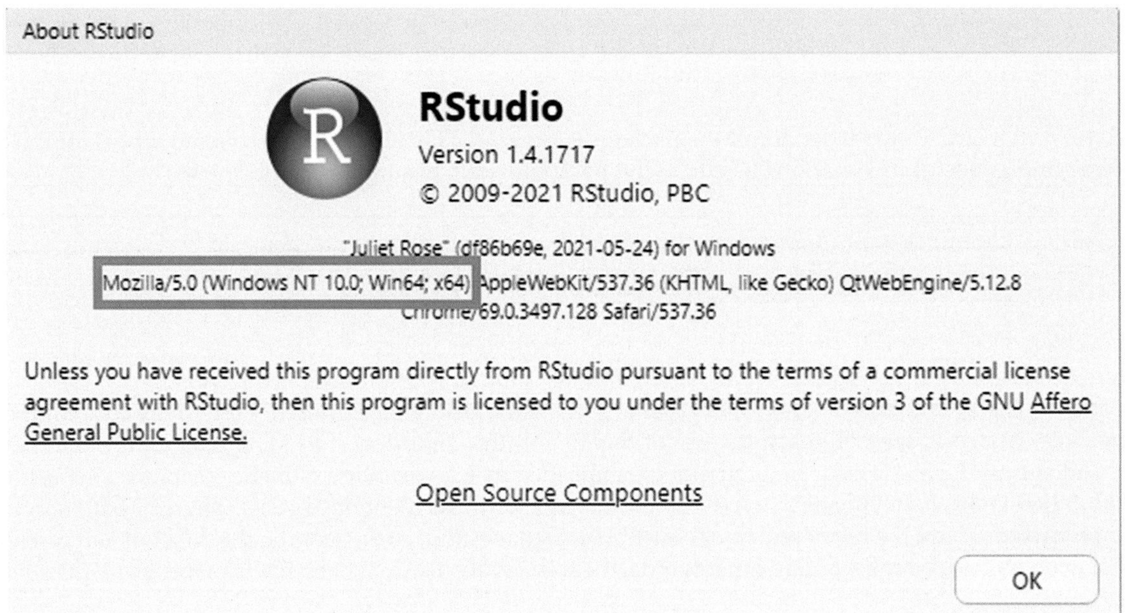

FIGURE 8.13 Checking the architecture of R-based language used.

The highlight in Figure 8.13 points out precisely what we need to know. For this case, the architecture used by the authors is ×64 (i.e., 64 bits). If the information present were ×86, then the architecture used would be 32 bits.

That said, the reader should go to the website https://www.java.com/en/download/, but there is another essential detail for users of *Microsoft Windows* or any *Linux* distribution! If the reader clicks on the "Agree and Start Free Download" button, the downloaded version will most likely be 32-bit. Thus if this is the architecture desired by the reader, just move on. If not, the reader must click on "See all Java downloads," as shown in Figure 8.14. In the case of users of any version of *Mac OS*, the button "Agree and Start Free Download" is satisfactory and will return the correct version to be used. Figure 8.14 also has arrows that highlight the points of interest narrated earlier.

FIGURE 8.14 The website for downloading the Java language.

After clicking on "See all Java downloads," scroll the new screen and choose the download version with the appropriate architecture. There remains, however, one last warning for *Microsoft Windows* users: if you are looking for the version with the 64-bit architecture, click on the "Windows Off-line (64-bit)" version; for any other choice ("Windows Online" or "Windows Offline"), the 32-bit version of Java will be downloaded.

After installing Java, we strongly recommend that the reader download one of the following Internet browsers in addition to the one he or she usually uses, for the robot to use: Internet Explorer, Google Chrome, Mozilla Firefox, or PhantomJS. If any of them are already installed, we ask the reader to make sure they are up to date and have the same architecture as the R-based and Java languages they are using.

Creating a robot with `RSelenium`

With the library `RSelenium` properly installed and loaded, the first function to be commanded will be `rsDriver()`. With this function, we will define which Internet browser the robot will use. Authors usually browse using Google Chrome, and for the purposes of this work, the robot will be designated the Mozilla Firefox browser.

```
browser_rselenium <- rsDriver(browser = "firefox")
```

The argument `browser = "firefox"` determines that R should use the Mozilla Firefox browser. If the reader prefers to use Google Chrome, he or she can use the argument `browser = "chrome"`; to use Internet Explorer, the reader can use `browser = "internet explorer"`; finally, if the reader wants to use the PhantomJS browser, he or she can argue `browser = "phantomjs"`.

Using the function `rsDriver()` usually takes a few seconds, and it is normal for the browser to be opened. We ask that if this occurs, the reader closes the currently open web browser and executes the following code:

```
remote_driver <- browser_rselenium[["client"]]
```

The previous command is responsible for making the browser obedient to R. After this, we can test if everything is running well by running the following:

```
remote_driver$open()
```

If all went well, the browser assigned to R will open immediately after the previous command. If nothing has happened, it is possible, but unlikely, that the version of `RSelenium` is out of date in relation to the adopted browser. Thus to adopt another browser, it is essential that R is closed, reopened, and that the previous routines are followed again.

Now we must define which web page our robot will navigate to. Always remember that our tool is mimetic, therefore we must teach it all the ways and artifices that we will use to navigate to the desired data.

Inspired by the example in the " Example 1: Using the Function `html_text()`" section, we will visit another site about scientific research, this time the Scopus portal. The URL containing the data of interest is https://www.scopus.com/home.uri?zone=header&origin=.

At the aforementioned web address, our objective will be to teach our robot to search and collect data about scientific journals that publish subjects in the area of artificial intelligence.

The first step will be to inform R about the URL of interest:

```
url_scopus <- "https://www.scopus.com/home.uri?zone=header&origin="
```

After this, we will make the browser that is under R's control (Mozilla Firefox, in our case) go to the URL of interest, as follows:

```
remote_driver$navigate(url_scopus)
```

As long as the R Console indicates the icon ●, it means that the web page is still loading. Just be patient until everything is finished. The process directly depends on the Internet connection speed.

Another interesting feature is that, as a rule, we declare the object that controls the browser (`remote_driver`, in our case), and followed by the operator `$`, there will be a function. For now, we will use the function `navigate()` to determine that the browser goes to a certain URL.

If the reader wants to observe the functions that can be used together with the object `remote_driver`, in *RStudio* it is enough to declare `remote_driver$`, and the possible functions will appear.

At the end of loading the previous command in R, the reader will verify that the browser assigned to the robot is already at the address of the page contained in the object `url_scopus`. We invite the reader, **using a different browser from the one used by the robot,** to visit the link https://www.scopus.com/home.uri?zone=header&origin=. Figure 8.15 presents the website's home page.

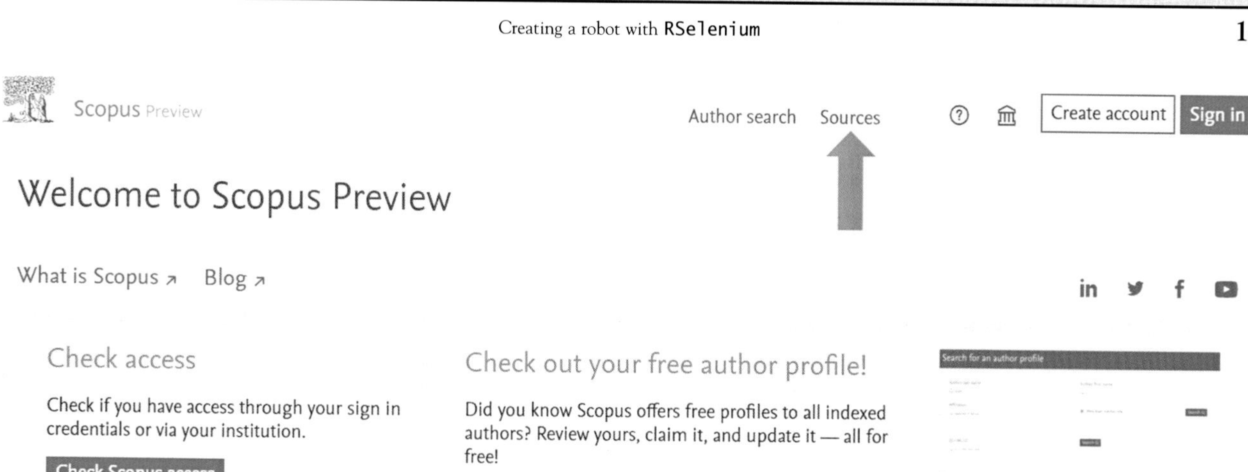

FIGURE 8.15 Clipping from the website of the Scopus portal.

To start fulfilling the objective of teaching our robot to search for scientific journals in the artificial intelligence area, the next step will be to teach the robot where the *Sources* option is located; then we must command the robot to access this option. In addition to illustrating a cutout of the homepage of the Scopus portal, Figure 8.15 highlights the *Source* option.

Before any action to be commanded by the robot, we must always teach the robot where the target element of the action is. At this point, we want to click on the *Source* option, so the first step is to make the robot "see" this option. This task must be done with the function `findElement()`. However, the function `findElement()` requires a path argument—preferably the CSS Selector path or the XPath path.

That said, it must also be said that we chose this task because for the case studied, the SelectorGadget tool has very limited functionality. So from here on, we will not use it.

Thus at the web address we are studying, **using a browser not linked to the robot,** we must click with the right mouse button on any field without links, without images, and without forms. After that, we must click with the left mouse button on an option next to *Inspect* or *Inspect Element* (naming needs to vary from browser to browser). A screen similar to the one shown in Figure 8.16 will open.

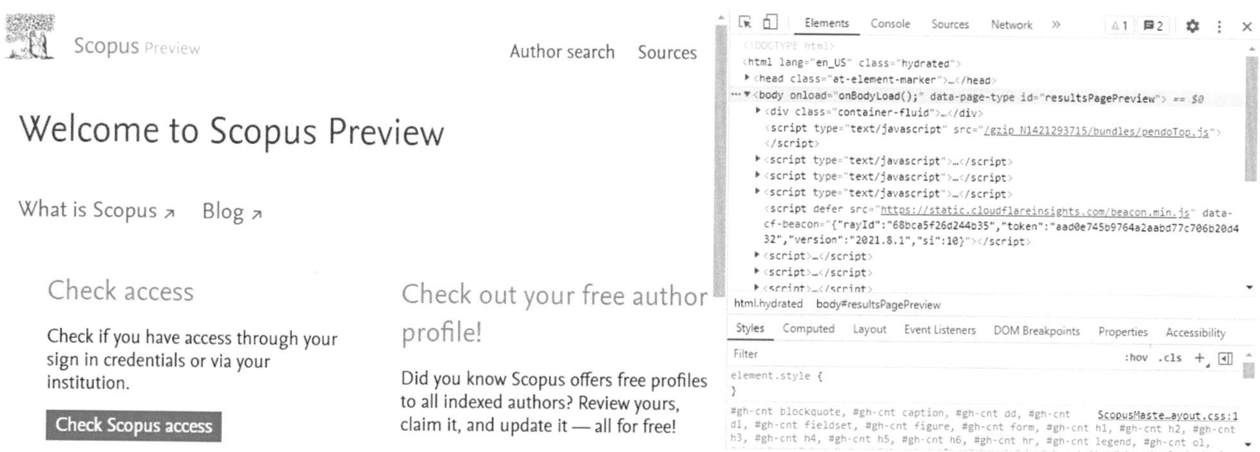

FIGURE 8.16 Manual inspection of web elements.

Regardless of the browser used, the screen will be divided into two parts, similar to the one shown in Figure 8.16. For didactic purposes, we will call the screen on the left (which in fact appears on the Scopus website) Screen A, and we will call the inspection environment (the screen where the web page's source codes appear) Screen B.

When inspecting codes manually, our main tool will be the button. Its location depends on the browser used, but it will certainly exist in the reader browser in the source code data screen (Screen B). An arrow, purposely placed in Figure 8.16, indicates on Screen B the position of the button in the Google Chrome browser (Fig. 8.17).

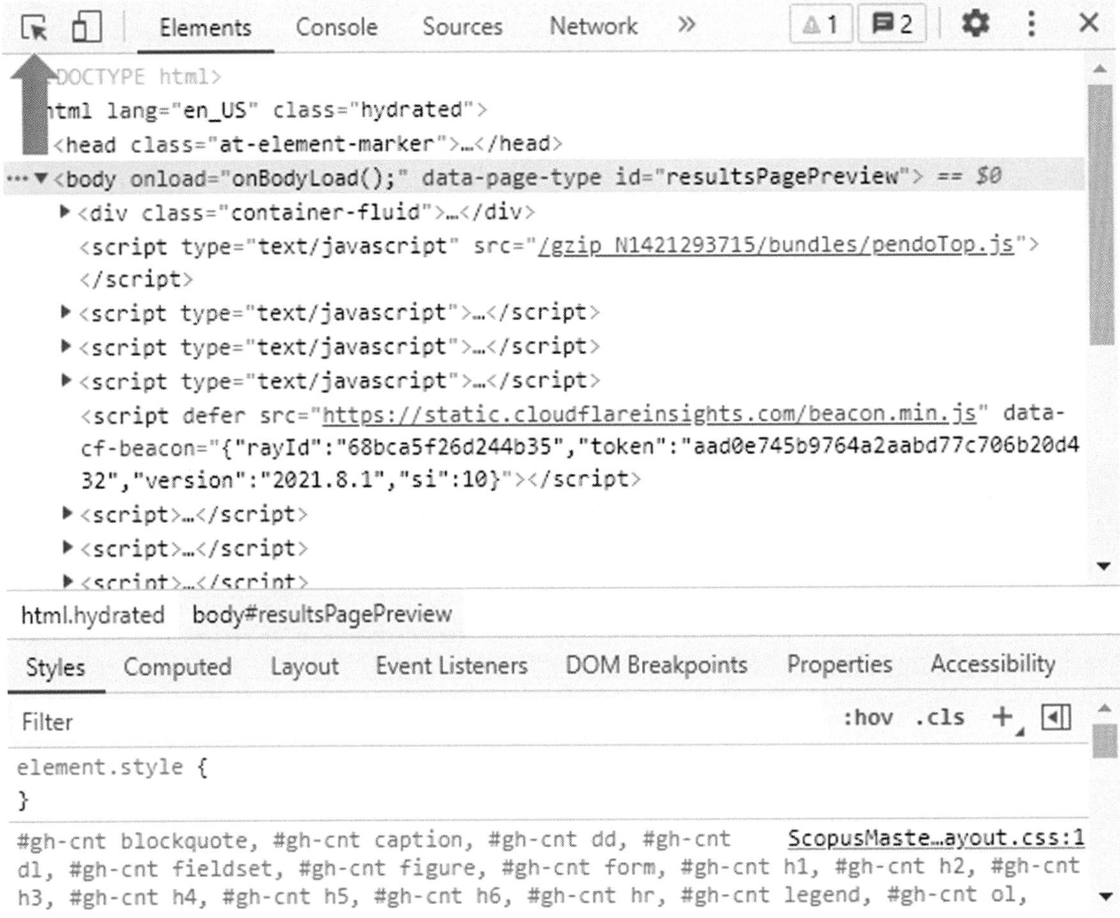

FIGURE 8.17 The position of the button in the Google Chrome browser.

The button holds the ability to enter CSS Selector or XPath paths. We ask the reader to click on the button present in the inspection environment (Screen B in Figure 8.16) and, after that, click on the *Source* option of the Scopus page (Screen A in Figure 8.16). Figure 8.18 shows us that, automatically, something new will be highlighted on Screen B (i.e., in the inspection environment), and this something new will point the way to the *Source* option of Screen A.

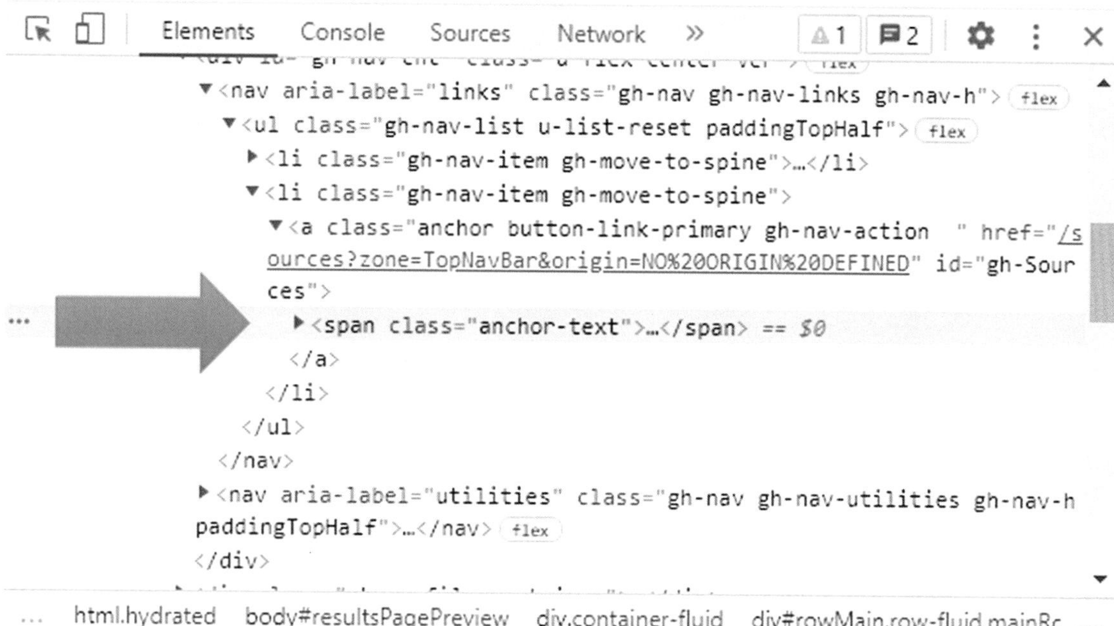

FIGURE 8.18 Manual inspection of web elements.

In the inspection environment (Screen B), just above the new selection shown by the orange arrow (purposely inserted in Figure 8.18), the reader must click the right mouse button and go to the option *Copy>>Copy Selector* or the analogous option for the chosen browser. We insist: CSS Selector path. By doing this, the CSS Selector path will be saved in the machine's Clipboard. Thus the reader can just run the paste command in any text editor to check the saved CSS Selector path, in this case, `#gh-Sources > span`.

Once this is done, we are able to inform R where the *Source* option is on the studied web page. As said, we will use the function `findElement()`:

```
scopus_source <- remote_driver$findElement(
        using = "css",
        value = "#gh-Sources > span")
```

It is important to note that in the previous command, the function `findElement()` was declared after the object that allows R to control the web browser (`remote_driver`, in our case), followed by the operator `$`. So that the reader can have access to other features of the browser controlled by R, he or she can just declare, in *RStudio,* `remote_driver$`.

It should also be said that in the previous command, for the function `findElement()`, we argued `using = "css"` to point out that we will use a path of type CSS Selector and `value` to indicate the value of the path adopted - as we said, `#gh-Sources > span`.

Still on the previous command, the application of the function `findElement()` was saved in a new object called `scopus_source`. This new object can use functions after the declaration of the operator `$`, similar to what we saw for the object `remote_driver`. By the way because the location for the *Source* option is contained in the object `scopus_source`, then to teach the robot to make a mouse click on this option, we must use the function `clickElement()` linked to that object:

```
scopus_source$clickElement()
```

We ask the reader to observe the browser controlled by R. In fact, we go to the *Sources* section. The next challenge will be to enter the term *Artificial Intelligence* into the form *Enter subject area,* highlighted in Figure 8.19.

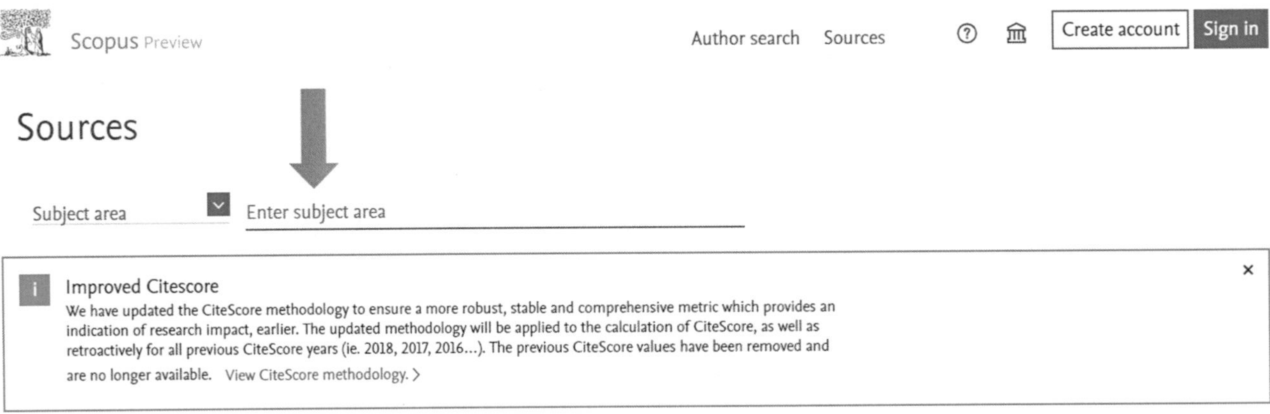

FIGURE 8.19 Clipping from the website of the Scopus portal.

To teach our robot to write the term *Artificial Intelligence,* we must first instruct it where the form *Enter subject area* is located, highlighted in Figure 8.19. **Thus with a browser other than the one used by R, we ask the reader to click on the form *Enter subject area,*** as shown in Figure 8.20.

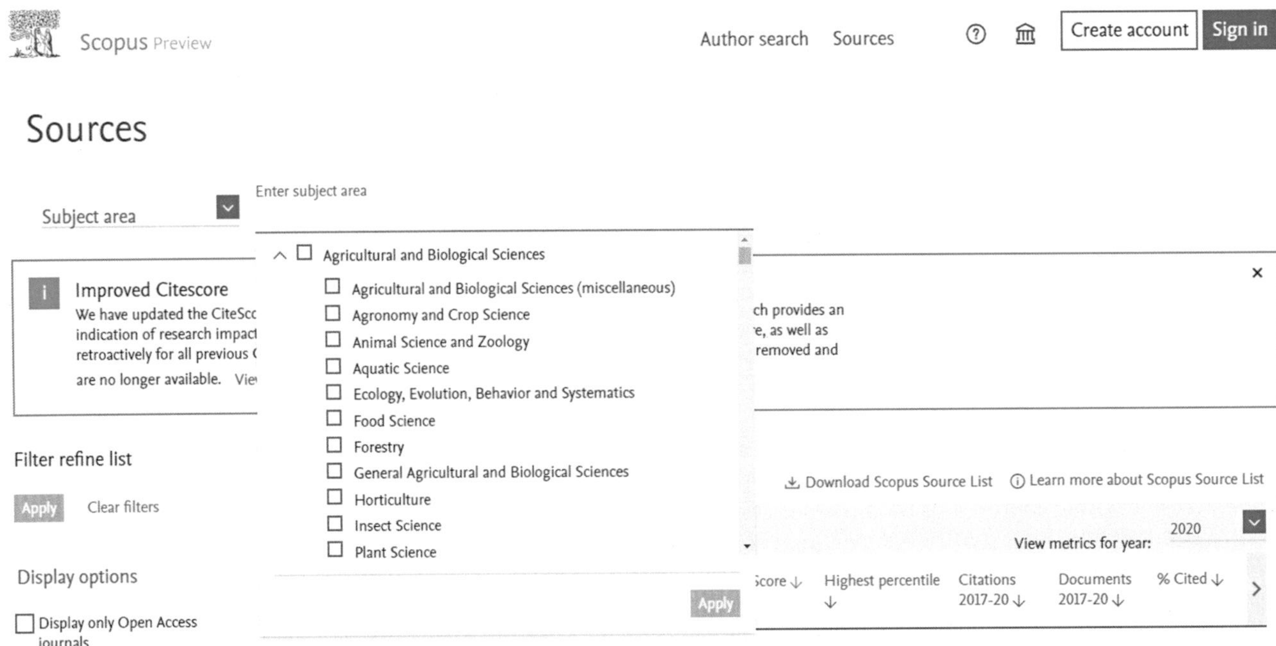

FIGURE 8.20 Clipping from the website of the Scopus portal.

From Figure 8.20, three tasks follow: (1) inform R where the form *Enter subject area* is located; (2) click on the form *Enter subject area*; and (3) enter the term of interest *Artificial Intelligence.*

As already learned, we can teach the robot where an element of a web page is with the function `findElement()`. From here, we will assume the premise that the reader has assimilated the use of the button.

```
scopus_area <- remote_driver$findElement(
        using = "css",
        value = "#search-term")
```

Then, we can click on the form *Enter subject area* with the help of the function `clickElement()`:

```
scopus_area$clickElement()
```

After the previous routine, the web page displayed by the robot-controlled browser should look similar to the one shown in Figure 8.20.

Now, we must teach the robot to type the term *Artificial Intelligence* into the open form. We can do this with the function `sendKeysToElement()`:

```
scopus_area$sendKeysToElement(
        list("Artificial Intelligence")
        )
```

If the reader observes the browser controlled by the browser, he or she will observe that the form *Enter subject area* was filled with the subject *Artificial Intelligence,* as shown in Figure 8.21.

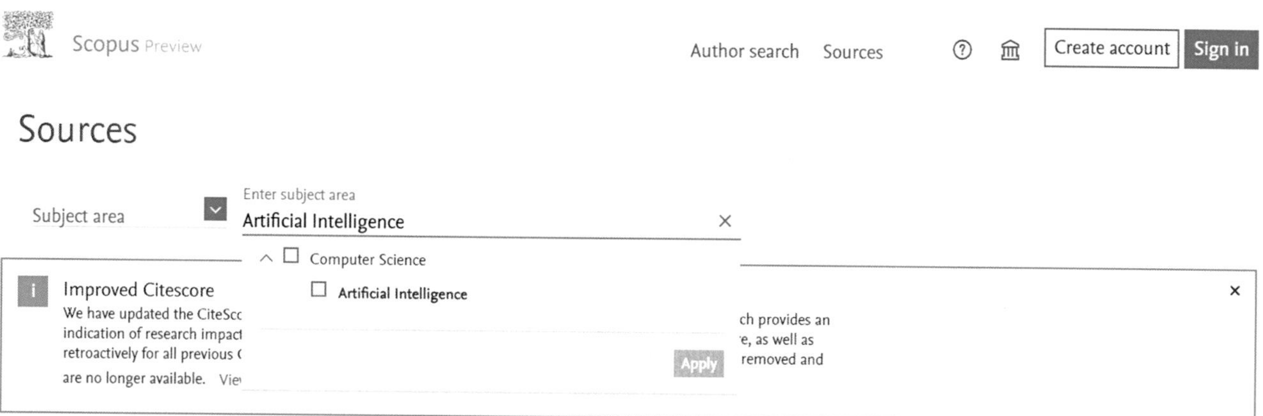

FIGURE 8.21 Clipping from the website of the Scopus portal.

The problem is that, according to Figure 8.21, the "Apply" button is not activated. On a keyboard, and absolutely manually, a combination of commands with the TAB and SPACE keys would be enough, but not our robot. In this case, we must click on the box corresponding to the term *Artificial Intelligence* to perform the search. Anyway, if the reader needs to teach some other robot to use commands coming from the keyboard keys, he could also use the function `sendKeysToElement()`, arguing `key` and the declaration in quotes of the desired key. For example:

```
#Do not command
#scopus_area$sendKeysToElement(list(key = "tab"))

#Do not command
#scopus_area$sendKeysToElement(list(key = "enter"))
```

However, as we have advanced, these commands will not solve our problem. In this way, we will teach the robot to click on the *Artificial Intelligence* option, which is highlighted in Figure 8.21. We can do this by commanding:

```
scopus_ia <- remote_driver$findElement(
        using = "css",
        value = "#body_autoSugg0 > ul > li > label > span > b")
```

Then:

```
scopus_ia$clickElement()
```

Next, we must teach where the "Apply" button, present in Figure 8.21, is:

```
scopus_apply <- remote_driver$findElement(
        using = "css",
        value = "#applyBox> div>input")
```

Soon after, we can click on the "Apply" button, as follows:

```
scopus_apply$clickElement()
```

At this point, in the browser used by the robot, the Scopus portal should return to the reader several scientific journals on the subject of *Artificial Intelligence*.

To gather the information, we must use the function `getElementText()` after obviously pointing to the R where the data of interest is. In this way, we will indicate to R where the names of scientific journals meet with the function `findElement()`:

```
scopus_results <- remote_driver$findElement(
        using = "css",
        value = "#sourceResults > tbody")
```

Then, we can finally capture the desired results with the function `getElementText()`:

```
results <- data.frame(scopus_results$getElementText())
```

However, if the reader declares the object `results`, he or she will notice that the organization of the data collected is far below acceptable, as explained in Figure 8.22.

FIGURE 8.22 The object `results`.

```
X.1.nIEEE.Transactions.on.Pattern.Analysis.and.Machine.Intelligence.
44.2.99..n1.548.nApplied.Mathematics.37.174.841.93.n2.nFoundations.a
nd.Trends.in.Machine.Learning.37.8.99..n2.389.nSoftware.604.16.75.n3
.nScience.Robotics.25.7.99..n1.111.nControl.an ...
1 1\nIEEE Transactions on Pattern Analysis and Machine Intelligence
44.2 99%\n1/548\nApplied Mathematics 37.174 841 93\n2\nFoundations and
Trends in Machine Learning 37.8 99%\n2/389\nSoftware 604 16
75\n3\nScience Robotics 25.7 99%\n1/111\nControl and Optimization
6.307 245 94\n4\nPhysics of Life Reviews 21.5 99%\n2/209\nGeneral
Agricultural and Biological Sciences 1.055 49 96\n5\nIEEE Transactions
on Neural Networks and Learning Systems 19.8 99%\n3/334\nComputer
Networks and Communications 30.901 1.562 91\n6\nIEEE Transactions on
Fuzzy Systems 18.3 99%\n2/260\nControl and Systems Engineering 17.049
931 90\n7\nInternational Journal of Information Management 18.1
99%\n1/235\nLibrary and Information Sciences 10.563 583 93\n8\nIEEE
Computational Intelligence Magazine 16.5 96%\n8/227\nArtificial
Intelligence 1.700 103 70\n9\nPattern Recognition 15.7
97%\n12/389\nSoftware 24.756 1.578 88\n10\nInternational Journal of
Computer Vision 15.0 96%\n13/389\nSoftware 6.069 404
81\n11\nInternational Journal of Intelligent Systems 14.8
97%\n4/120\nHuman-Computer Interaction 5.843 394 86\n12\nExpert
Systems with Applications 12.7 98%\n5/297\nGeneral Engineering 34.460
2.710 89\n13\nInternational Journal of Robotics Research 12.6
99%\n3/290\nModeling and Simulation 4.221 335 84\n14\nSoft Robotics
12.3 97%\n4/131\nBiophysics 2.781 226 91\n15\nInformation Sciences
12.1 95%\n33/693\nComputer Science Applications 37.189 3.086
88\n16\nKnowledge-Based Systems 11.3 95%\n6/114\nManagement
Information Systems 21.478 1.894 82\n17\nIEEE/CAA Journal of
Automatica Sinica 11.2 94%\n17/329\nInformation Systems 5.370 481
88\n18\nNeural Networks 10.9 97%\n3/96\nCognitive Neuroscience 10.252
943 79\n19\nJournal of Intelligent Manufacturing 10.6
95%\n15/336\nIndustrial and Manufacturing Engineering 5.780 543
94\n20\nNature Machine Intelligence 10.5 93%\n8/120\nHuman-Computer
Interaction 759 72 64
```

To start organizing the data, among many possible solutions, we suggest two initial steps: (1) save the object `results` in a *.csv extension file, and (2) open the *.csv extension file with the function `fread()` from the package `data.table`.

As learned in Chapter 2, to create a *.csv extension object, we must use the function `write.csv()`:

```
write.csv(results, "results_data.csv", row.names = F)
```

Next, for the second step, we will use the function `fread()`, which is one of the several possibilities for loading *.csv extension files:

```
final_results <- fread("results_data.csv", sep = "\n")
```

For the previous command, the argument `sep` defines what the column separator will be, and `"\n"` indicates that it will be a line spacing. Figure 8.23 demonstrates the results of the previous commands.

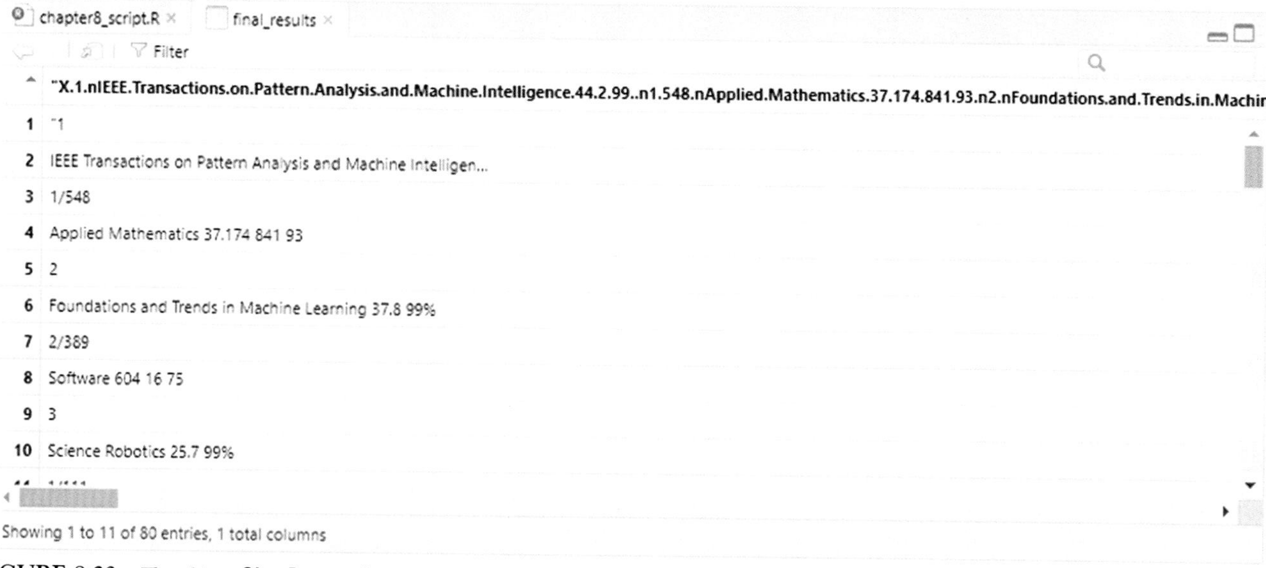

FIGURE 8.23 The object `final_results`.

Even though there has been an advance, Figure 8.23 insinuates that at least two more steps are still needed: (1) the journals are highlighted in even lines, therefore eliminate the odd lines, and (2) change the name of the column in which the journals appear.

After reading Chapter 2, the reader already has enough knowledge to solve the problems narrated.

To solve the first problem, that is, to filter the information regarding only the even lines, we can create a vector of odd values that later will indicate which lines will be eliminated:

```
odd_rows <- seq(from = 1, to = nrow(final_results), by = 2)
```

Then, using the operator `[]`, we can delete the unwanted lines from the object `final_results`:

```
final_results <- final_results[-odd_rows, ]
```

Finally, we can rename the column of our data frame with the help of the function `names()`:

```
names(final_results) <- "journals"
```

Figure 8.24 presents the final treatment for the object `final_results`.

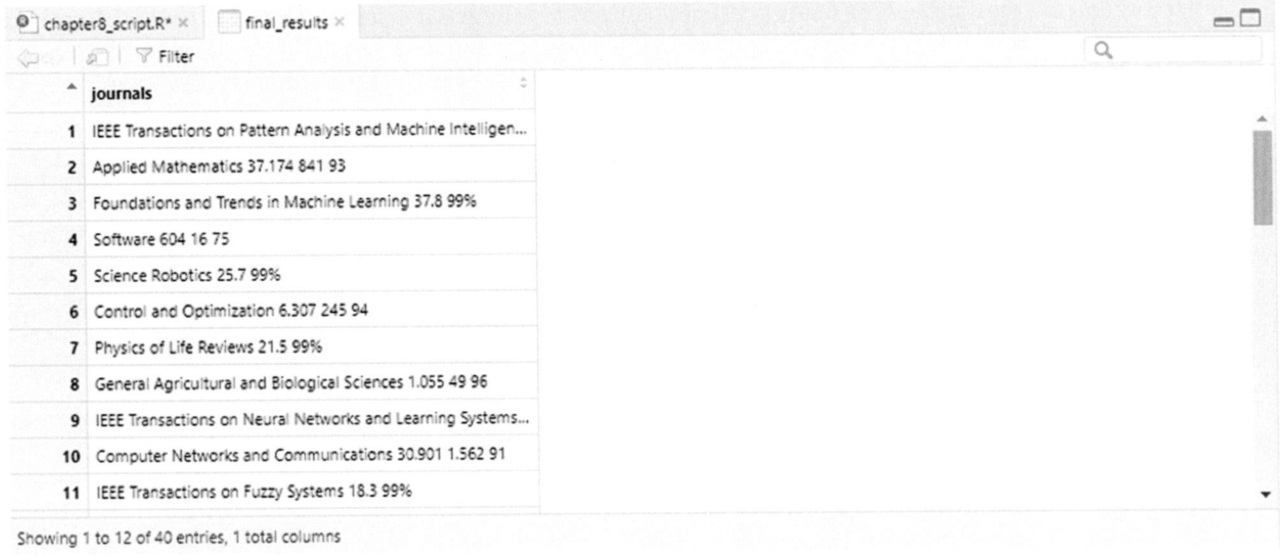

FIGURE 8.24 The object `final_results`.

The reader may say that there is still work to be done concerning the results of Figure 8.24 regarding data processing, and we agree! In Chapter 10, we will focus more on the manipulation, cleansing, and organization of data. In any case, we reinforce the tip of reading the book *R for Data Science*, especially Chapter 14. This reading is dedicated to explaining textual manipulation with pattern capture.

If the reader wants to impose an iterative routine with the demonstrated commands, collecting more data from more displayed pages, he or she can just follow, in an analogous way, the explicit commands for this kind of task in the "Example 1: Using the Function `html_text()`" and "Example 2: Using the Function `html_table()`" sections in this chapter.

Final remarks

In this chapter, we present interesting tools to facilitate the reader's data collection task, when this data is available on the Internet.

The use of packages `rvest` and `RSelenium` will bring security to the reader regarding the reliability of the collected data. Its use mitigates possible human error in the information gathering process.

As demonstrated in this section, it is also possible to automate the data collection task by combining the knowledge gained in Chapter 2 of this work.

We remind the reader that, as discussed in the "Creating a Robot with `RSelenium`" section, Chapter 10 of this work will intend to demonstrate new functionalities regarding the manipulation, cleansing, and organization of the collected data.

In Chapter 9, we will use another interesting form of data collection—Application Programming Interfaces (APIs).

Exercises

1. The Data.gov website (https://www.data.gov) calls itself the home of the US government's open data. Using what you learned in this chapter, try to solve what is asked:
   a. Create a robot that, from the Data.gov portal, searches for the term *rivers*.
   b. After performing the search for the term *rivers*, teach the robot to access data regarding the result *River Scientist Regions*.
   c. After fulfilling the objective in item "b," teach the robot to download data in *.csv present on the page.
2. On the Wikipedia page dedicated to the term *FIFA World Cup*, there is a table of tournament champions, as shown in Figure 8.25.

Rank	Team	Participations	Pld	W	D	L	GF	GA	GD	Pts	Titles
1	Brazil	21	109	73	18	18	229	105	124	237	5
2	Germany[120]	19	109	67	20	22	226	125	101	221	4
3	Italy	18	83	45	21	17	128	77	51	156	4
4	Argentina	17	81	43	15	23	137	93	44	144	2
5	France	15	66	34	13	19	120	77	43	115	2
6	England	15	69	29	21	19	91	64	27	108	1
7	Spain	15	63	30	15	18	99	72	27	105	1
8	Uruguay	13	56	24	12	20	87	74	13	84	2

FIGURE 8.25 World football champions table, according to FIFA World Cup Wikipedia page.

Using the knowledge acquired, capture in R the table presented in Figure 8.25.

3. On the Wikipedia page, dedicated to the term *Academy Award for Best Picture,* there is a table of the award-winning filmmakers, as shown in Figure 8.26.

Production Company	Nominations	Wins
20th Century Studios	62	9
Columbia Pictures	56	12
Metro-Goldwyn-Mayer	40	9
Universal Pictures	34	9
Warner Bros. Pictures	25	9
Paramount Pictures	20	11
Searchlight Pictures	19	5
Miramax Films	15	4
DreamWorks	13	4
RKO Pictures	11	1

FIGURE 8.26 Clipping of top 10 film producers who were Oscar winners in the best film category.

Using the knowledge acquired, capture in R the table presented in Figure 8.26.

CHAPTER

9

Using application programming interfaces to collect data

AT THE END OF THIS CHAPTER, YOU WILL BE ABLE TO:

- Teach the reader what Application Programming Interfaces (APIs) are and how they work in general.
- Demonstrate the use of APIs in R-based language.

R language packages used in this chapter

```
library(httr)
library(jsonlite)
library(lubridate)
library(tmap)
library(sf)
```

Don't forget to define the R working directory (the location where your datasets are installed):

```
setwd("C:/book/chapter9")
```

Introduction

In the previous chapter of this work, we presented some techniques for collecting data available on the web in its raw form. We also discussed some forms of webscraping, including the construction of handcrafted robots. However, as the reader can see, as a rule, the data collected in this way need cleansing, manipulation, and organization techniques to enable us to do something with them, and these techniques, whether collecting, cleansing, or organizing, require a considerable amount of mental effort and time.

In this chapter, we will introduce data collection via Application Programming Interfaces (APIs). APIs have the advantage of delivering data to the reader that is already properly organized and processed and is therefore ready for the application of machine learning algorithms.

Data Science, Analytics and Machine Learning with R
https://doi.org/10.1016/B978-0-12-824271-1.00021-4

Because this delivery of data is already organized and processed, it is possible to imagine that the data are already available on a given computer somewhere in the world, waiting for a request from another computer that belongs to someone interested in the data. In this sense, the APIs will provide interactions between the reader's machine, which is called the *client*, and the machine that contains the data of interest, called the *server*.

It is very common for large sites to provide connectivity via API. Common examples are World Bank portals, Facebook, Google, NASA, IBM, Microsoft, Amazon Web Services, Apple, Kaggle, the World Health Organization (WHO), national democratic Census offices, drug and drug regulatory agencies, drug control and disease-prevention agencies, and so on. Currently, the examples, in fact, tend to infinity.

In Chapter 8, to collect data, we used R packages to deal with other programming languages (e.g., HTML and Java). In this chapter, the reader must keep in mind that the data required from a server via API, as a rule, will be delivered following the syntax of a programming language called JavaScript (JS). It is also possible to find APIs that deliver data in HTML, XML, JPEG, or PNG format, however most of the data delivered via the API follow the JS format. Thus we will also use packages that facilitate our work, not forcing the reader to study, in addition to R-based language, the JS language.

Verbs about API

In Chapter 2, we drew a parallel between the functions of R and the verbs of a given human language. We said that the functions of R are analogous to verbs that denote human actions.

For APIs, these verbs also exist: GET, PATCH, POST, HEAD, PUT, and DELETE. For this work, we will focus on a single verb called GET. With the verb GET, we will be able to collect data available on a given server. As the objective, in fact, is to equip the reader with data collection via API, we thought it would not make sense to continue discussing about how to insert data into a server or how to modify or delete data from that server. Thus if the reader is interested in establishing a data repository and creating an API for other users to access his or her datasets, we recommend the package `plumber`.

Returning to the point, it will be with the verb GET that we will make our requests regarding data of interest to us. For this, we will use the package `httr` and its function `GET()`.

After using the function `GET()`, we will receive a response object. For this response object, which, as discussed earlier, commonly obeys JS syntax, we will use functions from the package `jsonlite` to extract the data of interest. The package `jsonlite` will be useful for handling JavaScript Object Notation (JSON) files (*.json extension files).

Even though it is not mandatory for the reader to become familiar with the JS language, it is necessary to know that *.json files are structured in *key-value pairs*. This means that each *key* is associated with a *value*.

To exemplify this concept, we ask the reader to imagine a dataset of students from a school. Thus taking the example of a student who was named Claire, there would certainly be a *key* that related to the name of the student, and, without a doubt, there would be a *value* that indicated the name of the student. There could also be a *key* regarding the mathematics course and a *value* regarding Claire's mathematics grade, and so on. Figure 9.1 illustrates the discussion.

```
{
"name": Claire Campbell
"mathematics": 9
"english": 10
"biology": 7
}
```

FIGURE 9.1 Examples of *key-value pairs* in *.json files.

Having made these considerations, we will start with a simple example and, step by step, we will deepen the lessons about data collection via API.

Example 1: Who is in the space stations?

This is one of the most basic examples for getting started with APIs. In this example, we will look for the names of the astronauts who are presently at the International Space Station (ISS) or at Tiangong.

The reader should be aware that the ISS was launched on November 20, 1998, and is approximately 400 km above the earth's ground, with an orbital speed of over 27,600 km/h. This means that, on average, it circles 15.49 times around our planet each day. Tiangong, the Chinese space station, orbits at an altitude ranging from 340 to 450 km above the earth's surface, and it circles the earth every 92.2 minutes on average.

It is also interesting to note that the last time all humans were on earth was on November 1, 2000. Since then, astronauts have always inhabited a space station, alternating with new ones who, perhaps, arrive to replace those who have been there longer.

The Open Notify website (http://open-notify.org) is an open-source project that provides an interesting interface with some NASA data via API.

To access data on how many people currently inhabit the ISS, the Open Notify website provides the following API: http://api.open-notify.org/astros.json.

Using R to collect the data in question, we will begin to use the function `GET()` from the package `httr`:

```
require_people <- GET(url = "http://api.open-notify.org/astros.json")
```

In the previous command, the function `GET()` required a single argument with respect to the API's URL. The object `require_people` is an object of type *list* that contains information about the reader's request regarding the number of humans in the ISS; it is our response object. Out of curiosity, the reader could declare the object `require_people` to R:

```
require_people
```

Figure 9.2 presents R's response to the previous command.

```
Response [http://api.open-notify.org/astros.json]
  Date: 2021-08-23 14:54
  Status: 200
  Content-Type: application/json
  Size: 494 B
```

FIGURE 9.2 The object `require_people`.

In Figure 9.2, we can see the URL for which we made our data request; we can note the date and time in Coordinated Universal Time (UTC) format regarding the request. You can also see that the data have a *.json extension as well as the size of the required data.

Also in Figure 9.2, regarding the information marked as `Status: 200`, this means that the request was successful. If the reader wants to know more about HTTP codes on data requests, we recommend the HTTP Status Codes website (https://httpstatuses.com).

An attentive reader may have explored the object `require_people` and would have noticed that the way it is in R, there is no way to extract the information about the humans present in the space stations. As Figure 9.2 already pointed out, there is *.json extension information there, so we must convert this object to R-friendly format so we can then extract the data of interest.

However, before this, we must instruct the reader about the function `rawToChar()` from the R-based language. The function `rawToChar()` performs the conversion to and from and the manipulation of objects of type "raw," both used as bits or "packed" 8 bits; the translation proposed by the discussed function is for the type *character*. For example, let's explore the component `content` of the object `require_people` (this is where the data of interest resides):

```
require_people$content
```

For the previous command, the reader will receive from R the answer presented in Figure 9.3.

```
  [1] 7b 22 70 65 6f 70 6c 65 22 3a 20 5b 7b 22 6e 61 6d 65 22 3a 20 22 4d 61 72 6b
 [27] 20 56 61 6e 64 65 20 48 65 69 22 2c 20 22 63 72 61 66 74 22 3a 20 22 49 53 53
 [53] 22 7d 2c 20 7b 22 6e 61 6d 65 22 3a 20 22 4f 6c 65 67 20 4e 6f 76 69 74 73 6b
 [79] 69 79 22 2c 20 22 63 72 61 66 74 22 3a 20 22 49 53 53 22 7d 2c 20 7b 22 6e 61
[105] 6d 65 22 3a 20 22 50 79 6f 74 72 20 44 75 62 72 6f 76 22 2c 20 22 63 72 61 66
[131] 74 22 3a 20 22 49 53 53 22 7d 2c 20 7b 22 6e 61 6d 65 22 3a 20 22 54 68 6f 6d
[157] 61 73 20 50 65 73 71 75 65 74 22 2c 20 22 63 72 61 66 74 22 3a 20 22 49 53 53
[183] 22 7d 2c 20 7b 22 6e 61 6d 65 22 3a 20 22 4d 65 67 61 6e 20 4d 63 41 72 74 68
[209] 75 72 22 2c 20 22 63 72 61 66 74 22 3a 20 22 49 53 53 22 7d 2c 20 7b 22 6e 61
[235] 6d 65 22 3a 20 22 53 68 61 6e 65 20 4b 69 6d 62 72 6f 75 67 68 22 2c 20 22 63
[261] 72 61 66 74 22 3a 20 22 49 53 53 22 7d 2c 20 7b 22 6e 61 6d 65 22 3a 20 22 41
[287] 6b 69 68 69 6b 6f 20 48 6f 73 68 69 64 65 22 2c 20 22 63 72 61 66 74 22 3a 20
[313] 22 49 53 53 22 7d 2c 20 7b 22 6e 61 6d 65 22 3a 20 22 4e 69 65 20 48 61 69 73
[339] 68 65 6e 67 22 2c 20 22 63 72 61 66 74 22 3a 20 22 54 69 61 6e 67 6f 6e 67 22
[365] 7d 2c 20 7b 22 6e 61 6d 65 22 3a 20 22 4c 69 75 20 42 6f 6d 69 6e 67 22 2c 20
[391] 22 63 72 61 66 74 22 3a 20 22 54 69 61 6e 67 6f 6e 67 22 7d 2c 20 7b 22 6e 61
[417] 6d 65 22 3a 20 22 54 61 6e 67 20 48 6f 6e 67 62 6f 22 2c 20 22 63 72 61 66 74
[443] 22 3a 20 22 54 69 61 6e 67 6f 6e 67 22 7d 5d 2c 20 22 6e 75 6d 62 65 72 22 3a
[469] 20 31 30 2c 20 22 6d 65 73 73 61 67 65 22 3a 20 22 73 75 63 63 65 73 73 22 7d
```

FIGURE 9.3 The object `require_people$content`.

It may sound bizarre, but, in fact, the data of interest to us resides in Figure 9.3! Let's apply the function `rawToChar()` to the object `require_people$content`:

```
rawToChar(require_people$content)
```

Figure 9.4 shows the result obtained from the application of the function `rawToChar()` to the object `require_people$content`.

```
[1] "{\"people\": [{\"name\": \"Mark Vande Hei\", \"craft\": \"ISS\"},
{\"name\": \"Oleg Novitskiy\", \"craft\": \"ISS\"}, {\"name\": \"Pyotr
Dubrov\", \"craft\": \"ISS\"}, {\"name\": \"Thomas Pesquet\",
\"craft\": \"ISS\"}, {\"name\": \"Megan McArthur\", \"craft\":
\"ISS\"}, {\"name\": \"Shane Kimbrough\", \"craft\": \"ISS\"},
{\"name\": \"Akihiko Hoshide\", \"craft\": \"ISS\"}, {\"name\": \"Nie
Haisheng\", \"craft\": \"Tiangong\"}, {\"name\": \"Liu Boming\",
\"craft\": \"Tiangong\"}, {\"name\": \"Tang Hongbo\", \"craft\":
\"Tiangong\"}], \"number\": 10, \"message\": \"success\"}"
```

FIGURE 9.4 The use of the function `rawToChar()`.

Figure 9.4 explains that, by applying the function `rawToChar()`, it is already possible to understand the results of our data request, even though we agree that the organization is still chaotic.

The reader will notice in Figure 9.4 that there is a structuring of the type *key-value pairs* in a way similar to that exemplified in Figure 9.1. We can see that there is a *key* "people" that indicates as *value* the name of the astronauts and the *key* "craft" with its corresponding *value* that indicates in which space module the astronaut is (on the ISS or Tiangong). It is also possible to observe the *key* "number" that indicates as value the number of people in the earth's orbit. **Obviously, depending on the date of reading this work, the results presented will be different.**

Finally, to organize the data presented in Figure 9.4, because we are working with a *.json extension file, we can use the function `fromJSON()` from the package `jsonlite`:

```
people_data <- fromJSON(txt = rawToChar(x = require_people$content))
```

Note that the object `people_data`, created from the function `fromJSON()`, is of type *list*. Out of curiosity, let's dec lare it to R:

```
people_data
```

R's answer is shown in Figure 9.5.

```
$people
                 name    craft
1    Mark Vande Hei      ISS
2    Oleg Novitskiy      ISS
3       Pyotr Dubrov     ISS
4    Thomas Pesquet      ISS
5    Megan McArthur      ISS
6   Shane Kimbrough      ISS
7   Akihiko Hoshide      ISS
8      Nie Haisheng Tiangong
9        Liu Boming Tiangong
10     Tang Hongbo Tiangong

$number
[1] 10

$message
[1] "success"
```

FIGURE 9.5 The object `people_data`.

The object `people_data` is much more organized than the object `require_people$content`, right?

Next, we will continue exploring another API from the Open Notify website. But this time, we will focus on finding the real-time position of the ISS.

Example 2: Where is the ISS now?

For this section, we will assume that the reader is already familiar with the functions `GET()`, `rawToChar()`, and `fromJSON()` presented in the "Example 1: Who is in the space stations?" section.

The API URL for ISS localization, according to the Open Notify website, is as follows: http://api.open-notify.org/iss-now.json.

The first step, as the reader may already imagine, is the application of the function `GET()` to the API URL in order to have our response object:

```
require_pos <- GET(url = "http://api.open-notify.org/iss-now.json")
```

When declaring the object require_pos to R, similar to what is shown in Figure 9.2, we will see that it is a file of type *.json.

Thus we also already know that the component content of the object require_pos can only be read in human language with the help of the function rawToChar(). Putting the aforementioned information together, we can apply the function fromJSON() to extract the ISS location in real time:

```
position_data <- fromJSON(txt = rawToChar(require_pos$content))
```

When declaring the object position_data to R, we will have an answer similar to the one presented in Figure 9.6.

```
$message
[1] "success"


$timestamp
[1] 1629734343


$iss_position
$iss_position$longitude
[1] "-46.6434"


$iss_position$latitude
[1] "26.9490"
```

FIGURE 9.6 The object position_data.

```
position_data
```

In Figure 9.6, the reader will note the ISS latitude and longitude coordinates when the authors executed the previous command, that is, latitude 26.9490 or 26° 56′ 56.4″ N and longitude –46.6434 or 46° 38′ 36.24″ W.

Also in Figure 9.6, the reader will notice an attribute called timestamp whose value is 1629734343. It contains the date and time of the query in Unix time format which, in other words, marks the number of seconds elapsed since January 1, 1970. If this is a nuisance, just use the function as_datetime() from the package lubridate:

```
as_datetime(x = 1629734343)
```

For the previous command, the reader will receive a UTC date and time. We can even plot the position of the ISS in relation to a world map. Next, we leave a routine for plotting the spatial type. These kinds of plots will be explored in depth in Chapters 23 to 26 of this work:

```
# Transforming ISS position data into a data frame
position_df <- data.frame(position_data$iss_position)
# Loading a world map
data("World")
# Georeferencing the position_df object
```

Continued

```
iss_location <- st_as_sf(x = position_df,
                         coords = c("longitude", "latitude"),
                         crs = 4326)

# Plotting the ISS position
tm_shape(shp = World) +
  tm_borders() +
  tm_shape(shp = iss_location) +
  tm_dots(size = 0.5,
          col = "orange")
```

Figure 9.7 shows the graph obtained from the previous routine.

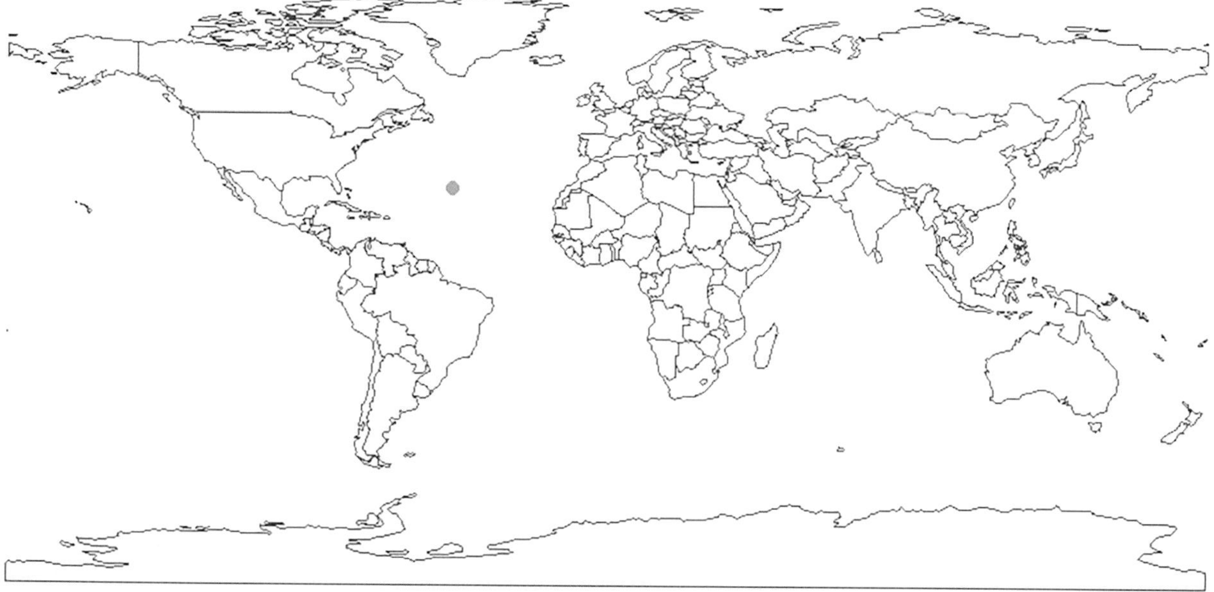

FIGURE 9.7 Plotting the geographic position of the ISS.

Next, we will explore one more example regarding the use of APIs with ISS data.

Example 3: When will the ISS fly over a certain point on the globe?

Another interesting API on the Open Notify site concerns the predictions of the geographic positions relative to the earth from the ISS. The API URL is as follows: http://api.open-notify.org/iss-pass.json.

We will start by making our data request with the function `GET()`, as usual. However, this time, we will add the argument `query` indicating the geographic position of interest for the ISS overflight in relation to the city of São Paulo, Brazil:

```
require_future <- GET("http://api.open-notify.org/iss-pass.json",
                      query = list(lat = -23.550520,
                                   lon = -46.633308))
```

If the reader intends to use geographic coordinates different from those used by the authors, he or she can use the LatLong website (https://www.latlong.net) to calculate, for example, the geographic position of his or her municipality of residence.

A fair question would be: How do we know what to inform to complement the function `GET()` request, as in the case of the argument `query`? When the reader chooses a site that contains an API regarding interesting data, we recommend reading that API's help/documentation page. Documentation regarding data requests is the responsibility of the websites that maintain these applications.

Next, as we have already learned, we will use the functions `rawToChar()` and `fromJSON()`:

```
future_position <- fromJSON(txt = rawToChar(require_future$content))
```

Once this is done, we can declare the object `future_position`:

```
future_position
```

Figure 9.8 contains the result of the previous codes.

```
$message
[1] "success"


$request
$request$altitude
[1] 100


$request$datetime
[1] 1629736801


$request$latitude
[1] -23.55052


$request$longitude
[1] -46.63331


$request$passes
[1] 5



$response
  duration   risetime
1      541 1629740528
2      640 1629746272
3      250 1629752324
4      303 1629770173
5      645 1629775854
```

FIGURE 9.8 ISS future positions.

In Figure 9.8, in its component `$response`, in the column `risetime`, we will have the next five ISS overflight dates in the city of São Paulo, in Unix time format. For the conversion to data and time in UTC format, the reader must use the function `as_datetime()` from the package `lubridate`, as discussed earlier in the "Example 2: Where is the ISS now?" section.

In the simple examples in the "Example 1: Who is in the space stations?", "Example 2: Where is the ISS now?", and "Example 3: When will the ISS fly over a certain point on the globe?" sections, we introduce the reader to the basics of extracting data via the API. In the "Example 4: Health indicators of the World Health Organization" section, we propose to extract a larger amount of data at once from the WHO.

Example 4: Health indicators of the World Health Organization

The Global Health Observatory (GHO) is a WHO data repository that has a series of APIs with extensive documentation. The website address is https://www.who.int/data/gho/info/gho-odata-api.

In the GHO, we can choose a series of indicators as a function of time, for a number of countries. The site has several examples of using its API.

For this section, we will learn how to download the WHO health indicator list and then choose one of these indicators. Then, with this chosen indicator, we will learn how to filter information from a given country in relation to that indicator.

The GHO website reports the following URL to the API that contains the list of indicators available for searching: https://ghoapi.azureedge.net/api/Indicator.

Thus we already know that everything starts with the application of the function `GET()`:

```
who_ind_list <- GET(url = "https://ghoapi.azureedge.net/api/Indicator")
```

Then we must use the functions `rawToChar()` and `fromJSON()`:

```
indicators_list <- fromJSON(txt = rawToChar(who_ind_list$content))
```

To save the list of indicators in a data frame, we can command:

```
indicators_df <- indicators_list$value
```

A curious reader will notice that our dataset `indicators_df` contains three columns: *IndicatorCode, IndicatorName, and Language*. Let's work with the indicator called *Per capita total expenditure on health (PPP int. $)*, whose code is WHS7_105. **We chose the indicator WHS7_105 at random. The reader can choose which indicator he or she wants to use the following codes, but must take care to use the correct coding given by the GHO regarding the chosen indicator.**

To collect data regarding our chosen indicator, the GHO provides the following URL to its API: https://ghoapi.azureedge.net/api/WHS7_105. **If the reader is using another indicator, we kindly ask him or her to change the end of the mentioned URL with the encoding of the desired indicator.**

```
expend_health <- GET(url = "https://ghoapi.azureedge.net/api/WHS7_105")
```

Then, as usual:

```
expend_data <- fromJSON(txt = rawToChar(expend_health$content))
```

To transform the object `expend_data` into a data frame, we can command:

```
expend_df <- expend_data$value
```

An attentive reader will notice that the object `expend_df` contains data about the WHS7_105 indicator for several countries. The following command highlights the name of the columns of the mentioned object:

```
names(expend_df)
```

Figure 9.9 presents the results obtained from the previous command.

Suppose we wanted our request to cover Thailand data only. Thus an attentive reader will notice that in the object `expend_df`, the column *SpatialDim* is a variable that contains acronyms of different countries. So, we can just make the request using the acronym of Thailand, that is, THA. **Obviously, the authors know that the data frame `expend_df` can be filtered directly. The example has didactic purposes so the reader is instructed to use APIs that return a high amount of data and that rework is not an advantageous option.**

```
 [1] "Id"                  "IndicatorCode"       "SpatialDimType"
 [4] "SpatialDim"          "TimeDimType"         "TimeDim"
 [7] "Dim1Type"            "Dim1"                "Dim2Type"
[10] "Dim2"                "Dim3Type"            "Dim3"
[13] "DataSourceDimType"   "DataSourceDim"       "Value"
[16] "NumericValue"        "Low"                 "High"
[19] "Comments"            "Date"                "TimeDimensionValue"
[22] "TimeDimensionBegin"  "TimeDimensionEnd"
```

FIGURE 9.9 The name of the columns of object `expend_df`.

To filter requests via API, the GHO website recommends the following **(once again we stress the importance of visiting the API help pages; each API has its own commands):**

- **API to get data about the WHS7_105 indicator:**

  https://ghoapi.azureedge.net/api/WHS7_105

- **API to filter data due to some variable (as informed, we will assume the variable *SpatialDim* with a value equal to THA):**

  https://ghoapi.azureedge.net/api/WHS7_105?$filter=SpatialDim eq 'THA'

The aforementioned website has spaces existing in the term SpatialDim eq 'THA'.

Did the reader notice the difference between the APIs? However, in R, the second API from the previous example (the API with filter) will not work! R will not know what to do with the spaces in the term SpatialDim eq 'THA'.

These spaces mentioned must be replaced by %20:

https://ghoapi.azureedge.net/api/WHS7_105?$filter=SpatialDim%20eq%20'THA'

Now we can command the function `GET()`:

```
expend_tha <- GET(
"https://ghoapi.azureedge.net/api/WHS7_105?$filter=SpatialDim%20eq%20'THA'")
```

Next, we will use the functions `rawToChar()` and `fromJSON()`:

```
expend_tha_data <- fromJSON(txt = rawToChar(expend_tha$content))
```

Finally, we can transform the object `expend_tha_data` into a data frame:

```
expend_tha_df <- expend_tha_data$value
```

Ready! We have a dataset with information on Thailand's indicator *Per capita total expenditure on health.*

Final remarks

In this chapter, we demonstrated a practical and quick way to collect data that has already been properly cleansed and organized: APIs.

Undoubtedly, data collection via API is much more advantageous than collection via webscraping with or without using robots. In APIs, the time required to manipulate the data for the application of a machine learning algorithm drops substantially, considering that the cleansing and organization of information will no longer be a problem.

Furthermore, APIs also carry the same advantage of the webscraping techniques seen in Chapter 8 of this work, including mitigating the human error factor in relation to data collection.

In the Chapter 10, we will study more sophisticated techniques for manipulating, cleansing, and organizing data using the universe `tidyverse`.

Exercises

1. Using the URL https://opendata.ecdc.europa.eu/covid19/virusvariant/json, the reader will have access to the tabulations of the SARS-CoV-2 virus variants in the United States and the countries that are part of the European Economic Area. The website is maintained by the European Center for Disease Prevention and Control. We ask the reader:
   a. Extract data on the variants of the SARS-CoV-2 virus in the United States and countries that are part of the European Economic Area.
   b. How many sequences of variable B.1.1.7 were in Belgium in the last week of 2021?
   c. How many new cases were in Bulgaria the last week of 2021?
2. Using the URL https://opendata.ecdc.europa.eu/covid19/vaccine_tracker/json, the reader will have access to data on vaccination against the SARS-CoV-2 virus in the United States and the member countries of the European Economic Area. The website is maintained by the European Center for Disease Prevention and Control. We ask:
   a. How many people were vaccinated with the first dose in Austria in the last week of 2021? How many people were vaccinated with the second dose?
   b. How many vaccination doses were denied in Spain in the last week of 2021?
   c. How many people who are in the 25 to 49 age group were vaccinated in France in the last week of 2021?

CHAPTER

10

Managing data

AT THE END OF THIS CHAPTER, YOU WILL BE ABLE TO:

- Present the basic features of the universe `tidyverse`.
- Understand how to organize and manipulate datasets.
- Learn how to rename, create, and select variables.
- Demonstrate how to filter and group information.
- Show ways of merging datasets.

R-based language packages used in this chapter

```
library(tidyverse)
```

Don't forget to define the R working directory (the location where your datasets are installed):

```
setwd("C:/book/chapter10")
```

Introduction

In Chapter 2, in addition to a presentation of R-based language, we demonstrated some ways to manipulate data.

The main objective of this chapter is to present more fluid ways of manipulating and organizing data beyond pure R-based language.

When it comes to data manipulation and organization in R, the discussion about two main packages naturally emerges: the DataTables (DT) library and the library `tidyverse`. Both packages have their merits and limitations. For this work, the library `tidyverse` was chosen because its statements have greater simplicity, in the authors' opinion. The reader will even notice that in many ways the syntax of the package `tidyverse` resembles the syntax of the Structured Query Language (SQL).

That said, we need to be absolutely honest with the reader. Even though we are referring to and will continue to refer to `tidyverse` as a package, it is actually a set of libraries that make up one large package. The packages `dplyr`, `ggplot2`, `forcats`, `tibble`, `readr`, `stringr`, `tidyr`, and `purrr` are part of the universe `tidyverse`. This is why, by the way, we commonly use the declaration `library(tidyverse)` when we want to use any of the packages mentioned here.

Data Science, Analytics and Machine Learning with R
https://doi.org/10.1016/B978-0-12-824271-1.00020-2

By the way, it must be said that there are a number of other packages, with more specific biases, that are part of the tidyverse collection, but we do not mention them here because they are not loaded directly when we declare library (tidyverse). Occasional examples are the packages haven (to load and save datasets from IBM *SPPS, Stata,* and *SAS* software), rvest (dedicated to webscraping tasks), and jsonlite (to manipulate data from JavaScript language).

In this sense, as it contains so many packages, it is correct to say that the large library tidyverse works with cleansing, manipulation, organization, and data visualization. It is also correct to say that, thanks to the package purrr, the universe tidyverse also contains syntaxes aimed at simplified functional programming. It is already a reality that the package tidyverse works with the estimation of some models, thanks to the package tidymodels, which is not the objective of this work.

As in Chapter 7, when we minimally introduced the package ggplot2, our intention in this chapter is not to exhaust the capabilities of the package tidyverse as this would require at least a book dedicated to its capabilities. On the other hand, we will give the reader subsidies so he or she can follow the statements used from this chapter onward, and we will try to generate curiosity so the reader is interested in the set of features that tidyverse offers.

Next, we will explore some data cleansing, manipulation, and organization functionalities present in the universe tidyverse.

The operator %>%

The operator %>% (read: *pipe*) has its origin in the package magrittr, an integral part of the universe tidyverse, and is a great facilitator in the fluidity of R-based language. The operator %>% allows several commands to be given in R-based language at once, following a chronological order of events.

Contrary to what we have studied so far, as a rule, the commands in R are given line by line, one by one. For example, in a first command, we create a variable; in a second command, we change its values; in a third command, we rename this variable; in a fourth command, we rearrange the dataset in alphabetical order; and so on. The operator %>% allows this logic to be broken, causing multiple commands to be nested and executed at once.

It is true that from version 4.1.0 of R-based language, R gained a native pipe operator (|>), but we will continue to use the operator %>% in this work because many readers may be using previous versions of R.

From now on, the operator %>% will be used continuously in our command routines.

The function rename()

To get started with the presentation of the function rename(), we ask the reader to open the file professors.RData:

```
load("professors.RData")
```

The dataset professors contains information about 1,242 fictitious teachers and their publications. With the command head(), we can see an interesting part of the dataset:

```
head(professors)
```

Figure 10.1 shows the clipping of the first six observations from the dataset professors.

```
  `Professor Name`   `Professor-ID` `Number of Docum~ `Subject Area`
  <chr>                       <int>             <dbl> <chr>
1 Corbett, Brenden                1                 5 "Biochemistry, Genetics and Mol~
2 el-Habib, Riyaal                2                 5 "Agricultural and Biological Sc~
3 Chambers, Ulysses               3                 5 "Engineering\nComputer Science\~
4 Miller, Delisa                  4                27 "Agricultural and Biological Sc~
5 Richard, Alejand~               5                 5 "Environmental Science\n"
6 Loughridge, Josh~               6                18 "Environmental Science\nDecisio~
```

FIGURE 10.1 Cutting from the dataset professors.

In Chapter 2, we learned how to select variables from a dataset with the help of the operator $ and how to rename these variables by combining the function names() with a new name for a given variable that already exists. For example:

```
#Please do not command

names(dataset$variable_A) <- "var1"
```

For the case of the previous fictitious codes, for a given object that contained a given database called dataset in which there was a given variable called *variable_A*, the function names() was applied, and from that, *variable_A* would be called *var1*.

The function rename(), which is part of the universe tidyverse, will be our favorite for renaming variables from now on. The reason we chose it is that it can rename variables directly, as in the previous example, or by position variable, which makes our work much easier.

In Figure 10.1, we can see that the names of the variables in the dataset professors are difficult to declare for future model estimation. The names of these variables have combinations of uppercase and lowercase letters, spaces, and hyphens. With the function rename(), we can rename them, for example, as follows:

```
professors %>%
  rename(professor_name = `Professor Name`,
         id = `Professor-ID`,
         articles = `Number of Documents`,
         area = `Subject Area`)
```

Figure 10.2 shows the result obtained from the previous command.

```
   professor_name       id articles area
   <chr>             <int>    <dbl> <chr>
 1 Corbett, Brenden      1        5 "Biochemistry, Genetics and Molecular Biology\n"
 2 el-Habib, Riyaal      2        5 "Agricultural and Biological Sciences\nEnvironme~
 3 Chambers, Ulysses     3        5 "Engineering\nComputer Science\n"
 4 Miller, Delisa        4       27 "Agricultural and Biological Sciences\nEarth and~
 5 Richard, Alejand~     5        5 "Environmental Science\n"
 6 Loughridge, Josh~     6       18 "Environmental Science\nDecision Sciences\nBusin~
 7 Sloan, Derek          7       14 "Agricultural and Biological Sciences\n"
 8 Hernandez, Jonat~     8       23 "Agricultural and Biological Sciences\n"
 9 Brewer, Takayla       9        5 "Social Sciences\nEarth and Planetary Sciences\n"
10 Davis, Derek         10        5 "Agricultural and Biological Sciences\n"
# ... with 1,232 more rows
```

FIGURE 10.2 Result obtained when applying the function rename().

With the help of Figure 10.2, we can see that the variable names were successfully changed. So when we turn our eyes to the codes that gave rise to the image, we can see that a possible syntax for the function rename() involves first arguing for the new variable name followed by the operator = and then the original variable name.

With the codes used, it is also possible to verify the application of the operator %>%. Note that first we declared the dataset professors, so the operator %>% was used, and finally we applied the function rename().

Thus it is possible to say that the operator %>% works as an additive conjunction "and." In other words, it was like saying to R something like: **R, access the dataset professors, AND rename the selected variables.**

An attentive reader will already imagine that a new operator %>% could be used for a new task after the end of the declaration of the function rename(). No doubt, this reader is absolutely right! It is also possible to conclude that, in most cases, the package tidyverse will not need the operator $ to access the variables of a given dataset.

An even more attentive reader will notice that, despite the use of the operator %>% and the syntax coming from the universe tidyverse, **the dataset professors was not modified.** The sentence is obvious because no assignment operator (<-) was used. **So, in addition to making declarations easier and nesting commands, the operator %>% allows us to check how the results of the commands are looking, one by one, before saving the changes to a given object.**

Another way to rename dataset variables can be achieved by declaring the position of these variables:

```
professors %>%
  rename(professor_name = 1,
         id = 2,
         articles = 3,
         area = 4)
```

The result of the previous command is identical to that shown in Figure 10.2. The "translation" to human language of what happened earlier was something analogous to: R, rename the variable that appears in the first column of the dataset `professors` with the name *professor_name;* R, rename the variable in the second column of the dataset `professors` with the name *id,* and so on.

If the reader is wondering if it is mandatory to rename all of the variables in the database at once, the answer is no. The reader can only rename the variables he or she chooses, no matter how many of them.

Next, we will introduce the function `mutate()`.

The function mutate()

The function `mutate()` has two great uses: (1) the creation of new variables and (2) the transformation of a given variable that already exists.

To illustrate the first case, that is, the creation of a variable, when using the dataset `professors`, we could create a column that would indicate a possible reference year for the data as follows:

```
professors %>%
  mutate(year = 2022)
```

```
   `Professor Name`   `Professor-ID` `Number of Docum~ `Subject Area`                year
   <chr>                       <int>             <dbl> <chr>                         <dbl>
 1 Corbett, Brenden                1                 5 "Biochemistry, Genetics ~     2022
 2 el-Habib, Riyaal                2                 5 "Agricultural and Biolog~     2022
 3 Chambers, Ulysses               3                 5 "Engineering\nComputer S~     2022
 4 Miller, Delisa                  4                27 "Agricultural and Biolog~     2022
 5 Richard, Alejand~               5                 5 "Environmental Science\n"     2022
 6 Loughridge, Josh~               6                18 "Environmental Science\n~     2022
 7 Sloan, Derek                    7                14 "Agricultural and Biolog~     2022
 8 Hernandez, Jonat~               8                23 "Agricultural and Biolog~     2022
 9 Brewer, Takayla                 9                 5 "Social Sciences\nEarth ~     2022
10 Davis, Derek                   10                 5 "Agricultural and Biolog~     2022
# ... with 1,232 more rows
```

FIGURE 10.3 Result obtained when applying the function `mutate()`.

Figure 10.3 shows the result obtained from the previous command.

In Figure 10.3, it is clear how to create a variable in which first we must declare the name of the new variable, followed by the operator = and, finally, the value or values of the new variable.

However, the creation of a new variable does not need to arise from something that was not previously present in the dataset. We could gather information from existing variables and create a variable, either working in a textual or algebraic way.

For example, imagine that we want to create a variable that would be a kind of identification of a given teacher's area of expertise, where this variable would correspond to the first three characters of the variable *Subject Area*. We will call this new variable *area_id:*

```
professors %>%
  mutate(area_id = substr(x = `Subject Area`, start = 1, stop = 3))
```

We remind the reader that the function `substr()` was already covered in Chapter 2. Figure 10.4 shows the result obtained from the previous command.

```
   `Professor Name`  `Professor-ID` `Number of Docum~ `Subject Area`           area_id
   <chr>                     <int>              <dbl> <chr>                    <chr>
 1 Corbett, Brenden              1                  5 "Biochemistry, Genetic~ Bio
 2 el-Habib, Riyaal              2                  5 "Agricultural and Biol~ Agr
 3 Chambers, Ulysses             3                  5 "Engineering\nComputer~ Eng
 4 Miller, Delisa                4                 27 "Agricultural and Biol~ Agr
 5 Richard, Alejand~             5                  5 "Environmental Science~ Env
 6 Loughridge, Josh~             6                 18 "Environmental Science~ Env
 7 Sloan, Derek                  7                 14 "Agricultural and Biol~ Agr
 8 Hernandez, Jonat~             8                 23 "Agricultural and Biol~ Agr
 9 Brewer, Takayla               9                  5 "Social Sciences\nEart~ Soc
10 Davis, Derek                 10                  5 "Agricultural and Biol~ Agr
# ... with 1,232 more rows
```

FIGURE 10.4 Result obtained when applying the function mutate().

Putting together what we have learned so far, let's join the functions rename() and mutate() with the help of the operator %>%:

```
professors %>%
  rename(professor_name = `Professor Name`,
         id = `Professor-ID`,
         articles = `Number of Documents`,
         area = `Subject Area`) %>%
  mutate(area_id = substr(x = area, start = 1, stop = 3))
```

Figure 10.5 shows the result obtained from the previous command.

```
   professor_name       id articles area                                               area_id
   <chr>             <int>    <dbl> <chr>                                              <chr>
 1 Corbett, Brenden      1        5 "Biochemistry, Genetics and Molecular Bi~ Bio
 2 el-Habib, Riyaal      2        5 "Agricultural and Biological Sciences\nE~ Agr
 3 Chambers, Ulysses     3        5 "Engineering\nComputer Science\n"          Eng
 4 Miller, Delisa        4       27 "Agricultural and Biological Sciences\nE~ Agr
 5 Richard, Alejand~     5        5 "Environmental Science\n"                  Env
 6 Loughridge, Josh~     6       18 "Environmental Science\nDecision Science~ Env
 7 Sloan, Derek          7       14 "Agricultural and Biological Sciences\n"   Agr
 8 Hernandez, Jonat~     8       23 "Agricultural and Biological Sciences\n"   Agr
 9 Brewer, Takayla       9        5 "Social Sciences\nEarth and Planetary Sc~ Soc
10 Davis, Derek         10        5 "Agricultural and Biological Sciences\n"   Agr
# ... with 1,232 more rows
```

FIGURE 10.5 Result obtained when combining the applications of the functions rename() and mutate().

An attentive reader will notice a substantial difference in the argumentation of the function mutate() that gave rise to Figure 10.5 and the application of the same function mutate() that gave rise to Figure 10.4.

The reader will remember that we noted at the beginning of "The operator %>%" section that the operator %>% follows a chronological order of events. Therefore for Figure 10.4 a new name for the variable *Subject Area* was not commanded. For the case of Figure 10.5, the first command was about renaming the variables, and the variable that was called *Subject Area* started to be called *area;* then we worked on top of a variable already named *area* and not *Subject Area* anymore.

For the case of the second utility of the function mutate(), that is, the transformation of an already existing variable, we can observe that both the variables *id* and *area_id*, shown in Figure 10.5, are being considered, respectively, as types *integer* (int) and *character* (chr). As they are identifying variables of something, they must naturally be categorical variables, and, as such, R must recognize them as a *factor* (fct). In this way, we can command the following:

```
professors %>%
  rename(professor_name = `Professor Name`,
         id = `Professor-ID`,
         articles = `Number of Documents`,
         area = `Subject Area`) %>%
  mutate(area_id = substr(x = area, start = 1, stop = 3),
         id = factor(id),
         area_id = factor(area_id))
```

Analogous to what is obtained for the function `rename()`, the function `mutate()` accepts multiple transformations and/or variable creations simultaneously. The great care to be taken, we insist, is with respect to the chronological order of commands. Figure 10.6 shows the result obtained from the previous commands.

```
   professor_name     id    articles area                                        area_id
   <chr>              <fct>    <dbl> <chr>                                       <fct>
 1 Corbett, Brenden   1            5 "Biochemistry, Genetics and Molecular Bi~ Bio
 2 el-Habib, Riyaal   2            5 "Agricultural and Biological Sciences\nE~ Agr
 3 Chambers, Ulysses  3            5 "Engineering\nComputer Science\n"         Eng
 4 Miller, Delisa     4           27 "Agricultural and Biological Sciences\nE~ Agr
 5 Richard, Alejand~  5            5 "Environmental Science\n"                 Env
 6 Loughridge, Josh~  6           18 "Environmental Science\nDecision Science~ Env
 7 Sloan, Derek       7           14 "Agricultural and Biological Sciences\n"  Agr
 8 Hernandez, Jonat~  8           23 "Agricultural and Biological Sciences\n"  Agr
 9 Brewer, Takayla    9            5 "Social Sciences\nEarth and Planetary Sc~ Soc
10 Davis, Derek       10           5 "Agricultural and Biological Sciences\n"  Agr
# ... with 1,232 more rows
```

FIGURE 10.6 Result obtained when combining the applications of the functions `rename()` and `mutate()`.

Next, we will introduce the function `filter()`.

The function `filter()`

The function `filter()` is responsible for filtering ***observations*** from logical operators.
Suppose we want R to return all of those professors in our dataset who have published fewer than 7 articles:

```
professors %>%
  rename(professor_name = `Professor Name`,
         id = `Professor-ID`,
         articles = `Number of Documents`,
         area = `Subject Area`) %>%
  mutate(area_id = substr(x = area, start = 1, stop = 3),
         id = factor(id),
         area_id = factor(area_id)) %>%
  filter(articles < 7)
```

For this case, R will return a clipping of the first 10 observations and will say that there are still 710 more that meet the condition. To access all of them, we can save the previous routine in some object. Figure 10.7 shows the top 10 teachers with fewer than 7 articles published.

```
   professor_name     id    articles area                                        area_id
   <chr>              <fct>    <dbl> <chr>                                       <fct>
 1 Corbett, Brenden   1            5 "Biochemistry, Genetics and Molecular Bi~ Bio
 2 el-Habib, Riyaal   2            5 "Agricultural and Biological Sciences\nE~ Agr
 3 Chambers, Ulysses  3            5 "Engineering\nComputer Science\n"         Eng
 4 Richard, Alejand~  5            5 "Environmental Science\n"                 Env
 5 Brewer, Takayla    9            5 "Social Sciences\nEarth and Planetary Sc~ Soc
 6 Davis, Derek       10           5 "Agricultural and Biological Sciences\n"  Agr
 7 Begay, Tallon      13           5 "Agricultural and Biological Sciences\n"  Agr
 8 Engstrom, Michel~  14           5 "Agricultural and Biological Sciences\n"  Agr
 9 el-Soliman, Nash~  17           5 "Social Sciences\n"                       Soc
10 al-Arif, Rashaa    18           5 "Agricultural and Biological Sciences\n"  Agr
# ... with 710 more rows
```

FIGURE 10.7 Result obtained when applying the function `filter()`.

We can combine logical data-filtering conditions. Let's assume that, in addition to teachers with less than 7 articles published, we also want those who have the values `Bio` or `Agr` in the variable *area_id:*

```
professors %>%
  rename(professor_name = `Professor Name`,
         id = `Professor-ID`,
         articles = `Number of Documents`,
         area = `Subject Area`) %>%
  mutate(area_id = substr(x = area, start = 1, stop = 3),
         id = factor(id),
         area_id = factor(area_id)) %>%
  filter(articles < 7 & area_id %in% c("Bio", "Agr"))
```

Note that in the previous statement, we combined logical conditions with the operator `&`, which means a conjunction, as learned in Chapter 2. We could also use the operator `|` in place of the operator `&` if we want a disjunction.

For the previous command, R will return the first 10 observations and warn the reader that there are still another 426 teachers who meet the stipulated filter parameters, as shown in Figure 10.8.

```
   professor_name      id    articles area                                      area_id
   <chr>               <fct>    <dbl> <chr>                                     <fct>
 1 Corbett, Brenden    1            5 "Biochemistry, Genetics and Molecular B~ Bio
 2 el-Habib, Riyaal    2            5 "Agricultural and Biological Sciences\n~ Agr
 3 Davis, Derek        10           5 "Agricultural and Biological Sciences\n" Agr
 4 Begay, Tallon       13           5 "Agricultural and Biological Sciences\n" Agr
 5 Engstrom, Michelle  14           5 "Agricultural and Biological Sciences\n" Agr
 6 al-Arif, Rashaa     18           5 "Agricultural and Biological Sciences\n" Agr
 7 Halling, Anthony    22           5 "Agricultural and Biological Sciences\n" Agr
 8 Danielson, Danvy    25           5 "Agricultural and Biological Sciences\n" Agr
 9 Morfin, Kevin       31           5 "Agricultural and Biological Sciences\n" Agr
10 al-Hussain, Mahde~  32           5 "Agricultural and Biological Sciences\n" Agr
# ... with 426 more rows
```

FIGURE 10.8 Result obtained when applying the function `filter()`.

Next, we will introduce the function `arrange()`.

The function arrange()

The function `arrange()` is intended to arrange a dataset based on increasing or decreasing values alphanumerically, based on one or more variables.

An extremely simplified form of declaration would be the alphabetical ordering of the teachers shown in Figure 10.8:

```
professors %>%
  rename(professor_name = `Professor Name`,
         id = `Professor-ID`,
         articles = `Number of Documents`,
         area = `Subject Area`) %>%
  mutate(area_id = substr(x = area, start = 1, stop = 3),
         id = factor(id),
         area_id = factor(area_id)) %>%
  filter(articles < 7 & area_id %in% c("Bio", "Agr")) %>%
  arrange(professor_name)
```

In the previous routine, when we argue a text variable for the function `arrange()`, the arrangement will be done alphabetically, as explained in Figure 10.9.

```
   professor_name      id    articles area                                          area_id
   <chr>               <fct>    <dbl> <chr>                                         <fct>
 1 Abeyta, Amanda      1206         5 "Agricultural and Biological Sciences\n"      Agr
 2 Adame, Daisy        932          5 "Agricultural and Biological Sciences\n"      Agr
 3 Aghanoury, Amery    956          5 "Agricultural and Biological Sciences\n~      Agr
 4 Aguilar, Savannah   199          5 "Agricultural and Biological Sciences\n~      Agr
 5 Ahluwalia, Elizab~  330          5 "Biochemistry, Genetics and Molecular B~      Bio
 6 al-Abed, Musheer    569          5 "Agricultural and Biological Sciences\n"      Agr
 7 al-Ahmed, Tahiyya   740          5 "Agricultural and Biological Sciences\n"      Agr
 8 al-Aly, Tahaani     1116         5 "Agricultural and Biological Sciences\n"      Agr
 9 al-Arif, Rashaa     18           5 "Agricultural and Biological Sciences\n"      Agr
10 al-Ashraf, Rihaab   1086         5 "Agricultural and Biological Sciences\n"      Agr
# ... with 426 more rows
```

FIGURE 10.9 Result obtained when applying the function `arrange()`.

To adopt the alphabetical order, but backwards, we must nest the function `desc()` with the function `arrange()`, as shown in Figure 10.10:

```
professors %>%
  rename(professor_name = `Professor Name`,
         id = `Professor-ID`,
         articles = `Number of Documents`,
         area = `Subject Area`) %>%
  mutate(area_id = substr(x = area, start = 1, stop = 3),
         id = factor(id),
         area_id = factor(area_id)) %>%
  filter(articles < 7 & area_id %in% c("Bio", "Agr")) %>%
  arrange(desc(professor_name))
```

```
   professor_name      id    articles area                                          area_id
   <chr>               <fct>    <dbl> <chr>                                         <fct>
 1 Zoucha, Brian       475          5 "Agricultural and Biological Sciences\n"      Agr
 2 Young, Wyatt        529          5 "Agricultural and Biological Sciences\n"      Agr
 3 Yeaman, Nicholas    1110         5 "Agricultural and Biological Sciences\nB~     Agr
 4 Wu, Rohit           1112         5 "Agricultural and Biological Sciences\n"      Agr
 5 Wu, Der             952          5 "Agricultural and Biological Sciences\n"      Agr
 6 Wright, Justine     71           5 "Agricultural and Biological Sciences\n"      Agr
 7 Worthington, Ric~   177          5 "Agricultural and Biological Sciences\nV~     Agr
 8 Woon, Hyun-Ah       368          5 "Agricultural and Biological Sciences\nE~     Agr
 9 Wolfert, Nastaran   1174         5 "Agricultural and Biological Sciences\n"      Agr
10 Winter, Marcus      1166         5 "Agricultural and Biological Sciences\n"      Agr
# ... with 426 more rows
```

FIGURE 10.10 Result obtained when applying the function `arrange()`.

We can also combine ways to organize the dataset with the function `arrange()`. For example, we can organize the dataset to consider the teachers who most publish by *area_id*, considering the filter of publications smaller than 7 and of the "Bio" and "Agr" areas:

```
professors %>%
  rename(professor_name = `Professor Name`,
         id = `Professor-ID`,
         articles = `Number of Documents`,
         area = `Subject Area`) %>%
  mutate(area_id = substr(x = area, start = 1, stop = 3),
         id = factor(id),
         area_id = factor(area_id)) %>%
  filter(articles < 7 & area_id %in% c("Bio", "Agr")) %>%
  arrange(desc(articles), area_id)
```

Next, we will introduce the function `group_by()`.

The function group_by()

The function group_by() aims to group individuals from the dataset according to their numerical or textual values present in a given variable.

Suppose we want the average of the professors' publications for each value of the variable *area_id:*

```
professors %>%
  rename(professor_name = `Professor Name`,
         id = `Professor-ID`,
         articles = `Number of Documents`,
         area = `Subject Area`) %>%
  mutate(area_id = substr(x = area, start = 1, stop = 3),
         id = factor(id),
         area_id = factor(area_id)) %>%
  group_by(area_id) %>%
  mutate(average_publications = mean(articles))
```

Figure 10.11 shows the result obtained from the previous command.

```
   professor_name    id    articles area                     area_id average_publicat~
   <chr>             <fct>    <dbl> <chr>                    <fct>               <dbl>
 1 Corbett, Brenden  1            5 "Biochemistry, Genetics~ Bio                 26.0
 2 el-Habib, Riyaal  2            5 "Agricultural and Biolo~ Agr                 18.6
 3 Chambers, Ulyss~  3            5 "Engineering\nComputer ~ Eng                  9.8
 4 Miller, Delisa    4           27 "Agricultural and Biolo~ Agr                 18.6
 5 Richard, Alejan~  5            5 "Environmental Science\~ Env                 23.2
 6 Loughridge, Jos~  6           18 "Environmental Science\~ Env                 23.2
 7 Sloan, Derek      7           14 "Agricultural and Biolo~ Agr                 18.6
 8 Hernandez, Jona~  8           23 "Agricultural and Biolo~ Agr                 18.6
 9 Brewer, Takayla   9            5 "Social Sciences\nEarth~ Soc                  8.28
10 Davis, Derek      10           5 "Agricultural and Biolo~ Agr                 18.6
# ... with 1,232 more rows
```

FIGURE 10.11 Result obtained when applying the function group_by().

The reader may notice that the function group_by() grouped individuals according to their categories present in the variable *area_id*. Then, with the function mutate(), we created a new variable called *average_publications* that corresponds to the averages of the professors' publications by reason of their areas of expertise given by the variable *area_id*.

It is important to say that after grouping due to a certain variable (e.g., group_by(area_id)), R will not forget this grouping and will consider them in the next groupings and eventual transformations and creations of variables commanded by the reader. After a given grouping, if the reader wants to make R forget this join, he or she must use the function ungroup():

```
professors %>%
  rename(professor_name = `Professor Name`,
         id = `Professor-ID`,
         articles = `Number of Documents`,
         area = `Subject Area`) %>%
mutate(area_id = substr(x = area, start = 1, stop = 3),
         id = factor(id),
         area_id = factor(area_id)) %>%
group_by(area_id) %>%
mutate(average_publications = mean(articles)) %>%
ungroup()
```

After using the function ungroup(), the reader can propose new kinds of groupings via the function group_by() if desired.

Next, we will introduce the function select().

The function select()

The function `select()` ***selects or excludes variables.*** We remind the reader that the selection of observations due to logical conditions must be performed with the function `filter()`.

The function `select()` is useful to extract only the variables that will be useful from a given dataset and/or to organize that given dataset.

Suppose we only wanted, in the following order, the variable *id*, the variable *professor_name*, and the variable created in the previous section, *average_publications:*

```
professors %>%
  rename(professor_name = `Professor Name`,
         id = `Professor-ID`,
         articles = `Number of Documents`,
         area = `Subject Area`) %>%
  mutate(area_id = substr(x = area, start = 1, stop = 3),
         id = factor(id),
         area_id = factor(area_id)) %>%
  group_by(area_id) %>%
  mutate(average_publications = mean(articles)) %>%
  ungroup() %>%
  select(id, professor_name, average_publications)
```

Figure 10.12 shows the result obtained from the previous command.

```
   id    professor_name       average_publications
   <fct> <chr>                               <dbl>
 1 1     Corbett, Brenden                     26.0
 2 2     el-Habib, Riyaal                     18.6
 3 3     Chambers, Ulysses                     9.8
 4 4     Miller, Delisa                       18.6
 5 5     Richard, Alejandre                   23.2
 6 6     Loughridge, Joshua                   23.2
 7 7     Sloan, Derek                         18.6
 8 8     Hernandez, Jonathan                  18.6
 9 9     Brewer, Takayla                       8.28
10 10    Davis, Derek                         18.6
# ... with 1,232 more rows
```

FIGURE 10.12 Result of applying the function `select()`.

We could also delete one or more variables with the help of the operator -. Suppose we do not want the variables *area* and *articles* from the variables present in Figure 10.11:

```
professors %>%
  rename(professor_name = `Professor Name`,
         id = `Professor-ID`,
         articles = `Number of Documents`,
         area = `Subject Area`) %>%
  mutate(area_id = substr(x = area, start = 1, stop = 3),
         id = factor(id),
         area_id = factor(area_id)) %>%
  group_by(area_id) %>%
  mutate(average_publications = mean(articles)) %>%
  ungroup() %>%
  select(-area, -articles)
```

Figure 10.13 shows the result obtained from the previous command.

```
   professor_name      id    area_id average_publications
   <chr>               <fct> <fct>                  <dbl>
 1 Corbett, Brenden    1     Bio                    26.0
 2 el-Habib, Riyaal    2     Agr                    18.6
 3 Chambers, Ulysses   3     Eng                     9.8
 4 Miller, Delisa      4     Agr                    18.6
 5 Richard, Alejandre  5     Env                    23.2
 6 Loughridge, Joshua  6     Env                    23.2
 7 Sloan, Derek        7     Agr                    18.6
 8 Hernandez, Jonathan 8     Agr                    18.6
 9 Brewer, Takayla     9     Soc                     8.28
10 Davis, Derek        10    Agr                    18.6
# ... with 1,232 more rows
```

FIGURE 10.13 Result of applying the function select().

Finally, let's assume that we want all of the variables, but the first one is necessarily the variable *id*. Thus after we declare the variable *id*, we could command the function everything() nested within the function select().

```
professors %>%
  rename(professor_name = `Professor Name`,
         id = `Professor-ID`,
         articles = `Number of Documents`,
         area = `Subject Area`) %>%
  mutate(area_id = substr(x = area, start = 1, stop = 3),
         id = factor(id),
         area_id = factor(area_id)) %>%
  group_by(area_id) %>%
  mutate(average_publications = mean(articles)) %>%
  ungroup() %>%
  select(id, everything())
```

Next, we will introduce the function summarise().

The function summarise()

The function summarise() works by summarizing information that was previously gathered by the function group_by().

In "The function group_by()" section, we saw how the function group_by() works by grouping our teachers according to the values present in the variable *area_id* and then, with the function mutate(), calculating the averages of the teachers' publications by area of expertise *(area_id)*. What the function mutate() did in this narrated case, and shown in Figure 10.11, was to create a new variable called *average_publications* in the existing dataset. On the other hand, the function summarise(), as said, will summarize the information about the variables grouped via the function group_by().

Suppose we want ***only*** a report on the median values of the publications of teachers in our dataset:

```
professors %>%
  rename(professor_name = `Professor Name`,
         id = `Professor-ID`,
         articles = `Number of Documents`,
         area = `Subject Area`) %>%
  mutate(area_id = substr(x = area, start = 1, stop = 3),
         id = factor(id),
         area_id = factor(area_id)) %>%
  group_by(area_id) %>%
  summarise(median_publications = median(articles))
```

Figure 10.14 shows the summary obtained with the previous commands.

```
   area_id median_publications
   <fct>                 <dbl>
 1 Agr                       5
 2 Art                       5
 3 Bio                       7
 4 Bus                       5
 5 Che                       5
 6 Com                       5
 7 Ear                       5
 8 Eco                       7
 9 Ene                       5
10 Eng                       5
# ... with 12 more rows
```

FIGURE 10.14 Result of applying the function summarise().

The function summarise() therefore ignores all variables that were not argued by the function group_by(). We therefore ask the reader to pay attention when using it.

The functions separate() and unite()

When we collect real-world data, it is very common to find datasets created by those who do not understand that the data can be modeled and studied in different ways. An example of this is the variable *Subject Area* (which we renamed *area*).

The reader may notice that the variable discussed has several values separated by a given delimiter (a one-line spacing, in this case discussed) and that, depending on the study to be done, it might make sense that each of these values were present in variables corresponding to these categories. For the case discussed, the function separate() can help the reader:

```
professors %>%
  rename(professor_name = `Professor Name`,
         id = `Professor-ID`,
         articles = `Number of Documents`,
         area = `Subject Area`) %>%
  mutate(area_id = substr(x = area, start = 1, stop = 3),
         id = factor(id)) %>%
  separate(area, paste0("area_", 1:16), sep = "\\n")
```

In the previous statement, we argued the variable of interest (*area*) to the function separate(); then we used the declaration paste0("area_", 1:16) to name the new variables that will appear. That way, there will be the variable *area_1* containing the first value of the original variable *area*, then the variable *area_2* containing the second position of the original variable *area*, and so on, until *area_16*. Finally, we declare the separator of knowledge areas, made by line spacing (\\n). If the spacing were the common spacing (made with the space bar key), we would declare \n. It is important to note that the function separate() excluded the original variable *area*.

If we want to go the other way around, that is, join values into a single variable, we would use the function unite(). To see how the function unite() works, let's save the previous routine in a new dataset called new_professors:

```
new_professors <- professors %>%
  rename(professor_name = `Professor Name`,
         id = `Professor-ID`,
         articles = `Number of Documents`,
         area = `Subject Area`) %>%
  mutate(area_id = substr(x = area, start = 1, stop = 3),
         id = factor(id)) %>%
  separate(area, paste0("area_", 1:16), sep = "\\n")
```

From the dataset `new_professors`, which contains 16 variables regarding the teachers' area of expertise (*area_1, area_2, ..., area_16*), we will join these 16 variables into a new variable called *new_area* using a comma (,) as an information separator:

```
new_professors %>%
  unite(new_area, area_1:area_16, sep = ",")
```

In the routine that used the function `unite()`, the reader will notice that the variables *area_1, area_2, ..., area_16* have been removed and replaced by the variable *new_area*.

The functions gather() and spread()

The functions `gather()` and `spread()` are interesting alternatives to the functions `melt()` and `dcast()` from the package `reshape2`.

In other words, the functions `gather()` and `spread()` can be alternatives to transform a dataset from wide format to long format, and from long to wide, respectively speaking.

Take the example of the dataset `new_professors` created. We will keep the original variables *id* and *professor_name,* but we will put the values present in the variables *area_1, area_2, ...* and *area_16* in a single variable in which each value of the original variables will appear in individual lines.

To make it easier to understand, we can go by steps. First, from the dataset `new_professors`, we will select 18 variables, that is, the variables *id, professor_name,* and the 16 other variables regarding the area of expertise of these professors:

```
new_professors %>%
  select(id, professor_name, area_1:area_16)
```

Figure 10.15 shows the result obtained from the previous command.

```
   professor_name  id    articles area_1   area_2   area_3   area_4  area_5  area_6  area_7
   <chr>           <fct>    <dbl> <chr>    <chr>    <chr>    <chr>   <chr>   <chr>   <chr>
 1 Corbett, Brend~ 1            5 Bioche~  ""        NA      NA      NA      NA      NA
 2 el-Habib, Riya~ 2            5 Agricu~  "Envir~  ""       NA      NA      NA      NA
 3 Chambers, Ulys~ 3            5 Engine~  "Compu~  ""       NA      NA      NA      NA
 4 Miller, Delisa  4           27 Agricu~  "Earth~  "Envir~  Multi~  ""      NA      NA
 5 Richard, Aleja~ 5            5 Enviro~  ""        NA      NA      NA      NA      NA
 6 Loughridge, Jo~ 6           18 Enviro~  "Decis~  "Busin~  Bioch~  "Agri~  Medic~  ""
 7 Sloan, Derek    7           14 Agricu~  ""        NA      NA      NA      NA      NA
 8 Hernandez, Jon~ 8           23 Agricu~  ""        NA      NA      NA      NA      NA
 9 Brewer, Takayla 9            5 Social~  "Earth~  ""       NA      NA      NA      NA
10 Davis, Derek    10           5 Agricu~  ""        NA      NA      NA      NA      NA
# ... with 1,232 more rows, and 10 more variables: area_8 <chr>, area_9 <chr>,
#   area_10 <chr>, area_11 <chr>, area_12 <chr>, area_13 <chr>, area_14 <chr>,
#   area_15 <chr>, area_16 <chr>, area_id <chr>
```

FIGURE 10.15 The first step of applying the function `gather()`.

Looking at Figure 10.15, we can see that the variable values we want to join, from the perspective of a long-format dataset, are from the 3rd position (3rd column) onward, up to the 18th position (18th column). Thus when commanding the function `gather()`, we must indicate a name for a new variable that will contain the names of the original variables that will be grouped, which we will call *original_variables;* then, the name of the new variable that will contain the values of the observations of the grouped variables, which we will call *areas_of_expertise*; and, finally, the variables to be grouped, those in positions 3 to 18:

```
new_professors %>%
  select(id, professor_name, area_1:area_16) %>%
  gather(key = "original_variable",
         value = "areas_of_expertise",
         3:18)
```

Figure 10.16 shows the result obtained from the previous command.

```
     id    professor_name      original_variab~ areas_of_expertise
     <fct> <chr>               <chr>            <chr>
   1 1     Corbett, Brenden    area_1           Biochemistry, Genetics and Molecular B~
   2 2     el-Habib, Riyaal    area_1           Agricultural and Biological Sciences
   3 3     Chambers, Ulysses   area_1           Engineering
   4 4     Miller, Delisa      area_1           Agricultural and Biological Sciences
   5 5     Richard, Alejandre  area_1           Environmental Science
   6 6     Loughridge, Joshua  area_1           Environmental Science
   7 7     Sloan, Derek        area_1           Agricultural and Biological Sciences
   8 8     Hernandez, Jonathan area_1           Agricultural and Biological Sciences
   9 9     Brewer, Takayla     area_1           Social Sciences
  10 10    Davis, Derek        area_1           Agricultural and Biological Sciences
# ... with 19,862 more rows
```

FIGURE 10.16 The final step of applying the function `gather()`.

An attentive reader will notice that the R in Figure 10.16 is pointing to a result with 19,872 lines, while the original base `new_professor` has 1,242 lines. This is due to the long format adopted.

It is also true to say that of these 19,872, there are many values `NA`, that is, missing values, something that Figure 10.15 already denounced. Another thing that Figure 10.15 denounces is the existence of blank cells, represented by the value "". The idea here is to, at the very least, demonstrate to the reader typical challenges of handling, cleansing, and organizing data.

In case the missing values are not needed, we can use the function `na.omit()`. **However, the reader needs to know that the function `na.omit()` does not belong to the universe `tidyverse`, and, therefore we must argue the operator . so R understands that its application is valid for the entire dataset, regardless of the considered variable.**

Another point we must take into account is the blank cells, represented by the value "". To overcome the situation, we can use the function `mutate()` and the function `ifelse()` (see Chapter 2) to replace the blank cells with the value `NA`.

```
new_professors %>%
  select(id, professor_name, area_1:area_16) %>%
  gather(key = "original_variable",
         value = "areas_of_expertise",
         3:18) %>%
  mutate(areas_of_expertise = ifelse(areas_of_expertise == "",
                                     yes = NA,
                                     no = areas_of_expertise)) %>%
  na.omit(.)
```

Figure 10.17 shows the result of the proposed routine, without considering the missing values, resulting in a dataset with 2,640 lines.

```
     id    professor_name      original_variab~ areas_of_expertise
     <fct> <chr>               <chr>            <chr>
   1 1     Corbett, Brenden    area_1           Biochemistry, Genetics and Molecular B~
   2 2     el-Habib, Riyaal    area_1           Agricultural and Biological Sciences
   3 3     Chambers, Ulysses   area_1           Engineering
   4 4     Miller, Delisa      area_1           Agricultural and Biological Sciences
   5 5     Richard, Alejandre  area_1           Environmental Science
   6 6     Loughridge, Joshua  area_1           Environmental Science
   7 7     Sloan, Derek        area_1           Agricultural and Biological Sciences
   8 8     Hernandez, Jonathan area_1           Agricultural and Biological Sciences
   9 9     Brewer, Takayla     area_1           Social Sciences
  10 10    Davis, Derek        area_1           Agricultural and Biological Sciences
 # ... with 2,630 more rows
```

FIGURE 10.17 The application of the function `na.omit()`.

To undo what we just did, that is, transform a dataset from long format to wide format, we will use the function `spread()`. However, first let's save the routine that generated Figure 10.17 in a new object called `spread_new_professors`:

```
spread_new_professors <- new_professors %>%
  select(id, professor_name, area_1:area_16) %>%
  gather(key = "original_variable",
         value = "areas_of_expertise",
         3:18) %>%
  mutate(areas_of_expertise = ifelse(areas_of_expertise == "",
                                     yes = NA,
                                     no = areas_of_expertise)) %>%
  na.omit(.)
```

Then, from the new base `spread_new_professors`, we will declare the variable *original_variable* to the function `spread ()`, whose categories will represent the new variables to be considered in a wide format dataset; then we will declare the variable *areas_of_expertise,* whose values will be the new values of the variables created from the variable *original_variable:*

```
spread_new_professors %>%
  spread(key = original_variable,
         value = areas_of_expertise)
```

The previous routine will undo what the function `gather()` did. In other words, the reader will return to a dataset close to the one shown in Figure 10.15, except for the absence of the variables *articles* and *area_id,* which were not covered by the function `select()` at the beginning of this section.

Join functions

The `join` functions are generally useful when we need to merge different datasets from one or more index variables. An index variable is a given variable present in the two datasets that one wants to merge, with the same nomenclature and with the same measurement scale. To elucidate this, see Figure 10.18.

id	name	city
1	Desiree Gonzales	Medelín
2	Jacob Hoan	Ottawa
3	Mila Kamau	Mombasa
4	Kevin Requa	Nashville
5	Khepri Gamal	Giza
6	Ulrich Weber	Hamburg
7	Ruiqi Liu	Beijing
8	Hiroshi Takahashi	Sapporo

id	name	age
1	Desiree Gonzales	22
2	Jacob Hoan	53
4	Kevin Requa	60
6	Ulrich Weber	17
7	Ruiqi Liu	29
9	Veronika Sidorov	41

FIGURE 10.18 Theoretical representation of joining two datasets.

Note that in Figure 10.18 we want to join two distinct datasets, but with variables in common. These common variables can serve as index variables from which the data merging process will occur. For this, as stated, they must have the same nomenclature and the same measurement scale (e.g., *character*, *factor*, *numeric*) in both datasets.

More than defining the index variables, most of the time, the reader should also assume a sense of orientation for data joining (e.g., from the left table, from the right table, from the union or intersection of the tables involved).

For the explanations to come, we will use the file `cities_and_ages.RData`. This file contains two objects, namely, `cities` and `ages`. In Figure 10.18, the object `cities` contains data from the table on the left, and the object `ages` contains data from the table on the right:

```
load("cities_and_ages.RData")
```

Another use of the `join` functions is the selection of observations from a given dataset based on their occurrence, or not, in another dataset.

We will cover six data functions of `join`: `left_join()`, `right_join()`, `full_join()`, `inner_join()`, `semi_join()`, and `anti_join()`. Of the functions presented, only the last two do not perform the data fusion procedure, being, therefore, used for the selection of observations, as narrated in the previous paragraph.

The function `left_join()`

Given Figure 10.18, the function `left_join()` will join the data from the perspective of the dataset on the left, considering the declared index variables. Figure 10.19 tries to exemplify the statement.

id	name	city
1	Desiree Gonzales	Medelín
2	Jacob Hoan	Ottawa
3	Mila Kamau	Mombasa
4	Kevin Requa	Nashville
5	Khepri Gamal	Giza
6	Ulrich Weber	Hamburg
7	Ruiqi Liu	Beijing
8	Hiroshi Takahashi	Sapporo

id	name	age
1	Desiree Gonzales	22
2	Jacob Hoan	53
4	Kevin Requa	60
6	Ulrich Weber	17
7	Ruiqi Liu	29
9	Veronika Sidorov	41

id	name	city	age
1	Desiree Gonzales	Medelín	22
2	Jacob Hoan	Ottawa	53
3	Mila Kamau	Mombasa	-
4	Kevin Requa	Nashville	60
5	Khepri Gamal	Giza	-
6	Ulrich Weber	Hamburg	17
7	Ruiqi Liu	Beijing	29
8	Hiroshi Takahashi	Sapporo	-

FIGURE 10.19 Theoretical representation of joining two datasets using the function `left_join()`.

In Figure 10.19, the reader will notice that, when using the function `left_join()` and based on the index variables *id* and *name*, R will necessarily merge the left table with the right table, in that order. This way, when R does not find values that index the merge in the table on the right, it will leave the resulting table with missing values regarding these observations. Incidentally, values that only exist in the table on the right (e.g., Veronika Sidorov) will not be considered in the merge via the function `left_join()`.

Figure 10.19 can be reproduced in R as follows:

```
cities %>%
  left_join(ages, by = c("id", "name"))
```

The above codes, from the perspective of human language, can be read as something close to: "R, access the dataset `cities`, and from the index variables *id* and *name*, perform a left join with the dataset `ages`".

The function `right_join()`

The function `right_join()` performs the perfect opposite of what we explained throughout "The function left_join()" section, with emphasis on Figure 10.19.

For the function `right_join()`, the orientation reference will no longer be the table on the left in Figure 10.18; it will be the table on the right in this figure.

Figure 10.20 shows the application of the function `right_join()`.

id	name	city
1	Desiree Gonzales	Medelín
2	Jacob Hoan	Ottawa
3	Mila Kamau	Mombasa
4	Kevin Requa	Nashville
5	Khepri Gamal	Giza
6	Ulrich Weber	Hamburg
7	Ruiqi Liu	Beijing
8	Hiroshi Takahashi	Sapporo

id	name	age
1	Desiree Gonzales	22
2	Jacob Hoan	53
4	Kevin Requa	60
6	Ulrich Weber	17
7	Ruiqi Liu	29
9	Veronika Sidorov	41

id	name	city	age
1	Desiree Gonzales	Medelín	22
2	Jacob Hoan	Ottawa	53
4	Kevin Requa	Nashville	60
6	Ulrich Weber	Hamburg	17
7	Ruiqi Liu	Beijing	29
9	Veronika Sidorov	-	41

FIGURE 10.20 Theoretical representation of joining two datasets using the function `right_join()`.

The reader will notice in Figure 10.20 that this time there are no missing values for the variable *age* because the reference is the table on the right in Figure 10.18. However, precisely because the table on the right is the reference, there will be no values in the variable *city* for the Veronika Sidorov observation.

The previous result can be produced in R with the following routine:

```
cities %>%
  right_join(ages, by = c("id", "name"))
```

The function `full_join()`

Starting from Figure 10.18, it can be said that the function `full_join()` does not adopt merging references, only following the index variables. In other words, it would be like the join sets operation. Figure 10.21 shows the application of the function `full_join()`.

id	name	city
1	Desiree Gonzales	Medelín
2	Jacob Hoan	Ottawa
3	Mila Kamau	Mombasa
4	Kevin Requa	Nashville
5	Khepri Gamal	Giza
6	Ulrich Weber	Hamburg
7	Ruiqi Liu	Beijing
8	Hiroshi Takahashi	Sapporo

+

id	name	age
1	Desiree Gonzales	22
2	Jacob Hoan	53
4	Kevin Requa	60
6	Ulrich Weber	17
7	Ruiqi Liu	29
9	Veronika Sidorov	41

id	name	city	age
1	Desiree Gonzales	Medelín	22
2	Jacob Hoan	Ottawa	53
3	Mila Kamau	Mombasa	-
4	Kevin Requa	Nashville	60
5	Khepri Gamal	Giza	-
6	Ulrich Weber	Hamburg	17
7	Ruiqi Liu	Beijing	29
8	Hiroshi Takahashi	Sapporo	-
9	Veronika Sidorov	-	41

FIGURE 10.21 Theoretical representation of joining two datasets using the function `full_join()`.

The reader may notice that in Figure 10.21, the left table in Figure 10.18 was not adopted as a reference, and neither was the table on the right. The process triggered by the function `full_join()` merged all of the data present in the datasets `cities` and `ages`, taking into account only the index variables.

If the reader wants to use the function `full_join()` in R, he or she can apply the following routine:

```
cities %>%
  full_join(ages, by = c("id", "name"))
```

The previous procedure, in fact, is equivalent to the operation of joining sets. If the reader is looking for a procedure that is similar to the intersection of sets, the function `inner_join()` should be used.

The function `inner_join()`

As for the function `full_join()`, the function `inner_join()` does not guide the merging of data based on which table will be on the left or on the right. However, as shown in Figure 10.22, contrary to what is proposed by the function `full_join()`, the function `inner_join()` proposes the selection of observations via a procedure similar to that of an intersection of sets.

id	name	city
1	Desiree Gonzales	Medelín
2	Jacob Hoan	Ottawa
3	Mila Kamau	Mombasa
4	Kevin Requa	Nashville
5	Khepri Gamal	Giza
6	Ulrich Weber	Hamburg
7	Ruiqi Liu	Beijing
8	Hiroshi Takahashi	Sapporo

+

id	name	age
1	Desiree Gonzales	22
2	Jacob Hoan	53
4	Kevin Requa	60
6	Ulrich Weber	17
7	Ruiqi Liu	29
9	Veronika Sidorov	41

id	name	city	age
1	Desiree Gonzales	Medelín	22
2	Jacob Hoan	Ottawa	53
4	Kevin Requa	Nashville	60
6	Ulrich Weber	Hamburg	17
7	Ruiqi Liu	Beijing	29

FIGURE 10.22 Theoretical representation of joining two datasets using the function `inner_join()`.

To replicate what is proposed by Figure 10.22, the reader will be able to command:

```
cities %>%
  inner_join(ages, by = c("id", "name"))
```

The functions `semi_join()` and `anti_join()`

Unlike everything exposed earlier in "The Function `left_join()`," "The Function `right_join()`," "The Function `full_join()`," and "The Function `inner_join()`," **the functions `semi_join()` and `anti_join()` do not merge two datasets.** They are ways of selecting observations, based on index variables, **always oriented from the left table.** Another way to explain it would be that these functions are ways of selecting the rows in the table on the left, based on index variables, regarding observations that are or are not included in the table on the right.

When looking at Figure 10.18 again, the function `semi_join()` will select the observations that exist in the left table and also exist in the right table, as proposed in Figure 10.23.

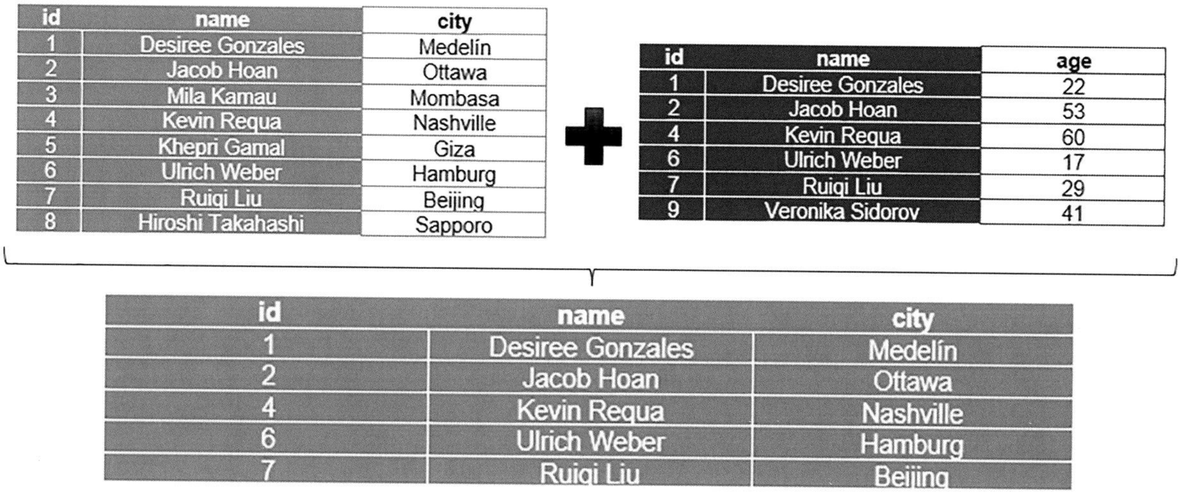

id	name	city
1	Desiree Gonzales	Medelín
2	Jacob Hoan	Ottawa
3	Mila Kamau	Mombasa
4	Kevin Requa	Nashville
5	Khepri Gamal	Giza
6	Ulrich Weber	Hamburg
7	Ruiqi Liu	Beijing
8	Hiroshi Takahashi	Sapporo

+

id	name	age
1	Desiree Gonzales	22
2	Jacob Hoan	53
4	Kevin Requa	60
6	Ulrich Weber	17
7	Ruiqi Liu	29
9	Veronika Sidorov	41

id	name	city
1	Desiree Gonzales	Medelín
2	Jacob Hoan	Ottawa
4	Kevin Requa	Nashville
6	Ulrich Weber	Hamburg
7	Ruiqi Liu	Beijing

FIGURE 10.23 Theoretical representation of selecting observations using the function `semi_join()`.

Figure 10.23 makes it clear that the function `semi_join()`, in fact, is not intended to merge datasets, but only to select common observations between two datasets, adopting the dataset on the left as a reference. The routine to use the function `semi_join()` in R can be given as follows:

```
cities %>%
  semi_join(ages, by = c("id", "name"))
```

The function `anti_join()`, on the other hand, does the opposite of the expected result when applying the function `semi_join()`; that is, **it will select the observations present in the left table that do not exist in the right table,** as shown in Figure 10.24.

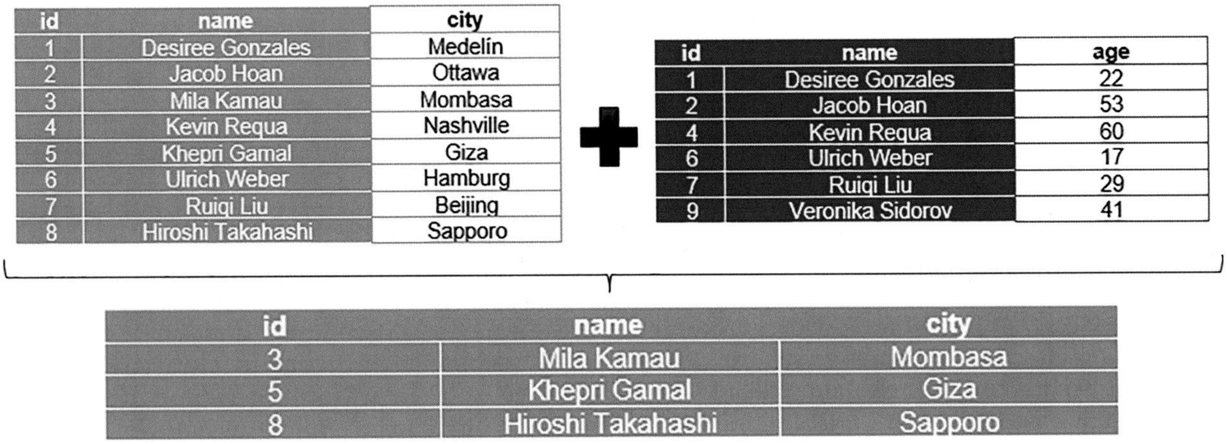

id	name	city
1	Desiree Gonzales	Medelín
2	Jacob Hoan	Ottawa
3	Mila Kamau	Mombasa
4	Kevin Requa	Nashville
5	Khepri Gamal	Giza
6	Ulrich Weber	Hamburg
7	Ruiqi Liu	Beijing
8	Hiroshi Takahashi	Sapporo

id	name	age
1	Desiree Gonzales	22
2	Jacob Hoan	53
4	Kevin Requa	60
6	Ulrich Weber	17
7	Ruiqi Liu	29
9	Veronika Sidorov	41

id	name	city
3	Mila Kamau	Mombasa
5	Khepri Gamal	Giza
8	Hiroshi Takahashi	Sapporo

FIGURE 10.24 Theoretical representation of selecting observations using the function `anti_join()`.

To replicate the result indicated in Figure 10.24, the reader can command the following:

```
cities %>%
  anti_join(ages, by = c("id", "name"))
```

Final remarks

In this chapter, the main idea was to present, albeit minimally, the functionalities of the universe `tidyverse` that are necessary for the continuity of the reading of this work. We also present some features that, even though they go beyond the scope of this work, we deem necessary for cleansing, manipulating, and organizing data.

The reader can rest assured about the organization of the datasets that will come in the next chapters. All of them are already properly cleansed and organized! However, in many topics we will manipulate these datasets or the results of estimated models, which will require the use of most of the functions presented in this chapter.

Therefore we believe it is necessary for the reader to become familiar with what is presented in the library `tidyverse` to have a greater understanding of data manipulation, the creation of graphs (see Chapter 7, as `ggplot2` is also an integral part of `tidyverse`), extracting insights, and presenting the results of a given model.

In addition to the intentions of this work, the authors firmly believe that this simple presentation of some functions of the package `tidyverse` will constitute an important asset in the reader's life regarding their use of R-based language. The authors also believe that the internalization of functionalities and syntaxes of `tidyverse` can smooth the R-based language learning curve.

Exercise

1. The file `exercise_chap10.RData` contains three datasets: `age_income_dataset`, `grades_dataset`, and `investor_dataset`. The three datasets are about the same individuals, and each dataset has a different size with different data. The object `age_income_dataset` contains information about 100 observations regarding the age and income of certain people, according to Table 10.1 (Fávero and Belfiore, 2019).

TABLE 10.1 Description of the variables present in the object `age_income_dataset` (Fávero and Belfiore, 2019).

Variable	Description
Name	Variable that contains the individual's name
Age	Variable that informs the individual's age
income	Variable that indicates the individual's monthly income

The object `grades_dataset`, on the other hand, comprises some information about the general averages of the high school age of 80 individuals (all present in the object `age_income_dataset`), whose variables are presented in Table 10.2.

TABLE 10.2 Description of the variables present in the object `grades_dataset` (Fávero and Belfiore, 2019).

Variable	Description
Name	Variable that contains the individual's name
math_course_grade	Variable that indicates the overall average of the mathematics subject
physics_course_grade	Variable that indicates the overall average of the physics discipline
english_course_grade	Variable that indicates the overall average of the English subject
chemistry_course_grade	Variable that measures the overall average of the chemistry discipline

Finally, despite having 300 lines, the object `investor_dataset` contains information about the investment profiles of the 100 individuals present in the object `age_income_dataset`, namely, how the person identifies as an investor, the type of investment in which the person most invests their income, and the marital status of that person. Table 10.3 explains the variables contained in the discussed dataset.

TABLE 10.3 Description of the variables present in the object `investor_dataset` (Fávero and Belfiore, 2019).

Variable	Description
Name	Variable that contains the individual's name
characteristic	Categorical variable that indicates characteristics about individuals, linked to the variable *investor_profile*, whose categories are: "profile," "application," and "marital_status"
investor_profile	Categorical variable related to the variable *characteristic*, whose values are: "conservative," "moderate," aggressive," "savings account," "investments funds," "stocks," "single," and "married"

Based on what we have learned in this section and using only resources present in the universe `tidyverse`, we would like you to:

a. Obviously, the dataset contained in the object `investor_dataset` is in long format. Transform the dataset into wide format in which each category of the variable *characteristic* is considered a variable whose values are those present in the variable *investor_profile*, **and save the result in an object called `investor_wide`.**

b. Reorder the variables present in the object `investor_wide` in the following order: *name, profile, application, marital_status,* and **overwrite the object `investor_wide`.**

c. Transform the variables present in the dataset `investor_wide` to variables of the type *factor,* and **overwrite the object `investor_wide`.**

d. Filter the observations present in the object `age_income_dataset` to highlight only individuals 35 years of age or younger. Next, present the mean, median, and standard deviation of their income. Do not overwrite the object **`age_income_dataset`.**

e. Organize the dataset `age_income_dataset` to account for the highest income. Who is the first individual to appear? **Do not overwrite the object `age_income_dataset`.**

f. Organize the dataset `age_income_dataset` to consider the highest age. Who is the first individual to appear? **Do not overwrite the object `age_income_dataset`.**

g. Rename all variables in the dataset `grades_dataset`, except for the variable *name*. The names of the variables should be, respectively, *math, physics, english,* and *chemistry*. **Overwrite the object `grades_dataset`.**

h. Create a variable in the dataset `grades_dataset` that indicates when a given individual has an overall average in English greater than or equal to 7.0. **Overwrite the object `grades_dataset`.**

i. Filter the dataset `grades_dataset` considering all English averages greater than or equal to 7.0 (use the new variable generated in item "h"). How many individuals meet the condition proposed by the filter? **Do not overwrite the object `grades_dataset`.**

j. Apply the function `right_join()` between the objects `age_income_dataset` and `grades_dataset`, in that order. Use the variable *name* as the index variable. **Save the results in an object called `join_1`.**
k. Delete the variable created in item "h" from the dataset saved in the object `join_1`. **Overwrite the object `join_1`.**
l. Apply the `left_join()` function between the objects `join_1` and `investor_wide`, in that order. Use the variable *name* as the index variable. **Save the results in an object called `join_2`.**
m. Using the object `join_2`, create a variable called *investor_characteristics* that corresponds to the joining of the values of the variables *profile, application,* and *marital_status*. The delimiter must be a semicolon (;). **Overwrite the object `join_2`.**
n. Using the object `join_2`, create a variable that represents the monthly income of each individual, that is, a variable that corresponds to *income* divided by 12, and make this variable occupy the third column. **Overwrite the object `join_2`.**

Supplementary data sets

```
professors.RData
cities_and_ages.RData
exercise_chap10.RData
```

Please access supplementary data files here: https://doi.org/10.17632/55623jkwrp.3

PART IV

Unsupervised machine learning techniques

CHAPTER

11

Cluster analysis

AT THE END OF THIS CHAPTER, YOU WILL BE ABLE TO:

- Calculate different measures of distance (dissimilarity) and similarity for metric variables.
- Understand the different hierarchical agglomeration schedules in cluster analysis and how to interpret dendrograms, with a focus on allocating observations in each group.
- Understand the nonhierarchical *k*-means agglomeration schedule, and learn how to differentiate it from a hierarchical schedule.
- Implement cluster analysis using R-based language, and interpret the outputs.

R-based language packages used in this chapter

```
library(tidyverse)
library(ggrepel)
library(cluster)
library(factoextra)
```

Don't forget to define the R working directory (the location where your datasets are installed):

```
setwd("C:/book/chapter11")
```

Cluster analysis with hierarchical and nonhierarchical agglomeration schedules in R

In this section, we will discuss the step-by-step process for elaborating our example in R-based language. The main objective is to offer the researcher an opportunity to run cluster analyses with hierarchical and nonhierarchical schedules in R, given how easy it is to use it and how didactical the operations are.

Elaborating hierarchical agglomeration schedules in R

Suppose that the marketing department of a retail company wants to study possible discrepancies in their 18 stores spread throughout three regional centers and distributed all over the country. To maintain and preserve its brand's image and identity, top management wants to know if their stores are homogeneous in terms of customers' perception of attributes, such as level of service (attendance), variety of goods (assortment), and organization. Research on

Data Science, Analytics and Machine Learning with R
https://doi.org/10.1016/B978-0-12-824271-1.00005-6

samples of clients was performed in each store to collect data regarding these attributes. These data were defined based on the average score obtained (0 to 100) in each store. The data can be found in the file `retail.RData` (Fávero and Belfiore, 2019) and in Table 11.1. In this section, we will carry out the cluster analysis using the Euclidian distance among the observations, considering only the single linkage method.

TABLE 11.1 Example: scores of attendance, assortment, and organization for 18 stores (Fávero and Belfiore, 2019).

Store	Regional_id	Attendance	Assortment	Organization
1	Regional 3	6	6	4
2	Regional 3	14	2	4
3	Regional 3	8	4	6
4	Regional 3	4	4	4
5	Regional 3	6	6	6
6	Regional 2	38	38	100
7	Regional 1	40	78	38
8	Regional 3	6	4	4
9	Regional 3	4	4	6
10	Regional 3	6	6	2
11	Regional 2	54	32	86
12	Regional 2	52	34	98
13	Regional 2	76	60	88
14	Regional 1	78	86	38
15	Regional 1	54	76	58
16	Regional 3	2	4	4
17	Regional 1	52	56	46
18	Regional 3	6	2	4

To implement a cluster analysis, we ask the reader to load the dataset as follows:

```
load("retail.RData")
```

We will now define a matrix of dissimilarities. In our particular case, as the magnitude of the measurement of the variables is the same (scores given by customers from 0 to 100), **there is no need to carry out Z-scores standardization**. If the reader must use standardization in other situations, Z-scores standardization is obtained by the function `scale()` in R-based language. If the reader still wants to standardize the variables with the Z-scores procedure in our current example, the results will be the same.

The dissimilarity matrix can be obtained through the function `dist()` in R-based language (in our case, using the Euclidean distance), as follows:

```
D_matrix <- dist(x = retail[, 3:5],
                 method = "euclidean")
```

In the previous routine, `D_matrix` is the name of the object that will contain the matrix of dissimilarities obtained through the function `dist()`. As arguments for the discussed function, we have: `x`, which concerns the metric variables that will be taken into account for clustering; and `method`, which indicates the distance that will be used to calculate the distances among the observations in the dataset. An attentive reader could command ?dist to check which types of distances are available in the function dist().

Once the matrix of dissimilarities D_matrix is built, we can elaborate the clustering. The R brings in its base language the algorithm hclust() that establishes hierarchical agglomerations; however we will use the function agnes() from the package cluster because it provides more information about the agglomeration schedule to be established:

```
cluster_retail <- agnes(x = D_matrix, method = "single")
```

For the function agnes(), we must declare two arguments: x, which will point to the similarity or dissimilarity matrix (the object D_matrix, in our example); and method, which indicates the linkage method to be used. We recommend that the reader view the documentation of the function agnes() to check other possible linkage methods.

An attentive reader will notice that the object cluster_retail has the following components:

- order: vector with dimension ($n \times 1$) that contains the order of agglomeration of observations defined by the algorithm for future plotting of the dendrogram, so as not to cross its ramifications;
- height: vector with dimension ($n-1 \times 1$) that contains the similarity or dissimilarity metrics calculated among observations of the dataset;
- merge: matrix with dimension ($n-1 \times 2$) that shows a kind of agglomeration schedule that is not very intuitive and whose logic is as follows: line i points out the stages of clustering. If a number k present in any column, j is negative, then cluster k is being combined at the precise stage identified by line i. However, if k is positive, then cluster considered in that line (stage) i is the result of the cluster previously formed in line $i=k$.
- diss: information about the considered similarity or dissimilarity matrix;
- call: points to the established command for clustering; and
- method: a redundancy that refers to the linkage method used in the routine.

R does not have an agglomeration schedule as intuitive as shown by some software like IBM *SPSS* or *Stata*, but nothing prevents us from creating something like that. For this, we can separate the similarity or dissimilarity metrics already calculated and present in the component height of the object cluster_retail:

```
coefficients <- cluster_retail$height
```

Next, we can sort the values present in the object coefficients in ascending order, as follows:

```
coefficients <- sort(x = coefficients, decreasing = FALSE)
```

Then, we can combine the object coefficients with the component merge present in the object cluster_retail:

```
agglomeration <- as.data.frame(cbind(cluster_retail$merge,
                                     coefficients))
```

To facilitate the interpretability of our agglomeration schedule, we can change the name of its columns, as follows:

```
names(agglomeration) <- c("cluster1", "cluster2", "distances")
agglomeration
```

Table 11.2 presents the agglomeration schedule built for the proposed example, which is identical to that contained in the object agglomeration.

In Table 11.2, as already discussed, in stage 1 of agglomeration we see two negative numbers, meaning that observations 8 and 18 come together to form a single cluster at that moment. In stage 2 of agglomeration, again, we see two negative numbers pointing to the combination of observations 4 and 16 in a single cluster at this precise moment. However, in stage 3 of agglomeration, we see a positive number and a negative number, meaning that the cluster formed in

TABLE 11.2 Agglomeration schedule.

Stage	Cluster 1	Cluster 2	Distances
1	–8	–18	2.000
2	–4	–16	2.000
3	2	–9	2.000
4	3	1	2.000
5	–1	–10	2.000
6	5	–5	2.000
7	6	4	2.000
8	7	–3	2.828
9	8	–2	6.633
10	–11	–12	12.329
11	–6	10	14.697
12	–15	–17	23.409
13	–7	12	24.495
14	13	–14	32.802
15	11	–13	35.665
16	15	14	40.497
17	9	16	78.256

stage 2 (in line 2, or the positive number 2, as you wish) is joining with observation 9 and forming a new cluster at that stage of the agglomeration, and so on.

Also in Table 11.2, we can verify that the biggest jump occurs between stages 16 and 17, which suggests, in a preliminary way, that the solution of two clusters seems to be interesting for the proposed exercise. To reinforce this analysis, it is interesting to study the dendrogram.

Based on how the observations are sorted in the agglomeration schedule and on the distances used as a clustering criterion, we can create the dendrogram shown in Figure 11.1. Note that the distance measures are rescaled to build the dendrograms in R. This makes it easier to interpret each observation allocation to the clusters and to mainly visualize the highest distance leaps. We can build a dendrogram using the function `fviz_dend()` from the package `factoextra`:

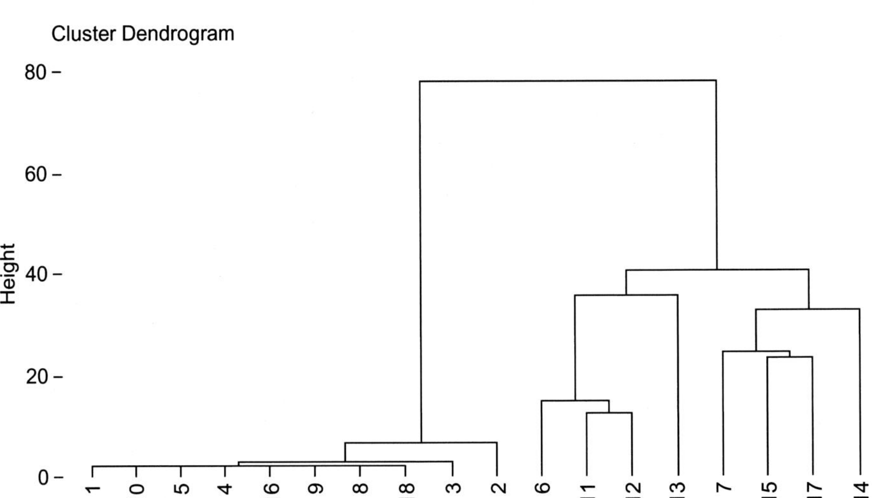

FIGURE 11.1 Dendrogram using single linkage method and rescaled Euclidian distances in R.

```
fviz_dend(x = cluster_retail)
```

If the reader wishes to make the dendrogram more elegant, showing the proposed solution of two clusters, the following commands can be entered:

```
fviz_dend(x = cluster_retail,
          k = 2,
          k_colors = c("orange", "darkorchid"),
          color_labels_by_k = FALSE,
          rect = TRUE,
          rect_fill = TRUE,
          lwd = 1,
          ggtheme = theme_bw())
```

In the previous routine, the number of clusters defined by the reader is declared to the argument `k`. Since `k = 2`, then we must declare two colors for the function `fviz_dend()` using the argument `k_colors`. The argument `color_labels_by_k = FALSE` indicates that we do not want store identification labels to follow the color scheme of the clustering. The argument `rect = TRUE` indicates that we want to highlight clusters formed with a rectangle, and the argument `rect_fill = TRUE` determines that the rectangle will be colored gray. Finally, to the argument `ggtheme` we must declare some function `theme()` from the package `ggplot2` (e.g., `theme_bw()`, `theme_classic`), which is studied in Chapter 7. The result is shown in Figure 11.2.

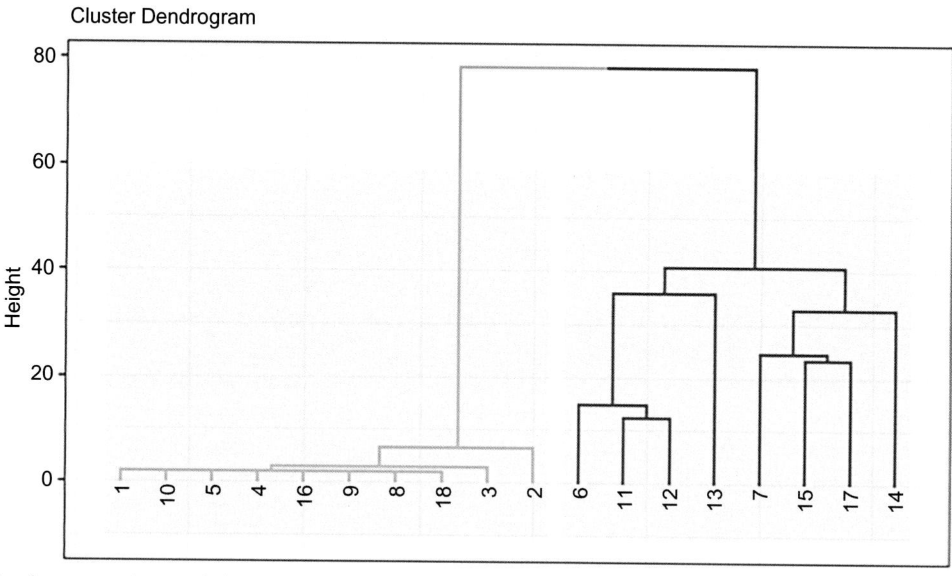

FIGURE 11.2 Dendrogram using single linkage method and rescaled Euclidian distances in R with colors.

The way the observations are sorted in the dendrogram corresponds to what was presented in the agglomeration schedule (see Table 11.2), and, from the analysis shown in Figure 11.2, it is possible to see that the greatest distance leap occurs when stores **1-10-5-4-16-9-8-18-3-2** merge with stores **6-11-12-13-7-15-17-14**. This leap could have already been identified in the agglomeration schedule found in Table 11.2 because a large increase in distance occurs when we go from the 16th to 17th stage, that is, when we increase the Euclidian distance from 40.497 to 78.256, so a new cluster can be formed by incorporating another observation. **The criterion for identifying the number of clusters that considers the clustering stage immediately before a large leap is very useful and commonly used.**

Figure 11.3 shows a dashed vertical line that "cuts" the dendrogram in the region where the highest leaps occur. At this moment, because two intersections with lines from the dendrogram occur, we can identify two corresponding clusters, respectively formed by stores **1-10-5-4-16-9-8-18-3-2** and **6-11-12-13-7-15-17-14**.

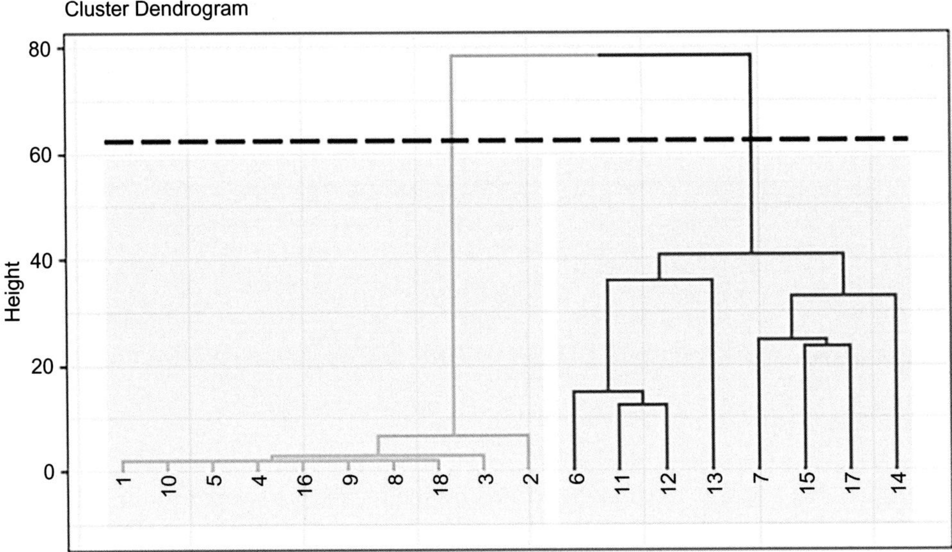

FIGURE 11.3 Dendrogram with cluster identification.

As discussed, **it is common to find dendrograms that make it difficult to identify distance leaps**, mainly because there are considerably similar observations in the dataset in relation to all of the variables under analysis. In these situations, it is advisable to use the **squared Euclidean distance** and the **complete linkage method** (furthest neighbor). **This criteria combination is very popular in datasets with extremely homogeneous observations.**

Having adopted the solution with two clusters, we can use the function `cutree()` of the R-based language to define which cluster each observation belongs to. To use the function `cutree()`, we must declare the object containing the clustering performed for the argument `tree` and the number of clusters we will adopt as a solution for the argument `k`:

```
retail["H_cluster"] <- cutree(tree = cluster_retail, k = 2)
```

The reader will notice that the variable *H_cluster* was created in the dataset `retail`, which identifies which cluster each observation belongs to, according to the adopted solution (`k = 2`, for our case). Although R, by default, creates metric variables with the function `cutree()`, there is no doubt that this is a nominal variable! The output of a clustering technique is **ALWAYS** a nominal categorical variable!

At this moment, the researcher may consider the cluster analysis with hierarchical agglomeration schedules concluded. Nevertheless, based on the generation of the new variable *H_cluster*, by using the one-way ANOVA test, the reader may still study if the values of a certain variable differ among the clusters formed, that is, if the variability among the groups is significantly higher than the variability within each group.

To do this, we must use the function `aov()` of the R-based language, as studied in Chapter 6, as follows:

```
anova_attendance <- aov(attendance ~ H_cluster, data = retail)
anova_assortment <- aov(assortment ~ H_cluster, data = retail)
anova_organization <- aov(organization ~ H_cluster, data = retail)
```

To access results from ANOVA tests, we must use the function `summary()`:

```
summary(anova_attendance)
summary(anova_assortment)
summary(anova_organization)
```

Figure 11.4 summarizes the three ANOVA tests. Diagram A shows the results for the variable *attendance*, diagram B shows the results for the variable *assortment*, and diagram C shows the results for the variable *organization*.

A – (*Attendance*)

	Df	Sum Sq	Mean Sq	F value	Pr (>F)	
factor (H_cluster)	1	10802	10802	108.5	1.56e-08	***
Residuals	16	1594	100			

B – (*Assortment*)

	Df	Sum Sq	Mean Sq	F value	Pr (>F)	
H_cluster	1	12626	12626	63.42	5.88e-07	***
Residuals	16	3186	199			

C – (*Organization*)

	Df	Sum Sq	Mean Sq	F value	Pr (>F)	
H_cluster	1	18547	18547	58.9	9.46e-07	***
Residuals	16	5038	315			

FIGURE 11.4 One-way analysis of variance: between groups and within groups variation, *F* statistics, and significance levels per variable.

Although we can see from diagrams A, B, and C in Figure 11.4 that there are mean differences of the variables *attendance*, *assortment*, and *organization* among the groups, these differences cannot be considered statistically significant at a significance level of 0.05 because we are dealing with a very small number of observations, and the *F* statistic values are very sensitive to the sample size. This analysis becomes very useful when we study datasets with a larger number of observations and variables.

Finally, researchers can still complement their analysis by elaborating a procedure known as **multidimensional scaling** because using the distance matrix may help them construct a chart that allows two-dimensional visualization of the relative positions of each observation, regardless of the total number of variables.

To do this, we will use the function `cmdscale()` of the R-based language. This function elaborates a classic multidimensional scaling, also known as *principal coordinates analysis*. The main idea is to use the metrics of the dissimilarity matrix to calculate coordinates in which the distances among them are approximately equal to the dissimilarities. For example, in ecology, this procedure is commonly called *ordination*. To do so, we will define `d` as the dissimilarity matrix and `k` as the number of dimensions we want to represent (we will use a biplot visualization):

```
multi_scaling <- cmdscale(d = D_matrix, k = 2)
```

Ready! The object `multi_scaling` now has the Cartesian coordinates we want! To view them graphically, we can use the package `ggplot2`, as discussed in Chapter 7:

```
data.frame(multi_scaling) %>%
  ggplot() +
  geom_point(aes(x = X1, y = X2,
                 color = retail$regional)) +
  geom_label_repel(aes(x = X1, y = X2,
                       color = retail$regional,
                       label = retail$store)) +
  scale_color_manual("Legend:",
                     values = c("orange",
                                "darkorchid",
                                "bisque4")) +
  labs(x = "Dimension 1",
       y = "Dimension 2") +
  theme_bw()
```

Figure 11.5 shows the chart with the relative positions of the observations projected on a plane.

This type of chart is very useful when researchers wish to prepare didactical presentations of observation clusters (e.g., individuals, companies, municipalities, countries) and to make the interpretation of the clusters easier, mainly when there is a relatively large number of variables in the dataset.

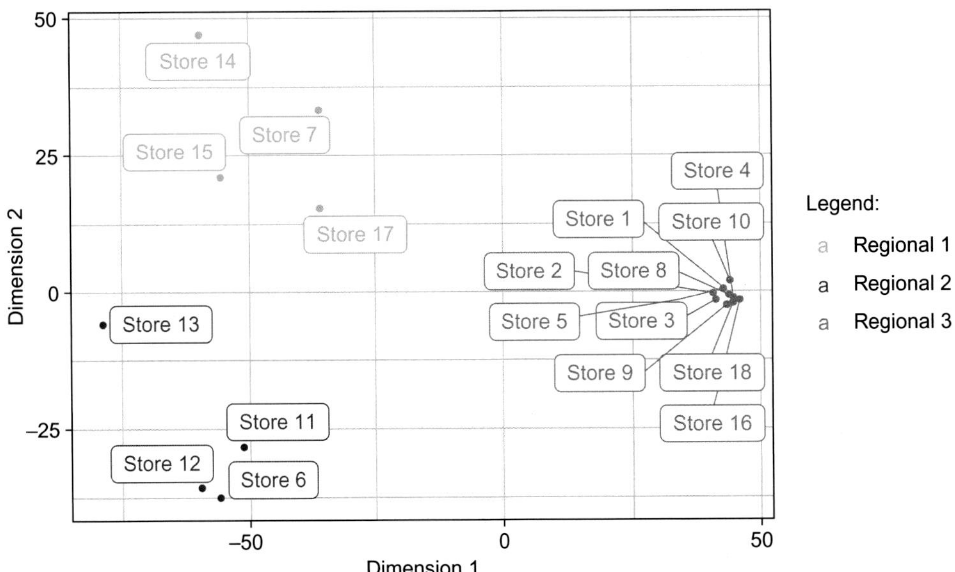

FIGURE 11.5 Two-dimensional chart with the projected relative positions of the observations.

Elaborating nonhierarchical *k*-means agglomeration schedules in R

Maintaining the same logic proposed in this chapter, from the same dataset we will develop a cluster analysis based on the nonhierarchical *k*-means agglomeration schedule. Thus, we must once again use the file `retail.RData`.

To do this, after elaborating the dissimilarity matrix (object `D_matrix`), we can use the function `kmeans()`, declaring the number of solutions (clusters) proposed for the argument `centers`:

```
cluster_kmeans <- kmeans(x = D_matrix, centers = 2)
```

The centroids calculated for each cluster can be verified by running `cluster_kmeans$centers`. The allocation of each observation in clusters can be verified by running `cluster_kmeans$cluster`, or as follows:

```
retail["K_cluster"] <- cluster_kmeans$cluster
```

An attentive reader will notice that, **for our case**, there was a correspondence between the hierarchical agglomeration method and the nonhierarchical *k*-means agglomeration method. This means that the **ANOVA** output (see Figure 11.4) will be identical for our proposed clustering.

As previously discussed, if one or more variables are not contributing to the formation of the suggested number of clusters, we recommend reapplying the algorithm without these variables. The researcher can even use a hierarchical procedure without the aforementioned variables before reapplying the *k*-means procedure.

Final remarks

It is strongly advisable for researchers to justify, clearly and transparently, the measure they choose and that will serve as the basis for the observations to be considered more or less similar, as well as the reasons that make them define nonhierarchical or hierarchical agglomeration schedules and, in this last case, determine the linkage methods.

In the past few years, the evolution of technological capabilities and the development of new software with extremely improved resources resulted in the development of new and better cluster analysis techniques. These techniques use more and more sophisticated algorithms and are aimed at the decision-making process in several fields of knowledge, always with the main goal of grouping observations based on certain criteria. However, in this chapter, we tried to offer a general overview of the main cluster analysis methods, also considered to be the most popular (Fávero and Belfiore, 2019) .

Exercise

(1) A greengrocer wants to monitor the sales of products for 16 weeks (4 months). The main objective is to verify if the sales behavior of three of their main products (bananas, oranges, and apples) is recurrent after a certain period as a result of weekly wholesale price fluctuations, prices that are passed on to customers and may affect sales. These data can be found in the file `veggiefruit.RData`, which have the following variables (Fávero and Belfiore, 2019):

Variable	Description
week	A string variable that varies from 1 to 16 and identifies the week in which the sales were monitored
week_month	A string variable that varies from 1 to 4 and identifies the week in each one of the months
banana	Number of bananas sold that week (un.)
orange	Number of oranges sold that week (un.)
apple	Number of apples sold that week (un.)

We would like you to:

(a) Run a cluster analysis using a hierarchical agglomeration schedule with the single linkage method (nearest neighbor) and Pearson's correlation measure. Present the matrix of similarity measures (Pearson's correlation) between each row in the dataset (weekly periods). **Reminder:** Because the variables are in the same unit of measure, it is not necessary to apply the Z-scores standardization procedure.

(b) Present and discuss the agglomeration schedule table.

(c) Based on the table found in the previous item and on the dendrogram, is there any indication that the joint sales behavior of bananas, oranges, and apples is recurrent in certain weeks?

Supplementary data sets

retail.RData
scholarship.RData
veggiefruit.RData

Please access supplementary data files here: https://doi.org/10.17632/55623jkwrp.3

C H A P T E R

12

Principal component factor analysis

AT THE END OF THIS CHAPTER, YOU WILL BE ABLE TO:

- Calculate and interpret the factor scores, and define the factors from them.
- Determine and interpret factor loadings and communalities.
- Build loading plots.
- Develop performance rankings based on the joint behavior of the variables.
- Implement principal component factor analysis using R-based language, and interpret the outputs.

R language packages used in this chapter

```
library(tidyverse)
library(ggrepel)
library(reshape2)
library(PerformanceAnalytics)
library(psych)
library(factoextra)
```

Don't forget to define the R working directory (the location where your datasets are installed):

```
setwd("C:/book/chapter12")
```

Principal component factor analysis in R

We now present the step-by-step procedure for developing our example in R. In this section, our main goal is not to discuss the concepts of principal component factor analysis. Instead, we offer the reader an opportunity to elaborate the technique by using the commands in this software.

That said, we ask the reader to load the dataset `demographic_atlas.RData` (Fávero et al., 2009). The file has socio-demographic indicators from the 96 districts belonging to the municipality of São Paulo, Brazil, whose variables are explained in Table 12.1.

Data Science, Analytics and Machine Learning with R
https://doi.org/10.1016/B978-0-12-824271-1.00006-8

TABLE 12.1 Sociodemographic variables from districts in the municipality of São Paulo, Brazil.

Variable	Description
id	Nominal categorical variable that represents an identification code for a given district belonging to the municipality of São Paulo
district	Nominal categorical variable that indicates the name of each district belonging to the municipality of São Paulo
income	Median household income of inhabitants, in $
m2_inhab	Ratio between the built area (m^2) and the number of inhabitants
scholarity	Mean years of schooling for the population 4 years of age and older
age	Median age of the population
child_mortality	Infant mortality rate (number of deaths of children younger than 1 year of age per 1,000 live births)
populational_growth	Average population growth (%)
externalcauses_mortality	Ratio between deaths by homicide and the population, multiplied by 100,000
shantytown	Population living in slums (% of population)
pop_density	Population density (population per unit area, in km^2)

We ask the reader to load the dataset, as follows:

```
load("demographic_atlas.RData")
```

We can access the univariate descriptive statistics for each variable of the dataset with the function `summary()`, which is shown in Figure 12.1.

```
       id           district             income          m2_inhab          scholarity
 1      : 1   Length:96          Min.   : 159   Min.   :  0.61   Min.   :4.800
 2      : 1   Class :character   1st Qu.:1150   1st Qu.: 12.40   1st Qu.:6.300
 3      : 1   Mode  :character   Median :1628   Median : 24.30   Median :7.000
 4      : 1                      Mean   :1856   Mean   : 30.48   Mean   :7.075
 5      : 1                      3rd Qu.:2316   3rd Qu.: 40.99   3rd Qu.:7.850
 6      : 1                      Max.   :5146   Max.   :104.73   Max.   :9.200
 (Other):90
      age        child_mortality populational_growth externalcauses_mortality
 Min.   :20.0   Min.   : 6.46   Min.   :-6.24000    Min.   : 22.68
 1st Qu.:23.0   1st Qu.:12.96   1st Qu.:-2.04250    1st Qu.: 56.42
 Median :27.0   Median :16.23   Median :-0.83500    Median : 70.39
 Mean   :27.4   Mean   :15.99   Mean   : 0.04115    Mean   : 71.09
 3rd Qu.:31.0   3rd Qu.:18.72   3rd Qu.: 1.34250    3rd Qu.: 82.37
 Max.   :36.0   Max.   :44.25   Max.   :18.12000    Max.   :127.37

   shantytown       pop_density
 Min.   : 0.000   Min.   :  0.37
 1st Qu.: 0.000   1st Qu.: 64.32
 Median : 3.015   Median : 96.17
 Mean   : 5.932   Mean   : 99.86
 3rd Qu.: 7.838   3rd Qu.:136.22
 Max.   :45.690   Max.   :249.60
```

FIGURE 12.1 Univariate descriptive statistics for each variable of the dataset `demographic_atlas`.

```
summary(demographic_atlas)
```

To establish a correlation matrix in R, the reader can use the function `color()`, as studied in Chapter 7. If the reader wants something more elaborate, we suggest using the function `chart.Correlation()` from the package

PerformanceAnalytics. Regardless of the path taken by the reader, remember that **Pearson's correlations can only be calculated from metric variables!** Therefore:

```
chart.Correlation(demographic_atlas[,3:11])
```

The function `chart.Correlation()`, as it was typed, must be applied to a dataset that contains metric variables, so we selected the variables in positions 3 to 11 with the operator `[ , ]`. The output from the previous routine is shown in Figure 12.2.

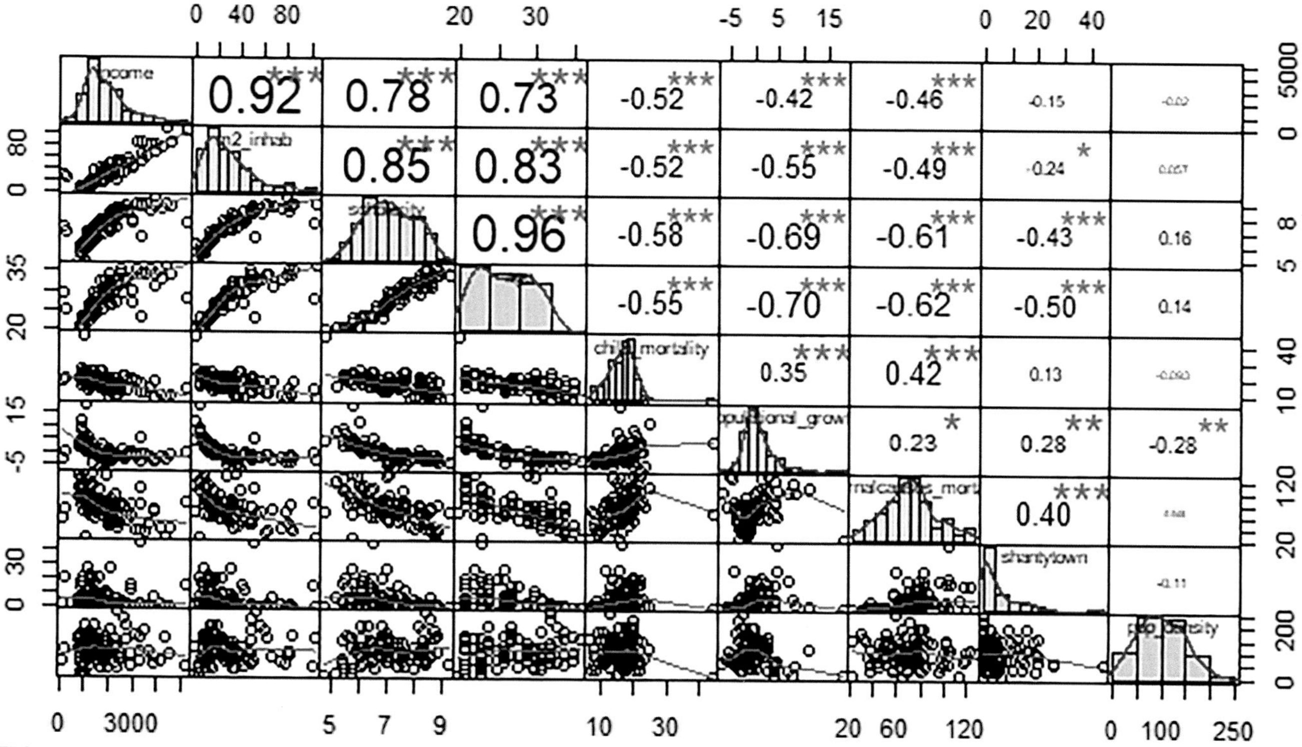

FIGURE 12.2 Output of the function `chart.Correlation()`.

In the upper-right portion of Figure 12.2, we can analyze the values of the correlations between the metric variables of the dataset `demographic_atlas`. An attentive reader will notice that the higher the value of the correlation, in module, the larger the typography used to highlight it. It must be said that the symbols next to the correlation values refer to the statistical significance of the calculated correlations, as follows:

- ***: $sig < 0.000$;
- **: $sig < 0.001$;
- *: $sig < 0.01$;
- .: $sig < 0.05$.

In Figure 12.2, its diagonal is filled by the histogram of each variable, and its lower left portion refers to a scatter among variables, with the respective fitted line (we will study fitted lines and fitted values from Chapter 14 onward).

As studied in Chapter 7, we could use a heat map to show the correlations among the variables of the object `demographic_atlas`, the result of which is shown in Figure 12.3.

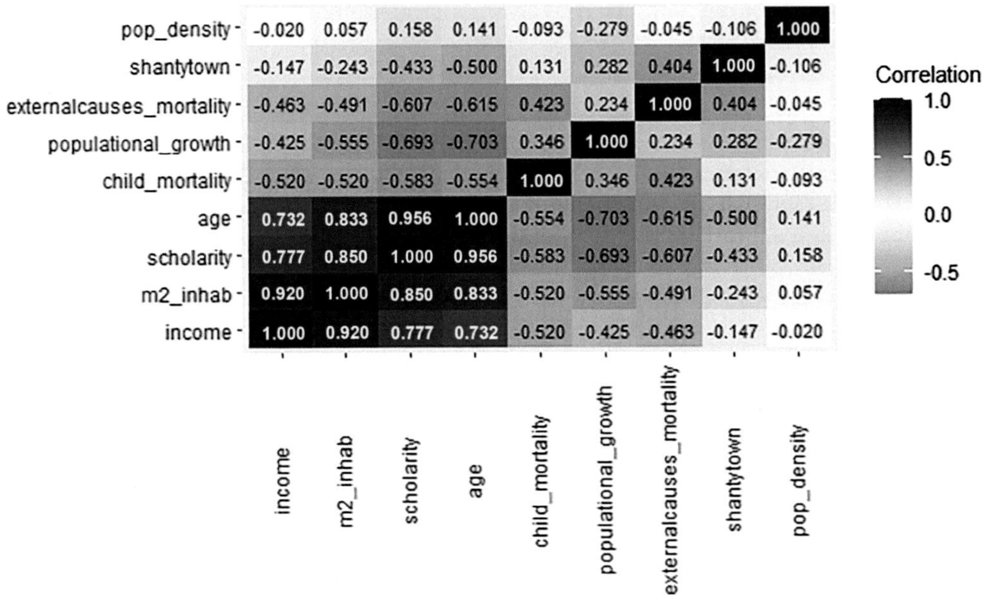

FIGURE 12.3 Heat map and correlations among the variables of the object `demographic_atlas`.

```
demographic_atlas %>%
  select(-id, -district) %>%
  cor() %>%
  melt() %>%
  rename(Correlation = 3) %>%
  ggplot() +
  geom_tile(aes(x = Var1, y = Var2, fill = Correlation)) +
  geom_text(aes(x = Var1, y = Var2, label = format(Correlation, digits = 2)),
            size = 3) +
  scale_fill_gradient2(low = "red",
                       mid = "white",
                       high = "darkblue",
                       midpoint = 0) +
  labs(x = NULL, y = NULL) +
  theme(axis.text.x = element_text(angle = 90))
```

The outputs of Figures 12.2 and 12.3 show that the correlations between the variables *shantytown* and *pop_density*, in module, are relatively low and not statistically significant at a significance level of 0.05 (level adopted as a rule). On the other hand, the correlations among the variables *income, m2_inhab, scholarity,* and *age*, in module, are reasonably high and statistically significant at a significance level of 0.05. Such a diagnosis is a preliminary indication that the factor analysis may group them in a certain factor without substantial loss of their variances, whereas the variables *shantytown* and *pop_density* can eventually have a higher correlation with other factors.

The overall adequacy of the factor analysis can be evaluated using the results of the KMO statistic and Bartlett's test of sphericity. We can use the function `KMO()` to obtain the KMO statistic, and we can use the function `cortest.bartlett()` to elaborate the Bartlett's test of sphericity, both functions in the package `psych`, whose results are shown in Figures 12.4 and 12.5, respectively.

```
KMO(demographic_atlas[,3:11])
cortest.bartlett(demographic_atlas[,3:11])
```

```
Kaiser-Meyer-Olkin factor adequacy
Call: KMO(r = demographic_atlas[, 3:11])
Overall MSA =  0.83
MSA for each item =
                     income                m2_inhab             scholarity
                       0.78                    0.82                   0.86
                        age         child_mortality    populational_growth
                       0.82                    0.95                   0.84
externalcauses_mortality              shantytown            pop_density
                       0.89                    0.79                   0.63
```

FIGURE 12.4 KMO Statistic

```
$chisq
[1] 748.1593

$p.value
[1] 5.607017e-134

$df
[1] 36
```

FIGURE 12.5 Bartlett's test of sphericity.

Based on the result of the KMO statistic (0.83), the overall adequacy of the factor analysis can be considered **meritorious**. However, more important than this piece of information is the result of Bartlett's test of sphericity. From the result of the χ^2_{Bartlett} statistic, with a significance level of 0.05 and 36 degrees of freedom, we can say that the Pearson's correlation matrix is statistically different from the identity matrix with the same dimension because $\chi^2_{\text{Bartlett}} = 748.159$ (χ^2 calculated for 36 degrees of freedom) and *Prob.* χ^2_{Bartlett} (*P*-value) < 0.05.

In R, to elaborate a factor analysis–principal component analysis, we will use the function `prcomp()` of the base `language`. That said, we can type:

```
fa <- prcomp(x = demographic_atlas[ ,3:11], scale. = TRUE)
```

The created object `fa` has the following components:

- `rotation`: corresponds to a matrix with dimensions ($k \times k$) of eigenvectors, where k represents the number of variables considered in the analysis
- `sdev`: corresponds to the square root of the eigenvalues
- `center`: refers to the means of the variables
- `scale`: refers to the standard deviations of the variables

We advise the reader to apply the function `summary()` to the created object `fa` to obtain the outputs presented in Figure 12.6:

```
summary(fa)
```

```
Importance of components:
                          PC1    PC2    PC3     PC4     PC5     PC6     PC7     PC8     PC9
Standard deviation     2.2262 1.0790 0.9982 0.85092 0.72753 0.63113 0.36010 0.25508 0.19196
Proportion of Variance 0.5507 0.1294 0.1107 0.08045 0.05881 0.04426 0.01441 0.00723 0.00409
Cumulative Proportion  0.5507 0.6800 0.7907 0.87120 0.93001 0.97427 0.98868 0.99591 1.00000
```

FIGURE 12.6 Square roots of the eigenvalues, the proportion of variance in each component, and the cumulative proportion of variance.

Figure 12.6 shows the values of the square root of the eigenvalues of the correlation matrix. We can analyze the proportion of variance of the data contained in each component in Figure 12.6, for example, Principal Component 1 (PC1) captured 55.07% of the variance of the data; Principal Component 2 (PC2) captured 12.94%, and so on. We can also analyze the cumulative proportion of variance captured by the components in the factor analysis. An attentive reader will remember two things already studied: that the sum of the eigenvalues is equal to k (number of variables) and that the variance captured in each factor is equivalent to the ratio between the eigenvalue and the number of variables used in the principal component analysis. To verify this, we can type:

```
sum((fa$sdev) ^ 2)
(fa$sdev ^ 2) / length(fa$sdev)
```

To better visualize the capture of variance by the components, we can build a scree plot with the function `fviz_eig()` from the package `factoextra`:

```
fviz_eig(X = fa,
         ggtheme = theme_bw(),
         barcolor = "black",
         barfill = "orange",
         linecolor = "darkorchid")
```

The arguments declared for the function `fviz_eig()` are: X, the object that contains the principal component factor analysis; `barcolor`, the color of the bar chart outline; `barfill`, the filling of the bars of the graph; `linecolor`, the color of the line graph; and `ggtheme`, a function `theme()` from the package `ggplot2`, as presented in Chapter 7. Figure 12.7 shows the scree plot prepared by the previous routine.

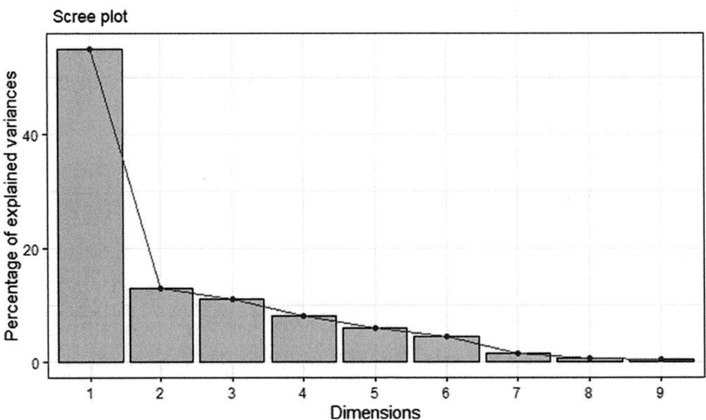

FIGURE 12.7 Scree plot.

Still using graph resources, we can visualize the contributions of the eigenvectors to the formation of each component using the rotation component of the created object `fa`:

```
data.frame(fa$rotation) %>%
  mutate(var = names(demographic_atlas[3:11])) %>%
  melt() %>%
  ggplot(aes(x = var, y = value, fill = var)) +
  geom_bar(stat = "identity") +
  facet_wrap(~variable) +
  labs(x = NULL, y = NULL, fill = "Legend:") +
  theme_bw() +
  theme(axis.text.x = element_text(angle = 90))
```

Figure 12.8 presents the result obtained from the previous code.

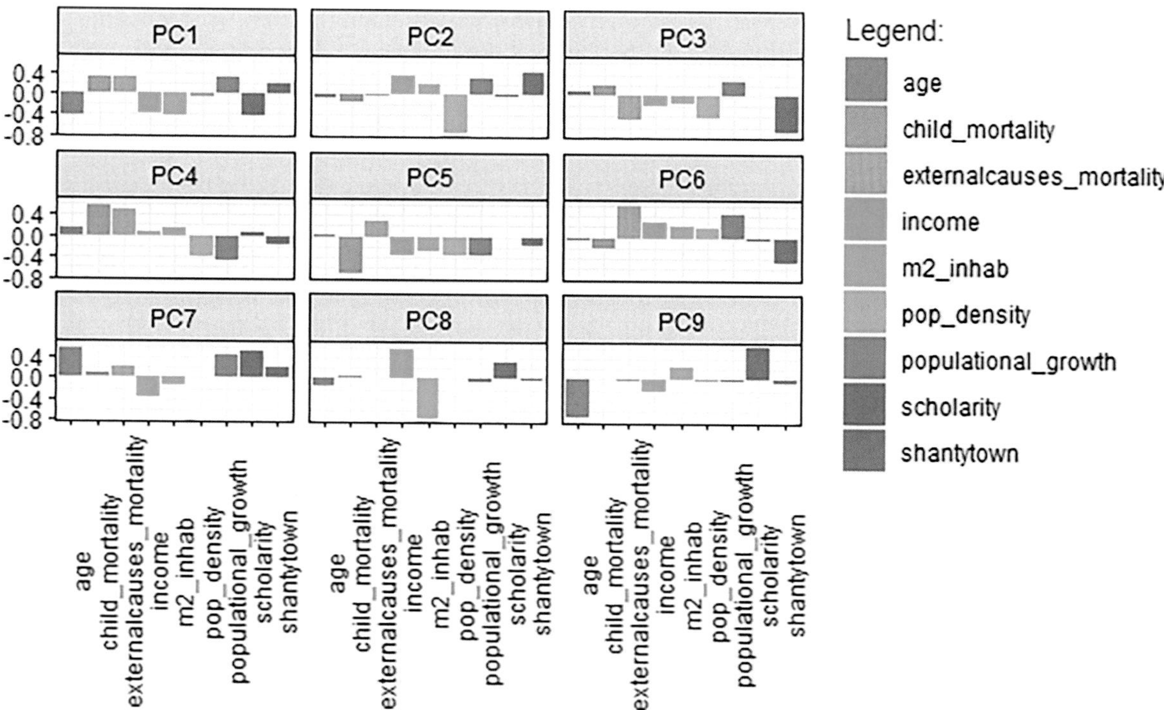

FIGURE 12.8 Contributions of the eigenvectors to the formation of each component.

According to Figure 12.8, in fact, the variables *income*, *m2_inhab*, *scholarity*, and *age* were predominant for the formation of the first component, although there is variance of these variables captured by the other components. On the other hand, the variables *pop_density* and *shantytown* had a large part of their variances captured by the second and third components, respectively.

Before extracting the factor loadings, the reader may have the following question: "How many principal components should I consider?" We adopt here the Kaiser criterion, that is, the selection of eigenvalues greater than 1. Thus, to extract the factor loadings, we can type:

```
eigen_greater_one <- sum((fa$sdev ^ 2) > 1)

loadings_fa <- fa$rotation[, 1:ncol(fa$x)] %*%
  diag(fa$sdev[1:ncol(fa$x)])

loadings_fa[ , 1:eigen_greater_one]
```

In the previous code, the first line seeks to capture how many eigenvalues are greater than 1, saving the response in the object `eigen_greater_one`. The second line of the code proposes multiplication of the matrix of eigenvectors whose eigenvalues are greater than 1 by the diagonal matrix of eigenvalues greater than 1. This procedure allows us to access to the factor loadings, which, as we already studied, relate to the correlations between the factors and the original variables. Figure 12.9 provides the factor loadings for the selected factors present so far in the object `loadings_fa`.

```
                              [,1]        [,2]
income                   -0.8321269  0.36897098
m2_inhab                 -0.9006058  0.22645316
scholarity               -0.9665432 -0.02459367
age                      -0.9601351 -0.06544713
child_mortality           0.6556993 -0.17663396
populational_growth       0.6967815  0.33744591
externalcauses_mortality  0.6665775 -0.04390999
shantytown                0.4571854  0.44283981
pop_density              -0.1662813 -0.79304783
```

FIGURE 12.9 Factor loadings.

Figure 12.9 shows that the variables *income*, *m2_inhab*, *scholarity*, and *age* have the highest correlations, in module, with the first factor. The variable *pop_density*, on the other hand, has a higher correlation, in module, with the second factor. We can calculate communalities, that is, the proportion of shared variance of each variable in each of the factors extracted, as follows:

```
communality <- rowSums(loadings_fa[ , 1:eigen_greater_one] ^ 2)
communality
```

ATTENTION: Following the latent root criterion adopted, that is, considering only eigenvalues > 1, if the reader extracts only one factor with an eigenvalue greater than 1, the function `rowSums()` of the previous routine must be disregarded, thus being commanded: `communality <- loadings_fa[ , 1:eigen_greater_one] ^ 2`.

If the reader wants to obtain the uniqueness, that is, the proportion of lost variance of each variable in each of the factors extracted, just type:

```
1 - communality
```

Table 12.2 summarizes the values of communality and uniqueness calculated by R.

TABLE 12.2 Communality and uniqueness.

Variable	Communality	Uniqueness
income	0.829	0.171
m2_inhab	0.862	0.138
scholarity	0.935	0.065
age	0.926	0.074
child_mortality	0.461	0.539
populational_growth	0.599	0.401
externalcauses_mortality	0.446	0.554
shantytown	0.405	0.595
pop_density	0.657	0.343

At this point, the loading plot of the rotated factor loadings can be obtained by typing the following code:

```
data.frame(unclass(fa_rotation$loadings)) %>%
  ggplot(aes(x = X1, y = X2)) +
  geom_point(color = "orange") +
  geom_hline(yintercept = 0, color = "darkorchid") +
  geom_vline(xintercept = 0, color = "darkorchid") +
  geom_text_repel(label = row.names(unclass(fa_rotation$loadings))) +
  labs(x = "Factor 1",
       y = "Factor 2") +
  theme_bw()
```

Figure 12.10 presents the loading plot obtained from the previous routine.

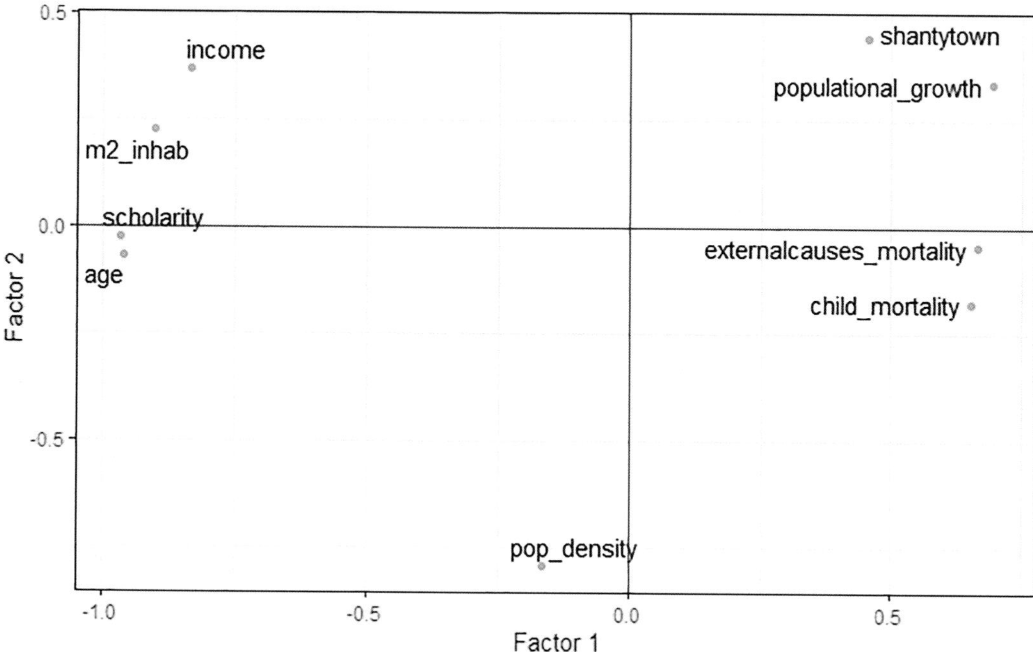

FIGURE 12.10 Loading plot with rotated loadings.

After developing these procedures, the reader may want to generate two new variables in the dataset, which correspond to the rotated factors obtained using the factor analysis.

For this, we must first calculate the factor scores, considering the adoption of two factors:

```
scores_fa <- t(fa$rotation[, 1:eigen_greater_one]) / fa$sdev[1:eigen_greater_one]
scores_fa
```

The factor scores calculated previously are shown in Table 12.3.

TABLE 12.3 Factor scores.

Variables	Scores PC1	Scores PC2
income	–0.168	0.317
m2_inhab	–0.182	0.194
scholarity	–0.195	–0.021
age	–0.194	–0.056
child_mortality	0.132	–0.152
populational_growth	0.141	0.290
externalcauses_mortality	0.134	–0.038
shantytown	0.092	0.380
pop_density	–0.034	–0.681

That said, we can type the following code to generate the new variables (which we call *F1* and *F2*),

```
demographic_atlas["F1"] <- rowSums(t(apply(X = scale(demographic_atlas[,3:11]),
                                           MARGIN = 1,
                                           FUN = function(x) -x * scores_fa[1, ])))
demographic_atlas["F2"] <- rowSums(t(apply(X = scale(demographic_atlas[,3:11]),
                                           MARGIN = 1,
                                           FUN = function(x) x * scores_fa[2, ])))
```

where *F1* and *F2* are the names of the corresponding variables to the first and second factors, respectively.

It is very important to mention that we multiplied the first factor scores by –1. Did you notice? This occurred in the arguments `FUN` of the functions `apply()`, when using the term –x. We use this resource for didactic purposes because the algorithm `prcomp()` generates factor loadings and scores with exchanged signals, in comparison, for example, with software such as *Stata* or IBM *SPSS*. In practice, the lack of this resource would generate the bias of identifying the district with the best score in our ranking with a negative sign. Furthermore, a curious reader could compare the graph in Figure 12.10 (generated in R) with another graph generated using the same procedure in *Stata* or IBM *SPSS*, and they will be "mirrored." **It is important to note that, compared to software such as *Stata* or *IBM SPSS*, R calculates the results of even factors (e.g., F2, F4, F6, F8) with the inverted sign, when the number of variables used is even; when the number of variables used is odd, in the factor analysis by principal components R inverts the signs of the odd factors (e.g., F1, F3, F5, F7). In this case, we used 9 variables, which explains the inversion of the signs of F1.**

From the factors extracted (variables *F1* and *F2*) and assuming them as performance indicators, we can establish a ranking. For this purpose, we will use the weighted rank-sum criterion in which a new variable is generated from multiplication of the values of each factor by the respective proportions of variance shared by the original variables. As we saw at the beginning of this section, the variance shared by the original variables can be obtained using the command `(fa$sdev ^ 2) / length(fa$sdev)`. Therefore we can type the following code:

```
shared_var <- (fa$sdev ^ 2 / length(fa$sdev))[1:eigen_greater_one]
```

What we did in the previous code was to save the shared variances for eigenvalues greater than 1 in an object. After this, we can type:

```
attach(demographic_atlas)
demographic_atlas["ranking"] <- F1 * shared_var[1] + F2 * shared_var[2]
```

With the previous routine, we just created a new variable called *ranking*. To order our observations in a decreasing way in relation to this new variable, we must type:

```
demographic_atlas <- demographic_atlas[order(demographic_atlas$ranking, decreasing = TRUE),]
demographic_atlas
```

Figure 12.11 shows the top 20 districts in our ranking according to the criteria adopted in this example.

```
demographic_atlas$district          demographic_atlas$ranking
 [1,] jardim paulista                1.41465734042385
 [2,] moema                          1.25438170051323
 [3,] santo amaro                    1.22730244960048
 [4,] alto de pinheiros              1.16624122791578
 [5,] morumbi                        1.02778323394175
 [6,] pinheiros                      1.02476341676112
 [7,] itaim bibi                     0.957764417736071
 [8,] consolacao                     0.895830135377558
 [9,] vila mariana                   0.891503847301929
[10,] perdizes                       0.885331130664469
[11,] campo belo                     0.778651794675638
[12,] lapa                           0.746737088695235
[13,] barra funda                    0.645776540894101
[14,] saude                          0.63256989157931
[15,] santana                        0.604366238821405
[16,] cambuci                        0.55186505943472
[17,] butanta                        0.539078578648445
[18,] socorro                        0.505814943921834
[19,] mooca                          0.50515571274276
[20,] tatuape                        0.454762491970609
```

FIGURE 12.11 Top 20 districts in our ranking.

In Chapter 27, we will revisit the results of the ranking shown in Figure 12.11 to establish an interactive choroplethic map of the 96 districts in the municipality of São Paulo.

Final remarks

Factor analysis allows us to improve decision-making processes based on the behavior and the interdependence among quantitative variables that have a relative correlation intensity. Because the factors generated from the original variables are also quantitative variables, the outputs of the factor analysis can be inputs in other multivariate techniques, such as the cluster analysis. The stratification of each factor into ranges may allow the association among these ranges and the categories of other qualitative variables to be evaluated using correspondence analysis.

The use of factors in confirmatory multivariate techniques may also make sense when researchers intend to elaborate diagnostics about the behavior of a certain dependent variable and use the extracted factors as explanatory variables, which eliminates possible multicollinearity problems because the factors are orthogonal. The consideration of a certain qualitative variable obtained from the stratification of a certain factor into ranges can be used, for example, in a multinomial logistic regression model, which allows preparation of a diagnostic on the probabilities each observation has of being in each range as a result of the behavior of other explanatory variables not initially considered in the factor analysis (Fávero and Belfiore, 2019).

Exercise

(1) The general manager of a store that belongs to a chain of drugstores wants to find out its consumers' perception of eight attributes, which are described as follows (Fávero and Belfiore, 2019):

Attribute (variable)	Description
assortment	Perception of the variety of goods
replacement	Perception of the quality and speed of inventory replacement
layout	Perception of the store's layout
comfort	Perception of thermal, acoustic, and visual comfort inside the store
cleanliness	Perception of the store's general cleanliness
services	Perception of the quality of the services rendered
prices	Perception of the store's prices compared with the competition
discounts	Perception of the store's discount policy

To do this, the general manager carried out a survey with 1,700 clients at the store for some time. The questionnaire was structured based on groups of attributes, and each question corresponding to an attribute asked the consumer to assign a score from 0 to 10 depending on his or her perception of that attribute, with 0 corresponding to an entirely negative perception and 10 corresponding to the best perception possible. Because the store's general manager is rather experienced, he decided in advance to gather the questions in three groups, such that the complete questionnaire would be as follows:

Based on your perception, fill out the questionnaire below with scores from 0 to 10, in which 0 means that your perception is entirely negative in relation to a certain attribute, and 10 means that your perception is the best possible.	***Score***
Products and Store Environment	
Please rate the store's variety of goods on a scale from 0 to 10.	
Please rate the store's quality and speed of inventory replacement on a scale from 0 to 10.	
Please rate the store's layout on a scale from 0 to 10.	
Please rate the store's thermal, acoustic, and visual comfort on a scale from 0 to 10.	
Please rate the store's general cleanliness on a scale from 0 to 10.	
Services	
Please rate the quality of the services rendered in our store on a scale from 0 to 10.	
Prices and Discount Policy	
Please rate the store's prices compared with the competition on a scale from 0 to 10.	
Please rate our discount policy on a scale from 0 to 10.	

The complete dataset developed by the store's general manager is shown in the file `drugstore_perception.RData` (Fávero and Belfiore, 2019). We would like you to:

(a) Present the correlation matrix between each pair of variables. Based on the magnitude of the values of Pearson's correlation coefficients, is it possible to identify any indication that the factor analysis may group the variables into factors?

(b) By using the result of Bartlett's test of sphericity, is it possible to state at the significance level of 0.05 that the principal component factor analysis is adequate?

(c) How many factors are extracted in the analysis considering the latent root criterion? Which eigenvalue(s) correspond(s) to the factor(s) extracted, as well as to the proportion(s) of variance shared by all of the variables to form this(these) factor(s)?

(d) What is the total percentage of variance loss of the original variables resulting from the extraction of the factor(s) based on the latent root criterion?

(e) For each variable, what are the loading and the proportion of shared variance to form the factor(s)?

(f) By demanding the extraction of three factors, to the detriment of the latent root criterion, and based on the new factor loadings, is it possible to confirm the construct of the questionnaire proposed by the store's general manager? In other words, do the variables of each group in the questionnaire, in fact, end up showing greater sharing of variance with a common factor?

(g) Discuss the impact of the decision to extract three factors on the communality values?

Supplementary data sets

```
atlasambiental.RData
demographic_atlas.RData
drugstore_perception.RData
```

Please access supplementary data files here: https://doi.org/10.17632/55623jkwrp.3

CHAPTER

13

Simple and multiple correspondence analysis

AT THE END OF THIS CHAPTER, YOU WILL BE ABLE TO:

- Know how to calculate and interpret the main partial and total inertia.
- Generate coordinates of the categories of variables, and build perceptual maps.
- Understand the differences between the binary matrix method and the Burt matrix method for the elaboration of the multiple correspondence analysis.
- Develop simple and multiple correspondence analysis techniques algebraically and using R, and interpret their results.

R-based language packages used in this chapter

```
library(plotly)
library(tidyverse)
library(sjPlot)
library(FactoMineR)
library(ggrepel)
library(amap)
```

Don't forget to define the R working directory (the location where your datasets are installed):

```
setwd("C:/book/chapter13")
```

Data Science, Analytics and Machine Learning with R
https://doi.org/10.1016/B978-0-12-824271-1.00013-5

Applications in R

For the following practical examples, we will use, for SCA, data regarding the contagion of the Sars-CoV-2 virus for the first 28 weeks of 2020 in the American continent. As for MCA, we will study the associations of some symptoms regarding typically tropical diseases, whose main vector of spread is the *Aedes aegypti* mosquito.

Correspondence Analysis

The data used in this section were taken from the European Centre for Disease Prevention and Control and can be found in the file `covid_28weeks.RData`. We ask the reader to load the dataset in R, as usual:

```
load("covid_28weeks.RData")
```

The basis concerns the spread of the Sars-CoV-2 virus during the first 28 weeks of 2020 in the American continent. It has three variables, which are described in Table 13.1.

TABLE 13.1 Description of the variables of the dataset present in the file `covid_28weeks.RData`.

Variable	Description
Schedule	Variable identifying the date regarding the data collected in *year, month, day* format. Some countries have more days considered than others because the Covid-19 pandemic hit the territories of the American continent asymmetrically.
Country	Polychotomic categorical variable identifying each country on the American continent.
let_q5	Polychotomic categorical variable regarding the level of lethality of the Sars-CoV-2 virus for each time period in each country on the American continent. Here, lethality is understood as the simple ratio between the number of deaths caused by Covid-19 and the number infected on the same day by the Sars-CoV-2 virus. After that, for each week considered, the lethality data were divided into their respective quintiles. Thus for a given period, L5 represents the highest level of lethality, L4 represents the second highest level of lethality, and so on until L1.

The function `summary()` can be used to give the reader an idea of the minimum and maximum dates to which the data refer, in addition to obtaining a kind of frequency table about the variables *country* and *let_q5*.

```
summary(covid_28weeks)
```

Getting straight to the point, if the reader has mastered the basics and just wants to implement a CA model, he or she can skip to the end of this section. R is very practical for execution of this kind of algorithm and, in short, the application of the function `CA()` from the package `FactoMineR` would suffice to a contingency table that will be established in the next code chunk. However, if the reader is interested in the fundamentals regarding the technique as well as knowing some routines that can make his or her work more elegant, we suggest reading this entire section.

That said, as demonstrated in the "Simple correspondence analysis" section, implementation of a CA starts with construction of a contingency table. The most direct way to build it is with the function `table()` from the base language of R:

```
tab <- table(covid_28weeks$country,
             covid_28weeks$let_q5)
```

Briefly, the function `table()` requires declaration of the variable whose categories will be considered in line and declaration of the variable to be placed in a column in the contingency table. The final result is fundamental for the future application of the algorithm `CA()`, however, visually speaking, the function `table()` does not bring such an attractive result, as shown in Figure 13.1.

```
Anguilla                          166   0   0   0   0
Antigua_and_Barbuda                21   0  36  40  76
Argentina                           3  18 106  57   2
Aruba                              24  36 110   0   0
Bahamas                            15  18  26   8 108
Barbados                           19   1   0  54 101
Belize                             13  33   2  26  95
Bermuda                            18   0   0 133  22
Bolivia                            17   0  17 132  14
Bonaire_Saint_Eustatius_and_Saba  160   0   0   0   0
Brazil                             21   7  32 109  27
British_Virgin_Islands             24   4   7   7 124
Canada                             44  28   8  21  95
Cayman_Islands                      1 147  10   3  12
Chile                              18  91  79   0   0
Colombia                           11  13  63  95   0
Costa_Rica                         11 174   0   0   0
Cuba                                4   1  63 109   1
Dominica                          170   0   0   0   0
Dominican_Republic                 10  47  69  56   0
Ecuador                             8   7   9  71  92
El_Salvador                        13  14 127  20   0
Falkland_Islands_(Malvinas)       158   0   0   0   0
Greenland                         173   0   0   0   0
Grenada                           170   0   0   0   0
Guatemala                           1   8  58 105   6
Guyana                              0   0  19  59 100
Haiti                              18  33  76  15  31
Honduras                           13   3  84  50  29
Jamaica                            12 128  20  19   1
Mexico                             13   8   5  11 148
Montserrat                         35   0   0   0 136
Nicaragua                           9   0  69  40  56
Panama                              1  12 167   1   2
Paraguay                            9 116  16  38   2
Peru                               12   9  84  80   0
Puerto_Rico                         0  64  34  67   0
Saint_Kitts_and_Nevis             167   0   0   0   0
Saint_Lucia                       178   0   0   0   0
Saint_Martin                        7   0   0  27 133
Saint_Vincent_and_the_Grenadines  169   0   0   0   0
Suriname                           15  58  41   1  58
Trinidad_and_Tobago                13  22  13  50  82
Turks_and_Caicos_Islands           12  38  23  12  83
United_States_of_America           40  16  15 123   2
United_States_Virgin_Islands       12  36  33  33  54
Uruguay                            15  21 142   0   0
Venezuela                          12 117  29  19   0
```

FIGURE 13.1 Contingency table built with the function `table()` from the base language of R.

If the reader wants to build a more elegant contingency table than the one shown in Figure 13.1, we suggest using the function `sjt.xtab()` from the package `sjPlot`. **In any case, we insist: for the logic followed in this work, it is absolutely necessary that the reader has created an object that contains a contingency table established by the function `table()`!** The function `sjt.xtab()` can be written by the following command:

```
sjt.xtab(var.row = covid_28weeks$country,
         var.col = covid_28weeks$let_q5,
         show.exp = TRUE,
         show.row.prc = TRUE,
         show.col.prc = TRUE)
```

In the previous routine, we chose to use the following arguments: `var.row` to assign to R which categories of the selected variable would appear in the lines of the contingency table; `var.col` to indicate which categories of the chosen variable would be arranged in columns; `show.exp` to highlight the expected values of each category; `show.row.prc` to explain the percentage values regarding the lines; and `show.col.prc` to point out the percentage values regarding the columns. The output of this command will only be found in the codes attached to this work because it is too large a figure and would therefore take several pages. However, an attentive reader will notice that the discussed algorithm, at the end of the established contingency table, presents the result of the χ^2 test, along with its degrees of freedom. That said, for the case in question, we have:

$$\chi^2 = \sum_{i=1}^{I} \sum_{j=1}^{J} \frac{\left[n_{ij} - \left(\frac{\sum c_{j\cdot} \sum r_i}{N}\right)\right]^2}{\left(\frac{\sum c_{j\cdot} \sum r_i}{N}\right)} = 14,903.029, \text{with 188 degrees of freedom.}$$

A more complete way to calculate the χ^2 test can be done with the function `chisq.test()`, which was studied in Chapter 7:

```
chi2 <- chisq.test(tab)
```

The previous routine will point out the corresponding *P*-value associated with the value of $\chi^2 = 14{,}903.029$, for 188 degrees of freedom, indicating that the association of the categories of the variables studied does not occur randomly, at a level of 5% of significance, *ceteris paribus*.

The function `chisq.test()` is more interesting because, in addition to pointing out the respective *P*-value for the case, when contained in an object, it also calculates the observed values (component `observed`), the expected values (component `expected`), the standardized residuals (component `residuals`), and adjusted standardized residuals (component `stdres`). We can use the operator `$` after the object created, which we call `chi2` to have access to everything described.

In fact, using the component `stdres`, we will establish a heat map that shows the values of positive adjusted standardized residuals greater than 1.96:

```
data.frame(chi2$stdres) %>%
  rename(country = 1,
         let_q5 = 2) %>%
  ggplot(aes(x = country, y = let_q5, fill = Freq, label = round(Freq,3))) +
  geom_tile() +
  geom_text(size = 3, angle = 90) +
  scale_fill_gradient2(low = "darkorchid",
                       mid = "white",
                       high = "orange",
                       midpoint = 0) +
  labs(x = NULL, y = NULL) +
  theme(legend.title = element_blank(),
        panel.background = element_rect("white"),
        legend.position = "bottom",
        axis.text.x = element_text(angle = 90))
```

Figure 13.2 presents the result of the previous routine.

	L1	L2	L3	L4	L5
Anguilla	22.969	-5.616	-6.507	-6.505	-6.507
Antigua_and_Barbuda	-3.767	-5.735	0.267	1.04	7.948
Argentina	-7.294	-2.283	12.75	3.673	-6.526
Aruba	-3.126	1.982	14.718	-6.584	-6.587
Bahamas	-4.901	-1.99	-1.72	-5.154	13.938
Barbados	-4.189	-5.559	-6.685	3.631	12.601
Belize	-5.084	1.381	-6.178	-1.513	11.886
Bermuda	-4.305	-5.735	-6.646	18.902	-2.421
Bolivia	-4.696	-5.853	-3.58	18.087	-4.145
Bonaire_Saint_Eustatius_and_Saba	22.542	-5.511	-6.386	-6.384	-6.386
Brazil	-4.486	-4.723	-1.302	12.615	-2.206
British_Virgin_Islands	-2.985	-4.754	-5.136	-5.133	17.791
Canada	-0.61	-0.551	-5.638	-3.286	10.079
Cayman_Islands	-7.35	25.303	-4.725	-6.067	-4.341
Chile	-4.76	12.464	7.632	-6.932	-6.934
Colombia	-5.804	-3.208	4.981	10.982	-6.82
Costa_Rica	-5.884	29.619	-6.877	-6.875	-6.877
Cuba	-6.933	-5.611	5.187	13.905	-6.554
Dominica	23.25	-5.684	-6.587	-6.584	-6.587
Dominican_Republic	-5.979	3.795	6.105	3.675	-6.82
Ecuador	-6.455	-4.545	-5.252	6.215	10.092
El_Salvador	-5.229	-2.805	17.654	-2.832	-6.665
Falkland_Islands_(Malvinas)	22.398	-5.476	-6.345	-6.343	-6.345
Greenland	23.458	-5.735	-6.646	-6.643	-6.646
Grenada	23.25	-5.684	-6.587	-6.584	-6.587
Guatemala	-7.462	-4.154	4.24	13.148	-5.607
Guyana	-7.639	-5.819	-3.145	4.435	12.194
Haiti	-4.305	1.232	7.948	-3.762	-0.693
Honduras	-5.371	-5.213	9.101	2.685	-1.286
Jamaica	-5.575	20.655	-3.015	-3.2	-6.593
Mexico	-5.538	-4.301	-5.948	-4.83	20.626
Montserrat	-1.179	-5.701	-6.606	-6.604	19.659
Nicaragua	-5.943	-5.752	6.547	0.998	4.058
Panama	-7.574	-3.437	24.36	-6.65	-6.466
Paraguay	-6.128	18.088	-3.796	0.341	-6.425
Peru	-5.711	-4.096	8.732	7.995	-6.877
Puerto_Rico	-7.349	8.232	0.195	6.686	-6.487
Saint_Kitts_and_Nevis	23.04	-5.633	-6.527	-6.525	-6.527
Saint_Lucia	23.802	-5.819	-6.743	-6.741	-6.743
Saint_Martin	-6.119	-5.633	-6.527	-1.248	19.458
Saint_Vincent_and_the_Grenadines	23.18	-5.667	-6.567	-6.564	-6.567
Suriname	-4.842	6.511	1.227	-6.451	4.492
Trinidad_and_Tobago	-5.399	-1.297	-4.333	2.64	8.662
Turks_and_Caicos_Islands	-5.236	2.489	-2.066	-4.206	9.622
United_States_of_America	-1.284	-2.935	-4.374	15.145	-6.722
United_States_Virgin_Islands	-5.236	2.061	-0.118	-0.115	3.973
Uruguay	-4.99	-1.447	20.147	-6.741	-6.743
Venezuela	-5.492	18.627	-1.217	-3.113	-6.724

0 10 20

FIGURE 13.2 Heat map of adjusted standardized residuals.

In the case of Figure 13.2, we chose the color orange to show positive values greater than 1.96 of the adjusted standardized residuals. The greater the color intensity, the greater the magnitude of the metric. So, we can check, for example, the dependence between the categories Anguilla *(country)* and L1 *(let_q5)*, between Antigua and Barbuda *(country)* and L5 *(let_q5)*, and so on because their adjusted standardized residuals are, respectively, 22,969 and 7,948 (positive and greater than 1.96).

Having verified the existence of a statistically significant association between the variables *country* and *let_q5* and identified the dependency relationships between their categories, we can type the command from the package `anacor`, which calculates the coordinates of each category from which the perceptual map can be constructed in R:

```
ca_covid <- CA(tab)
```

An attentive reader will notice that the function `CA()` has serious graphical limitations within the scope of a technique that is, by and large, visual. At the time of the previous command, R will immediately generate a perceptual map that is difficult to read because of the quantity of observations considered (Figure 13.3). In the following pages, we will continue to discuss what happens in the background of the algorithm, and the reader will have access to a much less polluted perceptual map at the end of the section.

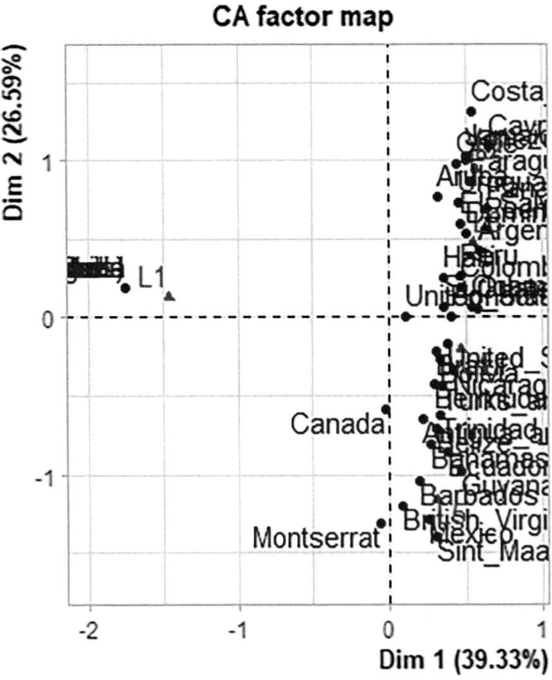

FIGURE 13.3 Perceptual map generated with the function `CA()`.

For the case studied, from a dataset of 8,458 observations, from Figure 13.3, we can say that dimensions 1 and 2 explain 39.33% and 26.59%, respectively, of the total principal inertia (I_T). If the reader wishes to verify *in loco* how the variance explained by dimension is calculated, the big step is defining the matrix **W**. However, an attentive reader will notice that it is necessary to find matrix **A** to define matrix **W**.

In R, to find matrix **A**, from a table of contingencies (our object `tab`), divide the terms of matrix $\mathbf{E}_{\mathbf{standardized}}$ by the square root of the sample size ($\sqrt{N}$). We will adopt the second path for didactic reasons, but if the reader wants the step by step to define the matrix **A** involving the calculation of the masses of the rows and columns, the definition of the matrices **P**, $\mathbf{D}_r$, $\mathbf{D}_c$ and $\mathbf{P} - rc'$, just type the following codes:

```
#P matrix
P <- 1/nrow(covid_28weeks) * tab

#Column profile
column_profile <- apply(tab, MARGIN = 1, FUN = sum) / nrow(covid_28weeks)

#Row profile
row_profile <- apply(tab, MARGIN = 2, FUN = sum) / nrow(covid_28weeks)

#Dr matrix
Dr <- diag(column_profile)

#Dc matrix
Dc <- diag(row_profile)

#rc matrix
rc <- column_profile %o% row_profile

#A matrix
A <- diag(diag(Dr) ^ (-1/2)) %*% (P - rc) %*% diag(diag(Dc) ^ (-1/2))
```

As we have already cautioned, the easiest way to determine matrix **A** would be to simply standardize matrix $\mathbf{E}_{\mathbf{standardized}}$ (present in the component `residuals` of the object `chi2`) by the square root of the sample size:

```
A_matrix <- chi2$residuals / sqrt(nrow(covid_28weeks))
```

Found matrix **A**, just perform the operation $\mathbf{W} = \mathbf{A}'\,\mathbf{A}$:

```
W_matrix <- t(A_matrix) %*% A_matrix
```

That said, in R, to extract eigenvalues from a given matrix, we must use the function `eigen()` from its base language:

```
eigenvalues <- eigen(W_matrix)
```

An attentive reader will notice that in addition to extracting eigenvalues from a given matrix, the function `eigen()` also extracts their respective eigenvectors, as shown in Figure 13.4.

```
eigen() decomposition
$values
[1] 6.930476e-01 4.685610e-01 3.693807e-01 2.310145e-01 1.221245e-15

$vectors
           [,1]        [,2]        [,3]         [,4]       [,5]
[1,]  0.8649353 -0.09290271 -0.01691918 -0.002144228 -0.4929150
[2,] -0.2720201 -0.54643866  0.66142026 -0.181444181 -0.3962463
[3,] -0.2955913 -0.30766011 -0.47105861  0.629307168 -0.4472665
[4,] -0.2513444  0.13218858 -0.45789243 -0.713973136 -0.4471343
[5,] -0.1653597  0.76200086  0.36149037  0.247564662 -0.4472665
```

FIGURE 13.4 Eigenvalues and eigenvectors of matrix **W**.

In Figure 13.4, we can see the existence of five eigenvalues from our matrix **W** at the top and their respective eigenvectors at the bottom. However, remember that the **perceptual map** is a **two-dimensional graph**, so in truth, the first two dimensions will be taken into account for its construction. This is why the explained variances, according to Figure 13.3, can be found algebraically by dividing the first two eigenvalues of the matrix **W** by the total inertia (I_T). To calculate I_T, we can:

```
It <- chi2$statistic / nrow(covid_28weeks)
```

So, to select the first two eigenvalues of the matrix **W** and divide by I_T, we can:

```
explained_var <- eigenvalues$values[1:2] / It
explained_var
```

After the previous command, the reader can confirm that the variances explained by dimensions 1 and 2 in Figure 13.3 are, in fact, 39.33% and 26.59%, respectively.

If the reader wants to know how the coordinates of the perceptual map present in Figure 13.3 were extracted, it is enough that the singular value is decomposed. For this, the reader must apply the function `svd()` in matrix **A**. However, we must remember an important detail! Although the perceptual map is a two-dimensional object, according to which it is detached, the dimensionality of our data is given by $m = \min(I-1, J-1)$ of our matrix **A**, which, for the case studied, has a 48×5 dimension:

$$m = \min(48-1,\ 5-1) = 4$$

Thus for decomposition of the singular value, we must consider a total of four dimensions:

```
dimensions <- min(nrow(A_matrix) - 1, ncol(A_matrix) - 1)
```

After that, we can type the command:

```
decomp <- svd(x = A_matrix,
              nu = dimensions,
              nv = dimensions)

decomp
```

The contents of the object `decomp` are shown in Figure 13.5.

The component `$d` at the top of Figure 13.5 shows the singular values.

```
#Row variable - abscissa coordinate
Xr_country <- diag((decomp$d[1]) * diag(diag(Dr)^(-1/2)) * decomp$u[,1])

#Row variable - ordinate coordinate
Yr_country <- diag((decomp$d[2]) * diag(diag(Dr)^(-1/2)) * decomp$u[,2])

#Column variable - abscissa coordinate
Xr_letq5 <- diag((decomp$d[1]) * diag(diag(Dc)^(-1/2)) * decomp$v[,1])

#Column variable - ordinate coordinate
Yr_letq5 <- diag((decomp$d[2]) * diag(diag(Dc)^(-1/2)) * decomp$v[,2])
```

A curious reader can compare the coordinates calculated by the previous routine with the coordinates existing in the components `row` and `col` of the object `ca_covid` and verify that they are exactly the same:

```
#Dimensions 1 and 2 row coordinates
ca_covid$row$coord

#Dimensions 1 and 2 column coordinates
ca_covid$col$coord
```

Finally, to obtain new access to the perceptual map present in the object `ca_covid`, the reader can type the function `plot()`, as follows:

```
plot(ca_covid)
```

```
$d
[1] 8.324948e-01 6.845152e-01 6.077670e-01 4.806397e-01 1.617933e-16

$u
             [,1]          [,2]          [,3]         [,4]
 [1,] -0.295290988 -0.0385738897  0.0079120741 -0.001267942
 [2,]  0.037263796  0.1359682164  0.0247196419  0.049460332
 [3,]  0.105276583 -0.0908998975  0.1816217225  0.084561833
 [4,]  0.055394226 -0.1581786357  0.0776415211  0.239757757
 [5,]  0.047041394  0.1691044103 -0.1098747807  0.128736463
 [6,]  0.034598342  0.2198347020 -0.0369860706 -0.052778420
 [7,]  0.051142104  0.1468766201 -0.1413191482 -0.002238940
 [8,]  0.050953040  0.0886549805  0.1619153109 -0.344464470
 [9,]  0.059171721  0.0568048047  0.1898218675 -0.302134366
[10,] -0.289905290 -0.0378703554  0.0077677689 -0.001244816
[11,]  0.056310689  0.0483360903  0.1438151222 -0.189670210
[12,]  0.015244416  0.2446963650 -0.1271003567  0.114781832
[13,] -0.005385212  0.1312195094 -0.1176675419  0.027945664
[14,]  0.111111321 -0.2275971469 -0.3284020909 -0.088398300
[15,]  0.079155823 -0.2122719450 -0.0888299042  0.114515063
[16,]  0.081964466 -0.0415068254  0.1887310225 -0.115795754
[17,]  0.096169932 -0.2826564910 -0.3815397526 -0.132601520
[18,]  0.094906764 -0.0137405756  0.2355194986 -0.144688040
[19,] -0.298827533 -0.0390358689  0.0080068329 -0.001283127
[20,]  0.088875213 -0.1149284801  0.0688378228 -0.023310942
[21,]  0.067470345  0.1862965504 -0.0046827522 -0.087722582
[22,]  0.081168330 -0.1242801125  0.1781008006  0.240596772
[23,] -0.288087684 -0.0376329214  0.0077190677 -0.001237012
[24,] -0.301452716 -0.0393787967  0.0080771725 -0.001294400
[25,] -0.298827533 -0.0390358689  0.0080068329 -0.001283127
[26,]  0.101138276 -0.0117315456  0.2017393908 -0.146506976
[27,]  0.080955176  0.2080505829 -0.0005255248 -0.020561516
[28,]  0.060762534 -0.0530544031  0.0216036343  0.146112928
[29,]  0.071841736 -0.0002132152  0.1493292621  0.089569475
[30,]  0.088670806 -0.2192923069 -0.2314085647 -0.101694089
[31,]  0.045023319  0.2785100469 -0.1525728949  0.112552233
[32,] -0.011121747  0.2734443904 -0.1487399019  0.129966195
[33,]  0.072279653  0.0699325803  0.0931522334  0.110052934
[34,]  0.114077913 -0.1501947050  0.2053811444  0.382931260
[35,]  0.093699876 -0.1865867406 -0.1850711506 -0.151699772
[36,]  0.082205620 -0.0569960630  0.2049088938 -0.022831287
[37,]  0.105817882 -0.1135704414 -0.0033554011 -0.155779847
[38,] -0.296179083 -0.0386899016  0.0079358699 -0.001271755
[39,] -0.305777940 -0.0399438011  0.0081930632 -0.001312972
[40,] -0.297947332 -0.0389208882  0.0079832487 -0.001279348
[41,]  0.052623461  0.2867158930 -0.1102055094  0.053346028
[42,]  0.062160787 -0.0143772052 -0.1346219180  0.105899147
[43,]  0.057735353  0.1334975393 -0.0502144263 -0.044331529
[44,]  0.058105618  0.0912628652 -0.1291804302  0.072762006
[45,]  0.019207754 -0.0001715351  0.1467125423 -0.293598508
[46,]  0.064473045  0.0332712781 -0.0479992045  0.012374956
[47,]  0.080218626 -0.1541425587  0.1542316369  0.322366559
[48,]  0.087481949 -0.2124568048 -0.1948364842 -0.073395710

$v
           [,1]        [,2]        [,3]         [,4]
[1,] -0.8649353 -0.09290271  0.01691918 -0.002144228
[2,]  0.2720201 -0.54643866 -0.66142026 -0.181444181
[3,]  0.2955913 -0.30766011  0.47105861  0.629307168
[4,]  0.2513444  0.13218858  0.45789243 -0.713973136
[5,]  0.1653597  0.76200086 -0.36149037  0.247564662
```

FIGURE 13.5 The decompositions of the singular values of matrix **A**.

However, if a more elegant perceptual map is desired, the reader can use the coordinates present in the components `row` and `col` of the object `ca_covid` next to the function `ggplot()` from the package `tidyverse`.

The first step is to join all of the coordinates of the perceptual map present in the object `ca_covid` in a single data frame that we will call `ca_coordinates`:

```
ca_coordinates <- rbind(ca_covid$row$coord, ca_covid$col$coord)
```

As in the object `ca_coordinates`, the coordinates regarding the categories of the variable in line and the categories of the variable in columns were mixed, so we must create some kind of indexer so R knows who each coordinate belongs to when we command the elaboration of the new perceptual map.

```
id_var <- apply(covid_28weeks[,c(1,15)],
                MARGIN = 2,
                FUN = function(x) nlevels(as.factor(x)))
```

Ready! Just join the object `ca_coordinates` and the object `id_var` in a single data frame that we will call `ca_coordinates_final`:

```
ca_coordinates_final <- data.frame(ca_coordinates,
                                   Variable = rep(names(id_var), id_var))
```

Finally, we can plot our perceptual map, identical to that of Figure 13.3, but more visually elegant:

```
ca_coordinates %>%
  rownames_to_column() %>%
  rename(Category = 1) %>%
  ggplot(aes(x = Dim.1, y = Dim.2, label = Category, color = Variable)) +
  geom_point() +
  geom_label_repel() +
  labs(x = paste("Dimension 1:", paste0(round(ca_covid$eig[1,2], digits = 2), "%")),
       y = paste("Dimension 2:", paste0(round(ca_covid$eig[2,2], digits = 2), "%"))) +
  scale_color_manual("Variable:",
                     values = c("darkorchid", "orange")) +
  theme_bw()
```

The perceptual map generated by the previously entered codes is shown in Figure 13.6.

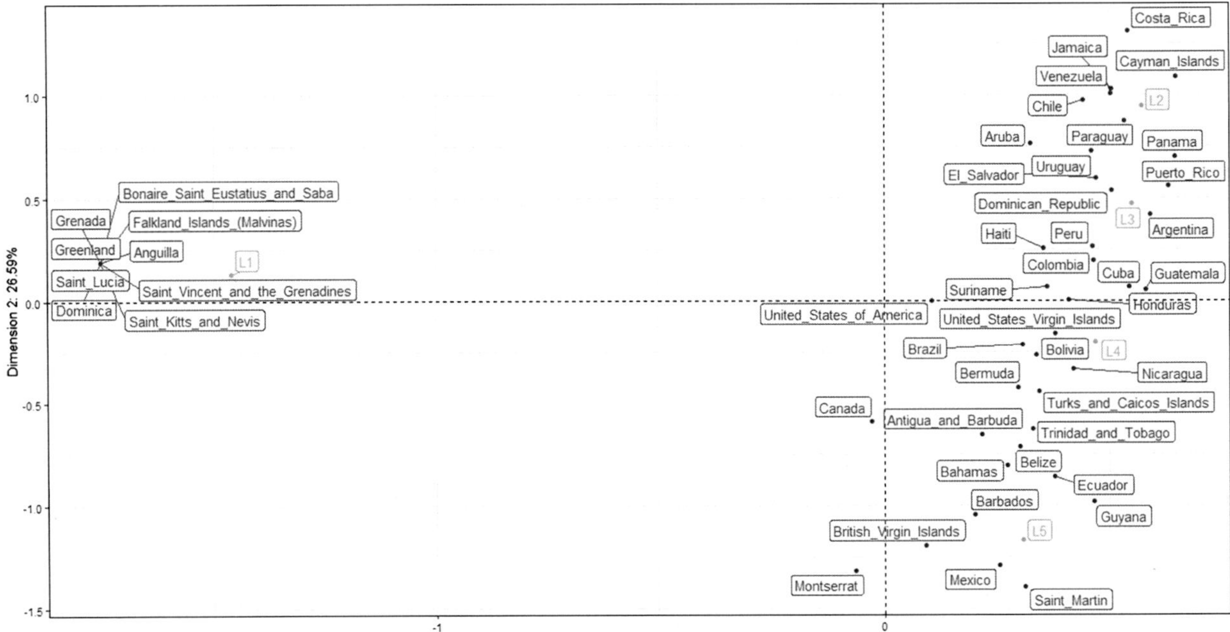

FIGURE 13.6 Perceptual map of the Covid-19 pandemic situation in American countries and territories after the first 28 weeks of 2020.

The analysis of a perceptual map arranged in its traditional form, that is, bidimensionally, must be done together with the calculated values of the adjusted standardized residuals (see Figure 13.2) to avoid hasty interpretations that lead to recurrent mistakes.

For example, because of the two-dimensional arrangement of the perceptual map present in Figure 13.6, we are commonly compelled to perceive the distances between the categories of the study variables in a purely Euclidean way. Thus we could be led to think that, although the results shown in Figure 13.2 indicate a strong association of Antigua and Barbuda with the category L5 of the variable *let_q5* because 22.969 > 1.96, Figure 13.6 also seems to indicate a strong association with the category L4 of the variable *let_q5*.

This situation is a kind of optical illusion. The reader should remember that the perceptual map present in Figure 13.6, being two-dimensional, represents only two of the four dimensions calculated for our data. In this case, dimension 1 explains 39.33% of the variances, and dimension 2 explains 26.59%. In other words, Figure 13.6 can explain 65.92% of the variances (39.33% + 25.59%). Therefore if Figure 13.6 can explain 65.92% of the variances, then 34.08% of the variances were not explained by our two-dimensional perceptual map. If we adopt one more dimension (i.e., three-dimensionality), it would be better to understand the distances between countries and the levels of lethality of Covid-19 in the first 28 weeks of 2020 in America. We will do this in the Appendix of this chapter, so when checking the three-dimensional perceptual map in the Appendix, we can be sure, for example, that the distance between Antigua and Barbuda and the L4 level is, in fact, higher than Figure 13.6 implies.

A good analogy to solidify an understanding of this explanation is the act of looking at the night sky with the naked eye. There will be countless stars, but the third dimension (i.e., depth) is impaired in this scenario. Thus it is not possible to state that the star immediately to the left of a reference star is necessarily closer to that celestial object of reference, than, for example, a third astronomical object considered. The package `anacor`'s algorithm loops around in the "sky of our perceptual map" and tries to take the best possible photograph, but in two-dimensionality there is a loss of depth.

Another possible example would be to hold a completely transparent acrylic cube. By observing it directly in its three-dimensional form, the observer can capture all information about its three-dimensionality; the observer would be able to notice, without exception, that the object is the union of segments of lines that, when united, form right angles to each other. However, when letting the light pass through this cube and observing the shadow formed by this object on any flat surface, the observer would start to see the projection of the cube in two-dimensional form, and by discarding one dimension (depth), he or she would have the impression that the observed object also has non-right angles (i.e., acute and/or obtuse) in addition to a very different shape from when observed directly. This is therefore one of the consequences of giving up a dimension.

Multiple correspondence analysis

As stated at the beginning of the "Applications in R" section, to exemplify the use of MCA in R-based language, we will use a dataset about the associations between symptoms of three tropical diseases transmitted by the same vector, that is, in this case, the *Aedes aegypti* mosquito. The data can be found in the file `symptoms.RData`, whose variables are presented in Table 13.2.

TABLE 13.2 Description of the variables of the dataset present in the file `symptoms.RData`.

Variable	Description
id	Identifying variable of the patient considered in the study.
disease	Polychotomic categorical variable in which each category represents a disease considered in the study that is transmitted by the *Aedes aegypti* mosquito: *dengue*, *chikungunya*, and *zika*.
fever	Polychotomic categorical variable that indicates the level of fever verified for each individual in the dataset at the time of the hospital visit: *no_fever* for a patient with normal body temperature; *low_fever* for a subfebrile patient (i.e., below 38°C); and *high_fever* for a patient with high fever (i.e., above 38°C at the time of measurement at the hospital).
itch	Polychotomic categorical variable that indicates the level of itchiness in the body reported to the doctor by the patient: *mild* for a mild level of reported itching; *moderate* for a moderate level of reported itching; and *intense* for an intense level of reported itching.
arthralgia	Polychotomic categorical variable that indicates the level of joint pain reported to the physician by the patient: *mild* for a mild level of joint pain; *moderate* for a moderate level of joint pain; and *intense* for an intense level of joint pain.

Obviously, the three diseases addressed have different fundamental characteristics and medical examinations for their correct identification. However, for didactic reasons, we will consider some common symptoms that occur in all of them, but we will take into account their different intensities for the application of an MCA. That said, we can load the dataset:

```
load("symptoms.RData")
```

If the reader uses the function `summary()`, he or she will check a table of frequencies regarding the variables present in Table 13.2.

```
summary(symptoms)
```

We can access the χ^2 tests regarding the variables of interest present in the object `symptoms`, considered two by two, with the function `sjt.xtab()`. Thus to verify the associations among the categories of the *disease* variable and the categories of the *fever* variable, we can type the following command:

```
sjt.xtab(var.row = symptoms$disease,
         var.col = symptoms$fever,
         show.exp = TRUE,
         show.row.prc = TRUE,
         show.col.prc = TRUE)
```

If we want the associations among the categories of the *disease* variable and the categories of the *itch* variable, we can type the following command:

```
sjt.xtab(var.row = symptoms$disease,
         var.col = symptoms$itch,
         show.exp = TRUE,
         show.row.prc = TRUE,
         show.col.prc = TRUE)
```

To check the associations between the categories of the *disease* variable and the categories of the *arthralgia* variable, we can type the following command:

```
sjt.xtab(var.row = symptoms$disease,
         var.col = symptoms$arthralgia,
         show.exp = TRUE,
         show.row.prc = TRUE,
         show.col.prc = TRUE)
```

In a similar way, if desired, the reader can check the associations between the other combinations not explored previously. Table 13.3 presents all possible combinations, the respective value of the χ^2 statistic, and their respective *P*-values.

TABLE 13.3 χ^2 tests to check the level of association among the categories of each pair of variables present in the object `symptoms`.

Combination of variables categories	Value of χ^2	*P*-value
disease × *fever*	296.581	0.000
disease × *itch*	405.455	0.000
disease × *arthralgia*	303.462	0.000
fever × *itch*	215.237	0.000
fever × *arthralgia*	25.587	0.000
itch × *arthralgia*	31.501	0.000

Through the outputs in Table 13.3, we can see that all pairs of variables have a statistically significant association, at the 5% significance level. **For a given variable to be included in an MCA, it must be associated in a statistically significant way with at least one of the other variables.**

Because all variables can be included in MCA, we could already start to elaborate the technique itself. However, if the reader is curious to observe a binary matrix made with R-based language for the implementation of MCA, he or she can use the function `matlogic()` from the package `amap`:

```
binary_matrix <- matlogic(symptoms[,2:5])
```

On the other hand, if the reader wants access to a Burt matrix, he or she must use the function `burt()` from the package `amap`:

```
binary_matrix <- matlogic(symptoms[,2:5])
```

That said, the MCA, in fact, can be obtained by the command `MCA()` from the package `FactoMineR`:

```
mca_symptoms <- MCA(symptoms[,2:5], method = "Indicator", graph = FALSE)
```

The reason for using a function of the package `FactoMineR` goes beyond the terms already used when implementing the package `anacor` in R. Your choice is given by its alignment with this work in respect to the calculation of the coordinates of the perceptual map. In other words, the function `MCA()` simultaneously calculates the standard coordinates and the principal coordinates.

However, from the point of view of graphic visualization, the function `MCA()` and the function `CA()` generate poor outputs and, depending on the dataset, generate images that do not reflect the correct calculations. The dataset present in the object `symptoms` is an example of this, which is why we argue `graph = FALSE` for the function `MCA()`. As a result, as we did with the package `ANACOR`, we will demonstrate to the reader how to generate elegant perceptual maps with the function `ggplot()` from the package `tidyverse`. If the reader wants to test other functions and packages with the capacity to implement an MCA, some examples we recommend are the function `mca()` from the package `MASS` or the function `dudi.acm` from the package (`ade4`).

The argument `method` concerns which type of matrix will be used for calculating the coordinates. When we argue `method = "Indicator"`, the algorithm will use the binary matrix **Z** (discussed in the "Multiple correspondence analysis" section), thus generating the standard coordinates. On the other hand, when arguing `method = "Burt"`, the function will use the Burt matrix **B** (also discussed in the "Multiple correspondence analysis" section) to generate the main coordinates $\mathbf{B} = \mathbf{Z}'\mathbf{Z}$.

Speaking directly of our new object `mca_symptoms`, which contains the implemented MCA, we think it would be interesting for the reader to explore some of its components that can be accessed by the operator `$`:

- `eig`: Contains data regarding the quantity of MCA dimensions, the values of the eigenvalues, the percentage of variance explained by each dimension, and the cumulative percentage of variance explained.
- `var$coord`: Contains the coordinates of the categories of the variables considered in column.
- `ind$coord`: Contains the coordinates of the categories of the variables considered in row.

That said, when accessing the component `eig` of the object `mca_symptoms`, typing the command `mca_symptoms$eig`, we can verify that the number of dimensions of the analysis is, in fact, equal to $J - Q$, where J refers to the sum of the number of categories of the variables considered in the analysis (in this case, 12), and Q refers to the number of variables (in this case, 4). So we have 8 dimensions.

From the 8 dimensions verified, in the component `eig`, we can access the $k = 8$ eigenvalues λ_k^2 calculated:

$$\begin{cases} \lambda_1^2 = 0.63315847 \\ \lambda_2^2 = 0.41264536 \\ \lambda_3^2 = 0.26313440 \\ \lambda_4^2 = 0.23738851 \\ \lambda_5^2 = 0.22181990 \\ \lambda_6^2 = 0.10489814 \\ \lambda_7^2 = 0.08784824 \\ \lambda_8^2 = 0.03910698 \end{cases}$$

The sum of the eigenvalues points to the total principal inertia I_T of the binary matrix **Z**, as studied earlier. Therefore $I_T = \lambda_1^2 + \lambda_2^2 + \lambda_3^2 + \lambda_4^2 + \lambda_5^2 + \lambda_6^2 + \lambda_7^2 + \lambda_8^2 = 2$. Another way to arrive at the value of I_T is:

$$I_T = \frac{J - Q}{Q} = \frac{12 - 4}{4} = 2.$$

That said, we can generate a perceptual map in three simple steps. The first step is to save the number of categories present in each variable in an object that we will call `categories`:

```
categories <- apply(symptoms[,2:5],
                    MARGIN = 2,
                    FUN = function(x) nlevels(as.factor(x)))
```

The second step is to create a data frame that will contain the coordinates regarding each category and dimension of the MCA. We will call this object `mca_df`:

```
mca_df <- data.frame(mca_symptoms$var$coord,
                     variable = rep(names(categories), categories))
```

The last step is to plot the perceptual map itself:

```
mca_df %>%
  ggplot(aes(x = Dim.1, y = Dim.2, label = rownames(mca_df), color = variable)) +
  geom_point() +
  geom_label_repel() +
  geom_hline(yintercept = 0, linetype = "dashed") +
  geom_vline(xintercept = 0, linetype = "dashed") +
  labs(x = paste("Dimension 1:", paste0(round(mca_symptoms$eig[,2][1], digits = 2), "%")),
       y = paste("Dimension 2:", paste0(round(mca_symptoms$eig[,2][2], digits = 2), "%"))) +
  theme(panel.background = element_rect("white"),
        panel.border = element_rect("NA"),
        panel.grid = element_line("gray95"),
        legend.position = "none")
```

The perceptual map generated by the previous commands is shown in Figure 13.7.

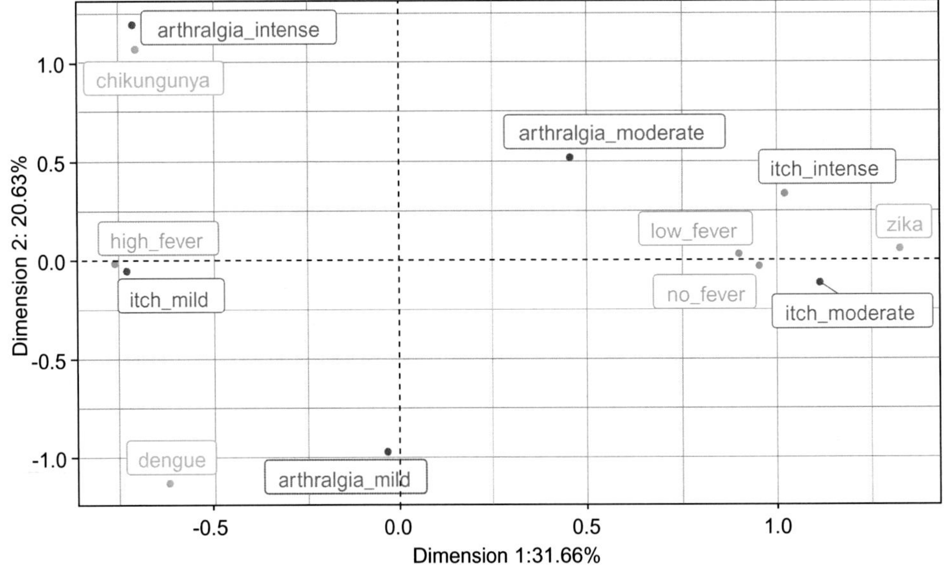

FIGURE 13.7 Perceptual map of the symptoms of the diseases studied in the "Multiple correspondence analysis" section.

In a similar way to what we discussed in the final part of the "Correspondence analysis" section, we recommend attention when analyzing the results of a two-dimensional perceptual map. In the Appendix of this chapter, the reader will also find a way to visualize a perceptual map coming from a three-dimensional MCA.

According to Figure 13.7, we can verify strong associations between *zika* disease and the symptoms of moderate or intense itching, non-existent or low fever, and moderate arthralgia. We can also verify, for example, that the associations between the symptoms of mild itching and high fever are very similar between the diseases *dengue* and *chikungunya*. In any case, the three-dimensional perceptual map present in the Appendix of this chapter will consider an additional dimension and will have greater explanatory power for the variances of the dimensions considered here.

Final remarks

The main objective of SCA and MCA techniques is to evaluate the significance of the association among categorical variables and among their categories, generate coordinates of the categories, and build perceptual maps from these coordinates. Although the first technique allows the researcher to assess the association between only two categorical variables and among their categories, the second is a multivariate technique in which the researcher can study the associations among more than two categorical variables and among each pair of categories. Therefore these techniques allow for improved decision-making processes based on behavior and the interdependent relationship among variables that present some form of categorization (Fávero and Belfiore, 2019).

Exercises

1. The Ministry of Health of a certain country wants to implement a campaign to alert a population about the importance of practicing physical exercise to reduce the low-density lipoprotein (LDL) cholesterol index (mg/dL). To this end, it conducted a survey of 2,304 people in which the following variables were raised (Fávero and Belfiore, 2019):

Variable	Description
cholesterol	Classification of LDL cholesterol index (mg/dL), namely: • Very high: greater than 189 mg/dL • High: 160 to 189 mg/dL • Borderline: 130 to 159 mg/dL • Suboptimal: 100 to 129 mg/dL • Optimal: less than 100 mg/dL
Sport	Number of times you practice physical activities weekly

When publishing the results of the research, the Ministry of Health presented the following contingency table, with the observed absolute frequencies for each crossing of categories of the two variables.

	Weekly physical activities (number of times)					
LDL cholesterol index classification (mg/dL)	**0**	**1**	**2**	**3**	**4**	**5**
Very high	32	158	264	140	40	0
High	22	108	178	108	58	0
Borderline	0	26	98	190	86	36
Suboptimal	0	16	114	166	104	54
Optimal	0	0	82	118	76	30

Note that although the *cholesterol* variable is a qualitative ordinal, the *sport* variable is quantitative but discrete and with few possibilities of response, therefore it can be considered categorical for the purposes of CA.

In this sense, we would like you to:

a. Present the expected absolute frequencies table.
b. Draw up the residuals table.
c. Present the total value of the χ^2 statistic.
d. Based on the calculated value of the χ^2 statistic and the degrees of freedom of the contingency table, is it possible to state that the LDL cholesterol index and the weekly amount of sports activities are not randomly associated, at the 5% significance level?

e. Build the dataset from the presented contingency table, and, through it, develop an SCA between cholesterol and sport. What percentages of total principal inertia are explained by dimension?

f. Based on the coordinates of the categories of the *cholesterol* and *sport* variables obtained from elaboration of the SCA, elaborate the two-dimensional perceptual map, and provide a brief discussion about the behavior of the points corresponding to the categories of each variable.

2. A survey of 500 executives from multinational companies was carried out to assess the perception of the general quality of the service provided and the perception of respecting the project deadlines of three major consulting companies (*Gabicks*, *Lipehigh*, and *Montvero*). Each executive answered about his or her perception in relation to each of the three companies, and the variables collected are as follows (Fávero and Belfiore, 2019):

Variable	Description
quality	Perception about the general quality of the service provided, namely: • Terrible • Bad • Regular • Good • Great
punctuality	Regarding project deadlines: • No • Yes

By analyzing the dataset present in the file `consultancy.RData` (Fávero and Belfiore, 2019), we would like you to:

- Present the contingency tables and the χ^2 test results for the variables *quality* and *company* and the variables *punctuality* and *company*. Is there an association between the *company* variable and the other variables, at the 5% significance level?
- If the answer in the previous item is yes, elaborate an MCA with the three variables. What are the principal and standard coordinates of the categories for each variable?
- Elaborate the two-dimensional perceptual map (with standard coordinates), and discuss the executive's reading about the three consulting companies.

Appendix

For the elaboration of a three-dimensional perceptual map, whether it comes from SCA or from an MCA, three things are sufficient: (1) that the analyzed data, in fact, have more than two dimensions; (2) that the reader has the package `plotly` installed and loaded; and (3) that the reader saves the coordinates, of each dimension, in line and in columns in different objects.

- **Example 1:** Three-dimensional perceptual map of the object `ca_covid` created in the "Correspondence analysis" section

For this case, in the "Correspondence analysis" section, we said that four dimensions were calculated for the data. In building Figure 13.6, we considered two of these dimensions. So, to start considering the next dimension with more explanation capacity for the phenomenon, let's first save the coordinates present in the object `ca_covid` in two new objects: `ca_row_coords` e `ca_col_coords`:

```
ca_row_coords <- ca_covid$row$coord

ca_col_coords <- ca_covid$col$coord
```

The next step will be to create an object with three-dimensional visual capability. We can do this with the function `plot_ly()` from the package `plotly`:

```
ca_covid_3D <- plot_ly()
```

Using the function add_trace() from the package plotly, we can indicate to the object that will compose our three-dimensional perceptual map the three dimensions to be plotted in the future, respectively, on the x, y, and z axes. We will start by extracting the data from our object ca_row_coords:

```
ca_covid_3D <- add_trace(p = ca_covid_3D,
                         x = ca_row_coords[,1],
                         y = ca_row_coords[,2],
                         z = ca_row_coords[,3],
                         mode = 'text',
                         text = rownames(ca_row_coords),
                         textfont = list(color = "orange"),
                         showlegend = FALSE)
```

If the reader is not an advanced R operator, the first contact with functions of the type of add_trace() can be shocking and confusing. When we use the assignment operator <- in R-based language on an object that has already been created, as a rule we are overwriting it (i.e., deleting its contents and adding a new value to it). This is not the case with the function add_trace(). This function adds information to objects that, for example, were created using the function plot_ly(), without necessarily deleting them.

In the previous command, to the function add_trace(), we argued in p the object created by the function plot_ly(); for the arguments x, y, and z, we declare the values that will appear on the x, y, and z axes of our future three-dimensional graphic. The other arguments, such as mode, text, textfont, and showlegend, concern the presentation of the graph's legends and their uses, due to their names, and are very intuitive.

Having exposed the curious characteristics of the function add_trace(), we will use it again, but this time to capture data about the object ca_col_coords:

```
ca_covid_3D <- add_trace(p = ca_covid_3D,
                         x = ca_col_coords[,1],
                         y = ca_col_coords[,2],
                         z = ca_col_coords[,3],
                         mode = "text",
                         text = rownames(ca_col_coords),
                         textfont = list(color = "darkorchid"),
                         showlegend = FALSE)
```

After that, we will identify the axes due to the three dimensions selected for the creation of the three-dimensional perceptual map using the function layout() from the package plotly. Analogously to the function add_trace(), the function layout() aims to add information to an object already created, for example, by the function plot_ly():

```
ca_covid_3D <- layout(p = ca_covid_3D,
                      scene = list(xaxis = list(title = colnames(ca_row_coords)[1]),
                                   yaxis = list(title = colnames(ca_row_coords)[2]),
                                   zaxis = list(title = colnames(ca_row_coords)[3]),
                                   aspectmode = "data"))
```

Ready! It is sufficient for the reader to declare to R the name of the object on which he or she saved the three-dimensional perceptual map. In our case, it would be sufficient:

```
ca_covid_3D
```

After declaring the object ca_covid_3D, the reader should receive a warning, and the three-dimensional graphic will appear in the *Viewer* tab of *RStudio* shortly thereafter. The three-dimensional perceptual map is interactive, and the reader can use the mouse to save, navigate, rotate, and zoom it. Figure 13.8 shows a cutout of the three-dimensional perceptual map we just created.

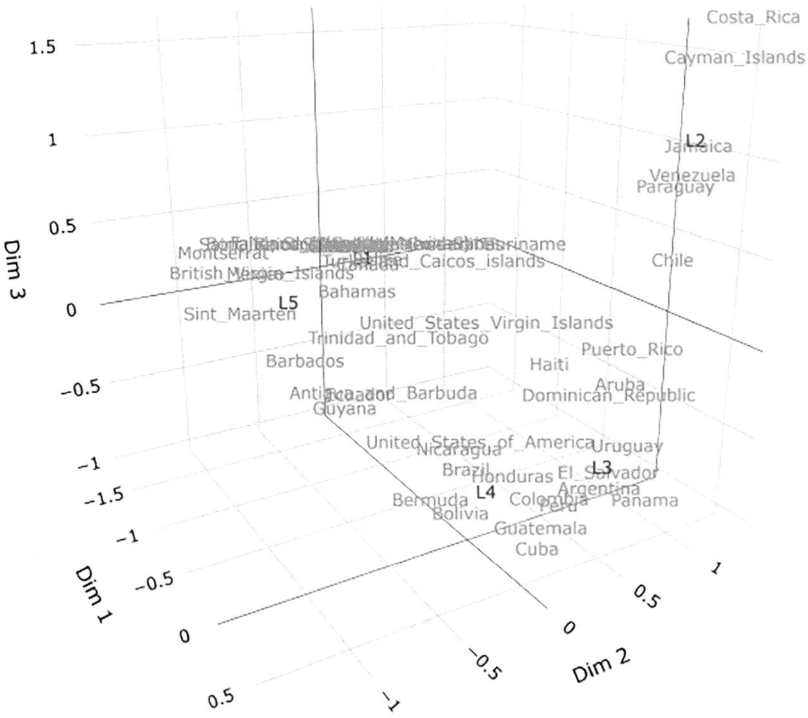

FIGURE 13.8 Cutout of the three-dimensional perceptual map created with the data studied in the "Correspondence analysis" section.

Unlike the perceptual map in Figure 13.6, which explained 65.92% of the variances studied, the ability of Figure 13.8 to explain the phenomenon is 86.89%.

- **Example 2:** Three-dimensional perceptual map of the object `mca_symptoms` created in the "Multiple correspondence analysis" section.

By the way we approach MCA, the construction of its respective three-dimensional perceptual map will be simpler. We will use the data frame contained in the object `mca_df`, which already contains all of the coordinates we need. This will make our way easier! The only detail we should be careful about is deleting the last column that we created so the package `ggplot2` will know what to select for the two-dimensional plot shown in Figure 13.7. This column, at this point, does not help at all. Therefore:

```
mca_coords <- mca_df[,-6]
```

Next, we will create an object that contains our three-dimensional perceptual map:

```
mca_symptoms_3D <- plot_ly()
```

In the new object `mca_symptoms_3D`, we will indicate which values will be plotted on the x, y, and z axes:

```
mca_symptoms_3D <- add_trace(p = mca_symptoms_3D,
                             x = mca_coords[,1],
                             y = mca_coords[,2],
                             z = mca_coords[,3],
                             mode = "text",
                             text = rownames(mca_coords),
                             textfont = list(color = "darkorchid"),
                             showlegend = FALSE)
```

Now we can name the axes:

```
mca_symptoms_3D <- layout(p = mca_symptoms_3D,
                          scene = list(xaxis = list(title = colnames(mca_coords)[1]),
                                       yaxis = list(title = colnames(mca_coords)[2]),
                                       zaxis = list(title = colnames(mca_coords)[3]),
                                       aspectmode = "data"))
```

Ready! Just declare the object `mca_symptoms_3D` to R. The reader should expect a warning, and the three-dimensional perceptual map will appear in the *Viewer* tab immediately afterward:

```
mca_symptoms_3D
```

Figure 13.9 shows a cutout of the three-dimensional perceptual map generated.

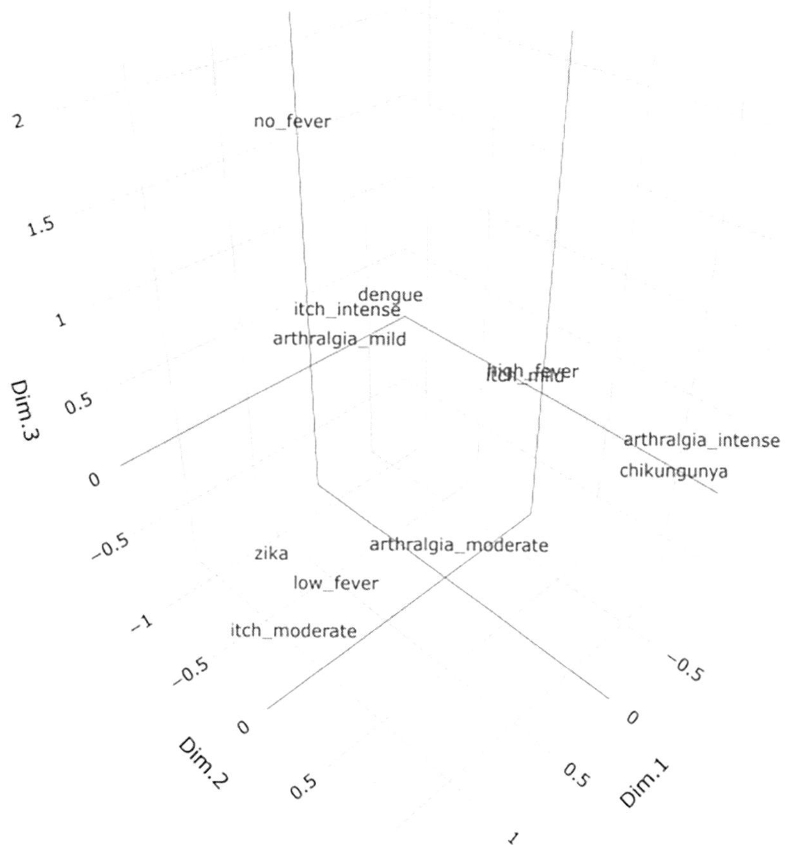

FIGURE 13.9 Cutout of the three-dimensional perceptual map created with the data studied in the "Multiple correspondence analysis" section.

For this case, unlike what the perceptual map present in Figure 13.7 explained (52.59% of the variances studied), the ability of Figure 13.9 to explain the phenomenon is 65.45%.

Supplementary data sets

Chapter13.Rproj
Chapter13_script.R
covid_28weeks.RData
symptoms.RData
consultancy.RData

Please access supplementary data files here: https://doi.org/10.17632/55623jkwrp.3

PART V

Supervised machine learning techniques

CHAPTER

14

Simple and multiple regression models

AT THE END OF THIS CHAPTER, YOU WILL BE ABLE TO:

- Estimate the parameters of the simple and multiple regression models.
- Evaluate the results of statistical tests pertinent to the regression models.
- Develop confidence intervals for the parameters of the forecasting models.
- Understand the assumptions of the regression models by the ordinary least squares (OLS) method.
- Specify non-linear regression models, and understand the Box-Cox transformation.
- Estimate simple and multiple regression models in R, and interpret their results.

R-based language packages used in this chapter

```
library(plotly)
library(tidyverse)
library(PerformanceAnalytics)
library(nortest)
library(olsrr)
library(lmtest)
library(sandwich)
library(fastDummies)
library(reshape2)
library(car)
```

Don't forget to define the R working directory (the location where your datasets are installed):

```
setwd("C:/book/chapter14")
```

Data Science, Analytics and Machine Learning with R
https://doi.org/10.1016/B978-0-12-824271-1.00007-X

Estimation of regression models in R

The objective of this section is not to again discuss the concepts inherent to statistics and the presuppositions of the regression technique, but to provide the researcher knowledge of the R commands and show its advantages in relation to other software in what can be said about confirmatory models.

For the following practical example, we collected data on annual medical expenditures (US$) of 200 individuals, considering the age (years), number of chronic diseases (unit), annual income (US$), and type of health plan used by the observation (silver, gold, or platinum). The data can be found in the file `medical_expenditure.RData` and are composed of the variables presented in Table 14.1.

TABLE 14.1 Description of the variables presented in the file `medical_expenditure.RData`.

Variables	Description
Id	Identity document
Expenditures	Annual medical expenditures (US$)
Age	Age of individual (years)
chronic_diseases	Number of chronic diseases that affect the individual (unit)
Income	Annual income of each individual (US$)
plan_type	Type of health plan used by the individual (silver, gold, or platinum)

We ask the reader to load the dataset file `medical_expenditure.RData`.

```
load("medical_expenditure.RData")
```

Next, we will propose the simple linear regression model, followed by the multiple regression model.

Estimation of a simple linear regression model in R

At first, let's investigate whether the medical expenditures of each individual are related to their respective annual incomes. To do this, the following model will be estimated:

$$exp\,enditures_i = a + b \times income_i + \varepsilon_i$$

The univariate descriptive statistics of the dataset can be obtained from the function `summary()`:

```
summary(medical_expenditure)
```

The results are presented in Figure 14.1.

```
       id        expenditures        age         chronic_diseases       income          plan_type
 1      :  1   Min.   : 887.3   Min.   :32.00   Min.   :0.000    Min.   :31600   platinum:72
 2      :  1   1st Qu.:1261.4   1st Qu.:38.00   1st Qu.:1.000    1st Qu.:38000   gold    :66
 3      :  1   Median :1550.0   Median :49.00   Median :2.000    Median :48800   silver  :62
 4      :  1   Mean   :1611.8   Mean   :50.01   Mean   :2.705    Mean   :50022
 5      :  1   3rd Qu.:1976.2   3rd Qu.:63.00   3rd Qu.:4.000    3rd Qu.:63200
 6      :  1   Max.   :2692.0   Max.   :68.00   Max.   :5.000    Max.   :68000
 (Other):194
```

FIGURE 14.1 Univariate descriptive statistics of each variable in the dataset `medical_expenditure`.

For the simple linear regression model, we will focus on the interrelationship between the dependent variable (*expenditures*) and its explanatory variable (*income*). However, before running the simple linear regression model, we can generate a graph that shows the relationship between the two mentioned variables. We can create the graph using the function `chart.Correlation()` from the package `PerformanceAnalytics` to provide a better understanding of how the variables are related, giving an indication about the best non-linear functional forms. Therefore we can type the following command:

```
chart.Correlation(medical_expenditure[,c(2,5)])
```

Figure 14.2 presents the correlation between the *expenditures* and *income* variables.

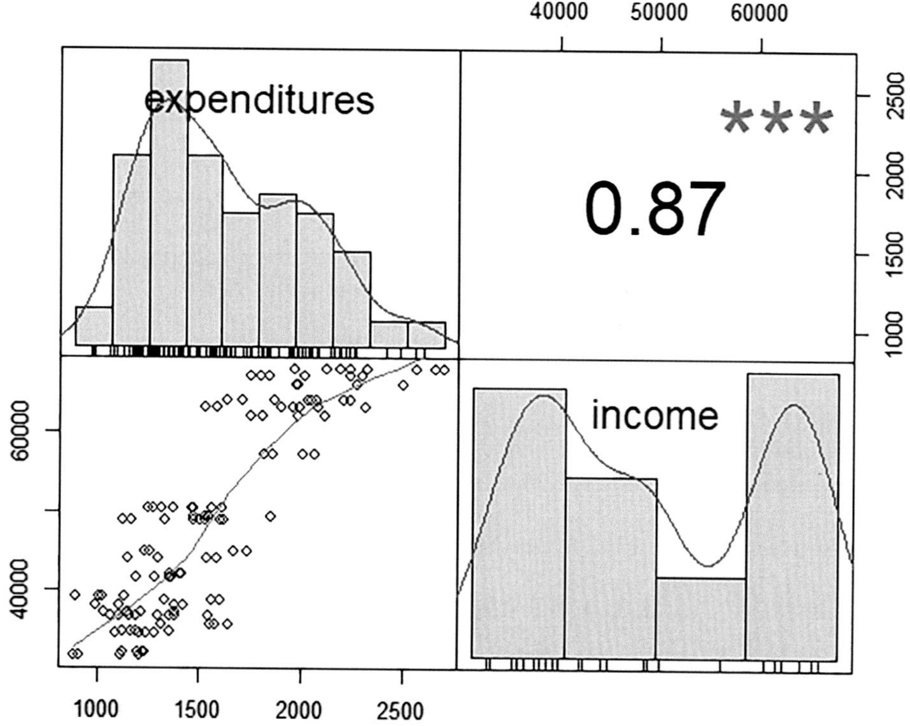

FIGURE 14.2 Interrelationship between *expenditures* and *income* variables.

We can see from this graph that the relationship between the *expenditure* variable and the *income* variable are positive and statistically significant. We can create a simple regression model using the function `lm()` (linear model) from R's base and stats package:

```
simple_reg <- lm(formula = expenditures ~ income,
                 data = medical_expenditure)
```

In the previous routine, the argument formula follows the sintax: $Y \sim X$, that is, the dependent variable is described as a function of the explanatory variable. The argument `data`, on the other hand, should indicate to which dataset the variables of the argument `formula` belong. To obtain the results of our first regression model, as shown in Figure 14.3, we can use the function `summary()` applied to our object `simple_reg` containing the following regression:

```
summary(simple_reg)
```

```
Call:
lm(formula = expenditures ~ income, data = medical_expenditure)

Residuals:
    Min      1Q  Median      3Q     Max
-463.92 -153.50   -3.07  132.02  557.13

Coefficients:
             Estimate Std. Error t value Pr(>|t|)
(Intercept) 1.565e+02  6.175e+01   2.535    0.012 *
income      2.909e-02  1.197e-03  24.304   <2e-16 ***
---
Signif. codes:  0 '***' 0.001 '**' 0.01 '*' 0.05 '.' 0.1 ' ' 1

Residual standard error: 213.2 on 198 degrees of freedom
Multiple R-squared:  0.7489,	Adjusted R-squared:  0.7477
F-statistic: 590.7 on 1 and 198 DF,  p-value: < 2.2e-16
```

FIGURE 14.3 Outputs of the simple linear regression model in R.

In Figure 14.3, we can see that the general statistics of the model, that is, the *F* test, has a value of 590.7, with 1 degree of freedom for the regression and 198 degrees of freedom for the residuals, and with a respective *P*-value < 0.05. As studied previously in this chapter, the *F* test indicates that we have at least one variable statistically different from zero, at a given significance level. For a simple linear regression model, when the *F* test is significant, necessarily, the *t* test of the single explanatory variable will also be—the reciprocal is true. The result of the *F* test allows us to conclude that the explanatory variable (*income*) is statistically significant, at a significance level of 5%, to explain the behavior of the *expenditure* variable because its *P*-value < 0.05.

Still with regard to Figure 14.3, we can see that the R^2 statistic is 0.7489, that is, the model proposed explains 74.89% of variability of the *Y* variable (*expenditures*), which is explained by the variation in behavior of the *X* variable (*income*). On the other hand, the adjusted R^2 has a value of 0.7477 and, as discussed earlier, it is relevant when there is an intention to compare models.

In Figure 14.3, we can also see a value of 156.5 for the intercept (α) and 0.02909 for the single slope (β) because there is only one explanatory variable in a simple regression model. Therefore we can say that each additional unit of the *income* variable increases in 0.02909, ***on average***, the variable *expenditures*.

Therefore the estimation of the proposed regression can be formally described by Expression (14.1).

$$\widehat{expenditures_i} = 156.5 + 0.02909 \times income_i. \tag{14.1}$$

Some statistics about the residuals are presented in the upper part of Figure 14.3. If the researcher wants more specific responses about them, we suggest accessing the component `residuals` of the object `simple_reg`, with the help of the operator `$`. We will study other components of the object `simple_reg` in parallel to other chapters, including the following:

- `coefficients`: vector of dimension $(k+1) \times 1$ that contains the value of α (always in the first position) and the values of β, where *k* refers to the number of variables used in the model. Considering the multiple linear regression model that will be estimated in "Estimation of a multiple linear regression model in R" section.
- `residuals`: vector of dimension $n \times 1$ that indicates the values of the model residuals, where *n* refers to the number of observations. It is important to note that, in the presence of missing values in the dataset, the estimations for these observations will not be calculated.
- `fitted.values`: vector of dimension $n \times 1$ that refers to the estimated values of the dependent variable for the observations present in the dataset, used for the regression model.

We can use the function `confint()`, which requires as an argument the appropriate profile object (`simple_reg`) and the confidence level desired:

```
confint(object = simple_reg, level = 0.95)
```

Figure 14.4 presents the outputs of the function `confint()`.

```
                   2.5 %       97.5 %
(Intercept) 34.77435957 278.31070772
income       0.02673241   0.03145364
```

FIGURE 14.4 CI estimated for the regression belonging to the object `simple_reg`.

From the results presented in Figure 14.4, we can describe Expressions (14.2) and (14.3), which correspond to the lower and upper bounds, respectively, of the model's CI in Expression (14.1).

$$\widehat{expenditures}_{i_{min}} = 34.774 + 0.027 \times income_i \tag{14.2}$$

$$\widehat{expenditures}_{i_{max}} = 278.311 + 0.031 \times income_i \tag{14.3}$$

We can have visual access to the estimation's CI, typing the function `geom_smooth()` as follows:

```
medical_expenditure %>%
  ggplot() +
  geom_point(aes(x = income, y = expenditures), color = "orange") +
  geom_smooth(aes(x = income, y = expenditures), color = "darkorchid",
              method = "lm", formula = y ~ x, level = 0.95) +
  labs(x = "Income",
       y = "Expenditures") +
  theme_bw()
```

Figure 14.5 shows the scatter plot between the variables under analysis (*expenditures* and *income*) in addition to a curve that represents the fitted values of the estimation, that is, the predicted value for the dependent variable. Furthermore, the hatched area around the regression curve represents the CI of the model. To view other CI levels, the researcher can just change the argument `levels` of the function `geom_smooth()` present in the previous routine.

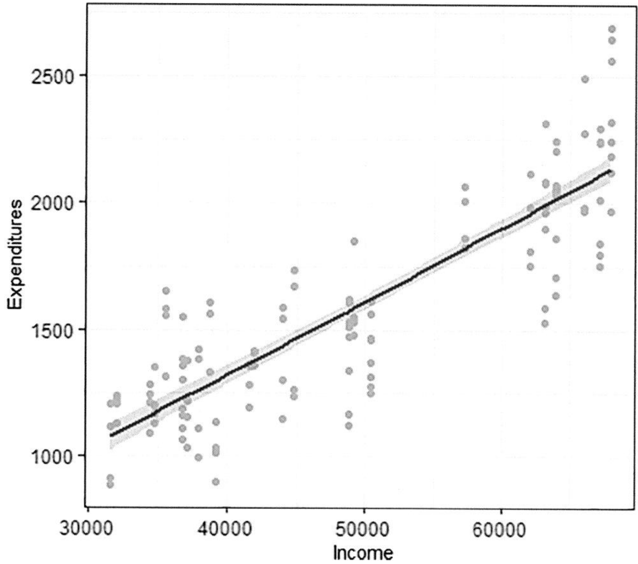

FIGURE 14.5 Fitted values of the regression present in the object `simple_reg`.

For an interactive plot, the researcher can just encapsulate the previous routine inside the function `ggplotly()` from the package `plotly`, as follows:

```
ggplotly(
  medical_expenditure %>%
    ggplot() +
    geom_point(aes(x = income, y = expenditures), color = "orange") +
    geom_smooth(aes(x = income, y = expenditures), color = "darkorchid",
                method = "lm", formula = y ~ x, level = 0.95) +
    labs(x = "Income",
         y = "Expenditures") +
    theme_bw()
)
```

Next, we will examine the assumptions of the regression model studied earlier in the "Presuppositions of regression models estimated by ordinary least squares" section.

Multicollinearity Problems: As studied earlier in the section entitled "The multicollinearity problem," multicollinearity is characterized by high correlation indices between the explanatory variables. In a simple regression model, there is only one explanatory variable, so that multicollinearity is not applicable, which we will study in the "Estimation of a multiple linear regression model in R" section.

Normality of Residuals: Adherence to the assumptions of normality of residuals can be verified by the Shapiro-Francia test (function `sf.test()` from the package `nortest`) because $n > 30$, as studied in Chapter 6. For cases in which $n \leq 30$, we recommend the Shapiro-Wilk test, whose corresponding function in R-based language is `shapiro.test()`. In this way:

```
sf.test(simple_reg$residuals)
```

An attentive reader will see that R's response is $W = 0.99085$ with a P-value of 0.2052. This result indicates that the residuals of the model present in the object `simple_reg` are possibly adhering to a Gaussian distribution. For didactic purposes, we can plot the residuals of our simple linear regression model together with a theoretical normal curve, typing the following command:

```
medical_expenditure["resids_simple_reg"] <- simple_reg$residuals

medical_expenditure %>%
  ggplot() +
  geom_histogram(aes(x = resids_simple_reg, y = ..density..),
                 fill = "orange",
                 color = "bisque") +
  stat_function(fun = dnorm,
                args = list(mean = mean(medical_expenditure$resids_simple_reg),
                            sd = sd(medical_expenditure$resids_simple_reg)),
                color = "darkorchid",
                size = 1.5) +
  labs(x = "Residuals of simple_reg object",
       y = "Residuals Density") +
  theme_bw()
```

In the previous routine, for the function `geom_histogram()`, we declare the function `aes()` with the argument `x` corresponding to the residuals that were saved in the `medical_expenditure` dataset. The argument `y`, on the other hand, has a different value compared with the others studied in Chapter 7 because we declare `y = ..density..` In other words, we declare in R code that we would like the density function of the variable listed by the argument `x` in the ordinate axis, that is, the residual's density function present in the model `simple_reg`. Still in relation to this routine, to draw the theoretical Gaussian curve, we used the function `stat_function ()`, arguing `fun = dnorm`, which explicitly informs to R that we want to plot a normal distribution whose values of its mean and standard deviation were informed by the argument `args`. Figure 14.6 shows the result of the previous codes.

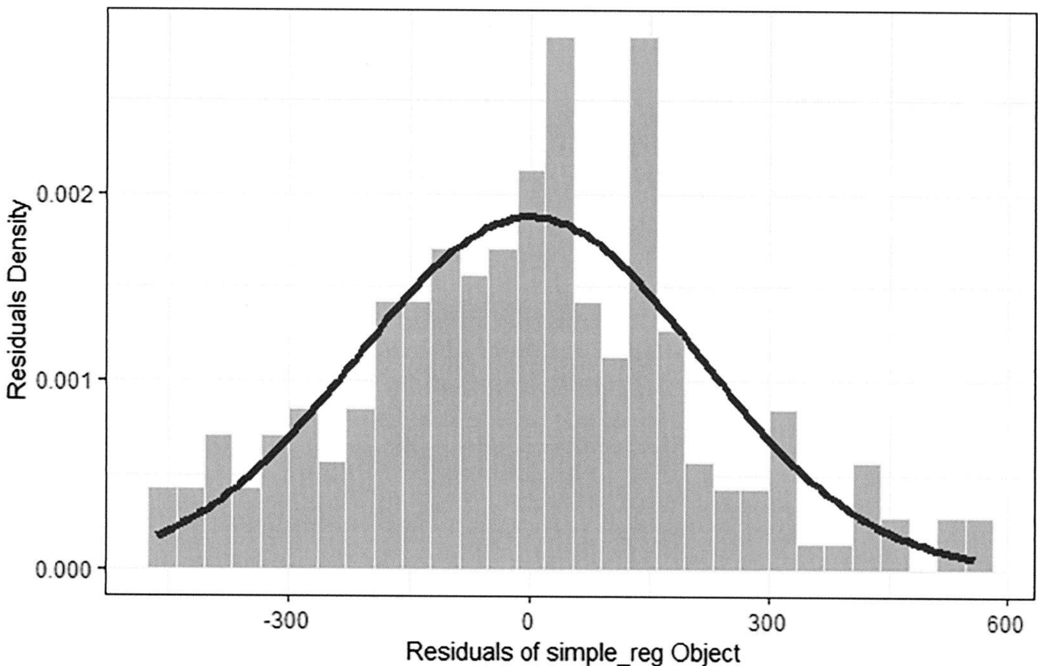

FIGURE 14.6 Residuals of the simple linear regression model.

Heteroskedasticity Problems: as discussed earlier in the section entitled "The problem of heteroskedasticity," the heteroskedasticity problem is the result of the correlation between the error terms and the explanatory variable, which provides the visual effect of a cone. Figure 14.5 does not provide preliminary evidence of this kind of problem for the model contained in the object `simple_reg`. To guarantee that our model is homoscedastic, we propose the use of the Breusch-Pagan/Cook-Weisberg test, present in the function `ols_test_breusch_pagan()` from the package `olsrr`:

```
ols_test_breusch_pagan(simple_reg)
```

The result of the previous command is $\chi^2_{BP}=8.612$ with P-value $= 0.003$. **This means that the model presents heteroskedasticity problems because its P-value < 0.05.**

To estimate a regression model using the weighted least squares method in the presence of a heteroskedastic model (as presented earlier in the "Weighted least squares method: A possible solution" section), it would be enough for the researcher to use the argument `weights` to declare the function `lm()`. On the other hand, to estimate a model with the adoption of the Huber-White method for Robust Standard Errors, the researcher could use the function `lm_robust()` from the package `estimatr`, arguing `se_type = "HC1"`:

```
simple_reg_rob <- lm_robust(formula = expenditures ~ income,
                            data = medical_expenditure,
                            se_type = "HC1")
```

In the previous routine, the argument `se_type = "HC1"` provides the estimation of robust standard errors by the Huber-White method. A curious researcher will find that, although the parameters are exactly the same, when we compare the models contained in `simple_reg` and `simple_reg_rob`, the values of the standard errors and, consequently, the *t*-tests are different. In this sense, the researcher should return to the "Huber-White method for robust standard errors" section and carefully review the implications caused by the procedure listed. In fact, for this case, heteroscedasticity can be an indicator of the omission of a relevant variable in the model. We will return to the case in the "Estimation of a multiple linear regression model in R" section, estimating a multiple regression model, that is, with more than one explanatory variable.

Finally, to make predictions, the researcher can use the function `predict()`, from R-based language, **but must always take care not to commit the problem of extrapolation!** Hence careful study of univariate descriptive statistics presented in Figure 14.3 is important.

According to Figure 14.3, the *income* variable has, respectively, minimum and maximum values of US $31,600 and US $61,000. Thus when we argue the value of the *income* variable to the function `predict()`, we should do it within this range of values. **A regression model has interpolation capabilities; not extrapolation.**

That said, if we want to know, **on average**, the expected amount of medical expenditures for an individual with an annual income of US$ 43,500, we should type the following command:

```
predict(object = simple_reg, newdata = data.frame(income = 43500))
```

In the previous routine, we declared the object `simple_reg` that contains our estimation. We also declared the argument `newdata` using the function `data.frame()` to simulate a test sample, that is, an observation not present in the dataset, but whose variables have values that do not extrapolate the data used to train our model.

Next, we will study the estimation and verification of the presuppositions of a multiple linear regression model in R.

Estimation of a multiple linear regression model in R

Still using the `medical_expenditure` dataset available in the `medical_expenditure.RData` file, this time we will estimate a multiple regression model to study the medical expenses (*expenditures* variable) according to the combined behavior of the variables *age, chronic_diseases, income,* and *plan_type* (see Table 14.1). Therefore initially, we will present the following model:

$$expenditures_i = a + b_1 \times age_i + b_2 \times chronic\_diseases_i + b_3 \times income_i + b_4 \times plan\_type_i + \varepsilon_i$$

First, for educational purposes, we request that the researcher open again the `medical_expenditure.RData` file to clear the changes made earlier in the "Estimation of a simple linear regression model in R" section:

```
load("medical_expenditure.RData")
```

Looking again at the univariate descriptive statistics obtained from the `medical_expenditure` dataset presented in Figure 14.3, it is clear that *age, chronic_diseases,* and *income* are metric variables. However, the *plan_type* variable, which indicates the type of plan hired by the individuals, is a categorical variable classified as polychotomous because it has more than two categories: silver, gold, and platinum. Thus, as presented earlier in the "Dummy variables in regression models" section, to avoid the problem of arbitrary weighting, we should resort to the n – 1 dummies procedure applied to the variable *plan_type*. The n – 1 dummies procedure can be done with the function `dummy_cols()` from the package `fastDummies`. For educational purposes and to allow the researcher to compare the before and after of the n – 1 dummies procedure applied to the `medical_expenditure` dataset, we will save the result of the function `dummy_cols()` in a new object called `medicalexp_dummies`:

```
medicalexp_dummies <- dummy_cols(.data = medical_expenditure,
                                 select_columns = "plan_type",
                                 remove_first_dummy = TRUE,
                                 remove_selected_columns = TRUE)
```

In the previous routine, for the function `dummy_cols()`, we declare the following:

- `.data` to indicate from which dataset the variables that will go through the n – 1 dummies procedure will be selected;
- `select_columns` to select (between quotes) to which variables the n – 1 dummies procedure will be applied. For two or more variables, we declare them with the help of function `c()`;

- `remove_first_dummy = TRUE` so R uses the first categories of each polychotomous variable selected as reference categories and therefore removes them from the dataset (it is also common to choose as reference the most used category of each variable present in the dataset and, if this path is desired, the researcher should argue `remove_most_frequent_dummy = TRUE` instead of `remove_first_dummy = TRUE`); and
- `remove_selected_columns = TRUE` to indicate that R should remove from the dataset the original variables in which the n – 1 dummies procedure was applied.

An attentive researcher would see that, in the object `medicalexp_dummies`, in fact, the polychotomous variable *plan_type* has been replaced by the dummy variables *plan_type_gold* and *plan_type_platinum*. There is no variable *plan_type_silver* because the first category of the original variable *plan_type* was the category "silver," which was assumed as a reference value.

That said, **if the researcher reloaded the `medical_expenditure.RData` file as requested at the beginning of this section**, we can proceed to the study of the correlations between the metric variables in our dataset (*expenditures, age, chronic_diseases,* and *income*), whose results are shown in Figure 14.7:

```
chart.Correlation(medicalexp_dummies[,2:5])
```

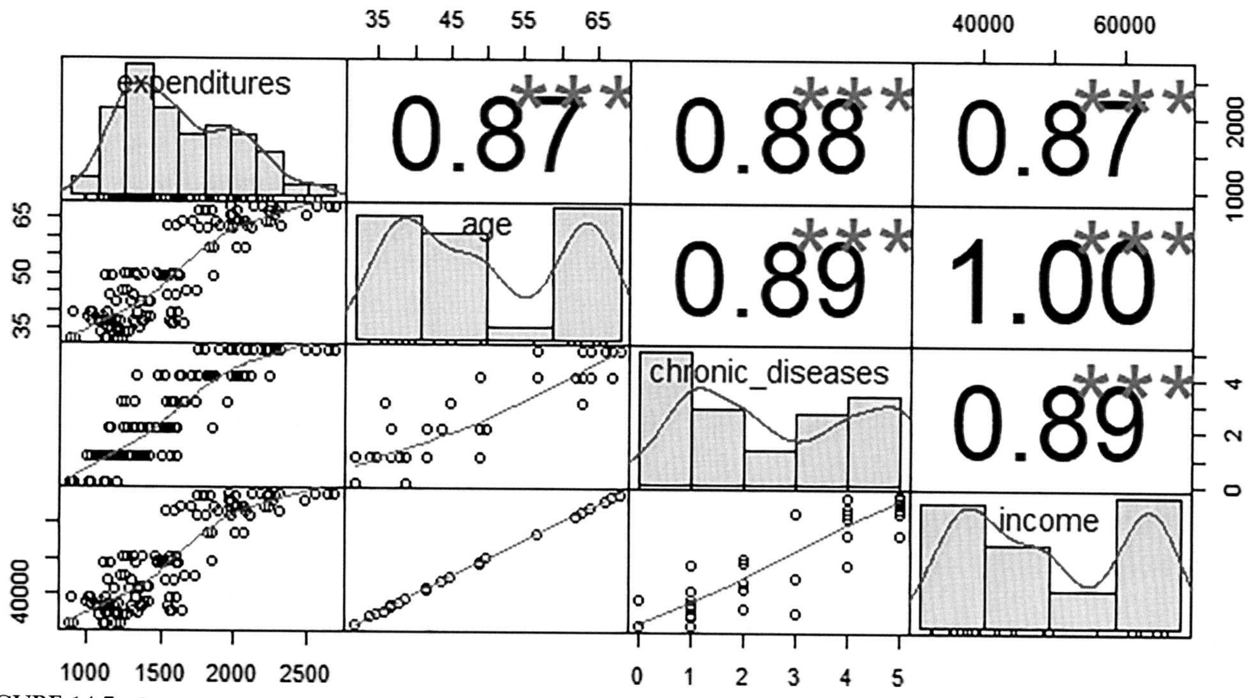

FIGURE 14.7 Interrelationship between variables.

Figure 14.7 gives us valuable insights. Note that all of the explanatory variables have high correlations and are statistically significant with the dependent variable *expenditures*. Also note that the *age* and *income* variables have a very high correlation between them ($\rho = 0.9999$, according to Figure 14.8). Also note that the relationship between the *expenditures* variable and the other metric variables does not seem to be linear. If desired, the researcher can establish a heat map between the correlations studied:

```
medicalexp_dummies %>%
  select(-id, -plan_type_gold, -plan_type_platinum) %>%
  cor() %>%
  melt() %>%
  rename(Correlation = 3) %>%
  ggplot() +
```

Continued

```
geom_tile(aes(x = Var1, y = Var2, fill = Correlation)) +
geom_text(aes(x = Var1, y = Var2, label = format(Correlation, digits = 4)),
          size = 3, color = "white") +
scale_fill_gradient2(low = "red",
                     mid = "white",
                     high = "darkblue",
                     midpoint = 0) +
labs(x = NULL, y = NULL) +
theme(axis.text.x = element_text(angle = 90))
```

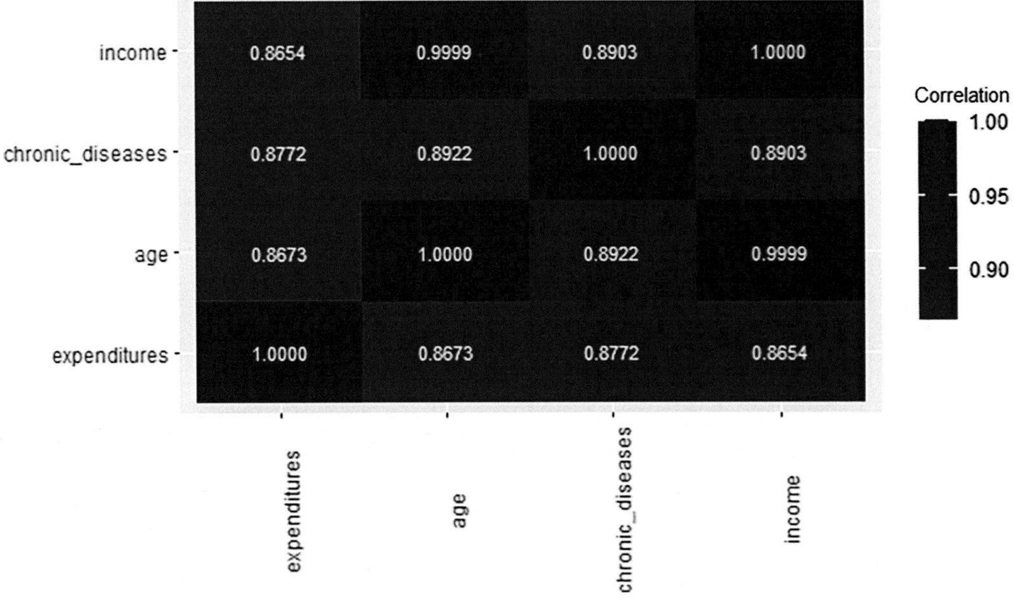

FIGURE 14.8 Heat map about the correlations of the metric variables of the dataset `medicalexp_dummies`.

After that, we can estimate our multiple regression model, with the help of the function `lm()`, as follows:

```
multi_reg <- lm(formula = expenditures ~ . -id,
                data = medicalexp_dummies)
```

In the previous routine, we informed R that the dependent variable would be the *expenditures* variable because it was declared to the left of the operator ~. To the right of the operator ~, it was declared the operator `.`, which indicates that all other variables in the variable base should be included in the model, except for the variable *id*, which is the reason we declare `-id`. Such a sequence of commands is very useful when we have a large number of variables that we must declare. Another way to establish the model is the following:

```
multi_reg <- lm(formula = expenditures ~ age + chronic_diseases +
                  income + plan_type_gold + plan_type_platinum,
                data = medicalexp_dummies)
```

For the previous routine, we followed the syntax $Y \sim X_1 + X_2 + \ldots + X_k$, which is a more laborious, and even dangerous, way to make an estimation. When declaring by hand variable by variable, there is a greater possibility of typing errors and even forgetting to declare some of them.

Similar to the simple linear regression model studied in the "Estimation of a simple linear regression model in R" section, we can access the parameters of the multiple regression model using the function `summary()`:

```
summary(multi_reg)
```

The outputs of the function `summary()` applied to the object `multi_reg` are shown in Figure 14.9.

```
Call:
lm(formula = expenditures ~ age + chronic_diseases + income +
    plan_type_gold + plan_type_platinum, data = medicalexp_dummies)

Residuals:
    Min      1Q  Median      3Q     Max
-377.07  -82.97   -4.76   84.22  540.74

Coefficients:
                    Estimate Std. Error t value Pr(>|t|)
(Intercept)        900.94283   85.04651  10.594  < 2e-16 ***
age                 89.22649   55.48810   1.608    0.109
chronic_diseases    67.23227   16.00230   4.201 4.04e-05 ***
income              -0.08442    0.05464  -1.545    0.124
plan_type_gold     237.46422   31.61618   7.511 2.09e-12 ***
plan_type_platinum 587.65304   60.75226   9.673  < 2e-16 ***
---
Signif. codes:  0 '***' 0.001 '**' 0.01 '*' 0.05 '.' 0.1 ' ' 1

Residual standard error: 154.3 on 194 degrees of freedom
Multiple R-squared:  0.8711,	Adjusted R-squared:  0.8678
F-statistic: 262.3 on 5 and 194 DF,  p-value: < 2.2e-16
```

FIGURE 14.9 Outputs of the multiple linear regression model in R.

According to Figure 14.9, we found that the *F*-test of our multiple regression model is statistically different from zero, with a significance level of 5% and 5 degrees of freedom for the regression and 194 degrees of freedom for the residuals; this means that at least one of the explanatory variables is statistically significant to explain the medical expenditures of our observations. We also verified that the value of the R^2 statistic is 0.8711, leading us to point out that the estimation made can explain 87.11% of the variation of the *expenditures* variable caused by the behavior of the other variables, *ceteris paribus*. For the purpose of comparison with other models with a different number of observations and/or variables, we must take into account the Adjusted R^2 statistic, whose value was 0.8678.

Speaking directly of the coefficients of the model contained by the object `multi_reg`, we can observe that, *ceteris paribus*, the variables *age* and *income* were not statistically different from zero at a 5% significance level. Thus a fair question from the researcher would be: **The dataset of the multiple regression model was the same dataset used to develop the simple regression model. In the simple model, the *income* variable alone was able to explain 74.89% of the variability of the *expenditures* variable. How did the *income* variable stop being significant?**

The first point to understand is that, at this moment, we are facing a multiple model. Thus we cannot simply say that the *income* variable is not significant because it has already been shown to be relevant in the simple model. We should say that it is not significant in the presence of the other explanatory variables that have been selected, *ceteris paribus*, that is, the other conditions are kept constant.

The second point is that, according to Figures 14.7 and 14.8, the explanatory variables have high correlation values between them, leading us to believe that we are facing the problem of multicollinearity.

A third situation that derives from the first observation is that the possible non-linear relationship between the *expenditure* variable and the other explanatory variables makes some of them insignificant in a multiple model.

Therefore we will start the study of the diagnostic of the multiple regression model present in the object `multi_reg`.

Multicollinearity Problems: The high correlations between the explanatory variables, presented by Figures 14.7 and 14.8, lead us to verify if the model existing in the object `multi_reg` has multicollinearity problems. For this, we can use the Variance Inflation Factor (VIF) and Tolerance tests, which can be performed simultaneously using the function `ols_vif_tol()` from the package `olsrr`:

```
ols_vif_tol(multi_reg)
```

Figure 14.10 explains the results of the previous command.

```
             Variables    Tolerance          VIF
1                  age 0.0002468853 4050.464684
2     chronic_diseases 0.1674016448    5.973657
3               income 0.0002514458 3977.000965
4       plan_type_gold 0.5388218598    1.855901
5 plan_type_platinum   0.1400378376    7.140927
```

FIGURE 14.10 Outputs of the VIF and Tolerance tests.

From the outputs present in Figure 14.10, we notice that there are too high values for the VIF statistic (and, consequently, very low values for the Tolerance statistic), with emphasis on the shared variances between the *age* and *income* variables, as we had already suspected. A possible treatment in this situation is the use of the Stepwise procedure, which excludes from the model variables whose parameters were not shown to be statistically significant. This can cause a problem of functional specification by omitting a relevant variable to explain the behavior of the dependent variable if there were no other explanatory variables in the final model. The Stepwise procedure, in R, can be performed by the function `step()` that will still deserve other considerations:

```
step_reg <- step(object = multi_reg,
                 k = qchisq(p = 0.05, df = 1, lower.tail = FALSE))
```

Before further discussing the function `step()`, we leave in Figure 14.11 the model after the Stepwise procedure that contains only variables that have been shown to be statistically significant at a significance level of 5%:

```
summary(step_reg)
```

```
Call:
lm(formula = expenditures ~ chronic_diseases + plan_type_gold +
    plan_type_platinum, data = medicalexp_dummies)

Residuals:
    Min      1Q  Median      3Q     Max
-381.61  -73.95  -14.25   73.25  557.89

Coefficients:
                   Estimate Std. Error t value Pr(>|t|)
(Intercept)         1066.05      24.83  42.934  < 2e-16 ***
chronic_diseases      85.83      13.34   6.436 9.20e-10 ***
plan_type_gold       253.34      30.78   8.230 2.58e-14 ***
plan_type_platinum   638.90      53.04  12.045  < 2e-16 ***
---
Signif. codes:  0 '***' 0.001 '**' 0.01 '*' 0.05 '.' 0.1 ' ' 1

Residual standard error: 155.5 on 196 degrees of freedom
Multiple R-squared:  0.8679,	Adjusted R-squared:  0.8658
F-statistic: 429.1 on 3 and 196 DF,  p-value: < 2.2e-16
```

FIGURE 14.11 Outputs of the multiple linear regression model in R, after the Stepwise procedure.

The function `step()` in R-based language, unlike algorithms that perform the Stepwise procedure in other software (e.g., *Stata* and IBM *SPSS*), uses the Akaike Information Criteria (AIC) instead of being guided by the *P*-values of variables.

Thus, for each variable that function `step()` considers as adherent to the model, the value of the AIC statistic is equivalent to a *P*-value of approximately 0.1573 (0.1572992, to be exact). Therefore when there is a comparison between models, which is essentially what the function `step()` does when testing estimations, removing and placing variables until only the statistically significant variables remain in the modeling, the discussed algorithm is comparing AIC statistics values, not *P*-values. That said, the function `step()` will prefer one model to another because of the lower AIC statistic found, adopting as a parameter $-2.\ LL_1-(-2.\ LL_2)>2$, where LL_1 is the value of the maximum likelihood logarithm of a given model, and LL_2 is the maximum likelihood logarithm of another model to which it is compared for the purpose of the Stepwise procedure.

There are two points to be considered: (1) when adopting as parameter $-2.\ LL_1 - (-2.\ LL_2) > 2$, we are facing a statistic, not a test; and (2) the value 2 adopted is in the 84.27th percentile of the probability distribution of the χ^2 test. This assumption can be confirmed with the following command:

```
pchisq(q = 2, df = 1, lower.tail = TRUE)
```

where the function `pchisq()` refers to the probability function of the χ^2 distribution; the argument `q` concerns the vector of quantiles; and the argument `df` concerns degrees of freedom.

Thus, when assuming the χ^2 distribution as a parameter, we are assuming Wilk's Theorem, according to which we must reject H_0 if a statistic exceeds the quantile of significance adopted in the χ^2 test. Thus, when adopting a proposal solution, that is, when we argue `k = qchisq(p = 0.05, df = 1, lower.tail = FALSE)` for the function `step()`, the model is chosen by the following parameter: $-2.\ LL_1 - (-2.\ LL_2) > \chi^2_c$.

On the other hand, the function `ols_step_both_p()` from the package `olsrr` performs the Stepwise procedure using the *P*-values of the variables as a criterion for removal or permanence:

```
ols_step_both_p(model = multi_reg, pent = 0.05, prem = 0.05)
```

where the arguments `pent` and `prem` point to which significance a variable should enter or be removed, respectively, from the model.

An attentive researcher will verify that the variables indicated by the previous routine coincide with those present in the model contained in the object `step_reg`, explained in Figure 14.11. Thus, Expression (14.4) indicates the multiple model after the Stepwise procedure:

$$\widehat{expenditures_i} = 1,066.05 + 85.83 \times chronic\_diseases_i + 253.34 \times plan\_type\_gold_i + 638.90 \times plan\_type\_platinum_i \quad (14.4)$$

From Expression (14.4), it is known that with each additional unit of the variable *chronic_diseases*, there is an average increase of 85.83 units with medical expenditures, keeping the other conditions constant. It is also clear that, if a given observation contracts a health plan of "gold" type, the medical expenditures increase, on average, by 253.34, *ceteris paribus*. Finally, hiring a health plan of "platinum" type, keeping the other conditions constant, generates an average increase of 638.90 in medical expenditures.

Similar to the "Estimation of a simple linear regression model in R" section, the CI of the model contained in the object `step_reg`, can be obtained with the aid of the function `confint()`:

```
confint(step_reg, level = 0.95)
```

From the previous routine, Expressions (14.5) and (14.6) appear, which refer to the lower and upper bounds, respectively, of the CI of the model `step_reg`.

$$\widehat{expenditures}_{i_{min}} = 1017.082 + 59.534 \times chronic\_diseases_i + 192.629 \times plan\_type\_gold_i + 534.288 \times plan\_type\_platinum_i \quad (14.5)$$

$$\widehat{expenditures}_{i_{max}} = 1115.020 + 112.133 \times chronic\_diseases_i + 314.043 \times plan\_type\_gold_i + 743.505 \times plan\_type\_platinum_i \quad (14.6)$$

Next, we will verify the adherence to normality of residuals.

Normality of Residuals: as discussed in Chapter 6 and in the "Estimation of a simple linear regression model in R" section, as $n > 30$, we will use the Shapiro-Francia test to verify whether $\varepsilon \sim N(0, \sigma^2)$:

```
sf.test(step_reg$residuals)
```

A careful researcher will verify that the result of the Shapiro-Francia test proposed by the previous routine was $W = 0.943$, with its corresponding *P*-value < 0.05, **resulting in violation of the assumption of normality of residuals**. This situation may be related to the suspicion of a non-linear relationship by the *expenditure* variable with the other metric explanatory variables.

As a curiosity and in parallel with the "Estimation of a simple linear regression model in R" section, the researcher can plot the residuals of the model `step_reg` together with a theoretical Normal curve, typing the following commands, whose results are shown in Figure 14.12:

```
medicalexp_dummies["resids_step_reg"] <- step_reg$residuals

medicalexp_dummies %>%
  ggplot() +
  geom_histogram(aes(x = resids_step_reg, y = ..density..),
                 fill = "orange",
                 color = "bisque") +
 stat_function(fun = dnorm,
               args = list(mean = mean(medicalexp_dummies$resids_step_reg),
                           sd = sd(medicalexp_dummies$resids_step_reg)),
               color = "darkorchid",
               size = 1.5) +
 labs(x = "Residuals of step_reg object",
      y = "Residuals Density") +
 theme_bw()
```

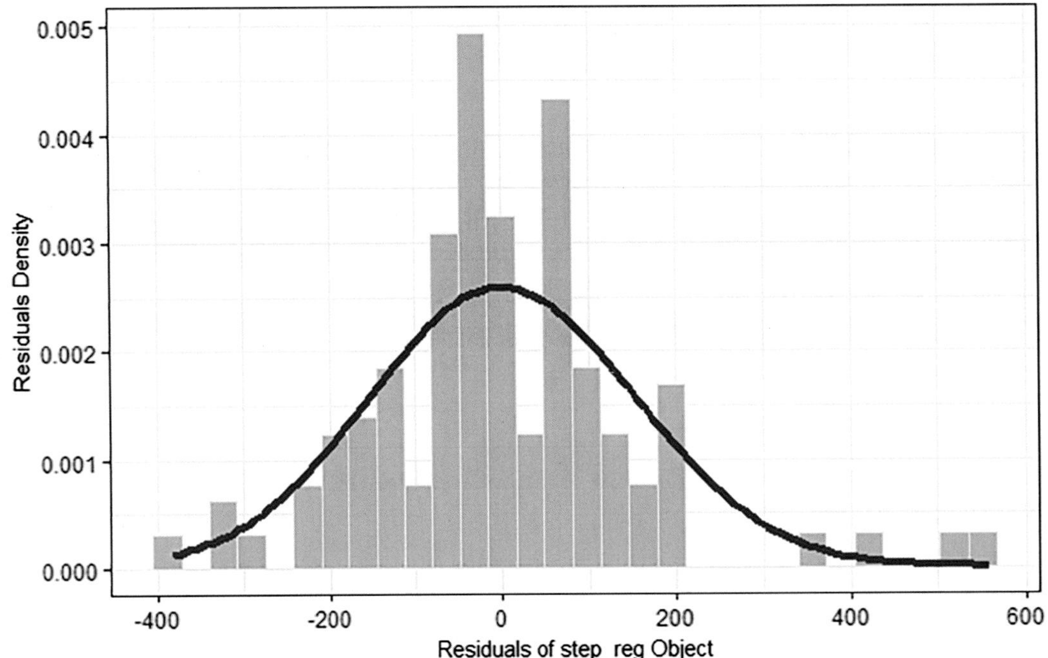

FIGURE 14.12 Residuals of the multiple linear regression model.

Heteroskedasticity Problems: to diagnose the violation of the presumption of homoscedasticity, once again, we will use the Breusch-Pagan/Cook-Weisberg test, present in the function `ols_test_breusch_pagan()` from the package `olsrr`:

```
ols_test_breusch_pagan(step_reg)
```

The test result shows that $\chi^2_{BP} = 60.802$, with 1 degree of freedom and with a P-value < 0.05, indicating **the existence of the heteroskedasticity problem at a significance level of 5%, *ceteris paribus***. Figure 14.13 shows the conical shape when we plot the residuals together with the fitted values of the model (the dashed lines are only a visual aid for the researcher).

```
medicalexp_dummies["fitted_step_reg"] <- step_reg$fitted.values

medicalexp_dummies %>%
  ggplot() +
  geom_point(aes(x = fitted_step_reg, y = resids_step_reg),
             color = "orange") +
  labs(x = "Fitted Values of step_reg",
       y = "Residuals of step_reg") +
  theme_bw()
```

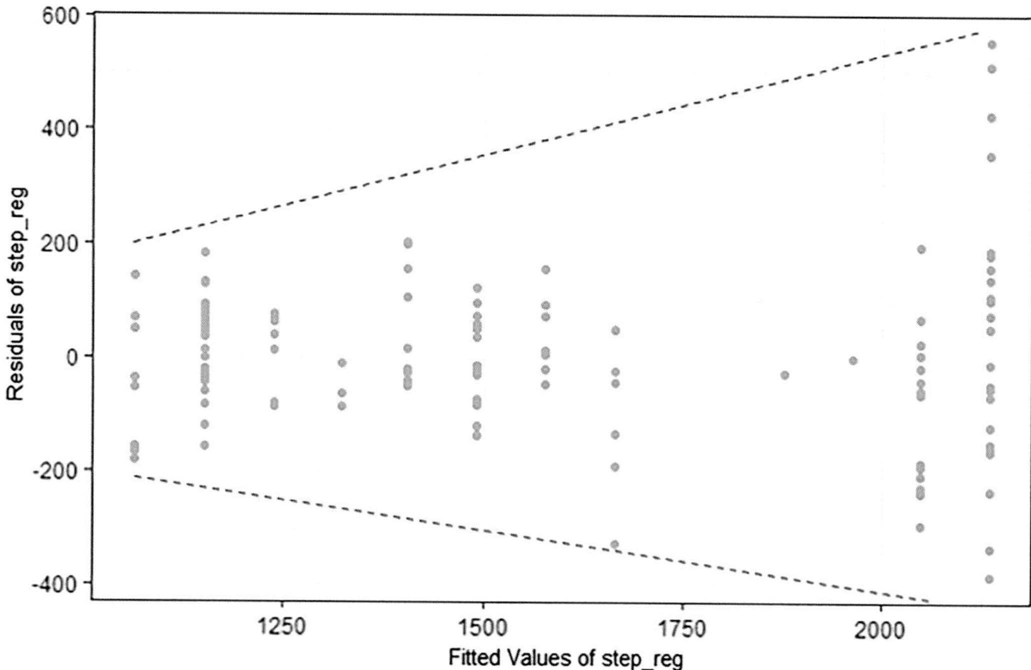

FIGURE 14.13 Conical shape commonly present in heteroskedastic models.

Next, we will discuss non-linear functional forms obtained with the Box-Cox transformation for the dependent variable. Until now, we found that the model contained in the object `step_reg`, estimated through the dataset `medicalexp_dummies`, violates the assumptions of normality of residuals and homoscedasticity. As a **possible** solution, but without guarantee that the procedure will work for all cases, we indicate the Box-Cox transformation of the dependent variable as discussed in the "Non-linear regression models" section. We will follow using the same dataset, continuing the study started in the "Estimation of a multiple linear regression model in R" section.

In view of the last result presented by the model contained in the object `step_reg` (problems of non-adherence of residuals to normality and problems of heteroskedasticity), we propose an attempt to transform the dependent variable *expenditures* according to the postulate by Box and Cox (1964). The transformation, discussed in the "Non-linear regression models" section, can be performed with the function `powerTransform()` from the package `car`:

```
lambda_BC <- powerTransform(medicalexp_dummies$expenditures)
lambda_BC
```

Thus we have:

$$bc\_expenditures_i = \left(\frac{expenditures_i^{\lambda} - 1}{\lambda}\right) = \left(\frac{expenditures_i^{-0.1443673} - 1}{-0.1443673}\right).$$

To transform the variable *expenditures*, we can type the following command:

```
attach(medicalexp_dummies)

medicalexp_dummies["bc_expenditures"] <- ((expenditures ^ lambda_BC$lambda) - 1) /
  lambda_BC$lambda
```

The following graph (Figure 14.14) shows how much the distribution of the *bc_expenditures* (Kernel density estimate) is close to the normal standard distribution and can be compared with the graph that considers the original *expenditures* variable (Figure 14.15). These graphs can be obtained using the following commands:

```
medicalexp_dummies %>%
  ggplot() +
  geom_density(aes(x = bc_expenditures), fill = "orange") +
  labs(x = "Expenditures Variable after Box and Cox (1964) Transformation",
       y = "Density") +
  theme_bw()
```

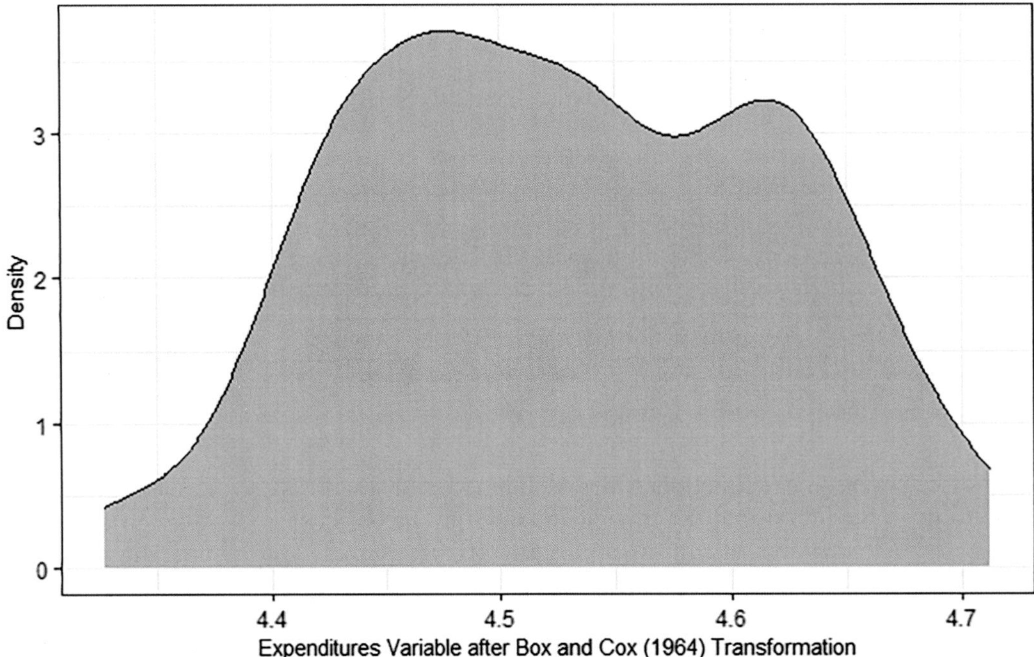

FIGURE 14.14 Kernel density estimate of *bc_expenditures*.

```
medicalexp_dummies %>%
  ggplot() +
  geom_density(aes(x = expenditures), fill = "darkorchid") +
  labs(x = "Expenditures Original Variable",
       y = "Density") +
  theme_bw()
```

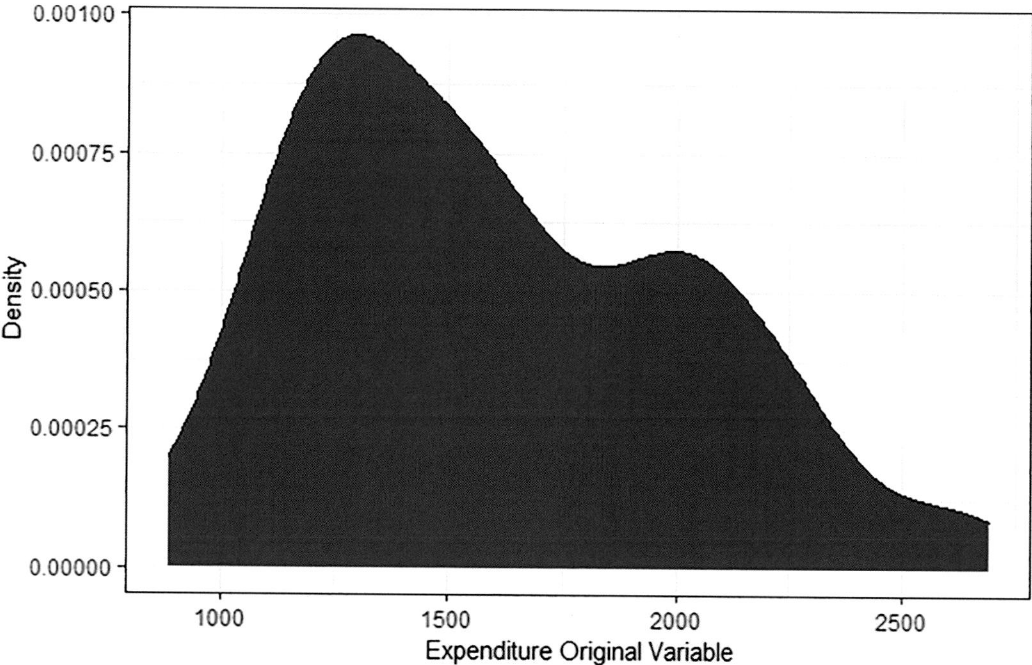

FIGURE 14.15 Kernel density estimate of *expenditures*.

Even though the two variables do not present a very close adherence to normality, it can be seen that the greatest proximity is given by the variable *bc_expenditures*. We can therefore estimate the following model:

$$bc\_expenditures_i = a + b_1 \times age_i + b_2 \times chronic\_diseases_i + b_3 \times income_i + b_4 \times plan\_type\_gold_i + b_5 \times plan\_type\_platinum_i + \varepsilon_i \quad (14.7)$$

As presented earlier, we can estimate the new multiple model with the transformed dependent variable (*bc_expenditures*), as follows:

```
multi_reg_bc <- lm(formula = bc_expenditures ~ age + chronic_diseases +
                     income + plan_type_gold + plan_type_platinum,
                   data = medicalexp_dummies)
```

Next, we can apply the Stepwise procedure:

```
step_reg_bc <- step(object = multi_reg_bc,
                    k = qchisq(p = 0.05, df = 1, lower.tail = FALSE))
```

The model parameters present in the object `step_reg_bc` can be accessed using the function `summary()` and are explained in Figure 14.16:

```
summary(step_reg_bc)
```

```
Call:
lm(formula = bc_expenditures ~ chronic_diseases + plan_type_gold + 
    plan_type_platinum, data = medicalexp_dummies)

Residuals:
      Min        1Q    Median        3Q       Max 
-0.076218 -0.017075  0.000068  0.016946  0.075196 

Coefficients:
                   Estimate Std. Error t value Pr(>|t|)    
(Intercept)        4.402643   0.004771 922.716  < 2e-16 ***
chronic_diseases   0.019429   0.002563   7.582 1.33e-12 ***
plan_type_gold     0.072174   0.005915  12.202  < 2e-16 ***
plan_type_platinum 0.136964   0.010193  13.437  < 2e-16 ***
---
Signif. codes:  0 '***' 0.001 '**' 0.01 '*' 0.05 '.' 0.1 ' ' 1

Residual standard error: 0.02987 on 196 degrees of freedom
Multiple R-squared:  0.892,	Adjusted R-squared:  0.8903 
F-statistic: 539.4 on 3 and 196 DF,  p-value: < 2.2e-16
```

FIGURE 14.16 Model parameter represented by the object `step_reg_bc`.

According to Figure 14.16, the non-linear model present in the object `step_reg_bc` contains the same variables that were present in the linear model, being statistically significant at a significance level of 5%. However, an attentive reader will notice that the parameter values are completely different from those previously shown in Figure 14.11. It is also important to point out that, although it did not occur, a variable that was previously disregarded could re-compose the new model with the transformed dependent variable because of the new functional form of the model, which directly implies the way the variables are related.

That said, we can test, again, the assumption of normality of residuals:

```
sf.test(step_reg_bc$residuals)
```

For the Shapiro-Francia test applied to the model kept by the object `step_reg_bc`, we have $W = 0.987$ with its P-value > 0.05, **indicating adherence of the residuals to normality, at a significance level of 5%.**

The plotting of the error terms of the model internal to the object can be obtained with the following routine and can be verified using Figure 14.17:

```
medicalexp_dummies["resids_step_bc"] <- step_reg_bc$residuals

medicalexp_dummies %>%
  ggplot() +
  geom_histogram(aes(x = resids_step_bc, y = ..density..),
                 fill = "orange",
                 color = "bisque") +
  stat_function(fun = dnorm,
                args = list(mean = mean(medicalexp_dummies$resids_step_bc),
                            sd = sd(medicalexp_dummies$resids_step_bc)),
                color = "darkorchid",
                size = 1.5) +
  labs(x = "Residuals of step_reg_bc Object",
       y = "Residuals Density") +
  theme_bw()
```

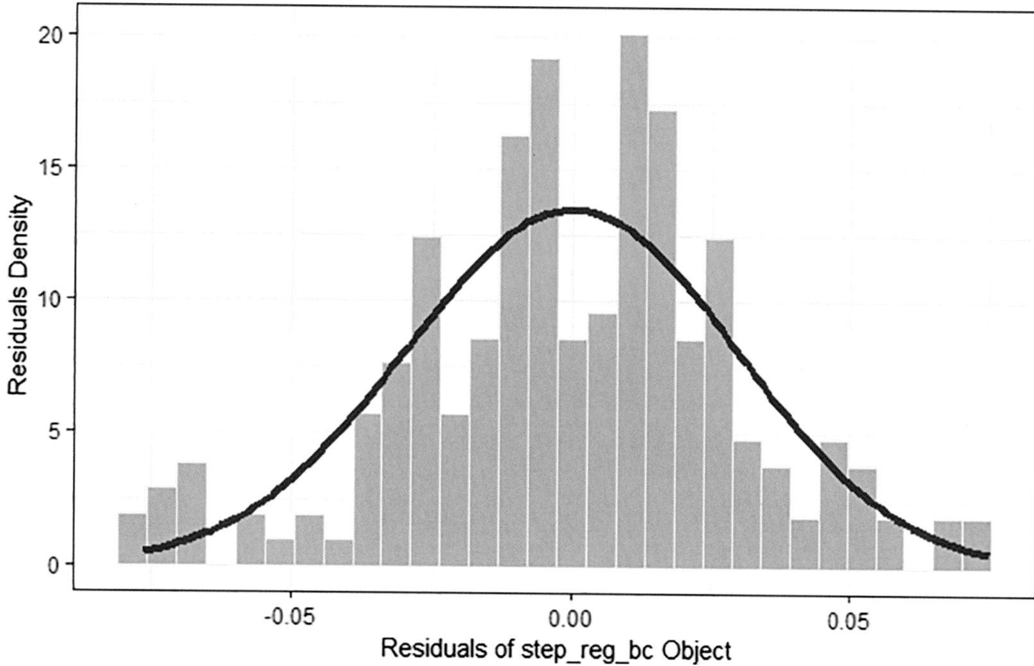

FIGURE 14.17 Residuals of the multiple regression model after a Box-Cox transformation in the dependent variable.

We should also verify if the new estimation presents the problem of heteroskedasticity:

```
ols_test_breusch_pagan(step_reg_bc)
```

The problem of heteroskedasticity has also been solved! Despite what happened, we reiterate that the Box-Cox transformation will not always be so successful, but we consider it an important skill to share with the researcher. The transformation proposed by Box and Cox (1964) can be a valuable resource to correct some models in which the error terms are not normally distributed. However, as demonstrated, there is no guarantee that the instrument will work in all cases. Figure 14.18 demonstrates the absence of the conical shape, commonly indicating a heteroskedastic model.

```
medicalexp_dummies["fitted_step_bc"] <- step_reg_bc$fitted.values

medicalexp_dummies %>%
  ggplot() +
  geom_point(aes(x = fitted_step_bc, y = resids_step_bc),
             color = "orange") +
  labs(x = "Fitted Values of step_reg_bc",
       y = "Residuals of step_reg_bc") +
  theme_bw()
```

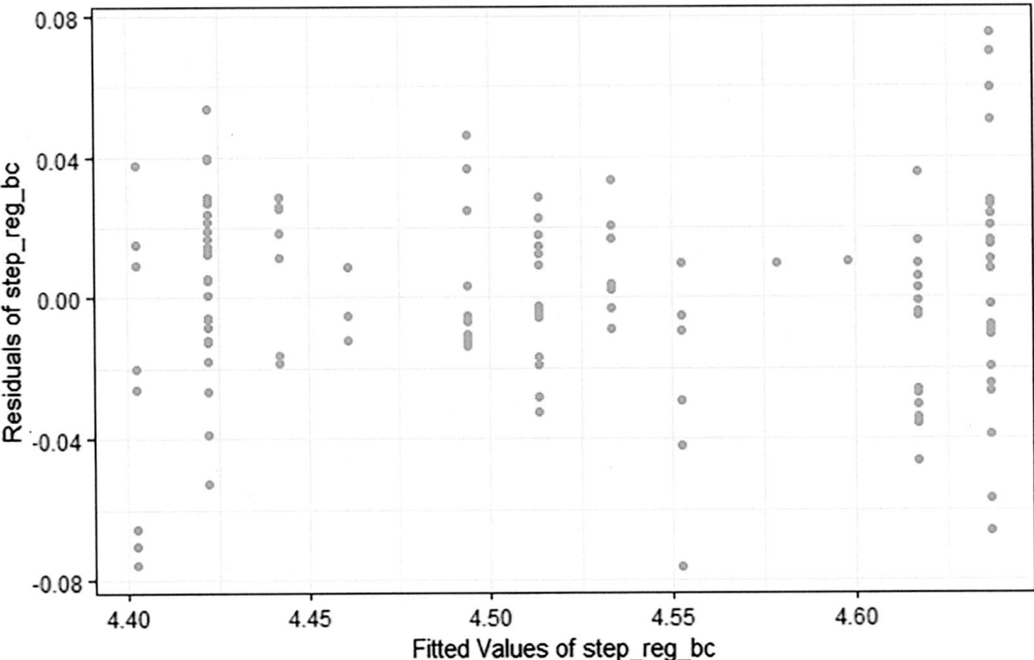

FIGURE 14.18 Plotting of residuals and fitted values of the model present in the object `step_reg_bc`.

The functional form of the model present in the object `step_reg_bc` is formally described in Expression (14.8).

$$\frac{\widehat{expenditures}_{i_{min}}^{-0.1443673} - 1}{-0.1443673} = 4.402 + 0.019 \times chronic\_diseases_i + 0.072 \times plan\_type\_gold_i + 0.137 \times plan\_type\_platinum_i \tag{14.8}$$

The confidence intervals can be displayed with the function `confint()`. Expressions (14.9) and (14.10) show the functional forms of the model for the lower and upper bounds of the CI, respectively, with a confidence level of 95% (5% significance level):

```
confint(step_reg_bc)
```

$$\frac{\widehat{expenditures}_{i_{min}}^{-0.1443673} - 1}{-0.1443673} = 4.393 + 0.014 \times chronic\_diseases_i + 0.061 \times plan\_type\_gold_i + 0.117 \times plan\_type\_platinum_i \tag{14.9}$$

$$\frac{\widehat{expenditures}_{i_{max}}^{-0.1443673} - 1}{-0.1443673} = 4.412 + 0.024 \times chronic\_diseases_i + 0.084 \times plan\_type\_gold_i + 0.157 \times plan\_type\_platinum_i \tag{14.10}$$

Finally, we find it interesting to discuss the commands for predictions in the estimations whose dependent variable was transformed. To make predictions, we just use the function `predict()`, as discussed in the "Estimation of a simple linear regression model in R" section. Thus, respecting the ranges of the explanatory variables present in the model contained by the object `step_reg_bc` (Figure 14.13), we can predict what the *expenditures* are for an individual who has three types of chronic diseases and who contracted the plan in the "platinum" category:

```
predict(object = step_reg_bc,
        newdata = data.frame(chronic_diseases = 3,
                             plan_type_gold = 0,
                             plan_type_platinum = 1))
```

Caution! Even though R returned the value of 4.597892, **this is the value of the *expenditures* variable after the Box-Cox transformation!** That said, according to our model, the estimated amount of *expenditures* for the simulation in the previous code **is not**, on average, US $4.597892, *ceteris paribus*, with a 95% confidence level!

We should therefore reverse the transformation by doing exactly the reverse of its steps. Algebraically:

$$\frac{\widehat{Y}^{-0.1443673} - 1}{-0.1443673} = 4.597892$$

so:

$$\widehat{Y} = 1901.165$$

or:

```
(1 / ((4.597892 * -0.1443673) + 1)) ^ (1 / 0.1443673)
```

Thus, for an individual who has three types of chronic diseases and who has contracted the plan in the "platinum" category, an average expenditure of US $1901.165 is expected, *ceteris paribus*.

Final remarks

The simple and multiple regression models estimated by the OLS method represent the group of regression techniques most used in academic and organizational environments, given the ease of application and interpretation of obtained results, besides being available in most software programs, even those in which there is no specific focus on the statistical analysis of data. It is also important to highlight the practicality of the techniques studied in this chapter for the purpose of preparing diagnoses and forecasts.

It is of fundamental importance that the researcher always evaluate and discuss the considerations of the technique presuppositions and, more than that, always reflect on the possibility that they are not necessarily models with linear functional forms.

We finally express that the researcher need not restrict the analysis of the behavior of a certain phenomenon based only and exclusively on the subjacent theory. The application of regression models requests, at times, that variables based on the experience and intuition of the researcher be included to generate ever more interesting and different models than traditionally proposed. In this way, new points of view and perspectives for the study of phenomena can always arise, which contributes to scientific development and the increase in ever more innovative empirical studies.

Exercises

1. The file `corruption.RData` provides data on 52 countries for a certain year, namely (Fávero and Belfiore, 2019):

Variable	Description
country	A string variable that identifies country *i*.
cpi	Corruption Perception Index that corresponds to citizen perception regarding the public sector abuse of a nation's private benefits, covering administrators and politicians (Source: Transparency International)
age	Average age of billionaires in a country (Source: Forbes)
hours	Average number of hours worked per week in a country, namely, the annual total of hours worked divided by 52 weeks (Source: International Labour Organization)

You wish to investigate if the perception of corruption in a country is as a function of the average age of its billionaires and average quantity of weekly hours worked and will therefore estimate the following model:

$$cpi_i = a + b_1 \cdot age_i + b_2 \cdot hours_i + u_i$$

We would like you to:

a. Analyze the significance level of the F-test. Is at least one of the variables (*age* and *hours*) statistically significant to explain the behavior of the *cpi* variable at the 5% significance level?

b. If the answer to the previous item is yes, analyze the significance level for each explanatory variable (t-tests). Are both statistically significant to explain the behavior of *cpi* at the 5% significance level 5%?

c. What is the final estimated equation for the multiple linear regression model?

d. What is R^2?

e. Discuss the results in terms of the signal coefficients of the explanatory variables.

f. Save the model residuals, and verify the existence of normality in these error terms.

g. Using the Breusch-Pagan/Cook-Weisberg test, check if there is evidence of heteroskedasticity in the final proposed model.

h. Present the VIF and Tolerance statistics, and discuss the results.

2. The file `corruption_emer.RData` provides the same data as the previous exercise, however with one more variable, namely (Fávero and Belfiore, 2019):

Variable	Description
emerging	Dummy variable corresponding to the fact that the country is considered either developed or emerging, according to the criteria of Compustat Global. In this case, if the country is developed, the variable *emerging* = 0, otherwise, the variable *emerging* = 1.

Initially it should be investigated if, in fact, the countries considered as emerging present lower *cpi* levels. Being thus:

a. What is the difference between the average *cpi* index for emerging countries against developed countries? Is this difference statistically significant to the 5% significance level?

b. Prepare, using the Stepwise procedure with a 10% significance level for rejection of the t-test's null hypothesis, an estimation of the model with the functional linear form that follows. Write the equation for the final estimated model.

$$cpi_i = a + b_1 \cdot age_i + b_2 \cdot hours_i + b_3 \cdot emerging_i + u_i$$

c. Based on this estimation, what would the forecast be, on average, of the *cpi* index for the country considered as emerging, with an average billionaire age of 51 and an average quantity of 37 hours worked weekly?

d. What are the minimum and maximum values for the confidence interval for the forecast of the previous item at a confidence level of 90%?

e. Imagine that a researcher proposes, for the problem under consideration, that the following non-linear model functional form be estimated. Write the final model equation estimated by the Stepwise procedure with a 10% significance level for the rejection of the t-test's null hypothesis.

$$cpi_i = a + b_1 \cdot age_i + b_2 \cdot \ln(hours_i) + b_3 \cdot emerging_i + u_i$$

f. Given that no problems were identified referent to the regression models in both cases, what would be the chosen functional form for forecasting purposes?

Supplementary data sets

```
cholesterol.RData
companies.RData
corruption.RData
corruption_emer.RData
medical_expenditure.RData
```

Please access supplementary data files here: https://doi.org/10.17632/55623jkwrp.3

CHAPTER

15

Binary and multinomial logistic regression models

AT THE END OF THIS CHAPTER, YOU WILL BE ABLE TO:

- Evaluate the results of statistical tests concerning logistic models.
- Develop confidence intervals of the model parameters for the purpose of prediction.
- Elaborate sensitivity analysis, and understand the concepts of cutoff, overall model efficiency, sensitivity, and specificity.
- Interpret the sensitivity curve and the ROC curve.
- Develop logistic and multinomial regression models in R, and interpret their results.

R-based language packages used in this chapter

```
library(plotly)
library(tidyverse)
library(jtools)
library(lmtest)
library(caret)
library(e1071)
library(ROCR)
library(fastDummies)
library(nnet)
library(reshape2)
```

Don't forget to define the R working directory (the location where your datasets are installed):

```
setwd("C:/book/chapter15")
```


https://doi.org/10.1016/B978-0-12-824271-1.00008-1

Estimation of binary and multinomial logistic regression models in R

The objective of this section is not to again discuss all concepts inherent to binary and multinomial logistic regression statistics, but to provide the researcher with an opportunity to prepare the same examples explored throughout the chapter with the use of R-based language.

Estimation of a binary logistic regression model in R

The data that will serve as an example for the estimation of the binary logistic regression are present in the file `barbecue.RData`. We ask the reader to load the dataset:

```
load("barbecue.RData")
```

The variables contained in the object `barbecue` are shown in Table 15.1.

TABLE 15.1 Variables contained in the object `barbecue`.

Variable	Description
income	Dependent binary variable that corresponds to the fact of the classifier represents a higher level of income (label 1) or a lower level of income (label 0).
beef	Annual expenditure on beef (x US$ 1000).
chicken	Annual expenditure on chicken (x US$ 1000).

The function `summary()` presents the univariate descriptive statistics of the variables present in the dataset `barbecue`:

```
summary(barbecue)
```

Figure 15.1 shows the results of the R-based language to the previous statement.

```
     income          meet           chicken
 Min.   :0.0   Min.   :1.479   Min.   :2.000
 1st Qu.:0.0   1st Qu.:3.929   1st Qu.:4.096
 Median :0.5   Median :4.860   Median :4.862
 Mean   :0.5   Mean   :4.785   Mean   :4.756
 3rd Qu.:1.0   3rd Qu.:5.543   3rd Qu.:5.435
 Max.   :1.0   Max.   :8.171   Max.   :6.856
```

FIGURE 15.1 Results from the function `summary()` for each variable in the dataset `barbecue`.

In R, a binary logistic regression model can be established using the function `glm()`, which is natively installed, whose minimum arguments must be `formula`, `data` and `family`:

```
logit_model <- glm(formula = income ~ .,
                   data = barbecue,
                   family = "binomial")
```

For the argument `formula`, we declare the variables that will be used in the modeling, reserving the first place for the dependent variable (*income*, in this case), followed by the operator ~ and, finally the operator . which indicates that all other variables in the dataset will be considered as predictors. For the argument `data`, we must indicate the dataset from which the variables declared by the argument `formula` come from. Finally, for the argument `family`, we must declare `"binomial"`.

Before exploring the model parameters, we will take a moment to discuss some important components of the object `logit_model`, which can be accessed using the operator `$`:

- `coefficients`: vector of dimension $(k+1)\times 1$ that contains the value of α (always in the first position) and the values of β, where k refers to the number of variables used in the model.
- `fitted.values`: vector of dimension $n\times 1$ that refers to the estimated values of occurrence probability of an event of the dependent variable for the observations present in the dataset, used for the regression model.

Similar to the one studied in Chapter 14, we can verify the estimation of the model parameters contained in the object `logit_model` using the function `summary()`, but as presented earlier in the "General statistical significance of the binary logistic regression model and each of its parameters," section there is no evidence of the general statistics of the model. Therefore we will give preference to use of the function `summ()` from the package `jtools`:

```
summ(model = logit_model, confint = TRUE , digits = 5)
```

In the previous code, we used the argument `model` in the function `summ()` to declare the object that contains the model that we want to observe; we used the argument `digits` to define the number of decimal places that will be considered for rounding parameters; and we indicated the logical value `TRUE` for the argument `confint` to have a 95% confidence interval (CI). For other confidence levels, it is enough for the researcher to argue `ci.width`, declaring the desired numeric value. Figure 15.2 explains the result of applying the function `summ()` from the object `logit_model`:

```
MODEL INFO:
Observations: 400
Dependent Variable: income
Type: Generalized linear model
  Family: binomial
  Link function: logit

MODEL FIT:
χ²(2) = 135.43218, p = 0.00000
Pseudo-R² (Cragg-Uhler) = 0.38296
Pseudo-R² (McFadden) = 0.24423
AIC = 425.08556, BIC = 437.05996

Standard errors: MLE
-----------------------------------------------------------------
---
                        Est.        2.5%       97.5%      z val.        p
----------------- ---------- ---------- ---------- ---------- -------
--
(Intercept)          6.03193     4.05437     8.00948     5.97827   0.00000
meet                 0.13443    -0.05567     0.32454     1.38601   0.16574
chicken             -1.39795    -1.71896    -1.07693    -8.53515   0.00000
-----------------------------------------------------------------
```

FIGURE 15.2 Results from function `summ()` of the object `logit_model`.

If, on one hand, Figure 15.2 brings interesting information about our model, even eliminating the need to use the function `confint()` to estimate the CI, on the other hand, the function `summ()` does not present standard errors referring to modeling. For that, we must use the function `export_summs()`, also available in the package `jtools`, which will be presented later.

The number of observations from the dataset used in the model, the dependent variable of the estimation, and the type of modeling that was performed is demarcated by the label `MODEL INFO` at the top of Figure 15.2.

In the part called `MODEL FIT`, we have access to the general statistics of the model, and we can see that $\chi^2_{2\ d.f.}=135.432$ with $p.\ value=0.000$, that is, we can say that there is some explanatory variable that is statistically different from zero to a 95% confidence level, keeping the other conditions constant.

The calculation of $\chi^2_{2\ d.f.}=135.432$ can be measured using the function `lrtest()` from the package `lmtest`. The function `lrtest()` is used for the application of the Log Likelihood Ratio (LLR) test which, in summary, compares two models seeking to verify whether or not they are different. In this way, the LLR test will indicate whether the increment of log likelihood (LL) proposed by one of the models, in relation to the other, is statistically different from zero at a given level of significance. Therefore to use the function `lrtest()`, in theory, we must declare two models; if we do not, the function will compare the only model declared to a non-conditional estimation, that is, a model estimated with the same dependent variable, but with only a single predictor parameter: the intercept.

```
lrtest(object = logit_model)
```

Figure 15.3 shows R's response to the previous command.

```
Likelihood ratio test

Model 1: income ~ meet + chicken
Model 2: income ~ 1
  #Df  LogLik Df  Chisq Pr(>Chisq)
1   3 -209.54
2   1 -277.26 -2 135.43  < 2.2e-16 ***
---
Signif. codes:  0 '***' 0.001 '**' 0.01 '*' 0.05 '.' 0.1 ' ' 1
```

FIGURE 15.3 Results from the function `lrtest()` from the package `lmtest`.

The results evidenced by the function `lrtest()`, at this point, are useful for two things. The first, somewhat obvious, is that the model contained in the object `logit_model` is better suited than a non-conditional model, which we already know because the general statistics of the model contained in the object `logit_model` proved to be statistically significant at 95% confidence, pointing out that any of our explanatory variables is different from zero, *ceteris paribus*, therefore generating a prediction capacity superior to that of a model that uses only the intercept. The second interesting situation is that the function `lrtest()` shows the LL values of each estimation, allowing us to calculate the general statistics of the model (χ^2) contained by the object `logit_model`:

$$\chi^2 = -2.[-277.26 - (-209.54)] = 135.44$$

Because the estimation contained in the object `logit_model` has two slope coefficients (β_1 and β_1), we therefore have 2 degrees of freedom (we can also reach this conclusion by subtracting the values referring to the degrees of freedom in Figure 15.3). Thus it would remain to calculate the critical value of the χ^2 statistic in case you want to verify, in a different way, its statistical significance. The situation can be solved with the function `qchisq()` in R-based language:

```
qchisq(p = 0.05, df = 2, lower.tail = FALSE)
```

When commanding the previous routine, we demand that R tells us the critical value of the χ^2 statistic, with a 5% significance level and 2 degrees of freedom. So, we will have the answer $\chi^2_c=5.991$. Thus as $\chi^2_{calc}>\chi^2_c$, in fact, it has that at least one of the two explanatory variables selected that can explain the behavior of the dependent variable, at a 5% significance level, keeping the others conditions constant. The *P*-value can be extracted as follows:

```
pchisq(q = 135.44, df = 2, lower.tail = FALSE)
```

With the outputs of Figure 15.3, we can also calculate the McFadden pseudo R^2:

$$pseudoR^2(McFadden) = \frac{-2.(-277.26) - [-2.(-209.5)]}{-2.(-277.26)} = 0.244$$

In the part `MODEL FIT` in Figure 15.2, we can also verify the estimated values for each parameter of the model, its CI, the values of Wald z statistics, and their respective *P*-values. Thus we will notice that only the variable *chicken* was statistically different from zero, at a 5% significance level, in the presence of the other variables. Therefore we can apply the Stepwise procedure to eliminate variables that are not significant to explain the behavior of the dependent variable *income*, and/or mitigate any multicollinearity problems of the model contained in the object `logit_model`.

```
step_logit_model <- step(object = logit_model,
                         k = qchisq(p = 0.05, df = 1, lower.tail = FALSE))
```

Soon after, we can apply the function `summ()` to the object `step_logit_model`:

```
summ(model = step_logit_model, confint = TRUE, digits = 5)
```

Figure 15.4 shows the outputs of the function `summ()` applied to our binary logistic model after the Stepwise procedure, now contained in the object `step_logit_model`.

```
MODEL INFO:
Observations: 400
Dependent Variable: income
Type: Generalized linear model
  Family: binomial
  Link function: logit

MODEL FIT:
χ²(1) = 133.49507, p = 0.00000
Pseudo-R² (Cragg-Uhler) = 0.37834
Pseudo-R² (McFadden) = 0.24074
AIC = 425.02267, BIC = 433.00560

Standard errors: MLE
-----------------------------------------------------------------
---
                        Est.       2.5%      97.5%     z val.       p
----------------- ---------- ---------- ---------- ---------- -------
--
(Intercept)          6.95214    5.43579    8.46848    8.98604  0.00000
chicken             -1.45369   -1.76502   -1.14237   -9.15177  0.00000
-----------------------------------------------------------------
```

FIGURE 15.4 Outputs from the function `summ()` from the object `step_logit_model`.

Looking at the results presented in Figure 15.4, we can see what we will consider our final model. If we want to access the standard errors of the model contained in the object `logit_model`, we could do so using the function `export_summs()` from the package `jtools`:

```
export_summs(step_logit_model, digits = 5)
```

Figure 15.5 explains the result of the previous command.

```
                                    Model 1
                         ------------------------
    (Intercept)                    6.95214 ***
                                  (0.77366)
    chicken                       -1.45369 ***
                                  (0.15884)
                         ------------------------
    N                            400
    AIC                          425.02267
    BIC                          433.00560
    Pseudo R2                      0.37834
    ---------------------------------------------
    *** p < 0.001; ** p < 0.01; * p < 0.05.

Column names: names, Model 1
```

FIGURE 15.5 Results from the function `export_summs()` from the package `jtools`.

In Figure 15.5, it is possible to see the estimated value for each model parameter contained by the object `step_logit_model`, in the same way as shown in Figure 15.4. The values regarding the standard errors of each parameter are shown in parentheses below each estimated value for the model parameters. Finally, the statistical significance of the estimation coefficients is given by the number of asterisks, whose legend is at the bottom of Figure 15.5.

After the foregoing, with the help of Figure 15.4, we can algebraically describe our final model:

$$p_i = \frac{1}{1 + e^{-(6.952 - 1.454 chicken_i)}}$$

Still with the aid of Figure 15.4, we can write the expressions for the lower (minimum) and upper (maximum) limits of the estimated probability with 95% confidence.

$$p_{i_{min}} = \frac{1}{1 + e^{-(5.436 - 1.765 chicken_i)}}$$

$$p_{i_{max}} = \frac{1}{1 + e^{-(8.468 - 1.142 chicken_i)}}$$

Therefore we can ask an important question: On average, what is the estimated expected probability of an individual belonging to a high-income group and with annual chicken consumption expenditure equal to US$ 2.594?

The command `predict()` allows the researcher to answer this question directly. To do this, we must type the following routine:

```
predict(object = step_logit_model,
        newdata = data.frame(chicken = 2.594),
        type = "response")
```

The reader may remember the measurement scale of the chicken variable—it represents the annual chicken consumption × US$ 1,000, hence the declaration is in decimal numbers. In response to the previous command, R will point to a 96.01% probability, on average, for the individual to belong to a group with a higher level of income.

It is important to say that the values calculated by the model parameters are used to calculate the probability of occurrence of a given event. To calculate the chance of occurrence for an event of interest in altering a unit of the corresponding explanatory variable, keeping the remaining conditions constant, we can use the function `coef()` internally to the function `exp()`, both natively installed in R, declaring the estimated model contained in the object `step_logit_model`:

```
exp(coef(object = step_logit_model))
```

The results of the previous command are shown in Figure 15.6.

```
 (Intercept)       chicken
1045.3810628     0.2337052
```

FIGURE 15.6 Results from the function `exp(coef())` from the object `step_logit_model`.

The only difference between the outputs in Figure 15.4 and those presented in Figure 15.6 is that now R presents the odds ratios for each explanatory variable. In what remains, it is asserted that the Wald z statistics and their respective P-values are exactly the same as those presented in Figure 15.4.

Now, we can propose another question: on average, by how much does the chance of an individual belonging to a high-income group decrease, when the variable *chicken* is increased by 1 unit, keeping other conditions constant?

The answer can now be given directly. The chance of an individual belonging to a group with higher level of income, when increasing the value of the variable *chicken* by 1 unit, may be multiplied by a factor of 0.766 (23.4% smaller), *ceteris paribus*.

The probability model being estimated, we can use the component `fitted.values` of the object `step_logit_model` to generate a new variable (*phat*) in the dataset. This new variable corresponds to the expected (predicted) values of the probability of an event occurrence for each observation, calculated based on the estimated parameters in the last modeling executed.

```
barbecue["phat"] <- step_logit_model$fitted.values
```

For teaching purposes, we will prepare three distinct graphs that relate the dependent variable and the *chicken* variable. These graphs are presented in Figures 15.7 to 15.9. The commands to obtain each are as follows:

```
#Figure 15.7

barbecue %>%
  ggplot(aes(group = 1)) +
  geom_point(aes(x = chicken, y = income),
             alpha = 0.5) +
  geom_smooth(aes(x = chicken, y = income, color = "Fitted Values"),
              method = "lm",
              formula = y ~ x,
              se = F) +
  labs(x = "Annual expenditure on chicken (US$)",
       y = "Income level") +
  scale_color_manual("Labels:", values = "darkorchid") +
  theme_bw()
```

```
#Figure 15.8

barbecue %>%
  ggplot() +
  geom_point(aes(x = chicken, y = income),
             alpha = 0.5) +
  geom_smooth(aes(x = chicken, y = phat, color = "Fitted Values"),
              method = "glm",
              formula =y ~ x,
              method.args = list(family = "binomial"),
              se = F) +
  labs(x = "Annual expenditure on chicken (US$)",
       y = "Income level") +
  scale_color_manual("Labels:", values = "darkorchid") +
  theme_bw()
```

```
#Figure 15.9

barbecue %>%
  ggplot() +
  geom_point(aes(x = chicken, y = phat),
             alpha = 0.5) +
  geom_smooth(aes(x = chicken, y = phat, color = "Fitted Values"),
              method = "glm",
              formula = y ~ x,
              method.args = list(family = "binomial"),
              se = F) +
  labs(x = "Annual expenditure on chicken (US$)",
       y = "Income level") +
  scale_color_manual("Labels:", values = "darkorchid") +
  theme_bw()
```

Although the graph in Figure 15.7 only presents the linear adjustment between the dependent and *chicken* variables, which does not provide much benefit to the analysis, the graph in Figure 15.8 gives the logistic adjustment based on the estimated probabilities while presenting the dependent variable in dichotomic form, therefore this graph is called the *deterministic logistic adjustment*. Finally, the graph in Figure 15.9, although similar to the previous graph, shows how the probabilities of occurrence for the event of interest behave as a function of alterations in the *chicken* variable and is therefore called the *probabilistic logistic adjustment*.

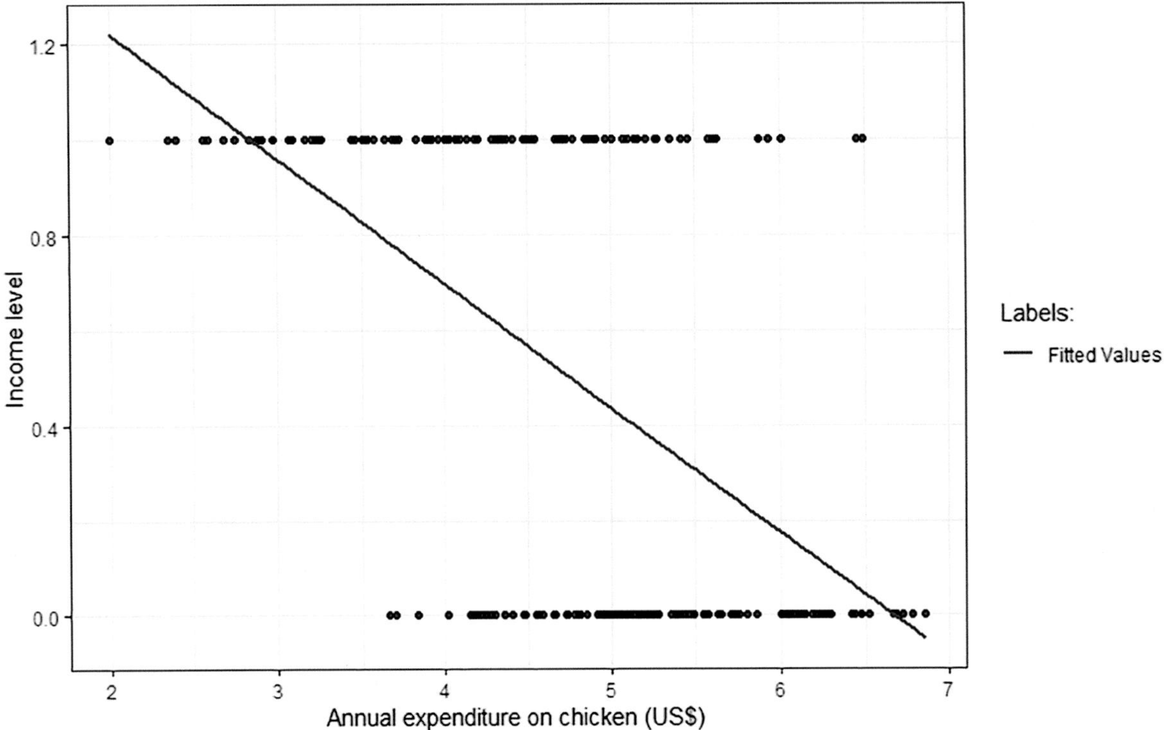

FIGURE 15.7 Linear adjustment between dependent and *chicken* variables.

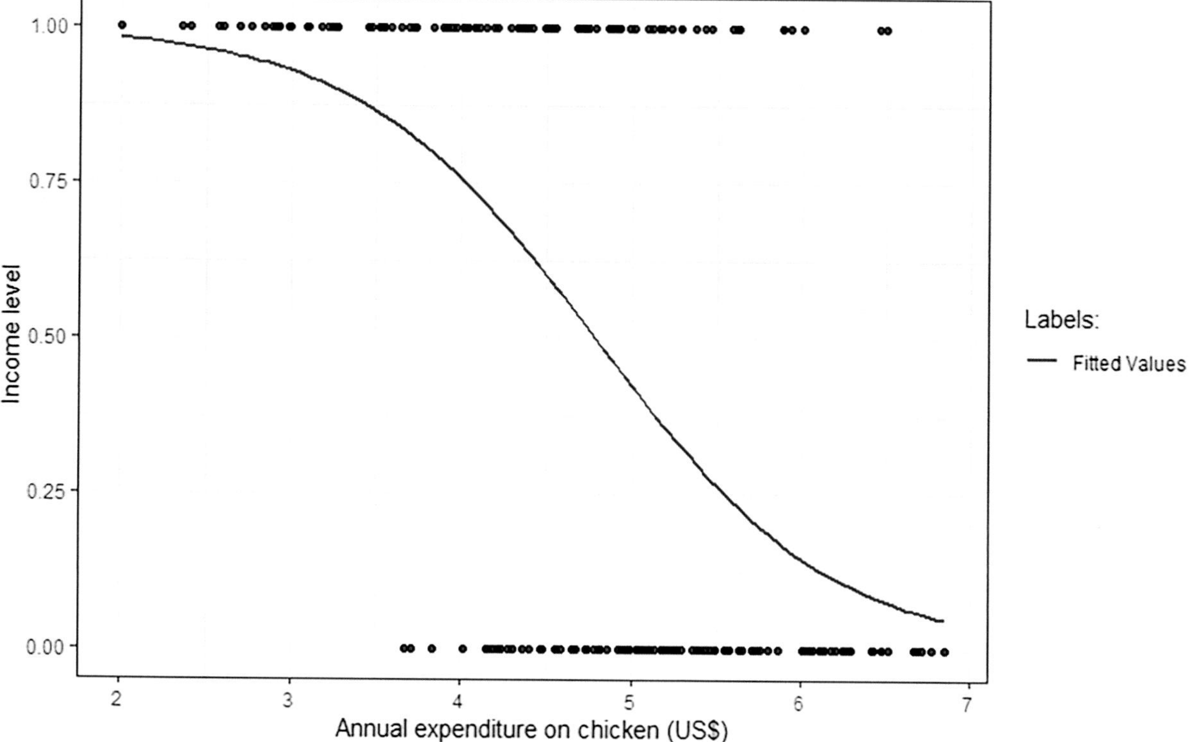

FIGURE 15.8 Deterministic logistic adjustment between dependent and *chicken* variables.

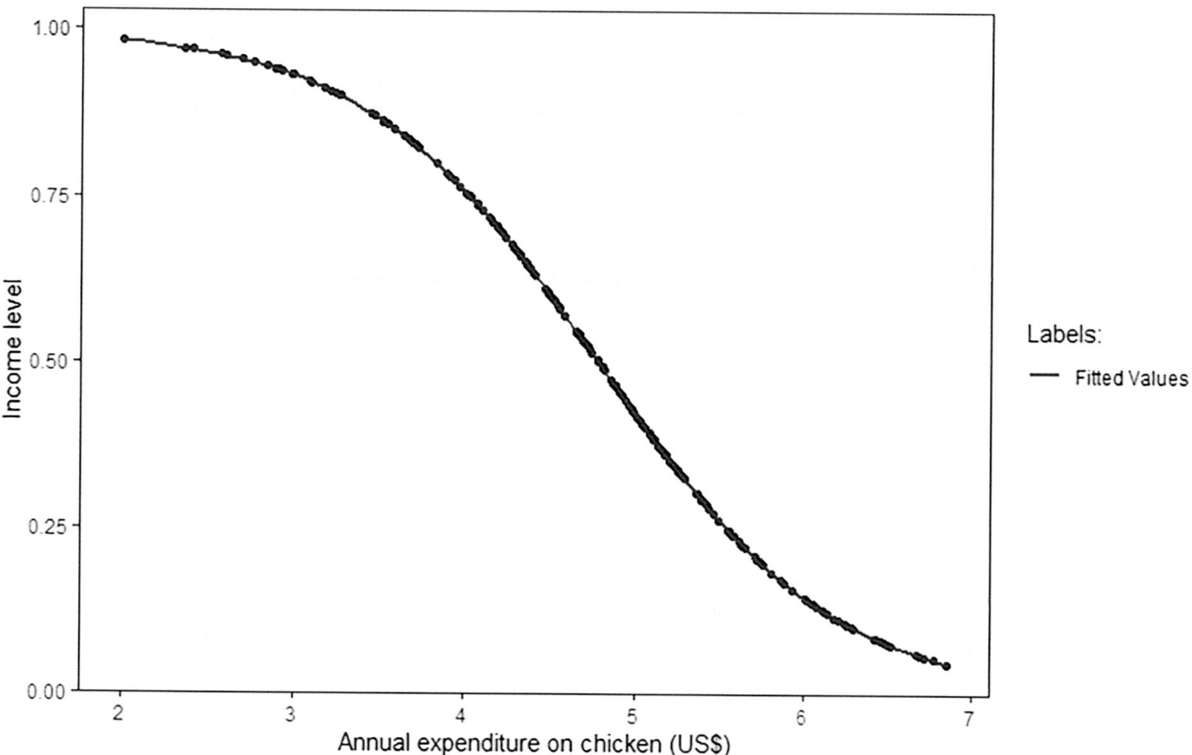

FIGURE 15.9 Probabilistic logistic adjustment between dependent and *chicken* variables.

Based on the final estimated model, we can now prepare the sensitivity analysis for the proposed model in accordance with what we presented in the "Cutoff, sensitivity analysis, overall model efficiency, sensitivity, and specificity" section. To do this, we can type the following command to create a variable called *classification*:

```
barbecue["classification"] <- predict(object = step_logit_model,
                                      newdata = barbecue,
                                      type = "response") > 0.5
```

We will begin the sensitivity analysis with a cutoff of 0.5 (hence the statement: `> 0.5`). After that, we can use the function `confusionMatrix()` from the package `caret` to evaluate a contingency table that crosses the observed values of an event (*income* = 1) with the predicted values classified as an event for a 50% cutoff (*classification* = TRUE):

```
confusionMatrix(
  data = table(barbecue$classification,
               barbecue$income == 1)[2:1, 2:1]
)
```

In the previous routine, the adjustment proposed by `[2:1, 2:1]` is for the algorithm `confusionMatrix()` to give answers according to what is proposed by this work, that is, event = 1 and non-event = 0. If the researcher does not make the adjustment, R will understand event = 0 and non-event = 1. The generated output is found in Figure 15.10.

```
Confusion Matrix and Statistics

       TRUE FALSE
TRUE    140    48
FALSE    60   152

               Accuracy : 0.73
                 95% CI : (0.6836, 0.7729)
    No Information Rate : 0.5
    P-Value [Acc > NIR] : <2e-16

                  Kappa : 0.46

 Mcnemar's Test P-Value : 0.2898

            Sensitivity : 0.7000
            Specificity : 0.7600
         Pos Pred Value : 0.7447
         Neg Pred Value : 0.7170
             Prevalence : 0.5000
         Detection Rate : 0.3500
   Detection Prevalence : 0.4700
      Balanced Accuracy : 0.7300

       'Positive' Class : TRUE
```

FIGURE 15.10 Sensitivity analysis (cutoff = 0.5).

We can then see that 292 observations were classified correctly, for a cutoff of 0.5, being that 140 were events and were in fact classified as such, and another 152 were not events and were not classified as events, for this cutoff. However, 108 observations were classified incorrectly (being 48 non-events classified as event; and 60 events classified as non-event).

R also offers OME in its outputs, also called *Accuracy* (overall percentage of hits), *Sensitivity* (percentage of hits considering only the observations that were actually events), and *Specificity* (percentage of hits considering only the observations that were not events), for a 0.5 cutoff. Therefore, we have, respectively:

$$OME = \frac{140 + 152}{400} = 73.00\%$$

$$Sensitivity = \frac{140}{200} = 70.00\%.$$

$$Specificity = \frac{152}{200} = 76.00\%$$

Figures 15.11 and 15.12 present the sensitivity analysis of the model for cutoff values equal to 0.1 and 0.7. The commands to obtain Figures 15.11 and 15.12 are as follows:

```
#Figure 15.11

barbecue["classification"] <- predict(object = step_logit_model,
                                      newdata = barbecue,
                                      type = "response") > 0.1

confusionMatrix(
  data = table(barbecue$classification,
               barbecue$income == 1)[2:1, 2:1]
)
```

```
#Figure 15.12

barbecue["classification"] <- predict(object = step_logit_model,
                                      newdata = barbecue,
                                      type = "response") > 0.7

confusionMatrix(
  data = table(barbecue$classification,
               barbecue$income == 1)[2:1, 2:1]
)
```

```
Confusion Matrix and Statistics

       TRUE FALSE
  TRUE   196   178
  FALSE    4    22

               Accuracy : 0.545
                 95% CI : (0.4948, 0.5946)
    No Information Rate : 0.5
    P-Value [Acc > NIR] : 0.03999

                  Kappa : 0.09

 Mcnemar's Test P-Value : < 2e-16

            Sensitivity : 0.9800
            Specificity : 0.1100
         Pos Pred Value : 0.5241
         Neg Pred Value : 0.8462
             Prevalence : 0.5000
         Detection Rate : 0.4900
   Detection Prevalence : 0.9350
      Balanced Accuracy : 0.5450

       'Positive' Class : TRUE
```

FIGURE 15.11 Sensitivity analysis (cutoff = 0.1).

```
Confusion Matrix and Statistics

        TRUE FALSE
  TRUE    98    14
  FALSE  102   186

               Accuracy : 0.71
                 95% CI : (0.6628, 0.754)
    No Information Rate : 0.5
    P-Value [Acc > NIR] : < 2.2e-16

                  Kappa : 0.42

 Mcnemar's Test P-Value : 6.597e-16

            Sensitivity : 0.4900
            Specificity : 0.9300
         Pos Pred Value : 0.8750
         Neg Pred Value : 0.6458
             Prevalence : 0.5000
         Detection Rate : 0.2450
   Detection Prevalence : 0.2800
      Balanced Accuracy : 0.7100

       'Positive' Class : TRUE
```

FIGURE 15.12 Sensitivity analysis (cutoff = 0.7).

Because the cutoff values vary between 0 and 1, it becomes operationally impossible to prepare a sensitivity analysis for each cutoff. Therefore it makes sense at this time to prepare the sensitivity curve and the ROC curve for all cutoff possibilities. First, we will view the sensitivity and specificity curves together using the functions `prediction()` and `performance()` from the package `ROCR`, which will facilitate our path.

First, we must declare the function `prediction()`:

```
predictions_barbecue <- prediction(predictions = step_logit_model$fitted.values,
                                   labels = barbecue$income)
```

As shown, for the function `prediction()`, we argue `predictions` to indicate the fitted values of our final model, and we argue `labels` to designate the values observed in the dataset. The object `predictions_barbecue` already contains a series of cutoffs for the subsequent construction of a graph in addition to information on which various values of sensitivity and specificity can be extracted. For this, we will use the function `performance()`:

```
sens_data <- performance(prediction.obj = predictions_barbecue, measure = "sens")
```

In the previous routine, the argument `prediction.obj` should refer to the object created by the function `prediction()` from the package `ROCR` (`predictions_barbecue`, in this case). For the argument `measure`, we declare `"sens"` to obtain data on the model sensitivity. There are other possibilities to be explored with the argument `"sens"`, and we encourage the researcher to read about the documentation of the function `performance()`. That said, we can type the following command:

```
sensitivity <- sens_data@y.values[[1]]
```

The previous routine extracted the sensitivity values for each cutoff proposed by the function `predictions()` present in the object `predictions_barbecue` and calculated by the function `performance()`. We will do a similar procedure to extract values regarding specificities as a result of the cutoffs proposed by the function `predictions()`:

```
spec_data <- performance(prediction.obj = predictions_barbecue, measure = "spec")
```

After that, we can extract the specificity values for each cutoff proposed by the function `predictions()` present in the object `predictions_barbecue` and calculated by the function `performance()`:

```
specificity <- spec_data@y.values[[1]]
```

Now we will highlight the cutoffs proposed by the function `predictions()` and saved in the object `predictions_barbecue`:

```
cutoffs <- predictions_barbecue@cutoffs[[1]]
```

The last step before plotting the sensitivity and specificity curves together is to combine the objects `sensitivity`, `specificity` and `cutoffs` in a single data frame:

```
plot_data <- cbind.data.frame(cutoffs,
                              specificity,
                              sensitivity)
```

Plotting can be done using the function `ggplot()` from the package `ggplot2`:

```
plot_data %>%
  ggplot() +
  geom_line(aes(x = cutoffs, y = specificity, color = "Specificity"),
            size = 2) +
  geom_point(aes(x = cutoffs, y = specificity),
             color = "orange", size = 1, shape = 15) +
  geom_line(aes(x = cutoffs, y = sensitivity, color = "Sensitivity"),
            size = 2) +
  geom_point(aes(x = cutoffs, y = sensitivity),
             color = "darkorchid", size = 1, shape = 16) +
  labs(x = "Cutoffs",
       y = "Sensitivity/Specificity") +
  scale_color_manual("Label:",
                     values = c("orange", "darkorchid")) +
  theme_bw()
```

Figure 15.13 shows the result of the plotting that combines, for all cutoffs, the sensitivity and specificity values of our final model.

An analysis of the sensitivity curve (see Figure 15.13) allows us to arrive at an approximate cutoff value that equals sensitivity to specificity. For our example, this cutoff is approximately equal to 0.18. The biggest problem that we see on the sensitivity curve deals with the behavior of the specificity curve. Although the sensitivity curve presents low percentages of hits for a minority of the cutoff values (up to about 0.15), the same cannot be said in relation to the behavior of the specificity curve, which presents high percentages of hits for most of the cutoffs (larger than about 0.25). In other words, although the percentage of hits for those that will be events is low (almost independently of the cutoff used), the percentage of those that will not be events is high for most cutoff values, which can hinder the overall model hit's efficiency for prediction. It is important for us to underscore, for our example, that the area below the ROC curve is 0.808 (Figure 15.14), which is considered very good for prediction!

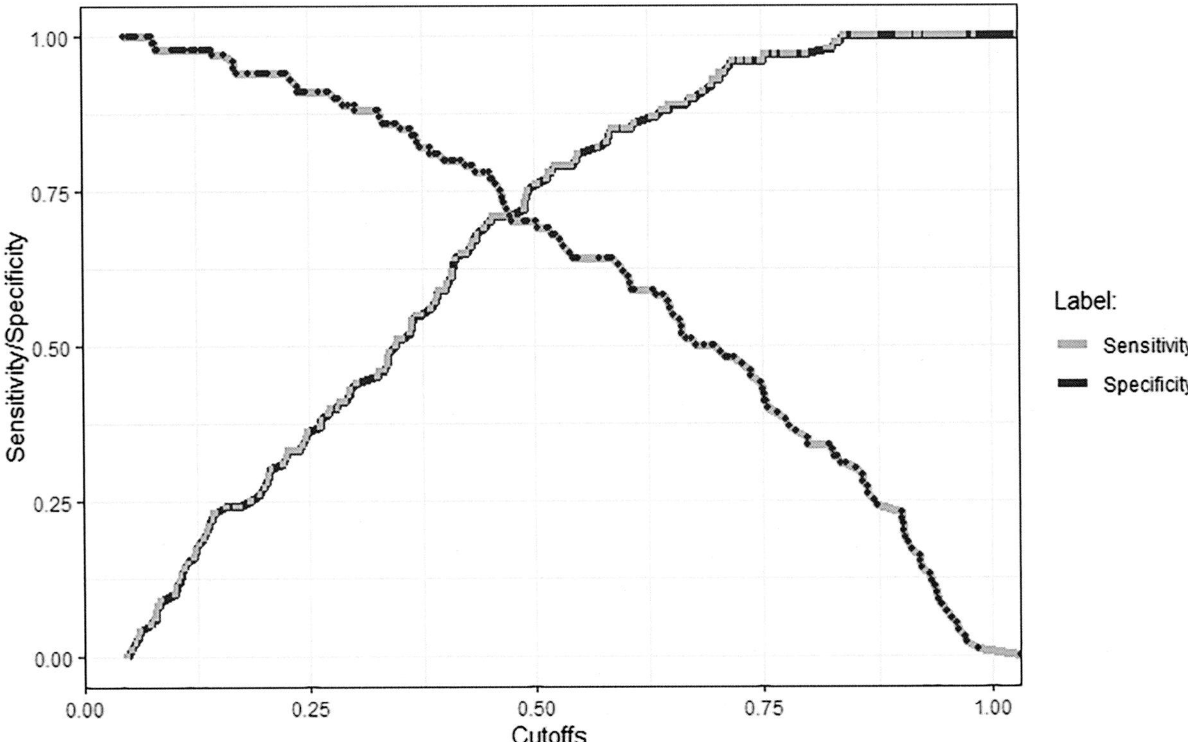

FIGURE 15.13 Sensitivity and specificity curve for the cutoff values.

For the construction of the ROC, we will use the values present in the object `sensitivity` in the ordinate axis, while `1-specificity` will be contained in the abscissa axis. This proposed graph is simple, but it poses a crucial problem: **What would be the precise value of the area under the ROC?** To overcome the obstacle, we will once again resort to the function `performance()` from the package `ROCR`, but arguing `measure = "auc"`:

```
au_roc <- performance(prediction.obj = predictions_barbecue, measure = "auc")
```

Ready! Here are the codes for building the ROC regarding our final model:

```
plot_data %>%
  ggplot() +
  geom_segment(aes(x = 0, xend = 1, y = 0, yend = 1),
               color="orange", size = 2) +
  geom_line(aes(x = 1 - specificity, y = sensitivity),
            color = "darkorchid", size = 2) +
  labs(x = "1 - Specificity",
       y = "Sensitivity",
       title = paste("Area under the curve:",
                     round(au_roc@y.values[[1]], 3))) +
  theme_bw()
```

Figure 15.14 shows an ROC created using the previous command.

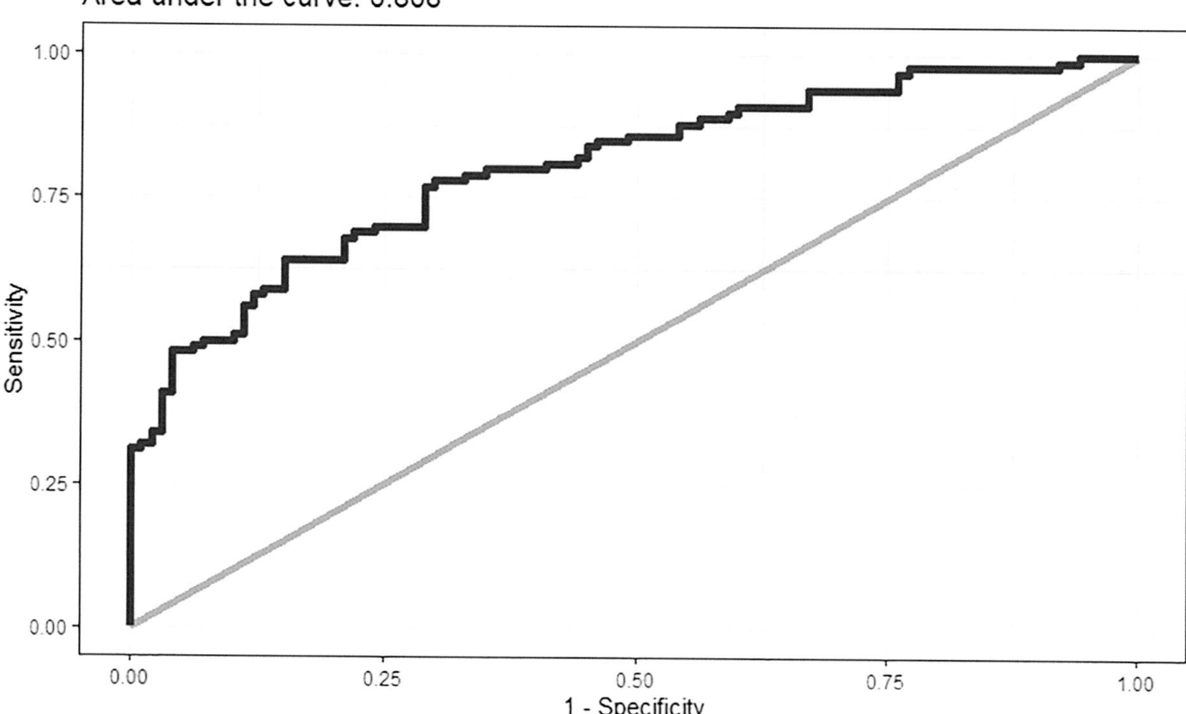

FIGURE 15.14 ROC curve for the final model.

In the following section, we will propose an example for the estimation of a multinomial logistic regression.

Estimation of a multinomial logistic regression model in R

For the following example, we will use real and open data. The dataset was built from the analysis of the website of the Brazilian Ministry of Education (MEC) and the positions of Brazilian Universities in 2018 present in the WEBOMETRICS academic ranking. Table 15.2 offers the description of variables present in the file `brazilian_universities.RData`.

TABLE 15.2 Description of variables present in the file `brazilian_universities.RData`.

Variables	Description
y4_webometrics	Polychotomous variable that indicates a classification, for a given Brazilian university, due to its position in the WEBOMETRICS academic ranking. For the case of the best positioned group, there is an "A" classification; for the second best positioned group, the label "B" was given, and so on, until the classification "D".
hei	Polychotomous variable that identifies the analyzed Brazilian university.
category	Polychotomous variable that indicates which academic stratum a given Brazilian university belongs to: *federal university* (for federal public universities); *state_university* (for state public universities); *municipal_university* (for municipal public universities); *private for-profit university* (for private for-profit universities); and, finally, *private non-profit university* (for private non-profit universities).
enade	Continuous variable that concerns the Brazilian higher education indicator. According to the Brazilian Ministry of Education (MEC), it is intended to assess the knowledge of graduating students in relation to curriculum guidelines. A curiosity: Enade stands for National Student Performance Exam.
cpc	The CPC, or Preliminary Course Concept, in our dataset is a continuous variable, which also concerns an indicator of Brazilian higher education. In this case, it is an indicator of Brazilian higher education that considers the performance of students, professors, physical infrastructure, and didactic-pedagogical resources of each university.
igc	The IGC, or General Course Index, is an indicator of undergraduate courses at Brazilian universities. In our dataset, it brings continuous values.
idd	The IDD, or Indicator of Difference between Observed and Expected Performance, points to the value added by the undergraduate course to the development of graduating students, considering their performance and their development characteristics when entering the undergraduate course evaluated. In our dataset, it brings continuous values.

We can see the descriptive statistics of the variables present in the object `brazilian_universities` using the function `summary()`, whose outputs are shown in Figure 15.15.

```
summary(brazilian_universities)
```

```
y4_webometrics      hei                                           category
enade
 A:45          Length:175         federal_university              :58
Min.    :1.260
 B:45          Class :character   municipal_university            : 4
1st Qu.:2.272
 C:44          Mode  :character   private_for_profit_university:19
Median :2.759
 D:41                             private_non_profit_university:62
Mean    :2.792
                                  state_university                :32
3rd Qu.:3.193

Max.    :5.000
      cpc              igc              idd
 Min.   :1.991   Min.   :2.162   Min.   :1.359
 1st Qu.:2.604   1st Qu.:2.704   1st Qu.:2.287
 Median :2.867   Median :3.042   Median :2.433
 Mean   :2.859   Mean   :3.097   Mean   :2.456
 3rd Qu.:3.101   3rd Qu.:3.423   3rd Qu.:2.607
 Max.   :4.453   Max.   :4.399   Max.   :5.000
```

FIGURE 15.15 Results from the function `summary()` of the object `brazilian_universities`.

When looking at Table 15.2 and Figure 15.15, we realize that the variable *category*, which will be used as an explanatory variable, is polyotomic. Thus as already studied in Chapter 14, we should apply the $n - 1$ dummies procedure using the function `dummy_cols()` from the package `fastDummies`:

```
brazil_univ_d <- dummy_cols(.data = brazilian_universities,
                            select_columns = "category",
                            remove_first_dummy = TRUE,
                            remove_selected_columns = TRUE)
```

In R, there is no native function for estimating a multinomial logistic model. Thus for this work, we will consider the function `multinom()` from the package `nnet`.

However, before estimating the model, the algorithm `multinom()` requires pointing out the reference category of the dependent variable to be considered, as studied earlier in "The Multinomial Logistic Regression Model." We can meet this demand with the function `relevel()` that is natively installed in R-based language. For this chapter, the "A" stratum will be considered as a reference category:

```
brazil_univ_d$y4_webometrics <- relevel(x = brazil_univ_d$y4_webometrics,
                                        ref = "A")
```

The function `relevel()` is very intuitive. First, we must declare our dependent variable. Then, in the argument `ref`, which will be the reference category adopted for the subsequent model, we can estimate our multinomial logistic regression model using the function `multinom()`:

```
mult_model <- multinom(formula = y4_webometrics ~ . -hei,
                       data = brazil_univ_d)
```

For models estimated by the function `multinom()`, the function `summ()` does not work, so we will use the function `summary()`. However, we ask the reader to be attentive regarding the outputs generated because they are not as similar as the outputs we have used until now.

```
summary(mult_model)
```

Figure 15.16 explains the result of the previous routine.

```
Call:
multinom(formula = y4_webometrics ~ . - hei, data = brazil_univ_d)

Coefficients:
  (Intercept)     enade      cpc         igc         idd
category_municipal_university
B    10.28456 -1.582246 4.754713  -6.338895  0.62141430
6.611803
C    15.30288 -2.585107 6.142232  -7.882316 -0.24215378
6.590745
D    21.09187 -4.123485 8.295990 -10.998950 -0.07233948
6.808599
  category_private_for_profit_university
category_private_non_profit_university
B                                 12.41801
0.7742694
C                                 13.85575
1.2636456
D                                 13.92740
1.5049594
  category_state_university
B                0.4609364
C                1.2124198
D                1.8026867

Std. Errors:
  (Intercept)     enade      cpc       igc      idd
category_municipal_university
B    4.187464 0.8234061 2.430771 1.722809 1.432727
0.9557166
C    4.575282 0.9221697 2.619323 1.980920 1.570958
0.9218848
D    5.112252 1.0540876 2.822050 2.235945 1.702620
0.9492096
  category_private_for_profit_university
category_private_non_profit_university
B                                0.5908037
0.9173456
C                                0.5143583
1.0060899
D                                0.6632751
1.2522564
  category_state_university
B                0.8315559
C                0.9443340
D                1.2617453

Residual Deviance: 301.7651
AIC: 355.7651
```

FIGURE 15.16 Results of the previous routine.

Figure 15.17 changes the reporting logic about the parameters of a GLM estimation that we were used to in R, right?

An attentive reader will notice that Figure 15.16 is divided into two parts: Coefficients and Std. Errors. Each line in the "Coefficients" section provides a logit for each category of the dependent variable, with the exception, of course, of the reference category. The "Std. errors" section informs the standard errors of each variable in each logit.

As the reader can see, the general statistics of the model (χ^2) is not presented in Figure 15.16. As we did in the "Estimation of a binary logistic regression model in R" section, we can calculate it using the outputs of the function `lrtest()`:

```
lrtest(mult_model)
```

The results of applying the function `lrtest()` in the model contained by the object `mult_model` are presented in Figure 15.17.

```
Likelihood ratio test

Model 1: y4_webometrics ~ (hei + enade + cpc + igc + idd +
category_municipal_university +
    category_private_for_profit_university +
category_private_non_profit_university +
    category_state_university) - hei
Model 2: y4_webometrics ~ 1
  #Df  LogLik  Df  Chisq Pr(>Chisq)
1  27 -150.88
2   3 -242.48 -24 183.19  < 2.2e-16 ***
---
Signif. codes:  0 '***' 0.001 '**' 0.01 '*' 0.05 '.' 0.1 ' ' 1
```

FIGURE 15.17 Results from the function `lrtest()` of the object `mult_model`.

Thus with the data shown in Figure 15.17:

$$\chi^2_{75\ d.f.} = -2 \times [-242.48 - (-150.88)] = 183.2$$

To calculate the critical value of the χ^2 statistic for 24 degrees of freedom and a 5% significance level, we can type:

```
qchisq(p = 0.05, df = 24, lower.tail = FALSE)
```

R will return the value 36.415, and because $\chi^2_{calc} > \chi^2_c$, at least one of the two explanatory variables selected can explain the behavior of the dependent variable at a significance level of 5%, keeping the other conditions constant. If the desire is to make a point of calculating the *P*-value regarding the general statistics of the model, the researcher must type the following command:

```
pchisq(q = 183.19, df = 24, lower.tail = FALSE)
```

Thus it is concluded that the general statistics of the model is given by $\chi^2_{24\ d.f.} = 183.20$, with a *P*-value equal to 0.000. With the outputs of Figure 15.17, it is also possible to calculate the McFadden pseudo R^2:

$$pseudoR^2(McFadden) = \frac{-2.(-242.48) - [-2.(-150.88)]}{-2.(-242.48)} = 0.378$$

Returning to the information presented in Figure 15.16, although the general statistic of the model informs us that there is at least one explanatory variable statistically significant at a 95% confidence level, to explain the behavior of our dependent variable, we have not yet been able to assess the Wald *z* statistics regarding each parameter or their respective *P*-values because R did not inform us of this.

Thus we can calculate the Wald *z* statistics using the ratio between the estimated value for each model parameter contained by the object `mult_model` and their respective standard errors:

```
zWald_mult_model <- (summary(mult_model)$coefficients /
                     summary(mult_model)$standard.errors)
```

Now that the Wald *z* statistics are saved in the object `zWald_mult_model`, we can calculate their respective *P*-values:

```
round(pnorm(q = abs(zWald_mult_model), lower.tail = FALSE) * 2, digits = 3)
```

Figure 15.18 presents the *P*-values regarding the parameters of the model contained in the object `mult_model`, and we can see that not all variables were significant in the presence of the others, at a 5% significance level, to explain the change in one category of the dependent variable for its corresponding reference category.

```
  (Intercept) enade   cpc igc   idd category_municipal_university
B       0.014 0.055 0.050   0 0.664                             0
C       0.001 0.005 0.019   0 0.877                             0
D       0.000 0.000 0.003   0 0.966                             0
  category_private_for_profit_university
category_private_non_profit_university
B                                      0
0.399
C                                      0
0.209
D                                      0
0.229
  category_state_university
B                     0.579
C                     0.199
D                     0.153
```

FIGURE 15.18 Significance of the parameters of the model in the object `mult_model`.

For example, the variables *idd* and *category_state_university* cannot explain (jointly and in the presence of the other variables) the changes from a university belonging to group "B" to group "A", *ceteris paribus*. In this way, we can apply the Stepwise procedure:

```
step_mult_model <- step(mult_model,
                        k = qchisq(0.05,1,lower.tail = F))
```

To access the model parameters, we will use the function `summary()`, whose outputs are shown in Figure 15.19:

```
summary(step_mult_model)
```

```
Call:
multinom(formula = y4_webometrics ~ enade + cpc + igc, data =
brazil_univ_d)

Coefficients:
  (Intercept)     enade      cpc        igc
B    11.68013 -1.798856 5.777874  -6.935645
C    16.55020 -2.925970 6.826511  -8.545385
D    23.18863 -4.290457 8.879187 -11.778399

Std. Errors:
  (Intercept)     enade      cpc      igc
B    3.513954 0.7990987 1.821762 1.480380
C    3.810159 0.8924524 1.945463 1.692567
D    4.171403 1.0087718 2.125254 1.907687

Residual Deviance: 309.9968
AIC: 333.9968
```

FIGURE 15.19 Results from the function `summary()` of the object `step_mult_ model`.

To measure Wald z statistics and their respective *P*-values, we will proceed as we did earlier. Thus we will first measure the Wald z statistics:

```
zWald_step_mult_model <- (summary(step_mult_model)$coefficients /
                          summary(step_mult_model)$standard.errors)
```

Then we can calculate the *P*-values regarding Wald z statistics contained in the object `zWald_step_mult_model`:

```
round(pnorm(q = abs(zWald_step_mult_model), lower.tail = FALSE) * 2, digits = 3)
```

Figure 15.20 shows the *P*-values of the model parameters that we consider the final model, that is, the internal estimation of the object `step_mult_model`.

```
  (Intercept) enade   cpc igc
B       0.001 0.024 0.002   0
C       0.000 0.001 0.000   0
D       0.000 0.000 0.000   0


C     16.55020 -2.925970 6.826511  -8.545385
D     23.18863 -4.290457 8.879187 -11.778399

Std. Errors:
  (Intercept)     enade      cpc      igc
B    3.513954 0.7990987 1.821762 1.480380
C    3.810159 0.8924524 1.945463 1.692567
D    4.171403 1.0087718 2.125254 1.907687

Residual Deviance: 309.9968
AIC: 333.9968
```

FIGURE 15.20 Significance of the model parameters in the final model.

In Figure 15.20, we can see that all parameters were statistically different from zero at a 5% significance level, except for the variable *enade*, to explain the differences regarding a university of group "B" in relation to a university of group "A". That said, we can write the logits (Z_i):

$$Z_{i_{University\ B}} = 11.680 - 1.798enade_i + 5.777cpc_i - 6.936igc_i$$

$$Z_{i_{University\ C}} = 16.550 - 2.926enade_i + 6.827cpc_i - 8.545igc_i$$

$$Z_{i_{University\ D}} = 23.189 - 4.290enade_i + 8.879cpc_i - 11.778igc_i$$

Having described the logits Z_i, we can express the final model:

Probability of the observation considered uma Universidade do Grupo A:

$$p_{i_{University\ A}} = \frac{1}{e^{Z_{i_{University\ B}}} + e^{Z_{i_{University\ C}}} + e^{Z_{i_{University\ D}}}}$$

Probability of the observation considered uma Universidade do Grupo B:

$$p_{i_{University\ B}} = \frac{e^{Z_{i_{University\ B}}}}{e^{Z_{i_{University\ B}}} + e^{Z_{i_{University\ C}}} + e^{Z_{i_{University\ D}}}}$$

Probability of the observation considered uma Universidade do Grupo C:

$$p_{i_{University\ C}} = \frac{e^{Z_{i_{University\ C}}}}{e^{Z_{i_{University\ B}}} + e^{Z_{i_{University\ C}}} + e^{Z_{i_{University\ D}}}}$$

Probability of the observation considered uma Universidade do Grupo D:

$$p_{i_{University\ D}} = \frac{e^{Z_{i_{University\ D}}}}{e^{Z_{i_{University\ B}}} + e^{Z_{i_{University\ C}}} + e^{Z_{i_{University\ D}}}}$$

If the researcher is interested in the construction of CI, simply apply the function `confint()` to the object `step_model_mult`, as studied in Chapter 14.

Having estimated the probability expressions, we will generate, in the dataset, six variables corresponding to the expressions of the average probability of the occurrence of each of the events, by typing in the following commands:

```
brazil_univ_d[c("A","B", "C","D")] <- step_mult_model$fitted.values
```

With regard to the routine previously established, it is imperative that the reader be attentive to what happens on the left side of the assignment operator <-. On the left side of the assignment operator, we are declaring to R the creation of six variables that correspond to each category of the dependent variable but must obey the following mandatory order: **first, the reference category used to establish the estimation and, after that, the other categories of the dependent variable, in the order established by the output of the function `summary()` applied to our model.**

Having generated the new variables, we are now able to construct two interesting graphs based on which we can come to some conclusions. Although the first graph (Figure 15.21) shows the behavior of the occurrence probabilities for each of the events as a function of the *enade* variable; the second graph (Figure 15.22) shows the behavior of these probabilities as a function of the *igc* variable:

```
#Figure 15.21

brazil_univ_d %>%
  select(y4_webometrics, enade, A, B, C, D) %>%
  melt(id.vars = c("y4_webometrics","enade"),
       value.name = "probabilities") %>%
  rename(categories = variable) %>%
  mutate(categories = factor(categories)) %>%
  ggplot() +
  geom_smooth(aes(x = enade, y = probabilities, color = categories),
              method = "glm", formula = y ~ splines::bs(x), se = F) +
  labs(x = "Enade Index of Brazilian Universities",
       y = "Probabilities") +
  theme_bw()
```

```
#Figure 15.22

brazil_univ_d %>%
  select(y4_webometrics, igc, A, B, C, D) %>%
  melt(id.vars = c("y4_webometrics","igc"),
       value.name = "probabilities") %>%
  rename(categories = variable) %>%
  mutate(categories = factor(categories)) %>%
  ggplot() +
  geom_smooth(aes(x = igc, y = probabilities, color = categories),
              method = "glm", formula = y ~ splines::bs(x), se = F) +
  labs(x = "IGC Index of Brazilian Universities",
       y = "Probabilities") +
  theme_bw()
```

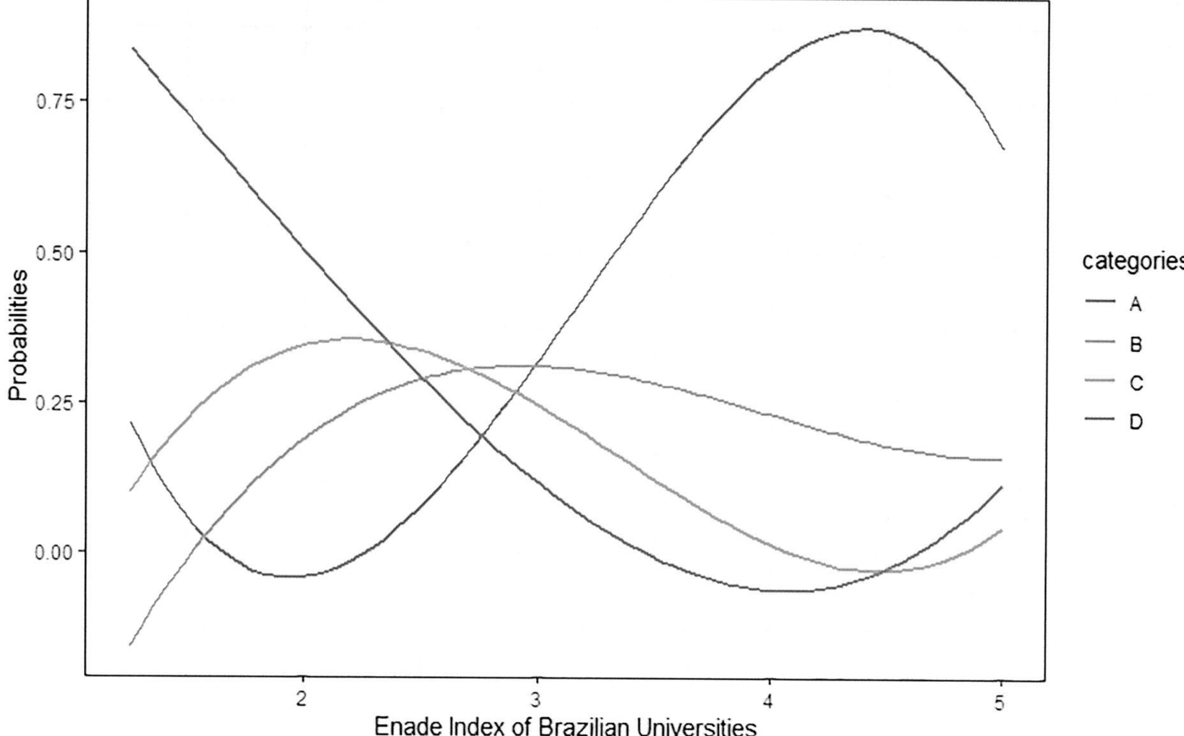

FIGURE 15.21 Occurrence probabilities for each event versus the behavior of Enade index.

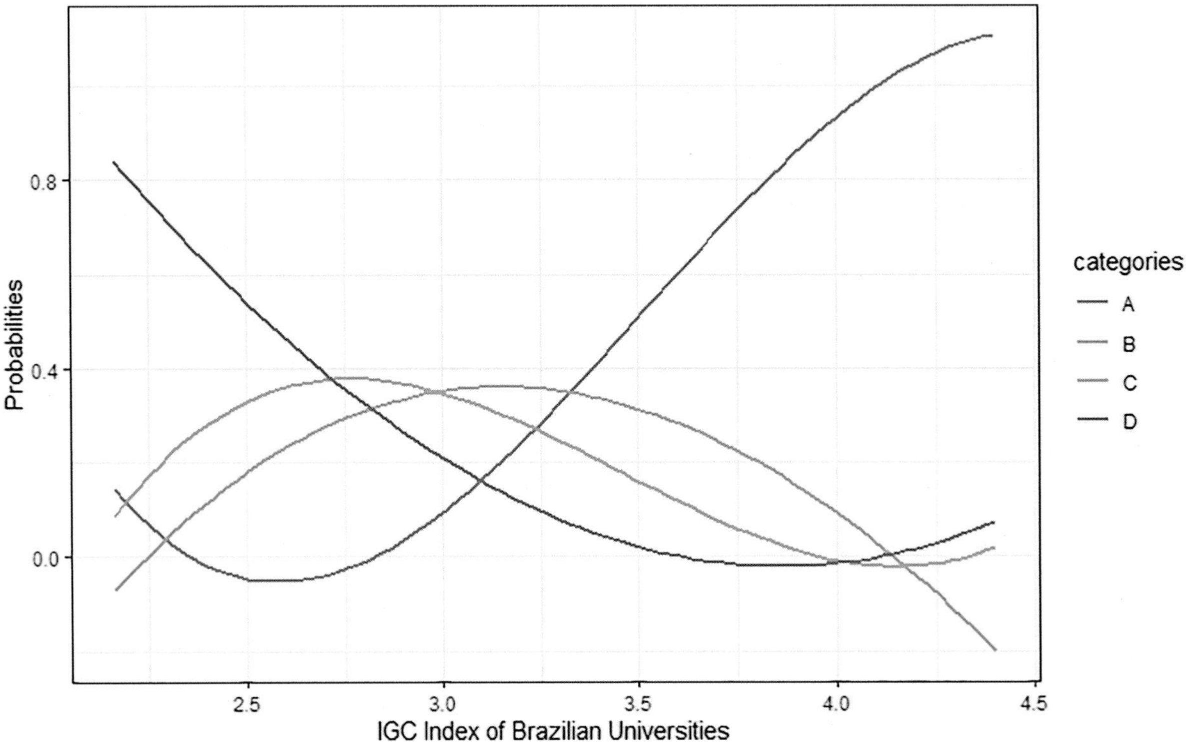

FIGURE 15.22 Occurrence probabilities for each event versus the behavior of IGC index.

The graph in Figure 15.21 shows that there are differences in the probabilities in the different categories of universities considered (B, C, and D) in relation to being classified as a group A university, when considering the increase in the Enade index (student knowledge in relation to curriculum guidelines), keeping the other conditions constant, with a 95% confidence level. We can observe that the probability of being a type A university, in relation to the variable *enade*, increases considerably after an approximate value of 3 for this predictor, keeping the other conditions constant. To obtain the classification of a type B university, in relation to the variable *enade*, we see that the probability of this categorization increases considerably after a value of the predictor variable equal to 2.5, approximately, *ceteris paribus*. Through Figure 15.21, it is also possible to affirm that low values of the studied indicator increase the probability of a university being categorized as type D for the WEBOMETRICS ranking, keeping the other conditions constant.

Figure 15.22 shows the differences in the probabilities between classifying a university as B, C, or D and having a university classified as A. As can be seen, values of the IGC index (indicator of undergraduate courses at Brazilian universities) higher than the value of 3.25, approximately, considerably increase the probability that a university will be classified as type A, *ceteris paribus*. On the other hand, lower values of this indicator lead to not so good rankings for Brazilian universities, keeping the other conditions constant.

Similar to what we learned thus far, if we were looking for predictions, we must use the function `predict()`. Thus if we want to calculate, on average, as probabilidades de classficação de uma dada universidade brasileira com valor de Enade igual a 3.2, CPC igual a 4, IGC igual a 5 e IDD igual a 3, tem-se:

```
predict(object = step_mult_model,
        newdata = data.frame(enade = 3.2,
                             cpc = 4,
                             igc = 5,
                             idd = 3),
        type = "probs")
```

When we argue `type = "probs"`, R will return the probability, on average, of diagnosis for each category of our dependent variable, *ceteris paribus*.

Unlike a binary logistic model, in multinomial logistic models there is no cutoff. Thus in terms of prediction, we must adopt the category with the highest probability of occurrence. That said, if the expressed values of the probabilities are not wanted, but rather the classification of the observation in any of the categories of the dependent variable, we can reapply the above routine, changing only the value of the argument `type` to `"class"`:

```
predict(object = step_mult_model,
        newdata = data.frame(enade = 3.2,
                             cpc = 4,
                             igc = 5,
                             idd = 3),
        type = "class")
```

On the other hand, if you want to evaluate the predictive capabilities of the model in question, similar to the confusion matrix of a binary logistic model (see Figure 15.11), we can create a classification table that contains the OME. First, we will save the classifications of our model for each observation of the dataset:

```
brazil_univ_d["y4_webometrics_fit"] <- predict(object = step_mult_model,
                                               newdata = brazil_univ_d,
                                               type = "class")
```

Then, we will create an object that we call `classification_table`, which will contain a type of contingency table that compares the observed categories of the dependent variable with the predicted categories by the model:

```
classification_table <- as.data.frame.matrix(table(brazil_univ_d$y4_webometrics,
                                                   brazil_univ_d$y4_webometrics_fit))
```

Next, we will create a row of totals for each row of the object `classification_table`:

```
classification_table["Total"] <- rowSums(classification_table)
```

To verify the correctness of the model, we will also need a column with the total of correct classifications for each category observed:

```
classification_table["True_Positives"] <- diag(as.matrix(classification_table))
```

After that, we can create a variable regarding OME as follows:

```
classification_table["OME"] <- classification_table$True_Positives /
  classification_table$Total
```

The *OME* variable of the object `classification_table` contains the level of accuracy of the step model for each category of the dependent variable. If the general accuracy of the model is desired, the researcher can type the following command:

```
round((sum(diag(table(brazil_univ_d$y4_webometrics,
                      brazil_univ_d$y4_webometrics_fit))) /
       sum(table(brazil_univ_d$y4_webometrics,
                 brazil_univ_d$y4_webometrics_fit))) * 100, 2)
```

The R capability to estimate models and execute statistical tests is enormous. We believe that what is given here can be considered required for researchers who have the intent of correctly applying the binary and multinomial logistic regression techniques.

Final remarks

The most adequate situation for applying the binary logistic regression model is when the phenomenon under study presents itself in a dichotomic way and the researcher has the intent of estimating an expression of the probability of an event occurrence defined between two possibilities as a function of determined explanatory variables. The binary logistic regression model can be considered a unique case of the multinomial logistic regression model, which variable also presents itself in a qualitative form, however now with more than two event categories, and an occurrence probability expression will be estimated for each category (Fávero and Belfiore, 2019).

Exercises

1. A lending institution that provides credit to individuals wants to evaluate the probability that its clients will default on their payment obligations (probability of default) (Fávero and Belfiore, 2019). Using a dataset with 2,000 observations of company clients who recently received credit, the institution intends to estimate a binary logistic regression model using age, gender (female = 0; male = 1), and monthly income ($) for each individual as explanatory variables. The dependent variable refers to the actual default (not default = 0, default = 1). The file `default_data.RData` gives this data, and using binary logistic regression model estimation, we would like you to:
   a. Analyze the significance level of the χ^2 test. Is at least one of the variables (age, gender, or income) statistically significant to explain the probability of default at the 5% significance level?
   b. If the answer to the previous item is yes, analyze the significance level of each explanatory variable (Wald z tests). Is each variable statistically significant to explain the probability of default at the 5% significance level?
   c. What is the final estimated equation for the average probability of default?
   d. On average, do individuals of male gender present a higher probability of default in credit obtained for personal consumption, keeping the remaining conditions constant?
   e. On average, do individuals with a higher age tend to present a higher probability of default for credit acquired for consumption, keeping the remaining conditions constant?
   f. What is the average estimated probability of default for a 37-year-old male with a monthly income of $6,850?
   g. On average, how much does the chance of default increase in a unit, keeping the remaining conditions constant?
   h. What is the OME with a cutoff of 0.5? What is the sensitivity and specificity for the same cutoff?

2. The health department for a determined country wants to launch a campaign to improve the citizen LDL (mg/dL) cholesterol index by encouraging the practice of physical activity and the reduction of tobacco use. Research on 2,304 individuals was conducted, from which the following variables were taken (Fávero and Belfiore, 2019).

Variable	Description
cholesterol	LDL (mg/dL) cholesterol index
cigarette	Dummy variable corresponding to the fact that an individual smokes or does not smoke (non-smoker = 0; smoker = 1)
sport	Number of times per week a physical activity is practiced

Because the cholesterol index is subsequently classified according the reference values, the health department has the idea of informing the population regarding the benefits of practicing physical activity and abstaining from tobacco to improve this classification. As such, the variable *cholesterol* will be transformed to the variable *colestquali*, to be described, which presents five categories and will be a dependent model variable whose results will be published by the health department.

Variable	Description
colestquali	LDL (mg/dL) cholesterol level classification • Very high: above 189 mg/dL (reference category) • High: 160 to 189 mg/dL • Borderline: 130 to 159 mg/dL • Near optimal: 100 to 129 mg/dL • Optimal: below 100 mg/dL

The dataset for this research is found in the file `colestquali_data.RData`. Using a multinomial logistic regression model estimation with *cigarette* and *sport* as explanatory variables, we would like you to:

a. Present the table of frequencies for the dependent variable categories.
b. Using multinomial logistic regression model estimation, is it possible to know that at least one of the explanatory variables is statistically significant to compose the probability expression of the occurrence of at least one of the proposed LDL cholesterol index classifications at the 5% significance level?
c. What are the final estimated equations for the average occurrence probabilities for the proposed LDL cholesterol index classifications?
d. What are the occurrence probabilities for each of the proposed classifications for an individual who does not smoke and who practices sporting activities once a week?
e. Based on the estimated model, prepare an occurrence probability graph for each event represented by the dependent variable as a function of the number of times physical activities are practiced weekly. At which weekly frequency does the practice of physical activity considerably increase the probability that the LDL cholesterol index will go to near-optimal or optimal levels?
f. On average, how much would one alter the chance of having a cholesterol index considered high, in relation to a level considered very high, by increasing by 1 unit the number of times weekly physical activities are performed, keeping all remaining conditions constant?
g. On average, how much would one alter the chance of having a cholesterol index considered optimal, in relation to a level considered near optimal, by quitting smoking, keeping all remaining conditions constant?
h. Prepare the classification table based on the estimated probability of each observation in the sample (predicted and observed classification for each category of the dependent variable).
i. What is the OME? What is the percentage of hits for each category of the dependent variable?

Supplementary data sets

```
barbecue.RData
brazilian_universities.RData
cholestquali_data.RData
default_data.RData
```

Please access supplementary data files here: https://doi.org/10.17632/55623jkwrp.3

CHAPTER

16

Count-data and zero-inflated regression models

AT THE END OF THIS CHAPTER, YOU WILL BE ABLE TO:

- Evaluate the results of statistical tests concerning count-data models.
- Differentiate negative binomial regression models from Poisson models.
- Understand the concept of overdispersion in data, and implement the test for identification of overdispersion in the data of the dependent variable, conditioned on its predictor variables (covariates).
- Estimate zero-inflated regression models, and implement the Vuong test to verify the existence of excessive amount of zeros in the dependent variable.
- Estimate count-data regression models in R, and interpret the results.

R-based language packages used in this chapter

```
library(tidyverse)
library(knitr)
library(kableExtra)
library(overdisp)
library(jtools)
library(lmtest)
library(MASS)
library(pscl)
```

Don't forget to define the R working directory (the location where your datasets are installed):

```
setwd("C:/book/chapter16")
```

Data Science, Analytics and Machine Learning with R
https://doi.org/10.1016/B978-0-12-824271-1.00012-3

Estimating regression models for count data in R

In this section, we will present the estimates studied in this chapter in R-based language and demonstrate the interpretation of each output obtained from the R codes.

For this, we will use the dataset `accidents_data.RData`, which brings the number of traffic accidents in 100 Brazilian municipalities over a period of 1 week, as shown in Table 16.1.

TABLE 16.1 Description of the variables present in the file `accidents_data.RData` (Fávero and Belfiore, 2019).

Variable	Description
accidents	Discrete quantitative variable that indicates the number of traffic accidents that occurred during the considered week
pop	Continuous quantitative variable that shows the total inhabitants of a particular municipality studied divided by 100,000
age	Average age of drivers in the considered municipalities
drylaw	Dummy variable that indicates whether or not the municipality studied adopted the dry law after 10:00 p.m.

As the reader should already know, we can access the univariate descriptive statistics of the metric variables (*accidents*, *pop*, and *age*) and the frequency table of the categorical variable (*drylaw*) using the function `summary()`, whose outputs are shown in Figure 16.1.

```
summary(accidents_data)
```

```
   accidents          pop                age          drylaw
 Min.   : 0.00   Min.   :0.6503   Min.   :24.00   no :58
 1st Qu.: 0.00   1st Qu.:1.3536   1st Qu.:47.77   yes:42
 Median : 0.00   Median :1.4635   Median :51.76
 Mean   : 3.01   Mean   :1.7742   Mean   :50.12
 3rd Qu.: 3.00   3rd Qu.:2.3005   3rd Qu.:54.95
 Max.   :33.00   Max.   :2.8675   Max.   :61.00
```

FIGURE 16.1 Univariate descriptive statistics and frequency table of the variables present in the object `accidents_data`.

From Figure 16.1, we can see that the mean of the dependent variable *accidents* is equal to 3.01. Thus to study, **in a preliminary way,** the existence of overdispersion in the dependent variable *accidents* conditioned on the predictor variables, we can demand that R presents its respective variance as follows:

```
accidents_data %>%
  summarise(Mean = mean(accidents),
            Variance = var(accidents))
```

The previous code presents the mean of the variable *accidents* (which we already knew) alongside its respective variance. If the reader wants to check the variance of the variable *accidents* more directly, it would be enough to use the function `var()`, that is, the command `var(accidents_data$accidents)`. Figure 16.2 shows the mean and variance of the dependent variable.

```
  Mean Variance
  <dbl>    <dbl>
1  3.01     43.0
```

FIGURE 16.2 Comparison between the mean and variance of the dependent variable *accidents*.

Figure 16.2 brings an interesting result: Mathematically speaking, the value of the variance of the variable *accidents* is more than 14 times greater than its mean. Let us repeat: ***Preliminarily,*** the diagnosis that compares the mean and variance of the dependent variable seems to indicate that we have a case of overdispersion.

Still preliminarily, to corroborate what we have perceived so far, we propose the elaboration of a histogram of the variable *accidents*.

```
accidents_data %>%
  ggplot() +
  geom_bar(aes(x = factor(accidents)), stat = "count", fill = "orange") +
  geom_text(aes(x = factor(accidents),label = ..count..),
            stat="count", vjust = -0.8, size = 2.5, color = "darkorchid") +
  labs(x = "Number of Accidents",
       y = "Frequency") +
  theme_classic()
```

An attentive reader will notice that, unlike what we discussed in Chapter 7, we used the function `geom_bar()` instead of the function `geom_histogram()` to construct the histogram. The idea is to present, in a didactic way, a histogram that contains the precise count of the number of traffic accidents in each of its boxes, by Brazilian municipality in a given week, **to highlight possible pitfalls in the estimation of count-data regression models, which the reader will fully understand at the end of this chapter**. Figure 16.3 shows the result of the previous command.

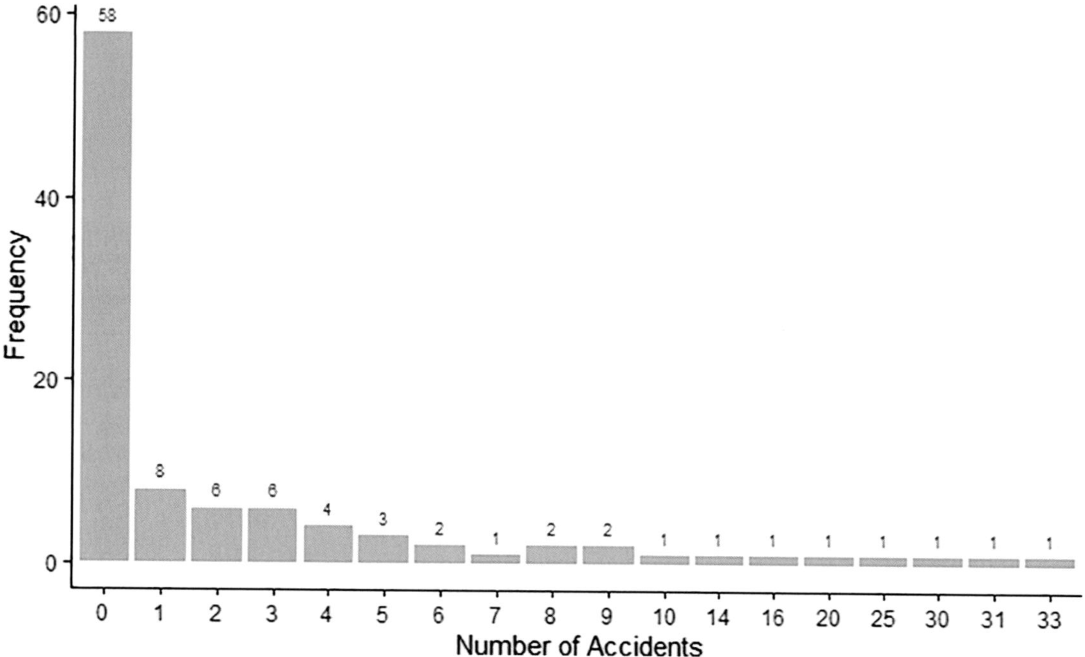

FIGURE 16.3 Histogram of the dependent variable *accidents*.

Figure 16.3 provides interesting preliminary insights. The first concerns the lengthening of the tail with respect to the occurrence of traffic accident counts in our data, which, together with the comparison between the mean and the variance (see Figure 16.4) leads us to believe in a **preliminary indication** of the existence of overdispersion in the dependent variable, conditioned on the predictor variables. **We are still able to guarantee that, in fact, there is a phenomenon of overdispersion in our data, and therefore an NB estimate would be the most appropriate, even if we have not yet performed any tests for this purpose.**

The second insight provided in Figure 16.5 concerns the number of counts with values equal to zero in our dataset. Thus in due course, we will also check if the zero-inflated models make sense for our data.

We encourage the reader to start the studies by detecting overdispersion or equidispersion in the count data. In R-based language, we indicate the function `overdisp()` from the package `overdisp` for the proposed task. Such an algorithm performs directly the Cameron and Trivedi test (Cameron and Trivedi, 1990), as discussed earlier in the "Test to verify overdispersion in Poisson regression models" section.

To the function `overdisp()`, we must command three parts of information: *x*, which represents the dataset; `dependent.position`, which is the position occupied by the dependent variable in the considered dataset; and `predictor.position`, which is the range of positions of the predictor variables to be considered. The result will, by default, take the significance of 5%; if the reader is interested in other levels of significance, just use the argument `sig` to do so.

```
overdisp(x = accidents_data,
         dependent.position = 1,
         predictor.position = 2:4)
```

Figure 16.4 shows the result of the previous command.

```
            Overdispersion Test - Cameron & Trivedi (1990)

data:  accidents_data
Lambda t test score: = 0.75134, p-value = 0.4542
alternative hypothesis: overdispersion if lambda p-value is less than or equal to the
stipulated significance level
```

FIGURE 16.4 Results of the overdispersion test proposed by Cameron and Trivedi (1990), obtained using the function `overdisp()`.

The *P*-value calculated by the function `overdisp()`, considering the variables *pop*, *age*, and *drylaw* as predictor variables of the dependent variable *accidents*, suggests that we cannot reject H_0 of the overdispersion test. **In other words, at a confidence level of 95%, we are facing an equidispersion diagnosis, and not overdispersion as the preliminary analysis of Figures 16.2 and 16.3 led us to think.** It is true that, for most cases, the reader will find consistency between the preliminary diagnosis (comparison of the mean with the variance) and the Cameron and Trivedi test (1990). However, the example chosen for this chapter reinforces the need for scholarship and care in establishing statistical models. In summary, the possible reason for the inconsistency is the excessive amount of zeros in the dependent variable, as we will see later.

Thus according to the results provided in Figure 16.4, we should estimate a Poisson model instead of an NB model, or, perhaps, a ZIP model because we have not yet implemented the Vuong test (1989) for the detection of the inflation of zeros in the dependent variable. Even so, we will go through the estimation of all models studied in this chapter, that is, Poisson, NB, ZIP, and ZINB.

Poisson regression model in R

In the introduction of the "Estimating regression models for count data in R" section, we found that there was a diagnosis of equidispersion of the dependent variable *accidents*, conditioned on the predictor variables *pop*, *age*, and *drylaw*.

To estimate Poisson regression models, we will use the function `glm()`, the same function used in Chapter 15 to estimate binary logistic regression models. However, we must now command `family = "poisson"` so R knows exactly what type of estimation we are looking for.

```
poisson_model <- glm(formula = accidents ~ .,
                     data = accidents_data,
                     family = "poisson")
```

Before exploring the model parameters, we will take a moment to consider some important components of the object `poisson_model`, which can be accessed using the operator `$`:

- `coefficients`: vector of dimension $(k+1) \times 1$ that contains the value of α (always in the first position) and the values of β, where k refers to the number of variables used in the model.
- `fitted.values`: vector of dimension $n \times 1$ that refers to the estimated values of occurrence probability of an event of the dependent variable for the observations present in the dataset, used for the regression model.

As discussed earlier, we can access the parameters of our model using the function `summary()`:

```
summary(poisson_model)
```

As in the estimations of binary logistic regression models (in fact, in any estimation generated by the maximum likelihood criterion), the reader will notice that the function `summary()` does not return the general statistics of the model. In this case, we prefer to use the function `summ()` from the package `jtools`.

```
summ(poisson_model, digits = 4, confint = TRUE)
```

After executing the previous command, the reader will obtain the same result as in Figure 16.5.

```
MODEL INFO:
Observations: 100
Dependent Variable: accidents
Type: Generalized linear model
  Family: poisson
  Link function: log

MODEL FIT:
χ²(3) = 631.9258, p = 0.0000
Pseudo-R² (Cragg-Uhler) = 0.9983
Pseudo-R² (McFadden) = 0.6463
AIC = 353.8909, BIC = 364.3116

Standard errors: MLE
-----------------------------------------------------------------------
                        Est.       2.5%      97.5%      z val.        p
-----------------  ---------  ---------  ---------  ----------  --------
(Intercept)           6.4118     5.7050     7.1186     17.7807    0.0000
pop                   0.1354    -0.0472     0.3181      1.4531    0.1462
age                  -0.1231    -0.1348    -0.1113    -20.5980    0.0000
drylawyes            -0.4627    -0.7372    -0.1882     -3.3043    0.0010
-----------------------------------------------------------------------
```

FIGURE 16.5 Outputs of the estimation related to the object `poisson_model`.

From Figure 16.5, we can calculate the value of the McFadden pseudo R^2:

$$pseudo\ R^2(McFadden) = \frac{-2.LL_0 - (-2.LL_{max})}{-2.LL_0}$$

$$pseudo\ R^2(McFadden) = \frac{-2 \times (-488.91) - [-2 \times (-172.95)]}{-2 \times (-488.91)} = 0.6463$$

It is also possible to calculate the χ^2 statistic of the model:

$$\chi^2 = -2 \times (LL_0 - LL_{max})$$

$$\chi^2_{(3df)} = -2 \times [-488.91 - (-172.95)] = 631.92$$

As discussed in Chapter 15, we can access the values of LL_0 and LL_{max} using the function `lrtest()` from the package `lmtest`. Remember that the function `lrtest()` shows the likelihood ratio test between models. When only one model is estimated, there will be a comparison of the log likelihood of the declared estimation against its respective null model (estimation of the dependent variable as a function of the intercept only).

```
lrtest(object = poisson_model)
```

Because the model contained in the object `poisson_model` uses three variables and therefore has three slope coefficients (β_1, β_2,and β_3), we have 3 degrees of freedom for the χ^2 statistic. The critical value of the χ^2 statistic for 3 degrees of freedom and at a significance level of 5%, can be found by typing:

```
qchisq(p = 0.05, df = 3, lower.tail = FALSE)
```

When commanding the previous code, the reader will obtain χ^2_c=7.815. Thus as $\chi^2_{calc} > \chi^2_c$, we can conclude, at a confidence level of 95%, that at least one of the parameters of our predictor variables is statistically different from zero in the presence of the others, *ceteris paribus*. The respective *P*-value can be obtained as follows:

```
pchisq(q = 631.92, df = 3, lower.tail = FALSE)
```

Even with the general statistics of the model indicating that, at a significance level of 5%, there is at least one predictor variable capable of explaining the behavior of the dependent variable, keeping the other conditions constant, we can see in Figure 16.5 that the parameter of the variable *pop* is not statistically different from zero, in the presence of the other variables, *ceteris paribus*. Thus we will apply the Stepwise procedure, as discussed in Chapters 14 and 15.

```
poisson_final_model <- step(object = poisson_model,
                            k = qchisq(p = 0.05,
                                       df = 1,
                                       lower.tail = FALSE))
```

After the previous routine, when typing `summ(poisson_final_model)`, we can access the outputs shown in Figure 16.6.

```
MODEL INFO:
Observations: 100
Dependent Variable: accidents
Type: Generalized linear model
  Family: poisson
  Link function: log

MODEL FIT:
χ²(2) = 629.8044, p = 0.0000
Pseudo-R² (Cragg-Uhler) = 0.9982
Pseudo-R² (McFadden) = 0.6441
AIC = 354.0122, BIC = 361.8277

Standard errors: MLE
-----------------------------------------------------------------
                      Est.      2.5%     97.5%      z val.       p
----------------- -------- --------- --------- ---------- --------
(Intercept)         6.8545    6.4756    7.2334     35.4574   0.0000
age                -0.1275   -0.1376   -0.1175    -24.8020   0.0000
drylawyes          -0.4239   -0.6921   -0.1557     -3.0981   0.0019
-----------------------------------------------------------------
```

FIGURE 16.6 Outputs of the estimation related to the object `poisson_final_model`.

After the Stepwise procedure, we will notice that the variable *pop* was removed, and the final expression of the model can be written as follows:

$$\widehat{accidents_i} = e^{\left(6.8545 - 0.1275 \times age_i - 0.4239 \times drylaw_i\right)}$$

or

$$\ln\left(\widehat{accidents_i}\right) = 6.8545 - 0.1275 \times age_i - 0.4239 \times drylaw_i$$

We can calculate the IRR for each variable in our Poisson regression model. Thus we can verify that, for example, for each increase of 1 unit in the variable *age*, we can expect, on average, that the rate of traffic accidents will be multiplied by a factor of 0.8803 ($e^{-0.1275}$) or that it will be approximately 11.97% lower, keeping the other conditions constant. Similarly, the adoption of the dry law after 10:00 p.m. (variable *drylaw*) causes, on average, the rate of traffic accidents to be multiplied by a factor of 0.6545 ($e^{-0.4239}$), that is, 34.55% lower, *ceteris paribus*.

If we are interested in the predictions using the estimation related to the object `poisson_final_model`, we can use the function `predict()` with the argument `type = "response"`. Thus if we are interested in knowing how many traffic accidents per week can be expected in a Brazilian municipality with 600,000 inhabitants whose average age of drivers is 37 years and when the dry law is not adopted after 10:00 p.m., we can type:

```
predict(object = poisson_final_model,
        newdata = data.frame(pop = 0.6,
                             age = 37,
                             drylaw = "no"),
        type = "response")
```

As a result of the previous command, the reader will obtain an average of 8.461 traffic accidents per week in a Brazilian municipality with 600,000 inhabitants whose average age of drivers is 37 years and when the dry law is not adopted after 10:00 p.m., *ceteris paribus*.

Next, contrary to the diagnosis of equidispersion of the dependent variable conditioned on the predictor variables, we will insist on an NB estimation in parallel so the reader can be aware of the consequences of this type of error and, in the presence of overdispersion, will in fact be able to estimate NB regression models in R.

Negative binomial regression model in R

Originally, R does not have an algorithm capable of estimating NB regression models. For this, we will use the function `glm.nb()` from the package `MASS`. **Once again, we recognize that it does not make sense to estimate an NB model for the example we present because of the diagnosis of equidispersion; the idea has didactic purposes only.** That said, we can command the following:

```
nb_model <- glm.nb(formula = accidents ~ .,
                   data = accidents_data)
```

Regardless of whether the reader chooses the function `summary()` or the function `summ()`, R will not report the general statistics of the model, as shown in Figure 16.7.

```
MODEL INFO:
Observations: 100
Dependent Variable: accidents
Type: Generalized linear model
  Family: Negative Binomial(1.1934)
  Link function: log

MODEL FIT:
χ²() = , p =
Pseudo-R² (Cragg-Uhler) = 0.5154
Pseudo-R² (McFadden) = 0.1863
AIC = 315.6199, BIC = 328.6457

Standard errors: MLE
--------------------------------------------------------------------
                      Est.      2.5%     97.5%    z val.        p
----------------- --------- --------- --------- --------- ---------
(Intercept)         6.4529    4.6218    8.2841    6.9070   0.0000
pop                 0.5666    0.1694    0.9637    2.7960   0.0052
age                -0.1381   -0.1700   -0.1063   -8.4992   0.0000
drylawyes          -1.1581   -1.7977   -0.5185   -3.5490   0.0004
--------------------------------------------------------------------
```

FIGURE 16.7 Outputs of the estimation related to the object `nb_model`.

If the reader is interested, alternative methods for presenting the general statistics of the NB model involve use of the function `lrtest()` or the function `logLik()`. In this case, the most interesting point of the function `lrtest()`, as shown earlier in the "Poisson regression model in R" section, is that it directly presents the values of LL_0 (LL of a null model) and LL_{max} (LL of the estimated model).

```
lrtest(object = nb_model)
```

From the outputs of the previous command we can calculate the general statistics of the model related to the object `nb_model`:

$$\chi^2 = -2 \times (LL_0 - LL_{max})$$

$$\chi^2_{(4df)} = -2 \times [-187.80 - (-152.81\ )] = 69.98$$

As for the number of degrees of freedom for an NB regression model, the reader should remember that, in addition to the slope coefficients, there is also the shape parameter θ. Thus for our case, in addition to β_1, β_2, and β_3, θ must be considered, which results in 4 degrees of freedom.

To find out if the general statistics of the model is statistically significant at a level of 5%, we must determine the critical value of χ^2 for 4 degrees of freedom, as follows:

```
qchisq(p = 0.05, df = 4, lower.tail = FALSE)
```

With the previous routine, we obtain that $\chi^2_c = 9.488$. Thus because $\chi^2_{calc} > \chi^2_c$, we can reject the null hypothesis H_0 of the test, that is, at least one of the parameters of the predictor variables is statistically different from zero, in the presence of the others, at a confidence level of 95%. To find out which P-value is associated with χ^2_{calc}, we can type:

```
pchisq(q = 69.98, df = 4, lower.tail = FALSE)
```

It is also possible to calculate the McFadden pseudo R²:

$$\text{pseudo R}^2(\text{McFadden}) = \frac{-2.\text{LL}_0 - (-2.\text{LL}_{\max})}{-2.\text{LL}_0}$$

$$pseudo\ R^2(McFadden) = \frac{-2 \times (-187.80) - [-2 \times (-152.81)]}{-2 \times (-187.80)} = 0.1863$$

According to the Wald z statistics in Figure 16.7, we can say that all parameters of the predictor variables are statistically different from zero and thus are significant to explain the behavior of the dependent variable *accidents*, at a confidence level of 95%, *ceteris paribus*. Therefore we can present the equation of the NB regression model, related to the object `nb_model`, as follows:

$$\widehat{accidents}_i = e^{(6.4529 + 0.5666 \times pop_i - 0.1381 \times age_i - 1.1581 \times drylaw_i)}$$

or

$$\ln\left(\widehat{accidents}_i\right) = 6.4529 + 0.5666 \times pop_i - 0.1381 \times age_i - 1.1581 \times drylaw_i$$

If the reader desires to obtain the value of the parameter θ, it is found in the component `theta` of the object `nb_model` and can be accessed using the operator `$`:

```
nb_model$theta
```

For our example, $\theta = 1.193429$. To verify its statistical significance, we can calculate the Wald z statistics by using the relationship between the estimated value of θ and its respective standard error. The standard error of `theta` can be found in the component `SE.theta` of the object `nb_model`. In this sense, we can type:

```
nb_model$SE.theta
```

In our example, the value calculated for the standard error of θ is 0.44235. Therefore the respective value of the Wald z statistics of the parameter θ is given by $\frac{1.193429}{0.44235} = 2.69854$. The same can be obtained by typing:

```
nb_model$theta / nb_model$SE.theta
```

For the case of Wald z statistics, we seek values greater than 1.96. **So, we have more apparently counterintuitive information here! If Cameron and Trivedi's (1990) test indicated the phenomenon of equidispersion, how could the shape parameter θ, which characterizes the long tail of the Poisson-Gamma distribution, have been statistically different from zero, *ceteris paribus*?**

What really happens, which we will see next, is that the excess of zeros in the dependent variable can cause a misdiagnosis of the statistical significance of the parameter θ (Cameron and Trivedi, 2013; Payne et al., 2018; Fávero and Belfiore, 2019), leading us to mistakenly consider, in this case, the best adequacy of the NB regression model.

By definition, the parameters of an NB regression model will naturally regress to the same parameters obtained by a Poisson estimation in the presence of equidispersion, and this did not occur here because of the apparent counterintuitiveness between the Cameron and Trivedi test (1990) and the statistical significance of θ, which, of course, is a mark of the existence of overdispersion of the dependent variable, conditioned on the predictor variables. **What has happened here is that, in fact, neither the Poisson estimation nor the NB estimation are adequate for the proposed example, as we will demonstrate throughout the next two sections.**

As for the interpretation of the parameters of an NB regression model, such as that in the object `nb_model`, this is similar to what we studied in the "Poisson regression model in R" section.

Therefore using the outputs presented in Figure 16.7, we can verify that the increase of 1 unit in the variable *pop* multiplies the incidence rate of accidents by a factor of 1.7623 ($e^{0.5666}$), keeping the other conditions constant. In other words, the increase of 1 unit of the variable *pop* generates, on average, an average increase of the incidence rate of the dependent variable of 76.23%, *ceteris paribus*. However, it is important to remind the reader that the increase of 1 unit in the variable *pop* is equivalent to considering 100,000 more inhabitants for a given municipality (see Table 16.1). A similar form of interpretation can be applied to the variables *age* and *drylaw*.

For NB regression models in R, predictions can also be made using the algorithm `predict()` with the argument `type = "response"`. Therefore if the intention is to know, on average, the expected weekly number of traffic accidents in a given Brazilian municipality with a population of 600,000 inhabitants whose average age of drivers is 37 years when the dry law is not adopted after 10:00 p.m., *ceteris paribus*, we just command the following:

```
predict(object = nb_model,
        newdata = data.frame(pop = 0.6,
                             age = 37,
                             drylaw = "no"),
        type = "response")
```

From the previous command, the reader will obtain an average of 5.379 traffic accidents per week in a Brazilian municipality with 600,000 inhabitants whose average age of drivers is 37 years and when the dry law is not adopted after 10:00 p.m., keeping the remaining conditions constant.

Next, we will detail the estimation of ZIP models in R.

Zero-inflated Poisson regression model in R

As for the NB regression models, R does not have a native algorithm for estimating models that take into account the existence of inflation of zeros in the dependent variable. Thus for both ZIP and ZINB models, we will use the function `zeroinf()` from the package `pscl`.

```
zip_model <- zeroinfl(formula = accidents ~ age | .,
                      data = accidents_data,
                      dist = "poisson")
```

In the previous routine, an attentive reader must have realized that, although the declaration of the argument `formula` is quite similar to those applied for estimating the supervised models studied so far, there is a simple difference: the use of the operator |.

The reader should remember that the ZI models are a combination of count-data and binary logistic regression models, but considering the occurrence of zeros as events, and the occurrence of other values as non-events.

That said, it is important that the reader pay attention to the order of variables declared in the argument `formula`. First, before the operator |, we must declare the variables for the count component; after the operator |, we must declare the variables for the logistic component. Therefore we would reach the same results by typing the following:

```
zip_model <- zeroinfl(formula = accidents ~ age | pop + age + drylaw,
                      data = accidents_data,
                      dist = "poisson")
```

If the reader declares nothing after using the operator |, R will assume that the same variables used for the count component should also be used for the logistic component. It is also important for the reader to be aware that if there is a polytomous predictor variable, regardless of whether it is before or after the operator |, the a procedure to create $n-1$ dummies must first be applied to it.

The other arguments used in the function `zeroinfl()` are intuitive: `data`, representing the dataset where the variables are, and `dist = "poisson"` to inform R that the fitted values of the estimation must follow a ZI Poisson distribution.

For models estimated using the function `zeroinfl()`, the command `summ()` does not work. Thus we must use the function `summary()`, which, as expected, will not report the general statistics of the model:

```
summary(zip_model)
```

Figure 16.8 presents the outputs of the ZIP model.

```
Count model coefficients (poisson with log link):
             Estimate Std. Error z value Pr(>|z|)
(Intercept)  5.815004   0.213476   27.24   <2e-16 ***
age         -0.094347   0.005804  -16.26   <2e-16 ***

Zero-inflation model coefficients (binomial with logit link):
            Estimate Std. Error z value Pr(>|z|)
(Intercept) -8.74089    3.43228  -2.547 0.010876 *
pop         -1.26875    0.52083  -2.436 0.014849 *
age          0.19661    0.06565   2.995 0.002747 **
drylawyes    3.04405    0.87804   3.467 0.000527 ***
---
Signif. codes:  0 '***' 0.001 '**' 0.01 '*' 0.05 '.' 0.1 ' ' 1

Number of iterations in BFGS optimization: 13
Log-likelihood: -131.7 on 6 Df
```

FIGURE 16.8 Outputs of the estimation related to the object `zip_model`.

Before discussing Figure 16.8, we remind the reader that functions `lrtest()` and `logLik()` are good ways to extract the general statistics of the models estimated throughout this chapter. When applying, for example, the function `lrtest()`, R informs the reader that $LL_0 = -295.79$ and $LL_{max} = -131.71$. We can calculate the value of the χ^2 statistic as follows:

$$\chi^2 = -2.(LL_0 - LL_{max})$$

$$\chi^2_{(6df)} = -2 \times [-295.79 - (-131.71)] = 328.16$$

For the ZIP model, the 6 degrees of freedom refer to the 6 parameters used in the estimation. So, in this case, we are talking about the coefficients α and β_1 (for the count component) and γ, κ_1, κ_2, and κ_3 (for the binary logistic component).

As discussed earlier, the critical value of the χ^2 statistics, for 6 degrees of freedom and a significance level of 5%, can be calculated with the function `qchisq()`, as follows:

```
qchisq(p = 0.05, df = 6, lower.tail = FALSE)
```

When using the function `qchisq()`, the reader obtains $\chi^2_c = 12.592$, and because $\chi^2_{calc} > \chi^2_c$, we can say that at least one of the parameters of the variables in the ZIP model is statistically different from zero, at a significance level of 5%, keeping the other conditions constant. If the reader wants to know the P-value related to the χ^2_{calc}, just type the following:

```
pchisq(q = 328.16, df = 6, lower.tail = FALSE)
```

Referring back to Figure 16.8, it is possible to see that, in fact, all variables have parameters statistically different from zero, at a confidence level of 95%, *ceteris paribus*. However, we want to discuss some relevant information regarding Figure 16.8.

The reader must have realized that the estimation outputs obtained using the function `summary()` are divided into two parts. The upper part, called `Count model coefficients (poisson with log link)`, presents the parameters of the Poisson (count) component. The lower part, called `Zero-inflation model coefficients (binomial with logit link)`, displays the parameters of the binary logistic component.

In addition, it is important to inform that the choice of the functional form present in Figure 16.8 was absolutely purposeful, for didactic purposes. An experienced reader will know that when modeling real-world data, a possible final model is rarely reached immediately. **Thus if any parameter is not statistically significant, in R-based language there is no implementation of the Stepwise procedure for models estimated using the function `zeroinf()`.**

A tip to try to mitigate this kind of problem, **but which is not guaranteed to work in all cases**, is to first try to estimate a binary logistic model (see Chapter 15) using the Stepwise procedure and then select those variables whose parameters are statistically different from zero at a significance level to compose the component of structural zeros of the ZIP model. The same can be said for the count part of the model because the reader can also estimate, in parallel, a Poisson model using the Stepwise procedure to choose the variables that will compose the count component of the ZIP model. That said, the ZIP regression model itself can be estimated.

At this point, we can therefore write the model shown in Figure 16.8:

$$p_{logit_i} = \frac{1}{1 + e^{-\left(-8.741 - 1.269 \times pop_i + 0.197 \times age_i + 3.044 \times drylaw_i\right)}}$$

and

$$\lambda_i = e^{\left(5.815 - 0.094 \times age_i\right)}$$

Even more directly, we can write the model as follows:

$$\lambda_{inf\,late} = \left\{1 - \frac{1}{1 + e^{-\left(-8.741 - 1.269 \times pop_i + 0.197 \times age_i + 3.044 \times drylaw_i\right)}}\right\} \times \left[e^{\left(5.815 - 0.094 \times age_i\right)}\right]$$

Because we are facing a model that combines two different types of estimation, we can use what we learned about relative risk ratio (RRR; see Chapter 15) to interpret the binary logistic component and what we learned about the IRR (see the "Construction of the confidence intervals of the parameters for the Poisson regression model" section) for the Poisson (count) component.

Thus we can say that **the chance of occurrence of structural zeros in the dependent variable** by increasing the variable *pop* 1 unit should be multiplied by a factor of 0.2811 ($e^{-1.269}$), that is, 71.89% lower, on average, *ceteris paribus*. The chance of occurrence of structural zeros in the dependent variable, with an increase of 1 unit in the variable *age*, should be, on average, 21.77% higher ($e^{0.197}$), keeping the other conditions constant. Finally, the chance of occurrence of structural zeros in the dependent variable, when adopting the dry law after 10:00 p.m. (variable *drylaw*) should be, on average, 1.998.90% higher ($e^{3.044}$), keeping the other conditions constant (Fávero and Belfiore, 2019).

Note that the previous results make sense because it is common that traffic accidents are more frequent in a city with a larger number of inhabitants, decreasing the chance of counts equal to 0, or that older age of drivers (usually linked to greater caution in traffic) increases the chance of counts equal to 0, or even that a ban on consumption of alcoholic beverages by drivers is linked to a reduction in traffic accidents, thus increasing the chance of counts equal to 0.

In the logistic component, we studied the occurrence of inflation of zeros, that is, the structural zeros. By definition, it is absolutely normal that there are values equal to zero in count-data models (sampling zeros), but when the occurrence of these zeros goes beyond the probabilities of their common occurrence of a Poisson distribution, we must estimate a ZIP regression model. The logistic component of a ZIP estimate is ideal for the study of this excess of zeros (Fávero and Belfiore, 2019).

As for the count component, we can say that the increase of 1 unit in the variable *age* generates, on average, **a decrease in the accident occurrence rate of 8.97% ($e^{-0.094}$), thus increasing the probability of occurrence of sampling zeros.**

Despite some interesting conclusions, **we are still unable to state that the ZIP model is more suitable for the proposed example than the Poisson estimation.**

We saw in the "Poisson regression model in R" section that the phenomenon of equidispersion exists in our dependent variable, according to the Cameron and Trivedi test (1990). However, as discussed in the "Negative binomial regression model in R" section, when insisting on estimating an NB regression model, the parameter θ was shown to be statistically significant, at a significance level of 5%, which should not occur in the presence of equidispersion. These two pieces of information, added to the histogram of the variable *accidents* (Figure 16.3), generate suspicion of the existence of inflation of zeros in our dependent variable. However, for such a diagnosis, we must apply the Vuong test (1989), as discussed earlier in the "Zero-inflated regression models" section.

For application of the Vuong test, we will use the function `vuong()` from the package `pscl`. The Vuong test aims to compare two models and we must compare the ZIP model with the Poisson model, typing:

```
vuong(m1 = poisson_final_model,
      m2 = zip_model)
```

The function `vuong()` can be applied without difficulty because we must declare the two models to be compared in `m1` and `m2`. The result of the Vuong test is shown in Figure 16.9.

```
Vuong Non-Nested Hypothesis Test-Statistic:
(test-statistic is asymptotically distributed N(0,1) under the
 null that the models are indistinguishible)
-------------------------------------------------------------
              Vuong z-statistic             H_A    p-value
Raw                   -4.088407 model2 > model1 2.1717e-05
AIC-corrected         -3.798410 model2 > model1 7.2814e-05
BIC-corrected         -3.420663 model2 > model1 0.00031234
```

FIGURE 16.9 Vuong test comparing the estimations related to the objects `poisson_final_model` and `zip_model`.

According to Figure 16.9, we can reject H_0 of the Vuong test, that is, the ZIP model is a better fit for the data in our example. Therefore the inflation of zeros in the dependent variable, conditioned on the predictor variables, is verified.

We verified that there was equidispersion in our data, with only verification of the existence or nonexistence of inflation of zeros. **Therefore, we can conclude that the ZIP model is a better fit and, in this sense, can be chosen as the best model for our case.** However, if the reader still wishes to compare a ZIP model with a ZINB model, considering the counterintuitive result of the parameter θ in the NB estimation proposed in the "Negative binomial regression model in R" section, or if the reader is curious about how to perform a ZINB estimation in R-based language, we recommend reading the following section.

Finally, if the reader wishes to make predictions, the function `predict()` can be used, commanding `type = "response"`. Therefore, considering the ZIP estimate, the expected weekly number of traffic accidents in a given Brazilian municipality with a population of 600,000 inhabitants whose average age of drivers is 37 years and when the dry law is not adopted after 10:00 p.m., *ceteris paribus*, should be obtained using the following command:

```
predict(object = zip_model,
        newdata = data.frame(pop = 0.6,
                             age = 37,
                             drylaw = "no"),
         type = "response")
```

As a result of the previous command, the reader can expect an average of 9.224 traffic accidents per week in a Brazilian municipality with 600,000 inhabitants whose average age of drivers is 37 years when the dry law is not adopted after 10:00 p.m., *ceteris paribus*.

Zero-inflated negative binomial regression model in R

First, we must remember that the first procedure implemented was the Cameron and Trivedi test (1990) and, through it, equidispersion in the dependent variable, conditioned on the predictor variables, was verified. **Given this result, there is no sense to estimate an NB regression model for our data; we did it in R for didactic purposes. Likewise, a ZINB estimation does not make sense.** What makes sense, and has been done, is that, given the diagnosis of equidispersion, we suspect and test the inflation of zeros and, after that, we adopt the ZIP estimation as the best model.

That said, for didactic purposes, we will now present how to estimate a ZINB regression model in R. To do this, we will again use the function `zeroinfl()`, but now with the argument `dist = "negbin"`, as follows:

```
zinb_model <- zeroinfl(formula = accidents ~ age | .,
                       data = accidents_data,
                       dist = "negbin")
```

To obtain the general statistics of the model related to the object `zinb_model`, we can use the calculated values of LL_0 and LL_{max} of the function `lrtest()`. That said, for our ZINB estimation, we have $LL_0 = -187.59$ and $LL_{max} = -131.71$. Thus we have:

$$\chi^2 = -2.(LL_0 - LL_{max})$$

$$\chi^2_{(7df)} = -2 \times [-187.59 - (-131.71)] = 111.76$$

An attentive reader will realize that the LL_{max} of our ZIP estimation is equal to the LL_{max} of the ZINB estimation, and this is not a coincidence (we will return to this discussion later). The reader will also notice that the general statistics of our ZINB model has 7 degrees of freedom, and this is due to the 7 parameters considered in the modeling: α, β_1, and θ (for the count component) and γ, κ_1, κ_2, and κ_3 (for the binary logistic component). To discuss the general statistics of our ZINB estimation, we must obtain the critical value of the χ^2 statistic, at a significance level of 5% and with 7 degrees of freedom, which can be defined as follows:

```
qchisq(0.05, df = 7, lower.tail = FALSE)
```

R will return $\chi^2_c = 14.067$. Because $\chi^2_{calc} > \chi^2_c$, at least one of the parameters of our variables is statistically significant to explain the behavior of the dependent variable, keeping the other conditions constant, at a significance level of 5%. We can reinforce this fact analyzing the P-value of the respective χ^2_{calc}, which can be obtained as follows:

```
pchisq(q = 111.76, df = 7, lower.tail = FALSE)
```

After that, we can use the function `summary()` to check the results of our ZINB estimation.

```
summary(zinb_model)
```

Figure 16.10 shows the results of the estimation related to the object `zinb_model`.

```
Count model coefficients (negbin with log link):
             Estimate Std. Error z value Pr(>|z|)
(Intercept)  5.815548   0.213501  27.239   <2e-16 ***
age         -0.094362   0.005804 -16.257   <2e-16 ***
Log(theta)  11.469631  48.824266   0.235    0.814

Zero-inflation model coefficients (binomial with logit link):
            Estimate Std. Error z value Pr(>|z|)
(Intercept) -8.73574    3.43301  -2.545 0.010939 *
pop         -1.27130    0.52135  -2.438 0.014750 *
age          0.19656    0.06567   2.993 0.002759 **
drylawyes    3.04730    0.87892   3.467 0.000526 ***
---
Signif. codes:  0 '***' 0.001 '**' 0.01 '*' 0.05 '.' 0.1 ' ' 1

Theta = 95762.9787
Number of iterations in BFGS optimization: 46
Log-likelihood: -131.7 on 7 Df
```

FIGURE 16.10 Outputs of the estimation related to the object `zinb_model`.

Similar to the ZIP estimation, whose outputs were presented in Figure 16.8, the outputs of the ZINB estimation (Figure 16.10) are also divided into two parts. The upper part, called `Count model coefficients (negbin with log link)`, presents the parameters of the NB (count) component. The lower part, called `Zero-inflation model coefficients (binomial with logit link)`, displays the parameters of the binary logistic component.

An attentive reader will notice that for ZINB estimates, the function `zeroinf()` offers the parameter `Log(theta)`, which is also common in other software (e.g., *Stata*). If we want the estimated value of θ, we can look at the final part of the outputs present in Figure 16.10, where it is shown that $\theta = 95{,}762.9787$. It is interesting to note that this parameter is not statistically significant (Pr(>|z|) = 0.814) at a significance level of 5%.

As for the Vuong test, we can compare the NB regression model with the ZINB regression model, as follows:

```
vuong(m1 = nb_model,
      m2 = zinb_model)
```

Figure 16.11 presents the result of the Vuong test, indicating the existence of inflation of zeros in the dependent variable.

```
Vuong Non-Nested Hypothesis Test-Statistic:
(test-statistic is asymptotically distributed N(0,1) under the
 null that the models are indistinguishible)
-------------------------------------------------------------
              Vuong z-statistic             H_A    p-value
Raw                   -3.295973 model2 > model1 0.00049041
AIC-corrected         -2.983522 model2 > model1 0.00142476
BIC-corrected         -2.576529 model2 > model1 0.00498989
```

FIGURE 16.11 Vuong test comparing the estimations related to the objects nb_`model` and `zinb_model`.

This fact can also be visualized graphically when comparing the outputs of Figure 16.8 with those of Figure 16.10. An attentive reader will remember that, in the absence of overdispersion (no statistical significance of θ), an NB estimation (classic or ZINB) will present outputs that will naturally regress to the Poisson estimation (classic or ZIP). Table 16.2 illustrates this.

TABLE 16.2 Comparison of the parameters of the ZIP and ZINB estimations.

Parameter	ZIP	ZINB
α	5.815[a]	5.816[a]
β_1	−0.094[a]	−0.094[a]
θ	–	95,762.979
γ	−8.741[a]	−8.736[a]
κ_1	−1.269[a]	−1.271[a]
κ_2	0.197[a]	0.197[a]
κ_3	3.044[a]	3.047[a]

[a] *Statistical significance at 5%.*

In fact, according to Table 16.2, the parameters present in the two models (ZIP and ZINB) are very similar. There is yet another factor that corroborates with everything said so far. The reader must remember that the LL_{max} of the ZIP estimate is equal to the LL_{max} of the ZINB estimate, and this is not a coincidence. We can apply the likelihood ratio test to compare these two models and see if there are any statistically significant differences between them.

```
lrtest(zip_model,
       zinb_model)
```

Figure 16.12 shows the results of the likelihood ratio test obtained from the function `lrtest()`.

```
Likelihood ratio test

Model 1: accidents ~ age | .
Model 2: accidents ~ age | .
  #Df  LogLik Df Chisq Pr(>Chisq)
1   6 -131.71
2   7 -131.71  1 9e-04     0.9765
```

FIGURE 16.12 Comparison between ZIP and ZINB models using the likelihood ratio test.

Due to the P-value obtained from the likelihood ratio test (Figure 16.12), there is no way to state that the two models are statistically different, at a significance level of 5%, even if the ZINB estimation has an additional degree of freedom related to the shape parameter θ.

As for interpretation of the parameters because they are extremely close to those estimated in the ZIP model, this must be done in a similar way to that presented in the "Zero-inflated Poisson regression model in R" section. As for the need for prediction, this must also be done using the function `predict()` with the argument `type = "response"`. Thus considering the ZINB estimate, the expected weekly number of traffic accidents in a given Brazilian municipality with a population of 600,000 inhabitants whose average age of drivers is 37 years and when the dry law is not adopted after 10:00 p.m., *ceteris paribus*, can be obtained by typing the following:

```
predict(object = zinb_model,
        newdata = data.frame(pop = 0.6,
                             age = 37,
                             drylaw = "no"),
        type = "response")
```

From the previous command, the reader obtains an average of 9.222 weekly traffic accidents in a Brazilian municipality with 600,000 inhabitants whose average age of drivers is 37 years and when the dry law is not adopted after 10:00 p.m., *ceteris paribus*. Unsurprisingly, the calculated value is very similar to that obtained from the ZIP estimate for this case.

Finally, if there is still the intention to observe the equation of the ZINB model estimated in this section, we can write it as follows:

$$p_{\log it_i} = \frac{1}{1 + e^{-\left(-8.736 - 1.271 \times pop_i + 0.197 \times age_i + 3.047 \times drylaw_i\right)}}$$

and

$$u_i = e^{\left(5.816 - 0.094 \times age_i\right)}$$

Even more directly, we can write the model as follows:

$$u_{\inf late} = \left\{1 - \frac{1}{1 + e^{-\left(-8.736 - 1.271 \times pop_i + 0.197 \times age_i + 3.047 \times drylaw_i\right)}}\right\} \times \left[e^{\left(5.816 - 0.094 \times age_i\right)}\right]$$

Final remarks

The Poisson and NB regression models are log-linear models (or semi-logarithmic to the left) and represent the best-known count-data models, being estimated by maximum likelihood. Although the correct estimation of a Poisson regression model demands the nonexistence of the overdispersion phenomenon in the dependent variable data, estimation by an NB regression model allows that the variance for a dependent variable be statistically higher than its mean (Fávero and Belfiore, 2019).

Before defining the most adequate and consistent regression model when there is count data, we recommended performing a diagnostic regarding the dependent variable distribution and the estimation of a Poisson regression model and, from that point, executing a test to verify the existence of overdispersion in the data. Should this be the case, an NB regression model should be estimated, and we recommended the NB2 type model (Fávero and Belfiore, 2019).

Exercise

1. The finance department for a large appliance retailer wants to know if consumer income and age explain the use installment closed-end credit financing when purchasing goods such as cellular phones, tablets, laptops, televisions, and video game systems so as to develop a marketing campaign for this form of financing based on consumer profile. To do this, the finance department marketing area randomly chose a sample of 200 consumers from its total client base, with the following variables (Fávero and Belfiore, 2019):

Variable	Description
id	String variable that varies between 001 and 200 and that identifies the consumer
purchases	Dependent variable corresponding to the amount of durable goods purchases using installment closed-end credit in the past year per consumer (count data)
income	Monthly consumer income (US$)
age	Consumer age (years)

By analyzing the dataset present in the `financing.RData` (Fávero and Belfiore, 2019) file, we would like you to:

a. Prepare a preliminary diagnostic regarding the existence of overdispersion in the purchases variable data. Present its mean and variance, and prepare a histogram.

b. Estimate a Poisson regression model and, based on the results, execute the test to verify the existence of overdispersion in the data. What was the test result at a significance level of 5%?

c. Execute an χ^2 test to compare the distribution of observed and predicted probabilities for the incidence of the annual use of installment closed-end credit. Does the test result, at a significance level of 5%, indicate a quality of adjustment for the Poisson regression model?

d. If the answer to the previous question is yes, present the final expression for the mean estimated quantity of annual use of installment closed-end credit when purchasing durable goods, as a function of the explanatory variables that show themselves to be statistically significant, at a confidence level of 95%.

e. What is the expected average quantity of installment closed-end credit use per year for a consumer with a monthly income of US $2,600 and who is 47 years of age?

f. On average, how much does the annual incidence rate of installment closed-end credit use change by increasing the average consumer monthly income by US $100, maintaining the remaining conditions constant?

g. On average, how does the annual incidence rate of installment closed-end credit use change by increasing the average consumer age by 1 year, maintaining the remaining conditions constant?

h. Construct a graph that shows the predicted value for the annual incidence of installment closed-end credit use as a function of consumer monthly income. Provide a brief discussion.

i. Estimate a multiple log-linear regression model by ordinary least squares, and compare the results predicted in this model with those estimated by the Poisson model.

j. If there is interest in increasing financing using installment closed-end credit, which consumers should be targeted in this financing market campaign?

Supplementary data sets

`accidents_data.RData`
`financing.RData`

Please access supplementary data files here: https://doi.org/10.17632/55623jkwrp.3

CHAPTER

17

Generalized linear mixed models

AT THE END OF THIS CHAPTER, YOU WILL BE ABLE TO:

- Know how to differentiate a multilevel model from a traditional regression model.
- Develop likelihood-ratio tests to compare estimations of different multilevel models.
- Estimate multilevel regression models in R software, and interpret their results.

R-based language packages used in this chapter

```
library(MASS)
library(pscl)
library(tidyverse)
library(glmmTMB)
library(lmtest)
library(gridExtra)
library(fastDummies)
```

Don't forget to define the R working directory (the location where your datasets are installed):

```
setwd("C:/book/chapter17")
```

Estimation of hierarchical linear models in R

The main objective of this section is to give researchers the opportunity to prepare multilevel modeling procedures using R software.

Estimation of a two-level hierarchical linear model (HLM2) with clustered data in R

We will now discuss an example that follows the same logic seen in Chapters 14 to 16, but this time with data that vary among individuals and among groups to which these individuals belong, characterizing a nested structure.

Data Science, Analytics and Machine Learning with R
https://doi.org/10.1016/B978-0-12-824271-1.00015-9

The data for the proposed example concerns the presence of a carcinoembryonic antigen (protein), in μg/mL of blood, in patients from different states for a given hospital. The increase in the presence of this protein is related to the existence of colorectal cancer. The variables present in the file `colorectal_cancer.RData` are presented in Table 17.1.

TABLE 17.1 Description of the variables present in the dataset `colorectal_cancer.RData`.

Variable	Description
patient_id	Level 1 categorical variable that identifies the studied patient.
state_id	Level 2 categorical variable that identifies the state of origin of the studied patient.
antigen	Continuous metric variable that indicates the amount of carcinoembryonic antigen, in μg/mL of blood, for a given patient studied. This will be the dependent variable of our models established throughout this section.
oil_fats_consumption	Level 1 metric variable that indicates the annual consumption of oils and fats, in kg, for each patient studied.
avg_income	Level 2 metric variable that indicates the average income of the inhabitants of a given state, in US dollars ($) × 10,000.

For educational purposes, we propose Table 17.2 to better explain the nestings present in the dataset used. Therefore our construct will be to study if the presence of carcinoembryonic antigens, in μg/mL of blood, is a function of the consumption of oils and fats as well as a function of characteristics of the place where the patient resides.

An attentive reader will notice the nesting of the observations in Table 17.2. For example, patients i are nested in states j. The reader will also notice that the variables *antigen* and *oil_fats_consumption* change due to each patient i, however the variable *avg_income* only changes due to changes in the variable *state* because they are level 2 variables. To open the dataset, we can type the following command:

```
load("colorectal_cancer.RData")
```

TABLE 17.2 Clipping of the dataset present in the file `colorectal_cancer.RData` showing patients' nestings in states.

patient i (Level 1)	**state j (Level 2)**	**antigen (Y_{ij})**	**oil_fats_consumption (X_{ij})**	**avg_income (W_{1j})**
1	1	3.33	11	3.6
2	1	6.93	23	3.6
			⋮	
140	4	9.27	27	5.5
141	5	2.47	17	1.9
			⋮	
357	10	1.87	7	3.9
358	10	5.53	24	3.9

The univariate descriptive statistics of the metric variables as well as the frequency tables of the categorical variables can be accessed using the function `summary()`:

```
summary(colorectal_cancer)
```

```
   patient_id       state_id       antigen          oil_fats_consumption    avg_income
1        :  1    3       : 48   Min.   : 0.870   Min.    : 4          Min.   : 1.900
2        :  1    5       : 48   1st Qu.: 2.800   1st Qu.:14          1st Qu.: 1.900
3        :  1    1       : 47   Median : 4.730   Median :20          Median : 3.600
4        :  1    9       : 44   Mean   : 5.541   Mean   :19          Mean   : 5.161
5        :  1    8       : 35   3rd Qu.: 7.870   3rd Qu.:24          3rd Qu.: 7.500
6        :  1    10      : 33   Max.   :13.330   Max.   :31          Max.   :13.000
(Other):352    (Other):103
```

FIGURE 17.1 Univariate descriptive statistics for metric variables and frequency tables for categorical variables.

Figure 17.1 shows the result of the previous command.

When observing, although in a minimal way, the behavior of the variable *state*, explained in Figure 17.1, the reader will notice that we are facing unbalanced data. Table 17.3 further stresses this statement when presenting the number of patients nested in states, resulting from the following code:

```
colorectal_cancer %>%
  group_by(state_id) %>%
  summarise(freq = n(),
            relative_freq = round(freq / nrow(.), digits = 3))
```

TABLE 17.3 Demonstration of the imbalance of patient nesting in states.

State	Frequency	Relative frequency
1	47	0.131
2	25	0.070
3	48	0.134
4	20	0.056
5	48	0.134
6	30	0.084
7	28	0.078
8	35	0.098
9	44	0.123
10	33	0.092

The average value of carcinoembryonic antigens, in μg/mL of blood, present in each patient, by state, can be calculated by the following routine, whose results are found in Table 17.4:

```
colorectal_cancer %>%
  group_by(state_id) %>%
  summarise(`average_antigen` = mean(antigen, na.rm = TRUE))
```

TABLE 17.4 Average amount of antigens present in patients by state.

State	Average of carcinoembryonic antigens
1	4.90
2	2.85
3	8.95
4	7.38

Continued

TABLE 17.4 Average amount of antigens present in patients by state—cont'd

State	Average of carcinoembryonic antigens
5	2.57
6	4.53
7	7.67
8	10.10
9	2.47
10	5.15

To conclude this initial diagnostic, we can create a chart that allows visualization of the average value of carcinoembryonic antigens, in μg/mL of blood, present in each patient, by state. This chart is shown in Figure 17.2 and can be obtained by typing the following command:

```
colorectal_cancer %>%
  group_by(state_id) %>%
  mutate(average_antigen = mean(antigen, na.rm = TRUE)) %>%
  ggplot() +
  geom_point(aes(x = state_id, y = antigen),color = "orange", alpha = 0.3) +
  geom_line(aes(x = state_id, y = average_antigen,
                group = 1, color = "Average Level of Carcinoembryonic Antigen by State"), size = 1.2) +
  scale_color_manual("Legenda:",
                     values = "darkorchid") +
  labs(x = "State",
       y = "Carconoembryonic Antigen in \u03bcg/mL") +
  theme(legend.title = element_blank(),
       panel.border = element_rect(NA),
       panel.grid = element_line("grey80"),
       panel.background = element_rect("white"),
       legend.position = "bottom")
```

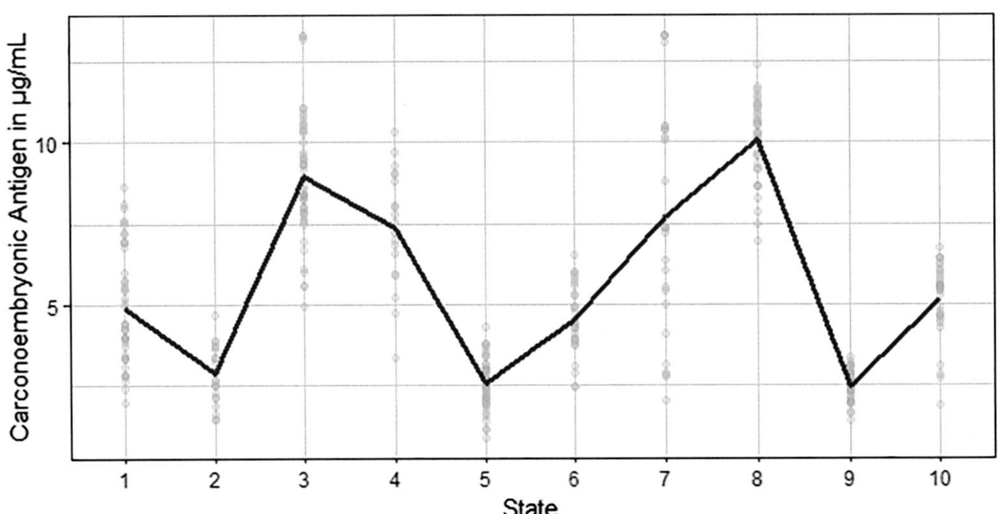

FIGURE 17.2 Average value of carcinoembryonic antigens, in μg/mL, present in each patient, by state.

Having characterized the nesting of patients in states based on our example's clustered data, we can now apply the multilevel modeling itself, constructing the procedures aiming at estimating a two-level hierarchical linear model (patients and states). In the states model, even though inclusion of dummy variables that represent states into the fixed effects component is possible, we will treat these level 2 units as random effects to estimate these models.

The first step is to establish a null model. The idea is to verify if consideration of a two-level state makes our model superior to an estimation that considers only one level, that is, to study if an estimation that considers the inclusion of random effects by state is superior, in predictive terms, to an estimation that considers the inclusion of only fixed effects.

To establish the multilevel models of this work, we will use the function `glmmTMB()` from the homonymous package. We choose the package `glmmTMB` because, for the time being, this approach considers the largest number of different possibilities of multilevel estimations in R language, even including zero-inflated multilevel models. In this first moment, as the reader already knows, we will study multilevel linear models.

That said, to establish our two-level null model, we must type the following command:

```
hlm2_nullmodel <- glmmTMB(formula = antigen ~ 1 + (1 | state_id),
                          family = gaussian,
                          data = colorectal_cancer,
                          REML = TRUE)
```

Depending on which date the reader installed the package `glmmTMB`, **after estimating the model, some warnings may occur regarding the disuse of some functions of the package `Matrix`** because some functions of the package `Matrix` are used in the background of the models that follow the approach proposed in this work. **For these cases, the situation does not indicate any reason for concern** because the model will normally appear in the *Global Environment* of the reader, with its parameters properly calculated as we will see later. Furthermore, as far as our knowledge goes, the situation has already been corrected in the development version, present on the GitHub of the authors of the package `glmmTMB`.

Related to the statement of the commands, although it is analogous to what we studied in Chapters 14 to 16, there are some points to clarify. In the argument `formula`, as the reader must be used to, we must declare the dependent variable first, followed by the operator ~, and the predictor variables interspersed by the operator +. To estimate a null model, that is, a model that considers only the intercept, in place of the predictor variables, we must declare the value `1`. All of the declaration discussed so far concerns the portion of the fixed effects of our model.

After declaring all variables that will be considered in the fixed effects of the estimation, we must use the operator `+`, and we must open parentheses. Within these parentheses, there will be a declaration regarding random effects, separating the variables considered at each level using the operator |. In our case, we will only consider the existence of random intercepts, without the presence of random slopes, so declaration `1` is inside the parentheses where the state level is declared. After this, we will declare | followed by the level to be considered. It is important to mention that each level must be considered individually within its own parentheses, and we must declare the levels from highest to the lowest, necessarily. This will become clearer when we estimate a multilevel model in the "Estimation of a three-level hierarchical linear model (HLM3) with repeated measures in R" section.

Another argument that deserves mention is the argument `family`. For linear models, we must consider `family = gaussian`. Other species of pet will therefore require the declaration of other arguments in `family`, as we will see in the following sections. If the reader wants to get ahead of this, we encourage reading the documentation for the function `glmmTMB()`using the command `?glmmTMB`.

Finally, the argument `REML = TRUE` determines that we will use the maximum likelihood restricted to estimate the coefficients regarding the random effects of our model. That said, the parameters of our first multilevel estimation can be viewed using the function `summary()`:

```
summary(hlm2_nullmodel)
```

Figure 17.3 presents the results of the previous command.

```
Family: gaussian  ( identity )
Formula:          antigen ~ 1 + (1 | state_id)
Data: colorectal_cancer

     AIC      BIC   logLik deviance df.resid
  1399.3   1410.9   -696.6   1393.3      356

Random effects:

Conditional model:
 Groups   Name        Variance Std.Dev.
 state_id (Intercept) 7.361    2.713
 Residual             2.540    1.594
Number of obs: 358, groups:  state_id, 10

Dispersion estimate for gaussian family (sigma^2): 2.54

Conditional model:
            Estimate Std. Error z value Pr(>|z|)
(Intercept)   5.6516     0.8625   6.553 5.65e-11 ***
---
Signif. codes:  0 '***' 0.001 '**' 0.01 '*' 0.05 '.' 0.1 ' ' 1
```

FIGURE 17.3 Parameters of the estimation contained in the object `hlm2_nullmodel`.

At the top of Figure 17.3, we have some interesting redundancies: we can check the arguments `family`, `formula`, and `data` declared for the construction of the estimation. After that, we can access some statistics regarding the goodness of fit of the model, being the statistics AIC, BIC, log-likelihood (*LL*), deviance ($-2 \times LL$), and degrees of freedom of the residues.

Next, in Figure 17.3, in the `Random effects` field, we have the values of the variance (τ_{00}) and the standard deviation of the error terms of the random intercepts (ν_{0j}) – 7.361 and 2.713, respectively. Right below, we have the variance (σ^2) and the standard deviation of the idiosyncratic error terms of the observations (ε_{ij}) – 2.540 and 1.594, respectively.

In the `Conditional Model` field in Figure 17.3, we have results that are similar to those studied in the models in Chapters 14 to 16. In other words, we will have the parameters regarding the fixed effects of the estimation, with their respective standard errors, *z* statistics, and *P*-values.

The parameters contained by the model presented in Figure 17.3 can be written algebraically, as follows:

$$antigen_{ij} = \beta_{0j} + \varepsilon_{ij},$$

where ε_{ij} refers to idiosyncratic error terms; $\beta_{0j} = \gamma_{00} + \nu_{0j}$, and ν_{0j} represents the error terms of level 2 random intercepts, resulting in:

$$antigen_{ij} = 5.652 + \nu_{0j} + \varepsilon_{ij}.$$

As mentioned earlier, Figure 17.3 does not bring the value of each ν_{0j} for each state considered; it brings the calculated variance of all error terms of the random intercepts (τ_{00}). To have access to each of the values of ν_{0j}, we must use the function `ranef()` from the package `glmmTMB`.

```
ranef(object = hlm2_nullmodel)
```

Table 17.5 shows the result of the previous routine.

TABLE 17.5 Values of ν_{0j}, of each state considered.

State	ν_{0j}—Values (random intercepts)
1	–0.7440238
2	2.7607073
3	3.2746353

TABLE 17.5 Values of ν_{0j}, of each state considered—cont'd

State	ν_{0j}—Values (random intercepts)
4	1.6956291
5	−3.0602385
6	−1.1095184
7	1.9941660
8	4.3627992
9	−3.1521201
10	−0.5006216

Despite the presentations made, we still do not have the answer to the following question: **Is the multilevel approach, for the considered dataset, a more interesting approach than an analogous estimation of a single equation (i.e., OLS estimation)?**

Over the past two decades, there have been extensive discussions in the literature about how to answer this question, going through anyone who advocates the need to calculate the standard errors of the variances of the terms of random errors, to obtain an eventual z statistic, therefore obtain statistical significance that defines whether or not the multilevel approach is worthwhile or whether or not a given level (s) is worth considering. On the other hand, there are those who advocate that it does not make sense to work with the previous procedure because it does not guarantee that the random effects, for each level considered, are adherent to a z curve or adherent to other distributions depending on the type of estimation adopted. In this work, we will use the LR test as a metric for comparing models to define the best estimate for predictive purposes.

Thus to carry out the LR test, we will necessarily establish a null OLS model, such as that learned in Chapter 14.

```
ols_nullmodel <- lm(formula = antigen ~ 1,
                    data = colorectal_cancer)
```

After that, we can command the function `lrtest()` from the package `lmtest` to achieve the LR test:

```
lrtest(ols_nullmodel, hlm2_nullmodel)
```

Figure 17.4 shows the results of the LR test between the estimations contained in the objects `ols_nullmodel` and `hlm2_nullmodel`.

```
Likelihood ratio test

Model 1: antigen ~ 1
Model 2: antigen ~ 1 + (1 | state_id)
  #Df  LogLik Df  Chisq Pr(>Chisq)
1   2 -912.13
2   3 -696.65  1 430.97  < 2.2e-16 ***
---
Signif. codes:  0 '***' 0.001 '**' 0.01 '*' 0.05 '.' 0.1 ' ' 1
```

FIGURE 17.4 LR test between the estimations contained in the objects `ols_nullmodel` and `hlm2_nullmodel`.

Figure 17.4 points out the highest *LL* for the multilevel approach, at a level of 1% significance, suggesting that considering state levels for the case studied makes sense. Directly, as shown in Figure 17.4, we can reject H_0 that the random intercepts are statistically equal to zero.

With this conclusion in mind, we can return to Figure 17.3 and notice that the parameter $\gamma_{00}=5.652$, which corresponds to the average amount of carcinoembryonic antigens expected in μg/mL of blood, by patient, by state (horizontal line estimated in the null model, or general intercept). The values of $Var(\nu_{0j})=\tau_{00}=7.361$ and $Var(\varepsilon_{ij})=\sigma^2=2.540$ must be considered for the calculation of the ICC:

$$ICC = \frac{\tau_{00}}{\tau_{00} + \sigma^2} = \frac{7.361}{7.361 + 2.540} = 0.7435.$$

The result suggests that approximately 74.35% of the total variance of the amount of carcinoembryonic antigens expected in μg/mL of blood, in patients, is due to changes among states, representing a sign that there is, in fact, variability in the amount of antigens per patients when they are from different states.

With the creation of a null model, having compared it with its analogous estimation looking for a statistically significant *LL* gain, we can propose a richer model, considering the other variables in the dataset.

```
hlm2_finalmodel <- glmmTMB(formula = antigen ~ oil_fats_consumption +
                    avg_income + oil_fats_consumption:avg_income +
                    (oil_fats_consumption | state_id),
                  family = gaussian,
                  data = colorectal_cancer,
                  REML = TRUE)
```

In the previous statement, an attentive reader will notice that in the argument `formula`, even before the use of parentheses, the argument of the variables of the fixed effects component is very similar to that studied in Chapters 14 to 16 of this work. However, there was the declaration `oil_fats_consumption: avg_income` in which the operator determines that we also want to check if the interactions between the variables *oil_fats_consumption* and *avg_income* make sense.

Inside the parentheses, we declare `oil_fats_consumption | state_id`, determining that R tries to calculate the random intercepts caused by the variable *oil_fats_consumption* due to the different states present in the dataset. The other stated arguments are identical to the one already discussed. The model parameters are presented by the function `summary()`:

```
summary(hlm2_finalmodel)
```

Figure 17.5 presents the parameters of the model contained in the object `hlm2_finalmodel`.

We can see from Figure 17.5 that in the fixed effects component, all variables declared were statistically different from zero at a level of 5% significance. As for the random effects component, we will notice a change in the variances: the variance of the error terms of the random intercepts ($Var(\nu_{0j})=\tau_{00}$), per state, is equal to 0.434, while the variance of the error terms of the random slopes ($Var(\nu_{1j})=\tau_{11}$), by state, as a function of the variable *oil_fats_consumption*, is equal to 0.005. The variance of idiosyncratic error terms ($Var(\varepsilon_{ij})=\sigma^2$) is 0.126.

Level 1 of the model can be written algebraically, as follows:

$$antigen_{ij} = \beta_{0j} + \beta_{1j}.oil\_fats\_consumption_{ij} + \varepsilon_{ij}.$$

The model's level 2 is algebraically represented as follows:

$$\begin{aligned} \beta_{0j} &= \gamma_{00} + \gamma_{01}.avg\_income_j + \nu_{0j} \\ \beta_{1j} &= \gamma_{10} + \gamma_{11}.avg\_income_j + \nu_{1j} \end{aligned}.$$

```
Family: gaussian  ( identity )
Formula:
antigen ~ oil_fats_consumption + avg_income + oil_fats_consumption:avg_income +
    (oil_fats_consumption | state_id)
Data: colorectal_cancer

     AIC      BIC   logLik deviance df.resid
   379.5    410.6   -181.8    363.5      354

Random effects:

Conditional model:
 Groups   Name                 Variance Std.Dev. Corr
 state_id (Intercept)          0.434070 0.6588
          oil_fats_consumption 0.005431 0.0737   -0.86
 Residual                      0.125570 0.3544
Number of obs: 358, groups:  state_id, 10

Dispersion estimate for gaussian family (sigma^2): 0.126

Conditional model:
                                 Estimate Std. Error z value Pr(>|z|)
(Intercept)                     -0.111187   0.400408  -0.278  0.78125
oil_fats_consumption             0.095033   0.042781   2.221  0.02632 *
avg_income                       0.211235   0.065014   3.249  0.00116 **
oil_fats_consumption:avg_income  0.030915   0.007021   4.403 1.07e-05 ***
---
Signif. codes:  0 '***' 0.001 '**' 0.01 '*' 0.05 '.' 0.1 ' ' 1
```

FIGURE 17.5 Parameters of the estimation contained in the object `hlm2_finalmodel`.

When we join the two levels in one equation, we have:

$$antigen_{ij} = \gamma_{00} + \gamma_{10}.oil\_fats\_consumption_{ij} + \gamma_{01}.avg\_income_j + \gamma_{11}.oil\_fats\_consumption_{ij}.avg\_income_j + \nu_{0j} + \nu_{1j}.oil\_fats\_consumption_{ij} + \varepsilon_{ij},$$

which is the same as:

$$antigen_{ij} = -0.111 + 0.095.oil\_fats\_consumption_{ij} + 0.211.avg\_income_j + 0.031.oil\_fats\_consumption_{ij}.avg\_income_j + \nu_{0j} + \nu_{1j}.oil\_fats\_consumption_{ij} + \varepsilon_{ij}.$$

To calculate the error terms of the intercepts and the random slopes of the proposed model (ν_{0j} and ν_{1j}, respectively) for the case studied, we must use the function `ranef()`, as discussed at the beginning of this section.

```
ranef(hlm2_finalmodel)
```

Table 17.6 displays the R response to the previous command.

TABLE 17.6 Values of ν_{0j} and ν_{1j}, for each state considered.

State	ν_{0j}: Values (random intercepts)	ν_{1j}: Values (random slopes: *oil_fats_consumption*)
1	−0.02916921	0.0585497413
2	0.17265033	−0.0371495094
3	0.81250709	−0.1039110685
4	−0.70184020	0.0601663454
5	−0.22672308	−0.0186018964
6	0.51702875	0.0005811613
7	−1.10382171	0.1212466111
8	−0.18008683	0.0289152056
9	0.49490027	−0.0809506589
10	0.24455458	−0.0288459315

In addition to the one proposed by Table 17.6, we can present the values of ν_{0j} and ν_{1j} graphically, as shown in Figure 17.6.

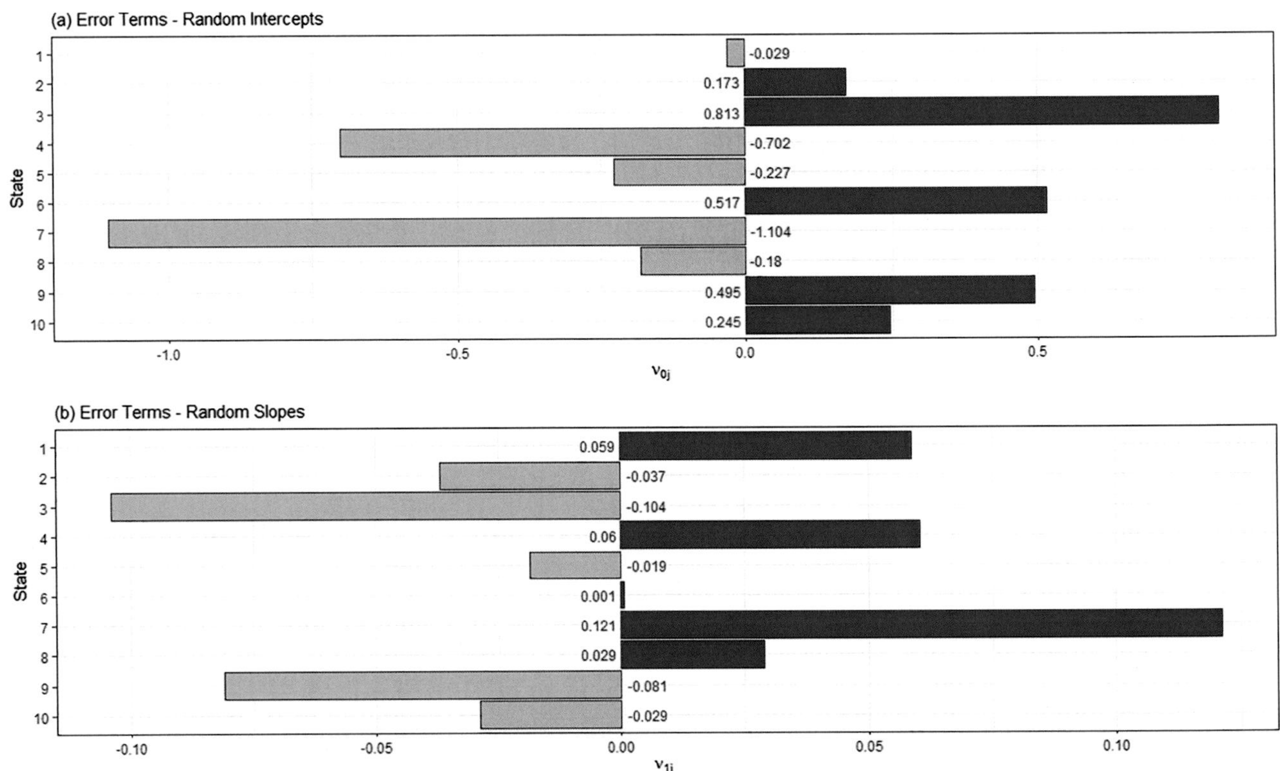

FIGURE 17.6 Graph of the values of ν_{0j} and ν_{1j} for the estimation contained in the object `hlm2_finalmodel`.

To elaborate Figure 17.6, we propose that the reader divide the task into three steps: (1) Save the values of the error terms of the components of the random effects in an object, together with color and legend adjustment settings; (2) save the graphs of the error terms of the intercepts and of the random slopes in different objects, both elaborated by the object mentioned in the first step; and (3) join the graphics resulting from the second step with the help of the function `grid.arrange()` from the package `gridExtra`.

So, for the first step in the elaboration of Figure 17.6, we will create a data frame called `plot_re_data` that will contain the random effects regarding the intercepts and slopes of our final model as well as color and legend adjustment settings for when the values are less than or greater than zero:

```
plot_re_data <- data.frame(ranef(hlm2_finalmodel)[1]) %>%
  rownames_to_column("state_id") %>%
  rename(random_intercepts = 2,
         random_slopes = 3) %>%
  mutate(color_re_intercepts = ifelse(test = random_intercepts < 0,
                                      yes = "less_than_zero",
                                      no = "greater_than_zero"),
         color_re_slopes = ifelse(test = random_slopes < 0,
                                  yes = "less_than_zero",
                                  no = "greater_than_zero"),
         hjust_re_intercepts = ifelse(test = random_intercepts > 0,
                                      yes = 1.15,
                                      no = -0.15),
         hjust_re_slopes = ifelse(test = random_slopes > 0,
                                  yes = 1.15,
                                  no = -0.15))
```

If the reader has difficulty understanding the previous syntax, we recommend reading Chapters 2 and 7 of this work.

Next, for the second step of the creation of Figure 17.6, we propose the creation of two objects: the object `v0j`, which will contain the graph regarding ν_{0j}, and the object `v1j`, which will contain the graph regarding ν_{1j}:

```
# #v0j - random intercepts
v0j <- plot_re_data %>%
  mutate(state_id = as.numeric(state_id),
         state_id = factor(state_id)) %>%
  arrange(state_id) %>%
  ggplot(aes(label = round(random_intercepts, digits = 3),
             hjust = hjust_re_intercepts)) +
  geom_bar(aes(x = fct_rev(state_id), y = random_intercepts, fill = color_re_intercepts),
           stat = "identity", color = "black") +
  geom_text(aes(x = state_id, y = 0), size = 3.1, color = "black") +
  coord_flip() +
  labs(x = "State",
       y = expression(nu[0][j]),
       subtitle = "(a) Error Terms - Random Intercepts") +
  scale_fill_manual(values = c("darkorchid","orange")) +
  theme(panel.background = element_rect("white"),
        panel.border = element_rect(NA),
        panel.grid = element_line("grey95"),
        legend.position = "none")

#v1j - random slopes(oil_fats_consumption)
v1j <- plot_re_data %>%
  mutate(state_id = as.numeric(state_id),
         state_id = factor(state_id)) %>%
  arrange(state_id) %>%
  ggplot(aes(label = round(random_slopes, digits = 3),
             hjust = hjust_re_slopes)) +
  geom_bar(aes(x = fct_rev(state_id), y = random_slopes, fill = color_re_slopes),
           stat = "identity", color = "black") +
  geom_text(aes(x = state_id, y = 0), size = 3.1, color = "black") +
  coord_flip() +
  labs(x = "State",
       y = expression(nu[1][j]),
       subtitle = "(b) Error Terms - Random Slopes") +
  scale_fill_manual(values = c("darkorchid","orange")) +
  theme(panel.background = element_rect("white"),
        panel.border = element_rect(NA),
        panel.grid = element_line("grey95"),
        legend.position = "none")
```

Finally, to replicate Figure 17.6, we can argue the two objects created (`v0j` and `v1j`) to the function `grid.arrange()`:

```
grid.arrange(v0j, v1j)
```

Calculation of the ICC of the estimation contained in the object `hlm2_finalmodel`:

$$ICC = \frac{\tau_{00} + \tau_{11}}{\tau_{00} + \tau_{11} + \sigma^2} = \frac{0.434 + 0.005}{0.434 + 0.005 + 0.126} = 0.7770.$$

From the ICC calculation of our last model, it appears that considering the random slopes of the variable *oil_fats_consumption* at the state level, there is an indication that 77.77% of the total variance of the amount of carcinoembryonic antigens expected in patients, in µg/mL of blood, is due to changes among states, representing a sign that there is variability, in fact, among the amount of antigens per patients when they are from different states.

Even so, the reader may not be convinced of the superiority of the multilevel approach for the case studied without comparing the estimation contained in the object `hlm2_finalmodel` with its OLS analogue estimation using dummies variables to represent each state. So, to carry out such an analysis, according to what we learned in Chapter 14, we will start generating dummies for each category of the variable *state_id* with the function `dummy_cols()` from the package `fastDummies`:

```
colorectal_cancer_d <- dummy_cols(.data = colorectal_cancer,
                                  select_columns = "state_id",
                                  remove_first_dummy = TRUE,
                                  remove_selected_columns = FALSE)
```

That said, for didactic reasons, we can estimate an OLS model considering all of the variables used in the estimation contained in the objective `hlm2_finalmodel`, including using the states as dummies and considering the interaction `oil_fats_consumption:avg_income`:

```
ols_finalmodel <- lm(formula = antigen ~ . + oil_fats_consumption:avg_income
                     -patient_id -state_id,
                     data = colorectal_cancer_d)
```

Next, we can apply the stepwise procedure:

```
step_ols_finalmodel <- step(object = ols_finalmodel,
                            k = qchisq(p = 0.05, df = 1, lower.tail = FALSE))
```

Having established the final version of the OLS estimation contained in the object `step_ols_finalmodel`, we can use the LR test to compare them:

```
lrtest(step_ols_finalmodel, hlm2_finalmodel)
```

Figure 17.7 presents the result of the previous command, demonstrating that, even with a lower amount of degrees of freedom, the multilevel estimation is superior to the OLS for this case study.

```
Likelihood ratio test

Model 1: antigen ~ oil_fats_consumption + avg_income + state_id_2 + state_id_3 +
    state_id_4 + state_id_5 + state_id_6 + state_id_7 + state_id_8 +
    state_id_9 + oil_fats_consumption:avg_income
Model 2: antigen ~ oil_fats_consumption + avg_income + oil_fats_consumption:avg_income
+
    (oil_fats_consumption | state_id)
  #Df  LogLik Df  Chisq Pr(>Chisq)
1  13 -265.87
2   8 -181.76 -5 168.21  < 2.2e-16 ***
---
Signif. codes:  0 '***' 0.001 '**' 0.01 '*' 0.05 '.' 0.1 ' ' 1
```

FIGURE 17.7 LR test among the estimation contained in the objects `step_ols_finalmodel` and `hlm2_finalmodel`.

For didactic reasons, we present in Table 17.7 the parameters of the two estimations (`step_ols_finalmodel` and `hlm2_finalmodel`) for the reader's comfort.

TABLE 17.7 Comparison of estimation parameters `step_ols_finalmodel` and `hlm2_finalmodel`.

	OLS model	HLM2 model
Fixed effects		
intercept	17.326[a] (1.491)	–0.111 (0.400)
oil_fats_consumption	0.111[a] (0.009)	0.095[b] (0.043)
avg_income	–4.427[a] (0.407)	0.211[a] (0.065)
oil_fats_consumption:avg_income	0.030[a] (0.002)	0.031[a] (0.007)
state_id_2 (dummy)	–8.495[a] (0.675)	–
state_id_3 (dummy)	42.207[a] (3.792)	–
state_id_4 (dummy)	8.458[a] (0.733)	–
state_id_5 (dummy)	–9.456[a] (0.751)	–
state_id_6 (dummy)	–1.319[a] (0.171)	–
state_id_7 (dummy)	20.341[a] (1.754)	–
state_id_8 (dummy)	17.710[a] (1.541)	–
state_id_9 (dummy)	–10.328[a] (0.761)	–
Random effects		
Var(ν_{0j}) – *intercept*	–	0.434
Var(ν_{1j}) – *slope (oil_fats_consumption)*	–	0.005
Another characteristics		
Observations	358	358
LL	–265.87 (df = 13)	–181.76 (df = 8)

[a] Statistically significantly different from zero at 99% confidence.
[b] Statistically significantly different from zero at 95% confidence.
Note: Standard errors are in parentheses.

In addition to a statistically significant *LL* gain at 1%, as shown in Figure 17.7, Table 17.7 explains that, for the case analyzed, a signal inversion occurs in the variable *avg_income* when we want to use a context as a dummy variable.

Figure 17.8 shows the adherence of the fitted values of the two estimations discussed in Table 17.7, by state. The curves of the fitted values of the OLS estimation are dotted. It is possible to note that the HLM2 estimation shows better adherence to the variable *oil_fats_consumption*, because of its intercepts and its slopes.

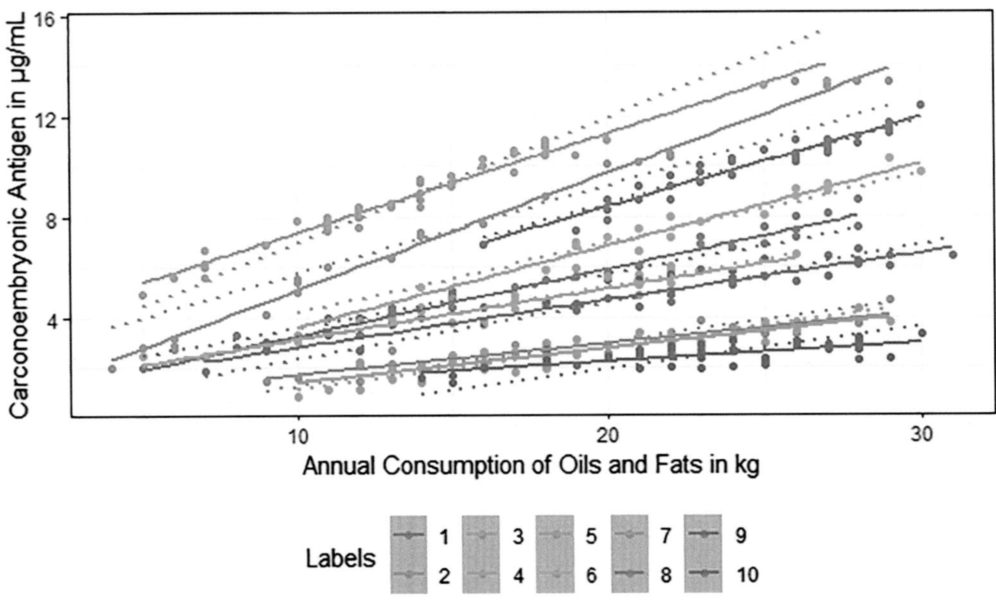

FIGURE 17.8 Graph showing adherence of the fitted values of the estimations contained in the objects `step_ols_finalmodel` and `hlm2_finalmodel`, in relation to the variable *oil_fats_consumption*. Note: The curves of the fitted values of the OLS estimation are dotted.

For the elaboration of Figure 17.8, the reader can command as follows:

```
colorectal_cancer_d %>%
  mutate(fitted_ols = predict(object = step_ols_finalmodel),
         fitted_hlm2 = predict(object = hlm2_finalmodel)) %>%
  ggplot(aes(group = state_id, color = state_id)) +
  geom_point(aes(x = oil_fats_consumption, y = antigen)) +
  geom_smooth(aes(x = oil_fats_consumption, y = fitted_ols),
              linetype = "dotted") +
  geom_smooth(aes(x = oil_fats_consumption, y = fitted_hlm2)) +
  labs(x = "Annual Consumption of Oils and Fats in kg",
       y = "Carconoembryonic Antigen in \u03bcg/mL",
      color = "Labels") +
  theme(panel.background = element_rect("white"),
        panel.border = element_rect(NA),
        panel.grid = element_line("grey95"),
        legend.position = "bottom")
```

To calculate the confidence intervals of the HLM2 estimation, the reader can use the function `confint()`, as discussed in Chapters 14 to 16.

```
confint(hlm2_finalmodel)
```

Finally, to establish predictions for the HLM2 model, the reader can use the function `predict()`. However, it is necessary for the reader consider some factors that we find interesting.

As we are facing a model that considers random effects, comprising two levels, the direct command of the function `predict()` will return to the reader the fitted values of a given observation, taking into account the values of the error terms of the intercepts and the random slopes that were explained by the function `ranef()`, as indicated by Table 17.6 and Figure 17.6. If that is the desire, then the reader can type the following command:

```
predict(object = hlm2_finalmodel)
```

In other words, the above command will take into account the calculated values of ν (in the case studied, ν_{0j} and ν_{1j}). On the other hand, if only the fitted values in relation to the fixed effects components are desired, the reader should argue `re.form = ~0` or `re.form = NA`, indicating disregard of the calculated ν values:

```
predict(object = hlm2_finalmodel, re.form = ~0)
```

Next, we will present and discuss an example of HLM estimation, but with three levels and repeated measures.

Final remarks

According to Fávero and Belfiore (2019), multilevel models allow us to identify and analyze individual heterogeneities and the heterogeneities among the groups to which these individuals belong, making it possible to specify random components in each analysis level. This fact represents the main difference of the traditional regression models estimated through OLS, which cannot consider the natural nesting of data and, consequently, generate biased parameter estimators.

To estimate multilevel models and for any other modeling technique, it is necessary for the application to be accompanied by methodological rigor and certain care when analyzing the results, mainly if these are meant for making forecasts. The use of a certain estimation method, to the detriment of another, can help researchers and managers choose the most suitable model, adding value to their research, and allowing new studies on the topic chosen to be carried out (Fávero and Belfiore, 2019).

Exercise

1. The organization of an international science competition for high school students from 24 countries ($j = 1,..., 24$) wishes to investigate participants' performance behavior based on their characteristics and on the characteristics of the countries they are from (Fávero and Belfiore, 2019). Although the event coordinators know that performance is a result of several factors, such as participants' dedication and the characteristics of the schools where they study, they wish to try to verify if there is a relationship among the scores obtained in the competition, students' social status (translated by median household income), and the importance given by their countries to issues such as scientific and technological development (translated by investments in research and development). The dataset collected contains data on the top 5 students from each country, which represents a total of 120 participants in the competition ($i = 1,..., 120$), and it generates a balanced clustered data structure. The dataset can be found in the file `science_competition.Rdata` (Fávero and Belfiore, 2019). The variables found in this dataset are as follows (Fávero and Belfiore, 2019):

Variable	Description
country	A string variable that identifies the country.
idcountry	Country code j.
resdevel	Country's investments in research and development, in % of the GDP (Source: World Bank).
idstudent	Student code i.
score	Science score obtained by the student in the competition (0 to 100).
income	Student's median household income per month (US$).

By using this dataset, we would like you to:

a. Elaborate a table that proves the existence of a balanced clustered data structure of students in countries.
b. Create charts that allow us to visualize the average score obtained in the science competition by the participants from each country.

c. Given the existence of two analysis levels, with students (level 1) nested into countries (level 2), estimate the following null model:

$$score_{ij} = \beta_{0j} + \varepsilon_{ij}$$
$$\beta_{0j} = \gamma_{00} + \nu_{0j}$$

which results in:

$$score_{ij} = \gamma_{00} + \upsilon_{0j} + \varepsilon_{ij}.$$

d. Through the estimation of the null model, is it possible to verify if there is variability in the scores obtained among students from different countries?

e. From the result of the likelihood-ratio test generated, is it possible to reject the null hypothesis that the random intercepts are equal to zero? That is, is it possible to rule out the estimation of a traditional linear regression model for these clustered data?

f. Also based on the estimation of the null model, calculate the ICC and discuss the result.

g. Create a chart that has a linear adjustment by OLS, for each country, of each student's science score behavior based on their median household income.

h. Estimate the following random intercepts model:

$$score_{ij} = \beta_{0j} + \beta_{1j} \cdot income_{ij} + \varepsilon_{ij}$$
$$\beta = \gamma_{00} + \nu_{0j}$$
$$\beta_{1j} = \gamma_{10}$$

which results in:

$$score_{ij} = \gamma_{00} + \gamma_{10} \cdot income_{ij} + \nu_{0j} + \varepsilon_{ij}.$$

i. Create a bar chart that allows us to visualize random intercept terms ν_{0j} per country.

j. Estimate the following random intercepts and slopes model:

$$score_{ij} = \beta_{0j} + \beta_{1j} \cdot income_{ij} + \varepsilon_{ij}$$
$$\beta_{0j} = \gamma_{00} + \nu_{0j}$$
$$\beta_{1j} = \gamma_{10} + \nu_{1j}$$

which results in:

$$score_{ij} = \gamma_{00} + \gamma_{10} \cdot income_{ij} + \nu_{0j} + \nu_{1j} \cdot income_{ij} + \varepsilon_{ij}.$$

k. Based on the estimations of the random intercepts model and random intercepts and slopes model, run a likelihood-ratio test, and discuss the result.

l. Estimate the following multilevel model:

$$score_{ij} = \beta_{0j} + \beta_{1j} \cdot income_{ij} + \varepsilon_{ij}$$
$$\beta_{0j} = \gamma_{00} + \nu_{0j}$$
$$\beta_{1j} = \gamma_{10} + \gamma_{11} \cdot resdevel_j$$

which results in:

$$score_{ij} = \gamma_{00} + \gamma_{10} \cdot income_{ij} + \gamma_{11} \cdot resdevel_j \cdot income_{ij} + \nu_{0j} + \varepsilon_{ij}$$

m. Present the expression of the last model estimated, with random intercepts and level 1 and level 2 variables.

n. Create a chart in which it is possible to compare the predicted values of the score obtained in the science competition, generated through this two-level hierarchical modeling (HLM2), to the real values obtained (observed values) by the students of the sample.

Supplementary data sets

colorectal_cancer.RData
science_competition.Rdata

Please access supplementary data files here: https://doi.org/10.17632/55623jkwrp.3

PART VI

Improving performance

CHAPTER

18

Support vector machines

AT THE END OF THIS CHAPTER, YOU WILL BE ABLE TO:

- Understand the reasons for using support vector machine algorithms.
- Understand the concepts of separating hyperplanes and maximal margin classifiers.
- Understand the differences between support vector classifiers and support vector machine algorithms.
- Implement support vector machine algorithms in R-based language, and interpret their results.

R-based language packages used in this chapter

```
library(e1071)
library(ROCR)
library(ISLR2)
library(plotly)
library(tibble)
library(caret)
```

Don't forget to define the R working directory (the location where your datasets are installed):

```
setwd("C:/book/chapter18")
```

Introduction

In this chapter, we will study support vector machines (SVMs), which are supervised algorithms used fundamentally to analyze data with a primary focus on classification. In these algorithms, the data are plotted in a multidimensional space, and the classification is given by the definition of hyperplanes (discussed in the next section) that best differentiate the classes of the phenomenon under study.

SVMs were developed by Cortes and Vapnik (1995) in the area of computer science for binary classification models, with the basic aim of defining an optimal hyperplane of separation between two groups by maximizing the margin between the closest points of these groups. Although the points belonging to the borders of the margin region are called support vectors, the region inside the margin contains the optimal separating hyperplane. According to these authors, the support vector is a machine learning algorithm for two-group classification problems, under the idea

Data Science, Analytics and Machine Learning with R
https://doi.org/10.1016/B978-0-12-824271-1.00032-9

that input vectors are non-linearly mapped to a very high-dimensional feature space where a linear decision surface is constructed. Figure 18.1 shows the logic behind the concepts of margin, separating hyperplane, and support vectors.

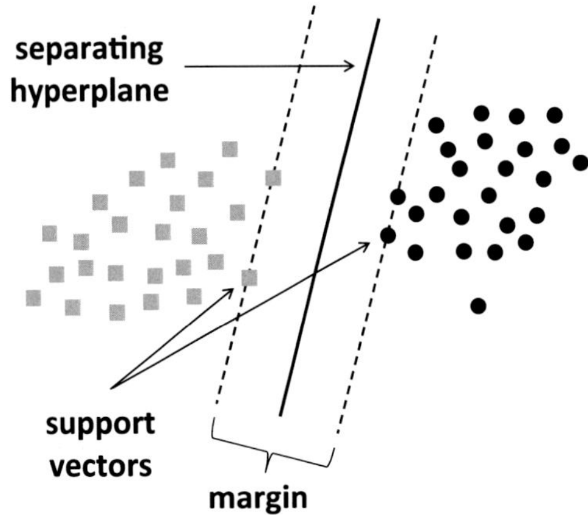

FIGURE 18.1 Concepts of margin, separating hyperplane, and support vectors.

SVMs represent a generalization of what are known as *maximal margin classifiers*, which we will discuss in later in this chapter in the "Maximal margin classifiers" section. Next, we will study support vector classifiers and the SVMs themselves in the "Support vector classifiers" and "Support vector machines" sections, respectively.

Separating hyperplanes

The mathematical definition of *hyperplane* is relatively simple, and, according to James et al. (2021a,b), for two dimensions the hyperplane equation can be defined by:

$$\alpha + \beta_1 X_1 + \beta_2 X_2 = 0 \tag{18.1}$$

which represents a line, since a hyperplane for two dimensions is, in fact, a line, as shown in Figure 18.2 for parameter values $\alpha = -10$, $\beta_1 = 2$, and $\beta_2 = 2.5$, for example.

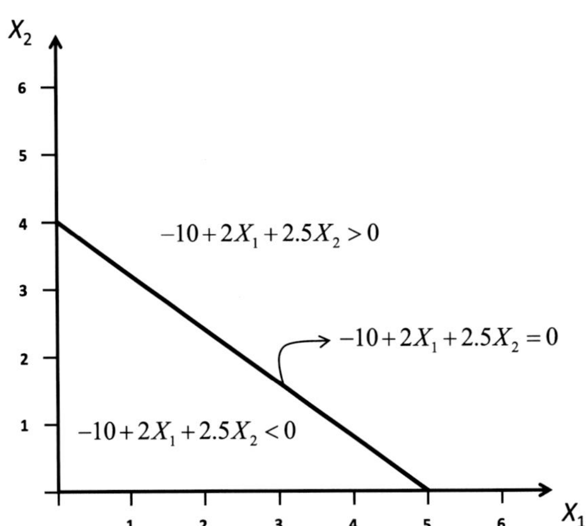

FIGURE 18.2 The hyperplane $-10+2X_1+2.5X_2=0$. The upper part refers to the region where $-10+2X_1+2.5X_2>0$, and the lower part refers to the region where $-10+2X_1+2.5X_2<0$.

In this sense, in an analogous way, we can expand our analysis by defining the equation of a hyperplane for a configuration with k dimensions as follows:

$$\alpha + \beta_1 X_1 + \beta_2 X_2 + \ldots + \beta_k X_k = 0 \quad (18.2)$$

which, in the same way, will divide the space into two regions with points that obey, respectively, the inequalities $\alpha+\beta_1X_1+\beta_2X_2+\ldots+\beta_kX_k>0$ and $\alpha+\beta_1X_1+\beta_2X_2+\ldots+\beta_kX_k<0$.

That said, let us consider a dataset with n observations and k predictor variables X, so our objective is to establish an algorithm that correctly classifies a new observation not initially present in the sample from the existing predictor variables, a fact that characterizes this algorithm as being supervised, similarly to the algorithms of logistic regression (Chapter 15), classification trees (Chapter 19), and artificial neural networks (Chapter 22). The difference is that, for this chapter, we will study an algorithm that establishes classification based on the definition of a separating hyperplane.

In other words, we will establish a criterion by which some observations from the original dataset will be classified in a certain group defined by a label, while the other observations will be classified in another group defined by a different label. Analogous to the logistic regression models, we can name these groups as, for example, $Y_i = 1$ and $Y_i = -1$, so:

$$\alpha + \beta_1 X_{1i} + \beta_2 X_{2i} + \ldots + \beta_k X_{ki} > 0 \text{ if } Y_i = 1 \quad (18.3)$$

and

$$\alpha + \beta_1 X_{1i} + \beta_2 X_{2i} + \ldots + \beta_k X_{ki} < 0 \text{ if } Y_i = -1 \quad (18.4)$$

where i represents a particular observation of the dataset, where $i = 1, \ldots, n$.

In general, as pointed out by James et al. (2021a,b), a hyperplane therefore has the following expression:

$$Y_i \cdot (\alpha + \beta_1 X_{1i} + \beta_2 X_{2i} + \ldots + \beta_k X_{ki}) > 0 \quad (18.5)$$

Returning to the case in which there are only two predictor variables, X_1 and X_2, we can classify the observations into two groups, as shown in Figure 18.3. In this same figure, three hyperplanes are defined among infinite possibilities, with emphasis on the separating hyperplane that indicates the decision rule established by a classifier based on this hyperplane.

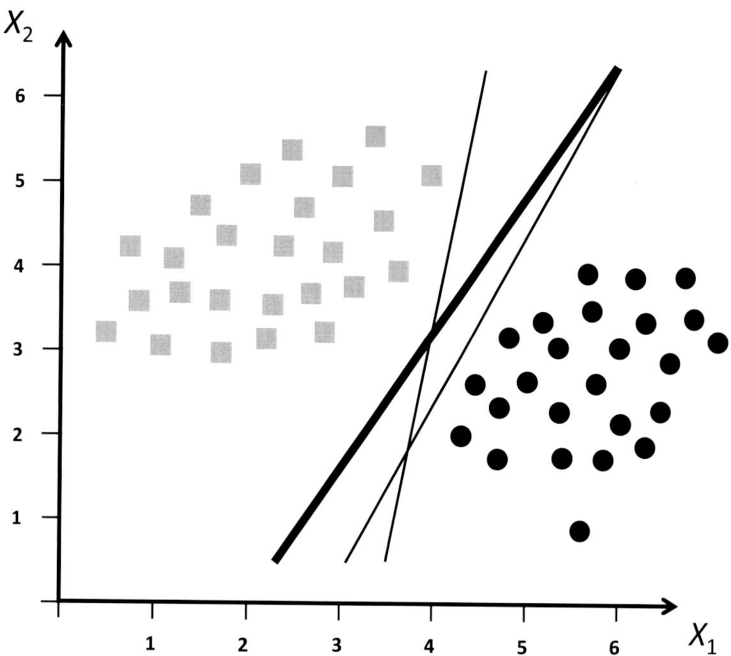

FIGURE 18.3 Classification of observations into two groups, based on two predictor (explanatory) variables X_1 and X_2 and through the definition of a separating hyperplane.

If, in fact, a separating hyperplane exists, we can use it as a classifier for other observations not initially present in the sample in order to respect the criterion established by the hyperplane for the creation of the two regions, or classes.

As shown in Figure 18.3, the classification criterion depends on the separating hyperplane, which will be chosen among infinite possibilities and, as pointed out by James et al. (2021a,b), a natural choice is to use a maximal margin hyperplane, whose concepts will be discussed in the next section.

Maximal margin classifiers

As shown in Figure 18.3, among infinite possibilities, a maximal margin hyperplane is one that is in a position farthest from the observations present in the sample. Following the logic proposed by James et al. (2021a,b), we can calculate the perpendicular distance of each observation for a given separating hyperplane, and the smallest of these distances will be the minimum distance of the observations to the hyperplane, known as the *margin*, as shown in Figure 18.1.

In this sense, the *maximal margin hyperplane* refers to the separating hyperplane in which the margin is as large as possible, that is, it offers the greatest minimum distance for dataset observations. And, in this way, we will be able to classify a given observation based on which side of the hyperplane it is on, which characterizes the maximal margin classifier. What we expect is that a classifier that offers a large maximal margin classifier for the observations initially already present in the dataset will also offer a large margin on new observations, which will lead to correct classification of these new observations. The biggest problem with this type of classifier, however, lies in the potential for overfitting when there are a large number of predictor variables (very large k).

Figure 18.4 shows the maximal margin hyperplane extracted from Figure 18.3, highlighting the greater minimal distance between the observations and the separating hyperplane *(arrows to the dashed lines)*, that is, the larger margin. As discussed earlier, the two observations on top of these dashed lines are known as *support vectors* because they are vectors in k-dimensional space (in our case, $k = 2$) and "support" the maximal margin hyperplane.

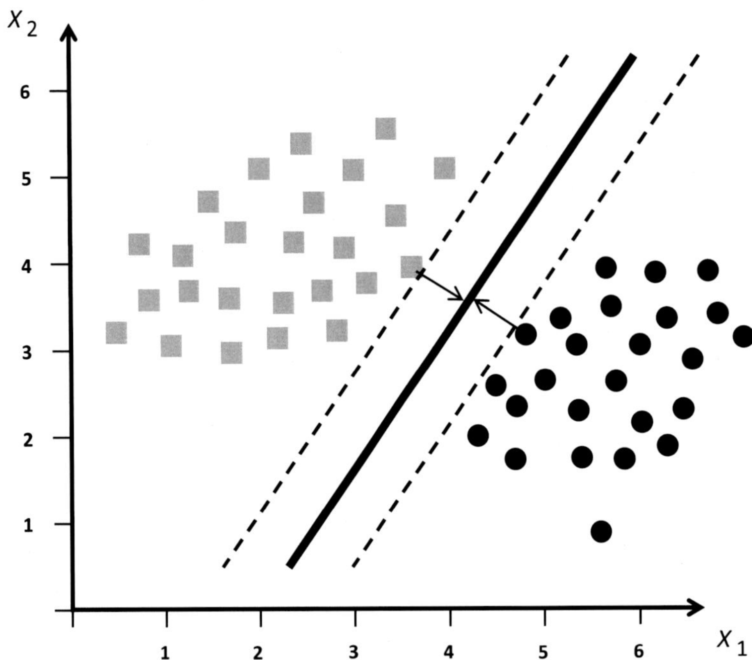

FIGURE 18.4 Definition of the maximum margin hyperplane.

In this sense, the maximal margin hyperplane depends fundamentally on support vectors, that is, on a very small number of observations (in the case of the example in Figure 18.4, only two observations define the maximal margin hyperplane), and the other observations do not affect the definition of the separating hyperplane. This feature is important for the discussion of support vector classifiers and SVMs, which we will discuss later in this chapter.

Quite simply, we can define the maximum margin hyperplane through an optimization problem, with the determination of an objective function that respects the condition that the value of the margin (M, hereinafter) is maximized. In other words, we must calculate the following:

$$\max_{\alpha,\beta_1,\ldots,\beta_k,M} \mathrm{M} \tag{18.6}$$

Subject to:

$$\sum_{j=1}^{k} \text{parameters}\left(\alpha^2, \beta_j^2\right) = 1 \tag{18.7}$$

and

$$Y_i \cdot (\alpha + \beta_1 X_{1i} + \beta_2 X_{2i} + \ldots + \beta_k X_{ki}) \geq M, \text{for all } i = 1, \ldots, n \tag{18.8}$$

The constraints (18.7) and (18.8) guarantee that each observation i is allocated on the correct side and at a minimum distance M from the hyperplane. Although the constraint (18.7) guarantees that each observation will be on the correct side of the hyperplane, provided that M is positive, the constraint (18.8) guarantees a perpendicular distance from the observation i to the hyperplane (James et al., 2021a,b).

In this sense, our problem is to choose the parameters $\alpha, \beta_1, \ldots, \beta_k$ that maximize M, a fact that characterizes the term **maximal margin hyperplane.**

In many situations, there may not be a separating hyperplane, and the optimization problem described by Expressions (18.6) to (18.8) may not have a solution for a positive value of M. In these cases, we can define a soft margin classifier, also known as a *support vector classifier,* which we will discuss in the next section.

Support vector classifiers

Figure 18.5 clearly shows that the definition of a perfect separating hyperplane is impossible. Sometimes, just a single observation makes the definition of a maximal margin hyperplane unfeasible. Because it is very sensitive to changes in the data, this can present overfitting when training the algorithm for the observations existing in the dataset.

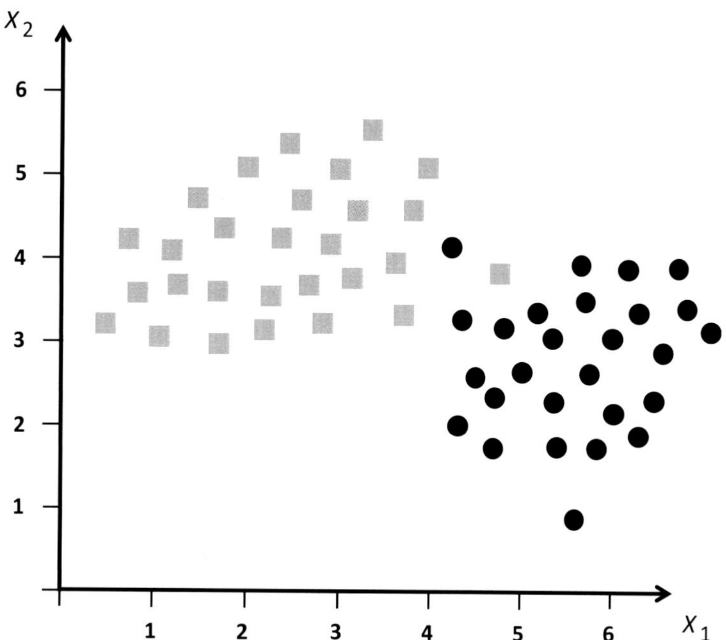

FIGURE 18.5 Two groups of observations not separable by a hyperplane (maximal margin classifier cannot be defined).

In these situations, we can be flexible and yield in the classification of a few observations, in favor of a correct classification for most of the observations present in the dataset, a fact that is considered in the support vector classifier algorithm, also known as *soft margin classifier.* In this algorithm, therefore, instead of defining the largest possible margin M, we can establish a criterion whereby some observations are allowed to be allocated on the wrong side of the hyperplane. Observations that are on the wrong side of the hyperplane correspond to those observations that are misclassified by the soft margin classifier, or by the support vector classifier.

Figure 18.6, created from the data in Figure 18.5, shows situations in which two observations are on the correct side of the hyperplane, but on the wrong side of the margin (A and B), and where two observations are on the wrong side of the hyperplane (C and D).

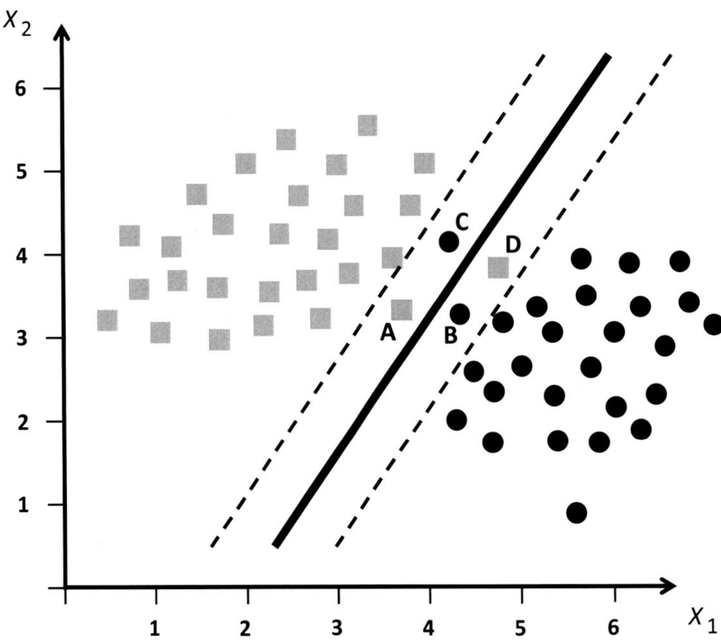

FIGURE 18.6 Observations A and B on the correct side of the hyperplane, but on the wrong side of the margin (A and B); observations C and D on the wrong side of the hyperplane.

Analogous to the optimization problem described in the previous section for the case of maximal margin classifiers using Expressions (18.6) to (18.8), we can define the optimization problem for the case of support vector classifiers, following the logic proposed by James et al. (2021a,b), as follows:

$$\max_{\alpha,\beta_1,\ldots,\beta_k,\varepsilon_1,\ldots,\varepsilon_n,M} \mathrm{M} \tag{18.9}$$

Subject to:

$$\sum_{j=1}^{k} \text{parameters}\left(\alpha^2,\beta_j^2\right) = 1 \tag{18.10}$$

$$Y_i \cdot (\alpha + \beta_1 X_{1i} + \beta_2 X_{2i} + \ldots + \beta_k X_{ki}) \geq M \cdot (1 - \varepsilon_i), \text{for all } i = 1,\ldots,n \tag{18.11}$$

$$\varepsilon_i \geq 0 \tag{18.12}$$

and

$$\sum_{i=1}^{n} \varepsilon_i \leq C \tag{18.13}$$

with $\varepsilon_1, \ldots, \varepsilon_n$ being slack variables that allow observations to be allocated on the wrong side of the margin or the hyperplane, that is, the slack variable ε tells us where observation i will be allocated relative to the margin and the hyperplane. In this sense, we must consider the following:

- If $\varepsilon_i = 0$, observation i will be placed on the correct side of the margin, as discussed in the previous section
- If $\varepsilon_i > 0$, observation i will be allocated on the wrong side of the margin
- If $\varepsilon_i > 1$, observation i will be allocated on the wrong side of the hyperplane

It is important to mention that observations that are allocated on the correct side of the margin do not affect the definition of the support vector classifier, and changes in their positions do not change the classifier. Only observations that fall on the wrong side of the margin, or directly on it, known as *support vectors*, affect the support vector classifier. In this way, the support vector classifier's decision rule is based only on a small quantity (subset) of the observations (support vectors) of the dataset, which means that the algorithm is not affected by the behavior of observations that are very far from the hyperplane. This fact is analogous to that studied in Chapter 15 when studying logistic regression models. In that case, the classification algorithms are also not very sensitive to changes in the behavior of observations with variables with extreme values (that consequently generate high values of logit in modulus) and therefore are very distant from a given decision threshold. This fact can be observed in Chapter 15, when we analyzed the behavior of the sigmoid probability curve, which becomes asymptotic for probabilities equal to 0 or 1 for logit values, in module, still close to zero.

Still in relation to Expressions (18.9) to (18.13), C can be defined as a non-negative adjustment parameter that limits the sum of slack variables ε_i, and, this way, determines the quantity and intensity of violations that we will be willing to tolerate for the classification of observations in relation to the margin and the hyperplane. This parameter is also called *cost* or *penalty parameter*, which controls the penalty of misclassification. Thus if $C = 0$, we will fall back on the particular case of optimization for the definition of the maximal margin classifier in Expressions (18.6) to (18.8), since $\varepsilon_1 = \ldots = \varepsilon_n = 0$, and violations will not occur in relation to the margin. On the other hand, if $C > 0$, no more than C observations can be allocated on the wrong side of the hyperplane because if a given observation i is on the wrong side of the hyperplane, we have $\varepsilon_i > 1$, causing it to obey the constraint represented by Expression (18.13), that is, that $\sum_{i=1}^{n} \varepsilon_i \leq C$.

In this sense, our tolerance for violations is associated with the parameter C, and the greater the value of C, the greater the tolerance and therefore the wider the margin. On the other hand, the smaller the value of C, the smaller our tolerance for violations and therefore the narrower the margin. Figure 18.7 shows two situations in which, for the same dataset, the margin *(dashed lines)* and the hyperplane *(solid line)* are shown. Note that a higher value of C (Figure 18.7A) sets up a greater tolerance for observations to be on the wrong side of the margin, which will be wider. On the other hand, a smaller value of C (Figure 18.7B), that is, a smaller tolerance for observations to be on the wrong side of the margin, makes the margin narrower.

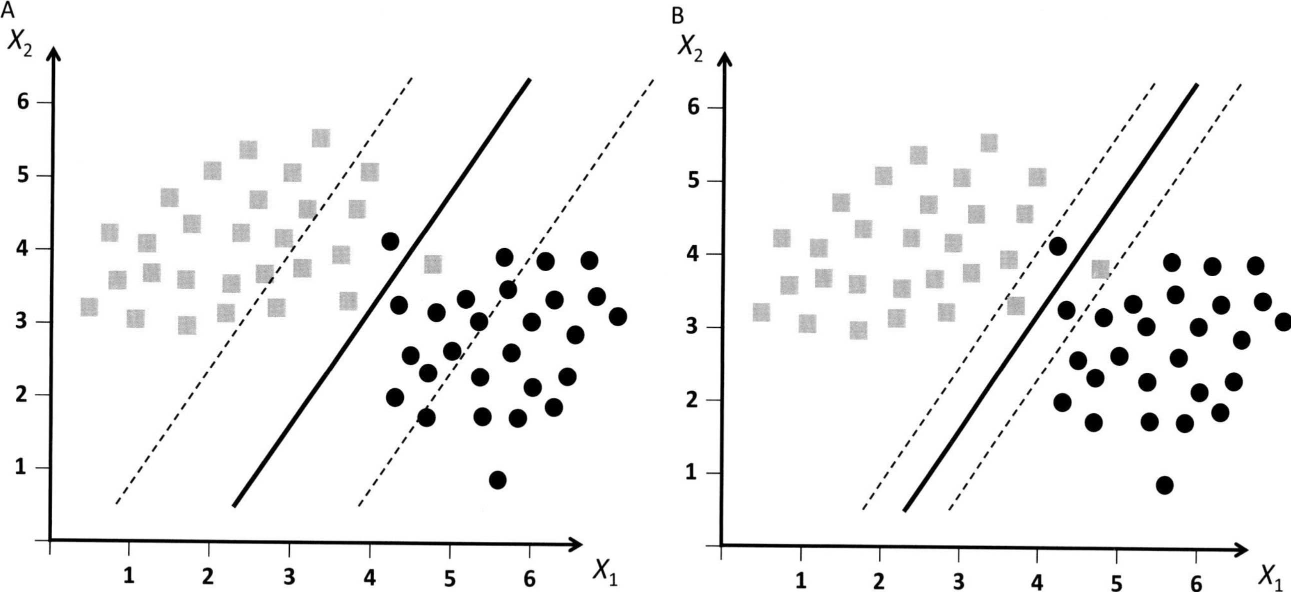

FIGURE 18.7 Different values of the non-negative adjustment parameter *(C)* for the definition of support vector classifiers. (A) Increase in the value of *C:* larger margin. (B) Decrease in the value of *C:* narrower margin.

Support vector machines

Sometimes, the boundary between two groups is presented in a non-linear way, and the definition of a support vector classifier separates the observations in these two groups very poorly. This fact can be seen in Figure 18.8.

Analogous to what we studied in Chapter 14 regarding the specification of non-linear regression models and the use of the Box-Cox transformation, here we can define a vector of predictor (explanatory) variables using the original ones ($X_1, \ldots, X_k$) and also non-linear specifications for the same variables (for instance, a quadratic specification, what generates $X_1^2, \ldots, X_k^2$). In this case, Expressions (18.9) to (18.13) of our optimization problem could be written as follows:

$$\max_{\alpha, \beta_{11}, \beta_{12}, \ldots, \beta_{k1}, \beta_{k2}, \varepsilon_1, \ldots, \varepsilon_n, M} M \tag{18.14}$$

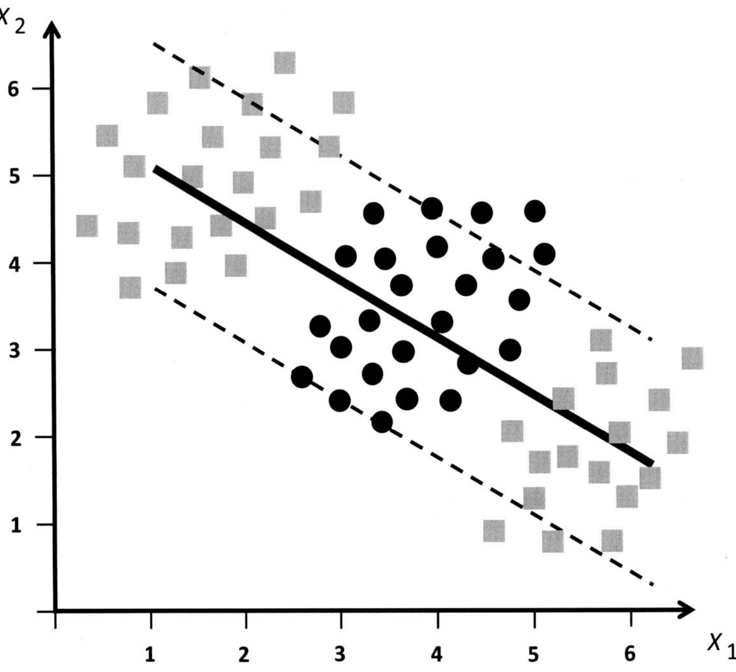

FIGURE 18.8 Poor performance of the support vector classifier with a linear boundary when observations define two groups with a clear non-linear boundary.

subject to:

$$\sum_{j=1}^{k} \text{parameters}\left(\alpha^2, \beta_{j1}^2, \beta_{j2}^2\right) = 1 \tag{18.15}$$

$$Y_i \cdot \left(\alpha + \sum_{j=1}^{k} \beta_{j1} X_{ji} + \sum_{j=1}^{k} \beta_{j2} X_{ji}^2 + \right) \geq M \cdot (1 - \varepsilon_i), \text{for all } i = 1, \ldots, n \tag{18.16}$$

$$\varepsilon_i \geq 0 \tag{18.17}$$

and

$$\sum_{i=1}^{n} \varepsilon_i \leq C \tag{18.18}$$

Obviously, Expressions (18.14) to (18.18) are a particular case using quadratic specification. Other specifications with higher-order polynomial terms can be used, and even interactions among predictor (explanatory) variables can be considered, but not without the need to increase computational capacity for algorithm convergence. This is where the great advantage of the SVM comes in, which makes use of kernels (discussed later) to increase the vector space of predictor variables in order to establish a non-linear boundary among groups of observations.

As discussed earlier, a function to define the linear support vector classifier can be written as follows:

$$f(x) = \alpha + \sum_{i=1}^{n} \beta_i \cdot \sum_{j=1}^{k} X_{ij} X_{i'j} \tag{18.19}$$

where there are n parameters β_i, for each observation $i = 1, \ldots, n$, and the term $\sum_{j=1}^{k} X_{ij} X_{i'j}$ is known as the *inner product* between two observations i and i', and whose nomenclature can also be given by $\langle X_i, X'_i \rangle$. In this way, Expression (18.19) can be rewritten as follows:

$$f(x) = \alpha + \sum_{i=1}^{n} \beta_i \cdot \langle X_i, X_{i'} \rangle \tag{18.20}$$

Therefore to estimate parameters α and $\beta_1, ..., \beta_n$, we must define the $\frac{n \cdot (n-1)}{2}$ inner products $\langle X_i, X'_i \rangle$ among all pairs of observations present in the dataset. In this sense, a linear support vector classifier can, in fact, be defined from the following function:

$$f(x) = \alpha + \sum_{i=1}^{n} \beta_i \cdot \langle X, X_i \rangle \tag{18.21}$$

that, to be estimated, we must define the inner product between a new observation and each of the observations i present in the original dataset.

Following the logic proposed by James et al. (2021a,b), we can generalize the inner product between two observations i and i' considering some function K (**kernel**) that quantifies the similarity between two observations, so that:

$$f(x) = \alpha + \sum_{i=1}^{n} \beta_i \cdot K(X, X_i) \tag{18.22}$$

Thus, as presented by Expression (18.19), we have, for a linear kernel

$$K(X_i, X_{i'}) = \sum_{j=1}^{k} X_{ij} X_{i'j} \tag{18.23}$$

which refers to a support vector classifier since a linear kernel presents a linear specification for the predictor variables. On the other hand, when a support vector classifier is combined with a non-linear kernel, the resulting classifier is known as an *SVM*. Expressions (18.24) and (18.25) present, for instance, a polynomial kernel of degree 2 and a radial kernel, respectively.

$$K(X_i, X_{i'}) = \left(1 + \sum_{j=1}^{k} X_{ij} X_{i'j}\right)^2 \tag{18.24}$$

$$K(X_i, X_{i'}) = e^{\left(-\gamma \cdot \sum_{j=1}^{k} (X_{ij} - X_{i'j})^2\right)} \tag{18.25}$$

being γ a positive constant. This parameter (in R, `gamma`) reshapes the decision boundary by trying to assemble and cluster similar data points.

Figure 18.9 shows an example of SVMs with a polynomial kernel of degree 2 (A) and with a radial kernel (B). We can see that these SVMs have good performance for the classification of observations into two groups considering

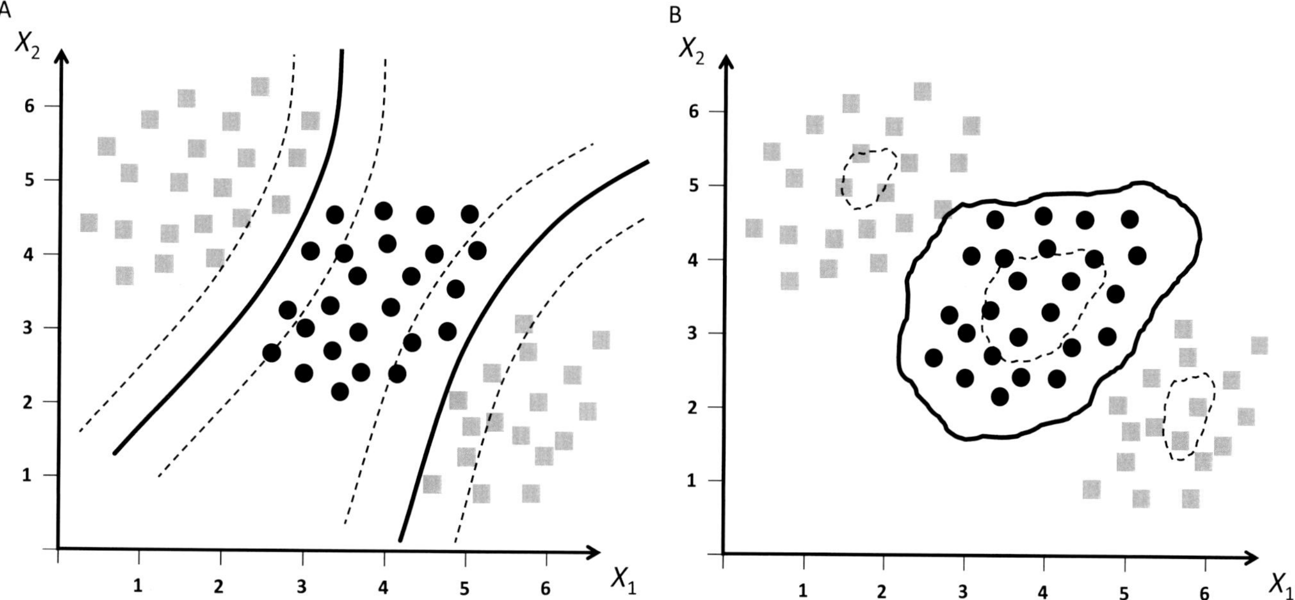

FIGURE 18.9 Good performance of a support vector machines considering non-linear boundaries (polynomial and radial kernels). (A) SVM with a polynomial kernel of degree 2. (B) SVM with a radial kernel.

non-linear boundaries, which represents a significant improvement on the fit over the linear support vector classifier considered in Figure 18.8.

The great advantage of using kernels to define nonlinear boundaries, compared with simply increasing the set of predictor (explanatory) variables by considering specifications with higher-order polynomial terms over these variables, as we did in Expressions (18.14) to (18.18), is purely computational because when using kernels, we only need to determine for all pairs of observations i and i'.

Support vector machines in R

Construction of a support vector machine classification plot in R

Generating an SVM classification plot in `ggplot2` (analogous to the plots shown in Figure 18.9) is not a simple task as there is no function in `ggplot2` that does this natively in R. This forces us to use the function `expand.grid()` as an artifice to achieve this goal. The function `expand.grid()` will generate a data frame using all possible combinations among the variables involved. Here is a teaching example:

```
x <- 1:3
y <- 4:6
expand.grid(x, y)
```

Note that the values of `x` and `y` were perfectly combined, generating a data frame with 2 columns and 9 lines, as shown in Figure 18.10. The idea here is to create a fill in the background of a plot yet to be drawn using `ggplot2`.

```
  Var1 Var2
1    1    4
2    2    4
3    3    4
4    1    5
5    2    5
6    3    5
7    1    6
8    2    6
9    3    6
```

FIGURE 18.10 Data frame generated from the function `expand.grid()`.

We will continue with an example that uses a greater number of observations. In this sense, we will create two variables x1 and x2, with 30 observations, with uniform distribution (function `runif()`), as follows:

```
set.seed(1)
x1 <- runif(30)
x2 <- runif(30)
```

Next, we will create a dichotomous categorical variable named y. Because of the small number of observations, trying to mitigate the possibility that there is no way to reasonably divide the individuals by a hyperplane, we will establish a higher probability of occurrence of one category than the other, so that:

```
y <- factor(sample(x = c(0,1), size = 30, replace = TRUE, prob = c(0.6, 0.4)))
```

Finally, we will join the variables y, x1, and x2 in a data frame called df1, as follows:

```
df1 <- data.frame(y, x1, x2)
```

As an example of what we are proposing, that is, creation of an SVM classification plot, we can estimate an SVM model, which we will name m1, where y represents the dependent variable, and x1 and x2 represent the explanatory variables. Therefore we can type the following code because, in R, for the estimation of an SVM model, we will use the function svm from the package e1071. Also, let's consider a linear kernel with cost equal to 10 and non-standard variables (argument scale = FALSE). Remember that cost is also called *penalty parameter,* which controls the penalty of misclassification.

```
m1 <- svm(formula = y ~ x1 + x2,
          data = df1,
          kernel = "linear",
          cost = 10,
          scale = FALSE)
```

Recall that the argument cost, as discussed in the "Support vector classifiers" section, can be defined as a non-negative adjustment parameter that limits the sum of slack variables and thus determines the amount and intensity of violations that we will be willing to tolerate for classification of observations in relation to the margin and the hyperplane. In our example, therefore, no more than 10 observations can be allocated on the wrong side of the hyperplane.

Thus, in R-based language, the SVM classification plot would be as shown in Figure 18.11.

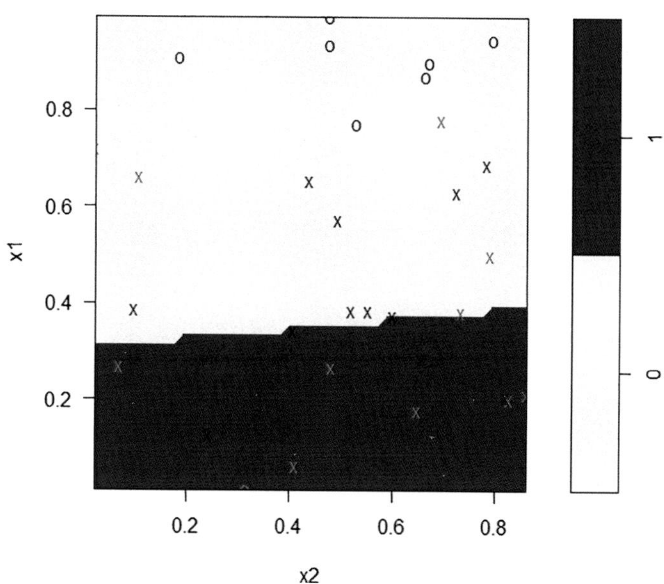

FIGURE 18.11 Support vector machine classification plot.

Using the function predict(), we will save the fitted values of our fictitious model m1 in our dataset df1, as follows:

```
df1["fitted"] <- predict(object = m1, newdata = df1)
```

Next, let's try to plot our variables x1 and x2, coloring them according to the fitted values of the model m1:

```
df1 %>%
  ggplot() +
  geom_tile(aes(x = x2, y = x1, fill = fitted))
```

The graph in Figure 18.12 is generated, and apparently there is nothing in it.

However, if we zoom in, we will notice that there are tiny (really tiny) points with different colors identifying the fitted values of categories 0 and 1 of m1. For greater visual comfort, we will replace the function geom_tile() with the function geom_point(), as follows:

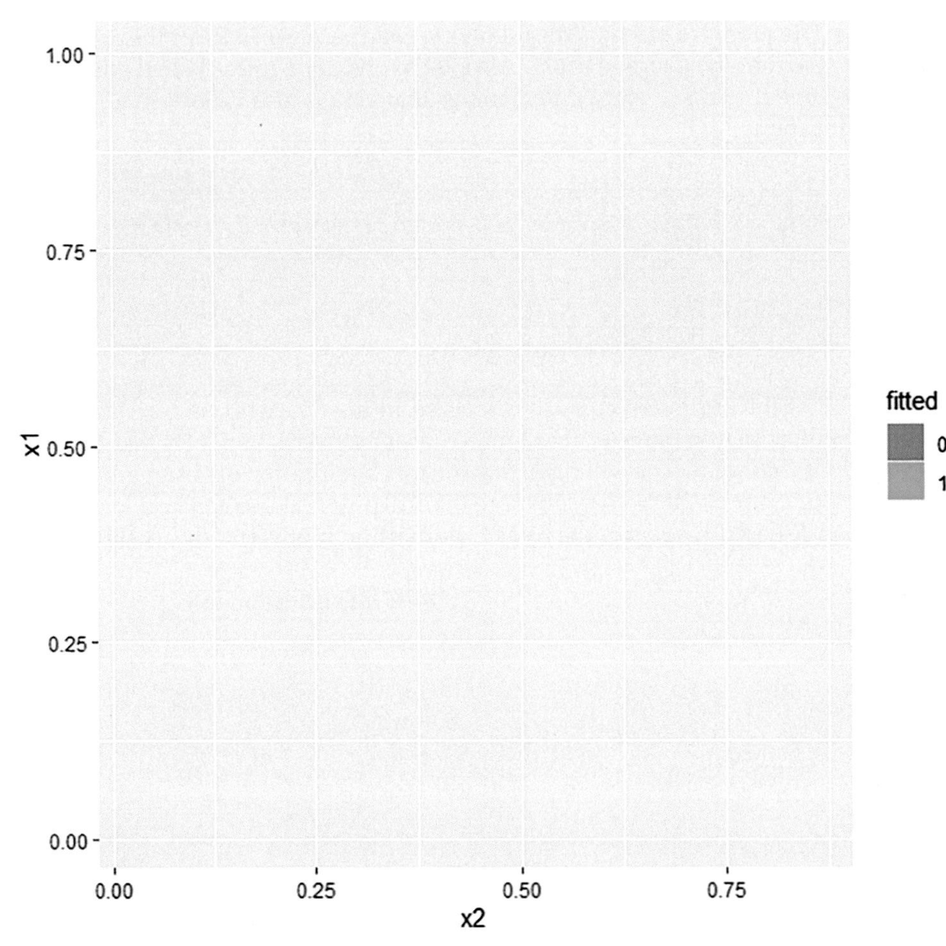

FIGURE 18.12 Plot with variables x1 and x2. Is something wrong?

```
df1 %>%
  ggplot() +
  geom_point(aes(x = x2, y = x1, color = fitted))
```

Figure 18.13 is generated!

The remarks are indeed there! However, later the function `geom_tile()` will be the most suitable for the task.

Using the knowledge gained in this chapter, let's try to imagine where a hyperplane would pass in Figure 18.13 so as to split it into two sides. It could be something like the one shown in Figure 18.14. So, we can enter the following code:

```
df1 %>%
  ggplot() +
  geom_point(aes(x = x2, y = x1, color = fitted)) +
  geom_segment(aes(x = 0, y = 0.32, xend = 1, yend = 0.425)) +
  scale_x_continuous(expand = c(0, 0), limits = c(0,NA)) +
  scale_y_continuous(expand = c(0, 0), limits = c(0, NA)) +
  theme_bw()
```

Based on Figure 18.14, let's try to color the opposite sides of the hyperplane with distinct colors. For this purpose, what if we use the function `expand.grid()` to generate an explosive combination of observations to just paint the background of our graph using the function `geom_tile()` instead of the function `geom_point()`? We will make the combinations between the `min` and `max` sequences of each variable with size equal to 50 (the combination will generate 2500 observations), through the following code that, again, uses the function `expand.grid()`, as follows:

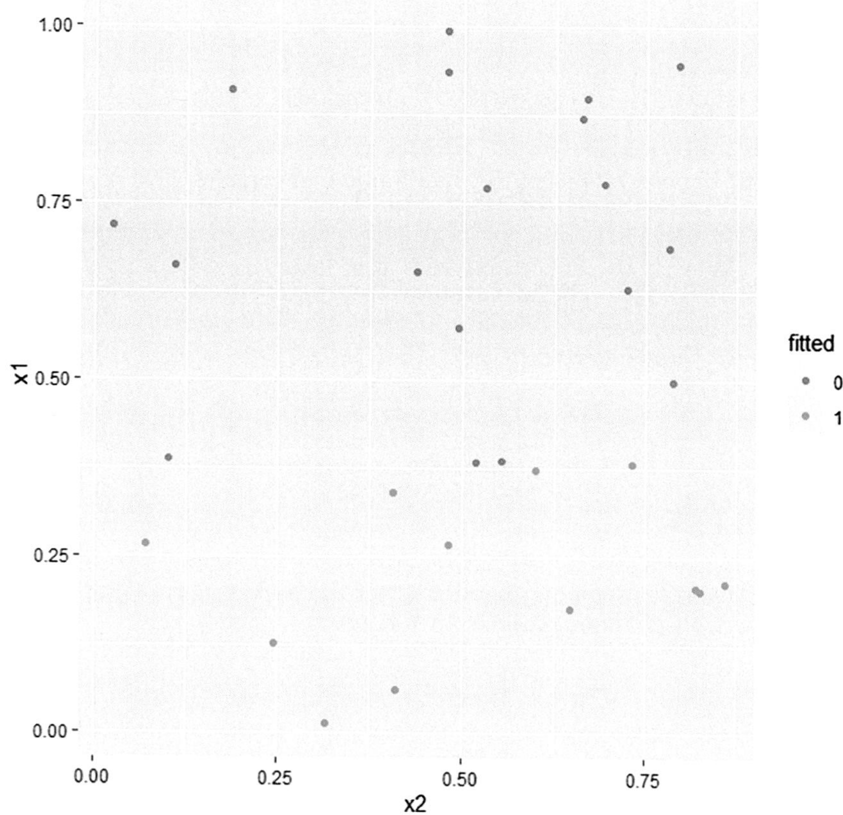

FIGURE 18.13 Plot with variables x1 and x2. Now it is clearer!

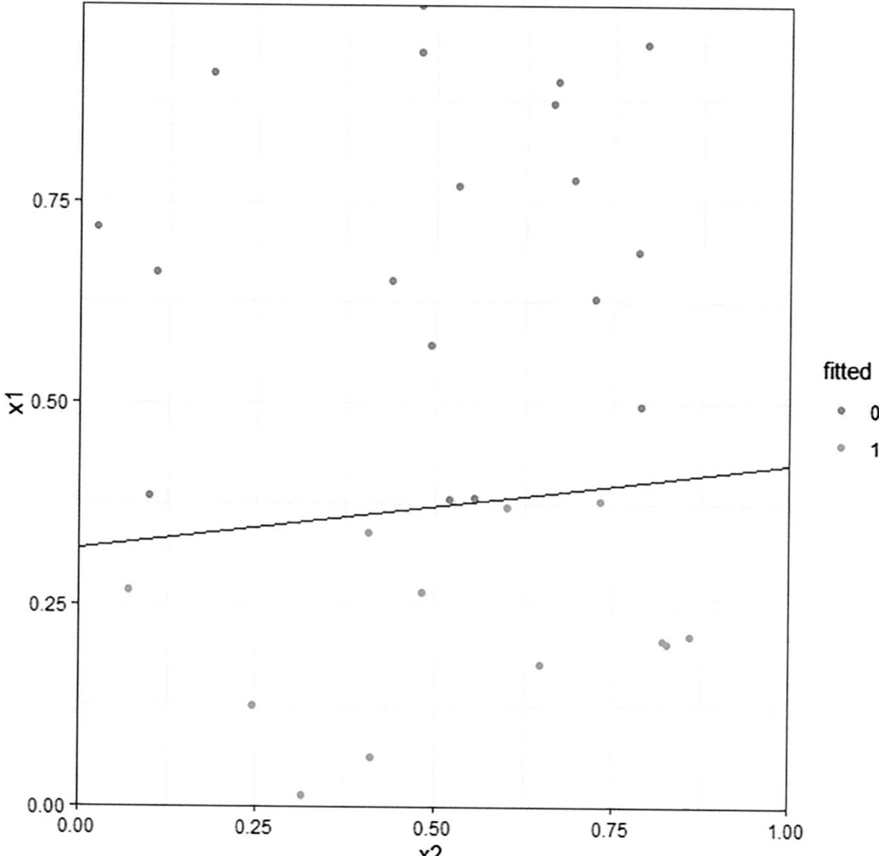

FIGURE 18.14 Plot with variables x1 and x2 and a separating hyperplane.

```
expand.grid(seq(from = min(df1$x1), to = max(df1$x1), length.out = 50),
            seq(from = min(df1$x2), to = max(df1$x2), length.out = 50))
```

Figure 18.15 shows the first 10 observations of the data frame that contains 2500 observations.

```
         Var1       Var2
1  0.01339033 0.02333120
2  0.03336004 0.02333120
3  0.05332975 0.02333120
4  0.07329946 0.02333120
5  0.09326917 0.02333120
6  0.11323888 0.02333120
7  0.13320859 0.02333120
8  0.15317830 0.02333120
9  0.17314801 0.02333120
10 0.19311772 0.02333120
```

FIGURE 18.15 First 10 observations from data frame cpm 2500 observations generated from the function `expand.grid()`.

Before creating a second dataset that will only serve to color the background of our SVM classification plot, let's create another variable `y`, also with 2500 observations, as follows:

```
set.seed(1)
y <- factor(sample(x = c(0,1), size = 2500, replace = TRUE))
```

To create a new data frame, which we will call `df2`, we can command:

```
df2 <- data.frame(expand.grid(
  x1 = seq(from = min(df1$x1), to = max(df1$x1), length.out = 50),
  x2 = seq(from = min(df1$x2), to = max(df1$x2), length.out = 50)),
  y)
```

Next, we will generate the fitted values for the data frame `df2` that will serve, solely and exclusively, to create a colored background on the graph—nothing more!

```
df2["fitted_color"] <- predict(object = m1, newdata = df2)
```

We are now going to plot the variables from the dataset `df2`, but we will use the function `geom_tile()` again, as follows:

```
df2 %>%
  ggplot() +
  geom_tile(aes(x = x2, y = x1, fill = fitted_color)) +
  theme_void()
```

Figure 18.16 is generated!

Now, using the dataset `df1`, we will highlight the support vectors, which are in the component `index` of the model `m1`, as shown in Figure 18.17 generated from the following code:

```
m1$index
```

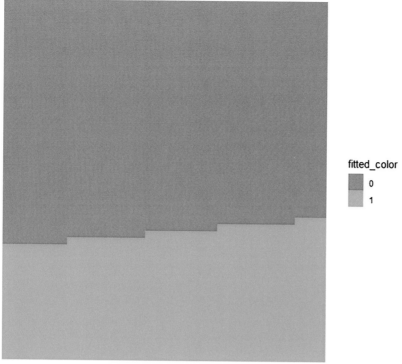

FIGURE 18.16 Plot with opposite sides of the hyperplane with distinct colors.

```
[1]  1  5  8 10 12 16 17 19 20 22 25  2  3  9 11 13 14 23 24 26 28 30
```

FIGURE 18.17 Component `index` of the model `m1`.

In this sense, to save the support vectors in our dataset `df1`, we must type:

```
df1 %>%
  rownames_to_column("index") %>%
  mutate(index = ifelse(index %in% m1$index,
                        yes = "support",
                        no = "not_support")) -> df1
```

Finally, the construction of the SVM classification plot can be elaborated as follows:

```
df2 %>%
  ggplot(aes(x = x2, y = x1)) + geom_tile(aes(fill = fitted_color)) +
  geom_point(data = df1, aes(x = x2, y = x1, color = y, shape = index), size = 3) +
  scale_color_manual(values = c("black","red")) +
  scale_shape_manual(values = c(1, 4)) +
  theme_void()
```

Figure 18.18 is generated!

We recognize that Figure 18.18 does not look fancy, but we will leave it this way on purpose! Note that the shapes' colors indicate which category each observation belongs to (*black* for category 0; *red* for category 1). The format of the shapes indicates whether or not the individual is a support vector (the X format for support vector; the O format otherwise). Finally, the colored areas of the background indicate how the observations were classified (category 0 of the dependent variable for the upper portion and category 1 for the lower portion).

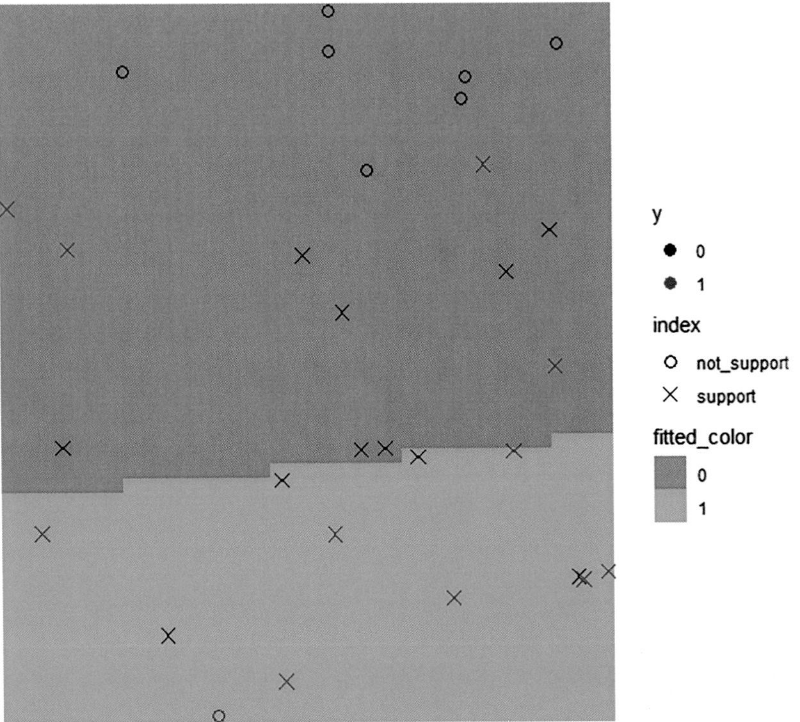

FIGURE 18.18 Support vector machine classification plot.

Support vector machines application with a linear kernel in R

Based on the considerations and criteria studied in the previous section, we will build an SVM classification plot for a specific dataset. In this section, we use the dataset present in the file `barbecue.RData`, composed by using the following variables presented in Table 18.1.

TABLE 18.1 Description of the variables presented in the File `barbecue.RData`.

Variable	Description
income	Dependent binary variable that corresponds to the fact of the classifier represents a higher level of income (group 1) or a lower level of income (group 2).
beef	Annual expenditure on beef (US$).
chicken	Annual expenditure on chicken (US$).

Now, let's open the dataset file `barbecue.RData`.

```
load("barbecue.RData")
```

Initially, we will elaborate a scatter plot with the variables *beef* and *chicken* on the ordinate and abscissa axes, respectively, highlighting the observations belonging to *income* groups 1 (circles) and 2 (triangles), through the following code that generates the graph in Figure 18.19:

```
ggplotly(
  barbecue %>%
    ggplot(aes(x = chicken, y = beef, color = income, shape = income)) +
    geom_point() +
    labs(x = "chicken",
         y = "beef",
```

Continued

```
        shape = NULL) +
    scale_color_manual("Labels:",
                            values = c("darkorchid","orange")) +
    theme_bw()
)
```

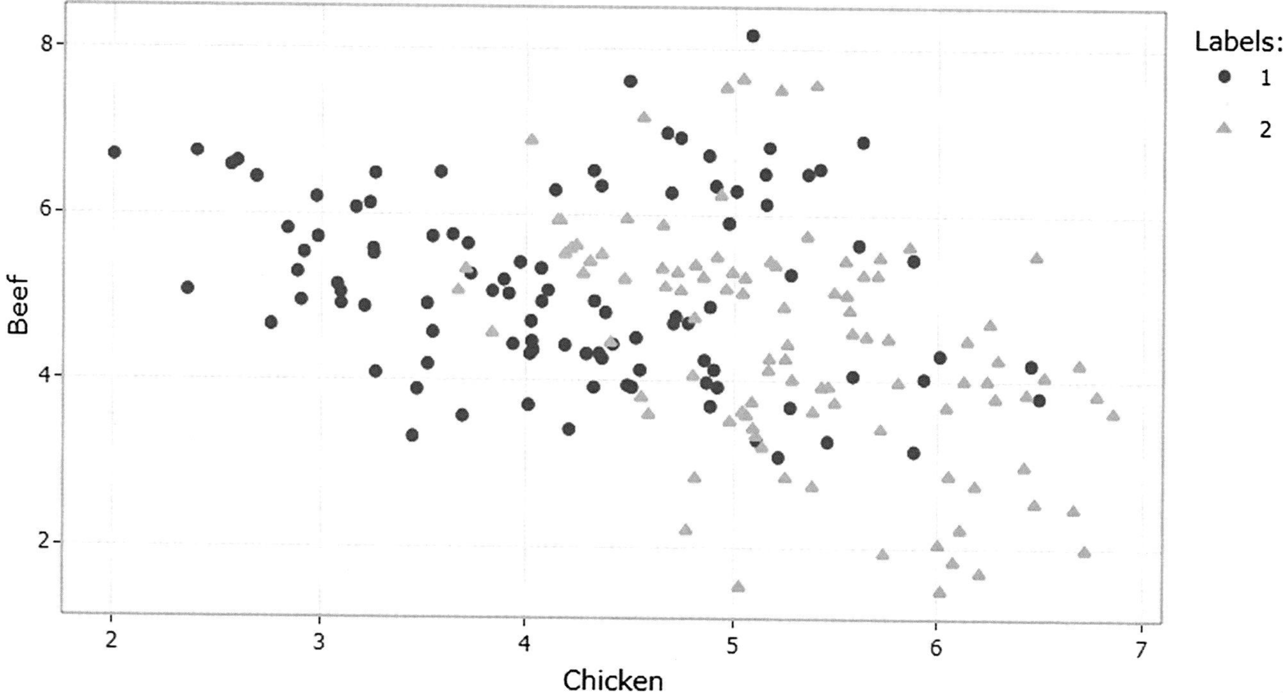

FIGURE 18.19 Scatter plot for the variables *beef* and *chicken*, with emphasis on *income* groups.

As discussed in the previous section, for the estimation of an SVM model in R, we can use the function `svm` from the package `e1071`. For our example, we will estimate a first model, which we will name `svmfit_1`, using the following code:

```
svmfit_1 <- svm(formula = income ~ beef + chicken,
                data = barbecue,
                kernel = "linear",
                cost = 10,
                scale = FALSE)
```

where the dependent variable of binary classification will be the group corresponding to the `income`, and the explanatory variables will be `beef` and `chicken`. Furthermore, we consider a linear kernel (argument `kernel = "linear"`), non-standard variables (argument `scale = FALSE`), and parameter C defined in Expression (18.13) equal to 10 (argument `cost = 10`), therefore not more than 10 observations are allocated on the wrong side of the hyperplane. This is because if a given observation i is on the wrong side of the hyperplane, we will have $\varepsilon i > 1$, causing the constraint represented by Expression (18.13) to be obeyed. As discussed in the "Support vector classifiers" section, the higher the value assigned to the argument `cost`, the greater the tolerance and therefore the wider the margin, a fact that allows greater tolerance for observations to be on the wrong side of the margin, as shown in Figure 18.7.

We can type the following code that will generate the graph in Figure 18.20, which shows a colored background divided by a hyperplane, with different colors for the different sides of the hyperplane.

```
plot(x = svmfit_1, data = barbecue)
```

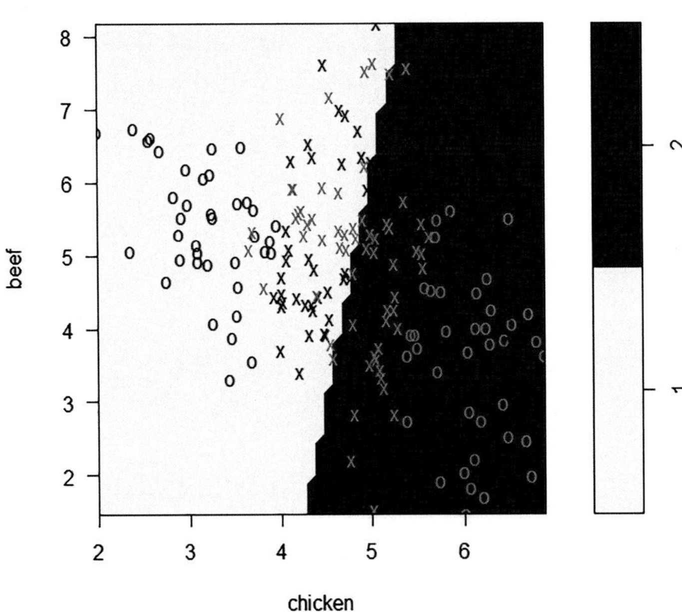

FIGURE 18.20 Support vector machine classification plot for the model svmfit_1.

As in the previous section, we are going to create a background for a future SVM classification plot, establishing all possible combinations of values from the observations of the variables of dataset barbecue, through the function expand.grid(). This time, we will use the argument length.out = 15, so we do not uselessly create too many combinations (this argument value will already generate a data frame with more than 50,000 lines!).

```
background <- expand.grid(expand.grid(
  beef = seq(from = min(barbecue$beef), to = max(barbecue$beef), length.out = 15),
  chicken = seq(from = min(barbecue$chicken), to = max(barbecue$chicken), length.out = 15))
  )
```

Now, let's add the fitted values of the model svmfit_1 to the dataset background. Note that this only serves to create a colored background for our graphic! In this way, we can enter the following code:

```
background["fitted_color"] <- predict(object = svmfit_1,
                                      newdata = background)
```

By typing the following code, we can see a preliminary result of the background of our SVM classification plot in Figure 18.21:

fitted_color
1
2

FIGURE 18.21 Creating the background of the support vector machine classification plot for the model svmfit_1.

```
background %>%
  ggplot() +
  geom_tile(aes(x = chicken, y = beef, fill = fitted_color)) +
  scale_fill_manual(values = c("cornsilk2", "aliceblue")) +
  theme_void()
```

Once this is done, we can save the fitted values of the model svmfit_1 as well as highlight the support vectors based on what we have studied so far, typing the following code:

```
barbecue %>%
  rownames_to_column("index") %>%
  mutate(index = ifelse(index %in% svmfit_1$index,
                        yes = "support",
                        no = "not_support"),
         fitted = predict(object = svmfit_1, data = .)) -> barbecue
```

Finally, the following code, based on the model svmfit_1, builds our SVM classification plot, shown in Figure 18.22:

```
background %>%
  ggplot(aes(x = chicken, y = beef)) + geom_tile(aes(fill = fitted_color)) +
  geom_point(data = barbecue, aes(x = chicken, y = beef, color = income, shape = index), size = 3) +
  scale_fill_manual(values = c("cornsilk2", "aliceblue")) +
  scale_color_manual(values = c("orange","darkorchid")) +
  scale_shape_manual(values = c(1, 4)) +
  theme_void()
```

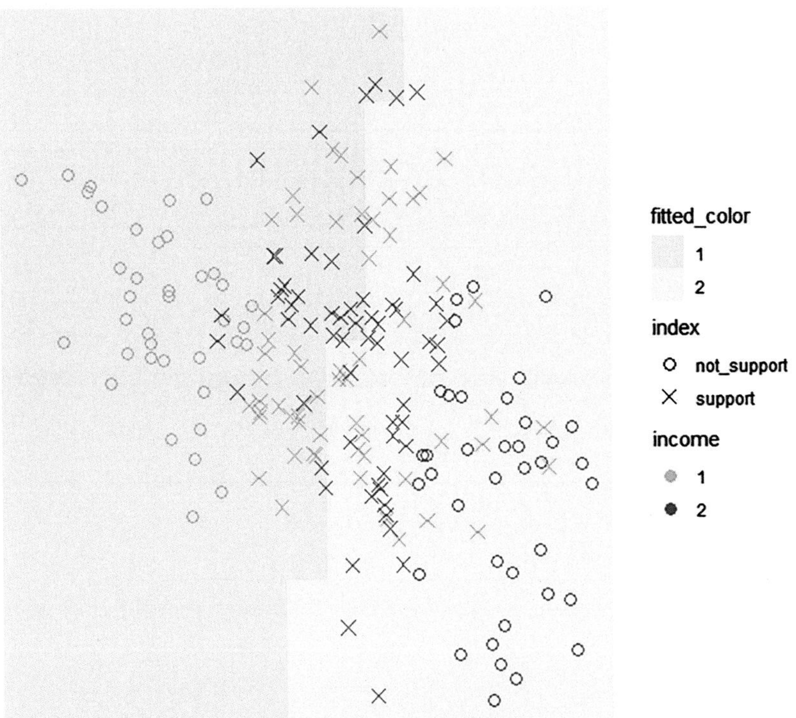

FIGURE 18.22 Support vector machine classification plot for the Model svmfit_1.

In Figure 18.22, we can see that the colors of the shapes indicate which category of the dependent variable (income classification) each observation belongs to. The format of the shapes indicates whether or not the individual is a support vector, with the X format for support vector and the O format otherwise. Finally, the colored areas of the background indicate how the observations were classified, with category 1 for the *left* part of the graph and category 2 for the *right* part. For a more elegant SVM classification plot, we suggest the following code, which builds the graph in Figure 18.23:

```
background %>%
  ggplot(aes(x = chicken, y = beef)) + geom_tile(aes(fill = fitted_color)) +
  geom_point(data = barbecue, aes(x = chicken, y = beef, color = income, shape = index), size = 3) +
  scale_fill_manual(values = c("cornsilk2", "aliceblue")) +
  scale_color_manual(values = c("orange","darkorchid")) +
  scale_shape_manual(values = c(1, 4)) +
  labs(x = "chicken",
       y = "beef",
       fill = "Predicted Category",
       shape = "SV",
       color = "Observed Category") +
  theme(panel.background = element_rect(NA),
      panel.border = element_rect(color = "black", fill = NA),
      legend.position = "bottom",
      legend.text = element_text(size = 8),
      legend.title = element_text(size = 8))
```

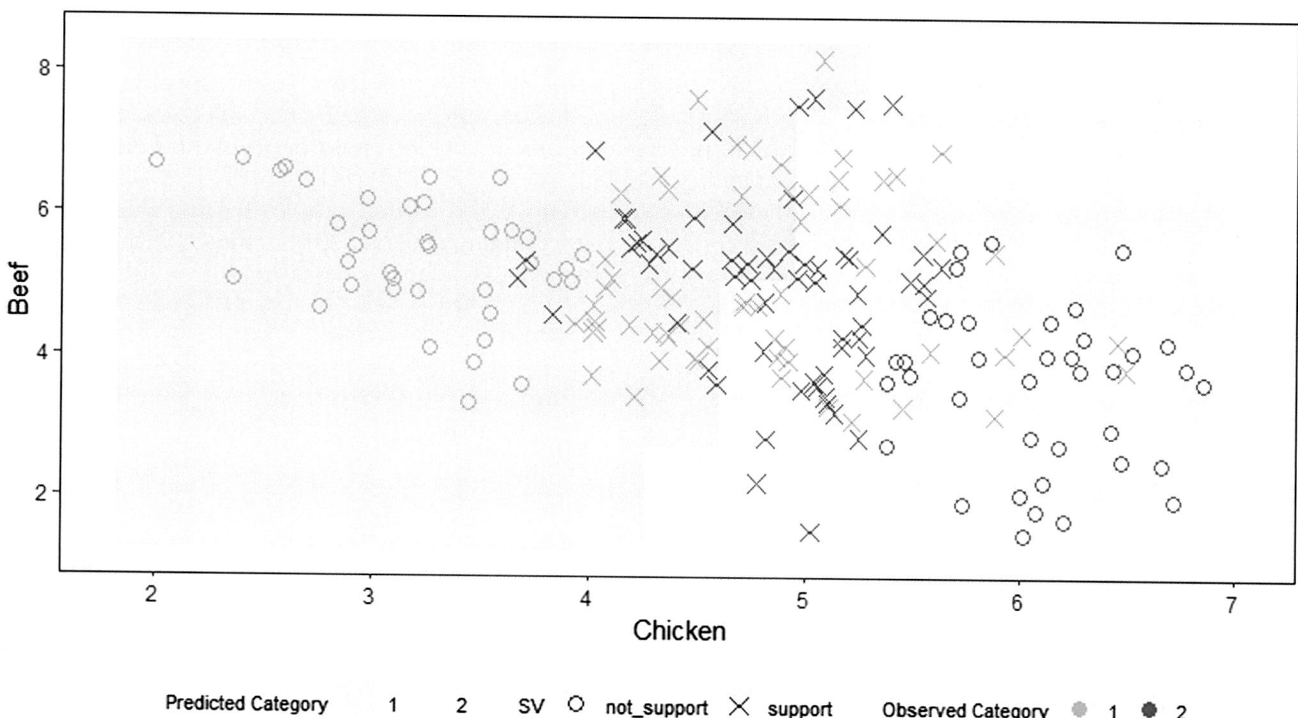

FIGURE 18.23 A more elegant support vector machine classification plot for the model `svmfit_1`.

Training and validation samples, tuning, and other support vector machine estimations in R

Adopting **sampling techniques by cross-validation** (i.e., creating subsets from the original set so there are **training and validation samples**) is a good practice when estimating SVM models and will help the reader determine whether or not the model is affected by the **overfitting** problem. We will also use this procedure in the next few chapters (such as Classification and Regression Trees, Bagging and Boosting, Random Forest, and Artificial Neural Network).The main reason for consideration of training and validation samples in SVM models is that we do not have an explicit predictive equation with parameters (betas) estimated through a deterministic optimization process in order to reach a high value of a log-likelihood function defined previously from a distribution function of the dependent variable, as is the case of supervised models in which the parameters of predictive equations are estimated from maximization of the logarithm of a certain likelihood function arising from the behavior of the outcome variable itself. This explains the fact that we do not use training and validation samples when estimating models such as the generalized linear model, or GLM (simple and multiple regression models, binary and multinomial logistic regression models, and count-data and zero-inflated regression models) and the generalized linear mixed model, or GLMM (multilevel models). In these cases, it made no sense to discuss the overfitting problem, and the complete dataset used for a given model could be considered, in essence, the training sample itself from which the chosen algorithm would be "trained."

In this section, we will elaborate three SVMs to illustrate the use of the technique. The first will be an SVM with a linear kernel, analogous to what we discussed in the previous section. Although the second will be an SVM with a polynomial kernel of degree 2, the last SVM to be estimated will be a model with a radial kernel, as discussed in the "Support vector machines" section. In the "Comparison of support vector machine models' performance to a binary logistic regression model" section, we will compare all models with the results obtained from an estimation of a binary logistic regression model because all of them have the same objective, that is, to reach better classifications of the observations for a dependent binary variable through use of predictor (explanatory) variables.

In addition to the foregoing, unlike the estimation methods for the supervised models studied in the previous chapters, this kind of algorithm has the random feature of built-in cross-validation, which means that, not necessarily, an

SVM will be identical to another SVM estimated from the same dataset. So, initially, it is important to introduce the function set.seed() to the reader.

The function set.seed() will ensure that the same random processes that occurred for the authors during the SVM estimation will also be replicated for the reader. If we did not use the function set.seed(), the reader would invariably estimate models with different characteristics and results from the models printed on the pages of this book. This procedure will also be adopted in the next few chapters.

Based on the procedures described, we will then define our training and validation samples, the first with 60% of the observations from the dataset barbecue and the second with the remaining observations, as shown in the following code. It is important to remember that the reader must have previously loaded the dataset barbecue using the code load(file = "barbecue.Rdata").

```
set.seed(1)
sample_index <- sample(x = 1:dim(barbecue)[1],
                       size = nrow(barbecue) * 0.6)

training_sample <- barbecue[sample_index, ]
validation_sample <- barbecue[-sample_index, ]
```

Having made these considerations, we will proceed to the estimation of an SVM with a linear kernel, but with different criteria from those adopted for the model svmfit_1 estimated in the previous section. Why should we use different criteria? In many data science applications, it is desirable to maximize the model's performance by defining specific criteria. The process of maximizing a model's performance without overfitting or creating a too-high variance is known as **tuning**. In analytics and machine learning, this procedure is accomplished by selecting appropriate hyperparameters that will define the best performance configuration for the model under analysis.

Despite being an optimization problem, tuning faces complex difficulties because as discussed earlier, the models do not explicitly present a functional form or a clearly defined mathematical formulation. In this sense, the definition of the set of hyperparameters is decisive and fundamental for machine learning model accuracy, but it can be computationally demanding. Hyperparameters are not automatically learned by the model through training methods, which makes them different from other model parameters, therefore we must manually set them.

For the definition of SVM with a linear kernel with the best performance (tuning model), we can proceed with the following code. An attentive reader will notice that we manually define the set of hyperparameters through the argument ranges = list(cost = c(0.001 , 0.01, 0.1, 1, 5, 10, 100)), with possible values for cost.

```
set.seed (1)
tune_out_linear <- tune(method = svm,
                        train.x = income ~ beef + chicken,
                        data = training_sample,
                        kernel = "linear",
                        ranges = list(cost = c(0.001, 0.01, 0.1, 1, 5, 10)
                                      )
                        )

summary(tune_out_linear)
plot(tune_out_linear)
```

The output of this procedure, obtained by the code summary(tune_out_linear), is shown in Figure 18.24.

For supervised learning, this function returns a table with *k*-fold cross-validated scores of the classification error as the evaluation metric along with a trained model object. In R, as a performance measure, the classification error is used for classification, and the mean squared error is used for regression models. Cross-validation randomizes the dataset before building the splits that, once created, remain constant during the training process (Meyer et al., 2021). By default, the fold is set to 10.

Through Figure 18.24, we can verify that the model with cost equal to 0.01 presents the smallest classification error, with its performance measure equal to 0.2208. Figure 18.25, obtained using the code plot(tune_out_linear), graphically presents the behavior of the classification error as a function of the cost hyperparameter values.

```
Parameter tuning of 'svm':

- sampling method: 10-fold cross validation

- best parameters:
 cost
 0.01

- best performance: 0.2208333

- Detailed performance results:
   cost     error dispersion
1 1e-03 0.4791667 0.07414638
2 1e-02 0.2208333 0.07095578
3 1e-01 0.2416667 0.06747199
4 1e+00 0.2458333 0.06349516
5 5e+00 0.2458333 0.06349516
6 1e+01 0.2458333 0.06349516
```

FIGURE 18.24 Parameter tuning of a support vector machine with a linear kernel.

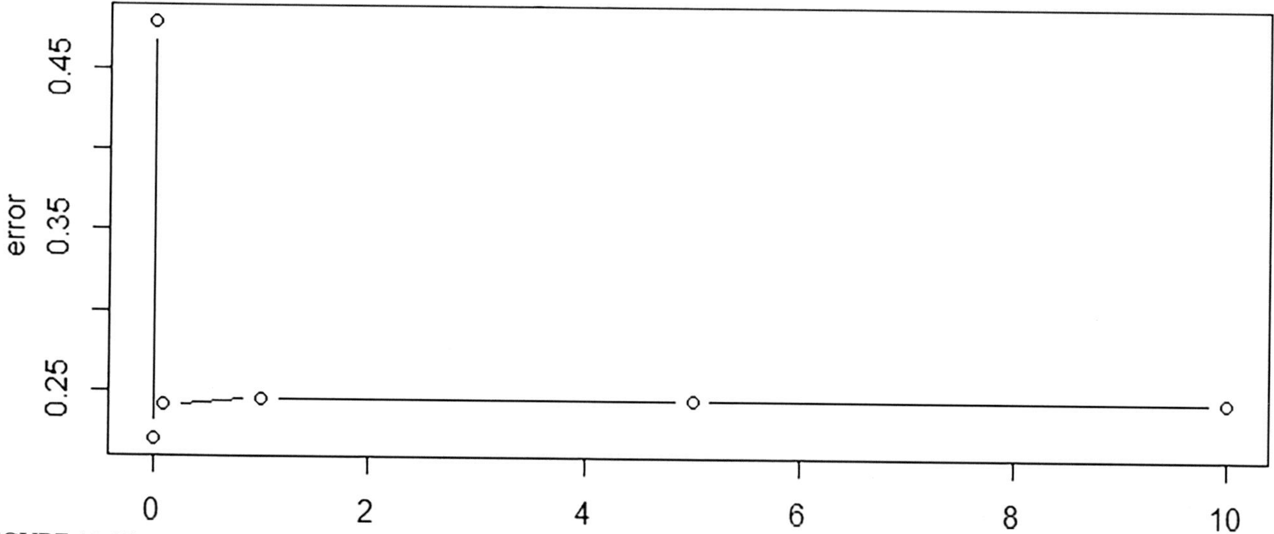

FIGURE 18.25 Performance of the support vector machine with a linear kernel.

In this sense, we will then estimate the model `svmfit_2` based on the concepts discussed and considering cost = 0.01. To do so, we can enter the following code. The argument `probability = TRUE` allows the probabilities of allocation to the observations in the groups to be calculated and, from the definition of a cutoff, the confusion matrix for the classifications of the observations in each of the groups existing in the dependent variable is constructed, exactly as we studied in Chapter 15.

```
set.seed(1)
svmfit_2 <- svm(formula = income ~ beef + chicken,
                data = training_sample,
                kernel = "linear",
                cost = 0.01,
                probability = TRUE)

summary(svmfit_2)
```

The output obtained through the code summary(svmfit_2) was purposely omitted. Next, we will build the SVM classification plot for the model svmfit_2. For this, it is necessary that the dataset background, with more than 50,000 lines, has already been defined (remember that this dataset was built when estimating the model svmfit_1 in the previous section!). In this sense, we can type the following code, which will generate the graph shown in Figure 18.26. Note that the following code also generates in the dataset barbecue two new variables: index_2 (support or not support for each observation) and fitted_2 (classification of each observation in group 1 or 2 as a result of the proposed model).

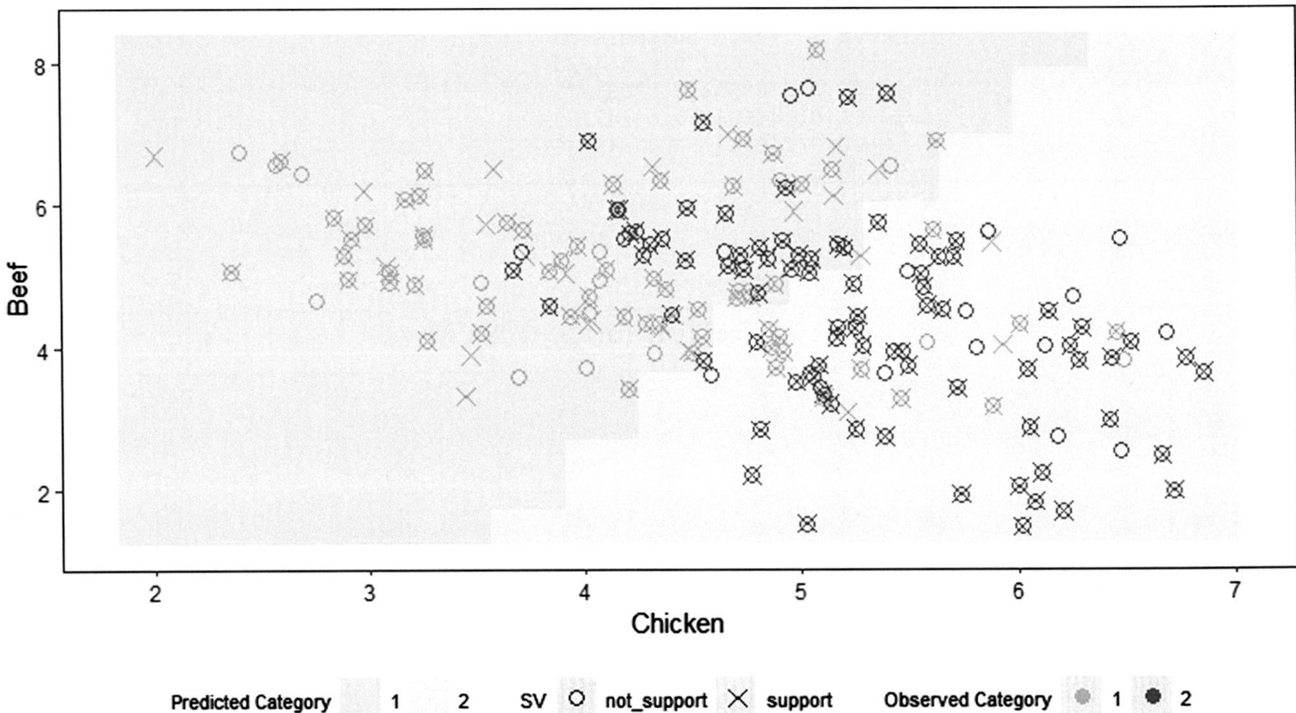

FIGURE 18.26 Support vector machine classification plot for the model svmfit_2.

```
background["fitted_color_2"] <- predict(object = svmfit_2,
                                        newdata = background)

barbecue %>%
  rownames_to_column("index_2") %>%
  mutate(index_2 = ifelse(index_2 %in% svmfit_2$index,
                          yes = "support",
                          no = "not_support"),
         fitted_2 = predict(object = svmfit_2, newdata = .)) -> barbecue

background %>%
  ggplot(aes(x = chicken, y = beef)) + geom_tile(aes(fill = fitted_color_2)) +
  geom_point(data = barbecue, aes(x = chicken, y = beef, color = income, shape = index_2), size = 3) +
  scale_fill_manual(values = c("cornsilk2", "aliceblue")) +
  scale_color_manual(values = c("orange","darkorchid")) +
  scale_shape_manual(values = c(1, 4)) +
  labs(x = "chicken",
       y = "beef",
```

Continued

```
        fill = "Predicted Category",
        shape = "SV",
        color = "Observed Category") +
  theme(panel.background = element_rect(NA),
        panel.border = element_rect(color = "black", fill = NA),
        legend.position = "bottom",
        legend.text = element_text(size = 8),
        legend.title = element_text(size = 8))
```

As we inserted the argument `probability = TRUE` when defining the object `svmfit_2`, we are able to build the confusion matrix for that model. To do so, we must command the following:

```
probs_fit_2 <- predict(svmfit_2,
                       newdata = validation_sample,
                       probability = TRUE)

pred_probs_fit_2 <- attr(x = probs_fit_2, which = "probabilities")[,1] <= 0.5

confusionMatrix(
  data = table(pred_probs_fit_2,
               validation_sample$income == 1)[2:1, 2:1]
  )
```

Note that we are considering, only for didactic purposes, the classification cutoff equal to 0.5, similar to the one elaborated in Chapter 15 when studying binary logistic regression models. The outputs obtained can be found in Figure 18.27, which shows, for this cutoff, an accuracy of the SVM model with a linear kernel equal to 0.7, as well as a sensitivity equal to 0.7067 and a specificity equal to 0.6941 for the validation sample, being the group 1 of the dependent variable *income* the considered event. We will not explore the results of this confusion matrix in detail because this is discussed in Chapter 15.

```
Confusion Matrix and Statistics


pred_probs_fit_2 TRUE FALSE
           TRUE    53    26
           FALSE   22    59

               Accuracy : 0.7
                 95% CI : (0.6226, 0.7698)
    No Information Rate : 0.5312
    P-Value [Acc > NIR] : 9.957e-06

                  Kappa : 0.3995

 Mcnemar's Test P-Value : 0.665

            Sensitivity : 0.7067
            Specificity : 0.6941
         Pos Pred Value : 0.6709
         Neg Pred Value : 0.7284
             Prevalence : 0.4688
         Detection Rate : 0.3312
   Detection Prevalence : 0.4938
      Balanced Accuracy : 0.7004

       'Positive' Class : TRUE
```

FIGURE 18.27 Confusion matrix for the model `svmfit_2` (validation sample and cutoff = 0.5).

Additionally, we will create a dataset, called `plot_data_linear`, from which it will be possible to build the graph to analyze the sensitivity and specificity values as a function of the cutoff as well as the receiver operating characteristic (ROC) curve referring to our SVM model with a linear kernel. To do so, we will command the following code:

```
predict(object = svmfit_2, newdata = barbecue, probability = TRUE)

probs_linear <- predict(object = svmfit_2,
                        newdata = barbecue,
                        probability = TRUE)

attr(x = probs_linear, which = "probabilities")[,1]

pred_probs_linear <- attr(x = probs_linear, which = "probabilities")[,1]

predictions_linear <- prediction(predictions = pred_probs_linear,
                                 labels = barbecue$income)

sens_data_linear <- performance(prediction.obj = predictions_linear,
                                measure = "sens")

sensitivity_linear <- sens_data_linear@y.values[[1]]

spec_data_linear <- performance(prediction.obj = predictions_linear,
                               measure = "spec")

specificity_linear <- spec_data_linear@y.values[[1]]

cutoffs_linear <- predictions_linear@cutoffs[[1]]

plot_data_linear <- cbind.data.frame(cutoffs_linear,
                                     specificity_linear,
                                     sensitivity_linear)
```

Similar to what we studied in Chapter 15, the first code of the previous command (`predict(object = svmfit_2, newdata = barbecue, probability = TRUE)`) generates, in the console, the classifications of each observation and the

```
 1  2  3  4  5  6  7  8  9 10
 1  1  1  2  2  1  1  2  1  1

11 12 13 14 15 16 17 18 19 20
 1  1  1  2  1  1  2  1  1  1


attr(,"probabilities")
            2          1
1  0.18383639 0.81616361
2  0.31299760 0.68700240
3  0.47385772 0.52614228
4  0.50246328 0.49753672
5  0.61803308 0.38196692
6  0.04506600 0.95493400
7  0.21911000 0.78089000
8  0.79821635 0.20178365
9  0.08111946 0.91888054
10 0.41625938 0.58374062
11 0.38157500 0.61842500
12 0.26659116 0.73340884
13 0.39881864 0.60118136
14 0.50137635 0.49862365
15 0.47996713 0.52003287
16 0.16387158 0.83612842
17 0.75958150 0.24041850
18 0.36694878 0.63305122
19 0.31417222 0.68582778
20 0.41838731 0.58161269
```

FIGURE 18.28 Classification and probabilities for the first 20 observations of the dataset `barbecue` for the model `svmfit_2`.

probabilities allocation in each of the dependent variable groups. Figure 18.28 shows these outputs for the first 20 observations of the complete sample with 400 observations (dataset barbecue), remembering that the classification of each observation in a given group is defined based on the highest probability (probability greater than 0.5) for that group.

Following the logic of Chapter 15, we will then build the graphs with the sensitivity and specificity curves for the cutoff values as well as the ROC curve for our SVM model with a linear kernel. The area under the ROC curve (AUC) will be used later for comparison with other models estimated throughout this chapter (the "Comparison of SVM models' performance to a binary logistic regression model" section). In this sense, we can command the following, which will generate the graphics in Figure 18.29:

```
plot_data_linear %>%
  ggplot() +
  geom_line(aes(x = cutoffs_linear, y = specificity_linear, color = "Specificity"),
            size = 2) +
  geom_point(aes(x = cutoffs_linear, y = specificity_linear),
             color = "orange", size = 2, shape = 15) +
  geom_line(aes(x = cutoffs_linear, y = sensitivity_linear, color = "Sensitivity"),
            size = 2) +
  geom_point(aes(x = cutoffs_linear, y = sensitivity_linear),
             color = "darkorchid", size = 2, shape = 16) +
  labs(x = "Cutoffs",
       y = "Sensitivity/Specificity") +
  scale_color_manual("Label:",
                     values = c("orange", "darkorchid")) +
  theme_bw()

au_roc_linear <- performance(prediction.obj = predictions_linear,
                             measure = "auc")

plot_data_linear %>%
  ggplot() +
  geom_segment(aes(x = 0, xend = 1, y = 0, yend = 1),
               color="orange", size = 2) +
  geom_line(aes(x = 1 - specificity_linear, y = sensitivity_linear),
            color = "darkorchid", size = 2) +
  labs(x = "1 - Specificity",
       y = "Sensitivity",
       title = paste("Area under the curve:",
                     round(au_roc_linear@y.values[[1]], 3))) +
  theme_bw()
```

We will now proceed to the estimation of an SVM model with a polynomial kernel of degree 2. Following the same logic adopted for the linear model, we will proceed with the definition of the best performance (tuning model) for the model, using the following code. An attentive reader will notice that we manually set the hyperparameters through the argument `ranges = list(cost = c(0.001, 0.01, 0.1, 1), gamma = c(0.1, 0.5, 1, 2, 3, 4))`, with the possibilities of values for cost and gamma. Although cost is also known as the *penalty parameter*, which controls the penalty of misclassification, as discussed earlier, gamma is the parameter that reshapes the decision boundary by trying to assemble and cluster similar data points.

```
set.seed (1)
tune_out_polyn <- tune(method = "svm",
                       train.x = income ~ beef + chicken,
                       data = training_sample,
                       kernel = "polynomial", degree = 2,
                       probability = TRUE,
                       ranges = list(
```

Continued

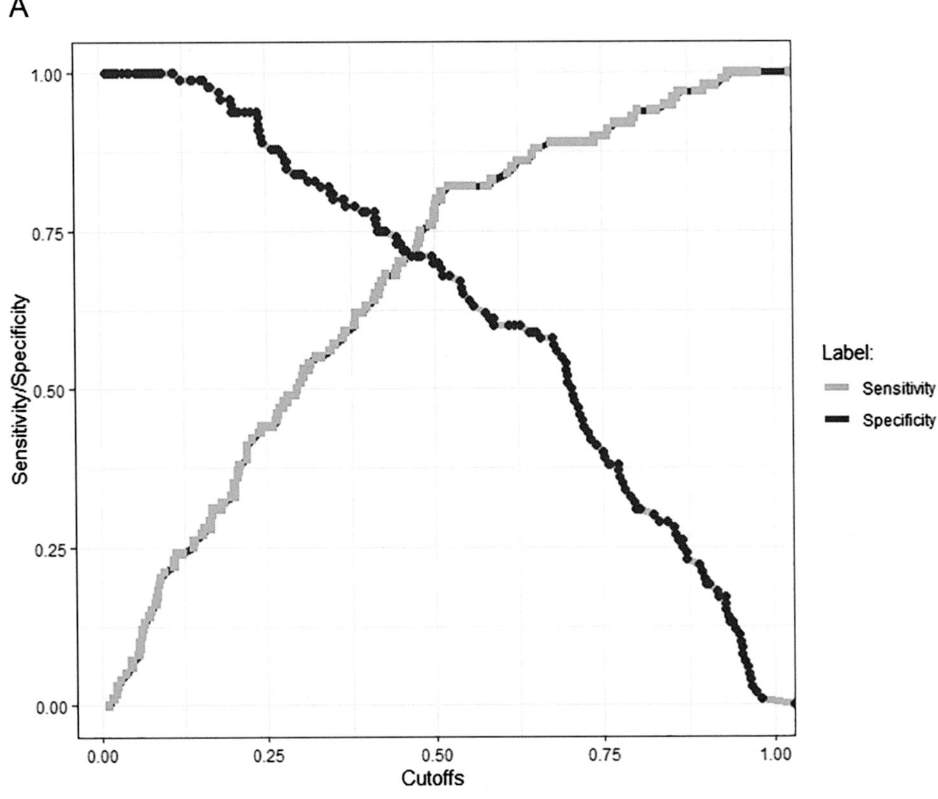

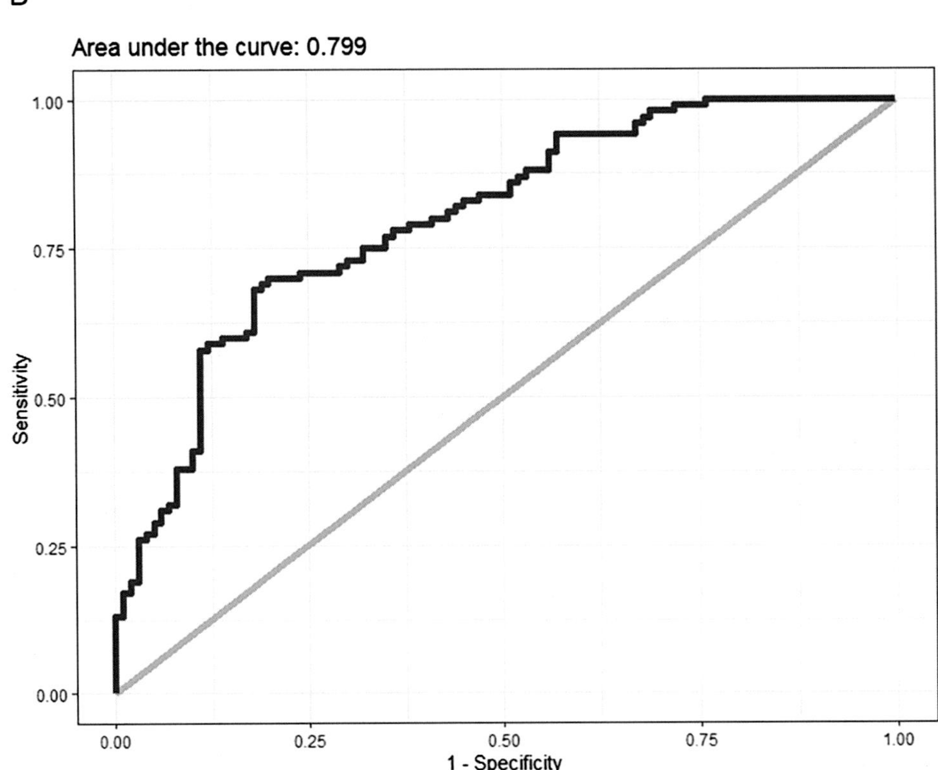

FIGURE 18.29 Sensitivity and specificity curve and ROC curve for the support vector machine model with a linear kernel. (A) Sensitivity and specificity curve for the cutoff values. (B) ROC curve.

```
        cost = c(0.001, 0.01, 0.1, 1),
        gamma = c(0.1, 0.5, 1, 2, 3, 4)
        )
        )
summary(tune_out_polyn)
plot(tune_out_polyn)
```

This code generates the outputs presented in Figure 18.30 and the graph shown in Figure 18.31. For the set of values of `cost` and `gamma` manually defined, we can verify, using Figure 18.30, that the model with `cost` equal to 0.1 and `gamma` equal to 0.5 presents the smallest classification error, with its performance measure equal to 0.3917.

```
Parameter tuning of 'svm':

- sampling method: 10-fold cross validation

- best parameters:
 cost gamma
  0.1   0.5

- best performance: 0.3916667

- Detailed performance results:
    cost gamma     error dispersion
1  0.001   0.1 0.4791667 0.07414638
2  0.010   0.1 0.4791667 0.07414638
3  0.100   0.1 0.4791667 0.07414638
4  1.000   0.1 0.4125000 0.07720523
5  0.001   0.5 0.4791667 0.07414638
6  0.010   0.5 0.4750000 0.07401618
7  0.100   0.5 0.3916667 0.09254628
8  1.000   0.5 0.4000000 0.08146043
9  0.001   1.0 0.4791667 0.07414638
10 0.010   1.0 0.4125000 0.07720523
11 0.100   1.0 0.4125000 0.09712297
12 1.000   1.0 0.4000000 0.08146043
13 0.001   2.0 0.4333333 0.06273105
14 0.010   2.0 0.3958333 0.07917885
15 0.100   2.0 0.4083333 0.08516505
16 1.000   2.0 0.4000000 0.08146043
17 0.001   3.0 0.4291667 0.07619926
18 0.010   3.0 0.4083333 0.09378857
19 0.100   3.0 0.4000000 0.08146043
20 1.000   3.0 0.4000000 0.08146043
21 0.001   4.0 0.4083333 0.06454972
22 0.010   4.0 0.4083333 0.08740074
23 0.100   4.0 0.4000000 0.08146043
24 1.000   4.0 0.4000000 0.08146043
```

FIGURE 18.30 Parameter tuning of a support vector machine with a polynomial kernel of degree 2.

Let's now estimate the model `svmfit_3` (SVM model with polynomial kernel of degree 2) considering `cost = 0.1` and `gamma = 0.5`, using the following code:

```
set.seed(1)
svmfit_3 <- svm(formula = income ~ beef + chicken,
                data = training_sample,
                kernel = "polynomial", degree = 2,
                gamma = 0.5,
                cost = 0.1,
                probability = TRUE)
summary(svmfit_3)
```

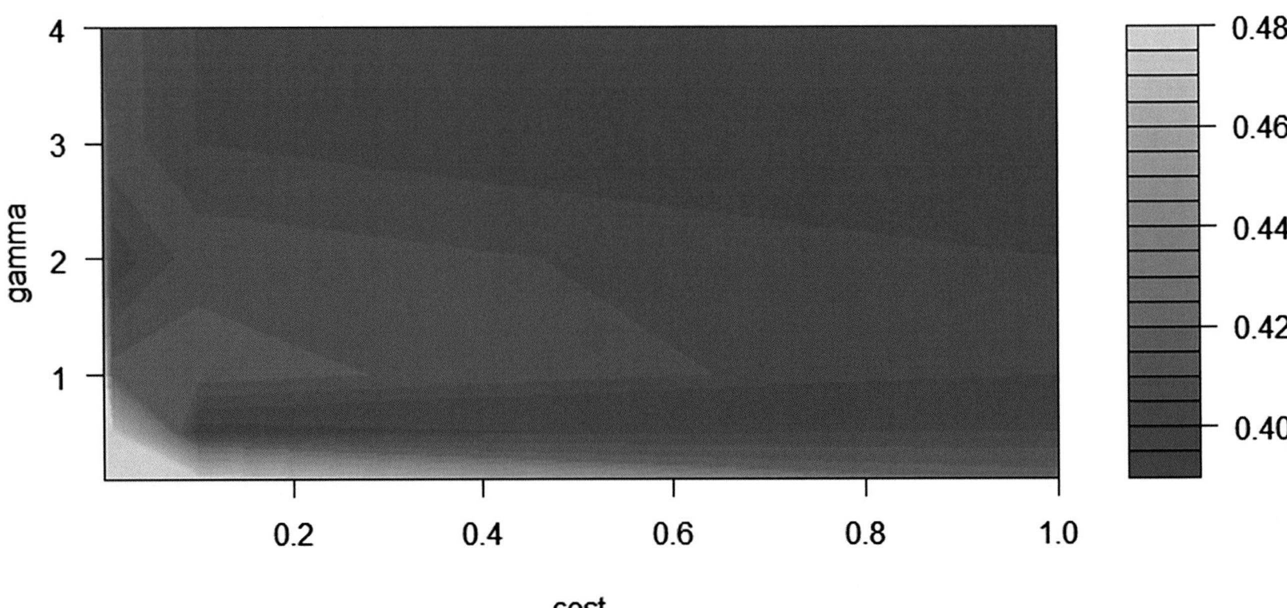

FIGURE 18.31 Performance of a support vector machine with a polynomial kernel of degree 2.

The output obtained through the code `summary(svmfit_3)` was purposely omitted. Next, we will build the SVM classification plot for the model `svmfit_3`. In this sense, we can type the following code, which will generate the graph shown in Figure 18.32. Note that the following code also generates in the dataset `training_sample` two new variables: `index_3` (support or not support for each observation) and `fitted_3` (classification of each observation in group 1 or 2 as a result of the proposed model).

```
background["fitted_color_3"] <- predict(object = svmfit_3,
                                        newdata = background)

training_sample %>%
  rownames_to_column("index_3") %>%
  mutate(index_3 = ifelse(index_3 %in% svmfit_3$index,
                          yes = "support",
                          no = "not_support"),
         fitted_3 = predict(object = svmfit_3, data = .)) -> training_sample

background %>%
  ggplot(aes(x = chicken, y = beef)) + geom_tile(aes(fill = fitted_color_3)) +
  geom_point(data = training_sample, aes(x = chicken, y = beef, color = income, shape = index_3), size = 3) +
  scale_fill_manual(values = c("cornsilk2", "aliceblue")) +
  scale_color_manual(values = c("orange","darkorchid")) +
  scale_shape_manual(values = c(1, 4)) +
  labs(x = "chicken",
       y = "beef",
       fill = "Predicted Category",
       shape = "SV",
```

Continued

```
    color = "Observed Category") +
  theme(panel.background = element_rect(NA),
        panel.border = element_rect(color = "black", fill = NA),
        legend.position = "bottom",
        legend.text = element_text(size = 8),
        legend.title = element_text(size = 8))
```

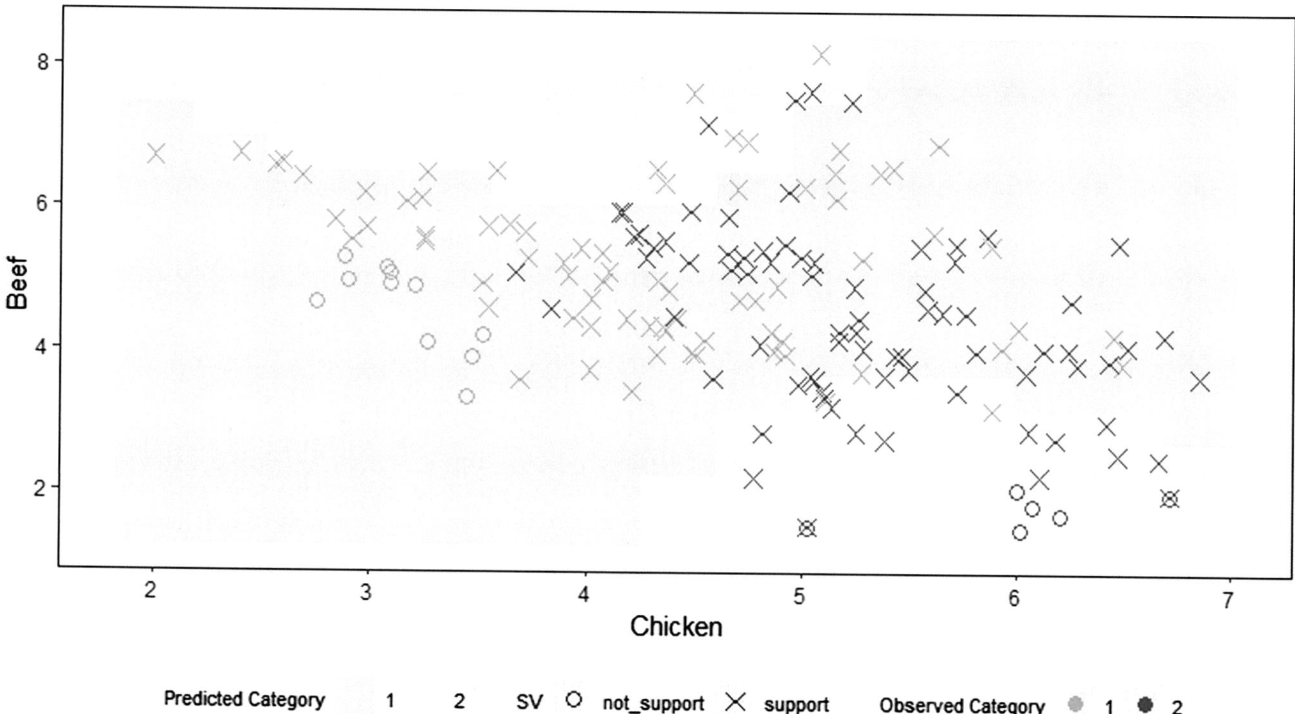

FIGURE 18.32 Support vector machine classification plot for the model `svmfit_3`.

Next, through the following code, we will build the confusion matrix for the model `svmfit_3`, considering a cutoff equal to 0.5. The confusion matrix generated with the indicators `accuracy`, `sensitivity`, and `specificity` can be found in Figure 18.33. We can verify that, for a cutoff of 0.5, the SVM model with a polynomial kernel of degree 2 is worse than the one obtained from the SVM model with a linear kernel (`svmfit_2`) estimated earlier. Despite this fact, we will compare these models through analysis of their respective areas under the ROC curves later in this chapter.

```
probs_fit_3 <- predict(svmfit_3,
                       newdata = validation_sample,
                       probability = TRUE)

pred_probs_fit_3 <- attr(x = probs_fit_3, which = "probabilities")[,1] <= 0.5

confusionMatrix(
  data = table(pred_probs_fit_3,
               validation_sample$income == 1)[2:1, 2:1]
)
```

```
Confusion Matrix and Statistics


pred_probs_fit_3 TRUE FALSE
           TRUE    33    37
           FALSE   42    48

               Accuracy : 0.5062
                 95% CI : (0.4262, 0.5861)
    No Information Rate : 0.5312
    P-Value [Acc > NIR] : 0.7622

                  Kappa : 0.0047

 Mcnemar's Test P-Value : 0.6527

            Sensitivity : 0.4400
            Specificity : 0.5647
         Pos Pred Value : 0.4714
         Neg Pred Value : 0.5333
             Prevalence : 0.4688
         Detection Rate : 0.2062
   Detection Prevalence : 0.4375
      Balanced Accuracy : 0.5024

       'Positive' Class : TRUE
```

FIGURE 18.33 Confusion matrix for the model svmfit_3 (validation sample and cutoff = 0.5).

Then, by creating a dataset called plot_data_polyn, we can build a graph to analyze the sensitivity and specificity values as a function of the cutoff and the ROC curve referring to our SVM model with a polynomial kernel with degree 2. The following code, similar to the one performed when estimating the SVM model with a linear kernel, has this purpose.

The first line of this code (predict(object = svmfit_3, newdata = barbecue, probability = TRUE)) generates the classifications of each observation as well as the allocation probabilities in each of the groups of the dependent variable. Figure 18.34 shows these outputs for the first 20 observations of the complete sample with 400 observations (dataset

```
 1  2  3  4  5  6  7  8  9 10
 2  1  2  2  2  2  1  2  2  2

11 12 13 14 15 16 17 18 19 20
 1  1  1  1  2  1  2  2  1  1

attr(,"probabilities")
           2         1
1  0.6202937 0.3797063
2  0.4411331 0.5588669
3  0.5045367 0.4954633
4  0.5048346 0.4951654
5  0.5271210 0.4728790
6  0.5013460 0.4986540
7  0.2974370 0.7025630
8  0.6192033 0.3807967
9  0.6287911 0.3712089
10 0.5031024 0.4968976
11 0.4186420 0.5813580
12 0.2647321 0.7352679
13 0.4917017 0.5082983
14 0.4973991 0.5026009
15 0.5045287 0.4954713
16 0.4675191 0.5324809
17 0.5575196 0.4424804
18 0.5020818 0.4979182
19 0.4369414 0.5630586
20 0.4893464 0.5106536
```

FIGURE 18.34 Classification and probabilities for the first 20 observations of the dataset barbecue for the model svmfit_3.

barbecue), remembering that the classification of each observation in a given group is defined based on the highest probability (probability greater than 0.5) for that group.

An attentive reader will notice how the probabilities and, consequently, the classifications differ from those obtained by estimating the SVM model with a linear kernel. An example of this occurs in the first observation of the dataset (while for the previous model, svmfit_2, the classification of the first observation indicates group 1, as shown in Figure 18.28, the same does not occur for the model svmfit_3, as shown in Figure 18.34). In fact, there are several differences between the classifications of the two models because of the change in fitted values from different kernels, which makes indicators of accuracy, sensitivity, specificity, and AUC quite different.

```
predict(object = svmfit_3, newdata = barbecue, probability = TRUE)

probs_polyn <- predict(object = svmfit_3,
                       newdata = barbecue,
                       probability = TRUE)
probs_polyn

attr(x = probs_polyn, which = "probabilities")[,1]

pred_probs_polyn <- attr(x = probs_polyn, which = "probabilities")[,1]

predictions_polyn <- prediction(predictions = pred_probs_polyn,
                                labels = barbecue$income)

sens_data_polyn <- performance(prediction.obj = predictions_polyn,
                               measure = "sens")

sensitivity_polyn <- sens_data_polyn@y.values[[1]]

spec_data_polyn <- performance(prediction.obj = predictions_polyn,
                               measure = "spec")

specificity_polyn <- spec_data_polyn@y.values[[1]]

cutoffs_polyn <- predictions_polyn@cutoffs[[1]]

plot_data_polyn <- cbind.data.frame(cutoffs_polyn,
                                    specificity_polyn,
                                    sensitivity_polyn)
```

In a similar way to the one performed for the SVM model with a linear kernel, we will build graphs with the sensitivity and specificity curves for the cutoff values as well as the ROC curve for our SVM model with polynomial kernel with degree 2. To do so, we will type the following code, which will generate the graphics in Figure 18.35:

```
plot_data_polyn %>%
  ggplot() +
  geom_line(aes(x = cutoffs_polyn, y = specificity_polyn, color = "Specificity"),
            size = 2) +
  geom_point(aes(x = cutoffs_polyn, y = specificity_polyn),
             color = "orange", size = 2, shape = 15) +
  geom_line(aes(x = cutoffs_polyn, y = sensitivity_polyn, color = "Sensitivity"),
            size = 2) +
  geom_point(aes(x = cutoffs_polyn, y = sensitivity_polyn),
             color = "darkorchid", size = 2, shape = 16) +
  labs(x = "Cutoffs",
       y = "Sensitivity/Specificity") +
  scale_color_manual("Label:",
                     values = c("orange", "darkorchid")) +
  theme_bw()
```

Continued

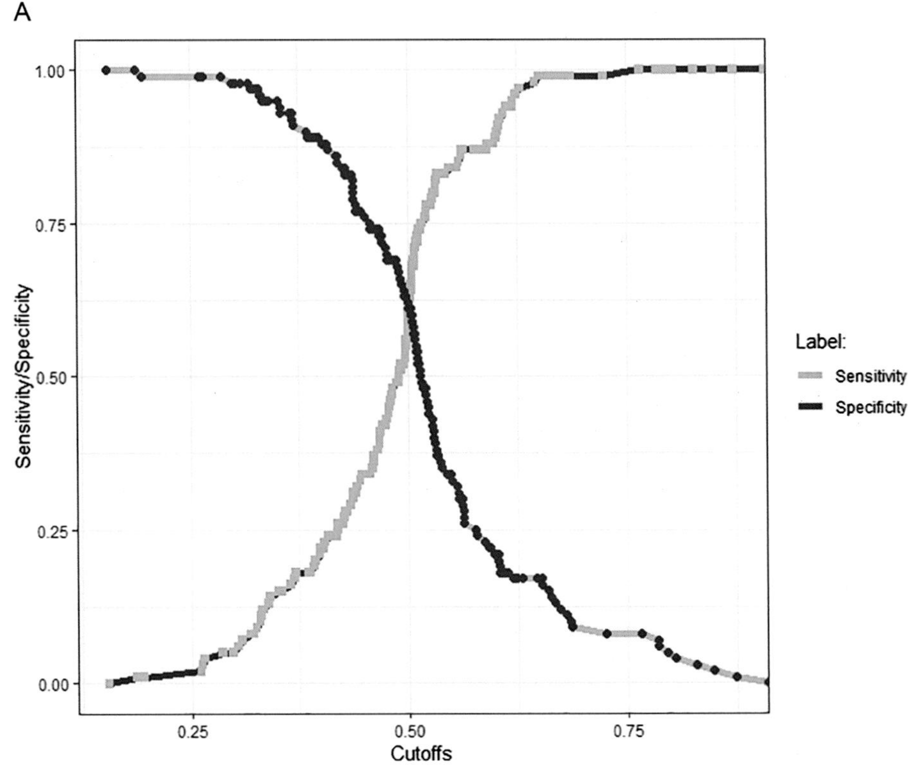

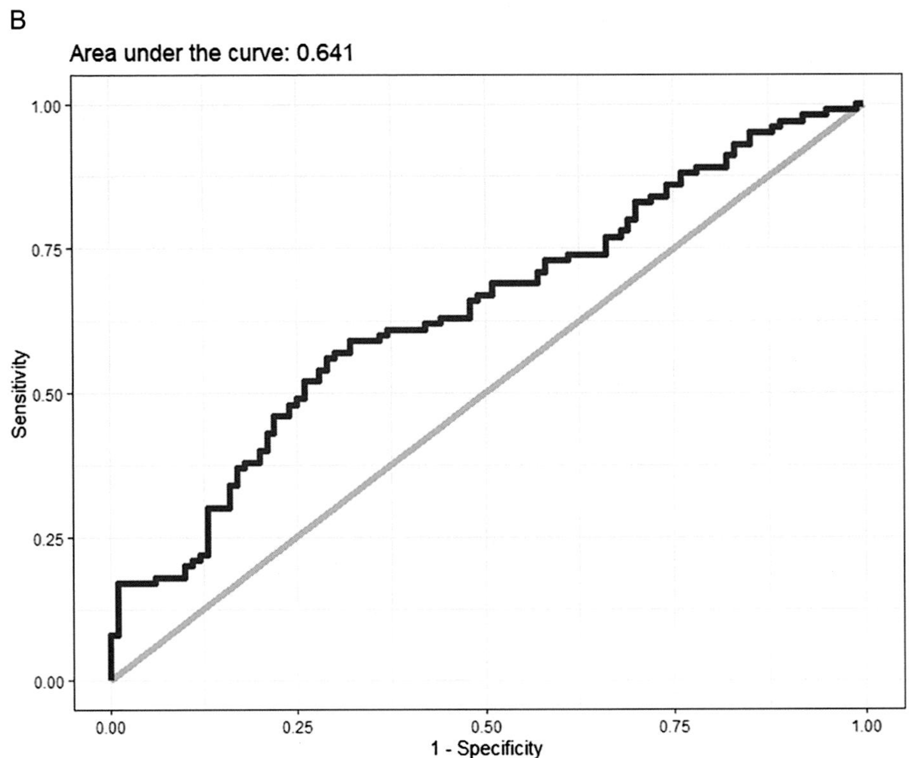

FIGURE 18.35 Sensitivity, specificity, and ROC curves for the support vector machine model with a polynomial kernel of degree 2. (A) Sensitivity and specificity curves for the cutoff values. (B) ROC curve.

```
au_roc_polyn <- performance(prediction.obj = predictions_polyn,
                            measure = "auc")

plot_data_polyn %>%
  ggplot() +
  geom_segment(aes(x = 0, xend = 1, y = 0, yend = 1),
               color="orange", size = 2) +
  geom_line(aes(x = 1 - specificity_polyn, y = sensitivity_polyn),
            color = "darkorchid", size = 2) +
  labs(x = "1 - Specificity",
       y = "Sensitivity",
       title = paste("Area under the curve:",
                     round(au_roc_polyn@y.values[[1]], 3))) +
  theme_bw()
```

Finally, we will estimate an SVM model with a radial kernel. Following the logic adopted in this section for the linear and polynomial kernel models with degree 2, we will proceed with the definition of the best performance (tuning model) for the radial model, using the following code. We will manually define the hyperparameters set through the argument `ranges = list(cost = c(0.001, 0.01, 0.1, 1, 10, 100), gamma = c(0.1, 0.5, 1, 2, 3, 4))`, with the value possibilities for `cost` and `gamma`.

```
set.seed (1)
tune_out_radial <- tune(method = "svm",
                        train.x = income ~ beef + chicken,
                        data = training_sample,
                        kernel = "radial",
                        probability = TRUE,
                        ranges = list(
                          cost = c(0.001, 0.01, 0.1, 1, 10, 100),
                          gamma = c(0.1, 0.5, 1, 2, 3, 4)
                          )
                        )

summary(tune_out_radial)
plot(tune_out_radial)
```

This code generates the outputs presented in Figure 18.36 and the graph shown in Figure 18.37. For the set of values of `cost` and `gamma` manually defined, we can verify, using Figure 18.36, that the model with `cost` equal to 10 and `gamma` equal to 4 presents the smallest classification error (0.1042), and these hyperparameters will be used for estimation of the SVM model with a radial kernel in the sequence.

In this way, we will estimate the model `svmfit_4` (SVM model with a radial kernel) considering the value of `cost = 10` and `gamma = 4`, as defined in the tuning (Figure 18.36), using the following code:

```
set.seed(1)
svmfit_4 <- svm(income ~ beef + chicken,
                data = training_sample,
                kernel = "radial",
                gamma = 4,
                cost = 10,
                probability = TRUE)

summary(svmfit_4)
```

As for the previous models, the output obtained through the code `summary(svmfit_4)` was purposely omitted. We will then prepare the SVM classification plot for the model `svmfit_4`, typing the following code, which will

```
Parameter tuning of 'svm':

- best parameters:
 cost gamma
   10     4

- best performance: 0.1041667

- Detailed performance results:
    cost gamma     error dispersion
1  1e-03   0.1 0.4791667 0.07414638
2  1e-02   0.1 0.4791667 0.07414638
3  1e-01   0.1 0.2333333 0.06860605
4  1e+00   0.1 0.2166667 0.07556373
5  1e+01   0.1 0.2083333 0.06514466
6  1e+02   0.1 0.1833333 0.04890782
7  1e-03   0.5 0.4791667 0.07414638
8  1e-02   0.5 0.4791667 0.07414638
9  1e-01   0.5 0.2083333 0.07349309
10 1e+00   0.5 0.1791667 0.06226809
11 1e+01   0.5 0.1500000 0.04025382
12 1e+02   0.5 0.1375000 0.05572890
13 1e-03   1.0 0.4791667 0.07414638
14 1e-02   1.0 0.4791667 0.07414638
15 1e-01   1.0 0.2041667 0.07466489
16 1e+00   1.0 0.1500000 0.02913358
17 1e+01   1.0 0.1208333 0.04988412
18 1e+02   1.0 0.1250000 0.06804138
19 1e-03   2.0 0.4791667 0.07414638
20 1e-02   2.0 0.4791667 0.07414638
21 1e-01   2.0 0.1666667 0.04811252
22 1e+00   2.0 0.1125000 0.05215273
23 1e+01   2.0 0.1166667 0.06148873
24 1e+02   2.0 0.1250000 0.06211300
25 1e-03   3.0 0.4791667 0.07414638
26 1e-02   3.0 0.4791667 0.07414638
27 1e-01   3.0 0.1500000 0.03513642
28 1e+00   3.0 0.1125000 0.05215273
29 1e+01   3.0 0.1083333 0.05957670
30 1e+02   3.0 0.1250000 0.05892557
31 1e-03   4.0 0.4791667 0.07414638
32 1e-02   4.0 0.4791667 0.07414638
33 1e-01   4.0 0.1416667 0.04479032
34 1e+00   4.0 0.1166667 0.06148873
35 1e+01   4.0 0.1041667 0.05973837
36 1e+02   4.0 0.1125000 0.05215273
```

FIGURE 18.36 Parameter tuning of a support vector machine with a radial kernel.

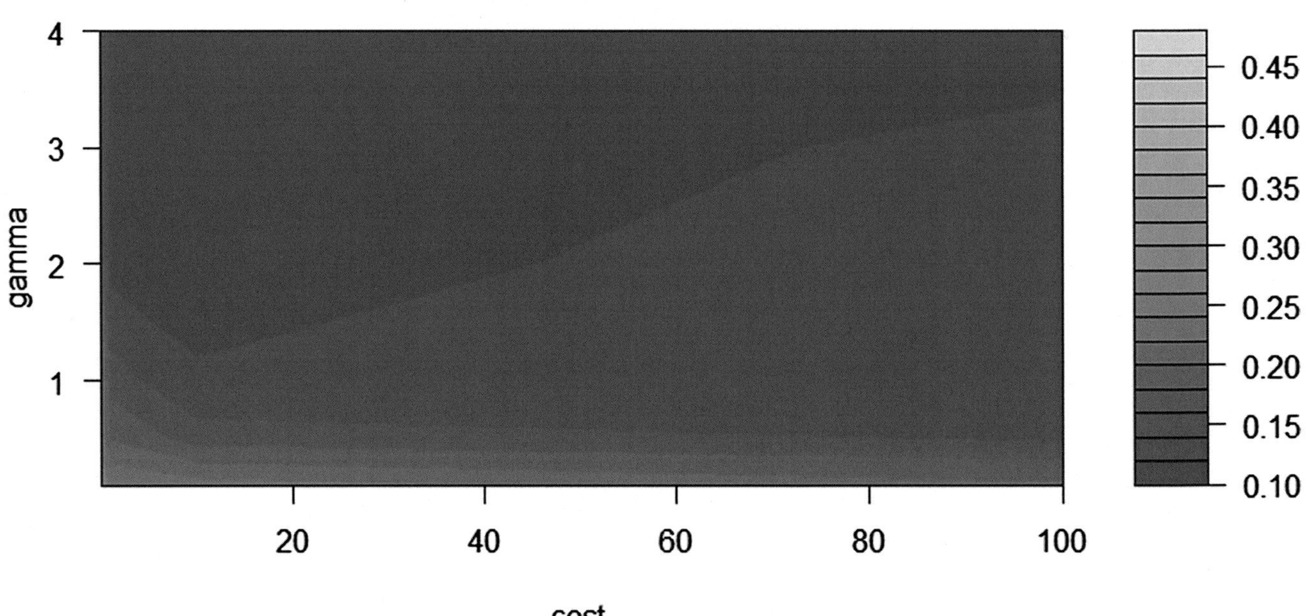

FIGURE 18.37 Performance of a support vector machine with a radial kernel.

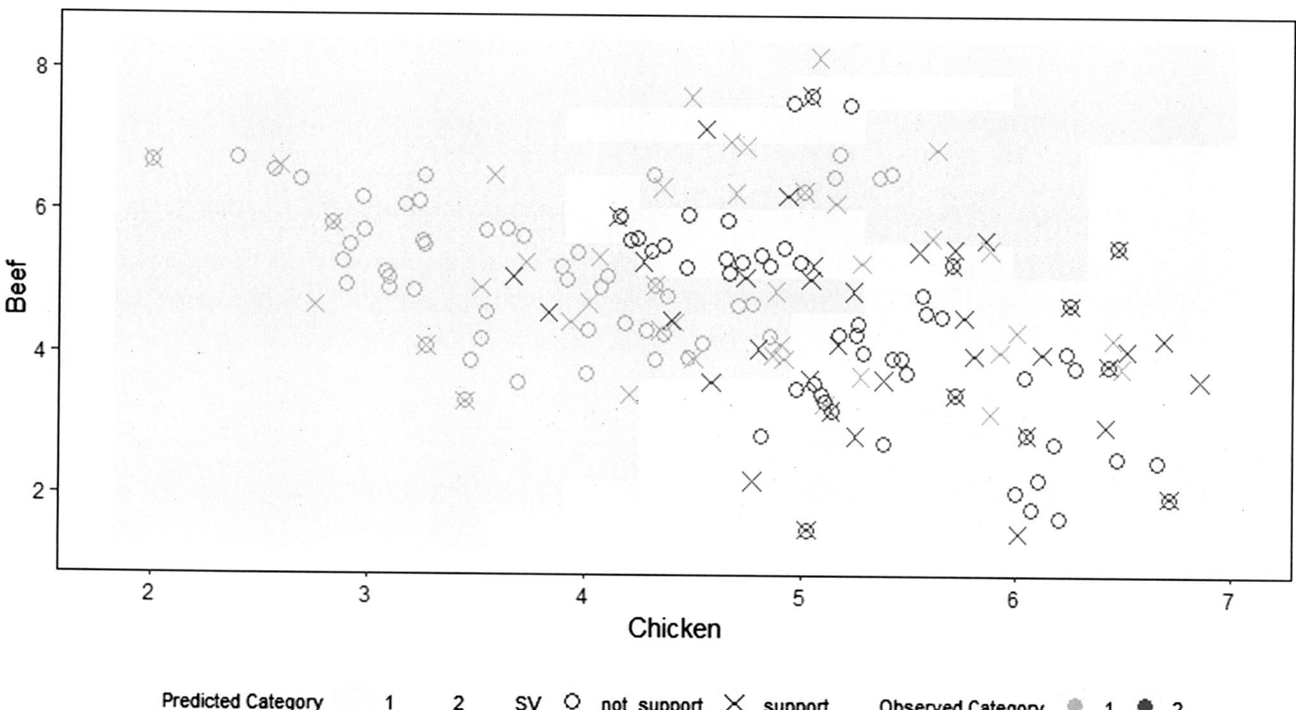

FIGURE 18.38 Support vector machine classification plot for the model `svmfit_4`.

generate the graph shown in Figure 18.38. Note that the following code also generates in the dataset `training_sample` two new variables: `index_4` (support or not support for each observation) and `fitted_4` (classification of each observation in group 1 or 2 as a result of the proposed model), with visible differences from to the corresponding variables `index_3` and `fitted_3` generated when estimating the SVM model with a polynomial kernel of degree 2.

```
background["fitted_color_4"] <- predict(object = svmfit_4,
                                        newdata = background)

training_sample %>%
  rownames_to_column("index_4") %>%
  mutate(index_4 = ifelse(index_4 %in% svmfit_4$index,
                          yes = "support",
                          no = "not_support"),
  fitted_4 = predict(object = svmfit_4, data = .)) -> training_sample

background %>%
  ggplot(aes(x = chicken, y = beef)) + geom_tile(aes(fill = fitted_color_4)) +
  geom_point(data = training_sample, aes(x = chicken, y = beef, color = income, shape = index_4),
  size = 3) +
  scale_fill_manual(values = c("cornsilk2", "aliceblue")) +
  scale_color_manual(values = c("orange","darkorchid")) +
  scale_shape_manual(values = c(1, 4)) +
  labs(x = "chicken",
       y = "beef",
       fill = "Predicted Category",
       shape = "SV",
```

Continued

```
        color = "Observed Category") +
  theme(panel.background = element_rect(NA),
        panel.border = element_rect(color = "black", fill = NA),
        legend.position = "bottom",
        legend.text = element_text(size = 8),
        legend.title = element_text(size = 8))
```

Following the same logic of the procedures adopted when estimating the previous models, we can build the confusion matrix for the model svmfit_4, also considering a cutoff equal to 0.5, using the following code.

```
probs_fit_4 <- predict(svmfit_4,
                       newdata = validation_sample,
                       probability = TRUE)

pred_probs_fit_4 <- attr(x = probs_fit_4, which = "probabilities")[,1] <= 0.5

confusionMatrix(
 data = table(pred_probs_fit_4,
              validation_sample$income == 1)[2:1, 2:1]
 )
```

The confusion matrix generated with the indicators accuracy, sensitivity, and specificity can be found in Figure 18.39. We can verify that, for a cutoff of 0.5, the SVM model with a radial kernel is better than those obtained from the SVM models with a linear kernel (svmfit_2) and with a polynomial kernel of degree 2 (svmfit_3).

```
Confusion Matrix and Statistics


pred_probs_fit_4 TRUE FALSE
           TRUE     59    14
           FALSE    16    71

               Accuracy : 0.8125
                 95% CI : (0.7433, 0.8698)
    No Information Rate : 0.5312
    P-Value [Acc > NIR] : 9.652e-14

                  Kappa : 0.6229

 Mcnemar's Test P-Value : 0.8551

            Sensitivity : 0.7867
            Specificity : 0.8353
         Pos Pred Value : 0.8082
         Neg Pred Value : 0.8161
             Prevalence : 0.4688
         Detection Rate : 0.3688
   Detection Prevalence : 0.4562
      Balanced Accuracy : 0.8110

       'Positive' Class : TRUE
```

FIGURE 18.39 Confusion matrix for the model svmfit_4 (validation sample and cutoff = 0.5).

From the creation of a dataset called plot_data_rad, it is possible to build a graph for analyzing the sensitivity and specificity values as a function of the cutoff and the ROC curve, referring to our SVM model with radial kernel, using the following code:

```
predict(object = svmfit_4, newdata = barbecue, probability = TRUE)

probs_rad <- predict(object = svmfit_4,
                     newdata = barbecue,
                     probability = TRUE)
probs_rad

attr(x = probs_rad, which = "probabilities")[,1]

pred_probs_rad <- attr(x = probs_rad, which = "probabilities")[,1]

predictions_rad <- prediction(predictions = pred_probs_rad,
                              labels = barbecue$income)

sens_data_rad <- performance(prediction.obj = predictions_rad,
                             measure = "sens")

sensitivity_rad <- sens_data_rad@y.values[[1]]

spec_data_rad <- performance(prediction.obj = predictions_rad,
                             measure = "spec")

specificity_rad <- spec_data_rad@y.values[[1]]

cutoffs_rad <- predictions_rad@cutoffs[[1]]

plot_data_rad <- cbind.data.frame(cutoffs_rad,
                                  specificity_rad,
                                  sensitivity_rad)
```

The first line of this code (`predict(object = svmfit_4, newdata = barbecue, probability = TRUE)`) generates the classifications of each observation and the allocation probabilities in each of the groups of the dependent variable. Figure 18.40 shows these outputs for the first 20 observations of the full sample with 400 observations (dataset `barbecue`).

```
 1  2  3  4  5  6  7  8  9 10
 1  1  1  1  1  1  1  2  1  2

11 12 13 14 15 16 17 18 19 20
 1  1  1  1  1  1  2  1  1  1

attr(,"probabilities")
            2          1
1  0.13608661 0.86391339
2  0.13212623 0.86787377
3  0.08657000 0.91343000
4  0.05449092 0.94550908
5  0.25479653 0.74520347
6  0.16898968 0.83101032
7  0.15468683 0.84531317
8  0.72720196 0.27279804
9  0.17052268 0.82947732
10 0.69878804 0.30121196
11 0.03402437 0.96597563
12 0.17052186 0.82947814
13 0.07804337 0.92195663
14 0.15062066 0.84937934
15 0.06375982 0.93624018
16 0.17044232 0.82955768
17 0.76028330 0.23971670
18 0.08803703 0.91196297
19 0.11635885 0.88364115
20 0.17046688 0.82953312
```

FIGURE 18.40 Classification and probabilities for the first 20 observations of the dataset `barbecue` for the model `svmfit_4`.

Here, we can also verify that the probabilities and, consequently, the classifications of the observations differ from those obtained by estimating SVM models with a linear kernel and a polynomial kernel of degree 2. This fact makes indicators of accuracy, sensitivity, specificity, and AUC quite different among models, as we will show in the next section.

Finally, we will build graphs with sensitivity and specificity curves for the cutoff values as well as the ROC curve for our SVM model with a radial kernel. To do so, we will type the following code, which will generate the graphs shown in Figure 18.41:

```
plot_data_rad %>%
  ggplot() +
  geom_line(aes(x = cutoffs_rad, y = specificity_rad, color = "Specificity"),
            size = 2) +
  geom_point(aes(x = cutoffs_rad, y = specificity_rad),
             color = "orange", size = 2, shape = 15) +
  geom_line(aes(x = cutoffs_rad, y = sensitivity_rad, color = "Sensitivity"),
            size = 2) +
  geom_point(aes(x = cutoffs_rad, y = sensitivity_rad),
             color = "darkorchid", size = 2, shape = 16) +
  labs(x = "Cutoffs",
       y = "Sensitivity/Specificity") +
  scale_color_manual("Label:",
                     values = c("orange", "darkorchid")) +
  theme_bw()

au_roc_rad <- performance(prediction.obj = predictions_rad,
                          measure = "auc")

plot_data_rad %>%
  ggplot() +
  geom_segment(aes(x = 0, xend = 1, y = 0, yend = 1),
               color="orange", size = 2) +
  geom_line(aes(x = 1 - specificity_rad, y = sensitivity_rad),
            color = "darkorchid", size = 2) +
  labs(x = "1 - Specificity",
       y = "Sensitivity",
       title = paste("Area under the curve:",
                     round(au_roc_rad@y.values[[1]], 3))) +
  theme_bw()
```

In the next section, we will estimate a binary logistic regression model using the same data so it will be possible to compare the models and their respective performance indicators.

Comparison of SVM models' performance to a binary logistic regression model

As studied in the "Estimation of the binary logistic regression model by maximum likelihood" section in Chapter 15, the parameters of a binary logistic regression model are estimated based on the definition of the probability of occurrence of a certain event defined in a qualitative dependent variable with two categories, as deduced in that chapter for the definition from Expression (15.10):

$$p_i = \frac{1}{1 + e^{-(Z_i)}} = \frac{1}{1 + e^{-(\alpha + \beta_1 \cdot X_{1i} + \beta_2 \cdot X_{2i} + \ldots + \beta_k \cdot X_{ki})}} \tag{18.26}$$

where the term in parentheses refers to what we call the logit (Z), α represents the constant, βj ($j = 1, \ldots, k$) are the estimated parameters for each explanatory variable, Xj are the predictor (explanatory) variables, and the subscript i represents each observation of the dataset ($i = 1, 2, \ldots, n$, where n is the size of the complete sample). It is important to highlight that Z does not represent the dependent variable, denominated by Y, and our objective with this

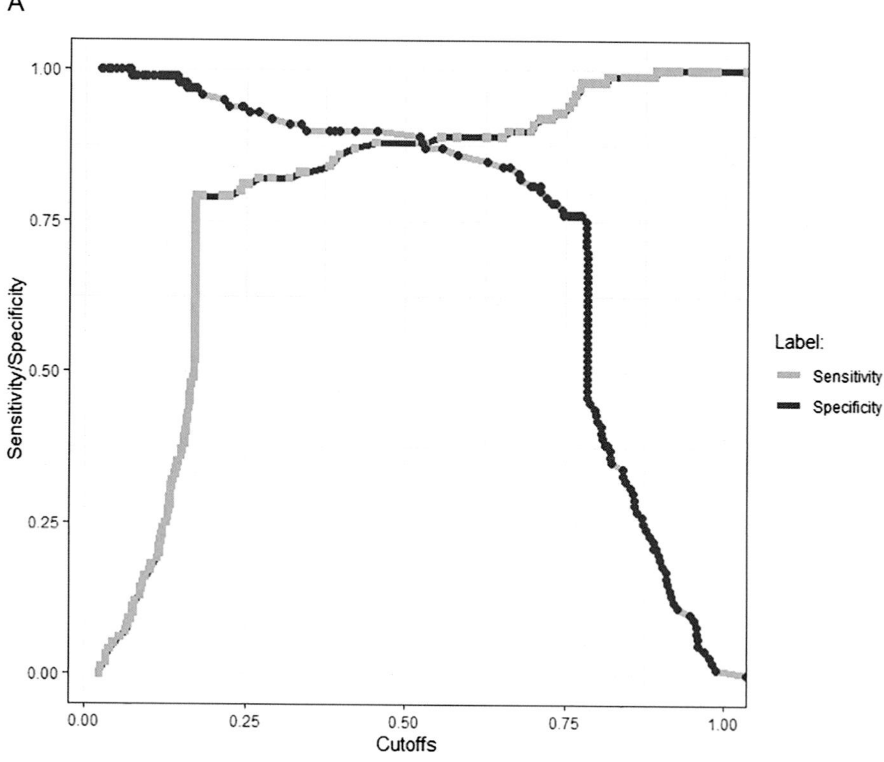

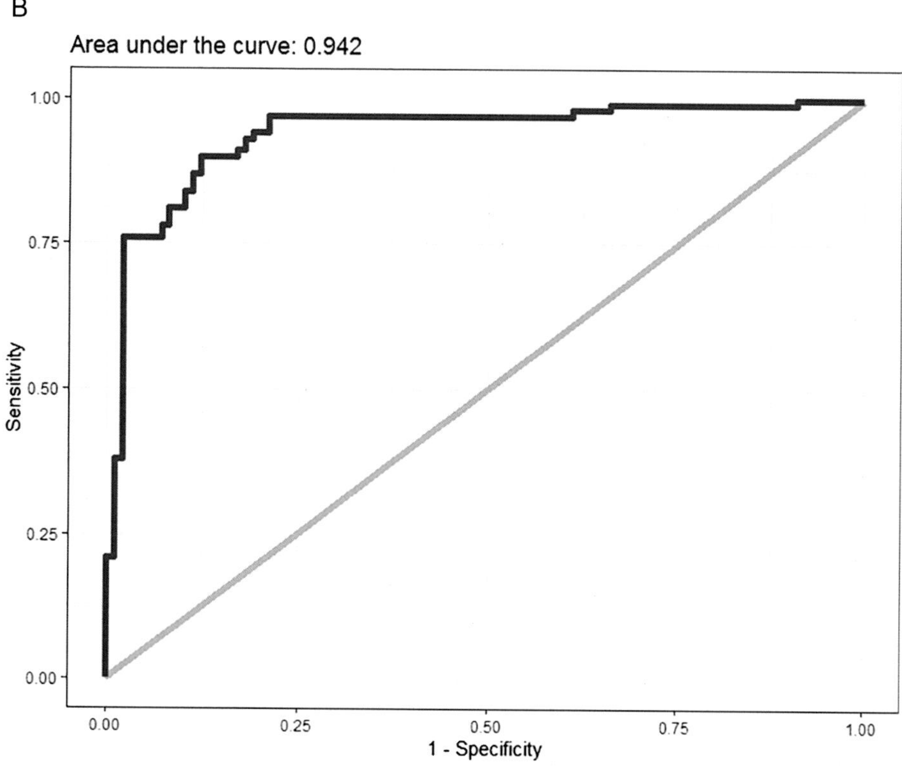

FIGURE 18.41 Sensitivity, specificity, and ROC curves for the support vector machine model with a radial kernel. (A) Sensitivity and specificity curves for the cutoff values. (B) ROC curve.

estimation is to define the *pi* probability expression for the occurrence of the event of interest for each observation, in function of logit *Zi*, or rather, in function of the estimated parameters for each explanatory variable.

Based on the Bernoulli distribution, we have defined in Chapter 15 the log likelihood function from Expression (15.15), from which the parameters of Expression (18.26) or Expression (15.10) can be estimated through its maximization:

$$LL = \sum_{i=1}^{n} \left\{ \left[(Y_i) \cdot \ln\left(\frac{e^{Z_i}}{1 + e^{Z_i}} \right) \right] + \left[(1 - Y_i) \cdot \ln\left(\frac{1}{1 + e^{Z_i}} \right) \right] \right\} = \max \tag{18.27}$$

This discussion is important because it shows the fundamental difference between the estimations of the SVM models and the binary logistic regression models. Although SVMs do not, in fact, present a predictive equation with parameters explicitly defined and estimated from a deterministic optimization method, as we have seen throughout this chapter, logistic regression models, which fall within the class of GLMs, clearly present the parameters estimated from the process of maximizing the log likelihood function.

In the estimation of the binary logistic regression model with the data from our example, it makes no sense to discuss the overfitting problem. In this section, we will not use the process of defining training and validation samples because the complete dataset `barbecue` will be considered the training sample itself from which the model will be estimated ("trained").

Having made these considerations, we will proceed to the estimation of the binary logistic regression model itself. Following the steps proposed in Chapter 15, we can enter the following sequence of commands. If the reader intends to analyze the outputs and parameters of the estimated model (object `logit_model`), which is purposely omitted here, he or she can just command `summary(logit_model)` after estimating the model, that is, after commanding the first line of the following code. Through this same sequence of commands, it is possible to build the confusion matrix for the estimated `logit_model` with a cutoff equal to 0.5 (outputs also omitted) as well as create a dataset entitled `plot_data_logit`, through which it will be possible to build the graph for analyzing the values of sensitivity and specificity as a function of the cutoff and the ROC curve referring to our binary logistic regression model.

```
logit_model <- glm(formula = income ~ beef + chicken,
                   data = barbecue,
                   family = "binomial")

confusionMatrix(table(predict(logit_model, type = "response") >= 0.5,
                      barbecue$income == 1)[2:1, 2:1]
               )

preds_logit_model <- prediction(predictions = logit_model$fitted.values,
                                labels = barbecue$income)

data_roc_logit <- performance(preds_logit_model, measure = "sens")

sensitivity_logit <- (performance(preds_logit_model, measure = "sens"))@y.values[[1]]

specificity_logit <- (performance(preds_logit_model, measure = "spec"))@y.values[[1]]

cutoffs_logit <- data_roc_logit@x.values[[1]]

plot_data_logit <- cbind.data.frame(cutoffs_logit,
                                    specificity_logit,
                                    sensitivity_logit)
```

Thus, similar to what we did for the SVM models estimated in the previous section, we will build the graphs with the sensitivity and specificity curves for the cutoff values as well as the ROC curve for our binary logistic regression model. To do so, we can type the following code, which will generate the graphics shown in Figure 18.42:

```
plot_data_logit %>%
  ggplot() +
  geom_line(aes(x = cutoffs_logit, y = specificity_logit,
                color = "Specificity"), size = 2) +
```

Continued

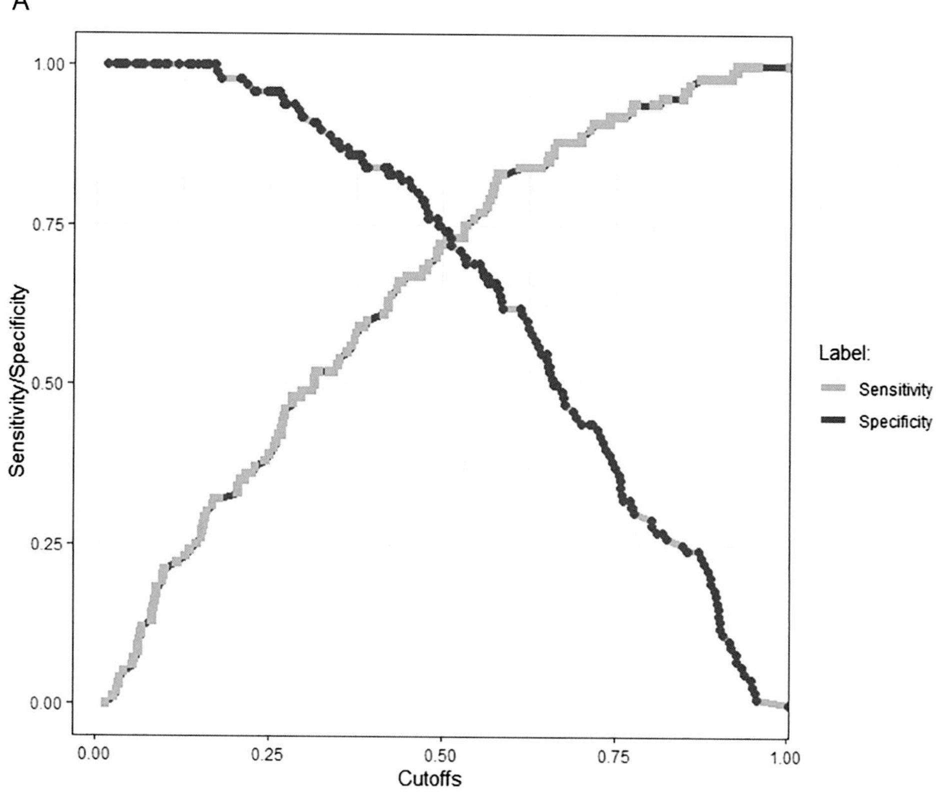

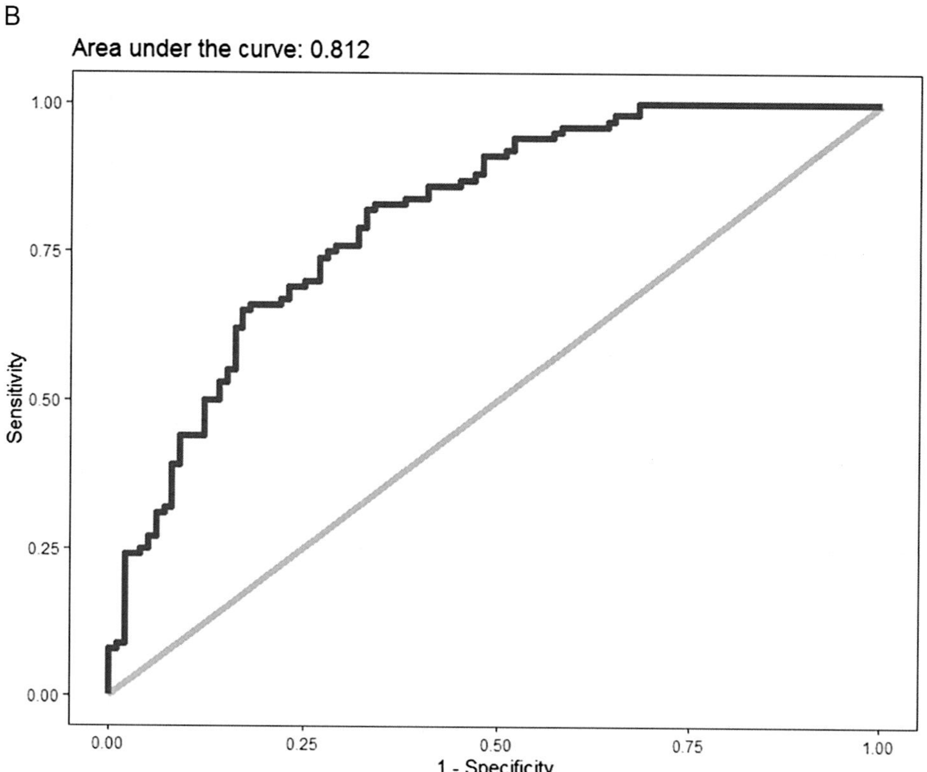

FIGURE 18.42 Sensitivity, specificity, and ROC curves for the binary logistic regression model. (A) Sensitivity and specificity curves for the cutoff values. (B) ROC curve.

```
  geom_point(aes(x = cutoffs_logit, y = specificity_logit),
             color = "orange", size = 2, shape = 15) +
  geom_line(aes(x = cutoffs_logit, y = sensitivity_logit,
             color = "Sensitivity"), size = 2) +
  geom_point(aes(x = cutoffs_logit, y = sensitivity_logit),
             color = "darkorchid", size = 2, shape = 16) +
  labs(x = "Cutoffs",
       y = "Sensitivity/Specificity") +
  scale_color_manual("Label:",
                        values = c("orange", "darkorchid")) +
  theme_bw()

au_roc_logit <- performance(prediction.obj = preds_logit_model,
                            measure = "auc")

  plot_data_logit %>%
    ggplot() +
    geom_segment(aes(x = 0, xend = 1, y = 0, yend = 1),
                 color="orange", size = 2) +
    geom_line(aes(x = 1 - specificity_logit, y = sensitivity_logit),
              color = "darkorchid", size = 2) +
    labs(x = "1 - Specificity",
      y = "Sensitivity",
      title = paste("Area under the curve:",
                        round(au_roc_logit@y.values[[1]], 3))) +
  theme_bw()
```

To compare the performance of the SVM models with the logistic model, we propose the following code, which allows the reader to analyze the sensitivity, specificity, accuracy (all for a cutoff equal to 0.5), and AUC for the four models estimated (SVM with a linear kernel, SVM with a polynomial kernel of degree 2, SVM with a radial kernel, and binary logistic regression model). We emphasize that the comparison of the first three indicators can generate misinterpretations when choosing the best model because sensitivity, specificity, and accuracy values can be quite sensitive to changes in the cutoff. It is for this reason that we have included the AUC in the analysis. Table 18.2 shows the consolidated results of the estimated models, obtained from the following code and through the use of the functions `data.frame()` and `rbind.data.frame()`:

TABLE 18.2 Sensitivity, specificity, accuracy (cutoff = 0.5), and AUC for estimated SVM and binary logistic regression models.

Model	Sensitivity	Specificity	Accuracy	AUC
SVM with a linear kernel	0.707	0.694	0.700	0.799
SVM with a polynomial kernel of degree 2	0.440	0.565	0.506	0.641
SVM with a radial kernel	0.787	0.835	0.812	0.942
Binary logistic regression model	0.280	0.260	0.270	0.812

```
df1 <- data.frame(Model = "SVM with Linear Kernel",
                  Sensitivity = round(confusionMatrix(data = table(pred_probs_fit_2,
                                                    validation_sample$income == 1)
                                      [2:1, 2:1])[["byClass"]][["Sensitivity"]],3),
                  Specificity = round(confusionMatrix(data = table(pred_probs_fit_2,
                                                    validation_sample$income == 1)
                                      [2:1, 2:1])[["byClass"]][["Specificity"]],3),
```

Continued

```
            Accuracy = round(confusionMatrix(data = table(pred_probs_fit_2,
                                                          validation_sample$income == 1)
                                                 [2:1, 2:1])[["overall"]][["Accuracy"]],3),
            AUC = round(au_roc_linear@y.values[[1]], 3))

df2 <- data.frame(Model = "SVM with Polynomial Kernel of Degree 2",
            Sensitivity = round(confusionMatrix(data = table(pred_probs_fit_3,
                                                          validation_sample$income == 1)
                                                 [2:1, 2:1])[["byClass"]][["Sensitivity"]],3),
            Specificity = round(confusionMatrix(data = table(pred_probs_fit_3,
                                                          validation_sample$income == 1)
                                                 [2:1, 2:1])[["byClass"]][["Specificity"]],3),
            Accuracy = round(confusionMatrix(data = table(pred_probs_fit_3,
                                                          validation_sample$income == 1)
                                                 [2:1, 2:1])[["overall"]][["Accuracy"]],3),
            AUC = round(au_roc_polyn@y.values[[1]], 3))

df3 <- data.frame(Model = "SVM with Radial Kernel",
            Sensitivity = round(confusionMatrix(data = table(pred_probs_fit_4,
                                                          validation_sample$income == 1)
                                                 [2:1, 2:1])[["byClass"]][["Sensitivity"]],3),
            Specificity = round(confusionMatrix(data = table(pred_probs_fit_4,
                                                          validation_sample$income == 1)
                                                 [2:1, 2:1])[["byClass"]][["Specificity"]],3),
            Accuracy = round(confusionMatrix(data = table(pred_probs_fit_4,
                                                          validation_sample$income == 1)
                                                 [2:1, 2:1])[["overall"]][["Accuracy"]],3),
            AUC = round(au_roc_rad@y.values[[1]], 3))

df4 <- data.frame(Model = "Binary Logistic Regression Model",
            Sensitivity = round(confusionMatrix(table(predict(logit_model, type = "response") >= 0.5,
                                                      barbecue$income == 1)
                                                [2:1, 2:1])[["byClass"]][["Sensitivity"]],3),
            Specificity = round(confusionMatrix(table(predict(logit_model, type = "response") >= 0.5,
                                                      barbecue$income == 1)
                                                [2:1, 2:1])[["byClass"]][["Specificity"]],3),
            Accuracy = round(confusionMatrix(table(predict(logit_model, type = "response") >= 0.5,
                                                      barbecue$income == 1)
                                                [2:1, 2:1])[["overall"]][["Accuracy"]],3),
            AUC = round(au_roc_logit@y.values[[1]], 3))

rbind.data.frame(df1, df2, df3, df4)
```

The results presented in Table 18.2 show that the best model for the global classification of observations based on the behavior of the data of the outcome variable *(income)*, conditional on the behavior of the predictor variables *beef* and *chicken* and regardless of the cutoff, is the SVM model with a radial kernel, which showed an AUC equal to 0.942. A curious reader may wish to compare the four models by constructing a graph showing the respective ROC curves. The following code serves this purpose, and the generated graph is shown in Figure 18.43:

```
plot_data_logit %>%
  ggplot() +
  geom_segment(aes(x = 0, xend = 1, y = 0, yend = 1),
               color="orange", size = 2) +
  geom_line(aes(x = 1 - specificity_linear, y = sensitivity_linear,
                color = paste("Linear:", "AUC =", round(au_roc_linear@y.values[[1]], 3))), size = 2) +
```

Continued

```
geom_line(aes(x = 1 - specificity_polyn, y = sensitivity_polyn,
            color = paste("Polynomial:", "AUC =", round(au_roc_polyn@y.values[[1]], 3))), size = 2) +
geom_line(aes(x = 1 - specificity_rad, y = sensitivity_rad,
            color = paste("Radial:", "AUC =", round(au_roc_rad@y.values[[1]], 3))), size = 2) +
geom_line(aes(x = 1 - specificity_logit, y = sensitivity_logit,
            color = paste("Logit:", "AUC =", round(au_roc_logit@y.values[[1]], 3))), size = 2) +
scale_color_viridis_d("Label:") +
labs(x = "1 - Specificity",
     y = "Sensitivity") +
theme(panel.background = element_rect(NA),
      panel.border = element_rect(color = "black", fill = NA),
      legend.position = "bottom",
      legend.text = element_text(size = 10),
      legend.title = element_text(size = 10)
      )
```

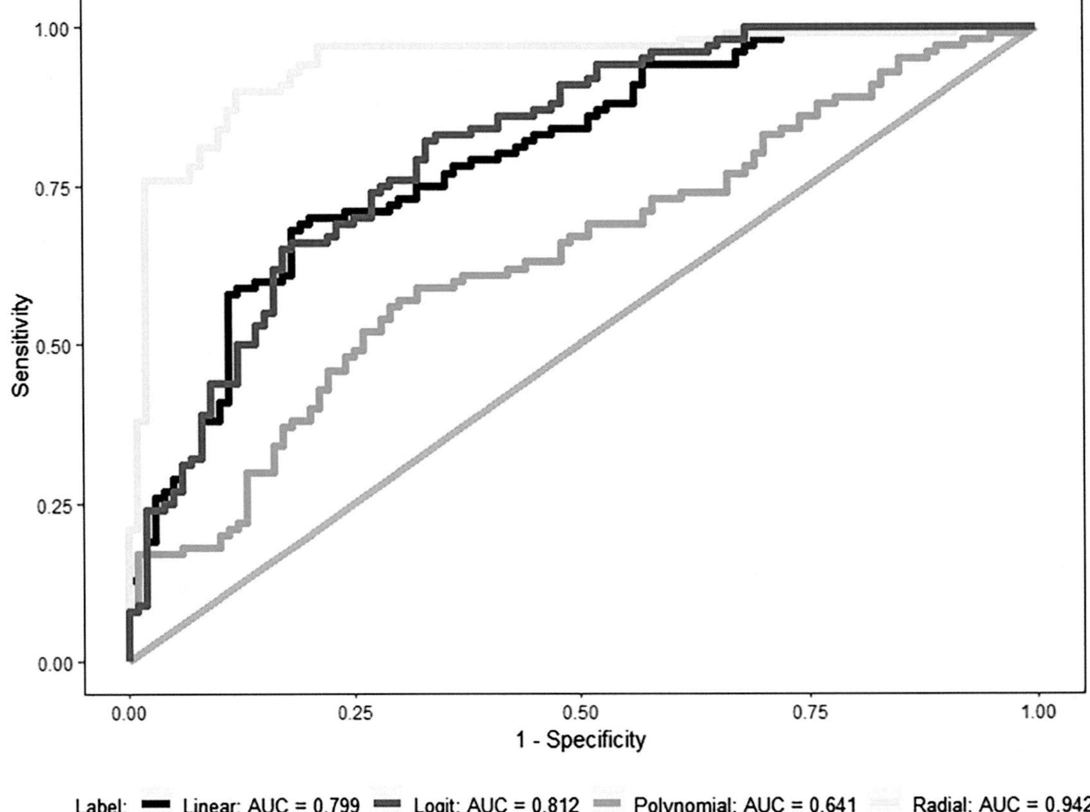

FIGURE 18.43 Comparison of ROC curves in support vector machine and binary logistic regression models.

Final remarks

SVM models are techniques with great predictive capabilities, especially when the aim is to classify observations based on a certain criterion established through a categorical outcome variable and based on the behavior of predictor (explanatory) variables.

These are interesting techniques, especially when the phenomenon under study does not present itself in a linear manner in relation to the behavior of predictor variables. However, unlike supervised models of the GLM or GLMM type studied in Chapters 14 to 17, it is a good practice for the estimation of SVM models to use sampling techniques by cross-validation, that is, creation of subsets from the original set (training and validation samples), because this procedure helps us evaluate the existence or nonexistence of the overfitting problem.

As mentioned earlier in this chapter, the process of maximizing a model's performance without overfitting or creating a too-high variance is known as *tuning*. In analytics and machine learning, this procedure is accomplished by selecting appropriate hyperparameters that will define the best performance configuration for the model under analysis.

Exercise

1. A group of enologists intended to assess wine label classification into two groups, from quantitative characteristics (predictor variables) related to the chemical composition and hue of the drinks. In this sense, based on the preliminary classification of 500 labels (variable *group*), the variables presented in the following table were raised.

Variable	Description
group	Dependent binary variable that corresponds to the fact that the classifier represents group 1 or group 2 for a specific wine (label).
flavonoid	Photochemical antioxidant and anti-inflammatory level of flavonoids. This variable presents the amount, in grams, of flavonoids per liter of wine.
hue	Measure of the color of the beverage through the hue angle. The hue angle starts on the positive axis of the abscissa and is expressed in degrees: 0 degrees corresponds to red, 90 degrees corresponds to yellow (positive axis of the ordinates), 180 degrees corresponds to green (negative axis of the abscissa), and 270 degrees corresponds to blue (negative axis of the ordinates). The interpretation of differences in wine tone can be done as follows: red (330 to 25 degrees), orange (25 to 70 degrees), yellow (70 to 100 degrees), green (100 to 200 degrees), blue (200 to 295 degrees), and violet (295 to 330 degrees). In this way, the hue angle refers to the color itself and is related to the wavelength of the visible spectrum.

The dataset for this research is found in the `wine.RData` file. In this sense, we would like you to:

a. Construct a scatter plot that shows the dispersion of observations in groups, with the *flavonoid* variable on the ordinate axis and the *hue* variable on the abscissa axis.

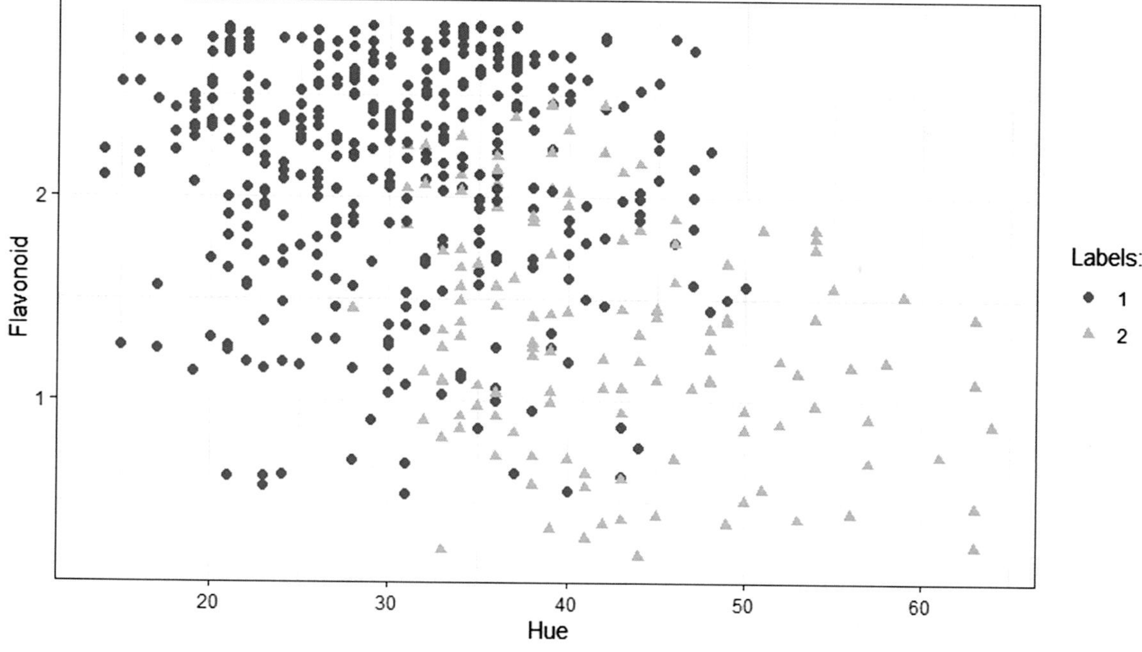

b. Create a training set containing a random sample of 60% of the observations and a validation set containing the remaining observations.

c. Using the function `tune()`, select an optimal cost for an SVM model with a linear kernel, considering *group* as the dependent variable and *flavonoid* and *hue* as the predictor variables, and considering values of `cost` equal to `(0.001, 0.01, 0.1, 1, 5, 10)`. What is the value of cost obtained in the tuning process? What is the value of the classification error for that value of cost?

d. Estimate an SVM model with a linear kernel, considering the hyperparameter cost equal to the value defined previously in the tuning process.

e. Repeat items (c) and (d) using an SVM with a polynomial kernel (set `degree = 2`), considering values of `cost` equal to `(0.001, 0.01, 0.1, 1)` and `gamma` equal to `(0.1, 0.5, 1, 2, 3, 4)`.

f. Repeat items (c) and (d) using an SVM with a radial kernel, considering values of `cost` equal to `(0.001, 0.01, 0.1, 1, 10, 100)` and `gamma` equal to `(0.1, 0.5, 1, 2, 3, 4)`.

g. Estimate a binary logistic regression model using the complete dataset `wine.RData`. To compare the performance of the SVM models, create a table with the sensitivity, specificity, accuracy (all of them for a cutoff equal to 0.5), and area under the ROC curve (AUC) for the four models estimated (SVM with a linear kernel, SVM with a polynomial kernel of degree 2, SVM with a radial kernel, and binary logistic regression model).

h. Create a graph that shows the ROC curves of the estimated models. Overall, which approach seems to give the best results on this data?

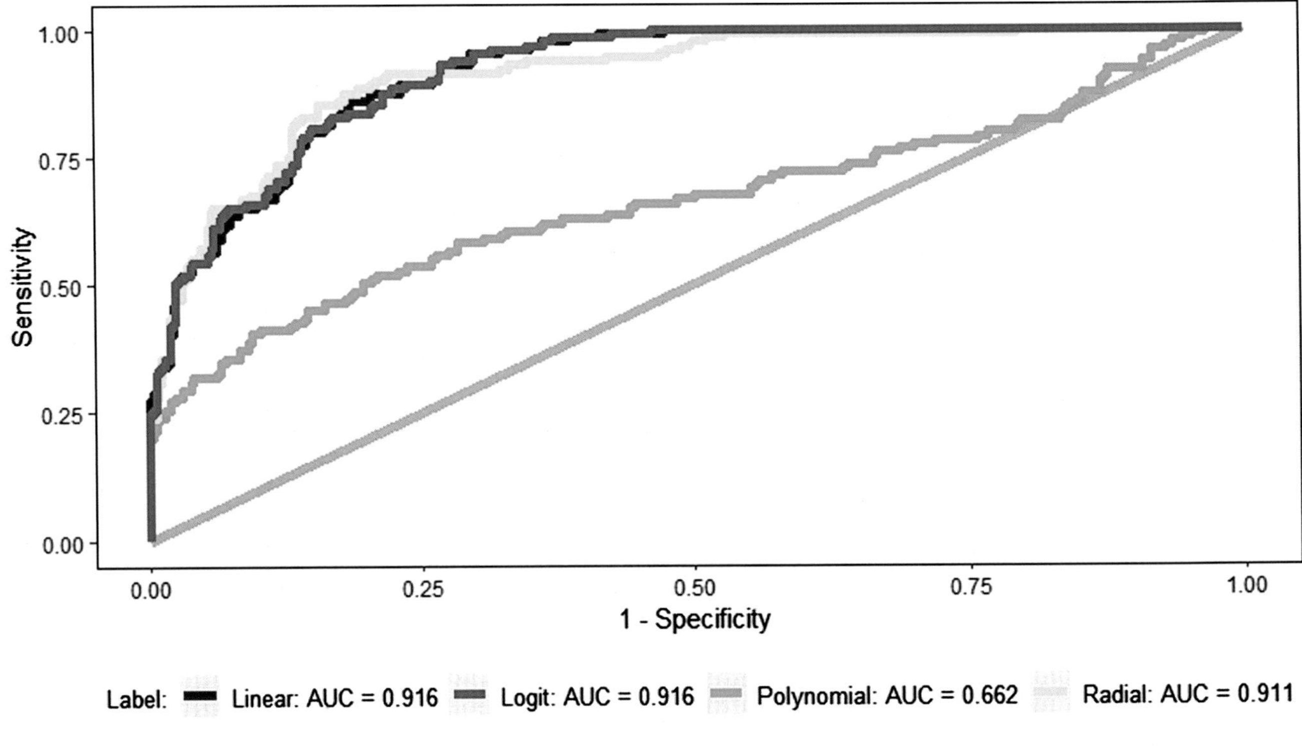

Supplementary data sets

```
barbecue.RData
wine.RData
```

Please access supplementary data file here: https://doi.org/10.17632/55623jkwrp.3

CHAPTER

19

Classification and regression trees

AT THE END OF THIS CHAPTER, YOU WILL BE ABLE TO:

- Understand the circumstances in which classification and regression trees (CARTs) can be used.
- Establish differences among estimation criteria via Shannon's entropy, the Gini index, and variance.
- Measure the impurity of a dataset.
- Understand the problem of overfitting and how to mitigate it with pruning techniques.
- Estimate CARTs in R, understand their differences, and interpret their results.

R-based language packages used in this chapter

```
library(tidyverse)
library(rpart)
library(rpart.plot)
library(caret)
library(e1071)
library(ROCR)
```

Don't forget to define the R working directory (the location where your datasets are installed):

```
setwd("C:/book/chapter19")
```

Introduction

Unlike the generalized linear models (GLMs), and generalized linear mixed models (GLMMs) we studied in Chapters 14 to 17 of this work, classification and regression trees (CARTs) are not estimated using the maximum likelihood criterion. Here, the choice of the estimation criterion will depend directly on the nature of the dependent variable.

CARTs are predictive techniques that can be used for the study of phenomena that manifest themselves both quantitatively and qualitatively. In them, the predictor variables can also be measured quantitatively or qualitatively. In decision trees, for categorical variables, the $n-1$ dummies procedure used in Chapters 14 to 17 would be meaningless.

Data Science, Analytics and Machine Learning with R
https://doi.org/10.1016/B978-0-12-824271-1.00016-0

In addition to the different estimation criteria, it must be said that CARTs are not described by an equation. Thus it is not the intention of this type of method to estimate, present, or discuss parameters (linear or angular coefficients) or to study the signs of these parameters or their respective marginal contributions, much less to address their statistical significance. The stepwise procedure would therefore make no sense here. This does not mean that it is not possible to point out, for example, which variables are most important for the model or which variables make sense for the model. Furthermore, if CARTs do not have parameters on the one hand, they will present what is termed *hyperparameters*.

It is necessary to say that, for the reader who has a background and a stronger connection with statistics, some concepts related to CARTs will sound different. For example, the literature usually refers to CARTs whose dependent variable is categorical (whether it be dichotomous or polychotomic) as *classification trees*. On the other hand, it is common for the literature to refer to CARTs whose dependent variable is metric as *regression trees*. These are all species of *decision trees*.

Another thing that may sound different is the nomenclature of the dependent variable. Synonyms for the term are not lacking in the typical computer science literature, being indicated as a *target variable*, *response variable*, *predicted variable*, and even a *label*. What's more, the term *label* is commonly referred to indistinctly whether the variable is categorical or metric. For the purposes of this work, we will only use the term *label* to indicate some kind of latent variable, that is, a variable of the categorical type.

That said, it can be pointed out that the CARTs are intended to study all of the phenomena exemplified in the course of Chapters 14 to 18. Therefore, we can study any behavior of a given phenomenon (metric or not) depending on one or more explanatory variables (metric or not). However, we make a voice so this last statement will not be used or internalized by the reader to assume what is called "the fallacy of the perfect technique" or to encourage a heard behavior, which is unfortunately very common in the world of data science and analytics. We hope that the reader sees CARTs and the other techniques in this work as an intellectual resource and that the choice of technique is directly linked to the underlying theory, to the operator's experience, and to better adherence to the data studied.

CARTs estimation methods

Initially, let's start by presenting a common example of a decision tree, as shown in Figure 19.1.

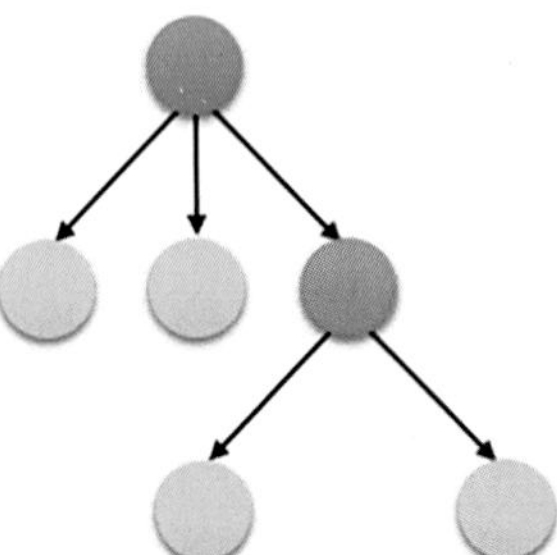

FIGURE 19.1 Theoretical visual example of a CART.

Basically, Figure 19.1 is a good example of a generic decision tree. As the reader can see, the technique, in fact, is configured in a set of branches (as in a tree) as to which decision to make based on the patterns and trends of the data that were captured by some estimation criterion.

In CARTs, each branch is called a *node*. We will always have only one root node; we may or may not have decision nodes; and we will have leaf nodes. The branches that connect the nodes to each other, from the root node to some leaf node, are called *branches*. Just like trees, which start their growth from their roots and develop a well-structured stem, branches, and then leaves, CARTs also lend this idea of biology to be built and understood.

In Figure 19.1, the only top node is the so-called *root node* (the blue node, if you are reading the color version of this work). This will be considered the most important variable for the model. Each branch will lead to a new node, but when the node has no more branches, it will be called the *leaf node*, that is, the predicted value for the phenomenon (the yellow nodes). Therefore, nodes that have branches (obviously the root node is excluded) will be called *decision nodes* (the orange node). Decision nodes will be variables with a lower degree of importance than the variable present in the root node.

An attentive reader will notice that the root node and decision nodes in Figure 19.1 have a common characteristic: they branch out, that is, from them, the directions taken by the algorithm are emerged to predict a given phenomenon. Each time a node branches, we will be facing a split.

That said, naturally, at least one fair question will arise: How will the algorithm be able to point out which variable will be the root node and which variables, and in what order, will the decision nodes be considered?

For this work, we will consider three estimation criteria commonly used in R-based language: (1) the entropy of information; (2) the Gini index; and (3) the variance. It will depend on these criteria, therefore, how the algorithm will build the CARTs and answer all of the questions raised previously.

The entropy of information

The idea of information entropy is commonly linked to physics and mathematics, and it derives directly from Shannon's Theory of Information (Shannon, 1948). In the simplest possible way, we can say that it concerns the attempt to measure chaos; more precisely, for the machine learning area, entropy is a way of measuring the impurity present in the dataset.

In the case of CARTs and the techniques that use them, which we will study in the following chapters of this work, **we will make use of Shannon's entropy when our phenomenon manifests itself in a qualitative way.** In this way, we will try to understand and organize the chaos (or mitigate the impurity of the data) present in our dataset so we can establish a decision tree, starting, therefore, from the most important characteristic of the sample, the *root node* (i.e., the variable that, a priori, has the greatest capacity to solve chaos or reduce impurity), passing through other slightly less important characteristics such as the *decision nodes* (i.e., interesting variables for the continuation of chaos mitigation), or impurity (previously softened by the variable that will be in the root node), until we are able to make inferences (leaf nodes).

To do so, we will follow the following four steps:

- **First step:** Calculate the entropy of information from the complete dataset (H), taking into account the categories of the dependent variable.
- **Second step:** For each explanatory variable individually considered, create splits due to the categories of the predictor variable with respect to the categories of the dependent variable, generating a number of sets equal to the number of categories of the analyzed explanatory variable. The proportionality of the number of observations present in each of these sets, due to the size of observations in the dataset, will be used to weigh what is called the *remaining entropy* (I), to be calculated for each predictor variable.
- **Third step:** Subtract the remaining entropy value (measured in step 2) from the total entropy value in the dataset (step 1). The result of this operation is called *information gain* (IG). The variable that promotes the greatest information gain will be considered the root node.
- **Fourth step:** Steps 1 to 3 must be iterated to define each of the decision nodes, taking into account the IG provided by the variable present in the root node and the decision nodes (if generated in previous steps), up to the lowest possible value of impurity calculated for the data, without causing the problem of overfitting (we will discuss this throughout the "Overfitting" and "Pruning" sections). This set of four steps will be demonstrated algebraically throughout the "Classification of trees in R" section.

That said, for the first step, the Shannon's entropy (H) of the vector of the dependent variable Y, in relation to the predictor variables, can be mathematically expressed by Expression (19.1).

$$H(Y,X) = -\sum_{i=1}^{m} p_i \times \log_2(p_i), \tag{19.1}$$

where Y refers to a dichotomous or polycotomic categorical dependent variable; X refers to the set of predictor variables X_k ($k=1,2,3,\ldots$), that is, to all explanatory variables X that will be considered to explain phenomenon Y; and p indicates the probability of the occurrence of a certain category m of Y.

A curious reader will notice that, when using Expression (19.1), we could verify that Shannon's entropy will be 0 when all observations of the dataset belong to the same category of the dependent variable and will be $\log_2 m$ when all m categories of the dependent variable are equally represented.

Figure 19.2 presents the theoretical distribution of probabilities proposed by Expression (19.1). Note that the lower the probability of occurrence of a given category of the dependent variable, the greater the value of the information entropy. The information is obvious, but it helps to internalize that the greater the impurity present in the data (i.e., the lower the probability of the occurrence of some category of Y) necessarily, the greater the entropy value will be.

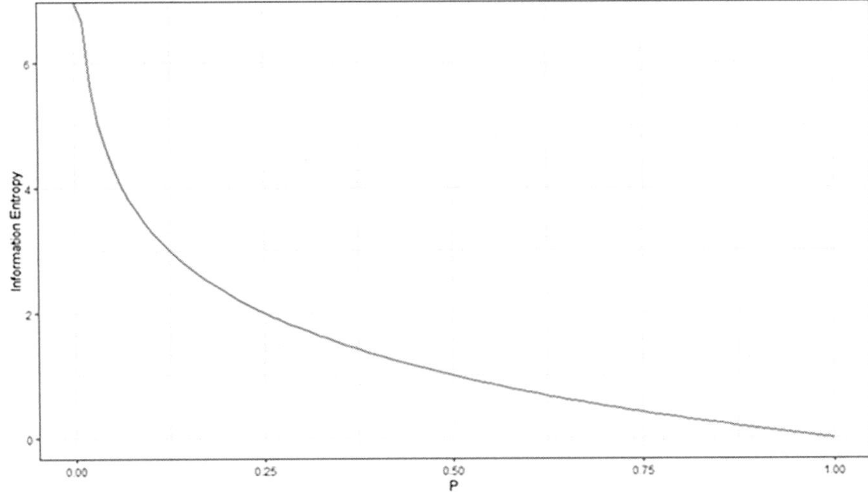

FIGURE 19.2 Theoretical distribution of probabilities for information entropy.

So, hypothetically, if we have a dependent variable with categories $m=2$, equally represented, we will have the probability distribution shown in Figure 19.3, in this case, $H=1$, since $\log_2 2=1$.

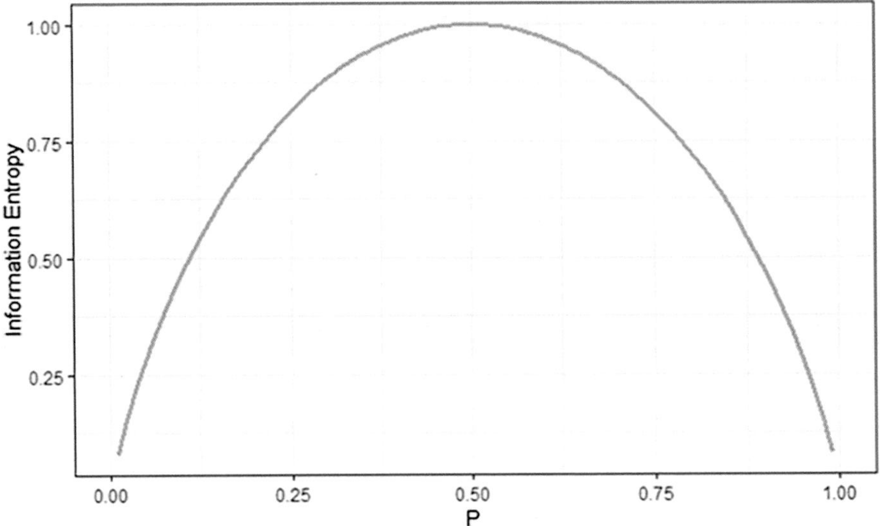

FIGURE 19.3 The entropy of information for a dichotomous dependent variable, with both categories equally represented.

After that, for the second step, we will calculate the remaining entropy (I) for each of the explanatory variables. **If a certain predictor variable (X_k) is categorical, we will immediately use the method proposed in Expression (19.2):**

$$I(Y, X_k) = \sum\nolimits_{l \in \text{categories}(X_k)} \frac{X_{k=l}}{N} \times H(Y, X_{k=l}), \tag{19.2}$$

where l represents each of the categories of a given predictor variable, where $l=1, 2, \ldots$, and N represents the number of observations in the dataset.

However, if any explanatory variable is quantitative, before applying Expression (19.2), we will need to create categories from the metric values so we can verify how much impurity is or is not eliminated when assuming that variable as a root node or decision node.

For this, the first step will be to order the dataset in an increasing way **in relation to the metric predictor variable considered**. Then, we should observe, between pairs, and from the first observation of the reordered dataset, when there is a change in the category of the target variable in relation to the change in value of the metric predictor variable studied. Thus for the pairs of observations of the quantitative predictor variable in which changes in categories were noted in the dependent variable, we should calculate the simple arithmetic mean, for each of these two observations, with respect to the metric values present in the explanatory variable. Finally, the simple arithmetic averages, calculated for these pairs of observations, will be assumed as thresholds to verify the remaining entropy (I). That done, we can use Expression (19.2).

In the third step, when we subtract the value of the general entropy of the model *(H)* by the remaining entropies *(I)* of each predictor variable, one by one, we will verify the information gains *(IG)* regarding each variable. The one with the highest information gain will be considered as the root node. Once this is done, the procedure is iterated, considering the entropy mitigated by the variable present in the root node, aiming to identify the decision nodes, until the value of H is the minimum possible. In the case of metric predictors, the threshold that provides the highest information gain will be assumed as the true threshold for the generated split, accompanied by the sign $\geq$.

Expression (19.3) presents the formula for information gain.

$$IG_{X_k} = H(Y,X) - I(Y,X_k) \tag{19.3}$$

Next, we will present another way to calculate the impurity of the data and to define the root node and decision nodes: the Gini index.

The Gini index

The Gini index is another method used to calculate the impurity present in a dataset **when the dependent variable is categorical.** Its use is analogous to that proposed later in this chapter in "The Entropy of Information," and in R-based language, it is usually the default option for elaboration of a CART, obviously, when the studied phenomenon manifests itself in a qualitative way.

Thus similar to what has been presented, the following four steps are proposed for calculation of the Gini index:

- **Step 1:** Calculate the value of the Gini index *(G)* for the entire dataset, in relation to the dependent variable.
- **Step 2:** For each explanatory variable individually considered, create splits due to the categories of the explanatory variable in respect of the categories of the dependent variable, generating a number of sets equal to the number of categories of the analyzed predictor variable. The proportionality of the number of observations present in each of these sets, due to the size of observations in the dataset, will be used to weigh what is called the *remaining Gini index (rem)* to be calculated for each predictor variable.
- **Step 3:** Subtract the remaining Gini index value (measured in step 2) from the total Gini index value of the dataset (measured in step 1). The result of this operation is called *information gain (IG).* The variable that promotes the greatest information gain will be considered the root node.
- **Step 4:** Steps 1 to 3 must be iterated to define each of the decision nodes, taking into account the *IG* provided by the variable present in the root node and in the decision nodes (if generated in previous steps), up to the lowest possible value of impurity calculated for the data, without causing the problem of overfitting (we will discuss this later throughout the "Overfitting" and "Pruning" sections).

Expression (19.4) explains the calculation of the Gini index for the entire dataset, which is important to comply with what was proposed by the first step previously enumerated.

$$G(Y,X) = 1 - \sum_{i=1}^{m} (p_i)^2, \tag{19.4}$$

where Y refers to a categorical dependent variable; X refers to the set of predictor variables X_k $(k=1,2,3,\ldots)$, that is, to all explanatory variables X that will be considered to explain the phenomenon Y; and p indicates the probability of the occurrence of a certain category m of Y.

According to Expression (19.4), the Gini index will be 0 when all observations i belong to the same class m, and $1-\frac{1}{m}$ when all m classes have the same probability of occurrence. Figure 19.4 demonstrates what was explained by showing the probabilities of occurrence of a dichotomous dependent variable when all of its categories have the same probability of occurrence.

Having performed the first step, we must calculate the remaining value of the Gini index *(rem)* similar to the way we did earlier in "The Entropy of Information." Similar to what we have seen, at this moment the reader must take different precautions for categorical predictor variables and for metric predictor variables. **For cases in which the explanatory variable is qualitative, we must use Expression (19.5) immediately.**

$$rem(Y,X_k) = \sum_{l \in \text{categories}(X_k)} \frac{X_{k=l}}{N} \times G(Y,X_{k=l}), \tag{19.5}$$

where l represents each of the categories of a given predictor variable, where $l=1,2,\ldots$; and N represents the number of observations in the dataset.

In the presence of a metric explanatory variable, the reader must identify thresholds for the calculation of *rem* (exactly as presented in "The Entropy of Information") to then be able to use Expression (19.5).

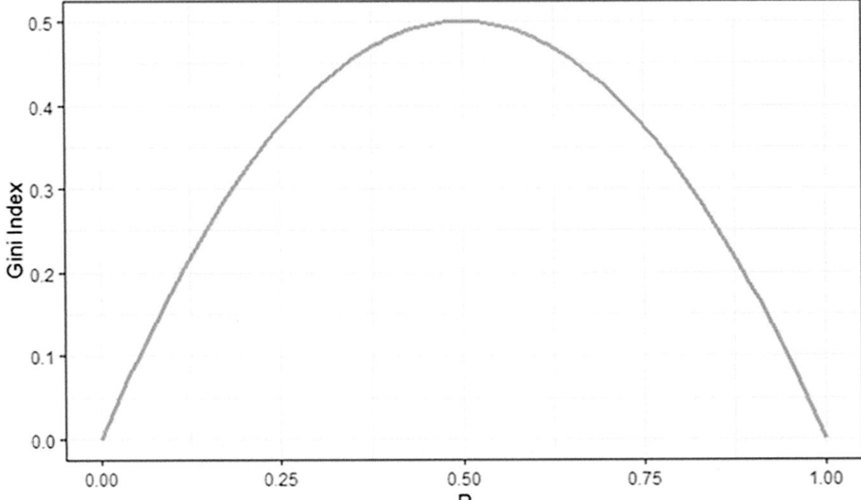

FIGURE 19.4 The Gini index for a dichotomous dependent variable, with both categories equally represented.

The information gain *(IG)* will therefore be the difference between *G* and *rem*, according to what is proposed by Expression (19.6).

$$IG_{X_k} = G(Y,X) - rem(Y,X_k) \tag{19.6}$$

Next, we will demonstrate a metric possibility for calculating the impurity of the dataset for cases in which the dependent variable is manifested in metric form.

Variance

When the reader is faced with a dependent quantitative variable, a possible way to measure the impurity present in the dataset is to use the variance calculation. To consider variance as an impurity metric, the procedures for defining a CART **will be reasonably different from the methods already studied.**

- **Step 1:** Calculate the variance of the dependent variable.
- **Step 2:** In the case of categorical predictor variables, for each predictor variable considered, create splits due to their categories, generating a number of sets equal to the number of categories of the analyzed predictor variable. Calculate the variances of the dependent variable in each set generated due to each split considered. Thus for each predictor variable, add the value of the variances of the dependent variable measured in each of the subsets, for each of the categories of the predictor variable of interest. Then divide this value by the total of categories of that explanatory variable considered. This procedure is called *weighted variance.* On the other hand, in the presence of a metric predictive variable, we must take into account the establishment of thresholds explored earlier in "The Entropy of Information" and "The Gini Index" so the weighted variance can be calculated after that.
- **Step 3:** Consider the variable with the lowest value of weighted variance, and adopt it as the root node.
- **Step 4:** Steps 1 to 3 must be iterated to define each of the decision nodes, taking into account the mitigation of the impurity of the data provided by the variable present in the root node, up to the lowest possible value of weighted variance, without causing the overfitting problem (we will discuss this throughout the "Overfitting" and "Pruning" sections).

The variance of the dependent variable must be calculated as we studied in the "Variance" section in Chapter 4. Expression (19.7) explains the calculation of the variance of the dependent variable.

$$var(Y,X) = \frac{\sum_{i=1}^{n}(Y_i - \overline{Y})^2}{n-1} \tag{19.7}$$

After this, we can proceed to the second step. Here, for each set generated in each split of each of the categorical predictor variables, we must recalculate the variance of the dependent variable. After that, for each predictor, we will add the variance of the dependent variable due to each category of the explanatory variable analyzed. We will then divide this value by the total of categories of the predictor variable of interest to obtain the weighted variance. For cases in which the explanatory variable is metric, the reader must proceed with the creation of thresholds, as studied earlier in "The Entropy of Information" and "The Gini Index." We will demonstrate these procedures in an algebraic manner throughout the "Regression trees in R" section.

Overfitting

Earlier in this chapter in "The entropy of information," "The Gini index," and "Variance" sections, we presented the reader with a step-by-step guide for elaboration of a CART, regardless of whether the dependent variable is categorical or metric. In the steps listed in each of these sections, we would like to make a special reservation to what, in all of them, we call **step 4: the excessive iteration of the mentioned instructions commonly leads to the problem of overfitting.**

The overfitting concept is given to the situation of excessive training of a certain algorithm, over a given dataset, so that the noises from the dataset are modeled. This situation, in CARTs, is generated when there are too many splits, implying a considerable loss in the model's predictive power. Figure 19.5 demonstrates, theoretically, the problem of overfitting.

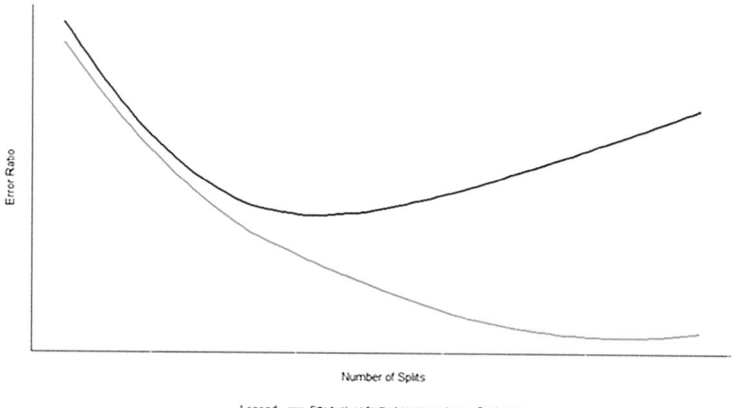

FIGURE 19.5 A theoretical example of overfitting.

The upper curve in Figure 19.5 (the purple curve, if you are reading the color version of this work) demonstrates the overfitting problem well when compared with the other curve in the graph. Figure 19.5 makes it clear that the greater the number of splits, the better our model will suit the data we provide for training the algorithm, but this will not necessarily guarantee good predictive power.

This occurs because, in the theoretical case discussed in Figure 19.5, the algorithm was overtrained in relation to the dataset provided for establishment of the model. Thus the algorithm began to model noise, errors, and residuals until it reached fitted values that best fit the observed values provided, but that will not necessarily have the same accuracy for the prediction of observations not present in the sample. Such situation occurred, for the case discussed, necessarily due to the amount of splits generated.

Thus a curious reader may ask the following question: "How do you know when to stop generating splits for a given CART?" To answer this question, we will need to discuss strategies of decision tree pruning.

Pruning

For the theoretical example present in Figure 19.5, the reader will notice that the two curves were very close during some splits, indicating a good model. However, as the number of splits started to increase, there was a better adequacy of the estimation to the patterns and trends captured for our dataset, with the evident tradeoff of worsening the prediction accuracy for observations not present in the dataset. So how do you know when to command an optimal number of splits? In other words, how do you know when your decision tree should stop growing? There is no single answer or pocket rule applicable to all cases. Next, we will deal with some good practices that the literature recommends to avoid the problem of overfitting.

To avoid the problem of overfitting in CARTs, we bring the idea of *pruning*, that is, the removal of subtrees from our decision tree. As a rule, the R algorithms we will use for this chapter usually mitigate the problem of overfitting automatically, for most cases. **To this practice and to any other type of control that occurred before estimating a CART, we will call it *pre-pruning*. The controls mentioned are what we will call *hyperparameters*. On the other hand, if a CART has already been estimated and the intention is to refine it, we will call this *post-pruning*.**

In any case, we affirm that the application of the algorithms selected for this work will help the reader avoid the problem of overfitting in most cases, **but we do not guarantee that they will work for all situations or that they will, in fact, generate the best model with its default values.**

In addition to pruning, adopting sampling techniques by *cross-validation* (CV), that is, creating subsets from the original set so there is a training sample and a test sample, is also a good practice in the estimation of a CART, and it will help the reader see whether or not the model is affected by the overfitting problem.

Hyperparameters

For CARTs, we will mention three main hyperparameters: (1) *minimum number of splits;* (2) *complexity parameter* (CP); and (3) *maximum depth.*

Setting values for these hyperparameters will affect both the size and complexity of the decision tree.

- **Minimum number of splits:** This hyperparameter concerns the minimum number of observations that must exist in a node for a split to be attempted. The default value is 20 for the algorithms we will use.
- **Complexity parameter:** This hyperparameter directly affects how large a CART can be, and the default value is 0.01. Its value comes from an iteration optimization function, which aims to minimize the model's error rates. R will do this automatically in the background, combining our commands with a CV strategy. If the reader wants more information, we suggest reading Breiman et al. (1984).
- **Maximum depth:** This hyperparameter concerns the maximum depth of any node of the final tree, that is, the maximum number of nodes between the root node and the leaf nodes, where the default value is 30 and the root node is considered as depth 0.

As mentioned earlier, as a rule, the default values of the algorithm will guarantee a good chance of not incurring overfitting, however it would be interesting for the reader to pay more attention to the second one (i.e., the CP) because its value will invariably affect the other two.

Without communicating to those who operate the CART algorithms for this work, R will use a *K-fold* CV technique in the estimation background to determine, among other things, the optimal CP values and model errors, aiming at greater accuracy of modeling.

The K-fold CV technique generally works as follows: (1) R randomly organizes the observations from the dataset used to establish a CART; (2) from this randomization, R divides the dataset provided by the reader into groups and creates a subsample; (3) R estimates a CART with the values not selected in the subsample from the previous step and tests it with the selected subsample; and (4) R iterates this process considering different amounts of splits, which will generate different errors for this CV process (R called `xerror`) as well as different CP values. Here, to mitigate the problem of overfitting, adopting the lowest CV value (`xerror`) is a good practice to choose the best CP.

Estimating CART models in R

In this section, we will elaborate two CARTs to illustrate the use of the studied technique. The first will be a *classification tree,* that is, the dependent variable will be categorical; the second will be a *regression tree,* that is, our variable will be metric.

As stated earlier in the "Hyperparameters" section, unlike the estimation methods studied so far, this kind of algorithm has the random feature of CV K-fold built in, which means that, not necessarily, a CART will be identical to a second CART estimated from the same dataset used when the first estimate was made. So, initially, it is important to introduce the reader to the function `set.seed()`.

The `set.seed()` function will ensure that the same random processes that occurred for the authors during CART estimation are also replicated to the reader. If we do not use the function `set.seed()`, the reader will invariably see models with characteristics that are different from the models printed on the pages of this work.

Classification trees in R

Because we will study the behavior of a categorical variable as a function of some predictor variables in this example, we will estimate a classification tree.

In our CART model, based on a survey of 200 amateur athletes who participated in a certain sprint-type triathlon competition, the objective is to indicate whether or not a certain athlete finished the competition, based on the average carbohydrates (in grams) ingested per kilogram of body weight, and if this athlete had been preparing for more than 90 days for the competition. Table 19.1 summarizes the variables in the database.

TABLE 19.1 Description of the variables that will be used to estimate a classification tree (Fávero and Belfiore, 2019).

Variable	Description
id	Variable identifying the athlete.
finished	Binary categorical variable indicating "yes" if the athlete was able to finish the triathlon competition or "no" if the athlete was unable to finish the competition.
carbs_consumption	Metric variable indicating the average intake of carbohydrates (in grams) per kilogram of body weight during the athlete's preparatory training for the competition.
training_days	Binary categorical variable that indicates whether the athlete has been preparing for more or less than 90 days for the triathlon competition.

The dataset presented in Table 19.1 can be found in the file `triathlon.RData` (Fávero and Belfiore, 2019):

```
load("triathlon.RData")
```

We can access the univariate descriptive statistics and frequency tables of our data by commanding the following:

```
summary(triathlon)
```

Figure 19.6 shows the result obtained from the previous code.

```
competitor_id finished  carbs_consumption              training_days
 1      :  1    no :141   Min.    : 0.400    less than 90 days:107
 2      :  1    yes: 59   1st Qu.: 1.144    more than 90 days: 93
 3      :  1              Median : 2.225
 4      :  1              Mean   : 2.670
 5      :  1              3rd Qu.: 3.944
 6      :  1              Max.   :10.325
 (Other):194
```

FIGURE 19.6 Univariate descriptive statistics and frequency tables of the dataset present in the object `triathlon`.

To estimate our classification tree, we will use the function `rpart()` from the package `rpart`. However, as stated at the beginning of the "Estimating CART models in R" section, it is important to define the command `set.seed()`:

```
set.seed(1)
```

Now we will have the guarantee that the outputs the reader will receive from R will be identical to those found in this work. Let's estimate our first CART:

```
CART_triathlon <- rpart(formula = finished ~ carbs_consumption + training_days,
                        data = triathlon,
                        control = rpart.control(minsplit = 20,
                                                cp = 0.01,
                                                maxdepth = 30),
                        parms = list(split = "information"),
                        method = "class")
```

The declaration of the function `rpart()`, demonstrated in the previous code, has the following argumentation:

- **`formula`**, similar to all of the models studied, indicates which dependent variable will be studied, according to certain predictor variables.
- **`data`** points to which object the variables declared in the argument `formula` belong.
- **`control`** indicates which hyperparameters will be used, using the function `rpart.control()`; here, the hyperparameters `minsplit`, `cp`, and `maxdepth` were used first with their default values.
- **`parms`** indicates which criteria will be used to measure the impurity of the data; `"information"` is equivalent to Shannon's entropy, while `"gini"` is equivalent to the Gini index.
- **`method`** indicates whether we want to estimate a classification tree (`"class"`) or a regression tree (`"anova"`).

We can view our CART with the algorithm `rpart.plot()`, from the package `rpart`.

```
rpart.plot(x = CART_triathlon)
```

Figure 19.7 shows the structure of our first CART.

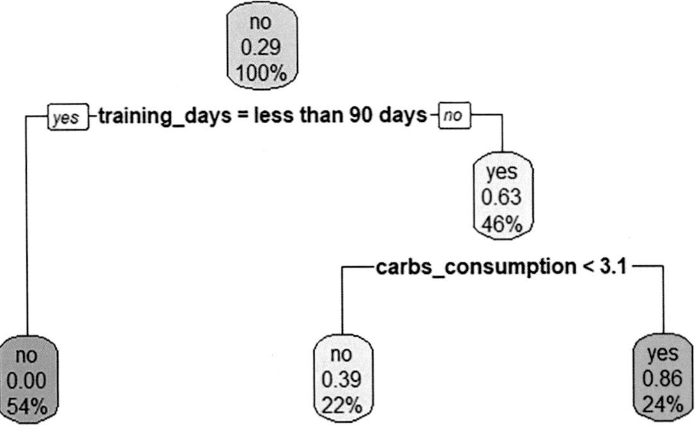

FIGURE 19.7 Classification tree estimated in the R-based language.

In Figure 19.7, we can see that there is a root node, a decision node, and three leaf nodes. To facilitate identification and explanations, we will call the root node of *r*, the single decision node of *d*, and the leaf nodes, considered from left to right, *l*1, *l*2, and *l*3.

The root node chosen *(r)* when adopting Shannon's entropy was the variable *training_days*, and if the tree stopped growing at this initial moment (adopting the answer "the triathlon competition is not finished"), we would have the value 0.29 (29%) of 200 observations mistakenly classified. The value of 100% is redundant and states that the entire dataset was considered at that specific moment.

In Figure 19.7, according to our initial model, when the athlete trained less than 90 days for the triathlon race, he or she was unable to finish the race. Leaf node *l*1 contains exactly these observations, and the value of 54% indicates the 107 athletes who, in fact, trained less than 90 days for the triathlon race. The reader can confirm the statement with the following routine:

```
triathlon %>%
  filter(training_days == "less than 90 days") %>%
  summarise(n = n(),
            percentage = n / nrow(triathlon))
```

Regarding leaf node *l*1, the value of 0.00 indicates the percentage of how many erroneous classifications the model had for athletes who trained less than 90 days for the triathlon race.

When we look at the only decision node of our model *(d)*, we realize that if we consider the end of our tree there, we would have 46% of our dataset (93 athletes) considered in that specific node; however, the tree does not stop there, and we will discuss this shortly. We can verify what has been said so far with the following codes:

```
triathlon %>%
  filter(training_days != "less than 90 days") %>%
  summarise(n = n(),
            percentage = n / nrow(triathlon))
```

Regarding *d*, the value of 0.63 (63%) concerns how many observations of value "yes" (the race ended) we have in this node, considering the 93 observations contained by it (59/63). The following routine is demonstrated as follows:

```
triathlon %>%
  filter(training_days != "less than 90 days" & finished == "yes") %>%
  count()
```

As stated earlier and in Figure 19.7, we can see that CART has not stopped growing in *d*. Because of the entropy of the calculated information, the variable *carbs_consumption* was used, using a threshold of 3.1. Thus the observations that trained more than 90 days but consumed, on average, less than 3.1 grams of carbohydrates per kilogram of body weight were contained by *l*2, under the classification of "no," that is, did not finish the race. On the other hand, the observations that trained more than 90 days and consumed, on average, more than 3.1 grams of carbohydrates per kilogram of body weight during training, were constituted by *l*3 under the classification of "yes," that is, they finished the race.

Speaking of *l*2, we noticed that 22% of the database is contained there (44 athletes), as shown in the following commands:

```
triathlon %>%
  filter(training_days != "less than 90 days" & carbs_consumption < 3.1) %>%
  summarise(n = n(),
            percentage = n / nrow(triathlon))
```

However, we will also notice that *l*2 has an error of 39% of classification, that is, 39% of the observations present in *t*2 ended the race (17 athletes):

```
triathlon %>%
  filter(training_days != "less than 90 days" &
           carbs_consumption < 3.1 &
           finished == "yes") %>%
  count()
```

The interpretations passed on *l*2 can be applied to *l*3 in a similar way. The caution here is that *l*3 classifies the observations as "yes," that is, the athlete finished triathlon race. Thus we realized that "yes" contains 24% of the observations in the dataset (49 athletes):

```
triathlon %>%
  filter(training_days != "less than 90 days" & carbs_consumption >= 3.1) %>%
  count()
```

However, of the 49 athletes present in *l*3, in fact, 14% (7 observations) did not finish the test:

```
triathlon %>%
  filter(training_days != "less than 90 days" &
           carbs_consumption >= 3.1 &
           finished == "no") %>%
  count()
```

At the end of this extensive explanation, we can agree that the default way in which Figure 19.7 is displayed makes analysis difficult. So we suggest a more elegant way of displaying our CART, declaring some arguments for the function `rpart.plot()`:

```
rpart.plot(x = CART_triathlon,
           type = 5,
           box.palette = "RdGn",
           extra = 2)
```

In the function `rpart.plot()`, the argument `type` controls some predefined layouts for displaying the CART (its values range from 0 to 5); `box.palette` indicates the colors to be used; and `extra` indicates the amount of information to be displayed on the graph.

We encourage the reader to command `?rpart.plot()` and explore other possible arguments. Figure 19.8 shows the results obtained from the previous command.

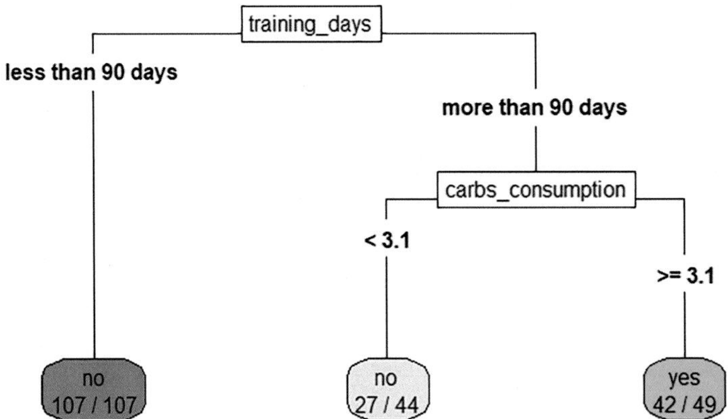

FIGURE 19.8 A more elegant presentation of a classification tree estimated in R-based language.

Going even deeper into the construction of the CART set out in Figure 19.8, we would like to demonstrate, according to Expressions (19.1), (19.2), and (19.3), the calculations for the definition of the root node and the decision node.

Following the logic proposed in "The Entropy of Information" (because our CART was prepared according to the Shannon entropy criterion), we must calculate $H(Y, X)$. Thus we can see that Figure 19.6 informs us that there are 141 observations that did not finish the race, while 59 athletes did. That way:

$$H(Y, X) = -\left\{\left[\sum_{i=1}^{yes} p_i \times \log_2(p_i)\right] + \left[\sum_{i=1}^{no} p_i \times \log_2(p_i)\right]\right\}$$

$$H(Y, X) = -\left\{\left[\frac{59}{200} \times \log_2\left(\frac{59}{200}\right)\right] + \left[\frac{141}{200} \times \log_2\left(\frac{141}{200}\right)\right]\right\} = 0.8750928.$$

Thus the impurity metric in our dataset is 0.8750928. The next step, therefore, will be to verify which variable will have the lowest remaining entropy *(I)*, implying a greater information gain *(IG)*. However, before using Expression (19.2), we must create sets due to the proposed splits for the two explanatory variables that we will use. For the variable *training days*, we will use the one proposed in Figure 19.9.

To make it easier, we already know that when the athlete trained less than 90 days, he or she did not finish the race. Thus for the first part of Figure 19.9 (the table indicated by the arrow with the label *less than 90 days*), we will have 107 observations with a value equal to "no" and 0 observations with a value equal to "yes." On the other hand, for the second part of Figure 19.9 (the table indicated by the arrow with the label *more than 90 days*), we will have 93 observations, in which 59 have the value "yes" and 34 assume the value "no." Thus we will have:

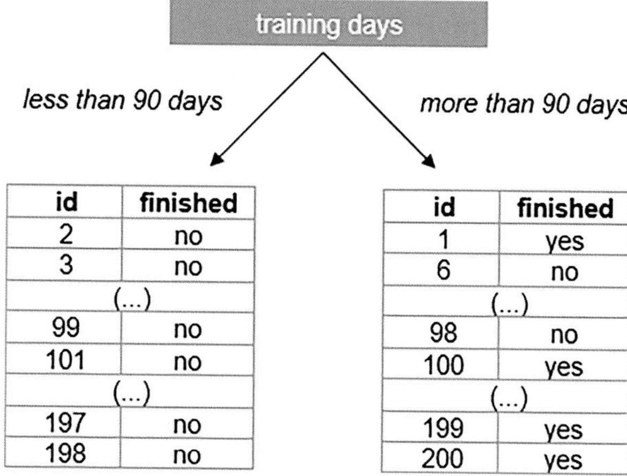

FIGURE 19.9 Subsets created due to the categories of the variable *training days*.

$$I(Y, training\ days) = \left[\frac{training\ days_{k=\text{less than 90 days}}}{N} \times H\left(Y, training\ days_{k=\text{less than 90 days}}\right)\right]$$

$$+ \left[\frac{training\ days_{k=\text{more than 90 days}}}{N} \times H\left(Y, training\ days_{k=\text{more than 90 days}}\right)\right]$$

$$I(Y, training\ days) = \frac{107}{200} \times \left\{-\left\{\left[\frac{107}{107} \times \log_2\left(\frac{107}{107}\right)\right] + [0]\right\}\right\} + \frac{93}{200}$$

$$\times \left\{-\left\{\left[\frac{34}{93} \times \log_2\left(\frac{34}{93}\right)\right] + \left[\left[\frac{59}{93} \times \log_2\left(\frac{59}{93}\right)\right]\right]\right\}\right\}$$

$$= 0.4404605.$$

To calculate the remaining entropy for the metric predictive variable *carbs_consumption*, we must first organize the dataset in an increasing way in relation to the variable discussed to follow the logic proposed earlier in "The Entropy of Information." Thus for educational purposes, we present a cutoff of the first 18 observations in a reordered way in Table 19.2.

TABLE 19.2 Cut of the dataset `triathlon`, reordered due to the variable *carbs consumption*, with 18 observations for didactic purposes (Fávero and Belfiore, 2019).

ID	Finished	carbs_consumption
23	No	0.400
62	No	0.400
102	No	0.400
126	No	0.400
128	No	0.400
66	No	0.475
68	No	0.525
31	No	0.550
137	No	0.550
190	No	0.550
61	No	0.575
70	No	0.575

Continued

TABLE 19.2 Cut of the dataset `triathlon`, reordered due to the variable *carbs consumption*, with 18 observations for didactic purposes (Fávero and Belfiore, 2019)—cont'd

ID	Finished	carbs_consumption
127	No	0.575
6	No	0.600
32	Yes	0.600
53	No	0.600
175	No	0.600
33	Yes	0.625
(...)		

That done, we should watch for a change in the category of our dependent variable. Note that the pairs of observations presented in Table 19.2 in which the category changes of the dependent variable occur are id 6 and id 32; id 32 and id 53; and id 175 and id 33. Obviously, there are other unrelated category changes in the clipping of Table 19.2, and we reinforce that the example has didactic purposes.

With the dataset increasingly reordered in relation to the metric predictor variable of interest, and **all** pairs of observations identified in which there is a change in the category of the predictor variable, we must calculate the simple arithmetic mean of the values of the studied metric explanatory variable, between these pairs. Thus we will have:

- id 6 e id 32: $\frac{0.600+0.600}{2}=0.600$
- id 32 e id 53: $\frac{0.600+0.600}{2}=0.600$
- id 175 e id 33: $\frac{0.600+0.625}{2}=0.6125$

After calculating the simple arithmetic mean of the values of the metric explanatory variable studied between pairs of observations in which there is a change in the category of the dependent variable, we must assume these averages as thresholds, using the sign $\geq$. Figure 19.10 explains the statement.

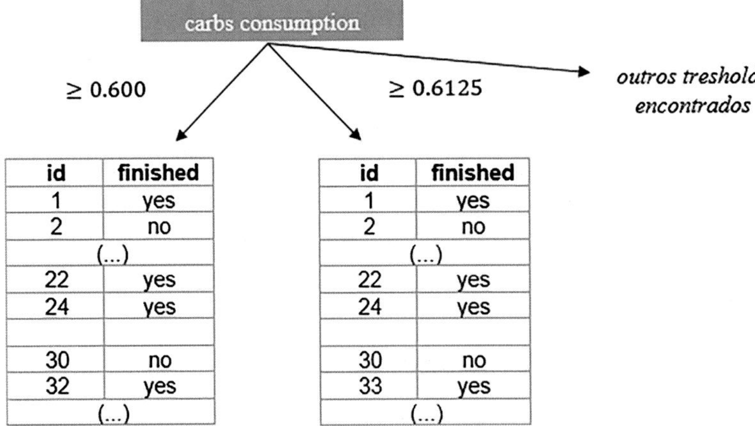

FIGURE 19.10 Subsets created due to the thresholds identified for the metric variable *carbs consumption*.

We also know that 59 observations, with carbohydrate consumption greater than or equal to 0.600, ended the race; and that, for the same premise, 128 athletes did not finish the test. We therefore have 187 individuals, and we can confirm this as follows:

```
#yes
triathlon %>%
  filter(carbs_consumption >= 0.6 & finished == "yes") %>%
  count()
```

Continued

```
#no
triathlon %>%
  filter(carbs_consumption >= 0.6 & finished == "no") %>%
  count()
```

On the other hand, we have no observation that ended the triathlon test by consuming less than 0.600 grams, on average, of carbohydrate per kilogram of body weight; and there are 13 competitors who did not finish the race consuming less than 0.600 grams. The following routines return to what we said earlier:

```
#yes
triathlon %>%
  filter(carbs_consumption < 0.6 & finished == "yes") %>%
  count()

#no
triathlon %>%
  filter(carbs_consumption < 0.6 & finished == "no") %>%
  count()
```

With the results of the previous routines, we have the possibility to calculate I, from the variable *carbs consumption*, for the threshold ≥ 0.600:

$$I(Y, carbs\ consumption\ ) = \left[\frac{carbs\ consumption_{k \geq 0.600}}{N} \times H\left(Y, carbs\ consumption_{k \geq 0.600}\right)\right] + \left[\frac{carbs\ consumption_{k<0.600}}{N} \times H(Y, carbs\ consumption_{k<0.600})\right]$$

$$\begin{aligned} I(Y, carbs\ consumption\ ) &= \frac{187}{200} \times \left\{-\left\{\left[\frac{59}{187} \times \log_2\left(\frac{107}{107}\right)\right] + \left[\frac{128}{187} \times \log_2\left(\frac{128}{187}\right)\right]\right\}\right\} + \frac{13}{200} \\ &\times \left\{-\left\{[0] + \left[\left[\frac{13}{13} \times \log_2\left(\frac{13}{13}\right)\right]\right]\right\}\right\} \\ &= 0.8409666 \end{aligned}$$

After the aforementioned procedure is done for all thresholds found, the reader will see that, for the definition of the root node, the value of I of the variable *training days* is less than any threshold of the variable *carbs consumption*.

That said, the information gain achieved by the variable *training days* is found as follows:

$$IG_{training\ day} = H(Y, training\ day) - I(Y, training\ day)$$

$$IG_{training\ day} = 0.8750928 - 0.4404605 = 0.4346323.$$

The next step will be to iterate the demonstrated procedures until there is no more information gain capable of improving our CART, trying to model, from that moment, the remaining entropy of 0.4346323.

If the reader is wondering if there is a package that demonstrates the calculations presented, we are forced to recognize that there are some that try to achieve this, but they have serious limitations and, in our modest opinion, would complicate rather than help the reader understand what CART algorithms do. Thus we propose the following function to help the reader calculate the Shannon entropy of a given database:

```
shannon.entropy <- function(y){
  tab <- base::table(y) / base::length(y)
  probs <- base::as.vector(tab)[tab > 0]
  -base::sum(probs * base::log2(probs))
}
```

However, if the reader's intention is to calculate the Gini index, then:

```
gini.index <- function(y){
   tab <- base::table(y) / base::length(y)
   probs <- base::as.vector(tab)
   1 - base::sum(probs ^ 2)
}
```

Both functions, `shannon.entropy()` and `gini.index()`, have a single argument called `y`. The dependent variable of the study must be declared for `y`:

```
#Shannon Entropy
shannon.entropy(y = triathlon$finished)

#Gini Index
gini.index(y = triathlon$finished)
```

If, on the other hand, the idea is to calculate the remaining entropy, then the reader can type the following command:

```
rem.entropy <- function(data, y.position, x.position){
   y <- base::names(data)[y.position]
   x <- base::names(data)[x.position]
   data <- data[!base::is.na(data[, x]), ]
   if(!base::class(data[, x]) %in% base::c("numeric","integer")){
      data %>% dplyr::group_by_at(x) %>% dplyr::summarise(
        shannon_entropy = shannon.entropy(base::get(y)),
        N = length(base::get(y)),
        .groups = "drop") -> terms
      terms["probs"] <- terms$N / base::nrow(data)
      base::abs(-sum(terms$probs * terms$shannon_entropy))
   }
   else{
      sorted_data <- data[base::order(data[, x]),]
      vessel <- base::list()
      for(i in 1:base::NROW(sorted_data)){
        if(i+1 > base::NROW(sorted_data)){break()}
        else{if(sorted_data[y][[1]][i] != sorted_data[y][[1]][i+1]){
          vessel[i][1] <- sorted_data[x][[1]][i]
          vessel[[i]][2] <- sorted_data[x][[1]][i+1]}}
      }
      vessel <- vessel[base::lapply(vessel, base::length) > 0]
      for(i in 1:base::length(vessel)){
        vessel[[i]][3] <- base::mean(base::c(base::as.numeric(vessel[[i]][1]),
                                         base::as.numeric(vessel[[i]][2])))
      }
      vector1 <- base::vector()
      for(i in 1:base::length(vessel)){
        vector1[[i]] <- vessel[[i]][3]
      }
      vessel2 <- base::list()
      for(i in 1:base::length(vector1)){
        data[base::which(data[x] >= vector1[i]),] %>% dplyr::summarise(
          shannon_entropy = shannon.entropy(base::get(y)),
```

Continued

```
        N = length(base::get(y)),
        .groups = "drop") -> terms
      terms["probs"] <- terms$N / base::nrow(data)
      vessel2[i][1] <- -base::sum(terms$probs * terms$shannon_entropy)
      data[which(data[x] < vector1[i]),] %>% dplyr::summarise(
        shannon_entropy = shannon.entropy(base::get(y)),
        N = length(base::get(y)),
        .groups = "drop") -> terms
      terms["probs"] <- terms$N / base::nrow(data)
      vessel2[[i]][2] <- -base::sum(terms$probs * terms$shannon_entropy)
    }
    for(i in 1:base::length(vessel2)){
      vessel2[[i]][3] <- -base::sum(vessel2[[i]])
    }
    vector2 <- vector()
    for(i in 1:base::length(vessel2)){
      vector2[[i]] <- vessel2[[i]][3]
    }
    base::abs(base::min(vector2))
  }
}
```

For application of the previous routine, the reader must declare three arguments: `data`, indicating the dataset; `y.position`, indicating the position of the column of the dependent variable in the dataset; and `x.position`, indicating the column position of the predictor variable in the dataset, regardless of whether categorical or metric. That said, to calculate the remaining entropy for the variables we use, it would be enough to type the command:

```
#carbs_consumption
rem.entropy(data = triathlon, y.position = 2, x.position = 3)
#training day
rem.entropy(data = triathlon, y.position = 2, x.position = 4)
```

If we want to evaluate the remaining value of the Gini index, we can use the following suggested algorithm:

```
rem.gini <- function(data, y.position, x.position){
  y <- base::names(data)[y.position]
  x <- base::names(data)[x.position]
  data <- data[!base::is.na(data[, x]), ]
  if(!base::class(data[, x]) %in% base::c("numeric","integer")){
    data %>% dplyr::group_by_at(x) %>% dplyr::summarise(
      gini_index = gini.index(base::get(y)),
      N = length(base::get(y)),
      .groups = "drop") -> terms
    terms["probs"] <- terms$N / base::nrow(data)
    sum(terms$probs * terms$gini_index)
  }
  else{
    sorted_data <- data[base::order(data[, x]),]
    vessel <- base::list()
    for(i in 1:base::NROW(sorted_data)){
      if(i+1 > base::NROW(sorted_data)){break()}
      else{if(sorted_data[y][[1]][i] != sorted_data[y][[1]][i+1]){
```

Continued

```
        vessel[i][1] <- sorted_data[x][[1]][i]
        vessel[[i]][2] <- sorted_data[x][[1]][i+1]}}
    }
    vessel <- vessel[base::lapply(vessel, base::length) > 0]
    for(i in 1:base::length(vessel)){
      vessel[[i]][3] <- base::mean(base::c(base::as.numeric(vessel[[i]][1]),
                                          base::as.numeric(vessel[[i]][2])))
    }
    vector1 <- base::vector()
    for(i in 1:base::length(vessel)){
      vector1[[i]] <- vessel[[i]][3]
    }
    vessel2 <- base::list()
    for(i in 1:base::length(vector1)){
      data[base::which(data[x] >= vector1[i]),] %>% dplyr::summarise(
        gini_index = gini.index(base::get(y)),
        N = length(base::get(y)),
        .groups = "drop") -> terms
      terms["probs"] <- terms$N / base::nrow(data)
      vessel2[i][1] <- -base::sum(terms$probs * terms$gini_index)
      data[which(data[x] < vector1[i]),] %>% dplyr::summarise(
        gini_index = gini.index(base::get(y)),
        N = length(base::get(y)),
        .groups = "drop") -> terms
      terms["probs"] <- terms$N / base::nrow(data)
      vessel2[[i]][2] <- -base::sum(terms$probs * terms$gini_index)
    }
    for(i in 1:base::length(vessel2)){
      vessel2[[i]][3] <- -base::sum(vessel2[[i]])
    }
    vector2 <- vector()
    for(i in 1:base::length(vessel2)){
      vector2[[i]] <- vessel2[[i]][3]
    }
    base::min(vector2)
  }
}
```

The declaration of the created function `rem.gini()` is analogous to the declaration of the function `rem.entropy()`:

```
#carbs_consumption
rem.gini(data = triathlon, y.position = 2, x.position = 3)

#training day
rem.gini(data = triathlon, y.position = 2, x.position = 4)
```

Once the CART is established, we can look for evidence of whether or not our `CART_triathlon` model incurs the overfitting problem. According to what was exposed in the "Hyperparameters" section, we can use the CV error (`xerror`) to check if the CP used by default is, in fact, the most appropriate. For this, we will use the command `printcp()` from the package `rpart`.

```
printcp(CART_triathlon)
```

Figure 19.11 shows the result obtained from the previous command.

```
Classification tree:
rpart(formula = finished ~ carbs_consumption + training_days,
    data = triathlon, method = "class", parms = list(split = "information"),
    control = rpart.control(minsplit = 20, cp = 0.01, maxdepth = 30))

Variables actually used in tree construction:
[1] carbs_consumption training_days

Root node error: 59/200 = 0.295

n= 200

       CP nsplit rel error  xerror     xstd
1 0.42373      0   1.00000 1.00000 0.109312
2 0.16949      1   0.57627 0.57627 0.090038
3 0.01000      2   0.40678 0.50847 0.085589
```

FIGURE 19.11 Outcome of the function `printcp()`.

As stated earlier, from Figure 19.11, we are interested in the lowest `xerror` value. We can verify that the lowest value is 0.50847, and it occurs for two splits (value of `nsplit`, and the reader must remember that the root node does not count as a split). Thus for our case, we must adopt the value of CP = 0.01.

Here, the reader can establish a second model directly or use the command `prune()`, from the package `rpart` to feel more secure. All results will be identical to the first tree because `xerror` of 0.50847 occurs for a CP of 0.01, the default value of the algorithm used for the first estimation.

```
#Direct way
CART_pruned <- rpart(formula = finished ~ carbs_consumption + training_days,
                     data = triathlon,
                     control = rpart.control(minsplit = 20,
                                             cp = 0.16949,
                                             maxdepth = 1),
                     parms = list(split = "information"),
                     method = "class")

#prune() function
pruned_triathlon <- prune(tree = CART_triathlon,
                          cp = CART_triathlon$cptable[which.min(
                          CART_triathlon$cptable[,"xerror"]),"CP"]
                          )
```

We can use the command `rpart.plot()` to view our pruned tree; we can use either the one contained in the object `CART_pruned` or the one contained in the object `pruned_triathlon` because both will be identical. In fact, as we said, they will be identical to the first CART because they use the same CP value and have the same depth. **This situation occurs because our model most likely does not have the problem of overfitting, and we advise the reader to give preference to the estimates after the pruning procedure. To achieve good modeling, we also recommend that the reader test the estimated model with data not present in the training sample and compare their fitted values with the actual observed values.**

```
rpart.plot(x = pruned_triathlon,
           type = 5,
           box.palette = "RdGn",
           extra = 2)
```

Figure 19.12 shows the classification tree internal to the object `pruned_triathlon`.

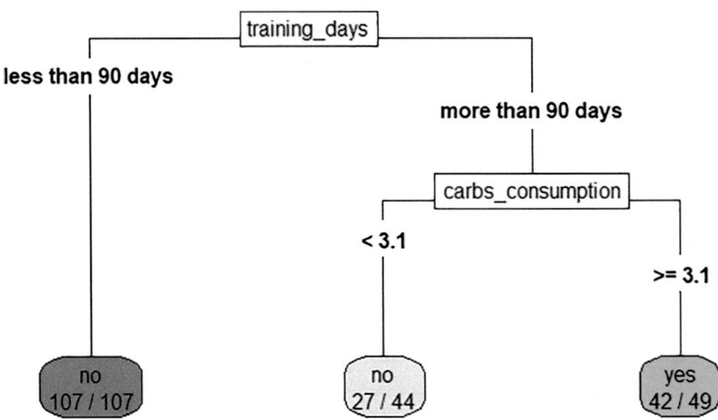

FIGURE 19.12 The final model of the classification tree.

Because we consider the CART presented in Figure 19.12 (identical to the model in Figure 19.8) as our final model, some things should already be clear to the reader. First, as we said in the introduction of this chapter, there are no linear or angular coefficients to analyze. On the other hand, we discussed the impurity metrics and the impurity size of the model, and we discussed hyperparameters, trying to find optimal CP and depth values from our decision tree. We can also see that no athlete who trained less than 90 days for the triathlon competition was able to finish the race. On the other hand, for those who trained more than 90 days, the consumption of carbohydrates in the period before the race was essential for the athlete to finish the race.

After establishing the best CART and understanding the way our model was conceived, we can proceed with the study of establishing a matrix of confusion because the studied phenomenon behaves in a dichotomous way. The construction of a matrix of confusion for a classification tree in R is done in a similar way to the one elaborated in Chapter 15 for binary logistics estimations. Even the cutoff concept already studied can be used here.

In this way, to facilitate the construction of a matrix of confusion for our classification tree, we can save the fitted values of the model, assuming a cutoff of 50%. However, it is important that the reader is aware of one of the differences in the use of the command `predict()` when applied to a CART: Unlike its use in binary logistics models, when we want to calculate the probability of an event, given a determined cutoff, we should not argue `type = "response"`, but instead should argue `type = "prob"`:

```
triathlon["classification"] <- predict(object = pruned_triathlon,
                                       newdata = triathlon,
                                       type = "prob") > 0.5
```

To establish the matrix of confusion after the previous command, we can use the function `confusionMatrix()` from the package `caret`, as studied in Chapter 15.

```
confusionMatrix(
  data = table(triathlon$classification[,2],
               triathlon$finished == "yes")[2:1, 2:1]
)
```

Figure 19.13 presents the matrix of confusion for the model contained in the object `pruned_triathlon`, assuming the cutoff value of 50%, considering as an event the fact that the athlete finished the race, that is `triathlon$classification[,2]` and `triathlon$finished == "yes"`. If we want to consider as an event the fact that the athlete did not finish the race, we can argue `triathlon$classification[,1]` and `triathlon$finished == "no"`.

```
Confusion Matrix and Statistics

       TRUE FALSE
  TRUE    42     7
  FALSE   17   134

               Accuracy : 0.88
                 95% CI : (0.8267, 0.9216)
    No Information Rate : 0.705
    P-Value [Acc > NIR] : 3.392e-09

                  Kappa : 0.6965

 Mcnemar's Test P-Value : 0.06619

            Sensitivity : 0.7119
            Specificity : 0.9504
         Pos Pred Value : 0.8571
         Neg Pred Value : 0.8874
             Prevalence : 0.2950
         Detection Rate : 0.2100
   Detection Prevalence : 0.2450
      Balanced Accuracy : 0.8311

       'Positive' Class : TRUE
```

FIGURE 19.13 Confusion matrix of a classification tree.

According to Figure 19.13, we can see that of the 59 observations (42 + 17) that ended the race, 42 were correctly classified as having finished the triathlon race, and of the 141 athletes who did not finish the race (7 + 134), 134 were correctly classified as not having finished the race. Thus knowing that we have 200 observations in the dataset, we can say that the accuracy of the model, assuming a cut of 50%, is 88%, since:

$$accuracy = \frac{42 + 134}{200} = 0.88.$$

Also according to Figure 19.13, the sensitivity of the model (see the "Cutoff, sensitivity analysis, overall model efficiency, sensitivity, and specificity" section in Chapter 15), that is, the correct classification of the observations as an event (the fact that the athlete has finished the race) due to the number of observed events is 71.19%:

$$sensitivity = \frac{42}{59} = 0.7119$$

Figure 19.13 also informs that the specificity of the model elaborated (see the "Cutoff, sensitivity analysis, overall model efficiency, sensitivity, and specificity" section in Chapter 15), that is, the ratio between the classification of the observations as non-event and the non-events observed, when assuming the 50% cutoff, is 95.04%:

$$specificity = \frac{134}{141} = 0.9504$$

In a similar way to the one studied in the "Cutoff, sensitivity analysis, overall model efficiency, sensitivity, and specificity" section in Chapter 15, we can also establish a receiver operating characteristic (ROC) curve for our classification tree present in the object `pruned_triathlon`. First, let's save the fitted values from the probabilities:

```
triathlon["fitted_probs"] <- predict(object = pruned_triathlon,
                                     newdata = triathlon,
                                     type = "prob")
```

Because the logic is exactly the same for the binary logistic models for elaboration of the ROC curve, we will present the commands directly to avoid incurring redundancy. For the reader to better understand what each command does, we ask you again to read the "Cutoff, sensitivity analysis, overall model efficiency, sensitivity, and specificity" section in Chapter 15.

```
#Predictions data
predictions_triathlon <- prediction(predictions = triathlon$fitted_probs[,2],
                                    labels = triathlon$finished)

#Sensitivity data
sens_data <- performance(prediction.obj = predictions_triathlon,
                         measure = "sens")

sensitivity <- sens_data@y.values[[1]]

#Specificity data
spec_data <- performance(prediction.obj = predictions_triathlon,
                         measure = "spec")

specificity <- spec_data@y.values[[1]]

#Cutoffs
cutoffs <- predictions_triathlon@cutoffs[[1]]

#ROC data
au_roc <- performance(prediction.obj = predictions_triathlon,
                       measure = "auc")

#Getting all together
plot_data <- cbind.data.frame(cutoffs,
                              specificity,
                              sensitivity)
```

Finally, to plot the ROC curve for the CART contained by the object `pruned_triathlon`, we can type the following command:

```
plot_data %>%
  ggplot() +
  geom_segment(aes(x = 0, xend = 1, y = 0, yend = 1),
               color="orange", size = 2) +
  geom_line(aes(x = 1 - specificity, y = sensitivity),
            color = "darkorchid", size = 2) +
  labs(x = "1 - Specificity",
       y = "Sensitivity",
       title = paste("Area under the curve:",
                     round(au_roc@y.values[[1]], 3))) +
  theme_bw()
```

Figure 19.14 shows the ROC of our final model.

Next, we will demonstrate the estimation of a regression tree, that is, of a CART whose dependent variable is represented in a metric form.

Regression trees in R

To present the estimation of a regression tree in R-based language, we will use data on the perception of corruption by the population of some countries of the globe, due to the average age of their billionaires, the average weekly workload worked by the population, and if the country is considered emerging or developed. The data can be found in the file `corruption.RData` (Fávero and Belfiore, 2019).

```
load("corruption.RData")
```

The variables that make up the dataset to be studied are described in Table 19.3.

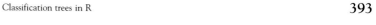

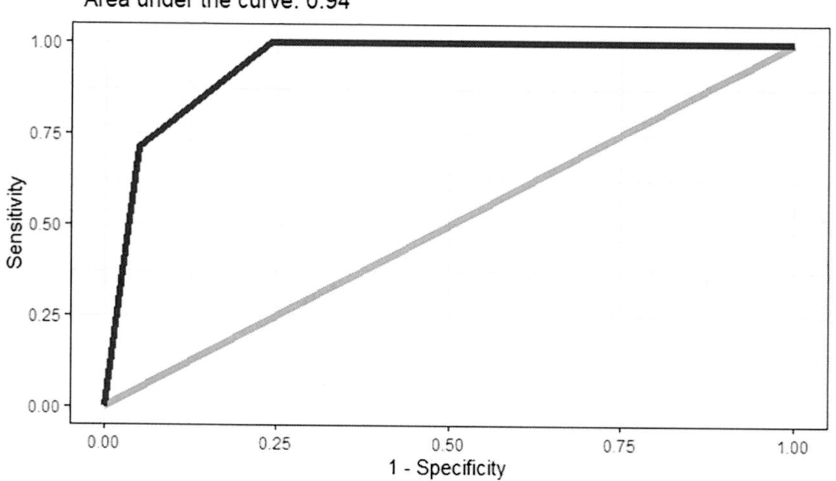

FIGURE 19.14 ROC of a classification tree.

TABLE 19.3 Description of the variables used to estimate the regression tree.

Variable	Description
country	String variable that identifies the country considered in the dataset.
cpi	Continuous metric variable about the perception of corruption in a country according to its population. The polarity of this indicator is that the greater it is, the smaller the corruption perceived by the people.
age	Metric variable that indicates the average age of billionaires in the country considered.
hours	Metric variable about the average weekly workload by the population of a given country.
emergent_country	Dichotomous variable with the value "yes" when the country is considered an emerging country and "no" when the country is considered developed.

For this case, we will estimate a CART using the variable *cpi* as the dependent variable. We can access the univariate descriptive statistics of the dataset with the command `summary()`:

```
summary(corruption)
```

Figure 19.15 shows the result obtained from the previous command.

```
     country          cpi              age             hours         emergent_country
 Argentina: 1   Min.   :2.000   Min.   :39.00   Min.   :26.80   no :21
 Australia: 1   1st Qu.:3.500   1st Qu.:58.75   1st Qu.:31.27   yes:31
 Austria  : 1   Median :5.300   Median :63.00   Median :32.95
 Belgium  : 1   Mean   :5.563   Mean   :61.73   Mean   :32.79
 Brazil   : 1   3rd Qu.:7.825   3rd Qu.:67.00   3rd Qu.:34.50
 Canada   : 1   Max.   :9.300   Max.   :79.00   Max.   :38.10
 (Other)  :46
```

FIGURE 19.15 Univariate descriptive statistics from the dataset present in the object `corruption`.

The reader must remember to use the function `set.seed()` to ensure that the results achieved are identical to those discussed in this work:

```
set.seed(1)
```

Because our dependent variable is quantitative, we will use variance as a metric criterion for data impurity, following the logic proposed earlier in the "Variance" section. That said, we can estimate this kind of CART as follows:

```
CART_corruption <- rpart(formula = cpi ~ age + hours + emergent_country,
                         data = corruption,
                         method = "anova")
```

An attentive reader will notice an important difference between the commands for estimating a regression tree and the commands for estimating a classification tree. Because the phenomenon manifests itself continuously, we argue `method = "anova"` to determine that R uses variance as a metric of impurity in the data. That said, we can use the command `rpart.plot()` to observe our CART.

```
rpart.plot(x = CART_corruption,
           type = 1,
           box.palette = "RdGn")
```

Figure 19.16 shows our regression tree contained in the object `CART_hate_crimes`.

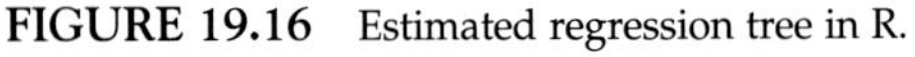

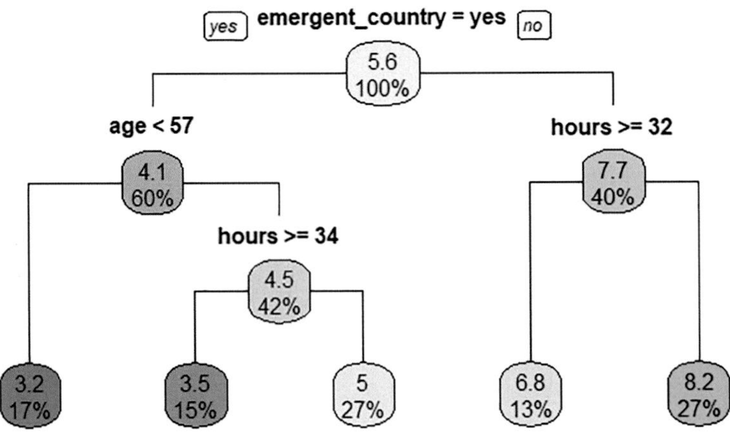

FIGURE 19.16 Estimated regression tree in R.

The reader will notice that, similar to the CART estimated in the "Classification trees in R" section, we let our tree grow freely, within the default settings of the function `rpart()`. In other words, this regression tree will not necessarily be our final model.

That said, we can access the variance of 5,530, of the variable *cpi*, using the command `var()` and Expression (19.7).

```
var(corruption$cpi)
```

Or yet:

$$var(Y,X) = \frac{\sum_{i=1}^{n}\left(Y_i - \overline{Y}\right)^2}{n-1} = \frac{282.0406}{52-1} = 5.530208.$$

For the case studied, we have two metric predictor variables and a categorical predictor variable. To define the root node, we must follow the logic of the weighted variance concept explained in the "Variance" section. First, we will use the variable *emergent_country*.

For subsets created due to the categories of the variable *emergent_country*, we must calculate their variances, as shown in Figure 19.17.

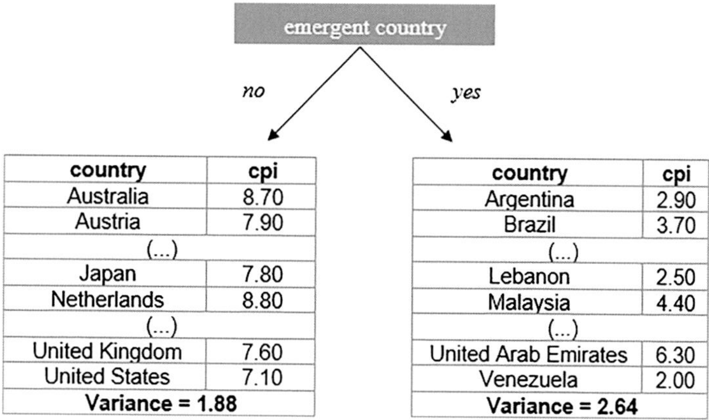

FIGURE 19.17 Subsets created due to the categories of the variable *emergent_country*.

According to Figure 19.17, for the category *no* of the variable *emergent_country*, the variance is 1.88, while for its category *yes* the variance is 2.64. The weighted variance is therefore given by:

$$weighted\ variance_{emergent\ country} = \frac{1.88 + 2.64}{2} = 2.26.$$

For the cases of the metric explanatory variables, the reader must organize the dataset in ascending order in relation to the explanatory variable of interest, observe the occurrence of changes in the value of the dependent variable, define thresholds, and check the weighted variance for each subset, in the same way explained in the "Classification trees in R" section. Then, to define the root node, **the reader must adopt the predictor variable with the smallest weighted variance**. The process must be iterated if there is a need to establish decision nodes.

Returning to Figure 19.16 to discuss each of its nodes, we can see that the value of 5.6 present in the root node refers to the average of the dependent variable *cpi*. The reader can verify the statement with the help of Figure 19.15 or by using the command:

```
mean(corruption$cpi)
```

It can also be said that the value of 100% stamped on the root node means that, at that moment in the tree, 100% of the observations were contained there.

To facilitate subsequent interpretations, similarly to the one elaborated in the "Classification trees in R" section, we will give names to the nodes of our regression tree, as shown in Figure 19.18.

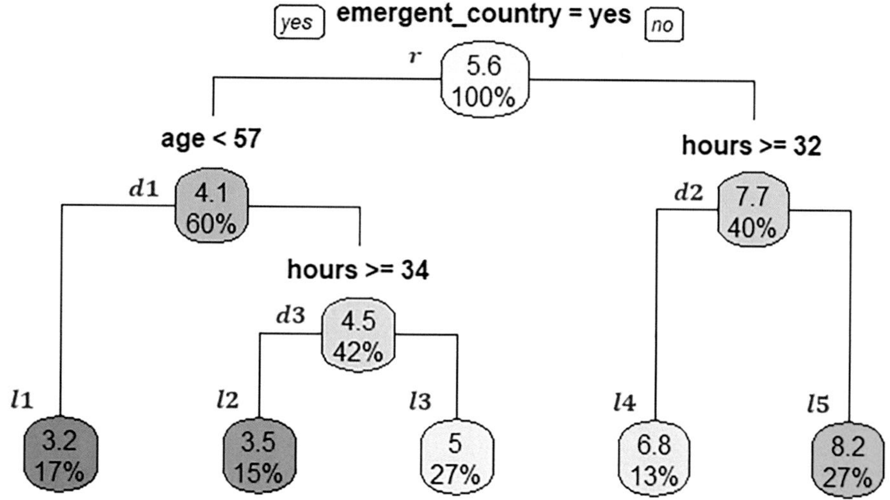

FIGURE 19.18 Naming the CART nodes.

For *d1*, the value of 4.1 represents the average value of the variable *cpi* for observations that are emerging countries, and the value of 60% indicates that 31 countries in the dataset were grouped there at that time. The reader can confirm the statement with the following routine:

```
corruption %>%
 filter(emergent_country == "yes") %>%
 summarise(mean = mean(cpi),
           n = n(),
           percentage = n / nrow(corruption))
```

Continuing with the split generated by *d1*, when we look at the case of *d3*, we can say that the value of 4.5 represents the average of those countries considered emerging, and whose average age of their billionaires is equal to or above 57 years of age. We also found that, at this specific moment of growth of our CART, 42% of our dataset (22 observations) were contained in *d3*. We can verify the aforementioned with the following routine:

```
corruption %>%
 filter(emergent_country == "yes" & age >= 57) %>%
 summarise(mean = mean(cpi),
           n = n(),
           percentage = n / nrow(corruption))
```

Following the proposed logic, in *l1* we can verify the fitted value (3.2) assumed for when the country is considered emerging and the average age of its billionaires is younger than 57 years of age. We can still say that 17% of the dataset (9 countries) received the fitted value discussed. The following routine reinforces what was exposed earlier:

```
corruption %>%
 filter(emergent_country == "yes" & age < 57) %>%
 summarise(mean = mean(cpi),
           n = n(),
           percentage = n / nrow(corruption))
```

We think the reader is already knowledgeable enough to explore the remaining nodes.

To prune the tree contained in Figure 19.16, let's go back to using the function `printcp()` from the package `rpart`, in search of the smallest CV error (`xerror`):

```
printcp(CART_corruption)
```

Figure 19.19 shows the R response for the previous command.

```
Regression tree:
rpart(formula = cpi ~ age + hours + emergent_country, data = corruption,
    method = "anova")

Variables actually used in tree construction:
[1] age              emergent_country hours

Root node error: 282.04/52 = 5.4239

n= 52

        CP nsplit rel error  xerror    xstd
1 0.585476      0   1.00000 1.02460 0.10998
2 0.039005      1   0.41452 0.43866 0.11416
3 0.034106      3   0.33651 0.47785 0.11196
4 0.010000      4   0.30241 0.42658 0.10351
```

FIGURE 19.19 Outcome of the function `printcp()`.

Figure 19.19 shows that the lowest value of xerror occurs with CP = 0.01 and nsplit = 4. With these hyperparameter values, we can prune our tree, and the result in this case will be the same as the original tree presented in Figure 19.16.

```
pruned_corruption <- prune(tree = CART_corruption,
                           cp = CART_corruption$cptable[which.min(
                             CART_corruption$cptable[,"xerror"]),"CP"]
                           )
```

As for the metric of how well the fitted values of the model adhere to the real data, we can use R^2 in a similar way to that used in Chapter 14 for a model estimated by OLS.

Thus we will add to our dataset corruption, the fitted values and the residuals of our CART:

```
#Fitted values
corruption["fitted"] <- predict(object = pruned_corruption,
                                newdata = corruption)

#Residuals
corruption["residuals"] <- corruption$cpi - corruption$fitted
```

That said, the R^2 value of 0.698 of our model can be found with the following command routine:

```
corruption %>%
 summarise(rss = sum((fitted - mean(fitted)) ^ 2),
           u = sum((residuals) ^ 2)) %>%
 summarise(r_squared = rss / (rss + u))
```

Figure 19.20 presents a scatter with the observed values of the variables *cpi* and *age*, together with the fitted values of the model, after typing the following codes:

```
corruption %>%
  ggplot() +
  geom_point(aes(x = age, y = cpi), color = "darkorchid") +
  geom_smooth(aes(x = age, y = fitted, color = "Fitted Values"), se = FALSE) +
  labs(x = "Billionaires' Mean Ages",
       y = "Corruption Perception Index") +
  scale_color_manual("", values = "orange") +
  theme(panel.background = element_rect("white"),
        panel.grid = element_line("grey95"),
        panel.border = element_rect(NA),
        legend.position = "bottom")
```

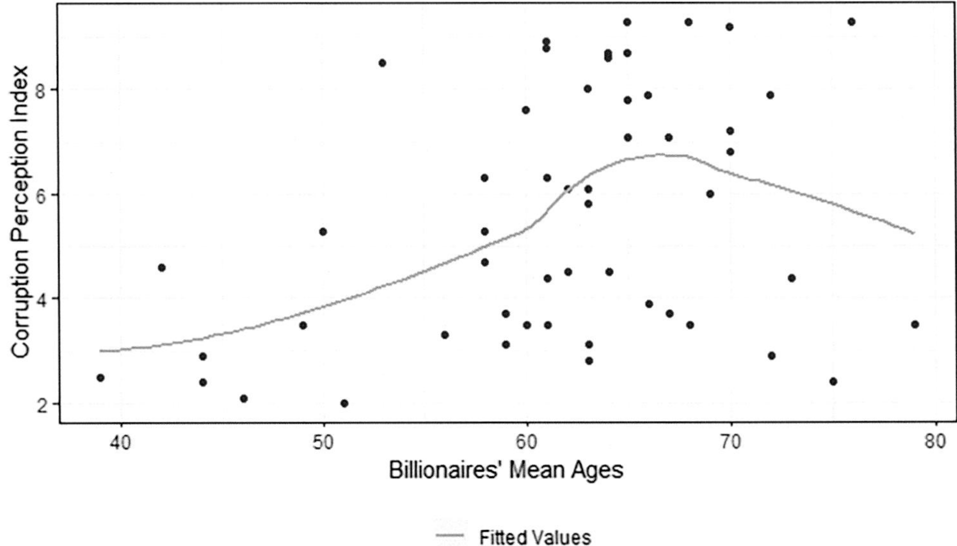

FIGURE 19.20 Graph showing the model's fitted values for the variables *cpi* and *age*.

It is also possible to see the adequacy of the model's fitted values in relation to the variable *hours*, with the following routine, whose result is explained in Figure 19.21.

```
corruption %>%
  ggplot() +
  geom_point(aes(x = hours, y = cpi), color = "darkorchid") +
  geom_smooth(aes(x = hours, y = fitted, color = "Fitted Values"), se = FALSE) +
  labs(x = "Average Hours Worked",
       y = "Corruption Perception Index") +
  scale_color_manual("", values = "orange") +
  theme(panel.background = element_rect("white"),
        panel.grid = element_line("grey95"),
        panel.border = element_rect(NA),
        legend.position = "bottom")
```

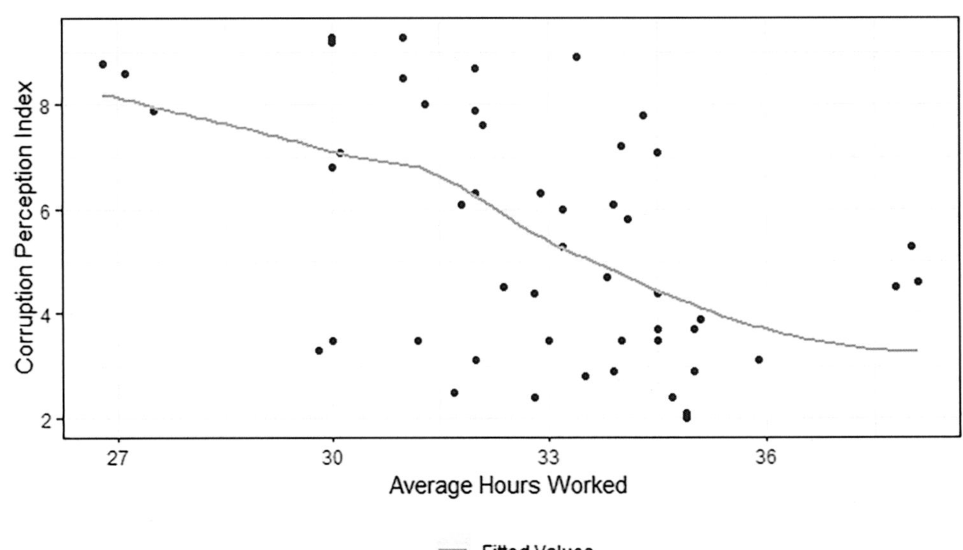

FIGURE 19.21 Graph showing the model's fitted values for the variables *cpi* and *hours*.

Finally, if the interest is to observe how the fitted values of the model behave in relation to the variable *emergent_country*, we can use the following codes, whose results are shown in Figure 19.22.

```
corruption %>%
  ggplot() +
  geom_point(aes(x = emergent_country, y = cpi), color = "darkorchid") +
  geom_smooth(aes(x = as.numeric(emergent_country),
                  y = fitted,
                  color = "Fitted Values"),
              se = FALSE) +
  labs(x = "Emergent Country",
       y = "Corruption Perception Index") +
  scale_color_manual("", values = "orange") +
  theme(panel.background = element_rect("white"),
        panel.grid = element_line("grey95"),
        panel.border = element_rect(NA),
        legend.position = "bottom")
```

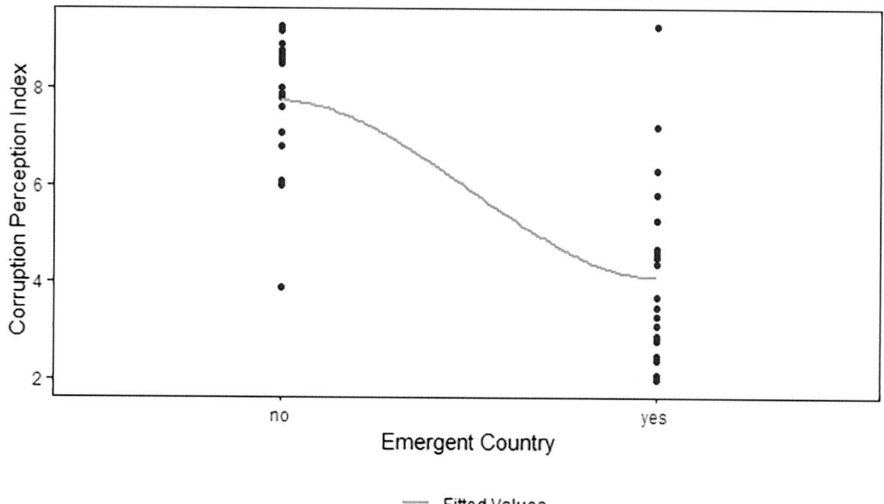

FIGURE 19.22 Graph showing the model's fitted values for the variables *cpi* and *emergent_country*.

Final remarks

Decision trees are predictive estimates that can be used for both metric and categorical dependent variables.

They are configured in models of reasonably simplified interpretation that, as initial care, it is recommended to study how the dependent variable manifests itself to better choose the data impurity mitigation criterion.

Although the command `rpart()` in R-based language has already been instrumentalized to, as a rule, avoid the overfitting problem in most cases, the reader must be aware of possible overfitting problems. For situations in which overfitting is detected, the tree can be pruned based on the smallest CV error, adopting the best coupled CP. It is also recommended that the operator of the algorithm continuously test the model against some observations not present in the training sample.

Exercises

1. With the idea of studying client fidelity, a supermarket group conducted research with 3,000 consumers at the time they were paying for their purchases. Being that the fidelity of a determined customer can be measured based on their return to the establishment, with their items paid for, within 1 year from the date of their previous purchase, monitoring is easy by means of their Social Security (SS) number. As such, if the SS number for a determined customer is in the store dataset, however no purchase is made under the same SS number within

the period of 1 year, this customer will be classified as having no establishment fidelity. On the other hand, if the SS for another customer is in the store dataset and is identified in another purchase within the period of 1 year, the customer will be classified in the establishment fidelity category. So to stipulate the criteria that increase the probability that a customer presents establishment fidelity, the supermarket group collected the following variables from each of the 3,000 customers and then followed them for 1 year from the date of the original purchase (Fávero and Belfiore, 2019).

Variable	Description
id	Variable that substitutes the SS due to security measures. It is a string variable, varies between 0001 and 3000, and will not be used in the modeling.
fidelity	Dependent binary variable corresponding to whether or not the customer returns to the store to effect a new purchase during a period of less than 1 year (no = 0; yes = 1).
gender	Customer gender (female = 0; male = 1).
age	Customer age (years).
service	Qualitative variable with five categories corresponding to the perceived level of service provided by the establishment at the time of the original purchase (terrible = 1; bad = 2; regular = 3; good = 4; excellent = 5).
assortment	Qualitative variable with five categories corresponding to the perception of quality of the assortment of goods offered by the establishment at the time of the original purchase (terrible = 1; bad = 2; regular = 3; good = 4; excellent = 5).
accessibility	Qualitative variable with five categories corresponding to the perception of quality of access to the establishment, such as parking and access to the sales area (terrible = 1; bad = 2; regular = 3; good = 4; excellent = 5).
price	Qualitative variable with five categories corresponding to product prices in relation to the competition at the time of the original purchase (terrible = 1; bad = 2; regular = 3; good = 4; excellent = 5).

By means of an analysis of the dataset present in the file `fidelity_data.RData`, we would like you to answer the following:

a. Among the metrics of data impurity studied in this chapter, which one should be used for the CART in question?
b. Present the estimated CART plot before a possible pruning, using the command `set.seed(111)` before estimation.
c. What is the lowest `xerror` value found?
d. For the lowest `xerror` value found, what is the CP value?
e. For the lowest `xerror` value found, what is the ideal number of splits?
f. After pruning the tree, present your new plot.
g. Present and interpret the confusion matrix of the pruned model.
h. What is the value of the area under the model's ROC curve?
i. Estimate the best possible binary logistic model with the data from this exercise. Which model should we choose in this specific case?

2. We will continue to investigate the dataset `audiology.RData`, discussed in the "Estimation of a multinomial logistic regression model in R" section in Chapter 15, which corresponds to the subset of the original dataset that can be found in the UCI Machine Learning Repository (Quinlan, 1992).

Variables	Description
Id	Variable indicating the code related to each observation.
age_gt_60	Dichotomous variable indicating if the observation is older than 60 years of age.
airbone_gap	Binary variable indicating if there is any air-bone gap in the observation.
bone_abnormal	Dummy variable indicating if there is any bone abnormality in the ear canal.
history_dizziness	Dichotomous variable indicating if there is a history of dizziness in the observation.
history_fluctuating	Binary variable indicating if there is a history of the sensation of fluctuation in the observation.
history_heredity	Dummy variable indicating if there is a history of hereditary hearing problems in the observation.
history_nausea	Dichotomous variable indicating if there is a recent history of nausea in the observation.
history_noise	Binary variable indicating if there is a recent history of hearing constant noise in the observation.
history_vomiting	Dichotomous variable indicating if there is a recent history of vomiting in the observation.
speech	Polychotomic variable regarding the speech level of the observation ("unmeasured"; "very poor"; "poor"; "normal"; "good"; and "very good").
viith_nerve_signs	Dummy variable indicating if there is a diagnosis of VIIth nerve palsy in the observation.
class	Polychotomic variable classifying whether the observation has normal hearing or if it fits into any possible hearing problems: "cochlear problems," "conductive problems," "otitis media," "possible brainstem disorder," or "possible menieres."

Using the variable *class* as the dependent variable of a classification tree, we ask you to answer the following:

a. Among the metrics of data impurity studied in this chapter, which one should be used for the CART in question?
b. Present the estimated CART plot before a possible pruning, using the command `set.seed(77)` before estimation.
c. What is the lowest `xerror` value found?
d. For the lowest `xerror` value found, what is the CP value?
e. For the lowest `xerror` value found, what is the ideal number of splits?
f. After pruning the tree, present your new plot.
g. Estimate the best possible multinomial logistic model with the data from this exercise. Which model should we choose in this specific case?
h. In a similar way to what we studied in the "Estimation of a multinomial logistic regression model in R" section in Chapter 15, what is the general effectiveness of the pruned CART?

Supplementary data sets

```
corruption.RData
triathlon.RData
```

Please access supplementary data files here: https://doi.org/10.17632/55623jkwrp.3

CHAPTER

20

Boosting and bagging

AT THE END OF THIS CHAPTER, YOU WILL BE ABLE TO:

- Understand the circumstances in which boosting and bagging estimations make sense.
- Establish differences between boosting and bagging approaches.
- Understand how to refine the combined estimates to mitigate the problem of overfitting and correlation among trees.
- Estimate boosting and bagging models, understand their differences, and interpret their results.

R-based language packages used in this chapter

```
library(plotly)
library(gbm)
library(ipred)
library(rpart)
library(tidyverse)
library(doParallel)
library(caret)
library(reshape2)
library(stringr)
library(vip)
library(gridExtra)
```

Don't forget to define the R working directory (the location where your datasets are installed):

```
setwd("C:/book/chapter20")
```

Introduction

In this chapter, we will study two kinds of estimations that consist of a combination of models with wide use in various areas of knowledge. We are talking about boosting and bagging techniques. It is appropriate to address the subject right after talking about classification and regression trees (CARTs) because the techniques in this chapter are mostly applied by combining decision trees, but they do not necessarily need to be; that is, they can be applied in the face of most supervised models used in this work.

https://doi.org/10.1016/B978-0-12-824271-1.00017-2

That said, **the combination of models proposed by the boosting and bagging methodologies** is inspired by the idea of collective intelligence narrated by Surowiecki (2005). The author, in his work, *The Wisdom of Crowds*, recalls a competition that took place commonly in the United Kingdom whose objective was to hit the weight of an ox. The entire population was free to participate, and the individual who matched the weight of the animal received it as a prize.

James Surowiecki narrates that Francis Galton realized that audience hunches had high variability when individually considered, including experts on the subject; however, the mean of the hunches, taken together, had strong accuracy, at 99% confidence! This conclusion indicates that the combined intelligence of the participants had a greater predictive power than an individual considered, even if that person was an expert on the subject. It is from this perspective that the idea of ensemble models arises.

A recent example of collective intelligence occurred in 2006, when Netflix offered a \$1 million prize in a kind of contest never seen before. The company shared a huge amount of anonymous data about the ratings its users gave its movies (from one to five stars) so contestants could better get their system called *Cinematch*. The data added up to more than 100 million ratings for more than 17,000 movies, given by 480,189 customers.

At the time, Cinematch tried to predict Netflix users' ratings of new movies based on what those people had already seen on the platform. The idea of the contest was to improve the predictive capacity of this algorithm by at least 10%.

The most interesting part is that the behavior of the human components of the teams participating in the contest started to resemble the main premise of the ensemble models, joint prediction, which is similar to what Francis Galton experienced in the 19th century: two of the contest's competing teams, BellKor and BigChaos, combined their predictive models and formed BellKor's Pragmatic Chaos team, which won the tournament. As Galton already imagined, the aforementioned teams, when combined, realized that collectively they would become more intelligent and managed to overcome the goal proposed by Netflix, increasing Cinematch's predictive power by 10.06%. The award was presented on September 21, 2009, and its story is still told in several pages of the scientific magazine *Chance* of the American Statistical Association.

It must be said that, regardless of the path chosen by the reader (boosting or bagging), there is considerable randomness in the iterative procedures internal to the algorithms; Therefore we will continue to use the function `set.seed()`, already discussed in Chapter 19, to allow the reader to obtain the same results presented here on his or her machine.

Boosting

As a rule, *boosting* refers to an estimation method of multiple combined models of the CART type. For example, if the reader desires, it is perfectly possible to perform boosting in generalized linear models (GLMs). However, for this work, we will cover the most common boosting applications, that is, those that use CARTs.

In this approach, each decision tree is purposely skewed to better fit the points where the immediately previous estimation was mostly incorrect. The idea is to aggregate models to assume a proxy for the collective intelligence narrated in the introductory section of this chapter. Therefore in each iterative step *(m)*, the boosting algorithm will give to the n observations of the original dataset a weight greater than or equal to 0 ($w_m \geq 0$), with the initial weight of $w_1 = \frac{1}{n}$.

The iterative procedure will be stopped when the maximum number of models commanded by the reader is reached. So, here, the amount of estimates to be combined with each other is configured in a hyperparameter.

The background of the boosting algorithm can be briefly explained in the following steps:

Step 1: Apply the weights $w_1 = \frac{1}{n}$ to each of the n observations in the dataset used to train the boosting algorithm, giving rise to the error term ε. However, in this case, ε will refer to the total sum of the weights w, where the predictions of the model are incorrect.

Step 2: For observations in which the predictions are incorrect, there will be an increase in the weights previously assigned, becoming $w_m = w_{m-1} \times \frac{1}{2\varepsilon}$; on the other hand, there will be a decrease in the weights previously attributed to good predictions, represented by $w_m = w_{m-1} \times \frac{1}{2 \times (1-\varepsilon)}$.

Step 3: Finally, a confidence factor *(α)* must be calculated so the higher the value of ε, the lower the value of α, and vice versa. The value of α can be measured using the formula $\alpha = \frac{1}{2}\ln\left(\frac{1-\varepsilon}{\varepsilon}\right)$.

Step 4: After the end of the iterations, for the case in which the dependent variable Y is categorical, its predictions will be made based on a weighted vote to rank the observations; however, if Y is metric, there will be a weighted average to predict the observations, with obviously higher weights for the last established trees.

In addition to its high predictive power, an interesting point of boosting is its ability to deal well with missing values of predictor variables without the need for value imputation; this is because several CARTs will be generated, and the weights for each observation will be revised during every iteration. On the other hand, because of the constant search to minimize errors, the risk for overfitting will always be present (see the "Overfitting" section in Chapter 19).

It is also necessary to point out that boosting techniques are usually computationally demanding and, like CART, cannot present a mathematical equation, which generates a limitation on the interpretability of the model.

It must be said that there are several possible types of optimization functions for models built with the boosting approach. In the "Boosting and bagging applications in R" section later in this chapter, we will focus on a generic optimization function called the *gradient descent algorithm.*

The choice of the gradient descent algorithm is due to its suitability to basically any cost function. If it is not obvious to the reader, cost function, in short, is a way to measure how much inaccuracy a given model has to measure the relationship of a given dependent variable to its predictor variables.

That said, for the gradient descent algorithm, unlike the maximum likelihood criterion seen in Chapters 14 to 17, it must reach the lowest possible value to minimize the cost function. This minimum value will directly depend on the hyperparameters used for the estimation.

Figure 20.1 exemplifies how the gradient descent algorithm works.

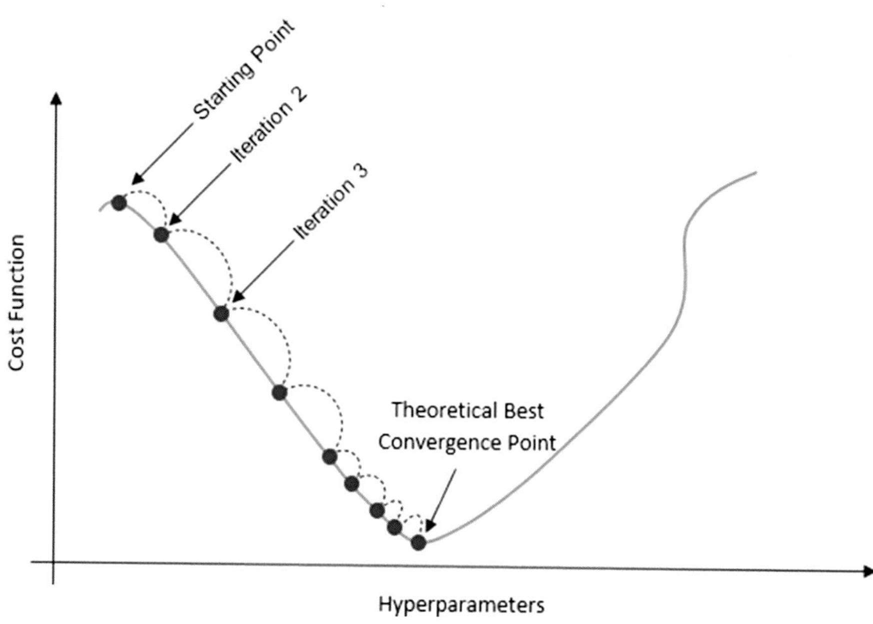

FIGURE 20.1 Theoretical behavior of the gradient descent algorithm.

Each point represents that an iteration *m* occurred as a result of the hyperparameters declared to R, aiming at reaching the lowest value that will necessarily cause the greatest decay of the cost function adopted.

Next, we will present the main hyperparameters for the boosting approach discussed in this chapter.

Main hyperparameters for boosting

There are different approaches that use boosting principles. For this work, we will emphasize the *generalized boosted regression modeling* (GBM) family. We are making this clear because there will be different hyperparameters to satisfy for each family of boosting techniques. Therefore we show the main hyperparameters for GBM-type estimations in the following sections.

Number of trees

Earlier in the "Boosting" section, we made clear one of the main hyperparameters of the boosting approach that we will work on in this book: the amount of CART to be estimated. Of course, this is not the only hyperparameter, but looking back at Figure 20.1, you can already see how important it is! The number of iterations will depend directly on this hyperparameter, and an unsuspecting reader can easily miss or even surpass a given optimum convergence point of the gradient descent algorithm.

There is no rule of thumb that determines how many iterations will be necessary for a better boosting model, but we will provide some important tips in the "Boosting and bagging applications in R" section later in this chapter to better guide the reader in search of the best fit.

Learning rate

The *learning rate,* also known in R as *shrinkage,* determines the contribution of each tree to the final result and controls how fast the algorithm will drive toward the minimum gradient value. Again, as noted in the dotted curves in

Figure 20.1, we can see how low values would increase the possibility of the algorithm finding the minimum gradient, which would generate robust models because of the lower error rate. However, depending on the number of trees established (see the "Number of trees" section), the iterations can stop before the ideal moment for an optimal gradient value.

Just as there is no general rule to determine the ideal number of trees, there is also no single path to determine what the learning rate of a given model should be. In any case, we will provide the reader with tools to help them find learning rates that make sense for their estimation.

Tree depth

It is also possible to determine the depth of the trees established in the predefined iterations. However, the reader should be aware of a possible tradeoff. As a rule, the ideal is to establish shallow trees, that is, decision trees in which the initial predictive power is low, comparable to the act of trying to guess the prediction.

When establishing shallow trees, there is an economy in computational demand and the expectation that, after establishing the first tree step by step, other CARTs to be estimated will add their predictive power to the immediately preceding model.

On the other hand, deep trees were able to achieve higher predictive power, but at the cost of greater computational demand. Furthermore, by definition, the boosting approach seeks the best model because of a better refinement of the error terms. Therefore overfitting becomes a constant problem, especially when opting for deep trees.

Minimum number of observations in leaf nodes

As discussed earlier, the boosting approach is performed on shallow trees as a rule, and this hyperparameter will rarely have a big impact on the model's performance within this perspective. However, higher values of the minimum number of observations in leaf nodes help the model capture the specific relationships of a given training sample, while lower values are more useful when the data is unbalanced.

Subsampling

The idea of subsampling during the boosting iterative processes aims to mitigate the overfitting problem by implementing a stochastic gradient descent to try to reduce error modeling. Adoption of this procedure also aims to contribute to the evidence of an optimal gradient value and, consequently, of the cost function.

Bagging

The word *bagging* comes from the expression *bootstrap aggregating* and refers to a method of estimating multiple models by combining the inferences of each model into a single aggregated prediction. A wide range of basic learners can be used to implement bagging, including CART, support vector machine (SVM), or GLM methods. However, Boehmke and Greenwell (2019) argue that for more stable algorithms (e.g., GLMs or generalized linear mixed models [GLMMs]), bagging does not usually provide much improvement. According to the authors, the approach discussed in this section makes great sense for CARTs because this kind of learner base is very sensitive to minor changes in the dataset, generating estimates with great variability among themselves in each iterative process.

Therefore, following the logic proposed earlier at the beginning of the "Boosting" section, we will also look at the bagging approach for CARTs.

Bagging uses the idea of bootstrap sampling, which is a type of random sampling with replacement in which each subset of the original data also has size n. Figure 20.2 demonstrates this proposal.

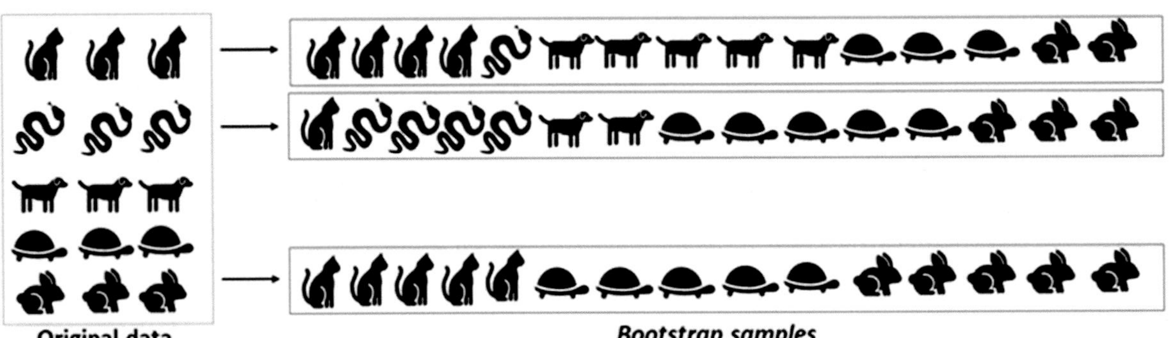

FIGURE 20.2 An example of bootstrap sampling.

The reader can see that, in fact, each new bootstrap sample in Figure 20.2 contains the same amount of elements as the original sample. Furthermore, by definition, there is replacement randomization, where each element of the original sample can be selected for the samples resulting from the procedure more than once or even not at all.

Given this, an attentive reader will question that, for example, there would be at least one repeated cat in the first bootstrap sampling. It could even be said that the four cats in the first subsampling refer to the same cat. Thus at times, when individually considered, each constructed tree would despise a good part of the sample. In the same sense, the reader may also notice that in the first bootstrap sampling, only one of the snakes was considered; in the last bootstrap sampling, snakes and dogs were not even considered, and so on.

In fact, an attentive reader can create an algorithm in R and propose these bootstrap sampling simulations for, say, 1 million times. The reader would conclude that the bootstrap samples contain repeated observations approximately 60% to 65% of the time, therefore when these samples are individually considered, they would disregard part of the original observations.

These observations not previously considered in each bagging step are called *out of bag* (OOB). The interesting part is that at each iteration, that is, at each tree created, the algorithm itself is tested for accuracy using, precisely, the observations not considered in that step; that is, the OOB will be a kind of training sample for the algorithm while the model is being refined. This situation will greatly facilitate the definition of how many iterations should be commanded in the hyperparameters of the bagging estimation. So for each iteration m, over each bootstrap sample b of the original dataset n, we can summarize the bagging procedure with the following steps:

- **Step 1:** Generate multiple bootstrap samples b from the n observations, where $b=1, 2, 3, \ldots$
- **Step 2:** Apply a given supervised algorithm to each of the samples b elaborated in Step 1, and produce results aimed at predictability.

That said, by assuming the predictions of the bagging approach as $\widehat{Y}_{bagging}$, one can playfully write how the approach works as $\widehat{Y}_{bagging} = \widehat{Y}_1 + \widehat{Y}_2 + \ldots + \widehat{Y}_b$.

In this sense, if the observed dependent variable Y is of the categorical type, $\widehat{Y}_{bagging}$ will be given by the greater amount of occurrence of the categories or by the greater probability of occurrence of a given category. On the other hand, if the observed dependent variable Y is of the metric type, $\widehat{Y}_{bagging}$ will be the mean of the $\widehat{Y}_b$ predictions.

When working with the bagging approach for CARTs, it is important to recognize that the estimated trees are not completely independent, even though the process is random in many of its steps. Thus by always using the same variables, the correlation among trees (with emphasis on the upper nodes) constitutes a limitation that can be mitigated by working with a similar technique called *random forests* (see Chapter 21 of this work).

According to Kelleher et al. (2015), bagging estimates are not usually as computationally demanding as boosting applications. The authors also mention that boosting estimates usually obtain superior predictive performance in datasets containing up to 4,000 observations; after this theoretical cutoff, bagging approaches, especially those of random forests, tend to stand out. Caruana et al. (2008) explain that this behavior occurs because boosted ensemble models are much more subject to the overfitting problem, and as there is a gradual increase in the number of variables, the probability of the existence of overfitting increases considerably.

Main hyperparameters for bagging

As presented earlier in the "Main hyperparameters for boosting" section, there are different approaches and families of techniques that use bagging assumptions. In Chapter 21, for example, we will look at random forests, which are a specific type of bagging. To follow the logic of this work, we will discuss the main hyperparameters based on the propositions of Breiman (1996).

Number of trees

Like boosting estimates, bagging approach estimates have the number of trees estimated as a hyperparameter. It is also possible to say that, similar to what was shown in the "Number of trees" section, there is no rule of thumb that predetermines an optimal number of iterations for the bagging approach. However, in the "Boosting and bagging applications in R" section later in this chapter, we will give some tips for the reader based on the outputs generated by the OOB error.

The *OOB error* refers to the errors calculated for observations not considered in each iteration (see the "Bagging" section). When the dependent variable is metric, according to the algorithms adopted by this work, the OOB error will be calculated using the root mean squared error (RMSE), given by $RMSE = \sqrt{\frac{1}{n}\sum_{i=1}^{n}\left(Y_i - \widehat{Y}_i\right)^2}$; on the other hand, when the dependent variable is categorical, classification errors will be considered. In both cases, the smallest error values are chosen for the purposes of comparison between estimates.

Minimum number of observations in leaf nodes

An attentive reader will notice that the minimum number of observations in leaf nodes is also a hyperparameter of the combination of models by boosting, but, in bagging, there will be no reoccupation with the tree depths.

The situation arises because, as studied in the "Bagging" section, overfitting is not the main concern that should be observed when combining models by bagging, but rather the correlation among the trees estimated at each iterative process of the algorithm.

Boosting and bagging applications in R

Before presenting the dataset used to apply the boosting and bagging approaches, we feel obliged to inform the reader that the following models will take much longer to obtain their convergences compared with those in the previous chapters. In this sense, we take care to explain the time we spend on the models that follow. It is important for the reader to know that the machine used had an Intel i5 processor and 32 MB of RAM.

In the following applications, we will use a single base that concerns the vulnerability to poverty of all 5,565 Brazilian municipalities due to educational issues and differences among regions to which each municipality belongs. We think using a single base will enable the reader to have a better idea of the differences between approaches and therefore be able to choose the best algorithm for the problems they want to model in their academic and/or professional life. It must be said that the data were obtained from the website of the United Nations Development Program (UNDP).

The variables present in the `brazilian_poverty.RData` file are highlighted in Table 20.1:

TABLE 20.1 Description of the variables used for model combinations via boosting and bagging.

Variable	Description
municipality	Variable identifying each of the 5,565 Brazilian municipalities.
state	Variable identifying to which of the 27 Brazilian states each of the 5,565 studied municipalities belongs.
poverty_index	Metric variable concerning an indicator of vulnerability to poverty. The index shows the proportion of individuals with a per capita family income of less than one-half the minimum wage.
illiteracy_rate	Metric variable indicating an illiteracy rate in the population, multiplied by 100.
elementary_school_rate	Metric variable indicating the rate of individuals older than 18 years of age who completed elementary school, multiplied by 100.
high_school_rate	Metric variable representing the rate of individuals older than 18 years of age who completed high school, multiplied by 100.
college_rate	Metric variable indicating the rate of individuals between 18 and 24 years of age who attended college, multiplied by 100.
region	Polychotomous variable considering the five largest regions in Brazil: midwest, north, northeast, south, and southeast.

The first step, therefore, will be loading the file `brazilian_poverty.RData`.

```
load("brazilian_poverty.RData")
```

After that, we can check the descriptive statistics for the metric variables and the frequency tables for the categorical variables:

```
summary(brazilian_poverty)
```

Figure 20.3 shows the results of the previous command. It is important for the reader to know that in Brazil there are several municipalities that use the same name, but it is not common for this to happen within the same state.

```
       municipality                     state          poverty_index    illiteracy_rate
bom jesus    :    5   Minas Gerais        : 853   Min.    : 1.97   Min.    : 1.10
são domingos:    5   São Paulo           : 645   1st Qu.:23.96   1st Qu.: 9.98
bonito       :    4   Rio Grande do Sul: 496   Median :42.23   Median :16.46
planalto     :    4   Bahia               : 417   Mean    :43.99   Mean    :20.52
santa helena:    4   Paraná              : 399   3rd Qu.:65.30   3rd Qu.:31.33
santa inês   :    4   Santa Catarina      : 293   Max.    :91.57   Max.    :57.18
(Other)      :5539   (Other)             :2462
elementary_school_rate high_school_rate  college_rate          region
Min.    :12.03        Min.    : 3.04    Min.    : 0.280   midwest   : 466
1st Qu.:31.53        1st Qu.:18.32    1st Qu.: 3.240   north     : 449
Median :38.44        Median :23.48    Median : 4.810   northeast:1794
Mean    :39.66        Mean    :24.75    Mean    : 5.496   south     :1188
3rd Qu.:46.43        3rd Qu.:30.01    3rd Qu.: 6.950   southeast:1668
```

FIGURE 20.3 Univariate descriptive statistics and frequency tables of the dataset present in the object `brazilian_poverty`.

A study of the outcomes of Figure 20.3 is important to prevent extrapolation problems at the moments of prediction. As with all the techniques studied so far, boosting and bagging approaches do not guarantee good functionality in the face of the extrapolation problem.

As discussed in the "Hyperparameters" and "Estimating CART models in R" sections in Chapter 19, the algorithms discussed in the following sections have a high rate of randomization in their procedures; therefore we will establish a training sample and a validation sample from the original dataset. The training sample will serve to train the algorithm and will concern 60% of the original data for the case studied. The rest of the data will be considered as a validation sample to verify the accuracy levels of our models, and in the case of boosting, it will help ensure that there is no overfitting problem.

An attentive reader will also notice that the dependent variable of the study *(poverty_index)* is of the continuous metric type. **If the reader variable were categorical, there is no doubt that the confusion matrices as well as the ROC curves (studied in Chapters 15 and 19), could be interposed with the same codes previously studied.**

That said, we can establish our training sample and our validation sample as follows:

```
set.seed(1)
sample_index <- sample(x = 1:dim(brazilian_poverty)[1],
                       size = nrow(brazilian_poverty) * 0.6)

train_sample <- brazilian_poverty[sample_index, ]

validation_sample <- brazilian_poverty[-sample_index, ]
```

As discussed earlier, the algorithms will be taught to recognize patterns using the same training sample, regardless of the approach used (boosting or bagging). After that, we will verify your prediction levels with the same validation sample. We can therefore proceed to the application of the combination of models via boosting.

Boosting in R

The model combination approach via boosting will use the algorithm `gbm()` from the package `gbm`. Our first estimate can be made as follows:

```
# 9,420 ms and 38.1 MB RAM
set.seed(1)
m1_boosting <- gbm(formula = poverty_index ~ region + illiteracy_rate +
                     elementary_school_rate + high_school_rate + college_rate,
                   data = train_sample,
                   distribution = "gaussian",
                   n.trees = 5000,
                   shrinkage = 0.1,
                   interaction.depth = 3,
                   n.minobsinnode = 10,
                   cv.folds = 10)
```

In the previous command of the function `gbm()`, we argued `formula` to define our dependent variable *(poverty_index)* and our predictor variables. We used the argument `data` to indicate where the data to train the algorithm will come from. We then argued `distribution = "gaussian"` because our dependent variable is a continuous metric. (Note that other distributions such as Bernoulli and Poisson are possible, and we ask the reader to take the time to study the algorithm documentation with the help of the command `?gbm`). Soon after, we established the combination of 5,000 CARTs (`n.trees`) and declared a learning rate (`shrinkage`) of 0.1, default value in the function `gbm()`. We then used the argument `interaction.depth` to indicate the depth of each CART to be combined and the argument `n.minobsinnode` to indicate a minimum number of observations in each leaf node. Finally, we used the argument `cv.folds` to determine how the subsamplings would occur; in this case, for each iterative step (each tree), 10 observations of the training sample will be reserved to verify the adequacy of the combined model by cross-validation.

Applying the function `summary()`to the created object `m1_boosting` gives us some interesting information, which is presented in Figure 20.4.

```
summary(m1_boosting)
```

```
                                             var   rel.inf
illiteracy_rate                  illiteracy_rate 55.348902
region                                    region 18.230989
high_school_rate                high_school_rate  9.740375
elementary_school_rate elementary_school_rate  8.394679
college_rate                        college_rate  8.285055
```

FIGURE 20.4 The importance of each variable in explaining the phenomenon, according to the combination of models present in the object `m1_boosting`.

According to Figure 20.4, the most important variable for the combined modeling via boosting, present in the object `m1_boosting`, is *illiteracy_rate* followed by *region*. We will see in the "Bagging in R" section that these results do not necessarily hold when we change the approach to bagging.

Despite an apparently well-estimated model, some doubts arise from the study of the "Main hyperparameters for boosting" section. For example, was the 5,000 CART combination a good idea or just a waste of time and computing power? Is the learning rate adequate? Are the CARTs' depths and the number of observations in each leaf node refined? We will try to answer these and other questions along the lines that follow.

Because we started with an interesting number of CARTs combined (5,000), we thought it would be interesting to check from which iteration there is the smallest error identified by the subsamplings (`cv.error`):

```
min_error <- which.min(m1_boosting$cv.error)

min_error
```

When doing this, R will present us the value of 227 as an answer, which refers to the amount of CARTs estimated to obtain the smallest error metric. **Because the algorithm we will study in the next section uses the RMSE as an accuracy metric, we will do the same here for our models estimated via boosting so we can compare them at the appropriate time.** Thus our RMSE for the estimation present in the object `m1_boosting` is given by the following:

```
sqrt(m1_boosting$cv.error[min_error])
```

The indicated value after the previous codes will be approximately 7.56. In fact, having this information, we can verify that when considering these same hyperparameters, there is no gain in prediction power after the 227th iteration. We can check what is stated with the help of a graphic, whose codes for its generation are as follows:

```
ggplotly(
  m1_boosting$cv.error %>%
    as.data.frame() %>%
    rownames_to_column(var = "trees") %>%
    rename(MSE = 2) %>%
```

Continued

```
    mutate(RMSE = sqrt(MSE),
           trees = as.numeric(trees)) %>%
    arrange(trees) %>%
    ggplot(aes(x = trees, y = RMSE)) +
    geom_line(color = "orange") +
    geom_vline(xintercept = min_error, color = "darkorchid", linetype = "dashed") +
    labs(x = "Amount of Trees",
         y = "RMSE") +
    theme_bw()
)
```

Figure 20.5 shows the results of the previous command and demonstrates that preliminarily, for this case, when considering the hyperparameters used, it does not resolve to combine 5,000 CARTs. In fact, according to Figure 20.5, a much smaller number of iterations (the intercept of the dashed line on the abscissa axis) would be enough for a good decrease in the RMSE. If the reader is using the complementary scripts while reading, he or she will see that 227 CARTs, in fact, already provide the value of 7.56 RMSE.

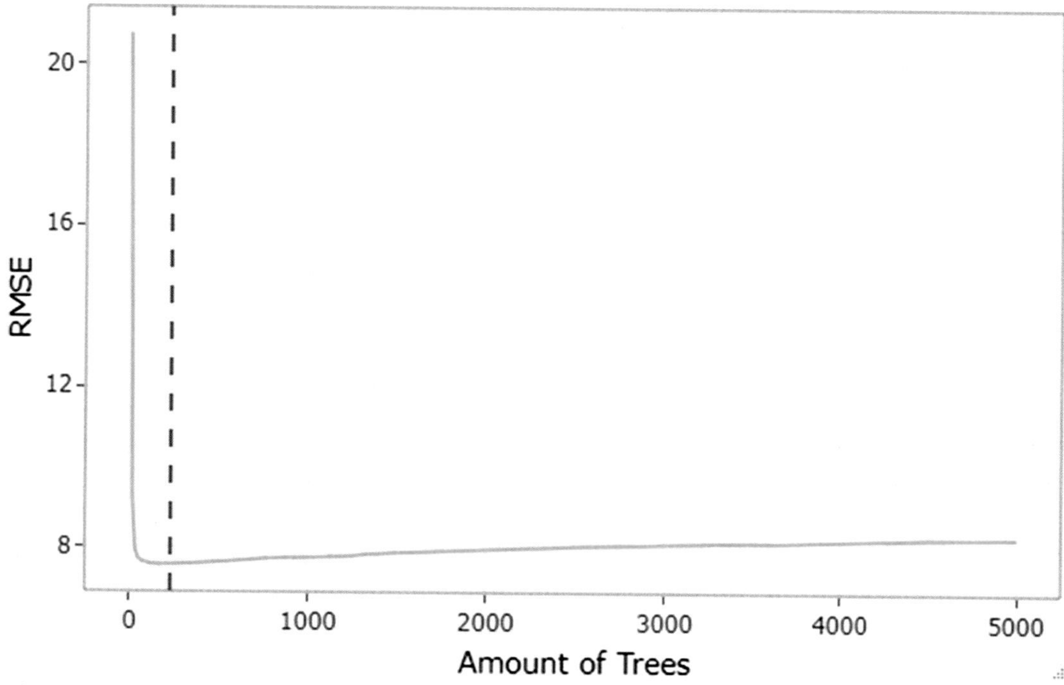

FIGURE 20.5 Graph showing the iterative moment when there is no more prediction power gain for the model `m1_boosting`.

From the insights promoted by Figure 20.5, we can begin trying to refine our initial model (`m1_boosting`) in search of more accurate hyperparameters. We can start by creating a data frame with random values of learning rate and leaving space to fill in the RMSE values, the amount of trees needed, and the time spent for each procedure. We will then save everything in an object we will call `tuning_step_1`:

```
tuning_step_1 <- data.frame(shrinkage = c(0.005, 0.01, 0.025, 0.05, 0.1, 0.15, 0.2),
                            RMSE = NA,
                            number_trees = NA,
                            time_spent = NA)
```

Next, we will do an iterative procedure that still considers the 5,000 CARTs but replaces the original value of the argument `shrinkage`, used in the estimation `m1_boosting`, with those we established in the object `tuning_step_1`. For this moment, the expectation is to find the shrinkage range in which a given learning rate value is found, which we will assume as optimal:

```
set.seed(1)
for(i in 1:nrow(tuning_step_1)) {
  tuning_model <- system.time({
    boosing_models <- gbm(
      formula = poverty_index ~ region + illiteracy_rate +
        elementary_school_rate + high_school_rate + college_rate,
      data = training_sample,
      distribution = "gaussian",
      n.trees = 5000,
      shrinkage = tuning_step_1$shrinkage[i],
      interaction.depth = 3,
      n.minobsinnode = 10,
      cv.folds = 10
    )
  })
 tuning_step_1$RMSE[i] <- sqrt(min(boosting_models$cv.error))
 tuning_step_1$number_trees[i] <- which.min(boosting_models$cv.error)
 tuning_step_1$time_spent[i] <- tuning_model[["elapsed"]]
}
```

To view the results, we can declare the object `tuning_step_1`, whose outcomes are shown in Figure 20.6:

```
tuning_step_1
```

```
  shrinkage     RMSE number_trees time_spent
1     0.005 7.518636         4054      22.52
2     0.010 7.543131         1730      20.60
3     0.025 7.533832          860      23.58
4     0.050 7.557014          446      20.94
5     0.100 7.543439          209      20.67
6     0.150 7.652017          134      19.32
7     0.200 7.588615           64      19.34
```

FIGURE 20.6 The object `tuning_step_1` after the iterative procedures.

In Figure 20.6, we can see that the lowest RMSE value appears for the 0.005 learning rate. From here, we will assume the argument `shrinkage`, used internally to the function `gbm()`, to equal 0.005 (no longer its default value of 0.1). There may be other more interesting learning rate values below this threshold. We will continue to adopt the mentioned value for educational purposes.

Still looking at Figure 20.6, by assuming the learning rate as 0.005, we realize that the combination of 4,054 CARTs was needed. We will continue to refine our modeling, and we will stress the number of CARTs combined to 7,000 to try to capture the best estimate. At this point, we will test new values for the depth of the tree (`interaction.depth`) and for the minimum number of observations in each leaf node (`n.minobsinnode`):

```
tuning_step_2 <- data.frame(number_trees = 7000,
                            shrinkage = 0.005,
                            interaction.depth = 2:7,
                            n.minobsinnode = 7:12)
```

Therefore if the object `tuning_step_1` served as a receptacle for capturing possible optimal values of the argument `shrinkage` in the past approach, when declared to the function `gbm()`, our new object `tuning_step_2` will serve to instruct the function gbm() on which hyperparameters to use. In this case, we intend to promote six combinations of models via boosting, considering values from 2 to 7 for CARTs depth and values from 7 to 12 for the minimum number of observations in each leaf node. In all cases, the amount of CARTs to be combined will be 7,000, with a learning rate of 0.005.

To be able to perform the proposed task, we can create a new algorithm that uses the function gbm() in its background. In addition, R will report the RMSE values to us:

```
tuning_step_2_fit <- function(n.trees, shrinkage,
                              interaction.depth, n.minobsinnode){
  boosting_models <- gbm(
    formula = poverty_index ~ region + illiteracy_rate +
      elementary_school_rate + high_school_rate + college_rate,
    data = training_sample,
    distribution = "gaussian",
    n.trees = n.trees,
    shrinkage = shrinkage,
    interaction.depth = interaction.depth,
    n.minobsinnode = n.minobsinnode,
    cv.folds = 10
  )
  sqrt(min(boosting_models$cv.error))
}
```

Obviously, R will not report anything after the previous command. We just created an algorithm called tuning_step_2_fit! The next step will be to propose an iterative process to actually establish the six combinations of models via boosting that consider the hyperparameters contained in the object tuning_step_2. To perform the iterations, we will use the function pmap_dbl() from the package purrr. If the reader has already commanded the package tidyverse, it is not necessary to load any package.

```
#243,425 ms
set.seed(1)
tuning_step_2["RMSE"] <- pmap_dbl(.l = tuning_step_2,
                          .f = ~ tuning_step_2_fit(n.trees = ..1,
                                                   shrinkage = ..2,
                                                   interaction.depth = ..3,
                                                   n.minobsinnode = ..4)
)
```

An attentive reader will notice that, in the previous routine, a variable called *RMSE* is being created inside the object tuning_step_2 that will capture the corresponding error metric of each one of the six combinations of CARTs via boosting. To access the information after the iterative procedure, we can use the following command:

```
tuning_step_2
```

Figure 20.7 shows R's response to the previous command.

FIGURE 20.7 The object tuning_step_2 after the iterative procedures.

```
  number_trees shrinkage interaction.depth n.minobsinnode     RMSE
1         7000     0.005                 2              7 7.568785
2         7000     0.005                 3              8 7.525533
3         7000     0.005                 4              9 7.501926
4         7000     0.005                 5             10 7.485483
5         7000     0.005                 6             11 7.479806
6         7000     0.005                 7             12 7.491954
```

Looking at Figure 20.7, we continue to look for the lowest RMSE value. We realize that, for a learning rate of 0.005, the lowest RMSE value occurs for a tree depth equal to 6, considering a total of 11 observations in each leaf node.

The final step, therefore, will be to declare the function `gbm()` to consider the 7,000 CARTs with a learning rate of 0.005, a tree depth equal to 6, and a minimum number of observations in each leaf node equal to 11:

```
#19,200 ms and 85.1 MB RAM
set.seed(1)
m2_boosting <- gbm(formula = poverty_index ~ region + illiteracy_rate +
                     elementary_school_rate + high_school_rate + college_rate,
                   data = training_sample,
                   distribution = "gaussian",
                   n.trees = 7000,
                   shrinkage = 0.005,
                   interaction.depth = 6,
                   n.minobsinnode = 11,
                   cv.folds = 10)
```

Using the function `summary()`, we can note that the boosting approach insists on considering the variable *illiteracy_rate* as the greatest predictor of vulnerability to poverty in Brazilian municipalities, followed by the variable *region*. It is noted, as shown in Figure 20.8, that the importance of the variable *illiteracy_rate,* according to the internal estimation of the object `m2_boosting` (74.48%), increased considerably in relation to the predictions of the model present in the object `m1_boosting` (55.35%) contained in Figure 20.4.

```
summary(m2_boosting)
```

```
                                          var   rel.inf
illiteracy_rate               illiteracy_rate 74.476724
region                                 region 13.770495
high_school_rate             high_school_rate  4.860035
college_rate                     college_rate  3.673621
elementary_school_rate elementary_school_rate  3.219125
```

FIGURE 20.8 The importance of each variable in explaining the phenomenon, according to the combination of models present in the object `m2_boosting`.

Following the same logic proposed for the estimation present in the object `m1_boosting`, we will identify the smallest error in the RMSE metric for the object `m2_boosting` as well as the number of iterations necessary for this:

```
min_error <- which.min(m2_boosting$cv.error)
min_error
```

After commanding the previous codes, considering that the hyperparameters adopted for our second estimation are constant, R will tell us that 2,449 iterations were necessary until the lowest RMSE value occurs. To calculate the RMSE, we can type the following command:

```
sqrt(m2_boosting$cv.error[min_error])
```

After the previous command, R will point out that the calculated RMSE for the estimation `m2_boosting` is approximately 7.48. To visualize the result graphically, we can type the following:

```
ggplotly(
  m2_boosting$cv.error %>%
    as.data.frame() %>%
    rownames_to_column(var = "trees") %>%
```

Continued

```
    rename(MSE = 2) %>%
    mutate(RMSE = sqrt(MSE),
           trees = as.numeric(trees)) %>%
    arrange(trees) %>%
    ggplot(aes(x = trees, y = RMSE)) +
    geom_line(color = "orange") +
    geom_vline(xintercept = min_error, color = "darkorchid", linetype = "dashed") +
    labs(x = "Amount of Trees",
         y = "RMSE") +
    theme_bw()
)
```

Figure 20.9 shows the graphic generated by the previous command.

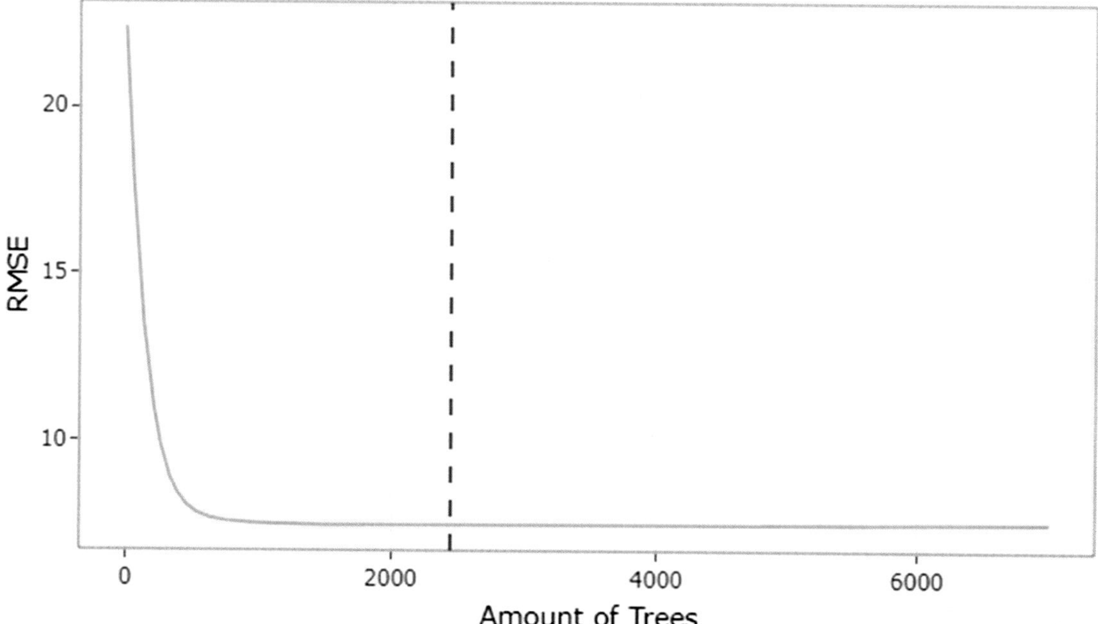

FIGURE 20.9 Graph showing the iterative moment when there is no more prediction power gain for the model `m2_boosting`.

We can access the fitted values for the validation sample with the help of the function `summary()`:

```
validation_sample["fitted_m2_boosting"] <- predict(object = m2_boosting,
                                                   newdata = validation_sample)
```

When executing this command, R will generate a warning informing the reader, **without any coincidence,** that it will only use the combination of 2,449 trees, as mentioned earlier.

Because our dependent variable *(poverty_index)* is a metric, we could explore the fitted values in a graph that compares the predicted values to the original values, the results of which are shown in Figure 20.10. **We repeat that, if the reader variable were of the categorical type, there is no doubt that the confusion matrices as well as the ROC curves (studied in Chapters 15 and 19) could be interposed with the same codes studied there.**

```
validation_sample %>%
  ggplot() +
  geom_line(aes(x = poverty_index, y = poverty_index), size = 1.2) +
  geom_smooth(aes(x = poverty_index, y = fitted_m2_boosting, color = "fitted values"),
              se = FALSE,
              size = 1.2) +
  scale_color_manual("Label:", values = "orange") +
  labs(x = NULL,
       y = NULL) +
  theme(panel.background = element_rect("white"),
        panel.grid = element_line("grey95"),
        panel.border = element_rect(NA),
        legend.position = "bottom")
```

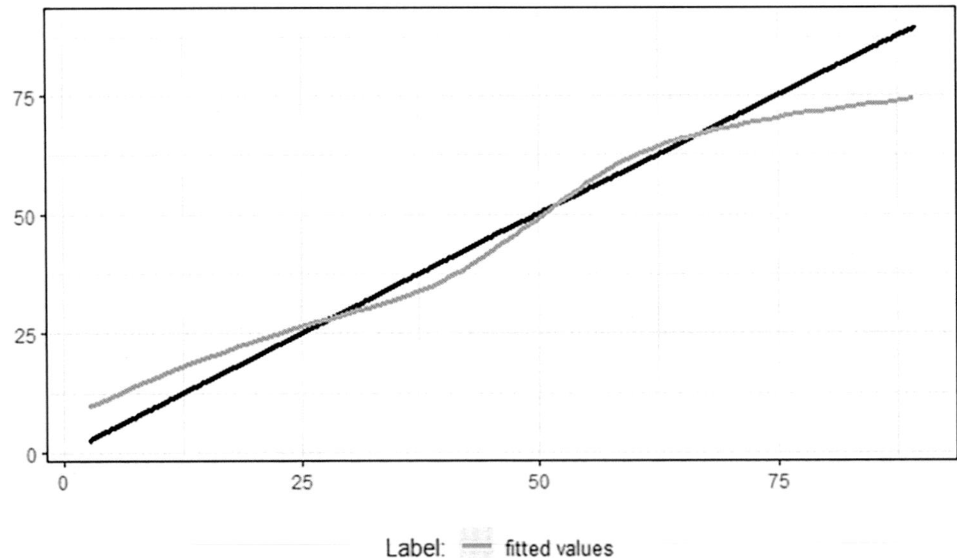

FIGURE 20.10 Graph comparing the estimated values by the model m2_boosting to the observed values (45-degree line).

Because our dependent variable is metric, drawing on the knowledge studied in Chapter 14, we can use Expression (14.18) to calculate the R^2 of the model contained in the object m2_boosting, whose value is 0.896.

```
validation_sample %>%
  mutate(ssr = ((poverty_index - mean(poverty_index)) ^ 2),
         rss = ((poverty_index - fitted_m2_boosting) ^ 2)) %>%
  summarise(r_squared = sum(ssr) / (sum(ssr) + sum(rss)))
```

If we are interested in graphically visualizing the adherence of fitted values to the variables *illiteracy_rate, elementary_school_rate, high_school_rate,* and *college_rate,* stratifying the information according to the variable region, we can type the following command:

```
# Illiteracy Rate
validation_sample %>%
  ggplot(aes(x = illiteracy_rate, y = fitted_m2_boosting, color = region)) +
  geom_point() +
  geom_smooth(aes(color = "Fitted Values"), se = FALSE) +
```

Continued

```
  scale_color_viridis_d() +
  labs(x = "Illiteracy Rate",
       y = "Poverty Index",
       color = "Label") +
  theme(panel.background = element_rect("white"),
        panel.grid = element_line("grey95"),
        panel.border = element_rect(NA),
        legend.position = "bottom") -> illiteracy_boosting

# Elementary School Rate
validation_sample %>%
  ggplot(aes(x = elementary_school_rate, y = fitted_m2_boosting, color = region)) +
  geom_point() +
  geom_smooth(aes(color = "Fitted Values"), se = FALSE) +
  scale_color_viridis_d() +
  labs(x = "Elementary School Rate",
       y = "Poverty Index",
       color = "Label") +
  theme(panel.background = element_rect("white"),
        panel.grid = element_line("grey95"),
        panel.border = element_rect(NA),
        legend.position = "bottom") -> elementary_boosting

# High School Rate
validation_sample %>%
  ggplot(aes(x = high_school_rate, y = fitted_m2_boosting, color = region)) +
  geom_point() +
  geom_smooth(aes(color = "Fitted Values"), se = FALSE) +
  scale_color_viridis_d() +
  labs(x = "High School Rate",
       y = "Poverty Index",
       color = "Label") +
  theme(panel.background = element_rect("white"),
        panel.grid = element_line("grey95"),
        panel.border = element_rect(NA),
        legend.position = "bottom") -> high_boosting

# College Rate
validation_sample %>%
  ggplot(aes(x = college_rate, y = fitted_m2_boosting, color = region)) +
  geom_point() +
  geom_smooth(aes(color = "Fitted Values"), se = FALSE) +
  scale_color_viridis_d() +
  labs(x = "College Rate",
       y = "Poverty Index",
       color = "Label") +
  theme(panel.background = element_rect("white"),
        panel.grid = element_line("grey95"),
        panel.border = element_rect(NA),
        legend.position = "bottom") -> college_boosting

grid.arrange(illiteracy_boosting, elementary_boosting,
             high_boosting, college_boosting)
```

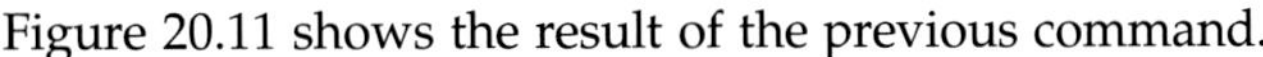

Figure 20.11 shows the result of the previous command.

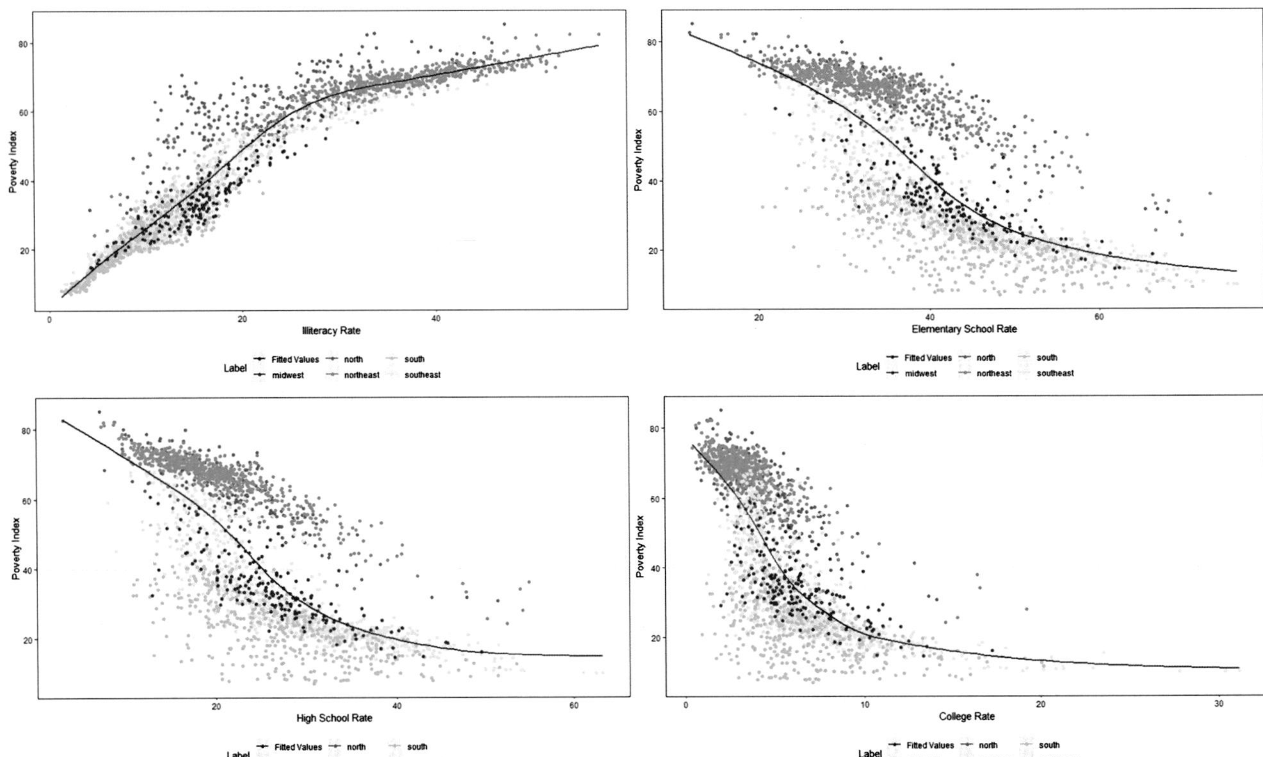

FIGURE 20.11 The adherence of the fitted values of the model `m2_boosting` to the *illiteracy_rate, elementary_school_rate, high_school_rate,* and *college_rate* variables stratified according to the *region* variable.

With the help of Figure 20.11, we can verify that the variable *poverty_index* keeps a positive correlation with the predictor variable *illiteracy_rate* and a negative correlation with the explanatory variables *elementary_school_rate, high_school_rate,* and *college_rate.* We can also verify that, for the dataset studied, Brazilian municipalities that are in a state of greater vulnerability to poverty are found in the north and northeast regions. On the other hand, municipalities that are less vulnerable to poverty are found in the south and southeast regions, where the number of individuals with a higher education degree is even greater.

Next, we will see the application of another approach to model mix: bagging techniques.

Bagging in R

For the combination of models by bagging, we will use the same dataset we used for the combination by boosting, due to didactic purposes, aiming at comparing the studied approaches.

Initially, we will estimate four different models that use 50, 100, 500, and 1000 CARTs combined, for two reasons: (1) so the reader perceives the computational demand as the number of iterations increases and (2) so the reader becomes used to the OOB error metric.

For the combination of models by the bagging approach, we will use the algorithm `bagging()` from the package `ipred`. That said, we can apply the following routine for the 50 CARTs combination using the same training sample and the same validation sample we used in the "Boosting in R" section. For illustrative purposes, on our machine, the time taken was 8,050 ms with 348.3 MB of RAM.

```
#8,050 ms and 348.3 MB RAM
set.seed(1)
m1_bagging <- bagging(formula = poverty_index ~ region + illiteracy_rate +
                          elementary_school_rate + high_school_rate + college_rate,
                      data = training_sample,
                      coob = TRUE,
                      nbagg = 50,
                      control = rpart.control(minsplit = 2, cp = 0))
```

For the function `bagging()`, we declare the argument `formula`, whose syntax is logical with all of the predictive model declarations studied so far; that is, we declare our dependent variable first and then the predictor variables. For the argument `data`, we declare the dataset used to train our model, that is, our training sample. Next, it is very important to use the argument `coob = TRUE` so R will inform us of the OOB error and we can decide which is the best model among the proposed estimates. Finally, there is the declaration of two hyperparameters, `nbagg` and `control`, which inform the amount of CARTs to be estimated and the minimum number of observations in the leaf nodes, respectively (see Chapter 19).

That said, we can declare the object that contains our model to have access to the OOB error:

```
m1_bagging
```

After the previous command, R will return the answer shown in Figure 20.12.

FIGURE 20.12 Estimation outputs via bagging present in the object `m1_bagging`.

```
Bagging regression trees with 50 bootstrap replications

Call: bagging.data.frame(formula = poverty_index ~ region + illiteracy_rate +
    elementary_school_rate + high_school_rate + college_rate,
    data = train_sample, coob = TRUE, nbagg = 50, control = rpart.control(minsplit =
2,
        cp = 0))

Out-of-bag estimate of root mean squared error:  7.9717
```

In Figure 20.12, we can see that the RMSE (because our dependent variable is metric) is 7.9717, for an estimation with 50 CARTs combined via the bagging approach. A fair question would be: Was using 50 CARTs appropriate or not?

There is no way to answer this question without establishing new estimates for comparison. So we will estimate three other models, as promised earlier, considering the combination of 100, 500, and 1,000 CARTs, respectively:

```
#15,110 ms and 711.0 MB RAM
set.seed(1)
m2_bagging <- bagging(formula = poverty_index ~ region + illiteracy_rate +
                        elementary_school_rate + high_school_rate + college_rate,
                      data = training_sample,
                      coob = TRUE,
                      nbagg = 100,
                      control = rpart.control(minsplit = 2, cp = 0))

#70,240 ms and 3,622.0 MB RAM
set.seed(1)
m3_bagging <- bagging(formula = poverty_index ~ region + illiteracy_rate +
                        elementary_school_rate + high_school_rate + college_rate,
                      data = training_sample,
                      coob = TRUE,
                      nbagg = 500,
                      control = rpart.control(minsplit = 2, cp = 0))

#144,220 ms and 7,267.8 MB RAM
set.seed(1)
m4_bagging <- bagging(formula = poverty_index ~ region + illiteracy_rate +
                        elementary_school_rate + high_school_rate + college_rate,
                      data = training_sample,
                      coob = TRUE,
                      nbagg = 1000,
                      control = rpart.control(minsplit = 2, cp = 0))
```

Given a reasonably small base in which we used only five predictor variables, the reader must have already noticed that the bagging approach charges time and computational power in exchange for the prediction power.

If we declared the estimations contained in m2_bagging, m3_bagging, and m4_bagging, we would have access to their OOB error metrics, being able to verify the following values, respectively: 7.859, 7.7806, and 7.7676.

```
m2_bagging
m3_bagging
m4_bagging
```

That said, for the case discussed, considering only the established models, we would probably have the estimation present in the object m4_bagging because it has the lowest RMSE. However, the choice of a model estimated by bagging often involves time and computational demand. Depending on the amount of memory or the time spent by the iterative procedures, perhaps we would prefer another estimation, even if its RMSE was significantly higher.

Appealing to this argument, in fact, the last two estimates would be very good competitors. On one hand, the model present in the object m4_bagging has the lowest RMSE, and on the other hand, the model m3_bagging required half the time with a RMSE that was only 0.013 higher. This means that in practical life, in the face of extensive and cumbersome databases, the RMSE metric (or hit rate for models with categorical dependent variables) should not be seen as an infallible rule of thumb without accounting for computational resources and available time.

If the intention is to capture the fitted values of the model (let's assume the estimation present in the object m4_bagging), we can use the function predict(), as follows:

```
predict(object = m4_bagging, newdata = train_sample)
```

An attentive reader will notice that the argument newdata was provided with the dataset with the training sample. We can save our fitted values from our validation sample as follows:

```
validation_sample["fitted_m4_bagging"] <- predict(object = m4_bagging,
                                                  newdata = validation_sample)
```

Because our dependent variable is metric, we could explore the fitted values in a graph in which we compare the predicted values to the original values, according to the following routine, whose results are shown in Figure 20.13.

```
validation_sample %>%
  ggplot() +
  geom_line(aes(x = poverty_index, y = poverty_index), size = 1.2) +
  geom_smooth(aes(x = poverty_index, y = fitted_m4_bagging, color = "fitted values"),
              se = FALSE,
              size = 1.2) +
  scale_color_manual("Label:", values = "darkorchid") +
  labs(x = NULL,
       y = NULL) +
  theme(panel.background = element_rect("white"),
        panel.grid = element_line("grey95"),
        panel.border = element_rect(NA),
        legend.position = "bottom")
```

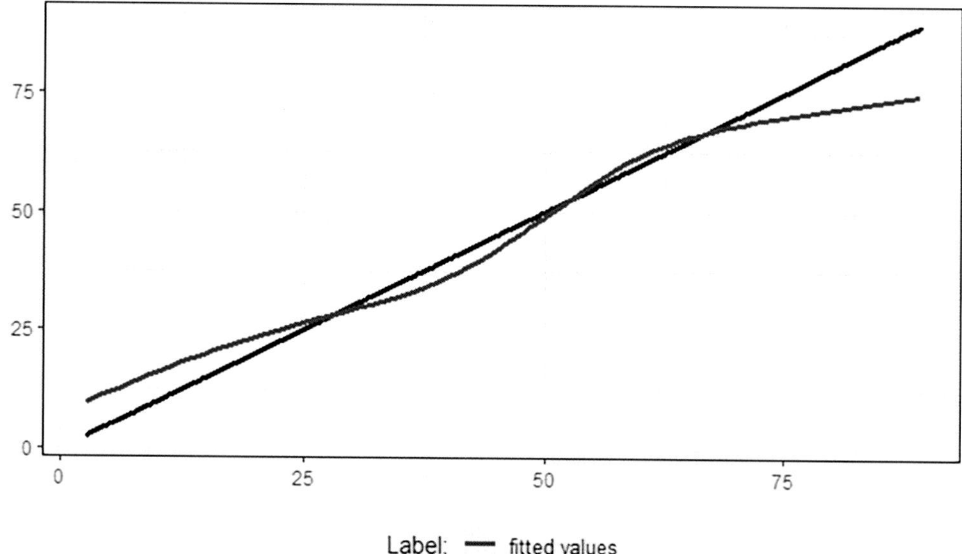

FIGURE 20.13 Graph comparing the values estimated by the model `m4_bagging` to the observed values (45-degree line).

On the other hand, if we want to see the adherence of the fitted values of the model present in the object `m4_bagging` to the predictor variables *illiteracy_rate, elementary_school_rate, high_school_rate,* and *college_rate,* stratifying the information by *region,* we can type the following command:

```
# Illiteracy Rate
validation_sample %>%
  ggplot(aes(x = illiteracy_rate, y = fitted_m4_bagging, color = region)) +
  geom_point() +
  geom_smooth(aes(color = "Fitted Values"), se = FALSE) +
  scale_color_viridis_d() +
  labs(x = "Illiteracy Rate",
       y = "Poverty Index",
       color = "Label") +
  theme(panel.background = element_rect("white"),
        panel.grid = element_line("grey95"),
        panel.border = element_rect(NA),
        legend.position = "bottom") -> illiteracy_bagging

# Elementary School Rate
validation_sample %>%
  ggplot(aes(x = elementary_school_rate, y = fitted_m4_bagging, color = region)) +
  geom_point() +
  geom_smooth(aes(color = "Fitted Values"), se = FALSE) +
  scale_color_viridis_d() +
  labs(x = "Elementary School Rate",
       y = "Poverty Index",
       color = "Label") +
  theme(panel.background = element_rect("white"),
        panel.grid = element_line("grey95"),
        panel.border = element_rect(NA),
        legend.position = "bottom") -> elementary_bagging

# High School Rate
validation_sample %>%
```

Continued

```
  ggplot(aes(x = high_school_rate, y = fitted_m4_bagging, color = region)) +
  geom_point() +
  geom_smooth(aes(color = "Fitted Values"), se = FALSE) +
  scale_color_viridis_d() +
  labs(x = "High School Rate",
       y = "Poverty Index",
       color = "Label") +
  theme(panel.background = element_rect("white"),
        panel.grid = element_line("grey95"),
        panel.border = element_rect(NA),
        legend.position = "bottom") -> high_bagging

# College Rate
validation_sample %>%
  ggplot(aes(x = college_rate, y = fitted_m4_bagging, color = region)) +
  geom_point() +
  geom_smooth(aes(color = "Fitted Values"), se = FALSE) +
  scale_color_viridis_d() +
  labs(x = "College Rate",
       y = "Poverty Index",
       color = "Label") +
  theme(panel.background = element_rect("white"),
        panel.grid = element_line("grey95"),
        panel.border = element_rect(NA),
        legend.position = "bottom") -> college_bagging

grid.arrange(illiteracy_bagging, elementary_bagging,
             high_bagging, college_bagging)
```

Figure 20.14 shows the result of the previous command.

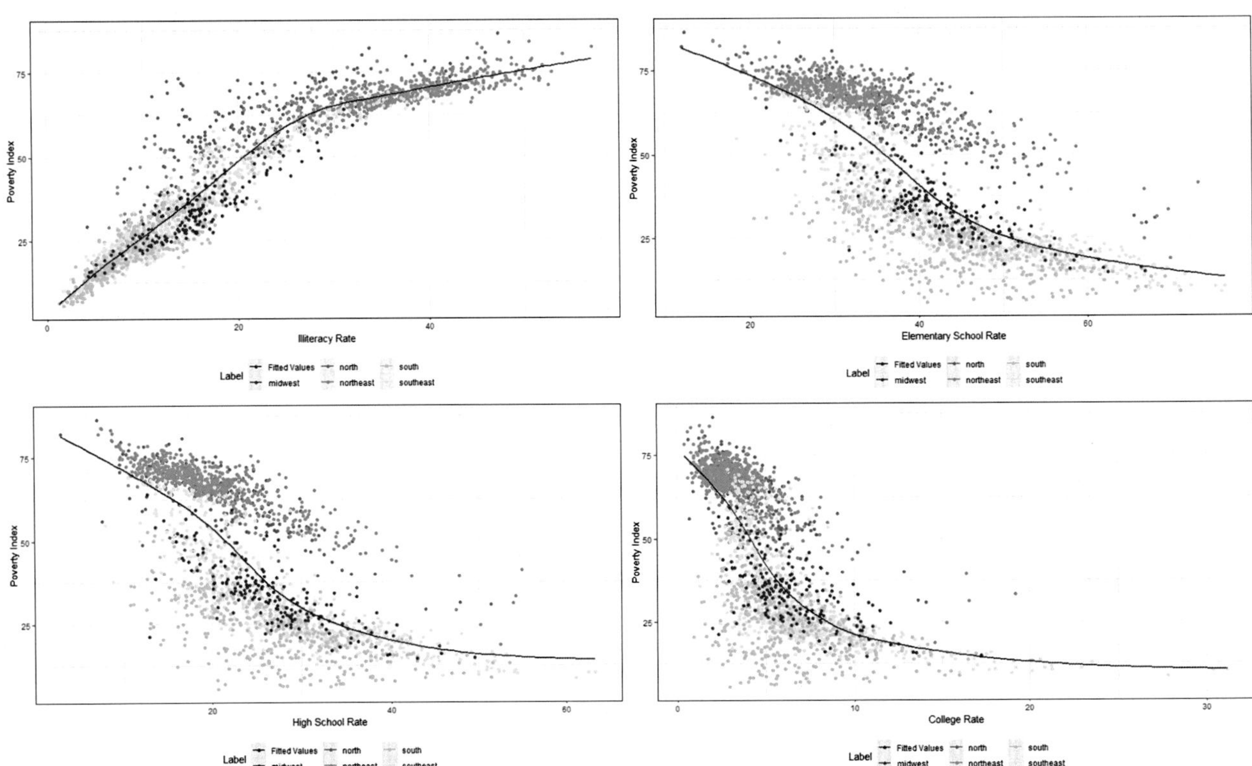

FIGURE 20.14 Adherence of the fitted values of the model `m4_bagging` to the variables *illiteracy_rate, elementary_school_rate, high_school_rate,* and *college_rate,* stratified according to the variable *region.*

Given everything presented throughout this section regarding computational and time demands, we will propose possible solutions that maximize the use of time, minimize the computational demand of the reader's machine, ands shed light on the determination of which model to adopt.

It must be said that the aforementioned solutions complement each other. The first solution concerns the use of parallel computing to reduce the time spent between estimations made via bagging; the second concerns estimation of a model that has a larger number of iterations but that makes use of parallel computing in which we will verify the decrease in the OOB error due to the number of these iterations. We think this will allow the reader to make better use of time and the processing power of his or her machine.

The second path will also be useful for the reader to verify *in loco* that a high number of iterations will not necessarily be the best solution. As in the approach via boosting, there comes a time when there is no relevant gain in predictive accuracy. Our job will therefore be to identify this moment.

Thus we will use the package `doParallel` which, in simplified language, will try to maximize the use of the reader's processor cores by emulating R parallel sections and segregating the tasks to be commanded.

To achieve this goal, we will use the function `makeCluster()`, which is nested within the function `registerDoParallel ()`. In our case, we will use eight parallel sections of R:

```
registerDoParallel(cl = makeCluster(spec = 8), cores = 4)
```

As we noticed that, apparently, there was no relevant decrease in the RMSE when we compared the internal estimations to the objects `m3_bagging` and `m4_bagging`, which used 500 and 1,000 iterations, respectively, we will propose an algorithm that captures the fitted values of the combination via bagging from 1 to 1,000 CARTs (in fact, it could be as many as the reader wants).

An attentive reader will notice that this time we will not use the algorithm `bagging()`. On the contrary, we will use the algorithm `rpart()` (discussed in Chapter 19) to establish our CARTs, and before its application, we will create a bootstrap sampling! In other words, we are building a bagging algorithm almost from scratch!

The interesting thing about this approach is that, despite saving up to 1,000 distinct combined models on our machine, the time taken is approximately 37 seconds. The reader should remember that when using the algorithm `bagging()` for combined 1,000 CARTs, we spent just over 144 seconds. RAM consumption also dropped from 7,267.8 MB to 100.0 MB.

```
fitted_values <- foreach(icount(1000),
                        .packages = "rpart",
                        .combine = cbind) %dopar% {
                          index <- sample(nrow(training_sample),
                                          replace = TRUE)
                          bagged_models <- rpart(formula = poverty_index ~
                                                   illiteracy_rate +
                                           elementary_school_rate +
                                             high_school_rate +
                                             college_rate,
                                         control = rpart.control(minsplit = 2,
                                                                 cp = 0),
                                         data = training_sample[index, ] )

                          predict(bagged_models, newdata = validation_sample)
}
```

Following the previous routine, the object `fitted_values` will therefore contain the predicted values of the established combinations of up to 1,000 CARTs. Once this is done, we can stop the parallel computing procedures as follows:

```
stopCluster(cl = makeCluster(spec = 8))
```

Soon after, we can already observe the decrease in the OOB error as follows:

```
fitted_values %>%
  as.data.frame() %>%
  mutate(id = 1:n(),
         observed = validation_sample$poverty_index) %>%
  melt(id.vars = c("id","observed")) %>%
  rename(trees = variable,
         predicted = value ) %>%
  group_by(id) %>%
  mutate(trees = str_extract(trees, '\\d+') %>% as.numeric(),
         fitted = cummean(predicted)) %>%
  group_by(trees) %>%
  summarize(RMSE = RMSE(fitted, observed)) %>%
  ggplot(aes(trees, RMSE)) +
  geom_line(color = "orange") +
  labs(x = "Amount of CART",
       y = "RMSE") +
 theme_bw()
```

Figure 20.15 presents the result of the previous routine.

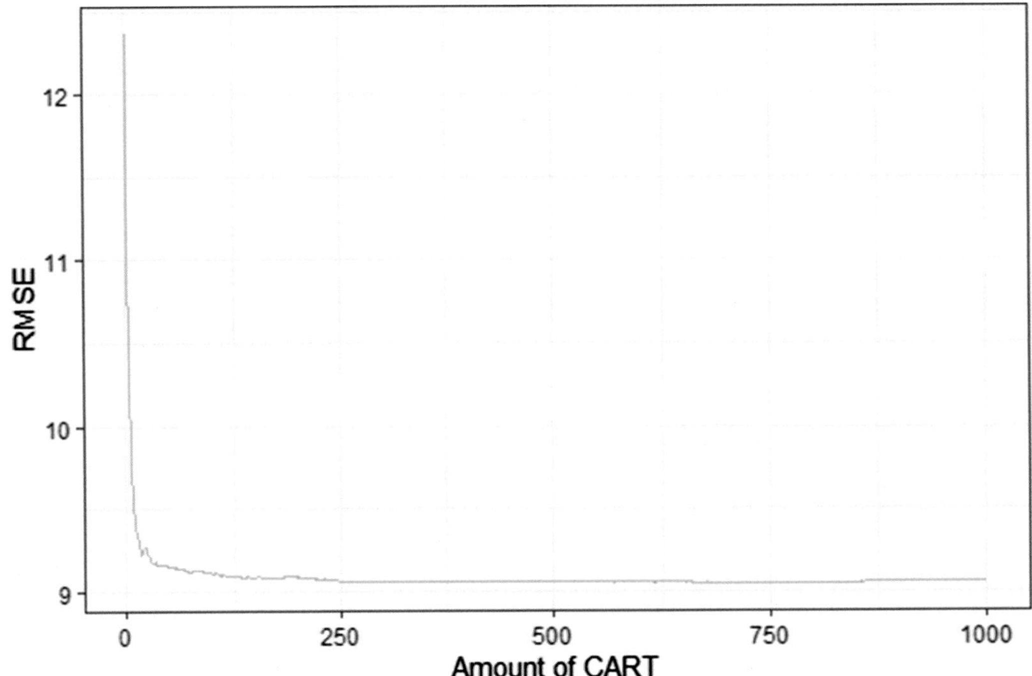

FIGURE 20.15 Graph showing the decrease in OOB.

Figure 20.15 explains well why predictive gain, when increasing from 500 to 1,000 iterations, is not relevant! As the reader can see, there comes a time when the bagging approach, like the boosting one, can no longer significantly refine itself. According to Figure 20.15, approximately 250 iterations would be enough to estimate a robust model, which combines a low RMSE and low consumption of time and memory.

That said, it is necessary to discuss the interpretability of an estimation via bagging. An attentive reader will notice that there are also no coefficients here that indicate marginal gains of a given predictor variable over the studied phenomenon.

Despite the insights provided by Figure 20.14, there is no way to measure the size of the marginal impact in the model, for example, of illiteracy rates on vulnerability to poverty. The same can be said for the boosting approach.

In this sense, we will try to propose to the reader a way to minimally evidence the most important variables for the estimation via bagging. The problem is that the most common function for this demand is the algorithm `vip()` from the package vip. This function is not compatible with the models elaborated with the help of the algorithm bagging(). As a possible solution, we present to the reader the function train() from the package caret. We voice the reader to carefully explore the documentation of the algorithm mentioned with the command ?train. **As the reader will notice, this algorithm allows the estimation of different kinds of model combinations via boosting and bagging.**

So first we will establish our last model with a previously discussed number of iterations of 250 CARTs, and then we will highlight the importance of the selected variables. There are some differences in the approach to be followed, apart from the selected algorithm. It must be said that the following command took approximately 135 seconds to run on our machine; moreover, by arguing trControl = trainControl(method = "cv", number = 10), we determine to R that, for each subsampling by bootstrap, 10 observations are reserved to verify the accuracy of the model during its iterative procedures.

```
#135,530 ms and 1,570.5 MB RAM
set.seed(1)
m5_bagging <- train(poverty_index ~ region + illiteracy_rate +
                      elementary_school_rate + high_school_rate + college_rate,
                    data = training_sample,
                    method = "treebag",
                    trControl = trainControl(method = "cv", number = 10),
                    nbagg = 250,
                    control = rpart.control(minsplit = 2, cp = 0))
```

We can see the results of the previous estimation with the following command, whose R responses are shown in Figure 20.16.

```
m5_bagging
```

FIGURE 20.16 Estimation outputs via bagging present in the object m5_bagging.

```
Bagged CART

3339 samples
   5 predictor

No pre-processing
Resampling: Cross-Validated (10 fold)
Summary of sample sizes: 3007, 3005, 3004, 3004, 3005, 3005, ...
Resampling results:

  RMSE      Rsquared   MAE
  7.885224  0.8773701  6.077803
```

Figure 20.16 shows us an RMSE value of 7.8852, close to the metrics found by the estimations m3_bagging and m4_bagging. The image also shows the model's R^2 of approximately 0.8774.

To check the importance of each variable, we can apply the function vip() to the object m5_bagging:

```
vip(m5_bagging,
    geom = "point",
    horizontal = FALSE,
    aesthetics = list(color = "orange")) +
 theme(panel.background = element_rect("white"),
      panel.grid = element_line("grey95"),
      panel.border = element_rect(NA),
      axis.text.x = element_text(angle = 90))
```

Figure 20.17 shows the result of the previous command.

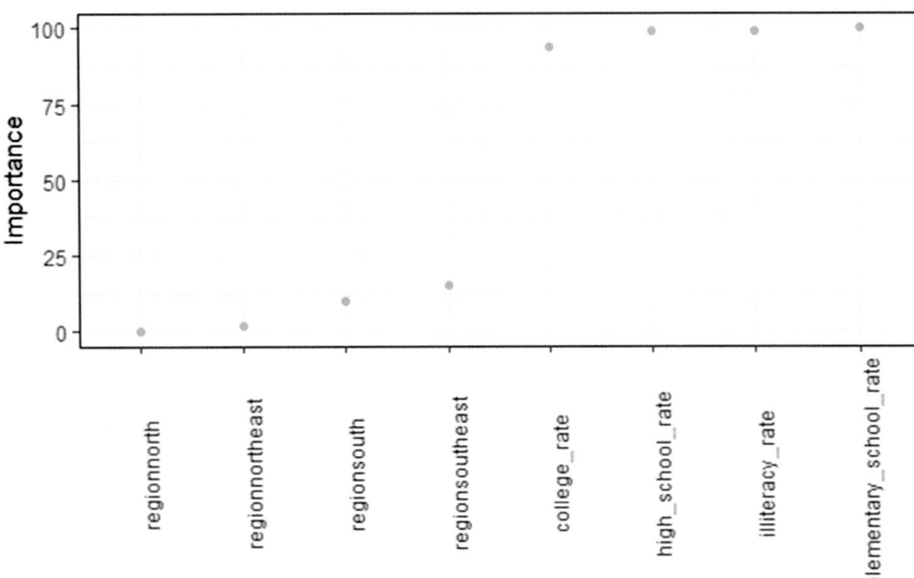

FIGURE 20.17 The importance of each variable for the model `m5_bagging`, according to the function `vip()`.

According to Figure 20.17, of the variables directly related to educational issues, the variable *elementary_school_rate* was most important in explaining the phenomenon studied for the combination of CARTs via bagging. Therefore we can assume that, as a rule, it was chosen as the root node in most decision trees, and looking at Figure 20.14, we can say that its low values indicate a high vulnerability to poverty, with emphasis in the north and northeast regions of Brazil.

On the other hand, still according to Figure 20.17, of the variables directly related to educational issues, the variable *college_rate* was the least important to predict vulnerability to poverty. When looking at Figure 20.14, we see that the statement makes sense as most municipalities have low rates of higher education, also called *post-secondary, third-level,* or *tertiary education.* Therefore from the point of view of establishing public policies, perhaps the levels of school to be emphasized for the case analyzed should be those that come before, that is, the elementary and secondary levels of education.

Final remarks

Model combinations via boosting and bagging are approaches capable of achieving a high predictive capacity, but they take their toll on the computational demand and available time of their users.

We could verify that the R^2 for the combination of models via boosting was significantly better (0.897) than for the approach via bagging (0.880). **This was expected, as according to Shmueli et al. (2018) and Kelleher et al. (2015), boosting estimates perform better on data with less variability when compared with bagging estimates.** Figures 20.11 and 20.14 make it clear that data on vulnerability to poverty in Brazil are not all that heterogeneous when educational issues are considered; if they were, estimations via bagging would probably perform better. The comparison between Figures 20.10 and 20.13 makes it clear that the difference was minimal.

We again warn the reader that, in view of the estimation of combined models, they maintain the practice of establishing training samples and validation samples to mitigate the problem of overfitting (in the case of boosting) and the correlation among trees (in the case of bagging). As for this last situation, in Chapter 21 we will study random forests, which are specific types of bagging that mitigate the problem of correlation among trees.

Exercise

(1) Considering the following data on some tourists around the world, develop a combination of bagging models that seek to predict whether or not a certain couple will travel to another country in the next year, **based only on their**

average age and number of children (Fávero and Belfiore, 2019). The data are found in the file `tourism_data.RData`, whose variables are as follows:

Variable	Description
country	Variable that identifies the nationality of the tourist.
tourism	Dummy variable that indicates whether or not a certain tourist made an international trip in the last year.
age	Metric variable that measures the average age of the considered couple.
children	Metric variable that indicates the number of children of the considered couple.

Remember that the dependent variable is categorical, so the prediction error metric is the classification error! Use `set.seed(1)`.

(a) Make a bagging estimate that considers the use of the 2,000 CARTs combination.
(b) What is the classification error present in the model elaborated in item (a)?
(c) Develop a bagging-type estimation with the algorithm `train()` that considers 500 CARTs and the use of the argument `trControl = trainControl(method = "cv", number = 10)`.
(d) What is the accuracy of the model estimated in item (c)?
(e) What is the order of importance of the variables present in the estimation made in item (c)?

Supplementary data sets

`brazilian_poverty.RData`
`fidelity_data.RData`
`tourism_data.RData`

Please access supplementary data files here: https://doi.org/10.17632/55623jkwrp.3

CHAPTER

21

Random forests

AT THE END OF THIS CHAPTER, YOU WILL BE ABLE TO:

- Understand when to use a mix of models via random forests
- Differentiate between a classic bagging approach and a random forest approach
- Learn to refine random forest models
- Estimate random forest models in R-based language and learn to interpret their results

R-based language packages used in this chapter

```
library(tidyverse)
library(randomForest)
library(gridExtra)
```

Don't forget to define the R working directory (the location where your datasets are installed):

```
setwd("C:/book/chapter21")
```

Introduction

In many ways, this chapter can be seen as an expansion of what we discussed throughout Chapter 19 and in the "Bagging" section in Chapter 20. Thus if the reader has chosen this section as the starting point for readings, we encourage him or her to go back to at least Chapter 19 and begin to study from there.

Random forests, as the name already seems to indicate, are configured as decision tree forests and can be considered a derivation and a combination of classification and regression trees (CARTs), but with even more intense stochastic effects. This is because random forests can also be seen as a particular kind of bagging model combination that uses bootstrap techniques. Here, however, the bootstrap approach only touches on sampling; the selection of the variables used in each iterative pass also goes through a choice via bootstrap, as we will see in the course of this section.

Random forests, as well as boosting and bagging approaches, are therefore part of the ensemble model family. They are algorithms with high predictive power and, contrary to the classic bagging approach, they do not usually have the problem of correlation among trees.

Data Science, Analytics and Machine Learning with R
https://doi.org/10.1016/B978-0-12-824271-1.00018-4

Its applications are already present in all fields of knowledge, and, like CARTs, they are flexible regarding the scale of measurement of the dependent variable. In other words, the target variable can be metric or categorical. However, like CARTs, these models do not have linear or angular coefficients to facilitate their interpretability or indicate marginal impacts. It should also be said that the high number of stochastic procedures, such as mo boosting and mo bagging, make it impossible to reproduce them, unless you call the function `set.seed()` or another analogous one.

Random forests

Random forests can be considered a recent technique, dating from 1996. They are supervised algorithms with a particular interesting use when directed to situations in which it is necessary to work with non-linear variables, being computationally less demanding than the classical boosting or bagging approaches (Du et al., 2015; Gislason et al., 2006).

As discussed by Belgiu and Dragut (2016), the idea of interposing random forests permeates the combination of decision trees in which m CARTs are generated, considering a given impurity measure (see Chapter 19), using bootstrap procedures for subsampling of the first to the m-th CART, where $m(m=1,2,3,\ldots,M)$. The authors also point out that if the dependent variable is metric, for each CART, $\frac{k}{3}$predictor variables will be randomly selected; if the dependent variable is categorical, $\sqrt{k}$ explanatory variables will be randomly selected. The use of k variables in their studies, but there was no considerable improvement in the prediction provided by the algorithm, and there was a substantial increase in time spent on the work.

That said, in each iterative step, each CART will obviously have a root node that possibly will not be the same for all m estimated trees. In addition to different compositions of leaf nodes, each tree may or may not have different forms of splits and therefore different (or even non-existent) decision nodes.

For the metric dependent variables, the calculation of their fitted values will concern the averages of the predicted values of all m CARTs iterated. For categorical dependent variables, their ratings will be given by the highest votes, considering all estimated m CARTs; it is also possible to obtain the probability of occurrence of each category of the qualitative target variable.

Figure 21.1 proposes the theoretical establishment of a random forest using, for educational purposes, 5 CARTs. In real world problems, as a rule, we would combine at least 500 CARTs.

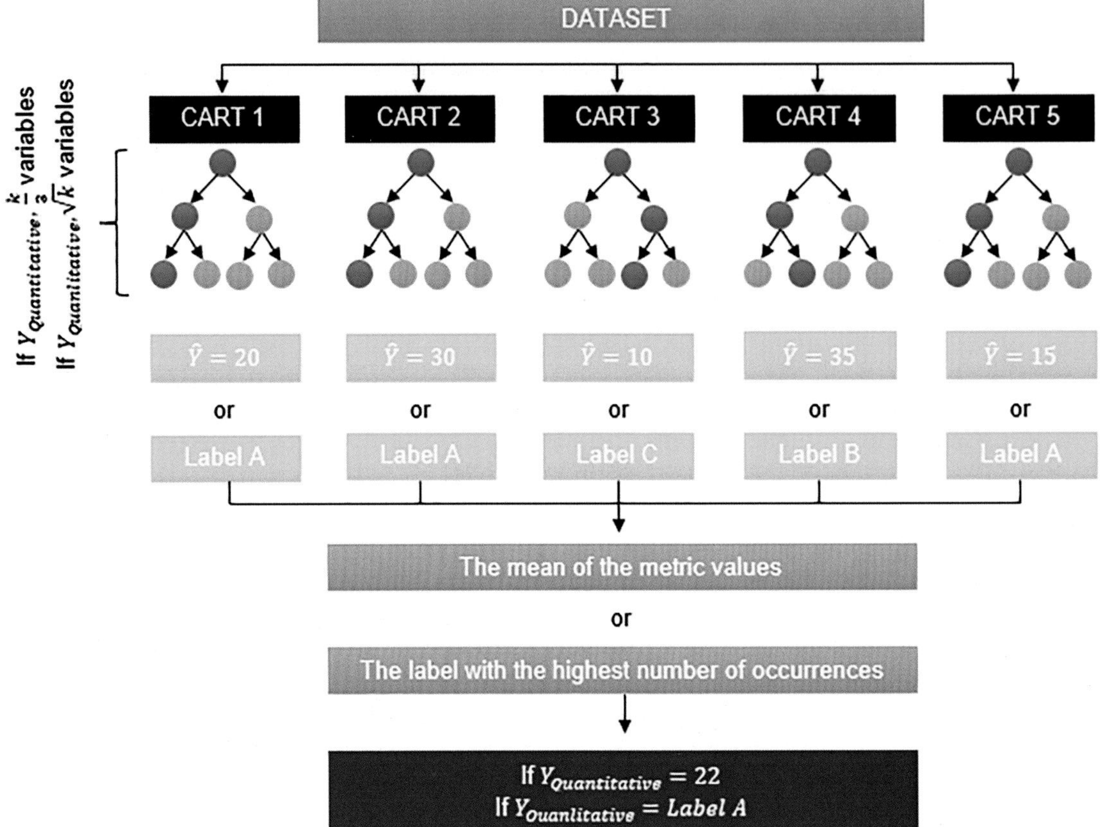

FIGURE 21.1 Framework that demonstrates the theoretical functioning of a random forest.

As shown in Figure 21.1, after randomly establishing the predictor variables, the random forests algorithm will start an iterative process by building m decision trees, whose optimal value for m is commonly referred to in the literature as between 500 and 3000 CARTs (Adelabu et al., 2013; Millard and Richardson, 2015). The default of most algorithms for estimating this technique in R-based language is 500 CARTs.

To further clarify what is demonstrated in Figure 21.1, we leave a kind of pseudo-algorithm of a random forest:

- **Step 1:** For each CART, generate samples via bootstrap (see the "Bagging" section in Chapter 20).
- **Step 2:** Define the number of variables to be used in each CART
- **Step 3:** Randomly select the variables for each CART based on the defined quantity.
- **Step 4:** Calculate the impurity measure of the dataset for each CART according to what was learned in Chapter 19.
- **Step 5:** After the end of the iterations, for the case in which the dependent variable Y is categorical, its predictions will be made based on a weighted vote to rank the observations; however, if Y is metric, there will be a weighted average to predict the observations, obviously with higher weights for the last established trees.

As a specific type of combination of CART models, random forests also do not have an equation to be analyzed. Furthermore, precisely because they are a combination of estimations via CART, there is no simplified analysis of the model, for example, as proposed in Figure 19.1 in Chapter 19.

On the other hand, the kind of models discussed in this section have a high predictive level, and, like boosting and bagging approaches, it is possible to verify which variables have the greatest impact on the estimation.

Furthermore, despite being a specific type of combination of models via bagging, because of the stochastic component in the selection of variables that will compose each combined CART, very little can be discussed about the problem of correlation among trees. On the other hand, due attention must be given to the problem of overfitting, as already presented in Figure 19.5 (see the "Overfitting" section in Chapter 19).

That said, as we did in Chapters 19 and 20 of this work, we will move on to the presentation of the main hyperparameters for a random forest estimation.

Hyperparameters

There are a number of hyperparameters that can be adjusted for a random forest model. As we will see in the "Random forests applications in R" section, we will use the function `randomForest()` from the package `randomForest` for the estimations of our models. Thus when commanding `?randomForest`, the reader will have access to a high level of possible customizations present in the algorithm documentation.

For the purposes of this work, our main concerns will be with the number of predictor variables randomly selected at each iteration and with the number of iterations of the model.

The number of predictive variables selected at each iterative step

By default, as already shown, R will work with a selection of $\frac{k}{3}$ explanatory variables in the case of a metric dependent variable and $\sqrt{k}$ predictor variables in the case of a categorical dependent variable. However, these predefined values will not necessarily make the best model emerge.

That said, the search for the ideal value of explanatory variables to be selected will be the reader's task. To help, we will provide some tips throughout the "Random forests applications in R" section.

As a rule, faced with a metric dependent variable, we will opt for the model with the lowest root mean squared error (RMSE; see Chapter 20). Faced with a categorical variable, we will opt for the estimation with the smallest classification error.

A hasty choice, therefore, of the number of selected predictor variables can generate models with low predictive power.

The number of model iterations

As pointed out earlier, R has as a predefined value of 500 iterations, that is, a combination of 500 CARTs. However, use of this default value will not always generate the best estimate via random forests.

In the course of the "Random forests applications in R" section, we will also help the reader monitor the decrease in the RMSE (for the case of metric dependent variables). If the dependent variable is categorical, the reader must monitor the decrease in classification error. For the case of stabilization of these metrics, it will not make sense to continue commanding more iterations.

Random forests applications in R

For this section, we will use the same dataset used in Chapter 20 of this work; this is because, as stated, random forests are specific types of bagging. Therefore the reader will have direct conditions of comparability among the techniques in relation to prediction levels, computational demand, and time spent on the model's refinement work.

The `brazilian_poverty.RData` file, whose variables were presented in Table 20.1, can be opened as follows:

```
load("brazilian_poverty.RData")
```

Next, we can get descriptive statistics for metric variables and frequency tables for categorical variables:

```
summary(brazilian_poverty)
```

Figure 20.3 in Chapter 20 shows the results of the previous command. It is important for the reader to know that in Brazil there are several municipalities that use the same name, but it is not common for this to happen within the same state.

Interpretation of the output in Figure 20.3 is important so we do not commit extrapolation problems at the time of prediction. As with all of the techniques studied so far, random forest approaches do not guarantee good functionality in the face of the extrapolation problem.

As presented at the beginning of this chapter, because of the intense stochastic processes present in the algorithms of random forests, we will use the function `set.seed()` to guarantee that the reader will obtain identical results to those present in this work.

An attentive reader will notice that the dependent variable of the study *(poverty_index)* is classified as continuous metric. **If the reader variable were categorical, there is no doubt that the confusion matrices as well as the ROC curves (both studied in Chapters 15 and 19) could be interposed with the same codes previously studied.**

That said, let's establish our training sample and our validation sample as follows:

```
set.seed(1)
sample_index <- sample(x = 1:dim(brazilian_poverty)[1],
                       size = nrow(brazilian_poverty) * 0.6)

training_sample <- brazilian_poverty[sample_index, ]
validation_sample <- brazilian_poverty[-sample_index, ]
```

To facilitate the reader's comparability with the traditional bagging model presented in Chapter 20, we will use the same training dataset to estimate the model via a random forest; the previous command `set.seed(1)` will guarantee this condition.

In this work, the estimation of a model via a random forest will be performed by the function `randomForest()` from the package `randomForest`. Its most basic statement is given by the following:

```
set.seed(1)
rf_brazilian_poverty_1 <- randomForest(formula = poverty_index ~ illiteracy_rate +
                                         elementary_school_rate +
                                         elementary_school_rate +
                                         college_rate + region,
                                       data = training_sample,
                                       importance = TRUE)
```

An attentive reader will notice that the arguments `formula` and `data` follow the same specifications of the predictive techniques studied in the course of Chapters 14 to 16 and 19 to 20, this chapter of this work. What is new is the argument `importance` in which we apply the logical value `TRUE` to ensure that the algorithm gives us conditions to assess the importance of each variable for the model.

When we declared the name of our model to R, we received interesting information about it, as shown in Figure 21.2.

```
rf_brazilian_poverty_1
```

```
Call:
 randomForest(formula = poverty_index ~ illiteracy_rate + elementary_school_rate +
elementary_school_rate + college_rate + region, data = training_sample,     importance
= TRUE)
               Type of random forest: regression
                     Number of trees: 500
No. of variables tried at each split: 1

          Mean of squared residuals: 58.9898
                    % Var explained: 88.34
```

FIGURE 21.2 The model `rf_brazilian_poverty_1`.

According to Figure 21.2, the random forest type is `regression` because the dependent variable is metric; for categorical dependent variables, R will return `classification`. It is also possible to see that 500 CARTs were combined, using 1 predictor variable for each of the decision trees because we declared 5 explanatory variables to the argument `formula`, and $\frac{5}{3} = 1,666\ldots$; in this case, R considers the number of variables as the value of the place of integers. Finally, the mean of squared residuals (mean squared error [MSE]) is equal to 58.9898 (RMSE = 7.6805, whereas MSE = RMSE^2), with an R^2 of 0.8834 (88.34%).

If we want to evaluate the importance of each explanatory variable, we can use the function `varImpPlot()` from the package `randomForest`.

```
varImpPlot(x = rf_brazilian_poverty_1)
```

When the function `varImpPlot()` is called according to the previous codes, it will output two graphs, as shown in Figure 21.3.

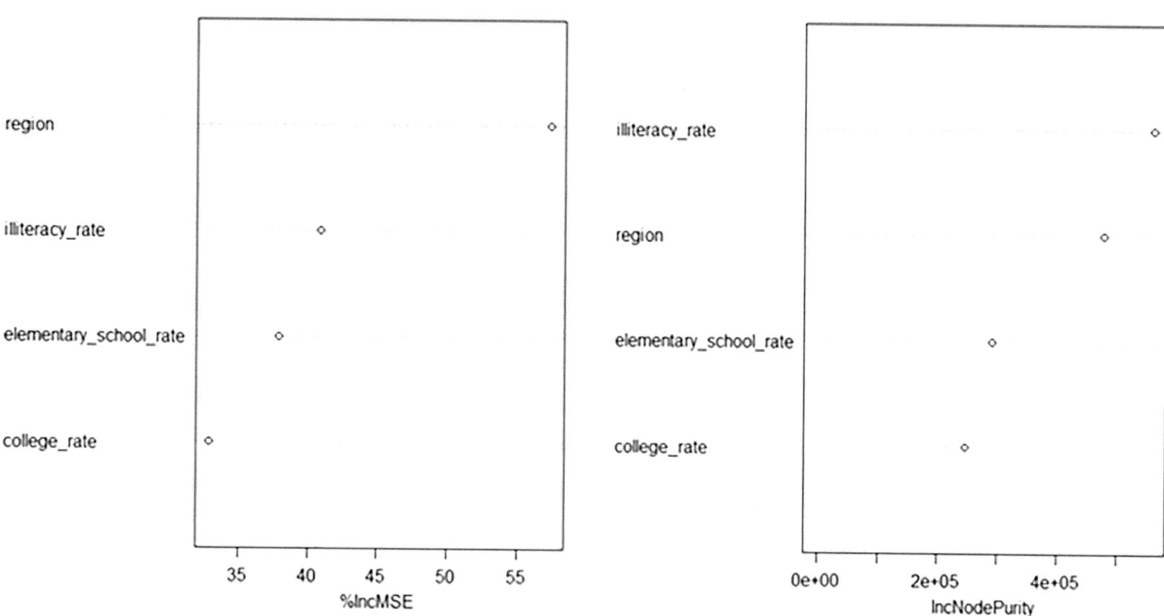

FIGURE 21.3 Applying the function `varImpPlot()` to the model `rf_brazilian_poverty_1`.

In Figure 21.3, the graph on the left shows the percentage of mean decrease in accuracy of the studied model; the graph on the right points to the mean decrease in node impurity (in this case, because the dependent variable is metric, impurity is measured by variance; see Chapter 19). That said, we can observe that the use of the explanatory variable *region* seems to have a greater impact on the decay of the MSE and, consequently, on the RMSE (we will use the RMSE with greater intensity by parallelism with Chapter 20). On the other hand, the variable *illeteracy_rate* seems to be the variable with the greatest capacity to decay the impurity of the subsamples of each CART.

If the reader is interested in obtaining the graphics present in Figure 21.3, but individually, he or she could type the following command:

```
# Mean decrease in accuracy
varImpPlot(x = rf_brazilian_poverty_1, type = 1)

# Mean decrease in node impurity
varImpPlot(x = rf_brazilian_poverty_1, type = 2)
```

If the reader is not interested in the graph shown in Figure 21.3, but rather in the importance values of each variable, the algorithm `importance()` from the package `randomForest` could be used.

```
importance(rf_brazilian_poverty_1)
```

In any case, it could be that the model `rf_brazilian_poverty_1`, which uses R's default hyperparameters, can still be refined because, for example, it used only 1 predictor variable for each combined CART. Next, we will estimate a random forest model that considers 4 of the 5 predictor variables in the dataset. To impute a predefined value of explanatory variables in a random forest model, we must use the argument `mtry`:

```
set.seed(1)
rf_brazilian_poverty_2 <- randomForest(formula = poverty_index ~ illiteracy_rate +
                                       elementary_school_rate +
                                         elementary_school_rate +
                                       college_rate + region,
                                       data = training_sample,
                                       mtry = 4,
                                       importance = TRUE)
```

To access the main information of the model, as already said, we can declare the name of the object that contains the estimation:

```
rf_brazilian_poverty_2
```

Figure 21.4 shows the results obtained from the previous command.

```
Call:
 randomForest(formula = poverty_index ~ illiteracy_rate + elementary_school_rate +
elementary_school_rate + college_rate + region, data = training_sample,      mtry = 4,
importance = TRUE)
               Type of random forest: regression
                     Number of trees: 500
No. of variables tried at each split: 4

          Mean of squared residuals: 62.5518
                    % Var explained: 87.64
```

FIGURE 21.4 The model `rf_brazilian_poverty_2`.

According to Figure 21.4, we still use the combination of 500 CARTs, but with 4 predictor variables per decision tree. In this situation, we can see that the RMSE was 7.9090 (higher than in the case of the model `rf_brazilian_poverty_1`) and with an R^2 of 0.8764 (lower than in the model `rf_brazilian_poverty_1`).

In the case studied, if on one hand, using the default amount of predictor variables may raise doubts about the accuracy of the model, on the other hand, using 4 explanatory variables does not seem to be the best solution. To solve this dilemma, we propose a routine analogous to the one studied for the techniques in Chapter 20, that is, we will estimate q random forest models in which q varies from the default value of predictor variables to the maximum number of explanatory variables present in the dataset.

Before we do this, to make the work easier, let's save our database in a new object called `new_database`, considering only the variables involved, in fact, in the modeling:

```
new_database <- brazilian_poverty %>%
  mutate(id = paste0(municipality,"|",state)) %>%
  column_to_rownames("id") %>%
  select(poverty_index, region, illiteracy_rate, elementary_school_rate,
         high_school_rate, college_rate)
```

After that, we will separate the training and validation samples so they are identical to those used in this chapter and in Chapter 20:

```
training_sample <- new_database[sample_index, ]

validation_sample <- new_database[-sample_index, ]
```

Next, let's create another object called `tuning_step`, which will contain the q `mtry` values and will serve as a receptacle for the subsequently calculated RMSE values:

```
tuning_step <- data.frame(mtry = as.integer(
  (ncol(new_database)-1)/3):(ncol(new_database)-1),
                          rmse = NA)
```

An attentive reader will notice that because the dependent variable is metric, q will range from $\frac{k}{3}$ to k. Once this is done, we can command the next routine:

```
for(i in min(tuning_step$mtry):max(tuning_step$mtry)){
  set.seed(1)
  tuning_model <- randomForest(formula = poverty_index ~ .,
                               data = training_sample,
                               mtry = i,
                               importance = TRUE)

mse = (training_sample$poverty_index - predict(tuning_model))^2

tuning_step$rmse[i] <- sqrt(sum(mean(mse)))
}
```

To access the results of the previous codes, we can command the following:

```
tuning_step
```

Figure 21.5 shows R's response to the previous routine.

```
mtry     rmse
   1  7.641899
   2  7.594631
   3  7.644969
   4  7.694150
   5  7.731056
```

FIGURE 21.5 The RMSE values for each q `mtry` value.

In Figure 21.5, we should look for the smallest RMSE value, which is 7.5946 for the case analyzed, when the number of randomly selected predictor variables for each CART is equal to 2.

Therefore we can interpose a new random forest model, arguing `mtry = 2`:

```
set.seed(1)
rf_brazilian_poverty_3 <- randomForest(formula = poverty_index ~ .,
                                       data = training_sample,
                                       mtry = 2,
                                       importance = TRUE)
```

To access the main features of the model, we can command the following:

```
rf_brazilian_poverty_3
```

Figure 21.6 shows the results obtained from the previous command.

```
Call:
 randomForest(formula = poverty_index ~ ., data = training_sample,
mtry = 2, importance = TRUE)
               Type of random forest: regression
                     Number of trees: 500
No. of variables tried at each split: 2

          Mean of squared residuals: 57.67842
                    % Var explained: 88.6
```

FIGURE 21.6 The model `rf_brazilian_poverty_3`.

Figure 21.6 indicates an RMSE of 7.5946 and an R^2 of 0.886. Both measures are superior to those verified in the models `rf_brazilian_poverty_1` and `rf_brazilian_poverty_2`.

To find out if there is no overfitting problem, we can calculate the RMSE and R^2 values for the validation database observations. However, first we must save the fitted values of the model for the validation sample, with the help of the function `predict()`:

```
validation_sample["fitted_rf_3"] <- predict(object = rf_brazilian_poverty_3,
                                            newdata = validation_sample)
```

The calculation of RMSE and R^2 can be done as follows:

```
validation_sample %>%
  mutate(ssr = ((poverty_index - mean(poverty_index)) ^ 2),
         rss = ((poverty_index - fitted_rf_3) ^ 2)) %>%
  summarise(rmse = sqrt(1/nrow(.) * sum(rss)),
            r_squared = sum(ssr) / (sum(ssr) + sum(rss)))
```

After the previous routine, for the validation sample, R should show RMSE and R^2 values of 7.59 and 0.89, respectively. Such values are close to the values originally calculated with the training sample and, as such, quite possibly indicate that there is no overfitting problem in the model `rf_brazilian_poverty_3`.

In Chapter 20, when we compared the boosting and bagging approaches for this same dataset, we explained why the boosting approach had superior performance in this case. Although this remains after the estimation of a random forest, it is possible to verify that the approach of this chapter proved to be superior to the classic bagging approach used in Chapter 20, both in relation to RMSE and R^2.

To verify the amount of estimated CARTs needed to minimize the RMSE value, the reader can apply the following routine:

```
data.frame(sqrt(rf_brazilian_poverty_3$mse)) %>%
  rownames_to_column("trees") %>%
  rename(rmse = 2) %>%
  mutate(trees = as.numeric(trees)) %>%
  arrange(trees) %>%
  ggplot() +
  geom_line(aes(x = trees, y = rmse), color = "orange", size = 1.2) +
  labs(x = "Amount of Trees",
       y = "RMSE") +
  theme_bw()
```

The previous commands will help guide the reader about the need for a greater number of CART iterations, as shown in Figure 21.7.

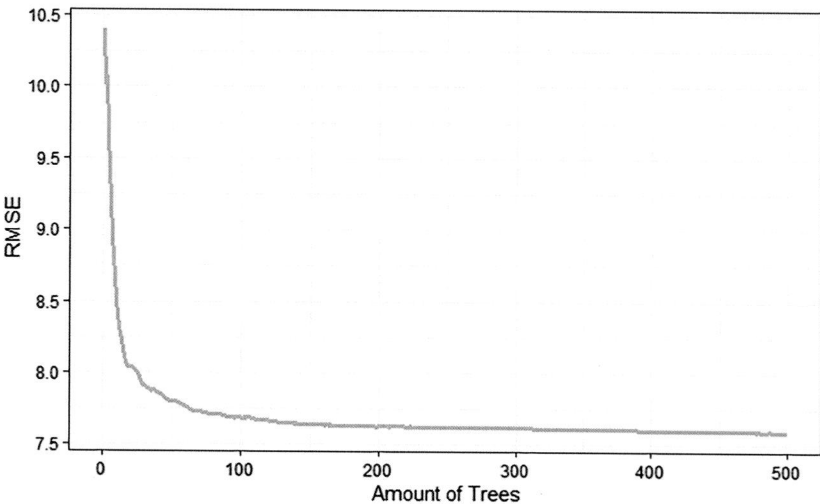

FIGURE 21.7 Graph showing the decrease in RMSE due to the number of decision trees iterated.

For the situation present in Figure 21.7, there is no reason to extrapolate the default number of CART iterations in the function `randomForest()`. If this were necessary, because of non-stabilization of the RMSE decrease resulting from the number of CARTs iterated, the reader could use the argument `ntree` with the desired value. However, when resorting to this resource, we suggest that the reader always do so in front of a training sample and a validation sample to be able to ascertain the existence, or non-existence, of the overfitting problem.

Finally, if the reader wants to verify the adequacy of the predicted values of the model `rf_brazilian_poverty_3` to the used predictor variables, he or she could do the following:

```
# Illiteracy Rate
validation_sample %>%
  ggplot() +
  geom_point(aes(x = illiteracy_rate, y = poverty_index, color = region)) +
  geom_smooth(aes(x = illiteracy_rate, y = fitted_rf_3), se = FALSE, color = "red") +
  scale_color_viridis_d() +
  labs(x = "Illiteracy Rate",
       y = "Poverty Index",
       color = "Label") +
  facet_wrap(~region) +
  theme(panel.background = element_rect("white"),
             panel.grid = element_line("grey95"),
```

Continued

```
        panel.border = element_rect(NA),
        legend.position = "none") -> illiteracy_rf

# Elementary School Rate
validation_sample %>%
  ggplot() +
  geom_point(aes(x = elementary_school_rate, y = poverty_index, color = region)) +
  geom_smooth(aes(x = elementary_school_rate, y = fitted_rf_3), se = FALSE, color = "red") +
  scale_color_viridis_d() +
  labs(x = "Elementary School Rate",
       y = "Poverty Index",
       color = "Label") +
  facet_wrap(~region) +
  theme(panel.background = element_rect("white"),
        panel.grid = element_line("grey95"),
        panel.border = element_rect(NA),
        legend.position = "none") -> elementary_rf

# High School Rate
validation_sample %>%
  ggplot() +
  geom_point(aes(x = high_school_rate, y = poverty_index, color = region)) +
  geom_smooth(aes(x = high_school_rate, y = fitted_rf_3), se = FALSE, color = "red") +
  scale_color_viridis_d() +
  labs(x = "High School Rate",
       y = "Poverty Index",
       color = "Label") +
  facet_wrap(~region) +
  theme(panel.background = element_rect("white"),
        panel.grid = element_line("grey95"),
        panel.border = element_rect(NA),
        legend.position = "none") -> high_rf

# College Rate
validation_sample %>%
  ggplot() +
  geom_point(aes(x = college_rate, y = poverty_index, color = region)) +
  geom_smooth(aes(x = college_rate, y = fitted_rf_3), se = FALSE, color = "red") +
  scale_color_viridis_d() +
  labs(x = "College Rate",
       y = "Poverty Index",
       color = "Label") +
  facet_wrap(~region) +
  theme(panel.background = element_rect("white"),
        panel.grid = element_line("grey95"),
        panel.border = element_rect(NA),
        legend.position = "none") -> college_rf

grid.arrange(illiteracy_rf, elementary_rf,
             high_rf, college_rf)
```

Figure 21.8 shows the result obtained from the previous command.

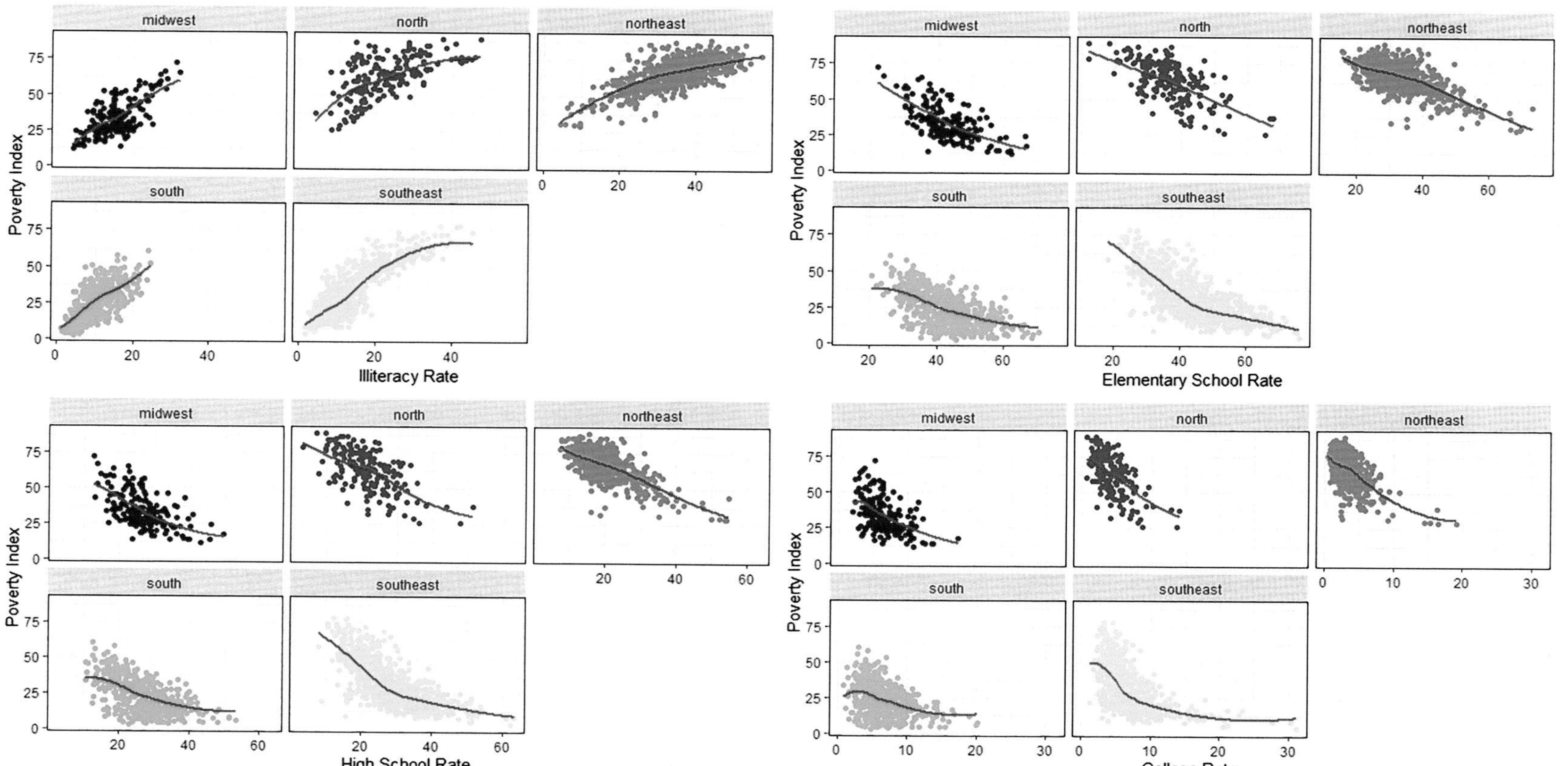

FIGURE 21.8 Adherence of fitted values of the model `rf_brazilian_poverty_3` to the variables *illiteracy_rate, elementary_school_rate, high_school_rate,* and *college_rate,* stratified according to the *region* variable.

Final remarks

Random forest estimations are models with high predictive capabilities, being considered specific types of bagging approach, however, without the problem of correlation among trees.

These are interesting techniques, especially for phenomena that do not manifest themselves in a linear way and that behave better in the face of data with less variability when compared with classic bagging approaches.

Despite the advantages mentioned, because of the high amount of stochastic procedures, we maintain the recommendation that the reader continue the practice of establishing training and validation samples for this kind of algorithm so, at a minimum, it is protected from the overfitting problem.

Exercise

(1) Considering the following data on some tourists around the world, develop a combination of bagging models that seek to predict whether or not a certain couple will travel to another country in the next year, **based only on their average age and number of children** (Fávero and Belfiore, 2019). The data are found in the file `tourism_data.RData`, whose variables are as follows:

Variable	Description
country	Variable that identifies the nationality of the tourist.
tourism	Dummy variable that indicates whether or not a certain tourist made an international trip in the last year.
age	Metric variable that measures the average age of the considered couple.
children	Metric variable that indicates the number of children of the considered couple.

Remember that the dependent variable is categorical, so the prediction error metric is the classification error! Use `set.seed(1)`.

(a) Make a random forest estimation with the default hyperparameters of R, and point out the variable with the greatest importance in relation to the mean decrease in accuracy.

(b) Make a random forest estimation with the default hyperparameters of R, and point out the variable with the greatest importance in relation to the mean decrease in node impurity.

(c) What is the `mtry` value that results in the smallest misclassification?

(d) Is the default value of `ntree` sufficient to stabilize the classification error?

(e) Create a graph that shows a good `ntree` value for stabilizing the classification error.

Supplementary data sets

```
brazilian_poverty.RData
fidelity_data.RData
tourism_data.RData
```

Please access supplementary data files here: https://doi.org/10.17632/55623jkwrp.3

CHAPTER

22

Artificial neural networks

AT THE END OF THIS CHAPTER, YOU WILL BE ABLE TO:

- Present the estimations of artificial neural networks of the multilayer feedforward networks type.
- Understand the need for the correct use of activation functions.
- Demonstrate the calculations of weights and bias values and the calculation of model errors for each iterative procedure.
- Estimate artificial neural network models in R-based language, and learn to interpret their results.

R language packages used in this chapter

```
library(tidyverse)
library(scales)
library(fastDummies)
library(neuralnet)
library(gridExtra)
library(caret)
library(e1071)
library(ROCR)
```

Don't forget to define the R working directory (the location where your datasets are installed):

```
setwd("C:/book/chapter22")
```

Introduction

So-called *artificial neural networks* are supervised models with high predictive capacity whose way of learning is inspired by the way human neurons learn.

Although the focus of this work refers to machine learning techniques, it must be said that the greatest field of application of neural networks is found in the field of deep learning, being commonly applied in the recognition of images, videos, and sounds. As a rule, when we see news about autonomous vehicles, machines capable of recognizing and

Data Science, Analytics and Machine Learning with R
https://doi.org/10.1016/B978-0-12-824271-1.00023-8

mimicking human facial expressions, and computers composing music or creating paintings, we are faced with a model of artificial neural networks applied to the field of deep learning.

However, as we said, the focus of this work is machine learning, and as such, we will work with these kinds of algorithms providing a dataset in the form of a matrix as a subsidy for their training, as we did for all of the algorithms of machine learning studied. For example, the objective of this chapter will not be the establishment of models aimed at facial recognition, the capture of video patterns, or the generation of automation for vehicles. We will continue working with the presence of a dependent variable Y and k predictor variables X, arranged in a two-dimensional way, that is, in a matrix form.

In addition to the assumptions made for this chapter, one more assumption must be defined. The reader must know that when talking about artificial neural networks, one is talking about a large family of algorithms with different specificities. For the development of this chapter, we will study the artificial neural networks of the type multilayer feedforward networks.

That said, the reader must know that neural network algorithms rely heavily on stochastic procedures and are very difficult (not to say impossible) to replicate. Thus we will return to using the function `set.seed()` so the reader can obtain the same results replicated in the images of this chapter on his or her computer.

For the algorithms discussed at this point to learn from their errors at each iterative step, it will also be necessary to define a given activation function. In this sense, if the phenomenon studied is characterized by linearity, it would be common for us to use an activation function analogous to the one studied for the simple and multiple regression models in Chapter 14 of this work. On the other hand, if the phenomenon manifests itself in a dichotomous way, the activation function could be very similar to that used in for the binary and logistic regression models studied in Chapter 15. Obviously, there are still other kinds of activation functions for when, for example, the phenomenon behaves in a polychotomous way or when the phenomenon behaves in an exponential, polynomial way, and so on.

Thus it should already be clear to the reader that artificial neural network algorithms work well, both with metric dependent variables and with categorical dependent variables.

It must also be said that, like the classification and regression tree (CART) and fandom forests, neural network models do not have a final equation. Therefore, there is nothing to talk about the interpretation of eventual linear and angular coefficients because they do not exist explicitly in this kind of estimation.

So, like CART and random forests, neural networks will depend on the calibration of so-called *hyperparameters* and, furthermore, on the correct choice of the activation function. Another necessary thing to mention is that, as the reader must have already suspected, overfitting will be a latent problem to be permanently taken care of as it is a kind of model that learns from its mistakes from stochastic processes.

In the sections to come, we will go deeper into the issues mentioned, addressing the specifics of this estimation in the presence of metric and categorical variables, regardless of whether they are dependent or predictor variables.

Artificial neural networks

Artificial neural network models are composed of a cluster of neurons distributed in layers. A generic theoretical model of a neural network is shown in Figure 22.1.

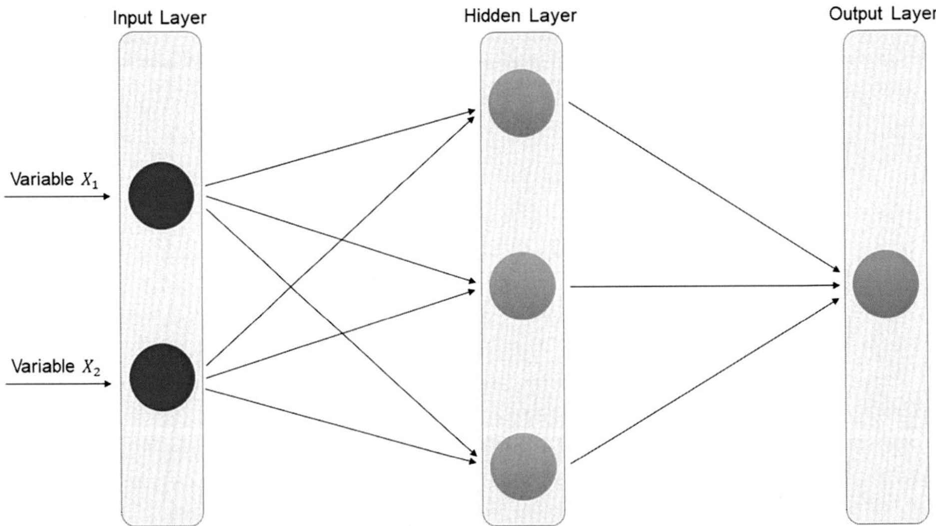

FIGURE 22.1 Theoretical model of an artificial neural network without iterations.

In Figure 22.1, there is a playful attempt to estimate a given phenomenon from two predictor variables (X_1 and X_2) without iterations, that is, without correcting errors due to the learning process. Each circle represents a neuron; each arrow represents the synapses, that is, the interconnections between neurons; each dashed rectangle emphasizes a layer of neurons.

For the first iterative step in Figure 22.1, the layer called *Input Layer* will concern the input values, that is, the values of the explanatory variables X_1 and X_2 for each observation $i(i=1,2,3,\ldots,n)$ of the dataset. The layer called *Hidden Layer*, on the other hand, will represent one or more hidden layers of neurons whose values will be estimated from the interactions between the values present in the input layer and their random weights present in the synapses, as well as the random bias values assigned to the hidden layer itself, as shown in Figure 22.2. Finally, the layer called *Output Layer* will present the estimated values of the phenomenon after the interactions between the hidden layer values, weighted by their random weights present in their synapses, as well as by a random bias value of the output layer itself, as shown in Figure 22.2.

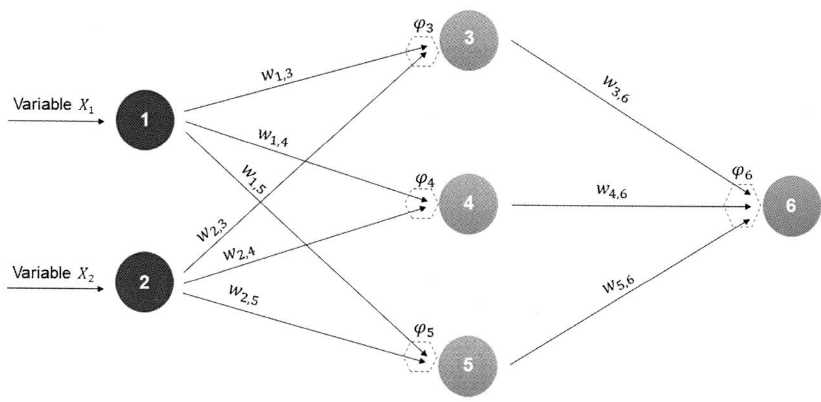

FIGURE 22.2 Theoretical model of an iteration-free artificial neural network, with emphasis on the weights attached to each layer.

In Figure 22.2, $w_{p,q}$ represents the random weights present in the synapses, where p is the anterior neuron, q is the present neuron, and φ_q represents the bias values of each layer.

In R, for the first iterative moment of a neural network of the multilayer feedforward networks type, the weights $w_{p,\,q}$ and the bias values φ_q receive random values composed, as a rule, but not always, in the range between -0.05 and $+0.05$.

Activation functions and estimations of the ouput values of each layer

The estimation of the output values of each layer depends on the choice of an activation function $g(.)$. Next, we present the most commonly used activation functions for the neural networks studied in this chapter.

Linear activation function

When assuming a phenomenon of linear behavior, the chosen activation function could be the one present in Expression (22.1).

$$Outcome_q = g\left(\varphi_q + \sum_{i=1}^{n} w_{p,q}.X_i\right) = \varphi_q + \sum_{i=1}^{n} w_{p,q}.X_i \quad (22.1)$$

An attentive reader will notice that Expression (22.1) refers to Expression (14.1), whose main difference points to the chosen unknowns. Figure 22.3 demonstrates a theoretical result of Expression (22.1) for hypothetical values of the predictor variable X between -5 and $+5$.

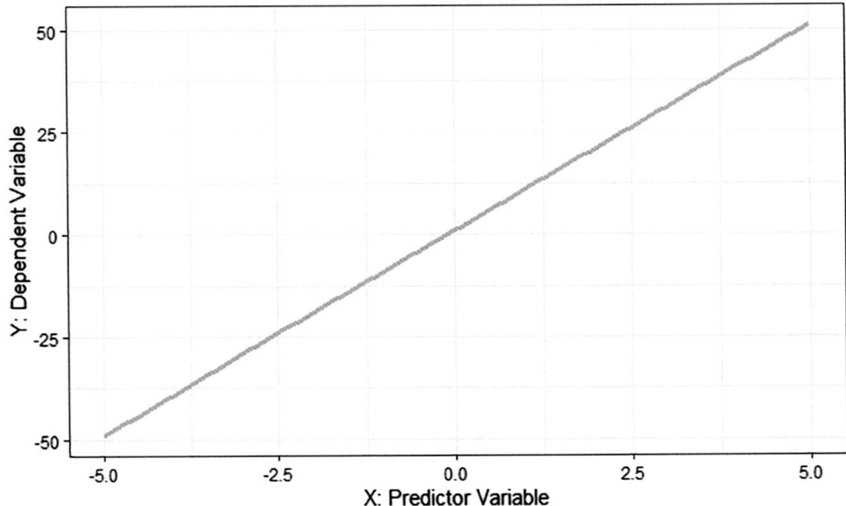

FIGURE 22.3 Theoretical example of using the linear activation function.

Sigmoid or logistic activation function

On the other hand, assuming a phenomenon of dichotomous manifestation (i.e., event, non-event), the activation function present in Expression (22.2), of the sigmoid type, could be the most adequate.

$$Outcome_q = g\left(\varphi_q + \sum_{i=1}^{n} w_{p,q}.X_i\right) = \frac{1}{1 + e^{-\left(\varphi_q + \sum_{i=1}^{n} w_{p,q}.X_i\right)}} \tag{22.2}$$

Again, an attentive reader will notice that Expression (22.2) looks a lot like Expression (15.10). Figure 22.4 provides a theoretical example of the use of a sigmoid activation function.

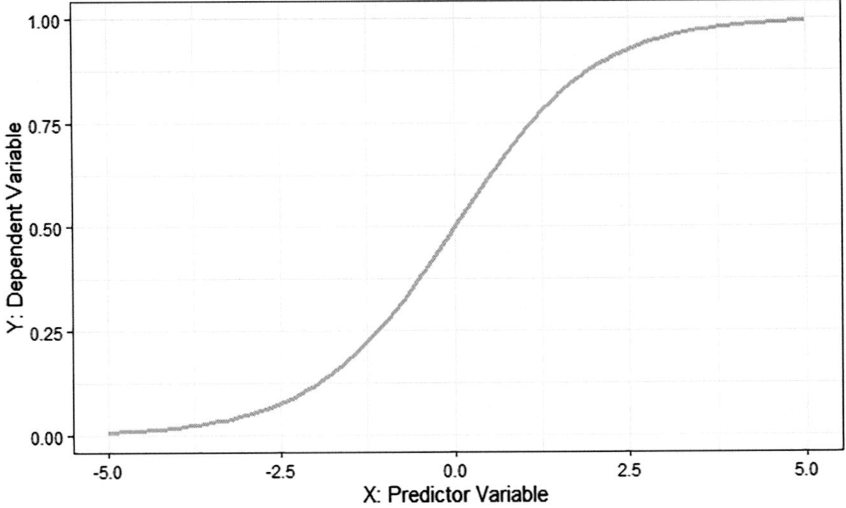

FIGURE 22.4 Theoretical example of using the sigmoid activation function.

Like the sigmoid curve studied in Chapter 15 of this work, the curve shown in Figure 22.4 is asymptotic between 0 and 1.

Hyperbolic tangent activation function

Differently, if the reader needed an asymptotic activation function between –1 and 1, he or she could choose the hyperbolic tangent activation function, described by Expression (22.3).

$$Outcome_q = g\left(\varphi_q + \sum_{i=1}^{n} w_{p,q}.X_i\right) = \frac{e^{\left(\varphi_q + \sum_{i=1}^{n} w_{p,q}.X_i\right)} - e^{-\left(\varphi_q + \sum_{i=1}^{n} w_{p,q}.X_i\right)}}{e^{\left(\varphi_q + \sum_{i=1}^{n} w_{p,q}.X_i\right)} + e^{-\left(\varphi_q + \sum_{i=1}^{n} w_{p,q}.X_i\right)}} \tag{22.3}$$

Figure 22.5 presents a theoretical example of the use of the hyperbolic tangent activation function.

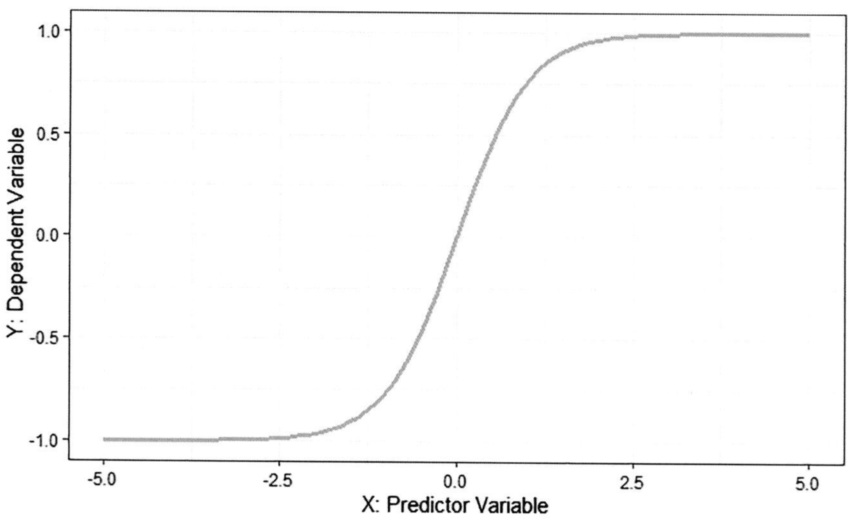

FIGURE 22.5 Theoretical example of the use of the hyperbolic tangent activation function

Softmax activation function

Imagining the reader's need for an activation function for phenomena that manifest themselves in a polychotomous way, the Softmax activation function could be a good alternative. The discussed function, for M categories of responses, is present in Expression (22.4) and refers to Expression (15.33).

$$Outcome_q = g\left(\varphi_q + \sum_{i=1}^{n} w_{p,q}.X_i\right) = \frac{e^{\left(\varphi_q + \sum_{i=1}^{n} w_{p,q}.X_i\right)_m}}{\sum_{m=0}^{M-1} e^{\left(\varphi_q + \sum_{i=1}^{n} w_{p,q}.X_i\right)_m}} \tag{22.4}$$

in that $m=0, 1, 2, \ldots, M-1$.

Figure 22.6 contains a possible theoretical example of the use of the Softmax activation function.

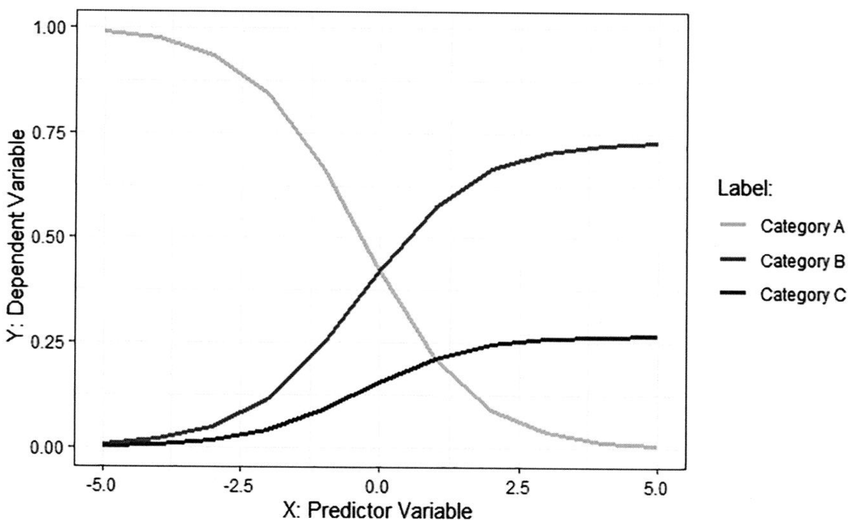

FIGURE 22.6 Theoretical example of using the Softmax activation function.

Softplus activation function

We would also like to mention the Softplus function, which is interesting for phenomena whose behavior is exponential, starting from 0, whose formula is presented by Expression (22.5).

$$Outcome_q = g\left(\varphi_q + \sum_{i=1}^{n} w_{p,q}.X_i\right) = ln\left[1 + e^{\left(\varphi_q + \sum_{i=1}^{n} w_{p,q}.X_i\right)}\right] \tag{22.5}$$

Figure 22.7 provides a possible theoretical example of the use of the Softplus activation function.

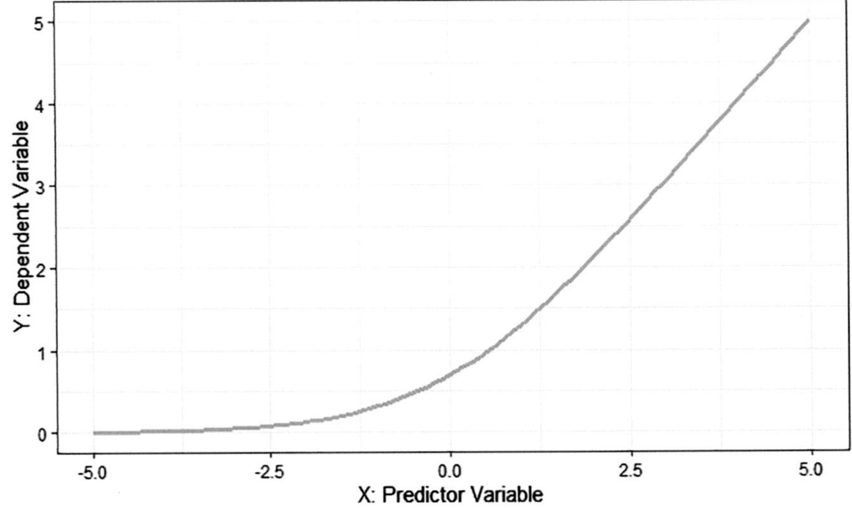

FIGURE 22.7 Theoretical example of using the Softplus activation function.

Rectifier linear unit activation function

Without intending to exhaust all possible neural network activation functions, we would like to present the last one, as an alternative to the Softplus activation function: the Rectifier Linear Unit (ReLU) function.

ReLU is an interesting alternative to Softplus as it is less computationally demanding because it does not have exponential calculations, as shown in Expression (22.6).

$$Outcome_q = g\left(\varphi_q + \sum_{i=1}^{n} w_{p,q}.X_i\right) = \begin{cases} 0, if\ \varphi_q + \sum_{i=1}^{n} w_{p,q}.X_i < 0 \\ \varphi_q + \sum_{i=1}^{n} w_{p,q}.X_i, if\ \varphi_q + \sum_{i=1}^{n} w_{p,q}.X_i \geq 0 \end{cases} \tag{22.6}$$

Figure 22.8 provides a theoretical example of the use of the ReLU activation function in comparison with the Softplus function.

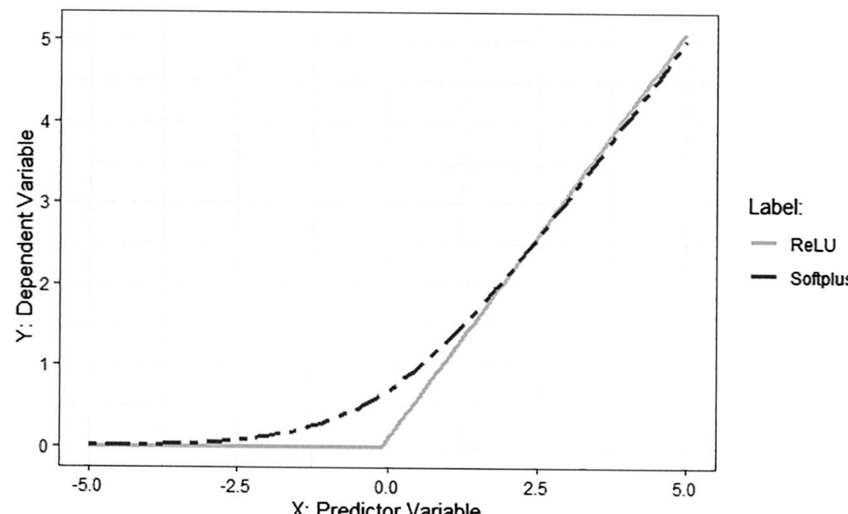

FIGURE 22.8 Theoretical example of the use of the ReLU activation function compared with the use of the Softplus activation function.

Demonstration of calculations of layer output values

Turning attention to the theoretical neural network proposed in Figure 22.2, we propose a small dataset to understand the calculation of the output values of the layers of the studied algorithm present in Table 22.1. Data refer to levels of hate crimes (low or high) in eight countries as a function of median income and percentage of unemployed. By hate crimes, the reader can understand as crimes motivated by religious, racial, gender and/or political ideology intolerance.

TABLE 22.1 Hate crimes dataset.

country_id	*median_income*	*share_unemployed*	*hate_crimes_level*
1	49,936	3.9	Low
2	62,283	4.7	High
3	70,489	4.3	High
4	62,539	3.9	Low
5	64,524	4.2	Low
6	42,781	4.8	Low
7	86,345	3.4	High
8	54,555	4.3	High

In the presence of metric variables, regardless of whether dependent or explanatory, the first step should be to standardize the values according to the variable's ranges. As a rule, the standardization of metric variables occurs between the values of 0 and 1, as shown in Expression (22.7).

$$Xstd_i = \frac{X_i - min\,(X)}{max\,(X) - min\,(X)} \tag{22.7}$$

On the other hand, if the reader wants a more adherent standardization to the hyperbolic tangent function, he or she can use Expression (22.8) to standardize the variables between –1 and 1.

$$Xstd_i = 2 \times \frac{X_i - min\,(X)}{max\,(X) - min\,(X)} - 1 \tag{22.8}$$

In the presence of categorical variables, regardless of whether dependent or explanatory, dummy variables must be carried out, regardless of whether the categorical variable is of the binary type. Table 22.2 presents the expected result of the indicated procedures.

TABLE 22.2 Dataset proposed by Table 22.1, with standardized variables.

country_id	*median_income_std*	*share_unemployed_std*	*hate_crimes_low*	*hate_crimes_high*
1	0.164	0.357	1	0
2	0.448	0.929	0	1
3	0.636	0.643	0	1
4	0.454	0.357	1	0
5	0.499	0.571	1	0
6	0.000	1.000	1	0
7	1.000	0.000	0	1
8	0.270	0.643	0	1

That said, we can revisit the proposed model Figure 22.2, adapting it to the dataset present in Table 22.2. Figure 22.9 explains the proposal.

Figure 22.9 demonstrates the first moment of establishing a neural network. **We repeat, in the first step, all values of $w_{p,q}$ and φ_q are randomly established.** For this example, we are using the Logistic Activation Function.

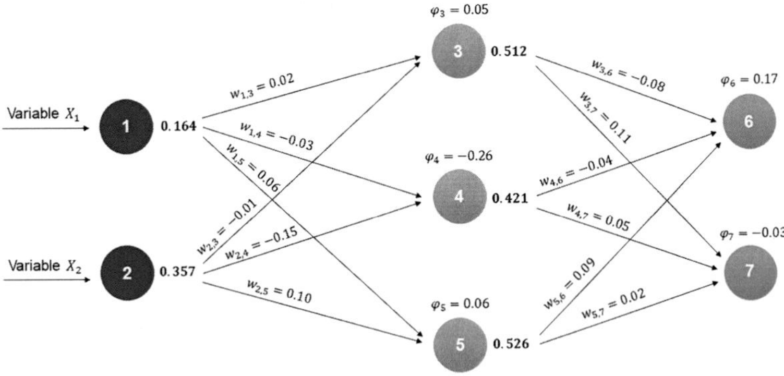

FIGURE 22.9 Theoretical example of the first step of a theoretical neural network using the dataset in Table 22.2.

In Figure 22.9, it is observed that for the first step, the values present in the input layer neurons refer to the observations of the first individual in the dataset present in Table 22.2, considering the two predictor variables. Then, using Expression (22.2) to calculate the output values of neurons 3, 4, and 5, we have:

$$Output_3 = \frac{1}{1 + e^{-(0.05+0.02\times0.164-0.01\times0.357)}} = 0.512$$

$$Output_4 = \frac{1}{1 + e^{-(-0.26-0.03\times0.164-0.15\times0.357)}} = 0.421$$

$$Output_5 = \frac{1}{1 + e^{-(0.06+0.06\times0.164-0.1\times0.357)}} = 0.526$$

Also in Figure 22.9, for calculating the output values of neurons 6 and 7:

$$Output_6 = \frac{1}{1 + e^{-(0.17-0.08\times0.512-0.04\times0.421+0.09\times0.526)}} = 0.540$$

$$Output_7 = \frac{1}{1 + e^{-(-0.03+0.11\times0.512+0.05\times0.421+0.02\times0.526)}} = 0.514$$

If we considered that there would be no iterations, that is, stopping the estimation after calculating the output values of neurons 6 and 7, **a careless reader might mistakenly think that the values 0.540 and 0.514 point to the probability of occurrence of the *low* and *high* categories of the dependent variable *hate_crimes_level*. These values are just scores, which can be transformed into values of the probability of occurrence of the categories mentioned as follows:**

$$hate\_crimes\_low = \frac{0.540}{0.540 + 0.514} = 0.512$$

$$hate\_crimes\_high = \frac{0.514}{0.540 + 0.514} = 0.488$$

That said, if we stopped our neural network in its first step, according to the proposed example, the probability of occurrence of a low rate of hate crimes for the first country in our dataset would be approximately 51.20%. Therefore, the probability of an occurrence of a high rate of hate crimes for that same country, under the same conditions proposed by the example, would be approximately 48.80%.

Anyway, when looking at Figure 22.9, an attentive reader will notice that after the output layer, the arrows (synapses) keep pointing to a continuity, that is, to a next step; this is an iterative process for the case of this chapter.

For the iteration to be carried out, it is necessary to discuss how to calculate the estimation errors at the present moment, so for the next iteration, the model can rearrange itself by learning from its own errors.

Method of calculation of estimation errors for iteration feeding

Among some possibilities for calculating model errors to update the weights $w_{p,\,q}$ and bias φ_q, at each iteration, is the criterion called *back propagation of error*.

By observing Figure 22.9, for this criterion, after estimating the output scores, we would use the errors arising from the back propagation of error technique. So, in a second iterative step, the values of $w_{p,q}$ and φ_q were reestimated, necessarily changing the score values presented by neurons 6 and 7. This procedure must be repeated at each iteration r.

The criterion discussed, in general, can be mathematically described by Expression (22.9).

$$error_{r,q} = \widehat{Y}_{r,q} \times \left(1 - \widehat{Y}_{r,q}\right) \times \left(Y_{r,q} - \widehat{Y}_{r,q}\right) \tag{22.9}$$

Assuming the q output values for the q neurons of our neural network, shown at the end of the "Demonstration of calculations of layer output values" section, for r iterative steps, we would have the update equations for $w_{p,q}$ and φ_q explained in Expressions (22.10) and (22.11).

$$w_{r+1,p,q} = w_{r,p,q} + l \times error_{r,q} \tag{22.10}$$

$$\varphi_{r+1,q} = \varphi_{r,q} + l \times error_{r,q} \tag{22.11}$$

where l indicates the learning rate.

In R, the default value of l is usually 0.5. If the reader is following the logic of this work chapter by chapter, he or she can associate l with the idea of shrinkage explored in Chapter 20. Figure 20.1 is a nice proxy for the idea of how l works. We will return to the idea of learning rate in the course of the "Hyperparameters" section.

That said, we can calculate the values of $\text{error}_{r,q}$ for the first iterative step of the model depicted in Figure 22.9, which will be used to update the values of $w_{p,q}$ and φ_q for a second iteration. Therefore, according to Expression (22.9), the error associated with neuron 6 during the first iteration is given by:

$$\text{error}_{1,6} = 0.540 \times (1 - 0.540) \times (0 - 0.540) = -0.134.$$

The error associated with neuron 7 during the first iteration is:

$$\text{error}_{1,7} = 0.514 \times (1 - 0.514) \times (1 - 0.514) = 0.121.$$

After calculating $\text{error}_{1,6}$ and $\text{error}_{1,7}$, with the help of Expressions (22.10) and (22.11), we can update the values of $w_{p,q}$ and φ_q for neurons 6 and 7 for the next iteration. First, considering the update of the values of φ_6, $w_{3,6}$, $w_{4,6}$, and $w_{5,6}$:

$$\varphi_{2,6} = 0.17 + 0.5 \times (-0.134) = 0.103$$
$$w_{2,3,6} = -0.08 + 0.5 \times (-0.134) = -0.147$$
$$w_{2,4,6} = -0.04 + 0.5 \times (-0.134) = -0.107$$
$$w_{2,5,6} = 0.09 + 0.5 \times (-0.134) = 0.023$$

Following the same logic, the new values of φ_7, $w_{3,7}$, $w_{4,7}$ and $w_{5,7}$, will be:

$$\varphi_{2,7} = -0.03 + 0.5 \times 0.121 = 0.031$$

$$w_{2,3,7} = 0.11 + 0.5 \times 0.121 = 0.171$$

$$w_{2,4,7} = 0.05 + 0.5 \times 0.121 = 0.111$$

$$w_{2,5,7} = 0.02 + 0.5 \times 0.121 = 0.081$$

The procedures narrated in this section should be expanded to the other neurons in the model, following the same logic. The iterations must cease in the event of at least one of the following situations: (i) when the number of iterations reaches the predefined value of iterative steps pointed out by the reader; (ii) when the update of the new values of $w_{p,q}$ and φ_q are not substantially different from their respective values in past iterations; or (iii) when the misclassification rate reaches a predefined threshold.

Next, we will present the most common hyperparameters for artificial neural networks of the multilayer feedforward networks type.

Hyperparameters

As with the kinds of estimations discussed in Chapters 19 to 21, we do not intend to exhaust the subject of all possible hyperparameters for the case of artificial neural networks. Therefore, following the same reasoning proposed for this work, we will present the most commonly used hyperparameters for the estimates studied in R-based language.

That said, an attentive reader will notice that there are at least six hyperparameters to be concerned with more intensely: (a) the definition of an activation function; (b) the choice of a number of hidden layers; (c) the definition of the number of neurons in hidden layers; (d) the value of the learning rate; (e) the value of a threshold to assess the misclassification rate; and (f) the number of iterations.

Defining an activation function

The definition of which activation function to use has direct relationships with the measurement scale of the model's dependent variable (i.e., whether Y is metric or categorical) as well as with the behavior of this dependent variable as a function of the selected predictor variables for the estimation.

In this sense, as discussed throughout this work, it would not make sense for the reader to choose the Linear Activation Function for a given variable of interest that was of the dichotomous type. In the same sense, the justification of a Logistic Activation Function for a given target variable of continuous type would be unlikely.

Choosing a number of hidden layers

Even though the reader is completely free to choose any amount of hidden layers in the case of the application of artificial neural networks in the field of machine learning, authors often point out that the choice of one or, at most, two hidden layers, is usually a good practice (Shmueli et al., 2018).

When looking at Figures 22.1, 22.2, and 22.9, keeping in mind the stochastic processes present at each iteration, it is not difficult to conclude that the greater the amount of hidden layers, the greater the expenditure of time and the greater the expenditure of computational power. Furthermore, the greater the amount of hidden layers, the greater the probability of model overfitting (Karsoliya, 2012). Thus in the reader's personal cases, we also agree with the authors mentioned and recommend the use of, at most, two hidden layers.

Defining the number of neurons in hidden layers

As pointed out in the "Choosing a number of hidden layers" section, here the general rule also applies that the greater the number of neurons in the hidden layer(s), the greater the probability of overfitting. However, there is an aggravating factor in this area: an uninteresting amount of neurons in hidden layers can lead to underfitting estimation.

Karsoliya (2012) asserts that the decision for the number of neurons in a given hidden layer is not necessarily something straightforward. The author, however, suggests that it is interesting that the amount of neurons used in more than one hidden layer is similar.

Boger and Guterman (1997) propose that the number of neurons in a hidden layer is between 70% and 90% of the number of neurons in the input layer. In a similar way, Berry and Linoff (1997) indicate that the number of neurons in a hidden layer must be smaller than the number of neurons in the input layer. Finally, Blum (1992) argues that the number of neurons in a given hidden layer must be between the number of neurons in the output layer and the number of neurons in the input layer.

That said, Shmueli et al. (2018) try to consider the narrated propositions and suggest that a first model be estimated with a number of neurons in the hidden layer equal to the number of k predictor variables X. Next, they propose to test the existence of overfitting in the estimated model. If overfitting is diagnosed, they propose the estimation of new models with a smaller amount of neurons in the hidden layer, until an estimation with good performance and without the overfitting problem is found.

Learning rate

Analogously to what we studied in Chapter 20, we can say that l will determine the contribution of each neuron, at each iterative step, to the determination of bias values, weights, and to the refinement of the fitted values of the model. Lower values of l increase the probability of the algorithm finding more accurate fitted values. However, depending on an insufficient predefinition of a maximum number of iterative steps by the reader, there may be an increase in the probability of the algorithm stopping its iterations before refining itself in the desired way. On the other hand, an excessive amount of iterations, combined with small values of l, will cost time and computational power. As said, R uses 0.5 as the default value for learning rate.

The threshold to evaluate the misclassification rate

This hyperparameter is associated with the use of a categorical dependent variable. For this work, we have already discussed this subject in the "Cutoff, sensitivity analysis, overall model efficiency, sensitivity, and specificity" section in Chapter 15, calling it the *cutoff*.

By assuming a model with a dichotomous dependent variable, it is often not enough to assume that if a given probability of an event (or non-event) is greater than 50%, then we will have a classification with a high accuracy rate.

A clear example of this would be an eventual diagnosis of cancer. Imagine a patient who had their clinical examinations submitted to a predictive model to assess the probability of the presence of cancer. Also imagine that the model resulted in a 30% probability of that patient having cancer. The question is: Would it be correct for the medical team to rule out the possibility of this disease because the probability is not greater than 50% or to go deeper into the study of the situation?

That said, this hyperparameter proposes to stop iterations from the moment when, for given threshold assumed by the reader, there is no better significance for the misclassification rate.

The number of iterations

Barring better judgment, we think this hyperparameter is self-explanatory. It will indicate the maximum number of iterative steps desired for the iterations to stop.

Next, we will present applications of artificial neural networks in R-based language.

Artificial neural networks applications in R

In this section, we will present two examples: one that considers the variable dependent of the metric type and another with the categorical dependent variable.

Estimation of an artificial neural network for a metric-type phenomenon

For this example, we will use data from 619 Brazilian municipalities. The objective will be to establish a predictive model on the life expectancy of residents of these cities. The data can be found in the file `life_expectancy_data.RData`. The variables used are described in Table 22.3.

TABLE 22.3 Description of the variables present in the file `life_expectancy_data.RData`.

Variable	Description
city_ibge_cod7	Variable that contains a unique identification code for a given municipality.
city	Variable that indicates the name of a given municipality.
state	Variable that indicates in which state a certain city is located.
life_expectancy	Continuous metric variable that measures the average life expectancy of residents in a given municipality.
mayor_educational_level	Polychotomous variable that indicates the level of schooling of the city's mayor, being *no_formal_education* for when the mayor has never attended school; *incomplete_elementary_school* for when the mayor has not completed elementary school; *complete_elementary_school* for when the mayor has as a maximum degree the complete elementary school level; *incomplete_high_school* for when the mayor has not completed high school; *complete_high_school* for when the mayor has as a maximum degree the complete high school level; *incomplete_higher_education* for when the mayor has started the tertiary level but has not completed his or her studies; and *complete_higher_education* for when the mayor has higher education.
urban_pop_share	Variable that measures the rate of citizens of a given city residing in the urban area of the municipality.
non_white_pop_share	Variable that indicates the rate of citizens who do not identify with the white color.
illiteracy_rate18	Variable that indicates the rate of illiterate citizens over 18 years of age.
prop_extremely_poor	Variable that measures the proportion of extremely poor citizens for a given municipality.
prop_households_running_water	Variable that indicates the proportion of houses with water supply.
prop_households_garbage_collection	Variable that indicates the proportion of houses with a garbage collection service.
prop_households_without_electricity	Variable that measures the proportion of homes without access to electricity.

To load the file `life_expectancy_data.RData` into R, we can command:

```
load("life_expectancy_data.RData")
```

Next, we can get descriptive statistics for metric variables and frequency tables for categorical variables:

```
summary(life_expectancy_data)
```

Figure 22.10 shows the results obtained from the previous command.

FIGURE 22.10 Univariate descriptive statistics and frequency tables of the dataset present in the object `life_expectancy_data`.

```
city_ibge_cod7          city                state              life_expectancy
 Length:619         Length:619         Length:619         Min.   :66.36
 Class :character   Class :character   Class :character   1st Qu.:73.52
 Mode  :character   Mode  :character   Mode  :character   Median :75.15
                                                          Mean   :74.78
                                                          3rd Qu.:76.22
                                                          Max.   :78.64

                     mayor_educational_level urban_pop_share
non_white_pop_share
 complete_higher_education   :449       Min.   :0.3268    Min.   :0.08126
 complete_high_school        : 88       1st Qu.:0.7928    1st Qu.:0.29313
 incomplete_elementary_school: 13       Median :0.9077    Median :0.48075
 incomplete_higher_education : 43       Mean   :0.8592    Mean   :0.47000
 complete_elementary_school  : 15       3rd Qu.:0.9619    3rd Qu.:0.64354
 incomplete_high_school      :  9       Max.   :1.0000    Max.   :0.90508
 no_formal_education         :  2
 illiteracy_rate18 prop_extremely_poor prop_households_running_water
 Min.   : 1.550    Min.   : 0.000      Min.   :51.59
 1st Qu.: 4.970    1st Qu.: 0.865      1st Qu.:92.29
 Median : 7.510    Median : 1.670      Median :96.79
 Mean   : 9.975    Mean   : 4.301      Mean   :94.19
 3rd Qu.:12.085    3rd Qu.: 5.075      3rd Qu.:98.77
 Max.   :43.090    Max.   :32.400      Max.   :99.99

 prop_households_garbage_collection prop_households_without_electricity
 Min.   : 68.22                     Min.   : 0.0000
 1st Qu.: 97.44                     1st Qu.: 0.0600
 Median : 99.12                     Median : 0.1700
 Mean   : 97.80                     Mean   : 0.6522
 3rd Qu.: 99.68                     3rd Qu.: 0.5150
 Max.   :100.00                     Max.   :14.1100
```

Attention to Figure 22.10 is essential for two reasons: (i) to avoid problems in extrapolation at the moments of prediction; and (ii) to verify the magnitudes of the metric variables and notice the existence of categorical variables.

As discussed in the "Demonstration of calculations of layer output values" section, metric variables must be standardized. For this case, we will standardize the quantitative variables between 0 and 1, with the help of the function `rescale()`, from the package `scales`:

```
life_expectancy_std <- life_expectancy_data %>%
  mutate(life_expectancy = rescale(life_expectancy,
                                   to = c(0, 1)),
         urban_pop_share = rescale(urban_pop_share,
                                   to = c(0, 1)),
         non_white_pop_share = rescale(non_white_pop_share,
                                       to = c(0, 1)),
         illiteracy_rate18 = rescale(illiteracy_rate18,
                                     to = c(0, 1)),
         prop_extremely_poor = rescale(prop_extremely_poor,
                                       to = c(0, 1)),
         prop_households_running_water = rescale(prop_households_running_water,
                                                 to = c(0, 1)),
         prop_households_garbage_collection = rescale(prop_households_garbage_collection,
                                                      to = c(0, 1)),
         prop_households_without_electricity = rescale(prop_households_without_electricity,
                                                       to = c(0, 1)))
```

The package `scales` is an integral part of the universe `tidyverse` and presents itself as an easy-to-use solution for standardizing variables, just declaring which variable you want to standardize, as well as the scale used (between 0 and 1, in this case). An attentive reader will also notice that we saved the default values in a new object called `life_expectancy_std`.

After standardizing the metric variables, we will proceed with the dummy variable for the categorical variable *mayor_educational_level*. The task can be performed using the function `dummy_cols()` from the package `fastDummies`, already presented in Chapter 14.

```
life_expectancy_std <- dummy_cols(.data = life_expectancy_std,
                                  select_columns = "mayor_educational_level",
                                  remove_first_dummy = FALSE,
                                  remove_selected_columns = TRUE)
```

In the previous routine, the reader must have noticed the argument `remove_first_dummy = FALSE`. This is because we are not performing a procedure of $n - 1$ dummies, but a complete dummization procedure.

After these procedures have been carried out, with a view to identifying and mitigating the overfitting problem, we will separate our database into a training sample to train the algorithm and a validation sample to verify the suitability of the model. So the reader can obtain the same results stamped in the images of this work, we will also use the function `set.seed()`:

```
set.seed(789)
sample_index <- sample(x = 1:dim(life_expectancy_std)[1],
                       size = nrow(life_expectancy_std) * 0.7)

training_sample <- life_expectancy_std[sample_index, ]
validation_sample <- life_expectancy_std[-sample_index, ]
```

Now we can estimate our first artificial neural network! For this, we can use the algorithm `neuralnet()` from the package `neuralnet`:

```
set.seed(789)
rn_life_exp_1 <- neuralnet(formula = life_expectancy ~ . -city_ibge_cod7
                           -city -state,
                           data = training_sample,
                           linear.output = TRUE,
                           hidden = 14)
```

For our first artificial neural network model, contained in the object `rn_life_exp_1`, we will use the default values for most hyperparameters for didactic purposes. The reader can query the different hyperparameter possibilities with the command `?neuralnet`.

The reader also should have noticed that we established the number of 14 neurons in the hidden layer as we have 14 predictor variables after standardization and dummization, as proposed by Shmueli et al. (2018). It is also possible to notice that the chosen activation function was of the linear type.

If the reader wants to visualize the topology of the estimated neural network, such as the theoretical scheme presented in Figure 22.9, he or she can command:

```
plot(rn_life_exp_1)
```

Figure 22.11 presents the result obtained from the previous command.

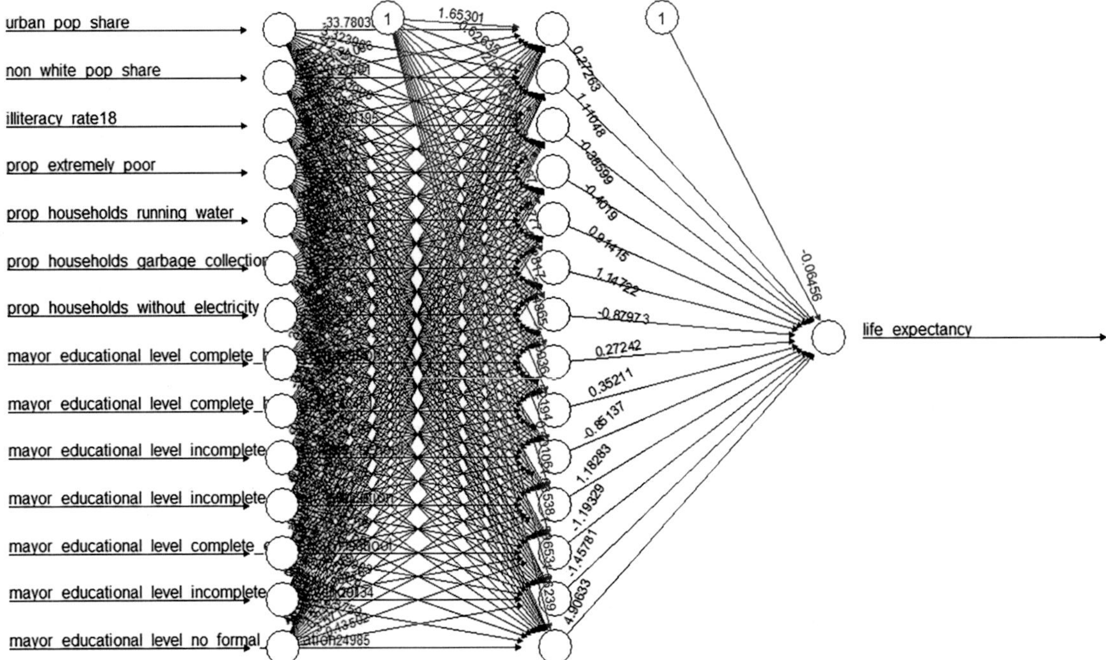

FIGURE 22.11 The artificial neural network contained in the object `rn_life_exp_1`.

The exposition of Figure 22.11 has didactic purposes because, given the amount of variables and synapses involved, the exposition of the values of $w_{p,q}$ and φ_q is difficult to visualize. If the reader wishes to observe the values of $w_{p,q}$ and $w_{p,q}$ calculated for the final iteration present in Figure 22.11, he or she can command:

```
rn_life_exp_1$weights
```

On the other hand, if the reader wishes to have access to the initial weights of the model, he or she can state the following:

```
rn_life_exp_1$startweights
```

To verify the existence, or not, of overfitting, we can use the root mean squared error (RMSE) and R^2 metrics, as studied in Chapters 14 and 19 to 21. First, let's save the fitted values of our first model with respect to the training dataset:

```
training_sample["fit_1"] <- predict(object = rn_life_exp_1,
                                    newdata = training_sample)
```

Then, to calculate the RMSE and R^2, we can command:

```
training_sample %>%
 mutate(ssr = ((life_expectancy - mean(life_expectancy)) ^ 2),
        rss = ((life_expectancy - fit_1) ^ 2)) %>%
 summarise(rmse = sqrt(1/nrow(.) * sum(rss)),
           r_squared = sum(ssr) / (sum(ssr) + sum(rss)))
```

After the previous routine, R will respond that the calculated RMSE is 0.070 and R^2 is 0.857. Once that's done, we can calculate the fitted values for the validation base to check if there are large discrepancies for the same statistics:

```
validation_sample["fit_1"] <- predict(object = rn_life_exp_1,
                                      newdata = validation_sample)

validation_sample %>%
  mutate(ssr = ((life_expectancy - mean(life_expectancy)) ^ 2),
         rss = ((life_expectancy - fit_1) ^ 2)) %>%
  summarise(rmse = sqrt(1/nrow(.) * sum(rss)),
            r_squared = sum(ssr) / (sum(ssr) + sum(rss)))
```

For the previous codes, R will inform the reader that the RMSE of the model contained by the object `rn_life_exp_1`, for the validation dataset, is 0.137; the R^2, 0.581. The exacerbated discrepancy between these statistics is a strong indication of model overfitting.

We propose to look at the fitted values of our first model in relation to the training base and the test base graphically. For the abscissa and ordinate axes, we will use the dependent variable to create a 45-degree straight line that will symbolize 100% correctness of the model. Then, we will overlay this first layer with another one that will use the model dependent variable on the abscissa axis and the fitted values of the estimation on the ordinate axis:

```
training_sample %>%
  ggplot() +
  geom_line(aes(x = life_expectancy, y = life_expectancy)) +
  geom_smooth(aes(x = life_expectancy, y = fit_1),
              se = FALSE, color = "darkorchid") +
  labs(subtitle = "Fitted values for the training sample",
       x = NULL,
       y = NULL) +
  theme_bw() -> training_plot

validation_sample %>%
  ggplot() +
  geom_line(aes(x = life_expectancy, y = life_expectancy)) +
  geom_smooth(aes(x = life_expectancy, y = fit_1),
              se = FALSE, color = "orange") +
  labs(subtitle = "Fitted values for the validation sample",
```

Continued

```
        x = NULL,
        y = NULL) +
  theme_bw() -> validation_plot

grid.arrange(training_plot, validation_plot)
```

Figure 22.12 presents the results obtained from the previous command and shows the existence of overfitting in the model.

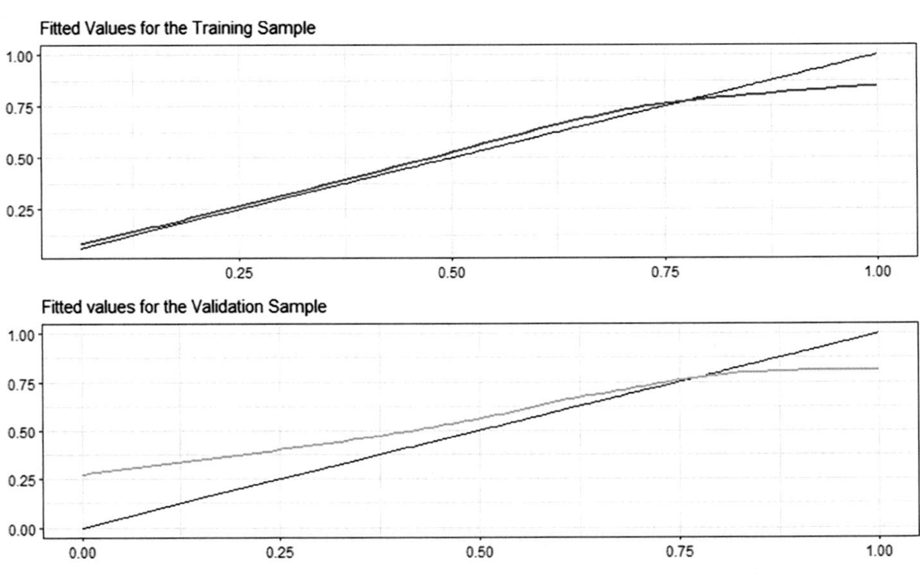

FIGURE 22.12 Comparison of the adherence of the fitted values of the model rn_life_exp_1 for the training sample and for the validation sample.

Next, we will elaborate an estimation with fewer neurons in the hidden layer; instead of 14 neurons, as in the model rn_life_exp_1, we will use 1 single neuron.

```
set.seed(789)
rn_life_exp_2 <- neuralnet(formula = life_expectancy ~ . -city_ibge_cod7
                           -city -state -fit_1,
                           data = training_sample,
                           linear.output = TRUE,
                           hidden = 1)
```

To check the overfitting in the new estimation contained in the object rn_life_exp_2, we will use RMSE and R^2 statistics again. First, let's save the fitted values of the new estimation in the dataset used to train the model contained in the object rn_life_exp_2:

```
training_sample["fit_2"] <- predict(object = rn_life_exp_2,
                                    newdata = training_sample)
```

Then, to calculate the RMSE and R^2 statistics in the training dataset, we must command:

```
training_sample %>%
  mutate(ssr = ((life_expectancy - mean(life_expectancy)) ^ 2),
         rss = ((life_expectancy - fit_2) ^ 2)) %>%
  summarise(rmse = sqrt(1/nrow(.) * sum(rss)),
            r_squared = sum(ssr) / (sum(ssr) + sum(rss)))
```

For the previous routine regarding the training dataset of the algorithm, the reader will receive from R values of RMSE equal to 0.092 and R^2 equal to 0.775.

To verify the overfitting, we will perform the same two procedures for the validation dataset, using the estimation present in the object `rn_life_exp_2`. So, let's save the fitted values of the new estimation against the model validation dataset:

```
validation_sample["fit_2"] <- predict(object = rn_life_exp_2,
                                      newdata = validation_sample)
```

We can then calculate the RMSE and R^2 statistics for the fitted values from the model `rn_life_exp_2` against the validation dataset:

```
validation_sample %>%
  mutate(ssr = ((life_expectancy - mean(life_expectancy)) ^ 2),
         rss = ((life_expectancy - fit_2) ^ 2)) %>%
  summarise(rmse = sqrt(1/nrow(.) * sum(rss)),
            r_squared = sum(ssr) / (sum(ssr) + sum(rss)))
```

For the above codes, the RMSE will be 0.091 and the R^2 will be 0.759—values very close to those verified for the training dataset.

As the one elaborated for the estimation contained by object `rn_life_exp_1`, we can verify a diagnosis for the overfitting in a visual way for the model `rn_life_exp_2`, as follows:

```
training_sample %>%
  ggplot() +
  geom_line(aes(x = life_expectancy, y = life_expectancy)) +
  geom_smooth(aes(x = life_expectancy, y = fit_2),
              se = FALSE, color = "darkorchid") +
  labs(subtitle = "Fitted values for the training sample",
       x = NULL,
       y = NULL) +
  theme_bw() -> training_plot_2

validation_sample %>%
  ggplot() +
  geom_line(aes(x = life_expectancy, y = life_expectancy)) +
  geom_smooth(aes(x = life_expectancy, y = fit_2),
              se = FALSE, color = "orange") +
  labs(subtitle = "Fitted values for the validation sample",
       x = NULL,
       y = NULL) +
  theme_bw() -> validation_plot_2

grid.arrange(training_plot_2, validation_plot_2)
```

Figure 22.13 shows the result obtained from the previous command.

By Figure 22.13, together with the comparison of RMSE and R^2, the reader can see that the overfitting problem was mitigated for the internal estimation of the object `rn_life_exp_2`.

To make predictions when using a neural network model with the dependent variable metric, the reader should remember that the dependent variable metric and all predictive metric variables have been standardized. For the case of the model `rn_life_exp_2`, we standardized the quantitative variables between 0 and 1. Furthermore, we dummied the categorical predictor variables.

This way, for inferences, we can use the function `predict()`, just like the one already used, or like the following routine:

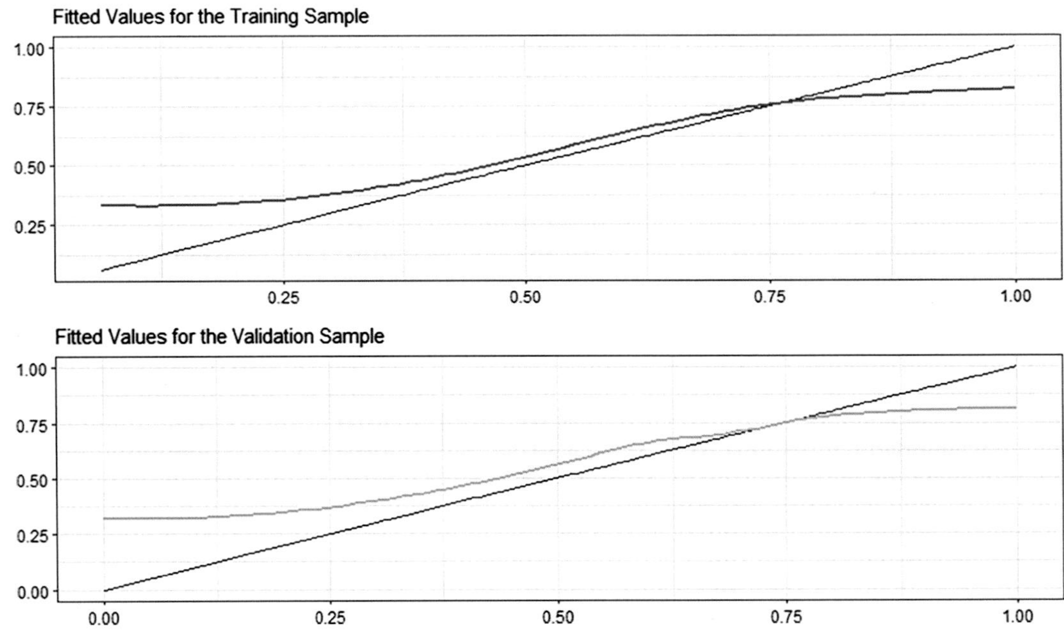

FIGURE 22.13 Comparison of the adherence of the fitted values of the model `rn_life_exp_2` for the training sample and for the validation sample.

```
life_expectancy_std["fitted"] <- predict(object = rn_life_exp_2,
                                         newdata = life_expectancy_std)
```

To compare the observed values of the dependent variable (*life_expectancy*) with the values predicted by the estimation present in `rn_life_exp_2` (*fitted*), we can command:

```
life_expectancy_std %>%
  select(city_ibge_cod7, city, state, life_expectancy, fitted)
```

Figure 22.14 shows the results obtained from the previous command.

```
   city_ibge_cod7 city                  state life_expectancy fitted
   <chr>          <chr>                 <chr>           <dbl>  <dbl>
 1 1100023        ariquemes             RO              0.570  0.653
 2 1100049        cacoal                RO              0.644  0.626
 3 1100056        cerejeiras            RO              0.536  0.659
 4 1100205        porto velho           RO              0.634  0.722
 5 1100304        vilhena               RO              0.581  0.741
 6 1100320        sao miguel do guapore RO              0.449  0.384
 7 1100452        buritis               RO              0.303  0.570
 8 1200401        rio branco            AC              0.529  0.634
 9 1302603        manaus                AM              0.666  0.727
10 1500602        altamira              PA              0.593  0.565
# ... with 609 more rows
```

FIGURE 22.14 Comparison between the observed values and the fitted values of the model `rn_life_exp_2`.

As shown in Figure 22.14, the reader can confirm that, in fact, the function `predict()` calculated standardized values between 0 and 1 of the dependent variable. To undo the transformation, for the case narrated, just revisit Expression (22.7), as explained by Expression (22.12):

$$X_i = Xstd_i \times [max\,(X) - min\,(X)] + min\,(X), \tag{22.12}$$

where $min(X)$ and $max(X)$ refer, respectively, to the original minimum and maximum values of the variable of interest.

Next, we will present an example of estimating an artificial neural network that uses a categorical variable as a dependent variable.

Estimation of an artificial neural network for a categorical type phenomenon

For the following example, we will use a dichotomous dependent variable, using data on sociodemographic issues in Venezuela collected by the United Nations between 2020 and 2021. Our dependent variable will be the variable *afford_food*, which will indicate whether or not a person will be able to buy food for themselves during the next 30 days. The data are found in the file `venezuela_data.RData`.

```
load("venezuela_data.RData")
```

The dataset present in the object `venezuela_data` has 94,225 observations and 17 variables described in Table 22.4.

TABLE 22.4 Description of the variables present in the file `venezuela_data.RData`.

Variable	Description
submission_id	Variable that contains a unique identification code for a given resident of Venezuela.
afford_food	Dichotomous variable that indicates whether a person will be able ("yes") or will not be able ("no") to provide food for themselves during the next 30 days.
gender	Polychotomous variable that indicates the respondent's gender: m for male; and *f* for female.
age	Polychotomous variable that points to age groups: *under16* for respondents under 16 years of age; *16to25* for respondents between 16 and 25 years of age; *26to35* for respondents between 26 and 35 years of age; *36to45* for respondents between 36 and 45 years of age; and *upper45* for respondents over 45 years of age.
geography	Polychotomous variable that indicates in which area of a municipality the respondent resides: *r*, rural area; *s*, suburban urban area; *d*, central urban area.
education	Polychotomous variable that indicates the maximum level of resident education: *no_formal_education* for residents without formal education; *primary_education_incomplete* for residents with incomplete primary education; *primary_education_complete* for residents with a complete elementary education level; *high_school_incompleted* for residents with incomplete high school; *high_school_completed* for residents who have completed high school; *college_university_incompleted* for residents with incomplete college education; and *college_university_completed* for college graduates.
employment_status	Polychotomous variable that indicates the respondent's current employment status: *unemployed* for unemployed residents; *disability* for residents unable to work due to long-term illness or disability; *domestic_tasks* for the housework resident, fulfilling domestic tasks, looking after children; *student* for residents who are only students; *student_and_work_part_time* for residents who are students and have some part-time paid activity; *community_or_military_service* for residents who carry out some community activity or who are serving in the country's Armed Forces; *employed_part_time* for residents who are not studying but who have some part-time paid activity; *employed_full_time* for residents who have some paid activity full time, but who do not work for themselves (e.g., their own company); *self_employed* for residents who work for themselves; *retired* for retired residents; and *others* for respondents who claim not to fit in any of the previous options.
submission_state	Polychotomous variable that identifies which Venezuelan state the respondent resides in.
uninterrupted_electricity	Dichotomous variable that indicates whether, at any given time of the current month, the respondent did not have any interruption in the supply of electricity in his or her home.
uninterrupted_electricity_7days	Discrete metric variable that measures the number of days in the last week in which the electricity supply was not interrupted for the respondent's home.
hours_interrupted_electricity_7days	Metric variable that indicates the number of hours during the week in which the electricity supply was interrupted for the respondent's home.
have_full_gas_cylinder	Dichotomous variable that indicates whether the respondent has a full gas cylinder at home.
changing_gas_cylinders	Polychotomous variable that indicates a frequency range of the offer of a gas cylinder exchange service in the respondent's home: *almost_never* for respondents who said that the service is almost never available; *at_least_once_per_week* for when the service is offered at least once a week; *every_15_days* for when the service is offered every 15 days; *once_per_month* for when the service is offered monthly; *other* for when the situation does not fit the previous possibilities.
gas_cylinders_near	Dichotomous variable that indicates whether there is a gas cylinder exchange service near the respondent's residence.

Continued

TABLE 22.4 Description of the variables present in the file `venezuela_data.RData`—cont'd

Variable	Description
other_means_of_cooking	Dichotomous variable that informs whether the respondent, in the last 30 days, used some other way of cooking their food due to lack of cooking gas.
garbage_collection_last_month	Polychotomous variable that indicates the availability of a household garbage collection service for the respondent's residence.
method_for_waste_disposal	Polychotomous variable that indicates which methods the respondent uses for residential waste disposal: *burn_it* for when the respondent burns residential waste; *public_roads* for when the respondent disposes of their residential waste on public roads; *dump* for when the respondent disposes of their residential waste in a landfill; *pay_for_it* for when the respondent pays a third party to get rid of their household waste; *public* for when household garbage collection is offered by the government; *other* for respondents who did not fit the previous options.

To have access to univariate descriptive statistics and eventual frequency tables, the reader can command:

```
summary(venezuela_data)
```

Figure 22.15 shows the results obtained from the previous command.

```
          submission_id    afford_food gender          age        geography
4503604953350144:     1    no :20647   f:47006   under16:  213    r:17206
4503656618786816:     1    yes:73578   m:47219   16to25 :20744    s:31019
4503735221616640:     1                          26to35 :25902    d:46000
4503900911828992:     1                          36to45 :23250
4503973234212864:     1                          upper45:24116
4504010125213696:     1
(Other)         :94219
                        education                    employment_status              submission_state
no_formal_education          :  314   employed_full_time        :28886   miranda        :23138
primary_education_incomplete :  677   employed_part_time        :25710   zulia          :19834
primary_education_complete   : 1652   unemployed                :12774   distrito_federal:19592
high_school_incompleted      : 9184   student                   : 6622   tachira        :18704
high_school_completed        :33892   student_and_work_part_time: 6404   lara           : 5393
college_university_incompleted: 7804  retired                   : 4960   anzoategui     : 3223
college_university_completed :40702   (Other)                   : 8869   (Other)        : 4341
uninterrupted_electricity uninterrupted_electricity_7days hours_interrupted_electricity_7days
no :38819                 Min.   :0.000                   Min.   :  0.000
yes:55406                 1st Qu.:1.000                   1st Qu.:  0.000
                          Median :3.000                   Median :  3.000
                          Mean   :3.272                   Mean   :  8.175
                          3rd Qu.:6.000                   3rd Qu.:  7.000
                          Max.   :7.000                   Max.   :168.000

have_full_gas_cylinder          changing_gas_cylinders gas_cylinders_near other_ways_of_cooking
no :47275               almost_never           :40403  no :73970          no :31144
yes:46950               at_least_once_per_week: 7025   yes:20255          yes:63081
                        every_15_days          :10552
                        once_per_month         :18465
                        other                  :17780


   garbage_collection_last_month method_for_waste_disposal
almost_never          :22633     burn_it     : 8904
at_least_once_per_week:26820     public_roads:15984
every_day             :13176     dump        :30712
once_a_month          :11429     pay_for_it  :22162
once_every_15_days    :14111     public      : 8349
other                 : 6056     other       : 8114
```

FIGURE 22.15 Univariate descriptive statistics and frequency tables of the dataset present in the object `venezuela_data`.

Analogous to what we studied in the "Estimation of an artificial neural network for a metric-type phenomenon" section, we will standardize the metric variables with ranges between 0 and 1, and we will dummy the categorical variables, **including the dummy variable for the dependent variable.**

As already studied, to standardize the metric variables, we can use the function `rescale()`:

```
venezuela_std <- venezuela_data %>%
  mutate(uninterrupted_electricity_7days = rescale(uninterrupted_electricity_7days,
                                                   to = c(0, 1)),
         hours_interrupted_electricity_7days = rescale(hours_interrupted_electricity_7days,
                                                       to = c(0, 1)))
```

To dummy the qualitative variables, including the dummy dependent variable, we must use the function `dummy_cols()`:

```
venezuela_std <- dummy_cols(.data = venezuela_std,
                            select_columns = c("afford_food","gender","age",
                                               "geography","education",
                                               "employment_status",
                                               "submission_state",
                                               "uninterrupted_electricity",
                                               "have_full_gas_cylinder",
                                               "changing_gas_cylinders",
                                               "gas_cylinders_near",
                                               "other_means_of_cooking",
                                               "garbage_collection_last_month",
                                               "method_for_waste_disposal"),
                            remove_first_dummy = FALSE,
                            remove_selected_columns = TRUE)
```

After the narrated procedures, the dataset present in the object `venezuela_std` should have 94,225 observations and 73 variables.

The next step will be the division of the dataset `venezuela_std` into a training sample and a validation sample:

```
set.seed(567)
sample_index <- sample(x = 1:dim(venezuela_std)[1],
                       size = nrow(venezuela_std) * 0.7)

training_sample <- venezuela_std[sample_index, ]
validation_sample <- venezuela_std[-sample_index, ]
```

That said, we can estimate our neural network. For educational purposes, we will use only three neurons in the hidden layer because the model is computationally demanding due to the amount of data and variables. **For the reader to have an idea, the routine to follow on an Intel i5 machine with 32MB of RAM took 1 hour to be estimated. If the reader does not want to spend that time, he or she can load the model estimated by the authors in the subsequent routine.**

```
set.seed(567)
rn_venezuela <- neuralnet(formula = afford_food_no + afford_food_yes ~ . -submission_id,
                          data = training_sample,
                          linear.output = FALSE,
                          hidden = 3)
```

We ask the reader to pay attention to the argument `formula` in the previous routine. The dependent variable *afford_food* is dichotomous and underwent the dummy variable, even though it was, strictly speaking, a binary variable.

In this sense, the dependent variable was partitioned into two: *afford_food_no* and *afford_food_yes*. An attentive reader will notice that the operator ~ was only declared after the declaration of the last category of the variable *afford_food*.

If the reader chooses to load the model estimated by the authors, he or she can command:

```
load("rn_venezuela.RData")
```

To make predictions, the reader can use the function `predict()`, as follows:

```
predict(object = rn_venezuela, newdata = training_sample)
```

However, it should be remembered that the original dichotomous dependent variable *afford_food* has been split into two: *afford_food_no* and *afford_food_yes*. In this way, R's response to the previous command will be a matrix with two

```
            [,1]      [,2]
 [1,] 0.141334681 0.8586660
 [2,] 0.039778483 0.9602213
 [3,] 0.214587464 0.7854117
 [4,] 0.214587464 0.7854117
 [5,] 0.039778483 0.9602213
 [6,] 0.214587476 0.7854116
 [7,] 0.046865390 0.9531353
 [8,] 0.520512908 0.4794884
 [9,] 0.214587464 0.7854117
[10,] 0.214587464 0.7854117
```

FIGURE 22.16 Probability of occurrence of *afford_food_no* and *afford_food_yes* for the first 10 observations of the training sample.

columns, as shown in Figure 22.16.

In Figure 22.16, the first column indicates the probability of the event occurring for the variable *afford_food_no*; the second column of Figure 22.16 indicates the probability of the event occurring for the variable *afford_food_yes*.

That said, we must remember that because we are dealing with a binary variable, we can draw up a confusion matrix and the receiver operating characteristic (ROC) curve.

The first step will be the construction of two confusion matrices: one regarding the training sample and the other regarding the validation sample. In addition to the overall efficiency of the model and the sensitivity and specificity metrics, we will seek to assess the existence, or not, of overfitting. Then, in a second step, we will establish the ROC curves for the training sample and the validation sample.

As studied in Chapters 15 and 19 of this work, the confusion matrix can be elaborated by the function `confusionMatrix()` from the package `caret`. But first, to help build a confusion matrix, we will recreate the original dependent variable *afford_food* in the training dataset:

```
training_sample["afford_food"] <- ifelse(training_sample$afford_food_yes == 1,
                                          yes = "yes",
                                          no = "no")
```

The following routine will construct the confusion matrix for the training sample, assuming a cutoff of 50%:

```
confusionMatrix(table(predict(object = rn_venezuela,
                              newdata = training_sample)[,2] >= 0.5,
                      training_sample$afford_food == "yes")[2:1, 2:1])
```

The confusion matrix for the training sample is shown in Figure 22.17.

```
Confusion Matrix and Statistics

        TRUE FALSE
  TRUE  45246  7598
  FALSE  6262  6851

               Accuracy : 0.7899
                 95% CI : (0.7867, 0.793)
    No Information Rate : 0.7809
    P-Value [Acc > NIR] : 1.297e-08

                  Kappa : 0.3647

 Mcnemar's Test P-Value : < 2.2e-16

            Sensitivity : 0.8784
            Specificity : 0.4742
         Pos Pred Value : 0.8562
         Neg Pred Value : 0.5225
             Prevalence : 0.7809
         Detection Rate : 0.6860
   Detection Prevalence : 0.8012
      Balanced Accuracy : 0.6763

       'Positive' Class : TRUE
```

FIGURE 22.17 Confusion matrix of the estimation `rn_venezuela` for the training sample.

To assess the presence or not of overfitting, we must compare the confusion matrix in Figure 22.17 with another confusion matrix elaborated through the validation sample:

```
validation_sample["afford_food"] <- ifelse(validation_sample$afford_food_yes == 1,
                                           yes = "yes",
                                           no = "no")

confusionMatrix(table(predict(object = rn_venezuela,
                              newdata = validation_sample)[,2] >= 0.5,
                      validation_sample$afford_food == "yes")[2:1, 2:1])
```

Figure 22.18 shows the confusion matrix for the validation sample.

```
Confusion Matrix and Statistics

        TRUE FALSE
  TRUE  19369  3381
  FALSE  2701  2817

               Accuracy : 0.7848
                 95% CI : (0.78, 0.7896)
    No Information Rate : 0.7807
    P-Value [Acc > NIR] : 0.04818

                  Kappa : 0.3458

 Mcnemar's Test P-Value : < 2e-16

            Sensitivity : 0.8776
            Specificity : 0.4545
         Pos Pred Value : 0.8514
         Neg Pred Value : 0.5105
             Prevalence : 0.7807
         Detection Rate : 0.6852
   Detection Prevalence : 0.8048
      Balanced Accuracy : 0.6661

       'Positive' Class : TRUE
```

FIGURE 22.18 Confusion matrix of the estimation `rn_venezuela` for the validation sample.

The reader may notice that the differences in accuracy, sensitivity, and specificity between Figures 22.17 and 22.18 are minimal, indicating that there is most likely no overfitting problem in the model `rn_venezuela`.

For elaboration of the ROC curves, we will use the algorithms from the package `ROCR`. If the reader does not master the features of the package presented, we ask the reader to return to Chapter 15 of this work for more detailed descriptions of each of the following functions used.

First, the ROC curve for the training sample:

```
pred_ven_training <- prediction(predictions = predict(object = rn_venezuela,
                                                      newdata = training_sample)[,2],
                                labels = training_sample$afford_food)

sens_data_training <- performance(prediction.obj = pred_ven_training, measure = "sens")

sensitivity_training <- sens_data_training@y.values[[1]]

spec_data_training <- performance(prediction.obj = pred_ven_training, measure = "spec")

specificity_training <- spec_data_training@y.values[[1]]

cutoffs_training <- pred_ven_training@cutoffs[[1]]

plot_data_training <- cbind.data.frame(cutoffs_training,
                                       specificity_training,
                                       sensitivity_training)

au_roc_training <- performance(prediction.obj = pred_ven_training, measure = "auc")

plot_data_training %>%
  ggplot() +
  geom_segment(aes(x = 0, xend = 1, y = 0, yend = 1),
               color="orange", size = 2) +
  geom_line(aes(x = 1 - specificity_training, y = sensitivity_training),
            color = "darkorchid", size = 2) +
  labs(x = "1 - Specificity",
       y = "Sensitivity",
       title = paste("Area under the curve:",
                     round(au_roc_training@y.values[[1]], 3)),
       subtitle = "Training Sample") +
  theme_bw()
```

Figure 22.19 shows the result obtained from the previous command.

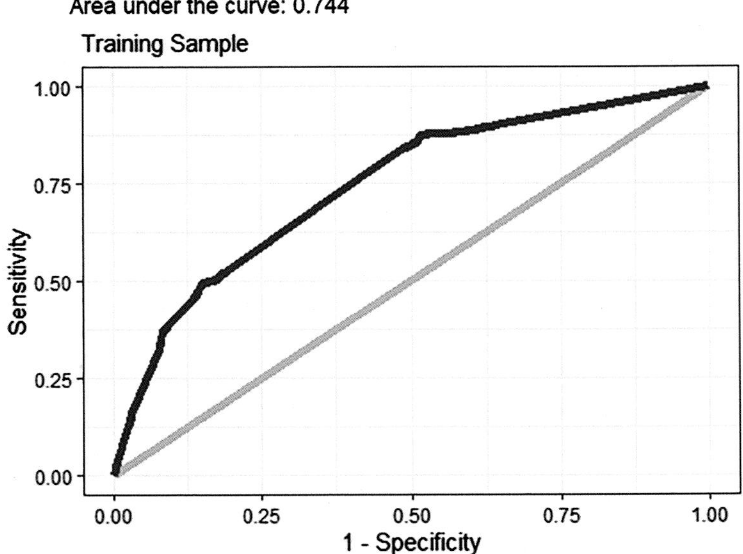

FIGURE 22.19 ROC curve of the estimation `rn_venezuela` for the training sample.

Similar to the one elaborated for Figure 22.19, we can construct the ROC curve for the validation sample as follows:

```
pred_ven_validation <- prediction(predictions = predict(object = rn_venezuela,
                                                        newdata = validation_sample)[,2],
                                  labels = validation_sample$afford_food)

sens_data_validation <- performance(prediction.obj = pred_ven_validation, measure = "sens")

sensitivity_validation <- sens_data_validation@y.values[[1]]

spec_data_validation <- performance(prediction.obj = pred_ven_validation, measure = "spec")

specificity_validation <- spec_data_validation@y.values[[1]]

cutoffs_validation <- pred_ven_validation@cutoffs[[1]]

plot_data_validation <- cbind.data.frame(cutoffs_validation,
                                         specificity_validation,
                                         sensitivity_validation)

au_roc_validation <- performance(prediction.obj = pred_ven_validation, measure = "auc")

plot_data_validation %>%
  ggplot() +
  geom_segment(aes(x = 0, xend = 1, y = 0, yend = 1),
               color="orange", size = 2) +
  geom_line(aes(x = 1 - specificity_validation, y = sensitivity_validation),
            color = "darkorchid", size = 2) +
  labs(x = "1 - Specificity",
       y = "Sensitivity",
       title = paste("Area under the curve:",
                     round(au_roc_validation@y.values[[1]], 3)),
       subtitle = "Validation Sample") +
  theme_bw()
```

Figure 22.20 contains the result obtained from the previous command.

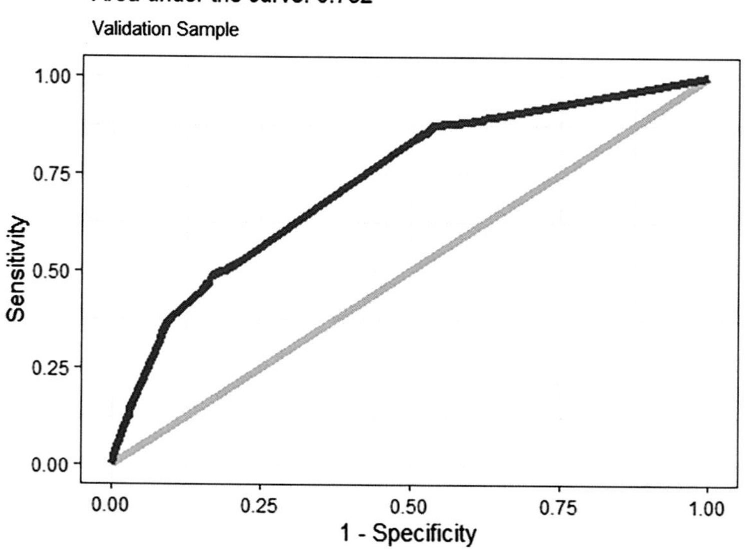

FIGURE 22.20 ROC curve of the estimation `rn_venezuela` for the validation sample.

A comparison between Figures 22.19 and 22.20 seems to reinforce the suspicion that there is no overfitting in the model `rn_venezuela`.

Final remarks

The estimations of artificial neural networks are a very useful asset in the field of machine learning techniques. Such models are flexible, being able to work, basically, with any kind of dependent variable, be it continuous metric or discrete metric, nominal categorical or ordinal categorical.

In this chapter, we demonstrated the use of these models in predicting a metric phenomenon and in predicting a dichotomous phenomenon. For the first case, in the "Estimation of an artificial neural network for a metric-type phenomenon" section, the activation function was the Linear Activation Function; for the second case, in the "Estimation of an artificial neural network for a categorical type phenomenon" section, the activation function was the Logistic Activation Function. We reinforce that correct application of this kind of model involves the correct specification of the activation function and that by no means are we saying that the functional forms present in the aforementioned sections are the best possible.

The intention, on the other hand, was to introduce and instruct the reader about artificial neural networks using the multilayer feedforward networks.

It is also necessary to reiterate that this type of model is usually computationally demanding and does not have an equation to be interpreted. In this sense, it is completely up to the reader to collect variables that, in fact, make sense for the phenomenon that is intended to be studied in order not to waste too much time or waste computational power.

Finally, for the two examples studied, we encourage the reader to improve them and compare them with the other algorithms studied in the course of this work.

Exercise

1. Consider the dataset studied in Chapters 20 and 21 on poverty in Brazil. The data can be found in the file `brazilian_poverty.RData`, whose description of the variables is shown in the following table.

Variable	Description
municipality	Variable that identifies each of the 5,565 Brazilian municipalities.
state	Variable that identifies to which of the 27 Brazilian states each of the 5,565 studied municipalities belongs.
poverty_index	Metric variable that concerns an indicator of vulnerability to poverty. The index shows the proportion of individuals with a per capita family income of less than one-half the minimum wage.
illiteracy_rate	Metric variable that indicates an illiteracy rate in the population, multiplied by 100.
elementary_school_rate	Metric variable that indicates the rate of individuals over 18 years of age who completed elementary school, multiplied by 100.
high_school_rate	Metric variable that represents the rate of individuals over 18 years of age who completed high school, multiplied by 100.
college_rate	Metric variable that indicates the rate of individuals between 18 and 24 years of age attending college, multiplied by 100.
region	Polychotomous variable that considers the five largest regions in Brazil: Midwest, North, Northeast, South, and Southeast.

Using *poverty_index* as the dependent variable and the function `set.seed(444)`, present the following:

a. Build a neural network with nine neurons in the hidden layer.

b. Are there signs of overfitting for the model estimated in item "a"?

c. Find the best artificial neural network estimation with one layer in the hidden layer. How many neurons in the hidden layer were needed?

d. What are the RMSE and R^2 values for the model found in item "c"?

e. Build a regression model estimated by ordinary least squares and compare with the model estimated in item "c."

f. Develop a multilevel regression model using the variable *region* as a level, and compare it with the models estimated in items "c" and "e."

Supplementary data sets

life_expectancy_data.RData
venezuela_data.RData
fidelity_data.RData
brazilian_poverty.RData

Please access supplementary data files here: https://doi.org/10.17632/55623jkwrp.3

PART VII

Spatial analysis

CHAPTER

23

Working on shapefiles

AT THE END OF THIS CHAPTER, YOU WILL BE ABLE TO:

- Understand what a shapefile is;
- Upload and edit shapefiles;
- Use, combine, and save shapefiles, including their visual presentation in R-based language.

R-based language packages used in this chapter

```
library(rgdal)
library(raster)
library(tidyverse)
library(nortest)
library(tmap)
library(RColorBrewer)
library(maptools)
```

Don't forget to define the R working directory (the location where your datasets are installed):

```
setwd("C:/book/chapter23")
```

Introduction

Although we do not intend to exhaust the subject, we will see in this chapter that we can use R to make spatial analysis (econometric or not) using the objects derived from them for statistical calculation or using R-based language in a similar way to Geographic Information Systems (GIS) software. We can even combine the knowledge learned in Chapters 8 and 9 to search, for example, georeferenced locations to enrich our databases.

Suppose we want to study a certain phenomenon in a neighborhood in any municipality, taking into account the impact of spatiality. Examples would not be lacking. We could use some kind of spatial analysis to study property

Data Science, Analytics and Machine Learning with R
https://doi.org/10.1016/B978-0-12-824271-1.00009-3

prices, crime rates, air quality, socioeconomic characteristics, saturation of the presence of certain commercial activities, and many other phenomena.

The examples cited do not need to stop in neighborhoods or municipalities. We could study the relationship among cities, states, and countries. Geographical boundaries would be necessary because, as we will still see in Chapter 26, we could study only the precise areas producing sugar cane or beef cattle or areas that have specific shoals or archaeological sites. The borders and their respective distances could even be pointed out in the vicinity according to the HDI (Human Development Index), GDP (Gross Domestic Product), and the creativity, supported by the underlying theory and by a thorough methodological approach, are the limits.

It is very common for beginners in this field of knowledge to assume that there is a need for an established type map. Obviously, this situation would be a facilitating factor, but a spatial analysis can be done with the use of a simple dataset as long as we know the geographic positions of our observations.

Given the latest information, an unsuspecting reader would mistakenly imagine that it is very difficult to obtain geographic coordinates. However, countless websites can help us obtain this kind of data, such as *Google Maps*, *LatLong.net*, and others. It would also be possible for a researcher to use a GPS to catalog desired coordinates and then carry out the spatial analysis.

In this chapter, however, we will work with shapefiles that, as discussed by Lansley and Cheshire (2016), provide geographic information, including location and format, commonly used in GIS software. In the following chapters, we will demonstrate how to use other devices to perform a spatial analysis, including combining it with the creation of a robot.

In the introductory approach proposed in this chapter, we will demonstrate how to use and perform spatial analysis on shapefiles at geographic points arranged in data frames and polygons. We emphasize that a minimum knowledge of R-based language is of fundamental importance for what follows, and we start from the premise that the reader understands the concepts studied in Chapter 2.

Furthermore, the reader will notice a purposeful difference between the structure of this chapter and the others. As a rule, we present the fundamentals of a certain technique and later demonstrate its proper application in R. However, because of the peculiarity of the subject, we will do everything together, that is, we will discuss the fundamentals and make applications in R at the same time.

Using shapefiles

Using a shapefile is comfortable and visually striking, but some basic care is necessary. The first is to make sure that the shapefile used comes from a trusted repository.

As we will see later, shapefiles contain more than spatial information. They are, as a rule, endowed with a preestablished georeferencing system that can consider geodesic or Euclidean distances, something that can make a lot of difference depending on the territorial size we study. Thus ensuring that your shapefile was obtained from a reliable repositor is of fundamental importance for the correct establishment of areas, distances, and centroids.

Another precaution to be taken with shapefiles is being aware that they may become computationally demanding, especially when used in conjunction with econometric techniques. In the case of this work, the reader will notice that his or her machine, depending on the functions used, will take a few seconds longer than normal to give answers.

Another precaution is that a shapefile usually comes with several other files that will be activated together with each new command on it. For example, in the contents of the `shapefile_sp` file folder, an attentive reader will notice a set of files whose nomenclature starts with "`state_of_sp`". They contain important data regarding the layers of the maps, the order of loading the polygons that make up the maps, and the geometries necessary for plotting and for statistical relationships. Therefore it is highly recommended to not edit them unless the reader has sufficient knowledge and expertise on the subject.

In the following sections, we will provide some basic knowledge for using shapefiles.

Carring a shapefile

Suppose that we want to study a phenomenon with spatial characteristics involving the municipalities of the state of São Paulo, Brazil. Thus we will open the file `state_of_sp.shp` from the Brazilian Institute of Geography and Statistics (IBGE) website (https://www.ibge.gov.br/).

That said, we can enter the following codes to load our shapefile:

```
sp_map <- readOGR(dsn = "shapefile_sp", layer = "state_of_sp")
```

In the previous routine, we used the function `readOGR()` from the package `rgdal` to load our first shapefile. We can also notice that we use the argument `dsn` to indicate which folder contains the files that were used and the argument `layer` to indicate which layers will be used.

As studied in Chapter 2, the functions `head()` and `View()` have limited effectiveness when applied directly to the object `sp_map`. This is because `sp_map` is not (just) a common dataset.

Initially, we propose a simplified view of the map present in the shapefile we are discussing, using the following command:

```
plot(sp_map)
```

The result of the previous command will be shown in the *Plots* tab, as shown in Figure 23.1. We add that it is absolutely normal for the computer to take a few seconds to display results from shapefiles.

FIGURE 23.1 The political map of the state of São Paulo present in the loaded shapefile.

Figure 23.1 shows the political map of the state of São Paulo divided by the borders of the municipalities that compose it. A curious reader can use the function `class()` on our new object, according to the following code.

```
class(sp_map)
```

The output of the above command is shown in Figure 23.2.

```
> class(sp_map)
[1] "SpatialPolygonsDataFrame"
attr(,"package")
[1] "sp"
```

FIGURE 23.2 Output of the command `class(sp_map)`.

Notice that the class of our object `sp_map` involves the existence of a map (spatial polygons, in this case) combined with a dataset (data frame). We can have direct access to the dataset present in the object `sp_map` using the operator `$`, but a curious reader would use the operator `@`. Figure 23.3 exemplifies the proposal.

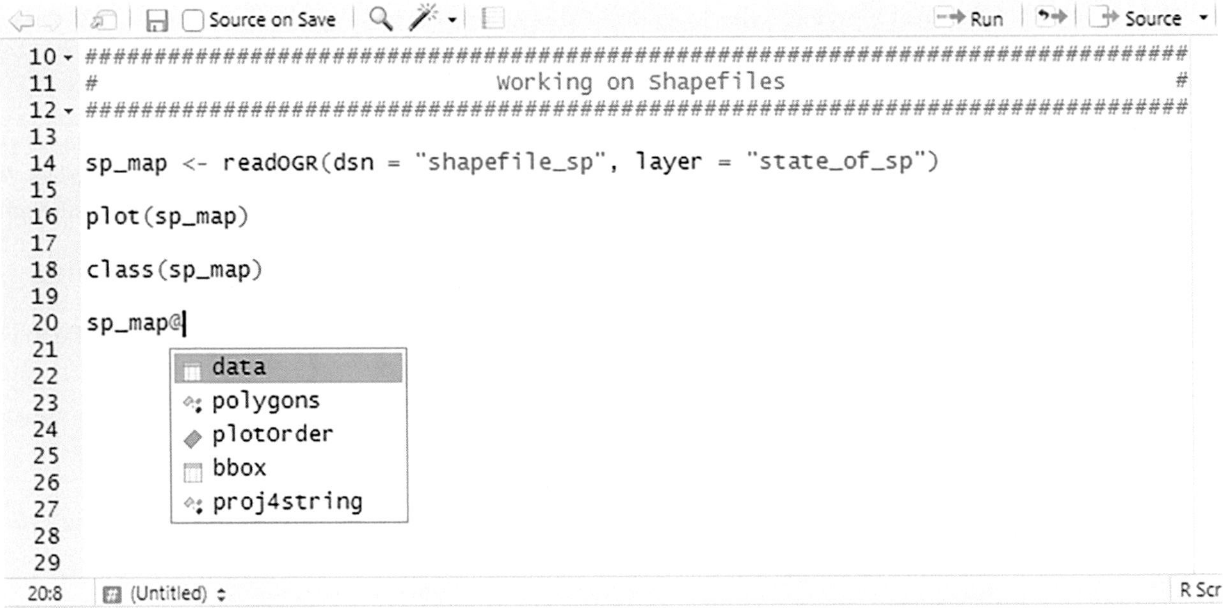

```
###############################################################################
#                           Working on Shapefiles                             #
###############################################################################

sp_map <- readOGR(dsn = "shapefile_sp", layer = "state_of_sp")

plot(sp_map)

class(sp_map)

sp_map@
        data
        polygons
        plotOrder
        bbox
        proj4string
```

FIGURE 23.3 The use of the operator @ in shapefiles.

Figure 23.3 shows that the object `sp_map` contains five attributes:

- **`data`**: A data frame that contains the dataset variables we want to work with. There are currently two variables: *NM_MUNICIP* refers to the name of the municipality, and *CD_GEOCMU* refers to a code that identifies the municipality.
- **`polygons`**: A list that contains information about the geographic position of the shapefile polygons.
- **`plotOrder`**: A vector of size $n \times 1$ that indicates to R the order in which the polygons of the shapefile should be plotted, where n is the number of observations present in `data`.
- **`bbox`**: An object that refers to the minimum and maximum coordinates occupied by the shapefile, imagining it in a Cartesian way.
- **`proj4string`**: An object that indicates to R the adopted coordinate system. In this case, the shapefile uses latitude and longitude coordinates (`longlat`), whose reference ellipsoid is GRS80 (`ellps = GRS80`). It is important for the researcher to be familiar with the coordinate system being used because some consider distances in geodesic ways, and others consider distances in Euclidian ways; some have metrics in miles, and others have metrics in meters, feet, or kilometers. This information will be important in the argument of some functions that will be presented.

Incorporating information into a shapefile

After making the necessary presentations, suppose we want to add some information about the municipalities of Sao Pãulo to our shapefile.

It would be interesting to measure the areas of each polygon (in this case, municipalities) on our map. Here, we would have two possible paths: we could find a dataset that contains this type of information (e.g. IBGE) and add it in `data` (`sp_map@data`), or we could obtain a good approximation from the package `raster`.

It is important to note that the package `raster` is not exactly intended for spatial analysis using shapefiles, but for this moment it is very useful! We will present some functionalities from the package in Chapter 25. Next, we can use the function `area()` to obtain the areas of our polygons in km^2:

```
sp_map$area_km2 <- area(x = sp_map) / 1000
```

The function area() works well for objects oriented by the latitude and longitude data internal to the shapefile used. For objects that are not oriented by the latitude and longitude attributes, we recommend the function gArea() from the package rgeos. The pointed artifice will not work with our shapefile because its projection obeys a geodesic metric; the function gArea() works with Euclidean coordinates.

We can proceed by adding external data to our shapefile. So we will first open the dataset sp_data.RData:

```
load("sp_data.RData")
```

Table 23.1 presents a description of the variables present in the object sp_data.

TABLE 23.1 Variables presented in the object sp_data.

Variable	Description
cod	Numeric variable that identifies each São Paulo municipality in the molds used by the IBGE
pop	Metric variable that indicates the population size of São Paulo municipalities
pop_density	Metric variable that measures the population density of São Paulo municipalities in inhabitants per km^2
hdi	Metric variable that presents the Human Development Index (HDI) of São Paulo municipalities
gdp	Metric variable that points to the Gross Domestic Product (GDP) per capita of each municipality in São Paulo

After that, we will use the function merge() to add the information from the dataset sp_data to the object sp_map, as shown in the following codes:

```
sp_merged <- merge(x = sp_map,
                   y = sp_data,
                   by.x = "CD_GEOCMU",
                   by.y = "cod")
```

In the proposed routine, the function merge() of the R-based language inserted the data present in the dataset extracted from the file sp_data.RData (object sp_data) in our shapefile. Note that the arguments by.x e by.y point out how the function should combine the two objects, that is, it pointed out variables whose observations were identical in sp_map and sp_data, respectively. It is also possible to verify that we have created a new object that we call sp_merged.

We could, from now on, use some functions related to descriptive statistics in our variables, which we have already presented in the past sections. We can therefore type the following command:

```
summary(sp_merged)
```

Figure 23.4 shows the results of the function summary() applied to the object sp_merged.

```
Object of class SpatialPolygonsDataFrame
Coordinates:
        min       max
x -53.11011 -44.16137
y -25.31232 -19.77966
Is projected: FALSE
proj4string :
[+proj=longlat +ellps=GRS80 +towgs84=0,0,0,0,0,0,0 +no_defs]
Data attributes:
  CD_GEOCMU           NM_MUNICIP           area_km2             pop
 Length:645         Length:645         Min.   :   3612   Min.   :     836
 Class :character   Class :character   1st Qu.: 158025   1st Qu.:    5688
 Mode  :character   Mode  :character   Median : 280697   Median :   13833
                                       Mean   : 384840   Mean   :   70603
                                       3rd Qu.: 511621   3rd Qu.:   41622
                                       Max.   :1977957   Max.   :12176866
  pop_density           hdi              gdp
 Min.   :    3.73   Min.   :0.6390   Min.   :  7310
 1st Qu.:   19.69   1st Qu.:0.7190   1st Qu.: 17954
 Median :   38.87   Median :0.7380   Median : 24499
 Mean   :  301.98   Mean   :0.7395   Mean   : 32181
 3rd Qu.:  108.87   3rd Qu.:0.7610   3rd Qu.: 35366
 Max.   :12536.99   Max.   :0.8620   Max.   :314638
```

FIGURE 23.4 Univariate descriptive statistics from the internal dataset to the object `sp_merged`.

We can also raise assumptions to be verified in the future. We may want to investigate whether the variable *hdi* adheres to a Gaussian distribution. As a curiosity, we could establish a histogram on the subject:

```
sp_merged@data %>%
  ggplot() +
  geom_histogram(aes(x = hdi),
                 color = "black",
                 fill = "orange",
                 bins = 30) +
  labs(x = "Municipal Human Development Index",
       y = "Frequency") +
  theme_bw()
```

Figure 23.5 presents a histogram of the variable *hdi*.

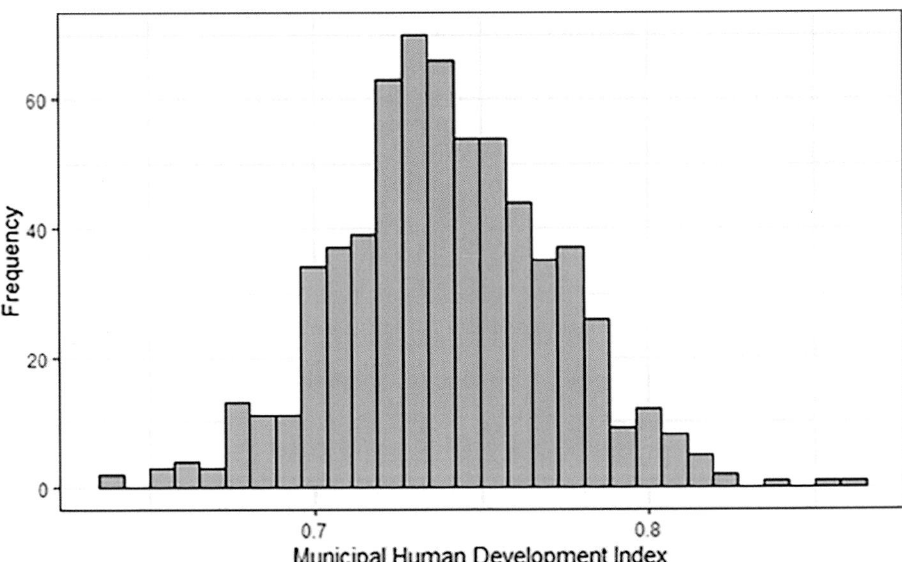

FIGURE 23.5 Histogram of the variable *hdi*.

Next, we could plot a theoretical density curve of the normal distribution in the histogram of Figure 23.5, with the following extension of commands:

```
sp_merged@data %>%
  ggplot() +
  geom_histogram(aes(x = hdi, y = ..density..),
                 color = "black",
                 fill = "orange",
                 bins = 30) +
stat_function(fun = dnorm,
              args = list(mean = mean(sp_merged$hdi),
                          sd = sd(sp_merged$hdi)),
              color = "darkorchid",
              size = 1.5) +
labs(x = "Municipal Human Development Index",
     y = "Frequency") +
theme_bw()
```

The result of the previous command is shown in Figure 23.6.

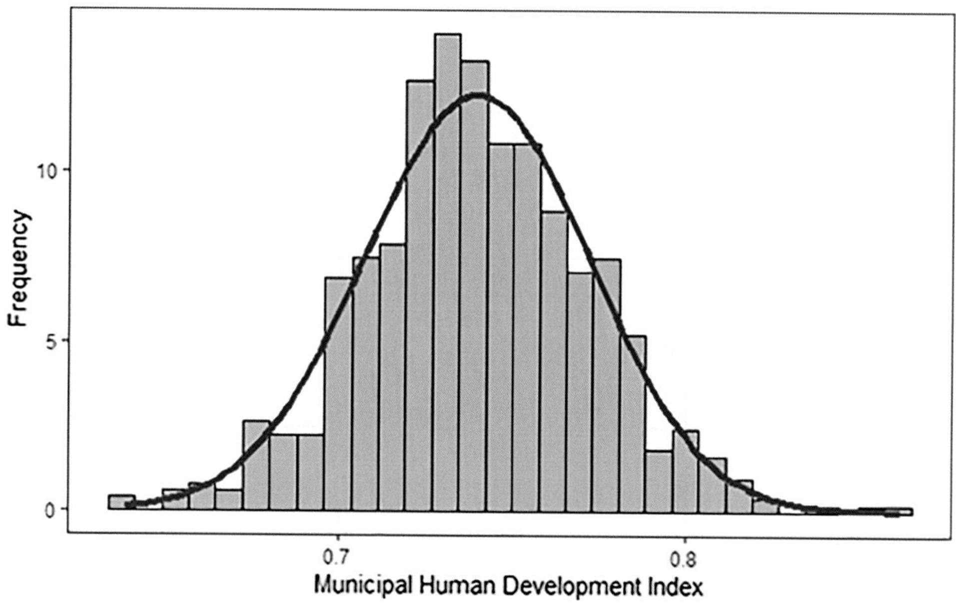

FIGURE 23.6 Comparison of the histogram of the variable *hdi* with a theoretical Gaussian distribution.

The final conclusion regarding adherence to the data normality of the variable *hdi* comes from the Shapiro-Francia test already presented in Chapter 6 because $n > 30$. This test is performed using the function `sf.test()` from the package `nortest`. We can perform the following:

```
sf.test(x = sp_merged$hdi)
```

To the previous command, R will answer that $W_{calc} = 0.99663$, with a respective $pvalue = 0.1733$ and, therefore because there is no rejection of H_0, it can be said that the variable *hdi*, present in the object `sp_merged`, presents normal distribution at a confidence level of 95%.

Next, we will present solutions for plotting data present in shapefiles.

Plotting information from a dataset on a map

Suppose we intend to plot the São Paulo map, highlighting the HDI of its municipalities. There are several paths that achieve this goal, and those that have greater visual capacity can be found in the packages `tidyverse` and `tmap`.

Although we recognize the potential of the package `tidyverse`, we prefer the visual capabilities of the package `tmap` because of its greater ease and intuitiveness in writing the routines, which provides a gain of time for the researcher.

That said, the HDI plotting of the municipalities of the State of Sao Pãulo can, for example, be performed using the function `qtm()` with the following command:

```
qtm(shp = sp_merged, fill = "hdi")
```

As the previous command demonstrates, the function `qtm()` from the package `tmap` is very intuitive. We just need to argue in the object `shp` that contains the map, followed by the variable that we seek to highlight with the argument `fill`. The expected result of the above command is shown in Figure 23.7.

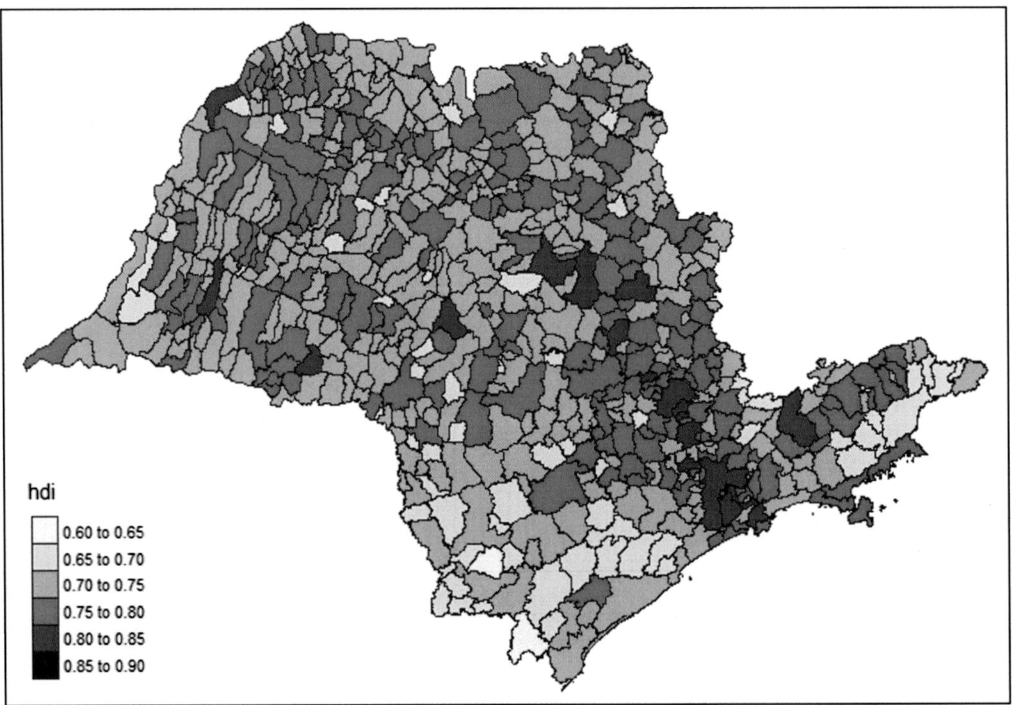

FIGURE 23.7 The HDI of the municipalities of the State of São Paulo.

There are also more elegant possibilities when plotting maps with the package `tmap`. We propose a different routine, again highlighting the HDI of the municipalities of São Paulo on a map as follows:

```
tm_shape(shp = sp_merged) +
  tm_fill(col = "hdi")
```

The result of the previous command is similar to that shown in Figure 23.7, but note the differences in the codes; there is a very useful breakdown! To the function `tm_shape()`, we must point the object that contains our map to the argument `shp`. After that, we add the operator + and indicate how we will fill this map using the function `tm_fill()` and the argument `col` to point to a color. However, when we declare a variable in place of a color, we can highlight the variable of interest in this map. Imagine that we prefer our maps by highlighting the variable of interest in blue tones. Thus it would suffice to type the following command:

```
tm_shape(shp = sp_merged) +
  tm_fill(col = "hdi", palette = "Blues")
```

In this code, an attentive reader will notice that the blue color was commanded in English, but in the plural: *Blues*. This is because we require R to use a color palette of blue tones to highlight the variable *hdi*. Figure 23.8 shows the result of the command.

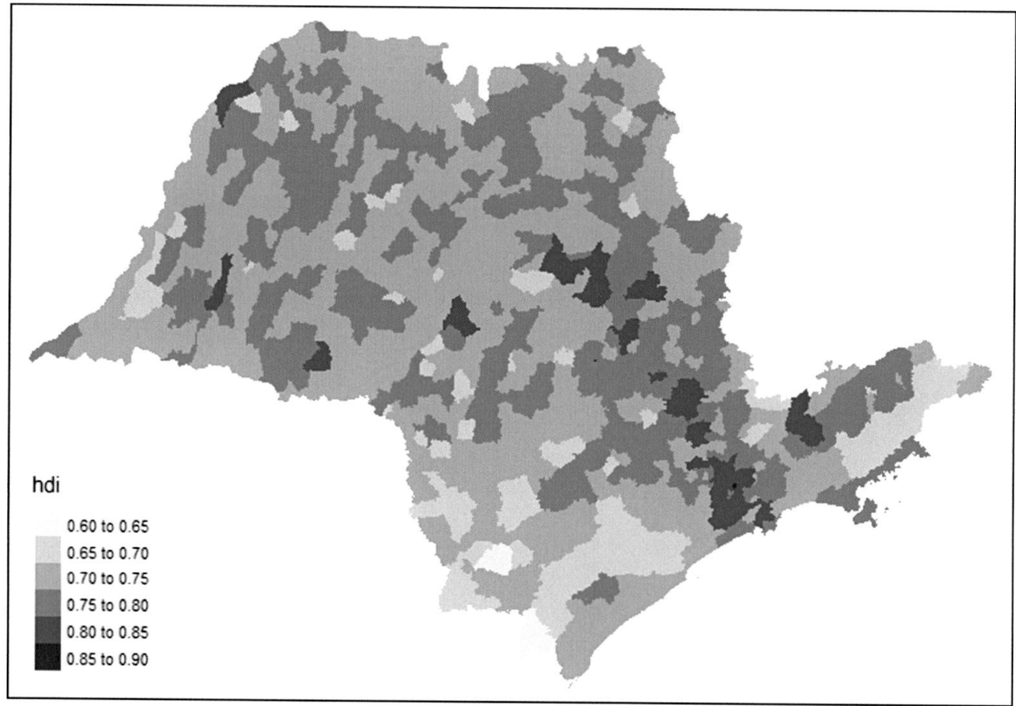

FIGURE 23.8 The HDI of the municipalities of the state of São Paulo plotted in shades of blue.

A curious reader can execute the following codes to view all color palettes available to use as an argument in the function `tm_fill()`:

```
display.brewer.all()
```

The result of the previous commands will be presented in the *Plots* tab and, for the researcher comfort, you can click on the *Zoom* button for a better view of the names of the color palettes that can be used. Figure 23.9 shows the result of the previous command.

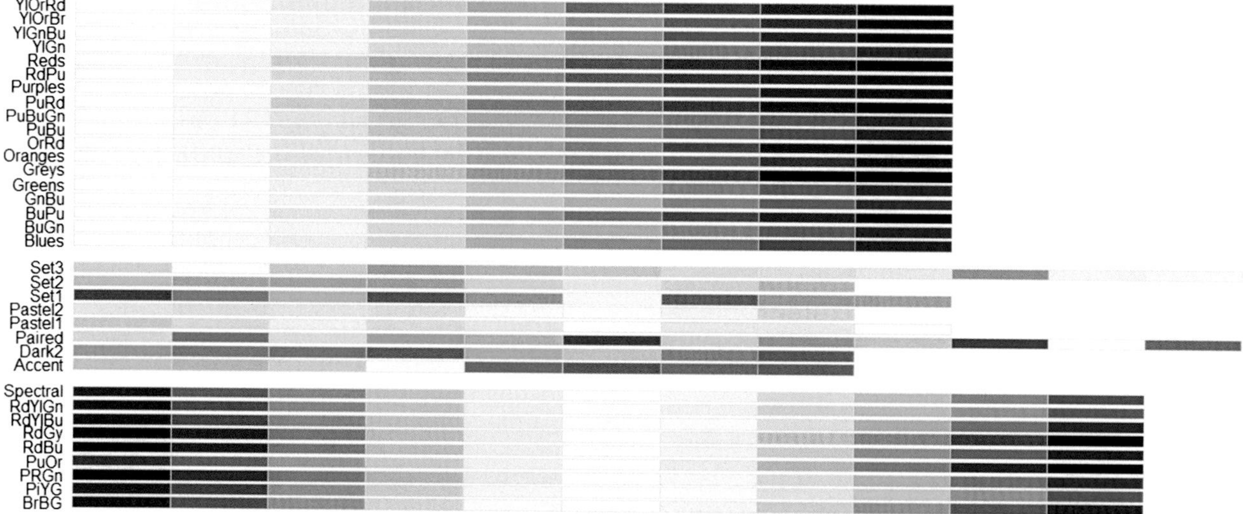

FIGURE 23.9 The color palettes applicable to the functions of the package `tmap`.

In Figure 23.8, we can see that there are six color ranges, and we can modify this by adding the argument `styles` to the function `tm_fill()`. Suppose we want the distribution of colors by quartiles of the values observed in the variable *hdi*. This way, we can run the following command:

```
tm_shape(shp = sp_merged) +
  tm_fill(col = "hdi",
          style = "quantile",
          n = 4,
          palette = "Greys")
```

As previously characterized, we divided the colors distribution into quartiles, arguing `style = "quantile"` and `n = 4`. If we wanted the distribution of the color's palette in quintiles, septiles, or deciles, we would change the value of the argument `n` to 5, 7, or 10, respectively. Figure 23.10 presents the result of the previous command.

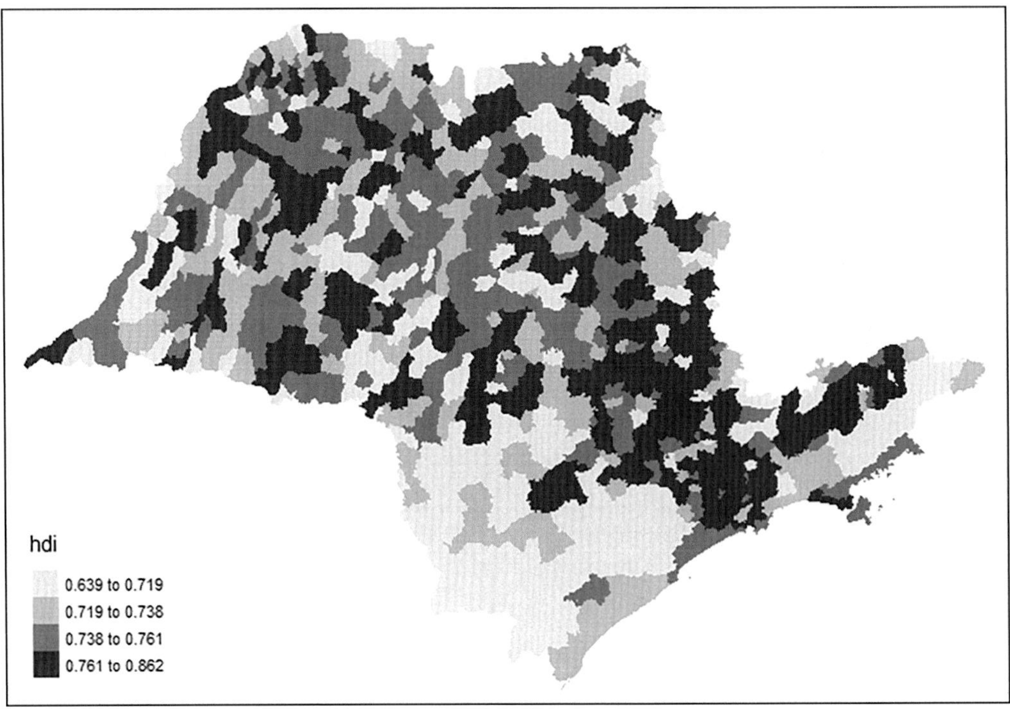

FIGURE 23.10 The HDI quartile division of the municipalities of the State of São Paulo.

We strongly recommend that the researcher execute the command `?tm_fill` and read the possibilities for arguing this function, with emphasis on the argument `styles`. Its possibilities go far beyond the stratification of observations in tertiles, quartiles, quintiles, and so on.

We can also make our map even more elegant, adding more information to it. We propose a different kind of legend, containing a histogram of the distribution of the variable *hdi*. The possibility can be executed with the following codes:

```
tm_shape(shp = sp_merged) +
  tm_fill(col = "hdi",
          style = "quantile",
          n = 4,
          palette = "Greens",
          legend.hist = TRUE)
```

Simple, right? It was enough that we argued `legend.hist = TRUE` in the function `tm_fill()`. Figure 23.11 demonstrates the result.

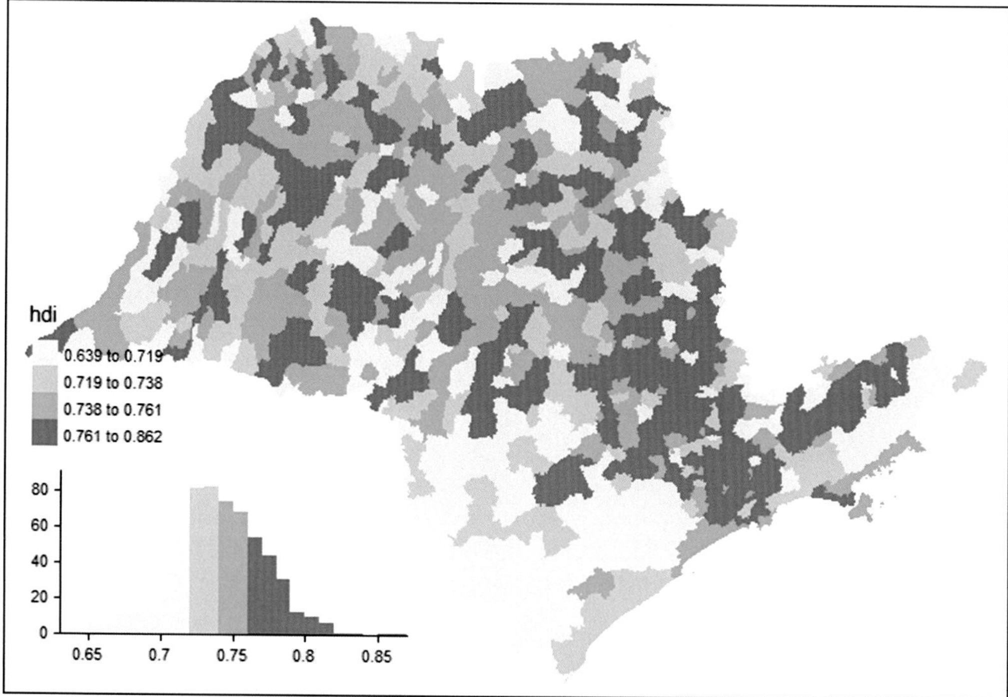

FIGURE 23.11 Inserting a histogram in the legend of a shapefile.

Although we fulfilled the proposed objective, as shown in Figure 23.11, note that the legend overlapped the map. To correct the situation, we will explore the arguments of the function `tm_layout()`, as suggested by the following codes:

```
tm_shape(shp = sp_merged) +
  tm_fill(col = "hdi",
          style = "quantile",
          n = 4,
          palette = "Greens",
          legend.hist = TRUE) +
  tm_layout(legend.outside = TRUE)
```

The argument `legend.outside = TRUE` applied to the function `tm_layout()` does precisely what the name *outside* suggests: it forces legends to leave the map, as shown in Figure 23.12.

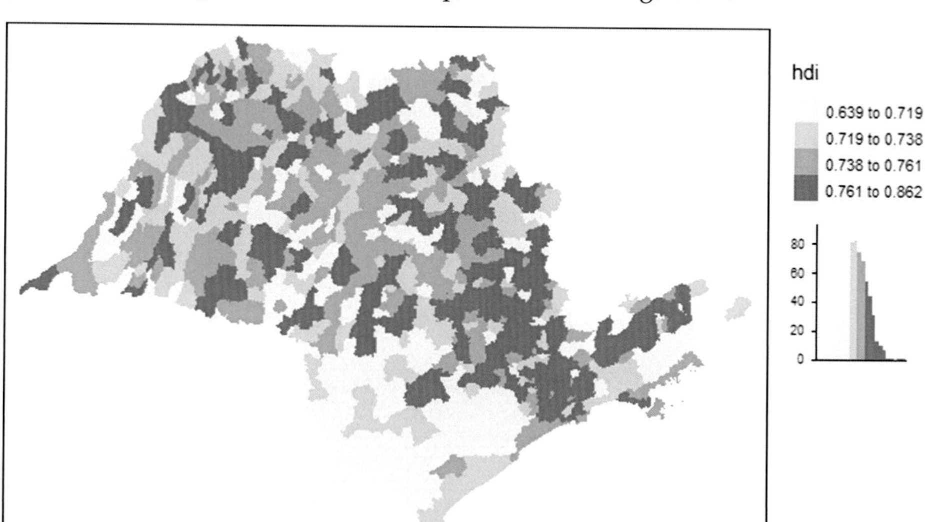

FIGURE 23.12 Repositioning legends on a map.

We can go further, exploring some other arguments of the function `tm_layout()`, as proposed:

```
tm_shape(shp = sp_merged) +
  tm_fill(col = "hdi",
          style = "quantile",
          n = 4,
          palette = "Set3",
          legend.hist = TRUE) +
  tm_layout(legend.text.size = 0.7,
            legend.title.size = 0.9,
            legend.hist.size = 0.5,
            legend.hist.height = 0.2,
            legend.hist.width = 0.3,
            frame = FALSE)
```

The values of the arguments of the function `tm_layout()` are not fixed and, without a doubt, should vary from map to map. In this case, the work is completely handmade, and the researcher must find the values that best suit his or her purposes. Figure 23.13 presents the result of the proposal.

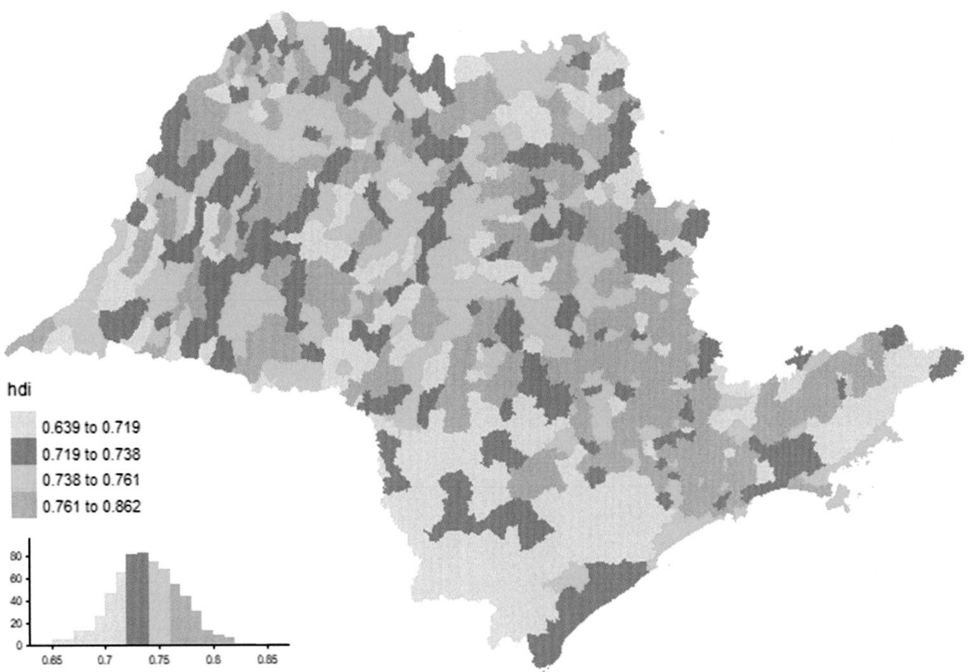

FIGURE 23.13 Exploring some arguments of legend of the function `tm_layout()`.

We can also add a title to our chart with the argument `main.title` applied to the function `tm_layout()`, as follows:

```
tm_shape(shp = sp_merged) +
  tm_fill(col = "hdi",
          style = "quantile",
          n = 4,
          palette = "BuPu",
          legend.hist = TRUE) +
  tm_layout(legend.text.size = 0.7,
            legend.title.size = 0.9,
```

Continued

```
         legend.hist.size = 0.5,
         legend.hist.height = 0.2,
         legend.hist.width = 0.3,
         frame = F,
         main.title = "The HDI Distribution in the Municipalities of SP")
```

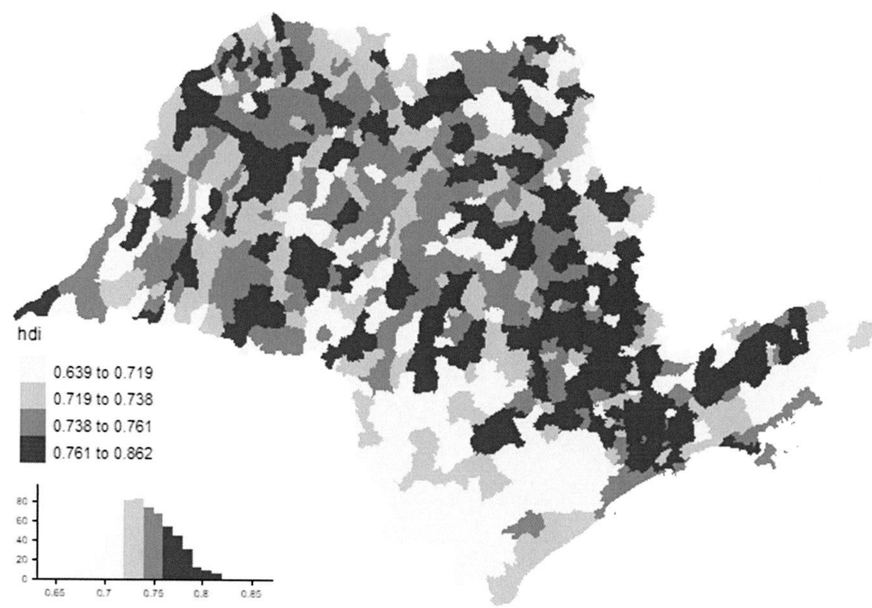

FIGURE 23.14 Adding titles in the shapefiles view.

Figure 23.14 shows the results of the previous coding.

If necessary, we can add borders to the polygons that make up our shapefile and also add a compass to our map, with the functions `tm_borders()` and `tm_compass()`, as follows:

```
tm_shape(shp = sp_merged) +
  tm_fill(col = "hdi",
          style = "quantile",
          n = 4,
          palette = "Reds",
          legend.hist = TRUE) +
  tm_layout(legend.text.size = 0.7,
            legend.title.size = 0.9,
            legend.hist.size = 0.5,
            legend.hist.height = 0.2,
            legend.hist.width = 0.3,
            frame = F,
            main.title = "The HDI Distribution in the Municipalities of SP") +
  tm_borders(alpha = 0.8) +
  tm_compass(type = "8star",
             show.labels = 3)
```

The results of the proposed codes are shown in Figure 23.15.

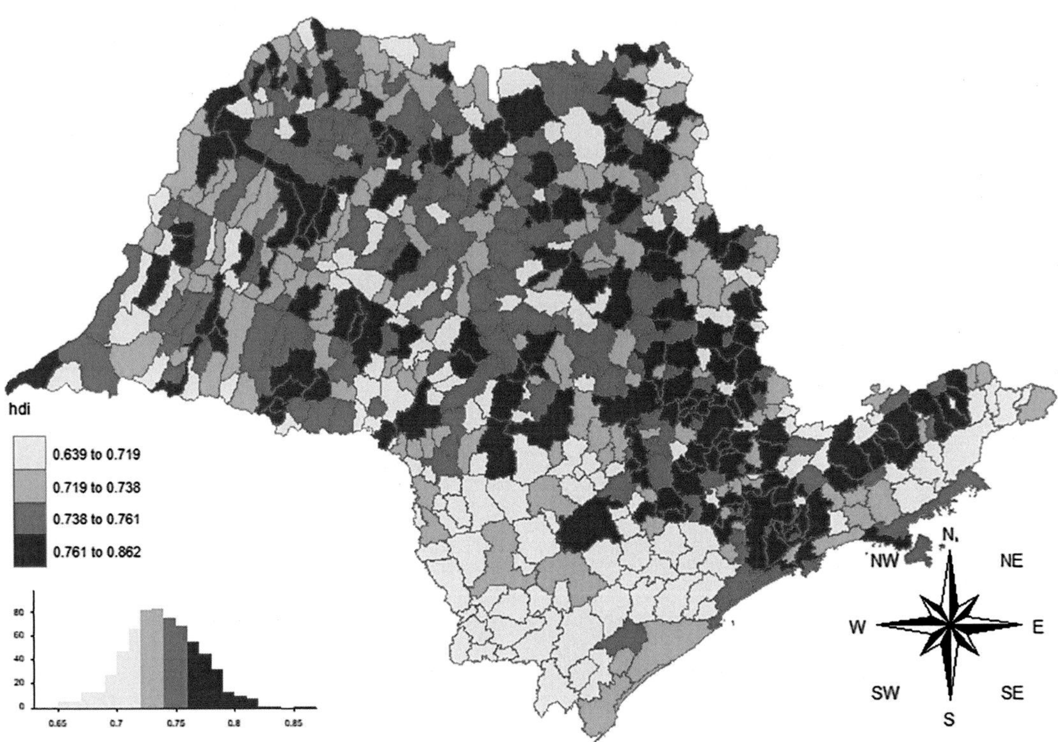

FIGURE 23.15 Changing the borders and adding compasses to the shapefile.

In the case of the function `tm_borders()`, the argument `alpha` will define the level of transparency of the borders: 80% in the example given. For the function `tm_compass()`, we recommend that the researcher explore its help file to see how many different compasses can be created using other arguments.

Finally, we can save our shapefile with the data inserted in it using the function `writeOGR()`, as follows:

```
writeOGR(obj = sp_merged,
         layer = "SP_new_shapefile",
         driver = "ESRI Shapefile",
         dsn = ".")
```

Dismembering shapefiles

Suppose a researcher wants to work with only part of a shapefile. A good example would be a researcher who needed a South American shapefile and who, hypothetically, found none available on the Internet. However, the researcher found a shapefile that contains all countries on the globe and therefore had the idea of extracting only the countries needed from that map.

As discussed in Chapter 2, recall that R-based language and many of its packages internally bring several datasets. The same is true with maps. For example, to have access to a world map, we can command the following:

```
data(wrld_simpl, package = "maptools")
```

An attentive reader will notice that a new object called `wrld_simpl` was created in the tab *Environment*, and its graphical visualization can be obtained as follows:

```
tm_shape(shp = wrld_simpl) +
  tm_borders()
```

Figure 23.16 shows the result of the previous command.

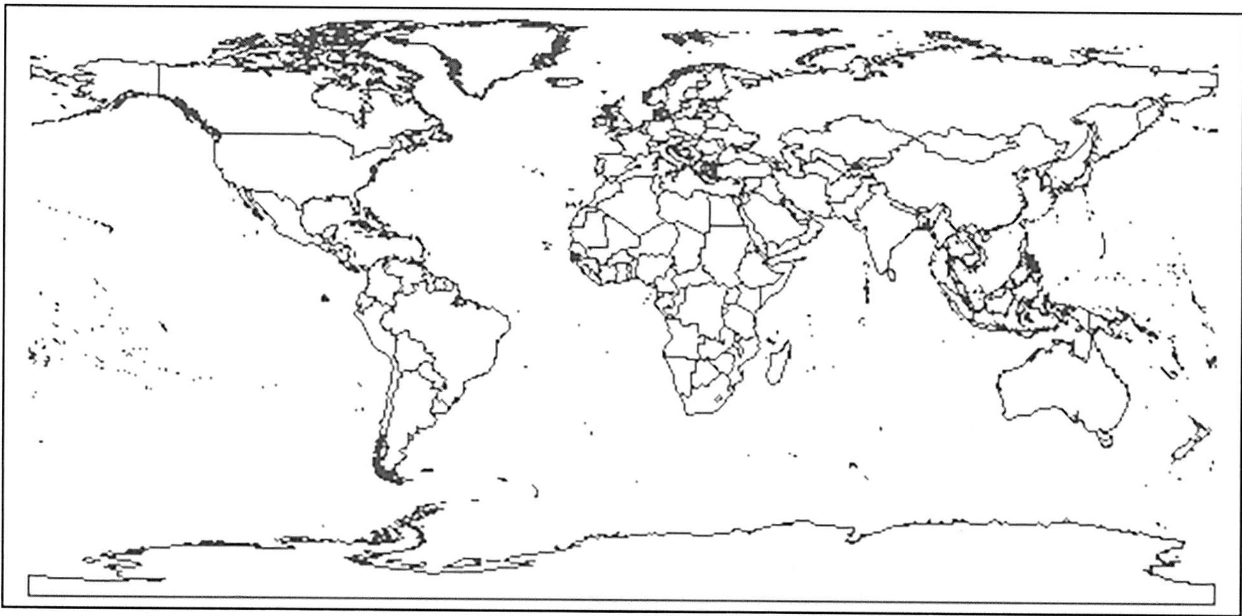

FIGURE 23.16 Shapefile of a world map from the package `maptools`.

A curious reader will also notice that our object `wrld_simpl` has some useful information in its dataset (`wrld_simpl@data`).

```
head(wrld_simpl@data)
```

Figure 23.17 demonstrates the variables and some data present in the object `wrld_simpl`.

```
    FIPS ISO2 ISO3 UN                NAME   AREA  POP2005 REGION SUBREGION     LON
ATG   AC   AG  ATG 28 Antigua and Barbuda     44    83039     19        29 -61.783
DZA   AG   DZ  DZA 12             Algeria 238174 32854159      2        15   2.632
AZE   AJ   AZ  AZE 31          Azerbaijan   8260  8352021    142       145  47.395
ALB   AL   AL  ALB  8             Albania   2740  3153731    150        39  20.068
ARM   AM   AM  ARM 51             Armenia   2820  3017661    142       145  44.563
AGO   AO   AO  AGO 24              Angola 124670 16095214      2        17  17.544
        LAT
ATG  17.078
DZA  28.163
AZE  40.430
ALB  41.143
ARM  40.534
AGO -12.296
```

FIGURE 23.17 Variables present in the dataset of the object `wrld_simpl`.

With the information present in the dataset of the object `wrld_simpl`, there are several solutions to obtain a map that contains only the countries of South America. We could cut out the world map informing the name of each country: *NAME* variable or their respective acronyms (e.g., FIPS, ISO2, or ISO3 variables). However, in this case, the simplest way to achieve the proposed objective is to use the *SUBREGION* variable, whose value 5 is the same for all countries in South America. Thus we can type the following command:

```
south_america <- wrld_simpl[wrld_simpl@data$SUBREGION == 5, ]
```

The reader should recall that in Chapter 2 we studied an analogous way of selecting data using the operator `[]`, but in data frames. In the previous code, we named a new object of `south_america`, which contains all information from the shapefile present in the object `wrld_simpl` with a value of 5 for the observations of the variable *SUBREGION*. We can verify the result by running the following command:

```
tm_shape(shp = south_america) +
  tm_borders()
```

The outcome of the previous command is shown in Figure 23.18.

FIGURE 23.18 Creation example of South America shapefile.

Next, we will describe the opposite process to that shown in this section: how to join shapefiles to form a single map.

Joining shapefiles

We immediately inform the reader that the practice of merging shapefiles is not advisable, **especially for those who are new to spatiality studies**. To do what we propose in this section, it is of fundamental importance that the attributes `proj4string` of the shapefiles to be used are, at least, compatible.

Even with the reservation made, there are certain difficulties in finding some customized shapefiles to meet the specificity of a given study (e.g., an unprecedented georeferencing of neighborhoods in a municipality). In any case, we advise the reader to first try to find a more comprehensive shapefile (e.g., the world map presented earlier in the "Dismembering Shapefiles" section and, from the shapefile found, proceed to dismember the regions needed, as already discussed. In the unlikely situation that the previous tip does not having an effect, we can fuse these kinds of objects. We ask the reader to upload the following shapefiles:

```
argentina <- readOGR(dsn = "shapefile_mercosul", layer = "argentina_shapefile")

bolivia <- readOGR(dsn = "shapefile_mercosul", layer = "bolivia_shapefile")

brazil <- readOGR(dsn = "shapefile_mercosul", layer = "brazil_shapefile")

chile <- readOGR(dsn = "shapefile_mercosul", layer = "chile_shapefile")
```

Continued

```
colombia <- readOGR(dsn = "shapefile_mercosul", layer = "colombia_shapefile")

ecuador <- readOGR(dsn = "shapefile_mercosul", layer = "ecuador_shapefile")

guyana <- readOGR(dsn = "shapefile_mercosul", layer = "guyana_shapefile")

paraguay <- readOGR(dsn = "shapefile_mercosul", layer = "paraguay_shapefile")

peru <- readOGR(dsn = "shapefile_mercosul", layer = "peru_shapefile")

suriname <- readOGR(dsn = "shapefile_mercosul", layer = "suriname_shapefile")

uruguay <- readOGR(dsn = "shapefile_mercosul", layer = "uruguay_shapefile")

venezuela <- readOGR(dsn = "shapefile_mercosul", layer = "venezuela_shapefile")
```

Imagine that we want to create a unique shapefile for countries that are effective members of Mercosur, and we obtained the shapefiles for each member country and want to join them.

As discussed earlier, the minimum attention we recommend is that the reader verify if the attributes `proj4string` of all shapefiles are at least compatible with each other. After that, we could use the function `bind()` from the package `raster`:

```
mercosul <- bind(argentina, bolivia, brazil, chile, colombia, ecuador, guyana,
                 peru, paraguay, suriname, uruguay, venezuela)
```

Visualization of the map present in the object `mercosul` can be obtained with the following code:

```
tm_shape(shp = mercosul) +
  tm_borders(lwd = 1) +
  tm_fill(col = "STATUS") +
  tm_layout(legend.width = 0.8)
```

The results of the previous routine are shown in Figure 23.19.

FIGURE 23.19 Results of creation of a shapefile from Mercosur member countries with the combination of individual shapefiles from each country.

Note that we did not tell R where each country should be or where they establish their borders. This was possible because the projection systems of the shapefiles used were compatible.

Final considerations

In this chapter, we introduced the use of shapefiles in R-based language. We saw tips on where to download them, how to load them, and how to use these objects. We also demonstrated how to customize them, that is, how to edit them and, if you are interested, how to save them.

Even though we have suggested some libraries, it is certain that they are not the only ones capable of working with shapefiles. A great example was the use of the package `tmap` instead of the package `ggplot2`, chosen for the ease and intuitiveness of its functions and arguments. If the reader is interested, we leave a tip for plotting three-dimensional maps: the package `rayshader`.

In the following chapters, we will demonstrate solutions for when you do not have a shapefile or, even if it is possible to obtain this type of object, it is not of interest to the researcher. For that, we can use georeferenced data frames (simple feature objects) or georeferenced images (raster-type objects).

Supplementary data sets

`sp_data.RData`

Please access supplementary data file here: https://doi.org/10.17632/55623jkwrp.3

CHAPTER

24

Dealing with simple feature objects

AT THE END OF THIS CHAPTER, YOU WILL BE ABLE TO:

- Understand what a simple feature object is
- Load and use simple feature objects
- Combine simple feature objects with shapefiles
- Perform the procedures of buffering, buffer union, and kernel density estimation
- Combine simple feature objects with other kinds of map layers
- Establish an algorithm for collecting geographic coordinates
- View simple feature objects in R-based language

R-based language packages used in this chapter

```
library(sf)
library(tmap)
library(rgdal)
library(rgeos)
library(sp)
library(adehabitatHR)
```

Don't forget to define the R working directory (the location where your datasets are installed):

```
setwd("C:/book/chapter24")
```

Introduction

Unlike a shapefile, a simple feature object does not constitute a set of georeferenced polygons that have a linked dataset. As discussed by Pebesma et al. (2017), simple feature objects refer, as a rule, to data frames that have vectors with geographic reference information.

Therefore this kind of object is an interesting alternative and less computationally demanding to work with spatialities. Even though there is no map *per se* linked to the file to be loaded, nothing prevents the researcher, after plotting

Data Science, Analytics and Machine Learning with R
https://doi.org/10.1016/B978-0-12-824271-1.00010-X

the vector geographic object, to also plot a secondary layer with a background map if it is of interest. These secondary layers of maps are easily found on the Internet and, as a rule, free of charge, as will be demonstrated throughout this section.

The reader will also notice that in R-based language, the classes of spatial objects (i.e., shapefiles, simple features, raster) are not consolidated things, and sometimes we will resort to transformations for other classes to achieve our goals, such as the class `Spatial Points`. As we did in the introductory section in Chapter 23, we emphasize that a minimum knowledge of R-based language is of fundamental importance for what follows.

Finally, as in Chapter 23, we will present the fundamentals together with the applications in R-based language.

Working with simple features

Let's assume that we need to identify on a map the locations of some shopping centers in the state capital of São Paulo. In the Chapter 23, we used shapefiles to introduce the reader to the field of spatial analysis. This time, we will take a different path.

First we will load data from shopping centers in the city. Suppose a researcher has collected data from 50 commercial establishments present in the `shoppings.RData` dataset. We ask the reader to open this file in R, according to the following codes:

```
load("shoppings.RData")
```

An attentive reader will notice that the object `shoppings` has data regarding the latitudes and longitudes of the observations, and this type of geographic referencing is essential for us to plot locations using a given dataset represented by a data frame. If the researcher wants to create a dataset for later georeferencing, this can be done in several ways. The most practical and commonly used are as follows:

- Use the package `ggmap` to connect to the Google Maps dataset, but since some years ago the service has created limitations for free users.
- Build a robot that visits specialized sites in informing the geographic coordinates sought (e.g., https://www.latlong.net) and collects the desired data. An interesting package for this solution, as discussed in Chapter 8, is `RSelenium`. Data mining packages, like `rvest`, can also provide interesting solutions.

We will now present suggestions on how to create a simple feature object from a data frame.

Creating a simple feature object

To proceed with the proposed task, we must use the function `st_as_sf()` from the package `sf`. This function can transform, for example, data frames into spatial objects. We therefore propose the following command:

```
shopping_locations <- st_as_sf(x = shoppings,
                               coords = c("longitude", "latitude"),
                               crs = 4326)
```

An attentive reader would compare the application of the function `class()` to the new object `shopping_locations`:

```
class(shopping_locations)
```

The outcomes of the previous commands are shown in Figure 24.1.

```
> class(shopping_locations)
[1] "sf"         "tbl_df"     "tbl"        "data.frame"
```

FIGURE 24.1 Classes of the object `pontos.shoppings`.

The content of Figure 24.1 informs us that, in fact, the new object `shopping_locations` belongs to the class `sf`, that is, the abbreviation for *simple feature*. In other words, it has become a spatial object.

We ask the reader to confirm the statement by typing the following command:

```
shopping_locations
```

The outcome of the previous command is shown in Figure 24.2.

```
Simple feature collection with 50 features and 3 fields
geometry type:  POINT
dimension:      XY
bbox:           xmin: -46.75752 ymin: -23.6783 xmax: -46.47064 ymax: -23.47987
geographic CRS: WGS 84
# A tibble: 50 x 4
   shopping          address                                 region              geometry
 * <chr>             <chr>                                   <fct>            <POINT [°]>
 1 Boavista Shopp~ Rua Borba Gato 59 Santo Amaro 047470~ south    (-46.7009 -23.65472)
 2 Bourbon Shoppi~ Rua Palestra Italia 500 Perdizes 050~ west    (-46.68082 -23.52655)
 3 Brascan Centur~ Rua Joaquim Floriano 466 Itaim Bibi ~ west    (-46.67502 -23.58434)
 4 Frei Caneca Sh~ Rua Frei Caneca 569 Consolacao 01307~ centr~  (-46.65259 -23.55414)
 5 Mais Shopping ~ Rua Amador Bueno 229 Santo Amaro 047~ south     (-46.71034 -23.653)
 6 Market Place    Avenida Doutor Chucri Zaidan 902 Vil~ south   (-46.69966 -23.62149)
 7 Mega Polo Moda  Rua Barao de Ladario 566 Bras 030100~ centr~   (-46.6185 -23.53686)
 8 Morumbi Shoppi~ Avenida Roque Petroni Junior 1089 Ja~ south   (-46.69884 -23.62336)
 9 Open Mall Pana~ Rua Jose Ramon Urtiza 975 Vila Andra~ south   (-46.72903 -23.63314)
10 Raposo Shopping SP-270 KM 14.5 Jardim Boa Vista 0557~ west    (-46.75106 -23.58805)
# ... with 40 more rows
```

FIGURE 24.2 Some features of the object `shopping_locations`.

The results at the top of Figure 24.2 reaffirm that the object `shopping_locations` is a spatial type, orienting itself geographically with data on the longitude and latitude of its information. The field `geometry type` tells us that this object corresponds to a set of points—a natural situation for simple feature files. **The geometry type vectors present in the object `sf` can also be a set of lines or even polygons.**

Still in Figure 24.2, an attentive reader will notice that the application of the function `st_as_sf()` of the object `shoppings` generated a new variable called *geometry*, and this variable will guide the plotting of the locations of the dataset observations on a map. We can plot the results of this operation with the following codes:

```
tm_shape(shp = shopping_locations) +
  tm_dots(size = 1)
```

Figure 24.3 shows the result obtained from the previous routine.

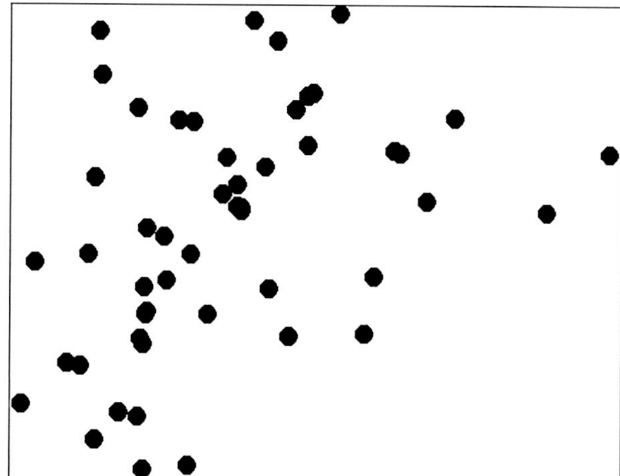

FIGURE 24.3 Plotting of the geographic points present in the geometry variable.

There is a good chance that the reader, a priori, found Figure 24.3 somewhat uninteresting. In the following sections, we will show the reader how to make it more visually appealing.

Using layers in simple feature objects

Although the georeferencing of 50 shopping centers in the city of São Paulo is correct, we agree that the map in Figure 24.3 could be more informative and elegant. Therefore we can add a layer with the streets of the city of São Paulo using the function `tmap_mode()` from the package `tmap`.

Use of the function `tmap_mode()` has two main arguments: `"plot"` for graphics without outer layers (e.g., Figure 24.3) and `"view"` for outer layers obtained from an Internet connection. Therefore **on a computer connected to the Internet**, we can type:

```
tmap_mode("view")
```

Then:

```
tm_shape(shp = shopping_locations) +
  tm_dots(col = "darkblue",
          border.col = "black",
          size = 0.2,
          alpha = 0.8)
```

The result of the previous command is shown in Figure 24.4.

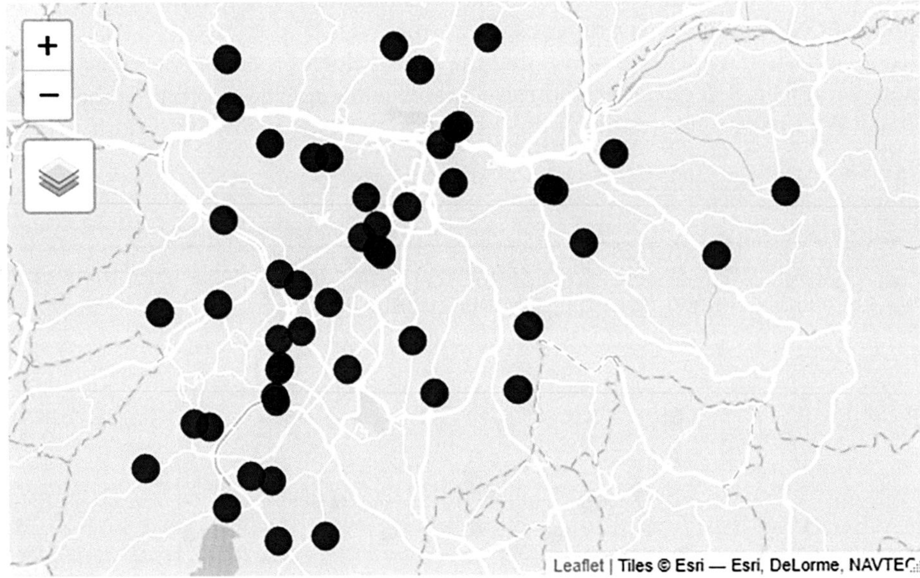

FIGURE 24.4 Using the function `tmap_mode()`.

It is interesting to note that points in Figure 24.4 are arranged exactly the same as in Figure 24.3. The big change was the addition of a layer with the map of the city of São Paulo.

The map in Figure 24.4 is interactive! The reader can zoom in or out of the image with the buttons that have a + and – sign. It is also interesting to note that when you click on any of the plotted points, a window opens with information about the location. The reader can also change the type of layer adopted using the button. Figure 24.5 shows an example of a layer that can be added.

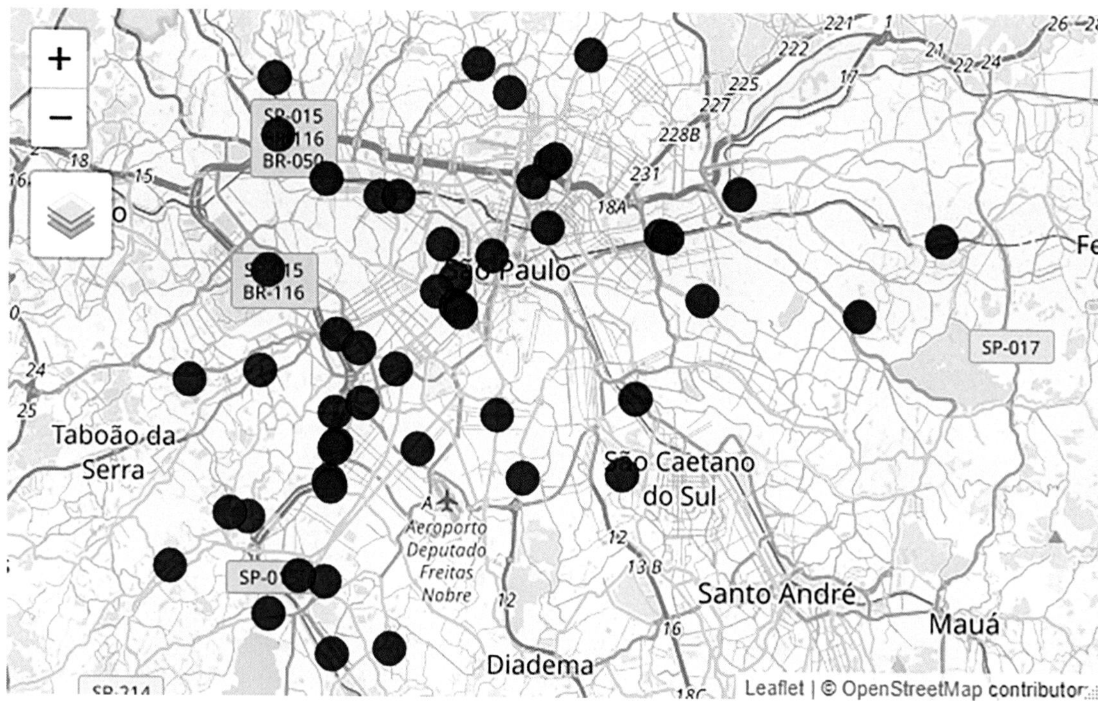

FIGURE 24.5 The addition of the layer OpenStreetMap.

The result of Figure 24.5 can also be obtained without using the mouse, with the following code:

```
tm_basemap(server = "OpenStreetMap.Mapnik") +
  tm_shape(shp = shopping_locations) +
  tm_dots(col = "darkblue",
          border.col = "black",
          size = 0.2,
          alpha = 0.8)
```

The arguments for the function `tm_basemap()` can be found at the following link: http://leaflet-extras.github.io/leaflet-providers/preview/. Figure 24.6 can help researchers by pointing out the location of the arguments in the previously mentioned Web address.

For R to return maps again without the presence of external layers of the Internet, the reader can type the following command:

```
tmap_mode("plot")
```

A different situation may be the researcher's interest in using a shapefile as a layer that represents a map of interest, and that is exactly what we will do next.

Combining simple feature objects with shapefiles

What if we wanted to plot the commercial establishments of the object `shoppings` in a shapefile? To do this, first we will load a shapefile from the municipality of São Paulo from its respective city hall, as discussed in Chapter 23:

```
sp_city <- readOGR(dsn = "shapefile_city", layer = "sp_city")
```

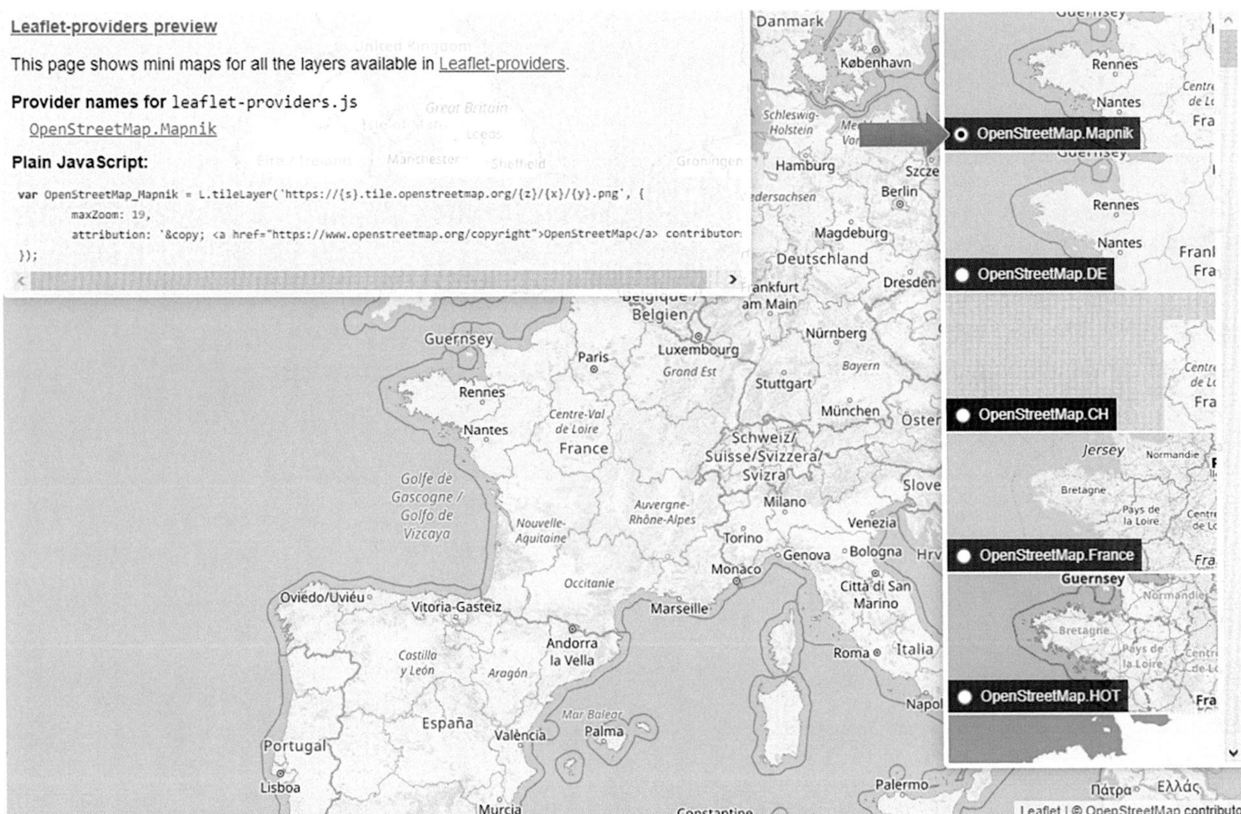

FIGURE 24.6 Internet address with possible arguments for the function `tm_basemap()`, with emphasis on the one used in Figure 24.5.

In the previous routine, the object `sp_city` started to contain a shapefile from the city of São Paulo. We can check this by typing the following command:

```
tm_shape(shp = sp_city) +
  tm_borders()
```

Figure 24.7 shows the result obtained from the previous code.

FIGURE 24.7 Shapefile of the city of São Paulo.

If the researcher were looking for more elegance in the presentation of Figure 24.7, use of tmap_mode() combined with the argument "view" would be sufficient, as discussed earlier:

```
tmap_mode("view")

tm_shape(shp = sp_city) +
  tm_borders()
```

Figure 24.8 shows the difference in the use of the arguments "plot" (see Figure 24.7) and "view" in the function tmap_mode().

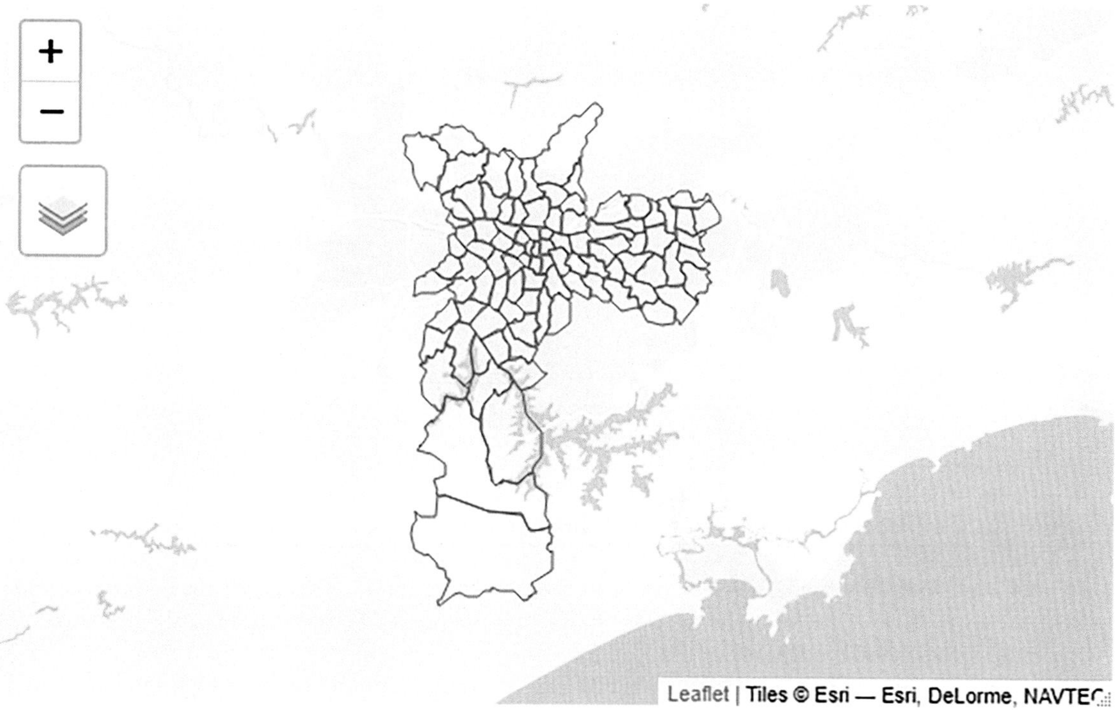

FIGURE 24.8 Shapefile of the city of São Paulo with the addition of an outer layer.

To plot the locations of the shopping centers surveyed in the object sp_city, we can combine the information from the object shopping_locations, as follows:

```
tm_shape(shp = sp_city) +
  tm_borders(alpha = 0.5) +
  tm_shape(shp = shopping_locations) +
  tm_dots(col = "region",
          size = 0.02)
```

Figure 24.9 shows the result of the previous codes. If the reader is working offline, that is, with the function tmap_mode("plot"), we suggest assigning the value 0.3 to the argument size of the previous code for a better view.

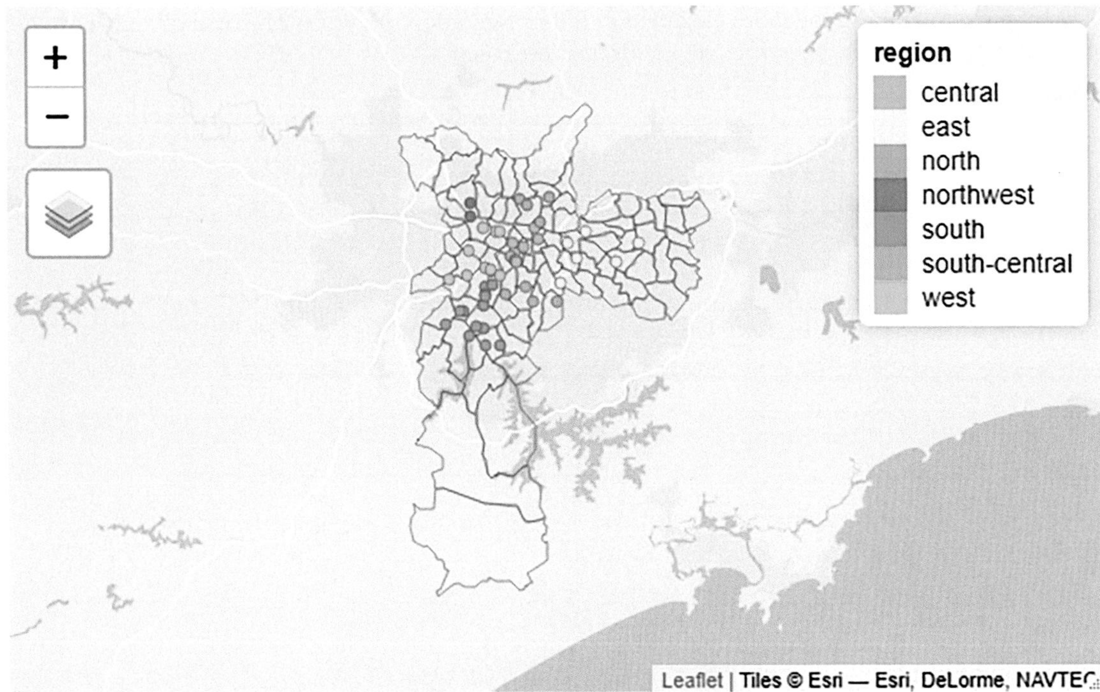

FIGURE 24.9 Plotting the 50 shopping centers of the municipality of São Paulo in a shapefile.

An attentive reader will notice that at the same time we are working with the object `sf` (another object of shapefile type) in addition to an external map layer (both with aggregated datasets). Still, the results are obtained quickly! The situation shows, reasonably, the capabilities of the R-based language.

Using R like geographic information systems software

According to Islam (2018), the choice of R for this type of task has two main advantages already highlighted: the first is that it is free software; the second concerns the possibility of writing scripts that can be saved and that make all the actions performed reproducible by any user.

In this section, we aim to give the reader some insight into the spatial capabilities of R. We choose to present three interesting and introductory techniques common to Geographic Information Systems (GIS) software: buffering, buffer union, and kernel density estimation.

The example set for the demonstration of techniques proposes the attempt to observe places for the establishment of a commercial point, but its capabilities do not stop there. An attentive reader, when searching for the term *spatial buffering* in Google Scholar, will quickly realize that these techniques are also used in the fields of medicine, cytology, hydrology, ecology, and others.

Buffering

Imagine that we work for a corporation that wants to install a new shopping center in the city of São Paulo, and the new establishment must be some distance from other shopping centers. Obviously, the proposition has didactic purposes and is disregarding social, economic, geographic, logistic, and other issues.

Then, assuming that the optimal distance proposed by the board is 1,500 meters, we could then use the function `gBuffer()` from the package `rgeos`. Thus we propose the first attempt to use the function `gBuffer()` as follows:

```
buffer_shoppings <- gBuffer(spgeom = shopping_locations,
                            width = 1500,
                            byid = TRUE)
```

Before exploring the arguments of the function `gBuffer()`, we would like to focus on the error that R returned to the reader. Figure 24.10 shows the description.

```
> ?gBuffer
> buffer_shoppings <- gBuffer(spgeom = shopping_locations,
+                             width = 1500,
+                             byid = TRUE)

Error in (function (classes, fdef, mtable)  :
  unable to find an inherited method for function 'is.projected' for signature '"sf"'
```

FIGURE 24.10 First error presented by the function `gBuffer()`.

The function `gBuffer()` will not work with objects of simple feature class. Looking at the documentation from the package `rgeos`, an attentive reader will realize that the function we want to use could be used for objects of the class `Spatial Points`. This is a problem of working with spatial analysis in R. There are a series of classes of objects (e.g., polygons, simple features, spatial points) that are not consolidated into a single or a few packages. Thus we must use the function `SpatialPoints()` from the package `sp`.

Next we propose to try to create an object of type `sp` so we can apply the function `gBuffer()`.

```
coordinates <- SpatialPoints(cbind(shoppings$longitude,
                                   shoppings$latitude),
                             proj4string=CRS("+proj=longlat"))
```

Note that the object created, called `coordinates`, is the result of the same basis used to create the object `shopping_locations`, that is, the data frame `shoppings`. We can view our new object with the following code, whose result will be identical to that already shown in Figures 24.3 and 24.4:

```
tm_shape(shp = coordinates) +
  tm_dots(size = 0.2)
```

With this transformation done, we could try to use the function `gBuffer()` again, as follows:

```
buffer_shoppings <- gBuffer(spgeom = shopping_locations,
                            width = 1500,
                            byid = TRUE)
```

Once again, R will report an error, as shown in Figure 24.11.

```
> buffer_shoppings <- gBuffer(spgeom = coordinates,
+                             width = 1500,
+                             byid = TRUE)
Warning message:
In gBuffer(spgeom = coordinates, width = 1500, byid = TRUE) :
  Spatial object is not projected; GEOS expects planar coordinates
```

FIGURE 24.11 Second error presented by the function `gBuffer()`.

The problem reported in Figure 24.11 concerns the impossibility of the function `gBuffer()` to work with objects that are oriented with geodesic distances.

Next, we will propose a transformation applied to the object coordinates so its distances are understood as Euclidean. **However, we reiterate that this is a proxy**; depending on the size of the territorial space studied, there may be serious divergences in the projection of distances among objects.

That said, a possible solution would be to find out which Universal Transversal Mercator (UTM) zone belongs to the territory of the city of São Paulo. After that, we can look for a smaller-scale projection system that meets the UTM zone. All of this can be done through the LatLong.net website.

Thus we verified that the municipality of São Paulo is in the UTM 23K Zone and that the smaller-scale projection system EPSG: 22523 could serve us with the least possible distortion in distance metrics. That said, we ask the reader to type the function `spTransform()` from the package `sp` as follows:

```
coordinates_UTM <- spTransform(x = coordinates,
                               CRSobj = CRS(projargs = "+init=epsg:22523"))
```

Visually, the object `coordinates_UTM` has an expected distortion compared with the object `coordinates` because we are comparing a flat projection with a geodesic projection, respectively, in a relatively extensive territorial space. To view the object `coordinates_UTM`, we can type the following command:

```
tm_shape(shp = coordinates_UTM) +
  tm_dots(size = 0.2)
```

We reiterate that what was exposed is a proxy. Figure 24.12, with the help of dotted lines, shows the discrepancies.

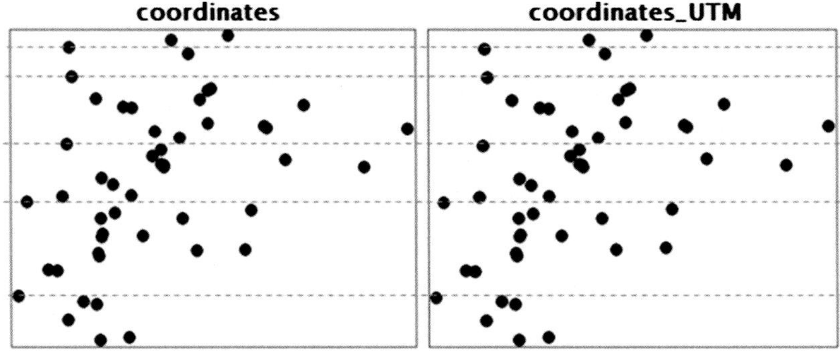

FIGURE 24.12 Georeferencing distortions between the objects `coordinates` and `coordinates_UTM`.

Now, finally, we can use the function `gBuffer()`:

```
buffer_shoppings <- gBuffer(spgeom = coordinates_UTM,
                            width = 1500,
                            byid = TRUE)
```

The results of the buffering procedure can be viewed according to the following:

```
tm_shape(shp = buffer_shoppings) +
  tm_borders()
```

Figure 24.13 shows the result of the previous code.

FIGURE 24.13 Results of the procedure buffering.

As shown in Figure 24.13, the function `gBuffer()` created circles, with diameters of 1,500 m each, whose centroids are the geographic coordinates of the commercial establishments present in the dataset `shoppings`. To achieve the objective proposed at the beginning of this section, simply type:

```
tm_shape(shp = sp_city) +
  tm_borders(alpha = 0.5) +
  tm_shape(shp = buffer_shoppings) +
  tm_borders(col = "black") +
  tm_shape(shp = shopping_locations) +
  tm_dots(col = "region",
          size = 0.02)
```

The final result of our buffering procedure is shown in Figure 24.14.

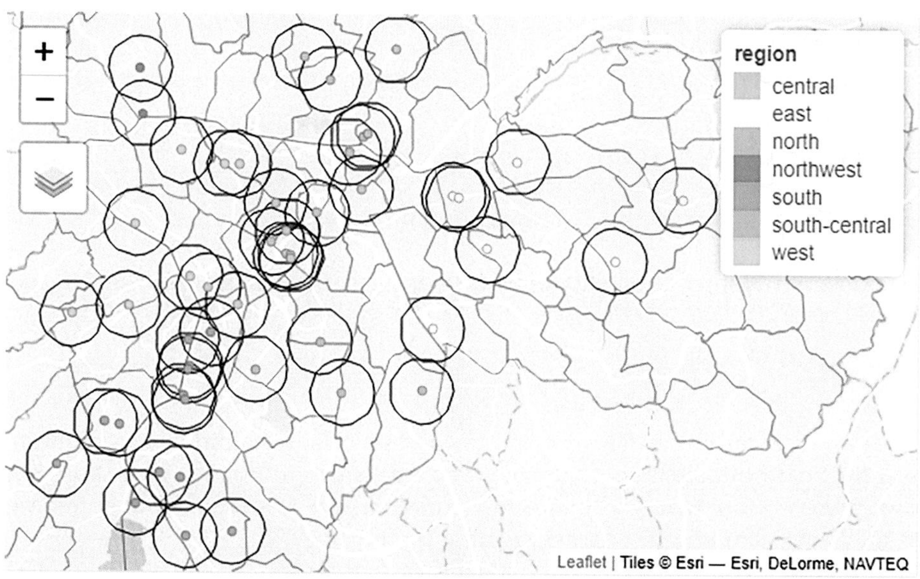

FIGURE 24.14 Results of the buffering procedure applied to 50 shopping centers in the city of São Paulo.

In the following section, we will demonstrate an interesting way of grouping the buffers due to their intersections.

Buffer union

The result present in Figure 24.14 can sometimes be quite troubled depending on the amount of observations in our database. An interesting solution to this possible visual problem is to join the circles generated by the buffering with the function `gUnaryUnion()`, also from the package `rgeos`. The command for the procedure is as follows:

```
buffer_union <- gUnaryUnion(spgeom = buffer_shoppings)
```

The final visual result can be achieved by the following codes:

```
tm_shape(shp = sp_city) +
  tm_borders(alpha = 0.5) +
  tm_shape(shp = buffer_union) +
  tm_borders(col = "black") +
  tm_fill(col = "gray",
          alpha = 0.5) +
  tm_shape(shp = shopping_locations) +
  tm_dots(col = "region",
          size = 0.02)
```

Figure 24.15 shows the resulting map of the technique.

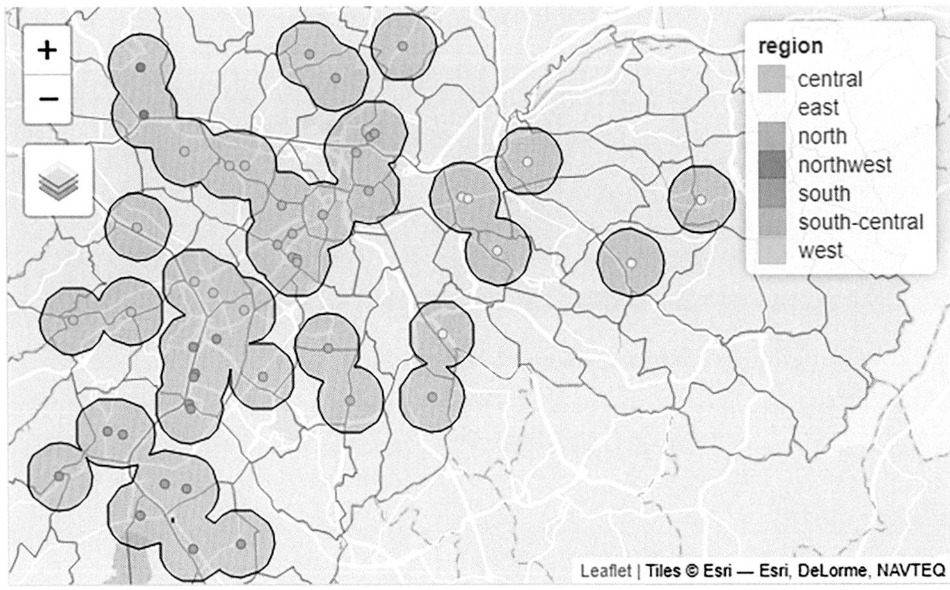

FIGURE 24.15 Results of the buffer union procedure applied to 50 shopping centers in the city of São Paulo.

In the following section, we will demonstrate another possibility of using R as a GIS instrument, establishing and plotting kernel density distributions.

Kernel densities

Following the proposed didactic line (i.e., disregarding social, economic, geographic, logistic, and other variables), we continue to follow the directions of the board of directors of our company that wants to install a new shopping center in the city of São Paulo. Thus we present a tool that can be directed to measure the saturation of the presence of certain types of establishment due to the calculation of the kernel distribution function.

Unlike buffering and buffer union techniques, there is no need to use planar data. In this way, we will use the dataset present in the object `shoppings` and their respective geographic coordinates present in the object `coordinates` to establish a new object of type Spatial Points Data Frame. In this way:

```
shoppings_dens <- SpatialPointsDataFrame(coords = coordinates@coords,
                                          data = shoppings,
                                          proj4string = CRS(
                                            projargs = "+proj=longlat"
                                            ))
```

To calculate the kernel densities of shopping centers in São Paulo, we will use the function `kernelUD()` from the package `adehabitatHR`. The letters *UD* refer to the abbreviation for *utilization distribution* because the listed package was primarily created to study the movement of wild animals around their dens or lairs. However, it proved to be very useful for other purposes, as we will see later!

Generally, the animals mentioned are monitored by a GPS collar. As a rule, this collar emits signals in predefined constant periods (e.g., every 1 hour or every 2 hours) and informs the monitoring team of the animal's position. For didactic purposes, we will call this position a *checkpoint*.

The more checkpoints sent in an area, the higher the saturation mark of the presence of that animal there, right? The idea is to use the algorithm `kernelUD()`, making the researcher understand that he or she is monitoring a single fictitious animal, whose checkpoints sent are, in fact, the real geographic positions of the shopping centers in the city of São Paulo. Thus the more commercial establishments identified in a given location, the higher the saturation mark of the presence of this type of company in a given location. To calculate the kernel distribution of the observations in the dataset shoppings, we will finally use the function kernelUD() as follows:

```
kernel_dens <- kernelUD(xy = shoppings_dens,
                        h = "href",
                        grid = 1000,
                        boundary = NULL)
```

In the previous command, the argument grid concerns the number of pixels that will be used on our map. An attentive reader could, for example, change the value 1000 to 50 and then plot the object to see what happens. In any case, we do not recommend very high values because the command is computationally demanding.

Still on the previous codes, the argument boundary = NULL establishes to the machine that we do not want to define movement boundaries because, obviously, shopping centers are immobile. The argument h = "href" is aimed at smoothing the graph curves that we will still establish.

We also thought it advisable to alert the reader that R will return a warning message that, depending on what we want, can be ignored because the object kernel_dens was correctly created in the Environment tab. In short, the error is caused by creating an object without arguing the animal identification vector.

Provisions made, we can visualize what we have done until now, typing:

```
plot(kernel_dens)
```

Figure 24.16 shows the result of the previous command.

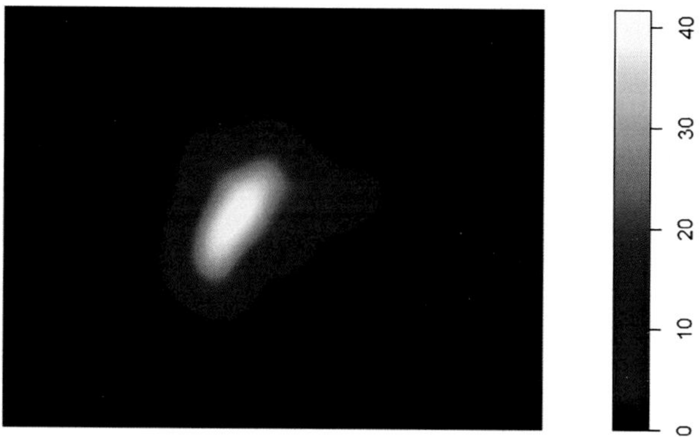

FIGURE 24.16 Calculation proposal for kernel densities distribution of 50 shopping centers in the city of São Paulo.

From the result obtained from Figure 24.16, we can establish areas of saturation due to the presence of shopping centers in the city of São Paulo, again making the reservation that the example has didactic purposes and disregards numerous important variables. Tthe objective is to present the technique! So, imagine that the board of our corporation has established that we must plot saturation zones due to the quintiles of the kernel distribution calculated. Thus we should type the function getverticeshr() from the package adehabitatHR, as follows:

```
zone1 <- getverticeshr(x = kernel_dens, percent = 20)

zone2 <- getverticeshr(x = kernel_dens, percent = 40)

zone3 <- getverticeshr(x = kernel_dens, percent = 60)

zone4 <- getverticeshr(x = kernel_dens, percent = 80)
```

To view the final result on the saturation map of the presence of shopping centers by region of the municipality of São Paulo, we propose the following command:

```
tm_shape(shp = sp_city) +
  tm_fill(col = "gray50") +
  tm_borders(col = "white", alpha = 0.5) +
  tm_shape(shp = shoppings_dens) +
  tm_dots(col = "region", size = 0.25) +
  tm_shape(shp = zone1) +
  tm_borders(col = "firebrick4", lwd = 2.5) +
  tm_fill(alpha = 0.4, col = "firebrick4") +
  tm_shape(shp = zone2) +
  tm_borders(col = "firebrick3", lwd = 2.5) +
  tm_fill(alpha = 0.3, col = "firebrick3") +
  tm_shape(shp = zone3) +
  tm_borders(col = "firebrick2", lwd = 2.5) +
  tm_fill(alpha = 0.2, col = "firebrick2") +
  tm_shape(shp = zone4) +
  tm_borders(col = "firebrick1", lwd = 2.5) +
  tm_fill(alpha = 0.1, col = "firebrick1")
```

Figure 24.17 shows the result of the previous routine.

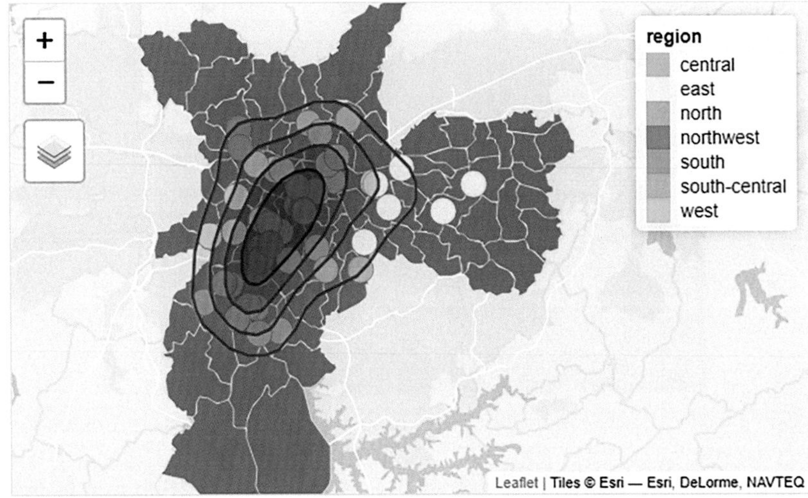

FIGURE 24.17 Saturation map of the presence of shopping centers by region of the municipality of São Paulo.

In the following sections, we will present more features regarding simple feature objects aimed at searching for research insight.

Combining simple feature layers and objects in search of insight

We can also plot different information from simple feature objects on the same map. Initially, we suggest viewing the main rivers in the world. We ask the reader to type the following command:

```
data(World, rivers)
```

The objects World and rivers belong to the package tmap and correspond to points in a georeferenced data frame, just like the object shopping_locations, that is, they are simple feature objects. To combine them, we must execute the following:

```
tm_shape(shp = World) +
  tm_borders() +
  tm_shape(shp = rivers) +
  tm_lines(col = "darkblue")
```

Figure 24.18 shows the result of the previous coding.

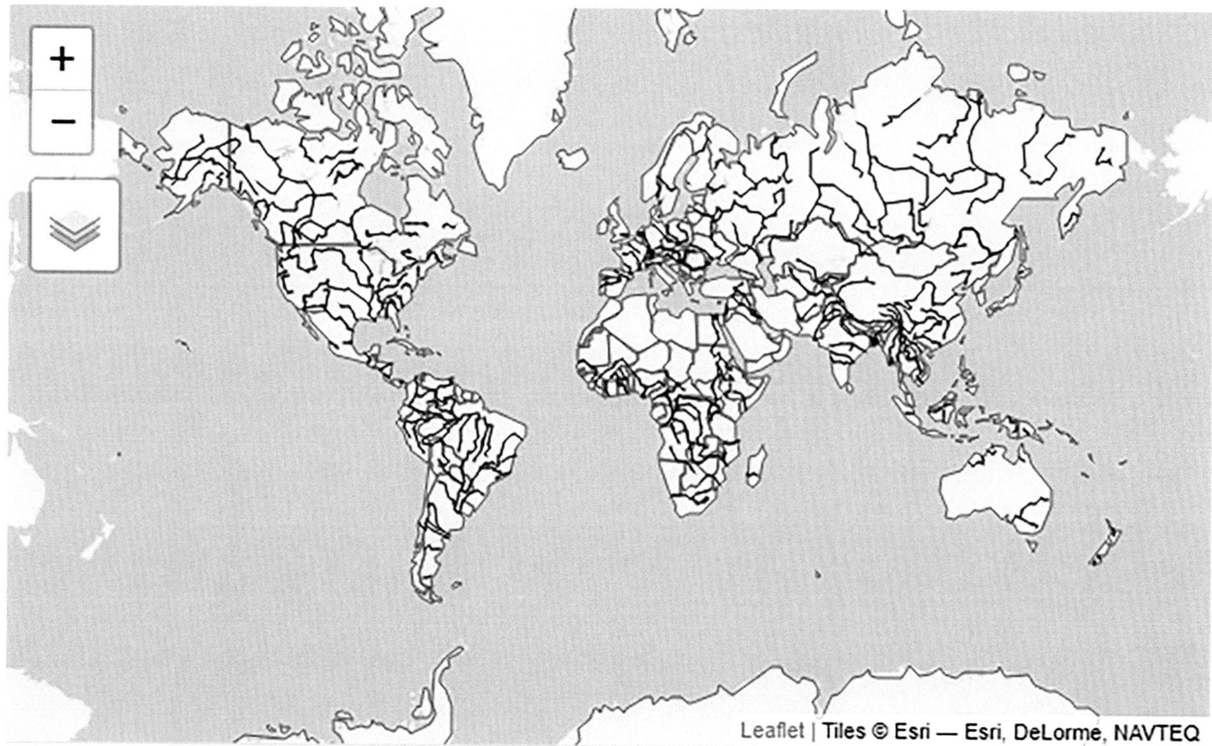

FIGURE 24.18 Visualization of a world map combined with the main rivers in the world.

The dataset of the object World brings interesting data, and the reader can type ?World to verify the statement. An example of this information is the so-called *Happy Planet Index* (HPI) found on the HappyPlanetIndex.org website. The HPI idea is to measure how well countries are able to provide their populations with a long, happy, and sustainable life; their polarity is: the bigger the better.

Suppose a researcher is looking for some insight for new research and wants to cross the HPI information with the presence of globally important rivers on a given map. Thus we could type the following command:

```
tmap_mode("plot")
```

Then:

```
tm_shape(shp = World, projection = "WGS84") +
  tm_fill(col = "HPI") +
  tm_shape(shp = rivers) +
  tm_lines(col = "darkblue")
```

Figure 24.19 demonstrates R's response.

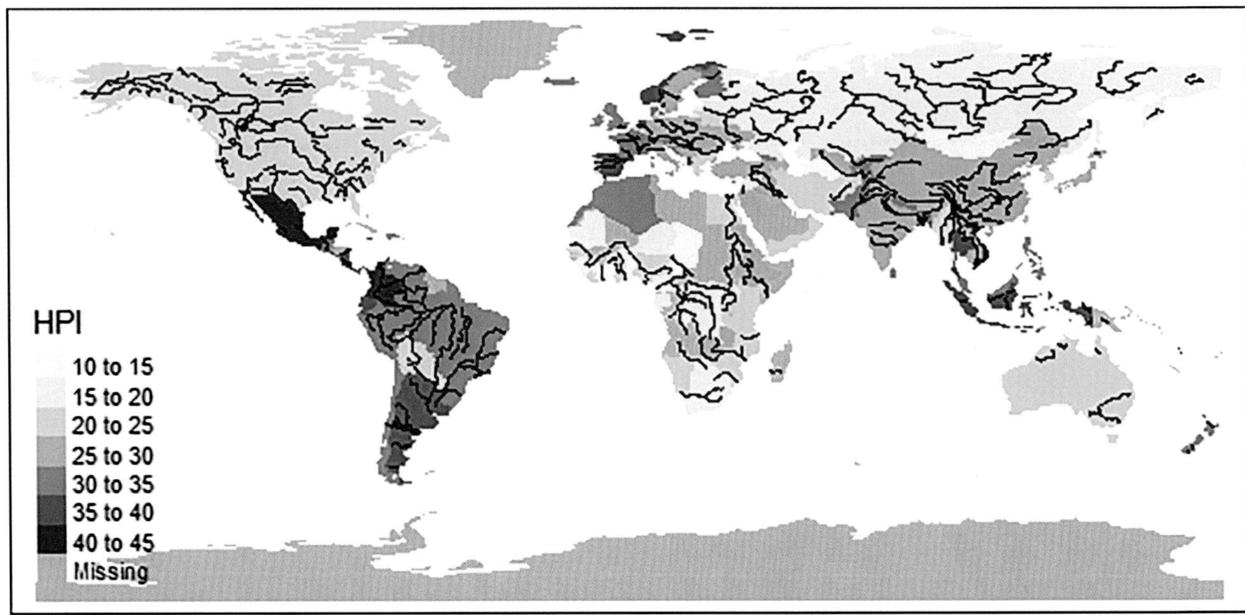

FIGURE 24.19 The combination of the HPI with the world map shown in Figure 24.18.

We could go further, pointing out cities that have a metro service. Thus the reader can type the following command:

```
data(metro)
```

To view the information together, we can:

```
tm_shape(shp = World, projection = "WGS84") +
  tm_fill(col = "HPI") +
  tm_shape(shp = rivers) +
  tm_lines(col = "darkblue") +
  tm_shape(shp = metro) +
  tm_dots(size = 0.07)
```

Figure 24.20 shows the result of the previous code.

Going further, the researcher could, in addition to everything demonstrated, emphasize the population size of the city in which the metro service is installed:

```
tm_shape(shp = World, projection = "WGS84") +
  tm_fill(col = "HPI") +
  tm_shape(rivers) +
  tm_lines(col = "darkblue") +
  tm_shape(shp = metro) +
  tm_bubbles(size = "pop2010", col = "darkorchid2")
```

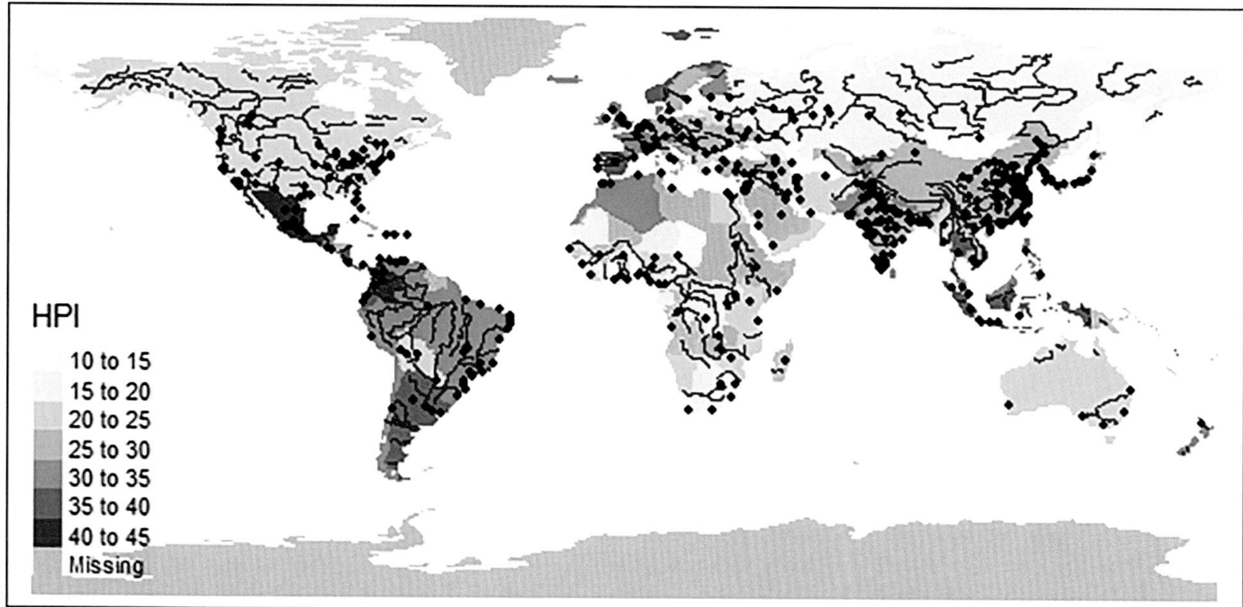

FIGURE 24.20 Cities with the metro service.

Figure 24.21 shows the outcome of the previous codes.

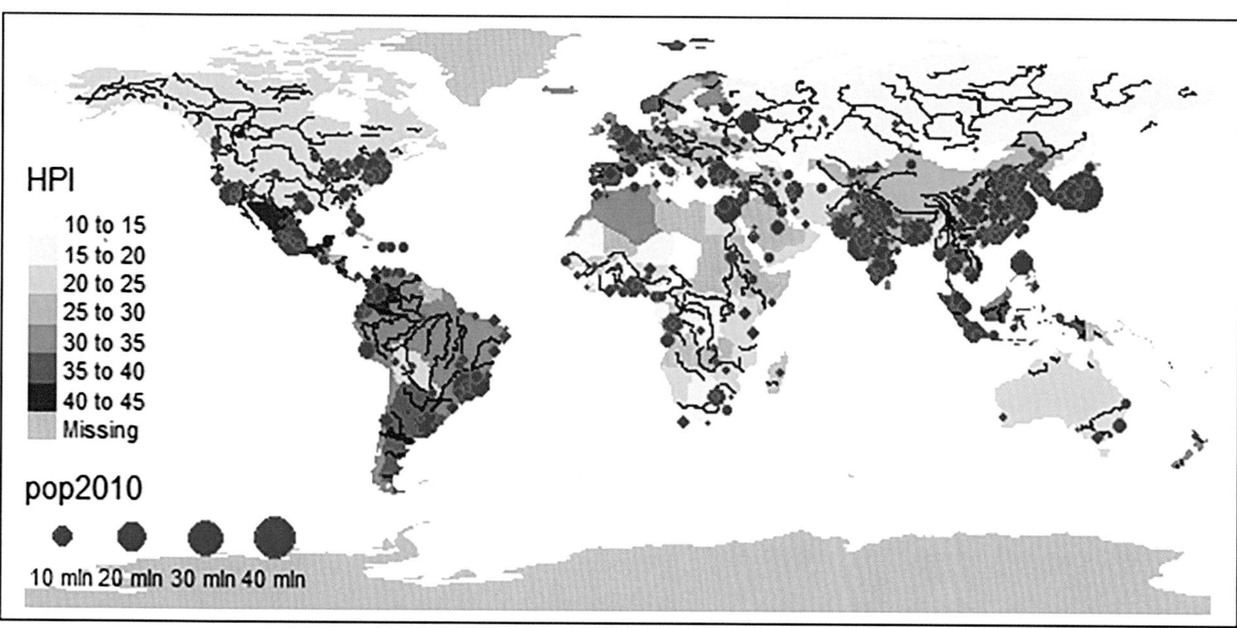

FIGURE 24.21 Combining the population size of each country with the existence of metro services in their cities.

Next, we will demonstrate an application in R, together with creation of a robot for the collection of geographic coordinates for observations in a common data frame.

Example of using a robot to capture space data

Oftentimes the researcher may experience the inconvenience of not finding a suitable shapefile or not being able to hand in time to collect GPS information to georeference a given dataset. In this sense, we propose the creation of a robot, with help from the package `RSelenium`, which will collect the location information of some Brazilian hospitals. **For the following example, we will assume that the reader has assimilated the knowledge in Chapters 2, 8, and 9 of this book, understood the limitations and dangers of the technique, and has a computer that is ready to use that package.**

In the same way presented during Chapter 8, we will assign the Mozilla Firefox browser to our robot. That way, we can type:

```
driver <- rsDriver(browser = "firefox")
```

Now that we have defined the browser, we will transform it into a remote browser, that is, we will give the robot authority to operate it according to our commands:

```
remote_driver <- driver[["client"]]
```

At this point, a chosen browser window should have opened. We ask the reader to close the browser window that just opened and type:

```
remote_driver$open()
```

A new browser window will open under the commands of the robot. As discussed in Chapter 8, if nothing happens, it is possible that the reader's version from the package `RSelenium` is out of date, there is an incompatibility between the architectures of the Java version and the installed R-based language, or the browser version used is not yet considered by the package `RSelenium`.

The next step will be to define which web page our robot will navigate to. Always remember that our tool is mimetic, and we must therefore teach all of the ways and devices we use to navigate to the desired data. The following codes suggest an example for collecting information on geographic coordinates of some locations on the LatLong.net website. First, we must create an object that contains the URL address from which we want to extract the data:

```
url <- "https://www.latlong.net"
```

The next step will be loading the dataset called `hospitals.RData`. The `hospitals.RData` file contains two unique variables: *hospital* and *address,* which, respectively, indicate the name of the health care institution and the address in Brazil. Therefore the dataset simulates the idea of a researcher who wants to collect GPS coordinates about some observations.

```
load("hospitals.RData")
```

To make it even easier, we will save the addresses of the hospitals contained in the object `hospitals` in a new vector:

```
hosp_address <- hospitals$address
```

We are almost ready to command the robot and collect GPS information about our dataset. We just need to create an object that will serve as a receptacle to contain the data on the latitude and longitude of the observations:

```
hosp_coordinates <- list()
```

Finally, using the knowledge acquired, mainly in Chapter 8 of this book, we can write the following algorithm that we will call `coords_extraction`:

```
coords_extraction <- function(x) {
  remote_driver$navigate(url)
  for(i in 1:length(x)) {
    remote_driver$navigate(url)
    Sys.sleep(1.5)
    place_name_form <- remote_driver$findElement(using = "id",
                                                 value = "place")
```

Continued

```
        place_name_form$sendKeysToElement(list(x[i]))
        find_button <- remote_driver$findElement(using = "id",
                                                 value = "btnfind")
        find_button$clickElement()
        Sys.sleep(3)
        latlong_results <- remote_driver$findElement(using = "id",
                                                     value = "latlngspan")
        hosp_coordinates[[i]] <<- latlong_results$getElementText()
    }
}
```

Ready! Just by having the computer connected to the Internet, we can type our function `coords_extraction`, arguing with it the vector of addresses of the hospitals of interest, that is, `hosp_address`:

```
coords_extraction(hosp_address)
```

As expected, the algorithm will take a few seconds to complete its work. As in Chapter 8, **we emphasize that the reader should not use R while the icon is visible on your console!** If you want, you can contemplate watching the browser commanded by the robot, **but we ask you not to do anything until the symbol disappears from the R console!**

When the symbol has disappeared, the latitude and longitude coordinates of our hospitals will be saved in the object `hosp_coordinates`. To add them to our dataset, we will use the function `ldply` from the package `plyr`:

```
hosp_latlong <- ldply(hosp_coordinates, data.frame)
```

An attentive reader will notice that, although the coordinate data are, in fact, in the object `hosp_latlong`, they are diagonally across the data frame. Therefore the final correction can be, for example:

```
hospitals["coordinates"] <- diag(as.matrix(hosp_latlong))
```

Finally, the reader can transform the object `hospitals` into a simple feature object in the same way as we demonstrated earlier in the "Creating a simple feature object" section.

Final considerations

In this chapter, we presented the possibilities of working in a spatial way without necessarily having an object that contains a pre-established map.

We also showed how to collect information about the latitude and longitude of observations in a common data frame, supported by a robot. After that, the reader could, for example, apply everything learned in this chapter, that is, creation of a simple feature object, application of buffering, buffer union, and kernel density techniques. The reader could also combine this object with other information he or she finds relevant by combining it, for example, with shapefiles and using everything learned in Chapter 23. In the next chapter, we will focus on another class of spatial objects: raster objects.

Supplementary data sets

```
shoppings.RData
hospitals.RData
```

Please access supplementary data files here: https://doi.org/10.17632/55623jkwrp.3

CHAPTER

25

Raster objects

AT THE END OF THIS CHAPTER, YOU WILL BE ABLE TO:

- Understand what a raster object is
- Load and use raster objects
- Combine raster objects with shapefiles
- Manipulate and cut out raster objects
- Use the raster objects in such a way as to demand less computational time for the execution of tasks
- View raster objects in R-based language

R-based language packages used in this chapter

```
library(raster)
library(tmap)
library(rgdal)
library(profvis)
```

Don't forget to define the R working directory (the location where your datasets are installed):

```
setwd("C:/book/chapter25")
```

Introduction

In this chapter, we will introduce the reader to a new kind of spatial object: raster files. Unlike a shapefile or a simple feature object, raster objects correspond to image files that contain information about each of the pixels that form them.

That said, raster files are ideal for numerous tasks. For example, they can be used when the researcher is interested in the topography of a given region, which does not have to be the surface above the sea or the surface of our planet. They can be used to establish thematic maps to analyze outbreaks of fire or deforestation or to better control areas of reforestation or environmental protection. Raster files can also be used to study phenomena resulting from tidal movements or events caused by seismologic phenomena. In short, as we have demonstrated in this book, the researcher's intuition and creativity will be the limits.

Data Science, Analytics and Machine Learning with R
https://doi.org/10.1016/B978-0-12-824271-1.00011-1

In R-based language, similar to shapefiles, raster objects are usually computationally demanding and, throughout this chapter, we will present a work proposal that can generate faster results for the reader.

We will also demonstrate how to manipulate and cut out this kind of file so the reader can best direct the computational power of his or her machine. As shown in Chapter 24, it should also be said that nothing prevents the researcher from designing a robot for the collection of data to further optimize time.

We advise the reader, whenever possible, to use the other techniques and species of objects that we present in the course of this book to enhance his or her capacity for insights, problem solving, and decision making.

Loading a raster file

To demonstrate the loading and subsequent manipulation of raster files, we will use the file `sp_geo_relief.tif`, which is located in the folder `sp_coast`. This file was taken from the public electronic collection of the Brazilian Agricultural Research Corporation (EMBRAPA), and refers to a part of the coast of the State of São Paulo, Brazil.

To load the file `sp_geo_relief.tif`, we can use the function `raster()` from the package `raster`:

```
sp_geo_relief <- raster("sp_coast/sp_geo_relief.tif")
```

As a curiosity, we ask the reader to declare the following command:

```
sp_geo_relief
```

Figure 25.1 shows the outcome of the previous command.

```
class      : RasterLayer
dimensions : 1200, 1800, 2160000  (nrow, ncol, ncell)
resolution : 0.0008333334, 0.0008333334  (x, y)
extent     : -46.50042, -45.00042, -24.00042, -23.00042  (xmin, xmax, ymin, ymax)
crs        : +proj=longlat +datum=WGS84 +no_defs
source     :
C:/Users/rafae/OneDrive/Stricto/Livro/chapter25/sp_coast/sp_geo_relief.tif
names      : sp_geo_relief
values     : 0, 1650  (min, max)
```

FIGURE 25.1 Main information about the object `sp_geo_relief`.

Figure 25.1 presents some interesting information, which we describe as follows:

- **dimensions:** refers to the dimensions of the file measured in pixels. The first value, `nrow: 1200`, indicates the number of lines that form the image. The second value, `ncol: 1800`, indicates the number of columns that form the image. The third value is `ncell: 2.160.000`, which is the result of multiplying the values of `nrow` and `ncol` and indicates how many pixels form the image.
- **resolution:** represents the size of the pixels that make up the image. As the file has a geodesic projection, oriented by longitude and latitude, it can be said that each pixel covers approximately a space of 0.0008333334 longitude by 0.0008333334 latitude.
- **extent:** concerns the total extension of the area covered by the raster file. To make it easier, when thinking in a Cartesian way, it means that the object `sp_geo_relief` concerns the area between the longitudes of 46° 30′ 1.512″ S to 45° 0′ 1.512″ S (–46.50042 to –45.00042) and latitudes 24° 0′ 1.512″ W to 23° 0′ 1.512″ W (–24.00042 to –23.00042).
- **crs:** concerns the geographic reference system used by the object.
- **values:** depend directly on the matter treated by the raster file. As our example is about the São Paulo relief, the attributes `min` and `max` relate to the altitudes, in meters, of the geographic formations.

Plotting the raster file information

To graphically view the object `sp_geo_relief`, we ask the reader to simply type the following command:

```
plot(sp_geo_relief)
```

Figure 25.2 shows the result of the previous command.

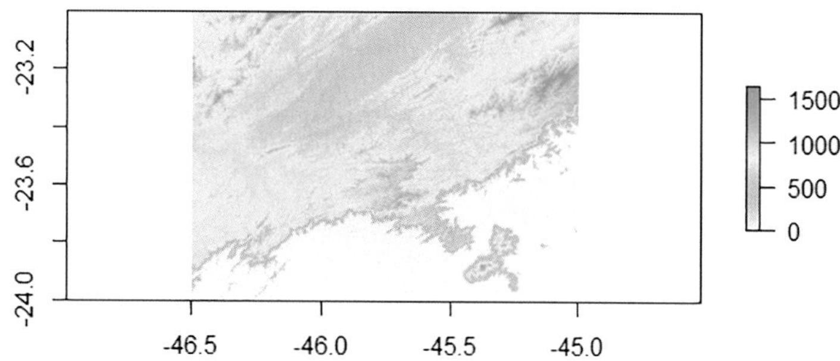

FIGURE 25.2 Object view `sp_geo_relief`.

Figure 25.2 shows the relief composition of part of the coast of the State of São Paulo evidencing, by color, the altitudes of the geographic formations; the figure also shows the geographic range covered by the object `sp_geo_relief`. From here, we can establish a histogram regarding the altitudes studied:

```
hist(x = sp_geo_relief,
     main = "",
     xlab = "Elevation",
     ylab = "Frequency",
     col = "orange",
     maxpixels = sp_geo_relief@ncols * sp_geo_relief@nrows)
```

Figure 25.3 shows the result of the previous code.

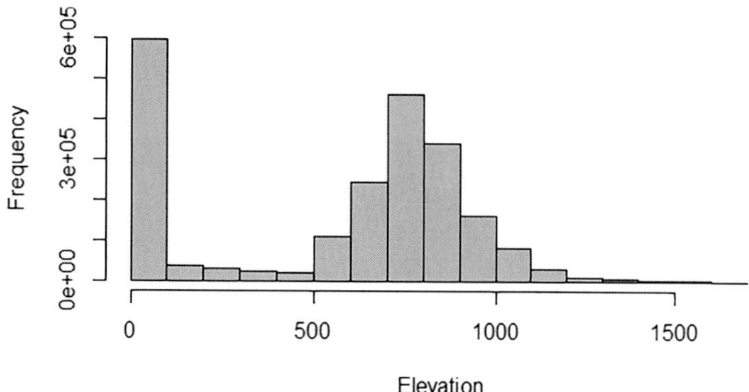

FIGURE 25.3 Histogram of the altitudes of the geographic formations present in the object `sp_geo_relief`.

Returning to Figure 25.2, although the function `plot()` accomplished what we expected, the `image()` function has greater visual capacity for working with images, being indicated for more robust raster objects. We ask the reader to execute the following command:

```
image(x = sp_geo_relief)
```

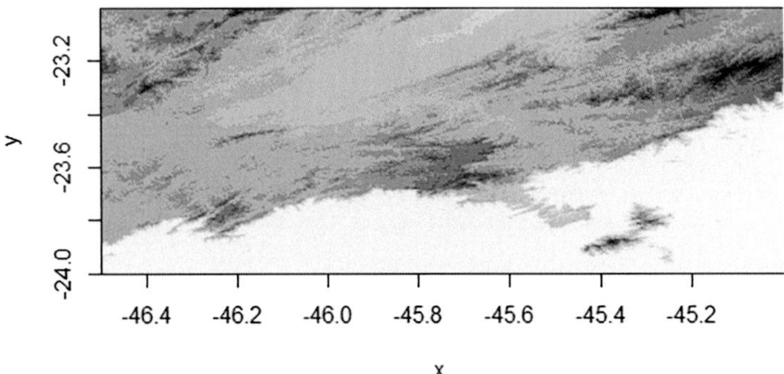

FIGURE 25.4 Using the function `image()`.

Figure 25.4 shows the result of the previous command.

We can make the visualization more elegant with the use of the attributes `xlab`, `ylab`, and `main`, according to the following code:

```
image(x = sp_geo_relief,
      xlab = "Longitude",
      ylab = "Latitude",
      main = "Part of The São Paulo's Coastline")
```

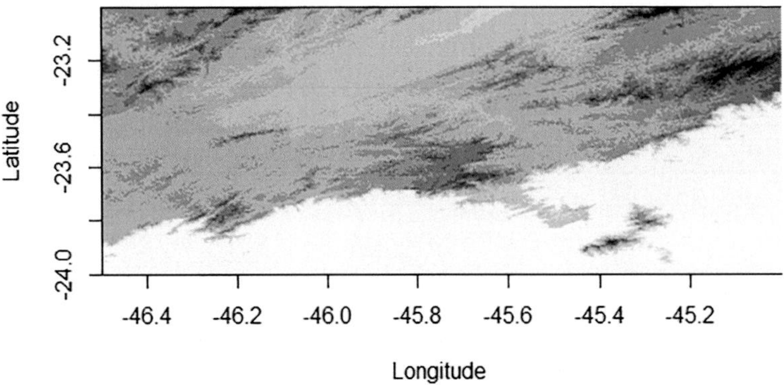

FIGURE 25.5 Adding information with the function `image()`.

Figure 25.5 shows the result, with a change in the nomenclatures of the graph and its respective axes.

The function `image()` also allows you to specify other colors in your results when combined with the function `terrain.colors()`. That way, we can type the following command:

```
image(x = sp_geo_relief,
      xlab = "Longitude",
      ylab = "Latitude",
      main = "Part of the São Paulo Coastline",
      col = terrain.colors(n = 10))
```

In the previous command, the argument `col` of the function `image()` tells R which colors to use, while a value of 10 argued to the function `terrain.colors()` tells the number of colors to be used. Figure 25.6 demonstrates the result of the previous command.

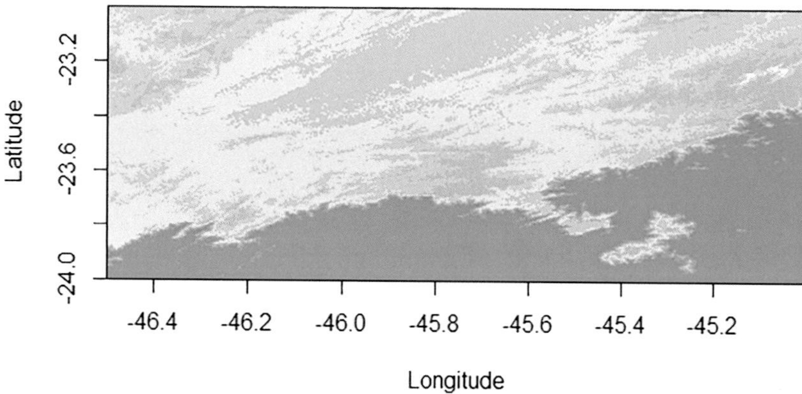

FIGURE 25.6 Changing colors with the function `image()`.

We can also delimit, for this case, the minimum and maximum altitudes to be plotted using the argument `zlim`. Suppose we are only interested in areas with a maximum altitude of 800 m. In this way, we can type the following command:

```
image(x = sp_geo_relief,
      xlab = "Longitude",
      ylab = "Latitude",
      main = "Part of the São Paulo Coastline",
      col = terrain.colors(n = 10),
      zlim = c(0,800))
```

The argument `zlim` delimited the visual presentation of the areas, so only those that are from 0 m to 800 m in altitude are presented. Figure 25.7 shows the result of the previous command.

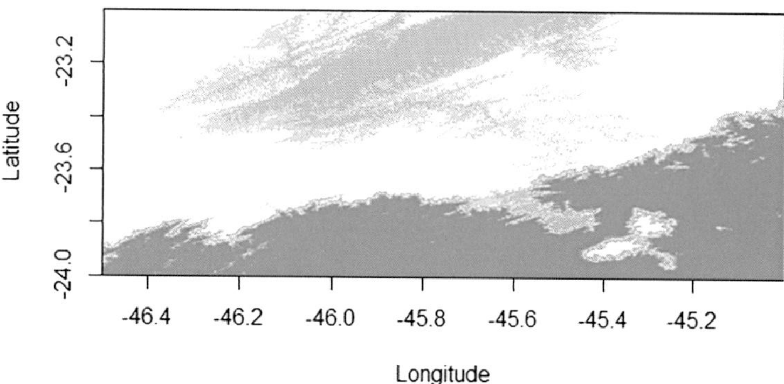

FIGURE 25.7 Delimiting values to be displayed with the function `image()`.

In Figure 25.7, the parts shown in white extrapolate, for more and less, the altitude limits imposed by the argument `zlim`.

For an even greater gain of information, we can use the function `tm_raster()` in a similar way to the set of functions from the package `tmap` previously presented, as proposed here:

```
tm_shape(shp = sp_geo_relief) +
  tm_raster(style = "quantile",
            n = 5) +
  tm_layout(legend.position = c("left", "bottom"),
            legend.outside = TRUE)
```

The commanded routine forced R to divide the altitudes into quintiles due to the combination of the arguments `style = "quantile"` and `n = 5` applied to the function `tm_raster()`. The function `tm_layout()`, on the other hand, helped us so the legend was not placed on our map. Figure 25.8 shows the result of the previous code.

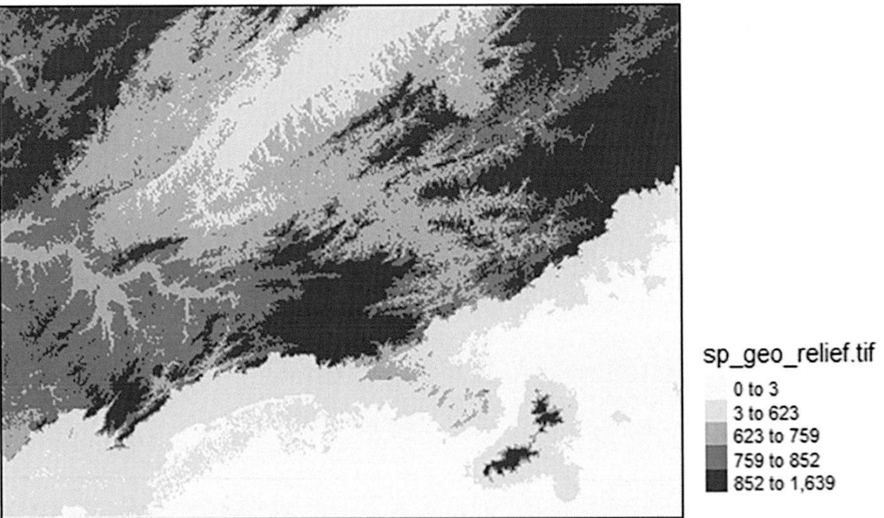

FIGURE 25.8 Implementation of features from the package `tmap` to a `raster` object.

Combining a raster object with a shapefile

Remember the São Paulo State shapefile we used in Chapter 23? We propose to combine it with visualization of the raster object `sp_geo_relief`. To recharge it, simply type the following command:

```
sp_map <- readOGR(dsn = "shapefile_sp", layer = "state_of_sp")
```

Next, we propose the following command that may take slightly longer to complete:

```
tm_shape(shp = sp_geo_relief) +
  tm_raster(style = "quantile", n = 5) +
  tm_shape(shp = sp_map) +
  tm_borders() +
  tm_layout(legend.position = c("left", "bottom"),
            legend.outside = TRUE)
```

Figure 25.9 shows the result of the previous command.

In addition to exposure of the division of municipalities, note how R knew precisely which part of the shapefile we should use to combine it with the raster object. Figure 25.9 also shows, more clearly, the municipality of Ilhabela (the big island on the map) and the Atlantic Ocean.

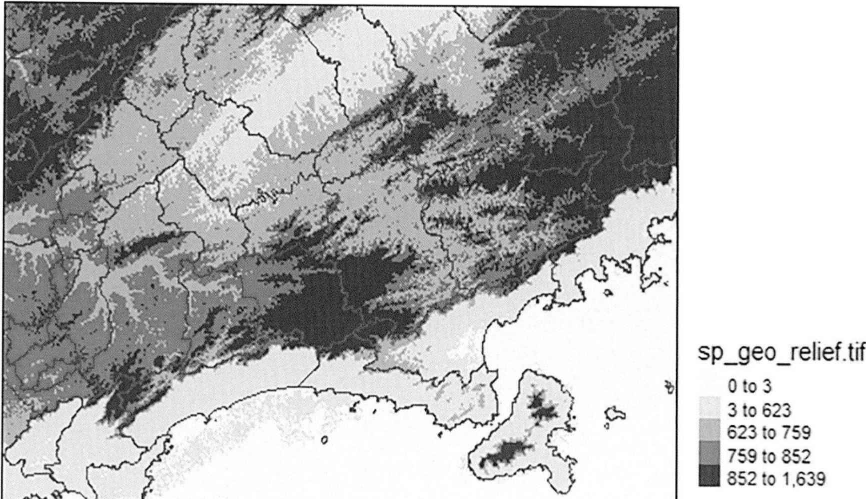

FIGURE 25.9 Combining a shapefile with a raster object.

Loading raster objects entirely into the computer's RAM

As we have already pointed out, the package raster does not usually load the raster objects in their completeness all at once. This device is interesting for machines that have too little RAM to do this type of spatial analysis, but there is a trade-off with an increase in time for execution of tasks.

The other examples belonging to this chapter require greater computational power, so we will teach the reader to force the package raster to open objects completely in the computer's RAM. We advise against the following procedure if the reader's machine has 6 GB or less of RAM in view of the high possibility of locking the machine. Even so, if you decide to go ahead, be aware that it is at your own risk.

If the reader has a computer with a larger amount of RAM, we suggest turning it off for a while, restarting it, and ensuring that no other program beyond RStudio is open. Remember to define the working directory, load the package raster, and load the object sp_geo_relief.

To check if the object sp_geo_relief is already completely open in the machine's RAM, we will use the function inMemory() from the package raster, typing the command as follows:

```
inMemory(x = sp_geo_relief)
```

After the previous command, R must answer the reader the logical value FALSE, indicating that the object sp_geo_relief is not completely loaded in the computer's RAM. For our objective to be fulfilled, we must use the function readAll() from the package raster:

```
mem_sp_geo_relief <- readAll(object = sp_geo_relief)
```

Next, we will use the function inMemory() again, but applied to the newly created object mem_sp_geo_relief:

```
inMemory(x = mem_sp_geo_relief)
```

If everything went well, this time the R will respond to the researcher with the logical value TRUE.

To demonstrate the time savings that the proposed device gives, we will use the package profvis. The package profvis has interesting resources to measure the time and memory spent for a given task in R. We propose a simple calculation of the univariate statistics of the altitudes of the geographic formations of the objects sp_geo_relief and mem_sp_geo_relief, just to evidence the gain of computational power obtained. We also propose that this simple calculation be repeated 10 times to stress the results:

```
#sp_geo_relief

info_sp_geo_relief <- profvis({
  for (i in 1:10) {
    summary(sp_geo_relief[])
    print(i)
  }
})
```

Next:

```
#mem_sp_geo_relief

info_mem_sp_geo_relief <- profvis({
  for (i in 1:10) {
    summary(mem_sp_geo_relief[])
    print(i)
  }
})
```

After that, the reader can type the following command:

```
info_sp_geo_relief
```

In the new open window, the reader can click *Data* to access the amount of memory and time used to build the object `info_sp_geo_relief`.

After that, the reader can type:

```
info_sp_geo_relief
```

Similar to what we did for the previous case, the reader should also click *Data* to observe the time and memory used for the object `info_mem_sp_geo_relief`.

Figure 25.10 compares the results obtained for the objects `info_sp_geo_relief` and `info_mem_sp_geo_relief`.

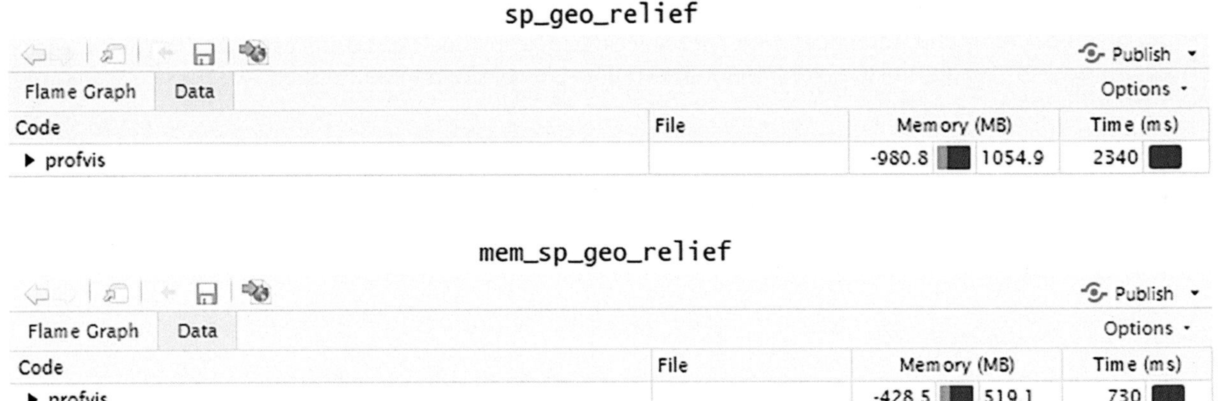

FIGURE 25.10 Comparison of RAM and time spent to calculate univariate statistics for objects `sp_geo_relief` and `mem_sp_geo_relief`, iterated 10 times.

Figure 25.10 shows the gain in processing and time. The *Memory* column is measured in MB and the *Time* column in milliseconds. The machine used for the test had 16 GB of RAM with an Intel Core i5-8265U processor.

After the operations presented in this section, it is not uncommon for R to present the error exposed by Figure 25.11,

```
Error in graphics::locator(n = 1, type = "p", pch = "+", col = col) :
  plot.new has not been called yet
```

FIGURE 25.11 Possible error presented by R after executing the commands of this chapter.

especially when we command a plot of a graph.

If the situation indicated by Figure 25.11 occurs, it will be sufficient to type the following command:

```
plot.new()
```

Then, you can return to using the graphical capabilities of R, as usual. If R insists on the error indicated in Figure 25.11, the reader should close RStudio and then reopen it.

Cutting out raster objects

There are some interesting ways to cut a raster object in R. We will quote below some ways that we think are more practical.

Cutting out raster objects with the aid of a mouse

The first way to cut out raster objects using the mouse is to use the function `drawExtent()` from the package `raster`, which will return rectangular shapes. Initially, you must plot the object `mem_sp_geo_relief` (if you have chosen not to command the codes in the "Loading raster objects entirely into the computer's RAM" section, just use the object `sp_geo_relief`) with the function `plot()`, as follows:

```
plot(mem_sp_geo_relief)
```

Next, you must create a new object, which we call `mouse_cut_1`, which contains the function `drawExtent()`:

```
mouse_selection_1 <- drawExtent()
```

At the precise moment of the previous command, the R console will indicate that the software is busy due to the icon ●. The reader should ignore the situation and place the mouse cursor on the *Plots* tab. Notice that the cursor, instead of the format ↖, has taken on the shape +. That said, you must click the upper-left part of the graph, indicating where the cutout should start, and then on the bottom right, indicating where it should end. Figure 25.12 demonstrates an example of the statement.

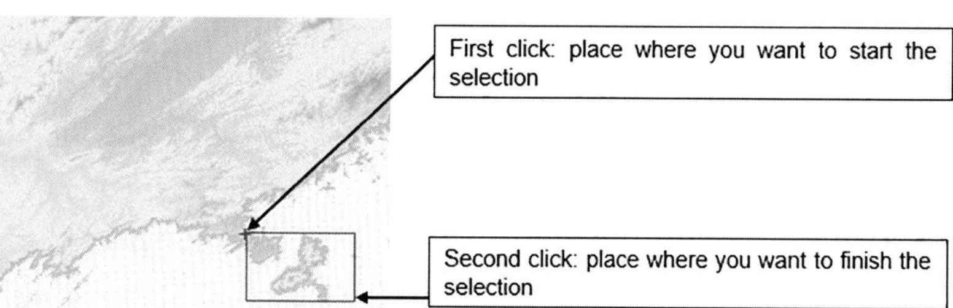

FIGURE 25.12 Cutting out raster objects in a rectangular shape.

Then, we must save the clipping as follows, using the function `crop()` from the package `raster`:

```
selection_1 <- crop(x = mem_sp_geo_relief, y = mouse_selection_1)
```

It can be verified that the proposed objective was reached by plotting the new object `selection_1`:

```
plot(selection_1)
```

Figure 25.13 shows the result of the previous command.

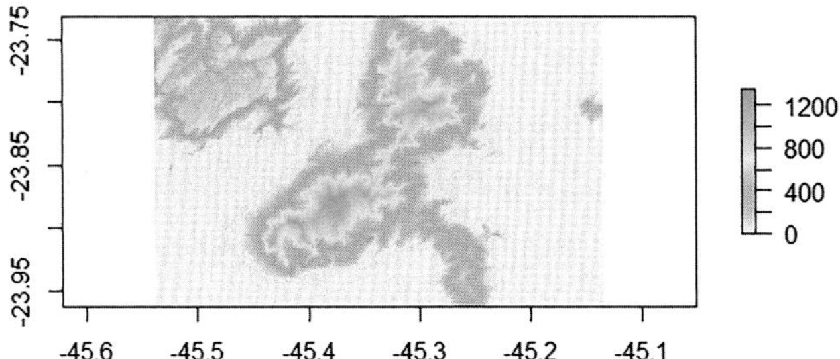

FIGURE 25.13 Example of a rectangular clipping of a raster object.

If you want a cutout in a format that is not necessarily rectangular, you can use the function `select()` from the package `raster`, combined with the argument `use = "pol"`. As a curiosity, the argument `use = "rec"` combined with the referenced function `select()` generates effects similar to the use of the function `drawExtent()`, mentioned earlier. That said, we must type the following command:

```
plot(mem_sp_geo_relief)
```

Then:

```
selection_2 <- select(x = mem_sp_geo_relief, use = "pol")
```

Immediately, after the command, R will indicate that it is busy with the icon present on your console. Similar to the previous technique, we will use the mouse cursor to click the vertices of the desired clippings on the *Plots* tab. Figure 25.14 demonstrates the previous example.

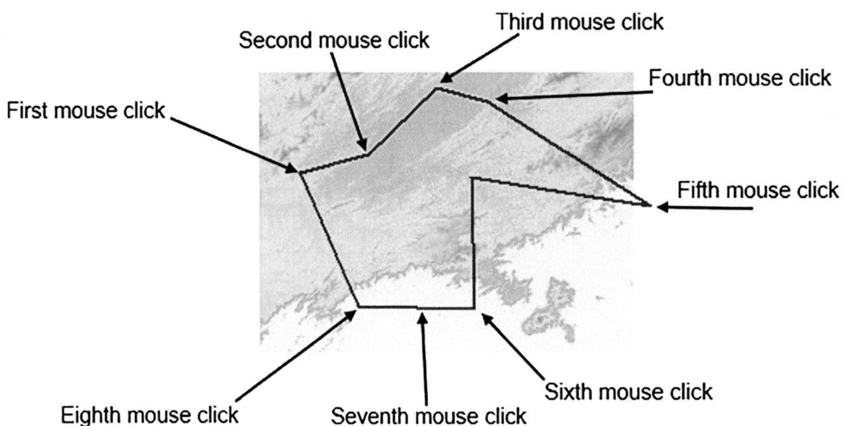

FIGURE 25.14 Clipping freeform raster objects.

You may have already noticed that R does not leave clicks marked on the screen while they are still occurring, which makes it very difficult to trace drawings with greater precision. Furthermore, because polygons are closed figures, that is, with connected vertices, the mentioned feature of R-based language makes use of the technique even more difficult.

So, when you are satisfied with the number of clicks, just press the Esc key on the keyboard. The final result can be viewed with the following code:

```
plot(selection_2)
```

Figure 25.15 shows the image present in Figure 25.14 already cropped.

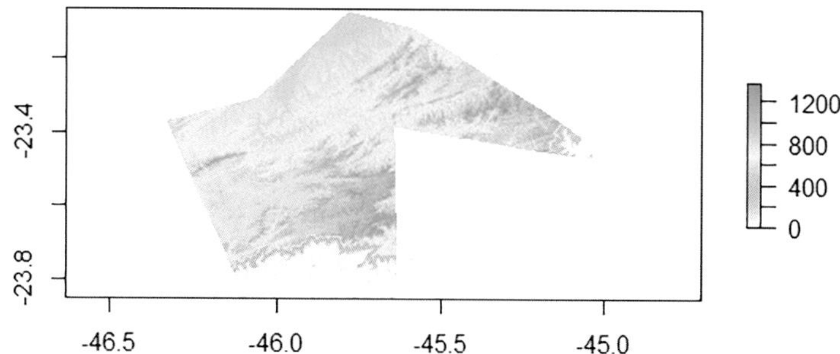

FIGURE 25.15 Example of free clipping of a raster object.

Cutting raster objects with vector aid

Another form of clipping can be done using, as delimiters, the geographical coordinates of the area to be cut. Thinking in a Cartesian way, we will first establish the minimum and maximum values of the abscissa axis—in our case, the longitudes. Then, we will establish the minimum and maximum values of the ordinate axis—the latitudes in the example used.

Suppose we want the area between the minimum longitudes 45° 30′ 37,512″ S and maximum longitudes 45° 11′ 13,488″ S and the minimum latitudes 23° 57′ 25,488" W and maximum latitudes 23° 44′ 28,500″ W. Thus:

```
coords.selection <- c(-45.51042, -45.18708, -23.95708, -23.74125)
```

Next, we must use the function `crop()`:

```
selection_3 <- crop(x = mem_sp_geo_relief, y = coords_selection)
```

To visualize the result, we will type the following command:

```
plot(selection_3)
```

Final considerations

In this chapter, we introduced the reader to a new kind of spatial object. We demonstrated its usefulness and the possibility of manipulation and combination with other spatial objects.

We also pointed out a way to explore your machine's RAM to save time in the results presented by R. We presented the customization techniques of clipping raster objects to decrease computational demand for analysis of these objects.

In any case, it is true that Chapters 23, 24, and this chapter only scratched the surface of what can be called an *exploratory spatial data analysis,* but the knowledge shared in this chapters will be essential to continue reading in the following chapters and choose the best ways to solve your research problems.

In the next chapters, regardless of the use of shapefiles, simple features objects, or raster files, the reader will learn to identify, analyze, and interpret spatial patterns.

CHAPTER

26

Exploratory spatial analysis

AT THE END OF THIS CHAPTER, YOU WILL BE ABLE TO:

- Understand the concept of neighborhood.
- Establish spatially weighted neighborhood matrices.
- Standardize spatially weighted neighborhood matrices, when necessary.
- Interpose an exploratory spatial analysis.
- Differentiate global autocorrelations from local autocorrelations.
- Measure and plot identified autocorrelations in thematic maps.

R-based language packages used in this chapter

```
library(rgdal)
library(sp)
library(spdep)
library(tmap)
```

Don't forget to define the R working directory (the location where your datasets are installed):

```
setwd("C:/book/chapter26")
```

Introduction

In the sections to come, we will present some econometrics techniques designed to study phenomena when researchers wish to take into account spatial aspects and biases. The central idea derives from the so-called *First Law of Geography*, postulated by Tobler (1970): "Everything is related to everything else, but near things are more related than distant things."

Starting from Tobler's First Law of Geography, with these techniques we could, for example, study poverty in a spatial way to understand whether and how poverty or wealth in neighboring municipalities affect our municipality. We could try to understand if and how the performance of sectors of a given company influence each other. We could

Data Science, Analytics and Machine Learning with R
https://doi.org/10.1016/B978-0-12-824271-1.00014-7

try to understand the adoption of animal migration routes or try to relate outbreaks of epidemics with income and education issues. There is no lack of possibilities, and the creativity linked to the well-defined methodology and the underlying theory will be great tools for the research that the reader wants to carry out.

It is clear from Tobler's First Law of Geography that a certain degree of influence of a phenomenon is due to proximity or distance. Thus we will present some ways to quantify these measures that go beyond the most usual metric systems. For example, it is true that we could measure the distance between São Paulo and Rio de Janeiro (the two biggest cities in Brazil) in kilometers or miles, but we could also verify this magnitude by their respective social, economic, political, or environmental differences. The choice of the metric for the distance between observations, in fact, will depend on the research purposes.

Despite the amount of econometric techniques available, our purpose here is to cover univariate and bivariate exploratory statistics in the sense of creating interest in the reader that allows continued study regarding this type of methodology.

First of all, as in any statistical study, it is essential to implement an exploratory analysis. When studying the spatialities of a given phenomenon, therefore, we must carry out what the literature calls *exploratory spatial data analysis* (ESDA). As discussed by Piatkowska et al. (2018), ESDA aims to facilitate the identification and visualization of spatial patterns of a given phenomenon, as shown in Figure 26.1.

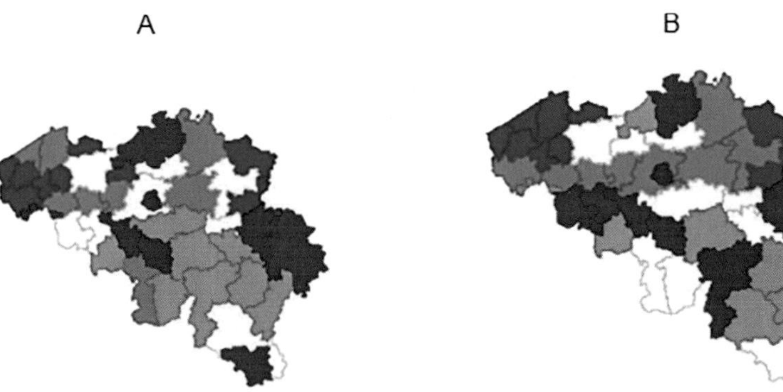

FIGURE 26.1 Evolution of crime in Belgium between 2006 and 2012. *Source: Piatkowska, S.J., Messner, S.F., Yang, T-C., 2018. Xenophobic and racially motivated crime in Belgium: exploratory spatial data analysis and spatial regressions of structural covariates. Deviant Behav. 39 (11), 1398–1418.*

Figure 26.1 addresses the evolution of crime rates in Belgium. Part A represents the period from 2000 to 2006, and part B represents the period from 2007 to 2012. Dark red indicates the areas with the highest crime rates, and dark blue indicates the areas with the lowest crime rates.

Some spatial patterns also can be seen in this figure. The reader may notice that areas with the highest crime rate commonly have neighboring areas with higher crime rates. Similarly, areas with low crime rates tend to cluster around areas with lower crime rates.

The construction of the maps was possible, first, because a neighborhood criterion was defined. A spatial weights matrix **W** must be proposed so it will be possible to study and verify the spatial autocorrelations of the phenomenon, globally and locally. This is precisely our proposal in this chapter.

There are many multivariate spatial econometric techniques, but they are not the target at this moment. The intention is to arouse the reader's curiosity for a data analytics area that has been developing strongly in recent years: *spatial analysis*.

Establishing neighborhoods

The first step to carry out an ESDA is establishment of the neighborhoods between the studied locations so, for example, we can verify the spatial autocorrelations, point out some heterogeneities, and even detect outliers.

As Anselin and Rey (2014) argue, the establishment of neighborhoods is done by a spatial weights matrix **W** that can assume several types, the most common of which are contiguity, geographic proximity, and socioeconomic proximity matrices. In the following section, we will demonstrate some possible examples of spatial weights matrices **W**.

Contiguity spatial weights matrix W

The idea of contiguity is based on the assumption that there is a common physical border between regions. In this sense, it can be said that Brazil is contiguous to Argentina, but not to China, for example. Based on this premise, a *contiguity spatial matrix* is a **W** matrix with binary values in which the value 1 is assigned in the presence of a common physical boundary, and zero is assigned for the absence of a common physical boundary. Mathematically, we can describe its terms w_{ij} as follows:

$$w_{ij} = \begin{cases} 1, \text{if there is contiguity between i and j;} \\ 0, \text{otherwise.} \end{cases} \tag{26.1}$$

where $w_{ii}=0$, by convention.

Contiguity between elements w_{ij} can be established by several criteria, and the definition of which one to use must take into account the reader's objectives, supported by an underlying theory. The most common conventions are the *queen*, the *bishop*, and the *rook (castle tower)*. The names are not coincidences and refer to contiguities based on the movement of the chess pieces.

In chess, the *queen* can, without distinction, move horizontally, vertically, and diagonally. Thus under the *queen* convention, all observations that share a physical boundary with these directions will be considered neighbors. In the case of the *bishop* convention in chess, the *bishop* moves only diagonally; thus there will be contiguity in observations that share physical boundaries by their vertices. Finally, the *rook* convention follows the movements of the chess *rook* to establish neighbors; the piece moves only horizontally or vertically, and, as such, there will be a neighborhood only when borders with sizes other than zero can be considered. Figure 26.2 exemplifies the establishment of *queen*, *bishop*, and *rook* neighborhoods.

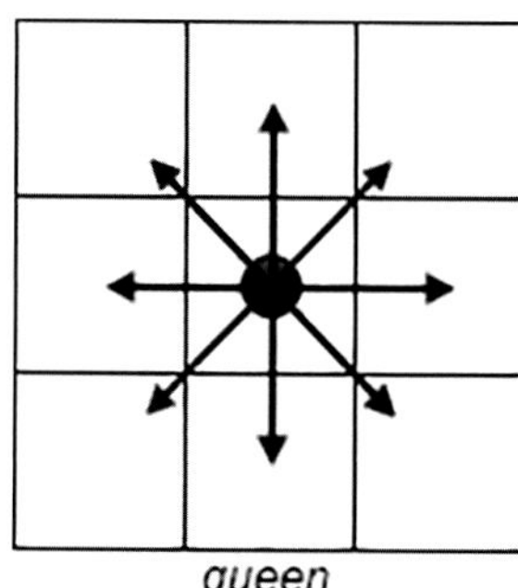

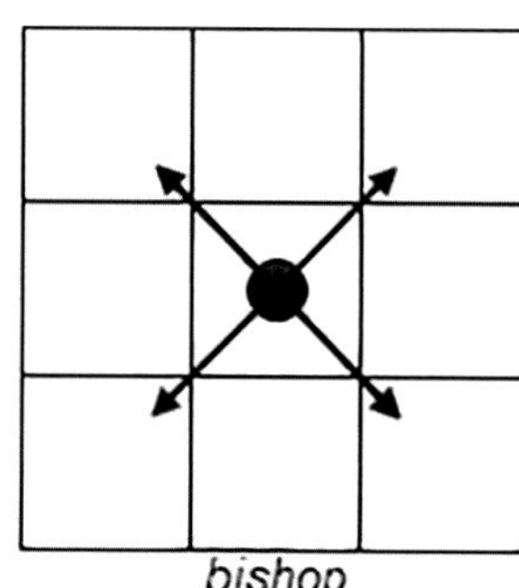

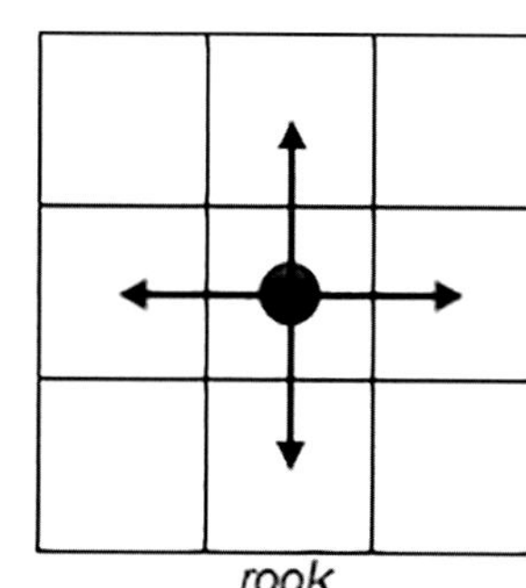

FIGURE 26.2 Establishment of neighborhoods, respectively, with the *queen*, *bishop*, and *rook* conventions.

Almeida (2012) raises the advantages and disadvantages of the spatial weights matrices **W** based on the contiguity criterion. According to the author, contiguity matrices have the advantage of defining, more clearly, the second- and third-order neighbors if one wants to consider them neighbors of neighbors and neighbors of neighbors of neighbors, respectively. Almeida continues pointing out that the main disadvantage of this type of artifice is that a balanced number of neighbors is not guaranteed for each observation, that is, the municipality of Ilhabela in the state of São Paulo, Brazil, has no physical borders with any other city because it is an island; thus its number of neighbors k is zero.

We propose an example of establishing neighbors by comparing *queen* and *rook* conventions. First, we ask the reader to load the same shapefile from the state of São Paulo (folder *shapefile_sp*) used in Chapter 23, as follows:

```
sp_map <- readOGR(dsn = "shapefile_sp", layer = "state_of_sp")
```

Next, we can use the function `poly2nb()` from the package `spdep` to establish our neighborhood matrix **W**, based on the *queen* criterion:

```
neighborhood_queen <- poly2nb(pl = sp_map,
                              queen = TRUE,
                              row.names = sp_map$NM_MUNICIP)
```

For the function `poly2nb()`, in the argument `pl`, we must indicate the set of polygons (i.e., a shapefile) in which the neighborhood is to be established. Additionally, in the argument `queen`, we must indicate `TRUE` if we want a matrix **W** with the *queen* contiguity criterion and indicate `FALSE` for a matrix **W** with the *rook* contiguity criterion. Finally, in the argument `row.names`, we point out the name of the municipalities present in the shapefile used to better verify the neighborhoods in the matrix form.

As for the visualization of the constructed matrix, we ask the reader for patience because of the specificities of R-based language. At this moment, the code that explains it is not intuitive at all. Later, in this section, we will demonstrate how the reader can visualize the constructed matrix **W**.

On the other hand, for the reader to visually join our shapefile to the neighborhood established by the *queen* criterion present in the object `neighborhood_queen`, we must type:

```
plot(sp_map, border = "lightgray")
```

And then:

```
plot(neighborhood_queen, coordinates(sp_map), add = TRUE, col = "orange")
```

Figure 26.3 shows the municipalities of the state of São Paulo, Brazil, that are first-order neighbors, according to the *queen* contiguity convention.

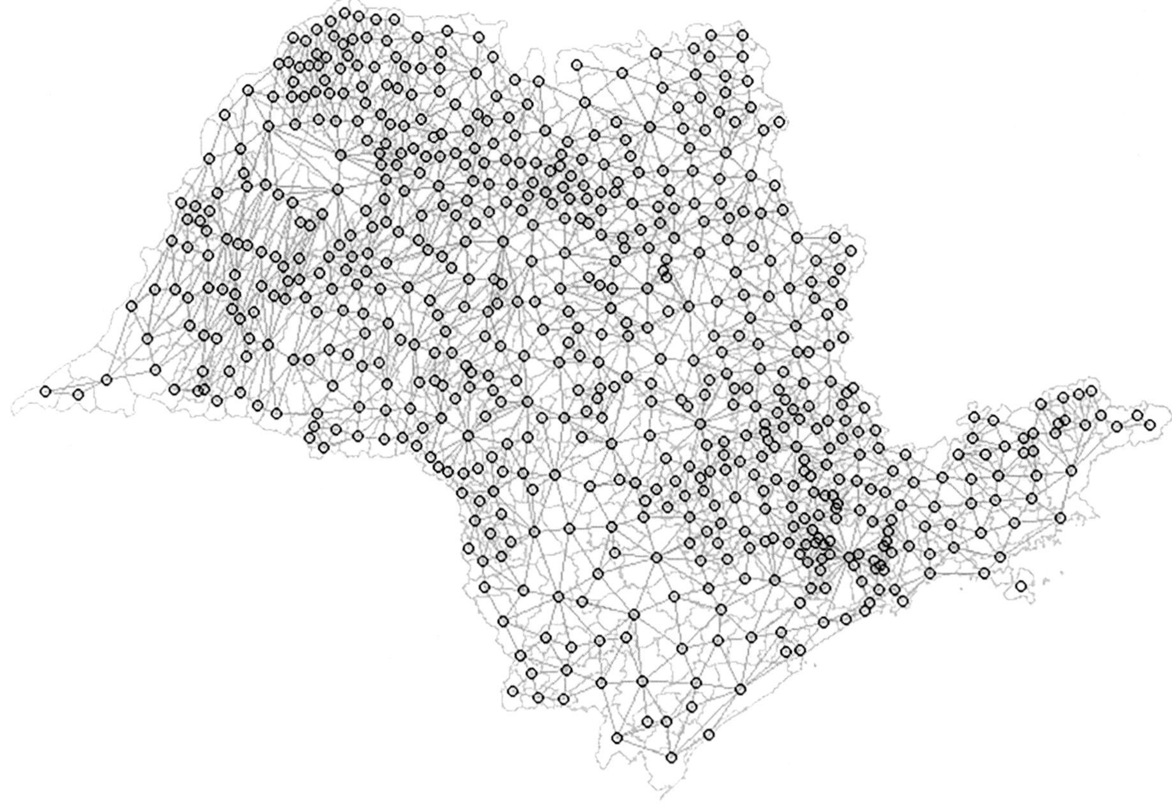

FIGURE 26.3 Neighborhood of municipalities in the state of São Paulo established by the *queen* convention.

In a preliminary analysis, it is possible to see that, in fact, there is an island without neighborhoods (the point without connecting lines to the right), as previously stated by Almeida (2012). It is possible to reinforce this fact by applying the function `summary()` to the object `neighborhood_queen`:

```
summary(neighborhood_queen)
```

Figure 26.4 shows the result of the previous command.

```
Neighbour list object:
Number of regions: 645
Number of nonzero links: 3664
Percentage nonzero weights: 0.8807163
Average number of links: 5.68062
1 region with no links:
ILHABELA
Link number distribution:

  0   1   2   3   4   5   6   7   8   9  10  11  12  14  23
  1   2  19  53 116 143 119  89  43  28  19   8   2   2   1
2 least connected regions:
ÁGUAS DE SÃO PEDRO ITIRAPUÃ with 1 link
1 most connected region:
SÃO PAULO with 23 links
```

FIGURE 26.4 Information on the neighborhood of the municipalities of the state of São Paulo established by the *queen* convention.

The outcomes in Figure 26.4 are very useful because they inform us that there are 645 locations on the map (`Number of regions`) and that the average number of neighbors, according to the *queen* convention, is 5.68062 (`Average number of links`). The results also show that the matrix **W** is 88.07% filled by the value 1 (`Percentage nonzero weights`) and that the municipality of Ilhabela has no neighbors (`1 region with no links`).

Figure 26.4 also shows a table of frequencies of the number of connections among observations (`Link number distribution`), that is, there is 1 location without neighbors, 2 locations with 1 neighbor, 19 locations with 2 neighbors, and so on.

Under the *queen* convention, R shows at the bottom of Figure 26.4 the municipalities with the lowest number of connections and the largest number of connections (those with no connection are not considered here). Águas de São Pedro and Itirapuã have the lowest number of connections with 1 connection, and the city of São Paulo has the largest number of connections with 23 connections.

Additionally, we can type the following:

```
View(neighborhood_queen)
```

Figure 26.5 shows the results of the previous command.

Name	Type	Value
vizinhos	list [645] (S3: nb)	List of length 645
[[1]]	integer [4]	6 12 16 17
[[2]]	integer [5]	13 23 632 639 641
[[3]]	integer [6]	11 14 17 18 26 640
[[4]]	integer [3]	20 24 642
[[5]]	integer [2]	19 25
[[6]]	integer [7]	1 7 14 16 17 22 ...
[[7]]	integer [5]	6 15 20 22 25
[[8]]	integer [5]	10 23 26 640 641
[[9]]	integer [3]	633 642 645
[[10]]	integer [4]	8 21 23 26
[[11]]	integer [5]	3 12 17 21 26

FIGURE 26.5 Result of the command `view(neighborhood_queen)`.

In the first column of Figure 26.5, the municipalities present in the object `sp_map` are sorted. In the last column are the cities with which the municipality in the left column establishes neighborhoods. Note that the *queen* convention, by itself, does not bring a balanced neighborhood because there are municipalities with different numbers of neighbors.

From here, we can establish and visualize our matrix **W** using the function `nb2mat()` from the package `spdep`:

```
W_matrix_queen <- nb2mat(neighbours = neighborhood_queen,
                         style = "B")
```

Note, however, that R returned an error! The error concerns the existence of polygons without a defined neighborhood, in this case, the municipality of Ilhabela. **The function `nb2mat()`, by default, does not accept drawing spatial weights matrices when there are observations without neighbors.** To force the algorithm to perform the task, we can use the argument `zero.policy`, as follows:

```
W_matrix_queen <- nb2mat(neighbours = neighborhood_queen,
                         style = "B",
                         zero.policy = TRUE)
```

The argument `style` refers to the type of weighting to be used. According to Expression (26.1), the value `"B"` indicates a basic binary matrix; the value `"C"` would return a globally standardized matrix; and the value `"W"` would determine the establishment of a matrix standardized in rows. For other types of weights for matrices **W**, we suggest that the reader type `?nb2mat`. **We will discuss the standardization of matrices W in the "Standardization of matrices" section, when different statements of the value `"B"` in the argument `style` will make more sense.**

If we wanted to establish a new neighborhood, but this time through the use of the *rook* criterion, we must type:

```
neighborhood_rook <- poly2nb(pl = sp_map,
                             queen = FALSE,
                             row.names = sp_map$NM_MUNICIP)
```

To plot the new type of neighborhood, we must type again:

```
plot(sp_map, border = "lightgray")
```

Right after, we must indicate our new object `neighborhood_rook` that follows the *rook* convention:

```
plot(neighborhood_rook, coordinates(sp_map), add = TRUE, col = "darkorchid")
```

Figure 26.6 presents the results of the previous codes, showing the neighborhoods among the municipalities of the state of São Paulo through the *rook* convention.

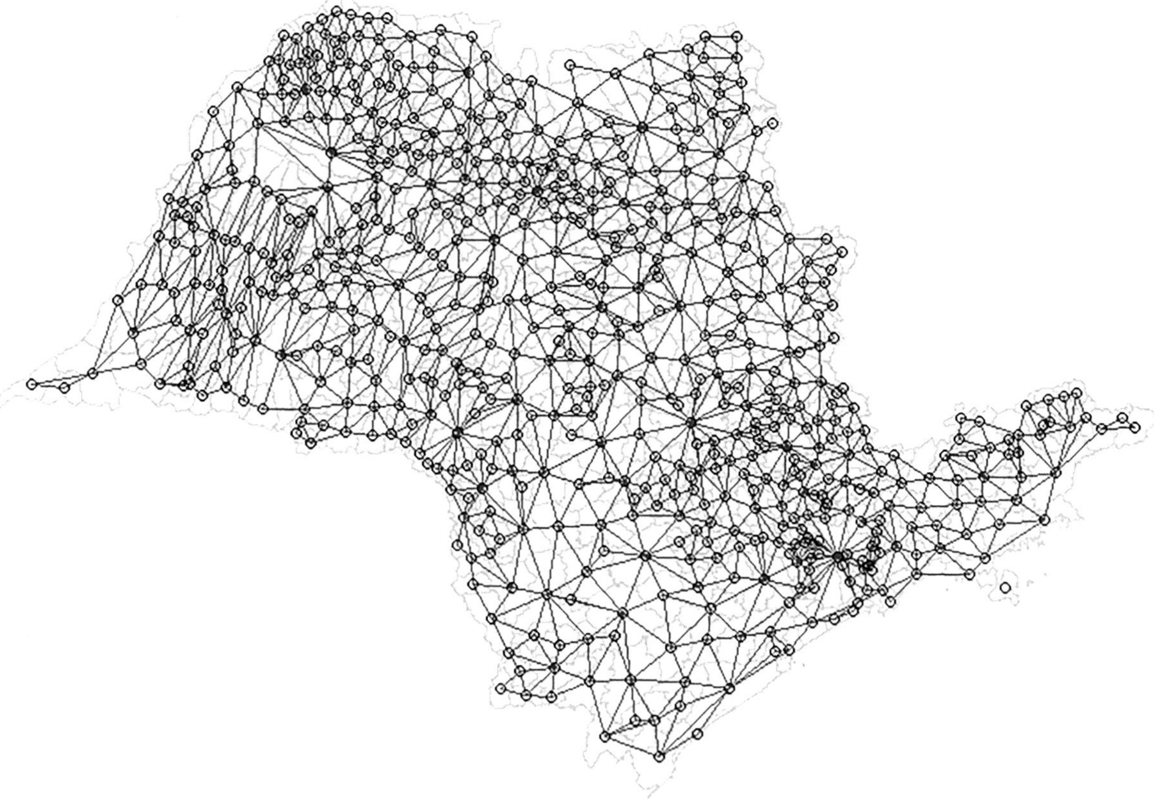

FIGURE 26.6 Neighborhood of municipalities in the state of São Paulo established by the *rook* convention.

Comparing Figure 26.3 with Figure 26.6, it is clear that the first is more visually polluted, and this is because the *rook* convention does not establish neighborhoods with observations that make physical boundaries only by its vertices. It is also noticable, without surprise, that the municipality of Ilhabela continues without the establishment of neighbors.

We can also compare the information of the object `neighborhood_rook` with the object `neighborhood_queen`, as follows:

```
summary(neighborhood_rook)
```

Figure 26.7 shows the results of the previous command.

```
Neighbour list object:
Number of regions: 645
Number of nonzero links: 3556
Percentage nonzero weights: 0.8547563
Average number of links: 5.513178
1 region with no links:
ILHABELA
Link number distribution:

  0   1   2   3   4   5   6   7   8   9  10  11  14  21
  1   2  19  64 120 149 119  84  36  26  16   6   2   1
2 least connected regions:
ÁGUAS DE SÃO PEDRO ITIRAPUÃ with 1 link
1 most connected region:
SÃO PAULO with 21 links
```

FIGURE 26.7 Information on the neighborhood of the municipalities of the state of São Paulo established by the *rook* convention.

As expected, the results present in Figure 26.7 point us to an average number of neighbors (`Average number of links`) lower than that showed in Figure 26.4. It is also less than the presence of values equal to 1 in the matrix **W** (`Number of nonzero links`) if it is elaborated based on the *rook* convention: approximately 85.48%.

Finally, we can establish and visualize our matrix **W** with the *rook* convention, as follows:

```
W_matrix_rook <- nb2mat(neighbors = neighborhood_rook,
                        style = "B",
                        zero.policy = TRUE)
```

Geographic proximity spatial weights matrix W

The criterion of the geographic distance can be an interesting way to promote the balance of neighbors among observations. From this perspective, a distance $d_i(k)$ should be established, which is the threshold for the establishment of k neighbors for a given region i. As Almeida (2012) points out, the idea of this type of matrix is the premise that geographically closer regions have greater spatial interaction.

For the geographic distance criterion, the elements w_{ij} of the matrix **W** can be mathematically defined by:

$$w_{ij}(k) = \begin{cases} 1, \text{for cases where } \mathrm{d}_{ij} \leq \mathrm{d}_i(k); \\ 0, \text{for cases where } \mathrm{d}_{ij} > \mathrm{d}_i(k). \end{cases} \tag{26.2}$$

where $w_{ii}=0$, by convention.

The greatest difficulty in establishing this type of matrix **W** is to define the ideal cutoff for $d_i(k)$. To avoid this problem, Anselin and Rey (2014) recommend that we define **W** based on the k-nearest neighbors criterion, where k is the same for all observations.

Next, we will present how to establish a geographic proximity spatial weights matrix **W**. Based on the objectives of research and supported by an underlying theory, suppose we conclude that observations distant from each other will be neighbors until the threshold of 40 km. For this activity, we can use the function `dnearneigh()` from the package `spdep`, as follows:

```
neighborhood_dist <- dnearneigh(x = coordinates(sp_map),
                                d1 = 0,
                                d2 = 40,
                                longlat = TRUE)
```

In the previous command, we used the function `coordinates()` in the function `dnearneigh()` to extract the longitude and latitude, respectively, of each municipality in the state of São Paulo present in the object `sp_map`. The arguments `d1` and `d2` indicate the range of distances from the centroid of each polygon; in this case, our shapefile has distances measured in kilometers, something that will not necessarily be the same for any other shapefile the reader decides to use. Finally, the argument `longlat` reinforces that we are currently working with longitudes and latitudes.

After the previous command, we must type:

```
plot(sp_map, border = "lightgray")
```

And:

```
plot(neighborhood_dist, coordinates(sp_map), add = TRUE, col = "steelblue")
```

Figure 26.8 shows the neighborhoods established by geographic distances with $d_i(k)=40$ present in the object `neighborhood_dist`.

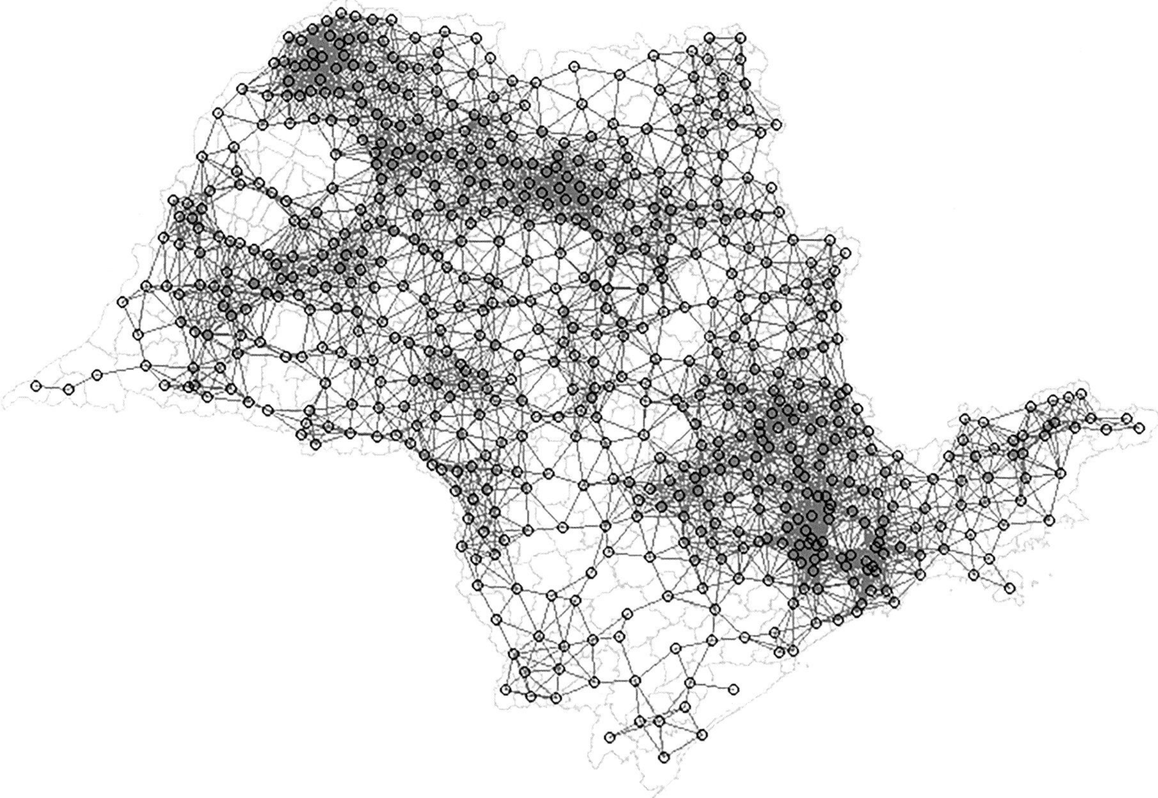

FIGURE 26.8 Neighborhood of the municipalities of the state of São Paulo established by the criterion of geographic distance, where $d_i(k) = 40$.

We can ask for a summary of the main information contained in the object `neighborhood_dist`, as follows:

```
summary(neighborhood_dist)
```

Figure 26.9 shows the results of the previous command.

```
Neighbour list object:
Number of regions: 645
Number of nonzero links: 8476
Percentage nonzero weights: 2.037378
Average number of links: 13.14109
Link number distribution:

 1  2  3  4  5  6  7  8  9 10 11 12 13 14 15 16 17 18 19 20 21 22 23 24 25 26 27 28
 2  4  9 16 26 12 27 30 42 52 58 60 42 36 30 23 31 24 28 19 21 12 13  5  3  6  4  6
29 30
 2  2
2 least connected regions:
19 246 with 1 link
2 most connected regions:
392 551 with 30 links
```

FIGURE 26.9 Information on the neighborhood of the municipalities of the state of São Paulo established by the criterion of geographic distance, where $d_i(k) = 40$.

This time, R did not name the municipalities of the state of São Paulo with the smallest and the largest number of neighbors, but offered reference numbers instead. If the reader is curious to know what these municipalities are, just type the following:

```
sp_map@data[19,]
sp_map@data[246, ]
sp_map@data[392, ]
sp_map@data[551, ]
```

Thus according to the previous codes, the municipalities whose names were omitted from the results shown in Figure 26.9 are Rosana, Iguape, Osasco, and São Paulo, respectively.

To create the matrix **W**, similar to what we discussed in the "Contiguity spatial weights matrix **W**" section, we must type:

```
W_matrix_dist <- nb2mat(neighbors = neighborhood_dist,
                        style = "B")
```

An attentive reader will notice that R did not return an error because of the absence of the argument `zero.policy` at this time. This is because we now consider the geographic distance criterion, and the municipality of Ilhabela (no matter how small an island is) is within the range established to make neighborhoods with at least one municipality.

k-Nearest neighbors spatial weights matrix W

Anselin and Rey (2014) argue that the matrix **W** weighted by the *k*-nearest neighbors convention, in addition to avoiding the existence of "islands" on the map, takes away the researcher's responsibility to arbitrate an optimal distance $d_i(k)$ among observations in the dataset. In contrast, in our opinion, it requires the researcher to decide the value of k neighbors. We emphasize, again, that $w_{ii}=0$, by convention.

Briefly, for the criterion discussed, a fixed number of neighbors is established, identical to all observations in the dataset. However, some problems arise when there is more than one observation j with the same distance as observation i. To create the balance for these cases, we will consider all *k*-order neighbors or randomly select some of them to be first-order neighbors.

In our example, we will use as a value of k the rounding of the average of neighbors calculated by the *queen* convention, as studied in the "Contiguity spatial weights matrix **W**" section, that is, $k=6$. That said, we should use the functions `knearneigh()` and `knn2nb()`, both from the package `spdep`. Thus:

```
knn_data <- knearneigh(x = coordinates(sp_map),
                       longlat = TRUE,
                       k = 6)
```

And:

```
neighborhood_knear <- knn2nb(knn = knn_data)
```

For this criterion, the visualization of the information present in the object `neighborhood_knear`, created through the function `knn2nb()`, is more friendly because one can declare to R the object itself, instead of using the function `summary()`. Therefore:

```
neighborhood_knear
```

Figure 26.10 shows the results of the previous command.

```
Neighbour list object:
Number of regions: 645
Number of nonzero links: 3870
Percentage nonzero weights: 0.9302326
Average number of links: 6
Non-symmetric neighbours list
```

FIGURE 26.10 Information on the neighborhood of the municipalities of the state of São Paulo established by the criterion of *k*-nearest neighbors, where $k=6$.

According to Figure 26.10, when establishing $k=6$ neighbors, notice that there will be an increase of values equal to 1 in the future matrix **W**. Before establishing it, we present the visualization of the neighborhood of the municipalities of the state of São Paulo through the *k*-nearest neighbors criterion; for this, we must type:

```
plot(sp_map, border = "lightgray")
```

And:

```
plot(neighborhood_knear, coordinates(sp_map), add = TRUE, col = "firebrick")
```

Figure 26.11 shows the results of the previous command.

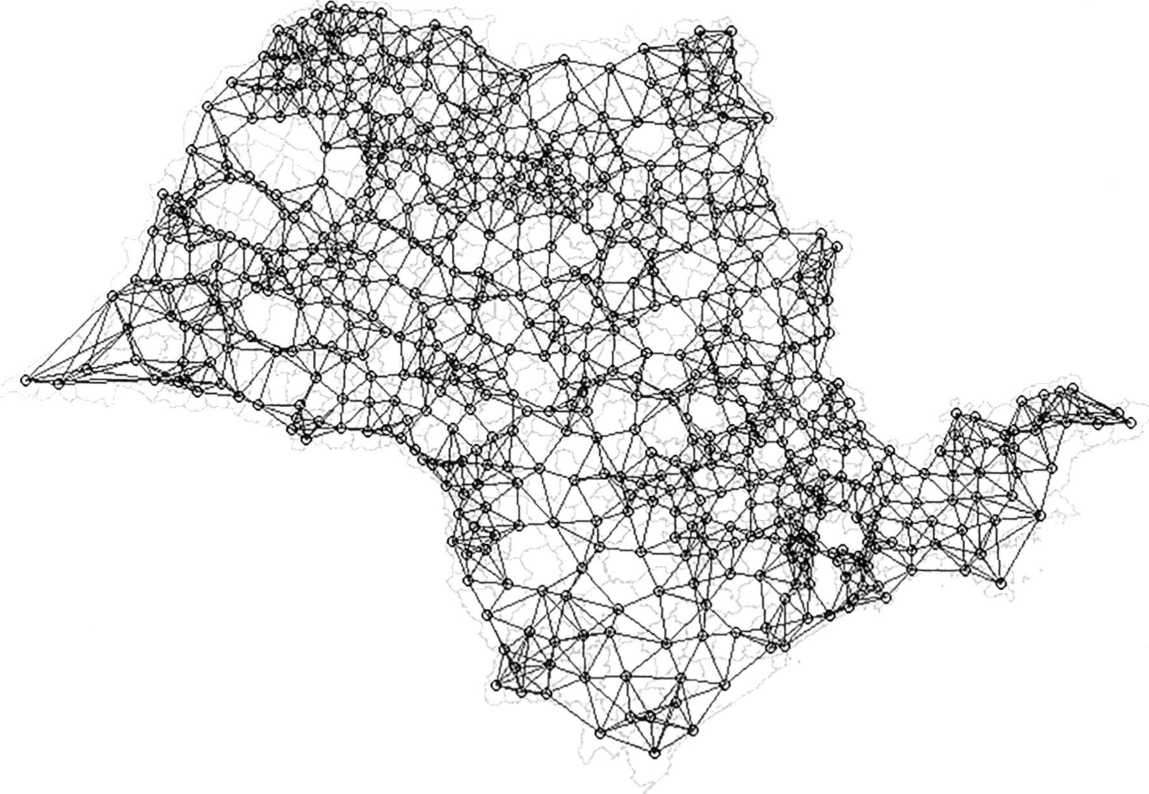

FIGURE 26.11 Information on the neighborhood of the municipalities of the state of São Paulo established by the criterion of *k*-nearest neighbors, where $k = 6$.

To create the matrix **W**, similar to what we already discussed, we must type:

```
W_matrix_knear <- nb2mat(neighbors = neighborhood_knear,
                         style = "B")
```

Socioeconomic proximity spatial weights matrix W

We can also establish a matrix **W** using social distances as a criterion for spatial weighting. We can understand social distances such as differences in the Human Development Index (HDI), the Gini Index, illiteracy rates, or infant mortality rates, among others. The problem is that, as far as we know, there is no direct algorithm in the R libraries that establishes this type of matrix. Thus later on, we will propose a routine for this kind of neighborhood estimation.

For the following example, we establish a spatial matrix **W** weighted by social distances among the GDP per capita of the municipalities of the state of São Paulo, present in the file `sp_data.RData`, already used in Chapter 23. To do so, we must type:

```
load(file = "sp_data.RData")
```

As discussed in Chapter 23, we can merge the data of the objects `sp_data` and `sp_map`, as follows:

```
sp_merged <- merge(x = sp_map,
                   y = sp_data,
                   by.x = "CD_GEOCMU",
                   by.y = "cod",
                   duplicateGeoms = TRUE)
```

To trace social distances, assuming the GDP per capita of municipalities in the state of São Paulo as a metric of social distance, we must stipulate a cutoff distance $d_i(k)$, as discussed earlier in the "Geographic proximity spatial weights matrix **W**" section. Thus we propose as a cutoff the variation of 0.003 standard deviations. Thus just to facilitate the calculation, we will standardize the variable *gdp* through the *zscores* procedure, as follows:

```
sp_merged$Zgdp <- scale(x = sp_merged@data$gdp,
                        center = TRUE,
                        scale = TRUE)
```

Using the previous commands, we created a new variable called *Zgdp* in the object `sp_merged`, which used the values of the variable *gdp*, transforming their respective values into new observations with a mean equal to zero and standard deviation equal to 1.

Now we propose a function that has the ability to establish a matrix **W** of social neighborhoods in the municipalities of the state of São Paulo, using the data on GDP per capita of these municipalities present in the object `sp_merged`, as follows:

```
social_distance <- function(x, dmin, dmax, style){
  transition.list <- list()
  vessel.list <- list()
  for(k in 1:length(x)){
    for(i in 1:length(x)){
      if(x[k] == x[i]){transition.list[[i]] <- 0}
      else{
        transition.list[[i]] <- dmin < abs(x[k] - x[i]) && abs(x[k] - x[i]) <= dmax}}
    vector <- unlist(transition.list)
    vessel.list[[k]] <- vector
  }
  data <- matrix(unlist(vessel.list), ncol = length(x), byrow = T)
  if(style == "W"){
    wdata <- data * 1/rowSums(data)
    wdata[is.nan(wdata)] <- 0
    return(wdata)}
  else if(style == "C"){
    sum.vector <- rowSums(data) == 0
    sum.verifier <- as.numeric(sum.vector)
    no.links <- sum(sum.verifier)
    links <- NROW(data) - no.links
    weightsC <- links / sum(data)
    vectorC <- gsub(1, weightsC, data)
    cdata <- matrix(vectorC, ncol = NCOL(data), nrow = NROW(data))
    return(cdata)}
  else if(style == "U"){
    sum.vector <- rowSums(data) == 0
    sum.verifier <- as.numeric(sum.vector)
    no.links <- sum(sum.verifier)
    links <- NROW(data) - no.links
```

Continued

```
    weightsC <- links / sum(data)
    weightsU <- weightsC / links
    vectorU <- gsub(1, weightsU, data)
    udata <- matrix(vectorU, ncol = NCOL(data), nrow = NROW(data))
    return(udata)}
  else if(style == "S"){
    step1 <- sqrt(rowSums(data^2))
    res.step1 <- data / step1
    res.step1[is.nan(res.step1)] <- 0
    step2 <- sum(res.step1)
    sum.vector <- rowSums(data) == 0
    sum.verifier <- as.numeric(sum.vector)
    no.links <- sum(sum.verifier)
    links <- NROW(data) - no.links
    step3 <- links / step2
    sdata <- res.step1 * step3
    return(sdata)
  }
  else if(style == "B"){return(data)}
  else {break()}
}
```

Having established the previous function in the tab *Environment*, we can point out its four main arguments: `x` concerns the pointing of a vector with social numeric data; `dmin` establishes the minimum value of the social distance to be considered; `dmax` establishes the maximum value of the social distance to be considered; and `style` defines the type of the matrix (e.g., binary, standardized in rows) following the same parameters as the homonymous argument of the function `nb2mat()`.

Thus assuming that we have established that the regions that will be neighbors to each other are within a variation of up to 0.003 standard deviations of their GDP per capita, the binary matrix **W** of social distances can be obtained as follows:

```
W_matrix_sociald <- social_distance(x = sp_merged$Zgdp,
                                    dmin = 0,
                                    dmax = 0.003,
                                    style = "B")
```

For a better observation of the matrix, we can insert the name of the regions, as follows:

```
colnames(W_matrix_sociald) <- sp_merged@data$NM_MUNICIP

rownames(W_matrix_sociald) <- sp_merged@data$NM_MUNICIP

View(W_matrix_sociald)
```

We can start to visualize the established neighborhoods using the following command:

```
neighborhood_sociald <- mat2listw(W_matrix_sociald)
```

The object `neighborhood_sociald` provides interesting information about the neighborhoods previously established:

```
summary(neighborhood_sociald, zero.policy = TRUE)
```

Figure 26.12 shows the results of the previous command.

```
Neighbour list object:
Number of regions: 645
Number of nonzero links: 1884
Percentage nonzero weights: 0.4528574
Average number of links: 2.92093
119 regions with no links:
7 13 19 20 25 36 39 46 53 57 60 67 70 72 76 87 89 92 96 101 104 108 111 116 125 146
155 159 162 170 179 192 200 208 209 214 227 229 231 232 233 241 247 248 255 259 271
279 285 288 289 290 292 297 305 316 319 322 323 326 328 334 342 344 354 363 377 380
381 383 384 388 390 391 392 396 398 399 411 412 418 421 442 450 455 457 462 465 468
469 487 488 501 502 512 515 520 525 527 531 532 534 535 550 551 561 565 567 574 589
591 596 605 620 621 623 632 641 644
Link number distribution:

  0   1   2   3   4   5   6   7   8   9  10
119 100  98  88  75  60  41  43  15   3   3
100 least connected regions:
6 9 11 23 31 34 35 47 48 65 69 73 81 82 90 99 105 106 109 115 118 124 126 130 133 139
144 147 150 151 154 156 175 176 181 184 197 202 221 223 226 228 239 261 266 270 272
275 281 282 294 302 303 314 336 339 340 343 352 353 358 360 382 386 387 393 397 402
408 416 432 434 438 441 444 446 458 473 475 479 482 489 518 521 528 530 536 544 546
549 562 570 571 572 581 590 594 608 631 643 with 1 link
3 most connected regions:
215 225 246 with 10 links

Weights style: M
Weights constants summary:
    n     nn   S0   S1    S2
M 526 276676 1884 3768 36280
```

FIGURE 26.12 Information on the neighborhood of the municipalities of the state of São Paulo established by the criterion of social distance.

The interpretation of Figure 26.12 must be done in a similar way to everything exposed in the establishment of previous matrices **W**. Visualization of the neighborhoods can be done using the following code:

```
plot(sp_merged, border = "lightgray")
```

Followed by:

```
plot(neighborhood_sociald, coordinates(sp_merged), add = TRUE, col = "green")
```

Figure 26.13 presents the map with the neighborhoods established by the criterion of social distance.

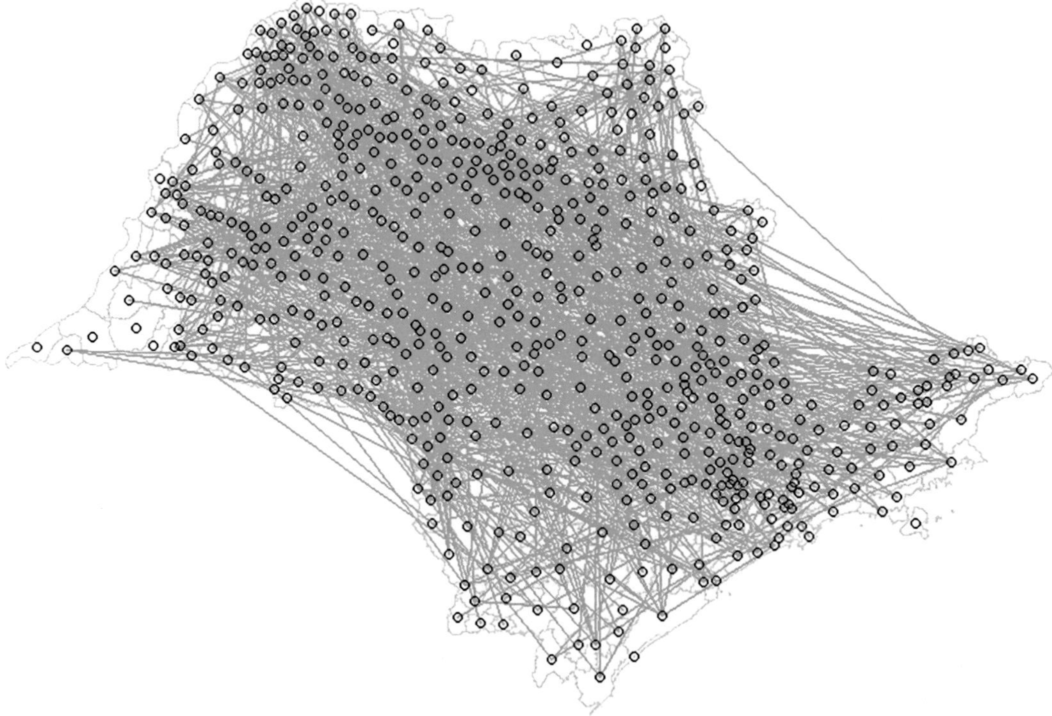

FIGURE 26.13 Neighborhood of the municipalities of the state of São Paulo established by the criterion of social distance.

We propose a minimum variation of 0.003 standard deviations in GDP per capita of municipalities in the state of São Paulo for didactic reasons, now explicit in Figure 26.13. The algorithm we developed proposes a rearrangement of the 645 municipalities in São Paulo, and similar municipalities may be very distant from the reference municipalities; hence the number of lines present. The idea was to leave the visualization with the lowest possible "pollution" so other metrics for `dmin` and `dmax` can be easily established.

Standardization of matrices

Wrongly, it is not difficult to find authors who call the following procedures *normalization* of space weights, when, in fact, what occurs is a *standardization*.

Anselin and Rey (2014) affirm that the use of a matrix **W** in its binary form is rare and suggest the adoption of some standardization of the matrix **W**, the most common being row standardization, double standardization, and variance stabilizing.

For the following discussions, we propose the use of a contiguity matrix with the first-order *queen* convention for the countries of South America, shown in Table 26.1.

TABLE 26.1 First-order binary matrix **W** of South American countries, spatially weighted by contiguity and established by the *queen* convention.

	ARG	BOL	BRA	CHL	COL	ECU	GUY	GUF	PRY	PER	SUR	URY	VEN
ARG	0	1	1	1	0	0	0	0	1	0	0	1	0
BOL	1	0	1	1	0	0	0	0	1	1	0	0	0
BRA	1	1	0	0	1	0	1	1	1	1	0	0	0
CHL	1	1	0	0	0	0	0	0	0	1	0	0	0
COL	0	0	1	0	0	1	0	0	0	1	0	0	1
ECU	0	0	0	0	1	0	0	0	0	1	0	0	0
GUY	0	0	1	0	0	0	0	0	0	0	1	0	1
GUF	0	0	1	0	0	0	0	0	0	0	1	0	0
PRY	1	1	1	0	0	0	0	0	0	0	0	0	0
PER	0	1	1	1	1	1	0	0	0	0	0	0	0
SUR	0	0	1	0	0	0	1	1	0	0	0	0	0
URY	1	0	1	0	0	0	0	0	0	0	0	0	0
VEN	0	0	1	0	1	0	1	0	0	0	0	0	0

The matrix presented in Table 26.1 is of the binary type, following Expression (26.1), and will serve as a basis for the standardizations described in the sequence.

Row standardization of the matrix W

Taking as an example of a neighborhood matrix the one presented in Table 26.1, a row standardization of the matrix **W** considers the sum of the binary spatial weights in each of its rows, dividing them by their respective w_{ij}. Mathematically, we have:

$$w_{ij\ row-s\tan dardized} = \frac{w_{ij}}{\sum_j w_{ij}}, \tag{26.3}$$

where the sum of the space weights of each row must be equal to 1, whereas the sum of all weights S_0 is given in Expression (26.4):

$$S_0 = \sum_i \sum_j w_{ij} = n, \tag{26.4}$$

where n is equal to the total number of observations. If there are q observations without neighbors, these must be subtracted from n, generating the exposed by Expression (26.5):

$$S_0 = \sum_i \sum_j w_{ij} = n - q. \tag{26.5}$$

In this sense, the row standardization of the matrix present in Table 26.1 would result in the exposed in Table 26.2.

TABLE 26.2 First-order matrix **W** of South American countries, spatially weighted by row.

	ARG	BOL	BRA	CHL	COL	ECU	GUY	GUF	PRY	PER	SUR	URY	VEN
ARG	0.00	0.20	0.20	0.20	0.00	0.00	0.00	0.00	0.20	0.00	0.00	0.20	0.00
BOL	0.20	0.00	0.20	0.20	0.00	0.00	0.00	0.00	0.20	0.20	0.00	0.00	0.00
BRA	0.14	0.14	0.00	0.00	0.14	0.00	0.14	0.14	0.14	0.14	0.00	0.00	0.00
CHL	0.33	0.33	0.00	0.00	0.00	0.00	0.00	0.00	0.00	0.33	0.00	0.00	0.00
COL	0.00	0.00	0.25	0.00	0.00	0.25	0.00	0.00	0.00	0.25	0.00	0.00	0.25
ECU	0.00	0.00	0.00	0.00	0.50	0.00	0.00	0.00	0.00	0.50	0.00	0.00	0.00
GUY	0.00	0.00	0.33	0.00	0.00	0.00	0.00	0.00	0.00	0.00	0.33	0.00	0.33
GUF	0.00	0.00	0.50	0.00	0.00	0.00	0.00	0.00	0.00	0.00	0.50	0.00	0.00
PRY	0.33	0.33	0.33	0.00	0.00	0.00	0.00	0.00	0.00	0.00	0.00	0.00	0.00
PER	0.00	0.20	0.20	0.20	0.20	0.20	0.00	0.00	0.00	0.00	0.00	0.00	0.00
SUR	0.00	0.00	0.33	0.00	0.00	0.00	0.33	0.33	0.00	0.00	0.00	0.00	0.00
URY	0.50	0.00	0.50	0.00	0.00	0.00	0.00	0.00	0.00	0.00	0.00	0.00	0.00
VEN	0.00	0.00	0.33	0.00	0.33	0.00	0.33	0.00	0.00	0.00	0.00	0.00	0.00

Note that in Table 26.1, Argentina had 5 neighbors indicated by the amount of numbers 1 in its row. We divided the value 1 by 5, thus each Argentine neighbor received the value 0.20, and we followed the same methodology for each observation.

Thus similar to using the data present in the object `sp_map` to define a matrix of spatial weights **W** standardized in rows, as studied in the "Contiguity spatial weights matrix **W**" section, we must first establish the neighborhood using the function `poly2nb()`:

```
neighborhood_queen <- poly2nb(pl = sp_map,
                              queen = TRUE,
                              row.names = sp_map$NM_MUNICIP)
```

After that, we must command the function `nb2mat()` with the argument `style = "W"` instead of the argument `style = "B"`, which would define a binary matrix:

```
W_matrix_rowstd <- nb2mat(neighbors = neighborhood_queen,
      style = "W",
      zero.policy = TRUE)
```

Double standardization of the matrix W

The idea of the double standardization procedure of the spatial weights matrix **W** is to transform it into a stochastic matrix whose sum of all of its weights S_0 is equal to 1, as shown in Expression (26.6):

$$w_{ij\ double-standardized} = \frac{w_{ij}}{\sum_i \sum_j w_{ij}} \tag{26.6}$$

Thus the matrix **W** present in Table 26.1 generates the matrix present in Table 26.3 when double standardized.

TABLE 26.3 First-order matrix **W** of South American countries, spatially weighted by the double-standardization criterion.

	ARG	BOL	BRA	CHL	COL	ECU	GUY	GUF	PRY	PER	SUR	URY	VEN
ARG	0.00	0.02	0.02	0.02	0.00	0.00	0.00	0.00	0.02	0.00	0.00	0.02	0.00
BOL	0.02	0.00	0.02	0.02	0.00	0.00	0.00	0.00	0.02	0.02	0.00	0.00	0.00
BRA	0.02	0.02	0.00	0.00	0.02	0.00	0.02	0.02	0.02	0.02	0.00	0.00	0.00
CHL	0.02	0.02	0.00	0.00	0.00	0.00	0.00	0.00	0.00	0.02	0.00	0.00	0.00
COL	0.00	0.00	0.02	0.00	0.00	0.02	0.00	0.00	0.00	0.02	0.00	0.00	0.02
ECU	0.00	0.00	0.00	0.00	0.02	0.00	0.00	0.00	0.00	0.02	0.00	0.00	0.00
GUY	0.00	0.00	0.02	0.00	0.00	0.00	0.00	0.00	0.00	0.00	0.02	0.00	0.02
GUF	0.00	0.00	0.02	0.00	0.00	0.00	0.00	0.00	0.00	0.00	0.02	0.00	0.00
PRY	0.02	0.02	0.02	0.00	0.00	0.00	0.00	0.00	0.00	0.00	0.00	0.00	0.00
PER	0.00	0.02	0.02	0.02	0.02	0.02	0.00	0.00	0.00	0.00	0.00	0.00	0.00
SUR	0.00	0.00	0.02	0.00	0.00	0.00	0.02	0.02	0.00	0.00	0.00	0.00	0.00
URY	0.02	0.00	0.02	0.00	0.00	0.00	0.00	0.00	0.00	0.00	0.00	0.00	0.00
VEM	0.00	0.00	0.02	0.00	0.02	0.00	0.02	0.00	0.00	0.00	0.00	0.00	0.00

In Table 26.3, we divided the total number of existing neighbors, that is, 47 (sum of values equal to 1 in Table 26.1) by 1. Thus the weight w_{ij} of each observation became 0.02 for situations in which the neighborhood is verified and zero for situations in which there is no neighborhood.

Following the logic proposed in the previous topic and using the *queen* neighborhood criterion present in the object `neighborhood_queen`, we can command the function `nb2mat()` using the argument `style = "U"`, as follows:

```
W_matrix_doublestd <- nb2mat(neighbors = neighborhood_queen,
                             style = "U",
                             zero.policy = TRUE)
```

Variance stabilizing of the matrix W

Standardization of the spatial weights matrix **W** by variance stabilizing was proposed by Tiefelsdorf et al. (1999). The standardized value of space weights is obtained in two basic steps. First, each original weight of row i must be divided by the square root of the sum of the squared weights of its respective row i, as shown in Expression (26.7), giving rise to a new weight w^*_{ij}, as follows:

$$w*_{ij} = \frac{w_{ij}}{\sqrt{\sum_j w_{ij}^2}}. \tag{26.7}$$

That said, each weight w^*_{ij} must be multiplied by the factor presented in Expression (26.8):

$$\frac{n-q}{Q}, \tag{26.8}$$

where n is the total number of observations, q is the total number of observations without neighbors, and Q is given by $\sum_i \sum_j w^*_{ij}$.

Thus if the spatial weights matrix **W** in Table 26.1 were standardized by variance stabilizing, it would become the matrix in Table 26.4.

TABLE 26.4 First-order matrix **W** of South American countries, spatially weighted by variance stabilizing criterion.

	ARG	BOL	BRA	CHL	COL	ECU	GUY	GUF	PRY	PER	SUR	URY	VEN
ARG	0.00	0.24	0.24	0.24	0.00	0.00	0.00	0.00	0.24	0.00	0.00	0.24	0.00
BOL	0.24	0.00	0.24	0.24	0.00	0.00	0.00	0.00	0.24	0.24	0.00	0.00	0.00
BRA	0.20	0.20	0.00	0.00	0.20	0.00	0.20	0.20	0.20	0.20	0.00	0.00	0.00
CHL	0.31	0.31	0.00	0.00	0.00	0.00	0.00	0.00	0.00	0.31	0.00	0.00	0.00
COL	0.00	0.00	0.27	0.00	0.00	0.27	0.00	0.00	0.00	0.27	0.00	0.00	0.27
ECU	0.00	0.00	0.00	0.00	0.38	0.00	0.00	0.00	0.00	0.38	0.00	0.00	0.00
GUY	0.00	0.00	0.31	0.00	0.00	0.00	0.00	0.00	0.00	0.00	0.31	0.00	0.31
GUF	0.00	0.00	0.38	0.00	0.00	0.00	0.00	0.00	0.00	0.00	0.38	0.00	0.00
PRY	0.31	0.31	0.31	0.00	0.00	0.00	0.00	0.00	0.00	0.00	0.00	0.00	0.00
PER	0.00	0.24	0.24	0.24	0.24	0.24	0.00	0.00	0.00	0.00	0.00	0.00	0.00
SUR	0.00	0.00	0.31	0.00	0.00	0.00	0.31	0.31	0.00	0.00	0.00	0.00	0.00
URY	0.38	0.00	0.38	0.00	0.00	0.00	0.00	0.00	0.00	0.00	0.00	0.00	0.00
VEM	0.00	0.00	0.31	0.00	0.31	0.00	0.31	0.00	0.00	0.00	0.00	0.00	0.00

In cases of standardization by variance stabilizing, we can point out that $S_0 = n - q$.

To define a matrix **W** standardized by variance stabilizing, after defining the neighborhoods according to the object `neighborhood_queen`, we must define the argument `style = "S"` in the function `nb2mat()`, as follows:

```
W_matrix_varstd <- nb2mat(neighbors = neighborhood_queen,
                          style = "S",
                          zero.policy = TRUE)
```

Techniques for verification of spatial autocorrelation

After establishing the neighborhoods and their respective spatial weights matrices **W**, we can verify if the observed data are distributed randomly or if they form a spatial pattern, that is, if there is a spatial autocorrelation involving the studied phenomenon.

Griffith (2003) points out that spatial autocorrelation can be understood as a measure of the existing correlation between the values of a single variable of interest in a geographic way. Next, we present the spatial autocorrelation tests most commonly referred to in the literature, and these measures are divided into two large groups: *global autocorrelation coefficients* and *local autocorrelation coefficients.*

The global spatial autocorrelation metrics aim to measure the degree of spatial relationship of a phenomenon in relation to all values observed in the dataset. Commonly, the literature references the Moran's *I* statistic as an effective coefficient of global spatial autocorrelation. Although not included in the scope of this work, we warn the reader about the existence of other coefficients of this kind, such as the Geary's *C* statistic and the Getis and Ord's *G* statistic.

The local spatial autocorrelation metrics, on the other hand, measure the autocorrelations of the observations, one by one, in relation to their neighborhood established by the spatial weights matrix **W**. Good examples of this kind of coefficients are the Local Moran's statistic and the Getis and Ord's *G* statistic.

Global autocorrelation: Moran's *I* statistic

Statistic *I* was first proposed by Moran (1948), and years later Cliff and Ord (1973, 1981) presented a more robust work on Moran's original ideas, defining the currently used formula presented in Expression (26.9):

$$I = \frac{n}{S_0} \cdot \frac{\sum_i \sum_j w_{ij} z_i z_j}{\sum_{i=1}^{n} z_i^2}, \tag{26.9}$$

where n represents the number of observations, z points to the standardized values of the dependent variable Y through the *zscores* procedure, w_{ij} are the spatial weights of matrix **W** for a given observation in row i and column j, and S_0 is the sum of all space weights w_{ij}.

In Expression (26.9), the null hypothesis H_0 refers to the spatial randomness and the expected value of the Moran's I statistic is $-\left[\frac{1}{n-1}\right]$. Thus when E(I) is statistically equal to I, for a given significance level, the values Y_i will be independent of the values of the neighboring observations, that is, H_0 cannot be rejected. However, when I is statistically greater than E(I), for a given significance level, we will see a positive global spatial autocorrelation; conversely, when I is statistically less than E(I), negative global spatial autocorrelation will be diagnosed.

As a rule, Moran's *I* statistic varies between −1 and 1, but such metrics can be extrapolated due to few observations in the dataset or due to the presence of outliers. For the calculation of Moran's *I* statistic in R, we propose the use of the function `moran.test()` from the package `spdep`. However, this function requires an object of type `listw`, resulting from the spatial weights matrices **W** generated in the "Contiguity spatial weights matrix **W**," "Geographical proximity spatial weights matrix **W**," "*k*-Nearest neighbors spatial weights matrix **W**," and "Socioeconomic proximity spatial weights matrix **W**" sections.

So, to transform the objects we have created and those that contain spatial weights matrices **W** (`W_matrix_queen`, `W_matrix_rook`, `W_matrix_dist`, `W_matrix_knear`, and `W_matrix_sociald`) into objects `listw`, we must use the function `mat2listw()`. For didactic purposes, in the following examples we will only use the object `W_matrix_queen`. But, if the reader wishes, any other type of matrices **W** can be considered in the following commands.

So, to convert our spatial weights matrices **W** into objects `listw`, we must type the following:

```
listw_W_queen <- mat2listw(W_matrix_queen)
```

Now we can obtain our Moran's *I* statistic! If we desire to verify if the phenomenon of global spatial autocorrelation occurs when we analyze the variable *hdi* present in the object `sp_merged`, we must type the following:

```
moran.test(x = sp_merged$hdi,
           listw = listw_W_queen,
           zero.policy = TRUE)
```

Figure 26.14 shows the results of the previous command.

```
        Moran I test under randomisation

data:  sp_merged$hdi
weights: listw_W_queen  n reduced by no-neighbour observations


Moran I statistic standard deviate = 10.092, p-value < 2.2e-16
alternative hypothesis: greater
sample estimates:
Moran I statistic       Expectation          Variance
     0.2328220224     -0.0015552100      0.0005393647
```

FIGURE 26.14 Moran's *I* statistic.

The results presented in Figure 26.14 indicate that $I = 0.2328$, while $E(I) = -0.0016$. Thus *a priori*, because $I > E(I)$, we verify the existence of a positive global spatial autocorrelation. Let's now study the *P*-value related to our of Moran's *I* statistic.

Assuming a significance level of 5% and a *P*-value equal to 2.2^{-16}, we can reject H_0. In other words, the variable *hdi* is spatially autocorrelated for the regions present in the dataset of the object `sp_merged`.

According to Almeida (2012), **positive global autocorrelations indicate "a similarity between the values of the studied attribute and the spatial location of the attribute."** On the other hand, the author states that **the negative global autocorrelations point to "dissimilarities between the values of the studied attribute and the spatial location of the attribute."**

Expanding on the previous explanations, according to Fotheringham et al. (2002), we can verify positive global spatial autocorrelations when relevant amounts of high values are grouped around high values as well as when low values tend to group with low values. In an inverse way, we can verify negative global spatial autocorrelations when we perceive a pattern in which high values are grouped with low values, and vice versa.

We hope the reader has understood the application of Moran's *I* statistic. Through its analysis, we can verify if data of the variable of interest are distributed randomly or not in relation to spatialities. We can also understand, by observing its signal, whether the autocorrelations (when they exist) occur in a positive or negative way. And, finally, we can observe its magnitude, which usually varies from −1 to 1; that is, the closer it is to the highest positive value, the more concentrated the data will be, and the farther it is, the more dispersed the data will be.

An interesting tool that helps us understand the results of Moran's *I* statistic is the so-called *Moran scatter plot*.

Moran scatter plot

The Moran scatter plot is a method of visualizing the global autocorrelations pointed out by Moran's *I* statistic, as presented earlier in the "Global autocorrelation: Moran's *I* statistic" section. This visual technique consists of a two-dimensional scatter plot with four quadrants, namely: High-High (HH), High-Low (HL), Low-Low (LL) and Low-High (LH), as shown in Figure 26.15.

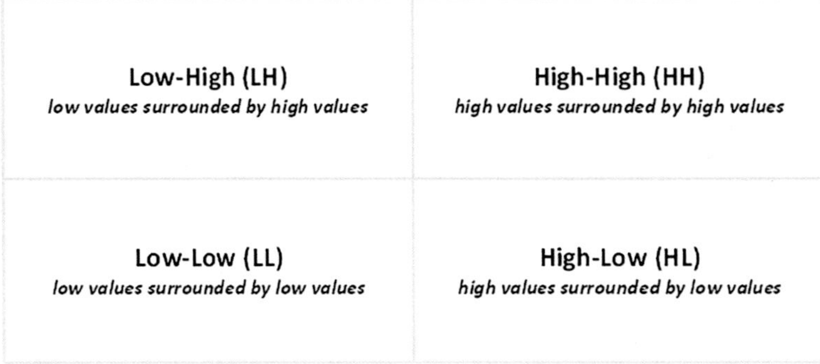

Low-High (LH)
low values surrounded by high values
High-High (HH)
high values surrounded by high values
Low-Low (LL)
low values surrounded by low values
High-Low (HL)
high values surrounded by low values

FIGURE 26.15 Quadrants of the Moran scatterplot.

The quadrant HH presents those observations (regions) of the studied variable that have high values and are spatially surrounded by other observations that also have high values. The quadrant HL shows the observations that have high values and are spatially surrounded by observations with low values. The quadrant LL presents the observations that have low values and are spatially surrounded by observations with low values. Finally, the quadrant LH contains the observations with low values that are spatially surrounded by observations with high values.

We can visualize the Moran scatter plot using the function `moran.plot()` from the package `spdep`. The proposed command is as follows:

```
moran.plot(x = sp_merged$hdi,
         listw = listw_W_queen,
         zero.policy = TRUE,
         xlab = "hdi",
         ylab = "HDI Spatial Lags",
         pch = 19)
```

Figure 26.16 shows the results of the previous command.

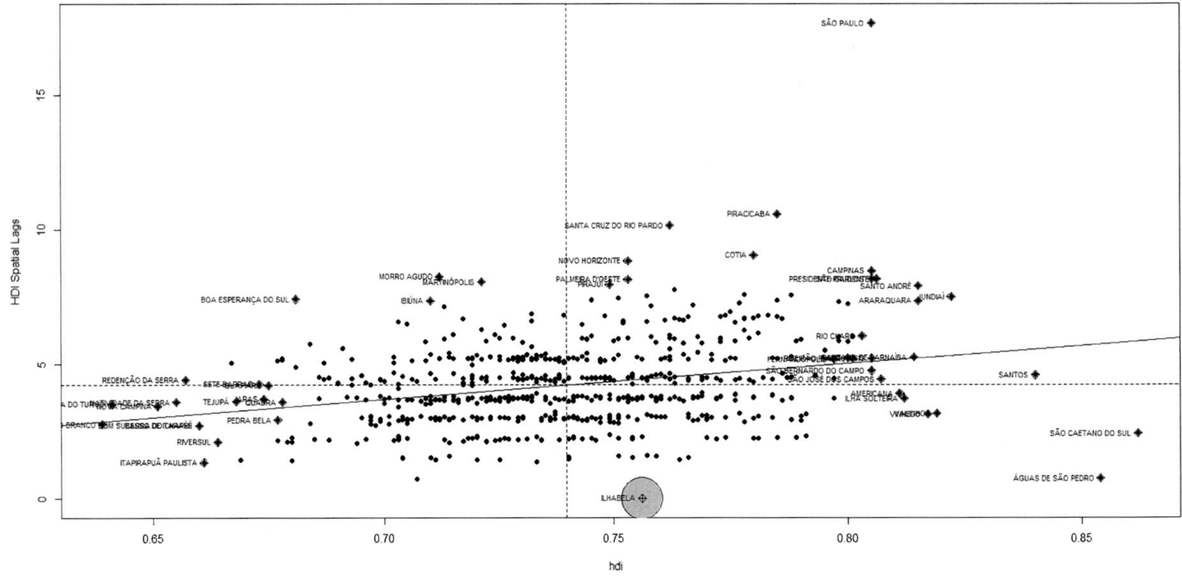

FIGURE 26.16 Moran scatter plot.

In Figure 26.16, the two dashed lines define the quadrants HH, HL, LL, and LH, following the logic presented in Figure 26.15. Thus it is possible to verify in the quadrant HH that, in fact, the municipalities of the state of São Paulo that have high values of the variable *hdi* are usually spatially surrounded by other municipalities with high *hdi* values, for example, Campinas (0.805), Presidente Prudente (0.806), and Santo André (0.815). The inverse can also be seen in the quadrant LL, that is, municipalities with low *hdi* values are usually spatially surrounded by other municipalities with low *hdi* values, for example, Riversul (0.664), Itapirapuã Paulista (0.661), and Pedra Bela (0.677).

Figure 26.16 also shows that the municipality of Ilhabela has no neighborhood, therefore considerations on this observation must be made with serious reservations. In fact, we recommend the definition of a new spatial weights matrix **W** that contains this observation. We have adopted this procedure to show the reader how the function `moran.plot()` works with observations without neighbors.

Another interesting outcome in Figure 26.16 is that the argument `labels = TRUE` is defined by default, even if the reader does not type it explicitly in the code. This argument is responsible for pointing out the name of certain observations, with an emphasis on those municipalities with the greatest influence on the adopted metric. We can suspect, **preliminarily,** that some municipalities, such as São Paulo, Santo André, Águas de São Pedro, and Itapirapuã Paulista, are outliers for the variable *hdi*.

Let's now discuss, finally, the continuous line that crosses the quadrants in the origin point in Figure 26.16. The reader should remember that Moran's I statistic defined in the "Global autocorrelation: Moran's I statistic" section was approximately 0.2328, and this partially explains the slope of the line because we are facing a positive global spatial autocorrelation. It can be obtained by the estimation, through ordinary least squares, of a simple regression model linked to the function `moran.plot()`, and its β is approximately the coefficient obtained using Expression (26.9), that is, the Moran's I statistic. In our case, the explanatory variable is *hdi,* and the dependent variable is represented by the spatial weights of the observations present in the matrix **W**. We must remember that all variables must be previously standardized by the *zscores* procedure.

Local autocorrelation: The local Moran's statistic

Anselin (1995) proposed a technique that aims to identify and measure local autocorrelations, known as *local indicators of spatial association* (LISA). According to the author, an indicator of local spatial autocorrelations must meet two criteria: (1) the pointing of spatial clusters must be statistically significant for each observation and (2) the sum of the local spatial autocorrelation indicators for each observation must be proportional to the global spatial autocorrelation indicator, according to a proportionality factor γ.

As discussed by Lansley and Cheshire (2016), the LISA technique investigates spatial relationships between data considering the established neighborhoods. Among the types of LISA proposed by Anselin (1995), such as Local Gamma and Local Geary, we will present the most commonly referenced type, the Local Moran, which is mathematically described in Expression (26.10).

$$I_i = z_i \sum_j w_{ij} z_j, \tag{26.10}$$

where, similarly to Moran's I statistic, discussed in the "Global autocorrelation: Moran's I statistic" section, z_i and z_j represent the standardized values of the dependent variable, and the sum considered includes only each neighbor j belonging to the neighborhood J_i established by the spatial weights matrix **W**. The spatial weights w_{ij} are preferably standardized in rows to facilitate the interpretation, without forgetting that, by convention, $w_{ii}=0$.

When adding the Local Moran values, we have:

$$\sum_i I_i = \sum_i z_i \sum_j w_{ij} z_j. \tag{26.11}$$

Starting from the Moran's I global statistic, shown in Expression (26.9), we can write Expression (26.12) as follows:

$$I = \frac{n}{S_0} \cdot \frac{\sum_i \sum_j w_{ij} z_i z_j}{\sum_{i=1}^{n} z_i^2} = \frac{\sum_i I_i}{\left[S_0 \left(\frac{\sum_i z_i^2}{n} \right) \right]}, \tag{26.12}$$

where $S_0 = \sum_i \sum_j w_{ij}$.

By calling the value of $\frac{\sum_i z_i^2}{n}$ as m (according to Cliff and Ord (1981) and assuming it as a consistent variance estimator, but biased), we can establish the proportionality factor γ, according to Expression (26.13).

$$\gamma = S_0 m. \tag{26.13}$$

As presented earlier in the "Row standardization of the matrix **W**" section, when adopting the suggested row standardization of the spatial weighs matrix **W**, we have $S_0 = n$. Therefore, the proportionality factor γ can be written according to Expression (26.14).

$$\gamma = \sum_i z_i^2 \tag{26.14}$$

Starting from the idea of standardizing the dependent variable through the *zscores* procedure, then $m = 1$. Thus we can write the proportionality factor γ according to Expression (26.15).

$$\gamma = S_0 = n \tag{26.15}$$

According to Anselin (1995), by randomization, the expected value of the Local Moran's statistic is given in Expression (26.16):

$$E(I_i) = -\frac{w_i}{(n-1)}, \tag{26.16}$$

where w_i is the value of the sum of the elements of the row i in the spatial weights matrix **W**.

Following the logic proposed by Anselin (1995), we must row standardize our spatial weights matrix **W**. Thus for didactic purposes, we will use the object `W_matrix_rowstd` because it is a row-standardized matrix **W**, created in the "Row standardization of the matrix **W**" section. In this way, we can generate an object `listw` from the object `W_matrix_rowstd`, as follows:

```
listw_W_stdrow <- mat2listw(W_matrix_rowstd)
```

That said, considering the variable *hdi* of the object `sp_merged`, we can check the Local Moran's statistic using the function `localmoran()` from the package `spdep`, as follows:

```
moran_local <- localmoran(x = sp_merged$hdi,
                          listw = listw_W_stdrow,
                          zero.policy = TRUE)
```

The new object `moran_local` is a matrix of size $n \times 5$. A curious reader can explore the data that compose it by typing `?local.moran`. For the moment, it is important that the reader knows that the first column, called `Ii`, contains the values of the Local Moran's statistic.

To view the results, we first must add the information present in the object `moran_local` to the object `sp_merged`, with the aid of the function `cbind()`:

```
map_moran_local <- cbind(sp_merged, moran_local)
```

After that, we can visualize what was done using the package `tmap`, as follows:

```
tm_shape(shp = map_moran_local) +
  tm_fill(col = "Ii", style = "quantile", n = 5)
```

Figure 26.17 presents the map of the Local Moran's statistic.

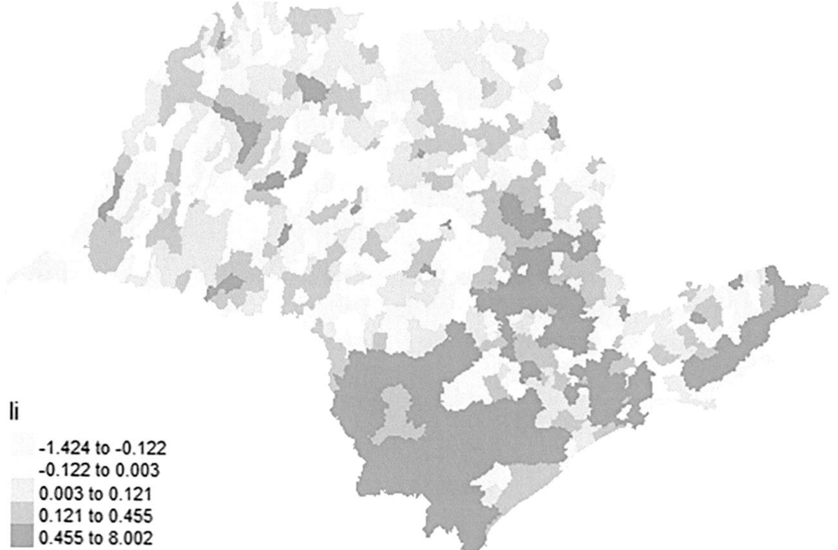

FIGURE 26.17 The Map of the Local Autocorrelations Defined by the Local Moran's Statistic.

From the legend and the colors of the map presented in Figure 26.17, it is evident that there is a variation in autocorrelation due to spatialities. It is also evident that there are several observations with similar values of the Local Moran's statistic spatially clustered. However, despite these insights, it is still not possible to interpret whether these spatial clusters of municipalities are formed by observations present in the quadrants HH, HL, LH, or LL of the variable *hdi*.

So, returning to our discussion of the matrix present in the object `moran_local`, we assert that its fifth (last) column refers to the *P*-values of the Local Moran's statistic for each observation. With this information, we can try to show the groups HH, HL, LH, or LL on a map, considering the values statistically different from zero, at a certain significance level. In this logic, we present the interesting solution proposed by Brunsdon and Comber (2019) for the creation of a LISA map of spatial clusters.

The first step, according to Brunsdon and Comber (2019), is to establish an object that will reserve spaces to contain, in the future, the quadrants HH, HL, LH, or LL. For this, we use the function `vector()` of the R-based language to create a numeric-type vector whose length is equal to the number of rows of the matrix present in the object `moran_local`, as follows:

```
quadrants <- vector(mode = "numeric", length = nrow(moran_local))
```

As expected, the created object `quadrants` comes down to a vector of size $n \times 1$ with values equal to zero. After that, Brunsdon and Comber suggest creating a vector that contains the center of the observations of the variable *hdi* around its mean. In other words, we subtract each observation of the variable from its respective mean, as follows:

```
center_hdi <- sp_merged$hdi - mean(sp_merged$hdi)
```

Then, similar to the previous command, we must create a vector that contains the center of the Local Moran's statistic values around its mean:

```
center_moran_local <- moran_local[,1] - mean(moran_local[,1])
```

After that, Brunsdon and Comber (2019) point out that we must create an object that contains the level of significance we want to adopt. In the following code, we assume a significance level of 10%:

```
sig <- 0.1
```

Now, according to the same authors, we are ready to allocate each of our observations in their respective quadrants (HH, HL, LH, or LL), as follows:

```
quadrants[center_hdi > 0 & center_moran_local > 0] <- "HH"
quadrants[center_hdi > 0 & center_moran_local < 0] <- "HL"
quadrants[center_hdi < 0 & center_moran_local > 0] <- "LH"
quadrants[center_hdi < 0 & center_moran_local < 0] <- "LL"
```

It is interesting to remember that we have established a significance level of 10%. Thus we must overlap the classifications made by the previous commands with the label "Statistically_not_significant" when the *P*-value of the Local Moran's statistic of a given observation is greater than the defined significance level. Thus:

```
quadrants[moran_local[,5] > sig] <- "Statistically_not_significant"
```

Finally, we will add the contents of our object `quadrants` to the object `sp_merged`, as follows:

```
sp_merged@data["quadrants"] <- factor(quadrants)
```

Ready! Our object `quadrants` offers the correct classification as to which spatial cluster each observation belongs to, at a significance level of 10%. To visualize the final results, we must type:

```
tm_shape(shp = sp_merged) +
  tm_polygons(col = "quadrants",
              pal = c(HH = "darkred",HL = "red", LH = "lightblue",
                      LL = "darkblue",Statistically_not_significant = "white"))
```

Figure 26.18 presents the map of spatial clusters, with a significance level of 10%, following the logic proposed by Anselin (1995) and the routine proposed by Brunsdon and Comber (2019).

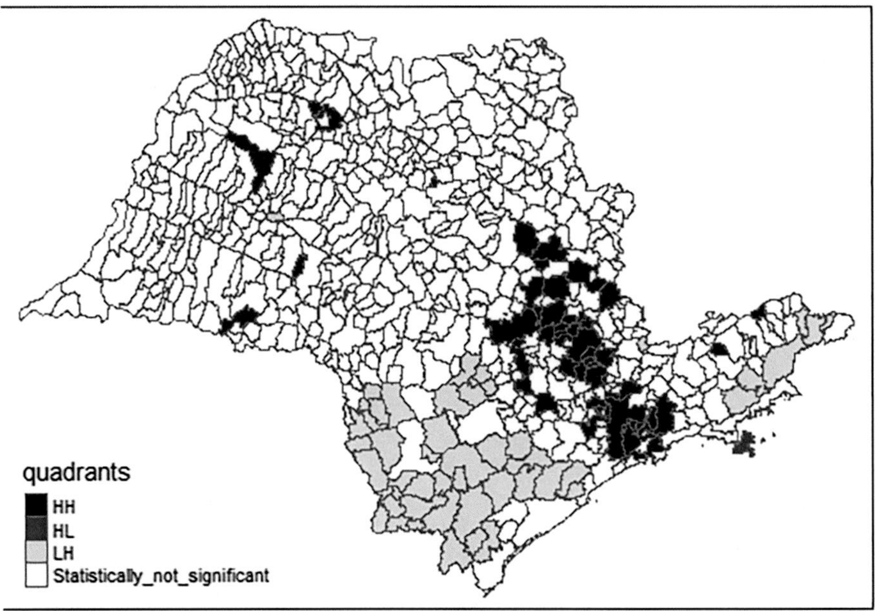

FIGURE 26.18 LISA map of spatial clusters.

The proposal of Figure 26.18 is to combine itself with the information from the Moran scatter plot shown in Figure 26.16, presenting statistically significant spatial clusters. In the LISA map, it is clear that there are patterns of grouping cities with high HDI values with other municipalities that follow the same behavior, such as São Paulo (0.805), São Bernardo do Campo (0.805), Campinas (0.805), São Caetano do Sul (0.862), and so on. It is also possible to verify the existence of an association pattern of municipalities with low HDI values, such as Barra do Turvo (0.641), Barra do Chapéu (0.660), Bom Sucesso de Itararé (0.660), and so on, with municipalities with higher HDI values, such as Capão Bonito (0.721), Angatuba (0.719), Torre de Pedra (0.714), and so on.

Local autocorrelation: The Getis and Ord's $\mathcal{G}$ statistic

Getis and Ord proposed another way of studying the spatial association of observations from a given dataset, based on spatial concentration. As discussed in the "Local autocorrelation: The local Moran's statistic" section, the Local Moran's statistic manages to define some clusters, but it fails to show what the authors classify as **hot spots** and **cool spots**.

According to Almeida (2012), for each observation i, the G statistic manages to define a metric that determines to what extent the individuals in the dataset are surrounded by observations with high values (the so-called *hot spots*) or observations with low values (the so-called *cool spots*). The G statistic can be mathematically expressed as follows:

$$G_i(d) = \frac{\sum_{j-1}^{n} w_{ij}(d) Y_j}{\sum_{j-1}^{n} Y_j}, \text{ being } j \neq i, \tag{26.17}$$

where w_{ij} represents the binary weights of a spatial matrix weighted by distances (see the "Geographic proximity spatial weights matrix **W**" section or the "Socioeconomic proximity spatial weights matrix **W**" section), remembering that $w_{ii}=0$ by convention; the numerator represents the sum of all neighboring values Y_j within the neighborhood established by the distance d of i, without including Y_i, and the denominator represents the sum of all neighboring values Y_j without including Y_i.

Thus to demonstrate the usefulness of the G statistic, we will follow the logic proposed by Getis and Ord and use the spatial matrix weighted by the geographic distances defined in the "Geographic proximity spatial weights matrix **W**" section: the object `W_matrix_dist`. Initially, we must create an object of type `listw` using the function `mat2listw()`, as follows:

```
listw_W_dist <- mat2listw(W_matrix_dist)
```

Recalling, our matrix **W** considers as neighbors the municipalities distant from each other up to the limit of 40 km. In this way, the G statistic can be calculated as follows, using the function `localG()` from the package `spdep`:

```
g_local <- localG(x = sp_merged$hdi, listw = listw_W_dist)
```

The object `g_local` will be a vector with size $n \times 1$ that will contain the G statistic of all observations in the dataset. In module, the higher the values, the greater the grouping intensity. And, finally, the positive signs indicate the highest spatial clusters, while the negative signs indicate the lowest spatial clusters.

To view the G statistic of the HDI of the municipalities of the state of São Paulo, we must first integrate their values into the dataset of the object `sp_merged`, as follows:

```
g_map <- cbind(sp_merged, as.matrix(g_local))
```

A curious reader will notice that the name of the column created in the new object `g_map`, regarding the G statistic of our observations, has a name that can make commands difficult:

```
head(g_map@data)
```

In this sense, we can type:

```
names(g_map)[dim(g_map)[2]] <- "G_Statistic"
```

We do not recommend compound names for the previous command. The new nomenclature can be verified as follows:

```
head(g_map@data)
```

That said, we can type the following command:

```
tm_shape(g_map) +
  tm_polygons("G_Statistic",
         palette = "-RdBu")
```

FIGURE 26.19 Getis and Ord's *G* statistic of the HDI of the municipalities of the state of São Paulo.

Figure 26.19 shows the map of the Getis and Ord's *G* statistic, showing the hot spots in red and the cool spots in blue. High values with a positive sign may indicate the possibility of a local cluster with high values of the observed variable. Similarly, high values, in module, with a negative sign may indicate the formation of local clusters with low values of the studied variable.

Final remarks

In the course of this chapter, we discussed ways to develop an exploratory spatial analysis based on Tobler's thoughts. First, we demonstrated that it is necessary to establish a neighborhood mathematically described by a spatial weights matrix, which is commonly referred to in the literature as *matrix* **W**. This matrix **W** can assume several contiguity criteria, depending on the researcher's objectives, such as the geographic distance among observations, the consideration of *k*-th-order neighbors, and even social distances.

After that, as a rule, the matrix **W** is subject to a standardization to allow the exploratory spatial analysis to look for patterns, insights, outliers, and/or clusters formed due to the phenomenon under study.

We then presented the differences between global and spatial autocorrelations, how to measure them, and how to visualize them on thematic maps with the use of R.

Exercise

The set of files in the folder *shapefile_india* refers to a shapefile that considers the 36 Indian states and territories and contains data on their respective literacy rates, according to the 2011 Census of the Republic of India. Table 26.5 shows the variables present in the data.

TABLE 26.5 Variables contained in the *shapefile_india*.

Variable	Description
ST_NM	Character variable that indicates the name of the Indian state or territory
ltrcy_r	Continuous variable that presents the literacy rates of each Indian state or territory, according to the 2011 National Census

Based on the knowledge acquired in the course of this chapter, we would like you to:

1. Establish a contiguity spatial weights matrix **W**, following the *queen* criterion for the Indian states and territories.
2. What is the average number of neighbors found?
3. When adopting the contiguity spatial weights matrix **W**, according to the *queen* criterion, how many regions were left without neighbors?
4. When adopting the contiguity spatial weights matrix **W**, according to the *queen* criterion, which Indian state has the largest number of neighbors?
5. When adopting the contiguity spatial weights matrix **W**, according to the *queen* criterion, disregarding the regions without neighbors, which regions have the least number of neighbors?
6. Establish a *k*-nearest neighbors spatial weights matrix **W** for Indian states and territories, considering $k=4$.
7. Demonstrate graphically the neighborhood when by adopting the $k=4$ criterion.
8. When using the *k*-nearest neighbors spatial weights matrix **W** for Indian states and territories, considering $k=4$ and with variance stabilizing, can one verify the value of Moran's I statistic for the variable *ltrcy_r*? What is the interpretation of the value found?
9. Based on the results of question 8, construct a Moran scatter plot using the variable *ltrcy_r*, and discuss the results.
10. Based on the methods adopted in question 8, construct a graph on the Local Moran's autocorrelation, and discuss the results.
11. Construct a graph with the Getis and Ord's autocorrelations, and discuss the results.

Supplementary data sets

`sp_data.RData`

Please access supplementary data files here: https://doi.org/10.17632/55623jkwrp.3

PART VIII

Adding value to your work

CHAPTER

27

Enhanced and interactive graphs

AT THE END OF THIS CHAPTER, YOU WILL BE ABLE TO:

- Understand the basic syntax of the package `plotly`
- Build bidimensional and tridimensional graphics in R-based language with the package `plotly`

R-based language packages used in this chapter

```
library(plotly)
library(tidyverse)
```

Don't forget to define the R working directory (the location where your datasets are installed):

```
setwd("C:/book/chapter27")
```

Introduction

In the course of Chapter 7 of this work, we introduced the reader to an indispensable tool for the elaboration of powerful graphics in the computational language R, the package `ggplot2`. In the appendix of Chapter 7, we demonstrated that some of the graphics generated by the package `ggplot2` can be combined with the features of the package `plotly`, making them interactive. However, the objective here is to instruct the reader to build interactive graphs from scratch with the package `plotly`, which, in addition, is also capable of constructing three-dimensional (3D) graphs. Later, we will see that this tool has great value when associated with the construction of dashboards.

Unlike the package `ggplot2`, the package `plotly` is not part of the universe `tidyverse` and as such has its own syntax. Next, we will present a good introduction to this set of tools that allow the creation of graphics that can be more informative and that interact with the information recipient.

Datasets used in this chapter came from the books Manual de Análise de Dados/Handbook of Data Analysis (Fávero and Belfiore, 2017, Portuguese Edition) and Data Science for Business and Decision Making (Fávero and Belfiore, 2019, English Edition; 2020, Korean Edition), published by Elsevier Academic Press.

The library `plotly`

Immediately, it must be said that the features provided by the package `plotly` may lead some beginners to R-based language to find its commands strange.

Data Science, Analytics and Machine Learning with R
https://doi.org/10.1016/B978-0-12-824271-1.00024-X

In Chapter 2 of this work, it became widespread that everything in R is an object and that when we use the assignment operator `<-`, we overwrite the contents of a given object.

For example, when we command the following routine, we will create an object called `test`, whose value is 22:

```
test <- 22
```

The reader should already know that the object `test` contains a numeric class value. However, if we want to assign a new value to the same object, this new value will overwrite the previous value:

```
test <- "data science"
```

As of the previous command, the numerical value 22 of the object `test` was lost forever, and from that moment on, this object will keep the textual value `"data science"`.

In the package `plotly`, this general R-based language mindset is, in some ways, subverted. With the functions of `plotly`, we can create and save a graph on a given object. In another moment, using the assignment operator `<-` applied to the object that contains the graphic, we can add colors, axis names, legends, new layers, and so on. For this case, we will not be overwriting the initial object, but adding new attributes to it. In fact, `plotly` will require a different mindset on the part of the reader, but we will present this step-by-step at appropriate times.

Figure 27.1 presents a basic syntax for building graphs with the package `plotly`. As we read, we will add new information and capabilities to this syntax.

```
some_object <- plot_ly(data = insert your database here,
                       x = ~ insert x-axis variable here,
                       y = ~ insert y-axis variable here,
                       type = desired chart type)
```

FIGURE 27.1 Explanation of the most basic theoretical syntax of the library `plotly`.

In Figure 27.1, an attentive reader will notice the operator ~, which must precede each of the variables that will be declared in the axes of the graphs. And yes, for the case of the package `plotly`, a Z axis is possible! In fact, in Chapter 13, there was already contact, albeit superficial, with the 3D graphics of the package `plotly`.

Within the basic syntax proposed in Figure 27.1, we will be able to add or modify colors, captions, titles, sizes, thicknesses, information, layers, and so on. For the case of the package `ggplot2`, we did this with the operator `+`; here, we will use the operator `%>%`, which is covered in Chapter 10 of this work.

In Figure 27.1, the argument `type` must be declared in quotes, which indicates the type of graph the reader wants R to elaborate. There are a multitude of different types of two-dimensional and 3D graphics that are possible. After reading this chapter, the reader may be interested in the page https://plotly.com/r/plotly-fundamentals/ and in the documentation of the package `plotly`.

Another point that deserves to be highlighted in Figure 27.1 is that when we worked with the package `ggplot2` in this work, it was not common for us to save the graphics in objects. This is because, as a rule, this practice for `ggplot2` is a little more work. In this chapter, for the case of `plotly`, we will always save the graphs created with it in objects; it is not a mandatory procedure, but it will be more didactic due to change in mindset of the algorithms that make up the package, as already discussed.

It is also necessary to say that, as proposed in Chapter 7, we will return to using the datasets studied in Chapter 4 for the construction of interactive graphs. It is also true that we will introduce the reader to other datasets.

That said, we can start building our first charts with the help of the package `plotly` features. Probably the most basic initial chart format in `plotly` is the scatter plot. Let's go to it.

Scatter plot with `plotly`

The first step will be to load a dataset in which it makes sense to use a scatter plot. We ask the reader to open the well-known file `papermisto.RData` (Fávero and Belfiore, 2019). The dataset variables were presented in Table 4.14 and are replicated here.

```
load("papermisto.RData")
```

Following the instructions presented in Figure 27.1, we can create a scatter plot with the following routine:

```
scatter_plotly <- plot_ly(data = papermisto,
                          x = ~ time_min,
                          y = ~ weight_kg,
                          type = "scatter")
```

The reader should be sure not to forget the declaration of the operator ~ before the variables declared to the abscissa and ordinate axes. To access the graphic, just declare the object that contains it:

```
scatter_plotly
```

Figure 27.2 shows the result obtained from the previous command.

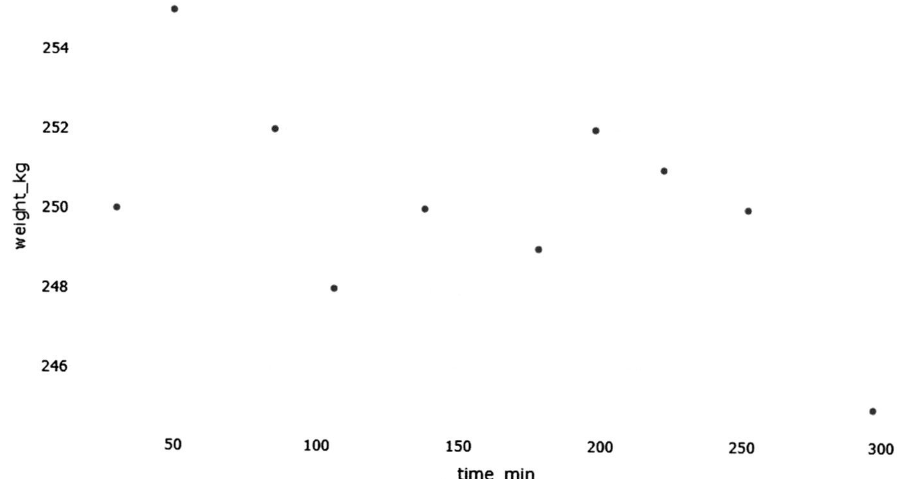

FIGURE 27.2 Scatter plot created with the package `plotly`.

A fair question would be: Why are we paying attention to a graphics generation package that, *a priori,* presents results so close to those achieved by the package `ggplot2`? As mentioned earlier, the package `plotly` is capable of generating 3D graphs, and its graphs are naturally interactive. By the way, we invite the reader to hover his or her mouse cursor over the graphic displayed in RStudio.

The reader will notice that the graphs created by the package `plotly` are, in fact, interactive. Such a feature is very well-regarded for use in building web pages with R and building dashboards (see Chapter 28).

Another interesting feature is the possibility to use a zoom effect on the image, and **we are *not* talking about the button Zoom in RStudio.** Such functionality is one of the most interesting in graphics that can be polluted by the excess of plotted information. To zoom in on a graph built with `plotly`, just click and hold the left mouse button on an area of interest, and drag and drop to another point where you want to enlarge the image. To return the graph to its original size, simply double-click on any white area of the graph.

Suppose the reader wanted to customize the colors of the scatter plot points which, by default, are shown in steel-blue. Assuming the reader wants the color goldenrod (see the appendix in Chapter 7 for a list of colors that can be used in R-based language):

```
scatter_plotly <- plot_ly(data = papermisto,
                          x = ~ time_min,
                          y = ~ weight_kg,
                          type = "scatter",
                          marker = list(color = "goldenrod"))

scatter_plotly
```

For the proposed objective, we use the argument `marker`, declaring the function `list()` to it. The idea here is to organize the codes. So, for the scatter plot points, using the function `list()`, we will (literally) list their attributes. In this case, it was just a color change, as shown in Figure 27.3, but as we will see later, it could be changing the stitch size, the stitch outline color, the stitch outline thickness, and so on.

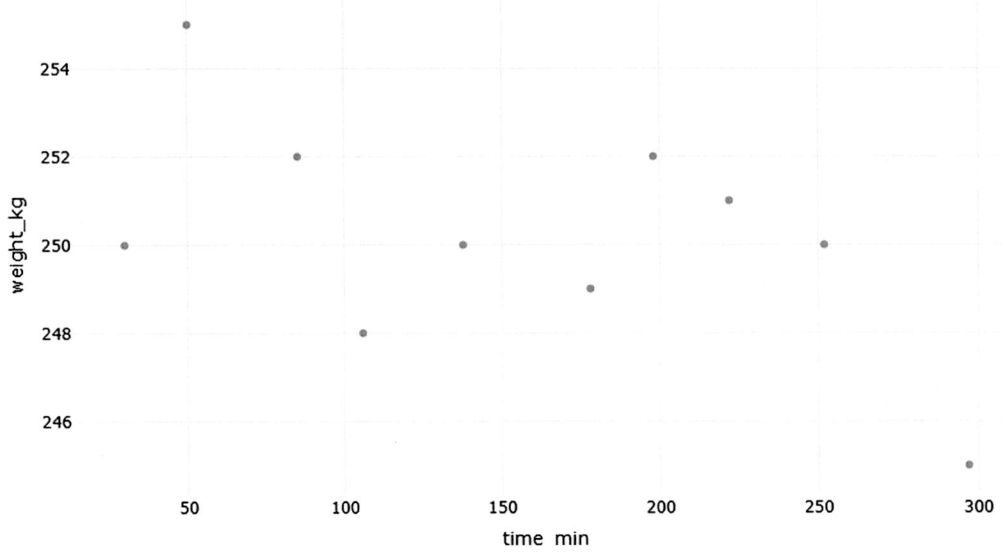

FIGURE 27.3 Scatter plot created with the package `plotly`.

To change the size of the points on the graph in Figure 27.3, just use the argument `size`, internally to the function `list()` declared to the argument `marker`:

```
scatter_plotly <- plot_ly(data = papermisto,
                          x = ~ time_min,
                          y = ~ weight_kg,
                          type = "scatter",
                          marker = list(color = "goldenrod",
                                        size = 15))

scatter_plotly
```

Figure 27.4 shows the result obtained from the previous command.

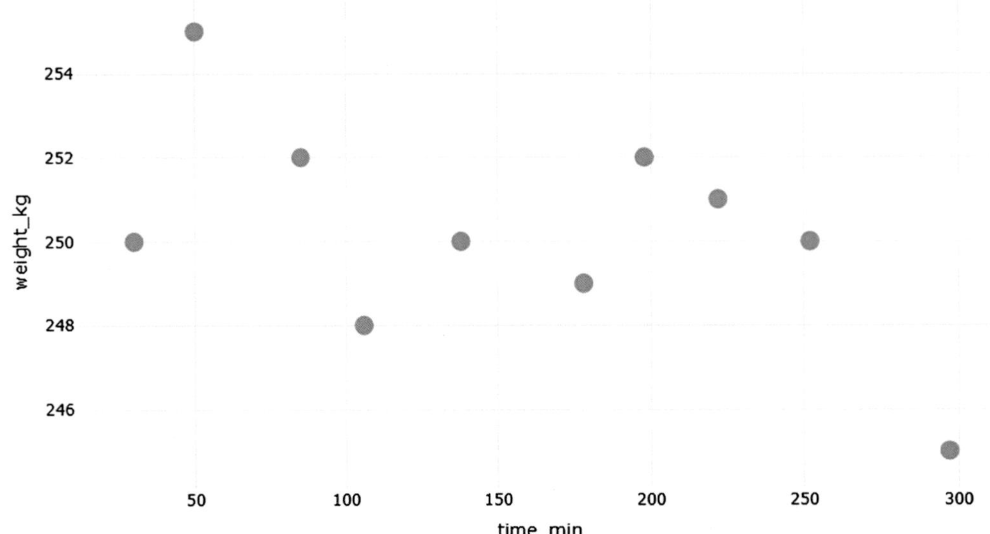

FIGURE 27.4 Scatter plot created with the package `plotly`.

In a similar way to what is done for dot colors and sizes, we can add an outline color for these dots to our attribute list. However, the detailing of the contours of the points must always be linked to the declaration of the thickness of this contour:

```
scatter_plotly <- plot_ly(data = papermisto,
                          x = ~ time_min,
                          y = ~ weight_kg,
                          type = "scatter",
                          marker = list(color = "goldenrod",
                                        size = 15,
                                        line = list(
                                          color = "darkred",
                                          width = 3)))
scatter_plotly
```

An attentive reader will notice that the outline of the points was elaborated by the argument `line`. Because the outline of the points depends on a color and a thickness, we go back to using the function `list()` to list the desired attributes. Figure 27.5 shows the result obtained from the previous command.

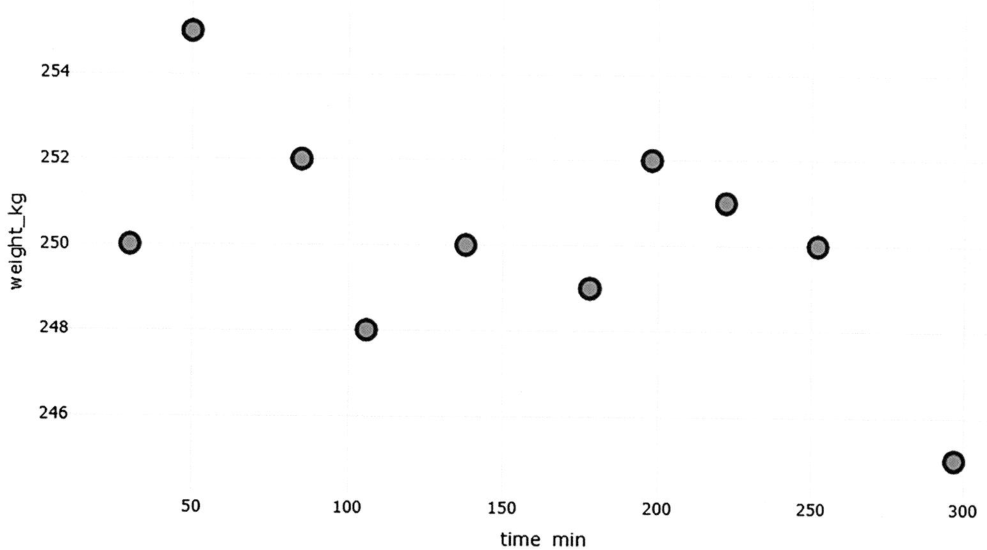

FIGURE 27.5 Scatter plot created with the package `plotly`.

Once this is done, we will move on to inserting a title in our scatter plot. **This is where the mindset shift discussed in "The library `plotly`" section begins to make practical sense.** We will not revisit the last routine; instead, we will add a title to the already existing object `scatter_plotly`:

```
scatter_plotly <- scatter_plotly %>%
  layout(title = "Evolution of the weight throughout time")
scatter_plotly
```

Looking at the previous routine, it is normal to imagine that a beginner in R-based language could be confused. In this routine, we are not overwriting the object `scatter_plotly`; we are just adding a new attribute to the chart, namely, a title.

To add a title, we are starting from the object `scatter_plotly` at its previous stage, using the operator `%>%` and, with the help of the function `layout()`, we are arguing a textual value to the argument `title`. Figure 27.6 shows the result obtained from the previous command.

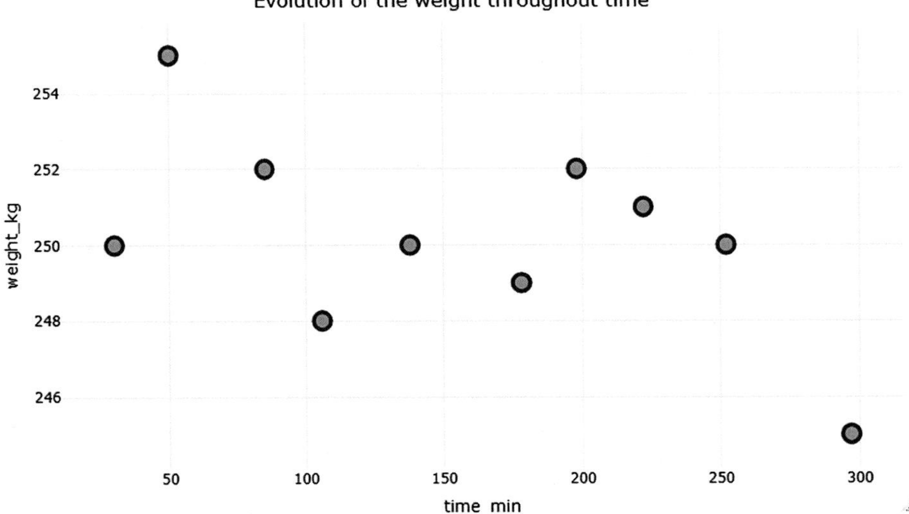

FIGURE 27.6 Scatter plot created with the package `plotly`.

To add or modify the names of the X and Y axes, we must use the arguments `xaxis` and `yaxis`, respectively. Internally to these arguments, we must list the desired attributes, as follows. Figure 27.7 shows the result obtained from the previous command.

```
scatter_plotly <- scatter_plotly %>%
  layout(yaxis = list(title = "Weight (kg)"),
         xaxis = list(title = "Time (min)"))
```

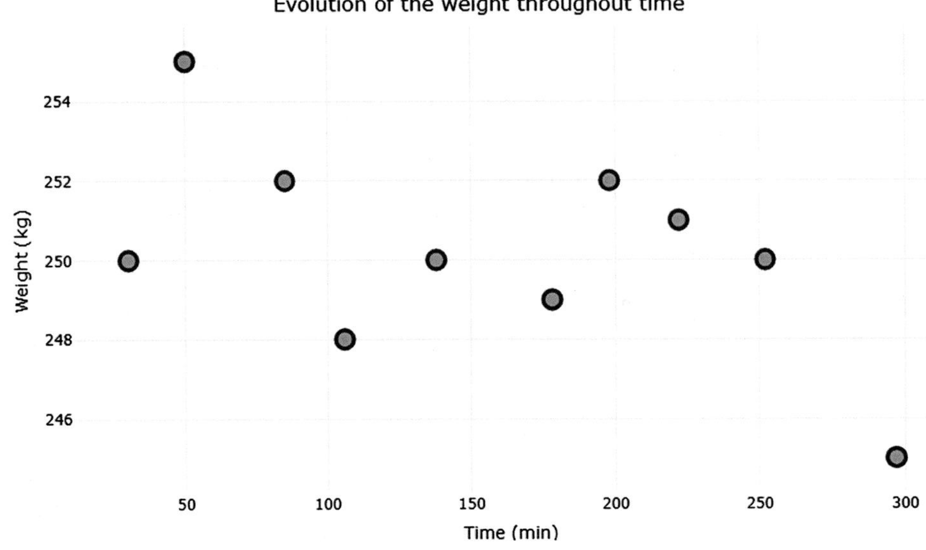

FIGURE 27.7 Scatter plot created with the package `plotly`.

Let us assume that the reader is willing to establish a 3D scatter plot—something similar to the one presented in the appendix of Chapter 13 of this work (Figures 13.8 and 13.9). The novelty in relation to what has been studied so far in this section will be the declaration of the variable that will occupy the Z axis and the argument `type = "scatter3d"`.

A fair question might be: Why, in constructing the 3D graphs in the appendix to Chapter 13 of this work, did the authors not argue type = `"scatter3d"` for the function `plot_ly()`? We did not do it at the time because we know that the algorithm `plot_ly()` has well-defined rules for most cases, so it is smart to recognize the most common needs of its users. The intention in this chapter, however, is to teach the reader about the capabilities of `plotly` (assuming that he or she knows little about this package) in order to be able to read Chapter 28 of this work and, from it, create more elegant dashboards. If you are new to `plotly`, we recommend declaring the argument `type` to build your graphs.

That said, we ask the reader to open the dataset `demographic_atlas.RData` (Fávero and Belfiore, 2019), which we used in Chapter 12 of this work, whose variables are described in Table 12.4:

```
load("demographic_atlas.RData")
```

Imagine that we want to visualize a 3D scatter plot that demonstrates the joint behavior of the variables *income*, *m2_inhab* and *scholarity*. Using the knowledge gained so far, we can command the following:

```
demographic_plotly <- plot_ly(data = demographic_atlas,
                              x = ~ income,
                              y = ~ m2_inhab,
                              z = ~ scholarity,
                              type = "scatter3d")

demographic_plotly
```

Figure 27.8 shows the graph obtained from the previous codes.

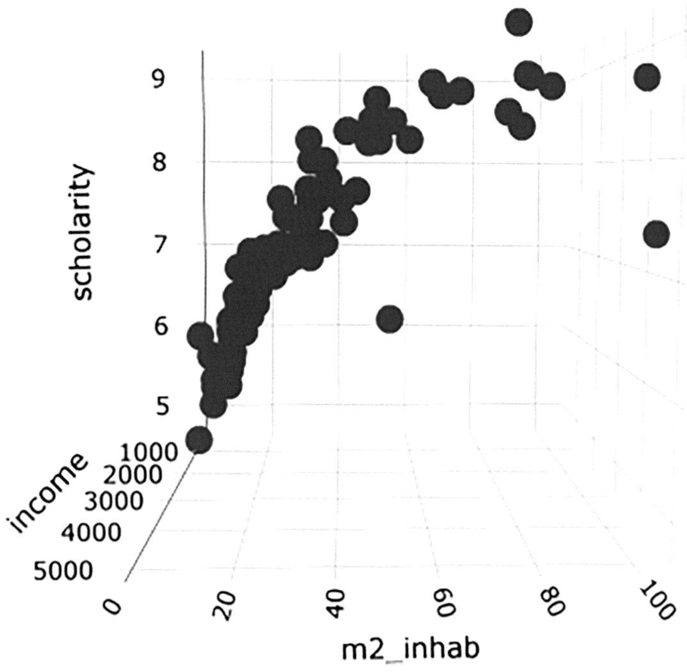

FIGURE 27.8 3D scatter plot created with the package `plotly`.

To add some aesthetic attributes, in order to make the graphic in Figure 27.8 more elegant, we can command:

```
demographic_plotly <- plot_ly(data = demographic_atlas,
        x = ~ income,
        y = ~ m2_inhab,
        z = ~ scholarity,
        type = "scatter3d",
        marker = list(color = "darkgreen",
                      size = 5,
```

Continued

```
                    line = list(color = "black",
                                width = 1))) %>%
layout(scene = list(xaxis = list(title = "Household Income"),
                    yaxis = list(title = "Built area (m²) / number of inhabitants"),
                    zaxis = list(title = "Years of Schooling")))

demographic_plotly
```

Figure 27.9 shows the 3D graphic obtained from the previous command.

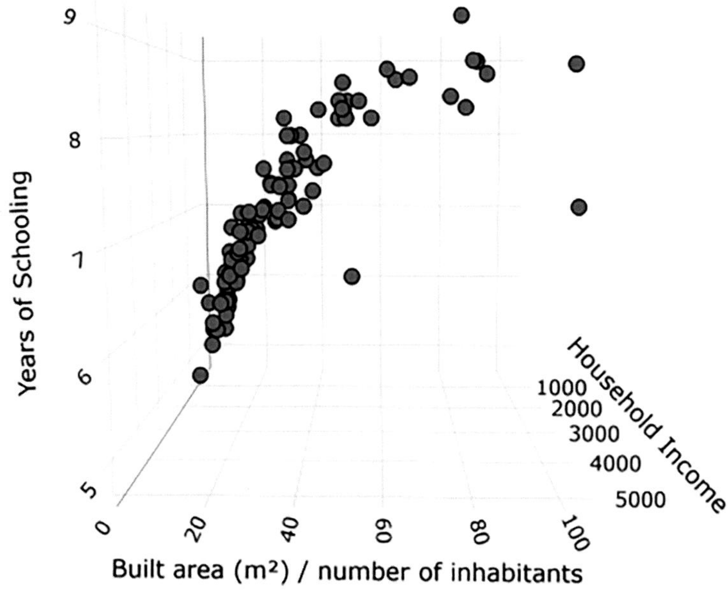

FIGURE 27.9 3D scatter plot created with the package `plotly`.

An interesting thing to do next might be to define a variable to stratify the observations in Figure 27.9. Therefore, let's imagine that we want to stratify the individuals in our chart into two groups: (1) those with a population density *(pop_density)* less than or equal to 96.17 inhab/km^2; and (2) those with a population density *(pop_density)* above 96.17 inhab/km^2.

To accomplish this goal, we will need two new arguments to the function `plot_ly()`: `color` to define which variable will generate the stratification, and `colors` to define which colors will be used in each group after layering. Because the colors of the observations will be defined by a stratification given from a variable, it makes no sense to continue declaring a color for each point of the scatter plot to the argument `marker`:

```
demographic_plotly <- plot_ly(data = demographic_atlas,
                              x = ~ income,
                              y = ~ m2_inhab,
                              z = ~ scholarity,
                              color = ~ pop_density > 96.17,
                              colors = c("darkgreen","orange"),
                              type = "scatter3d",
                              marker = list(size = 5,
                                            line = list(color = "black",
                                                        width = 1))) %>%
 layout(scene = list(xaxis = list(title = "Household Income"),
                     yaxis = list(title = "Built area (m²) / number of inhabitants"),
                     zaxis = list(title = "Years of Schooling")))
```

Figure 27.10 shows the result obtained from the previous command.

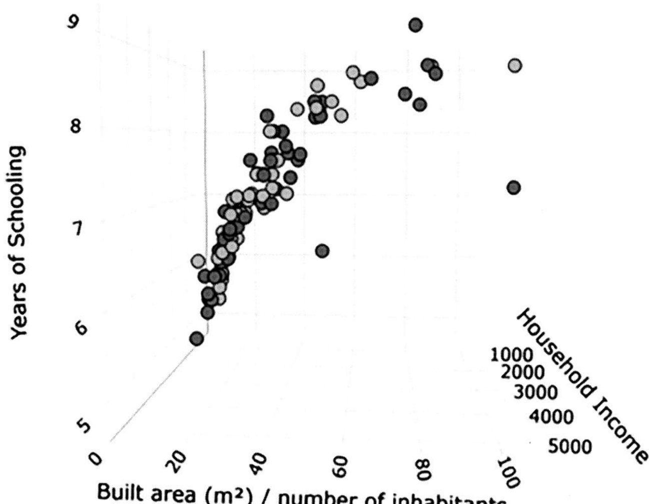

FIGURE 27.10 3D scatter plot created with the package plotly.

Next, we will demonstrate creating a line chart with the package plotly.

Line graph with plotly

For this example, we will use the dataset present in the file cheap_easy.RData (Fávero and Belfiore, 2019) again, whose variables are described in Table 4.13.

```
load("cheap_easy.RData")
```

Creating a line chart with the package plotly for the first time is not so intuitive. If we followed the logic proposed in Figure 27.1, plotly would imply the creation of a bar graph for the case. In order for the situation not to occur and for the graph created to be a line graph, we must argue type = "scatter" and mode = "lines". The idea is that the lines of the graph, given by the argument mode = "lines", cross the markers given by the argument type = "scatter":

```
lines_plotly <- plot_ly(data = cheap_easy,
                        x = ~ month,
                        y = ~ losses,
                        type = "scatter",
                        mode = "lines")
lines_plotly
```

Figure 27.11 shows the result obtained from the previous commands.

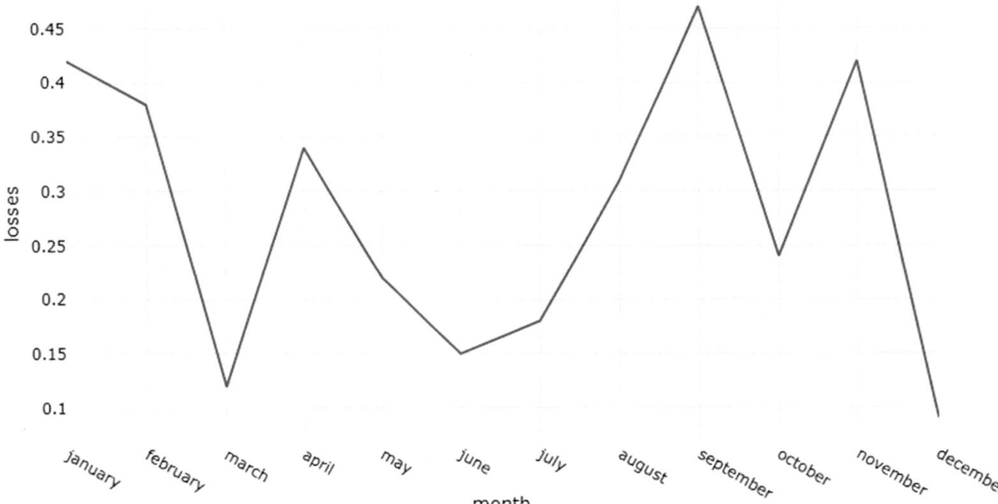

FIGURE 27.11 Line chart created with the package `plotly`.

If the reader wishes to highlight the markers that show where the coordinates of the abscissa and ordinate axes meet, he or she can command the following:

```
lines_plotly <- plot_ly(data = cheap_easy,
                        x = ~ month,
                        y = ~ losses,
                        type = "scatter",
                        mode = "lines + markers")
lines_plotly
```

The reader will have noticed that we changed the value of the mode argument to `"lines + markers"`. The syntax `plotly` therefore allows for the combination of attributes for graphing. Figure 27.12 shows the result obtained from the previous command.

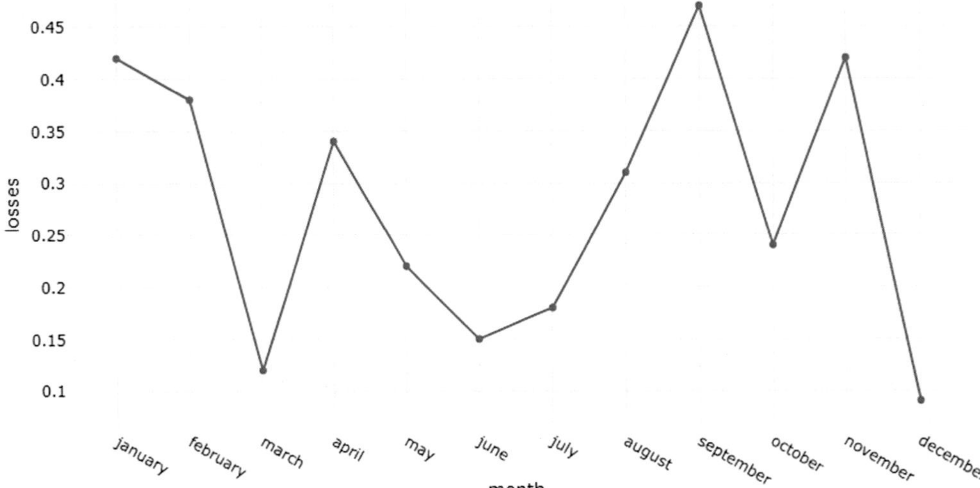

FIGURE 27.12 Line chart created with the package `plotly`.

Even though we can combine some arguments (i.e., mode = "lines + markers"), the declarations for any changes in color and size/thickness of graphic components must be declared individually, as follows:

```
lines_plotly <- plot_ly(data = cheap_easy,
                        x = ~ month,
                        y = ~ losses,
                        type = "scatter",
                        mode = "lines + markers",
                        marker = list(color = "chartreuse",
                                      size = 10),
                        line = list(color = "deepskyblue",
                                    width = 3))
lines_plotly
```

The graph resulting from the combination of the above codes is contained in Figure 27.13.

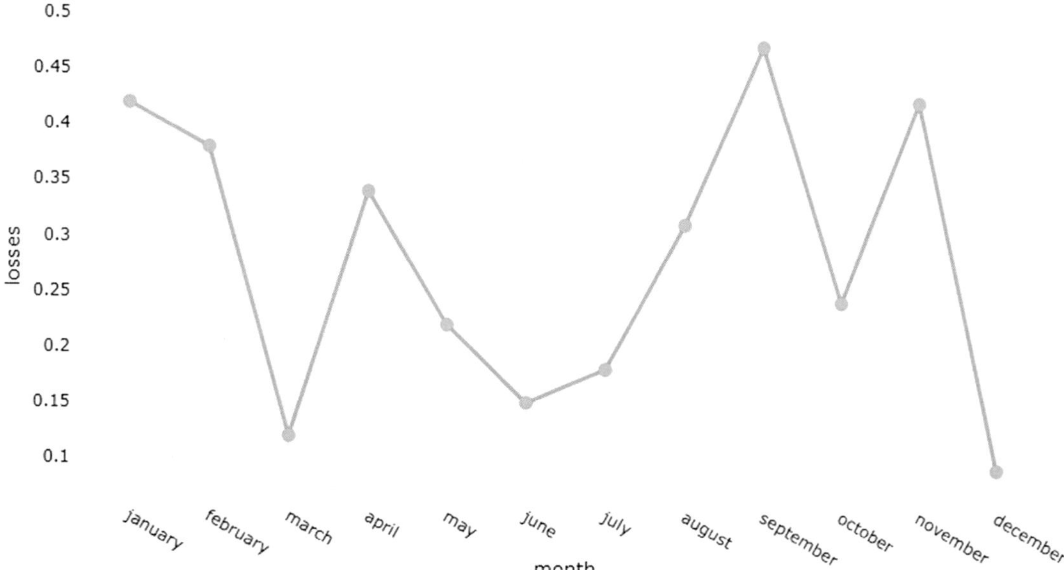

FIGURE 27.13 Line chart created with the package plotly.

In Figure 27.13, an attentive reader will notice that we used the argument marker to set the attributes of the points on the graph, and we used the argument line to set the attributes of the graph lines.

The addition of a possible title and the insertion of names for the axes follows the logic studied in the "Scatter plot with plotly" section earlier in this chapter:

```
lines_plotly <- lines_plotly %>%
  layout(title = "Losses x Months",
         yaxis = list(title = "Losses (%)"),
         xaxis = list(title = "Months"))
  lines_plotly
```

Figure 27.14 shows the result obtained from the previous command.

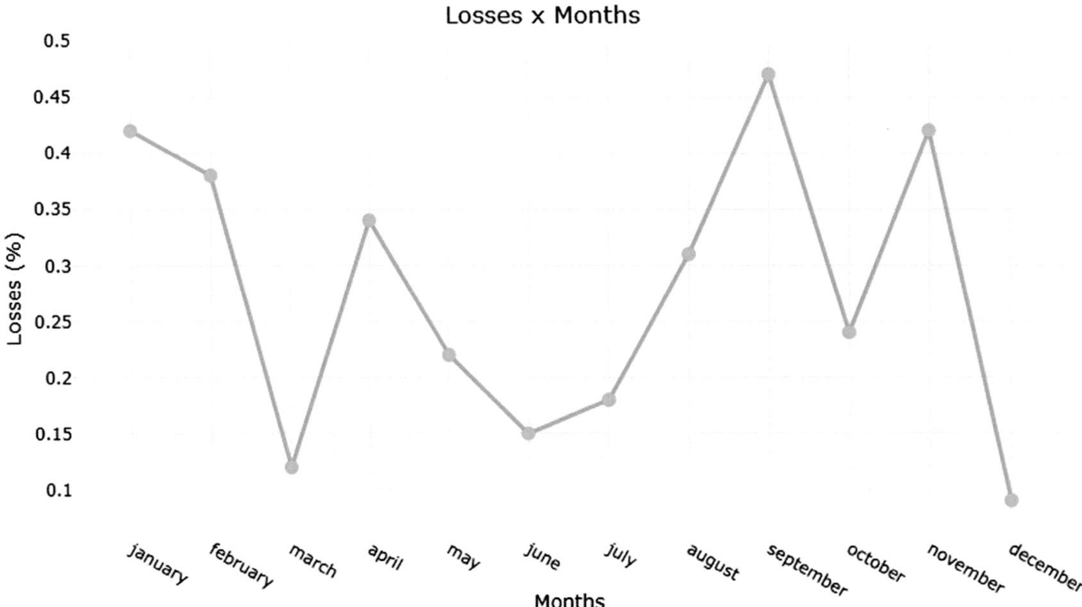

FIGURE 27.14 Line chart created with the package `plotly`.

Line graphs are very interesting for observing trends, and `plotly` can plot, for the same graph, trends in different situations. We propose that the reader open the `public_finances.RData` (Fávero and Belfiore, 2019):

```
load("public_finances.RData")
```

The dataset contained by the object `public_finances` presents some expenses of a certain Brazilian university, between the years 2008 and 2020, as described in Table 27.1:

TABLE 27.1 University expenses between 2008 and 2020.

Year	Payroll expenses	Other expenses
2008	79,575,753.66	17,885,827.34
2009	88,092,777.96	18,572,535.80
2010	101,657,278.88	26,658,622.36
2011	113,214,560.42	20,051,731.04
2012	123,736,965.63	25,749,439.63
2013	141,243,043.24	32,454,348.25
2014	196,361,592.28	36,868,663.57
2015	229,915,213.84	42,353,287.19
2016	250,484,306.11	37,689,089.45
2017	277,911,804.36	41,547,211.93
2018	284,540,280.34	36,462,842.79
2019	303,749,556.03	38,219,691.30
2020	334,381,791.98	39,419,360.65

Suppose that the interest is to compare the growth of personnel expenses in relation to other expenses between the years 2008 and 2020. Directly, our objective will be to plot, in the same graph, two different types of data: personnel expenses and other expenses.

Therefore, we will start by commanding the creation of a graph of spending on people as a function of time, whose output is shown in Figure 27.15. Because a second layer (of the variable *Other Expenses*) will be added in the future, we have already gone ahead and used the argument name, to name the line created at that moment. This procedure, at first, does not seem to be the most important; however, when we add the second layer, its importance will become clear.

```
public_finances_plotly <- plot_ly(data = public_finances,
                                  x = ~ year,
                                  y = ~ payroll_expenses,
                                  name = "Payroll Expenses",
                                  type = "scatter",
                                  mode = "lines + markers")

public_finances_plotly
```

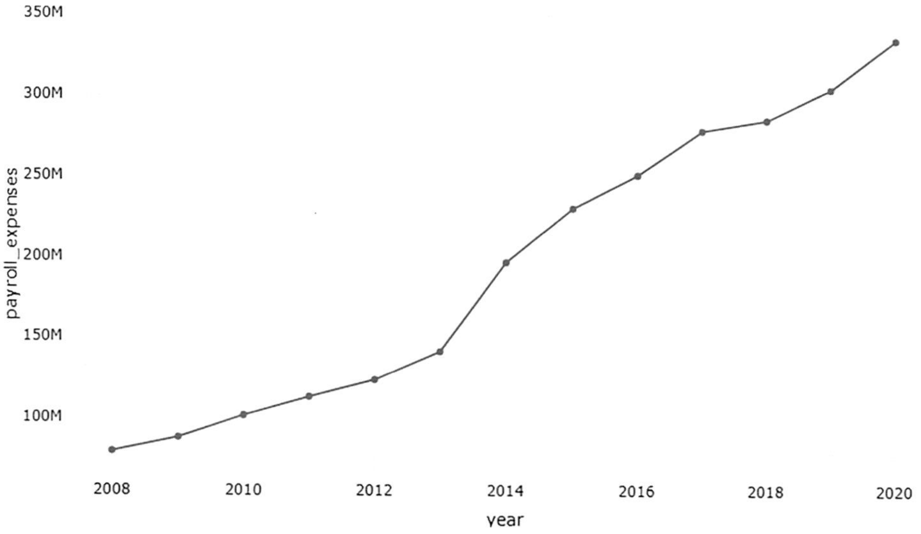

FIGURE 27.15 Line chart created with the package plotly.

To add a line with the values of the variable *Other Expenses*, we must use the function add_trace() from the package plotly. The argument to be declared for the function add_trace() is very similar to that declared for the algorithm plot_ly():

```
public_finances_plotly <- public_finances_plotly %>%
  add_trace(y = ~ other_expenses,
            name = "Other Expenses",
            mode = "lines + markers",
            line = list(dash = "dot"))

public_finances_plotly
```

In the previous routine, we did not have to re-declare the data source (i.e., the object public_finances) or the variable that would occupy the abscissa axis, as previously discussed. Thus, to create a new layer, it was enough to use the function add_trace(), declaring which other variable would be present in the ordinate axis (the variable *Other Expenses*).

We also added an aesthetic detail with the argument dash = "dot". Another useful value option for the argument dash can be the eponymous "dash", enclosed in quotes.

Finally, it is important to point out that we use the argument name to identify the new line created. Figure 27.16 shows the result obtained from the previous command.

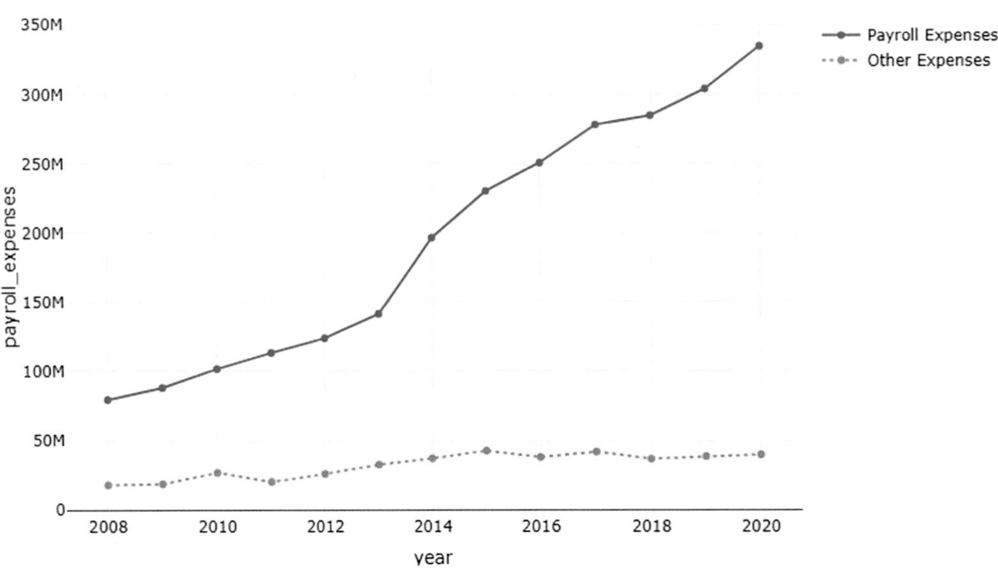

FIGURE 27.16 Line chart created with the package `plotly`.

Recall the routine that gave rise to Figure 27.15. There, we introduced the reader to the argument `name`. If the reader did not use it, there would be no identification that the solid line (in blue, for those who are reading the color version of this work) in the caption of Figure 27.16 refers to the *Payroll Expenses* variable.

If the caption is not in a satisfactory location, we can move it or even hide it with the function `layout()`. To hide it, we can declare the value `FALSE` for the argument `showlegend`:

```
public_finances_plotly <- public_finances_plotly %>%
  layout(showlegend = FALSE)

public_finances_plotly
```

Although we agree that the absence of a legend in a given graph can be a problem for the information recipient, it must be considered that the package `plotly` creates naturally interactive graphs, just by hovering the mouse over them, to know what handles each component of the graph. Figure 27.17 shows the graph in Figure 27.13 without subtitles.

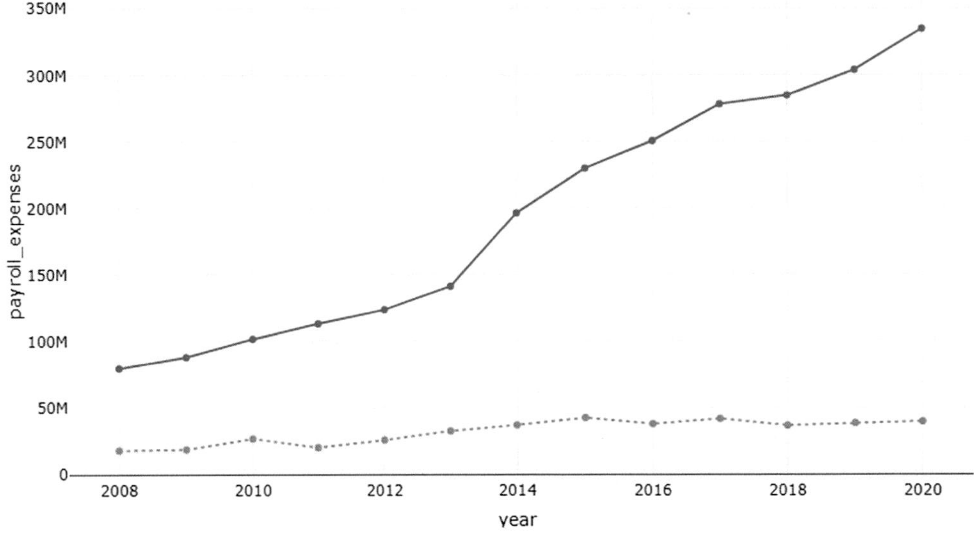

FIGURE 27.17 Line chart created with the package `plotly`.

On the other hand, if the intention is to change the subtitle's orientation, we can command the following:

```
public_finances_plotly <- public_finances_plotly %>%
  layout(showlegend = TRUE,
         legend = list(orientation = "h"))

public_finances_plotly
```

Note that we had to change the value of the argument `showlegend` to `TRUE` as we previously assigned it the value `FALSE`! If this was not done, the legend, which was hidden for the construction of Figure 27.17, would not appear again!

It is also possible to notice the creation of a list for the argument `legend`. For the mentioned list, it was argued `orientation = "h"` for a horizontal positioning of the legend; to return to vertical positioning, we can change the value of the argument `orientation` to `"v"`. Figure 27.18 shows the result obtained from the previous command.

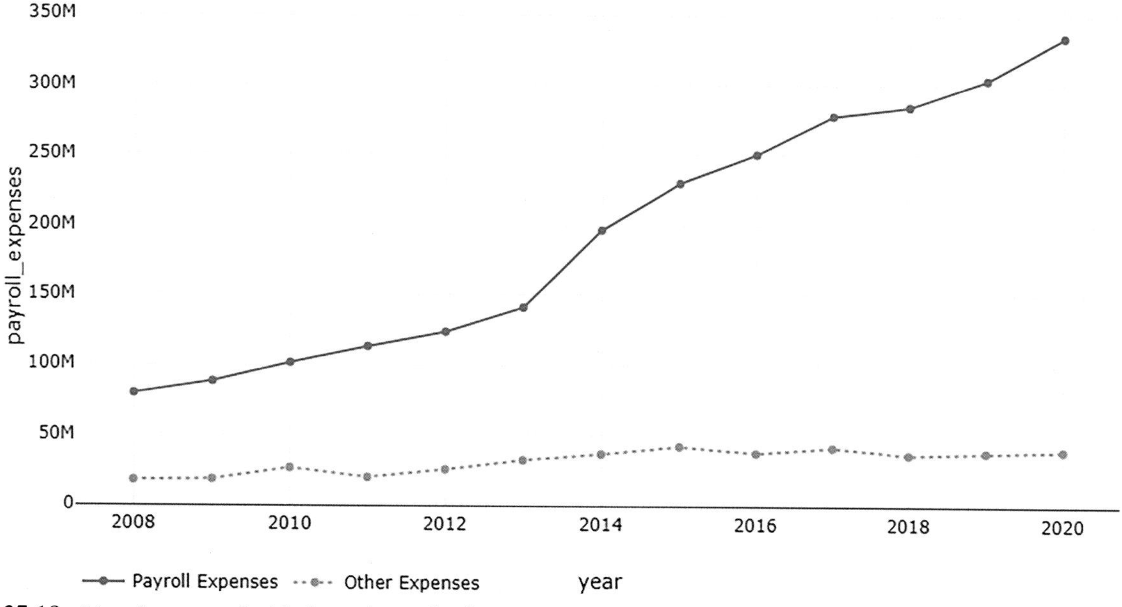

FIGURE 27.18 Line chart created with the package `plotly`.

Next, we will assist the reader in building a bar plot.

Bar chart with `plotly`

To establish a bar chart, we will use the file `satisfaction_survey.RData` (Fávero and Belfiore, 2019).

```
load("satisfaction_survey.RData")
```

The variables present in the object were presented in Table 4.9 and are replicated here.

The reader will notice that the object `satisfaction_survey` is a dataset that does not present the frequencies of each of the categories of the *satisfaction* variable. In order for the intended graphic to be correctly prepared, we first propose the following command:

```
new_survey <- satisfaction_survey %>%
  group_by(satisfaction) %>%
  count()
```

The previous command saved, in a new object called `new_survey`, the occurrence counts of the *satisfaction* variable. The reader can be sure of what happened when declaring the name of the new object for R:

```
new_survey
```

Figure 27.19 shows the counting structure present in the new object called `new_survey`.

```
  satisfaction      n
  <fct>         <int>
1 poor             12
2 satisfactory     32
3 good             18
4 excellent        58
```

FIGURE 27.19 The object `new_survey`.

According to Figure 27.19, the object `new_survey` has two variables: (1) *satisfaction*, whose description is still the same as in Table 4.9, and (2) *n*, which indicates the frequency of occurrence of each category.

Once this is done, we can proceed with the construction of our bar chart, as follows:

```
bar_plotly <- plot_ly(data = new_survey,
                      x = ~ satisfaction,
                      y = ~ n,
                      type = "bar")
bar_plotly
```

Figure 27.20 shows the result obtained from the previous command.

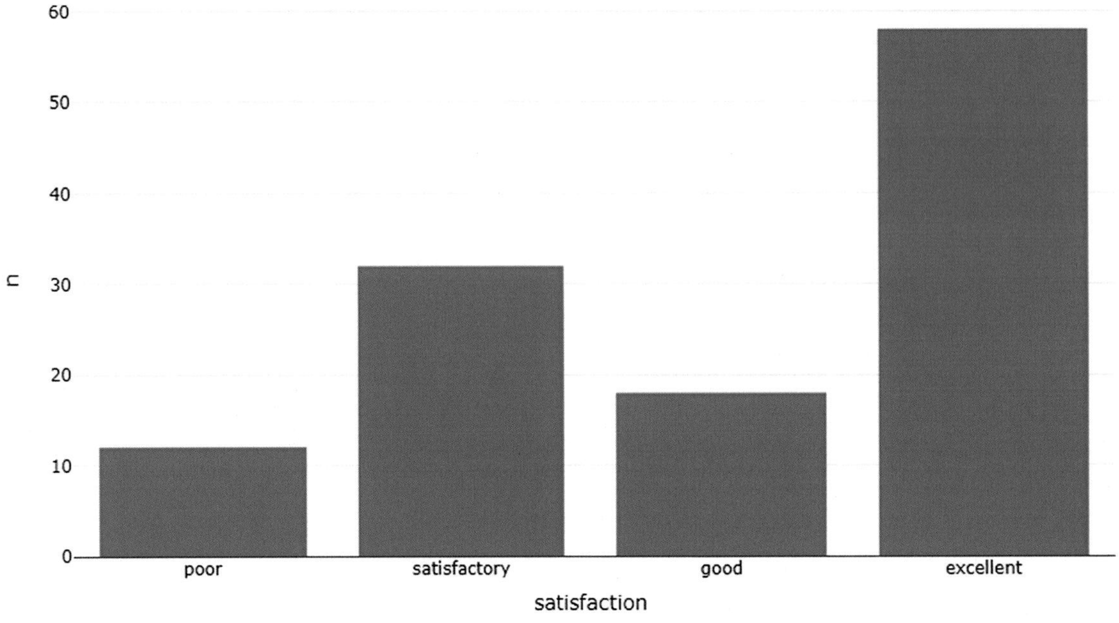

FIGURE 27.20 Bar chart created with the package `plotly`.

If the reader feels the need to present the total labels of each category of the *satisfaction* variable in each bar, he or she could use the arguments `text` and `textposition`:

```
bar_plotly <- plot_ly(data = new_survey,
                      x = ~ satisfaction,
                      y = ~ n,
```

Continued

```
                      type = "bar",
                      text = new_survey$n,
                      textposition = "auto")
bar_plotly
```

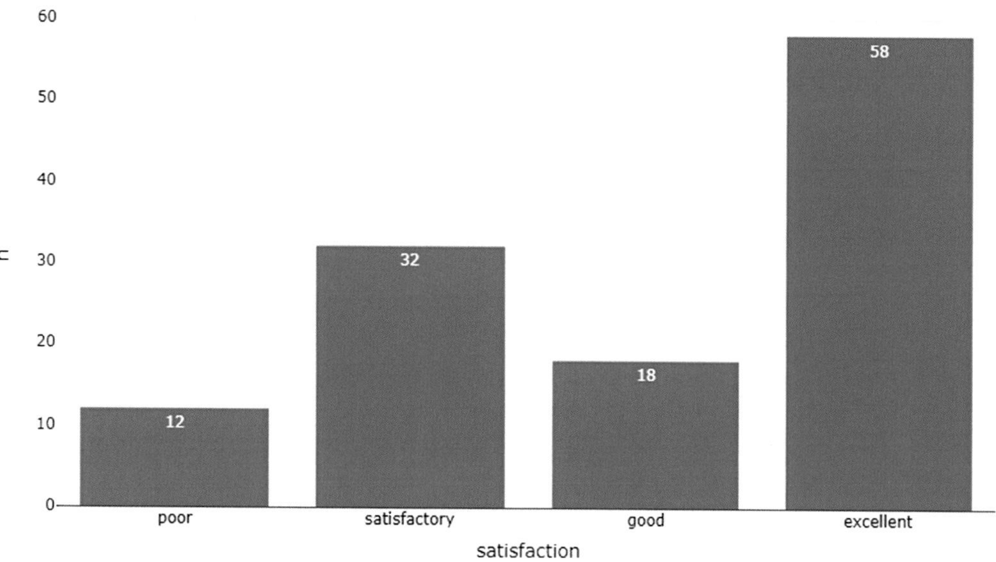

FIGURE 27.21 Bar chart created with the package `plotly`.

In the previous routine, the argument `text` requires presentation of the source of the labels for the totals of the given variable category (*satisfaction*, in this case); for the argument `textposition`, however, we must indicate the values `"inside"` or `"outside"`; we indicated `"auto"` so the algorithm will suggest what it judges to be the best place to display the totals labels. Figure 27.21 demonstrates the generated graph.

Suppose you wanted to emphasize the category with the highest count. We could give it a different color from the others, as follows:

```
bar_plotly <- plot_ly(data = new_survey,
                      x = ~ satisfaction,
                      y = ~ n,
                      type = "bar",
                      text = new_survey$n,
                      textposition = "auto",
                      marker = list(color = c("steelblue",
                                              "steelblue",
                                              "steelblue",
                                              "red")))
bar_plotly
```

Figure 27.22 shows the proposed graph with an emphasis on the category with the highest total.

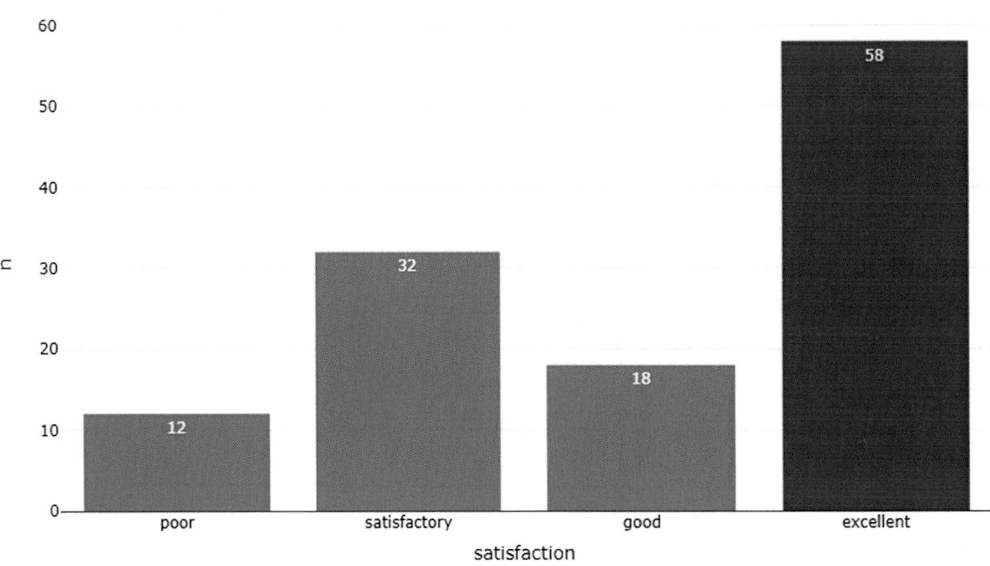

FIGURE 27.22 Bar chart created with the package `plotly`.

If the reader wants a horizontal bar graph, it would be enough to argue `orientation = "h"`, not forgetting to change the declarations of which variable will occupy the ordinate axis and which will occupy the abscissa axis; in relation to the graph in Figure 27.22, we invert the positions of the variables involved. Figure 27.23 shows the result obtained from the previous command.

```
bar_plotly <- plot_ly(data = new_survey,
                      x = ~ n,
                      y = ~ satisfaction,
                      type = "bar",
                      text = new_survey$n,
                      textposition = "auto",
                      orientation = "h",
     marker = list(color = c("steelblue",
                            "steelblue",
                            "steelblue",
                            "red")))

bar_plotly
```

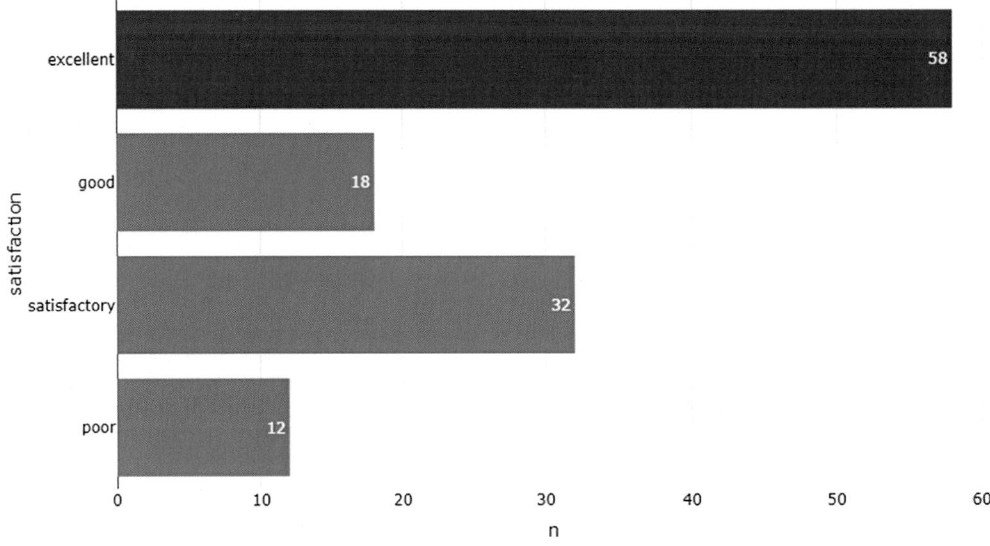

FIGURE 27.23 Bar chart created with the package `plotly`.

Suppose further that the idea was to use bar charts to compare two distinct groups using grouped bars or stacked bars. In this case, we would go back to using the function `add_trace()`, as studied in the "Line graph with `plotly`" section of this work. We ask the reader to open the file `banks_comparison.RData` (Fávero and Belfiore, 2019), whose structure is shown in Table 27.2.

```
load("banks_comparison.RData")
```

For this case, Table 27.2 presents the satisfaction levels among 120 account holders who have, at the same time, accounts in Bank A and in Bank B.

TABLE 27.2 Satisfaction levels among 120 account holders who have accounts in Bank A and Bank B at the same time.

Satisfaction	Bank A	Bank B
Poor	12	19
Satisfactory	32	27
Good	18	62
Excelent	58	12

To create a grouped bar chart, or a stacked bar chart, based on the data in Table 27.2, we must first choose one of its columns (*Bank A* or *Bank B*) to establish a common bar chart, as already studied. Then, using the function `add_trace()`, we will add the data from the other variable. This practice, therefore, is very similar to the one studied for the second case in the "Line graph with `plotly`" section:

```
banks_plotly <- plot_ly(data = banks_comparison,
                        x = ~ satisfaction,
                        y = ~ bank_a,
                        type = "bar",
                        text = banks_comparison$bank_a,
                        textposition = "auto",
                        name = "Bank A")
banks_plotly
```

The result of the above codes, visually speaking, should be identical to Figure 27.21. After that, using the function `add_trace()`, we will add the *Bank B* information:

```
banks_plotly <- banks_plotly %>%
  add_trace(y = ~ bank_b,
            name = "Bank B",
            text = banks_comparison$bank_b,
            textposition = "auto")
banks_plotly
```

By default, the plotly package will generate a grouped bar graph, as shown in Figure 27.24. Note also that the ordinate axis still holds the name of the first variable declared to it (*Bank A*, in this case).

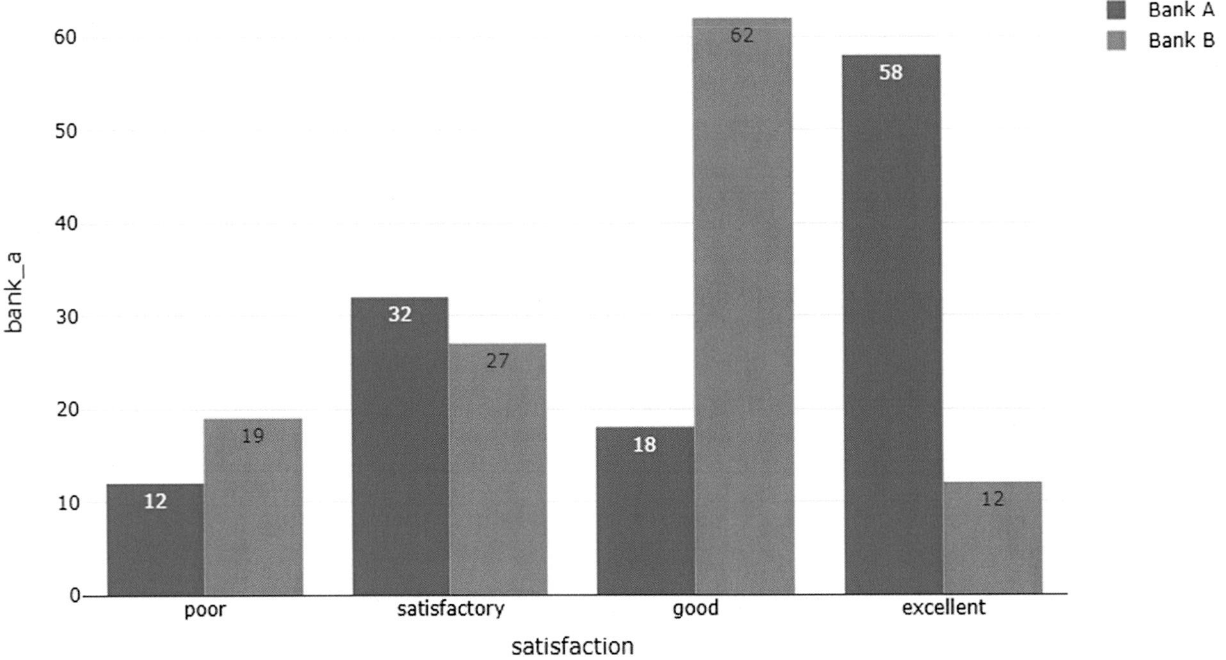

FIGURE 27.24 Grouped bar chart created with the package `plotly`.

If the reader wants a stacked bar chart, he or she can use the function `layout()`, arguing `barmode = "stack"`:

```
banks_plotly <- banks_plotly %>%
  layout(barmode = "stack",
         yaxis = list(title = "Count"),
         xaxis = list(title = "Satisfaction Level"))
banks_plotly
```

Figure 27.25 shows the result obtained from the previous command. If the reader wants to go back to the grouped bars format, he or she can argue `barmode = "group"` for the function `layout()`. The logic for renaming axes and adding titles is the same as discussed earlier in this chapter.

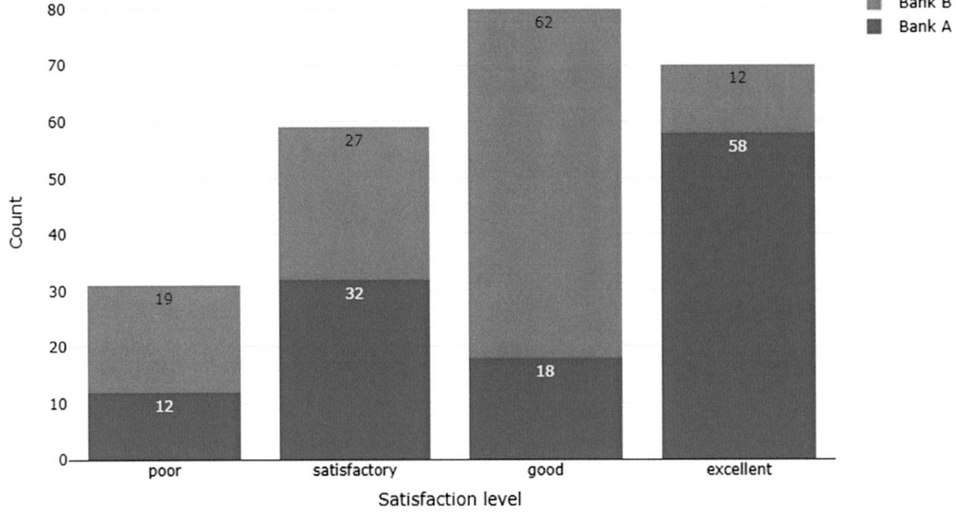

FIGURE 27.25 Stacked bar chart created with the package `plotly`.

Next, we will present the construction of a Pareto chart, which involves the knowledge acquired earlier in this chapter in the "Scatter plot with plotly," "Line graph with plotly," and "Bar chart with plotly" sections.

Pareto chart with plotly

As stated, the making of a Pareto chart will involve knowledge acquired in the "Scatter plot with plotly," "Line graph with plotly," and "Bar chart with plotly" sections. In this sense, we imagine that the reader is already able to do so.

We will start by loading the file cards.RData (Fávero and Belfiore, 2019), already used in Chapters 4 and 7 of this work:

```
load("cards.RData")
```

The data present in the object cards were presented in Table 4.11 and are replicated here.

Similar to what we discussed in Chapters 4 and 7 of this work, for the construction of a Pareto chart, there is a need to organize the dataset in a descending way. However, instead of using the base language of R, we will do so using the data manipulation knowledge of the package tidyverse, which we studied in Chapter 10.

```
cards <- cards %>%
  arrange(desc(absolute_frequency))
```

After that, we will be able to fulfill the first part of our goal of building a Pareto chart: establishing a bar graph, shown in Figure 27.26.

```
pareto_plotly <- plot_ly(data = cards,
                         x = ~ type_of_defect,
                         y = ~ absolute_frequency,
                         type = "bar",
                         name = "Absolute Frequency")

pareto_plotly
```

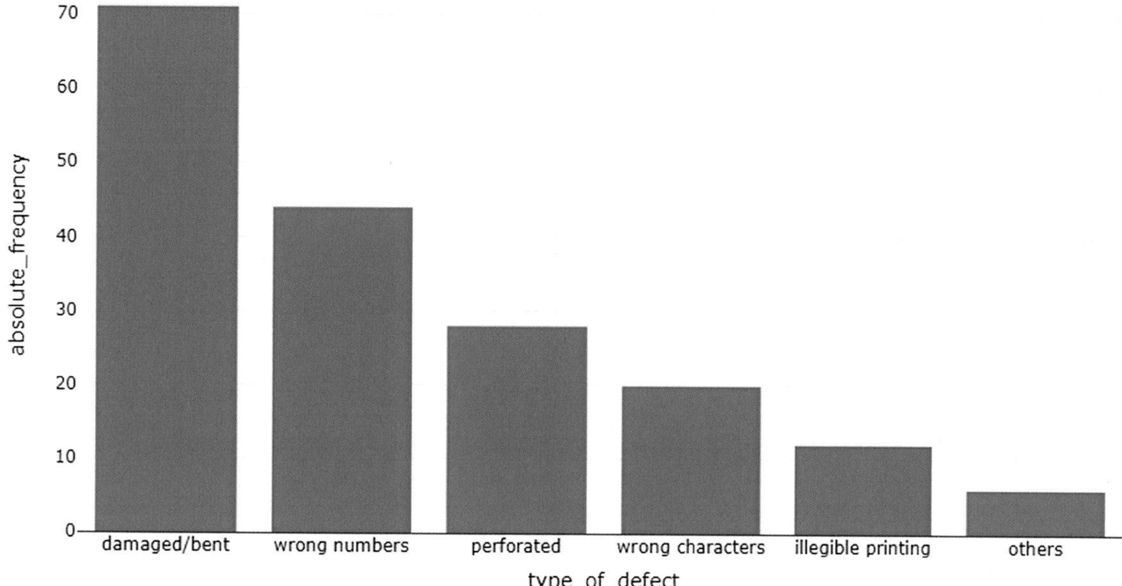

FIGURE 27.26 Vertical bar graph of absolute frequencies created with the package plotly.

The next step will be to create a variable, in the dataset cards, that indicates the cumulative count, as er did in Chapters 4 and 7:

```
cards <- cards %>%
  mutate(cumulative_count = cumsum(
    prop.table(absolute_frequency)
    ) * 100)
```

Finally, we will add the layer with points and lines at once. To add layers, the reader must already foresee the use of the add function add_trace():

```
pareto_plotly <- pareto_plotly %>%
  add_trace(y = ~ cumulative_count,
            type = "scatter",
            mode = "lines + markers",
            name = "Cumulative Count")

pareto_plotly
```

Figure 27.27 shows the graph obtained from the previous command.

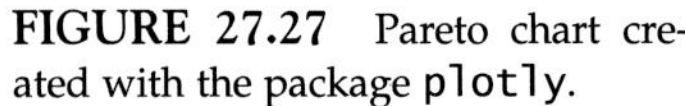

FIGURE 27.27 Pareto chart created with the package plotly.

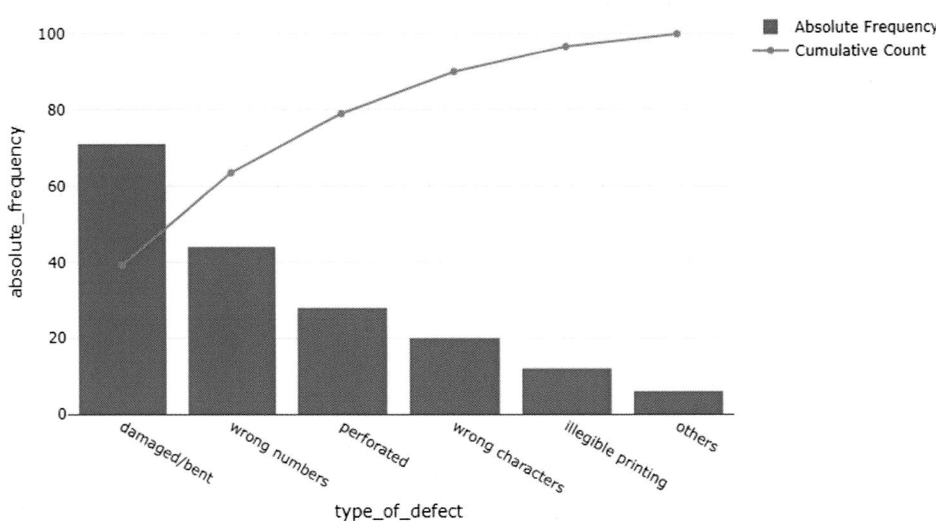

Finally, we can adjust some aesthetic aspects of the chart with the knowledge already acquired in this chapter. The final result is shown in Figure 27.28.

```
pareto_plotly <- pareto_plotly %>%
  layout(yaxis = list(title = ""),
         xaxis = list(title = "Type of Defect"),
         legend = list(orientation = "h"))

pareto_plotly
```

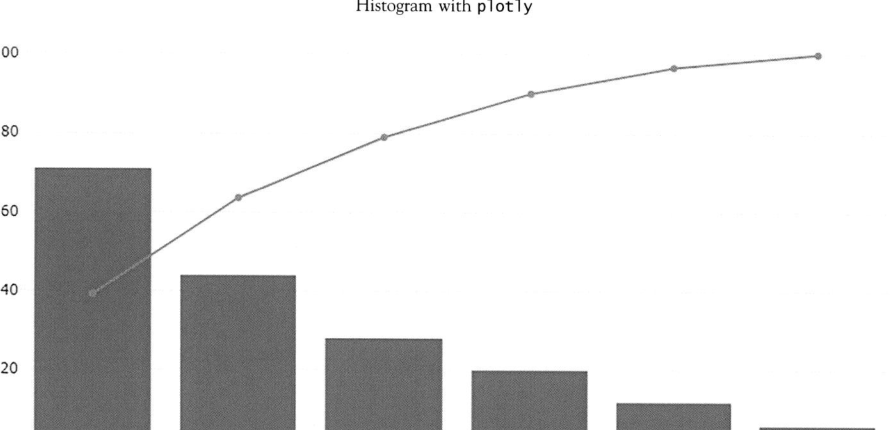

FIGURE 27.28 Pareto chart created with the package `plotly`.

Histogram with `plotly`

With all of the information that has been presented, the construction of a histogram with the package `plotly` will not be difficult for the reader. By the way, for the function `plot_ly()`, the reader must have already guessed that we will apply the argument `type = "histogram"`.

We will reload the file `bank.RData` (Fávero and Belfiore, 2019), whose data were presented in Table 4.15 and are replicated here.

```
load("bank.RData")
```

Once this is done, a histogram can be easily constructed with the package `plotly`, as follows, the result of which is shown in Figure 27.29.

```
hist_plotly <- plot_ly(data = bank,
                       x = ~ number_of_companies,
                       type = "histogram")

hist_plotly
```

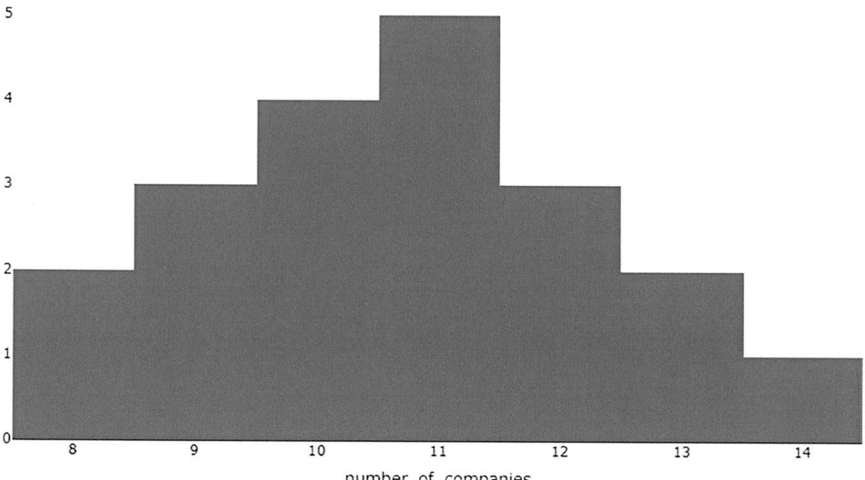

FIGURE 27.29 Histogram created with the package `plotly`.

Simple, right? The great difficulty in building this kind of graph in the package `plotly` is when we want to add a new layer, that is, compare two histograms of phenomena or distinct groups. **For this case, the function `add_trace()` will not help the reader, who should make use of the function `add_histogram()`.**

Suppose we wanted to compare the histograms of the data presented in Table 4.15 with data from a second bank. Thus, we ask the reader to upload the file `banks.RData` (Fávero and Belfiore, 2019):

```
load("banks.RData")
```

The loaded dataset has two variables: *Bank V* (the same data presented in Table 4.15) and *Bank W* (new data). Thus to compare the histograms of the data from the two datasets, the first step is to create an object with the function `plot_ly ()` using only two arguments: an argument that indicates a transparency (`alpha`) and another that indicates the dataset where we will extract the plots:

```
banks_plotly <- plot_ly(data = banks,
                        alpha = 0.5)
```

The idea of the previous routine is to reserve an object, in the case `banks_plotly`, which will keep a minimum structure to support the graphics of the package `plotly`. However, for the graphs that will be commanded in the future, there will be an attribute of transparency given by the argument `alpha` because we will overlay histograms; this way, it will be possible to calmly observe the two distributions.

That said, let's add our first histogram (regarding *Bank V*—Table 4.15):

```
banks_plotly <- banks_plotly %>%
  add_histogram(x = ~ bank_v,
                name = "Bank V")

banks_plotly
```

The result obtained from the previous command should be identical to Figure 27.29, but with an opaque color. Next, we will add the information from the other variable, that is, from *Bank W*:

```
banks_plotly <- banks_plotly %>%
  add_histogram(x = ~ bank_w,
                name = "Bank W") %>%
 layout(barmode = "overlay",
        xaxis = list(title = ""))

banks_plotly
```

The reader will notice that, in addition to the function `add_histogram()`, we use the function `layout()`, arguing `barmode = "overlay"` to it, in order to guarantee the overlapping of the histograms of the two distributions. Figure 27.30 presents the generated graph.

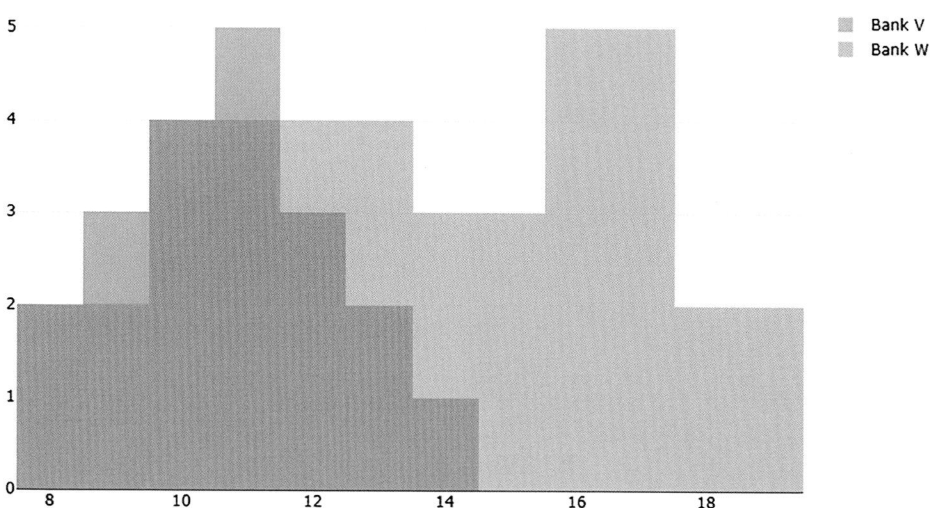

FIGURE 27.30 Overlaid histograms created with the package `plotly`.

If the reader wants the histograms to be stacked, he or she can use the function `layout()`, arguing `barmode = "stack"`, as shown earlier in the "Pareto chart with `plotly`" section.

Boxplot with `plotly`

Creating a boxplot with the package plotly is easy. For the task, we will use the file `cheap_easy.RData` (Fávero and Belfiore, 2019) again, presented in the "Line graph" section in Chapter 4 and the "Line graph with `ggplot2`" section in Chapter 7 of this work, whose variables are shown in Table 4.13.

```
load("cheap_easy.RData")
```

The construction of a boxplot can be done as follows:

```
boxplot_plotly <- plot_ly(data = cheap_easy,
                          y = ~ losses,
                          type = "box",
                          name = "")

boxplot_plotly
```

Figure 27.31 shows the result obtained from the previous command. If the reader wants to add other layers, that is, other boxplots of other variables, he or she must use the function `add_trace()`, already presented earlier in this chapter.

A feature that can be useful for the reader is the addition of jittered points to the boxplot. To do so, just argue `boxpoints = "all"` for the function `plot_ly()`:

```
boxplot_plotly <- plot_ly(data = cheap_easy,
                          y = ~ losses,
                          type = "box",
                          boxpoints = "all",
                          name = "") %>%
  layout(yaxis = list(title = ""))

boxplot_plotly
```

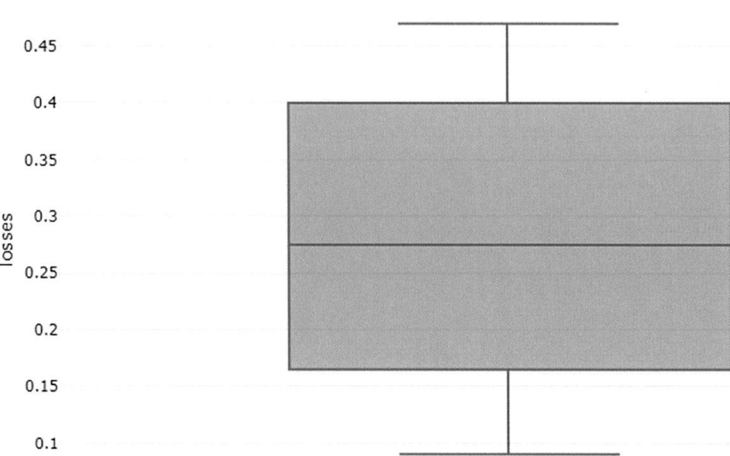

FIGURE 27.31 Boxplot created with the package `plotly`.

The previous command will add a point cloud of the observations used to construct the boxplot. The horizontal distance between the points is mere deliberate disorganization of the algorithm in order to avoid data overlapping. The graph is shown in Figure 27.32.

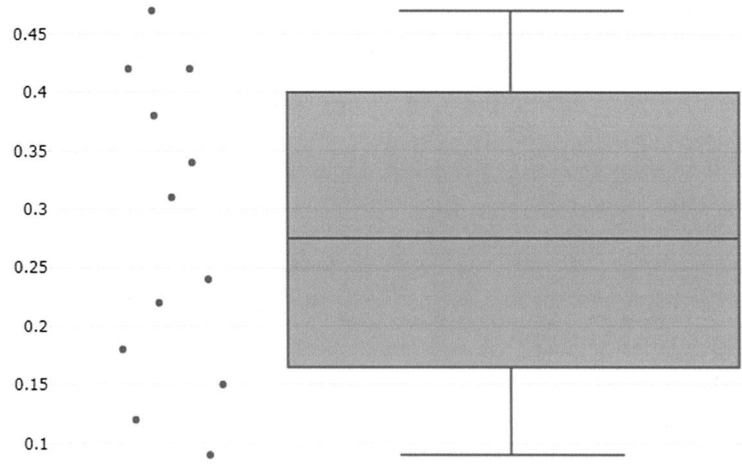

FIGURE 27.32 Boxplot created with the package `plotly`.

Pie charts with `plotly`

In the appendix of Chapter 7 we talked about the limitations of the package `ggplot2` in the elaboration of pie charts. Even though we have proposed a solution, we suggest that, for this kind of graph, the package `plotly` could be a less traumatic path.

Thus, in the appendix of Chapter 7, we suggested a routine for pie charts, but we did not adequately explore the arguments declared to the function `plot_ly()`. In this section, we will precisely equip the reader for this kind of graph using the syntax of `plotly`. To do so, we ask the reader to load the file `notebooks.RData` (Fávero and Belfiore, 2019).

```
load("notebooks.RData")
```

Table 7.2 presents the data present in the file `notebooks.RData`, which refers to five brands of notebooks and their respective market shares.

For the creation of a pie chart, with the package `plotly`, there will be a value `"pie"` for the argument `type`, but there will be no declarations about variables for the abscissa and ordinate axes because this would not make sense. On the other hand, we must declare the values of interest, which will delimit the pie chart slices, as well as whether or not we want labels for these areas. It was precisely because of this that we proposed in the appendix to Chapter 7 a routine similar to the following:

```
notebooks_plotly <- plot_ly(data = notebooks,
                            labels = ~ brand,
                            values = ~ market_share,
                            type = "pie",
                            textinfo = "label + percent",
                            showlegend = TRUE)

notebooks_plotly
```

In the commanded routine, the argument `labels` will receive the variable that will identify the calculated area for each pie chart slice; the argument `values` will receive the metric variable with the values that will be used to calculate the previously labeled areas; the argument `textinfo` will make explicit the values of the metric variable declared to the argument `values`; finally, the argument `showlegend = TRUE` will be responsible for displaying a legend. The result is shown in Figure 27.33.

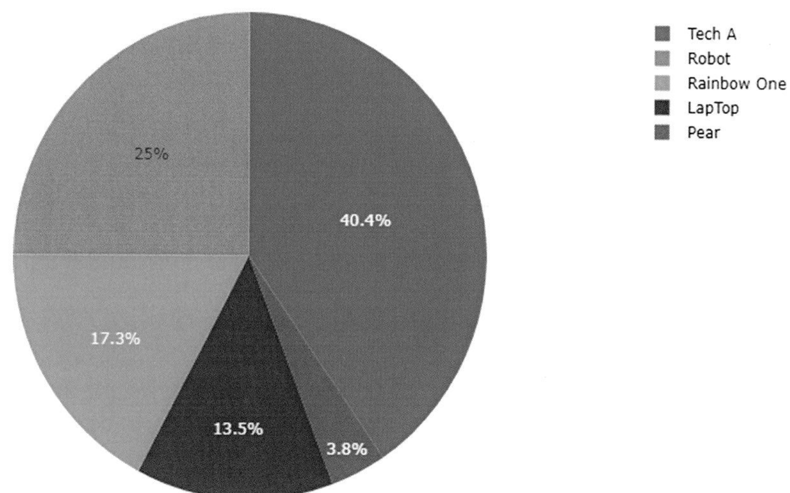

FIGURE 27.33 Pie chart created with the package `plotly`.

An interesting aesthetic variation of the chart shown in Figure 27.33 is the donut chart. To build one, we can argue the desired percentage size of opening, that is, `hole = 0.5`:

```
notebooks_plotly <- plot_ly(data = notebooks,
                            labels = ~ brand,
                            values = ~ market_share,
                            type = "pie",
                            textinfo = "percent",
                            showlegend = TRUE,
                            hole = 0.7)

notebooks_plotly
```

The donut chart created is contained in Figure 27.34.

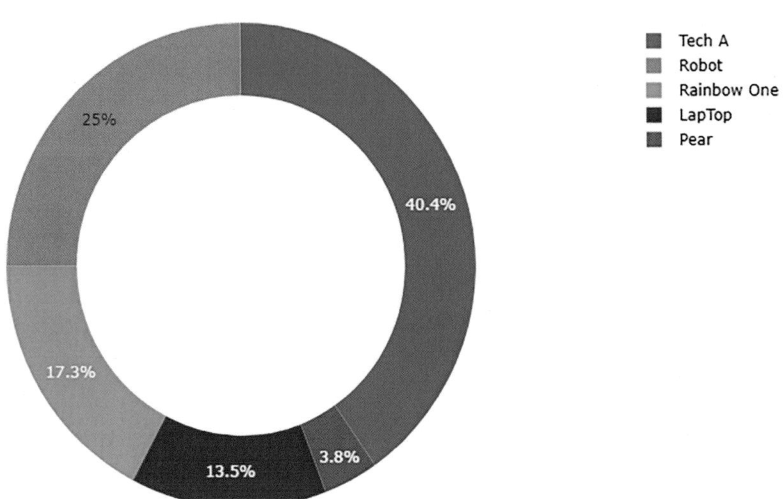

FIGURE 27.34 Donut chart created with the package `plotly`.

Final remarks

In this chapter, our intention was to introduce the capabilities of the package `plotly` to the reader. Here we do not advocate against the package `ggplot2`. This would not make sense as we have devoted an entire chapter to it. What we propose is to use these two powerful tools together whenever possible. In Chapter 7, we introduced the function `ggplotly()` from the package `plotly` and its capabilities to create some interactive graphics of `ggplot2`.

The point is that not all graphics in the package `ggplot2` are receptive to the function `ggplotly()`. Furthermore, the package `ggplot2` has its own limitations (i.e., not creating 3D graphics). Interactivity and three-dimensionality are usually welcome features in web-based reports, web pages, and dashboards.

By the way, this is exactly why we chose the penultimate chapter of our work to present `plotly` in a deeper way. So far, throughout the book, our primary objective was to instruct the reader on the concepts of mathematics, statistics, and optimization techniques. Whenever we use graphics, we try to make them as simple as possible, focusing on demonstrating the results of the techniques in a didactic way and without abusing the reader's computational capabilities. This is because, as a rule, the reader will be using a personal notebook. From here, it makes sense to bring `plotly` in with more intensity, presenting it as an interesting tool to inhabit the dashboards we will build in the course of Chapter 28.

Exercises

(1) At an electrical appliance factory, in the door component production phase, the quality inspector verifies the total number of parts rejected per type of defect (lack of alignment, scratches, deformation, discoloration, and oxygenation), as shown in Table 4.44 (Fávero and Belfiore, 2019).

We ask the reader to create a Pareto chart using the library `plotly` with the dataset available in the file `electrical_appliances.RData`.

(2) To preserve *açaí*, it is necessary to carry out several procedures, such as, whitening, pasteurization, freezing, and dehydration. The file `dehydration.RData` shows the processing times (in seconds) in the dehydration phase throughout 100 periods. We ask the reader to construct a histogram and a boxplot for the variable being studied using the library `plotly` (Fávero and Belfiore, 2019).

(3) In a certain bank branch, we collected the average service time (in minutes) from a sample with 50 customers regarding three types of services. The data can be found in the file `services.RData`. We ask the reader to construct a 3D scatter plot, an overlayed histogram, a line graph, and a boxplot for each variable (Fávero and Belfiore, 2019).

(4) A passenger collected the average travel times (in minutes) of a bus in Vila Mariana, on the Jabaquara route, for 120 days (Table 4.45). The data are found in the file `bus_travel.RData` (Fávero and Belfiore, 2019).

We ask the reader to construct a bar chart, a histogram, and a boxplot using the library `plotly`.

Supplementary data sets

```
papermisto.RData
demographic_atlas.RData
cheap_easy.RData
public_finances.RData
satisfaction_survey.RData
banks_comparison.RData
cards.RData
bank.RData
banks.RData
notebooks.RData
electrical_appliances.RData
dehydration.RData
services.RData
bus_travel.RData
```

Please access supplementary data files here: https://doi.org/10.17632/55623jkwrp.3

CHAPTER

28

Dashboards with R

AT THE END OF THIS CHAPTER, YOU WILL BE ABLE TO:

- Introduce the basic features of the package `shiny`
- Understand building dashboards using the package `shiny`
- Learn to integrate the knowledge from this work in dashboards made with the package `shiny`

R-based language packages used in this chapter

```
library(shiny)
library(plotly)
library(tidyverse)
```

Don't forget to define the R working directory (the location where your datasets are installed):

```
setwd("C:/book/chapter28")
```

Introduction

This chapter aims to add value to everything learned by the reader throughout this work, adding an expository and explanatory potential to information users who perhaps do not know how to program; have not mastered the machine learning techniques presented; or are even trying to learn about the work developed by the researcher.

In this sense, imagine that the reader has developed extensive research on the spatial impacts of fires on the fauna and flora of a given biome. More than presenting a model, the reader could establish, in a single place, graphics that address the study variables, in a univariate, bivariate, and/or multivariate manner.

Still on the narrated example, the reader could create in his or her dashboard sections that present descriptive statistics, frequency tables, possible correlations or associations, maps, and models of his or her research. It could even enable the reader to download his or her dataset, partially or completely. If the reader desires, all of this can be published on the Internet.

For these kinds of narrated demands, the computational language R has a powerful package: the `shiny` one.

https://doi.org/10.1016/B978-0-12-824271-1.00025-1

The objective of this chapter is to present some functionalities of `shiny` that are directly linked to the essence of the knowledge shared in this work. If the reader wants to delve into the details of this interesting package, we recommend reading *Mastering Shiny* (Wickham, 2021).

Datasets used in this chapter came from the books Manual de Análise de Dados/Handbook of Data Analysis (Fávero and Belfiore, 2017, Portuguese Edition) and Data Science for Business and Decision Making (Fávero and Belfiore, 2019, English Edition; 2020, Korean Edition), published by Elsevier Academic Press.

First steps in the library `shiny`

During the course of this work, the reader must have noticed in the support material that there is always a single script for the subjects developed per chapter. For this chapter, we will simultaneously work with two scripts: one is named `ui.R`, and the other is named `server.R`.

The purpose of segregation is organization! In the `ui.R` script, we will make the statements regarding the construction of the dashboard *User Interface*—hence the chosen nomenclature for the script. So it is true to say that layouts, themes, colors, buttons, scrollbars, and other aspects that make our dashboard a friendly environment will be in charge of this script.

The `server.R` script, on the other hand, will be reserved for the background of what will be happening when using the dashboard, so to speak. In this sense, the declarations for the creations of objects that will contain datasets, graphics, models, or the part about data manipulation, and so on, will be in this script.

That said, the reader may wonder how to make two distinct scripts work concurrently to generate a single final product: the dashboard. The package `shiny` will make these two scripts communicate and work in perfect harmony.

Next, we will show a first example of a simple dashboard, which comes ready-made with R, so the reader can feel comfortable about what will come during this chapter.

Creating the first dashboard in the library `shiny`

The most basic example for creating a dashboard with the package `shiny` can be done by clicking on the tab *File* >> *New File* >> *Shiny Web App...* in the *RStudio* software, as shown in Figure 28.1.

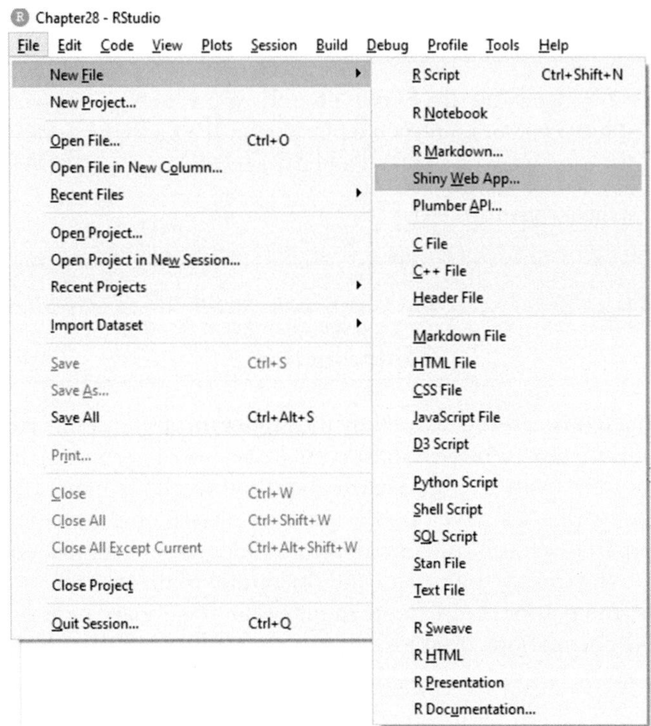

FIGURE 28.1 Creating *Shiny Web App* scripts in *RStudio*.

Clicking on *Shiny Web App*, as shown in Figure 28.1, will open a pop-up window, as shown in Figure 28.2.

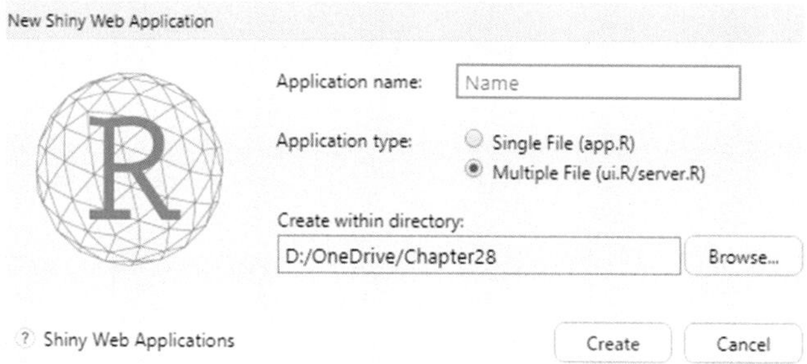

FIGURE 28.2 Creating scripts of type Shiny Web App in *RStudio*.

In Figure 28.2, the reader should name the dashboard in the field "Application name:". In the field "Application type:", the reader must select the option "Multiple File (ui.R/server.R)". Finally, in the field "Create within directory:", the reader must confirm where he or she wants the dashboard to be saved. After this, the reader can just click on the "Create" button.

After applying the proposed settings and clicking on the "Create" button, two scripts will appear in the reader's Script Editor: `ui.R` and `server.R`. For this first case, they are already filled in by default. To see them working, just click on the button ▶ Run App ▾, in any of the scripts, in the upper corner of the Script Editor screen.

When clicking on the button ▶ Run App ▾, the *RStudio* software will be occupied, and a new pop-up window will appear. This will be where our dashboard will appear. Figure 28.3 shows the expected result.

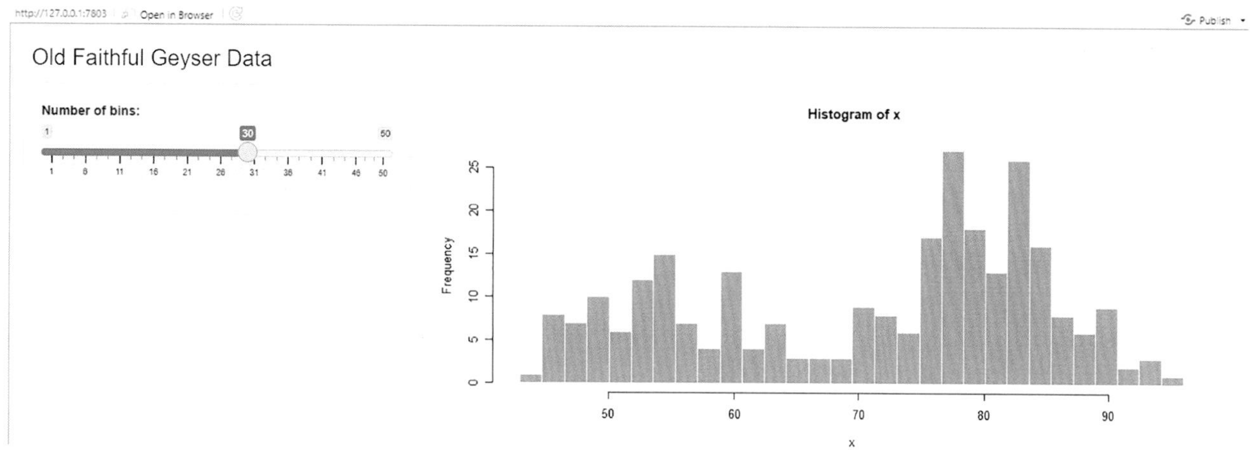

FIGURE 28.3 The first dashboard in R.

For this first example, shown in Figure 28.3, the reader may note that the data refer to the Old Faithful geyser, located in Yellowstone National Park, Wyoming, USA. It is also possible to notice that the field "Number of bins" is interactive and that the histogram that accompanies the dashboard communicates directly with this field.

If the reader closes the dashboard and starts looking at the Script Editor, with an emphasis on the `ui.R` and `server.R` scripts, he or she will notice a series of functions and declaration types that, at first, may seem not very intuitive.

The purpose of the upcoming sections will be to present a smooth way to use the main features of `shiny`, according to the authors' opinion.

Reactive programming

In the "Creating the first dashboard in the library `shiny`" section, we realized that our first dashboard is interactive, and the accompanying graphic instantly reacts to our interactions. This is possible thanks to the paradigm called *reactive programming*.

For the reader to feel this paradigm, we propose creating a new Shiny Web App, going to *File >> New File >> Shiny Web App…*, and configuring the section as shown in the "Creating the first dashboard in the library `shiny`" section.

In this new Shiny Web App, we ask the reader to delete the codes that appear by default and to copy and paste the following:

- In the `ui.R` script:

```
fluidPage(
    textOutput("first_message")
)
```

- In the `server.R` script:

```
function(input, output){
    output$first_message <- renderText("This is a test!")
}
```

After that, just save and click on the button Run App. As expected, a new window will open containing the message *This is a test!*.

The reader may notice that, for the `ui.R` script, we use the function `fluidPage()`. This function is commonly used for most simple dashboards, as it has the objective of what is called a more fluid presentation, that is, one that adapts to different computer screen sizes of the information user.

Later on, we will present a function that we think is more interesting to start the `ui.R` script, generating more elegant and organized outputs; but for now, let's continue with this simple syntax of the function `fluidPage()`.

Also note that, for the `ui.R` script, we argue `textOutput("first_message")` for the function `fluidPage()`. When we want to display texts in our dashboards, as a rule, we can use the function `textOutput()`.

However, note that the argument `"first_message"` acts as an indexer for the text we want to display. And this indexer must be declared without quotes, as if it were a component of a given output in the `server.R` script.

In the `server.R` script, we must start with the function `function()`, indicating, at a minimum, the future existence of input and output arguments. Do you remember that what we type in the *User Interface* appears in the `server.R` script? So, for the expected outputs, we must declare the indexer of what is expected to be present in the `ui.R` script, plus the codes themselves. Look at the syntax of the `server.R` script again:

```
function(input, output){
    output$first_message <- renderText("This is a test!")
}
```

Note that the indexer `"first_message"` from the `ui.R` script will become the component of an object called `output` in the `server.R` script. More: exactly where this indexer `"first_message"` was placed, in the `ui.R` script, the message *This is a test!* will be displayed, thanks to the use of the function `renderText()`.

That said, everything that we want to present in the user-friendly environment of the *User Interface* must be indexed with a certain possible and unambiguous name in the `ui.R` script. This indexing name present in the `ui.R` script will be a component of the given object (usually, the object called `output`) to be created and/or manipulated in the `server.R` script. Figure 28.4 tries to explain the reactivity between the code in the `ui.R` and `server.R` scripts.

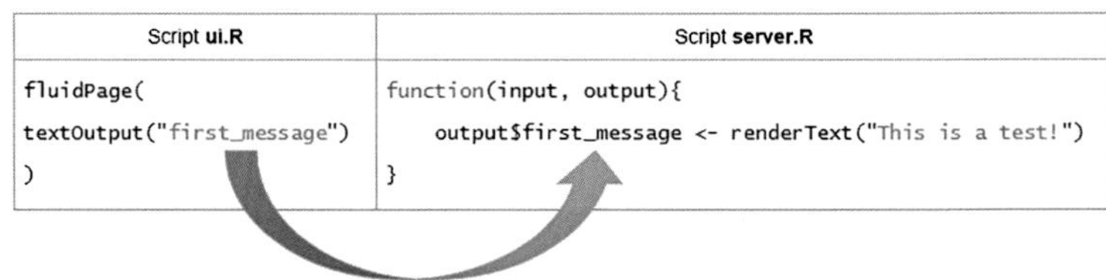
Script ui.R
Script server.R
fluidPage(
textOutput("first_message")
)
function(input, output){
output$first_message <- renderText("This is a test!")
}

FIGURE 28.4 Reactivity between the `ui.R` and `server.R` script codes.

The argument `input` of the function `function()`, present in the `server.R` script, will be used internally to the `server.R` script itself. Imagine a situation in R, in an ordinary script, in which the reader saves a model to a given object called `model`. However, imagine that the reader's interest, in this example, is with respect to a given coefficient of the object `model`. So, in another line of code, the reader would declare something close to `new_object <- model$coefficient`, and in that `new_object` the reader would capture the desired result, right?

With the argument `input`, from the `server.R` script, the reader will be able to elaborate this step by step until reaching the value that, in fact, interests him or her (the coefficient, in this case) and declare it as an `output`, whose indexer appears in the `ui.R` script. Further ahead will be a practical example of the situation.

The reader must have already understood that for everything you want to insert in your *User Interface* (e.g., scrollbars, buttons, texts, images, maps, templates), there must be an unambiguous indexer. This unambiguous indexer will be present in the `server.R` script together with an object that will contain what is wanted to be presented to the user of the information.

Construction of a complex dashboard

From here, we will create a much more interesting dashboard than the one presented in the "Creating the first dashboard in the library `shiny`" section. However, we will assume that the reader already has knowledge of the "Introduction," "First steps in the library `shiny`," "Creating the first dashboard in the library `shiny`," and "Reactive programming" sections as well as some machine learning and data manipulation techniques presented throughout this work.

In Chapter 14, we studied simple and multiple regression models. In this chapter, we present the dataset `corruption_emer.RData` that was presented in exercise 3 of Chapter 14. As a reminder, the dataset brings data from 52 countries regarding their Corruption Perception Index (variable *cpi*). Table 28.1 presents a description of the variables that make up the mentioned dataset.

TABLE 28.1 Description of the variables of the dataset `corruption_emer.RData` (Fávero and Belfiore, 2019).

Variable	Description
country	A string variable that identifies country *i*.
cpi	Corruption Perception Index, which corresponds to citizen perception regarding the public sector abuse of a nation's private benefits covering administrators and politicians (Source: Transparency International).
age	Average age of billionaires of a country (Source: Forbes).
hours	Average number of hours worked per week in a country, namely, the annual total of hours worked divided by 52 weeks (Source: International Labour Organization).
emerging	Dummy variable corresponding to the fact that the country is considered either developed or emerging, according to the criteria of Compustat Global. In this case, if the country is developed, the variable *emerging* = 0, otherwise, the variable *emerging* = 1.

The objective will be to create a dashboard that presents the following items to a hypothetical user of the information: the dataset used, the univariate descriptive statistics and variable frequency tables, the histograms of the dataset variables, and a model predictive.

We will divide the task into parts. Our first step will be to prepare the structuring of the `ui.R` and `server.R` scripts to receive our dashboard.

First step: Preparing the `ui.R` and `server.R` Scripts

We assume that the reader has read and understood the "Introduction," "First steps in the library `shiny`," "Creating the first dashboard in the library `shiny`," and "Reactive programming" sections.

That said, throughout the "Reactive programming" section, we inform the reader that the function `fluidPage()` is commonly used in the *User Interface* of dashboards generated in R, with the package `shiny`. We also said that we would use a function with more attractive results and greater possibilities for organization. This will be the function `navbarPage()`.

The function navbarPage() will allow us to create, very easily, tabs/sections for our dashboard, allowing greater organization of the content to be integrated into it. In this way, we will have a section for the presentation of the dataset, another section for univariate descriptive statistics and variable frequency tables, another section for variable distributions, and so on.

In this way, we can create a Shiny Web App, as discussed in the "Creating the first dashboard in the library shiny" section. We should delete the default encoding and replace it with the following syntaxes:

- In the script ui.R:

```
navbarPage(
    title = "CPI Dashboard"
)
```

- In the script server.R:

```
function(input, output){

}
```

Then just save the changes and click on the button Run App. An attentive reader will notice that a blank dashboard will be generated whose title will be *CPI Dashboard*, as shown in Figure 28.5.

FIGURE 28.5 Building a dashboard on corruption in 52 countries.

Ready! We can move on to the next step, which will be to present the dataset to information users.

Second step: Introducing the dataset

Now we will add a section called *Database* to the dashboard shown in Figure 28.5. To do this, we will need to nest some functions. First, we will introduce the proposed syntax for the ui.R script, and then we will discuss it. Note that we will not need to change anything in the server.R script as we are not yet manipulating any data.

- In the script ui.R:

```
navbarPage(
    title = "CPI Dashboard",
    mainPanel(
        tabsetPanel(
            type = "tab",
            tabPanel(title = "Database")
        )
    )
)
```

The function mainPanel() will be responsible for reserving an area for a main panel in the *User Interface*. The function tabsetPanel(), on the other hand, will be responsible for creating a tabset that can take several different forms (see the function documentation with the command ?tabsetPanel). We argued type = "tab" because our desire was to divide our dashboards into tabs. Finally, the function tabPanel() will actually create a tab that, using the argument title, we will call *Database*. The result is shown in Figure 28.6, where an arrow was purposely inserted to highlight the change proposed with the previous codes.

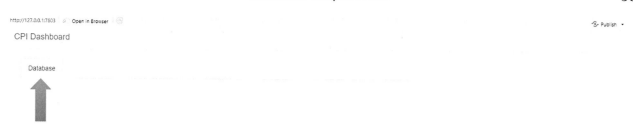

FIGURE 28.6 Building a control panel on corruption in 52 countries.

Now it is time for us to start entering relevant information into our dashboard! Our first information will be the presentation of our dataset.

The first step will be to add an indexer to our dataset in the `ui.R` script. We will call this indexer `database`, and to display our dataset in the future, we will use the function `uiOutput()`:

- In the `ui.R` script:

```
navbarPage(
    title = "CPI Dashboard",
    mainPanel(
        tabsetPanel(
            type = "tab",
            tabPanel(title = "Database",
                     uiOutput("database"))
            )
    )
)
```

If a curious reader presses the button ▶ Run App ▾, he or she will notice that, from a visual point of view, our dashboard will still look identical to Figure 28.6.

To add our dataset after the previous modifications, we must first declare it in the `server.R` script. Next, we will use three functions: (1) `renderDataTable()`; (2) `dataTableOutput()`; and (3) `renderUI()`:

- In the script `server.R`:

```
load("corruption_emer.RData")

function(input, output){
    output$table <- renderDataTable(corruption_emer)

    output$database <- renderUI({
        dataTableOutput("table")
        })
}
```

The first function, `renderDataTable()`, is an interesting way to generate a reactive version of a data frame or array. This function will allow the information user to organize and search for data of interest in our dataset. Also note that we are creating the table component in the output object to save this first change.

Then, to extract the outputs from the component `table`, we use the function `dataTableOutput()`. Finally, to render the final result in our *User Interface*, we use the function `renderUI()`. This entire procedure was saved as the component `database` of the object `output`. Note that the component `database` is what we want to display in our *User Interface;* therefore in the `ui.R` script, it was given the same name (but enclosed in quotes). Figure 28.7 shows a cutout of the result.

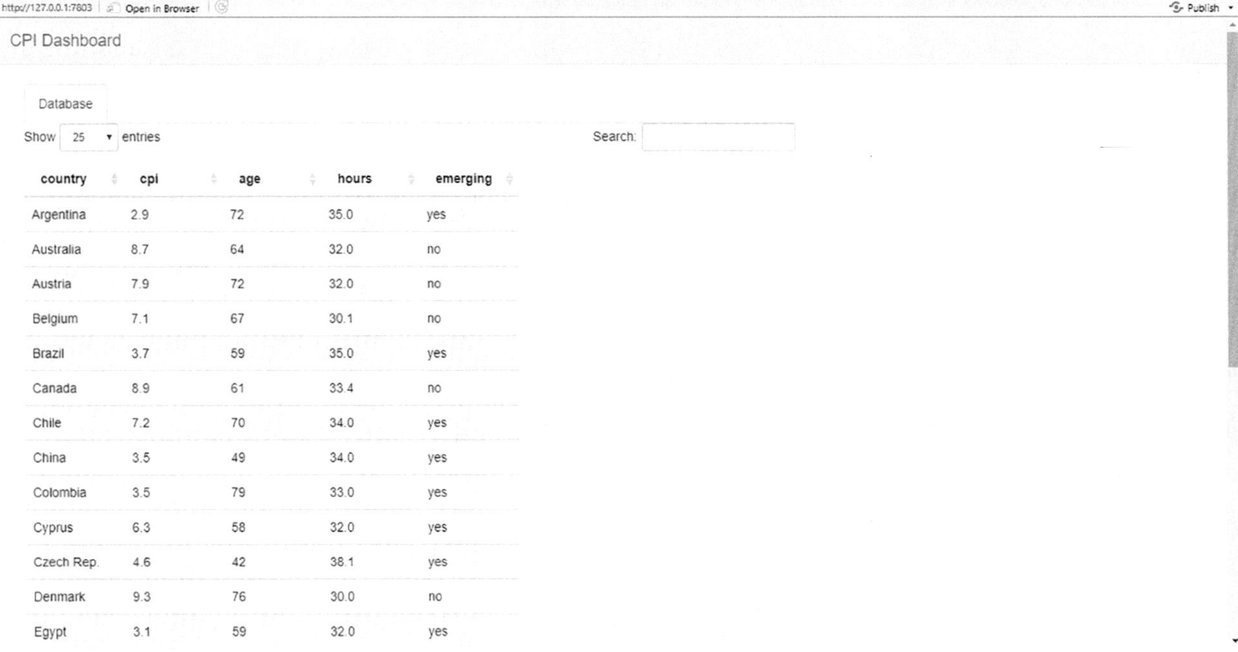

country	cpi	age	hours	emerging
Argentina	2.9	72	35.0	yes
Australia	8.7	64	32.0	no
Austria	7.9	72	32.0	no
Belgium	7.1	67	30.1	no
Brazil	3.7	59	35.0	yes
Canada	8.9	61	33.4	no
Chile	7.2	70	34.0	yes
China	3.5	49	34.0	yes
Colombia	3.5	79	33.0	yes
Cyprus	6.3	58	32.0	yes
Czech Rep.	4.6	42	38.1	yes
Denmark	9.3	76	30.0	no
Egypt	3.1	59	32.0	yes

FIGURE 28.7 Building a dashboard on corruption in 52 countries.

In Figure 28.7, due to the aforementioned combination of functions for displaying our dataset, it is possible to see a search field, an option field for the number of lines to be displayed, in addition to the possibility of organizing the dataset in ascending or descending order of alphanumeric values.

Suppose variable names spelled in lowercase in Figure 28.7 are a problem. To correct the situation, we will use the knowledge of the package `tidyverse` presented in Chapter 10. Note the following routine:

- In the script `server.R`:

```
library(tidyverse)

load("corruption_emer.RData")

function(input, output){

    output$table <- renderDataTable(
        corruption_emer %>%
            rename(Country = 1,
                   CPI = 2,
                   Age = 3,
                   Hours = 4,
                   Emerging = 5)
        )

    output$database <- renderUI({
        dataTableOutput("table")
        })
}
```

Figure 28.8 shows a cutout of the result.

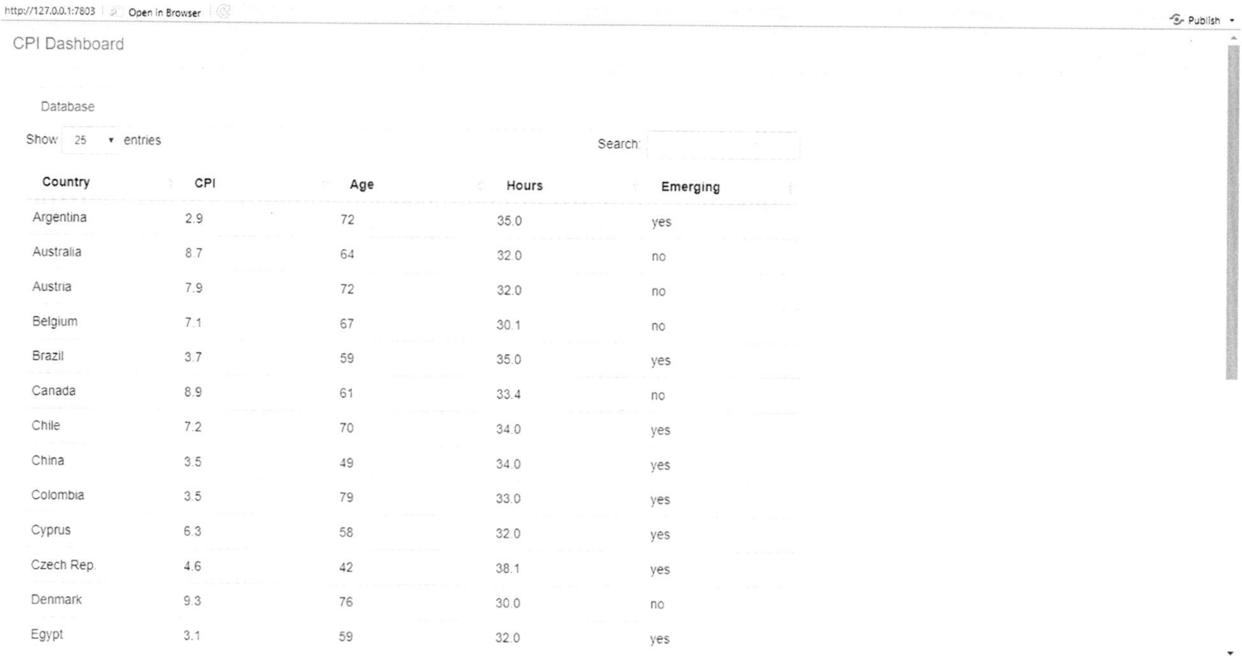

http://127.0.0.1:7803 | Open in Browser | Publish

CPI Dashboard

Database

Show 25 entries Search:

Country	CPI	Age	Hours	Emerging
Argentina	2.9	72	35.0	yes
Australia	8.7	64	32.0	no
Austria	7.9	72	32.0	no
Belgium	7.1	67	30.1	no
Brazil	3.7	59	35.0	yes
Canada	8.9	61	33.4	no
Chile	7.2	70	34.0	yes
China	3.5	49	34.0	yes
Colombia	3.5	79	33.0	yes
Cyprus	6.3	58	32.0	yes
Czech Rep.	4.6	42	38.1	yes
Denmark	9.3	76	30.0	no
Egypt	3.1	59	32.0	yes

FIGURE 28.8 Building a dashboard on corruption in 52 countries.

Next, we will create a second tab in our dashboard that will contain the univariate descriptive statistics and frequency tables from our dataset.

Third step: Introducing univariate descriptive statistics and frequency tables of the dataset variables

After all the structure of our dashboard built, to add new tabs we must add new functions `tabPanel()` in the script `ui.R`:

- In the script `ui.R`:

```
navbarPage(
    title = "CPI Dashboard",
    mainPanel(
        tabsetPanel(
            type = "tab",
            tabPanel(title = "Database",
                    uiOutput("database")),
            tabPanel(title = "Summary")
        )
    )
)
```

An attentive reader will notice that we have named this new *Summary* tab. The result is shown in Figure 28.9, where an arrow was purposely inserted to highlight the newly created tab.

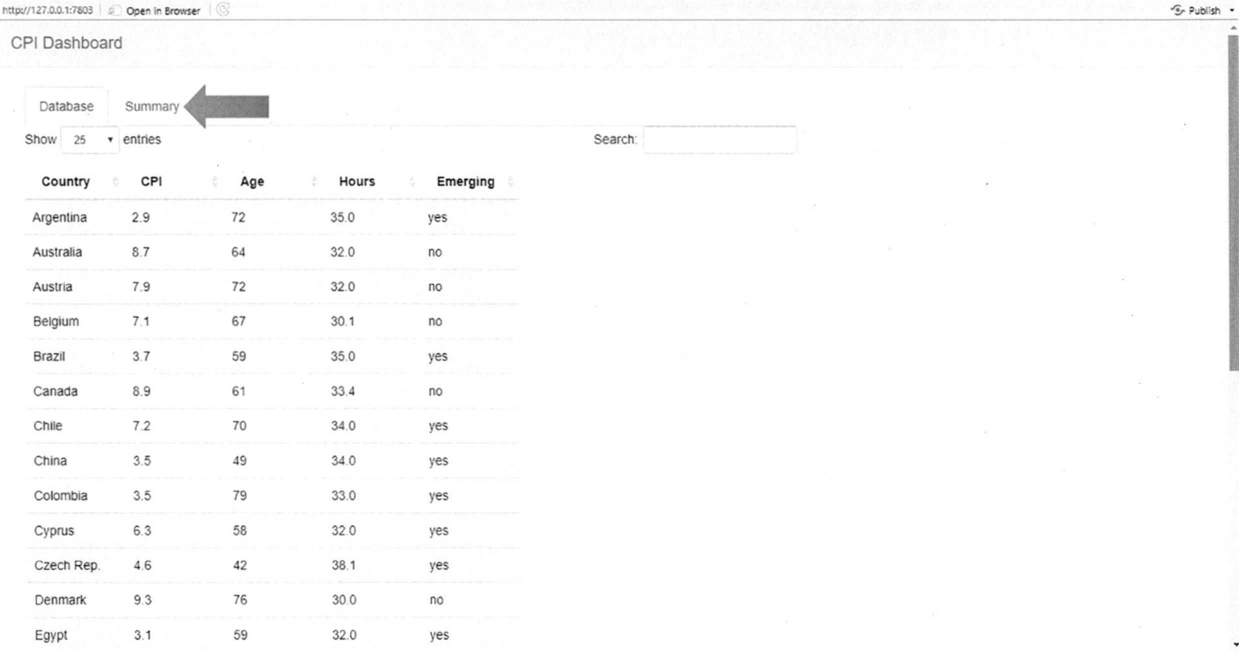

Country	CPI	Age	Hours	Emerging
Argentina	2.9	72	35.0	yes
Australia	8.7	64	32.0	no
Austria	7.9	72	32.0	no
Belgium	7.1	67	30.1	no
Brazil	3.7	59	35.0	yes
Canada	8.9	61	33.4	no
Chile	7.2	70	34.0	yes
China	3.5	49	34.0	yes
Colombia	3.5	79	33.0	yes
Cyprus	6.3	58	32.0	yes
Czech Rep.	4.6	42	38.1	yes
Denmark	9.3	76	30.0	no
Egypt	3.1	59	32.0	yes

FIGURE 28.9 Building a dashboard on corruption in 52 countries.

Obviously, at this point, if the reader clicks on the new *Summary* tab, he or she will notice that the content is empty because we have not indexed what is to be displayed yet or manipulated the results to be worked on in the script `server.R`.

First, let's create an indexer for the expected results in the script `ui.R`. We will call this indexer `"summary"`, with the help of the function `verbatimTextOutput()`:

- In the script `ui.R`:

```
navbarPage(
    title = "CPI Dashboard",
    mainPanel(
        tabsetPanel(
            type = "tab",
            tabPanel(title = "Database",
                     uiOutput("database")),
            tabPanel(title = "Summary",
                     verbatimTextOutput("summary"))
        )
    )
)
```

We use the function `verbatimTextOutput()` on purpose.

To display the dataset, in the script `ui.R`, we use the function `uiOutput()`, which generates more beautiful texts that are adaptable to the size of the reader's window. The function `uiOutput()` in the script `ui.R` is commonly associated with the function `renderUI()` in the script `server.R`.

When we want results explained with fixed patterns, similar to the R console, we must use the function `verbatimTextOutput()`. When declared to the script `ui.R`, this function is associated with the function `renderPrint()` in the script `server.R`, as shown here:

- In the script `server.R`:

```
library(tidyverse)

load("corruption_emer.RData")

function(input, output){

    output$table <- renderDataTable(
        corruption_emer %>%
            rename(Country = 1,
                   CPI = 2,
                   Age = 3,
                   Hours = 4,
                   Emerging = 5)
        )

    output$database <- renderUI({
        dataTableOutput("table")
        })

    output$summary <- renderPrint({
        summary(corruption_emer)
    })
}
```

Figure 28.10 shows the result obtained from the previous command.

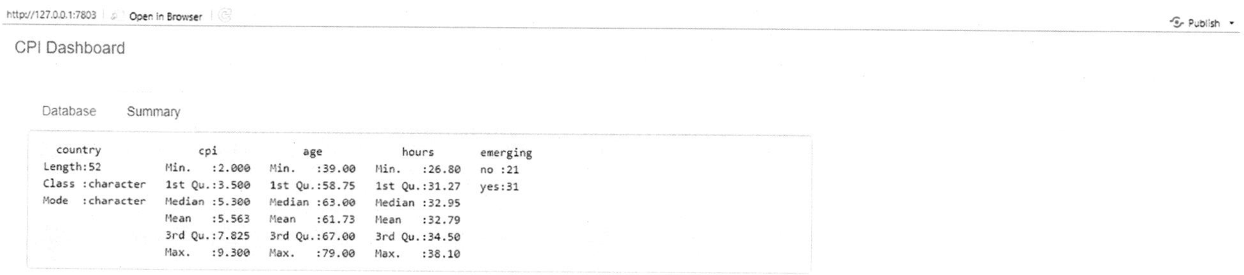

FIGURE 28.10 Building a dashboard on corruption in 52 countries.

Next, we will show you how to insert graphics about the variables in the dataset.

Fourth step: Variable distributions graphics

First, let's create a tab on our dashboard that we will call *Histograms*:

- In the script `ui.R`:

```
navbarPage(
    title = "CPI Dashboard",
    mainPanel(
        tabsetPanel(
            type = "tab",
            tabPanel(title = "Database",
                     uiOutput("database")),
            tabPanel(title = "Summary",
                     verbatimTextOutput("summary")),
            tabPanel(title = "Histograms")
        )
    )
)
```

Figure 28.11 shows the result obtained from the previous command.

To index a graph made by ggplot2, we must use the function plotOutput(). We will index our graph with the name

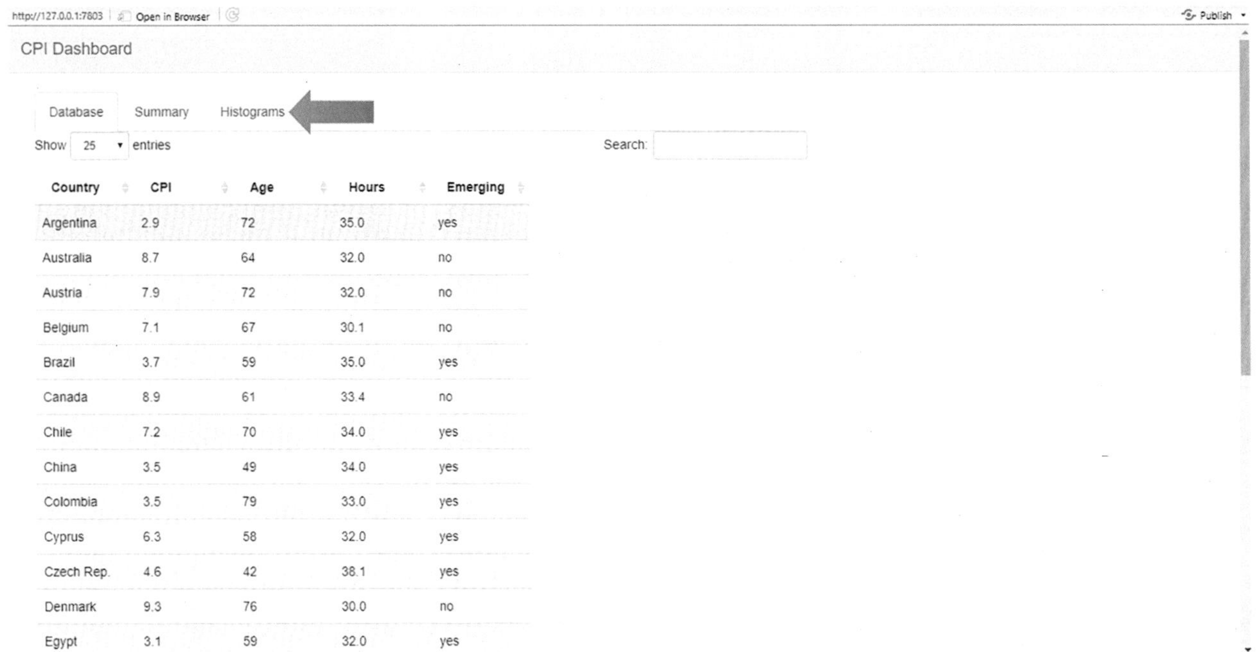

FIGURE 28.11 Building a dashboard on corruption in 52 countries.

hist_cpi because at first, we only will create a histogram of the variable *cpi.*

- In the script ui.R:

```
navbarPage(
    title = "CPI Dashboard",
    mainPanel(
        tabsetPanel(
            type = "tab",
            tabPanel(title = "Database",
                     uiOutput("database")),
            tabPanel(title = "Summary",
                     verbatimTextOutput("summary")),
            tabPanel(title = "Histograms",
                     plotOutput("hist_cpi")),

        )
    )
)
```

Then, in the script server.R, we will associate the function renderPlot() with the function plotOutput() from the script ui.R. The construction of this first graph follows what we studied in Chapter 7:

- In the script server.R:

```
library(tidyverse)

load("corruption_emer.RData")

function(input, output){

    output$table <- renderDataTable(
        corruption_emer %>%
            rename(Country = 1,
                   CPI = 2,
                   Age = 3,
                   Hours = 4,
                   Emerging = 5)
        )

    output$database <- renderUI({
        dataTableOutput("table")
        })

    output$summary <- renderPrint({
        summary(corruption_emer)
    })

    output$hist_cpi <- renderPlot({
        corruption_emer %>%
            ggplot(aes(x = cpi)) +
            geom_histogram(fill = "orange",
                           color = "black",
                           bins = 15) +
            labs(x = "Corruption Perception Index (CPI)",
                 y = "Frequency") +
            theme_bw()
    })
}
```

Figure 28.12 shows the result obtained from the previous command.

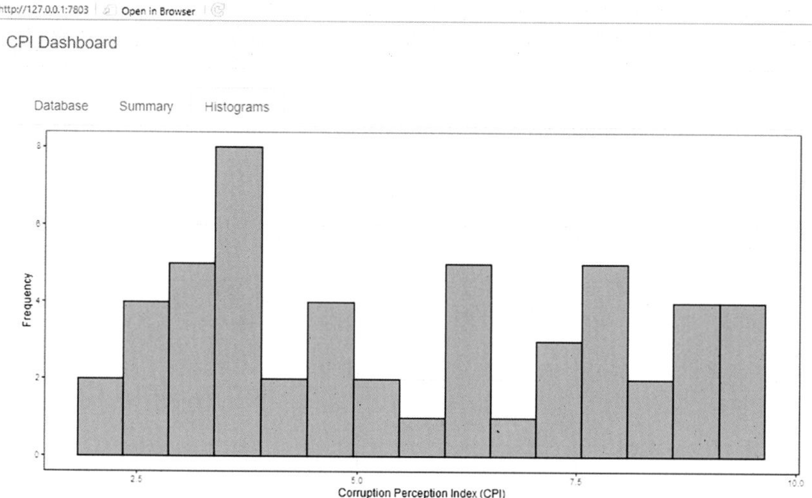

FIGURE 28.12 Building a dashboard on corruption in 52 countries.

However, we agree that the graph shown in Figure 28.12 is quite simple. Perhaps it would be more interesting if the information user had the option to choose the variable that he or she wants to check the distribution. So we must insert a scrollbox and, from this choice, explain to `shiny` to generate a histogram.

Thus, we will undo the changes proposed throughout this section, and we will index two objects, in the script `ui.R`: (1) one that identifies the variable for which the histogram is desired and (2) the histogram about the chosen variable.

- In the script `ui.R`:

```
navbarPage(
    title = "CPI Dashboard",
    mainPanel(
        tabsetPanel(
            type = "tab",
            tabPanel(title = "Database",
                     uiOutput("database")),
            tabPanel(title = "Summary",
                     verbatimTextOutput("summary")),
            tabPanel(title = "Histograms",
                     uiOutput("choosed_var"),
                     plotOutput("histogram")),

        )
    )
)
```

Note that for the function `tabPanel()` regarding the *Histograms* tab, we declare two indexers: (1) one with the statement `uiOutput("choosed_var")`, which will point to the variable to be chosen; and (2) another with the statement `plotOutput("histogram")`, which will present the histogram of a chosen variable. Also note that after this change, the *Histograms* tab will no longer show results. This is absolutely normal.

In the script `server.R`, our first concern is creating a variable selection box. We index this result as `"choosed_var"` in the script `ui.R`, using the function `uiOutput()`, and as we have seen, for the script `server.R`, the function `renderUI()` is commonly associated with the function `uiOutput()`:

- In the script `server.R`:

```
library(tidyverse)

load("corruption_emer.RData")

function(input, output){

    output$table <- renderDataTable(
        corruption_emer %>%
            rename(Country = 1,
                   CPI = 2,
                   Age = 3,
                   Hours = 4,
                   Emerging = 5)
        )

    output$database <- renderUI({
        dataTableOutput("table")
        })

    output$summary <- renderPrint({
        summary(corruption_emer)
    })
```

Continued

```
    output$choosed_var <- renderUI({
        selectInput(inputId = "indicated_var",
                    label = "Select a variable:",
                    choices = as.list(
                        names(corruption_emer[,-c(1,5)])
                        ),
                    multiple = FALSE)
    })
}
```

In the previous command, the function `selectInput()` will generate an options box that will contain the variables to be selected for creating the histogram. The argument `inputId` asks for a pseudo name that will replace the name of the chosen variable, whatever it is. Therefore it works like a wild card; we call it `indicated_var`. On the other hand, the argument `label` will generate a label for the variable options box; it is merely an aesthetic attribute. The argument `choices` must be declared in list format, and we will point to it the name of the variables that make sense in the construction of a histogram (note that a histogram for the *country* variable or the *emerging* variable does not make sense). Finally, the argument `multiple = FALSE` prevents more than one variable from being selected at the same time.

Figure 28.13 shows the preliminary result.

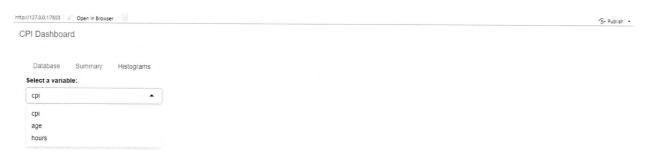

FIGURE 28.13 Building a dashboard on corruption in 52 countries.

This way, as discussed earlier, when the user of the information clicks with a mouse on any of the variables presented in Figure 28.13, its name, no matter which one, will be replaced by the name `indicated_var`. From this information, in theory, we could build the graph. However, when we want this level of interactivity, or better, **reactivity**, we must transform the objects that are the source of our data with the function `reactive()`. In this case, the source of information for the graphics is the dataset, `corruption_emer`. So, let's transform it with the function `reactive()`:

- In the script `server.R`:

```
library(tidyverse)

load("corruption_emer.RData")

function(input, output){

    output$table <- renderDataTable(
        corruption_emer %>%
            rename(Country = 1,
                   CPI = 2,
                   Age = 3,
                   Hours = 4,
                   Emerging = 5)
```

Continued

```
        )

    output$database <- renderUI({
        dataTableOutput("table")
        })

    output$summary <- renderPrint({
        summary(corruption_emer)
    })

    output$choosed_var <- renderUI({
        selectInput(inputId = "indicated_var",
                    label = "Select a variable:",
                    choices = as.list(
                        names(corruption_emer[,-c(1,5)])
                        ),
                    multiple = FALSE)
    })

    reactive_database <- reactive({
        data.frame(x = corruption_emer[[input$indicated_var]])
    })
}
```

First of all, it must be said that the function `reactive()` leaves objects reactive, that is, interactive. It will be the enabler to assume the name `indicated_var` as the name of any variable chosen by the user. Remember, `indicated_var` is our wild card.

It is interesting to note that what we call `indicated_var` becomes a component of an object called `input`. We already commented on this at the beginning of this section.

It is also important to note that every time the information user chooses a variable on the *Histograms* tab of our dashboard, a new reactive dataset, called `reactive_database`, will be generated and overwrite the previous one. This dataset will be a data frame with a single variable inside it, called *x* (it could be any other name, as long as possible and unambiguous).

Another extremely important point is that, when we create an object with the function `reactive()`, it is no longer a common object and becomes a function! So when we return to declaring the object `reactive_database`, in order to extract some information from it, we should declare it as `reactive_database()`!

Once these alerts are done, we can declare the creation of graphics, in the script `server.R`, as follows:

- In the script `server.R`:

```
library(tidyverse)

load("corruption_emer.RData")

function(input, output){

    output$table <- renderDataTable(
        corruption_emer %>%
            rename(Country = 1,
                   CPI = 2,
                   Age = 3,
                   Hours = 4,
                   Emerging = 5)
        )

    output$database <- renderUI({
        dataTableOutput("table")
```

Continued

```
    })

    output$summary <- renderPrint({
        summary(corruption_emer)
    })

    output$choosed_var <- renderUI({
        selectInput(inputId = "indicated_var",
                    label = "Select a variable:",
                    choices = as.list(
                        names(corruption_emer[,-c(1,5)])
                        ),
                    multiple = FALSE)
    })

    reactive_database <- reactive({
        data.frame(x = corruption_emer[[input$indicated_var]])
    })

    output$histogram <- renderPlot({
        reactive_database() %>%
            ggplot(aes(x = x)) +
            geom_histogram(fill = "orange",
                           color = "black",
                           bins = 15) +
            labs(x = NULL,
                 y = "Frequency") +
            theme_bw()
    })
}
```

Figure 28.14 shows the final result of the *Histograms* tab, in our dashboard, with an emphasis on the *age* variable.

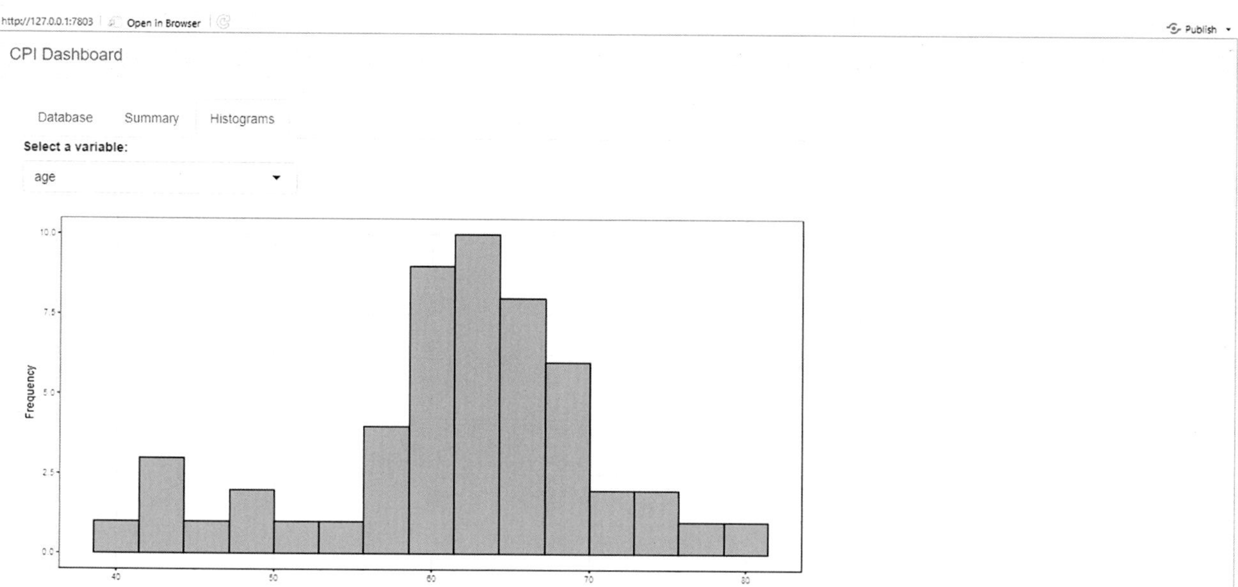

FIGURE 28.14 Building a dashboard on corruption in 52 countries.

If the reader is willing to use the graphics from the package `plotly`, the indexing function for the script `ui.R` will be the function `plotlyOutput()`, although its associated function in the script `server.R` will be the function `renderPlotly()`:

- In the script `ui.R`:

```
navbarPage(
    title = "CPI Dashboard",
    mainPanel(
        tabsetPanel(
            type = "tab",
            tabPanel(title = "Database",
                     uiOutput("database")),
            tabPanel(title = "Summary",
                     verbatimTextOutput("summary")),
            tabPanel(title = "Histograms",
                     uiOutput("choosed_var"),
                     plotlyOutput("histogram")),

        )
    )
)
```

- In the script `server.R`:

```
library(plotly)
library(tidyverse)

load("corruption_emer.RData")

function(input, output){

    output$table <- renderDataTable(
        corruption_emer %>%
            rename(Country = 1,
                   CPI = 2,
                   Age = 3,
                   Hours = 4,
                   Emerging = 5)
    )

    output$database <- renderUI({
        dataTableOutput("table")
    })

    output$summary <- renderPrint({
        summary(corruption_emer)
    })

    output$choosed_var <- renderUI({
        selectInput(inputId = "indicated_var",
                    label = "Select a variable:",
                    choices = as.list(
                        names(corruption_emer[,-c(1,5)])
                    ),
                    multiple = FALSE)
    })

    reactive_database <- reactive({
        data.frame(x = corruption_emer[[input$indicated_var]])
    })
```

Continued

```
    output$histogram <- renderPlotly({
        plot_ly(data = reactive_database(),
                x = ~ x,
                type = "histogram",
                marker = list(color = "orange",
                              width = 3,
                              line = list(color = "black",
                                          width = 1))) %>%
            layout(yaxis = list(title = "Frequency"),
                   xaxis = list(title = ""))
    })
}
```

By way of comparison with the result shown in Figure 28.14, Figure 28.15 shows the presence of a graph prepared with the package `plotly` in our dashboard.

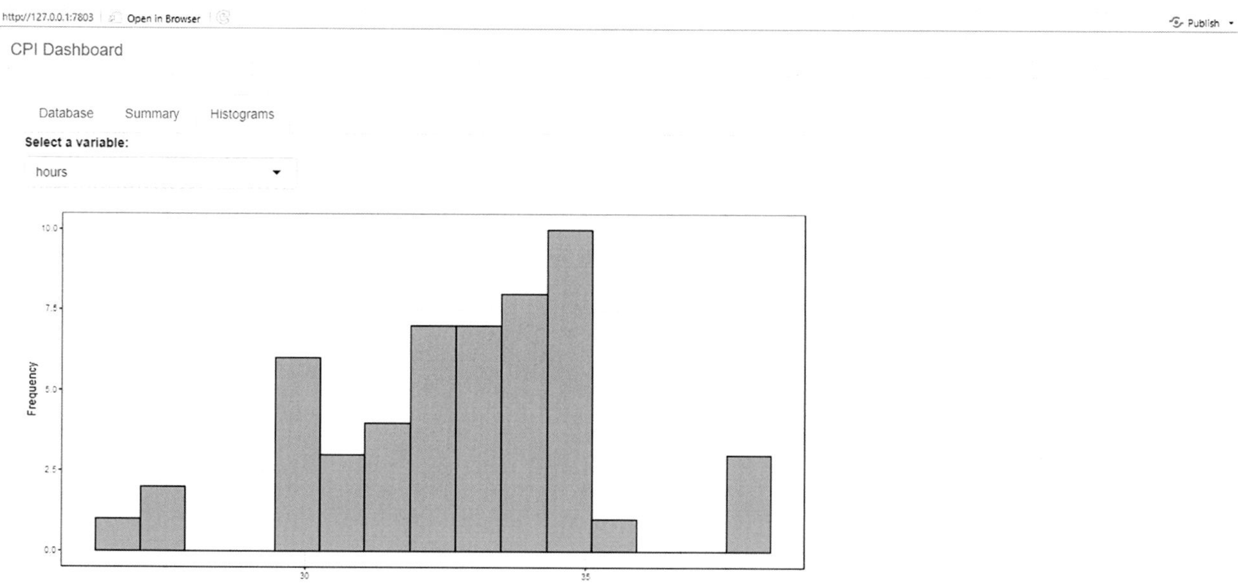

FIGURE 28.15 Building a dashboard on corruption in 52 countries.

Next is the inclusion of a predictive model in our dashboard.

Fifth step: Including a predictive model

As usual so far, we will start by adding a new tab to our dashboard, which will be called *Final Model*.

- In the script `ui.R`:

```
navbarPage(
    title = "CPI Dashboard",
    mainPanel(
        tabsetPanel(
            type = "tab",
            tabPanel(title = "Database",
                     uiOutput("database")),
            tabPanel(title = "Summary",
```

Continued

```
                  verbatimTextOutput("summary")),
            tabPanel(title = "Histograms",
                  uiOutput("choosed_var"),
                  plotOutput("histogram")),
            tabPanel(title = "Final Model")

        )
    )
)
```

Figure 28.16 shows the insertion of the *Final Model* tab.

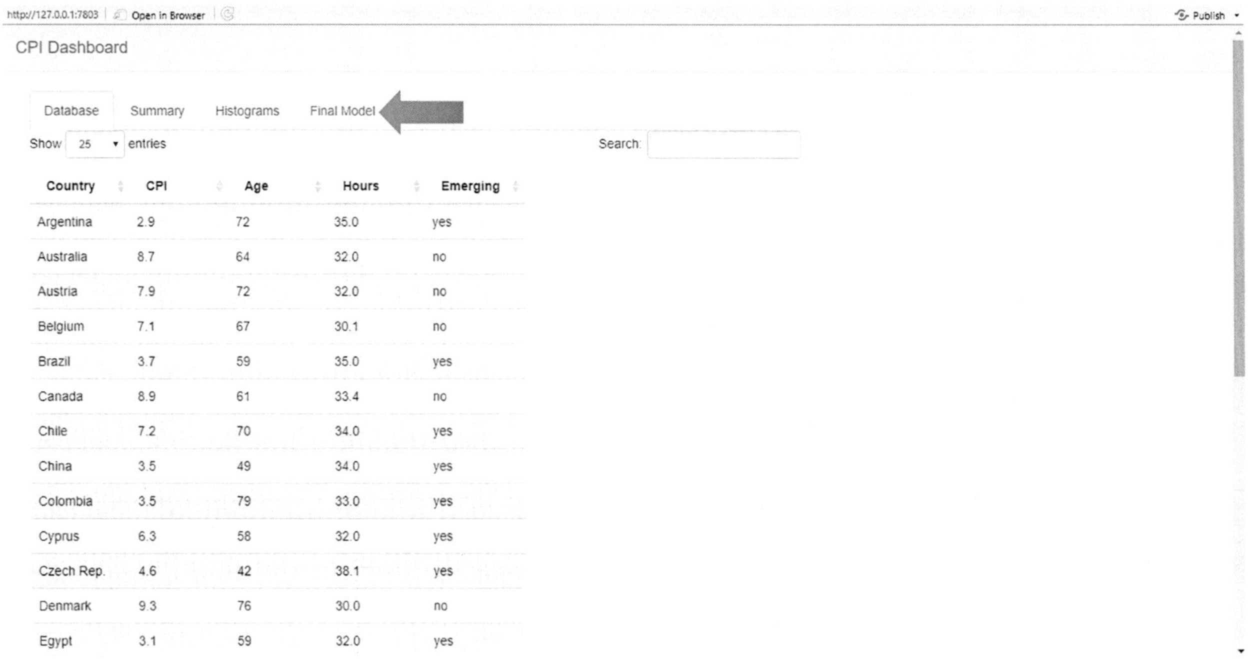

http://127.0.0.1:7803 Open in Browser Publish

CPI Dashboard

Database Summary Histograms Final Model

Show 25 entries Search:

Country	CPI	Age	Hours	Emerging
Argentina	2.9	72	35.0	yes
Australia	8.7	64	32.0	no
Austria	7.9	72	32.0	no
Belgium	7.1	67	30.1	no
Brazil	3.7	59	35.0	yes
Canada	8.9	61	33.4	no
Chile	7.2	70	34.0	yes
China	3.5	49	34.0	yes
Colombia	3.5	79	33.0	yes
Cyprus	6.3	58	32.0	yes
Czech Rep.	4.6	42	38.1	yes
Denmark	9.3	76	30.0	no
Egypt	3.1	59	32.0	yes

FIGURE 28.16 Building a dashboard on corruption in 52 countries.

To index the explicitness of our final predictive model, in the script `ui.R`, we can declare:

- In the script `ui.R`:

```
navbarPage(
    title = "CPI Dashboard",
    mainPanel(
        tabsetPanel(
            type = "tab",
            tabPanel(title = "Database",
                     uiOutput("database")),
            tabPanel(title = "Summary",
                     verbatimTextOutput("summary")),
            tabPanel(title = "Histograms",
                     uiOutput("choosed_var"),
```

Continued

```
                    plotOutput("histogram")),
            tabPanel(title = "Final Model",
                    verbatimTextOutput("model"))

        )
    )
)
```

For this case, we index our final predictive model with the nomenclature `model`, as we declare `verbatimTextOutput ("model")`.

In the script `server.R`, we can insert the establishment of a final regression model, assuming a significance level of 5%, as discussed in Chapter 14:

- In the script `server.R`:

```
library(tidyverse)

load("corruption_emer.RData")

function(input, output){

    output$table <- renderDataTable(
        corruption_emer %>%
            rename(Country = 1,
                   CPI = 2,
                   Age = 3,
                   Hours = 4,
                   Emerging = 5)
        )

    output$database <- renderUI({
        dataTableOutput("table")
        })

    output$summary <- renderPrint({
        summary(corruption_emer)
        })

    output$choosed_var <- renderUI({
        selectInput(inputId = "indicated_var",
                    label = "Select a variable:",
                    choices = as.list(
                        names(corruption_emer[,-c(1,5)])
                        ),
                    multiple = FALSE)
    })

    reactive_database <- reactive({
        data.frame(x = corruption_emer[[input$indicated_var]])
    })

    output$histogram <- renderPlot({
        reactive_database() %>%
            ggplot(aes(x = x)) +
            geom_histogram(fill = "orange",
                           color = "black",
```

Continued

```
                                bins = 15) +
            labs(x = NULL,
                 y = "Frequency") +
            theme_bw()
    })

    output$model <- renderPrint({
        summary(
            step(object = lm(formula = cpi ~ age + hours + emerging,
                             data = corruption_emer),
                 k = qchisq(p = 0.05, df = 1,lower.tail = FALSE),
                 trace = 0)
        )
    })
}
```

Out of curiosity, the argument `trace = 0`, in the function `step()`, silences the messages of that particular algorithm.

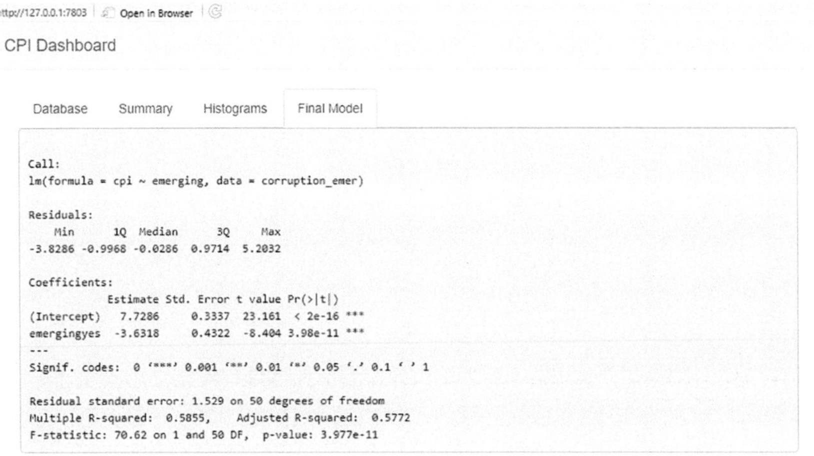

FIGURE 28.17 Building a dashboard on corruption in 52 countries.

Figure 28.17 shows the result obtained from the previous command.

Final remarks

The purpose of this chapter was to demonstrate to the reader the integration of the package `shiny` with the essence of the knowledge shared throughout this work.

By demonstrating the possibility of creating a dashboard that enables, from the display of a manipulated dataset, through the study of its descriptive univariate statistics and frequency tables, the display of graphs as well as the estimation of models, the authors try to demonstrate ways to add value to research, academic or otherwise, created by readers.

The authors have no doubt that everything shown in this work can be rigorously reproduced on a dashboard made with `shiny`, including maps and three-dimensional graphics.

We hope that shared knowledge can be used in favor of the propagation of scientific knowledge and as a facilitating bridge for third parties regarding the assimilation of the content explained in the dashboards.

Exercise

(1) Using the dataset `demographic_atlas.RData` (Fávero and Belfiore, 2019), which contains sociodemographic indicators from the 96 districts belonging to the municipality of São Paulo, Brazil (whose variables were described in Table 12.4), build a dashboard using the package `shiny` that contains:

a. A dataset display tab
b. A tab with univariate descriptive statistics of the dataset
c. A tab containing a heat map of Pearson correlations among metric variables
d. A tab showing the factor loadings arising from a factor analysis (see Chapter 12), considering two factors
e. A tab showing the communalities present in the factor analysis elaborated in item d.

Supplementary data sets

```
ui.R
server.R
corruption_emer.RData
demographic_atlas.RData
```

Please access supplementary data files here: https://doi.org/10.17632/55623jkwrp.3

Answers

Chapter 3

4.

a. Continuous
b. Ordinal
c. Continuous
d. Discrete
e. Continuous
f. Nominal
g. Ordinal
h. Ordinal
i. Continuous
j. Nominal
k. Binary
l. Ordinal
m. Discrete
n. Ordinal
o. Binary

Chapter 4

1.

Vehicles sold	F_i	Fr_i (%)	F_{ac}	Fr_{ac} (%)
5	4	13.33	4	13.33
6	5	16.67	9	30
7	4	13.33	13	43.33
8	6	20	19	63.33
9	4	13.33	23	76.67
10	4	13.33	27	90
11	3	10	30	100
Sum	**30**	**100**		

2.

Patients' weight	F_i	Fr_i (%)	F_{ac}	Fr_{ac} (%)
54.7 ├ 61.7	4	8.0	4	8.0
61.7 ├ 68.7	4	8.0	8	16.0
68.7 ├ 75.7	10	20.0	18	36.0
75.7 ├ 82.7	17	34.0	35	70.0
82.7 ├ 89.7	6	12.0	41	82.0
89.7 ├ 96.7	7	14.0	48	96.0
96.7 ├ 103.7	2	4.0	50	100.0
Sum	**50**	**100**		

3.

Type of defect	F_i	Fr_i (%)	F_{ac}	Fr_{ac} (%)
Lack of alignment	98	39.2%	98	39.2%
Scratches	67	26.8%	165	66.0%
Deformation	45	18.0%	210	84.0%
Discoloration	28	11.2%	238	95.2%
Oxygenation	12	4.8%	250	100.0%
Sum	**250**	**100**		

4.

a. $\overline{X} = 39.192$, $Md = 40$, $Mo = 40$.

b. $Q_1 = 35$; $Q_3 = 42$; $D_4 = 38$; $P_{61} = 41.4$ and $P_{84} = 43$.

c. There are no outliers.

d. $R = 20$; $S^2 = 20.560$; $S = 4.534$; $S_{\overline{X}} = 0.414$.

e. $g_1 = -0.317$; $g_2 = -0.279$ (Negative asymmetrical distribution and platykurtic curve).

5.

a. $\overline{X} = 133.56$, $Md = 136.098$, $Mo = 137.826$.

b. $Q_1 = 106.463$; $Q_3 = 163.611$; $D_2 = 97.317$; $P_{13} = 97.317$ and $P_{95} = 198.636$.

c. There are no outliers.

d. $R = 180$; $S^2 = 1{,}505.508$; $S = 39.944$; $S_{\overline{X}} = 2.526$.

e. $Sk_1 = -0.107$; $k = 0.253$.

Chapter 5

1.

a.

company	motivation: Very demotivated	Demotivated	Little motivated	Motivated	Very motivated	Total
Petrobras	36 72 % 78.3 %	8 16 % 16.3 %	6 12 % 10.2 %	0 0 % 0 %	0 0 % 0 %	50 100 % 20 %
Bradesco	0 0 % 0 %	0 0 % 0 %	3 6 % 5.1 %	16 32 % 28.6 %	31 62 % 77.5 %	50 100 % 20 %
Fiat	0 0 % 0 %	8 16 % 16.3 %	32 64 % 54.2 %	9 18 % 16.1 %	1 2 % 2.5 %	50 100 % 20 %
Vivo	10 20 % 21.7 %	33 66 % 67.3 %	7 14 % 11.9 %	0 0 % 0 %	0 0 % 0 %	50 100 % 20 %
Wallmart	0 0 % 0 %	0 0 % 0 %	11 22 % 18.6 %	31 62 % 55.4 %	8 16 % 20 %	50 100 % 20 %
Total	46 18.4 % 100 %	49 19.6 % 100 %	59 23.6 % 100 %	56 22.4 % 100 %	40 16 % 100 %	250 100 % 100 %

$\chi^2=375.066 \cdot df=16 \cdot$ Cramer's $V=0.612 \cdot p=0.000$

b. 18.4%.
c. 78.3%.
d. 0%.
e. 64%.
f. 77.5%.
g. Yes.
h. 375.066, *sig* = 0.000.
i. Yes.

2.
a. Strong positive correlation; $\rho = 0.794$.

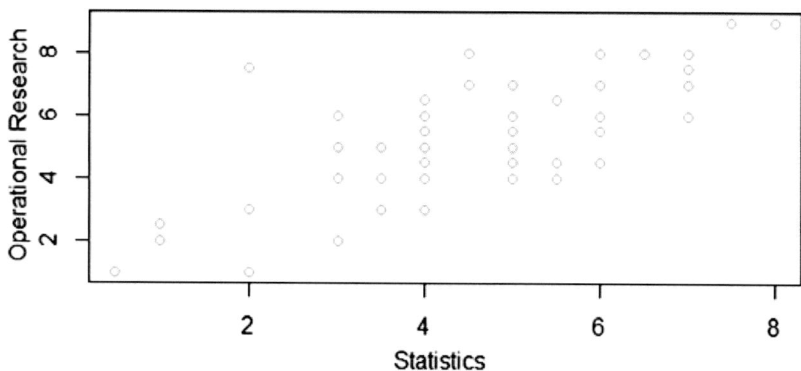

b. Positive correlation; $\rho = 0.689$.

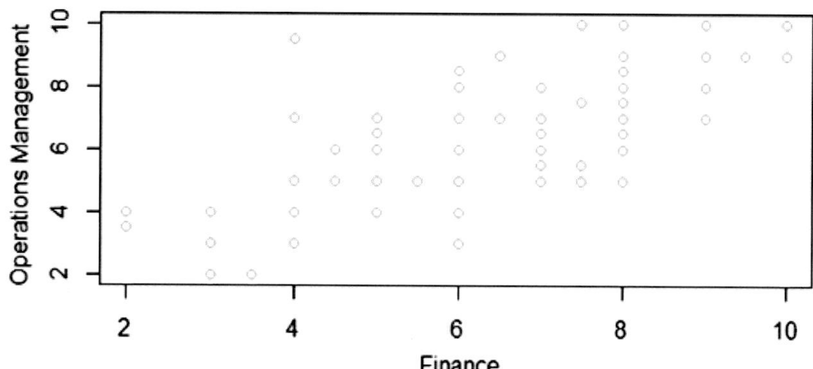

c. Strong positive correlation; $\rho = 0.962$.

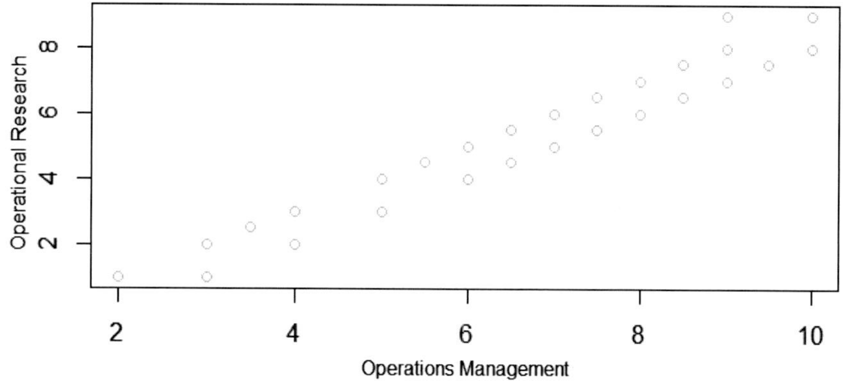

3.

a.

Case 1: Considering all 30 Brazilian supermarket chains.

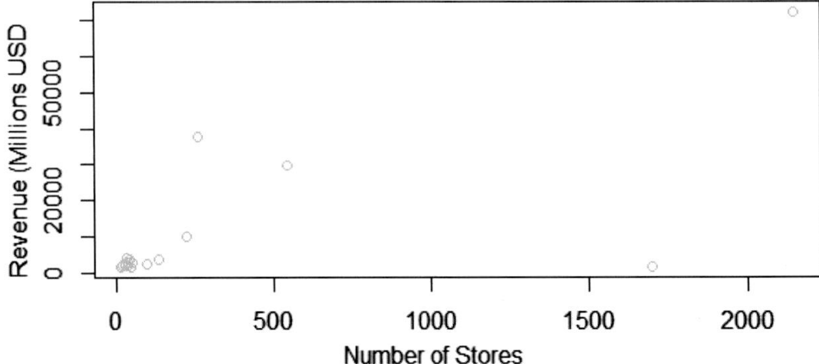

b. $\rho = 0.692$.

c.

Case 2: Excluding the four largest Brazilian supermarket chains.

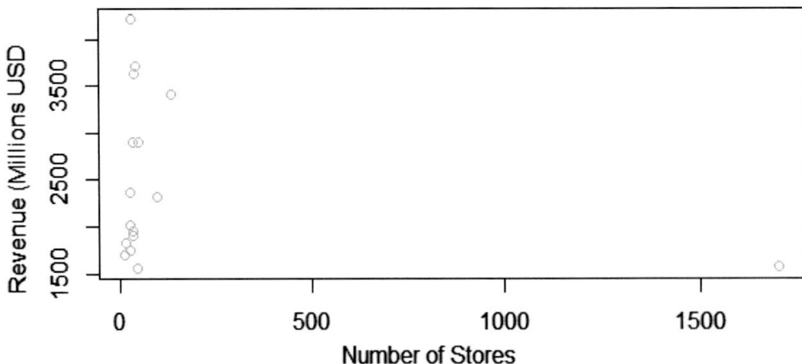

d. $\rho = -0.259$.

Chapter 6

1.

Kolmogorov-Smirnov test: $D = 0.150$, $P = 0.949$;
Shapiro-Wilk test: $W = 0.898$, $P = 0.151$.
Therefore, since P > 0.05, the distribution of data is normal.

2.

$P = 0.228 > 0.05$. The data follow the Normal distribution.

3.

Levene's F-test: $F = 0.025$, $P = 0.876$. The variances are homogeneous.

4.

$T_{cal} = 6.921$, $P = 0.000$. Thus, we reject H_0 ($\mu_1 \neq \mu_2$).

5.

$F_{cal} = 2.476$, $P = 0.1 > 0.05$. Thus, we do not reject H_0 ($\mu_{Factory\ 1} = \mu_{Factory\ 2} = \mu_{Factory\ 3}$).

Chapter 7

1.
Histogram:

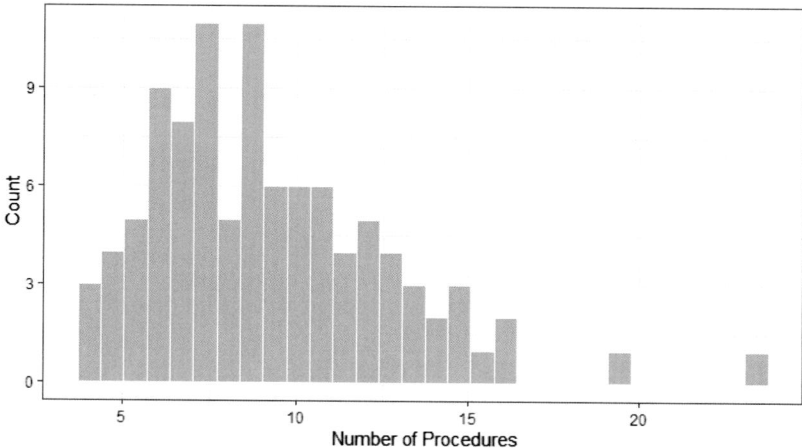

Boxplot:

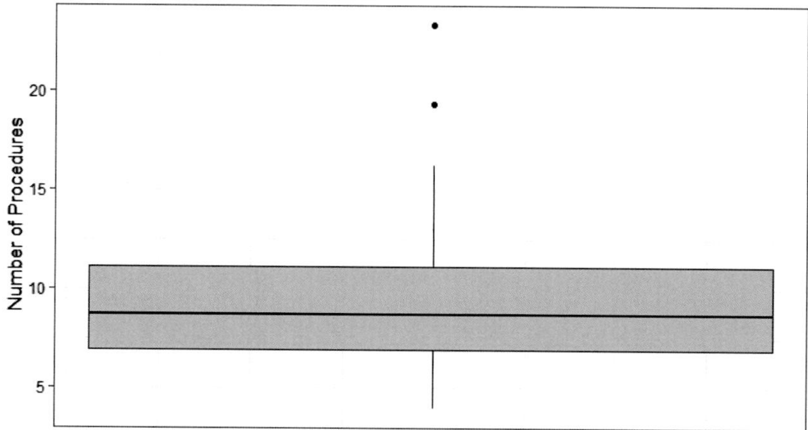

2.
Histogram (bins = 11):

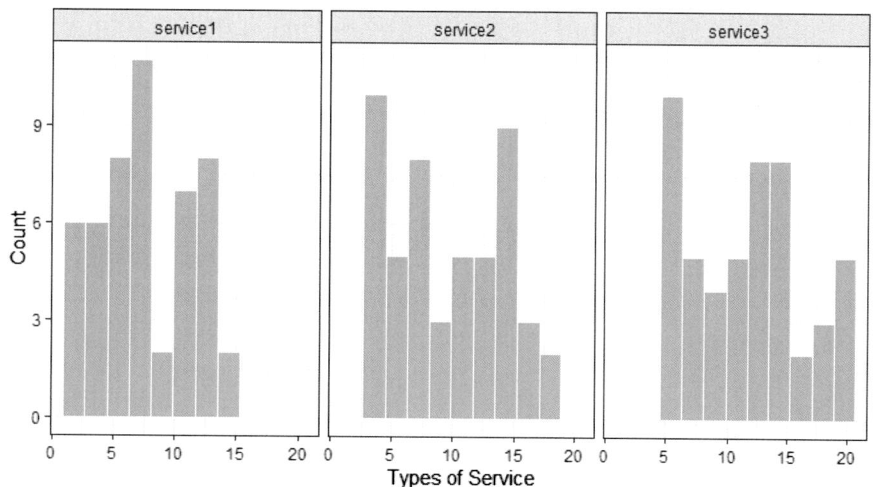

Boxplot:

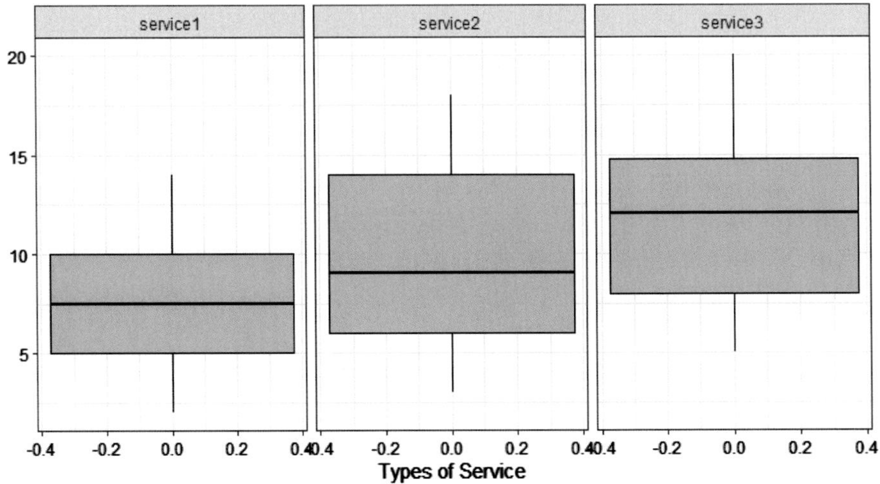

Chapter 11

1.

a.

```
 1.000  0.866 -1.000  0.000  0.998  0.945 -0.996  0.000  1.000  0.971 -1.000 -0.500  0.999  0.997 -1.000  0.327
 0.866  1.000 -0.866 -0.500  0.896  0.655 -0.908 -0.500  0.866  0.721 -0.856 -0.866  0.891  0.822 -0.881 -0.189
-1.000 -0.866  1.000  0.000 -0.998 -0.945  0.996  0.000 -1.000 -0.971  1.000  0.500 -0.999 -0.997  1.000 -0.327
 0.000 -0.500  0.000  1.000 -0.064  0.327  0.091  1.000  0.000  0.240 -0.020  0.866 -0.052  0.082  0.030  0.945
 0.998  0.896 -0.998 -0.064  1.000  0.922 -1.000 -0.064  0.998  0.953 -0.996 -0.554  1.000  0.989 -0.999  0.266
 0.945  0.655 -0.945  0.327  0.922  1.000 -0.911  0.327  0.945  0.996 -0.951 -0.189  0.926  0.969 -0.935  0.619
-0.996 -0.908  0.996  0.091 -1.000 -0.911  1.000  0.091 -0.996 -0.945  0.994  0.577 -0.999 -0.985  0.998 -0.240
 0.000 -0.500  0.000  1.000 -0.064  0.327  0.091  1.000  0.000  0.240 -0.020  0.866 -0.052  0.082  0.030  0.945
 1.000  0.866 -1.000  0.000  0.998  0.945 -0.996  0.000  1.000  0.971 -1.000 -0.500  0.999  0.997 -1.000  0.327
 0.971  0.721 -0.971  0.240  0.953  0.996 -0.945  0.240  0.971  1.000 -0.975 -0.277  0.957  0.987 -0.963  0.545
-1.000 -0.856  1.000 -0.020 -0.996 -0.951  0.994 -0.020 -1.000 -0.975  1.000  0.483 -0.997 -0.998  0.999 -0.346
-0.500 -0.866  0.500  0.866 -0.554 -0.189  0.577  0.866 -0.500 -0.277  0.483  1.000 -0.545 -0.427  0.526  0.655
 0.999  0.891 -0.999 -0.052  1.000  0.926 -0.999 -0.052  0.999  0.957 -0.997 -0.545  1.000  0.991 -1.000  0.277
 0.997  0.822 -0.997  0.082  0.989  0.969 -0.985  0.082  0.997  0.987 -0.998 -0.427  0.991  1.000 -0.994  0.404
-1.000 -0.881  1.000  0.030 -0.999 -0.935  0.998  0.030 -1.000 -0.963  0.999  0.526 -1.000 -0.994  1.000 -0.298
 0.327 -0.189 -0.327  0.945  0.266  0.619 -0.240  0.945  0.327  0.545 -0.346  0.655  0.277  0.404 -0.298  1.000
```

b.

```
   Cluster1 Cluster2     Distances
1        -1       -9 0.00000000000
2        -4       -8 0.00000000000
3        -5      -13 0.00006755768
4        -3      -11 0.00019811788
5       -15        4 0.00046136104
6         1        3 0.00137457110
7        -7        5 0.00183148943
8       -14        6 0.00338410446
9        -6      -10 0.00412940511
10        8        9 0.01281601283
11      -16        2 0.05508881748
12       -2       10 0.10374184047
13      -12       11 0.13397459622
14       12       13 0.38141042587
15        7       14 0.42344333980
```

From the agglomeration schedule, it is possible to verify that a big Euclidian distance leap occurs from the 16th stage (when only two clusters remain) to the 17th stage. Analyzing the dendrogram also helps in this interpretation.

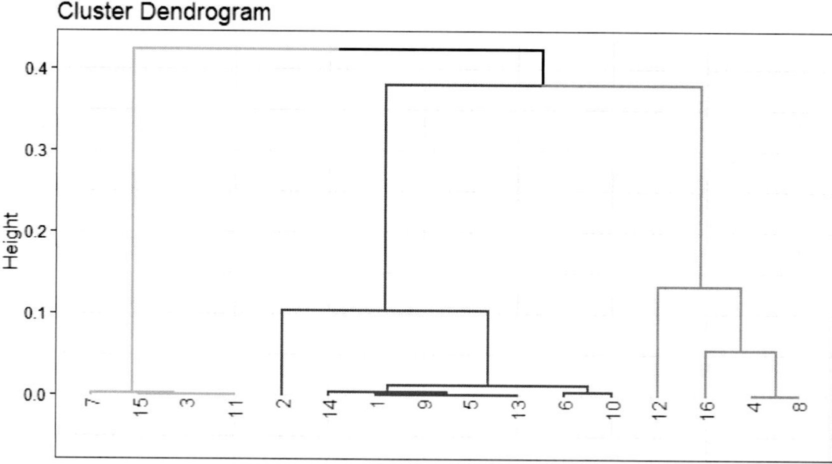

In fact, there are indications of two clusters of stores.

Chapter 12

1.

a.

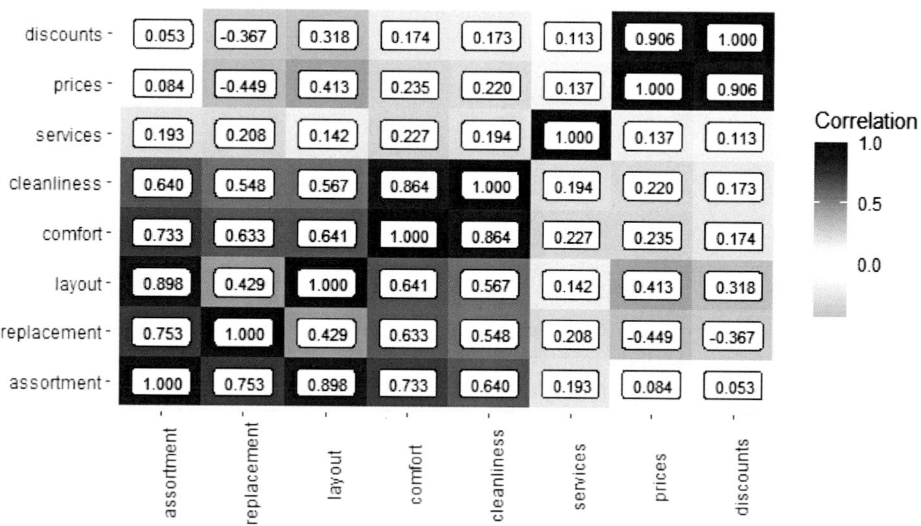

Yes. Based on the magnitude of some Pearson's correlation coefficients, it is possible to identify a first indication that the factor analysis may group the variables into factors.

b.

```
$chisq
[1] 13752.94

$p.value
[1] 0

$df
[1] 28
```

Yes. From the result of the $\chi^2_{Bartlett}$, it is possible to reject that the correlation matrix is statistically equal to the identity matrix with the same dimension, at a significance level of 0.05 and based on the hypothesis of Bartlett's test of sphericity, since $\chi^2_{Bartlett}=13{,}752.94$ ($Sig.\ \chi^2_{Bartlett}<0.05$ for 28 degrees of freedom). Therefore, the principal component analysis can be considered adequate.

c.
Considering the latent root criterion, two factors are extracted, with the respective eigenvalues:

Factor 1: 3.825
Factor 2: 2.254

The proportion of variance shared by all variables to form each factor is:

Factor 1: 47.812%
Factor 2: 28.174%

Thus, the total proportion of variance shared by all variables to form both factors is equal to 75.99%.

d.
The total proportion of variance lost by all variables to extract these two factors is:

$$1-0.7599=0.2401\ (24.01\%)$$

e.
Factor Loadings:

```
             Component1  Component2
assortment  -0.9179228  0.17358884
replacement -0.6921685  0.65956728
layout      -0.8552432 -0.18455871
comfort     -0.9090551  0.02924618
cleanliness -0.8488383  0.01020367
services    -0.3105135 -0.06475223
prices      -0.2736408 -0.95034455
discounts   -0.2316529 -0.91999037
```

Communalities:

```
assortment replacement      layout     comfort cleanliness    services
 0.8727153   0.9141263   0.7655028   0.8272365   0.7206306   0.1006115
    prices   discounts
 0.9780340   0.9000454
```

Note that the loadings and communality of the variable *services* are considerably low. This may demonstrate the need to extract a third factor, which mischaracterizes the latent root criterion.

f.
Factor Loadings:

```
             Component1  Component2   Component3
assortment  -0.9179228  0.17358884  0.119311288
replacement -0.6921685  0.65956728 -0.050840580
layout      -0.8552432 -0.18455871  0.195862787
comfort     -0.9090551  0.02924618  0.021148058
cleanliness -0.8488383  0.01020367  0.032634707
services    -0.3105135 -0.06475223 -0.941641098
prices      -0.2736408 -0.95034455  0.010633819
discounts   -0.2316529 -0.91999037  0.003096998
```

Communalities:

```
assortment replacement      layout     comfort cleanliness    services
 0.8869505   0.9167110   0.8038651   0.8276837   0.7216956   0.9872994
    prices   discounts
 0.9781471   0.9000550
```

Yes, it is possible to confirm the construct of the questionnaire proposed by the store's general manager because the variables *assortment*, *replacement*, *layout*, *comfort*, and *cleanliness* have a stronger correlation with a specific factor, the variables *price* and *discount* with another factor, and, finally, the variable *services* with a third factor.

g.

To the detriment of the extraction based on the latent root criterion, the decision to extract three factors increases the communalities of the variables, highlighting the variable *services*, now more strongly correlated with the third factor.

Chapter 13

1.

a.

ldl_classification	*physical_activities* 0	1	2	3	4	5	*Total*
very_high	32	158	264	140	40	0	634
	15	85	203	199	100	33	634
high	22	108	178	108	58	0	474
	11	63	151	149	75	25	474
borderline	0	26	98	190	86	36	436
	10	58	139	137	69	23	436
suboptimal	0	16	114	166	104	54	454
	11	61	145	142	72	24	454
optimal	0	0	82	118	76	30	306
	7	41	98	96	48	16	306
Total	54	308	736	722	364	120	2304
	54	308	736	722	364	120	2304

χ^2=539.357 · df=20 · Cramer's V=0.242 · p=0.000

b.

```
                     0          1          2          3          4          5
very_high    17.140625  73.246528  61.472222 -58.675347 -60.163194 -33.020833
high         10.890625  44.635417  26.583333 -40.536458 -16.885417 -24.687500
borderline  -10.218750 -32.284722 -41.277778  53.371528  17.118056  13.291667
suboptimal  -10.640625 -44.690972 -31.027778  23.730903  32.274306  30.354167
optimal      -7.171875 -40.906250 -15.750000  22.109375  27.656250  14.062500
```

c.

```
        Pearson's Chi-squared test

data:  tab
X-squared = 539.36, df = 20, p-value < 2.2e-16
```

d.

Since $Sig.\chi^2_{cal} < 0.05$, we can reject the null hypothesis that the two variables are randomly associated, that is, there is a statistically significant association, at a 5% significance level, between the LDL cholesterol index and the weekly number of sports activities.

e.

We have, for dimension, the following values of the total principal inertias:

$$\lambda_1^2 = 0.2255$$

$$\lambda_2^2 = 0.0050$$

$$\lambda_3^2 = 0.0025$$

$$\lambda_4^2 = 0.0011$$

Therefore, the total principal inertia is 0.2341. The four dimensions explain, respectively, 96.3% (0.2255/0.2341), 2.1% (0.0050/0.2341), 1.1% (0.0025/0.2341), and 0.5% (0.0011/0.2341) of the total principal inertia.

f.

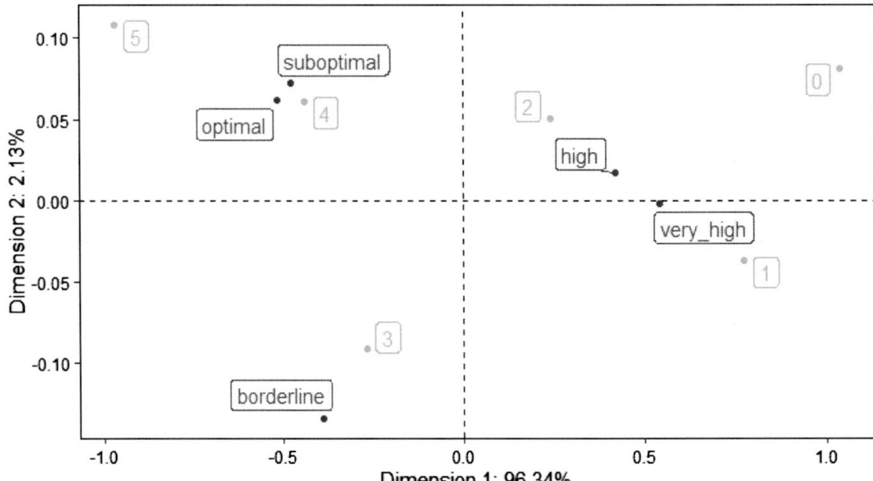

From the perceptual map, we can verify the existence of an association between the variables *cholesterol* and *sport* and, more than that, the association between their categories, since people who practice sport more often tend to have lower levels of LDL cholesterol.

2.

a.

Quality x Company

quality	*company* Gabicks	Lipehigh	Montvero	*Total*
terrible	0	263	0	263
bad	183	237	0	420
regular	150	0	0	150
good	167	0	244	411
great	0	0	256	256
Total	500	500	500	1500

χ^2=1785.553 · df=8 · Cramer's V=0.771 · p=0.000

Punctuality x Company

punctuality	*company* Gabicks	Lipehigh	Montvero	*Total*
no	270	317	183	770
yes	230	183	317	730
Total	500	500	500	1500

χ^2=74.010 · df=2 · Cramer's V=0.222 · p=0.000

Based on the results of the χ^2 tests, we can verify that there is an association between the *company* variable and the other variables (*quality* and *punctuality*), at a significance level of 5%, therefore all variables will be included in the correspondence analysis.

b.

Standard Coordinates

```
                Dim 1       Dim 2
terrible -1.29298035 -1.08086962
bad      -0.71933959  0.27042314
regular  -0.07041242  2.03303061
good      0.74474191  0.26562372
great     1.35409920 -0.95091776
no       -0.39077918  0.03347822
yes       0.41219173 -0.03531265
Gabicks  -0.05826405  1.27440597
Lipehigh -1.14134177 -0.68875346
Montvero  1.19960583 -0.58565251
```

Principal Coordinates

```
                Dim 1       Dim 2
terrible -1.05029473 -0.79606164
bad      -0.58432332  0.19916693
regular  -0.05719638  1.49732923
good      0.60495776  0.19563216
great     1.09994189 -0.70035195
no       -0.31743197  0.02465675
yes       0.33482551 -0.02600780
Gabicks  -0.04732820  0.93860137
Lipehigh -0.92711791 -0.50726767
Montvero  0.97444611 -0.43133370
```

c.

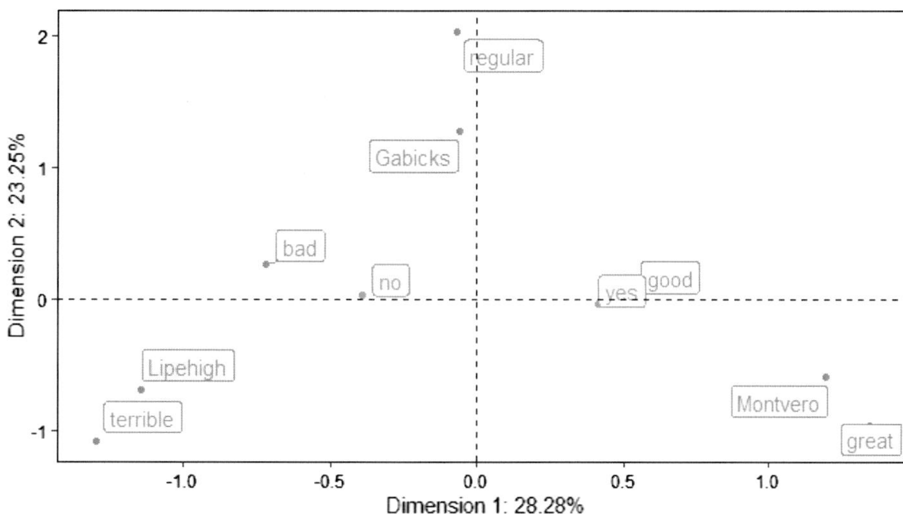

Chapter 14

1.

```
Call:
lm(formula = cpi ~ . - country, data = corruption)

Residuals:
    Min      1Q  Median      3Q     Max
-3.2815 -1.4753  0.0621  1.6076  3.6473

Coefficients:
            Estimate Std. Error t value Pr(>|t|)
(Intercept) 15.15894    4.75438   3.188 0.002493 **
age          0.07005    0.03277   2.138 0.037568 *
hours       -0.42453    0.11692  -3.631 0.000674 ***
---
Signif. codes:  0 '***' 0.001 '**' 0.01 '*' 0.05 '.' 0.1 ' ' 1

Residual standard error: 1.982 on 49 degrees of freedom
Multiple R-squared:  0.3177,	Adjusted R-squared:  0.2899
F-statistic: 11.41 on 2 and 49 DF,  p-value: 8.549e-05
```

a. Yes, since the *P-value* of the *F* statistic < 0.05, we can state that at least one of the explanatory variables is statistically significant to explain the behavior of variable *cpi,* at a significance level of 0.05.

b. Yes, since the *P-value* of both *t* statistics < 0.05, we can state that their parameters are statistically different from zero, at a significance level of 0.05. Therefore, the Stepwise procedure would not exclude any of the explanatory variables of the final model.

c. $\widehat{cpi_i} = 15.15894 + 0.07005.age_i - 0.42453.hours_i$.

d. $R^2 = 0.3177$.

e. By analyzing the signs of the final model's coefficients, for this cross-section, we can state that countries with billionaires with lower average ages have lower *cpi* indexes. That is, there is a higher corruption perception from society. Besides, on average, a greater number of hours worked per week has a negative relationship with variable *cpi*. That is, countries with a higher corruption perception (lower *cpi*) have a higher workload per week. It is important to mention that countries with a lower *cpi* are those considered emerging countries.

f.

Shapiro-Francia:

```
	Shapiro-Francia normality test

data:  m1$residuals
W = 0.96864, p-value = 0.1614
```

Shapiro-Wilk:

```
	Shapiro-Wilk normality test

data:  m1$residuals
W = 0.95835, p-value = 0.06638
```

By using the Shapiro-Francia test, the most suitable for the size of this sample, we can see that the residuals follow a normal distribution, at a significance level of 0.05. We would have arrived at the same conclusion if the test used had been the Shapiro-Wilk test.

g.

```
Breusch Pagan Test for Heteroskedasticity
-----------------------------------------
 Ho: the variance is constant
 Ha: the variance is not constant

              Data
 -------------------------------
 Response : cpi
 Variables: fitted values of cpi

          Test Summary
 -------------------------------
 DF            =    1
 Chi2          =    0.0002974765
 Prob > Chi2   =    0.9862392
```

From the Breusch-Pagan/Cook-Weisberg test, it is possible to verify if there is homoskedasticity in the model proposed.

h.

```
h.
  Variables Tolerance      VIF
1       age 0.9419066 1.061676
2     hours 0.9419066 1.061676
```

Since the final model obtained does not have very high VIF statistics ($1-Tolerance=0.058$), we may consider that there are no multicollinearity problems.

2.

```
Call:
lm(formula = cpi ~ emerging, data = corruption_emer)

Residuals:
    Min      1Q  Median      3Q     Max
-3.8286 -0.9968 -0.0286  0.9714  5.2032

Coefficients:
            Estimate Std. Error t value Pr(>|t|)
(Intercept)   7.7286     0.3337  23.161  < 2e-16 ***
emergingyes  -3.6318     0.4322  -8.404 3.98e-11 ***
---
Signif. codes:  0 '***' 0.001 '**' 0.01 '*' 0.05 '.' 0.1 ' ' 1

Residual standard error: 1.529 on 50 degrees of freedom
Multiple R-squared:  0.5855, Adjusted R-squared:  0.5772
F-statistic: 70.62 on 1 and 50 DF,  p-value: 3.977e-11
```

a. The difference between the average *cpi* value for emerging and for developed countries is –3.6318. That is, while emerging countries have an average $cpi=4.0968$, developed countries have an average $cpi=7.7286$. This is exactly the value of the *cpi* regression intercept based on variable emerging, since the dummy emerging for developed countries = 0.

Yes, this difference is statistically significant, at a significance level of 0.05, since the *P-value* of the *t*-statistic < 0.05 for the variable emerging.

b.

```
Call:
lm(formula = paste(response, "~", paste(preds, collapse = " + ")),
    data = l)

Residuals:
    Min      1Q  Median      3Q     Max
-3.1846 -1.1748 -0.0467  1.0853  4.7284

Coefficients:
            Estimate Std. Error t value Pr(>|t|)
(Intercept) 13.17009    3.07829   4.278 8.70e-05 ***
emergingyes -3.22385    0.48135  -6.698 1.95e-08 ***
hours       -0.17338    0.09753  -1.778   0.0817 .
---
Signif. codes:  0 '***' 0.001 '**' 0.01 '*' 0.05 '.' 0.1 ' ' 1

Residual standard error: 1.497 on 49 degrees of freedom
Multiple R-squared:  0.6106, Adjusted R-squared:  0.5947
F-statistic: 38.42 on 2 and 49 DF,  p-value: 9.224e-11
```

c.

$$\widehat{cpi}_i = 13.17009 - 3.22385.emerging_i - 0.17338.hours_i$$

$$\widehat{cpi}_i = 13.17009 - 3.22385.(1) - 0.17338.(37) = 3.53414$$

d.

$$\widehat{cpi}_{min} = 8.009177 - 4.030851.emerging_i - 0.336882.hours_i$$

$$\widehat{cpi}_{max} = 18.331000457 - 2.416839514.emerging_i - 0.009869259.hours_i$$

Obviously, the confidence interval is extremely broad and makes no sense. This happened because the value of R^2 is not so high.

e.


```
Call:
lm(formula = paste(response, "~", paste(preds, collapse = " + ")),
    data = l)

Residuals:
    Min      1Q  Median      3Q     Max
-3.1846 -1.1748 -0.0467  1.0853  4.7284

Coefficients:
            Estimate Std. Error t value Pr(>|t|)
(Intercept) 13.17009    3.07829   4.278 8.70e-05 ***
emergingyes -3.22385    0.48135  -6.698 1.95e-08 ***
hours       -0.17338    0.09753  -1.778   0.0817 .
---
Signif. codes:  0 '***' 0.001 '**' 0.01 '*' 0.05 '.' 0.1 ' ' 1

Residual standard error: 1.497 on 49 degrees of freedom
Multiple R-squared:  0.6106, Adjusted R-squared:  0.5947
F-statistic: 38.42 on 2 and 49 DF,  p-value: 9.224e-11
```


$$\widehat{cpi}_i = 27.4048 - 3.2133.emerging_i - 5.7138.\ln(hours_i)$$

f.

Since the adjusted R^2 is slightly higher in the model with non-linear functional form (logarithmic functional form for variable *hours*) than in the model with linear functional form, we choose the non-linear estimated model seen in item **e.** Since, in both cases, neither the number of variables nor the sample size used changes, such analysis could be carried out directly based on the values of R^2.

Chapter 15

1.

```
Call:
glm(formula = default ~ ., family = "binomial", data = default_data)

Deviance Residuals:
    Min        1Q    Median        3Q       Max
-2.3090   -0.6518   0.5219    0.6998    1.7247

Coefficients:
               Estimate Std. Error z value Pr(>|z|)
(Intercept)  2.97507265  2.623e-01  11.341  < 2e-16 ***
age         -0.02432932  6.965e-03  -3.493 0.000478 ***
gender       0.74149654  1.135e-01   6.532 6.47e-11 ***
income      -0.00025601  1.703e-05 -15.030  < 2e-16 ***
---
Signif. codes:  0 '***' 0.001 '**' 0.01 '*' 0.05 '.' 0.1 ' ' 1
```

a. Yes. Since the *P-value* of the χ^2 statistic < 0.05, we can state that at least one of the explanatory variables is statistically significant to explain the probability of default, at a significance level of 0.05.

b. Yes. Since the *P-value* of all Wald z statistics < 0.05, we can state that their respective parameters are statistically different from zero, at a significance level of 0.05. Therefore, no explanatory variable will be excluded from the final model.

c. $p_i = \dfrac{1}{1 + e^{-(2.97507265 - 0.02432932.age_i + 0.74149654.gender_i - 0.00025601.income_i)}}$

d. Yes. Since the parameter estimated for the variable gender is positive, on average, male individuals (dummy = 1) have higher probabilities of default than female individuals, as long as the other conditions are kept constant. The chances of the event occurring will be multiplied by a factor greater than 1.

e. No. Older people, on average, tend to have smaller probabilities of default, maintaining the remaining conditions constant, since the parameter of the variable *age* is negative, that is, the chances of the event occurring is multiplied by a factor less than 1, as age increases.

f. $p_i = \dfrac{1}{1 + e^{-[2.97507265 - 0.02432932.(37) + 0.74149654.(1) - 0.00025601.(6{,}850)]}} = 0.7432.$

The average probability of default estimated for this individual is 74.32%.

g.

$$age: e^{-0.02432932} = 0.9759643$$

$$gender: e^{0.74149654} = 2.099075$$

$$income: e^{-0.00025601} = 0.999744$$

The chance of being default as the income increases by 1 unit is, on average and maintaining the remaining conditions constant, multiplied by a factor of 0.999744 (a chance 0.0256% lower).

h.

```
Confusion Matrix and Statistics

          TRUE FALSE
   TRUE   1392   360
   FALSE    92   156

               Accuracy : 0.774
                 95% CI : (0.755, 0.7922)
    No Information Rate : 0.742
    P-Value [Acc > NIR] : 0.0005056

                  Kappa : 0.2893

 Mcnemar's Test P-Value : < 0.00000000000000022

            Sensitivity : 0.9380
            Specificity : 0.3023
         Pos Pred Value : 0.7945
         Neg Pred Value : 0.6290
             Prevalence : 0.7420
         Detection Rate : 0.6960
   Detection Prevalence : 0.8760
      Balanced Accuracy : 0.6202

       'Positive' Class : TRUE
```

Although the overall model efficiency is 77.40%, the sensitivity is 93.80% and the specificity is 30.23% (for a cutoff of 0.5).

2.

a.

```
                 n     %  val%  %cum val%cum
very high      634  27.5  27.5  27.5    27.5
high           474  20.6  20.6  48.1    48.1
borderline     436  18.9  18.9  67.0    67.0
near optimal   454  19.7  19.7  86.7    86.7
optmimal       306  13.3  13.3 100.0   100.0
Total         2304 100.0 100.0 100.0   100.0
```

b.

Model:

```
Call:
multinom(formula = cholestquali ~ . - cholesterol, data =
cholestquali_data)

Coefficients:
             (Intercept)  cigarette     sport
high          -0.4165745 -0.3074251 0.1608636
borderline    -2.6223817 -0.4097294 1.0089338
near optimal  -2.4572009 -1.4064853 1.1260647
optmimal      -2.8566764 -1.6684912 1.1554804

Std. Errors:
             (Intercept) cigarette      sport
high           0.1694834 0.1299829 0.06264927
borderline     0.2105744 0.1391029 0.06931333
near optimal   0.2101977 0.1402708 0.07142414
optmimal       0.2389271 0.1602054 0.07922159

Residual Deviance: 6552.877
AIC: 6576.877
```

P-values:

```
P-values:
             (Intercept) cigarette sport
high               0.014     0.018  0.01
borderline         0.000     0.003  0.00
near optimal       0.000     0.000  0.00
optmimal           0.000     0.000  0.00
```

Yes. Since the P-value of the χ^2statistic < 0.05, we can reject the null hypothesis that all parameters $\beta_{jm}(j=1,2;$ $m=1,2,3,4)$ are statistically equal to zero at a significance level of 0.05. That is, at least one of the explanatory variables is statistically significant to form the occurrence probability expression of at least one of the classifications proposed for the LDL cholesterol index.

c. Since all of the parameters are statistically significant for all of the logits (Wald z tests at a significance level of 0.05), the final equations estimated for the average occurrence probabilities of the classifications proposed for the LDL cholesterol index can be written the following way:

Probability of an individual *i* having a very high LDL cholesterol index:

$$p_i = \frac{1}{1 + e^{(0.42-0.31.cigarette_i+0.16.sport_i)} + e^{(-2.62-0.41.cigarette_i+1.01.sport_i)} + e^{(-2.46-1.41.cigarette_i+1.13.sport_i)} \cdots}$$

$$\cdots \overline{+ e^{(-2.86-1.67.cigarette_i+1.16.sport_i)}}$$

Probability of an individual *i* having a high LDL cholesterol index:

$$p_i = \frac{e^{(0.42-0.31.cigarette_i+0.16.sport_i)}}{1 + e^{(0.42-0.31.cigarette_i+0.16.sport_i)} + e^{(-2.62-0.41.cigarette_i+1.01.sport_i)} + e^{(-2.46-1.41.cigarette_i+1.13.sport_i)} \cdots}$$

$$\cdots \overline{+ e^{(-2.86-1.67.cigarette_i+1.16.sport_i)}}$$

Probability of an individual *i* having a borderline LDL cholesterol index:

$$p_i = \frac{e^{(-2.62-0.41.cigarette_i+1.01.sport_i)}}{1 + e^{(0.42-0.31.cigarette_i+0.16.sport_i)} + e^{(-2.62-0.41.cigarette_i+1.01.sport_i)} + e^{(-2.46-1.41.cigarette_i+1.13.sport_i)} \cdots}$$

$$\cdots \overline{+ e^{(-2.86-1.67.cigarette_i+1.16.sport_i)}}$$

Probability of an individual *i* having a near-optimal LDL cholesterol index:

$$p_i = \frac{e^{(-2.46-1.41.cigarette_i+1.13.sport_i)}}{1 + e^{(0.42-0.31.cigarette_i+0.16.sport_i)} + e^{(-2.62-0.41.cigarette_i+1.01.sport_i)} + e^{(-2.46-1.41.cigarette_i+1.13.sport_i)} \cdots}$$

$$\cdots \overline{+ e^{(-2.86-1.67.cigarette_i+1.16.sport_i)}}$$

Probability of an individual *i* having an optimal LDL cholesterol index:

$$p_i = \frac{e^{(-2.86-1.67.cigarette_i+1.16.sport_i)}}{1 + e^{(0.42-0.31.cigarette_i+0.16.sport_i)} + e^{(-2.62-0.41.cigarette_i+1.01.sport_i)} + e^{(-2.46-1.41.cigarette_i+1.13.sport_i)} \cdots}$$

$$\cdots \overline{+ e^{(-2.86-1.67.cigarette_i+1.16.sport_i)}}$$

d. For an individual who does not smoke and only practices sports once a week, we have:
Probability of having a very high LDL cholesterol index = 41.32%.
Probability of having a high LDL cholesterol index = 31.99%.
Probability of having a borderline LDL cholesterol index = 8.23%.
Probability of having a near optimal LDL cholesterol index = 10.92%.
Probability of having an optimal LDL cholesterol index = 7.54%.

e.

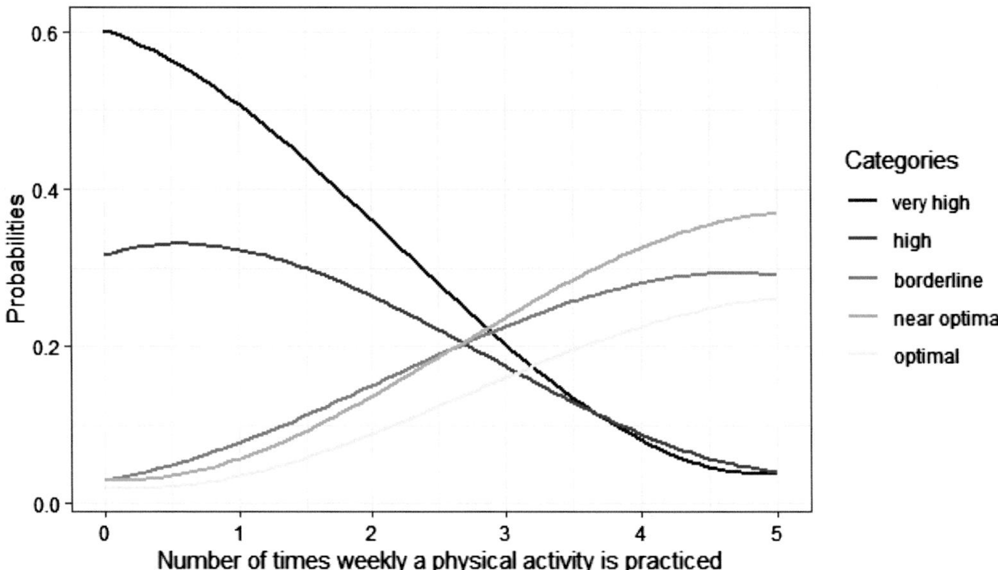

If people start practicing sports twice a week, they will considerably increase their probability of having near-optimal or optimal levels of LDL cholesterol.

f.

```
             cigarette    sport
high         0.7353379 1.174525
borderline   0.6638299 2.742675
near optimal 0.2450029 3.083498
optmimal     0.1885313 3.175549
```

The chances of having a high cholesterol index in comparison with a level considered very high are, on average, multiplied by a factor of 1.1745 (17.45% higher) when we increase the number of times physical activities are done weekly by 1 unit and maintaining the remaining conditions constant.

g. The chances of having an optimal cholesterol index on average and in comparison with a level considered near optimal are multiplied by a factor of 1.2995 (0.2450029/0.1885313) when people stop smoking and maintaining the remaining conditions constant. That is, the chances are 29.95% higher.

h. and i.

```
             very high high borderline near optimal optmimal Total True_Positives       OME
very high          542    0         34           58        0   634            542 0.8548896
high               380    0         34           60        0   474              0 0.0000000
borderline         236    0         74          126        0   436             74 0.1697248
near optimal       182    0         58          214        0   454            214 0.4713656
optmimal           114    0         30          162        0   306              0 0.0000000
```

Accuracy: 36.02%

Chapter 16

1.

a.

```
  Mean Variance
 <dbl>    <dbl>
1 1.02     1.13
```

Even if in a preliminary way, we can see that the mean and variance of the variable *purchases* are quite close.

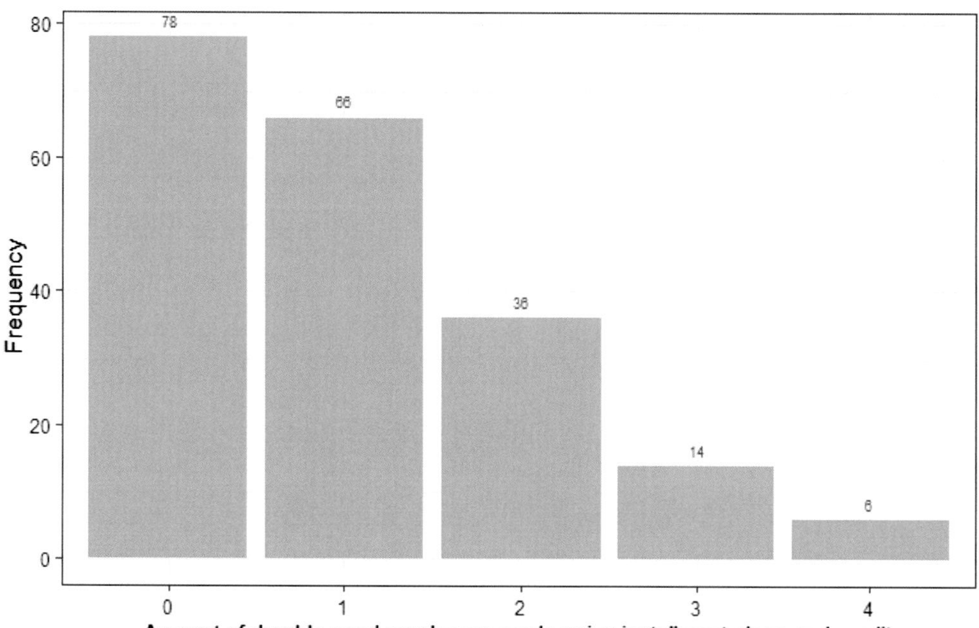

b.

```
Call:
glm(formula = purchases ~ . - id, family = "poisson", data = financing)

Deviance Residuals:
    Min       1Q   Median       3Q      Max
-1.4820  -0.9637  -0.1592   0.3973   3.2299

Coefficients:
              Estimate Std. Error z value Pr(>|z|)
(Intercept)  7.0483781  0.8047050   8.759  < 2e-16 ***
income      -0.0011246  0.0001498  -7.506 6.08e-14 ***
age         -0.0864971  0.0173831  -4.976 6.49e-07 ***
---
Signif. codes:  0 '***' 0.001 '**' 0.01 '*' 0.05 '.' 0.1 ' ' 1


        Overdispersion Test - Cameron & Trivedi (1990)

data:  financing
Lambda t test score: = -1.6538, p-value = 0.09974
alternative hypothesis: overdispersion if lambda p-value is less than
or equal to the stipulated significance level
```

Since the *P-value* of the *t*-test that corresponds to the β parameter of *lambda* is greater than 0.05, we can state that the data of the dependent variable *purchases* **do not present overdispersion**. So, the Poisson regression model estimated is suitable due to the **presence of equidispersion in the data**.

c. $purchases_i = e^{[7.0483781 - 0.0011246.\ (2{,}600) - 0.0864971.\ (47)]} = 1.06$

We recommend that this calculation be carried out with a larger number of decimal places.

```
   income       age
0.9988760 0.9171382
```

d.

The annual use incidence rate of closed-end credit financing when there is an increase in the customer's monthly income of US\$1.00 is, on average and as long as the other conditions are kept constant, multiplied by a factor of 0.9988 (0.1124% lower). Consequently, at each increase of US\$100.00 in the customer's monthly income, we expect the annual use incidence rate of closed-end credit financing to be 11.24% lower, on average and provided the other conditions are kept constant.

e. The annual use incidence rate of closed-end credit financing when there is an increase of 1 year in consumers' average age is, on average and as long as the other conditions are kept constant, multiplied by a factor of 0.9171 (8.29% lower).

f.

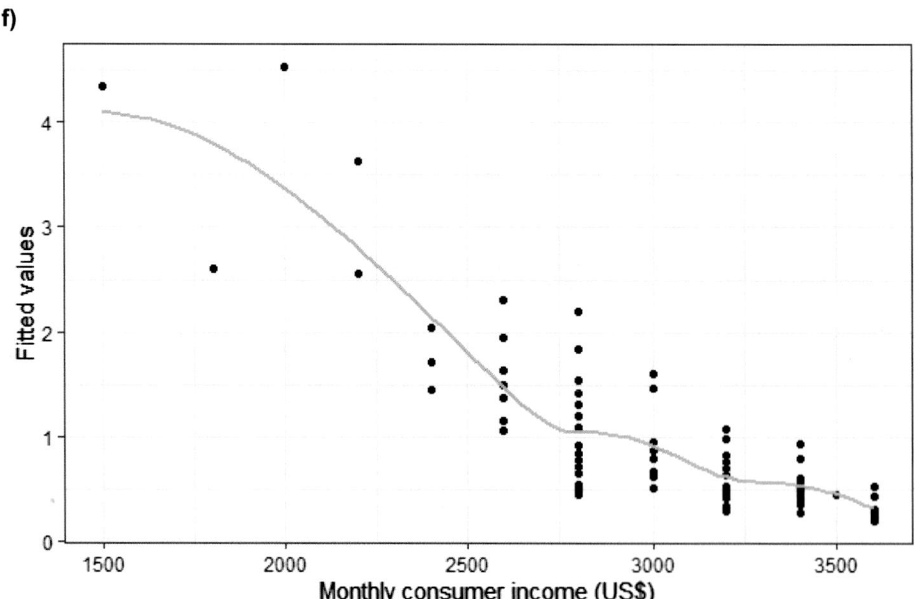

In the constructed chart, it is possible to see that higher monthly incomes lead to a decrease in the expected annual use of closed-end credit financing when purchasing durable goods, with an average reduction rate of 12.0% at each increase of US\$100 in income.

g.

```
Call:
lm(formula = lnpurchases ~ income + age, data = financing_log)

Residuals:
     Min       1Q   Median       3Q      Max
-0.64801 -0.28001 -0.07398  0.19650  1.45081

Coefficients:
              Estimate Std. Error t value Pr(>|t|)
(Intercept)  3.01336709  4.756e-01   6.336 4.37e-09 ***
income      -0.00057517  9.911e-05  -5.803 5.50e-08 ***
age         -0.02289243  9.463e-03  -2.419   0.0171 *
---
Signif. codes:  0 '***' 0.001 '**' 0.01 '*' 0.05 '.' 0.1 ' ' 1

Residual standard error: 0.4033 on 119 degrees of freedom
Multiple R-squared:  0.2646,	Adjusted R-squared:  0.2522
F-statistic: 21.41 on 2 and 119 DF,  p-value: 1.145e-08
```

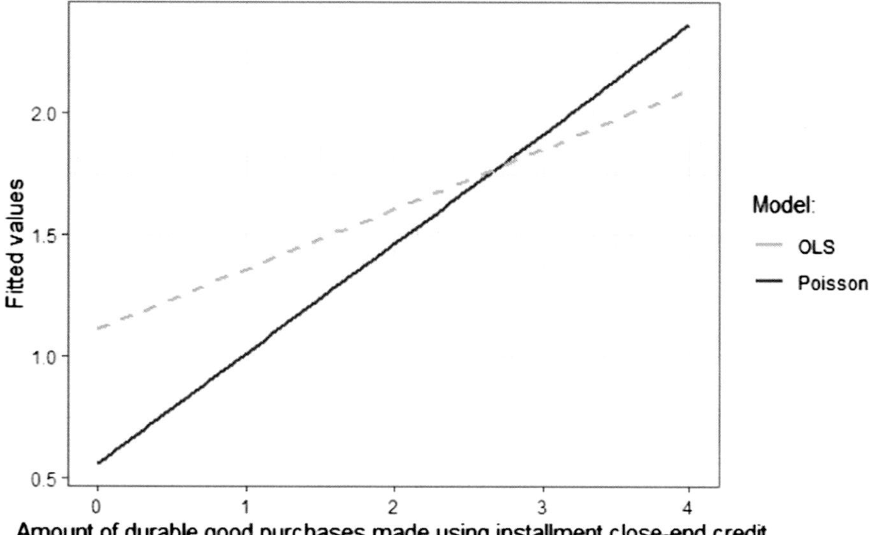

h. Young people and with lower monthly income.

Chapter 17

1.

a.

```
   country      Freq
   <fct>       <int>
 1 Argentina       5
 2 Australia       5
 3 Brazil          5
 4 Canada          5
 5 Chile           5
 6 China           5
 7 Denmark         5
 8 Finland         5
 9 France          5
10 Germany         5
11 Iceland         5
12 Italy           5
13 Japan           5
14 Mexico          5
15 Netherlands     5
16 Portugal        5
17 Singapore       5
18 South Korea     5
19 Spain           5
20 Sweden          5
21 Switzerland     5
22 UK              5
23 Uruguay         5
24 USA             5
```

In fact, this is a balanced clustered data structure.

b.

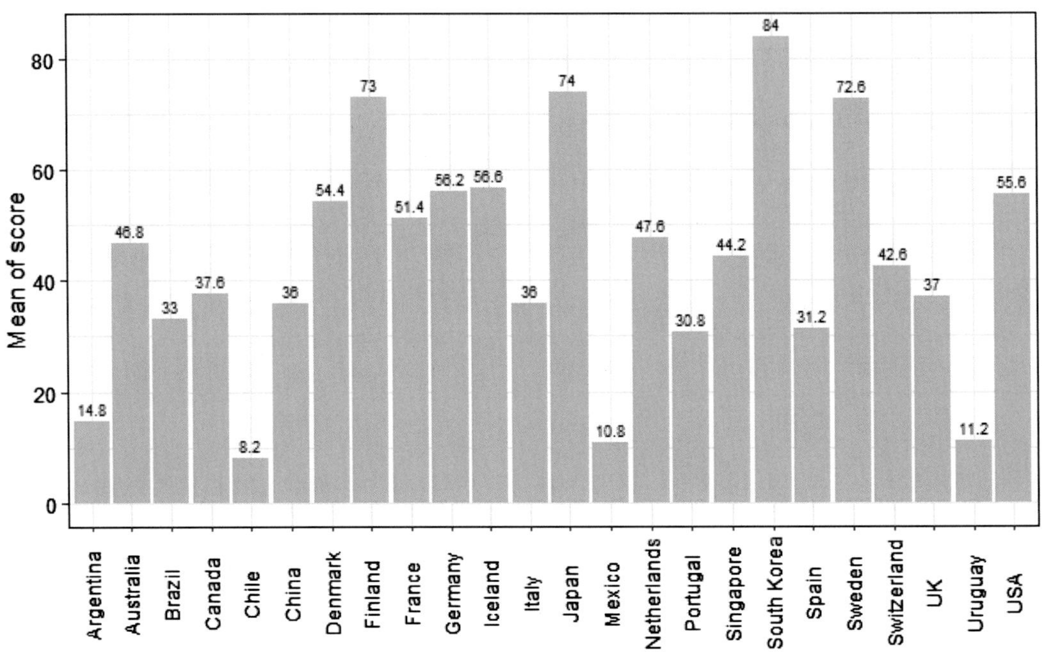

c.

```
Family: gaussian  ( identity )
Formula:          score ~ 1 + (1 | country)
Data: science_competition

     AIC      BIC   logLik deviance df.resid
   756.6    765.0   -375.3    750.6      118

Random effects:

Conditional model:
 Groups   Name        Variance Std.Dev.
 country  (Intercept) 422.6    20.558
 Residual              11.2     3.346
Number of obs: 120, groups:  country, 24

Dispersion estimate for gaussian family (sigma^2): 11.2

Conditional model:
            Estimate Std. Error z value Pr(>|z|)
(Intercept)   43.567      4.207   10.36   <2e-16 ***
---
Signif. codes:  0 '***' 0.001 '**' 0.01 '*' 0.05 '.' 0.1 ' ' 1
```

d.

```
Likelihood ratio test

Model 1: score ~ 1 + (1 | country)
Model 2: score ~ 1
  #Df  LogLik Df  Chisq Pr(>Chisq)
1   3 -375.30
2   2 -532.13 -1 313.67  < 2.2e-16 ***
---
Signif. codes:  0 '***' 0.001 '**' 0.01 '*' 0.05 '.' 0.1 ' ' 1
```

Since *Sig.* $\chi^2 = 0.000$, it is possible to reject the null hypothesis that the random intercepts are equal to zero ($H_0: \nu_{0j} = 0$), which makes the estimation of a traditional linear regression model be ruled out for these clustered data.

e.

$$ICC = \frac{\tau_{00}}{\tau_{00} + \sigma^2} = \frac{422.6}{422.6 + 11.2} = 0.9742$$

This suggests that approximately 97% of the total variance in students' grades in science is due to differences between the participants' countries of origin.

f.

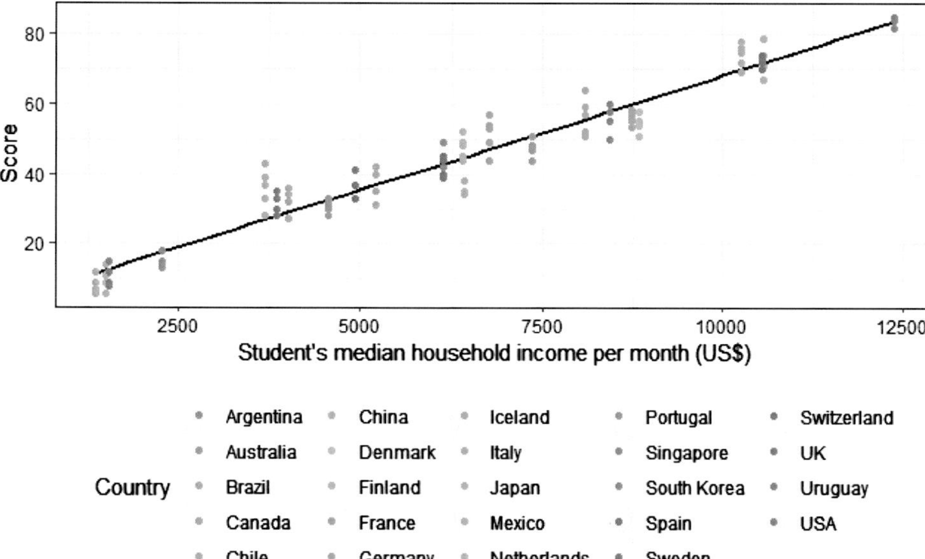

g.

```
Family: gaussian  ( identity )
Formula:          score ~ income + (1 | country)
Data: science_competition

     AIC      BIC   logLik deviance df.resid
   723.0    734.2   -357.5    715.0      118

Random effects:

Conditional model:
 Groups   Name        Variance Std.Dev.
 country  (Intercept) 13.08    3.617
 Residual             14.70    3.834
Number of obs: 120, groups:  country, 24

Dispersion estimate for gaussian family (sigma^2): 14.7

Conditional model:
            Estimate Std. Error z value Pr(>|z|)
(Intercept) 4.407935   1.999089   2.205   0.0275 *
income      0.006245   0.000291  21.463   <2e-16 ***
---
Signif. codes:  0 '***' 0.001 '**' 0.01 '*' 0.05 '.' 0.1 ' ' 1
```

h.

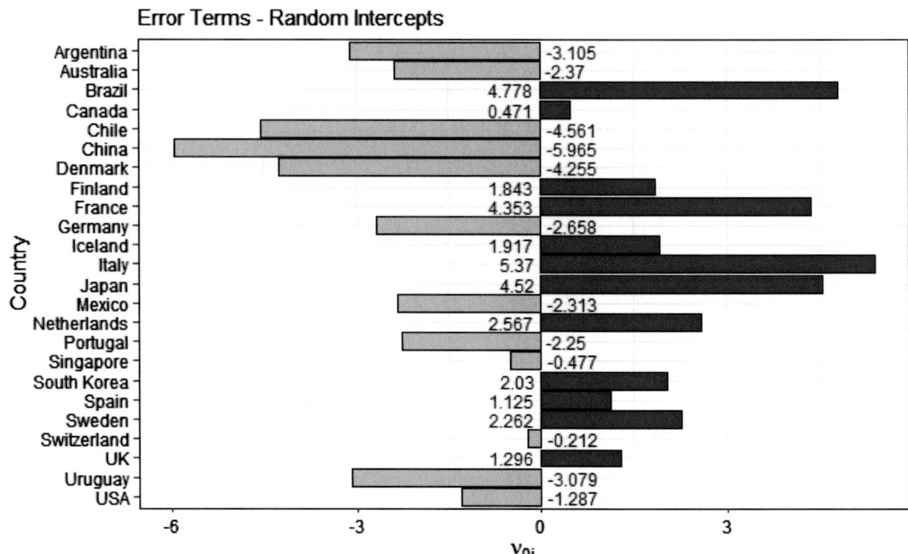

i.

```
Family: gaussian  ( identity )
Formula:          score ~ income + resdevel + income:resdevel + (1 |
country)
Data: science_competition

     AIC      BIC   logLik deviance df.resid
   706.5    723.2   -347.2    694.5      118

Random effects:

Conditional model:
 Groups   Name        Variance Std.Dev.
 country  (Intercept) 12.13    3.483
 Residual             11.07    3.327
Number of obs: 120, groups:  country, 24

Dispersion estimate for gaussian family (sigma^2): 11.1

Conditional model:
                   Estimate Std. Error z value Pr(>|z|)
(Intercept)      3.47294365  2.914e+00   1.192    0.233
income           0.00119013  9.845e-04   1.209    0.227
resdevel        15.78275761  3.023e+00   5.221 1.78e-07 ***
income:resdevel  0.00002033  2.283e-04   0.089    0.929
---
Signif. codes:  0 '***' 0.001 '**' 0.01 '*' 0.05 '.' 0.1 ' ' 1
```

j. $score_{ij} = 3.47294365 + 0.00119013 \cdot income_{ij} + 15.78275761.resdevel_j + 0.00002033 \cdot resdevel_j \cdot income_{ij} + \nu_{0j} + \varepsilon_{ij}$

k.

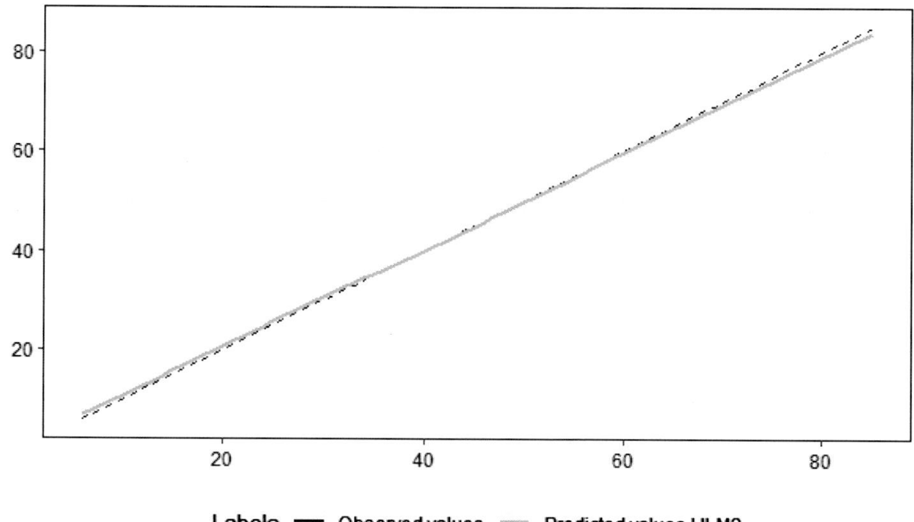

Chapter 18

1.

a.

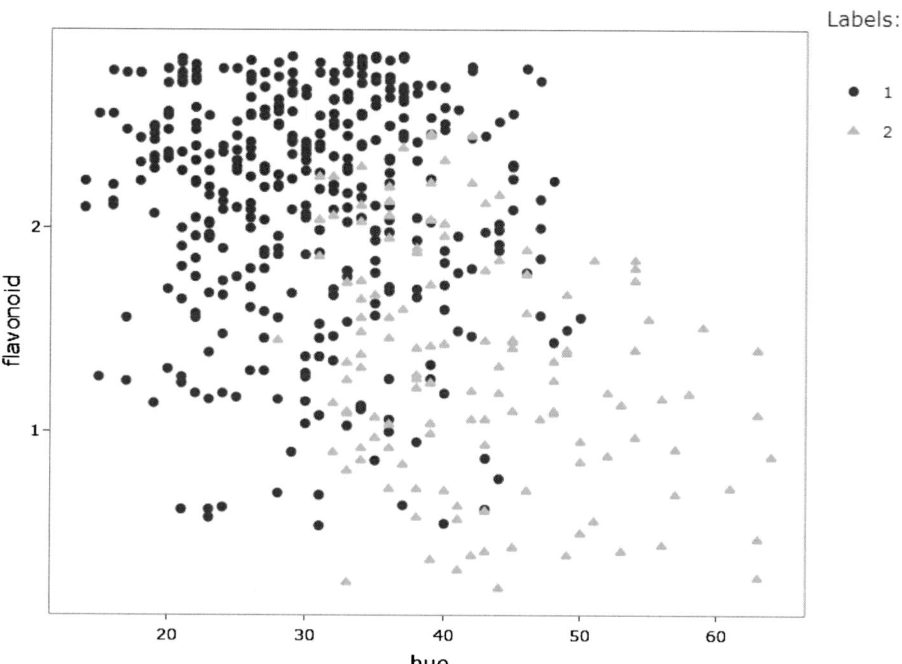

c. SVM with linear kernel:
cost = 0.1
classification error = 0.14

e. SVM with polynomial kernel of degree 2:
cost = 1

gamma = 1
classification error = 0.207

f. SVM with radial kernel:
cost = 10
gamma = 0.1
classification error = 0.133

g.

Model	Sensitivity	Specificity	Accuracy	AUC
SVM with Linear Kernel	0.920	0.560	0.830	0.916
SVM with Polynomial Kernel of Degree 2	0.973	0.280	0.800	0.660
SVM with Radial Kernel	0.940	0.480	0.825	0.911
Binary Logistic Regression Model	0.073	0.357	0.146	0.916

h. Overall, the SVM model with linear kernel and the binary logistic regression model seem to give the best results, since they have the higher values for the area under the ROC curve (AUC = 0.916).

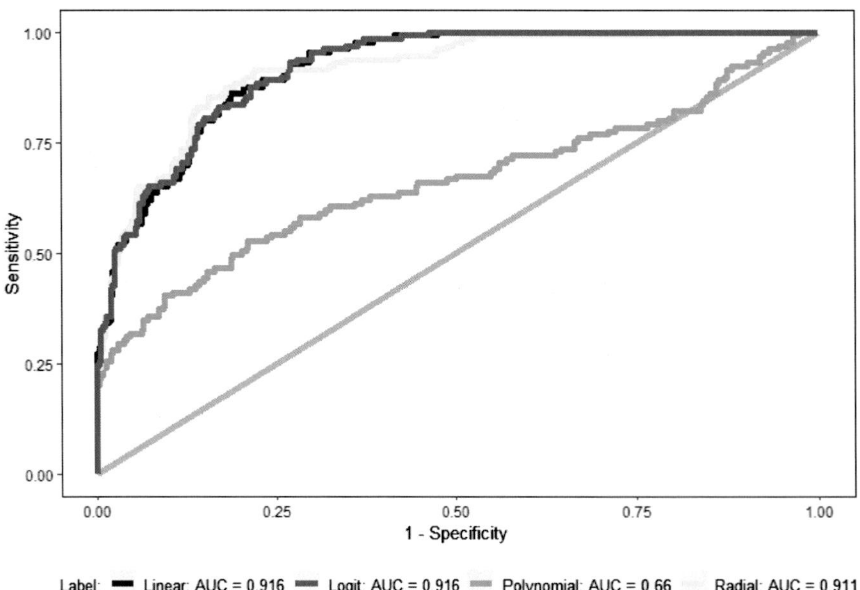

Chapter 19

1.

a. Entropy or Gini Index.

b. Entropy was used.

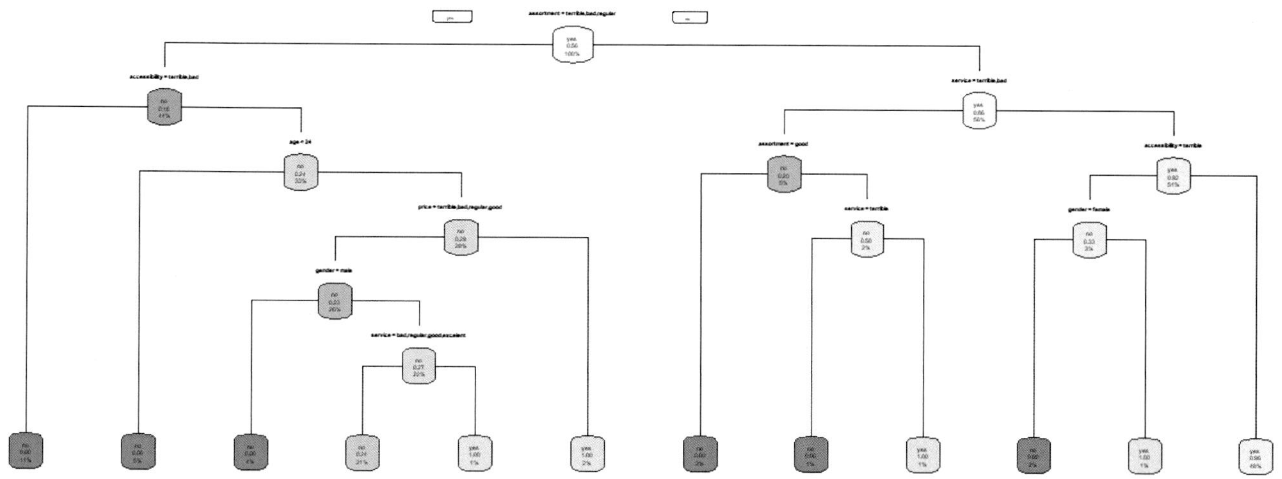

c. 0.18788 (Entropy was used).
d. 0.01(Entropy was used).
e. 11 (Entropy was used).
g. (Entropy was used).

```
Confusion Matrix and Statistics

        TRUE  FALSE
  TRUE  1530     60
  FALSE  150   1260

               Accuracy : 0.93
                 95% CI : (0.9203, 0.9389)
    No Information Rate : 0.56
    P-Value [Acc > NIR] : < 2.2e-16

                  Kappa : 0.859

 Mcnemar's Test P-Value : 8.17e-10

            Sensitivity : 0.9107
            Specificity : 0.9545
         Pos Pred Value : 0.9623
         Neg Pred Value : 0.8936
             Prevalence : 0.5600
         Detection Rate : 0.5100
   Detection Prevalence : 0.5300
      Balanced Accuracy : 0.9326

       'Positive' Class : TRUE
```

h. 0.961.

Chapter 21

1.

a. *country* variable.
b. *country* variable.
c. mtry = 3 (AUC = 0.991).

Chapter 22

1.

a. Hint: use stepmax = 1e7.

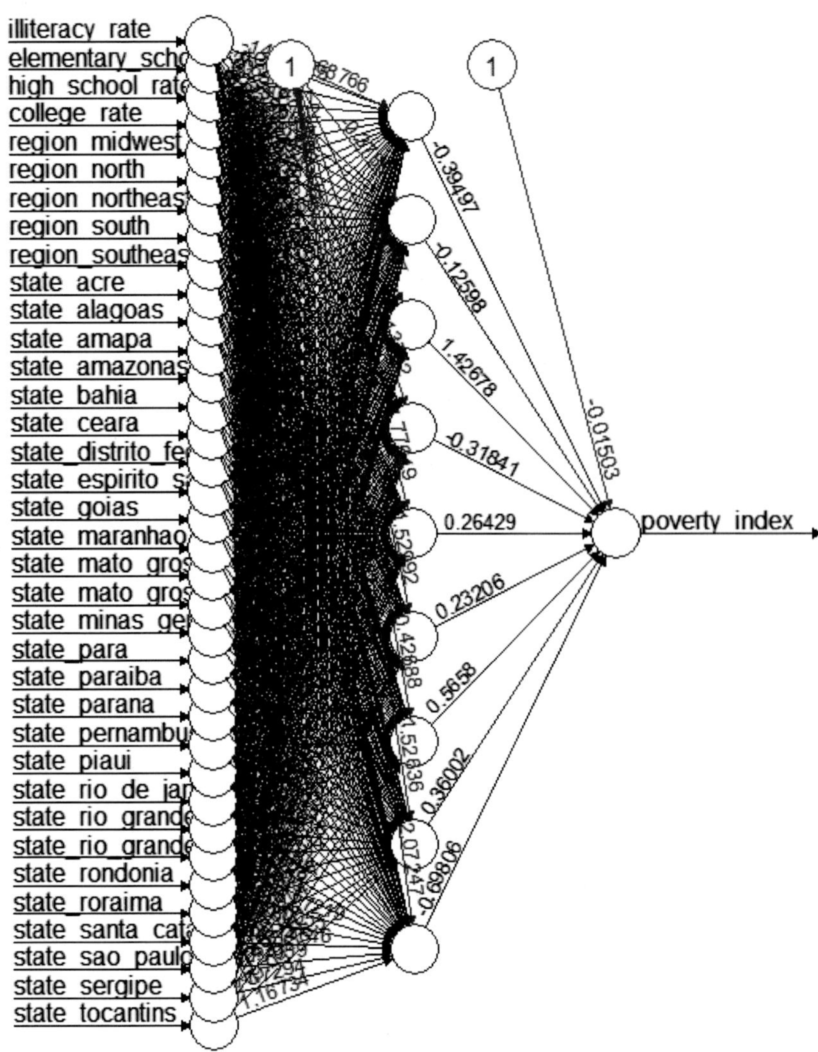

b.
Training sample: RMSE = 0.0694; R^2 = 0.928;
Validation sample: RMSE = 0.0811; R^2 = 0.906.

The RMSE and R^2 values are very close. There does not seem to be any overfitting in the model.

Chapter 26

1.

a.

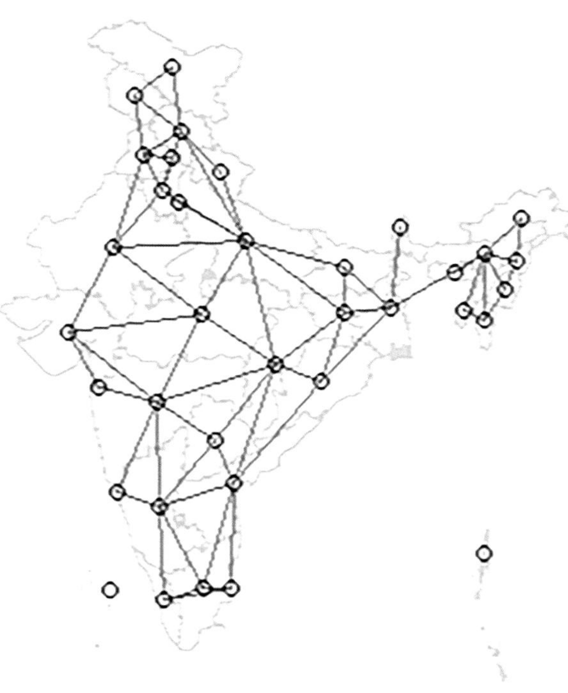

b. 3.72.

c. 2.

d. Uttar Pradesh.

e. Meghalaya and Sikkim.

f.

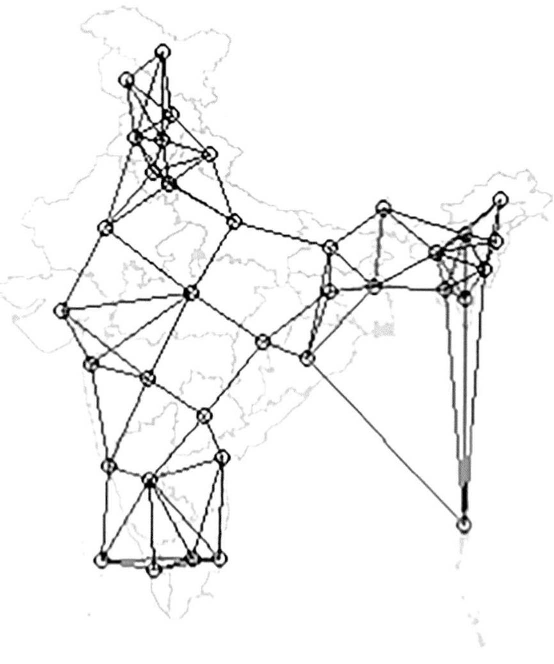

h. $I = 0.25517$.

i.

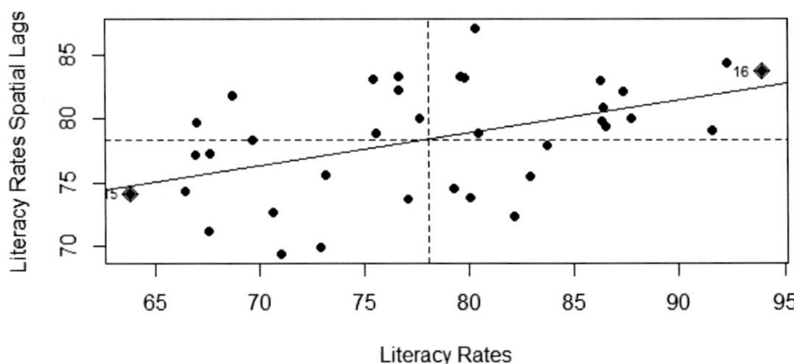
Literacy Rates Spatial Lags
70
75
80
85
65
70
75
80
85
90
95
Literacy Rates
16

j.

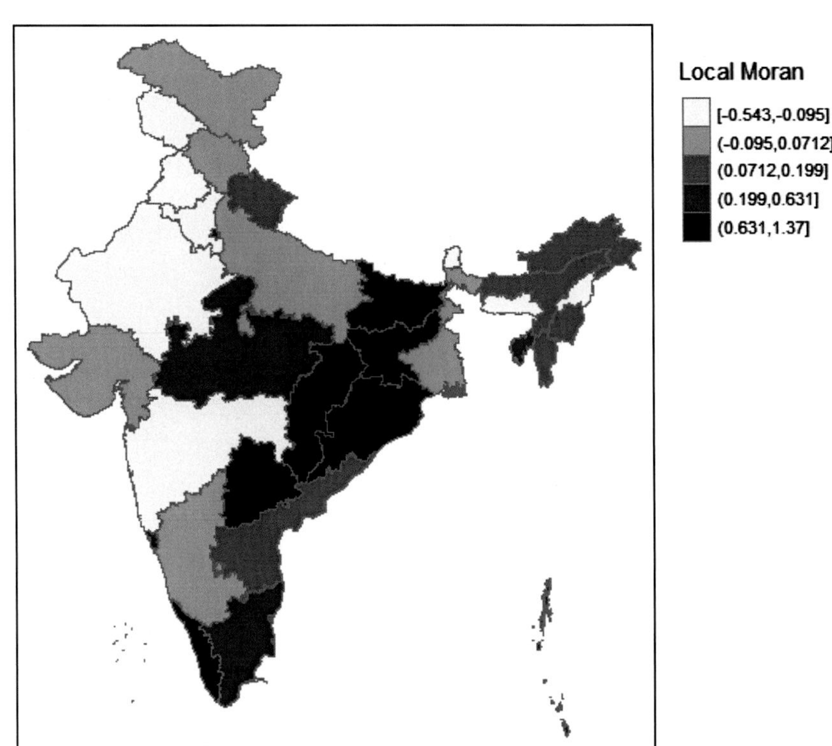
Local Moran
[-0.543,-0.095]
(-0.095,0.0712]
(0.0712,0.199]
(0.199,0.631]
(0.631,1.37]

k.

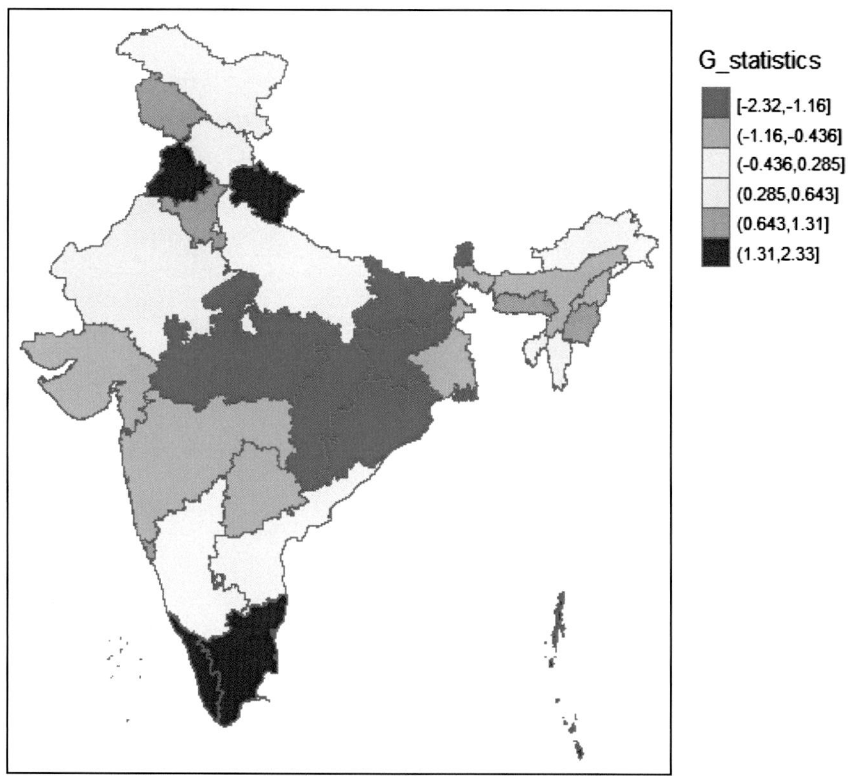

Chapter 27

1.

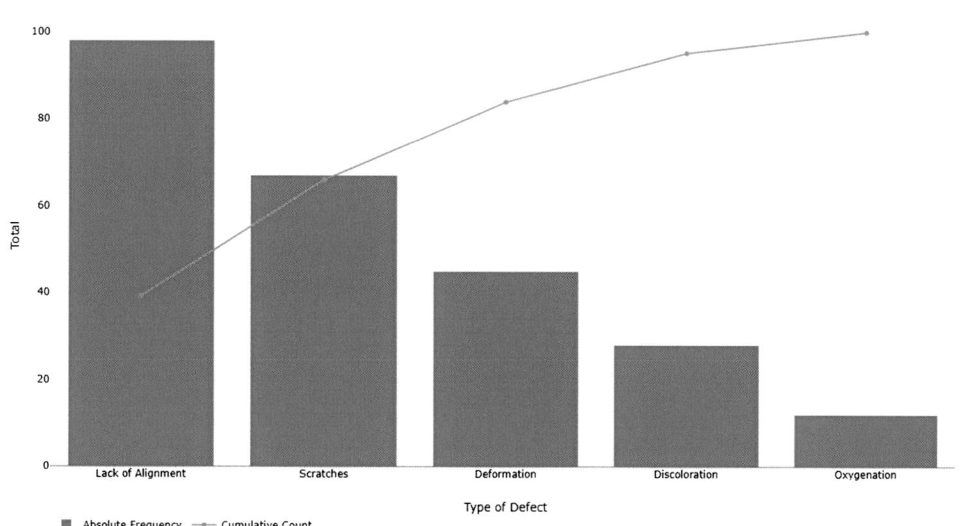

2.

Histogram:

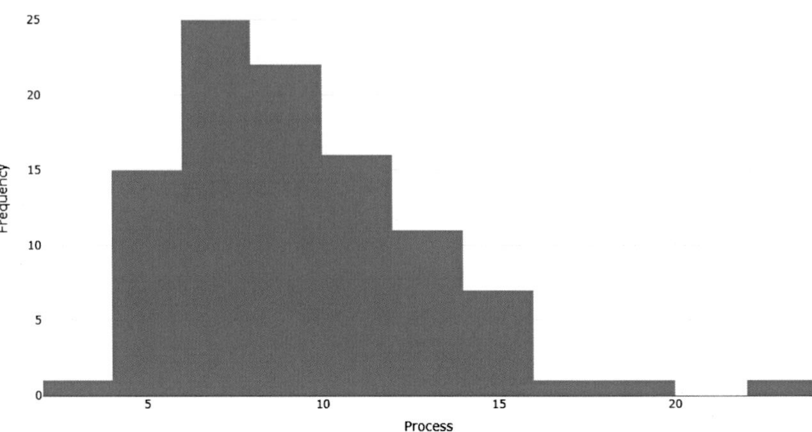

Boxplot:

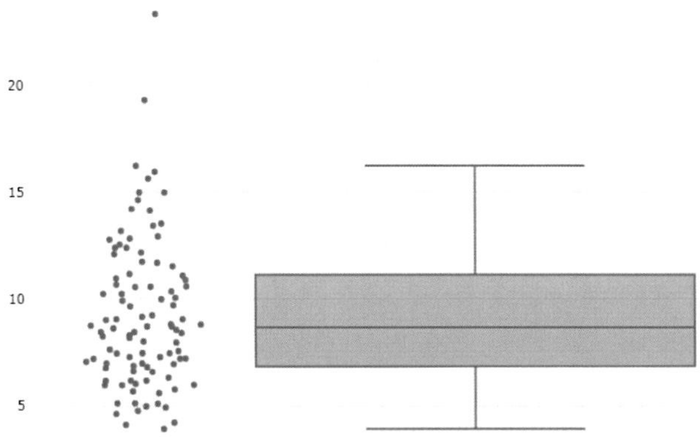

3.
Histogram:

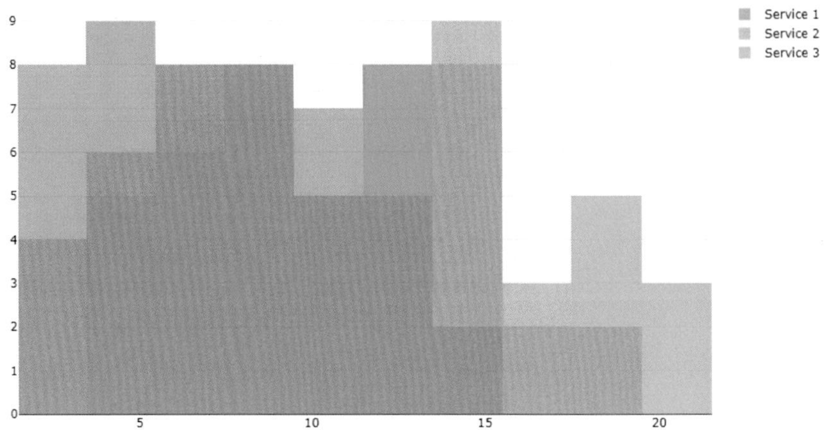

Boxplot:

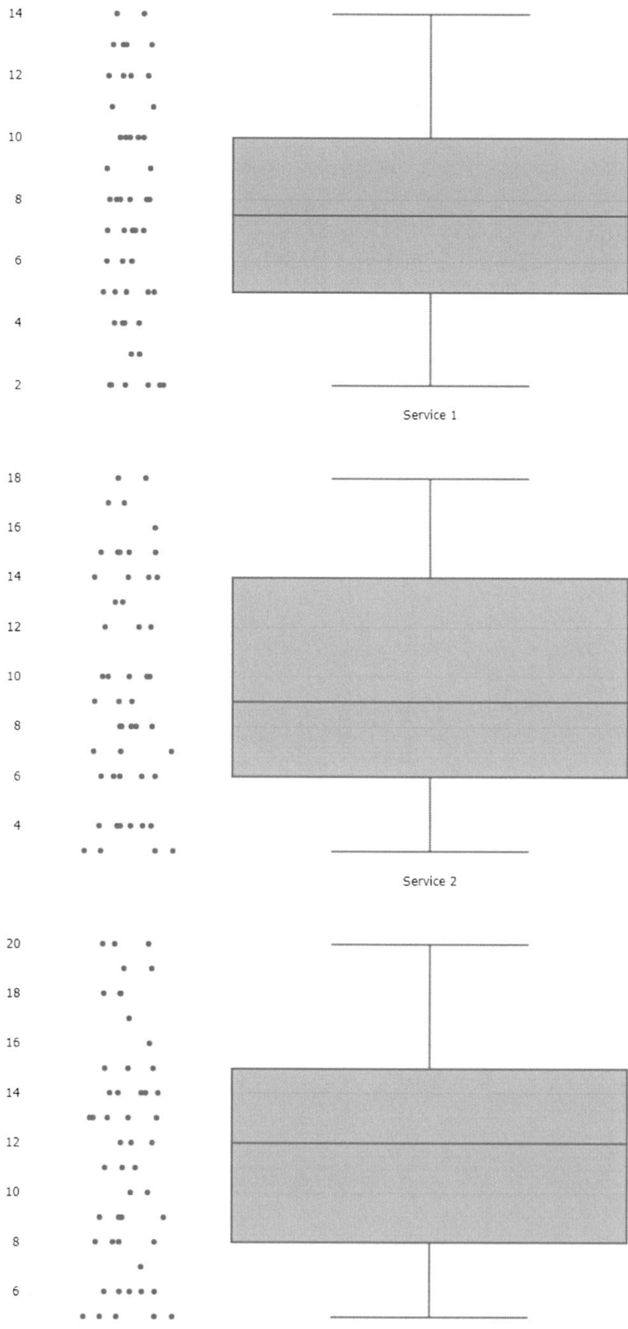
14
12
10
8
6
4
2
Service 1
18
16
14
12
10
8
6
4
Service 2
20
18
16
14
12
10
8
6
Service 3

4.

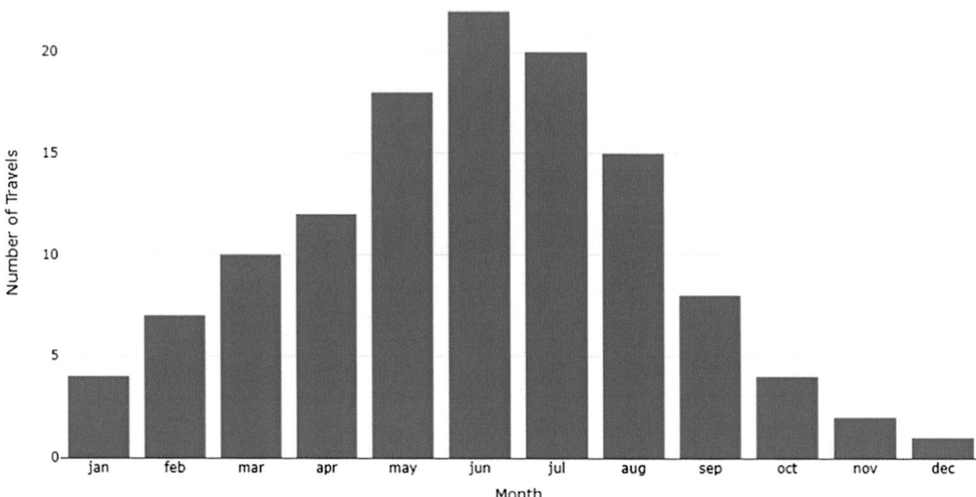

Number of Travels
20
15
10
5
0
jan
feb
mar
apr
may
jun
jul
aug
sep
oct
nov
dec
Month

References

Adelabu, S.A., Mutanga, O., Adam, E.M., Sebego, R., 2013. Spectral discrimination of insect defoliation levels in mopane woodland using hyperspectral data. IEEE J. Sel. Top. Appl. Earth Obs. Remote Sens. 7 (1), 177–186.

Almeida, E., 2012. Econometria espacial aplicada. Alínea, São Paulo.

Anselin, L., 1995. Local indicators of spatial association—LISA. Geogr. Anal. 27 (2), 93–115.

Anselin, L., Rey, S.J., 2014. Modern Spatial Econometrics in Practice: A Guide to Geoda, Geodaspace and Pysal. Geoda Press LLC, Boston.

Belgiu, M., Dragut, L., 2016. Random forest in remote sensing: a review of applications and future directions. ISPRS J. Photogramm. Remote Sens. 114, 24–31.

Berry, M.J., Linoff, G.S., 1997. Data Mining Techniques: For Marketing, Sales, and Customer Support. John Wiley & Sons, New York.

Blum, A., 1992. Neural Networks in C++. John Wiley & Sons, New York.

Boehmke, B., Greenwell, B., 2019. Hands-On Machine Learning With R. Chapman & Hall/CRC Press, London.

Boger, Z., Guterman, H., 1997. Knowledge extraction from artificial neural network models. In: Proceedings of the Conference on Systems, Man, and Cybernetics, pp. 1–13.

Box, G.E.P., Cox, D.R., 1964. An analysis of transformations. J. R. Stat. Soc. Ser. B 26 (2), 211–252.

Breiman, L., 1996. Bagging Predictors. Springer, New York.

Breiman, L., Friedman, J.H., Olshen, R.A., Stone, C.J., 1984. Classification and Regression Trees. Routledge, New York.

Brunsdon, C., Comber, L., 2019. An Introduction to R for Spatial Analysis and Mapping. Sage Publications, Thousand Oaks.

Bussab, W.O., Morettin, P.A., 2017. Estatística básica, ninth ed. Saraiva, São Paulo.

Cameron, A.C., Trivedi, P.K., 1990. Regression-based tests for overdispersion in the Poisson model. J. Econ. 46 (3), 347–364.

Cameron, A.C., Trivedi, P.K., 2013. Regression Analysis of Count Data, second ed. Cambridge University Press, Cambridge.

Caruana, R., Karampatziakis, N., Yessenalina, A., 2008. An empirical evaluation of supervised learning in high dimensions. In: Proceedings of the 25th International Conference on Machine Learning. ACM, pp. 96–103.

Chang, W.R., 2013. Graphics Cookbook. O'Reilly Media, Sebastopol, CA.

Cliff, A.D., Ord, J.K., 1973. Spatial Autocorrelation. Pion, London.

Cliff, A.D., Ord, J.K., 1981. Spatial Processes: Models and Applications. Pion, London.

Cortes, C., Vapnik, V., 1995. Support-vector network. Mach. Learn. 20, 1–25.

Du, P., Samat, A., Waske, B., Liu, S., Li, Z., 2015. Random forest and rotation forest for fully polarized SAR image classification using polarimetric and spatial features. ISPRS J. Photogramm. Remote Sens. 105, 38–53.

Fávero, L.P., Belfiore, P., 2017. Manual de análise de dados: estatística e modelagem multivariada com Excel®, Stata® e SPSS®. Elsevier, Rio de Janeiro.

Fávero, L.P., Belfiore, P., 2019. Data Science for Business and Decision Making. Academic Press, Cambridge.

Fávero, L.P., Belfiore, P., Silva, F.L., Chan, B.L., 2009. Análise de dados: modelagem multivariada para tomada de decisões. Campus Elsevier, Rio de Janeiro.

Fotheringham, S., Brunsdon, C., Charlton, M., 2002. Geographically Weighted Regression: The Analysis of Spatially Varying Relationships. Wiley, West Sussex.

Gislason, P.O., Benediktsson, J.A., Sveinsson, J.R., 2006. Random forests for land cover classification. Pattern Recogn. Lett. 27, 294–300.

Griffith, D.A., 2003. Spatial Autocorrelation and Spatial Filtering. Springer, New York.

Grolemund, G., 2014. Hands-On Programming With R: Write Your Own Functions and Simulations. O'Reilly Media, Sebastopol, CA.

Hyndman, R.J., Fan, Y., 1996. Sample quantiles in statistical packages. Am. Stat. 50, 361–365.

Islam, S., 2018. Hands-On Geospatial Analysis With R and QGIS: A Beginner's Guide to Manipulating, Managing, and Analyzing Spatial Data Using R and QGIS. Packt Publishing.

James, G., Witten, D., Hastie, T., Tibshirani, R., 2021a. An Introduction to Statistical Learning, second ed. Springer, New York.

James, G., Witten, D., Hastie, T., Tibshirani, R., 2021b. ISLR2: Introduction to Statistical Learning. R Package Version 1.3.

Karsoliya, S., 2012. Approximating number of hidden layer neurons in multiple hidden layer BPNN architecture. Int. J. Eng. Trends Technol. 3, 714–717.

Kelleher, J.D., Namee, B.M., D'arcy, A., 2015. Machine Learning for Predictive Analytics. MIT Press.

Lansley, G., Cheshire, J., 2016. An Introduction to Spatial Data Analysis and Visualisation in R. CDRC Learning Resources.

Meyer, D., Dimitriadou, E., Hornik, K., Weingessel, A., Leisch, F., Chang, C.-C., Lin, C.-C., 2021. e1071: Misc Functions of the Department of Statistics, Probability Theory Group. R Package Version 1.7-9.

Millard, K., Richardson, M., 2015. On the importance of training data sample selection in random forest image classification: a case study in Peatland ecosystem mapping. Remote Sens. 7 (7), 8489–8515.

Moran, P.A., 1948. The interpretation of statistical maps. J. R. Stat. Soc. Ser. B 10 (2), 243–251.

Payne, E.H., Gebregziabher, M., Hardin, J.W., Ramakrishnan, V., Egede, L. E., 2018. An empirical approach to determine a threshold for assessing overdispersion in Poisson and negative binomial models for count data. Commun. Stat. Simul. Comput. 47 (6), 1722–1738.

Pebesma, E., Bivand, R., Cook, I., Keitt, T., Sumner, M., Lovelace, R., Wickham, H., Ooms, J., Racine, E., 2017. sf: Simple Features for R. R Package Version 1.0-4.

Piatkowska, S.J., Messner, S.F., Yang, T.-C., 2018. Xenophobic and racially motivated crime in Belgium: exploratory spatial data analysis and spatial regressions of structural covariates. Deviant Behav. 39 (11), 1398–1418.

Quinlan, J.R., 1992. Learning with continuous classes. In: Proceedings of the Australian Joint Conference on Artificial Intelligence. World Scientific, Singapore, pp. 343–348.

Shannon, C.E., 1948. A mathematical theory of communication. Bell Syst. Tech. J. 27 (3), 379–423.

Shmueli, G., Bruce, P.C., Yahav, I., Patel, N.R., Lichtendahl, K.C., 2018. Data Mining for Business Analytics: Concepts, Techniques, and Applications in R. John Wiley & Sons, New York.

Stevens, S.S., 1946. On the theory of scales of measurement. Science 103 (2684), 677–680.

Surowiecki, J., 2005. The Wisdom of Crowds. Anchor Books, New York.

Tiefelsdorf, M., Griffith, D.A., Boots, B., 1999. A variance-stabilizing coding scheme for spatial link matrices. Environ. Plan. A 31 (1), 165–180.

Tobler, W.R., 1970. A computer movie simulating urban growth in the Detroit region. In: Economic Geography, v. 46, Supplement: Proceedings, International Geographical Union, Commission on Quantitative Methods, pp. 234–240.

Vuong, Q.H., 1989. Likelihood ratio tests for model selection and non-nested hypotheses. Econometrica 57 (2), 307–333.

Wickham, H., 2009. ggplot2: Elegant Graphics for Data Analysis. Springer, New York.

Wickham, H., 2021. Mastering Shiny: Build Interactive Apps, Reports, and Dashboards Powered by R. O'Reilly Media, Sebastopol, CA.

Wickham, H., Grolemund, G., 2017. R for Data Science: Import, Tidy, Transform, Visualize, and Model Data. O'Reilly Media, Sebastopol, CA.

Index

Note: Page numbers followed by *f* indicate figures, *t* indicate tables, and *b* indicate boxes.

C

D

E

T

U

V

W

Z

Printed in the United States
by Baker & Taylor Publisher Services